The Human Expression

A History of Peoples and Their Cultures

PAUL THOMAS WELTY

J. B. LIPPINCOTT COMPANY
PHILADELPHIA • NEW YORK • SAN JOSE

ABOUT THE AUTHOR: PAUL THOMAS WELTY

Dr. Paul Welty has long believed that basic world history books should stress the cultural approach. He feels that a student will come to a deeper and broader understanding of our human heritage after studying the many cultural expressions of humanity. The books he has authored and edited reflect this belief. Besides writing *The Human Expression*, Dr. Welty is also the author of *The Asians: Their Heritage and Their Destiny* and *Man's Cultural Heritage*. He is the editor of *World Cultures Sourcebooks* (8 volumes), *Pageant of World Cultures*, and *Readings in World Cultures*. Dr. Welty teaches at Northeastern Illinois University. He is a member of a number of professional organizations including the American Historical Association, Association for Asian Studies, and the American Political Science Association.

STANLEY E. DIMOND, Consultant

Dr. Dimond has served as Divisional Director, Department of Social Studies, Detroit Public Schools, and is Professor Emeritus of Education in the School of Education, University of Michigan. Dr. Dimond is the author of *Schools and the Development of Good Citizens*, and co-author of *Our American Government* and *Civics for Citizens*.

Design of cover, maps, charts, and graphs by Sulpizio Associates

THE COVER: TIME IS WHAT WE MAKE OF IT

This book is about people and time. People live in time and by time. They are of the times in which they live, yet they make those times. Many peoples have expressed their feelings about time. This is just one example:

> *For everything there is a season,*
> *and a time for every matter under heaven:*
> *a time to be born, and a time to die;*
> *a time to plant, and a time to harvest...*
> *a time to weep, and a time to laugh;*
> *a time to mourn, and a time to dance...*
> *a time to keep silence, and a time to speak;*
> *a time to love, and a time to hate;*
> *a time for war, and a time for peace.*

Peoples have also measured time in many ways. The earliest peoples measured their lives by the sun and the moon. Modern people hurry to the flash of their digital watches. Ancient Romans, like many other peoples, moved to the tempo of the shadow on a sundial (tempus means time). Aztecs marked their seasons by a calendar stone. Later Europeans watched their empires rise and fall as time ticked away on their grandfather clocks. Traditional Asians count minutes and hours, but measure true time in eras. Athletes compete with the seconds on a stopwatch. Seconds, minutes, hours, days, months, years, eras — time for us all.

Contents

To The Reader   1

A Note About This Book   2

Beginnings: *The Study of Culture*   4

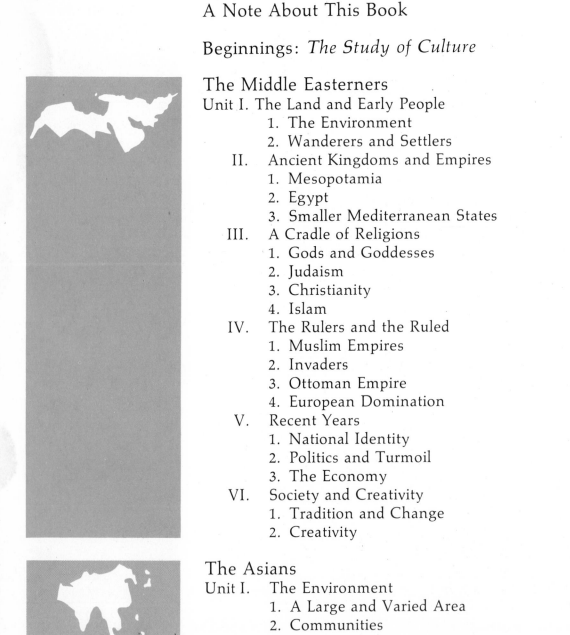

The Middle Easterners   24
Unit I. The Land and Early People   26
    1. The Environment   27
    2. Wanderers and Settlers   33
  II. Ancient Kingdoms and Empires   38
    1. Mesopotamia   39
    2. Egypt   47
    3. Smaller Mediterranean States   52
  III. A Cradle of Religions   58
    1. Gods and Goddesses   59
    2. Judaism   62
    3. Christianity   66
    4. Islam   71
  IV. The Rulers and the Ruled   76
    1. Muslim Empires   77
    2. Invaders   81
    3. Ottoman Empire   84
    4. European Domination   92
  V. Recent Years   98
    1. National Identity   99
    2. Politics and Turmoil   106
    3. The Economy   114
  VI. Society and Creativity   124
    1. Tradition and Change   125
    2. Creativity   130

The Asians   138
Unit I. The Environment   140
    1. A Large and Varied Area   141
    2. Communities   145
  II. India—Pakistan—Bangladesh   150
    1. Ancient India   151

    2. Early Indian Religions 152
    3. Creativity 158
    4. Society 166
    5. Independence 171
    6. Pakistan and Bangladesh 175
III. China 180
    1. Ancient China 181
    2. Thoughts and Beliefs 182
    3. Creativity 190
    4. Society 199
    5. Revolutions 205
    6. Korea—A Meeting Place 213
IV. Japan 216
    1. Early Japan 217
    2. Creators and Adapters 218
    3. Artistry 222
    4. Traditional Society and Social Change 230
    5. Modern Japan 234
V. Southeast Asia 242
    1. Spread of a Culture—The Hoabinhians 243
    2. Religious Beliefs 244
    3. Mainland Nations 245
    4. Part Island, Part Mainland—Malaysia 252
    5. Island Countries 254
    6. Society 260

The Africans 264
Unit I. The Land and the People 266
    1. Environment and Development 267
    2. Early People 275
II. Kingdoms, Empires, and States 280
    1. The Northeast 281
    2. Central and South Africa 284
    3. East Africa 291
    4. West Africa 296
III. Colonialism 306
    1. European Impact on African Trade 307
    2. Scramble for Africa 311

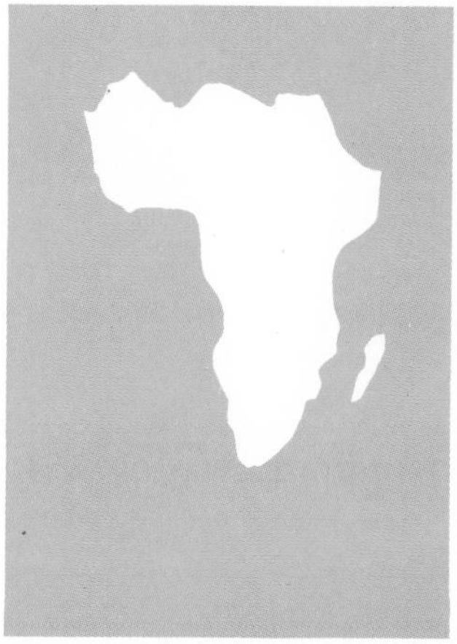

Contents, *cont.*

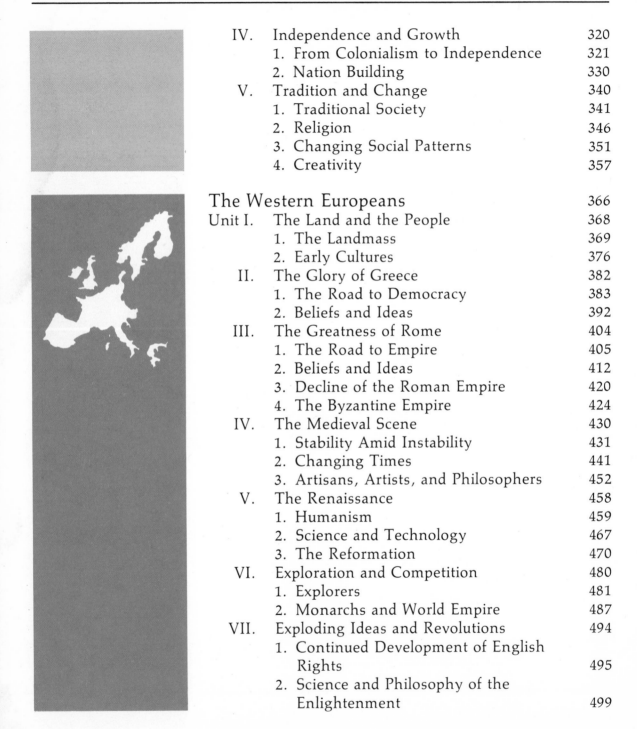

IV.	Independence and Growth	320
	1. From Colonialism to Independence	321
	2. Nation Building	330
V.	Tradition and Change	340
	1. Traditional Society	341
	2. Religion	346
	3. Changing Social Patterns	351
	4. Creativity	357

The Western Europeans — 366

Unit I.	The Land and the People	368
	1. The Landmass	369
	2. Early Cultures	376
II.	The Glory of Greece	382
	1. The Road to Democracy	383
	2. Beliefs and Ideas	392
III.	The Greatness of Rome	404
	1. The Road to Empire	405
	2. Beliefs and Ideas	412
	3. Decline of the Roman Empire	420
	4. The Byzantine Empire	424
IV.	The Medieval Scene	430
	1. Stability Amid Instability	431
	2. Changing Times	441
	3. Artisans, Artists, and Philosophers	452
V.	The Renaissance	458
	1. Humanism	459
	2. Science and Technology	467
	3. The Reformation	470
VI.	Exploration and Competition	480
	1. Explorers	481
	2. Monarchs and World Empire	487
VII.	Exploding Ideas and Revolutions	494
	1. Continued Development of English Rights	495
	2. Science and Philosophy of the Enlightenment	499

	3. The French Revolution and Napoleon	504
	4. The Arts	513
VIII.	Machines and Materialism	522
	1. The Industrial Revolution	523
	2. The Machine and Change	527
	3. Scientific and Philosophic Thought	533
	4. From Romanticism to Post-impressionism	537
IX.	Europe Warred and the World Followed	548
	1. The Forces of War	549
	2. The Rise of Dictators	560
X.	The New Europe	570
	1. Cooperation—Legacy of World War II	571
	2. Contemporary Technology and Thought	581
	3. The Contemporary Arts	586
	4. Changing Social Patterns	596

The Russians and Eastern Europeans 604

Unit I.	Russian Land and Early People	606
	1. The World's Largest Nation	607
	2. A Sweep of Peoples	614
II.	The Rise of the Russian State	618
	1. Kiev and Moscow	619
	2. Expansion Abroad—Unrest at Home	625
III.	Communism in Russia	634
	1. The Fight for Power	635
	2. Party and Government	642
	3. Change in Direction	645
IV.	Life in the Soviet Union	654
	1. The Economy	655
	2. Society	660
	3. Religion	668
	4. The Arts	672
V.	Eastern Europe	678
	1. The Nations	679
	2. Life	690

Contents, *cont.*

The Latin Americans		700
Unit I.	The Land and Ancient Peoples	702
	1. The Environment	703
	2. Early Peoples	710
II.	Pre-Columbian Civilizations	714
	1. Mesoamerica	715
	2. The Andes	723
III.	Coming of the Europeans	730
	1. The Spanish	731
	2. The Portuguese	737
IV.	Wars of Independence	742
	1. Spanish South America	743
	2. Mexico's Struggle	747
	3. Brazil's Development	751
	4. Independence in the Caribbean	754
V.	The Evolving Political Scene	762
	1. Rise of Caudillos	763
	2. Radical versus Conservative Change	766
	3. Hemispheric Relations	773
VI.	Society in Transition	780
	1. Social Patterns	781
	2. Economic Development	789
	3. Creativity	795
Social Studies Vocabulary / Glossary		808
Acknowledgements		816
Index		818

Maps, Charts, and Graphs

Beginnings: *The Study of Culture*

Indo-European Language Family   10

The Middle Easterners

Locator Map   27
A Physical Map of the Middle East   28
A Political Map of the Middle East   29
Fertile Crescent   31
Ancient Cities   36
Sumerian Civilization, c. 2800 B.C.   39
Akkadian Empire, c. 2300s B.C.   41
Babylonian Empire, c. 1760 B.C.   41
Assyrian Empire, c. 671 B.C.   43
New Babylonian Empire, c. 570 B.C.   43
Persian Empire, c. 500s B.C.   45
Seleucid Dynasty, c. 200s B.C.   46
Old Kingdom, c. 3000 B.C.   47
Empire Period, c. 1450 B.C.   48
Phoenician Sphere of Influence, c. 500s B.C.   53
Kingdom of David and Solomon,
    c. 1000-900 B.C.   56
Hebrews, c. 933-912 B.C.   56
Major World Religions   63
Muslim Empire Under Muhammad,
    c. 632 A.D.   77
Ommaid Dynasty, c. 661-750 A.D.   79
Abbasid Dynasty, c. 1200s A.D.   80
States of the Crusaders   82
Mongol Invasions, c. 1200s A.D.   84
Ottoman Empire, c. 1683   87
Safavid Empire, 1600s   87
Middle East, 1914   94
Mandates   95
Israel, 1948   111
Israel, 1967   112
Israel, 1973   113
Natural Resources   116
Land Use   116
GNP of OPEC vs Non-OPEC Countries   118

The Asians

Locator Map   141
A Physical Map of Asia   142
A Political Map of Asia   143
Indus Valley Civilization, c. 2500-1500 B.C.   151
Maurya Empire Under Asoka, c. 250 B.C.   158

Gupta Dynasty, c. 400 A.D.   159
Imperialism in India, 1857   172
Natural Resources   178
Land Use   178
Chou Dynasty, c. 1000 B.C.   181
Han Dynasty, c. 100 A.D.   185
Manchu Dynasty, 1800s   196
Natural Resources   210
Land Use   210
Women in the Labor Force   231
Natural Resources   233
Land Use   233
Japanese Empire: 1895-1942   237
Mon Migrations   246
Burman Migrations   246
Chin, Naga, Kachin Migrations   246
Thai Migrations   248
Khmer Migrations   248
Vietnamese Migrations   250
Malay Migrations   253
Major Exports and Imports   258
Natural Resources   259
Land Use   259

The Africans

Locator Map   267
A Physical Map of Africa   268
A Political Map of Africa   269
Nok Culture, c. 300 B.C.-200 A.D.   278
Kingdom of Kush, c. 500 B.C.   281
Kingdom of Axum, c. 400 A.D.   283
Bantu Migrations   285
Kingdoms of Luba and Lunda   287
Kingdom of the Congo, 1400s   288
Monomotapa Empire, 1400s   291
East Coast Cities   292
Empire of Ghana, c. 300-1076   296
Empire of Mali, 1300s   298
Empire of Songhai, 1500s   299
Empire of Kanem-Bornu, c. 1550   300
Yoruba City-States   302
The Ashanti Union, c. 1700   303
Africa, 1914   311
Guide to African Nations   322
Natural Resources   334
Land Use   335
Rural-Urban Shift in Ghana   354

Maps, Charts, and Graphs, *cont.*

The Western Europeans

Locator Map	369
A Physical Map of Western Europe	370
A Political Map of Western Europe	371
Athens in the Age of Pericles, c. 450 B.C.	389
Empire of Alexander the Great	392
Ancient Italy	405
Roman Republic, c. 133 B.C.	407
Roman Empire at Its Peak, c. 117 A.D.	413
Invasions of the Huns, c. 300s-500s A.D.	422
Invasions of the Visigoths, c. 300s-500s A.D.	423
Invasions of the Ostrogoths, c. 300s-500s A.D.	423
Invasions of the Vandals, c. 400s A.D.	423
Byzantine Empire Under Justinian	424
Charlemagne's Empire	431
Invasions of the Vikings, c. 700s-1000s A.D.	432
Holy Roman Empire, c. 1000	451
Empire of Napoleon, 1812	510
Europe After the Congress of Vienna, 1815	512
Prussia, 1866	553
German Empire, 1871	553
Italy in 1852 Before Unification	554
European Alliances, 1914	559
Europe After the Treaty of Versailles, 1919	559
Allied and Axis Powers, 1939	566
The United Nations and its Specialized Agencies	573
Natural Resources	577
Land Use	577
Selected Health Care Over a 15-Year Period	601

The Russians and Eastern Europeans

Locator Map	607
A Physical Map of the USSR and Eastern Europe	608
A Political Map of the USSR and Eastern Europe	609
Kievan Russia, 1054	620
Russia, 1613	625
Russia, 1914	632
Party and Government Structure	643
Natural Resources	657
Land Use	657

Production Increases of Selected Consumer Goods Over 10 Years	663
Migrations, 500-1000 A.D.	681
Natural Resources	693
Land Use	693

The Latin Americans

Locator Map	703
A Physical Map of Latin America	704
A Political Map of Latin America	705
Olmec Civilization, c. 1200s-200s B.C.	715
Mayan Civilization, c. 500s B.C.-1200s A.D.	718
Toltec Civilization, c. 750 A.D.	719
Aztec Civilization, c. 1200s-1520 A.D.	720
Chavin Civilization, c. 1000s-400s B.C.	723
Huari Empire, 600-1000 A.D.	724
Mochica-Chimu Civilizations	725
Inca Empire, c. 1200s-1533 A.D.	728
Spanish Colonial Administration, 1790	736
Portuguese Colonial Administration, 1790	739
Independent South America, 1825	743
Mexico and United Provinces of Central America, 1825	751
Empire of Brazil, 1825	752
Literacy by Age Group in Selected Countries	783
Natural Resources	790
Land Use	791
Employment by Industry in Selected Countries	793

To The Reader

The Human Expression: A History of Peoples and Their Cultures was written to introduce you to the cultural history of the peoples of the world. This book reflects the belief that a meaningful introduction should show the many expressions of what it means to be human.

In the following pages, therefore, you will see people at work and at play. You will learn about their religions, philosophies, and ideals. You will read about their family and social patterns. You will see their works in art, literature, music, technology, and in many other areas of creativity. You will observe them as political and economic beings. And you will follow the changing patterns of peoples' lives as they move through the late 20th century. As you read, you will discover the many sides of the past and present cultural expressions of those with whom we share our planet. A deeper knowledge of yourself and others should come as you realize that a close and continuing connection exists between the past, present, and future.

In reality all humanity shares its cultures. We have much in common for we are all of the human family. But for one reason or another, people in different regions of the world developed differing ways of life and of looking at life.

You should know, however, that not all people within culture regions are alike. For example, as different regions of the United States enjoy different local foods and use different slang expressions so other cultures have variety. There are great differences among those who share the culture of Asia, for example. Those who live in India are culturally different from those who live in Japan. The same can be said about the other major regions of the world. As you read, you will see that attention has been given to these differences within regions.

It is also important for you to know that cultures influence each other. Through such things as trade, conquest, and missionary work, features of one culture are carried to other cultures. The Byzantine Empire of the 400s through the 1400s, for example, influenced the development of Eastern Europe and Russia. Most recently it has been Western Europe and the U.S. that have deeply influenced other areas of the world. This is what we mean by cultural diffusion, a theme which runs throughout this book.

Finally you should know that a number of talented people helped me to make this book. And you were always in our minds as we worked. The words were written, the maps drawn, the illustrations chosen, the questions written—for you. We shall feel that our task was well done if you find this book has broadened and deepened your understanding and knowledge of our shared cultural heritage.

Paul Thomas Welty

A Note About This Book

We, the author and editors of *The Human Expression*, thought it would be helpful if you knew how this textbook is arranged. It is divided into seven sections. The first, called *Beginnings: The Study of Culture*, introduces you to the terms and methods of anthropologists. It contains all the basic vocabulary you will need to study each culture region. It also contains various anthropologists' theories on the development of humankind.

Each of the remaining six sections deals with a culture region. They are *The Middle Easterners*, *The Asians*, *The Africans*, *The Western Europeans*, *The Russians and Eastern Europeans*, and *The Latin Americans*. Because you take courses in United States history, geography, economics, society, and the arts there seemed no need to provide an historical-cultural study of the United States.

Unit page

Illustrations that relate directly to the text

Captions that will help you understand the relation-ship between picture and text; they sometimes ask discussion questions

Unit summary

Social Studies Vocabulary/ Glossary words appear in bold type

Unit II

Pre-Columbian Civilizations

The Castillo at Chichen Itza has 91 steps on each of its four sides. They lead to a temple. What other peoples built pyramids? Were they temples too?

Millions of people lived in Middle and South America before Columbus arrived. They represented hundreds of **tribes**, cultures, and language groups. Where the people had settled down to farming, the food supply had become more certain and plentiful. As a result, the population increased. More people lived in larger settlements.

Permanent farming made possible the development of the complex **civilizations** of southern Middle America and the Andes Mountains. These two areas became the two most intensely farmed regions of pre-Columbian America. Trade played an important role in these civilizations.

However, not all pre-Columbian peoples were farmers or traders. Many—like the Puelches (PWEL-chays) of the pampas and the Araucanians (uh-raw-KAHN-ee-uhns) of the southern Andes—were nomads. They lived by hunting, fishing, and seed gathering. In the rain forests of Brazil and the Caribbean islands, people such as the Arawaks (AR-uh-wahks) and the Caribs used slash-and-burn farming.

714

2

Each section dealing with a culture region is divided into units, chapters, and topics. Below you will find sample pages from the textbook. They are pages 714 and 715 of *The Latin Americans*. They are reproduced here to show you the features that we hope will help you to use and enjoy this book.

Additional features are "Summing Up the Unit," which includes study material, discussion questions, and project ideas, and "For Further Study," which is a bibliography of non-fiction and fiction works. A "Social Studies Vocabulary/Glossary" and an index have also been provided. Charts and graphs are used to help clarify political structures and economic concepts. Biographical sketches are sprinkled throughout the text to make the reading more interesting. This text is above everything a book about people for people. We hope that we have succeeded in making it readable, interesting and informative.

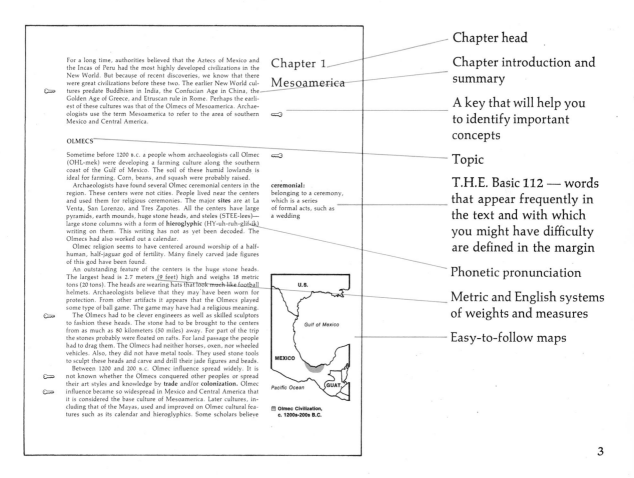

For a long time, authorities believed that the Aztecs of Mexico and the Incas of Peru had the most highly developed civilizations in the New World. But because of recent discoveries, we know that there were great civilizations before these two. The earlier New World cultures predate Buddhism in India, the Confucian Age in China, the Golden Age of Greece, and Etruscan rule in Rome. Perhaps the earliest of these cultures was that of the Olmecs of Mesoamerica. Archaeologists use the term Mesoamerica to refer to the area of southern Mexico and Central America.

OLMECS

Sometime before 1200 B.C. a people whom archaeologists call Olmec (OHL-mek) were developing a farming culture along the southern coast of the Gulf of Mexico. The soil of these humid lowlands is ideal for farming. Corn, beans, and squash were probably raised.

Archaeologists have found several Olmec ceremonial centers in the region. These centers were not cities. People lived near the centers and used them for religious ceremonies. The major sites are at La Venta, San Lorenzo, and Tres Zapotes. All the centers have large pyramids, earth mounds, huge stone heads, and steles (STEE-lees)— large stone columns with a form of hieroglyphic (HY-uh-ruh-glif-ik) writing on them. This writing has not as yet been decoded. The Olmecs had also worked out a calendar.

Olmec religion seems to have centered around worship of a half-human, half-jaguar god of fertility. Many finely carved jade figures of this god have been found.

An outstanding feature of the centers is the huge stone heads. The largest head is 2.7 meters (9 feet) high and weighs 18 metric tons (20 tons). The heads are wearing hats that look much like football helmets. Archaeologists believe that they may have been worn for protection. From other artifacts it appears that the Olmecs played some type of ball game. The game may have had a religious meaning.

The Olmecs had to be clever engineers as well as skilled sculptors to fashion these heads. The stone had to be brought to the centers from as much as 80 kilometers (50 miles) away. For part of the trip the stones probably were floated on rafts. For land passage the people had to drag them. The Olmecs had neither horses, oxen, nor wheeled vehicles. Also, they did not have metal tools. They used stone tools to sculpt these heads and carve and drill their jade figures and beads.

Between 1200 and 200 B.C. Olmec influence spread widely. It is not known whether the Olmecs conquered other peoples or spread their art styles and knowledge by trade and/or colonization. Olmec influence became so widespread in Mexico and Central America that it is considered the base culture of Mesoamerica. Later cultures, including that of the Mayas, used and improved on Olmec cultural features such as its calendar and hieroglyphics. Some scholars believe

Chapter 1
Mesoamerica

ceremonial:
belonging to a ceremony,
which is a series
of formal acts, such as
a wedding

Chapter head

Chapter introduction and summary

A key that will help you to identify important concepts

Topic

T.H.E. Basic 112 — words that appear frequently in the text and with which you might have difficulty are defined in the margin

Phonetic pronunciation

Metric and English systems of weights and measures

Easy-to-follow maps

3

Beginnings: The Study of Culture

Culture, as anthropologists use the term, means all the ways of life and knowledge—the learned behavior—of a people. This man is making sun-dried bricks the way his ancestors have done for centuries. But culture is not static. He is working to the music of a transistor radio.

The family, work, and belief in higher or supernatural values are parts of all cultures. Left is a Buddhist wedding in Cambodia; right is a team of Nigerian surveyors. Below are churchgoers at Chartres Cathedral in France.

The world of the late 20th century is more than ever one of interdependence. The 1970s saw oil prices set by the Arabs affecting the cost of oil all over the world. Fighting between Turkish and Greek Cypriots affected the North Atlantic Treaty Organization which affected the defense system of Western Europe and the United States.

Why do the Arabs raise oil prices? Why do Greeks and Turks fight? The answers are not simply **economic** or **political**. A complex of social, **religious**, political, and economic reasons that are centuries old underlie these actions. They fall within the area we call **culture**.

In order to deal with the world of today and tomorrow, it is necessary that we know about each other's cultures. Whether we live in the United States, China, Russia, Iran, Tanzania, Denmark, or Costa Rica, we need to know about each other's past as well as present. We should know not only about the influences that shaped political **institutions** and economies, but society and **the arts** too. Without this knowledge, we will never be able to appreciate the different **customs** and attitudes about life in other parts of the world. As this knowledge helps us to understand other peoples, it should also help us to understand ourselves.

That is the goal of this book. Through it we examine the origins and development of social groups. We study past successes and failures in **government**. We look at the way people express themselves in their art. We see them exploring their inner selves, the natural world, and the supernatural in attempts to fulfill their spiritual needs.

Writers of **history** must depend upon the research and analysis of scholars in other fields. Writers of cultural history are especially dependent upon findings in the fields of **anthropology**, **archaeology**, **linguistics**, **sociology**, and **geography**, among others. In the following pages a brief survey is given of the findings and terms of those studies.

ANTHROPOLOGY

The term anthropology comes from two Greek words: anthropos, which means man; and logos, which means word. In modern usage, anthropos might be translated more acceptably as people. Anthropologists use the word man to mean both men and women. Anthropology is literally words about people. It is the study of people, their place in the natural world, their cultural development, and their differing ways of living and behaving. Two major divisions are physical anthropology and cultural anthropology.

Physical anthropologists study the physical development of humans since their first appearance in **prehistoric** time, that is, since before writing was developed. They also study the biological variations of human populations. Cultural anthropologists study the development of human culture and the ways social groups behave. They may study dead cultures or living ones. Anthropologists use comparisons between peoples to study physical and cultural similarities and differences. From these studies they form general ideas about the nature of human development, both in the present and in the past.

The field of anthropology is so large and all-embracing that it has been further subdivided into various special branches of study. One of these special branches is called archaeology. Archaeo means ancient. Archaeologists investigate the cultures of both historic and prehistoric peoples by studying the materials they have left behind. These remains include anything people made or created such as tools, pottery, buildings, and writings.

SPECIAL TERMS   Like all sciences, anthropology uses special terms. To anthropologists, objects made by people, either by hand or machine, are called **artifacts**. Some ordinary words have very exact meanings. For example, dig means an excavation **site**.

Archaeology studies the material remains of past cultures. The diver on the left is an archaeologist investigating a sunken ship off Cyprus. The center photo shows archaeologists working at Leptis Magna, Libya. And today's fad is tomorrow's artifact. What do you think an archaeologist 1,000 years from now would think of the Mickey Mouse watch? Do you think he or she might think the figure represented a god? possibly one connected with time?

When anthropologists speak of a culture, they mean all the ways of life and knowledge—the learned behavior—of a people. A culture includes the tools and other objects that people make and use, their language, their religious beliefs, customs, values, **folklore**, ways of eating and dressing, and their everyday activities.

Culture is the way a particular group of people has adapted to its particular **environment** and background. All people have a culture. But people around the world have different cultures; they do not share the same one.

As anthropologists use the term, culture does not mean achievements in arts, letters, or scientific thought. Anthropologists do not think in terms of one person or group being more cultured than another. All people are cultured in the sense that they grow up learning their own culture. This is so that as adults, they can function more or less effectively within their group. For example, some peoples learn to eat with forks; some learn to eat with chopsticks. Each way is efficient for the people who use it. These are different **culture traits**—objects, behaviors, and characteristics of a culture. But anthropologists can and sometimes do evaluate a culture by how it does or does not meet the needs of all its members.

Anthropologists also speak of a **culture region**. By this they mean an area in which people of different cultural groups have adapted to their surroundings in similar ways. Thus many culture traits are held in common. Most farmers in central and southern China grow paddy rice for a living. So do most farmers in Vietnam. For over a thousand years the two peoples have shared a common written **language**. Most have lived in small **villages**. Most were or are Buddhists. Because they have so many common ways of life, the Vietnamese and Chinese can be said to belong to the same culture area.

Throughout history there has been a flow of culture traits from one cultural group to another. This process is known as **cultural diffusion**. An example of this process was the movement of Buddhism from India to Sri Lanka and Southeast Asia and from India across Central Asia to China, Korea, Japan, and Vietnam. Americans also use a great many objects and foods that came from other cultures.

All cultures experience change. Sometimes this change is slow and may not be noticed for many years. In modern times this is true of those cultural groups which have not been greatly influenced by the **technological revolutions** of the West. Sometimes the change is rapid, as in the **industrialized nations**. In such areas the changes in a way of life are noticeable within 10 to 20 years, or perhaps less. In these nations the ever-increasing pace of technology brings about a rather rapid change in some areas of the cultural life of the people.

Anthropologists use the term acculturation to describe a process

Cultural anthropology is a relatively new social science and Margaret Mead (left) was one of the first to work in it. This photo shows her in Samoa in the 1920s. Why do you think cultural anthropologists live as their subjects do?

of change that takes place when two cultural groups have contact with each other over a long period of time. In this process each may influence the cultural life of the other. The relationship between the U. S. and England since the **industrial revolution** is such an example. There are also times when one culture may strongly influence the other without being greatly affected itself. European **colonial** governments greatly changed the **traditional** ways of African societies while being influenced very little in return.

LANGUAGE FAMILIES

The scientific study of language is called linguistics. Language—either written or spoken—is a way of communicating that can be understood by all members of a group. Language is an important part of a culture.

Not all people who speak the same language are necessarily of the same national origin. Many people in the U. S. have parents who came from China, Africa, India, or Europe. All these people may speak English today, yet their parents came from different geographic areas of the world. In addition, even though people may live in the same geographic area they may not speak the same language. For example, the Chinese and the Japanese are Asians but they speak different languages.

Many languages of the world belong to the same **language families**. They have words that come from the same source and that can be recognized in each of the languages of the same family. For example, the Latin word mater is madre in Spanish, mutter in German, and mother in English. All these languages belong to the Indo-European language family. Each developed from an ancient language called Proto-Indo-European. Proto means before.

In the world of the late 20th century, Western clothes, foods, attitudes, and values have spread around the world. This is an example of cultural diffusion. Here a Japanese mother and daughter window-shop. Few young Japanese women wear kimonos anymore. What specific Western culture has influenced Japan?

9

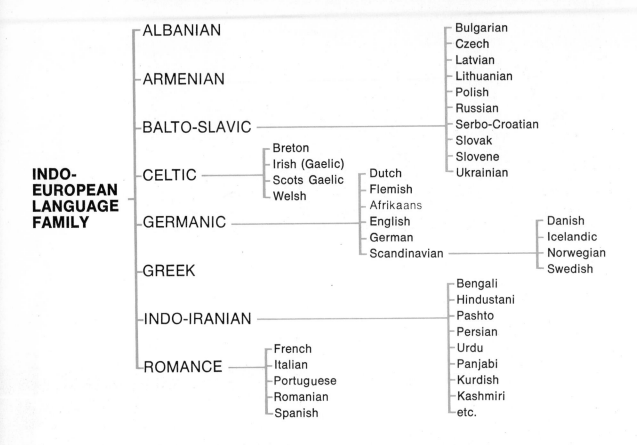

INDO-EUROPEAN LANGUAGE FAMILY

- ALBANIAN
- ARMENIAN
- BALTO-SLAVIC — Bulgarian, Czech, Latvian, Lithuanian, Polish, Russian, Serbo-Croatian, Slovak, Slovene, Ukrainian
- CELTIC — Breton, Irish (Gaelic), Scots Gaelic, Welsh
- GERMANIC — Dutch, Flemish, Afrikaans, English, German, Scandinavian — Danish, Icelandic, Norwegian, Swedish
- GREEK
- INDO-IRANIAN — Bengali, Hindustani, Pashto, Persian, Urdu, Panjabi, Kurdish, Kashmiri, etc.
- ROMANCE — French, Italian, Portuguese, Romanian, Spanish

Indo-European languages include most of the languages of Western and Eastern Europe. Hindustani of India and the Persian language of Iran also belong to this family.

Through the study of ancient languages and languages that are related to one another, it is often possible to tell something about the movements or the origins of people. People carry their language with them as they move from place to place.

For example, the original home of the Gypsies has been determined through their language. Over the many centuries of their **migrations** throughout Europe and elsewhere, they still keep a few words of Sanskrit, an ancient Indian language. Thus linguists have been able to establish that the Gypsies came from India, not Egypt as once thought.

SOCIETY AND SOCIAL GROUPINGS

People are social beings. They have always lived together in small, medium, or big groups. Anthropologists have developed a number of terms to describe social groupings.

The basic unit of human social contact is the family. The unit

The family is the basic unit of society. In rural areas the usual grouping is the extended family, such as this one from a Greek fishing village. Why?

may be either a **nuclear** or an **extended family**. The nuclear family is made up of a father, mother, and their children. It is the usual type of family unit found in industrialized **urban** areas. An extended family includes close relatives or perhaps another nuclear family. Such a family might include grandparents, aunts, uncles, and cousins. This type of family is quite common in Asia and Africa. It is also found in many **rural** areas of the world.

Everyone is related to someone. This relationship is called **kinship**. A person usually is part of both a nuclear family and an extended family. Kinship has been and still is very important in many cultural groups. Members of societies regulate their behavior according to their kinship to others.

Some societies have traditionally large kinship systems that include all those who are descended from a common ancestor. Those who trace their line of descent from one or both sides of the family—mother and/or father—make up a **lineage**. Sometimes several families claiming an often remote, perhaps even **mythical**, common ancestor will form a **clan**. The clan system was once very important in China. Lineage and clans are still important for many Africans.

These various kinship groupings influence the behavior patterns of their members in many ways. For instance, within some cultures the members of a family, lineage, or clan may marry only someone from outside the group.

Families live in households. When larger numbers of people cluster together they are said to live in villages. Not everyone lives a settled way of life. Some people are nomads. They wander from place to place usually looking for grasslands for their herds. Such groups are called bands.

Many bands and villages may occupy the same **territory**. When they share a similar culture they are known as **tribes**. The term tribe has taken on a negative or misleading meaning in recent years. For

Villages are composed of many families. They may be either nuclear or extended families. This is a village in the Cotswold Hills, England.

that reason, we prefer to refer to this larger grouping as a **people**. If more than one grouping, we call them peoples. Groups of peoples may organize themselves into a larger political, economic, and social unit defined by territorial boundaries. This is called a nation or country.

Another common term in anthropology is **society**. Any group of people who have a shared culture and identity are known as a society. Generally the group also occupies the same territory. The size of the group does not matter. An isolated village, a small band of nomads, or a nation of millions can be a society. When speaking of nations, however, one must be very careful.

origin: beginnings

Some nations in the world are made up of people who share a common tradition, language, and origin—a common culture. Such countries are said to have a single society. England is an example. Other nations contain many societies within their geographic borders. For example, the Soviet Union has over 100 different societies.

THE MEANING OF RACE

Race is a term that has been misused so frequently that its real meaning is lost to most people. Race is not based upon religion, language, or any other cultural concept. These are learned characteristics of a people. And it is not based upon the intelligence of a particular group of people. Nor is race based upon the myth of a pure blood line.

To anthropologists, race is a biological concept. All organisms of the same species, whether animals or plants, have the same basic form. For example, all members of the human species, Homo sapiens sapiens (HOH-moh SAP-ee-uhns SAP-ee-uhns) have two eyes, two ears, two hands, and two feet. Male and female organisms of the same species can reproduce.

But there are differences within species. Birds of the same species may differ in color, and each bird has a slightly different size or shape. There are also differences among people. Eye and skin color, shape of skull, hair texture, and nose shapes may vary among individuals and among groups.

Many anthropologists think of race as an interbreeding population of persons who share a common **gene pool** and who marry only others of the same group. Their skin color, hair texture, or eye color varies from that of other populations. However, they remain relatively the same for the population over long periods of time. To achieve this result, populations must be isolated from each other to a degree.

Some anthropologists use a classification of races which distinguish human populations according to geography. Interbreeding is the basis of this concept. A geographical race includes populations that are isolated from other populations by natural barriers such as water, mountains, or deserts. For example, Asians are a geographical race. They are separated from other populations by great barriers of desert, mountains, and water. Africans south of the Sahara Desert are considered a geographical race.

Anthropologists do not agree on the number of races because human beings do not fit into exact categories. All people are similar in some ways and different in other ways. But scientists agree that every race belongs to the same species—Homo sapiens sapiens.

EARLY INHABITANTS OF EARTH

There is still much mystery about the **hominids**—humanlike creatures —who lived in the prehistoric period. Time and decay have destroyed most of the bones and artifacts that anthropologists need to reconstruct the beings and cultures of the past. They are forced to develop theories based on evidence which is often scanty. This is especially true of very ancient times. Anthropologists are like detectives who arrive at conclusions from a few clues. Later evidence may prove them right or wrong.

Therefore, anthropologists—especially those working in the prehistoric period—must keep an open mind. Their accounts of prehistoric life are always subject to change and modification. Their conclusions are based on the current amount of knowledge in their fields. What is said here is the generally accepted theory of anthropologists at present. Future discoveries may change these ideas.

Anthropologists place the hominids under a genus called Australopithecus (aw-STRAY-loh-pith-uh-kuhs). Fossils of two species of these beings were found in eastern and southern Africa. One species of Australopithecus was large and appears to have walked upright. The other species was small and slender. This being apparently walked and hunted on two legs, and possibly used pebble tools.

At Olduvai (OHL-duh-way) Gorge in Tanzania, Dr. Louis S. B. Leakey and Mary Leakey, found fossil remains of a being they called Homo habilis (HAB-uh-luhs), skillful one. Some simple pebble tools were found with the fossil remains which are believed to be between one million and 1.8 million years old.

Since the discovery of Homo habilis, other creatures have been found that may push the origins of humans even farther back in time. In 1972 Richard E. Leakey—son of the Homo habilis discoverers—found in Kenya fossil fragments of a being between 2.6 and 2.8 million years old. It is called 1470 skull.

Two years later, Dr. Donald C. Johanson discovered remains of humanlike creatures in the Awash (AH-wahsh) Valley of north-central Ethiopia which are possibly three million years old. The following year, 1975, while working in Tanzania, Mary Leakey uncovered

One of the most famous physical anthropologists is Dr. Louis S. B. Leakey. Here he is shown in Olduvai Gorge, Tanzania, the site of his and Mary Leakey's most startling finds. Why is their work considered to be theory?

humanlike fossils which are even older. Her finds date back from 3.35 million to 3.75 million years.

Scientists do not agree on whether these recent finds are of the genus Homo or advanced forms of Australopithecus. If they are determined to be true Homo, they will push the origins of humans back to well over three million years ago.

HUMANS Anthropologists generally place two species within the genus called Homo. One is known as **Homo erectus** (uh-REK-tus), upright person. Specimens of Homo erectus have been found in Africa, Europe, and Asia. Among the most widely known of these specimens are the Java forms found in Indonesia and the Peking forms found near Peking, China. The Java people may go back 700,000 years. The Peking people are believed to have lived around 400,000 years ago.

Homo erectus walked upright. At least some among this species knew how to use fire. They made crude stone tools. From the distances that separated their fossil sites it appears that they covered thousands of kilometers in their wanderings.

The other species is called **Homo sapiens**. Sapiens means wise or intelligent. Several early types of Homo sapiens have been uncovered throughout the world. Probably the best known is **Neanderthal** (nee-AN-der-tahl). The first skeleton discovered was found in the Neander Gorge in Germany in the 1850s. Since that time a number of other Neanderthal remains have been found in Europe, Asia, the Middle East, and Africa. Neanderthal people lived as early as 100,000 years ago. They used fire. Around 30,000 years ago, they vanished. No one knows why.

About 40,000 years ago, humans appeared that looked much like the people of today. They were called **Cro-Magnon** (kroh-MAG-nuhn) after the place in southern France where their remains were first found. Cro-Magnon tools were improvements over earlier ones. Spear throwers for hunting and sewing needles were developed. The

By the time the type Cro-Magnon had developed, about 40,000 years ago, artwork began to appear. Anthropologists theorize that the art may have been connected with a ritual or religious ceremony asking for good luck on the hunt. Above is a molded clay figure of a bison found in France. Below are cave paintings. The one on the left shows bison, and the one on the right is of oxen. The latter are part of the famous paintings at Lascaux, France.

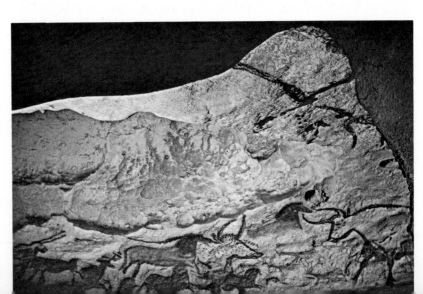

spear thrower enabled hunters to hurl spears farther and with greater force than simple throwing would have done. Cro-Magnon people buried their dead with ceremony.

Pictures of animals painted by Cro-Magnon people have been found on the walls of caves in Spain and France. These paintings may have been part of a magic **ritual** used to bring good luck to hunters. Cro-Magnon people made clay figures and used heat to bake and harden them. The figures were of animals as well as people. Animal statues were also carved from bone and reindeer antlers. One of the oldest known musical instruments is a bone flute or whistle dating from Cro-Magnon times.

Cro-Magnon and later varieties of Homo sapiens multiplied and spread. Today Homo sapiens sapiens, the type we call ourselves, dominates this planet.

DATING PREHISTORIC REMAINS　　One of the greatest problems in archaeology is deciding the age of remains and the cultures they represent. About 1949, **radiocarbon dating** began to be used for this purpose. The method worked fairly well. But it was based on the assumption that the amount of radiocarbon in the atmosphere had always remained constant.

In the 1960s this assumption was found to be false. By dating the growth rings of the bristlecone pine—a tree that reaches an age of over 4,000 years—scientists learned that radiocarbon in the earth's atmosphere has varied throughout time. Discoveries dating to before the 1200s B.C. had to be extended earlier into time. Tree-ring dating—called dendrochronology (den-droh-kruh-NAHL-uh-jee)—is not completely accurate. However, when matched with radiocarbon dating, it is possible to narrow dates to a range of one or two hundred years. When dealing with a span of thousands of years, this is helpful.

The new dating has had an important effect on anthropology. It has upset theories about the development and spread of older cultures in prehistory, especially European cultures. The change has been so recent that anthropologists are still not in agreement about many dates and about certain cultural developments.

As a result, it is likely that years may go by before a clearer picture of prehistory emerges. It is also likely that other and perhaps more accurate methods of dating will be developed.

STAGES OF CULTURE

Anthropologists describe the cultural development of early prehistoric people according to the type of tools used. The **Stone Age**, when all tools were made of stone, is divided into three stages.

Archaeologists are detectives of a kind. They fit together pieces of pottery like these Israeli amphorae or jars.

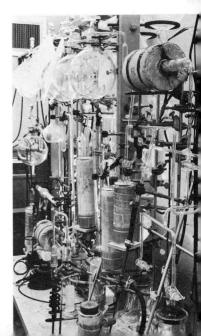

Archaeologists can date objects by using such methods as dendrochronology and carbon-14. This is a radiocarbon-dating laboratory.

This cave painting of a horse was found in France. Does its appearance differ in any way from horses today? Horses were first domesticated during the New Stone Age, when people began to grow crops. Why do you think people domesticated horses? How might they have done it?

During the oldest stage, called Paleolithic or **Old Stone Age**, the simplest forms of pebble tools were used. These have a few large flakes or chips knocked off one side to form a crude cutting edge. Pebble tools have been dated to two million years ago. The earliest evidence of the use of fire—in China—dates to between 400,000 and 500,000 or more years ago. A stone hand ax was also developed.

Around the middle of the Old Stone Age, the quality and variety of stone tools advanced. Some groups of early people built rock shelters and apparently began the ceremonial burying of their dead. Neanderthals lived in this period. They had improved weapons for hunting, scrapers for cleaning animal skins, and better methods for making stone tools. Offerings found in their graves indicate some belief in life after death.

Toward the end of the Old Stone Age, many cultural advances were made by the Cro-Magnon people. A number of their skills were mentioned earlier. In addition, they probably had a system of social grouping. Old Stone Age people hunted wild game and gathered some food. Their tools and weapons for hunting improved with time.

The second stage, called Mesolithic or the **Middle Stone Age**, began as the last great Ice Age came to an end, about 12,000 years ago. People gradually became more dependent upon plant gathering for food. They added wild grain to their diet of fish and wild game. The bow and arrow was developed during this period. Groups of people began to stay longer in an area.

This is a Neolithic or New Stone Age tool-sharpener. The label Stone Age means that all the tools of the period were stone. How would a hunter sharpen a stone tool on another stone? Would the edge be very sharp?

During the third stage, called Neolithic or the **New Stone Age**, people began to grow crops and to **domesticate** cattle, horses, and sheep. Among the earliest grains grown in various parts of the world were millet, wheat, rice, corn (maize), and barley. Other crops included peas, beans, potatoes, and squash. Agriculture as a way of life made it important to know the seasons. It was later during the New Stone Age that calendars were developed. People also began to make pottery and weave baskets, reed mats, and fishing nets. They also wove cloth from wool, flax, or cotton on handlooms. Generally speaking, the New Stone Age ended with the discovery of metalworking. The **Copper Age** began.

Around 5000 B.C. people were smelting and making copper, silver, and gold into ornaments and weapons in eastern and central Europe, the Middle East, and perhaps in other parts of the world. The **Bronze Age** began about 3000 B.C. with the making of bronze from a mixture of copper and tin. Bronze was harder and stronger than copper and made better weapons. Whenever people learned to make iron, the **Iron Age** of their culture began. The people of Asia Minor, in what we today call Turkey, probably began their Iron Age around 1000 B.C.

A word of caution is necessary. When speaking about the various stages of cultural development, we are really considering stages in the development of each culture. Not all groups of people arrived at the same cultural stage at the same time. For example, the Eskimos did not use metal until it was introduced by Europeans. In the early 1970s a Stone-Age people were found living in the Philippines. The stages in cultural development listed here describe the way of life of a particular people at a given time. They are not precise historical or calendar periods for the world as a whole.

Numerous reasons explain why all cultures did not reach the same stage of development at the same time. **Climate**, soil type, and water supply affect the growing of crops. Food supply affects the number of people an area can support, which affects the economic capacity of the area. Geographical features—such as mountains, plains, valleys, and location, for example, near a sea or navigable river—may help determine contacts with other cultures. **Natural resources**—mineral deposits, fur-bearing animals, forests—influence trade and therefore culture. Relations with neighbors affect cultural development.

FARMING Exactly how people made the change from food gathering to farming is not known. Perhaps a group of hunter-gatherers stayed in one place to guard a patch of wild grain until it was ready to be harvested. They may have remained after the harvest which

---

Different cultures entered the various metal ages at different times. Some areas skipped periods. Africa as a whole, for example, never had a bronze age. The copper scoop is from Latin America and the iron pot, from Western Europe.

could have yielded enough food to feed a small group for a year. Perhaps they supplemented the grain and game by gathering wild fruits and berries and by fishing.

At some time a few seeds of the harvested wild grain may have fallen into favorable soil in or near the semipermanent camp. Grain may have grown. In time these early people noticed that grain grew where the seeds had fallen. The hunters may have scattered some seeds and then more and more and more each year. The change would have been gradual. Hunting and gathering may have continued for a time along with farming. Early cultivation was done by using pointed sticks to loosen the soil. Grain was harvested first by hand, later with knives or sickles made of flint, a stone.

The lives of some nomadic hunter-gatherers changed. Some settled in permanent camps. In the Old Stone Age hunters built huts of branches and lean-to shelters. Dwellings now became more permanent.

Improvements in tools occurred simultaneously with changes in methods of living. Farming first brought about improved stone and wooden tools and then metal ones such as these bronze sickles. Below is a painting from an Egyptian tomb showing farmers breaking ground, sowing and plowing.

Because life was easier for the farmers, the population increased. A piece of land can support a limited number of people. When an area became crowded, groups would break away and settle in another place. Every 10 or 15 years a whole settlement would need to shift its location as the soil became less fertile from constant use.

With the growing of crops came the domestication of various animals. The dog was the first animal to be tamed. This took place among the hunting people in northern Europe, long before the first farmers. The horse was domesticated in Central Asia. Sheep and goats were domesticated in the Middle East about 9000 B.C. and cattle in Greece about 6500 B.C. When archaeologists study a site, they can tell whether the bones they find are those of wild or domesticated

With farming and a settled way of life the making of pottery developed. Here an archaeologist fits together pottery shards or fragments. What can pottery tell archaeologists about a culture?

animals. Changes take place in the structure of bones and horns when animals are domesticated.

In farming villages there was no need for a daily hunt for food. This allowed time for other things. **Crafts** and the arts developed. The making of statues and ornaments increased. Pottery making became important. More and bigger vessels were needed to store grain and water and for cooking. As pottery making developed, pottery was fired in ovens. Ovens were also used for baking bread. Each culture developed its own style of pottery. The shape and decoration of pottery is one of the ways archaeologists identify a culture.

GEOGRAPHY AND THE STUDY OF CULTURES

The way a people's culture grows is affected by geography. Geography is more than the study of physical characteristics of the land. It is also the study of how these characteristics influence people and are changed by people.

Cultural geography divides the earth into regions on the basis of similar history, race, language, and way of life of its people. The culture area is studied in relation to its location on earth, its climate, and natural features. Cultural geography also includes economic and social aspects of the environment. In this study people and how they use their environment are most important.

Also important to the development of any region is its closeness to water—rivers and oceans. Rivers provide water for drinking, irrigation, and power. They provide cheap transportation for people and goods. As a result, some of the oldest known **cities** and **towns** were located along rivers. Cities have also developed where two different geographical areas come together. Such an example is a river valley. There people were able to grow food on the fertile land and then transport it down the river.

A balance of suitable land, climate, and water is found only in small areas of the world. Huge sections of the world are underpopulated. Where the environment is harsh and lacks some of these basics, the people do not develop so rapidly. They generally have a low **standard of living**.

The industrialization of a nation depends in part on its geography. Sources of power and transportation and a supply of natural resources are necessary.

Political affairs are also influenced by geography. Natural barriers such as mountains and oceans can protect a country from invasion. **Overpopulation** or shortages of food or resources have been used by leaders to justify expanding their territory. In the event of war, the terrain and climate of a region can prove an ally or an enemy. Geographical conditions may also influence **international alliances**. National boundaries have long been a source of friction and tension.

Geography often determines where people settle. Many cities have grown up on rivers, along seacoasts, or where rivers and oceans meet. Why? This is Neuburg, West Germany, on the Danube.

CIVILIZATION AND CITIES

Many anthropologists avoid the terms **civilization** or civilized when referring to cultures or peoples. If they do use the term civilization they intend to describe a very complex level of cultural development. Such a development would include the following factors: (1) a food-producing base which makes possible a high population density; (2) increasing **centralization** of political and religious authority; (3) monumental buildings; and often, but not always, (4) the development of writing and written records. Other factors may be added, but are not essential. They would include development of arts and advanced manufacturing techniques.

Large cities are not self-sufficient. They have to rely on trade for materials they do not grow or make. This is a market in a Romanian city.

There is a close relationship between the words civilization and city. Both words come from the same root Latin word civis meaning inhabitant of a city. The word city can be traced even farther back in time to a Greek word that can be broadly translated "to settle down in." Where people settled down, towns developed. Some towns grew into cities and civilizations developed.

Perhaps the most important fact about early towns and cities is that they required a highly organized social life. Many people have to work together in order to build a town or city. Specialists are needed to build houses, to undertake public works such as sewer systems, to manufacture goods, to carry on trade, and to protect the citizens against enemies. Cities require a food supply. This can be obtained by local agriculture or through trade.

Urban life requires government. A means of regulating social life is needed so that many people can live and work together. The administration of city governments in ancient times, as in modern times, required the keeping of records. This may have been the origin of writing. And with the use of written records, history begins.

These few pages have taken you from stone tools to sophisticated trade networks. Would our culture be possible without writing? This is an example of one of the earliest forms of writing—Egyptian hieroglyphics.

21

Summing Up the Unit

Social Studies Vocabulary

Define: anthropology; archaeology; linguistics; prehistoric; artifacts; site; culture traits; culture region; cultural diffusion; traditional; language families; lineage; clan; peoples; gene pool; hominids; Homo sapiens; radiocarbon dating; Stone Age; Copper Age; Bronze Age; Iron Age; B.C.

Names

Identify: Indo-European; Cro-Magnon

Words

Define: dig; acculturation; geographical race; interbreeding; dendrochronology

⌐ Questions

1. a. What do physical anthropologists study? b. What do cultural anthropologists study?
2. a. To an anthropologist, what is the meaning of the term culture? b. Why don't anthropologists think of some people as being more cultured than others?
3. How are languages identified as being members of a language family?
4. What is the difference between a nuclear and an extended family?
5. What is a single society?
6. Why are kinship groupings important?
7. Why is race regarded not as a cultural or social concept but as a biological concept?
8. Why must people keep open minds about anthropologists' theories about the origins of people?
9. a. When did what anthropologists call the earliest Homo sapiens live? b. Where have their remains been found?
10. What marks the end of the New Stone Age?
11. a. Did all groups of people arrive at the same cultural stage at the same time? b. Why or why not?
12. As people became farmers and village life developed, in what ways was life changed?
13. a. Name three areas of life in which the geography of a region plays an important role. b. Why did most cities and towns develop near water?

14. When the term civilization is used, what factors are often included?
15. How can a city obtain a food supply to feed its population?

Discussion Topics

1. Anthropology is divided into several branches. How can each contribute to our understanding of present-day humanity?
2. People who do not read and write pass their culture along by word of mouth. This body of knowledge is called oral tradition. What might be some advantages and disadvantages of writing as a means of transmitting a culture from one generation to another?
3. The physical characteristics of a culture region affect the ways in which its people make a living, but so do the skills and attitudes of the people themselves. Which do you think are more important in shaping the development of a region: natural resources or human resources?
4. The extended family is found most often in rural areas. Why is it found less often in cities? What might urban people gain or lose by not being part of an extended family?

Project Ideas

1. Using reference materials, compile a report on one of the following: discoveries of the Leakey family in Africa; the Tasaday people of the Philippines; Neanderthal people; Cro-Magnon people.
2. Make an illustrated time chart showing the stages of human development and the lengths of time that elapsed in each stage.
3. Using illustrations from magazines or your own drawings, make a poster showing the achievements of humans in each of the Stone Ages.
4. Using an atlas or encyclopedia for reference, draw a population distribution map for one of the culture regions in the text. Include the major rivers and mountains that are on the physical map in the text for that region. Form a general statement about the relationship of population to geographical features within the region.

For Further Study

General Readings

1. *Adventures with the Missing Link* by Raymond A. Dart. Houghton Mifflin Company, 1972. Paperback. Dart startled the world in the 1920s with his finds of Australopithecine.

2. *African Genesis* by Robert Ardrey. Atheneum Publishers, 1961. Examines scientific evidence about the origins of humans and advances the author's own theory. Clear, interesting style.

3. *Ancient Ruins and Archaeology* by L. Sprague de Camp and Catherine C. de Camp. Doubleday & Co., Inc., 1964. About ruins and the legends surrounding them.

4. *Archaeology* by Walter Shepherd. New American Library, Inc., 1966. Paperback. Describes the methods and findings of archaeologists and sites of ancient civilizations. Illustrated.

5. *Archaeology* ed. by Samuel Rapport and Helen Wright, Washington Square Press, 1968. Paperback. Various distinguished archaeologists discuss their techniques and discoveries.

6. *The Ascent of Man* by Jacob Bronowski. Little, Brown and Company, 1973. A history of science, developed from the author's BBC television series. Focuses on people's ability to understand nature and to control it by means of inventions. Highly readable.

7. *Back of History: The Story of Our Own Origins* by William W. Howells. Doubleday & Co., Inc., 1954. Paperback. An informal and readable account of human prehistory.

8. *The Birth of Civilizations* ed. by Paul Thomas Welty. J. B. Lippincott Company, 1973. Readings on development of the human species and civilization. Inquiry format.

9. *Everyday Life in Prehistoric Times* by Marjorie C. Quennell and Charles H. B. Quennell. G. P. Putnam's Sons, rev. ed., 1959. A detailed description of how prehistoric people lived.

10. *Gods, Graves, and Scholars: The Story of Archaeology* by C. W. Ceram. Bantam Books, Inc., 2nd rev. ed., 1972. Paperback. Archaeologists, their work, and scientific methods. Reviews archaeological discoveries in Egypt, Greece, Italy, Mexico, and Central America.

11. *Invitation to Anthropology* by Douglas L. Oliver. Natural History Press, 1964. Paperback. Explains the fundamentals of anthropology.

12. *On the Track of Prehistoric Man* by Herbert Kuhn. Random House, Inc., 1955. Paperback. Discusses the famous caves in France and Spain—their physical features, discovery, and later history.

13. *Man's Way: From Cave to Skyscraper* by Ralph Linton and Adelin Linton. Harper & Row Publishers, 1947. Uses anthropological findings to show how human culture has changed with new ways of making a living. Easy reading.

14. *People and Places* by Margaret Mead. World Publishing Company, 1972. The author is a cultural anthropologist.

15. *Prehistoric Men* by Robert J. Braidwood. Scott, Foresman & Co., 8th edition, 1975. Paperback. A short, clear survey and introduction to the study of ancient and primitive human-kind.

Fiction

The Caves of the Great Hunters by Hans Baumann. Pantheon Books, Inc., rev. ed., 1962. Story of the discovery of the Lascaux Cave and other caves in France and Spain.

Pictorial History

1. *Cro-Magnon Man* by Tom Prideaux. (*The Emergence of Man* Series) Time-Life Books, Div. of Time, Inc., 1973. Beautifully illustrated, readable, informative text.

2. *Early Man* by F. Clark Howell. (Life *Nature Library* Series) Time-Life Books, Div. of Time, Inc., rev. ed. 1973.

3. *The First Farmers* by Jonathan N. Leonard. (*The Emergence of Man* Series) Time-Life Books, Div. of Time, Inc., 1973.

4. *The March of Archaeology* by C. W. Ceram. Alfred A. Knopf, Inc., 1970. Paperback. Superb text. Illustrated.

5. *The Wonderful World of Archaeology* by Ronald F. Jessup. Doubleday & Co., Inc., 1956. Explains archaeologists' work, difficulties, and accomplishments. Illustrated.

The Middle Easterners

Archaeologists learn about peoples from many different sources. One of the most important sources for students of ancient Egypt is its tombs. This tomb painting shows Nakt, a priest to the pharaoh Thutmose IV in the 1400s B.C., and his family. The scene on the right shows Nakt with a boomerang. On the left he is about to spear a fish, but the artist never finished painting.

Unit I

The Land and Early People

Most of Libya is part of the Sahara Desert. How much of the Middle East is desert? What physical features explain this fact?

The Middle East is sometimes called the Near East, Mideast, or Southwest Asia. **Geographically** it extends from Afghanistan in the east to the Mediterranean Sea in the west. To the north are the Black and Caspian seas, to the south, the Gulf of Aden and the Arabian Sea.

Because we are discussing regions culturally rather than geographically, we are including in this section on the Middle East the North African countries of Morocco, Tunisia, Libya, and Algeria. Their peoples are predominantly Muslim. These **nations** stretch across the top of Africa from the Atlantic Ocean in the west to Egypt in the east. The Sahara Desert borders them on the south and the Mediterranean Sea on the north.

Geographically Egypt too is part of Africa. Originally it was African in **culture**. Since the 700s A.D., however, it has been closer to the Islamic culture of the Middle East than to the African culture of its southern neighbors. Today, because of its Muslim religious and cultural ties, Egypt is considered a Middle Eastern nation.

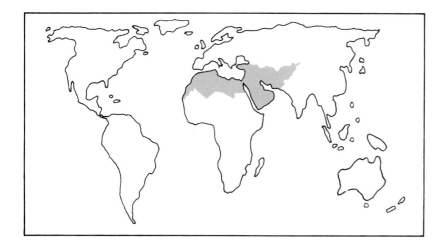

The largest single land feature of the Middle East is the Arabian **Peninsula**. Millions of years ago the area was completely attached to the African continent. But a weakness in the earth's crust caused a part to split from Africa. This section became a peninsula—land that is almost surrounded by water. The resulting rift or crack filled with water. What we now call the Red Sea and the Gulf of Aden were created. Today the artificially-made Suez Canal cuts through the remaining tip of land. It joins the Red Sea to the Mediterranean.

The nations of the Arabian Peninsula are: Kuwait, Oman, Qatar, Saudi Arabia, United Arab Emirates, People's Democratic Republic of Yemen (Yemen), and the Yemen Arab Republic (South Yemen). The island-nation of Bahrain lies off the peninsula in the Persian Gulf. To the north are Jordan and Iraq. On the west and north Israel, Lebanon, Syria, Turkey, and Egypt border the peninsula.

East of the peninsula is Iran—once known as Persia. It lies between the Persian Gulf and the Gulf of Oman on the south and the Caspian Sea and the Union of Soviet Socialist Republics on the north. Next to Iran is Afghanistan, the easternmost country of the Middle East. Afghanistan is landlocked.

STEPPES AND DESERTS

Parts of Turkey, Iran, and some mountain and coastal areas, especially in Syria, Lebanon, and Israel, receive large amounts of rain. The north and west coasts of Turkey receive the most rain. Little, if any, rain falls over great parts of Egypt, the Arabian Peninsula, Iraq, and the North African nations. Mountain ranges along the coast stop the rain-bearing winds that blow in from the seas. The area between the mountains and the seas receive the most rainfall. The vast stretches behind the mountains are very dry. For this reason most North

Chapter 1
The
Environment

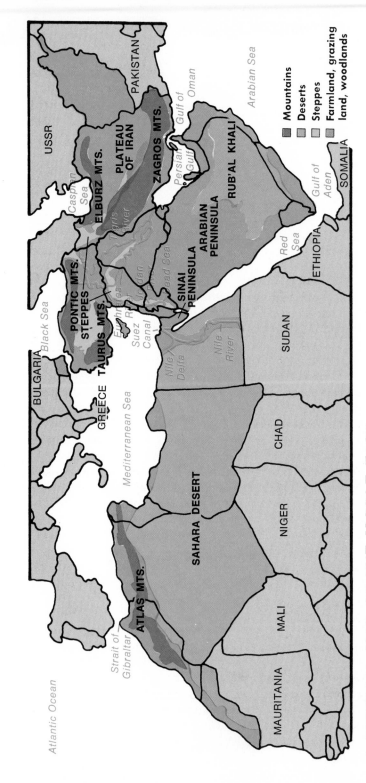

A PHYSICAL MAP OF THE MIDDLE EAST

Mountains
Deserts
Steppes
Farmland, grazing
land, woodlands

Atlantic Ocean

Strait of Gibraltar

MAURITANIA

MALI

NIGER

CHAD

SUDAN

ATLAS MTS.

SAHARA DESERT

Mediterranean Sea

Nile Delta

Nile River

ETHIOPIA

SOMALIA

Gulf of Aden

Red Sea

Arabian Sea

RUB'AL KHALI

ARABIAN PENINSULA

SINAI PENINSULA

Suez Canal

Euphrates River

Jordan R.

Dead Sea

Tigris River

Persian Gulf

Gulf of Oman

ZAGROS MTS.

PLATEAU OF IRAN

ELBURZ MTS.

Caspian Sea

PAKISTAN

USSR

BULGARIA

Black Sea

GREECE

PONTIC MTS.

STEPPES

TAURUS MTS.

28

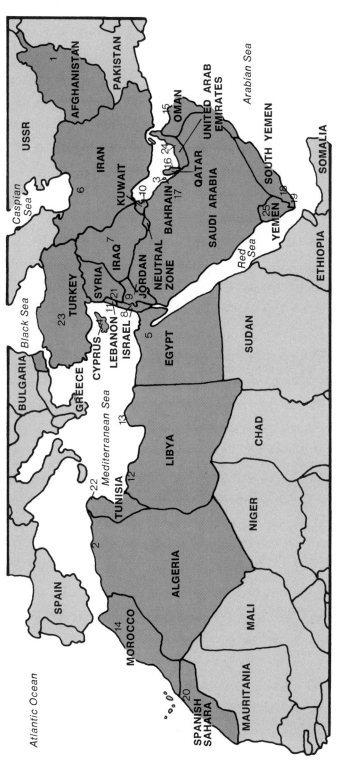

A POLITICAL MAP OF THE MIDDLE EAST

Capitals:

1. Kabul
2. Algiers
3. Manama
4. Nicosia
5. Cairo
6. Tehran
7. Baghdad
8. Jerusalem
9. Amman
10. Kuwait
11. Beirut
12. Tripoli
13. Bengasi
14. Rabat
15. Masqat
16. Doha
17. Riyadh
18. Aden
19. Madinat ash Sha'b
20. El Aiun
21. Damascus
22. Tunis
23. Ankara
24. Abu Zaby
25. Sana

29

Turkey's borders are mostly mountainous. This area is near the western border. Using the map on page 28 as reference, what is to the west of these mountains?

Africans live on a narrow ribbon of land between the mountains and the Mediterranean.

Because of the dryness there are vast stretches of steppe and desert. In the steppe area enough rain falls for some grasses and trees to grow. Nomads—wandering herders—roam the steppes with their camels, sheep, and goats. The best steppe lands are in Turkey, Iran, Afghanistan, Syria, Jordan, and Iraq.

The Middle East has some of the most barren deserts in the world. The Rub'al Khali (rub-al KAHL-ee) in southern Saudi Arabia is often called the empty quarter. Little life exists there. Other deserts lie in central Iran, northern Saudi Arabia, and on the Sinai (SY-ny) Peninsula, which is located at the northern end of the Red Sea. Part of the Sahara, the largest desert in the world, stretches across Egypt and the other North African countries.

Until recently most of Egypt was desert. An exception was the narrow Nile Valley. In 1960 Egypt began a program of dam construction on the Nile. After the Aswan High Dam was completed in 1968, the Nile Valley was widened. An additional 800,000 hectares (about two million acres) of desert were opened to farming.

MOUNTAINS AND PLATEAUS

Beginning on the Afghanistan-Iran border and zigzagging west, the Elburz and Pontic mountains run along the northern borders of Iran and Turkey. On the higher slopes are forests. Strung between some of the mountains are plateaus. Much of Turkey and Iran is plateau. Along the southern and western borders of Iran are the Zagros Mountains. In ancient times, passes in Iran's mountains provided invasion routes into the Middle East from the north and east.

Smaller mountains run through Jordan, Israel, Lebanon, and Syria. Southeast of these, along the western edge of the Arabian Peninsula, is a highland region. Where the highlands meet the sea along the western coast, steep cliffs have been formed. To the east of the highlands is a plateau that slopes gradually to the Persian Gulf. The Atlas Mountains cut across parts of North Africa.

RIVERS

The major rivers of the Middle East are the Tigris, Euphrates (yu-FRAYT-ees), and Nile. For many centuries, Middle Easterners have used these rivers to irrigate their fields and ship their goods.

The Tigris and Euphrates rivers begin in the mountains of Turkey. They flow southeast through Syria and Iraq. Before they empty into the Persian Gulf, the two rivers join to form one large waterway. Through the centuries these rivers have often overflowed their banks. As the floodwaters recede, they leave deposits of rich soil on the lands along the rivers. The Greeks named the whole area washed by the rivers Mesopotamia (mes-uh-puh-TAY-mee-uh). This means land between the rivers.

The land between the rivers and the green land bordering the Mediterranean are often called the Fertile Crescent. When pictured on a map, the area looks like the curved shape of a new moon. This region is the home of the earliest **civilization** for which we have written records. Today the area lies in parts of Iran, Iraq, Syria, Turkey, Lebanon, Jordan, and Israel.

The Nile River, which flows north from deep in Africa to the Mediterranean, is vital to the Egyptians. It is the central crop-producing area in the country. Once the Nile regularly overflowed its banks. This left rich soil deposits on the lands bordering it. Where the river enters the sea, these deposits formed a triangle of fertile land called the Nile Delta.

In ancient times, the Fertile Crescent and the Nile River Delta were the two most fertile areas in the Middle East. Today much of the Crescent has been made unproductive by the invasion of salt water. The Delta, however, continues to have some of the best farmland.

■ **Fertile Crescent**

The Jordan is another important Middle Eastern river. It flows southward between Jordan and Israel and empties into the Dead Sea. The river forms part of the border between Jordan and Israel.

AGRICULTURE

About three-fourths of the people of the Middle East earn their living by some form of agriculture. However, as much as 90 percent of the land cannot be farmed. The people struggle to produce what they can on the remaining 10 percent. The Nile Valley and Delta and the Fertile Crescent are good farmland. Farming is possible in parts of Turkey and Iran and along the coastal regions of the Black and Mediterranean seas. In North Africa the land is worked in areas where farmers can use underground water sources for irrigation. But much of this land is covered with rocks.

Among the items grown are wheat, barley, rice, rye, corn, and dates. Most of the world's dates come from Iraq. Iran and Afghanistan grow melons and other fruits. Olive groves are part of the landscapes of Turkey, Lebanon, and Syria. Figs, peaches, and citrus fruits are grown along the eastern Mediterranean.

Middle Easterners also raise animals. Camels—the carriers of the desert—are still needed for transportation despite the increasing use of cars, trucks, and planes. When camels have outlived their usefulness as beasts of burden, they are killed and eaten as food. Their hides are made into tent covers. Sheep and goats, however, are the main sources of meat for Middle Easterners. Their hair is spun into yarn and woven into cloth. Their skins are made into coats and other articles of leather.

Although the nomadic way of life is disappearing, many Middle Easterners are still herders. Here a goatherd watches over his flock.

The major source of income in the Middle East today is oil. This is a refinery at Port el-Ahmadi, Kuwait. What other countries in the Middle East have large oil reserves? How are they using the income from oil?

MINERAL RESOURCES

Almost two-thirds of the known oil reserves of the world are in the Middle East. The growing world energy crisis has called attention to the new economic and political importance of these countries. The major oil-producing countries are Saudi Arabia, Iran, Kuwait, and Iraq. They are grouped around the Persian Gulf and on the Arabian Peninsula. Algeria and Libya in North Africa also have oil. Libyan oil is especially valuable because of its low sulphur content. This clean-burning oil is important in keeping down air pollution.

Egypt, Turkey, and Iran have some coal deposits. In general, however, the nations of the Middle East lack large amounts of minerals other than oil. The area did have large deposits of copper and tin. But these deposits have been exploited for thousands of years and are almost gone.

The **peoples** of the Middle East are a product of the blending of peoples from Europe, Asia, and Africa. From very early times, migrants and conquerors crisscrossed the area. Peoples from Europe passed back and forth across the Mediterranean Sea. Peoples from Asia and Africa used the Middle East as a **land bridge**.

LANGUAGES

We can tell something about the **history** of these people by studying their **languages**. As people move, they carry their language with them. When they conquer other peoples, they often force the conquered to use their language. But the conquerors often take words from the

Chapter 2
Wanderers
and Settlers

language of the conquered. **Linguists** can tell us about the movement of a people by studying how one language is related to another. Several major **language families** have thus been identified in the Middle East: Afro-Asian, Ural-Altaic, and Indo-European.

Most Middle Eastern languages belong to one of two groups within the Afro-Asian family: Semitic and Cushitic. Semitic languages include Arabic, Ethiopic, Aramaic, and Canaanite. These groups may be further subdivided. Canaanite, for example, includes Hebrew and Phoenician. The Cushitic group includes languages spoken in parts of North Africa.

A language family does not necessarily represent a **gene pool**. A common gene pool means that members of a group of people share physical characteristics like blood type. Language is part of a people's culture. Arabic is the chief language spoken in the Middle East today. But many different culture groups speak it. The Arabic language has become a key link in the concept of Arab unity. To identify as an Arab usually means to speak Arabic, to practice the Islamic **religion**, and to want to be part of the Arab community.

In Israel the national language is Hebrew, a Semitic language. Hebrew was spoken by an ancient people who were among the ancestors of modern Jews. The modern Jewish people, however, are of many cultures. This is a result of the many centuries that Jews lived away from the Middle East. Modern Jews hold their religion in common, but not necessarily their languages or nonreligious **customs** and **traditions**.

In the Middle East today there are several non-Arabic-speaking groups. The Turks speak a branch of the Ural-Altaic language. Ural-Altaic languages are spoken across Central Asia as far east as China. Iranians speak Persian, an Indo-European language. Indo-European languages are also spoken throughout Europe and in India.

EARLY PEOPLES

No remains of any beings up to and including **Homo erectus** have been found in the Middle East. But **archaeologists** have uncovered there **artifacts** of the kind Homo erectus used in other parts of the world. Archaeologists believe, therefore, that Homo erectus at least traveled through the area, possibly coming up from Africa. With more digging, however, Homo erectus skeletons may be found.

In Israel and Iraq **Neanderthal** remains have been found. Archaeologists are especially interested in the fossils discovered on Mt. Carmel in Israel. The remains of 11 individuals have been unearthed. **Anthropologists** have carefully examined and analyzed the physical features of these so-called Skulh people. Some experts believe that the Skulhs show a direct line of descent from Neanderthal to Homo sapiens sapiens. The skeletons seem to have physical features of both

Neanderthal and **Cro-Magnon** people. Other experts are not so sure.

In any event, by 25,000 B.C. people of the Cro-Magnon type were living throughout the Middle East. Cro-Magnon **sites** have been found around the Mediterranean from Egypt to Turkey. No sites have been found yet in Saudi Arabia.

JERICHO

Some of the world's oldest **towns** have been found in the Middle East. The oldest settlement so far discovered has been named Jericho (JER-ih-koh). It is near the modern **village** of Jericho, north of the Dead Sea in Jordan.

Archaeologists have found layer upon layer of towns there. A fresh-water spring made it an ideal place to settle. The site was used at least ten times. At each level different types of buildings, tools, and pottery have been found.

The earliest remains of towns date to between 9000 and 8000 B.C. Evidence suggests that cave-dwellers from nearby hills visited the area as early as 9500 B.C. Archaeologists believe that these early people were plant gatherers. Stones for pounding and grinding grains have been found at the lowest levels of Jericho.

Around 7000 B.C. Jericho was a **trade** center. Several thousand people lived within its walls. Salt from the Dead Sea was the basis of its trade. Among the goods Jericho received in return was obsidian (uhb-SID-ee-uhn). Obsidian is shiny black glass made by volcanic

Over 11,000 years of history can be seen in this photo. In the background is the Dead Sea. Next are the remains of an "old" town, then mounds that reveal ancient settlements. In the foreground is a deserted Palestinian refugee camp. Why do you think this site was so popular?

Ancient Cities

action. It is hard enough for knife blades and other cutting tools.

Obsidian was plentiful in the Middle East, and trade in obsidian was especially important in the development of the region. The obsidian trade provided a way for nonagricultural areas to grow and prosper. At various times between 8000 and 2500 B.C., the trade in obsidian linked what are modern Turkey, Israel, Iraq, Armenia (ahr-MEE-nee-uh, now part of Turkey, Iran, and the USSR), Bahrain in the Persian Gulf, and the Mediterranean island of Crete.

CATAL HUYUK

In south-central Turkey, archaeologists have found ruins of a **city** dating to about 6500 B.C. This site is called Catal Huyuk (CHAH-tuhl hoo-YUK). The city covered approximately 13 hectares (32 acres) and probably housed 6,000 people. Murals, burial shrines, and other artifacts have been uncovered. The figure of a bull appears often. It may have been central to the religion of Catal Huyuk. Traders from this city may have carried their religion along with their trade goods to distant places. Some artifacts found at the site indicate that trade was carried on with places as distant as 160 kilometers (100 miles). The religion of the later Cretan civilization (c. 5000-1100 B.C.) of the Mediterranean may have been influenced by Catal Huyuk. The figure of a bull appears to have been important there too.

Catal Huyuk was an especially important find. It was discovered in 1961. Until then most experts believed that **urban** life did not evolve until an area had reached the **Bronze-Age** level of development. For Catal Huyuk that would have been around 3000 B.C. But discoveries at the site show an urban way of life before 5000 B.C. In addition, Catal Huyuk was built on a trade **economy** and not on agriculture. Previously authorities believed that a farming economy had to develop in an area before urban life.

OTHER SITES

These two sites, plus others recently unearthed in the Middle East, have greatly changed archaeological theory. Until these discoveries were made, many archaeologists had believed that Middle Eastern civilization began with the Sumerians around 5000 B.C.

Jarmo, in northern Iraq, is thought to have been settled around 6700 B.C. and lasted for about 400 years. Obsidian from eastern Turkey has been found there. The first evidence of farming in Iraq has also been discovered there. Goats appear to have been the only **domesticated** animals. Wild cattle, pigs, and sheep were hunted. About 5700 B.C., a people were cultivating grain and making pottery at Hassuna (ha-SOO-nuh), also in northern Iraq. The remains of bake ovens and brick houses have been found.

Summing Up the Unit

Social Studies Vocabulary

Define: geographical; nation; culture; peninsula; peoples; land bridge; history; language; linguist; gene pool; religion; Homo erectus; archaeologist; Neanderthal; anthropologist; Cro-Magnon; village; trade; city; economy

Places

Locate: Arabian Peninsula; Sahara Desert; Red, Mediterranean, Arabian seas; Rub'al Khali; Sinai Peninsula; steppes; Elburz, Pontic, Zagros, Atlas mountains; Plateau of Iran; Fertile Crescent; Jericho; Catal Huyuk; Jarmo; Hassuna

Words

Define: Near East; Mideast; Southwest Asia; nomads; Mesopotamia; Semitic; Hebrew

Questions

1. Why do most North Africans live between the mountains and the sea?
2. a. Why are there vast stretches of steppe and desert in the Middle East? b. What effect does this environment have on some peoples? c. How has the Egyptian desert been opened to farming?
3. What mountains provided invasion routes into the Middle East from the north and east?
4. a. How have Middle Easterners used their rivers? b. Why was flooding of the Tigris and Euphrates rivers important? c. Why is the Nile River vital to Egyptians?
5. a. What portion of Middle Easterners earn their living by some form of agriculture? b. What percent of the land cannot be farmed? c. Where is the best farmland?
6. Why are camels important to some Middle Easterners?
7. How much of the world's oil reserves are in the Middle East?
8. Middle Easterners are a product of the blending of the peoples from where?
9. a. What can we learn about a people by studying their language? b. Why?
10. What is the difference between a language family and a gene pool?

11. What is the chief language spoken in the Middle East today?
12. How is a person identified as an Arab?
13. a. What do modern Jews hold in common? b. What things are not common to all Jews?
14. a. Why do archaeologists believe that Homo erectus at least traveled through the Middle East? b. What further proof will be needed before they can say Homo erectus lived there?
15. a. What is the oldest settlement discovered so far in the Middle East? b. Why was it an ideal place to settle?
16. a. How did archaeologists arrive at the conclusion that early people in Jericho were plant gatherers? b. What was the basis of Jericho's trade?
17. What evidence suggests that Cretan religion was influenced by Catal Huyuk?
18. How have the discoveries at places such as Jericho, Catal Huyuk, and Jarmo changed previous theories about the beginning of Middle Eastern culture?

Discussion Topics

1. From very early times, migrants and conquerors have crisscrossed the Middle East. How did the location and environment of the Middle East encourage migration and conquest? Why is the Middle East a great crossroads?
2. The natural resources of the Middle East are unevenly distributed. What are some examples? What have been some historical results?
3. Some of the world's oldest towns have been found in the Middle East. What do archaeological discoveries at Jericho, Catal Huyuk, and Jarmo tell us about the ways in which people made a living in early towns? Why did each of these towns have its particular location?

Project Ideas

1. Write a report on: farming today in Egypt; building the Aswan High Dam; desalinization; nomadic peoples of the Middle East.
2. Learn about obsidian: how it was used in making tools; what kinds of tools it was used for; how the tools were constructed; what their uses were.

Unit II

Ancient Kingdoms and Empires

Darius the Great receives an official on this bas relief or carving found on a wall at Persepolis. Persepolis was the capital of Persia under Darius and later kings. Alexander the Great destroyed much of it in 331 B.C.

Like other cultures, the Sumerians and the Egyptians built their civilizations where there was water and fertile soil. Both are found along the Tigris and Euphrates in Mesopotamia and in the Nile River Valley in Egypt. Later, Semitic-speaking peoples wandered up from the south and settled the narrow coastal lands around the Mediterranean. Members of the Indo-European language group settled the eastern and western sections of Persia (modern Iran) and parts of Asia Minor (that part of modern Turkey in Asia).

These civilizations grew slowly over thousands of years. The work of hundreds of generations contributed to their development. These early Middle Easterners were skilled **artisans**, builders, and writers. They were also scientists. Much of Western Europe's later scientific knowledge was based on the work of ancient Middle Easterners.

One of the earliest civilizations of the Middle East arose where the Tigris and Euphrates rivers join. This was the civilization of Sumer (SOO-muhr). It seems to have begun at a site called Tell Al Ubaid (tel-al-oo-BAYD) in southern Iraq.

The people of Tell Al Ubaid probably came to the area some time between 5000 and 4500 B.C. They may have come from the southwest. As Tell Al Ubaid prospered, settlements grew up around it. About 4000 B.C. herders wandered north from the desert of the Arabian Peninsula. Other migrants came from Central Asia or Iran. Within the next 500 years these people blended their cultures into what is now known as Sumerian (soo-MER-ee-uhn) culture.

SUMER

Agriculture and herding were the foundations of Sumerian wealth. The Sumerians grew barley, wheat, dates, and other crops. They built dikes to contain the floodwaters of the Tigris and Euphrates. This water was used to irrigate their fields. The Sumerians raised cattle, sheep, goats, and oxen. The oxen were used to pull plows. Oxen as well as donkeys pulled carts and chariots. The first known use of the wheel was in this area. These early wheels were made of wood and had leather or copper tires.

Around 3000 B.C. the Sumerians began to build walled cities. They became the **political, economic,** religious, and cultural centers of Sumerian life. The center of each city was the temple. The temple was a business center, a storehouse for grains, and a bank. From the temple, the priest-king administered the city and surrounding land. Much of the farmland around the cities was owned by the **deities,** but managed for them by the priest-king. Ordinary citizens owned the rest of the land.

As cities grew, trade developed. Sumerians **exported** textiles, wool, and grain. They **imported** gold, silver, copper, lead, woods of various kinds, ivory, and jewels. Sumerian land routes reached east into Iran. Sumerian traders sailed down the Persian Gulf to Bahrain and beyond into the Arabian Sea. They went as far east as the Indus Valley of India. They went west to Africa.

Among the great **city-states** of Sumer were Ur (UHR), Erech (EE-rek), Nippur (nip-UHR), and Lagash (LAY-gash). These cities often warred among themselves. At times one city would become powerful enough to conquer several of its neighbors. A small **empire** would be set up. However, none lasted very long.

We know so much about the life of the Sumerians for two reasons. First, some of their **architectural** inventions were copied by later peoples. The arch, vault, and dome were Sumerian inventions that are still used in modern buildings.

The Sumerians were the first to build ziggurats (ZIG-uh-rats). These were temple towers built to look like mountains. Ziggurat

□ **Sumerian Civilization, c. 2800 B.C.**

means peak. A ziggurat's sides were ramps that inclined upward like mountain slopes. The top was flat. A representation of a Sumerian deity was placed there. Sumerians may have built ziggurats because in their original homeland they had worshiped their deities on hills and mountains. Since there were no hills or mountains in Sumer, the ziggurat was substituted. One ziggurat in Ur rose to a height of 21 meters (70 feet).

We also know about the Sumerians because they developed the oldest known form of writing. Sumerians used a sharpened stick or the tip of a reed to scratch wedge-shaped marks on soft clay tablets. This type of writing is called cuneiform (kyoo-NEE-uh-form). The word means having the shape of a wedge. The tablets were baked in large ovens until they hardened.

Libraries of these clay tablets have been found in the remains of Mesopotamian temples and palaces. Some tablets are account records. Others tell of Sumerian work in mathematics, **astronomy**, and medicine. The Sumerians used a mathematical system based on the number 6. This system was the basis for our 60-minute hour and 360-degree circle.

AKKAD

For hundreds of years, the Sumerians farmed, traded, and fought with each other. Then around 2400 B.C. they were conquered by the Semitic-speaking Akkadians (uh-KAYD-ee-uhns) from the north. The Akkadian leader King Sargon I united the Mesopotamian city-states into one empire. At its peak the new empire extended from the Persian Gulf to the Mediterranean Sea. With this conquest, the decline and disappearance of the Sumerians as a people began. However, elements of their civilization survived in that of their conquerors.

The Akkadians had not developed a form of writing. They adapted the Sumerian writing system to their own language. Akkadian became the official language for **diplomacy** and **commerce**. But the Sumerian system of weights and measures was used.

At various times either a Sumerian or an Akkadian ruled. The old Sumerian city of Ur was the major city of the empire for 100 years. The empire came to an end around 2000 B.C. Amorites overran it.

☐ **Akkadian Empire,**
c. 2300s B.C.

BABYLONIA

The Amorites (AM-uh-ryts) were originally from an area northwest of Mesopotamia. They spoke a Semitic language similar to that of the Akkadians. Around 2000 B.C. various Amorite groups began setting up small **kingdoms** between the Tigris and Euphrates rivers. About 1894 B.C., Amorites occupied a small town on the Euphrates called Babylon (BAB-uh-luhn). During the next 300 years the city became so powerful that all Mesopotamia came to be known as Babylonia (bab-uh-LOH-nee-uh).

The most famous Babylonian king was Hammurabi (ham-uh-RAHB-ee) who lived in the 1700s B.C. He is remembered as one of the first great lawmakers. Codes or systems of laws had been used before Hammurabi. A code of laws known as the Sumerian code of Ur-Nammu was written around 2100 B.C. Without laws an orderly society cannot exist. But the earlier laws had been those of individual cities. Hammurabi researched past and present laws and customs. He selected those that seemed to be important. To these he added new laws he felt were needed. They were then arranged into a code and proclaimed as law for his entire empire.

☐ **Babylonian Empire,**
c. 1760 B.C.

Hammurabi's code covered the daily lives of his subjects. Many laws were based on the principle of an eye for an eye and a tooth for a tooth. For example, if a house fell and killed the owner, the builder of the house could be put to death. Some scholars believe, however, that judges generally stressed the spirit rather than the letter of the law. Laws dealt with military service, business, marriage, divorce, alimony, child welfare, and the rights of women. The laws regarding women guaranteed the rights to own property, work, and receive equal pay.

Over the next 200 years, invaders from outside Mesopotamia poured in, conquered, and ruled. Among them were peoples known as Hittites (HIH-tyts), Hurrians (HUR-ee-uhns) who were later known as Mitanni (mih-TAN-ee), and Kassites (KAS-syts). The Hittites and Hurrians probably came from Central Asia. Both groups spoke Indo-European languages.

41

Beginning around 1600 B.C., the Hurrians built a group of kingdoms in northern Syria. They eventually spread into Babylonia. The Hittites settled in part of Turkey. Their empire came to rival that of Egypt. In the 1500s, the Hittites raided Babylonia and destroyed Babylonian power. The Hittites were among the earliest known people in the Middle East to make and use iron weapons. These were harder than the copper and bronze weapons used by other Middle Easterners.

Next the Kassites took Babylonia and ruled the empire for about 400 years. The Kassites came from the Zagros Mountain region of Iran. Under Kassite rule, which lasted until around the 1170s B.C., Babylonia grew weaker. At the same time, a new empire began to rise along the upper Tigris where the river runs out of the mountains. This empire was known as Assyria (uh-SIR-ee-uh).

Assyrians conquered much of the Middle East because of the superiority of their weaponry. But they did not invent all their weapons. They borrowed some ideas, such as the horse and chariot. From whom did they take this idea? The above bas relief was found at Nineveh.

ASSYRIA

The first known Assyrian settlements were along the Tigris about 320 kilometers (200 miles) north of Babylon. The area had rich soil and abundant rain. By 5000 B.C., small villages dotted the region. Sometime before 3000 B.C., groups of Semitic-speaking peoples began moving there from the south. People from the lowlands of Sumer also wandered into Assyria. The Assyrians became a mixture of a number of peoples.

During this time, Assyria suffered a series of invasions by neighbors such as the Babylonians. The Assyrians fought constantly to survive. Beginning around 1200 B.C., however, the Assyrians started their own conquests. They had learned much from their centuries of battle experience.

From the Hittites the Assyrians had learned to make iron weapons.

From the Hurrians they had learned to use the horse and chariot in battle. The Assyrians themselves invented weapons. Battering rams, armored towers on wheels, and other siege equipment were first used by the Assyrians. For almost 600 years the Assyrian empire dominated the Middle East.

The warlike nature of the Assyrian people is reflected in their art. Bravery, struggle, and death are frequent themes. The best-known examples of Assyrian art are wall carvings of hunting scenes and battles. The Assyrians admired bigness. They judged beauty and usefulness by this standard. Their capital at Nineveh (NIN-uh-vuh) was surrounded by huge brick walls that ran for several kilometers along the Tigris River. The city itself was filled with palaces and tower temples. In building these, the Assyrians borrowed the idea of arches and domes from the Sumerians.

The Assyrians also borrowed the cuneiform style of writing from the Sumerians. But they greatly simplified it by reducing the number of signs and symbols. They also preserved much of the culture of the Sumerians and Babylonians. In the 700s B.C. King Sargon II started a library of Sumerian and Babylonian clay tablets. The following century King Ashurbanipal (ahsh-uhr-BAHN-uh-pahl) built a library to house some 22,000 cuneiform tablets. He also had a Sumerian dictionary compiled.

As rulers, the Assyrians were stern and greedy. Assyrian cities paid very low taxes and had special privileges. Beyond Assyria, the empire was divided into **provinces**. The conquered provinces paid heavy taxes. The Assyrians took their gold, silver, jewels, and any other valuable and useful items. Men, women, and children were forced into **slavery**.

The Assyrians reached the peak of their empire under Sargon II. However, their authority was constantly challenged by revolts in the provinces. Thus the Assyrians were forced to keep large armies. Over the centuries this constant warfare drained Assyrian strength. Finally, in 612 B.C., Nineveh was destroyed. A **coalition** of Medes from northern Iraq and Chaldeans (kal-DEE-uhns) from the south marched against the Assyrians.

NEW BABYLONIAN EMPIRE

Around 1000 B.C. the Chaldeans, a Semitic-speaking people, established the base of their empire in southern Babylonia near the Persian Gulf. For centuries they warred against the Assyrians. With the fall of Nineveh, the New Babylonian Empire of the Chaldeans became dominant in the Middle East.

Under the rule of Nebuchadnezzar (neb-yuh-kuhd-NEZ-uhr, 605-565 B.C.), the empire reached the height of its glory. The city of Babylon was rebuilt and covered almost 39 square kilometers (15 square miles) along both sides of the Euphrates River. The city's walls were so wide that chariots could be driven on the road that ran along their

□ Assyrian Empire, c. 671 B.C.

□ New Babylonian Empire, c. 570 B.C.

This is a late European version of the Hanging Gardens of Babylon. The large building on the left is a temple. Around it are the gardens. The river in the foreground is the Euphrates.

top. Beside the road were covered walks. One hundred bronze-plated gates opened through the huge walls.

Within the city Nebuchadnezzar built his palace. Its sides were covered with brilliantly decorated glazed tiles. Around the palace were terraces, one above the other. On the terraces many varieties of trees, plants, and shrubs were planted. They grew in such numbers and to such length that they hung down like tapestries from terrace to terrace. These were known as the Hanging Gardens of Babylon.

Besides their architecture, the Chaldeans are also remembered for their knowledge of astronomy. They accurately recorded eclipses and other heavenly phenomena. They used a seven-day week in which the days were divided into 12 hours of 120 minutes each. They knew the length of the year to within less than one-half hour.

The New Babylonian Empire did not last long after Nebuchadnezzar. In 539 B.C., it fell to the armies of Cyrus the Persian.

PERSIAN EMPIRE

Between 1000 and 900 B.C. the Persians settled in parts of what are now Iran and Afghanistan. They came from somewhere to the north and spoke Aryan, an Indo-European language. Around 550 B.C. Cyrus became king. He was a man of great military and administrative ability. Under his leadership the Persians conquered a great part of the Middle East. Their empire extended from the Iranian plateau to the Mediterranean Sea. In 529 B.C. Cyrus's son Cambyses (kem-BY-seez) succeeded him. Four years later Cambyses added Egypt to the empire. Cambyses was murdered and the throne was taken by a man who came to be known as Darius the Great.

Darius (521-486 B.C.) continued to expand the empire. Under him the empire reached from the Indus River in India northward to the Black Sea and into Turkey and northeastern Greece. Southward the empire included parts of modern Israel, Jordan, Egypt, and Libya.

The Persian Empire was divided into provinces and governed by

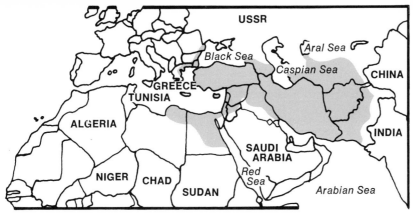

☐ **Persian Empire, c. 500s B.C.**

Persian officials. They were tolerant rulers. Persian subjects could follow their own religions and traditions so long as they accepted Persian authority and paid taxes.

The Persians also established a system of standard weights and measures throughout the empire. One of their outstanding architectural accomplishments was a 2,570-kilometer (1,600-mile) highway. It ran from Susa near the Persian Gulf to Sardes near the Mediterranean. Under Darius, the Persians also rebuilt the ancient Egyptian canal which joined the Nile River to the Red Sea.

Under later rulers, the Persian Empire declined. The armies of Alexander the Great finally conquered it around 330 B.C.

MACEDONIA

Alexander the Great was king of Macedonia, (mas-uh-DOH-nee-uh), a region north of ancient Greece. Today Macedonia is part of Yugoslavia, Bulgaria, and Greece. Alexander's father had conquered the Greek section. Alexander continued his father's conquests. He built an empire that eventually extended across the Middle East to India.

As a youth, Alexander had been taught by Aristotle, the Greek philosopher. By the time of Alexander's youth—the mid-300s B.C.— the Greeks had made great advances in **philosophy**, **the arts**, and science. Alexander valued these ideas. As a conqueror, he wanted to spread Greek knowledge.

Alexander and the Macedonian generals who followed him founded cities that became centers of Greek thought and science in the Middle East: Alexandria in Egypt, Antioch (ANT-ee-ahk) in Syria, and Seleucia (suh-LOO-shee-uh) along the Tigris. Greek became the language of the educated and the ruling class. Greek philosophy, education, art, and science became known throughout the Middle East.

The exchange of knowledge worked both ways, however. Alexander did not want to force Greek ideas on the peoples he conquered. He wanted to merge the various cultures. In fact, some experts believe

standard: a rule established by authority, custom, or general consent as a model or example

45

**Seleucid Dynasty,
c. 200s B.C.**

that Middle Eastern thought and ways had more impact on the Greeks than Greek thought and ways had on Middle Easterners.

After Alexander died in 323 B.C., his generals fought over control of his empire. No one was able to gain complete control. Eventually the empire was broken into three parts. Egypt came under the control of Ptolemy (TAHL-uh-mee) who founded the Ptolemaic **dynasty** (DY-nuh-stee). Members of a family who rule in succession are called a dynasty. The Ptolemaic dynasty lasted until the death of Cleopatra in 30 B.C. Egypt then became a Roman province.

Syria and portions of Asia Minor came under the rule of Seleucus (suh-LOO-kuhs) who began the Seleucid dynasty. Macedonia came under the rule of Antigonus (an-TIG-uh-nuhs). These two parts also later came under Roman rule.

LATER PERSIANS

In Persia, a people known as Parthians (PAHR-thee-uhns) revolted against their Seleucid governor. From about 250 B.C. to 226 A.D., the Parthians ruled Persia. From their homeland in northeastern Iran, they carved out a great empire that stretched from Mesopotamia to China.

Around the 50s B.C., the Parthians began fighting with the Romans. The Romans were trying to expand their empire eastward. This warfare along the western frontier eventually weakened Parthian power. In 226 A.D. the Parthians were overthrown by Ardashir I (AHR-duh-shuhr), a district governor. He claimed to be descended from earlier Persian kings. He began the Sassanian (suh-SAY-nee-uhn) dynasty.

After Rome fell, the Persians were still not free of warfare. Fighting continued with the Byzantines. Sassanian power steadily weakened. Finally the dynasty was overthrown in 641 by Arab Muslim armies. This event marks the end of ancient Persian civilization. From this time on, we will use the terms Iranian (ir-AY-nee-uhn) and Iran (ih-RAN) to describe these people, their culture, and land.

ROMAN RULE

Between 146 and 30 B.C. the Romans extended their rule into the Middle East. They had already conquered the western Mediterranean, including Spain, and North Africa. The Romans respected the arts, science, and learning of the people they conquered. They generally allowed the peoples to live as they wished so long as they accepted Roman authority.

Although Roman rule lasted in some places in the Middle East for 600 years, little evidence of them remains. There are some aqueducts for carrying water and some buildings and monuments. In North Africa, scattered ruins of temples, villas, and coliseums still stand. In some places Roman laws are the basis of the present legal systems.

Chapter 2
Egypt

The history of ancient Egypt is the history of dynasties and kingdoms. The monument above is called a sphinx and represents the ruler as having the strength of a lion. In the background is the pyramid of Khafre.

Perhaps as early as 5000 B.C. an ancient people known today as Egyptians settled along the Nile River. They spoke a language related to Semitic. From evidence found at various sites it is known that these people built canals and irrigation ditches and farmed. They wove linen and cotton cloth. Gold and silver ornaments and pottery were also made. These early Egyptians also developed a form of writing. Sometime before the 3100s B.C. two separate **government** units began to emerge. In the Nile Delta area the Kingdom of Lower Egypt arose. Farther south along the Nile, the Kingdom of Upper Egypt was formed.

FIRST TWO DYNASTIES AND OLD KINGDOM

Around 3100 B.C. a leader from Upper Egypt named Menes (MEE-nees) united the two kingdoms. Menes built his capital at Memphis, near the Nile Delta. As the ruler of all Egypt, Menes took the name pharaoh (FER-oh). Pharaoh means royal house. According to tradition, the pharaoh was a direct descendant of a god. Pharaohs usually married members of their own family, because they believed that if deities married humans, they would have human, not divine, children.

During the first 400 years (c. 3100-2700 B.C.), pharaohs of the First and Second Dynasties ruled. Little is known about them. The few tombs and inscriptions that have been found from this period indicate that the Egyptians enjoyed peace. For the time being, the deserts

■ **Old Kingdom, c. 3000 B.C.**

protected them from invaders. The period from about 2700 to 2200 B.C. is known as the Old Kingdom.

MIDDLE KINGDOM

After 2200 B.C. internal struggles tore Egypt apart. Princes and nobles fought for more power. It was only when a new dynasty of pharaohs came to the throne around 2050 B.C. that some unity was restored. The new dynasty marked the beginning of the Middle Kingdom. During the 250 years of the Middle Kingdom, nobles grew more powerful and wealthy. In return for favors and services that the nobles provided, the pharaohs had to grant them land. Gradually, under a series of weak rulers, the office of pharaoh lost much of its power.

During the Middle Kingdom, additional irrigation systems and reservoirs were built. In the 1800s B.C. Amenemhet III (AH-men-em-het) built a canal that linked a branch of the Nile to the northern end of the Red Sea.

HYKSOS ERA

The Middle Kingdom ended around 1800 B.C. Until around 1570 B.C. various groups of invaders known as Hyksos (HIK-sohs)—Princes of the Desert—seized power. They may have come from Asia Minor. Egyptian weaponry was no match for their war chariots. However, just as the Assyrians learned from their conquerors, the Egyptians learned from theirs. The Egyptians added horses and chariots to their stock of weapons.

The invasions of the Hyksos taught the Egyptians another lesson. They learned that in order to overcome an invader they had to put aside disagreements among themselves. They found, as others have, that disunity results in weakness. Toward the end of the 1600s B.C., Egyptians were able to unite. Gradually the conquerors were driven out. By around 1570 B.C. Egypt was free of the Hyksos. A new pharaoh, Ahmose I (AH-mohs), took the throne and began the Empire Period.

EMPIRE PERIOD

From around 1570 to 1165 B.C., Egypt played the dominant role in the Middle East. The power of ancient Egypt rose to its greatest heights and then declined. In the 1400s B.C., during the reign of Thutmose III (thoot-MOH-suh), the Egyptian empire was extended in the northeast to Palestine and Syria and in the south to Nubia. The wealth of the conquered lands poured into the Egyptian treasury.

The Egyptians made many enemies by their conquests. Their wealth attracted more enemies. A major conflict with the Hittites in the 1300s B.C., during the reign of Amenhotep IV (ah-men-HOH-tep), greatly weakened Egyptian power. Ramses III (ram-SEES) is considered the last of the great pharaohs. His death in 1165 B.C. marks the beginning

☐ Empire Period, c. 1450 B.C.

*Ramses II
was pharaoh in the 1200s
B.C. He used the labor
of enslaved Israelites
on public works projects
such as the buildings
at Luxor (left).*

of a long line of unfit rulers. Internal fights for power left Egypt without strong defenses. Enemies began to attack. Around 945 B.C. a Libyan ruler from the west seized the throne. In the 700s B.C. Nubians from the south drove the Libyans out. In 663 B.C. the Assyrians conquered Egypt. The Egyptians regained their independence, but lost it to the Persians in 525 B.C. Egypt remained a Persian province until 332 B.C., when Alexander the Great conquered it.

SCIENCE AND ART

The Egyptians were a practical people. This quality is reflected in their science and **technology**. Egyptians were able to compute the area of squares, triangles, rectangles, and circles. This knowledge enabled them to measure fields and construct pyramids and other buildings. They were also able to figure accurately the amount of supplies needed by their armies and workers.

As astronomers, the Egyptians made careful observations of the heavens. These observations too were turned to practical use. Because they were farmers, they depended on the yearly flooding of the Nile. They observed that the Nile overflowed its banks soon after the star Sirius (SIR-ee-uhs) appeared on the horizon before dawn. They made the rising of Sirius the beginning of their year. The Egyptian year was divided into 12 months of 30 days each. The five extra days were saved at the end of the year for feasts. The Egyptians used their astronomical knowledge in building. Their pyramids, temples, and other monuments were built so that they were in line with the rising of Sirius and other important stars.

horizon: the visual meeting point of earth and sky

During the Old Kingdom, the Egyptians built pyramids as tombs for pharaohs. The earliest is called the Step Pyramid. Larger and larger ones followed. The pyramid of the Pharaoh Khufu is the largest. Dated to the 2600s B.C., it contains over two million blocks of limestone.

49

Each weighs almost two metric tons (two tons). Except for a few chambers in the center and a few passages and airshafts, the pyramid is solid stone. An estimated 100,000 workers labored 20 years to complete it.

When a pyramid was finished and the dead pharaoh was placed in the tomb, the entrance was sealed and hidden. Nothing was supposed to disturb the peace of the pharaoh. The Egyptians believed that as long as their pharaoh enjoyed peace, the kingdom would too. However, over the centuries, tomb robbers discovered the hidden entrances.

The Egyptians stopped building pyramids after the Old Kingdom. However, they continued to create huge stone temples. The temples at Karnak and Luxor are the most famous examples. Egyptian architects were the first to use stone columns and pillars to support roofs. Egyptian sculptors carved huge statues of their pharaohs. Some statues are over 21 meters (70 feet) high. The Egyptians also carved obelisks (AHB-uh-lisks)—tapered stone pillars—which weigh as much as 900 metric tons (1,000 tons). Great stone sphinxes (SFINK-suhs)—statues with a lion's body and a man's head—were also built. They represent pharaohs as having the strength of lions.

Egyptian artisans worked in many materials: ivory, ebony, wood, gold, silver, copper, bronze, and glass. Necklaces, bracelets, pendants, containers for jewelry and cosmetics, and many other decorative objects were made. Egyptians were also painters. Murals such as those found in the tombs at Thebes (THEEBZ) caught the delicateness of nature. Often their artwork had religious themes. Egyptians also painted portraits.

WRITING   Writing had developed even before Menes united Egypt. Pictures which represented objects were the earliest form of Egyptian writing. This system is called **hieroglyphics** (hy-ruh-GLIF-iks). In time a kind of writing developed in which part of each picture represented a syllable. From these syllables words were formed. They might be different from what the separate pictures represented. Thus parts of two pictures would make a new word. Groups of two or more picture-words would make a sentence. Writing for ordinary business was done with pictures in abbreviated form. People called scribes were specially trained for this job.

Egyptian hieroglyphics were not decoded until the 19th century. In 1799 French soldiers with Napoleon discovered a stone in Egypt with three inscriptions. One was in Greek, one in hieroglyphics, and one in a later form of Egyptian. Twenty years later, a French scholar

The Book of the Dead *(top) contained magical charms and was supposed to guarantee a happy life in the next world. The statue is of a scribe. Could everyone in Egyptian society read and write? Do people who can read and write have an advantage in gaining power over those who can't?*

reasoned that all three inscriptions said the same thing. The knowledge gained by comparing the languages and decoding the hieroglyphics helped unlock many mysteries of Egypt's past. The stone—known as the Rosetta (roh-ZET-uh) Stone—was discovered near the Rosetta, a branch of the Nile.

During the Old Kingdom period, the Egyptians began to write long documents and books. They wrote on papyrus (puh-PY-ruhs), paper made from reeds that grew along the Nile. They wrote about surgery, engineering, mathematics, geography, and astronomy. The oldest known books on medicine and surgery were written by Egyptians.

During the Middle Kingdom, some of the finest classical Egyptian literature was written. Much of it was religious. It included hymns to the sun god Re (RAH) and poetry which told of eternal life and the ways to gain it. Ancient Egyptian literature also included love poetry, tales of adventure, and fables. Some of these later became part of a collection of stories, *Arabian Nights Entertainment.*

SOCIETY

Ancient Egypt had a rigid social system. Pharaohs, priests, nobles, and government officials held the highest positions. Below them in descending rank were scribes, merchants, and artisans. Still further down were the farm workers. Lowest of all were the slaves.

Egyptian nobles lived comfortably in large, cool villas along the river. For privacy, the houses were surrounded by high walls. Within the walls, trees shaded the house, walks, and gardens. A typical villa had two stories and was built of brick and wood. The floors were tiled. Tapestries decorated the walls. Soft leather cushioned the chairs and couches. The wooden frames were inlaid with ivory and ebony. On the roof of the house was a garden. A linen awning shaded it.

A man of noble rank wore a linen kilt. A noblewoman wore a long, sleeveless dress of linen. It was starched and pleated. She also wore necklaces and bracelets. She used a black powder to darken her eyebrows and eyelashes. She also used green eye shadow. The juice of the henna plant was used to color her nails. She kept her

These sandstone figures were made during the Hyksos or Empire Periods. The statues are of an official and his wife. What was the role of women in upper-class Egyptian society?

This Egyptian wall painting shows workers winnowing grain with wooden scoops. They are throwing it up in the air so that the waste matter— dirt and chaff—will be separated from the usable grain.

own hair short, but wore wigs of various styles and colors.

In ancient Egypt, women generally enjoyed a good position in society. Women were consulted in family and business matters. No man could have more than one legal wife. Descent was **matrilineal**— that is, it was traced through the woman's side of the family. Women of the royal family often exercised great influence in affairs of state. During the Empire Period, women were pharaohs. An example is Hatshepsut (hat-SHEP-soot) who ruled jointly with her brother, Thutmose III, in the 1400s B.C.

In a noble's home, guests dined with elaborate tableware and glasses. Wine and many kinds of meats and vegetables were served. All this comfort, beauty, and abundance was made possible by the labor of farmers and slaves.

Farmers had to struggle to survive. Their lives were a weary routine of planting, irrigating, and harvesting. Some farmers had oxen for their plows. A few had donkeys for carrying their produce. They used river water to irrigate their fields.

The farmers paid high rents to nobles or priest landowners. Their possessions were few: some cooking pots, a wooden bed, and an outdoor brick oven for baking. Their diet was barley or wheat bread and beer. They also planted flax for linen thread. Farmers ate little meat, except when they were lucky enough to catch a wild duck in the marshes. Fish, however, was plentiful. These farmers had little time to entertain friends, or money to buy jewelry or fine clothes. They felt themselves lucky if they were not forced to work on public works projects.

These examples of different social **classes** could be found throughout Mesopotamia too. Only some slight changes in the nobility's home and dress would be needed.

Chapter 3
Smaller Mediterranean States

While the empires of Mesopotamia and Egypt were rising and declining, other Middle Easterners were founding kingdoms. They were conquering and being conquered. These peoples had settled along the eastern and southern coasts of the Mediterranean. The Hittites and Hurrians (Mitanni) have already been mentioned. Smaller **states** were founded by the Phoenicians, Aramaeans, and Hebrews.

PHOENICIANS

The Phoenicians (fi-NISH-uhns) lived in several independent cities along the eastern Mediterranean coast. A single state known as Phoenicia did not exist. Phoenician is a term used by the early Greeks to describe the people of this region who lived by trading.

Much of the area where the Phoenicians lived is part of the modern nations of Lebanon, Syria, and Israel. The section of their land between the Jordan River and the coast was known to the ancients as Canaan. (KAY-nuhn). The ancestors of the Phoenicians probably **migrated** to this area around 2000 B.C. Their original homeland is not known. But they spoke a Semitic language. Over the centuries they were influenced by the cultures of the Egyptians, Mesopotamians, and Hittites among others. Often the Phoenicians were targets for invasion by these peoples. Then, between 1200 and 1100 B.C., the Phoenicians began their own period of expansion.

The Phoenicians expanded their holdings through trade, not war. They were excellent sea traders. They traveled the Mediterranean coast of Africa as far west as the Strait of Gibraltar (juh-BROL-tuhr). They built settlements all along the coast. Carthage (KAHR-thij) was their most famous North African site. The Phoenicians also sailed through the Strait and down the coast of West Africa. They went north to the British Isles and perhaps beyond. Cadiz in Spain was one of their important European ports.

From their trading trips, Phoenicians brought back tin, copper, ivory, and silver. Artisans fashioned the **raw materials** into decorative or useful objects. These items then became Phoenician trade goods and were exchanged for more raw materials. The Phoenicians also traded their own glass objects and wool cloth as well as lumber from cedar trees that grew along the coast (modern Lebanon). The Phoenicians also used cedar trees for their own ships.

From their trade centers, Phoenician ways spread through the lands around the Mediterranean and beyond. Phoenicians from the city of Ugarit—Ras Shamra in modern Syria—were in contact with the Mediterranean island of Crete as early as 1900 B.C. The word Bible comes from a Greek word meaning book. This word was taken from the name of the Phoenician city of Byblos (the modern Lebanese

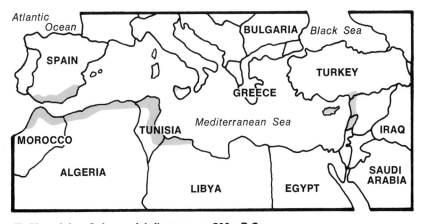

■ **Phoenician Sphere of Influence, c. 500s B.C.**

city, Jubayl). It was an ancient trading center for papyrus.

The Phoenicians borrowed the Egyptian alphabet which contained only consonants. This alphabet was later adapted by the Greeks. The Greeks added symbols for vowels. In addition some of the Phoenician consonant signs were used as vowels. In this form the alphabet was adopted by the Romans. It became the basis of the modern Latin alphabet used for the Indo-European language family.

Between 800 and 700 B.C., the Assyrians harassed the Phoenicians. Later, in the 500s B.C., Phoenician cities were taken over by Nebuchadnezzar's empire and then the Persian empire.

ARAMAEANS

Sometime before 1500 B.C., after the Phoenicians settled along the eastern Mediterranean, a desert people called Aramaeans (ahr-uh-MEE-uhns) were migrating into Syria from the south. By 1200 B.C. they dominated much of the area. Aramaeans were divided into small kingdoms centered around trading cities. Damascus (duh-MAS-kuhs) was the most famous center. It lay on the main trade routes of the Middle East.

The Aramaeans traded in a wide variety of goods from many places—dye from the Phoenicians, ivory from Africa, pearls from the Persian Gulf. They spread their goods and language throughout Mesopotamia.

Their language and alphabet may have been the Aramaeans' greatest contribution to Middle Eastern culture. The use of Aramaic allowed for an easy and rapid exchange of goods and ideas among Middle Easterners. Originally the Aramaeans borrowed the Phoenician alphabet and adapted it to their own language. In this form they transmitted it to their neighbors. Between 700 B.C. and 700 A.D. Aramaic (ahr-uh-MAY-ik) was the common language of the Fertile Crescent. The Assyrians used Aramaic in addition to their own language. Under Darius the Great (521-486 B.C.), it was the official language of the Persian government in dealing with its provinces.

transmitted: sent or transferred from one person or place to another; caused or allowed to spread; passed on

HEBREWS

Although the Hebrews (HEE-broos) later spoke Aramaic, their earliest language was Hebrew. Their first historical writings are believed to have been recorded between 1000 and 800 B.C. They tell of the beginnings of the Hebrew people, the great flood, Abraham, Isaac, Jacob, and the journey out of Egypt. Modern archaeologists have found evidence that supports much of these historical writings. For example, an inscription on a monument of the Pharaoh Merneptah (MER-nep-tah), who ruled in the 1200s B.C., confirms that the Hebrews were in Egypt as mentioned in the Old Testament of the Bible.

THE PROMISED LAND   The early Hebrews were nomadic herders who worshiped many gods. Between 2000 and 1600 B.C. they left their home in the land of Ur (modern Iraq) in Mesopotamia. Under the leadership of Abraham—who told them there was only one God—they went into the land of Canaan. This is approximately the modern nation of Israel. According to Jewish tradition, this land was promised to them by their God.

In time Abraham's grandson, Jacob, became leader. Jacob changed his name to Israel. It is from his name that the Jewish people derived the name Israelites (IZ-ree-uh-lyts)—children of Israel. Jacob or Israel had 12 sons. Their descendants later became known as the Twelve **Tribes** of Israel.

From the land of Canaan, a number of Israelites traveled to Egypt. The Old Testament tells of Joseph, a son of Jacob, who was sold into slavery in Egypt by his brothers. He became a favorite of the pharaoh and was set free. He brought his father and brothers to Egypt. Later pharaohs made the Israelites slaves. They were forced to work on building projects for Seti I and his son, Ramses II, in the 1300s and 1200s B.C.

During the 1200s B.C., a man named Moses was born among the Israelites in Egypt. According to the Old Testament, he was a messenger of God and a prophet—a foreteller of the future. He told the Israelites that God would deliver them from slavery. After threatening the pharaoh with God's anger, Moses was able to lead the Israelites out of Egypt and back toward Canaan. This journey is known as the Exodus (EK-suhd-uhs). It is remembered today in the Jewish feast of the Passover.

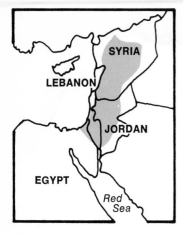

Kingdom of David and Solomon, c. 1000-900 B.C.

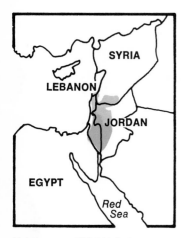

Hebrews, c. 933-912 B.C.
■ **Kingdom of Israel**
■ **Kingdom of Judah**

After the Israelites left Egypt, they wandered in the wilderness between Egypt and Canaan for 40 years. During this time God gave Moses the Ten Commandments. After Moses died, Joshua took over the leadership of the Israelites. He finally led them into Canaan. He divided the land among the 12 tribes.

Once in Canaan the Israelites had to fight to survive. Under military leaders called Judges, they fought such enemies as the Philistines (FIL-uh-steens), Canaanites (Phoenicians), and Aramaeans. It was from the name Philistine that the land of Canaan later became known as Palestine.

The years between 1000 and 900 B.C. were a great period in Israel's history. During this time David and then Solomon ruled. Israel dominated a large part of the surrounding area. David, a powerful warrior, was also a poet. His Book of Psalms (SAHMS) contains some of the most beautiful poetry in the Bible. David's son, Solomon, built the first Temple in Jerusalem.

THE JEWS   Around 925 B.C., after Solomon died, a division occurred among the Israelites over taxation. As a result, two kingdoms were formed. The two southern tribes became the Kingdom of Judah (JOOD-uh). Its capital was Jerusalem (juh-ROO-suh-luhm). It is from the name Judah that the word Jew comes. The ten tribes in the north made up the Kingdom of Israel.

Around 721 B.C. the Assyrians overran the Kingdom of Israel. The ten tribes were scattered across the Middle East. Their identity as a people was lost. They are known as the Ten Lost Tribes of Israel. This event marks the end of Hebrew history.

In 586 B.C. the Chaldean king, Nebuchadnezzar, destroyed Jerusalem and the Temple. He deported most of the people to Babylon. This period in Jewish history is known as the Babylonian Captivity. After Cyrus of Persia conquered Babylon, he allowed the Jews to return to their homeland. Around 539 B.C. they rebuilt Jerusalem and the Temple.

Unfortunately their troubles were not over. Around 332 B.C. they came under the rule of Alexander the Great. In 168 B.C. the Jews revolted against the Seleucid dynasty that had taken control of part of Alexander's empire. The Jews were fighting for their religious freedom. They won and founded their own Hasmonean (haz-muh-NEE-uhn) dynasty of the Maccabees. Chanukah (HAHN-uh-kuh)— the Feast of Lights—commemorates Israel's victory over the Seleucids.

Around 63 B.C. the Romans took control of Palestine and its people. During Roman rule there were many revolts. One, which lasted from 66 to 70 A.D., ended in the second destruction of the Temple. The Jews revolted again in 135 A.D. This time the Romans scattered the Jews throughout the empire. This is known as the Diaspora (dy-AS-puh-ruh). From then until 1948, when the independent state of Israel was established, Jews remained without a country.

Summing Up the Unit

Social Studies Vocabulary

Define: artisan; deity; city-state; empire; architecture; diplomacy; commerce; kingdom; coalition; philosophy; the arts; dynasty; hieroglyphics; states

People

Identify: Sargon I; Hammurabi; Sargon II; Nebuchadnezzar; Cyrus; Darius the Great; Alexander the Great; Ptolemy; Ardashir I; Menes; Thutmose III; Ramses III; Hatshepsut; Abraham; Jacob; Moses; David; Solomon

Words

Define: ziggurat; cuneiform; pharaoh; obelisk; sphinxes; scribe; Rosetta Stone; papyrus; Aramaic; Exodus; Diaspora; Ten Lost Tribes of Israel; Babylonian Captivity

Questions

1. a. What were the foundations of Sumerian wealth? b. What special methods did they use in their agriculture?
2. a. What was the base of Sumerian trade? b. How do we know so much about the life of the Sumerians?
3. a. Who conquered the Sumerians? b. How did elements of Sumerian civilization survive?
4. Why are laws important to a society?
5. Describe Hammurabi's code.
6. a. Who were among the earliest users of iron weapons in the Middle East? b. What was the advantage of iron over copper and bronze?
7. What did the Assyrians learn from: a. the Hittites? b. the Hurrians?
8. How is the warlike nature of the Assyrians reflected in their art?
9. How did the Assyrians control the provinces they conquered?
10. Describe Chaldean achievements in: a. architecture; b. astronomy.
11. What kind of rulers were the Persians?
12. a. How did Alexander the Great merge Greek culture with the cultures of the Middle East? b. Did Middle Eastern thought and ways have more

impact on the Greeks than Greek thought and ways had on the Middle Easterners?
13. Describe how the Romans treated their conquered peoples.
14. a. Why did the Egyptians apparently enjoy peace during the period of the Old Kingdom? b. How do we know this?
15. How did the nobles gain power in Egypt's Middle Kingdom?
16. What two lessons did the Egyptians learn from the Hyksos invaders?
17. How did the Egyptians make practical use of: a. mathematics? b. astronomy?
18. Describe Egypt's social system.
19. What was a woman's role in Egyptian society?
20. What goods did the Phoenicians trade?
21. a. What was the greatest contribution of the Aramaeans? b. Why?
22. What example is given of evidence archaeologists have found to support Hebrew writings?
23. a. How did the Jewish people come to be called Israelites? b. What happened to the Kingdom of Israel? c. What happened to the Ten Tribes of Israel? d. What events are commemorated in Passover? e. in Chanukah? f. What caused the Diaspora?

Discussion Topics

1. A long succession of invaders conquered and ruled Mesopotamia. Why were so many kingdoms and empires established by invaders from surrounding areas? Why was invasion and conquest less frequent in Egypt than in Mesopotamia?
2. Early Middle Easterners discovered many principles of astronomy, mathematics, physics, chemistry, and medicine. How might their location or ways of making a living have influenced their scientific research?

Project Ideas

1. Make a chronological chart of kingdoms and empires that ruled Mesopotamia. Give their dates of rule and accomplishments.
2. Arrange a bulletin board display showing pictures of some of the structures mentioned in this unit.

Unit III

A Cradle of Religions

Within the city of Jerusalem are places sacred to Jews, Christians, and Muslims. Among them are the Jewish Wailing Wall, the Christian Church of the Holy Sepulchre, and the Muslim Dome of the Rock.

Early Middle Easterners, like people in other parts of the world, looked beyond themselves for answers to their problems. At first they worshiped the many expressions of nature: the sun, stars, wind, rain, and animals among others. Gradually some of them came to believe that there was only one God. This one God they thought was supreme above nature and humans.

Nearly 4,000 years ago the Hebrews began to teach belief in one God. Christianity came from the same base 2,000 years later. Islam built on both earlier religions. Islam began in the 600s A.D.

Many of the practices, traditions, and moral laws of each religion are different. But Judaism, Christianity, and Islam have certain common basic beliefs. All teach that the one God who created the universe is independent of creation and above it. This God is also all-powerful and all-knowing. Besides religious influence, each religion had great social and political influence on its followers.

The Sumerians, the various Semitic-speaking peoples of the Middle East, and the Egyptians believed in many gods and goddesses. Some deities were thought to be more powerful than others. Deities were represented in many forms and worshiped in many different ways. Often the ruler was looked on as a representative of the chief deity. Sometimes rulers themselves were considered divine. This was true in Egypt.

Chapter 1
Gods and
Goddesses

EARLY DEITIES

Because Sumerians and Semitic-speaking peoples depended on farming for their living, nature was very important to them. Nature and agriculture became the bases of their religions. Among the greatest of their deities were Entil, the storm god; Enten, the god of farming; and Ishtar, the goddess of love and fertility. During the 1800s B.C. and later, the Babylonian god Marduk and the Assyrian god Ashur became important.

The Sumerians and Semitic-speaking peoples were afraid of their deities. The people thought their gods and goddesses were able to feel the same violent emotions that humans felt. To protect themselves, the people made sacrifices and gave gifts to their deities. When one deity became angry, the people asked other gods and goddesses for help.

Evidently deities often became angry. One example is found in the *Gilgamesh Epic* (GIL-guh-mesh) of Babylonia. The deities became so angry that they threatened to destroy humanity with a flood. A man who was liked by one of the gods was warned. He was told to build a boat to save himself and a few others. This story is similar to the Old Testament account of Noah and the ark.

Interest in life after death was not an important part of the religions of these early Middle Easterners. They were more concerned with their lives on earth. They did not build elaborate tombs or monuments for their dead. But they did show concern for them. They buried them in cemeteries or under the floors of their houses.

EGYPTIAN DEITIES

With the beginning of the Old Kingdom, the sun god Re became the most important Egyptian deity. He became the state god and worship of him became the **state religion**. The pharaoh was supposedly his representative on earth. Re was not concerned with the welfare of individuals. He preserved the state and the people as a whole. Most Egyptians felt closer to the special deities of their cities and regions than to Re.

Gradually Osiris (oh-SY-ruhs), the god of the Nile and of life, became more important than Re. Osiris supposedly taught the Egyptians how to farm, and helped them in many ways. Osiris had a jealous

This alabaster figurine of a Sumerian worshiper was made between 2800 and 2550 B.C. Why was sacrifice an important part of Sumerian religion?

59

This wall painting shows Osiris and the gods of burial. Osiris was the chief god of the underworld. What did belief in him include? Why would belief in a life after death appeal to Egyptians?

brother named Set. Set hacked Osiris to pieces and scattered his body across the earth. Isis (EYE-suhs), who was both Osiris' wife and sister, brought him back to life. Osiris' son Horus (HOHR-uhs) avenged his father by killing Set. To the Egyptians this was a story of the triumph of good over evil, of life over death. Its promise that death was not the end appealed to them.

By the time of the Middle Kingdom, Horus had become the god concerned with people's lives on earth. Osiris had become the god who judged the goodness or badness of the dead.

By the beginning of the Empire Period, priests sold magical charms which were supposed to fool Osiris. If people who had led bad lives bought these charms, they would be able to enter the kingdom of light, peace, and pleasure instead of the kingdom of darkness.

THE ONE GOD OF IKHNATON   In the 1300s B.C. Amenhotep IV tried to reform Egyptian religion. As a young man he worshiped Re. But he turned away from Re and announced a new god—Aton (AH-tuhn). According to Amenhotep, Aton had created the world and was the god of light and truth. At their deaths all those who led good lives would be rewarded.

In honor of Aton, Amenhotep changed his name to Ikhnaton (ik-NAHT-uhn). He moved his capital away from Thebes which was the center of worship for Re. Ikhnaton proclaimed Aton the only god of the Egyptians. Worship of Aton became the state religion. Ikhnaton became the high priest.

Ikhnaton tried to wipe out all traces of Re. The temples were closed. The name and images of Re were removed from monuments. New paintings and **sculptures** showed Ikhnaton and his family receiving life from Aton. They were pictured as his chosen representatives.

Ikhnaton devoted most of his time to spreading the worship of Aton. He neglected the Egyptian empire, especially its holdings in Syria. Hittite invaders overran the land. The loss of Syria and other parts of the eastern empire caused political trouble within Egypt. This increased resistance to the worship of Aton. After Ikhnaton's death, the Egyptians quickly returned to the worship of the old deities.

ZOROASTRIANISM

For many centuries the Persians practiced a religion called Zoroastrianism (zohr-uh-WAS-tree-uh-niz-uhm). A man named Zoroaster (ZOHR-uh-was-tuhr) had received the truths of this religion from the creator of goodness and light—Ahura-Mazda (uh-hur-uh-MAZ-duh). This was sometime between 1000 and 600 B.C. The sacred book of Zoroastrianism is the *Zend-Avesta* (zen-duh-VES-tuh).

Zoroastrianism emphasized social justice. People should be good to their neighbors and fight evil. According to Zoroastrianism, good and evil are waging a powerful battle for control of the universe and humanity. One force is Ahura-Mazda. The other is the creator of evil and darkness, Ahriman (AHR-ih-man). The battle will end in a final judgment. The dead will rise and be judged. Those who led good lives will be rewarded with eternal happiness. The evil will receive eternal punishment.

Under Darius the Great, Zoroastrianism became the state religion of the Persian Empire. Religious freedom, however, was allowed. Even after Persia was defeated by Alexander the Great around 330 B.C., Zoroastrianism continued to spread. Like other religions, though, some of its basic beliefs changed with time. Different groups or **sects** arose.

One such sect was the Manichaeanist (man-uh-KEE-uh-nizt). The group took its name from Manes (MAY-neez), who lived in the 200s A.D. Manes taught that all that was spiritual, good, and bright came from the good God. All that was material and evil was created by the Spirit of Evil, also a god. To be saved, people had to separate good and evil in themselves. They had to repress their desires. The influence of Manes' teachings was widespread in Asia. It lasted into the 900s.

Zoroastrianism was largely replaced by Islam. This occurred when the Muslims conquered Persia in the 600s. A few thousand Iranians still practice Zoroastrianism. A larger group lives in India. They are descendants of Zoroastrians who fled Persia to escape the Muslims. They are known today as Parsis (PAHR-sees), from the Persian word for Persians.

Queen Nefertiti was Ikhnaton's wife. She greatly influenced his religious ideas. Why did she and Ikhnaton try to change the religious practices of their subjects? Do you think this is wise policy for leaders to follow?

repress: to hold in by self-control

61

Chapter 2
Judaism

A man blows the shofar or ram's horn to mark the beginning of Rosh Hashanah, the Jewish New Year. The shofar is also used at the end of Yom Kippur, the Day of Atonement. Ancient Hebrews used it as a battle signal.

The first of the three great world religions to begin in the Middle East is Judaism (JOOD-uh-iz-uhm). The ancient Hebrews gave to the world a knowledge of the one God whom they called Yahweh (YAH-way) or Jehovah (jih-HOH-vuh). For almost 4,000 years Hebrews and their descendants—the Jewish people of today—have preserved knowledge of this one God. Their writings make up the Jewish Bible. It is part of the sacred writings of both Christianity and Islam.

THE BIBLE

The Jewish Bible consists of three parts: Pentateuch (PENT-uh-tyook), Prophets, and Hagiographa (hag-ee-AHG-ruh-fuh). The Pentateuch, or Five Books of Moses, is also known as the Torah (TOHR-uh). The first book is Genesis (JEN-uh-suhs). It begins with the creation of the world and ends with Joseph in Egypt. The other four books concern Moses and the covenant—or agreement—made between the Hebrews and God. Exodus, the second book, relates the journey of the Israelites out of Egypt. Leviticus (lih-VIT-ih-kuhs) is a set of instructions for worship. Numbers is an account of the Hebrews' 40 years of wandering in the desert. In Deuteronomy (dyoot-uh-RAHN-uh-mee) Moses summarizes the Law that God gave to the Hebrews. The book ends with his death at the edge of the Promised Land.

The second part of the Jewish Bible, the Prophets, is an account of the activities, sermons, and words of the prophets. Hagiographa means sacred writings. It is a collection of psalms, poems, **proverbs**, and history.

In the Christian Bible, these three parts are called the Old Testament. Testament also means covenant. Christians believe that after the coming of Jesus Christ, a new covenant was made with God. The New Testament—the second half of the Christian Bible—is an account of the teachings of Jesus and his disciples.

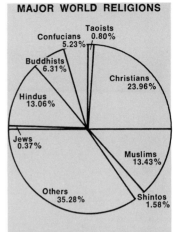

MAJOR WORLD RELIGIONS

Taoists 0.80%
Confucians 5.23%
Buddhists 6.31%
Hindus 13.06%
Jews 0.37%
Christians 23.96%
Muslims 13.43%
Others 35.28%
Shintos 1.58%

Source: Reprinted with permission from the *1975 Britannica Book of the Year,* copyright 1975 by Encyclopedia Britannica, Inc., Chicago, Ill.

THE TORAH   Throughout their history, the Jews have carefully preserved the Torah, or Five Books of Moses. Copies of it, written in Hebrew on parchment scrolls, can be found today in the ark of every synagogue (SIN-uh-gahg). A synagogue is the Jewish place of worship.

The term Torah is also used in a broader sense. It can mean all the laws found in the Jewish Bible for personal and community conduct. Torah also describes all the revealed instructions and guidance which are the basis of the Jewish way of life. Teachings of the Torah direct the spiritual, social, and physical lives of Jews.

THE TALMUD   Moses received many laws besides the Ten Commandments. Over the centuries, these laws had been handed down among the Jews by word of mouth. They are oral laws. The Bible is known as the Written Law. With the passing of time, Jews found it necessary to enlarge on or reinterpret the oral laws in accord with changing times. After the first destruction of the Temple in 586 B.C., a number of Jews went to Babylonia. There they were allowed to preserve their ancient traditions. By the late 400s A.D., Babylonia had become an important Jewish religious and cultural center. Scholars working there collected the oral laws into a collection of books known as the Talmud (TAHL-mud).

The Talmud contains more than laws. It has a wealth of other knowledge as well: biographies, stories, debates and discussions with unbelievers, practical wisdom, and a code of ethics. The code considers such things as personal conduct, manners, family living, work, friendship, and virtue. The Talmud provides a look at Jewish life up to that time. It also plays a vital role in the education of the Jewish people today.

ORTHODOX, CONSERVATIVE, REFORM

Over the centuries, divisions have taken place among Jews over the interpretation of Jewish laws. Modern Judaism is made up of three major groups: Orthodox, Conservative, and Reform.

Orthodox Judaism emphasizes tradition and observance of **ritual**. Extremely Orthodox Jews believe in the actual coming of the Messiah (muh-SY-uh)—the promised leader. They believe the Messiah will forgive their sins and begin the Kingdom of God on earth. This will be a time of peace and harmony. To most Jews, however, the coming of the Messiah is not the coming of one person. It means a time when all humanity will begin to work together for peace and harmony.

Orthodox Jews strictly observe Saturday as the Sabbath—the day of rest and worship. No business, work, or travel is allowed. The Hebrew language is used for prayers and ceremonies. Women sit in separate places in the synagogue. Dietary laws, which were given in the Book of Leviticus, are carefully followed. These laws are called kosher (KOH-shuhr)—that is, correct according to ritual. These dietary laws show a deep concern for not inflicting pain on living creatures. Animals for food must be killed painlessly and quickly. Jewish laws also forbid eating the meat of animals that hurt or kill other animals. Killing animals for sport is forbidden.

Conservative Jews follow many of the practices of Orthodox Jews. But they are less strict about it. Conservative Jews observe the Sabbath, holy days, and traditional festivals. However, they believe that it is sometimes necessary to change traditions. They are more flexible in their hours of religious service and in the use of Hebrew for prayers. Women may sit with men at services.

Reform Jews depart more from tradition than do Conservative Jews. They allow women equality in the synagogue. Prayers are said mostly in the **vernacular** (ver-NAK-yuh-luhr)—the language of the region. Among Reform Jews there are many viewpoints. For example, the more **liberal** Reform Jews worship on Sunday instead of Saturday.

Although Orthodox, Conservative, and Reform Jews differ on various points of law, they all agree basically on the ethical and moral

A family observes Passover with the traditional seder meal. Passover commemorates the deliverance of the Jews out of Egypt. The flat brownish squares are matzot, an unleavened bread. They symbolize both enslavement and freedom.

A boy becomes a man when he has his Bar Mitzvah. What other religions mark the change from child to adult with religious ceremonies?

teachings of Judaism. They also agree on the need for prayer, worship, and belief in the one God to whom the Hebrews are the chosen people.

TEACHERS AND STUDENTS

Early Jewish scholars came to be known as rabbis (RAB-eyes). This is a Hebrew word meaning teachers. The term is used today to describe those in the Jewish community who pass along learning to others. Judaism has no religious **hierarchy**. Rabbis are trained at schools called yeshivas (yuh-SHEE-vuhs). Rabbis preach, conduct religious services, and offer guidance to members of their congregation when needed. They also perform religious ceremonies concerned with birth, confirmation, marriage, and death.

Cantors are also important in Jewish worship. Jewish prayers are not spoken. They are chanted. As the cantor begins each prayer, the congregation takes up the chant. The cantor also helps with the religious education of the congregation, especially in preparing a young man for his Bar Mitzvah (bahr-MITS-vuh). This is a Hebrew term meaning son of the Law.

When a Jewish boy reaches the age of 13, he is ready to take on the responsibilities of adulthood. During the ceremony which marks this event, the boy promises to live up to the highest ideals of his religion. He also promises to dedicate himself to the Torah. It is a time of joy and celebration. Among some Reform and Conservative congregations, a similar service—a Bas Mitzvah—is held for girls.

Philo (FY-loh) of Alexandria worked to blend Greek and Jewish thought. He lived sometime between 100 B.C. and 100 A.D. During the 900s A.D., Saadia Gaon (sah-DEE GAH-ohn) translated most of the Bible into Arabic. He also wrote poetry as well as religious works.

By the end of the 900s, Spain had become a center of Jewish learning and culture. Some Jews had been living there since the Diaspora. In the early 700s, Islam reached Spain. The Muslims practiced religious tolerance. This attracted Jewish scholars to Spain. Among the great thinkers of this golden age was Moses Maimonides (my-MAHN-uh-deez) who worked to reconcile Judaism with the Greek philosophy of Aristotle. He is widely regarded as the greatest of Jewish philosophers.

The Jews in Spain at this time also served as a cultural bridge between the ancient Middle East and **medieval** Europe. They helped to preserve and translate early Greek writings. Some made translations from Greek to Arabic. Later other scholars made translations from Arabic to Latin, and passed the works along to the Christians of medieval Europe.

The golden age ended in the 1400s when Queen Isabella expelled Jews from Spain. By then the Muslims had lost control and Christianity had become dominant. Many Spanish Jews went to Italy, Poland, Turkey, Holland, and later to the New World.

Chapter 3
Christianity

Christ is shown blessing the faithful in this enamel picture. During the 1000s, the Christian Church became divided into the Roman Catholic and Greek, or Eastern Orthodox, branches. This artwork is from an Orthodox church.

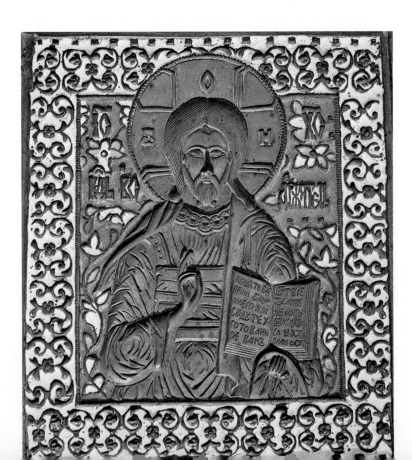

Christianity was founded by Jesus Christ almost 2,000 years ago. He was a Jew who was born in Palestine. What we know of his life and teachings is found mainly in the first four of the 27 books of the New Testament. They are the Gospels of Matthew, Mark, Luke, and John. Gospel means good news.

According to the Gospels, Jesus grew to adulthood in Nazareth. When he was about 30 years old, he began what can be called his public life. For the next several years he preached about the way God wanted people to act toward one another. Those who heard and saw him believed that he had extraordinary powers. In the third year of preaching, Jesus went to Jerusalem to celebrate Passover. His arrival caused great excitement. When word that he claimed to be the Messiah and Son of God reached the Sanhedrin (san-HED-ruhn), he was arrested. The Sanhedrin was a group of Jews who had legal, civil, and religious authority. Jesus was charged with blasphemy—irreverence to God. Under Jewish law this was a crime that demanded the death penalty.

Jesus was found guilty. He was crucified and died. Crucifixion was a common form of punishment at the time. Most of his followers scattered. The few who remained buried him. Two days later the tomb was empty. According to his followers, an angel had told them that Jesus had risen from the dead. They began to teach that Jesus was the Messiah who had been promised in the Old Testament.

TEACHINGS OF JESUS

Everything Jesus said and did centered on God's love for humanity and the love people should have for each other. He sometimes used parables—stories—to make his point. He told his followers to love everyone. There were no exceptions to this love because God made no exceptions. Christians had to show by their actions this love. Jesus once told his followers to sell their possessions and divide the money with the poor. The real treasures, he said, were in Heaven. Because of such teachings, early Christianity had great appeal for the poor.

Not all Christians today agree on how the teachings of Christ should be interpreted. There is, however, agreement on a number of beliefs. Most Christians believe in the Trinity: three separate persons in God—Father, Son, and Holy Spirit—all with one nature. Each is fully God. Christians consider Jesus to be the Messiah who came to earth to make up for humanity's sins. Most Christians accept the word of God as revealed through the Bible. As mentioned earlier, Christians believe that the coming of Jesus marked a new covenant with God. For that reason, they place special emphasis on the New Testament.

SPREAD OF CHRISTIANITY

Many people were drawn to the warmth, sincerity, and goodness of Jesus. He chose 12 of his followers to spread his teachings. These special messengers were called Apostles (uh-PAHS-uhls). Chief among them was Peter. Small groups of Jews began to accept Jesus as the Messiah and follow his teachings.

Within a few years after his death, Christianity began to reach Gentiles (JEN-tyls) or non-Jews. One of those responsible for this was Saul of Tarsus. He had once fought against the Christians. But after seeing a vision from God, he became a Christian. He changed his name to Paul and spent the rest of his life preaching. Through his efforts, Christian communities were set up in Syria, Asia Minor, Greece, Egypt, and even Rome itself. Paul kept in touch with the various groups of Christians by epistles (ih-PIS-uhls). This is another word for letters. In these he interpreted Christian teachings. These messages and those of the Apostles make up the Epistles—21 of the books of the New Testament. The other two books are Acts and Revelation. Revelation, also known as Apocalypse (uh-pahk-uh-LIPS), is the last book of the New Testament. It is a book of prophecy.

EARLY CHRISTIAN CHURCH In the beginning Christians saw little need for organization. Some expected the kingdom of God to come within their lifetimes. They achieved a sense of unity by observing common rituals called sacraments. These sacraments were signs of God's love for them. Originally, the most important sacraments were Baptism and the Eucharist, or Communion. Through Baptism, one became a Christian. Through the Eucharist (YOO-kuh-ruhst)—taking bread and wine—early Christians commemorated the death and resurrection of Christ.

Eventually five other sacraments developed. They still exist within some Christian churches. They are Confirmation, in which the bonds of Baptism are strengthened; Penance, the forgiving of sins; Anointing the Sick; Matrimony; and Holy Orders, ordaining the clergy.

In actuality the early Christian Church spread quickly along the

Central to Christian worship is communion. Here a young woman drinks the wine and a man gives the host, a wafer of unleavened bread. What are the different beliefs about the nature of Communion held by the various denominations?

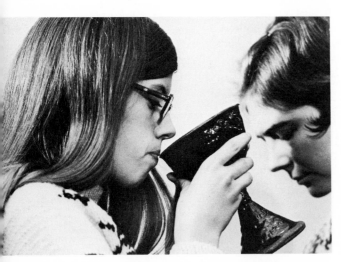

trade and communication networks of the huge Roman Empire. Roman authorities saw Christianity as a threat to their rule. Many Christians were persecuted or killed. Finally the Emperor Constantine ended the persecution. He said that he had received a vision from God that had helped him in battle. In 313 A.D. he issued an order, the Edict of Milan, which granted freedom of worship to Christians. By 400 Christianity was the official religion of the Roman Empire. Worship of all other deities was illegal.

As the number of Christians increased, the need for organization became clear. By around 200 A.D., an official clergy began to develop. The clergy—priests and ministers—were trained to handle the ceremonies and administration of the Church. As the early Church spread, it became necessary to divide it into sections called provinces. Each was headed by a member of the clergy called an archbishop. In some areas, such as Antioch and Alexandria, the title patriarch was used instead of archbishop.

Provinces—or archdioceses—were later divided into dioceses (DY-uh-suh-suhz). Each was headed by a bishop. Dioceses were further divided into parishes. Priests were in charge of these. Each level of clergy was responsible for giving the sacraments, preaching, and looking after the welfare of the Christian community. The Bishop of Rome came to be looked upon by many Christians as holding a special position. He later became known as the pope. The clergy were recognized as the successors of the Apostles.

DIFFERENCES ARISE   During the first centuries of the Christian Church, a number of differences arose over the interpretation of Church teachings. A number of sects grew up. Among them were the Manichaeans and Monophysites. Defining the Trinity was a special source of disagreement. In 325 A.D. the first Church **council** was held to settle the argument over the nature of the three persons in the

Baptism brings a person into Christianity. Some denominations have infant baptism, and others believe a person should not be baptized until they are older. This is a baptism in the Roman Catholic Church.

Trinity. Once a Church council defined a teaching, Christians were obliged to accept it. If people doubted or denied the definition, they were considered heretics (HER-uh-tiks). Heretics were excommunicated. All rights of Church membership were taken from them.

Certain clergy—who became known as Church Fathers—argued against heresies. One of the early Church Fathers was St. Ambrose, the archbishop of Milan. In the 300s he wrote *Duties of the Clergy,* which became a guide for the clergy for centuries. St. Jerome, who lived at the same time, translated the Bible into Latin, the Church language of that time. Known as the *Vulgate,* it became the only approved version of the Bible.

Among the greatest of the early Church Fathers was St. Augustine, bishop of Hippo in North Africa (in modern Algeria). He wrote *City of God* and *Confessions.* Both writings had a major impact on Christian theology because of their emphasis on original sin and salvation.

DIVISIONS WITHIN CHRISTIANITY

While Emperor Constantine granted religious freedom, he set the stage for a split within the Christian Church. He divided the Roman Empire into two parts: east and west. He built a new capital in the east on the site of the ancient city of Byzantium. It was later named Constantinople in his honor. The western half of the empire declined and finally fell apart in the 400s. The eastern section remained until the 1400s.

Starting with Constantine, the Byzantine (BIZ-uhn-teen) emperor was head of both **Church and State**. He dominated all religious issues. His people regarded him as God's agent on earth. As a result, rivalry developed between the pope in Rome and the emperor in the east. Religion and politics became mixed.

Ordinary Christians of the two parts of the former empire began to drift apart. In culture and language the two regions were very different. People in the west spoke Latin. Those in the east spoke Greek. The eastern region also contained a greater mixture of people and cultures. In time the Christians in the east began to call their church the Eastern Orthodox or the Greek Orthodox Church. This was to distinguish it from the Roman church which later became known as the Roman Catholic Church. Catholic means universal.

Over the centuries a number of differences in **doctrine** arose. A formal split between the two churches occurred in the 1000s. The Roman Church had excommunicated the eastern patriarch over a new problem in defining the Trinity. Also involved was the question of who had final authority—the pope or the emperor. In the 1400s an attempt was made to bring the two groups together, but it failed.

Christianity—both eastern and western—continued to grow. In Western Europe corrupt practices began to creep into the Church. A reform movement developed in the 1500s. This led to formation of the Protestant branches of the Christian Church.

Chapter 4
Islam

Muslim places of worship are called mosques. This one is in Damascus. Muslims also believe the world is a mosque and they, therefore, may pray wherever they are when the call to prayer is sounded five times each day.

The third great world religion to begin in the Middle East is Islam (is-LAHM). It started on the Arabian Peninsula. Much of this region is controlled today by the Kingdom of Saudi Arabia.

By the 500s A.D. the peninsula was dominated by Arabian nomads known as Bedouins (BED-uh-wuhns). They lived mostly by herding. A few towns and cities dotted the trade routes between Asia and Europe. One of the largest was Mecca (MEK-uh), on the Red Sea.

Mecca was also a religious center. It was the site of the Kaaba (KAHB-uh) and a holy well. The Kaaba housed an ancient black stone said to have come from Heaven. The shrine also contained several hundred statues of deities that were worshiped by the peoples of the region. Each year hundreds of Arabs visited the Kaaba. The holy well, which stands nearby, dates to the time of Abraham.

Abraham fathered a son—Ishmael (ISH-mee-uhl)—by his wife's maid Hagar. But Abraham's wife, Sara, later had a son, Israel. To protect Israel's legal rights, Ishmael and Hagar were sent away. While wandering in the desert, they were saved by the angel Gabriel (GAY-bree-uhl) who showed them the well. Gabriel also promised that Ishmael's descendants would create a great nation. Arabs trace their ancestry to Ishmael.

MUHAMMAD

The story of Islam begins with Muhammad (moh-HAM-uhd). He was born in Mecca around 570 A.D. Muhammad was orphaned at an early age and raised by relatives. During his youth he worked as a herder. He married Khadijah, a rich widow. For many years he managed her business and was a successful merchant.

Muhammad was also a religious man. He often went to a cave near Mecca to meditate. According to Islamic teaching, it was there one night in 610 that God began speaking to him. The revelations—or messages—came through the voice of the angel Gabriel.

At first Muhammad told only his family and close friends what he heard. Later he began preaching publicly in Mecca. He gained followers among the poor because he taught that the rich should share their wealth. But when he preached against the deities in the Kaaba, he made enemies. He threatened the economic security of those who profited from the pilgrimages. They turned against him. Muhammad was forced to flee Mecca in 622. He went to Medina (muh-DEE-nuh), a city farther north. This flight is known as the Hegira (hih-JY-ruh). The event marks the beginning of the Islamic calendar.

Muhammad wanted all Arab people to know the one God of the Jews and the Christians. The revealed teachings he preached came to be known collectively as the religion of Islam. The word Islam means submission—that is, to Allah (AL-uh) or God. Followers of Islam took the name Muslim. Muslim means one who submits.

In Mecca, Muhammad had preached a religious message of social justice and equality. In Medina he found himself in a new role—political leader. He was called on to settle arguments and make laws.

Later Muhammad took on a third role. In 624 fighting broke out between Mecca and Medina. Muhammad led a group of Muslims in battle against Mecca. They were victorious. Muhammad proved himself to be a military as well as a religious and political leader. By 630 he had an army strong enough to seize Mecca. He marched on the city and ordered all the statues removed from the Kaaba. Only the black stone was to remain.

After that many people converted to Islam. Muhammad sent missionaries all over Arabia to preach. Muhammad returned to Medina where he died in 632. His tomb lies in the Mosque (MAHSK) of the Prophet in that city.

TEACHINGS OF MUHAMMAD Muhammad taught that there is only one God—Allah. Allah is the creator of all things. Muslims believe that Allah is the same God who spoke through the prophets Abraham, Moses, Jesus, and their own prophet Muhammad. Muslims believe that Muhammad was chosen to complete and seal this long series of revelations. To Muslims, Muhammad is known as the Seal of the Prophets.

Muhammad's revelations were recorded in a sacred book called the Koran (kuh-RAN). It contains many references to the Old and New Testaments of the Bible. It speaks of a day of judgment and of a heaven and hell. It stresses a belief in angels and spirits, especially an evil spirit. The Koran also contains laws governing the daily life of Muslims.

Following in the path of Muhammad became an important goal for Muslims. But problems of interpretation arose through the years. Muslims also found difficulties in handling situations that were not covered in the Koran. As a result another authority developed. It is based on tradition and stories which describe what Muhammad did, said, or tolerated among his followers. This authority is called the Hadith or Sunna. The Hadith supplements the Koran and is equally authoritative in matters which were not treated in the Koran.

Muslims look to the Hadith not merely as an historical document but as a basic element of their faith. The collections of the Hadith are a guide for conduct and a legal source. They direct the faithful Muslims in following the Sunna or example of Muhammad and other early holy Muslims.

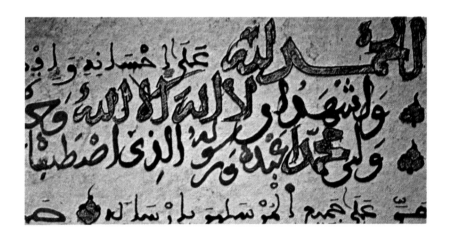

The Koran is the holy book of Islam. The copy from which this page comes dates to the 1400s. What are the major teachings of Islam?

FIVE BASIC PILLARS

Islamic devotion is based on five articles of faith. They are known as the Five Pillars of Islam.

The first pillar is recital of the words: There is no God but Allah; and Muhammad is His Prophet. Muslims say this many times a day. They believe that the oneness of God must be engraved in their minds and hearts. A sincere public recital of this creed is all that is necessary to become a Muslim. In repeating these words, Muslims will be reminded that Muhammad was only a prophet. He was a human and must not be worshiped.

The second pillar of Islam is prayer. Muslims are required to pray five times a day: at dawn, noon, midafternoon, sunset, and nightfall. Services are held at noon on Fridays in mosques. Mosques are Muslim places of worship. If there is no mosque available, Muslims may pray wherever they happen to be. Muslims are told that the whole world

One of the Five Pillars of Islam is a pilgrimage to Mecca. These Muslims are fulfilling this part of their law. What is the purpose of the pilgrimage? Do other religions encourage pilgrimages? Are they voluntary?

is their mosque. When Muslims do come together at the mosque, any Muslim may lead the prayers. Islam has no organized clergy. When Muslims pray, they face the direction of Mecca. This is to remind them of the unity within Islam.

The third pillar is charity. Muslims are required to share what they have with others. This is to show appreciation for God's generosity. Muslims are asked to pay a tax each year on all their possessions. The tax is used for charitable purposes. Islam also tries to give its followers a social conscience—a sense of obligation to help ease the suffering of others.

The fourth pillar is fasting during Ramadan (RAM-uh-dahn). This is the ninth month of the Muslim calendar. It was during Ramadan that Muhammad first received God's revelations. It was also in this month, several years later, that Muhammad fled to Medina. During Ramadan, Muslims fast each day from sunrise to sunset. Fast means to avoid eating, drinking, or earthly pleasures such as smoking. Fasting is supposed to remind Muslims that they are weak and need the constant help of God. It is also supposed to remind them to be sympathetic and helpful to the less fortunate.

pilgrimage: a journey, especially to a shrine or sacred place

The fifth pillar is a pilgrimage to the Kaaba, the shrine in the Great Mosque of Mecca. Islam teaches that Muslims should visit this shrine at least once, if possible. The pilgrimage will strengthen their faith. In the mosque at Mecca, no distinctions are made because of a person's wealth or status. All are equal before Allah. All pilgrims dress alike in plain white cloth. This coming together of Muslims from all over the world symbolizes the **international** community of Islam.

All Muslims are expected to practice the five pillars of Islam. Some try to reach the highest form of Islam—Sufism (SOO-fiz-uhm). Its followers, called Sufis, strive for a personal experience of God. They seek a personal union with their creator. In the early days of Islam, they founded monasteries where they lived lives of prayer, meditation, and self-sacrifice. Sufis have also been the great missionaries of Islam.

Summing Up the Unit

Social Studies Vocabulary

Define: state religion; sculpture; sect; proverb; vernacular; liberal; medieval; council; Church and State; doctrine

People

Identify: Amenhotep IV; Zoroaster; Manes; Philo of Alexandria; Saadia Gaon; Moses Maimonides; Saul of Tarsus; Constantine; St. Ambrose; St. Jerome; St. Augustine; Ishmael

Words

Define: *Gilgamesh Epic*; Yahweh; Jehovah; covenant; synagogue; Messiah; kosher; rabbi; yeshiva; cantor; Bar Mitzvah; Sanhedrin; blasphemy; Trinity; epistle; Revelations; Edict of Milan; clergy; archbishop; patriarch; diocese; pope; *Vulgate*; Hegira; Koran; mosque

☞ Questions

1. a. What were the bases of the religions of Sumerian and Semitic peoples? b. Why? c. Why did these peoples fear their deities?
2. What was the function of Re?
3. How did Ikhnaton's worship of Aton weaken the Egyptian Empire?
4. What religion became the state religion of the Persian Empire?
5. a. Name the three parts of the Jewish Bible. b. What are they called in the Christian Bible? c. List the five books of Moses.
6. What things are considered in the code of ethics found in the Talmud?
7. a. Name the three major groups within modern Judaism. b. What do all three agree on basically? c. How do they differ?
8. a. Where did the Jews serve as a cultural bridge between the ancient Middle East and medieval Europe? b. What attracted them to that area? c. What caused them to leave?
9. What was the charge against Jesus that led to his crucifixion?
10. a. What did the teachings of Jesus center on? b. Why did they appeal to the poor?
11. a. Why did early Christians see little need for organization? b. Why did organization become necessary? c. Describe the organization that developed.
12. How did Constantine's division of the Roman Empire affect the Christian Church?
13. a. Where did Islam originate? b. Why was Mecca important at that time?
14. a. Why was Muhammad forced to flee Mecca? b. What religious message did Muhammad preach?
15. List and explain the Five Pillars of Islam.

Discussion Topics

1. Judaism, Christianity, and Islam originated in the Middle East. What do these religions have in common? In what ways are they different? What human needs do they meet? Why do they rank among the world's greatest religions?
2. The story of the flood appears in both the *Gilgamesh Epic* and the Bible. How might the inclusion of a great flood in both works be explained?
3. The conflict between good and evil is emphasized by many religions. Why? How is a religious concept of God related to its beliefs about good and evil? What beliefs about good and evil have been emphasized by Judaism and Christianity?

Project Ideas

1. Prepare a report on: the history of Zoroastrianism; the origins of Jewish religious traditions; the early spread of Christianity; the origins of Islam.
2. Write an essay on revelations and their significance in Judaism, Christianity, and Islam.
3. Stage a panel discussion on the various teachings of Judaism, Christianity, and Islam about conduct for daily living. Have one person represent each of the three religions.
4. Using the chart on page 63 and library references, make a similar chart on religions in the U.S. Compare the two charts.

Unit IV

The Rulers and the Ruled

In this fresco found in Isfahan, Iran, Shah Tahmasp receives a foreign delegation. In the 1500s Iranian Muslims fought Turkish Muslims for power. Each side tried to gain allies. What attracts allies to one side or the other?

The teachings of Muhammad inspired his followers with a missionary spirit. They determined to spread the will of Allah and their own power as far as possible. Within a century after Muhammad's death, most Middle Easterners and many North Africans were Muslims. As Islam spread, peoples of many different backgrounds were tied together by a shared religion and culture. A vast civilization was created which at one time reached from the Philippine Islands to Spain.

In the 1000s, the Muslims were overrun by non-Arabic invaders from the east—Turkish nomads. The Turks quickly accepted Islam and continued to spread its teachings. They also spread Turkish power. They invaded areas of southeastern Europe. In the 1400s they overthrew the Byzantine Empire. In the 1500s, the Ottoman Turks penetrated deeper into Europe. Their expansion was finally checked in the late 1600s near Vienna. After that, Turkish power slowly declined. In the 1920s the Ottoman Turkish Empire finally collapsed.

By this time, Western nations dominated the Middle East. In 1923 Turkey became an independent nation. This event began a movement toward independence among other Middle Eastern nations.

From the beginning Islam was more than a religious force. Its impact was felt in social, political, and economic areas. When Muhammad died in 632, most of the Arabian Peninsula was under his control. His successors continued to exercise political power. They directed the material lives of the people as well as their spiritual lives.

SUCCESSORS TO MUHAMMAD

After the death of his first wife, Khadijah, Muhammad took other wives. One of them was an African. According to tradition, this was to teach Muslims that Islam preaches racial equality. Some of these marriages were for political reasons: to unite the Arab peoples. Muhammad and his wives had daughters but no sons. Under Arab law, daughters could not inherit his position. When Muhammad died, he had not chosen a successor. His followers chose Abu Bakr (ah-boo-BEK-uhr). He was Muhammad's closest friend and the father of Muhammad's wife, Ayesha. Abu Bakr was given the title caliph (KAY-luhf). The word is Arabic for successor. He ruled until 634. Omar (OH-mahr) succeeded him. During his 12 years in power, Omar created a strong civil and military government. When he died, he was succeeded by Othman (oth-MAHN).

Othman was a member of the Ommaid (oh-MY-ad) clan. Muhammad, Abu Bakr, and Omar had been members of the Hashemite (HASH-uh-myt) **clan**. Both clans were part of a larger **kinship group** —sometimes called a tribe—known as the Quraysh (kuh-RYSH). During his rule, Othman tended to favor his own clan over that of Muhammad's. This caused jealousies which eventually led to Othman's murder in 656.

In that year, Ali (ah-LEE), Muhammad's son-in-law, was elected fourth caliph. Muawiyah (moo-AH-wih-yah), the governor of Syria and a relative of Othman, led a revolt against Ali. He blamed him for Othman's death. For the next several years, there was bitter fighting among the Muslims. In 661 Ali was murdered. Muawiyah declared himself caliph and established the Ommaid dynasty. He moved the capital from Medina to Damascus, Syria. This was closer to the geographical center of the empire.

DIVISIONS   Besides a political division, Ali's death created a religious split within Islam. Two major groups emerged: Sunni (SUN-ee) and Shia (SHEE-ah). They still exist. The Sunnis consider the caliph's position to be elective. Sunnis follow closely the Koran and the traditions of the *Sunna,* from which they take their name. They also follow the teachings of those whom they consider the rightful successors of Muhammad. The majority of Muslims today are Sunni.

The Shia sect began in Persia as a political group. They were Ali's supporters. The Shi'ites (SHEE-ytes) believe that Muhammad intended his successors to be descendants of Ali. Ali was married to

■ **Muslim Empire Under Muhammad, c. 632 A.D.**

Although Iranian Muslims fought Turkish Muslims for power, they also had a religious motive. What was it? This mosque is in Iran. To what sect do most Iranian Muslims belong?

Muhammad's daughter, Fatima. Thus his descendants were direct descendants of Muhammad.

 Shi'ites honor Ali as a holy man. The Shi'ites call Muhammad's

legitimate: legal legitimate successors imams (ih-MAHMS). Imam means leader of all Muslims. According to the Shi'ites, imams inherited Muhammad's power both to interpret and to enforce Islamic law. In 878 the 12th imam disappeared. His return—as the Mahdi (MAHD-ee), or Messiah—will come before the end of the world.

Today more than half of Iraqi and most Iranian Muslims are Shi'ites. Within the Shia sect several subgroups arose. These stemmed from differences in interpreting the role of the imam. Most important of these are the Twelvers. They take their name from the 12th imam. In the absence of a legitimate imam, they recognize the shah of Iran as the guardian of Islam.

SPREAD OF ISLAM

When Muawiyah took control of the Muslim empire, Islam took a new direction. To the missionary spirit were added material goals. The Muslims already controlled Syria, Palestine, (today part of Israel and Jordan), Iraq, and Iran. They expanded into Egypt and along the coast of North Africa into Libya, Tunisia, Algeria, and Morocco.

People have long lived in North Africa. These early people were mostly nomads. Many of their descendants came to be known as Berbers (BUHR-buhrs). Around the 1100s B.C. Phoenicans traded along the coast. In the 700s B.C., the Phoenician trading center of

Carthage was founded. In time Carthage (in modern Tunisia) grew to be a great power in the Mediterranean region. It rivaled the Roman Empire. In 146 B.C. Rome destroyed Carthage. The Roman Empire controlled the region for 600 years. The Vandals replaced them in the 400s A.D. They were a Germanic people who had moved southwest into Spain and then south into North Africa. Next in the series of rulers were the Byzantines a hundred years later. In the 600s they were swept away by Muslim Arabs.

Within a century most North Africans were Muslims. Islam brought to these people the beginning of a new and brilliant civilization. Schools and universities were founded that became great centers of learning.

Berbers who married Arabs became known as Moors. The name Moor comes from Mauritania (mor-uh-TAY-nee-uh)—an ancient region of North Africa that was once part of the Carthaginian Empire. The Moors moved into Spain and brought Islam with them. They carried it into France, almost as far as Paris. Charles Martel and his army of Franks turned them back at Tours in 732. The Moors retreated into Spain where their rule lasted for over 700 years. In 1492 Granada, the last Moorish stronghold in Spain, fell.

OMMAID DYNASTY

Besides territorial gains, Muawiyah's most important changes in the Muslim empire were administrative. He organized the empire into provinces. Each was headed by a governor who reported to the caliph. Governors were allowed to appoint their own deputies. These changes led to a decline in central authority.

Also during the Ommaid dynasty a class system emerged. Four major social classes developed. At the top were nobles. They were usually soldiers and were descended from the most important families of Mecca and Medina. They were the ruling class. Much of their

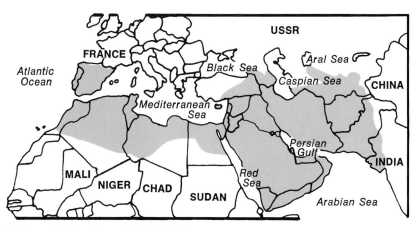

□ **Ommaid Dynasty, c. 632-750 A.D.**

wealth came from land given to them by the caliph.

Directly below the nobles were non-Arabs called mawali (muh-WAH-lee). They formed an urban middle class of craftworkers, merchants, and storekeepers. As their numbers increased, their power grew. They became especially important in the government. The third group were non-Muslims who believed in one God. These included Christians and Jews. Muslims wanted to convert those who worshiped many gods. But religious freedom existed for monotheists—those who believed in one God.

The lowest group were the slaves. Generally they were treated fairly. In fact, Muslims improved the life of slaves. Under Muslim rule it became possible for them to rise in society.

Eventually a group of Shi'ite Muslims in Iran and Iraq revolted against the Ommaid dynasty. They brought about its downfall in 750. The new caliph was Abdul Abbas (ab-DOOL uh-BAS), of the Hashemite clan. He began the Abbasid (AB-uh-suhd) dynasty.

ABBASID DYNASTY

Under Abbasid rule (750-1258), the Muslim empire reached its peak. Al-Mansur (al-man-SOHR), the second Abbasid caliph, established a new capital at Baghdad (BAG-dad). Today it is the capital of Iraq. The splendor of Baghdad was known throughout east and west. The court and nobles lived in luxury. They dined off gold and silver plates decorated with jewels. Such luxury was possible because of the empire's profits from trade. Baghdad had an excellent geographical position. It was located on the trade routes between Asia and Europe.

TURNING POINT The Abbasid dynasty marked a turning point in Arab control and rule. Through conquests, the empire had acquired a variety of peoples. The Arabs took these various peoples into their culture and, in turn, profited much from the knowledge that these new people had. The Iranians especially began to exercise considerable influence in the Arab world. Islam and the use of Arabic as the official language gave the empire unity.

Eventually the wealth and luxury of Baghdad corrupted the caliphate (KAY-luhf-ayt). The caliph's political power fell into the hands of Iranian **prime ministers** and their paid Turkish soldiers. Although the Abbasids ruled until 1258, their power had declined long before.

Besides being unable to deal with trouble at home, the Abbasids could not control the outer areas of the empire. In Spain a member of the Ommaid clan set up a caliphate at Cordova. In North Africa, the governor of Tunisia established a separate state known as an emirate (ih-MIR-uht). The Tunisians set out on their own territorial conquests. They captured Sicily from the Byzantines in 902 and held it for almost 200 years. The Egyptians pulled away from Abbasid

■ **Abbasid Dynasty, c. 1200s A.D.**

control in 968 and set up the Fatimid (FAT-ih-mid) dynasty. Their caliph was a descendant of Ali and Fatima. This independent state lasted until 1171. In that year the Seljuk Turks took control.

HOLY WARS

The unusually rapid growth of the Muslim empire did not result, as some have said, from a command of Muhammad to go forth and convert by the sword. The opposite is true. Muhammad tried to prevent his followers from rushing into aggressive battle. In the Koran he stated: Defend yourselves against your enemies, but attack them not first; for God does not love transgressors.

Muhammad wanted to limit the horrors of war. But conversion to a religion does not always end the desire for power and plunder. Arabs gave their allegiance to Islam. And the Arab world gained because of its teachings. But **environment**, circumstances, temptations, and traditions sometimes prevented them, as they have others, from living ideals completely and constantly.

The Arabs who spread Islam lived in an area and at a time when fighting was a part of life. For example, control of a water hole or grazing land was often the cause for battle. These desert peoples were used to having to fight to survive.

Chapter 2
Invaders

During the disunity of Abbasid rule, people from the steppes of Central Asia began moving into the Middle East. They were a nomadic people who spoke a Turkic language and came to be called Seljuk (SEL-jook) Turks. They took their name from an early leader, Seljuk. The Turkic peoples were no strangers to Muslims. As early as the Ommaid dynasty, Arabs had used Turks as slaves and soldiers.

SELJUK TURKS

Under Togrul Beg, Seljuk's grandson, the Seljuk Turks began a conquest of the Middle East. In 1055 they captured Baghdad. The Abbasid caliph was allowed to keep his religious authority. But the Seljuk Turks took political control. Their leader took the name sultan (SUHL-tuhn). This means he who has authority. The Seljuk Turks eventually became Muslims.

In their continued campaign for **territory**, the Turks overran Armenia and Georgia (part of the modern USSR). In 1071 they crushed the Byzantine army stationed in Asia Minor and took much of the region. They next turned south and took Jerusalem. The city was then under the rule of the Fatimids of Egypt. The Byzantine emperor appealed to Rome for help.

States of the Crusaders

THE CRUSADES

In 1096 Urban II, the Roman Catholic pope, answered the emperor's appeal. He called for rich and poor, knights and peasants, men, women, and children to drive the Turks out of the Holy Land—Jerusalem and the area surrounding it. It is so called because most of the events mentioned in the Bible took place there. The Pope's call resulted in a series of crusades. These were religious-military expeditions. The crusades became holy wars for both Muslims and Christians. Religious leaders on each side promised their soldiers that if they died in battle, they would go directly to Heaven. In all, eight major crusades were launched. The fighting continued off and on for 200 years.

In 1099 the crusaders took Jerusalem with savage fury. Many of the city's residents were mercilessly killed. The crusaders kept control for 88 years. In 1187 Jerusalem fell to the Turks under Saladin (SAL-uhd-uhn). He recaptured several other cities.

By this time, the Seljuk Turks had lost some of their original force. A number of military leaders had set up their own dynasties and small states. In 1171 Saladin had taken over the Fatimid dynasty and created his own Ayyubid (eye-YOOB-uhd) dynasty. Saladin, however, recognized the authority of the Abbasid caliph in Baghdad. Again, part of the Muslim world was unified for a time.

Before the end of the 1100s, the crusaders had been driven from most of the Holy Land. They had failed as much because of their own greed as because of the bravery and skill of Muslim warriors. Many crusaders were more interested in easy wealth than in religion. They were greedy, treacherous, and cruel. For example, in 1204, the fourth crusade went not to the Holy Land but to Constantinople, the Byzantine capital. There, crusaders looted the city and destroyed or stole thousands of art treasures and manuscripts. This event seriously weakened the Byzantine Empire.

CONSEQUENCES   Many Middle Eastern cities were destroyed and people killed during the crusades. However, the crusaders left little physical evidence of their presence. They did leave in the Middle East a distrust of Westerners.

The greatest material impact of the crusades was felt in Europe. Crusaders took back with them knowledge of the **intellectual** accomplishments of Middle Easterners. The crusaders had learned much about the history, arts, literature, technology, and way of life of Muslims and Byzantines. They learned of ancient Greek philosophies and sciences that had been preserved and added to by these peoples. Among practical applications, they learned how to build a pointed arch. This was to be important to European architecture.

The crusaders also carried home a taste for many of the luxuries they had discovered: spices, sugar, fine fabrics, exotic foods, and many other things. To fill the demand for these goods, European trade

exotic: unusual, foreign

This fresco or wall painting shows two crusaders in camp. Thousands of men, women and children joined the crusades. What were the consequences of the crusades, both in the Middle East and in Western Europe?

with the Middle East became important. Middle Easterners were a link in the chain between European and Asian merchants. Great city-states such as Venice and Genoa grew up. Eventually this trade led to the colonial empires of Western Europe.

MONGOLS

Control of the Middle East by the Seljuk Turks finally collapsed in the 1200s. Mongols (MAHN-guhls), also a nomadic group from Central Asia, invaded the area. They had begun their **campaign** of conquests in the late 1100s under Genghis Kahn (JEN-guhs KAHN). They overran much of what is modern China, Mongolia, Tibet, and parts of the USSR and Eastern Europe. At its peak the Mongol Empire extended from the Pacific Ocean to the borders of Hungary.

Mongol conquest of the Middle East was accomplished by one of Genghis Khan's grandsons, Hulagu (hoo-LAH-goo). In 1258 he captured and destroyed Baghdad and ended the Abbasid caliphate. The Mongol-Muslim empire he created included lands that are today parts of Iran, Iraq, Turkey, and Syria. Additional Mongol expansion in the region was checked near Jerusalem in 1260 by an army of Mamelukes (MAM-uh-looks), Turkish soldiers who had been slaves.

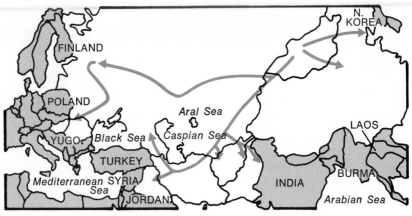

Mongol Invasions, c. 1200s A.D.

In 1238, an Ayyubid sultan had purchased several thousand Mamelukes. They were bought when they were very young and trained as warriors and palace guards. Within a few years, the Mamelukes had murdered the sultan and installed their own leader. They stopped Mongol expansion and also fought the crusaders. Under the leadership of Baybars, the Mamelukes drove the crusaders from the last of their holdings in Syria. The Mamelukes controlled Egypt until 1517, when Ottoman Turks took over.

After Hulagu's defeat, he and his successors settled in Iran. They accepted Islamic beliefs and culture. Mongol influence gradually faded. By 1335 a number of small dynasties had risen in what had once been Hulagu's Mongol empire.

But other Mongols were still engaged in conquests. In the late 1300s Tamerlane, the last of the major Mongol conquerors, swept westward from Central Asia. He seized much of the Middle East. His empire ended with his death in 1405.

Chapter 3
Ottoman
Empire

In the 1300s, while Mongol influence was fading, another group of people—the Ottomans (AHT-uh-muhns)—began their rise to power. Their empire eventually lasted for 600 years. During that time it played a dominant role in the affairs of the Middle East and southeastern Europe.

The Ottomans were a group of nomadic Turks from Central Asia. They began migrating westward as early as the 1100s. In a part of Asia Minor known as Anatolia (an-uh-TOH-lee-uh, now part of Turkey), the Ottoman Turks were hired by the Seljuk Turks to protect their borders against Mongol invaders. In exchange for this service, the Ottomans were given a small piece of land.

OTTOMAN EXPANSION

In 1299 Osman I (or Othman I), one of the Turkish chiefs, began to expand this territory. He is considered the founder and first sultan of the Ottoman Empire. When Osman died in 1323, he had extended Ottoman land to the Black Sea. His grandson, Murad I, extended the territory north of the Sea of Marmara. He seized Adrianople from the Byzantines and renamed it Edirne (ay-DIR-nuh). The Ottomans continued to eat away at the weakened Byzantine Empire.

By the mid-1400s Constantinople was almost surrounded by Ottoman lands. In 1453, under Mehmed II (meh-MET), the Ottomans captured the city and made it the capital of their empire. The Byzantine Empire had been declining steadily since the crusades. The Byzantines had regained control of Constantinople after it had been looted by crusaders in 1204, but their power had been greatly reduced. The year 1453 marks the end of the Byzantine Empire.

With Constantinople, the Ottomans now had control of a strategic area: the Bosporus (BAHS-puh-ruhs) and the Dardanelles (dard-uhn-ELZ). The Bosporus is a narrow strait that connects the Black Sea on the north with the Sea of Marmara on the south. The Dardanelles is another strait. It connects the Sea of Marmara with the Aegean Sea on the south. These two straits and Marmara form a link between the Black and Mediterranean seas. Possession of these waterways played a critical role in the destiny of the Ottoman Empire. Whoever controlled them also controlled the traffic between Russia and the Mediterranean.

PEAK OF POWER   In 1512 Selim I (seh-LEEM) began his rule. He was an ambitious leader who dreamed of an Ottoman Empire that connected Europe and Asia. He used the defense of Islam as an excuse for his campaigns. The first campaign was against the Safavids (sa-fa-VIDS) of Iran.

The Safavids had restored order among the Iranians after earlier Mongol invasions. The Safavids were Shi'ite Muslims. Their shah, Ismail (is-ma-EEL, 1500-1524), built a large army that grew daily because of converts. The Safavids began to spread their influence beyond Iran into Syria and Iraq.

Selim was a Sunni Muslim. He saw the Shi'ite Safavids as a religious as well as political threat. He set out to destroy them. The Safavids were badly defeated but were able to hold Iran.

Selim turned his attention to Syria. In 1516 he conquered that country. The next year the Ottoman Turks swept into Egypt. The Mameluke sultanate in Cairo was overthrown. North Africa came under Ottoman control. In 1517 when the Ottomans finally took Mecca and Medina in Arabia, the two holy cities of Islam, the Turkish sultan became caliph of all Muslims. The Ottomans now controlled the trade routes between Europe and Asia.

Selim was succeeded by his son Suleiman I (SOO-lay-mahn) in

European Turkey and Asian Turkey are divided by a narrow passageway of water or strait called the Dardanelles. At its narrowest the strait is only 1.6 kilometers (one mile) wide. At the fall of the Byzantine Empire Turkey took control of the strait. What once made this strait and the Bosporus so important?

Under Suleiman the Magnificent, the Ottoman Empire reached its peak. How did his successors go about delegating authority? How did their policies weaken the central government?

1520. He became known as the Magnificent. Suleiman led a number of campaigns against the Iranians. He was unable to defeat them completely. But he did gain territory along the Iranian borders and on the Arabian Peninsula. But he finally had to sign a peace **treaty** with the shah.

Suleiman then turned to Europe. At the time the Hapsburgs ruled the Holy Roman Empire. The empire was made up of Germany, Spain, the Netherlands, Switzerland, Austria, and parts of Czechoslovakia, France, and Italy. On land the Hapsburgs stopped the Ottomans at Vienna, Austria, in 1529.

The two empires then shifted their warfare to the Mediterranean. The Ottomans built a powerful navy and eventually controlled the eastern Mediterranean for many years. In the western part of the Mediterranean, the Hapsburgs made some gains. They took Tunis from the Turks for a time. The Turks regained it in

A SLOW DECLINE

Suleiman's rule marked the peak of Ottoman co   With his death in 1566, a period of slow decline set in. N   Ottoman sultan was as capable a leader as Suleiman. Appoint   o government positions came to be based on political favorit   nd bribery. The once-efficient Ottoman administration became i   asingly corrupt. As the central government grew weaker, local   rs began to exercise more authority.

One of the reasons for the decline of the Ottoman Turks was their expansionist policies. This representation shows the Turks beseiging Vienna, Austria.

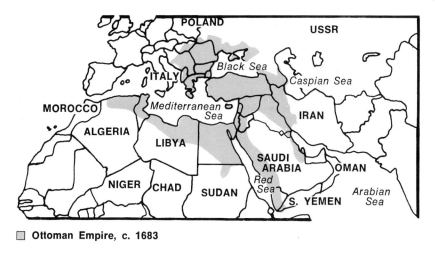

□ Ottoman Empire, c. 1683

□ Safavid Empire, 1600s

As matters grew worse, subjects rioted. Attempts were made at reform. But the efforts were either too limited or too temporary to do any good.

Ottoman sultans survived as long as their problems remained inside the empire. Old fears of the military might of the Turks saved them from outside interference. But as conditions within the empire worsened, powers on all sides began to attack. The Hapsburgs, Venetians (vuh-NEE-shuhns), Iranians, Egyptians, and Russians took up arms against the Ottoman Empire.

Under Suleiman's son, Selim II (1566-1574), the Ottomans experienced the first of a long series of setbacks. Selim's fleet was defeated in a major battle at Lepanto, Greece, by a holy **league** of Spanish, Venetian, and papal ships. They destroyed Turkish naval superiority in the eastern Mediterranean.

In 1683 the Ottomans tried again to take Vienna. John Sobieski (soh-BYES-kee), the Polish king, united with the Holy Roman emperor to save the city. Sobieski pushed the Turks back into Hungary. By 1699 the Turks had been driven from Hungary back to the Danube. In the 1700s the Ottomans fought a series of wars with Russia. They were defeated and forced to give up their lands along the Black Sea.

REFORM ATTEMPTS

Although the Ottomans had lost some of their lands, their empire was still vast. At the beginning of the 1800s, the empire was made up of peoples of many **nationalities**. The Turks were the dominant group. They were Muslims. So were the Arabs of the eastern Mediterranean, Egypt, and North Africa. The subject peoples of southeastern Europe were mostly Christian, however. They were often singled out for economic or religious persecution. Any rebellion on their part was harshly put down. Today this region of Europe is made up of

Romania, Bulgaria, Albania, and parts of Greece, Yugoslavia, and Turkey. This area is known as the Balkan Peninsula.

Under Selim III (1789-1807) **reform** attempts were made. The government was streamlined along European lines. Selim organized a **cabinet** of 12 **ministers**. He also tried to create an army like those of European powers. Schools were opened to teach the ideas of the Enlightenment movement of Western Europe. Some of these reforms made him unpopular. He was deposed in 1807. However, his efforts marked the end of Ottoman isolation.

In 1808 Mahmud II (mah-MOOD) came to the throne. His goal was complete **modernization**. He opened schools and emphasized the importance of education. Many Turks were sent abroad to study. He tried to reorganize the central government so that the sultan had supreme power.

Mahmud was not very successful. Allegiance to traditional ways within Ottoman society was strong. Continuing problems, especially among Balkan peoples, also held back his efforts. However, Mahmud did create a base for later reforms. The young men who had been educated abroad continued the process of modernization. But it was too late. Ottoman foreign affairs were growing worse.

A CRUMBLING EMPIRE

During the early 1800s, the Turks came to be dominated more and more by European powers. The weakness of the Ottoman Empire attracted foreign intervention. The Ottoman Turks became pawns in the political struggles of Europe. Only rivalry among the different European nations saved them from total destruction.

At first the Hapsburgs, Venetians, and Russians formed an anti–Ottoman coalition. The French and Swedes backed the Turks. The British and the Dutch wanted a **balance of power**.

THE RUSSIAN THREAT   At one point, Austria and Russia hoped to divide the Ottoman Empire. But the other European powers stopped them. By the mid-1800s Russia had become a threat to the European powers. It was also apparent that Russia posed the greatest threat to the Ottomans. Austria, France, Britain, and Prussia (eventually part of Germany) decided to use this threat for their own gain. They plotted to use the Ottomans to stop Russian expansion.

By expanding into Turkish territory, the Russians hoped to gain more territory and a way to the Mediterranean Sea. They also wanted to increase their **sphere of influence**. But the Russians needed an excuse to move against the Ottomans. They used their claim as Protector of Orthodox Christians in Ottoman territory as the reason. The Turkish sultan had granted a similar claim to the French. Russia insisted on the sole right to maintain holy places in Palestine and protect all Christians living in or visiting Ottoman lands. The sultan

disagreed. War broke out between the Russians and the Turks. The Russians quickly crushed the Turks. Britain and France rushed to Turkey's aid. The result was the Crimean (kry-MEE-uhn) War. Named for the Crimean Peninsula on the Black Sea where the fighting occurred, the war lasted from 1853 to 1856.

A **compromise** agreement was reached at the Congress of Paris in 1856. Russian expansion was halted. Despite this setback, the Russians were not stopped. Czar Alexandar II refused to abide by the treaty. Using the slogan "All Slavs are Brothers," the Russians aided revolts in the Balkans. They helped to fan the fires of increasing **nationalism** among the various Balkan peoples. Nationalism is a feeling of loyalty not to a local region or **ethnic group**, but to a nation.

Russia's interference led to another war: the Russo-Turkish War of 1877-1878. This time the Russians defeated the Ottomans. By the terms of the peace treaty, the Turks lost huge sections of Balkan territory to Russia. Serbia, Romania, and Montenegro (MAHNT-uh-NEE-groh) received their independence (Serbia and Montenegro are today part of Yugoslavia). A Bulgarian state, under Russian domination, was created.

Other European powers rejected the treaty. They were not pleased with the extension of Russian influence. The major European powers called the **Congress** of Berlin in 1878 to redistribute land in the Balkans. The Austro-Hungarians received Bosnia and Herzegovina (hert-suh-goh-VEE-nuh). The British were allowed to occupy the island of Cyprus. The Russians, however, continued to promote Pan-Slavism. This meant political and cultural unity among Slavs.

The Turks were also victims of other nations' expansionist policies. This representation shows Turkish troops marching out to meet Russian invaders at Constantinople.

REBELLION

deposed: removed from a position of power

During the time of these wars, the situation within the Ottoman Empire continued to worsen. The empire faced bankruptcy. Finally Midhat Pasha (mid-HAHT pah-SHAH), a reform leader, deposed the sultan. Midhat and the new sultan, Abdul Hamid (ahb-dool-hah-MEED), framed a new **constitution** in 1876. A **parliament** was set up. All citizens were considered equal.

Abdul Hamid soon grew tired of sharing his power. Declaring a state of emergency, he abolished the constitution and the parliament. Midhat was sent into exile. Censorship was imposed.

To gain popularity and justify his actions, Abdul Hamid promoted nationalism and an Islamic revival. He directed religious and nationalistic feeling against Balkan Christians. Abdul Hamid earned the name Red Sultan for his role in the Armenian massacres—a series of horrible bloodbaths. Accusing them of helping the Russians, the sultan tried to wipe out the entire Armenian people. Armenia was once a kingdom, but had been overrun by the Turks in the 1500s. Armenia today is part of the USSR, Turkey, and Iran.

The drawing on the left shows Abdul Hamid opening a session of the Turkish Parliament. Hamid soon tired of sharing his power. A group of reformers known as the Young Turks (right) took over the government in 1909. Were they any more successful than Hamid had been in reforming the Turkish government?

YOUNG TURKS While Abdul Hamid ruled, many reformers fled. Others remained and organized a **revolutionary** group of officers and students. This group and the exiles became known as the Young Turks.

The Young Turks were nationalists. But they disagreed among themselves as to the type of government they wanted. Some sought a nation in which many nationalities lived as equals. Others wanted a nation that included only Turks who could trace their roots back to the Turanians (tyoo-RAY-nee-uhns), a people of Central Asia.

Turks, however, were a minority in the empire.

The Young Turks gained control of the government in 1909. They attempted to restore order, but the problems by then were overwhelming. Their efforts were generally ineffective. They were opposed from without and from within. Economically, the empire was on the edge of collapse. Only European money was holding it together. The Turks had never built a **commercial** or industrial base for their economy. They thus allowed Europeans and non-Muslims to control their economy and trade. The leaders of Islam refused to accept anything that they thought was non-Muslim and thus opposed most of the reform measures. Furthermore, efforts at social reform rarely reached the people. A rigid class system and official corruption were in the way.

The Balkan situation continued to be critical. Nationalism and efforts for control by competing powers made it impossible for the Turks to handle the Balkans. Matters reached a crisis in 1912-1913 when the Balkan Wars erupted. In the first war, Serbia, Bulgaria, Greece, and Montenegro defeated the Turks. They took all the Ottoman Empire in Europe except Constantinople. The second war broke out when Romania, Serbia, and Turkey joined forces against the Bulgarians over a territorial disagreement. Bulgaria lost.

WORLD WAR I   Serbia then declared plans to form a **union** of Slavic peoples south of the Danube. This would include Austrian territory. The Austro-Hungarians said they would not allow such an action. In 1914 the heir to the Austro-Hungarian throne, Archduke Franz Ferdinand, was assassinated by a Serbian sympathizer. The Austrians moved against the Serbs. The Serbs asked for Russian aid.

Because of a complex system of **alliances** among the major European powers, the conflict—World War I—soon included all of Europe. Russia responded to Serbia's plea. Germany, an ally of Austro-Hungary, declared war on Russia. Russia was at that time part of an alliance known as the Triple **Entente** (ahn-TAHNT). The other two members were France and Britain. With Russia in the war, France and Britain were soon dragged into the fighting. The Triple Entente nations, joined by Belgium and Serbia, became known as the Allies. Later, the United States joined them. Germany and Austro-Hungary became known as the Central Powers. Under Enver Pasha, a Young Turk general, the Ottoman Turks allied themselves to the Central Powers. This was partly because the Turks feared the Russians.

As a result, the Turks fought on the losing side in World War I. They lost all their lands except those which today make up Turkey. The Turks would have lost more except for Mustafa Ataturk, a Turkish army officer. After the war, he led a resistance movement of Turkish nationalists. He resented the Treaty of Sevres which stripped the Ottoman Turks of everything except their holdings in Asia Minor and their capital, Constantinople.

When the Greeks invaded Asia Minor in 1919, Ataturk led the fight. His forces took Constantinople, deposed the sultan, and forced the Allies to negotiate a new treaty—the Treaty of Lausanne (1923). The Turks kept possession of all of Asia Minor, Constantinople, and the strategic Dardanelles. The Turkish military force was not limited. Turkey did not have to pay damages. Turkey did lose its Arab territories, however.

Chapter 4
European
Domination

Almost every Middle Eastern nation has been dominated to some degree by Europeans. Western nations used this control for their own benefits. These benefits were economic, nationalist, and/or military. Control of the Middle East meant control of the trade routes to Asia and around the Mediterranean. The 1700s and 1800s were also the time of European **colonialism**. Europeans were busy building world empires. Rulers believed that territory abroad made them more powerful in the eyes of their European rivals. Eventually world opinion, economic problems at home, and nationalist movements within the Middle East forced Europeans to give up their holdings.

EGYPT

In 1798 the French under Napoleon tried to seize Egypt. They were defeated by the Ottoman Turks and the British near Alexandria. In 1805 Mehemet Ali (or Muhammad Ali) seized control. He was a Turkish soldier who had been appointed governor by the Ottomans. Mehemet Ali killed the Mameluke rulers and drove the remaining British from Egypt. He began a dynasty that ruled Egypt until 1952.

Although a new dynasty had been created, Egypt was still a part of the Ottoman Empire in name. However, Egypt came increasingly under the domination of Western powers. The French and British were the most active. Between 1859 and 1869 a French company built the Suez Canal. The canal connected the Mediterranean and Red seas through the Gulf of Suez. Most of the stock that financed the project was owned by France and the Ottoman Empire. By 1875, as a result of trying to move Egypt too quickly into the modern world, the king was forced to sell Egypt's share to Britain. Continued financial problems brought the Egyptian economy under greater British management.

Between 1883 and 1907 Egypt was essentially under British control. The local ruler did as the British council-general ordered him. When the Ottoman Empire joined the Germans in World War I, the British made Egypt a **protectorate**. Increased nationalist sentiment among Egyptians forced Britain to give Egypt its independence in 1922. The British agreed to withdraw all troops except those in the Suez Canal Zone. During World War II, British troops used Egypt as a base for fighting the Italians and Germans in North Africa. After the war British troops remained in the Suez Canal Zone until the mid-1950s.

NORTH AFRICA

As early as the 1490s the Christian Spanish and Portuguese tried to take North Africa from the Muslims. They managed to capture some Moroccan ports, but they were never able to keep them. In the 1500s, during the rule of Selim I, the Ottoman Turks took a large part of the region stretching from Egypt to Morocco. However, the region remained fairly independent. Local governors paid **tribute** to the Ottoman Turks, but they governed much as they pleased.

During the next 200 years, North Africa was a stronghold for pirates. Morocco, Algeria, Tunisia, and Libya became known as the Barbary (BAR-buh-ree) States. The name probably came from the word Berber. Barbary pirates, and indirectly their rulers, demanded money from the major sea powers. In return for this money, the ships of these countries were given safe passage through the Mediterranean. This action eventually led to the Tripolitan (trip-AHL-uh-tuhn) Wars. The infant navy of the U.S. finally broke the power of the Barbary pirates in the early 1800s.

Later in the 1800s the North African states came under Western domination. European powers began claiming parts of the area and making them colonies.

In 1830 the French took the port city of Algiers and overthrew the local ruler. The French destroyed Arab resistance and took the rest of the area in the 1850s. The French used it as a base for their later movement into sub-Saharan Africa. In 1881 Tunisia's ruler was forced to sign a treaty making that state a French protectorate. France's control lasted into the 1950s.

When the French seized Algeria, the Ottoman Turks began to take a greater interest in their Libyan territory. The Turks feared it too would fall to the French. In 1912, after a war with Italy, the Turks had to give Libya to the Italians. The Libyans fought this action but with little success. During World War II, Italy fought on the losing side. As a result its empire was taken apart. Libya remained under French and British control until 1951.

France, Spain, Britain, and Germany all were interested in Morocco. Its location makes it especially important. It has coastline along the

The Suez Canal was originally a joint project between a French company and the Egyptian government. Later the Egyptians had to sell their stock to the British. Egypt came increasingly under British domination.

Mediterranean Sea, the Strait of Gibraltar, and the Atlantic Ocean. In 1912 Morocco became a protectorate of France and Spain. The idea was to allow outsiders to deal equally with the Moroccans. The area was divided into French Morocco, Spanish Morocco, Spanish Sahara, and an international zone—Tangier (tan-JIR). Tangier was singled out because it sits at the Strait of Gibraltar.

OUTSIDE INTEREST IN IRAN

Iran never was conquered by the Ottoman Turks. But during the 1800s and early 1900s Russia and Britain became interested in Iran. The British were interested because it was near India which they controlled. The Russians were interested because they wanted an outlet on the Persian Gulf. The Qajar rulers of Iran found Russia and Britain eager to lend them money. In return for loans, the outside powers gained increasing control of the internal affairs of Iran.

chaos: total confusion

In 1901 oil was discovered in Iran. The British began to develop Iran's rich oil fields. Together with the Iranians, they formed the Anglo-Iranian Oil Company. Within Iran, however, there was political, economic, and social chaos. The people had become dissatisfied with the shah's rule. They forced him to grant them a constitution in 1906. A parliament of two houses was set up.

In 1907 Russia and Britain signed an agreement dividing Iran into spheres of influence. The Russians took the north. The British took the south. A small area was left between the two for the shah. The Iranians reacted bitterly. But World War I intervened. During the war, the Russians, British, and Germans among others schemed for

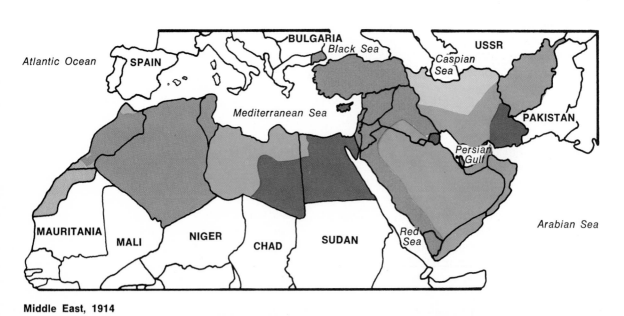

Middle East, 1914

■ British ■ French ■ Italian ■ Spanish □ Russian ■ Ottoman Empire ■ Independent control of Iran. None were successful. After the end of World War I, Britain and Russia canceled their agreement. A new dynasty took over the Iranian government in the 1920s.

WARS OVER AFGHANISTAN

The British and Russians were also rivals in neighboring Afghanistan. Both saw the region as a possible threat to their growing empires. The British invaded Afghanistan in 1839. They controlled much of India and wanted to protect their possession on the north. Russia reacted to Britain's move. The Afghans and Russians shared a common boundary. For many years the Russians and British fought the Afghans and each other in a series of Afghan Wars. Finally, in 1879, the British gained the dominant role. They controlled Afghan foreign affairs until 1919. In that year, after another war, the British granted Afghanistan its independence.

THE MANDATES

When the Ottoman Empire collapsed after World War I, the breakup of its territory led to the creation of several **mandates** along the eastern Mediterranean. These mandates were orders granted by the League of Nations to member nations. The League of Nations was an international organization created after World War I to keep peace. The mandates required that the nations set up governments over lands formerly controlled by the Central Powers.

Syria and Lebanon became French mandates in 1920. The Syrians did not accept this action. They worked for independence using riots, revolts, and strikes. As a result the French allowed them some **self-government**. But they did not gain their full independence until after World War II.

Iraq and Palestine became mandates of the British. Soon after, Iraqi nationalists began the fight for independence. The British ended the mandate in 1932. However, the British continued to influence Iraqi policies in order to protect their economic investments. The Palestine mandate was divided by the British into Transjordan and Palestine in 1922.

Mandates
- British
- French
- Independent

PERSIAN GULF STATES

Although most European nations had withdrawn from the Middle East by 1960, Britain continued to dominate a number of small states. Under the role of protecting these states, Britain was really protecting its own political and commercial interests. Britain finally withdrew when the expense of keeping up its defense agreements became too much of a financial burden. The states involved were the United Arab Emirates, Bahrain, Qatar, Kuwait, and Oman.

The United Arab Emirates were once a series of small sheikhdoms.

The Pirate Coast made shipping in the Persian Gulf dangerous. This print shows pirates attacking a ship of the British East India Company. How did the British finally solve the problem with the sheikhs?

Sheikh (SHEEK) is an Arabic word for chief. The area they covered was called the Pirate Coast. In the late 1700s and 1800s, pirates sailing from the Pirate Coast were attacking ships of the British East India Company. Britain signed an agreement with the various sheikhdoms. They would protect British shipping against future pirate attacks. In return the British guaranteed the sheikhs protection from outsiders.

North of this area is Bahrain (bah-RAYN), a series of islands in the Persian Gulf. In 1507 the Portuguese set up a trading base among these, but they were driven out. Later the islands fell under Iranian domination. In 1820 the local ruler made an agreement with the British to protect the islands from outside interference. This included interference from the Iranians, Ottoman Turks, and Arabs living on the peninsula. A British agent was appointed to act as advisor to the local sheikh.

Qatar (KAHT-uhr), south of Bahrain, had been under Ottoman Turkish control from 1872 to 1915. In 1916 it signed a defense agreement with Great Britain.

The agreements between Britain and these various Persian Gulf States remained in force until 1971. In that year Britain freed itself of its defense commitments east of the Suez. The states talked about joining together in a **federation**. But Bahrain and Qatar decided to seek independence as separate countries. The other states formed the United Arab Emirates. Some of these Persian Gulf states have rich oil reserves.

North of these states is Kuwait (kuh-WAYT). It was once part of the Ottoman Empire. However, the Turks interfered little with its rule. In 1899 the sheikh asked for the protection of Great Britain. As with other small states in this region, the ruler feared domination by outsiders. For 62 years the agreement remained in force. In 1961 Britain recognized Kuwait's independence.

After independence, Britain and Kuwait signed a new defense agreement. This agreement proved useful when Iraq tried to invade Kuwait in 1961. Iraq's ruler claimed Kuwait because, under the Ottoman Turks, it had once been part of Iraq. Kuwait called on Britain for help. The British acted promptly and Iraq was defeated. Britain ended the defense agreement in 1968. In 1972 Iraq invaded Kuwait. This time the Iraqi were turned back when nearby Iran threatened to aid Kuwait.

On the southeastern edge of the Arabian Peninsula is the Sultanate of Oman. It was formerly known as Muscat and Oman. In the early 1800s, the sultan had great power along the east coast of Africa, the Arabian Sea, and the Gulf of Oman. In 1798 the sultan signed a trade agreement with the British through the British East India Company. It gave the British a **monopoly**. No other Western nation could trade with Oman. The two powers also signed a defense agreement. Over the years the sultans of Oman have used British aid in putting down local disturbances.

Summing Up the Unit

Social Studies Vocabulary

Define: clan; kinship group; territory; nationality; cabinet; minister; balance of power; sphere of influence; nationalism; ethnic group; congress; constitution; parliament; revolutionary; entente; colonialism; protectorate; mandate

People

Identify: Abu Bakr; Ali; Muawiyah; Fatima; Abdul Abbas; Al-Mansur; Seljuk; Togrul Beg; Urban II; Saladin; Genghis Khan; Hulagu; Baybars; Tamerlane; Osman I; Mehmed II; Selim I; Sulëiman the Magnificent; Mahmud II; Midhat Pasha; Abdul Hamid; Ataturk; Mehemet Ali

Words

Define: caliph; Sunni; Shia; imam; Moors; monotheists; sultan; Holy Land; crusades; Mamelukes; Pan-Slavism; Treaty of Sevres; Barbary States; League of Nations

Questions

1. a. Why did Muhammad marry an African? b. Why were some of his marriages made for political reasons?
2. What problems did Ali's death cause?
3. How do the Sunnis and Shi'ites regard the position of the caliph?
4. What administrative changes did Muawiyah make in the empire?
5. a. What was Muhammad's attitude toward the war? b. Why was fighting part of Middle Eastern life?
6. a. Why did Urban II begin the crusades? b. When? c. How long did they last?
7. Why did crusaders fail in their attempts to free the Holy Land?
8. a. Where was the greatest material impact of the crusades felt? b. How?
9. What event marked the end of the Byzantine Empire?
10. What is the strategic importance of the Bosporus, Sea of Marmara, and the Dardanelles?
11. Why did Selim I view the Safavids as both a political and a religious threat?
12. What caused Ottoman power to weaken?
13. Subject peoples of the Ottoman Empire in southeastern Europe were mostly of what religion?
14. a. What reform attempts did Selim III make? b. What effect did his reforms have on Ottoman isolation?
15. What excuse did the Russians use to move against the Ottomans?
16. Why did Abdul Hamid try to wipe out the Armenian people?
17. Why were the Young Turks ineffective?
18. What developments that grew out of Pan-Slavism brought on World War I?
19. a. How did Britain obtain part ownership of the Suez Canal? b. How long did British troops remain in the Suez Canal Zone?
20. What parts of North Africa came under control of: a. France? b. Italy? c. Spain?
21. Why was Tangier an international zone?
22. How did Russia and Britain gain increasing control of Iran's internal affairs?
23. What was Britain's interest in the Persian Gulf States?

Discussion Topics

1. The crusades were holy wars for both Muslims and Christians. Are holy wars different from other wars? If so, how?
2. What was Turkey's role in the Balkans? What led to World War I? Did Turkey's weakness in the Balkans make a clash there between Russia and Austria inevitable?
3. Middle Easterners developed a distrust of Westerners. What historical reasons do Middle Easterners have for this distrust?

Project Ideas

1. Write a report on: the Moors; Baghdad; the Seljuk Turks; Saladin; Constantinople; Suleiman the Magnificent; the Battle of Lepanto; the Barbary Pirates; the Crimean War; Pan-Slavism; the Young Turks; Ataturk.
2. Make a chart of the various Muslim dynasties. Briefly describe the importance of each.

97

Unit V

Recent Years

Independence movements in the Middle East have brought about great changes in the social welfare of the people. This student attends Saudi Arabia's new University of Petroleum and Minerals. Why is petroleum important?

As we have seen, the Ottoman Empire collapsed after World War I. Western European nations increased their control of the Middle East. For their convenience in governing, the Western powers divided the region without regard for the peoples living there. Middle Easterners were angered by these acts of colonialism and **imperialism**. Over the years, this anger was expressed through increasingly violent words and actions. Beginning with the 1920s, the Middle East has been the scene of many fights for and since independence.

The movement toward nationalism was late starting in the Middle East. Most Middle Easterners had been part of the Ottoman Empire for centuries. During that time they identified themselves not with a nation but with Islam. By its very nature, Islam knows no national boundaries. Before they could form a **national identity**, Middle Easterners had to adapt Islam to the modern world. A national identity is a sense of the oneness of a people who hold a common land, economy, culture, and language. Many leaders have found the process of blending the old and the new a long, slow one.

MODERNIZATION OF TURKEY

Turkey was the first Middle Eastern nation to move toward modernization. The changes were brought about by the resistance leader Mustafa Kemal Ataturk (moos-tah-FAH kuh-MAHL ah-tah-TOORK). When Turkey was declared a **republic** in 1923, Ataturk became the first president.

Ataturk gave the Turkish people purpose and direction. Because he hoped to achieve many of his goals within his lifetime, he moved his people along as rapidly as possible.

ATATURK'S SIX PRINCIPLES   Ataturk was guided by six principles. These were nationalism, secularism, populism, republicanism, statism, and revolutionism.

By nationalism, Ataturk meant a sense that all people within the borders of Turkey were Turks. The origins, physical appearance, or beliefs of the people did not matter. All would be treated alike.

Secularism meant separating religion from the government. When Ataturk began his reforms, Turkey was a religious state. The legal system was based on Islamic law. All parts of daily living—manner of dress, education, politics, and so on—were closely tied to Islam. Ataturk realized that to carry out his reforms, he must separate religion from the state. His first step was to abolish the caliphate in 1924. He then changed the legal system. Laws were no longer to be interpreted according to the Koran, Sunna, or other Islamic sources. Instead, they would be based on European legal codes. Religious shrines and monasteries were closed. Sunday replaced Friday as the day of rest.

Education too was separated from Islam. Schools were placed under government control. Schools no longer taught religion. Many new schools were opened. By the time Ataturk died in 1938, Turkey had become, in name at least, a **secular** state.

Populism meant the popular will. The national **assembly**—the governing body—was to work for the good of all the people. Republicanism was the form of government Ataturk wanted Turkey to adopt. Representatives were elected.

Statism was concerned mostly with improving the Turkish econ-

Mustafa Kemal Ataturk headed the Turkish Republic from 1923 to 1938. What reforms did Ataturk begin? Aware that it is not easy for people to change their age-old traditions, he tried to explain the reasons for his reforms.

Besides actively working for social and welfare benefits for Turkish citizens, the government has entered the field of business. This is a sugar refinery built by the Turkish government.

omy. State aid was granted to private **industry**. People were trained for management positions. Railroads, shipping, banks, and other businesses were taken over by the government. This is called **nationalization**. To help the economy, Ataturk promoted **industrialization** in every way. Additional railroads were built to transport raw materials and finished goods more efficiently. The state entered into the manufacture of such items as sugar, tobacco, textiles, and matches.

Revolutionism meant making and accepting changes in political, social, and economic life. Few parts of Turkish life were unchanged. But Ataturk knew it was not easy for his people to give up their old ways. But change was necessary to bring Turkey into the mainstream of the modern world. For example, Ataturk felt that the Arabic **script** used by the Turks was not suited to modern business. In 1929 he ordered that it be replaced with the Latin alphabet. This is the alphabet used by Western nations. Typewriters then came into widespread use in Turkey.

Ataturk did much to improve the status of women. **Polygyny**—having more than one wife—was discouraged. Women were given the right to vote and encouraged to seek political office. They were also encouraged to pursue careers in science and the arts.

IRAN'S NATIONALISM

Ataturk's reforms influenced many other nations. One example in particular is Iran. The first major attempts at reform began when Riza Khan seized control of Iran in 1921. In 1925 he was proclaimed shah and founded the Pahlevi (PAHL-uh-vee) dynasty. During his rule, Riza Shah gave the Iranians direction and a strong sense of nationalism.

Riza Shah forced the various peoples throughout the country to acknowledge the authority of the central government. He broke the power of Muslim religious leaders who opposed reforms. European codes of law replaced Islamic laws. An educational system was set up patterned after that of France. Riza Shah encouraged industry and built factories and railroads. Banks and currency controls were created to put the nation's finances in order.

acknowledge: recognize, accept

Religious and social customs that Riza Shah considered too extreme were abolished. Women in particular benefited from such reforms. Polygyny was discouraged. A man was not allowed to take a second wife unless the first and the prospective wives agreed. Nor could girls marry before the age of 15.

During the early days of World War II, Riza Shah tried to keep Iran **neutral**. He resisted Soviet and British demands for a supply line through Iran. In 1941 the Soviets invaded from the north. The British invaded from the south. Riza Shah was forced to step down. The British sent him to South Africa. He was succeeded by his son, Mohammad Riza Pahlevi.

In 1942 Britain, the USSR, and Iran signed the Tripartite (try-PAHR-tyt) Treaty of Alliance. The treaty guaranteed the withdrawal of all outside troops from Iran after the war. As part of the agreement, Iran declared war on Germany. Iran became the crossroads for the movement of military supplies and equipment from the Persian Gulf to the USSR. The Iranian people resented the Soviet and British troops in their country. They feared that these foreign powers would again try to divide the country between them. Moreover, the war resulted in shortages of food and **consumer goods**. The Iranians became restless. **Communists** became active. In 1946 a revolt broke out in northern Iran. The USSR used this as an excuse to keep Soviet troops in the north. The U.S. backed Iran. The United Nations Security Council condemned the Soviet action. The Soviets withdrew.

Since that time the Iranians have had a series of national crises. One was caused when Prime Minister Mohammad Mossadegh nationalized the oil industry, dissolved the parliament, and tried to overthrow the shah. From 1951 to 1953 Mossadegh ruled like a **dictator**. In 1953 a coalition of nationalists and army officers removed him from office. The shah returned to power.

In 1961-1962 the shah began a program of **land reform**. Large amounts of royal land were divided into small farms and given away. Shah Mohammad Riza has encouraged health-care and **literacy** programs. Economic reforms and industrial development have been stressed. Some of the profits from the huge oil reserves are used for economic and social reforms. In recent years the shah has also built a modern military force. Since the early 1970s a definite improvement in the economic growth of Iran can be seen. However, it will be a number of years before the success of Mohammad Riza Pahlevi's reforms can be accurately judged.

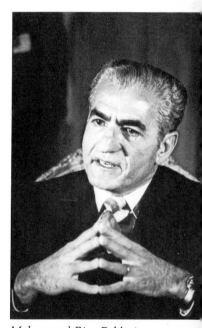

Mohammad Riza Pahlevi —the Shah of Iran— has done much to improve the lives of his subjects. What reforms has he undertaken?

Gamal Abdul Nasser was a controversial leader. What tactics did he use to gain and keep power? What reforms did he bring about? Did the end justify the means?

EGYPTIAN NATIONALISM

After World War II feelings of discontent erupted into violence in Egypt. Egyptian nationalists resented British troops in the Suez Canal Zone. In 1952 a group of army officers led a **revolution** and expelled King Farouk. The following year Egypt was proclaimed a republic. General Mohammad Naguib was the first president. In 1954 Colonel Gamal Abdel Nasser (juh-MAHL AHB-dool NAH-suhr) became prime minister. He was elected president in 1956 and led the country until his death in 1970.

Nasser wanted to improve the political, economic, and social conditions of his people. He also wanted to bring political, economic, and social improvements to all Arab peoples. The name Arab socialism has been given to this goal. Nasser believed that the peoples of most Arab nations wanted unity based on their shared Islamic religion, language, culture, and history. He did not wish to force this unity on Arab nations, however. He wanted to encourage a spirit of cooperation among them.

NASSER'S IMPROVEMENTS   After the revolution of 1952, Nasser was determined to rid Egypt of British troops. In 1954 he signed an agreement with the British to remove their troops from the Canal Zone by June 1956. In July 1956 he nationalized the Suez Canal. Nasser also nationalized the trade and industrial holdings of most foreigners.

Nasser pushed hard to improve the lives and working conditions of Egyptian farmers. One of his first steps was land reform. He broke up large landholdings and reduced land rents. The Egyptian government loaned money at low interest rates to farmers to buy land. Irrigation projects were improved, expanded, and paid for by the government. Nasser sought to increase agricultural production. **Cooperatives** were set up to distribute farm supplies and machinery. Nasser accepted **foreign aid** from both the East and the West. Perhaps his greatest project was the huge Aswan High Dam. It was built with the aid of the USSR.

Nasser worked to improve health-care services. He provided a better education for Egyptian youth. The growth of industries such as iron, steel, chemicals, textiles, and petroleum products were encouraged. Nasser aimed to make Egypt as self-supporting as possible.

Women gained from Nasser's reforms as well as men. They gained the vote in 1956. Nasser did much to liberalize the role of women in Egyptian society. Today many attend universities or have professional careers.

For almost 20 years Nasser controlled Egypt with a firm hand. He destroyed threats to his political control by breaking the power of any organization or group that opposed him. He sometimes exercised the power of a dictator. He was determined to make Egypt a democratic socialist country.

The Aswan High Dam is one of the chief accomplishments of Nasser's domestic reforms. What improvements resulted from the dam?

When Nasser died in 1970, he was succeeded by Vice-President Anwar Sadat (suh-DAHT). Sadat had been a leading figure in the 1952 revolution. As president, Sadat began extensive political and economic reforms. He called for a new constitution to guarantee individual rights. He also entered into an agreement with Israel which was negotiated by the U.S. This pact brought a period of peace between Egypt and Israel.

SAUDI ARABIA'S RELIGIOUS NATIONALISM

By the 1500s the Ottoman Turks had conquered parts of the western Arabian Peninsula. The rest of the peninsula was occupied by various people who were bound together by **kinship** ties. In the 1700s Abd-al-Wahhab (ahb-dool-wah-HAHB) began a reform movement within some of these groups. His followers became known as Wahabis. He felt that Islam had been corrupted. He wanted a return to the strict interpretation of the teachings of Islam as given in the Koran. The prophet Muhammad had taught that gambling, drinking wine, smoking, wearing luxurious dress, and using tombstones for

103

Saudi Arabian nationalism is built on Islamic traditions. How does this differ from Egyptian nationalism? King Faisal (above) used profits from oil to move the technology and industry of his country into the 20th century while keeping Islam strong.

the dead were wrong. Abd-al-Wahhab wanted to enforce these teachings. He also wanted Muslims to follow the teachings of the Koran with regard to prayers, fasting, and the pilgrimage to Mecca.

THE SAUD FAMILY   Eventually Abd-al-Wahhab made an alliance with the Saud (sah-OOD) family of central Arabia. By 1814 King Saud III controlled a great state on the Arabian Peninsula. From 1818 until the end of World War I, the Ottoman Turks controlled most of the area. Gradually, the Sauds regained the power they once had. By 1926 the Saud family under King ibn Saud had expanded its control to the present boundaries of Saudi Arabia. In 1932 Saudi Arabia (SOWD-ee uh-RAY-bee-uh) became the official name of the country. Mecca became the religious capital. Riyadh (ree-YAHD) became the political capital.

Ibn Saud died in 1953. His son Saud ibn-Abdul Aziz succeeded him. He proved to be an irresponsible ruler. Soon Saudi Arabia was nearly bankrupt. Saud appointed his brother, Prince Faisal (FY-zal), prime minister in 1958. In 1964 the Saud family made Faisal king. He began a program of gradual social and economic reform. One of his first acts was to abolish slavery. Some of the profits from the sale of the country's vast oil resources were spent for free medical services and free schools. Faisal ruled until his assassination in 1975. A family council selected his brother Khalid (KAH-lid) as successor.

STRENGTH OF ISLAM   Religion is the very heart of Saudi Arabian life. Islamic teachings are considered law. In fact, the law of Islam is the only law. As a result, Saudi Arabian nationalism is based entirely on religion. The first pillar of Islam is written on the flag. Most national holidays are religious holidays. Any nonreligious ideas of national identity have been held back by the very **conservative** Wahabi Muslims. In Saudi Arabia nationalism involves more modernization than reform. The people do not want to give up their Islamic teachings. They want better health care, transportation and **communications** systems, and agriculture. Most of all, they want better education. But always these improvements must be kept within the framework of Islamic tradition.

NORTH AFRICA

Although there had been earlier attempts, the nationalist movement in North Africa did not become a real political force until the 1950s and 1960s. Unlike other areas of the Middle East, large numbers of Europeans had settled in North Africa. These Europeans formed separate communities from the Muslims. The Europeans dominated their colonies' economies. Attempts at creating independence movements were usually quickly put down. In Morocco, for example, the ruler was deposed by the French in 1953 in an attempt to discourage the growing independence movement.

Morocco did gain its independence as a **monarchy** in 1956, however. Tangier, an international zone since 1912, was restored to the country. A constitution went into effect in 1962. However, the king continued to have absolute power. In 1970 a new constitution went into effect and a parliament was elected by popular vote. But the king dissolved parliament in 1972. In 1975 Morocco took control of most of the territory known formerly as the Spanish Sahara. Mauritania took over southern portions of this territory.

Unlike Morocco, Algeria's drive for independence was a long, bloody struggle. Before the fighting ended, an estimated one million people had died. Since France had taken the area in the 1850s, many French colonists had settled in Algeria. It was also a base for the French army in North Africa and the French Foreign Legion. After World War II, some Algerians wanted to remain tied to France. Others wanted complete independence. Widespread fighting began in 1954. For the next seven years, Algeria was torn by **civil war**.

The Algerian conflict tore apart France's government and former French President Charles de Gaulle returned to power. He negotiated Algeria's independence. In 1961 Algeria became independent. Internal political struggles continued until 1962. In 1965 the government was overthrown by a military revolt and a revolutionary council was set up to rule.

Tunisia also felt the impact of growing nationalism after World War II. Civil turmoil in 1952 prompted France to give the Tunisians

The fight for independence in North Africa was late in beginning but was a long and bloody one. This is a street scene in Algiers in 1962.

a degree of independence. In 1956 Tunisia was declared fully independent and made a republic. Its first elected president was Habib Bourguiba (boor-GEE-buh), a hero in Tunisia's struggle for independence. He has been reelected several times.

Chapter 2
Politics
and Turmoil

A military coup in Iraq ended the monarchy in 1958, and crowds cheered the new premier, General Abdul Karim Kassem. Later, Kassem himself was overthrown. What are the historic roots of military rule in the Middle East?

When independence came, most Middle Easterners lacked the political knowledge to deal with it. They had lived for centuries as part of a society in which they placed their trust in particular political and/or religious leaders. Or they were part of a colonial system in which European nations held political power.

Since independence, people in some countries have put their faith in leaders who did not deserve such trust. Others thought that independence would bring instant equality or prosperity. Middle Easterners have also learned that independence is no guarantee of political stability. In recent years military takeovers have become common in the Middle East. In some countries the greatest threat to political stability has been internal disagreement over how to handle the Arab-Israeli situation.

MILITARY TAKEOVERS

Like Egypt, Iraq and Libya were once monarchies. Iraq gained its independence from Britain in 1932 as a constitutional monarchy—a state ruled by a hereditary leader according to a constitution. In 1958 the king, several of his ministers, and some members of the royal family were executed by revolutionaries. The country became a republic. But that did not end the unrest. Since 1958 Iraq has had several military **coups** or takeovers.

Libya was under Italian rule until World War II. Afterward, two of Libya's three provinces were placed under British control. The third province was placed under French control. The entire area was granted its independence in 1961 as a monarchy. A great gap existed between the very rich and the very poor. Younger, educated Libyans demanded more equal distribution of the wealth. Little progress was made. Consequently, a military **junta** (HUN-tuh) overthrew the king in 1969.

Turkey also experienced a military takeover. The nation had run smoothly from Ataturk's death in 1938 until the 1950s. In the 1950s, however, the government overextended the nation's economy. The government undertook many construction and development projects that it did not have the money to finance. The Turks began to suffer from shortages of food and consumer goods. Riots broke out. As criticism mounted in the newspapers, the government made mass arrests. Press censorship was imposed. An opposition party was formed. However, it was unable to gain enough support in the elections of 1957 to unseat the government. Finally in May 1960 the military junta took over. They claimed their action was necessary to prevent civil war. A Committee of National Unity governed Turkey. A new constitution was written and approved by the voters. A two-house legislature—a national assembly and a **senate**—was set up.

Syria also has had a hectic political history since gaining its independence from the French in 1942. The military has emerged often as the strongest force in the country. The government changed hands and philosophies on a seesaw basis. Some Syrians prefer the old path of political control by one or a few. Others are extreme **rightists, leftists**, or those who borrow doctrines from both conservatives and **radicals**.

The strongest and only legal party in Syria is the Socialist Baath (BAHTH). The Baathists seek freedom of speech, assembly, and elections. These are characteristics of a **democracy**. The Baathists also want **socialism** which, they believe, will improve the welfare of the people and the economic strength of the country. Syrians are experiencing not only political but also economic instability. Syria is a land of few **natural resources**.

In 1942 Lebanon changed its status from mandate to independent nation. It is officially a democracy but violence has often limited the rights of individuals. A revolt in 1958 caused the Lebanese president to call on the U.S. for help. Fourteen thousand marines were sent. After the 1958 crisis, the new president instituted reforms. Efforts were made to improve the economy. Civil wars continued, however. Conflict broke out in 1975 between Muslims and Christians.

As we have seen, under a mandate given to Britain, Jordan was part of Palestine. In 1922 the Palestine mandate was divided into Palestine proper (now Israel) and Transjordan. Transjordan became independent in 1946. Four years later, the country's name was changed to the Hashemite Kingdom of Jordan. In 1951 Jordan's King Abdullah was assassinated by a Palestinian nationalist. Palestinian (pal-uh-STIN-ee-uhn) is the name given to Arabs who lived in the area of Palestine before it became the state of Israel in 1948. Jordan's throne passed to Abdullah's grandson, Hussein (hoo-SAYN). Hussein's rule has been marked with endless difficulties. Attempts to kill him and overthrow his government have been repeated. One of his most serious problems has been the refugees from Arab-Israeli conflicts.

WHY THE MILITARY   Independence and modernization attempts have created uncertainty for many Middle Easterners. Given their historical background in Islam, it is not surprising that in times of change they should turn to strong leaders. The people have traditionally placed their faith in one leader. Often that person has been a military as well as spiritual leader. Military officers may be the only ones who have the organizational abilities, respect, and education to govern. Ataturk, Riza Shah, Nasser, and Sadat among others were once army officers. All carried their countries through periods of major reform.

Some people complain that military leaders are dictatorial. Under their control **representative government** is lost. For these nations,

Part of the Egyptian armed forces lines up for inspection. Why do Middle Eastern nations devote so much of their budgets to military expenses?

representative government may come in time. But leaders feel that education and economic programs are needed before the people can control their political futures.

OTHER INTERNAL STRUGGLES

At the southwestern end of the Arabian Peninsula are two nations with similar names: the Democratic Republic of Yemen and the Yemen Arab Republic. To distinguish between the two nations, the Democratic Republic of Yemen is referred to as Southern Yemen. The other is called simply Yemen. Both nations have experienced internal struggles in recent years as the people have sought more representative governments.

The Ottoman Turks tried twice to control Yemen: in the 1500s and the 1800s. When the Ottoman Empire fell after World War I, the local ruler, the imam, regained control. The people were not content with his rule, however. In 1948 the imam was assassinated. But reformers were not able to overthrow the existing government. From 1962 to 1969 the country experienced a civil war between **republicans** and **royalists**—supporters of the imam. In 1969 the republicans declared the civil war over. The following year, a republican form of government was established.

Southern Yemen was once the British colony of Aden. Britain gained control of the area in the 1800s. Aden was the headquarters for British troops stationed in the Middle East. To guarantee the **colony's** defenses, the British began to extend their influence over the small states surrounding Aden. Six of these states were formed into a protectorate.

Pressured by violence and revolts, the British gave the area its independence in 1967. But the new government was troubled by internal struggles. In 1970 the country finally came together as one: The People's Democratic Republic of Yemen. It has a leftist government. Both the People's Republic of China and the USSR have given Southern Yemen military and economic aid.

ARAB-ISRAELI CONFLICT

Perhaps the greatest conflicts in the Middle East in recent years have centered around the Arab-Israeli struggle over possession of the land once known as Palestine.

The Diaspora in 135 A.D. caused most of the Jewish people living in Palestine to be scattered throughout the world. Only a few managed to stay. Of those who left and their descendants, many believed they could never return until the coming of the Messiah. But some later Jews did not want to wait for that indefinite day.

In the 1800s Jews were being persecuted in Russia and its territories in Eastern Europe. Many fled, especially to the U.S. Some of the

Immigrants crowd a ship's deck for their first sight of the new state of Israel. The year was 1948. When did the movement to return to Palestine begin? Why?

younger ones, however, slipped quietly into Palestine. The first **migration** back to the promised land had begun.

ZIONISM During the late 1800s, a movement to reestablish Palestine as the Jewish homeland was founded. The movement came to be known as Zionism (ZY-uh-niz-uhm). Publication of a pamphlet called *The Jewish State* and other articles by Theodore Herzl (HERT-suhl) helped the cause of Zionism. Herzl was disturbed by the European **prejudice** against Jews. He believed the solution was a mass exodus of Jews from Europe to a place where they could live in freedom. In 1897 Herzl and others held the First Zionist Congress in Basel, Switzerland. There they organized the World Zionist Organization.

Further attacks against Jews in Eastern Europe and Russia started the second migration to Palestine in the early 1900s. Among the migrants was David Ben-Gurion (ben-goor-YON), a Polish Jew who later became Israel's first prime minister.

During World War I, Chaim Weizmann (hy-YIM VYTS-mahn), won British recognition for Zionism. In 1917, in a paper by Arthur J. Balfour (BAL-fuhr), the British Foreign Secretary, Britain formally stated the historical connection of the Jews with the land of Palestine. This statement is known as the Balfour Declaration. It was made part of the League of Nations' orders that gave Britain authority to govern Palestine. From the 1920s on, many Jews migrated to Palestine. Their numbers increased greatly in the 1930s and early 1940s. Jews from Germany and German-occupied countries fled there to escape Adolf Hitler's persecutions.

Palestinian Arabs resented their coming. The mass migrations represented an economic and social threat to them. During the many centuries of the Diaspora, Arabs had become the majority in Palestine. They claimed that their centuries of work on the land gave them a right to the area. They saw the Jews as invaders. They would have to be put out—with violence, if necessary. On the other hand, the Jews regarded Palestine as their land by ancient right. Their ancestors had been removed by force.

The Palestinian Arabs and the Jews were both determined to push their claims. Violence, bloodshed, and misery resulted.

PARTITION   After World War II, Britain continued to rule Palestine. The British tried to satisfy the Arabs. They limited the number of Jews who could enter Palestine each year. But violence increased. Arabs attacked Jews. The Jewish underground stepped up its **terrorist** attacks against both the British and the Arabs. An underground is a secret organization usually created for revolutionary purposes. The Jews refused to obey the immigration limits. In spite of British patrols many Jews were smuggled into Palestine. Finally in 1947 the problem of Palestine was submitted to the UN.

The UN General Assembly recommended the **partition** of Palestine into three parts: a Jewish state, an Arab state, and the city of Jerusalem. Jerusalem would be administered by an international body. The British were to withdraw in eight months.

In May 1948 the new state of Israel came into being. Chaim Weizmann was the first president. David Ben-Gurion was prime minister.

WAR   The Arabs refused to recognize the new state of Israel. Fighting broke out as soon as the British troops left. The Palestinian

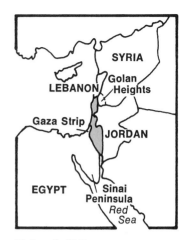

Israel, 1948

From the very beginning, the new nation of Israel was a war zone. This was once a shop in Jerusalem.

111

Arabs were supported by troops from Egypt, Iraq, Lebanon, Syria, Jordan, and later Saudi Arabia and Yemen. The UN sent Count Folke Bernadotte of Sweden to negotiate. He was assassinated. Ralph Bunche of the U.S. replaced him. A **truce** was signed. This happened in part because of the diplomacy of these two men and in part because the Arab armies had been badly defeated by the Israelis.

The Arab nations boycotted Israel—that is, they refused to allow commercial goods to be sent there. Egypt stopped Israel from using the Suez Canal. In 1956 Israeli forces invaded Egypt to gain a way to the canal. Britain and France demanded that the fighting stop. Egypt refused. Britain and France invaded Egypt. Again the UN intervened. Another truce was arranged. British, French, and Israeli forces withdrew. A UN peacekeeping force was set up.

War broke out again in June 1967. Within six days the Israelis had overrun the Sinai Peninsula and occupied the east bank of the Suez Canal. The Egyptians closed the canal. The Israelis took Old Jerusalem and the west bank of the Jordan River. They also occupied the neighboring Golan Heights of Syria. The extent of Soviet aid to the Arabs was revealed when the Israelis captured or destoyed huge quantities of Soviet military equipment. During the Six-Day War, the U.S. supported Israel. Many Arab nations broke off diplomatic relations with the U.S. because of this action.

☐ **Israel, 1967**

THE PALESTINIANS During all these periods of terror and war, hundreds of thousands of Palestinian Arabs fled to neighboring countries. They lived in refugee camps where misery was the lot of most. Many went to Jordan where they soon presented a serious problem for King Hussein. They were restless, discontented, and politically powerful. They practically formed a state within a state.

After the Arab defeat in the Six-Day War, Palestinians organized commando units—specially trained military raiding parties—to attack Israel. These commandos based their activities in Jordan. Known as Fedayeen (fy-da-YEEN)—those who are prepared to sacrifice their lives—they were determined to liberate Palestine. Two of the largest groups are Al Fatah (ahl-fah-TAH) headed by Yasir Arafat (YAH-sir AHR-uhf-aht) and Front for the Liberation of Palestine led by George Habash.

The Fedayeen staged a number of raids into Israel. They also began a program of terrorist activities throughout the world. The Israelis responded by attacking Palestinian bases and camps. Since many of the commando groups were based in Jordan, Israel often attacked there. In more recent years, the Palestinian commandos have come from Lebanon. Israelis have counterattacked by air, land, and sea.

As the Fedayeen grew stronger, they began to pose a threat to Hussein's power. In 1970 conflict broke out in Jordan between the Palestinian commandos and the Jordanian army. At first Syria came to the aid of the Palestinians. But the Syrians withdrew under pressure

counterattacked: attacked to offset an enemy's attack

112

This is a Palestinian refugee camp. The settlement of Arab refugees became a major issue in the Arab-Israeli conflict. Explain both sides of the question.

from the Jordanian army. Within a few weeks Arafat agreed to a truce. Order was restored. In 1971, however, the terrorists murdered two of Hussein's closest associates. After that he was determined to drive them from Jordan. He did this in a series of short but violent campaigns.

CONTINUING UNREST   In October 1973, on Yom Kippur—the Jewish Day of Atonement—fighting broke out between Egypt and Israel along the Gaza Strip and on the Sinai Peninsula. At the same time, fighting began between Syria and Israel on the Golan Heights. Each side received foreign aid.

During an uneasy cease-fire, U.S. Secretary of State Henry Kissinger traveled back and forth between the Arabs and the Israelis carrying peace offers and counteroffers. In what became known as shuttle diplomacy, he was finally able to achieve a truce between Egypt and Israel. An agreement for removing troops and reopening the Suez Canal was reached. Arrangements were made to reopen the canal in 1975, after removing mines and sunken ships. Agreements were also reached with Syria.

U.S. President Richard Nixon's visit to major Arab nations in 1974 symbolized an improvement in Arab-U.S. relations. Additional peace talks were set for Geneva, Switzerland. Arab leaders met in Morocco in late 1974 to decide on who was to represent the Palestinians at the talks. The establishment of a Palestinian government-in-exile was agreed upon in an effort to create an independent Palestinian state. Arafat headed it. He had become chairman of the Palestinian Liberation Organization (PLO) in 1969. The PLO is an overall organization of Fedayeen. Arafat addressed the UN General Assembly in late 1974 and called for the creation of a democratic state in Palestine. He stated that Christians, Jews, and Muslims would be welcome.

The peace remained an uneasy one. Each side expected the other to attack. Terrorist activities continued while diplomats talked.

☐ **Israel, 1973**

113

Chapter 3
The Economy

Kuwait City is the capital of Kuwait and one of the country's largest and most prosperous cities. In the foreground is a new hospital. What is the source of Kuwait's wealth? Is it a source that will one day disappear?

In ancient times the Middle East was a prosperous land. But over the centuries, Middle Easterners have not been fortunate. Careless handling of irrigation systems, destructive invasions, changing trade routes, and the interference of foreign powers caused the Middle East's prosperity to fade. Today poverty is widespread. Lack of education and **capital** keeps the people from exploiting their resources fully.

National governments are trying to change the situation. They feel they are the only agencies with enough money and education to make decisions that can improve the economies. As a result they are involved in all economic decisions. Areas that are receiving special attention are land management and industrialization. The Middle Eastern nations that are making the most rapid progress are those with vast oil reserves.

LAND MANAGEMENT

The majority of Middle Easterners earn their living by farming. But only a small percentage of the land is tillable. The region is not self-sufficient. Great quantities of food must be imported. In Iraq, much of the area that was once part of the lush Fertile Crescent is now barren. Perhaps as much as 90 percent can no longer be farmed.

Over-irrigating, floods, and poor drainage have caused the soil to become salted and unworkable. It is possible to desalinate—unsalt— the land. However, the process takes time, money, and work. Programs are underway, but it will be many years before the land is completely reclaimed.

The most critical problem facing Middle Eastern farmers is lack of water. In recent years, several governments have begun major irrigation projects. The Aswan High Dam in Egypt is one such project. These dams serve many purposes. They provide flood control, water for irrigation, hydroelectric power, and fishing reservoirs.

A few nations, primarily Saudi Arabia and Kuwait, have built desalinization plants to make use of seawater. In many areas, however, the only water that can be used for farming comes from below the ground's surface. In some places this source—called groundwater— cannot be replaced. For example, in North Africa, the groundwater was left from the last ice age.

Another great problem for Middle Eastern farmers is control or ownership of land. In some Middle Eastern nations much of the land is controlled by a few large landowners. They divide their holdings into small plots and rent them at high prices. Several Middle Eastern governments—for example, Iran and Egypt—are working toward a more equal distribution of land.

Lack of knowledge of modern farming technology also hampers Middle Eastern farmers. Efforts have been made in Egypt and elsewhere to set up community development centers. Through these centers, new crops and farming techniques are introduced.

Much of North Africa is desert, but oases like this one in Libya make possible limited agriculture. What is the source of water for an oasis?

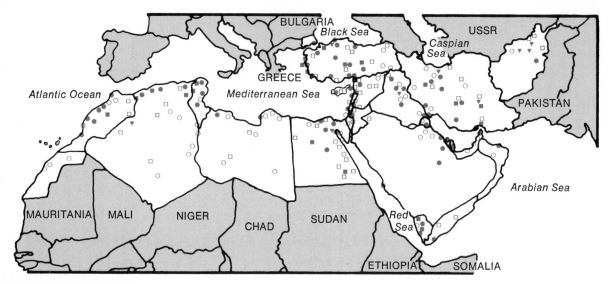

Natural Resources

● **Industrial** ▼ **Coal** ■ **Iron** ○ **Oil** □ **Minerals**

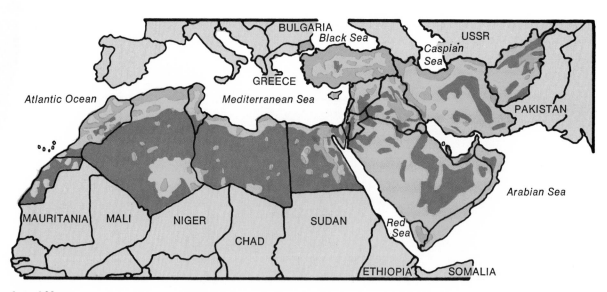

Land Use

■ **Farming**   ■ **Grazing**   ■ **Nonproductive**

INDUSTRIALIZATION

Many Middle Eastern nations are placing emphasis on increasing industrialization. With the exception of oil and oil-related industries such as refining, little **heavy industry** exists in the Middle East. Heavy industry involves the manufacture of such things as steel, machines, transportation equipment, and the machinery used for making machines. Most Middle Eastern industry is considered **light**: textiles, food canning, handcrafted articles, and so on.

refining: purifying

The governments of both Turkey and Egypt have strongly promoted industrialization. Turkey has some heavy industry, including iron and steel processing, transportation equipment, and chemicals. Egypt is producing cotton textiles. Iran is moving toward industrialization too.

The economic development of the Middle East lags for several reasons. Many countries do not have trained technicians because of a lack of educational systems. The kind and size of a country's labor force is important too. Most often, however, the reason is a lack of capital—the money, machines, and goods used to produce other goods. Except for Turkey, most Middle Eastern nations do not have important **raw materials** and power sources. Because most Middle Easterners are poor, they do not have much money to buy locally made goods. Industries have not been able to build up capital. One way a country can increase its capital is by exporting goods. But to make goods for export, a country that lacks natural resources has to import raw materials first. To import raw materials a country needs capital.

IMPACT OF OIL

Oil is the one major industry of the Middle East. It accounts for a major portion of the **gross national product** of 11 countries of the Middle East. It is highly developed and of international importance because oil is the major source of energy for industrialized nations. Western Europe and Japan are heavily dependent on Middle East oil. By the early 1970s, the U.S. was importing as much as 13 percent of its oil from the Middle East.

Most of the Middle Eastern oil industry is concentrated in the Persian Gulf region in Iran and on the eastern Arabian Peninsula. Oil is the primary source of income for Iran, Iraq, Saudi Arabia, Kuwait, Oman, and the United Arab Emirates. In North Africa, Libya and Algeria also are major oil producers.

SAUDI ARABIA: AN EXAMPLE   Saudi Arabia is an example of the development of the Middle Eastern oil industry. Oil was first discovered there in the late 1930s by Standard Oil of California. Until that time, Saudi Arabia's economy was based on the export of a few items such as horses, dates, and animal hides.

117

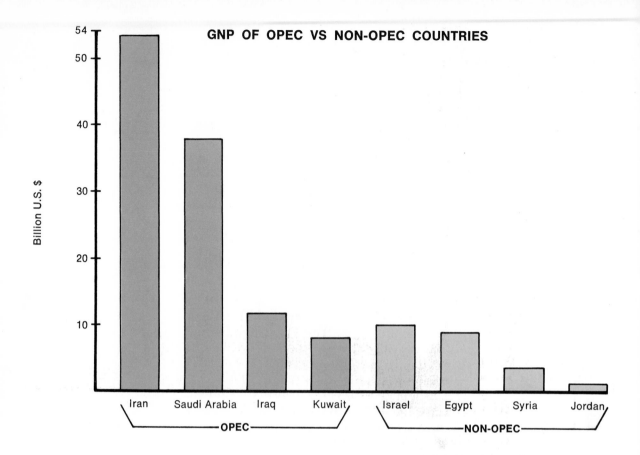

GNP OF OPEC VS NON-OPEC COUNTRIES

Billion U.S. $

OPEC: Iran, Saudi Arabia, Iraq, Kuwait

NON-OPEC: Israel, Egypt, Syria, Jordan

Eventually Standard Oil joined with several other U.S. oil companies to form the Arabian American Oil Company (Aramco). Aramco developed and marketed the oil. Saudi Arabia received a percentage on each barrel sold. But Saudi Arabia began to take control of Aramco. First it was 25 percent. Then in the early 1970s it was 60 percent. Finally plans were made for Saudi Arabia to own 100 percent. Aramco then took on a new role. It became a partner with Saudi Arabia in developing and building industries to make use of oil byproducts.

OIL AS A WEAPON   In the early 1960s, Saudi Arabia, Kuwait, Iraq, and the non-Arab nations of Venezuela and Iran joined to form the Organization of Petroleum Exporting Countries (OPEC). Their goal was to gain a greater financial return for their oil. Later, other oil-producing nations joined OPEC. In 1973 the OPEC nations decided to set their own prices for oil. The cost of a barrel zoomed from $3.00 to over $11.00.

Over the years there arose within OPEC a subgroup consisting of Arab petroleum exporting nations (OAPEC). After the Arab-Israeli war of 1973, OAPEC imposed an oil embargo. An embargo is a government order forbidding ships from entering or leaving a port. Oil shipments to the U.S. and the Netherlands were halted for a time because of the pro-Israeli positions of these countries.

Since 1973 OPEC has continued to raise prices and limit production. The increase in oil prices in the 1970s worsened the already existing problem of world **inflation**. As their money reserves grow, the oil-producing nations are becoming increasingly powerful in international politics and economics.

OIL AND PROSPERITY Within individual oil-producing nations, remarkable changes have occurred. Kuwait has probably the highest **standard of living** of any nation anywhere. There is a general policy of sharing profits of oil with the people. Medical and health-care services, education, and housing are free. Food and clothing are provided to students.

Besides investing in social programs, oil-producing nations have invested heavily in military equipment. Almost half of Oman's income from oil is used on defense spending. Oman has constant border fights with neighboring Southern Yemen. One cause of the fighting is Southern Yemen's support of a rebel group within Oman.

Oil nations realize that oil is a nonrenewable natural resource. Someday the wells will run dry. Depending on the size of their reserves, countries may have 90 to 100 years before this happens. But many nations are already making plans against that day. They are investing in foreign countries and working to make their own countries more self-sufficient. Saudi Arabia set up a series of **five-year plans** beginning in 1969. Highways, schools, hospitals, desalinization plants, and social security are among the areas being carefully developed. At the end of the five years, the projects are reviewed and either kept, enlarged, or dropped.

ISRAEL'S ECONOMY

Since the creation of Israel, immigrants from all over the world have poured into the country. Over 1.5 million people have entered Israel since 1948. Immigrant Jews are automatically granted citizenship.

Many of the immigrants have technical skills needed for advancing the country's economy. But many are poor, illiterate, and unskilled. The government has undertaken housing, job training, and educational programs for them. New citizens are immediately given courses in Hebrew, the language of Israel.

Israel lacks most raw materials and energy resources and must import these. In spite of these limitations, Israel has one of the most advanced economies in the Middle East. Israel produces aircraft, fertilizers, chemicals, and textiles. Food and beverage industries—such as coffee, chocolate processing, and winemaking—are also important to the economy.

Grants and loans from other countries and foreign investments are encouraged. Jews living elsewhere in the world have poured large sums of money into Israel. This capital has brought a rapid expansion of Israel's economy. Immigrants have also boosted the nation's economy. They have enlarged the home market for goods and added to the labor force. But they have also strained the economy. Government expenses for their resettlement have increased as their numbers have grown.

Israel has economic problems too because of its large defense and military needs. A major portion of Israel's budget is devoted to defense. Each time war breaks out, the whole country is mobilized—that is, called into military service. Industry suffers. Israel does not have enough people or money to keep both sectors working at a peak level at the same time.

AGRICULTURE Israel has made its largest gains in agriculture. The Israelis have almost reached their goal of complete food self-sufficiency. Their most serious farming problem is lack of water. Israel has tried to expand its usable land through large irrigation projects. Water resources are strictly controlled and new methods of irrigation are constantly being researched. Israel has introduced some crops new to the region, such as cotton. Its citrus fruits, especially Jaffa oranges and grapefruits, are famous throughout the world.

An unusual and experimental element of Israel's agriculture is the kibbutz (kib-OOTS) plural: kibbutzim. Although only about four percent of the population live on kibbutzim, these village collectives have played an important role in Israel's history. The kibbutz began with the early Zionist settlers.

Israel's greatest economic gains have been made in agriculture. This is a wheat field. Why has Israel attempted to make itself agriculturally self-sufficient?

120

This kibbutz was founded in 1922. Today its income comes from light industry as well as agriculture. What is the difference between light and heavy industry? Why do you think kibbutzim have turned to light industry?

All property is collectively owned on a kibbutz. All work is shared equally. In return for food, housing, clothing, and social services, members give their labor and talent. No one is forced to do anything. Members work because they want to do so. The kibbutz is their home. Women share fully and equally in the work and running of the kibbutz. Children are educated together. All eat in a central dining room.

Although the kibbutzim were originally agricultural, they have branched out in recent years. They also have some light industry such as assembling televisions.

EDUCATION AND ECONOMIC GROWTH

Education still remains one of the most critical problems in the Middle East. **Illiteracy** rates vary from one country to another. In Yemen, 95 percent of the people are not able to read. Lebanon has the lowest illiteracy rate of any Arab country. Only 20 to 25 percent of the Lebanese are considered illiterate.

Middle Eastern governments are committed to education for everyone. Each country has a **centralized** school system. And each country has at least one university. But Middle Eastern governments face many problems in providing education. There are not enough qualified teachers. In addition, Islam has traditionally stressed learning by memorizing—especially memorizing the Koran. Muslims are taught the Koran by hearing it read. Thus it has not been necessary to learn to read. In addition, many young people still must quit school to work and support their families. Some students do not want to take certain subjects, such as the sciences. But these subjects are needed to create a modern society. If a country is to develop, it needs scientists,

This is a class of bedouin children. What problems do Arab governments face in educating the children of nomads? What other problems do Arab governments face in raising the literacy level of their citizens? What is education in Israel like?

engineers, and architects among other professionals.

The absence of **skilled** and educated people continues to hold back economic and political growth. It also tends to create rule by a few. The few are not the wealthy so much as the educated. Except for the countries with monarchies—where family and wealth are important—education is the key to **social mobility**. Social mobility means movement from one social class to another. Thus the military with their officer-training backgrounds have been able to advance. In the socialist countries, the power of the military is shared with educated **civil servants**. In other countries, the military shares power with the business middle class.

ISRAEL   The Israelis are very aware of the importance of education to their future economic growth. Free public education is available to everyone. For children, schooling is compulsory between the ages of five and 16. Over 90 percent of the people are able to read. Israel, although a new nation, has several universities. Emphasis is placed on scientific research. A major research center is the Weizmann Institute.

TOWARD ARAB UNITY

Arab culture springs from its religion. Arabs, regardless of their nationalities, share a common language. They all have the same social system. The Arab nations realize that if they are to prosper, they need to develop unity among themselves. As we have seen, Arab oil-producing nations united in OAPEC and won greater profits from their oil.

Nasser, Egypt's late president, was dedicated to the advancement of Arab unity. He saw Egypt as part of an Arab union in which member nations worked together to improve the political, economic, and social lives of their people. He attempted to join Egypt and Syria into an Arab state in 1958. Yemen later became part of the union. But the union did not last. Syria withdrew in 1961. A second federation of Iraq, Syria, and Egypt was proposed in 1963. That union was never formed. In 1971 Egypt, Libya, and Syria joined in the Federation of Arab Republics. Its purpose was to work toward developing the economies and foreign policies of the member nations.

THE ARAB LEAGUE   The Arab League was organized in 1945. It began as a union of Egypt, Yemen, Saudi Arabia, Lebanon, Syria, Jordan, and Iraq. With independence, other Arab nations joined.

Member nations cooperate on military, social, cultural, and economic matters. Within the League, various agencies coordinate Arab scientific efforts, telecommunications, tourism, postal rules, publications, and exchange of the latest agricultural methods. The League also provides a common front in publicizing Arab concerns in the fight against Israel.

Summing Up the Unit

Social Studies Vocabulary

Define: national identity; republic; secular; assembly; industry; script; land reform; conservative; monarchy; rightist; leftist; democracy; representative government; prejudice; capital; heavy industry; light industry; standard of living; five-year plan

People

Identify: Riza Shah; Mohammad Riza Pahlevi; Nasser; Sadat; Saud family; Bourguiba; Herzl; Ben-Gurion; Weizmann; Arafat

Words

Define: Arab socialism; Wahabis; Palestinian; Zionism; Balfour Declaration; underground; boycott; Fedayeen; Al Fatah; Yom Kippur; PLO; groundwater; OPEC; OAPEC; embargo; nonrenewable natural resource; kibbutz; Arab League

Questions

1. Why did Middle Easterners' identification with Islam cause their movements toward nationalism to be delayed?
2. Describe Ataturk's six principles.
3. How did Ataturk influence Riza Shah's steps toward nationalism?
4. a. How was the status of Middle Eastern women influenced by a. Ataturk? b. Riza Shah? c. Nasser?
5. What reforms has Shah Mohammad Riza Pahlevi made?
6. Why did Nasser seek to promote both Egyptian and Arab socialism?
7. a. How did Nasser help Egyptian farmers? b. How did he rule Egypt? c. How was his successor, Sadat, different from him?
8. What is Islam's strength in Saudi Arabia?
9. Why was the nationalist movement slower in North Africa than elsewhere in the Middle East?
10. a. List two reasons why most Middle Easterners lack the political knowledge to deal with independence. b. Why have they turned to strong military leaders in times of change?

11. What have the greatest conflicts in the Middle East centered around in recent years?
12. Why did Herzl help to found the Zionist movement?
13. Why did both the Palestine Arabs and the Jews argue their claims to Palestine?
14. What happened to the Palestine Arabs during the Arab-Israeli fighting?
15. a. Why is the once-prosperous Middle East no longer that way? b. List three factors that hamper Middle Eastern farmers.
16. a. Where is most of the Middle East's oil located? b. How has oil been used as a weapon? c. What use have Middle Easterners made of the income from their oil? d. How are they preparing for the future? e. Why?
17. What is the key to social mobility in the Middle East?
18. Why do Arab nations feel that they need to develop unity among themselves?

Discussion Topics

1. How might changes as drastic as those made by Ataturk affect people? Think of changes that could be made in your own society that might be equally shocking to many people. Do you think they could be made without great resistance?
2. Saudi Arabian nationalism is based almost entirely on religion. How has its nationalism brought modernization without disturbing Islamic traditions? Compare relationships between religion and state in Turkey and Saudi Arabia.

Project Ideas

1. Using library resources, report on oil exploitation in an Arab nation.
2. Write a brief biographical sketch of: Ataturk; Riza Shah; Mohammad Riza Pahlevi; Nasser; Sadat; Faisal; Hussein; Ben-Gurion; Weizmann.
3. With class members representing different Middle Eastern nations, stage a debate on Arab-Israeli issues or on oil prices.
4. Point out the historical events behind current news stories about the Middle East.

Unit VI

Society and Creativity

These stained glass windows were designed by Marc Chagall for the government of Israel. Like many artists everywhere, Chagall has chosen a religious theme.

The late 20th century has brought changes to the people of the Middle East. More land is being made available for farming. Industry is creating new kinds of jobs. The nomadic way of life is gradually disappearing. Cities are taking on a new look. But the most dramatic changes have been in the status of women.

In the areas of arts and sciences, Muslims have given much to the world. They have been preservers, adaptors, and creators. They have preserved the accomplishments of earlier people. Moreover, they have adapted the works of their contemporaries. And Muslims have made their own contributions.

Most Middle Easterners live in **rural** areas. Only about one-fourth of the population lives in cities. The percentage varies from country to country. In Lebanon, for example, 40 percent of the people are city dwellers. But on the Arabian Peninsula, only 10 percent are. Besides villagers and city dwellers, some nomadic peoples still wander through the Middle East. Today they are few in number.

Chapter 1
Tradition and Change

VILLAGE LIFE

Most Middle Easterners are farming people who live in villages. Surrounding the villages are the fields. A few nonfarming villagers, such as shopkeepers, provide services for the others.

Villagers do not have an easy life. There are few modern conveniences. Most people live in small one- or two-room houses made of mud or sun-dried bricks. The houses often have dirt floors and usually are windowless. The people have little furniture. The family may sleep on mats. Women cook outside on a community oven. Since most villages have no electricity, villagers use oil lamps for light. Usually there is no running water or indoor plumbing. Water must be carried from wells. The average lifespan of Middle Easterners is short—under 48 years. This will increase, however, as health-care services become more widely available.

The diet of village people consists mainly of grains. Millet is usually eaten as a cooked cereal. Rice, barley, and wheat are also eaten where available. Wheat and barley are baked into bread. Rice is boiled. Locally grown fruits and vegetables are also important to the diets of Middle Eastern villagers.

NOMADS

Nomads represent less than 5 percent of the Arab people of the Middle East. The nomads who live in Saudi Arabia and parts of Iraq, Jordan, Syria, Egypt, and North Africa are called bedouins. The word means desert dwellers. Bedouins have lived in the Middle East since **prehistoric** times.

Nomads travel from place to place grazing their herds. They own little except their animals, tents, and a few personal items. For their livelihood, they depend on their animals: sheep, goats, and camels. Camels provide transportation as well as clothing and housing. Nomads exchange wool, milk, meat, or their services as herders to villagers for items such as grain, fruits and vegetables, coffee, utensils, or tools.

Milk and milk products—yogurt and cheese—are important parts of the diet of nomads. Middle Eastern people in general eat little meat. Goats or sheep may be slaughtered for special occasions. Cattle is scarce, so beef is not part of the diet. Muslim people are forbidden to eat pork. Coffee and tea are popular drinks.

Bazaars such as this one in Marrakech, Morocco, are still the marketplaces of Arab countries. How has modernization affected the old cities? How have people adapted to the needs that make modern cities necessary?

CITY LIFE

The Middle East has a long history of urban life. Some of the great cities dating from ancient times are located there: Alexandria, Baghdad, Damascus, Cairo, Istanbul, and Jerusalem. Traditionally the city has served as the center of political and economic activity. The rich and the powerful have always lived in cities.

The general pattern of many Middle Eastern cities today is an old Arab city next to a modern one. The old cities were built around a fortress and the major mosque. These were surrounded by covered bazaars or marketplaces such as the Casbah in Algiers, the Golden Bazaar in Istanbul, or the Mushi in Cairo. Sellers on the narrow, crowded streets of the bazaars are grouped by occupation. All the leather workers are on one street, goldsmiths on another, and so on. The Middle Eastern custom of bargaining for goods is still practiced in these places. Surrounding the bazaars are food markets, public baths, and private homes. The old cities are usually enclosed by high walls with several gates.

The new cities look like cities of the Western world. The architecture is international in style. There is a central business and shopping district. Residential areas surround it. On the outskirts of the city are slums.

In recent years, Middle Eastern cities have experienced an extremely rapid growth. People seeking better jobs or educational opportunities come to urban areas in large numbers. This often creates problems: housing shortages, overcrowding in the schools, strains on the transportation systems, and lowered health standards. The new arrivals expect the cities to provide jobs, education, water, housing, and health services. Most often the cities do not have the funds for these services.

In some instances people have not left their villages, yet find themselves living in an urban setting. In a short time, oil prosperity has changed some villages of the Persian Gulf region into urban areas complete with highrises and paved highways. The capital of Abu Dhabi (ahb-oo DAB-ee), one of the United Arab Emirates, experienced such growth. The newly created oil cities are not faced with the problems of other Middle Eastern urban areas. They have the money to cope with rapid **urbanization**. Services such as schools, housing, and health care are available because of the wealth brought by the oil boom.

FAMILY TIES

The family is the key unit of Middle Eastern society. Middle Easterners traditionally have considered themselves first as members of an **extended family**. Several generations of the same family live in one household. Relationships then reach beyond the extended family to a **lineage**—a group in which all the people trace their families back to a common ancestor. Lineages that live together form kinship groups. These larger groups are sometimes known as tribes.

Nomads identify themselves as part of the kinship group. Sometimes the group contains several hundred families. Among the bedouins the group leader is called a sheikh or sayyid (SAY-id). The leader is responsible for solving problems and maintaining law and order. Nomads live under severe conditions. To cope with their harsh environment, strict discipline is required of all group members. The kinship group as a whole is responsible for the behavior of each member. Members are expected to give loyalty to the group and to offer help when it is needed. In return, individuals may call on the group when they need help. Because of their unsettled way of life, nomads lack a sense of national identity. Their loyalty stops at their kinship group.

CHANGING PATTERNS   Today the number of nomads is decreasing. Nations such as Saudi Arabia are working to settle them into villages. Some have taken jobs in the oil industry. As these people become settled in villages, they depend less on the kinship group. Keeping law and order or dealing with matters that affect the whole community is handled by local people or organizations. These people—employers, municipal workers, and elected officials—may not be part of the kinship group. As outsiders take over duties once handled by the kinship group, the political and economic functions of the group are fading.

The extended family today is more the ideal than the reality. In the past it was more economical and convenient to live as part of an extended family, especially for nomads. But today this arrange-

The Middle East, like so many other regions, is undergoing rapid change. Apartment buildings dot Istanbul's skyline while nomads still ride the desert. What problems are nomads having in adjusting to modernization?

127

ment is the exception. For Middle Easterners, poverty is common. Managing a large household is impossible for most of them. The trend is toward the **nuclear family** in which the husband and wife and their children live together. Beyond the nuclear family, people feel loyalty to a few generations of their family—grandparents and grandchildren. They are also aware of belonging to a certain lineage.

City dwellers, especially those who are educated, are more independent of family ties than are villagers or nomads. By moving to the city, members of a kinship group have less contact with each other. In an urban, industrialized environment, more emphasis is placed on a person's achievements than on family background. People are more likely to make their own way without depending on their **kinfolk**. This independent attitude is beginning to extend to the choice of a mate, a decision traditionally made by the families.

MARRIAGE

Traditionally, marriages among Middle Easterners have been arranged by male members of families. The bride leaves her family to live with her husband and his family. Marriages frequently take place between relatives. Often the bride marries the son of her father's brother.

At the time of the marriage, the husband or his family has to provide a sum of money—a bride-price—for the bride. The bride uses it to buy clothing, articles for her home, or items that will insure her future financial security, such as jewelry or livestock.

If a husband divorces his wife, she is allowed to keep the bride-price. However, if she divorces him and he objects to the divorce, he can demand that the amount of the bride-price be returned.

The Koran permits a man to have four wives at one time. But a man who takes more than one wife must be able to support, love, and treat all equally. Because of Islam's strict rules, the majority of Muslim men rarely have more than one wife.

Under Islamic law divorce is easy to obtain. A husband divorces his wife simply by stating three times "I divorce you" before two witnesses. In recent years many Arab countries have instituted divorce laws. More and more, as women seek social equality, divorces are becoming matters for the court. In nations such as Egypt and Algeria a husband must now appear in court and give reasons for wanting a divorce.

WOMEN

The prophet Muhammad did much to improve the lives of women. A woman could not be left without support by her father or her husband. Islamic law requires that she share with male heirs in her father's property. As mentioned earlier, at the time of her marriage,

This young woman is a nomad in Iran. She has little chance to obtain an education or to be paid for her work. Why?

a woman is provided with a bride-price to guarantee her financial independence.

Over the centuries, Muslim women in the higher levels of Islamic society began to veil their faces from men other than family members. This practice was more common in larger towns and cities. It was not practiced among some bedouins and farming people. In urban areas, marriageable Muslim women began to be isolated socially from men. By the beginning of the 1800s, these Muslim women were living a life apart from men.

During the 1800s and early 1900s, the British, French, and other Europeans came to dominate much of the Middle East. They criticized the way Arab women were treated. These Westerners claimed the women were given little respect and no social equality. Muslims who visited Europe began to speak out about the treatment of Arab women too. By the 1920s a few women were appearing in city streets without their veils. Some began attending secondary schools and colleges.

The greatest changes in the **status** of Arab women have been made since the late 1940s. Since then, many Middle Eastern women have gained the right to vote. Increasingly large numbers of women are attending secondary schools and universities. In Egypt, Syria, and elsewhere, they are becoming doctors, lawyers, and engineers.

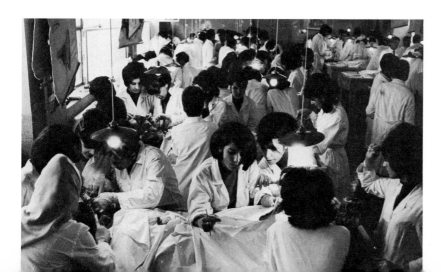

These women are medical students at Tehran University. Why are their opportunities greater than those of the young woman above? What cultural differences explain this?

In spite of some opposition from conservative Muslims, women are making gains. Today Middle Eastern governments realize that women can contribute to the economic growth of their nations. Women's traditional **roles** as mothers and housekeepers are being reevaluated. Women in the Middle East, as elsewhere, are being recognized as important human resources. They are becoming a valuable part of the Middle Eastern labor force.

ISRAEL   The status of women in Israel is very different from that of women in Muslim nations. Israeli women work alongside men in fields and factories. Their equality is guaranteed by law. Generally, however, women receive less pay than men.

Women serve with men in the armed forces, although no longer in combat. As in most Western countries, fewer women than men become doctors and lawyers. And few women hold government positions. One notable exception is the former prime minister of Israel, Golda Meir (me-IHR). She held that office from 1969 until her defeat in the elections of 1974.

Chapter 2
Creativity

Muslim conquests extended their influence from Spain to India. In these diverse areas, the Muslims took what interested them from the arts and sciences of the various cultures. They blended these with their own ideas and developed a creative expression that is uniquely Islamic. Early Muslim scholars also acted as the link between the ancient Greeks and the Europeans of the Middle Ages. After the fall of the Roman Empire, many ancient works would have been lost. But beginning in the 700s Muslims worked carefully to preserve them.

EARLY ISLAMIC ARTS

When the Arab followers of Muhammad set out to convert the world, they had not yet developed a strong artistic style. As a result, the style that we call Islamic is really made up of many different styles. For this reason, Muslim art is called a composite (kahm-PAHZ-uht) art style. By examining Muslim architecture, we can see how this blending of styles occurred.

ARCHITECTURE   Muslim buildings throughout the empire were usually built by the conquered people. Thus the materials, size of the structures, degree of ornamentation, and features such as domes vary from place to place. These characteristics depend on the skill of the peoples who built them and the materials available.

The major Muslim buildings are mosques, tombs, fortresses, and palaces. The most common is the mosque, the place of worship. On the wall that faces Mecca is the mihrab. All Muslims turn toward

Mecca when they pray. The mihrab is a central point of worship much like an altar in a Christian church. Outside the mosque is a tower called a minaret. Some mosques may have several such towers. The minaret may be part of the mosque or a separate structure. Five times a day a man climbs the steps of the minaret to call faithful Muslims to prayer.

Early mosques were simple wooden structures without the mihrab or minaret. But as Muslim power and wealth grew and spread, the buildings became more elaborate. First the mihrab was added. Later the minaret was included. Eventually domes became a part of the design. Stone, brick, or marble replaced wood. Ornately carved stone columns replaced wooden pillars. Sometimes these columns had been taken from Roman or Byzantine buildings or ruins. The Great Mosque at Kairouan (ker-WAHN), Tunisia, contains many such columns.

Gradually the mosques began to rival Christian cathedrals in splendor. Among the most famous are the Great Mosques at Cordova, Spain, and Damascus, Syria. Today the Cordova mosque is a Christian church. In Istanbul, however, this process was reversed. The Byzantine Cathedral of St. Sophia, once a Christian church, has been a mosque since the 1400s.

Orthodox Islam does not allow the pictures of any creatures—human or animal—to be used in architecture or art. Early Muslim leaders feared the people would return to the practice of worshiping statues. Instead artists were encouraged to decorate buildings and art objects with geometric and floral patterns. Often Arabic script was used. The writing usually was a passage from the Koran. The patterns that result are called arabesques (ar-uh-BESKS). The ban on living figures in art was not strictly followed, however. For example, carved marble lions were used as part of a fountain in the courtyard of the Alhambra, a Moorish fortress in Spain.

The building materials used varied greatly. In India white marble was used in the Taj Mahal, a tomb built in the 1600s by Shah Jahan (SHAH ja-HAHN), a Mogul ruler. The Moguls were Muslim rulers of India. In Egypt and North Africa, stone of various colors was used. Iranians used brick and glazed tile in their buildings. They also made wide use of ornamentation.

The domes that Muslim builders used also took a variety of forms. The Taj Mahal has an onion-shaped dome. It tapers delicately to a point. The tombs of the Mamelukes in Cairo, Egypt, have domes shaped like half an egg. The Great Mosque at Kairouan has semicircular ribbed domes.

OTHER VISUAL ARTS Islamic creativity was not limited to buildings. Muslims made colorful carpets, silks, and tapestries. Their painted pottery, leather goods, and objects of brass, copper, ivory, gold, and silver were in demand as trade goods. Steel swords made in Damascus, Syria, and Toledo, Spain, were also valuable trade

This is an example of a mihrab or prayer niche in a mosque.

This is the courtyard of the Alhambra in Spain. What elements of Islamic art styles can you find in it?

items. Linens woven in Damascus were of such fine quality that they took the name of that city—damask.

When Islam was introduced into Persia (Iran) in 641 A.D., the people had a civilization that was already hundreds of years old. Art and science continued to flourish under Islam. Iranians were not as strict as other Muslims in not using creatures in their art. They painted miniatures of people and landscapes which included animals. The peak of Iranian—sometimes called Persian—miniature art was reached in the 1400s. This form had great impact on the art of India. In the 1500s there arose at the Mogul court in India an Indo-Iranian school of miniature painting.

LITERATURE   Early Muslim literature was mostly poetry. Poets writing in the Arabic language composed verses on many subjects and for every occasion. They also enjoyed compiling and hearing folktales. An early work that is well known to Western readers is the *Thousand and One Nights*, sometimes called *Arabian Nights Entertainments*. These 200 tales were taken from many peoples—Iranians, Indians, Arabs, Egyptians, and others. The collection was first put together in Arabic translations, probably during the 900s. Among the more popular stories are "Ali Baba and the Forty Thieves," "The Magic Carpet," "Sinbad the Sailor," and "Aladdin." Although considered fiction, the stories give us a picture of life in Baghdad during Abbasid rule (750-1258). One of the important characters is Harun al-Raschid (hah-ROON al-RASH-id), a real caliph of the Abbasid dynasty, who ruled in the late 700s.

Most early Islamic literature was in Arabic. But by the 900s, Iranians began using their own Persian language to express their ideas. They used Arabic script and many Arabic words, however. Omar Khayyam (ky-YAHM), author of the *Rubaiyat* (ROO-bee-aht), is one of the most famous Iranian writers. In his own time, however, he was better known as an astronomer and mathematician. The Iranian poet Firdausi (fir-DOO-see) is also famous. He wrote an **epic** story of the early Persians, *Shah-nama (Book of Kings).* It covers the history of his people from their creation to the Sassanian dynasty (226-641).

Other Iranian poets whose works are well known are Saadi (sah-DEE) and Hafiz (hah-FIZ). Saadi wrote the *Bustan (Fruit Garden)* and the *Gulistan (Rose Garden)*. His works have great humor and wisdom. Hafiz wrote a collection of poems, *Divan of Hafiz,* which is considered a spirtual guide for Muslims.

EARLY SCIENCE AND TECHNOLOGY

During the rule of the Abbasids, the capital of Baghdad was a dazzling city. Many artists, poets, and musicians came there. It was a time of great creative expression and intellectual development. Muslim astronomers understood that the earth rotates on its axis and revolves around the sun. This was centuries before Western Europeans accepted these facts. Omar Khayyam was commissioned by the sultan to revise the solar calendar. He devised one that was more accurate than the Gregorian calendar used today in the Western world.

These early Muslims were also navigators. They made improvements on the astrolabe, an earlier Greek invention. The astrolabe is a navigational device used for observing the position of stars. By the 1100s Arab Muslim scholar al-Idrisi (al-ih-DREE-see) had mapped the lands from Spain to Indonesia with great accuracy and detail.

Of all the sciences, medicine was the area in which the Muslims made their greatest contributions. Al Razi (RAY-zee) or Rhazes (RAY-zeez), an Iranian, wrote over 200 books on medicine. One of his works was a medical encyclopedia. It was later translated into Latin and used by European doctors. Muslim doctors were able to diagnose stomach cancer. They knew antidotes for poison as well as ways to stop bleeding and infection.

Avicenna (av-ih-SEN-uh), another Iranian doctor, knew that diseases could be spread by dirt or contaminated water. Around the year 1000, he wrote *Canon of Medicine.* This work was used by Muslims for centuries. When translated, it became a highly respected work in Europe. Avicenna also wrote works on physics, mathematics, as well as other scientific subjects.

Arab Muslims built hospitals, clinics, and medical libraries. Medical students learned through practical experience. When they had completed their training to the satisfaction of their teachers, they were allowed to practice on their own.

As well as being creators, Muslims learned from other peoples. Baghdad and other great Islamic centers attracted scholars from as far away as China. Chinese inventions such as paper, printing, and the compass were first known in the West through Arab Muslims. The system of numbers known as Arabic was passed along to the Western world by way of the Middle East. The system apparently began among the Hindus of India. Al Khwarizmi (al-KWAH-riz-mee), an Iranian mathematician who lived in the 800s, made use of the numbers when he compiled a textbook on algebra. He and other Muslim mathematicians also transmitted the decimal system and concept of zero to the rest of the world.

IMPACT ON WESTERN CULTURE

Muslim contributions to Western culture are many and varied. Europeans learned to sing their songs to music played on the guitar and lute. These instruments as well as their names were originally Arabic. Many everyday English words as well as the objects they name have come by way of the Arabs. Cotton, lemon, syrup, almanac, sofa, and coffee are just a few.

The Muslims also made important contributions to the West by

The astrolabe is a navigational instrument that originally came from the ancient Greeks. Middle Easterners improved it, and it was their instrument that Western Europeans used on their voyages around the world in the 1500s.

compiled: collected into a volume

acting as preservers of the past. After the fall of the Roman Empire in the 400s A.D., much of the great learning of the ancient Greeks would have been lost were it not for Arab Muslim scholars. Other conquering peoples might have destroyed or burned the manuscripts of those whom they conquered. The Arabs did not. Instead they tried to learn as much as they could from the ancient writings. They carefully translated the Greek manuscripts they found at Antioch and elsewhere. Among the works translated were those of the philosophers Aristotle and Plato who lived in the 300s and 400s B.C. The works of Galen (GAY-luhn), a physician and writer who lived in the 100s A.D., were also preserved and translated.

Many non-Muslim people were working under Arab direction at this time. These included Christians in Syria and Jews in Spain. At a time when there was not much intellectual activity in Europe, scholars writing in Arabic were actively preserving works of the past and adding to them. Beginning in the 1000s Christian monks began translating the works from Arabic into Latin. They thus became available to later European scholars.

THE ARTS TODAY

Modern Islamic creativity is a mixture of religious tradition and folk art. The Middle East is still mostly a traditional society. Over the centuries, people have expressed themselves most often through literature and handcrafts. These forms are being encouraged today because they are so much a part of the peoples' cultural **heritages**.

LITERATURE   In recent times, the Middle East has produced some excellent poets. The one probably best known to Western readers is Kahlil Gibran of Lebanon. He wrote *The Prophet.* Maruf ar-Rusafi, who wrote in the first half of the 1900s, was an Iraqi poet who described the changing modern world. Two well-known Syrian poets are Mahmud Adwan and Ali Ahmed Said. Said writes under the name Adonis. His works reflect a French influence.

Besides poetry, other literary forms have become popular among Arabic writers in recent years. In Egypt Abd-al-Rahman-ash-Sharqawi used the novel *The Earth* to describe Egypt after the fall of Farouk's regime. Another Egyptian novelist, Eshan Abdel Kuddous, wrote of the 1956 Suez crisis in *Don't Shut Off the Sun.* Egypt has also produced a number of playwrights, including Tewfiq-al-Hakim, whose subject matter ranges from symbolic to modern, and Mahmud Taymur who writes comedies.

VISUAL ARTS   Handcrafted objects remain an important part of Middle Eastern creativity. Iranians, especially, are famous for their beautifully designed carpets. Middle Eastern rugs are of such fine quality that they are often hung on walls. The artistry of Middle Eastern craftworkers is also evident in articles of gold, silver, and brass, particularly jewelry. The region is also well known for colorful

One of the most beautiful examples of Middle Eastern art is the Persian rug. Not all rugs of this type are made in Persia (Iran) today, but the name remains. Compare this to the use of the word china for porcelain. This rug was woven in Turkey in the 1500s.

pottery, glassware, and ceramics. Other **crafts** include embroidery and, particularly in North Africa, leatherwork.

Islam has influenced the direction of visual arts in those countries with strong Arab ties. Oman, Yemen, and Saudi Arabia are among the nations where **orthodox** beliefs still forbid using figures in art. In some nations today, however, this ban is not rigidly followed. Now Jordanian art includes sculptures and paintings that depict human and animal forms.

MUSIC　　Singing, dancing, and instrumental music are very much a part of Middle Eastern Muslim life. As with other peoples, music expresses emotion and is a form of entertainment. Traditional ballads and hudas—songs of camel drivers—are still very popular. In Egypt folk singers and musicians travel throughout the countryside singing old melodies and playing such stringed instruments as the lute, zither, and kanoun. Folk dances are very popular.

Middle Eastern music may sound strange to Western ears because the musical scale is different. Arabic music uses many more notes within the range of a Western octave. Recently some efforts have been made to develop a musical style more like that of Europe. Syria has been especially prominent in this effort with such musicians as Wadi Sabra and Alexis Butros. Sabra is a composer of operas. Butros, a talented violinist, founded the Syrian National Conservatory of Music. Turkey has a number of fine music schools too.

ISRAEL'S ARTS

The arts of Israel are active and varied. There has been much emphasis on preserving Jewish **folklore** and art. As the Israelis seek to trace their past, archaeology has become a major national pastime.

Traditional folk songs and dances are important. The country supports several symphony orchestras including the Israel Philharmonic. There are also dance companies such as the Batsheva. A number of internationally known performing artists and conductors live in Israel. Composers include Mordechai Seter and Ami Maayani.

In literature and the theater Israel has produced Nobel Prize winner Shmuel Yosef Agnon and playwright Nissim Aloni. Poetry is popular. Among those whose works are famous are Abba Kovner and Yehuda Amichai.

A number of Israeli artists have turned to their Jewish past for inspiration. Marc Chagall (shah-GAL), a Russian Jew and member of the Paris school of Jewish painters, has been very influential in depicting Jewish folklore. Two of the best-known Israeli painters are Mordechai Ardon and Joseph Zaritsky. Ardon frequently uses Judaism as a theme of his works. Zaritsky's abstracts make powerful use of color. Of Israel's sculptors, the foremost in Yitzhak Danziger. His works are abstract in form. Anna Ticho and Jacob Steinhardt are widely known graphic artists.

Traditional music is still an important part of Middle Eastern Arab culture. Musicians, such as those above, travel through the countryside singing, dancing, and playing the old music.

school: a group of artists under a common influence

135

Summing Up the Unit

Social Studies Vocabulary

Define: rural; prehistoric; urbanization; extended family; lineage; nuclear family; kinfolk; status; role; epic; heritage; crafts; orthodox; folklore

People

Identify: Golda Meir; Shah Jahan; Omar Khayyam; Firdausi; Saadi; Hafiz; al-Idrisi; Al Razi; Avicenna; Al Khwarizmi; Gibran; Chagall

Words

Define: bedouins; bazaar; sayyid; bride-price; composite art; mihrab; minaret; arabesque; damask; astrolabe; *Canon of Medicine*; hudas

⚷ Questions

1. a. Where do most Middle Easterners live? b. What portion of the population lives in cities? c. What percent are nomads?
2. Describe the life of: a. village people; b. nomadic people.
3. a. What is the general pattern of many Middle Eastern cities? b. What problems are the cities facing today? c. Why?
4. What identity and loyalty do bedouins have?
5. a. Why is the number of nomads decreasing? b. What happens when they settle in villages?
6. Why are city dwellers more independent of extended family ties than villagers and nomads?
7. Why do Muslim men usually have no more than one wife?
8. a. How did Muhammad improve the lives of women? b. What effect did Europeans have on the way Arab women were treated?
9. How is the status of women different in Israel than in Muslim nations?
10. What are the major Muslim buildings?
11. a. Why were human and animal forms not used in Islamic architecture? b. What forms were used instead?
12. a. What collection of folktales of many Middle Eastern peoples is well known throughout the world? b. Which of its characters was a real caliph?
13. When was Baghdad a center of creativity?
14. What area of the world had al-Idrisi mapped in the 1100s?
15. What Chinese inventions were introduced to the West through the Arab Muslims?
16. Where did Arabic numbers apparently begin?
17. What musical instruments were originally Arabic?
18. How did Arab scholars preserve the past?
19. Why are Middle Eastern governments encouraging preservation of arts and crafts?
20. Why does Middle Eastern music sound strange to Western ears?
21. Why has archaeology become a major national pastime in Israel?

Discussion Topics

1. Iranians have made many cultural contributions to the world. How did Iran's geographic location make it a logical place for the blending of Eastern and Western knowledge? With modern transportation and communication, does the geographic location of a country still play a major part in its development?
2. What do the arts and crafts tell us about the life of a people in the past times? What forms of art do we have today that might be of interest to historians a thousand years in the future?

Project Ideas

1. Read some of the stories in the *Thousand and One Nights*. Organize a panel discussion about what these tales reveal about Muslim life and values. What do the stories confirm that you have learned in the study of Middle Easterners? What do they add?
2. Collect illustrations of Middle Eastern art and architecture for the bulletin board. Or prepare a display of your own sketches that show typical Muslim art.
3. Assemble a display of Israeli art. Add notes explaining the cultural values or historical references that are portrayed in the selections.

For Further Study

General Readings

1. *Ancient Kingdoms of the Nile* by Walter A. Fairservis, Jr. New American Library, Inc. Paperback. Covers all the ancient kingdoms bordering on the Nile. Emphasis on Egypt.

2. *Ancient Near East in Pictures with Supplement* ed. by J. Pritchard. Princeton University Press, 2nd ed., 1969. To 1700 B.C.

3. *Ancient Worlds of Asia: From Mesopotamia to the Yellow River* by Ernest Diez. G. P. Putnam's Sons, 1961. Begins in 5000 B.C.

4. *Arab Cold War 1958–1970: A Study of Ideology in Politics* by Malcolm Kerr. Oxford University Press, Inc., 3rd ed., 1971. Paperback. The politics of Gamal Abdul Nasser and his rivals, 1958-1970.

5. *Building the Suez Canal* by S. C. Burchell and C. Issawi. Harper & Row, Publishers, 1966. Illustrated volume on the construction of the canal.

6. *Everyday Life in Babylon and Assyria* by Georges Contenau. W. W. Norton & Co., Inc., 1966. Paperback. Basic to understanding human life during this era.

7. *Historical Sites in Israel* by Moshe Pearlman and Yannai Yaacov. Vanguard Press, Inc., 1965. Guide to biblical history. Illustrated.

8. *History of the Arabs* by Philip K. Hitti. St. Martin's Press, Inc., 10th ed., 1970. Paperback. From earliest times to the fall of the Ottomans.

9. *How the Great Religions Began* by Joseph Gaer. New American Library, Inc., rev. ed. Paperback. A useful aid to understanding.

10. *Islamic Art* by David Talbot Rice. Praeger Publishers, Inc., 1975. Paperback. 600 to 1600 A.D.

11. *Israel: Years of Challenge* by David Ben-Gurion. Holt, Rinehart & Winston, Inc., 1963. Jews in Palestine up to the proclamation of the state of Israel.

12. *Istanbul and the Civilization of the Ottoman Empire* by Bernard Lewis. University of Oklahoma Press, 1968. Paperback. Istanbul as the center of the empire.

13. *The Land and the People of Egypt* by Zaki Naguib Mahmoud. J. B. Lippincott Company, rev. ed., 1972.

14. *The Land and People of Israel* by Gail Hoffmann. J. B. Lippincott Company, rev. ed., 1972.

Introduction to Israel. Clearly written.

15. *The Land and People of Turkey* by William Spencer. J. B. Lippincott Company, new rev. ed., 1972. Introduction to the Turkish people.

16. *Letters from Mesopotamia: Official, Business, and Private Letters on Clay Tablets from Two Millenia* by A. Leo Oppenheim. University of Chicago Press, 1967. These letters are original translations. Their style and content suggest letters today.

17. *Middle Eastern Cultures* ed. by Paul Thomas Welty. J. B. Lippincott Company, 1973. Readings. Inquiry format.

18. *New Light on the Most Ancient East* by V. Gordon Childe. W. W. Norton & Co., Inc., 4th ed., 1969. Paperback. Discusses the beginning of civilization in the Middle East.

19. *Peoples and Cultures of the Middle East* by Louis Sweet. Vols. I and II. Doubleday & Co., Inc., 1970. Paperback. Volume I, *Depth and Diversity*, focuses on the historical heritage of the area. Volume II, *Life in the Cities, Towns, and Countryside*, concentrates on the effects of urbanization and change on traditional institutions.

20. *Politics in Lebanon* by Leonard Binder. John Wiley & Sons, Inc., 1966. Response to change.

21. *Pyramids of Egypt* by I. E. Edwards. Penguin Books, Inc., 1975. Paperback. Monuments to the mighty dreams of the pharaohs.

Fiction

1. *Carpet of Solomon* by Sulamith Ish-Kishor. Pantheon Books, Inc., 1966. Story of King Solomon.

2. *Foreigner* by Gladys Malvern. David McKay Co., Inc., 1954. Story of Ruth.

3. *The Gate of Hell* by Alfred Coppel. Pinnacle Books, 1975. Paperback. War in the Middle East.

4. *Land of Foam* by Ivan Yefremov. Houghton Mifflin Co., 1959. A slave in ancient Egypt.

5. *Three Brothers of Ur* by Jennifer G. Fyson. Coward, McCann and Geoghegan, Inc., 1966. Daily life of the Sumerians.

The Asians

Love of nature is often expressed in Asian art. These trees were painted on a silk screen by a Japanese artist. His name was Nonomura Sotatsu, and he painted from about 1600 to 1630. Many Japanese and Chinese artists of this period painted on folding screens and sliding panels. Sliding panels are still used instead of doors in many homes in Japan.

Unit I

The Environment

One of Asia's busiest ports is Singapore, a major center of banking and trade.

The **environment** in which people live plays an important role in influencing the kind of **culture** they develop. The area we call Asia has many different land features and **climates**. The Asians have had to learn to live with these differences over thousands of years. In China and Indonesia, **anthropologists** have found evidence of ancient inhabitants that date to 300,000, 500,000, or even a million years ago.

Today two billion people—about half the world's population—are Asians. These Asians speak hundreds of **languages** and **dialects**. They belong to numerous **ethnic groups** or **nationalities**. The Asians are not one; they are many. And they can be distinguished from one another by differences in attitude, culture, and physical appearance.

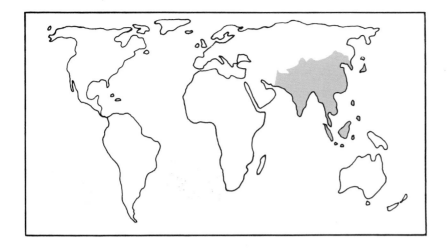

The **geographical** area of Asia that we are considering is made up of almost 30 **nations**. It is spread over an enormous mainland and thousands of islands. The mainland is part of the Eurasian landmass. Some geographers consider the Asian mainland to reach north to the Arctic Circle and west to the Red Sea.

However, the Asian mainland we will study is that part bounded on the north by the Soviet Union, on the east by the China Sea and the Sea of Japan, on the west by the Middle Eastern countries of Iran and Afghanistan, and on the south by the Indian Ocean. The islands included in the region stretch from the tip of Malaysia down to Australia and west to the Philippines.

Wherever the land can be cultivated it is crowded. The greatest numbers of people are found near the coasts and rivers.

Chapter 1
A Large and Varied Area

RIVERS

For centuries Asians, like people elsewhere, have gathered near water. As early as 3000 to 2700 B.C., a widespread **civilization** was centered around the Indus River in India and Pakistan. Ancient cultures also developed on the broad plain around the Ganges (GAN-jeez) in India and the Brahmaputra (brahm-uh-PYOO-truh) in India and Bangladesh. People still crowd around these two rivers. The Chinese began their early civilization along the Yellow River and its tributaries. Today the Chinese continue to live in large numbers around their rivers—the Yangtze (YAHNG-SEE), the Pearl, the Red, the West, and others. The Irrawaddy in Burma and the Mekong which flows through Cambodia, Laos, and Vietnam have large populations along their banks.

Sometimes the river is the only means of **communication** between one place and another. It is also the main means of transportation for many Asians. In all but the **industrialized** areas, the roads are

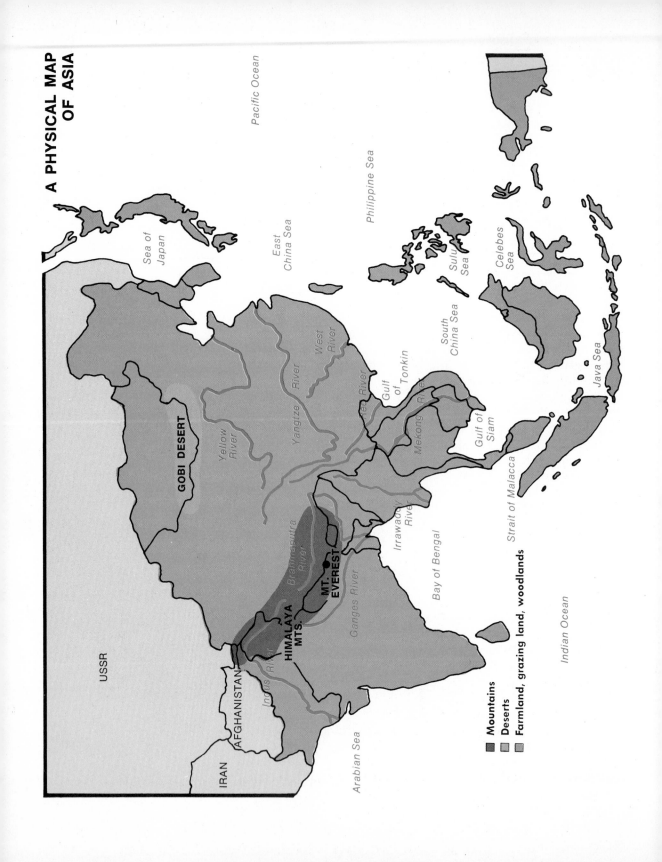

A PHYSICAL MAP OF ASIA

Pacific Ocean

Sea of Japan

East China Sea

Philippine Sea

USSR

GOBI DESERT

Yellow River

Yangtze River

West River

Gulf of Tonkin

South China Sea

Sulu Sea

Celebes Sea

Java Sea

IRAN

AFGHANISTAN

HIMALAYA MTS.

MT. EVEREST

Brahmaputra River

Ganges River

Indus River

Mekong River

Irrawaddy River

Bay of Bengal

Gulf of Siam

Strait of Malacca

Arabian Sea

Indian Ocean

■ Mountains
Deserts
Farmland, grazing land, woodlands

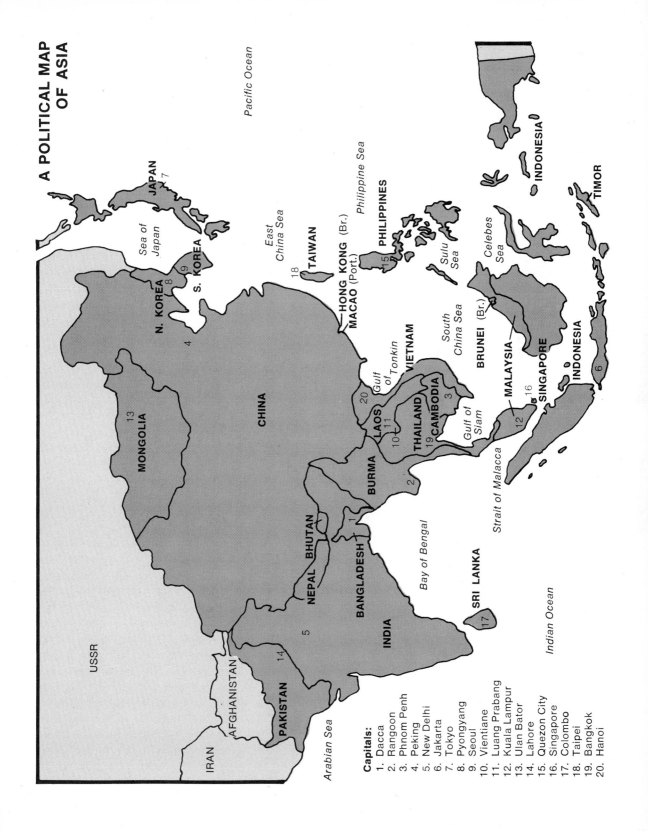

A POLITICAL MAP
OF ASIA

Pacific Ocean

USSR

JAPAN 7

Sea of
Japan

N. KOREA

S. KOREA 8 9

East
China Sea

TAIWAN 18

4

MONGOLIA 13

CHINA

HONG KONG (Br.)
MACAO (Port.)

Philippine Sea

PHILIPPINES

15

Sulu
Sea

VIETNAM

Gulf
of Tonkin 20

LAOS 11
10
THAILAND
CAMBODIA 19
3

South
China Sea

Celebes
Sea

BRUNEI (Br.)

INDONESIA

TIMOR

BURMA

2

Gulf of
Siam

MALAYSIA 16
12
SINGAPORE

INDONESIA 6

NEPAL
BHUTAN

BANGLADESH 1

5

INDIA

Bay of Bengal

SRI LANKA

17

Strait of Malacca

Indian Ocean

AFGHANISTAN

PAKISTAN 14

IRAN

Arabian Sea

Capitals:
1. Dacca
2. Rangoon
3. Phnom Penh
4. Peking
5. New Delhi
6. Jakarta
7. Tokyo
8. Pyongyang
9. Seoul
10. Vientiane
11. Luang Prabang
12. Kuala Lampur
13. Ulan Bator
14. Lahore
15. Quezon City
16. Singapore
17. Colombo
18. Taipei
19. Bangkok
20. Hanoi

Where electricity to run pumps is not available, Indians use the age-old method of lever and counterbalance to fill irrigation ditches.

few, mostly dirt, and in poor condition. Rivers have become the roads. To handle the resulting **trade**, great **cities** have grown up along the rivers. Most of Asia's largest cities are either on rivers, the coast, or where the sea and river meet. Calcutta, India; Shanghai, China; and Tokyo, Japan are a few examples.

The river itself has been home for many generations of Asians. These are the boat people. They are born, grow up, marry, have children, and die on their boats. The river is also a shopping center, where boats serve as floating stores. When the boats are moored together beside a wharf or the river bank, people can walk across them for miles without touching land or wetting their feet.

Rivers can also be destructive. Frequently they break from their banks and flood the land, bringing hunger, sickness, and death. For centuries the Asians have fought to keep the rushing waters behind dikes. It is an endless task. As rivers flow, they pick up silt or mud and carry it along. As more silt is picked up, the mud at the bottom of the flowing water drops to the riverbed. In this way the riverbed builds up and raises the level of the river. Then the Asians must construct higher and higher dikes. When the dikes weaken, as they can in heavy rain, the water pours out. Then the river becomes a river of sorrow, as the floodwaters destroy homes and crops.

Despite the frequent floods, Asians always return to the land near the rivers. They have little choice. They need the river water to irrigate their fields so they can grow food.

In recent years the rushing waters of rivers have been harnessed to improve the life of the Asians. Japan and the People's Republic of China, among others, are tapping their river systems to provide cheap hydroelectric power to heat and light homes and operate factories.

MOUNTAINS

Much of the land area of Asia is made up of mountains. Walls of mountains run from a core called the Pamir Knot in Central Asia, to Pakistan, India, Southeast Asia, and China. They cut across Korea and appear again in Japan. In Indonesia, Japan, and the Philippines, the mountains are occasionally active volcanoes.

The Himalaya Mountains range across northern India and Nepal. One of them, Mount Everest, is the highest mountain in the world. The Himalayas stop the moisture-bearing winds that blow inland from the Indian Ocean. As a consequence, the grass-covered lands of Mongolia, Sinkiang (SHIN-jee-ahng), and Tibet to the north of the mountains are dry and can be farmed only by using irrigation.

The early people who inhabited these lands led a nomadic existence. They roamed from place to place in search of food for themselves and their animals. They were constantly drawn to the settlements along the rivers and the greener fields which lay beyond the mountains. Year after year these **peoples** journeyed through the passes of the mountains to the better land to the south. The **history** of India is in great part the history of those who came there through mountain passes—the Khyber, the Gumal, the Bolan, and others.

The mountains occupy so much of Asia that there is little flat land for farming. But Filipinos, Indians, Nepalese, Southeast Asians, Japanese, and Chinese have learned to farm the mountains. They found that they could cultivate the side of the mountains that stopped the wind and caused the rain to fall. They met the challenge of the mountains by terracing the slopes.

MONSOONS

Many Asians depend for water not only upon rivers but also upon seasonal circulations of the winds called monsoons. In the Asian summer, from May to October, the air over the land becomes hot. This hot air rises, causing a low-pressure area under it. Cooler air from over the ocean moves into the low-pressure area, bringing rain to the land.

In winter, from November to April, this process is reversed. Air over the ocean is warmer than air over the land. The warm air over the ocean rises, and cooler air from the land flows out to the low-pressure ocean areas. The winds blowing out to sea from the land do not carry rain. But as the winds pass over water, the ocean water evaporates into the air, forming clouds. This becomes rain as the winds push the clouds over land again.

For example, winds from China blowing toward the ocean pass over the Sea of Japan. They bring rain to the west coast of Japan. Winds from the Asian continent blowing over the Bay of Bengal bring rain in winter to the southeast coasts of India and Sri Lanka (formerly Ceylon). The Philippines and Indonesia also reap the benefits of winter rains.

When the monsoons come late or bring too little rain, many Asians suffer. Their rivers and wells cannot supply enough water for crops, adding to the problem of hunger in Asia.

For thousands of years Asians have lived in **rural villages**. It is estimated that today there are almost two million villages in Asia. However, for centuries Asians have also known the conveniences of city life. Today some Asian cities are among the largest in the world.

VILLAGE LIFE

Asian villages are not planned; they just grow. A village is frequently a network of tiny lanes and alleys winding through closely packed houses. These passages are often filled with garbage and sewage and are seldom covered with anything but mud. Sometimes cobblestones

Chapter 2
Communities

This village of bamboo is in China's Yunnan Province. The area borders Southeast Asia. What culture traits does this village share with those of Southeast Asia?

thatched: covered with straw or palm leaves

are laid, but they are usually uneven and irregularly spaced. The narrow lanes of the village permit only the passage of people and their beasts.

Some villages, particularly in Japan and southern China, are stretched out like a string. They are laid out in rows on one or both sides of a river, canal, or highway.

For centuries many Asians have lived in farmhouses made of mud or mud bricks. Frequently the roof is thatched with grass tied down with bamboo strips. Rooms are small and few. The tiny, barred windows are covered with paper, but seldom with glass. The villagers are poor and thieves are greatly feared. Any loss can be a disaster. It is not uncommon for Asian villagers to share their house with their animals, especially at night, for animals are valuable.

In many parts of Southeast Asia, houses are thatched and raised above ground on stilts. They sit in the middle of a compound, among shade trees of fruit and palm. The houses have roofed porches which provide shade during the hot days. The animals live beneath the house. This kind of house suits a warm climate because it permits good air circulation.

The furniture of a villager is simple and essential: an earthen stove, some brass pots, tin cans, and clay dishes. The bed is made of rope, wooden planks, or simply a mat on the floor. There are a few benches or chairs and a table. The Asian villager may also own a scroll, a vase for flowers, a picture or two, and little else.

The number of Asians who live in a village varies from several hundred to over a thousand. They may all bear the same family name and be descendants of a common ancestor who founded the village, as in China. Other villages are made up of families with several different names, although they are often related through many generations. Or the people of a village may be separated by great social barriers, as in India.

Around the villages lie the fields, which the villagers cultivate. The Asians are still primarily farmers. Their principal crops are rice and wheat. But they also grow barley, millet, sorghum, corn, soybeans, many kinds of vegetables, and sweet potatoes. During the working season, the villagers walk each day to the fields carrying their tools. Often they lead or drive before them a water buffalo, a cow, or a bullock.

The village is not completely self-sufficient. Some items must be bought—salt, sugar, cooking oil, implements of iron and metal, and dyes for cloth. To obtain these necessities, the villagers raise crops such as peanuts and other vegetables which can be sold for cash. The villagers were more self-supporting in the past than they are today. Machine-made products and a **cash economy** are changing village life.

In some villages, electric lights shine in almost every house, filtered water pours from modern faucets, and blaring radios and an occasional television antenna intrude dramatically on the **traditional** Asian scene. Such villages are found in Japan and in the model villages of the People's Republic of China. They may be seen in small numbers in Thailand, India, Malaysia, the Philippines, and elsewhere.

The life of the villagers in most of Asia, however, is not so easy. There are too many villagers trying to obtain a living from little plots of earth. The rains may not come or too much rain may bring floods. Locusts or other insects may destroy the crops.

But the villagers have their moments of happiness. In the past, wandering storytellers would stop and entertain. Today a group of players may stage dramas that tell of honored and heroic people. In every Asian country there are festivals which give temporary relief from daily problems. There are marriages and funerals, which are always occasions for visiting, gossiping, and eating.

CITIES

As long ago as 2700 B.C. people were living in cities on the South Asian subcontinent—India, Pakistan, and Bangladesh. Cities also flourished in ancient China. Then as now, cities were the centers of **commerce** and culture. Today more than 40 Asian cities have populations of over a million.

Many of these cities are ports and look to trade and to the sea for their livelihoods. Some of these Asian cities have become Western in attitude and appearance. It is in the cities that new ways of life develop and from the cities that changes and **reforms** spread.

But Asian cities are contributing increasingly to environmental problems in their nations. Wherever there is **urban** growth and industrialization, there is also growing **pollution** of all kinds: air, water,

Like many large cities, Tokyo has problems of congestion, noise, and smog.

noise, land. The cities of Asia also have some of the worst traffic problems in the world.

THE QUALITY OF LIFE

The Asians are trying to adapt to the **economic** and social changes that have revolutionized the West in the last few centuries. But most of the Asian nations are troubled by problems of **overpopulation**, **illiteracy**, and poor health care. One of the reasons most nations have difficulty in improving the **standard of living** is a lack of **capital**— money and machines—for industrialization. Without money people cannot buy machinery. Without machinery, **raw materials**, or a **surplus** of food to sell, more capital cannot be produced.

Many observers believe that overpopulation is the major problem. Overpopulation plagues every Asian nation except rice-surplus areas like Thailand and upper Burma. Elsewhere, there is not enough fertile land to feed the fast-increasing population. China and India both show increases of several million people per year.

Most Asians do not starve to death, but many are victims of malnutrition. They get enough food to keep themselves alive and working. Often, however, it is not enough to keep them healthy and working effectively. As a result, many Asians are easy victims for disease. At birth, most Asians cannot expect to live much beyond 45 years of age.

Illiteracy is prevalent everywhere in Asia except in Japan. In India, it is estimated that 71 percent of the population cannot read or write. As Asian nations launch programs of industrialization, a reading and writing public is needed. More people will need to be trained for technical jobs. More doctors and nurses are needed to give improved health care. In many Asian nations education is compulsory.

Summing Up the Unit

Social Studies Vocabulary

Define: environment; culture; climates; anthropologists; languages; dialects; nations; civilization; communication; industrialized; trade; cities; peoples; rural; villages; cash economy; tradition; commerce; reforms; urban; pollution; overpopulation; illiteracy; standard of living; capital; surplus; raw materials

Places

Locate: the countries and bodies of water that border the Asian mainland; Ganges, Yellow, Irrawaddy, Mekong rivers; Calcutta; Tokyo; Himalaya Mountains

Words

Identify: boat people; hydroelectric power; monsoons; river of sorrow; model villages

Questions:

1. a. In what ways do Asians depend on their rivers? b. What problems have rivers created for Asians? c. Why do they return to the land near the rivers?
2. Where are most of Asia's largest cities located?
3. a. Why do some Asian farmers have so little room to farm? b. How have they solved this problem?
4. a. Explain how monsoons are helpful to Asians. b. harmful. c. What are the seasonal patterns of monsoons?
5. Describe the possessions of a typical Asian villager.
6. How is the Asian village not self-sufficient?
7. Why does the typical Asian villager have a hard life?
8. Where in Asia are the new ways of life developing?
9. Name the three problems most Asian nations face today.
10. Why do most nations have difficulty in improving the standard of living of their people?

Discussion Topics

1. Asians speak hundreds of languages and dialects. And they belong to numerous national and ethnic groups. How has Asian geography contributed to this variety?
2. Almost all the known civilizations of the world originally developed around rivers. Using the material in the text as a basis, what explanation can you give for this?
3. Rivers, mountains, and monsoons are all important in Asia. How has each of these aided Asians? How has each been a hindrance?
4. Almost half of the world's population lives in Asia. How has the geography of Asia made it possible for the total population to be so large?
5. The Asians are trying to adapt to the economic and social changes that have revolutionized the West in the last few centuries. Do you think this adaptation is necessary? What would happen if the Asians resisted change? Is change always good even if necessary?

Project Ideas

1. Using an atlas, almanac, or encyclopedia, make a chart or graph comparing the population figures of major cities of the U.S. with those of major cities of Asia.
2. Write a short story describing what it would be like to: live on a boat in Hong Kong; live in an Asian village; climb Mount Everest; live through a monsoon; visit an Asian city, either as a tourist or a villager.
3. Report on the relationship between geography and the way of life of a typical Asian in any of the nations discussed in this section.
4. Prepare two maps of Asia showing the seasonal patterns of monsoons.
5. Draw a sketch of an Asian village or a villager's house.
6. Using salt dough or clay, make a relief map of a region of Asia showing mountains, plateaus, river valleys, and the slope of the land.
7. Collect pictures of Asian village and city life. Arrange them in a collage. Your collage could sample the variety of Asian life or it could show the contrast between modern and traditional ways.

149

Unit II

India–Pakistan–Bangladesh

The Taj Mahal, one of the world's most beautiful buildings, was built as a tomb for Mumtaz Mahal. She was the favorite wife of Shah Jahan, who ruled the Mogul Empire from 1628 to 1658. The monument is in Agra, India.

The Indo-Pakistan-Bangladesh subcontinent lies between Europe, Africa, and the Middle East on one side and the Far East and the Pacific regions on the other. The subcontinent's central location early exposed it to many outside contacts. The northern part was convenient to the mainland trade routes between Asia and western Europe. Southern India lay across the great water routes between the Pacific, Mediterranean, and Atlantic areas.

Because of its strategic position, the subcontinent received cultural and **ideological** contributions from both east and west. The Indians adapted some and created others of their own. In many instances, they acted as go-betweens transmitting to east and west the knowledge, beliefs, and ideas they had gathered.

On the Indo-Pakistan-Bangladesh subcontinent, the practice of agriculture began around 4000 B.C. Gradually villages and **towns** developed. By around 2700 B.C., some of these villages had become cities. They were the centers of civilizations covering 1.3 million square kilometers (500,000 square miles) or more.

In the 1920s two long-buried cities were uncovered in Pakistan—Mohenjo-Daro (moh-hen-joh-DAH-ro) on the Indus River north of Karachi, and Harappa, southwest of Lahore. The widespread civilization these cities represent is variously called Indus Valley civilization, Harappan culture, or Indus culture.

Chapter 1
Ancient India

INDUS VALLEY CIVILIZATION

Capital cities of the Indus Valley civilization were well-planned. Their streets ran north-south and east-west in regular fashion. One- and two-story houses, their blank walls facing outward, lined these streets. Doorways were on the sides of the houses. The houses were built around open interior courtyards.

These ancient people worked with gold, copper, silver, and bronze. They created artfully designed seals and imaginative toys. The Indus Valley civilization possessed a written language which has been partially deciphered. Their **religion** was centered on the fertility and life-giving features of the earth.

The people of the Indus Valley civilization used their skills as builders and engineers to provide themselves with what we call modern conveniences. They had private and public baths and toilets. These were connected to a network of sewers lined with baked brick. At intervals, shafts for inspection led to the sewers.

Trade was carried on both inside and outside the Indus Valley region. At Lothal, on the Gulf of Cambay, near the present city of Bombay a dock extended more than 210 meters (700 feet) into the water. This made it possible to load and unload cargoes during both high and low tides.

Several settlements of Indus peoples have also been discovered along the northern coast of the Arabian Sea. These settlements were probably trading and stopping places for Indus ships en route to Persian Gulf ports or farther west to southern Mesopotamia in the Middle East. Indus ships were carrying timber, ivory, and other goods there before 2000 B.C.

The Indus Valley civilization declined sometime between 1700 and 1500 B.C. Skeletons and the remains of buildings suggest that war may have been the cause. However, the civilization carried on in modified forms in southern and central India for some time after that.

It was around this time that nomadic people from Central Asia invaded the region. These were the Aryans (AIR-ee-uhns). The Indus Valley people, the Aryans, and others who came between 1700 and 500 B.C., laid the cultural foundations of the later Indian people.

☐ **Indus Valley Civilization, c. 2500-1500 B.C.**

Chapter 2
Early Indian Religions

Diwali, *or Festival of Lights, celebrates the happy ending of the epic,* Ramayana. *The epic is no longer regarded merely as a story. The main characters have become examples of what good women and men should be.*

The Indians have talked, thought, and written much about their relationship with others, with nature, and with their **deities**. From them came the religions of Hinduism and Buddhism. These religions have played a great part in making the Asians what they are today.

ANCIENT BELIEFS

Sometime between 1700 and 1500 B.C. the Aryans invaded the Indian subcontinent. These fierce warriors from Central Asia are named after the form of an early Indo-European language they spoke. The Aryans took over much of what is present-day Pakistan and India. Their influence left a deep mark on the development of the Indians.

The name Aryan means noble one. The Aryans thought that those outside their group were inferior. Perhaps it was the Aryans, by insisting on their superiority and separateness, who planted the seed of a **caste** system in India.

But the principal contribution of the Aryans to Indian culture was through their religion. Aryan deities represented the beauty and forces of nature. The Aryans honored Ushas, goddess of the dawn, Indra of the storm, Agni of the fire, and Varuna of the sky. The ruler of the stars was Soma, the moon god. Religious **rituals** included sacrifices of animals as well as offerings of milk and grain.

What is known about the religious practices, **customs**, and **institutions** of the Aryans comes from sacred writings called *Vedas* (VAY-duhs). Veda means divine knowledge. The *Vedas* consist of hymns, prayers, rituals, and **myths**. They were collected and written down sometime between 1500 and 500 B.C. This is known as the Vedic period.

Over the years, other works were added to the original *Vedas.* Some dealt with ritual and law. Others were interpretations of the original religious themes of the *Vedas.* Among the best known of these additional works are the *Upanishads.* Upanishad means sitting near. A knowledge of the truths of the *Vedas* was learned while sitting around wise teachers. The *Vedas* and *Upanishads* are the basic scriptures of Hinduism, the religion which evolved from Aryan beliefs.

Other Aryan writings are also important to the religious life of Hindus. Among the best known are two **epics**, the *Mahabharata* (muh-HAH-BAH-rah-tuh) and the *Ramayana* (rah-MAH-yuh-nuh). The events and characters described in these stories reach far back into India's past. It is believed that the two works were finally written down around the second or third centuries B.C.

The *Mahabharata* describes a war between two Indian families. They fight over control of a kingdom in northern India near the modern city of Delhi. The war is a savage one, and many are killed.

Within the poem is the *Bhagavad-Gita* (BAHG-uh-vahd GEE-tuh), The Lord's Song. It is a dialogue between Arjuna, a member of one of the warring families, and the god Krishna. Its basic thought—duty should be done without emotion or desire—became fundamental to the religion of the Hindus. Scenes from the *Mahabharata* are still told by village storytellers, dramatized on the Indian stage, and repeated in books.

The second epic, the *Ramayana,* is about Prince Rama and his devoted wife, Sita. They were exiled because of the jealousy of a stepmother. The *Ramayana* tells of their wanderings in the jungle and of the kidnaping of Sita by a demon king. Sita is rescued by Prince Rama with the help of the monkey king, Hanuman. The story ends with the return of Sita and Rama to their native land.

HINDUISM

Other people came to India after the Aryans, and other deities replaced the Aryan deities of nature. Three of these became supreme: Brahma, the Creator; Vishnu, the Preserver; and Siva, the Destroyer. They are still honored today in Hinduism—the religion that is practiced by the majority of the Indian people.

In Hinduism, the Indians found a religion which seeks to meet the needs of all people. It is tolerant and adaptable. To the mystic, it offers meditation. For those who prefer the more tangible, it provides temples, ritual, and a choice of many deities.

In its efforts to meet human wants, the Hindu religion has become almost bewildering in its variety. Religious practices vary from region to region, and even from home to home. But beneath the face of Hinduism there lies a basic unity of thought and action.

153

ONE ULTIMATE REALITY   Hinduism teaches that reality is one. The many statues and pictures of deities displayed in temples, the countryside, and homes are merely symbols of one Ultimate Reality, which the Hindus call Brahma. But this reality cannot be limited to a name, a form, or a person. All the statues and pictures only represent the limited efforts of peoples to show what can never be truly shown. Brahma, the Ultimate Reality, must be forever formless and nameless.

Everything in the universe—people, deities, animals, nature—is part of Brahma, the Ultimate Reality. We are all related through this Ultimate Reality. We are all one. Nothing, living or nonliving, stands apart from anything else. Within every human being there is an essential self, similar perhaps to what is called the soul. The Hindus call it Atman. This Atman is one with Brahma. An individual is simply one of the countless evidences of Brahma.

SALVATION   Hinduism teaches that deities and temples, rituals and creeds, are not important in themselves. They are merely means to aid the individual in being delivered from a particular body. The essential self, or Atman, is imprisoned in a confining, ignorant, self-centered body.

The senses limit the body's awareness. It does not know it is part of everything else that exists. The body is self-centered in thinking of itself as something special. The final goal of the self is to realize that it is one with the Ultimate Reality. To reach this goal, each person must escape from the idea of being an individual, separate from others.

Those who finally realize that they are one with the Ultimate Reality become free. They are no longer confined by the body and the bonds of an individual existence. But this is not an easy task. Often the individual must live through a series of separate lives before salvation from material existence is reached.

REBIRTH   The Hindus believe that an individual may be reborn again and again. This is called reincarnation. The essential self does not die when the body dies. As part of the Ultimate Reality, it has no beginning and no end. Nor is the self restricted to the human form when it is reborn. In succeeding lives, the self may rule as a god, bloom as a flower, or crawl as a snake.

The form taken when a person is reborn is determined by the law of karma. According to karma acts that an individual performs while living determine that person's future state. Our present state itself is the result of all our previous acts. Good acts done now will raise a person to a higher level in the next rebirth. Bad acts will lower a person's status in the next life.

The purpose of reincarnation is spiritual progress. The final goal is reached when a person is liberated from the cycle of birth and rebirth. The system of caste is one way in which Hindus measure the individual's progress toward liberation.

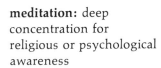

STAGES OF LIFE   Hinduism divides the life of each individual into four progressive stages. These stages of life are marked by the movement of the individual from material to spiritual occupations. In ascending order, these stages are: student, householder, anchorite, and sannyasi.

The stage of the student is one of preparation, study, and discipline. The householder stage is one in which the individual undertakes responsibilities to family, **society**, community, and nation. When these responsibilities are fulfilled, the individual should withdraw from the world and enter the third stage, anchorite. This is a period of study and meditation.

Finally, there comes the complete denial of all that is material, the sannyasi stage. During this period, a person may become a hermit, living in some remote place, satisfied to be alone with thoughts of Brahma. Or sannyasis may wander among the people, asking nothing of anyone nor caring if they receive anything. These holy ones are greatly honored by the Hindus.

A GUIDE FOR LIFE   The duties and rules of conduct for a Hindu are called dharma. If the rules of dharma are followed faithfully, every act furthers an individual's progress toward liberation from rebirth. Ideally people should act without attachment to the act. They should not be concerned with whether or not they will profit by what they do. The Hindu aims to destroy the desire that goes with action—but not action itself.

These are some of the basic beliefs that lie beneath the many faces of Hinduism. But another religion was born in India. That religion is Buddhism.

meditation: deep concentration for religious or psychological awareness

The Ganges River is sacred to Hindus. Each year thousands come to bathe in its waters. Some come to purify their souls. Others believe that the holy river will cure them of illness.

155

BUDDHISM

Much that has been said about Hinduism can also be said about Buddhism. Each has influenced the teachings of the other. Buddhism began in the 500s B.C. In a sense it was an offshoot of Hinduism. In another real sense, it was a protest against certain teachings and practices of the Hindu priests called Brahmans.

Gautama Siddhartha (GOW-tah-mah sid-DAHR-tuh), the historical founder of Buddhism, is generally known as Gautama Buddha (BOOD-uh). Sometimes he is simply called Buddha or the Enlightened One. What we do know about Gautama comes to us through **tradition**. Much of this tradition is accepted as fact.

Gautama was the son of a wealthy and powerful local chief. His people lived in the foothills of the Himalaya Mountains, perhaps near the present borders of Nepal. Gautama was married and, at the age of 29, became a father. During this same year he was shocked into changing his life by meetings with an old man, a sick man, a dead man, and a beggar. He was struck by the misery, sorrow, and decay of life. Gautama left his family and his home to find the cause and the solution of human sufferings. For six years he searched for the answers.

Then one day he suddenly understood. He had received enlightenment. Gautama Buddha gave up his life of meditation and began preaching his message to the people of India.

TEACHINGS OF BUDDHISM Buddha believed that there is always change. Nothing that we see today is the same tomorrow. While things are changing, they are decaying. The young become old and finally die. The fresh flower of the dawn droops at sunset. Nothing is permanent, not even the essential self or soul. The only thing that might be said to endure is the ever-turning wheel of change and decay. Basic to Buddhism are the Four Noble Truths.

The first is that everyone suffers. There is no one who does not suffer in some way almost daily. Even pleasure is a cause of suffering because we know that it will not last. This knowledge in itself is a sorrow. These sorrows will go on and on, rebirth after rebirth, until all desires and attachments to people and things are ended.

The second Noble Truth states that desire is the cause of suffering. Unless people suppress all desires, they will go on forever, chained to the wheel of a changing and decaying life. Humans must stop wanting things—happiness, pain, individuality, existence—in short, everything. They must realize that their feeling of individuality is an illusion and that all things are temporary and changing. Individual existence can only result in suffering. Only when a person comes to realize these things will that person become enlightened—a Buddha. Rebirth will end and the individual will escape to nirvana.

According to the third Noble Truth, nirvana is a condition or state in which all desires are extinct. Nirvana is the ultimate goal of all good Buddhists. It is a condition of not suffering. Nirvana cannot be described because it can be known only by those who are enlightened.

Gautama Buddha offered guidelines for entering nirvana in the fourth Noble Truth. These guidelines are known as the Noble Eightfold Path: (1) right knowledge of the cause and ending of suffering; (2) high and worthy intentions; (3) kind, frank, truthful speech; (4) right conduct; (5) right livelihood that does not injure any living thing; (6) right effort to train oneself; (7) a keen and active mind; and (8) meditation. If people followed these ethical guidelines carefully and well, they would find nirvana.

BUDDHISM SPREADS: MAURYA DYNASTY   Many of the people of India, especially of northern India, heard and believed the teachings of Gautama Buddha and his disciples. They built monasteries, and many became monks or nuns. They were seeking enlightenment and eventually nirvana. This beginning of monastic life occurred as the Persians, under Darius, conquered northwest India in 518 B.C.

Buddhism continued expanding for the next 200 years. It reached its greatest heights in India during the Maurya (MOWR-yuh) **dynasty** (322-185 B.C.). Dynasty generally means a succession of rulers who are of the same family. This dynasty was founded by a clever, cunning person named Chandragupta. The Maurya dynasty was the first to unite most of the Indians under one ruler. Chandragupta was an efficient ruler, with a well-organized spy system, a fine network of roads, and an effective **government** structure.

ASOKA: TOLERANT BUDDHIST KING   Under Asoka, the grandson of Chandragupta, the Maurya **empire** reached its greatest extent. During this time Buddhism flourished in India and expanded abroad. Asoka (273-232 B.C.) is regarded by the Indians as one of their most remarkable rulers.

At first Asoka embarked upon an expansion of the empire left him by his grandfather and his father. But the awful, bloody price of his conquest was paid by the death of hundreds of thousands of his people. This realization turned him from violence and war. Asoka became a fervent disciple and teacher of Buddhism. He forgave his former enemies, pardoned many, and gave up his favorite pastime of hunting. Asoka became concerned with the welfare of his people. He improved their medical services and gave much attention to irrigating their lands. He eased the life of the traveler with rest houses and beautified the landscape.

All over India he proclaimed his rules and laws by having them carved on stones and on pillars. Some of these pillars still stand, rising 15 meters (50 feet) above the ground.

Asoka's personal example, his moral teachings, and the direction of his government all served to publicize Buddhism throughout his

The Buddhist ruler Asoka publicized his laws by carving them on stone pillars for all to see.

Maurya Empire Under Asoka, c. 250 B.C.

empire. Toward the end of his life, Asoka held the first council of Buddhists. This group, known as the Council of Patna, met at Pataliputra, the capital. It settled the basic texts of Buddhism.

Asoka wanted those beyond his empire to hear and accept the truths of Buddhism. His own brother was sent to Sri Lanka where he converted the king of that country. Missionaries were also sent to Burma and Nepal, and from there Buddhism spread to other parts of Southeast Asia. Today, with the exception of Indonesia, Malaysia, and the Philippines, the majority of Southeast Asians are Buddhists.

The Maurya dynasty ended with the assassination of the last ruler in 185 B.C. But Buddhism continued to advance abroad. It entered China around the first century A.D. From there it spread to Korea and Japan. During the 700s A.D., Buddhism was introduced into Tibet.

Chapter 3
Creativity

The Indians have been moved by religious beliefs, by nature, and by their feelings for other people to express themselves in the creative arts. They have carved, painted, written and created music, dance, and drama. Many of their creations still remain, preserved in temples, in paintings, in literature, and in the theater.

EARLIEST ARTS

Religion has influenced the art, **architecture**, literature, music, and dance of India from very early times. The earliest known Indian writings are the *Vedas,* the sacred books of Hinduism. Then there are epics like the *Mahabharata* and the *Ramayana* that became part of Hindu thought. Other Indian religious and **philosophical** works explained, extended, and praised the religions of India.

The technique and art of advising and teaching moral lessons through **fables** originated in India. The *Panchatantra* (PAHN-chuh-tahn-truh) is a collection of stories for the instruction of young people. In the stories, animals characterize human failings and weaknesses. The tales in *The Arabian Nights* and Aesop's *Fables* are almost identical with some of these Indian stories.

The Buddhist stupa is one of the oldest types of monuments in India. A stupa is a hemispheric mound of brick or stone which houses a sacred relic. Stupas were considered sacred and Buddhists gained merit by merely walking around them.

An outstanding example, the Sanchi Stupa, dates from the time of Asoka (273-232 B.C.). This stupa is a stone with a flattened top. It sits on a raised terrace and is encircled by a stone railing. The railing has four large gateways facing north, east, south, and west. These gateways are elaborately carved with symbolic figures of men, women, animals, and plants. Buddha is represented by the wheel,

158

the lotus, the lion, the footprint, and the sacred tree, but never in human shape.

Later, Indians carved temples from solid rock. They imitated structures of wood and masonry by carving beams from the stone. Pillars of stone carved along the sides of the temple appear to hold up the beams. In the most holy place, the sanctuary, a stupa was placed.

Gradually statues of Buddha began to replace the stupa. These statues were not supposed to resemble Buddha. They were sculptured to portray his peace of mind, calmness, and happiness which went beyond the pleasures of the senses. Many of these statues have a swelling or bulge on top of the head to signify wisdom. Buddha's earlobes are long and pierced to remind the viewer that Buddha at one time wore jeweled earrings of such weight that they stretched the lobes of his ears. This symbol is a reminder that wealth is of little value. A mark was placed on the forehead between the eyes to represent a third eye of virtue and spirituality. The statue of Buddha preaching in the Deer Park at Sarnath is regarded as one of the finest examples of this type of art.

symbol: a word or object that stands for another object or idea

A few early Indian paintings survived the weathering of the centuries because they were painted inside caves. Among these paintings are those in the caves of Ajanta in central India. From around 200 B.C. to 500 A.D. a religious community lived in an isolated jungle above the Wardha River.

From cliffs of solid rock the monks chiseled and dug halls of worship and living quarters. The walls of these temple-caves were graced with **sculpture** and paintings. The unknown artists painted the variety of Indian life: beggars, the rich, peasants, kings, flowers, children, animals of the earth, and forms that are not earthly. All are painted in vivid greens, browns, reds, blues, and white.

CLASSICAL PERIOD: GUPTA DYNASTY

From the fall of the Maurya dynasty (185 B.C.) until the establishment of the Gupta dynasty (320 A.D.), the Indians were invaded many times by the peoples of Central Asia. During this period many of the early artistic achievements of the Indians were lost. But during the Gupta dynasty (320 A.D.-c.500 A.D.) there was a revival of **the arts**. A Chinese Buddhist pilgrim who visited India during this period described the **political** and cultural atmosphere as flourishing. Religious tolerance was practiced. The government was mild, and the ruler appeared to have a real interest in the people's welfare.

Although tolerant of Buddhism, the Gupta kings were Hindus. During this period Hindu themes and representations of deities were fashioned in stone, bronze, and gold. Hindu temples were cut from solid rock. One of the most famous is Kailasa Temple. Another is the cave of Elephanta in the Bay of Bombay, which is dedicated to Lord Siva.

Thousands of interpretations of the three great Hindu gods Brahma,

☐ **Gupta Dynasty, c. 400 A.D.**

Siva, the god of destruction and creation, is one of the most important Hindu gods. This bronze statue of Siva is more than 700 years old.

Siva, and Vishnu, and other Hindu deities have been carved, sculptured, and painted. Brahma is sometimes represented with four heads and four arms holding the *Vedas.* Siva is sometimes portrayed in a dancing pose to show his powers of creation and destruction. He is often shown with his wife Parvati, who can also destroy or save people. Vishnu is sometimes represented with four arms holding a shell, a staff of authority called a mace, a lotus flower, and a disk indicating the sun. He rides a bird which is part human and part eagle.

Over the centuries most Indian artists have had to work within detailed and strict rules. There were rules, for example, for the length and width of the nostril. Even the placement of the hands was spelled out. The artists used no living models. Before painting or carving, they thought carefully of what they were about to describe. Finally they identified themselves with the idea they were about to portray. It is a mark of the genius of the Indian artists that they were able to produce an art of magnificence and beauty within these limitations.

Indians combined poetry and drama to write drama in poetic form. The greatest of the poetic dramatists was Kalidasa, who wrote his drama *Sakuntala* in the 400s A.D. Sakuntala, the heroine, is shy like the animals of the forest in which she lives. She is also tender, merciful, generous, and faithful. Sakuntala has strength of character and beauty of form. She represents an ideal vision of woman.

SCIENTIFIC THOUGHT

The Maurya and Gupta periods were golden ages of science and discovery in India. During the Gupta period there were great universities at Nalanda and at Valabhi. The university at Nalanda included eight colleges and three libraries.

Indian scientific thought had made great advances long before those times, and it continued for many years afterward. Many of the discoveries made by the Indians were later made known to Western Europeans by contact with the Arabs. Through scholars, Western Europeans began to learn that Indian scientific knowledge was often older and more accurate than that of the ancient Greeks.

The Indians knew of the earth's movement around the sun and its rotation on its axis centuries before Western Europeans accepted the fact. The Indians could also explain eclipses. Their mathematicians used the zero and the decimal system. They developed algebra, working with negative quantities, quadratic equations, and square root.

eclipse: the loss of light which occurs on earth when a heavenly body passes in front of the sun and blocks its light

Indians studied anatomy and knew that certain characteristics are transmitted through heredity. Medicinal properties of plants in treating diseases were known to them. They used inoculation against such diseases as smallpox. Other Indian scientific achievements included knowledge of the theory of atoms and the transmission of sound waves. They developed systems for classifying plants, animals, and minerals based upon observation and experiment.

MORE WAVES OF PEOPLE

After the fall of the Gupta dynasty, there followed a period of chaos. Then another great king, Harsha (606-617), arose to bring peace, unity, and security to the land. He was a tolerant and responsible ruler who worked hard to improve the life of his people.

With the death of King Harsha a mist envelops the history of India for more than 500 years. This period serves as a dim divider between old and modern India. Hinduism survived in a modified form. Buddhism was almost completely lost to the Indians sometime during this period. Empires existed in India, but they are like formless shadows passing hurriedly. There were notable people, but we know of them mostly through **folklore**.

During this time there were also vast and continuous **migrations** of people from Central Asia into India. They were **assimilated** and given their places in the layers of Indian caste system.

In the 1000s, a people came to India who stamped a cultural and political impression that is still visible today. These new invaders were mostly Turkish in origin. They were a restless people who burst from Central Asia to make themselves rulers in the Middle East. There they became Muslims and were greatly influenced by Persian culture.

But this culture had not penetrated deeply when they began their raids into India.

Toward the end of the 1100s the invaders had established a capital at Delhi. By the beginning of the 1200s most of north and northwest India were under their control. This was the first time that India had been united since the Gupta empire in the 400s A.D. The new empire lasted from 1192 to 1398. During this time, the newcomers engaged in a holy war. They destroyed Hindu and Buddhist temples and tried to convert the Indians to Islam.

Islam teaches that there is only one God, who is the same as the God of the Jews and Christians. Muslims believe that Muhammad, the historical founder, was a prophet, as were Jesus, Moses, Abraham, and others. They believe that divine teachings were revealed to Muhammad, as they had been revealed to other prophets before him. These revelations are contained in a book called the Koran. The Koran is regarded by Muslims as a sacred book.

In the 1200s, to the north of India, Mongols under Genghis Khan (JENG-guhs KAHN) and his descendants ruled from the Yellow Sea in China to the Dnieper (NEE-puhr) River in Russia. Although the Mongols attempted to invade India, they could not overcome the empire there. Then, at the end of the 1300s, divisions weakened it.

Timur, sometimes called Tamerlane, invaded India in 1398. He had taken advantage of the quarrels among the Mongol successors of Genghis Khan to build a great empire. Timur's invaders left death and destruction behind. It is said that in Delhi not even a bird moved its wings until months after they had left. Timur did not linger in India but returned to his homeland in Central Asia.

MOGUL EMPIRE

After Timur withdrew, India remained divided for more than a hundred years. Then in 1526 Babur, a descendant of Timur, invaded India and founded the Mogul Empire. Mogul is an Indian pronunciation of Mongol. This name is given to the Muslim Indian empire because Timur and Babur, although mostly Turkish, claimed legal and family descent from the Mongols.

Babur was much different from Timur. He was human, warm, and witty. He was sensitive to beauty, a poet, and author of prose. He was a rare figure amid the trouble, deceit, and pride of his time. In 1530 Babur was succeeded by Humayun, his eldest son. Humayun was a good man, but a weak ruler. When he died, he left a son, Akbar.

Akbar was only 13 when his father died in 1556. With the help of able and loyal followers, and later under his own leadership, Akbar brought the greater part of India under his rule. More than a military leader, he was a fine **diplomat** and a magnificent organizer. He also

Akbar's son, Jahangir, ruled the Mogul Empire from 1605 to 1627. During this time, the art of Muslim painting reached its peak in India. This painting shows Jahangir on his throne receiving gifts from both Europeans and Indians.

cared about the welfare of his people. He set up land taxes that were fair and just and established a **civil service**. Under his rule, the Muslim tax on nonbelievers was removed, and Hindu temples were protected.

Persian had been the official language of the court before Akbar's reign but he made it the language of the common people as well. From the mixture of Persian and Hindi languages came the Urdu language. Urdu is still spoken by many people in India and is the official language of modern Pakistan.

Under Akbar and his successors, the culture of Persia (Iran) merged with that of the Hindus. From this union, there flowered the art of the Moguls.

The Moguls encouraged painting. Artists made realistic and detailed landscapes and portraits in miniature. They often decorated the borders and bindings of their books with gold. The Moguls hon-

163

The sitar was developed around the 1200s A.D. It has 6 or 7 strings that are plucked and 12 to 20 that vibrate. Metal strips called frets are used to adjust string tension.

ored people whose handwriting was beautiful. The emperor Aurangzeb (1658-1707) enjoyed making copies of the Koran. It was probably the Moguls who first introduced the Indians to the use and manufacture of paper, a knowledge which had been passed to them by the Chinese.

In building their places of worship called mosques, their palaces, and their tombs the Moguls used arches and graceful bulb-shaped domes. Soaring, delicate buildings of marble and red sandstone were often surrounded by landscaped parks and mirrored in lakes and lagoons.

The Moguls delighted in poetry. It was a great honor to come before the emperor and recite one's own poetry. Often this was in praise of the emperor's reign. But the Moguls would also improvise lines of poetry when moved by an event, an emotion, or the beauty of the landscape.

But like all empires the Mogul Empire too was destined to decline. In the 1600s and 1700s Mogul control of India was gradually weakened by divisions within and by the growing power of the Europeans who were coming.

THE ARTS TODAY

Some ancient Indian artistic forms such as music and dance are performed today as they were thousands of years ago. In other areas of the arts, Western influences are being felt. Artists are blending traditional and Western ideas to develop new ways of expressing themselves.

Indian music uses scales somewhat different from those to which most Westerners are accustomed. Although the Indian tone system of 12 notes is much like ours, certain notes are sharper or flatter. Consequently, Indian music is likely to sound out of tune or strange to our ears.

Indian music does not use harmony as we know it, except where it has been influenced by Western music as in films. Instead, melody, rhythm, mood, and even the time of day or night are all-important, especially to the performance of the raga. The raga is a traditional musical form of which there are thousands of variations.

Instruments native to India include several types of flutes and pipes and the sitar and the vina. These are plucked with the fingers. The drum is also used as well as a kind of horn or trumpet, made from a conch shell and used on ceremonial occasions.

Like Indian art and music, the dance is highly formal. It uses a great deal of symbolism that is meaningless to those unfamiliar with the ancient traditions. In all classical dancing, every position of the body, every expression of the face, every gesture of the arms and hands, every tempo has a meaning. With such elaborate symbolism, the dance can convey unlimited ideas and emotions to the audience. The dancer intends to entertain, but he or she also wishes to uplift, to express to the audience a mood and an idea. The dancer seeks, through the dance, to become one with the universal spirit who controls all.

There are several schools of classical dance. They originated in various parts of India as temple dancing. One type is dance drama. The great epics of Hinduism including the *Ramayana* and the *Mahabharata* are often performed in this way. The dancers mime the story while a chorus chants the verses.

Nearly every age of Indian history has produced outstanding writers. Today Indian authors are writing in English as well as in their native languages, for India is a nation of many languages and many dialects. There is no single common tongue.

One of India's greatest modern writers was Rabindranath Tagore (ruh-BIN-druh-naht tuh-GOR), who died in 1941. He was a man of many talents and a winner of the Nobel Prize for literature. In 1921 he founded a university that has become a center for Indian arts and a means for spreading his ideal of world unity.

India is a leading film center. It is second only to Japan in the total footage of films produced. (The United States is third.) Indians are enthusiastic film-goers. Costume romances and dance sequences are the most popular films.

The colorful saris of these present-day Indian women represent an old tradition. Indian art takes many forms, from classical dance to modern films.

This scene is from the film Two Daughters, *directed by Satyajit Ray. His realistic films of daily life in India have won prizes all over the world.*

A very different note is sounded, however, by the films of Satyajit Ray. This director has won **international** recognition for films that portray modern Indian life with sensitivity and realism.

Chapter 4
Society

The caste and the family are basic social institutions in India. Although changes are occurring in these institutions, they still remain important features of Indian life.

CASTE

Indians are born into different groups within their society. This division of groups is known in English as the caste system. The word caste is borrowed from the Portuguese who used it to describe the divisions of people they observed when they first came to India in the 1500s.

STRUCTURE The system groups the people into four castes: Brahman, Kshatriya (kuh-SHA-tree-yuh), Vaisya (VEESH-yuh), and Sudra (SHOO-druh). The Brahman or priestly caste ranks first. The Kshatriya or warrior caste ranks second. The Vaisya or merchant and farming caste ranks third. Those of the lowest rank are the Sudra, who originally were supposed to serve the other three castes. In addition to these four castes, there are those with no caste. They belong to the lowest levels of Indian society and are called such names as outcastes, pariahs, and untouchables.

This ranking according to caste had both an occupational and a religious significance. The Brahmans were held in the highest esteem because of their spiritual and educational work. They were traditionally the teachers of India. Of next importance came the function of governing and protecting the land. Then came food production and commerce and trade. The least important function was that of service to the other three castes.

The outcastes or untouchables are so called because they generally perform those jobs which the Hindus regard as most degrading: sweeping the streets and floors; removing trash; and working with leather. In India, the cow is sacred, and **orthodox** Hindus consider unclean those who work with its hide to make leather goods. The other castes believe that outcastes could not touch anything without contaminating the item so the other castes could not use it. To be contaminated is, for the Hindu, to be spiritually unclean. Contamination is not necessarily a matter of being physically dirty.

This ranking of castes is supported by the Hindu religion. A person's caste is considered an indication of the distance from final salvation or liberation. The Brahman is nearest to salvation, followed in descending order by the Kshatriya, the Vaisya, and the Sudra castes. The most removed, of course, are the outcastes.

This rigid caste structure remains the ideal system to those who believe strictly in Hinduism. In Hindu society castes are still considered honorable social divisions. But the caste system in reality has evolved in a flexible way.

DEVELOPMENT   Perhaps the caste system began with the Aryans who came to northern India between 1700 and 1500 B.C. from Central Asia. In any event the Indian people came to be separated by the kinds of work they did. Those who followed the same occupation developed a closely knit community. Sometimes groupings grew out of religious differences. There were also instances of whole groups of people being placed within certain castes. The Rajputs (RAHJ-poots) were an example of this process.

The Rajputs, whose ancestors were also invaders from Central Asia, were powerful in northern and central India from about 650 to 1150 A.D. They remained important politically until the 1800s. They were warriors—brave, clannish, and **aristocratic**. They proclaimed themselves royal ones. The name Rajput means the sons of kings. Sometimes, when defeat was inevitable, the Rajputs would kill their women and children before dying themselves on the sword of their conquerors.

The Brahmans could not withstand such valiant warriors, so they linked the Rajputs to themselves by means of the caste system. Some of the Rajput priests became Brahmans. The Rajput chiefs became members of the warrior caste and their followers became members of the farming caste.

During the long course of India's history, a continuous flow of new physical types, occupations, and foreign elements found places within the caste system. Thus a complicated social structure arose. Castes died out and new castes formed, but always the caste system remained the basis of the social order. Over the centuries even the outcastes have organized themselves on a graduated social scale into many groups. Today there are thousands of castes and subcastes— separate groups within a large group—in the Hindu community.

CHARACTERISTICS   The caste system has three main characteristics: (1) members should marry within their caste; (2) caste members should eat and drink with members of the same caste and not with members of an inferior caste; and (3) all members should practice the same occupation which is generally **hereditary**, that is, passed from one generation to another within the same family.

There are some exceptions today to these requirements, especially the last one. But the first two remain generally common to most castes and subcastes.

ADVANTAGES—DISADVANTAGES—CHANGE   Some Hindu writers have claimed that the caste system has helped preserve Indian culture and civilization. Over thousands of years, India has experienced many invasions. The people have seen rulers come and go. But always they have kept their loyalty to the caste system. It has maintained the stability and continuity of their culture. It has created cooperation instead of competition. Each individual has a special duty in society. There is neither reason nor opportunity to compete.

Other Indian writers say that the caste system has weakened India, especially in today's world. Rabindranath Tagore stated that there can be no real political unity possible until all Indians are permitted to mingle freely. Some Indian leaders have declared that real social progress is impossible while so many millions remain **segregated** and bound by the rigid caste system. The spiritual father of modern India, Mahatma Gandhi, pleaded for more tolerance and justice for the outcastes whom he called Children of God.

There have been changes. Officially the outcastes are now called Scheduled Castes. Some members of the Brahman caste are even willing to marry those of another caste. These are mostly of the younger generation who probably plan to live in cities where their **radical** step may be less noticed.

Industry, transportation systems, hospitals, schools, and colleges throw the various castes and outcastes together. From this association, of necessity, there will eventually come changed attitudes. But when emotions, traditions, and religion are involved, change comes slowly.

THE FAMILY

The traditional Indian family is a joint or **extended family**. It generally consists of the parents, all unmarried children, and the married sons with their wives and their children. It often includes other persons such as grandparents and even some distant relatives.

The oldest male is usually the head of the family and possesses all authority. This system is known as a patriarchal family. He supervises family property and finances. The members pool their resources and their income, and the head of the family spends it according to the needs of each. He is, however, bound by tradition, custom, and public opinion to preserve and not to waste the family holdings. He consults with the elders of the family, and he seeks advice from his mother and his wife, if they are living. This is not to say that individuals do not possess personal property. They do.

For example, the jewelry that a bride receives from her family remains her personal property. Most women in India, except widows, wear gold or silver bracelets, earrings, nose rings, necklaces, and other jewelry. This is generally all they can call their own except the clothes they wear. Widows are not supposed to wear jewelry, bright clothing, or cosmetics. It is assumed that all brightness has left their lives when husbands die. Society frowns upon their seeking another husband.

Traditionally, the woman occupies a position subordinate to the

A bride and her family prepare for a wedding. Is marriage as much a family concern in the U.S. as in India? Why or why not?

male in Indian society. The ideal wife is one who is submissive, obedient, modest, retiring, and loyal. She serves her husband and her family quietly, efficiently, and without complaint. When she is the wife of the family head and mother of his children, she is respected. Her advice on household and other matters is asked for and often followed.

 One of the most serious responsibilities of Indian parents is the marriage of their children. Traditionally, marriage in India is not a private romantic affair between two people. It is a family matter of grave importance. Two people are being brought together to preserve and continue the family, not merely to satisfy their own emotions.

The Indians take the view that love should follow marriage, not precede it. As a consequence, the couple may not see each other before their engagement, and sometimes not before their marriage day. They may see only a picture of each other.

It is not always easy for parents to find suitable mates for their children. Many social concerns surround marriage in India. There is the question of caste, reputation, and the economic position of the families. The bride must have a trousseau and a dowry. These items are important to the family of the groom, for these are new resources she brings to his family.

dowry: money or goods that a woman brings to a marriage

There is also the question of matching the horoscopes of the prospective couple. The horoscope of each was cast at birth. If their stars and signs do not harmonize, it would be foolish to chance marriage. In the face of all these difficulties, parents usually ask the help of a third person to find a suitable mate. The matchmaker undertakes all the arrangements and is usually paid.

 A successful marriage traditionally results in children. These children are primarily members of the joint family and are the responsibility of the joint family rather than of the parents alone. Children thus absorb a sense of responsibility toward the entire family which rarely deserts them. Indian history is filled with stories of sacrifice and suffering undertaken on behalf of the family.

There is some change in family life today, especially in the cities and among those educated along Western patterns. The growth of industrialization in India has attracted many people from the villages to the cities. In the cities, crowded conditions and cramped living quarters do not permit the joint families of the countryside. Some Indian young people are seeking greater choice in the selection of a mate. Sometimes individuals personally suggest a candidate for their parents' consideration.

WOMEN IN MODERN INDIA

The position of women in Indian society is slowly changing. Women have voted since 1919, but with some notable exceptions few women have held high offices. By the early 1970s, 80 percent of Indian women

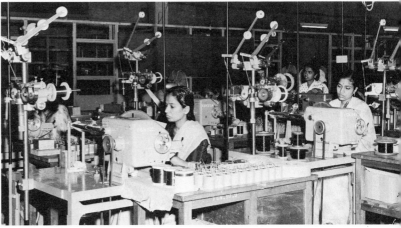

were still illiterate, but changes were becoming evident.

Indian political parties were encouraging women to run for office. More and more women were attending high schools and universities. More than ten million Indian women had entered professional or technical careers by the early 1970s. Supported by education, Indian women were beginning to take a place in society outside the home and family. How fast their progress will be and how it will affect Indian society is still to be seen.

As in the case of caste, traditional attitudes are still held firmly by the vast majority of Indians. As India passes through its economic and political transitions, change is inevitable. But no one can say to what extent these changes will penetrate and modify Indian attitudes toward the **role** of women.

Education is required for children 6 to 14. Although lack of teachers and money is a problem, educational opportunities are increasing, especially for women. These women work in an electronics plant.

People from the West had visited Asia since early times. In 327-26 B.C., Alexander the Great opened up trade between India and the West. From that time Westerners made their way to India and other Asian countries. They came mostly to trade for gems, cotton, spices, and drugs. A few sought Asian knowledge.

Chapter 5
Independence

WESTERN DOMINANCE

After the early 1500s, Westerners started to come to India in great numbers. They came for spices, especially pepper, that could be obtained only from Asia. In the days before refrigeration and canning, meat was often half spoiled by the time it was eaten. Spices improved the flavor and made the meat easier to eat. The spices had to travel over a long land route from Asia through the Middle East to Europe. During the journey the spices passed through the hands of many

Imperialism in India, 1857

- ● **Foreign Ports**
- ▢ **British Possessions**
- ▢ **Independent States**

bribery: giving money or something of value to an official in return for favors

merchants. As the European market for spices grew larger and more profitable, these merchants grew increasingly numerous and demanding. The cost of spices continually rose. Europeans began to search for a sea route which would allow them to obtain spices directly from the Asians.

The Spanish and Portuguese were the first to look for a sea route. The Spanish tried sailing west and reached America instead. Vasco da Gama, a Portuguese captain, found a way to India by sailing south around the tip of Africa and across the Indian Ocean. His ship brought a cargo of spices back to Portugal in 1499.

In 1520, Ferdinand Magellan sailed west and made his way around the southern tip of South America. He crossed the Pacific Ocean as far as the Philippines where he died. His ship, however, continued the voyage and reached Spain in 1522. The voyage had shown that the world was round and had also uncovered another sea route to Asia.

COLONIAL EMPIRES   From that time onward more and more Westerners came to Asia and they came to stay, not just to trade. The British, French, and Dutch were interested mainly in the area for the economic rewards they could get. The Portuguese and Spanish were also interested in converting the Asians to Christianity. In all cases Europeans gained greater and greater political control over the Asians. By the 1800s, most of Asia was directly or indirectly under the rule of Westerners.

The Portuguese were among the first Westerners to come to India, and the last to leave. In 1961 the Indian army chased them from the district of Goa, south of Bombay. Following the lead of the Portuguese, the British, French, and Dutch began establishing trading posts in India. There were the inevitable jealousies and clashes among them. The British were the biggest winners. With the help of discontented and ambitious Indians, through bribery, and by military force, they were able to take advantage of Indian disunity.

By the beginning of the 1800s, the British East India Company held control over most of India. This company was an association of British merchants and manufacturers who had been given a **monopoly** of the Asian trade by the British crown. The company was a profit-making organization. In order to control its profits, the company recruited and kept armies in India. The company's agents ruled and lived like kings. Greed and mismanagement within the company led to civil strife and even mutiny by its Indian soldiers. In 1858 control of India was taken from the company and given to the British Parliament.

ASIAN REACTION   In their coming, Westerners laid the foundations for the political structure of Indians and other Asians. When Westerners took control of much of Asia's land and replaced the former native rulers, they brought with them ideas about **nationalism, representative forms of government**, and the worth and rights of the individual. From Westerners, Asians learned to think of their rulers as servants rather than masters of the people. From Westerners, the Asians also learned about **communism, socialism**, and **capitalism**.

Some Asians went to study and observe in Western nations where **democracy**, socialism, and communism were practiced. Many Indians and other Asians leaned toward a democratic socialism, but some embraced communism. Others borrowed the outer forms of the West but retained much of the traditional Asian ruling spirit.

Many Asians began to dislike the Western rulers who were democratic at home and undemocratic in Asia. They resented the Western view that they were unfit and unready to govern themselves. The Asians were angered that their resources and products went to foreigners rather than to their own people. Many of the Western governors showed by their attitudes that they thought Asians were racially inferior.

Spurred by anger, resentment, and a desire to be free, the Asians acted. Some like Tilak preached violence, and their foreign rulers were imprisoned. Some rioted, and there was bloodshed. A more realistic and moderate approach was taken by Gokhale. He understood that the British were too strong at the time to be overcome by force. He preached a slower, less bloody path to freedom.

MAHATMA GANDHI

In 1869 a man was born in northwestern India who was destined, more than any other single person, to unify the Indians and gain their freedom. He was a Hindu named Mohandas K. Gandhi (GAHN-dee). Later an adoring Indian people called him Mahatma (muh-HAHT-muh) which means great soul. It is by Mahatma that he is generally known to India and to the world.

Gandhi went to London to study law and returned to India to practice. In 1893 he went to South Africa on a law case and stayed to fight the discrimination there against Indians. During this time he conceived and put into practice the idea of mass resistance through nonviolence. He called this soul-force. Soul-force came from certain basic beliefs he held. He believed in injuring no living being and in returning love for hate, good for evil and unselfishness for selfishness. Gandhi believed in conquering by the power of goodness. He was tormented by his enemies and imprisoned. He was handled roughly by the police but he never struck back. He suffered all in silence and patience. In the end, the government of South Africa agreed to change the practices Gandhi had fought against by nonviolence.

Gandhi returned to India in 1914. From that time until he was assassinated in 1948, he worked for peace, unity, and the freedom of the Indian people. This little man dressed in a simple piece of

Mahatma Gandhi led the way to India's independence. His teachings influenced people around the world.

white cloth, ate little, owned little, and asked little for himself. If his people rioted, if they fought with guns or clubs, or even with their bare hands, he pleaded for them to stop. When they did not listen, he fasted. He continued to fast until his wishes were met and they were always met. He was very special to the Hindu people.

The British had never before encountered nonviolent protest, or **civil disobedience**—a term Gandhi borrowed from the American philosopher Henry David Thoreau. Women and children lay down on railroad tracks and on streets and highways. They accepted passively the beatings of those who tried to remove them. Gandhi was jailed for civil disobedience, but he did not give up. Resistance stiffened. The British were left with no choice except to talk and negotiate. The talking went on for years. Finally in 1947 the British announced that they would leave India in June 1948.

India was to be a democracy with a **government** patterned somewhat after the British system. There is a **prime minister**, a president, judges, and a legislature. The members of the legislature are elected by the people. But unlike Great Britain, India is a **federal** system. Each state has a legislature whose members are chosen by the people.

Despite the peace efforts of Gandhi, the Indians did not achieve independence without bloodshed. With the announcement that the British intended to leave, wild emotions and long-restrained hatreds erupted. Muslims and Hindus fought. Sikhs and Muslims fought.

More than eight million Sikhs live in the Punjab region of northwestern India. Their religion, Sikhism, teaches that there is only one God. It was founded by Guru Nanak (1469-1538), who wanted to unite Hindus and Muslims into a single community. His efforts failed, and the history of the Sikhs has been a long struggle to maintain independence. For many years the Sikhs had supported the British. They feared that when the British withdrew, they might be overcome by the Muslims.

In the struggle that resulted many Muslims, Sikhs, and Hindus inflicted great cruelty and brutality upon each other. Mahatma Gandhi pleaded, begged, and finally fasted almost to death in his efforts to bring a halt to the suffering. He succeeded in saving thousands of lives. But he came to be hated by a few Hindu fanatics. One of them shot and killed him as he walked in the midst of a crowd on January 30, 1948.

JAWAHARLAL NEHRU

Gandhi was succeeded as leader of the Indian people by his long-time supporter Jawaharlal Nehru (juh-WAH-huhr-lahl NAY-roo). A brilliant, versatile man of the Brahman caste, he had been educated at home and at some of England's best schools. His thinking was not so simple and direct as Gandhi's, but he had worked closely with Gandhi for many years. Nehru became the first prime minister of

Here Nehru is shown speaking at the UN. He supported a policy of neutrality in world politics. What are some advantages and disadvantages of neutrality?

India's new **parliamentary** government. He remained in that position until his death in May 1964.

INDIRA GANDHI

Nehru was succeeded by Lal Bahadur Shastri. After Shastri's death in 1966, Indira Gandhi was elected prime minister. The daughter of Nehru, she and her husband (not related to Mahatma Gandhi) had been active in the fight for Indian **self-government**. She had been an advisor to her father, president of the Indian National Congress party, and when chosen prime minister, was **minister** of information and broadcasting.

Indira Gandhi took office in the midst of food shortages and unemployment as well as disputes with Pakistan. As prime minister, she encouraged modern agricultural programs and industrialization.

Regardless of her programs poverty continued to be the central problem in India. Most of the people live at less than **subsistence** level. New crops and improved irrigation almost doubled food production in ten years. New industries have been introduced and factories that employ millions have been built. But India's population grows at a faster rate than food production, industrialization, and employment. The population increases by about 13 million people every year. This increase pushes more people below the poverty level each year. Unemployment continues to increase and feeds unrest among workers.

In foreign affairs too Prime Minister Gandhi changed India's policies. Formerly Indian leaders maintained a policy of **nonalignment** with both East and West. This policy ended in 1971 when she signed a **treaty** of friendship with the Soviet Union. The Soviet-Indian **alliance** confronts the China-Pakistan front.

In 1975 Prime Minister Gandhi was convicted of election irregularities in her 1971 campaign for her home seat in Parliament. She was deprived of her seat and given 20 days to appeal. Blaming an atmosphere of violence in India, she suspended **civil liberties**. Thousands of her political opponents were arrested. Press censorship was imposed. Her appeal was upheld and her conviction dismissed.

As prime minister, Indira Gandhi became a controversial leader. She ended India's neutrality by signing a treaty with the USSR in 1971. In 1975 she was accused and found guilty of election fraud. She had the laws changed so she could keep her power.

As we have seen, the Muslims began to come to northern India in force around the 1000s A.D. Under a succession of able military leaders, they gradually conquered most of India and established the Mogul Empire. The Muslims were different from previous invaders because they had a religion of Middle Eastern origin and a Persian culture. They felt that their culture and religion were equal, if not superior, to that of the Indians. The Muslims refused to be assimilated into the Indian population as other invaders before them had been. They remained distinct and separate.

Chapter 6
Pakistan and Bangladesh

Further, the Islamic culture and religion had a real impact upon the Indians. Persian language, literature, art, and architecture became part of Indian culture and society. This was particularly true among the middle and upper **classes**. Millions of Indians were also attracted to the teachings of Islam. Islam denied caste, gave women a better status, and preached racial equality. Many Indians converted to Islam.

After the decline of the Mogul Empire in the 1700s, the Muslims lacked spirit and direction. They were a minority surrounded by a Hindu majority and governed by the foreign British.

THREE MUSLIM VOICES

Direction, purpose, and spirit were given to the Muslims by three men. These men led Indian Muslims to dream of and eventually to realize a country of their own.

The first voice was that of Sir Sayyid Ahmad Khan (1817-1898). He urged Muslims to learn from the West so that they might become strong once again. He emphasized their feeling of separateness from the Hindus and reminded them that in an independent India they would be outnumbered three to one.

Next was the great Punjabi poet, Sir Mohammed Iqbal (1873-1938). He inspired Muslims to study modern science. He was among the

Thousands of Muslims jammed trains for Pakistan during the relocation of people during the 1947 partition of India. What historical events and religious and social customs made the partition seem necessary?

176

first to present them with the dream of a separate homeland which he called Pakistan, meaning land of the pure.

The third voice was that of Mahomed Ali Jinnah, a lawyer (1876-1948). He led the Muslims to their new homeland and is called the father of Pakistan. He leaned toward Western ideas and was carefully Western in dress. But he was also a Muslim, a nationalist, and, in the beginning, a supporter of the Hindu-dominated Congress party.

At first Mahomed Ali Jinnah did not intend to seek a division of India when the British left. He thought in terms of a **coalition** government in which Muslims would participate. It was his aim to guarantee individual and group rights of Muslims and to prevent cultural, economic, and political domination by the Hindu majority. But the Hindu-dominated Congress party refused to part with any of its power. Party leaders underestimated the determination and ability of Jinnah and his supporters. They did not understand how much the Muslim minority feared Hindu domination. Nor did they understand the need Muslims felt for a nation of their own.

The Muslims asked for **partition**, and they stood firm on their demand. The British and Congress party leaders finally gave in. In August 1947, Great Britain gave dominion **status** to both India and Pakistan.

Mahomed Ali Jinnah is considered the founder of Pakistan. He began working for the partition of India in 1940.

A DIVIDED COUNTRY

Pakistan began as a nation divided into two parts which were separated by over a thousand miles of land and sea. Although Muslims are found throughout the South Asian subcontinent, they are concentrated in the eastern and western portions. When Pakistan became independent, these two widely separated Muslim areas were joined into the new state. They were called East Pakistan and West Pakistan. Islam was the tie that held them together.

Although the partition of India followed roughly the concentration of Muslim population, millions of people were uprooted. Many Muslims lived in **territory** assigned to India, and many Hindus in lands assigned to Pakistan. Great numbers of people had to travel long distances to their new homeland. Thousands did not survive the journey. Caravans of refugees were ambushed and many people were killed. Property on both sides of the new borders was confiscated. Often entire villages were burned to the ground.

Over the years West Pakistan came to dominate the nation. West Pakistan military men governed. They generally favored certain business and landlord groups who cooperated with them and supported their policies. The people in both areas of Pakistan came to resent the methods of these rulers and their supporters. They showed their resentment from time to time in speeches, riots, and strikes. The East Pakistanis began to call for more self-rule. They could not be quieted even though the military took harsh measures against them.

177

BANGLADESH

In early December 1971, the armies of India invaded East Pakistan to aid the East Pakistanis. In a short time their superior military forces defeated the West Pakistani troops stationed there. East Pakistan became a new country called the People's Republic of Bangladesh. Sheikh Mujibur Rahman, leader of the majority party in former East Pakistan, became the first head of Bangladesh. In 1975, he was assassinated and replaced by a more pro-Western military government.

After the separation of Bangladesh, the West Pakistani military leader, President Yahya Khan, was replaced by Zulfikar Ali Bhutto. Bhutto was the elected leader of the Pakistan People's party. West Pakistan retained the old name of Pakistan.

Like India, both Bangladesh and Pakistan suffer from unemployment, poverty, and the lack of capital to encourage industrialization. Moreover, Bangladesh is one of the most densely populated countries in Asia. This condition has resulted in widespread malnutrition and the ever-present threat of starvation. Bangladesh is further troubled by recurring floods, drought, and typhoons. In 1974 a particularly bad flood placed half of the country underwater. Almost all the nation's crops were destroyed. Pakistan is more fortunate. It is able to produce enough food to feed its people. Under President Bhutto, Pakistan has raised the standard of living and given people a greater voice in their government.

Bangladesh has few products for **export**. Jute, used in the making of burlap and rope, makes up about four-fifths of its foreign trade. Because its resources are limited, Bangladesh's economy has been slow to develop. Bangladesh has had to rely on large amounts of **foreign aid** since its independence.

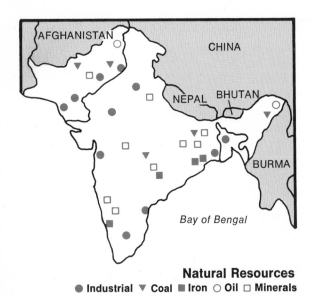

Natural Resources

● Industrial ▼ Coal ■ Iron ○ Oil □ Minerals

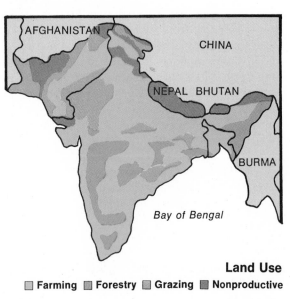

Land Use

□ Farming ■ Forestry ■ Grazing ■ Nonproductive

Summing Up the Unit

Social Studies Vocabulary

Define: deities; institutions; myths; dynasty; assimilate; civil service; caste; segregate; monopoly; civil disobedience; nonalignment; partition; foreign aid

People

Identify: Gautama Buddha; Asoka; Moguls; Babur; Mahatma Gandhi; Indira Gandhi; Mohamed Ali Jinnah.

Places

Locate: Indus River; Pakistan; Bangladesh

Words

Identify: Indus Valley civilization; *Vedas*; *Upanishads*; Hinduism; reincarnation; karma; householder; anchorite; sannyasi; dharma; Buddhism; nirvana; Four Noble Truths

☞ Questions

1. What was the principal contribution of Aryans to Indian culture?
2. In attempting to meet the needs of all people, what has happened to Hinduism?
3. a. What is the teaching of Hinduism on reality? b. salvation? c. rebirth?
4. According to the rules of dharma, should people seek to profit from their actions?
5. a. According to Buddha's Four Noble Truths, what is the greatest problem that faces everyone? b. What is its cause? c. When the cause is eliminated, what goal is reached?
6. What influence has religion had on the arts?
7. What qualities are the statues of Buddha sculptured to portray?
8. a. How might the Aryans have contributed to the development of the Indian caste system? b. Into what four groups does the caste system divide people? c. What is the occupational function of each caste?
9. a. What are the three main characteristics of the caste system? b. What are supposedly the advantages of the system? c. disadvantages?
10. a. Describe the traditional family pattern in India. b. Describe changes.
11. a. What factors led to the partition of India? b. the birth of Bangladesh?
12. What are the greatest problems facing modern India, Pakistan, and Bangladesh?

Discussion Topics

1. How are Hindu beliefs interconnected? How have they affected the life of India? Is Hinduism well-suited to the religious needs of India? What are its advantages and disadvantages when compared with other religions?
2. Artists in India have worked within detailed and strict rules. Why do you think Indian artists were so restricted by tradition? Has this hampered what they created? Or merely made their works undeniably Indian?
3. Buddha based his teachings on the Four Noble Truths and offered the Noble Eightfold Path as a guide for entering nirvana. What solution do these offer for human suffering? Does Buddhism seem to be pessimistic or hopeful?
4. Does a caste system exist in your society? If so, in what way? If not, how are the classes in your society unlike the castes of India?
5. Mass resistance through nonviolence was Mahatma Gandhi's way of opposing British discrimination. How do Gandhi's methods compare with those of Martin Luther King, Jr. in the U.S.?

Project Ideas

1. Using reference materials, prepare a report on one of the following: the Mogul Empire; Ajanta cave art; the caste system in India today; India's music; India's film-making industry.
2. Imagine you are a reporter. Write an interview with one of the following: Buddha; Mahatma Gandhi; Nehru; Indira Gandhi; Tagore.
3. Create a bulletin board display or poster showing one of the following aspects of India-Pakistan-Bangladesh creativity: arts and crafts; foods; architecture; dance.
4. Write a brief history of Bangladesh. Explain how the nation's past was influenced by the Moguls. Include recent events.

Unit III

China

At a May Day parade in Peking, workers carry banners with political slogans and the names of places where they work. The front banner says "Peking Press." May Day is an international holiday for socialist and Communist workers.

China is the outstanding geographic feature of Asia. It covers almost 9.6 million square kilometers (3.7 million square miles) and has a population of nearly 800 million people. Because of the natural barriers of mountain, desert, jungle, and ocean, China grew and matured largely independent of other cultures. It was in the fertile region of the north that China's earliest civilization began.

The origins of the Chinese are hidden in mystery. But there is evidence that their ancestors were probably making pottery as long ago as 6000 or 7000 B.C., and cultivating plants as early as 4500 B.C. They also **domesticated** animals. By 3000 B.C. the Chinese were raising silkworms to provide fibers for cloth.

The Chinese say that their first dynasty started around 2000 B.C. and lasted until about 1766 B.C. It was called the Hsia (shee-AH) dynasty. We know of the Hsia dynasty chiefly through **legends**. No **archaeological** or historical proof of it has been uncovered so far. However, bits of truth are frequently found in legends and future archaeological diggings may give us more knowledge of the earlier Chinese.

■ Chou Dynasty, c. 1000 B.C.

SHANG DYNASTY

The first great historical dynasty, the Shang, arose in China around 1766 to 1122 B.C., and is known for its fine bronze work. Written records from this period reveal the Chinese living under a ruler who combined both religious and political duties. Under the Shang emperors, the culture and political influence of the Chinese spread north, south, east, and west.

During the Shang dynasty, the Chinese refined ideographic writing. This is writing in which pictures or symbols stand for ideas. They do not spell the sounds of the words as Westerners do with their alphabet. It is not known definitely when this type of writing began. But Chinese tradition states that a sage known as Huang Ti (HWAHNG DEE) invented writing around 2500 B.C.

In Anyang (AHN-yahng), a major city during the Shang dynasty, archaeologists have dug up tortoise shells and animal bones carved with characters of the old Shang ideographic writing. The ideographs were usually answers to questions put by the king to his diviners or prophets. The bones or shells were heated which caused a pattern of cracks in them. The diviner interpreted the cracks and carved his answer in the shell or bone. The Chinese still use an ideographic form of writing. There are great differences, however, between ancient writing and modern Chinese characters.

CHOU DYNASTY

The Shang dynasty was overthrown by members of the House of Chou (JOH). They justified this act by declaring that it was right to overthrow an emperor who was not a good ruler. By doing this, the Chinese used a **revolutionary** theory that has been followed by many since. The Chou dynasty lasted from about 1122 to approximately 249 B.C. The early Chou emperors started the **feudal** system. Under this system the emperor gave parts of his land to subordinates—usually **kinfolk**—called **vassals**. In return the vassal lords were

181

obliged to pay tribute, give military service, and full obedience in all questions concerning the kingdom. The right to rule was hereditary and supported by spiritual authority. Certain spirits had to be sacrificed to if the empire was to be prosperous.

During the Chou period the use of iron became widespread in China. Iron plows and swords were used. More important, during the later stage of the Chou dynasty, the great Chinese philosophies of Confucianism, Taoism, and Legalism were born. They were to influence the Chinese for hundreds of years.

Chapter 2
Thoughts and Beliefs

Missionaries and travelers carried Buddhism to China about the first century A.D. However, the Chinese had already developed ideas that were quite different from the concepts of Buddhism. Unlike the Indians, the Chinese were optimistic about the possibilities of finding some happiness here and now. They wanted to improve society. They were not too much concerned with what might happen after death, although they did think about it.

The practical quality of the great Chinese philosophies—Confucianism, Taoism, and Legalism—may have been due to the troubled times in which they developed. These troubled times led to the Warring States Period, between 400 and 200 B.C. The feudal kingdoms of the Chou dynasty had been replaced by a group of independent **states**.

The Great Wall of China winds across northern China for 2,400 kilometers (1,500 miles). It was begun during the Warring States Period. Han rulers lengthened the Wall in an effort to keep out Mongol invaders from Central Asia. The final sections were added under the Ming dynasty (1368-1644).

These states fought among themselves for control of China. It was a time of bloodshed and the breakdown of customary ways of life.

CONFUCIANISM

Confucius (kuhn-FYOO-shuhs) was born in 551 B.C. and died around 479 B.C. His proposals for society were based on a return to the past. This gave Chinese society a backward-looking **conservatism** which lasted to the present century. Actually some of the ideas of Confucius were new, but he clothed them in much of the ritual and formality of the past. For example, ancestor worship had been practiced for centuries before Confucius added it to his philosophy. The basic writings of Confucianism have been grouped into a collection known as the *Confucian Canon*.

SYMPATHY   People, Confucianists said, are by nature social creatures. To live apart from others is unnatural and harmful. To live with others is natural and will further the growth and development of humanity. The quality, which makes people social creatures, is called jen. It is often translated as human-heartedness, sympathy, or benevolence. It means all of these things, and more. Jen relates each human being to every other human being.

social creatures: beings who enjoy the company of others

This relationship is so close that whatever affects one affects all others. Through jen we share the feelings, interests, and humanity of others. Jen lies at the very root of society. Without it there could be no society, and jen can only exist when there is a society.

Since all people have jen, they merely have to look within themselves to find the solutions to the problems of others. Thus, understanding oneself will give an understanding of others. The person who truly understands the importance and nature of jen will want to help others. In helping others, people are really helping themselves. Jen will always say, "Do not do unto others what you do not wish done to yourself." The Confucianists taught that jen must be expressed in action, and they defined some of these actions.

RIGHT ACTION   Confucianists insisted that individuals must play definite roles if they are to live in harmony with themselves and with others. They taught that there were five fundamental social relationships. These are between: ruler and subject; father and son; elder brother and younger brother; husband and wife; and between friend and friend.

In these relationships there were duties and responsibilities which each person owed to the other. In each case, except between friends, one person had authority over the other. The subordinate should give loving obedience to the superior. The superior should be lovingly responsible for the subordinate. If there was any doubt about an ac-

Compare the beliefs of Confucianism with those of Hinduism and Buddhism. How important is the individual person in each of these religions?

tion, one had merely to ask oneself: If I were a ruler, how would I wish my subject to serve me? If I were a friend, how would I want my friend to act toward me?

HUMANENESS Any just action, Confucianists said, is filled with a humane feeling for others. Confucianists did not doubt the need for written laws, but they doubted that just decisions could always come from strict obedience to the letter of the law. Custom, circumstances, and human relationships should be considered.

Confucianists also believed that it was quite normal and correct for people to express openly their feelings of sorrow, respect, sympathy, and reverence. For instance, they approved of ceremonies through which people showed respect to their ancestors. But these rituals meant nothing if the individual did not experience the sorrow or reverence. Used properly, ceremony and ritual were considered important in the moral growth of humanity.

FAMILY Confucianists taught that the family was basic to society. Within the family, individuals learned to play their correct social roles. If people learned their roles well, they would naturally be good members of the community and good government officials. For the state was an extension of the family. The individual Chinese owed the same obedience and loyalty to political authorities as was owed to senior family members.

The emperor was considered the father of all the Chinese. He was responsible to an impersonal force called Heaven for the welfare of all his children. He was responsible in much the same way that the father of a family was responsible to his ancestors.

If the emperor did not maintain a proper relationship with Heaven, he and his people would suffer. This proper relationship demanded that the ruler be a morally good example for his large family and an able administrator. Also he must give his people peace, order, and prosperity. Otherwise, Heaven would disown him. This very insistence upon the responsibility of the ruler for the welfare of his people was totally Confucian.

BETTER SOCIETY THROUGH GOVERNMENT   Confucianists believed that virtue of those who ruled was basic to good government. Both the emperor and his ministers had to understand that people could be changed by their example. It was the duty of government officials to reduce corruption by moral teachings and by leading moral lives. This was just as important as maintenance of irrigation systems, the empire's defense, and other affairs of state—perhaps of greater importance.

Because of the supreme importance of men—women had no official status—to good government, Confucianists urged that only the best and wisest should govern. Those who wanted to govern should be educated in all subjects. Confucianists wanted to establish a tradition in government of morally sound, educated men who worked solely in the people's interests. If such a tradition could be established, society would improve and the state would prosper. Then the people would be happy.

Confucianists taught that if the emperor did not give the people good government, they could overthrow him. If their revolution succeeded, they would know that they had received a **mandate** from Heaven to change rulers. Theoretically, there was no absolute king in China. The king's authority was checked by Confucianist principles and the will of the people. This was ultimately the will of Heaven.

INFLUENCE ON THE CHINESE   Starting with the Han dynasty (202 B.C.-220 A.D.), Confucianism came to be a powerful force in the society and government of China. For almost 2,000 years it dominated the thinking and actions of Chinese scholars and officials. Knowledge of it became necessary for advancement. Confucianism became the core and substance of all Chinese education.

Thus learning in China was largely ethical in character. The rightness or wrongness of acts became the basis of education. Confucianism gave unity but also a conservative slant to Chinese civilization. Confucian leaders were not inclined to accept other ideas of government and society. They were somewhat contemptuous of those outside China.

☐ **Han Dynasty, c. 100 A.D.**

But during the Period of the Philosophers, from 551 to 233 B.C., Confucianism was not yet the generally accepted philosophy of the Chinese. Some philosophers looked at life, society, and politics from other points of view. Much of what they taught also entered into the developing Chinese way of life and influenced literature, customs, and attitudes. Among the most influential of these philosophies were Taoism and Legalism.

TAOISM

Taoism (DOW-is-uhm) originated sometime during the 400s and 300s B.C. Its name comes from the Chinese word tao meaning the way. Lao-tzu (LOW-dzuh), is traditionally believed to be the founder of Taoism and the author of the original sourcebook of this philosophy, the *Tao Te Ching.* Two other people, Chuang-tzu and Tang Chu, also contributed to the teachings of Taoism.

NATURALNESS   Taoists taught that suffering pain, bloodshed, and chaos were a result of the unnaturalness of people's lives. People, they said, had been chained by the conventions and restrictions of an unnatural society. At one time people had lived and moved about freely and naturally like wild deer. They were unhampered by the artificial restraints that society now placed upon their movements and actions. In this natural state, people had been happy and in harmony with their nature and the tao.

The tao could not be defined, Taoists said, but it could be suggested. It is beyond measure, endless, and unceasing. Its shape is without a shape, its features are featureless, like the uncarved block. It moves along, like nature, unconsciously, without motive and without effort. The sun shines, clouds drift, and rain falls. There is no purpose to these happenings in nature; they just happen. This is the tao or like the tao.

THE ESSENTIAL QUALITIES   The tao gives life and their special nature to all things. It is the tao that sustains the nature of all things; and all things are different in their natures. A duck differs from a fish, a dog from a cat, a horse from a cow, and so on. The tao is constantly changing these things but always in accord with the nature of each animal or thing.

To act contrary to the particular nature of an animal is to harm it by blocking the preserving flow of the tao. It is harmful to place halters on horses or whip them to work. These things are artificial and contrary to their nature.

Taoism is a belief in the naturalness of all things. To show this, Taoists use plants and animals as examples. According to Taoism, bamboo stalks like those on the left grow in their own way, according to their own nature.

SOCIAL CONVENTIONS   Taoists taught that social conventions such as ceremonies are artificial and not part of human nature. They are harmful. People should be free to express themselves spontaneously and naturally. These practices are forced upon people by the inventors of social conventions and rules. Taoists condemned the Confucianists, who urged people to harness themselves with rituals and ceremony. Taoists believed that each person should withdraw from society, although not from other humans.

Taoists had doubts about the usual notions of right and wrong, good and evil. They felt that the idea of one thing being good and another evil had been created by the false standards of society. Taoists said that locks and seals encourage people to steal and be dishonest. Both the person of great virtue and the person of great evil are abnormal and unnatural, they said.

This symbol represents the basic Taoist philosophy— Yin/Yang. According to Taoism, two forces are at work in the world. White represents Yin, the passive principle. Black is Yang, the active principle. Taoists believe that the interaction of these two opposite forces influence everything that happens.

ONE WITH EVERYTHING   People are led astray, Taoists said, because they think things outside themselves—things perceived by the senses—have an independent existence. Because of this, people either want to own these things, or they fear them, or they seek a knowledge of them. The Taoist sage, on the other hand, already possessed all these outward-appearing things because of his union with the tao. He had no illusion that they were separate. Therefore he did not fear, want, or seek a knowledge of them. He had no intention of seeking anything. Therefore he could have no frustration.

Taoists were imaginative and poetic. They wanted to free people from routine thinking. They tried to stimulate and excite new thought by statements that seemed to express impossible ideas, such as "Do nothing, and there is nothing you cannot do." They applied this type of thinking to politics. One who was in union with the tao would govern without appearing to govern. The proper ruler would fill the people's stomachs and free their minds. Everyone would be happy.

EVOLUTION OF TAOISM   As time went on, Taoism took a religious turn. Chinese peasants began to associate Taoism with the world of spirits. Gods close to the daily life of the Chinese—the gods of rain, fire, agriculture, and the kitchen arose from Taoism. Taoists were called upon to select lucky days for weddings and funerals and to select good sites for houses and shops. Eventually, Taoism and Chinese Buddhism influenced each other in the development of ritual ceremony, and priesthood.

In their arts, the Chinese are more Taoist than Confucianist. Taoism is mirrored in many of their poems, paintings, and books, and in the great appeal that nature has for the Chinese.

LEGALISM

Legalism is another important philosophy of the Chinese. The main collections of Legalist writings are found in three works written between 350 and 100 B.C. They are the *Book of Lord Shang,* written by Shang Yang; *Han Fei-tzu,* written by Han Fei-tzu, and the *Kuan Tzu,* attributed to Kuan I-wu.

THE ABSOLUTE RULER   In Legalism the ruler was all-powerful. He was subordinate to no one, neither Heaven nor the people. Law was the ruler's main way to control the people, secure his power within the state, and expand it abroad. The law was not intended to protect individuals and their rights. Individuals existed to serve the ruler and the state. They had no privileges except what the ruler might give them. The laws dealt mostly with punishment. Legalists believed that the Confucianists were foolish to think that kindness and compassion could keep order.

THE LAW IS THE LAW   Human beings are selfish animals, Legalists said. People will obey a ruler only in hope of reward or fear of punishment. People, naturally, were blind to the welfare of other people and of the state and would fight among themselves for goods and power.

The solution, Legalists said, was to set up a strong, **centralized** state under the firm hand of one ruler. Then the ruler should publish a detailed list of laws, stressing the penalties for lawbreakers. Nothing should excuse offenders from punishment. Even the smallest offenses should be dealt with in a severe manner. For example, Legalists recommended that the hand that threw ashes into the street be cut off. They believed that if the ruler was harsh in small offenses, the people would not dare break the more important laws.

Following their idea of human nature, Legalists recommended the state encourage only war and agriculture. This was because food was essential and war was the way to control all China. Life must be made bitter for those who did not farm or soldier. Thus, people would choose agriculture and war and shun other occupations.

After publishing laws and organizing the people into war or agriculture, the ruler should select officials. To these officials would be given full responsibility for carrying out laws. The ruler then would do nothing more. Borrowing the words of the Taoists, Legalists said that the ruler could rule by doing nothing; yet there would be nothing that was not done.

legacy: inheritance

LEGACY OF LEGALISM   The methods of the Legalists were quite successful at first. The rulers of the small state of Ch'in used them to conquer the other states and unify China. The first Ch'in ruler became the emperor of China around 221 B.C. He divided China into various administrative districts and published very harsh laws and penalties for lawbreakers.

The people could not endure these severe laws and penalities, and

188

finally, about 207 B.C., they revolted. The Ch'in ruler was toppled from his throne. The Han (HAHN) dynasty succeeded the Ch'in and lasted from about 202 B.C. to 220 A.D. With the coming of the Han, Confucian philosophy began to dominate the social and political scene. However, the law codes of later dynasties reflected the influence of Legalism.

BUDDHISM BECOMES CHINESE

Buddhism appeared in China about the middle of the Han dynasty and was not welcomed. The Buddhist idea of rebirth seemed like nonsense. The practice of encouraging people to give up marriage and become monks or nuns was considered disgraceful. The Chinese felt strongly that every person should have descendants. It was the duty of children to look after their parents in old age and to honor them after death. Finally, there was the question of the family, which was the backbone of the Chinese state. What would happen to the state if Buddhism was accepted by the people? Besides, Buddhism was a foreign religion. Its spread might undermine the authority of Chinese officials.

Representations of Buddha are highly stylized. The knot on his forehead symbolizes wisdom. The foot pointing toward heaven shows that Buddha is meditating. This figure dates from the Yuan dynasty (1280-1368).

Despite its early rejection, Buddhism stayed in China and gradually became acceptable. By the 500s A.D., it had become a part of Chinese life and thought. There are several important reasons why Buddhism became Chinese.

After the Han dynasty fell in 220 A.D., China was split once again into a number of rival kingdoms. For over 400 years, the land and people of China suffered from bandits, famines, plagues, and **civil wars**. This period is sometimes referred to as the Dark Ages. While the Chinese fought among themselves, invaders poured into China from the north. Among the invaders were the Huns, a warrior people that later invaded Europe. The Chinese grasped for hope and release from their troubles. Buddhism offered them this hope.

THERAVADA AND MAHAYANA BUDDHISM   Even before Buddhism spread to China from India, it had divided into two major forms. These two divisions were known as Theravada (ther-uh-VAHD-uh)—sometimes called Hinayana (hee-nuh-YAH-nuh) Buddhism—and Mahayana (mah-huh-YAH-nuh) Buddhism.

Theravada Buddhism followed closely the original teachings of Gautama Buddha. It taught that each person must find one's own way to nirvana. For this reason many adult male Buddhists became monks for short, and sometimes long, periods of their lives. During this time they studied, meditated, taught, and performed good works.

The original teachings of Buddha, as practiced in Theravada Buddhism, were too difficult for many individuals. These Buddhists were looking for the heart and compassion of their great teacher. The result was Mahayana Buddhism. It was the compassion and comfort of Ma-

189

hayana Buddhism which gave hope to the people of China. This type of Buddhism emphasized the example of Gautama Buddha, who had delayed his entrance into nirvana so that he might help others to learn the way there.

Those Buddhists who delay their entrance into the bliss of nirvana are called bodhisattvas (boh-dih-SUHT-vuhs). Those who enter nirvana become Buddhas. Gautama Buddha had accumulated great merit as a bodhisattva in many previous existences before he finally entered nirvana.

Mahayana Buddhists urged all to follow the example of Buddha: to feel compassion for those who suffer, to feed the hungry, and to soothe the troubled. They taught that the true followers of Buddha chose the path of unselfishness and sought enlightenment in order to aid others. The Chinese began to rely more and more upon the mercy and compassion of these holy ones. Buddhas and bodhisattvas were represented in figures of bronze, gold, and jade. Temples and pagodas were built for them. Buddhas and bodhisattvas became gods and goddesses in the minds and hearts of the Chinese.

BLENDING OF BELIEFS

By the end of the 300s A.D., most of the Chinese living in northwestern China had become Buddhists. And Buddhism had become very Chinese. It had gradually blended with Taoism and Confucianism. The Buddhists adopted certain ideas and practices of Taoism. The many similarities between Buddhist and Confucian morality were emphasized. Confucius was regarded as a bodhisattva and temples were named for him. Buddhists stressed the duty of children to their parents. They set up plaques in special halls to honor their dead monks. This continued the Chinese practice of showing respect toward ancestors.

This blending of three views of life continued through the Sui (SWIH) dynasty (589-618 A.D.) and peaked in the T'ang dynasty (618-906 A.D.)

Not all Chinese art was religious or practical. Some, like this bronze bear tamer of the Chou period, was decorative.

Chapter 3
Creativity

The Chinese have been sculpturing, painting, working in metal, carving, and building from the earliest period of their history. Fortunately, some of their creations have survived the decay and destruction of the ages.

Since ancient times Chinese inventions have been passed along to people of other parts of the world. The Romans traded with China for silks; Chinese porcelains and lacquerware have been prized all over the world for centuries; and modern physicians have studied the Chinese technique of acupuncture as an aid in treating disease or relieving pain.

Chinese archaeologists found this mysterious bronze horse in the tomb of a Han general. The horse is galloping, and one hoof brushes the back of a swallow in flight. The bird looks up in amazement at the flying horse.

EARLY WORKS OF ART

Among the oldest surviving pieces of Chinese art are works of bronze produced during the Shang dynasty (c. 1766-1122 B.C.) The Chinese made bronzes for a variety of uses. For drinking they made tall slender cups. To hold their food, they made vessels of bronze with handles and three legs. To hold their wines, they fashioned containers of bronze, sometimes in the shape of owls and other animals.

During the Chou dynasty (1122-c. 249 B.C.), the Chinese continued to make objects in the shape of bells, cups, and bowls. On their bronzes they carved birds and animals, imaginative dragons, and abstract symbols. Some of the Chou bronze bowls were made for use in rituals honoring ancestors and important family and state events.

In their tombs, the ancient Chinese placed small reproductions of houses and other objects of bronze, gold, shell, and pottery. On the walls of tombs they carved scenes from daily life. We have learned much about the early Chinese from their tombs, particularly those of the Han dynasty (202 B.C.-220 A.D.)

Many of the early Chinese buildings had curved roofs which overhung the walls. The roofs were supported by pillars. Walls filled the spaces between the pillars and kept out harsh weather, but did not support the roofs. Roofs were made of tiles of various colors, mostly blue and green, but the tiles of the royal palace were yellow. This was the royal color. The Chinese were fond of colors and used them lavishly. Wooden beams and pillars were carved and brightened with gold, lacquer, and a variety of inlays. These were the homes of the wealthy or the palaces of kings and nobles. The average Chinese could not afford the luxury of art.

From the earliest times, the Chinese have worked in jade. Jade is a hard stone that is found in a number of colors, of which green is the most common. Ornaments such as rings, buckles, and hooks, as well as cups, bowls, vases, seals, and badges of authority were carved from jade. Articles of jade were also made for use in religious ceremonies.

When Buddhism entered China around the first century A.D., it brought its own art forms. A new art combining both Indian and Chinese styles developed. The evolution of this new art can be viewed as Buddhism slowly made its way eastward. For example, in northern China, caves called grottoes were dug in sandstone and limestone cliffs. In these caves were placed Buddhas and religious scenes cut from marble. These statues and carvings expressed the spiritual beauty, compassion, and mercy of Mahayana Buddhism. Among the most famous works are those of the 500s A.D. in the caves of Lung-Men.

This glazed pottery figure is a larger-than-life portrait of a lohan. A lohan is a Buddhist monk. This figure was made in the style of T'ang pottery in the 900s A.D. It was discovered during this century in a cave near Peking.

T'ANG DYNASTY: ARTISTIC PEAKS

The T'ang dynasty (618-906) is one of the greatest periods of Chinese history. Its cultural and political influence extended westward into Central Asia and southward into Southeast Asia and beyond. This was the period during which the Chinese dazzled the Japanese with their arts, their **crafts**, and their achievements in many fields.

Some time before the 700s, the Chinese developed the art of printing with wood blocks. A written page was first pasted on a smooth block of wood. Then the wood was carved away, leaving the writing or characters raised. The raised characters were inked and then pressed on paper. One of the oldest printed books dates from this period. It is a Buddhist text printed in 868 A.D.

The Chinese continued to value calligraphy, the art of beautiful writing. Painting and calligraphy were connected because the same type of brush was used for both. The force and skill that gave character and feeling to Chinese ideographs also gave meaning, strength, and beauty to Chinese paintings.

Little remains of the paintings of the T'ang Chinese. But we know about them from copies and descriptions written by people who lived at the time. Then, and later in the Sung (SOONG) dynasty which followed, the Chinese painted mostly scenes from nature. Sometimes they portrayed horses, flowers, birds, and butterflies in fine detail. But they were especially talented in painting misty landscapes. Mountain peaks in their paintings were veiled with fog and clouds, and often a river, stream, or lake would be linked with the mountain or the cloud by mist. The line and the stroke, not the use of color, were important to T'ang artists. Sometimes people were introduced into these landscapes, but they were generally small and insignificant amid the grandeur of nature. The Chinese rarely painted portraits.

Chinese artists often painted on scrolls. This painting, Plum Blossoms, *was painted on silk. Many families did not display their scrolls on their walls, but kept them rolled up in a safe place. From time to time the scrolls would be brought out for a leisurely viewing.*

The Chinese have a vast literature, much of it nonfiction. At the Chinese court, scribes were kept busy taking down in great detail everything that was said and done by the emperor. There were also histories of dynasties, of **provinces**, of localities, and detailed histories of various events. The past and its preservation have always been of great importance to the Chinese.

The Chinese compiled dictionaries and genealogies or family histories, and they wrote at length on Confucianism, Taoism, and Buddhism. They wrote essays, romances, and poetry. Some of their finest poets lived and wrote during the T'ang dynasty.

congenial: agreeable

One was Li T'ai-po (LEE TY-BOO) who was fond of parties and congenial companions. His unconventional ways eventually led to his exile from the court of the emperor. His poetry shows a delicateness and sadness that do not seem to match his behavior.

Another poet of the period was Tu Fu. He was interested in the state of the society in which he lived, and he sorrowed over the sufferings of the poor and afflicted. He wrote of them with warmth and sympathy. Tu Fu was a sharp critic of the government which permitted the miseries of the poor.

The poems of Po Chu-i (BO JOO-EE) who also wrote during the T'ang period were less lyrical than those of the other two. They were written to teach moral lessons. By command of the emperor Po Chu-i's poems were carved on stone tablets.

The T'ang Dynasty is also noted for its pottery. Graceful, dramatic figures of dancers, musicians, and animals such as horses and camels were modeled in clay and glazed in rich colors of green, yellow, and brown. Thousands of these lively, colorful figures were placed in tombs. Their variety, colors, and design are further evidence of the imaginative, highly developed culture of the T'ang dynasty.

SUNG AND YUAN DYNASTIES

The next great dynasty in China was the Sung (960-1279). Between the decline of the T'ang dynasty and the rise of the Sung, there were years of fighting among rival Chinese states. The Sung emperors were never able to rule an area as great as that of the T'ang dynasty. During the 1100s they were forced to move to southern China, where they located their capital in the city of Hangchow.

During the Sung dynasty the Chinese continued to write histories and poetry. They also wrote works on medicine, botany, **astronomy**, and mathematics. The highly glazed and translucent porcelains of the Sung dynasty have rarely been equaled. Their porcelains are so striking that since then all similar works have been called china. But the Sungs are best remembered through their paintings. The artists did not wish to paint an exact copy of what they saw. They tried, rather to express the ebb and flow of life within nature. They painted an impression of what they saw.

It was during the Sung period that Genghis Khan, chief of a Mongol tribe of Central Asia, started on his far-reaching conquests. He conquered much of northern China, most of Central Asia, and extended his rule as far as modern Russia and the eastern borders of Europe. His grandson, Kublai Khan (KOO-bly), overthrew the Sungs about 1279, and the Mongols ruled China until 1368.

In Chinese history the period of Mongol rule is known as the Yuan (yoo-AHN) dynasty. Kublai Khan established his capital on the present site of Peking and called it Cambaluc. It was during this reign that Marco Polo, the Venetian, visited China. Polo won the favor of the emperor and eventually returned to Italy, where he published an account of his travels and his observations. The Europeans of that day were so far behind the culture and the achievements of the Asians that they could not believe what Marco Polo told them.

During the rule of the Mongols, the Chinese turned to writing novels and dramas. The Chinese generally date their development of these literary forms from this period.

This bowl was made in China during the Ming period, when China became a sea power. The bowl was made for sale to Arabs. The Arabic writing is a wish for good luck and power. Using the text as reference, trace on a map China's trade routes during the Ming period.

MING PERIOD

The Chinese overthrew the Mongols and the Ming or Glorious dynasty (1368-1644) was established. During this period China became a sea power. Chinese ships traded as far as Cambodia, Thailand, Sumatra, Java, India, and Sri Lanka. Fleets of Chinese ships reached as far as the Persian Gulf, Aden, and the east coast of Africa.

Peking became one of the world's imposing capitals with its great walls, its temples, and its palaces. The emperor's palace was so huge that it was like a city within a city and was named the Forbidden City. Inside its walls were spacious courtyards, great halls, lovely gardens, and waterways.

During the Ming dynasty, the Chinese continued to turn out many

195

histories, essays, poems, and prose fiction. They began to paint portraits as well as landscapes and to introduce color into their paintings. Porcelain cups, bowls, and vessels of every variety became more and more sought after beyond the borders of Ming China.

MANCHUS

The Mings were overthrown by people of Manchuria called Manchus. They ruled China from 1644 to 1912. Their dynasty is known in Chinese history as the Ch'ing.

During this period the Chinese wrote much but not with the originality and power of some of the earlier Chinese. However, one of the greatest novels of China was written at this time, *The Dream of the Red Chamber.* It is a love story about a large, rich family. During the Ch'ing dynasty, the Chinese continued to paint, carve, and make fine porcelain, but the works did not equal those of the great artists of their past.

In the latter part of the Ming dynasty, Christian missionaries had begun coming to China. Traders and adventurers from Europe began to come in greater numbers during the Ch'ing dynasty. In this period European ideas and culture were beginning to influence the traditional patterns of the Chinese way of life.

TECHNOLOGY AND SCIENCE

Throughout their history the Chinese have amassed a long list of **technological** and scientific achievements. Most of their discoveries were made long before the Europeans began their scientific and technological revolutions.

The Chinese invented paper, gunpowder, the crossbow, paddle boats, the wheelbarrow, mechanical clocks, cannons, grenades, and heavy armor for soldiers. The Chinese invented printing with movable type as well as wood block printing. Deep drilling techniques, the use of natural gas, silk spinning, and immunization techniques were all known to the Chinese. They built suspension bridges, segmental-arch bridges, and canals with locks. They used water mills and chain pumps, and made high-quality hard steel. Among Chinese scientific achievements were also the development of the seismograph, a calendar, an astronomical clock, devices for showing the location of sun, moon, and planets, and the observation and recording of such phenomena as eclipses.

THE ARTS TODAY

The modern Chinese have not lost pride and appreciation for their past artistic achievements. They have carefully preserved their artistic

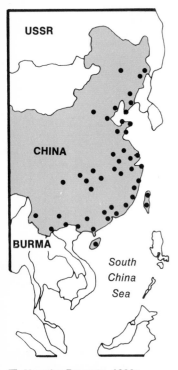

□ Manchu Dynasty, 1800s
● Foreign Treaty Ports

treasury in museums. Many Buddhist temples and pagodas have been made into national monuments supported by the state. Many of the **artifacts** dug up recently by their archaeologists have been sent abroad so that other people might admire the works of the Shang, Chou, Han, and other dynasties. The modern Chinese, however, are developing new artistic forms and techniques.

Although China has a literary legacy that goes back centuries before the Christian **era**, writings of pre-Communist China are—at least officially—treated only as negative examples. The classics show what not to write about. Official policy has, however, moved back and forth between almost complete rejection and qualified approval of certain past writers. Chairman Mao Tse-tung (MOW dzuh-DOONG) wrote many poems in a traditional style and form. He has even borrowed phrases from classical poets to express his ideas.

For the most part, writers, however, must conform to the ideals of the party. Criticism of the government is not tolerated except when movements such as the Cultural Revolution (1966-1968) explode in the country. Chinese art today is almost without exception used only for **propaganda** purposes. It tends to be realistic and to glorify the peasants and the workers of modern China.

The Chinese have a five-tone musical scale which is melodic, not harmonic. That is, the melody, or tune is not accompanied by chords or combinations of other notes to complement it.

Instrumental music is performed on flutes, bowed and plucked

Silk-making is thought to have begun in China around 2700 B.C. It remained a national secret for 3,000 years. This scroll shows one stage of the process, pressing the silk. The scroll itself is silk, and dates from the Sung dynasty.

In the ballet called White-Haired Girl, a young woman's hair turns white from poverty and hardship. In this scene, she meets enemies of her class while searching for food. Burning with hate, she attacks them. Why is class struggle an important idea in China?

stringed instruments, gongs, drums, and cymbals. Traditionally, Chinese vocal music is sung in a nasal voice without resonance. Foreign influences have affected instrumental and vocal styles, but the traditional form of Chinese music has been kept. Today, however, orchestras are encouraged to play only Chinese music composed since the Cultural Revolution. Orchestras were limited in the early 1970s to less than a dozen pieces. Following the philosophy that the group rather than the individual is important, the *Yellow River* Concerto was composed by a committee. Chinese opera is still popular but it is limited to revolutionary themes.

At one time the dance in China was part of the drama. It has now become a separate art. Furthermore, folk dancing has become popular throughout the country. The Chinese government encourages and supports ethnic and regional dance groups, and contests are popular. A more formal type of dancing is the ballet. One of the best-known ballets is *White-Haired Girl*. The chief theme of this ballet as of other modern works is class struggle. Other forms of Chinese dancing are highly stylized. Makeup is often deliberately unrealistic, and the audience can know the type of person the dancer is portraying by his or her makeup.

China has been making films since 1917, and the principal centers of production are in Shanghai and Peking. Since 1949 photography, sound, and color have improved greatly. Cartoons as well as feature-length films are popular. Projectors with generators are made so films can be shown in rural areas that do not as yet have electricity.

Family and **clan**, peasants, gentry, and scholars were important groups in traditional China. Under the government of the People's Republic, many features of traditional Chinese society have disappeared. New social patterns have evolved.

Chapter 4
Society

FAMILY

Traditionally, the family was so important to Chinese society that even the state was regarded as an extension of it. The Chinese customarily expressed this thought in the phrase, "Within the four seas [China] all men are brothers." Confucius stressed the importance of the family in his philosophy. Three of the five basic social relations he described were concerned directly with the family.

To the Chinese each individual was regarded as a member of some family. The success or failure of the individual was the success or failure of the family. Individuals were responsible to the family and it was responsible for them. If they stole, the family had to pay back what was taken. If they offended another, apology had to come from the family. If they revolted against the government, the family was punished. If they became honored officials, it was a family honor.

The ideal family was the joint family which contained a number of generations all within one household. But only the wealthy could achieve this ideal of 20, 30, 40 or more people within a single household. Poor people had to be content with fewer people under one roof, generally five to seven.

As in Indian families, it was the duty of parents and elders to teach young members their proper roles. Boys were taught to perform ancestral rites and prepared for their future responsibilities as family heads and village and community elders. Families that could afford it started their boys early on the road to scholarship. Only the educated could obtain service in the Chinese government thus bringing prestige and wealth to the family.

Girls learned the care and supervision of the household. They were destined for marriage and motherhood. Before marriage a woman's life was limited to the household of her parents. After marriage she moved to the household of her husband's parents. Peasant girls learned to work in the fields. Since ancient times, the peasant women of China have worked beside their husbands and children.

peasant: poor farm person

The oldest male in the family was its official and formal head. He represented the family in all matters outside the household. Within the family, he held all authority. In practice, his wife or his mother had great power in domestic matters. From behind the scenes, women also had influence in public matters. For instance, a mother had much to say about the choice of a bride for her son. And this bride came directly under the authority of her husband's mother. The social position of a family was affected by the marriages of its members. Marriages were usually arranged by parents or by a third party.

199

Children in traditional Chinese society were required to give their parents loving obedience and support while they lived. After death, it was the children's duty to carry out the ceremonial rites to ancestors. The Chinese did not fear old age, especially if they had sons, for this was the best period of life. They were respected and supported. The burdens and work had shifted to others. They could now rest and prepare to become ancestors.

CLAN

The clan was an extended family of all those people who traced their **lineage** back to a common ancestor. The line of descent was traced from the father's side, not the mother's. Some clans had thousands of members. Proof of membership in a clan was demonstrated by means of a family record. This record, or genealogy, listed the members in each generation descended from the common ancestor. These were elaborate records and often included biographies of individuals, a history of the locality, and many other details.

The clan had an ancestral center where there was usually an ancestral hall. The family graves were there. In the hall, personal data about each clan member was kept. On a rectangular piece of wood the name, title, and birth and death dates for each ancestor were written. The ancestor's spirit was in the tablet, especially when ancestral ceremonies were being performed. It was very important to have male descendants who would perform these necessary rites. This custom is sometimes called ancestor worship, but it is not worship in the usual sense of the term.

The clan also held property, often in the form of fields. The income from the property was used for the clan members. The clan had, in effect, its own welfare system. It supported orphans, widows, and childless older members and put promising students through school.

GENTRY AND SCHOLAR

Those who held much of the wealth in traditional China made up a special class called gentry. The members of the gentry were usually well-educated. The governing officials generally came from this group. The gentry dominated China until the Communists came to power in 1949.

The gentry stressed etiquette and ritual. They were not expected to do physical labor. They were teachers, governors, and patrons of the arts, writers of poetry and prose, historians, and professional people. They were dedicated to preserving the system of thought and practice by which they had benefited. Thus they were the greatest supporters of Confucianism and the traditional ways.

The gentry was a flexible class. Families might enter and leave it within the space of three or four generations. There were always forces of separation at work within the large families. Jealousies and disagreements among the brothers and their wives frequently forced a division of the family property. In many cases the separated families could not live on their smaller share of the property in the same manner as before. Sometimes families became so large that they could not be supported adequately by the land they owned and they were forced to sell. This reduced their wealth and usually led to loss of gentry status. But there were always those rising from the peasant class to take the places of those who sank from the gentry.

adequately: well enough

PEASANT

Throughout China's history peasants have made up the vast majority of the Chinese. Their income came from the land which they cultivated. It was supplemented by handicraft work such as basketmaking, embroidery, or weaving. Chinese peasants often lived on the edge of hunger and sometimes starvation. They have had one main purpose—to get enough to eat. There was little time for literature, the arts, theater, or elaborate ritual. Often the peasants were illiterate. However, they appreciated the finer things of life and wanted these things for themselves and their children. They followed traditional etiquette and rituals to the best of their ability and means.

There was always the hope for a peasant family that perhaps one day, through its children, it might rise to the gentry class. The peasant

Below, workers on the Muyu People's Commune in southeast China weed their rice paddies. What are some advantages and disadvantages of commune living?

family would struggle and save in order to educate one or more of its sons. Sometimes the peasants of a village would pool their resources to provide a tutor for one or more promising boys. If a boy passed the state examinations and obtained an official position, the entire village would share in this good fortune. The history of China is filled with examples of peasant boys who rose in status and carried their families along with them. Few gentry families did not have a peasant origin, and few peasant families did not have ancestors of the gentry class.

CHANGES

 After Europeans began to trade and live in China changes were gradually introduced into Chinese society. The Chinese who lived in cities and large ports were the first to be influenced by Western social thought and customs. It was in these places that most Europeans lived and worked. Western missionaries too brought change when they carried the teachings of Christianity to China. Many of the young were introduced to Western social attitudes in the schools and universities established by the government or through Western books and periodicals. Some students went abroad.

attitudes: ways of thought, action, or feelings

In the first half of the 1900s, one of these Chinese students, Sun Yat-sen (SOON YAHT-SEN), proposed a new political, economic, and social system for China. This system was a combination of Chinese and Western ideas. From that time until the Communists established the People's Republic in 1949, social change was rapid, especially among the young, the educated, and the city dwellers.

Since 1949 under Communist leadership, substantial and radical social change has taken place. The state set about weakening the family's hold on the individual. Individuals were commanded to give their loyalty to the state rather than to their immediate families.

The traditional avenues to family wealth through its children have been removed. Parents no longer exercise the same control over their children as they did in the past. Parents are still responsible for preparing their children to fill certain roles in society. However, institutions operated and supported by the state are also performing this function. Schools, youth groups, official clubs, and **unions** are used to shape the values and behavior of the young.

Few extended families remain except in rural areas where tradition is not easily erased. In cities the Chinese live mostly in **nuclear families**. In villages, the Communists resettled groups of several thousand households into communes. The people live in dormitories and share communal dining rooms. The state has also taken over the welfare duties of the clans. There is no longer a gentry class because the land is the property of the government. Individual families are allowed only small plots for their personal use.

  Education is now open to everyone. The People's Republic has

City officials from Peking attend a lecture on the works of Marx and Lenin at a government school. The students are administrators, health officials, and educators. They will spend six months studying political theory. Some will spend part of their time doing manual labor on communes.

shortened schooling from 12 years to nine. The school year is $8^1/_2$ months with two vacation periods of a month each, one in the summer and one in the winter. Students must spend six weeks working in factories or on communes. University education has been reduced from four years to three. Students may not enter a university until they have spent two years as a worker or a soldier.

STATUS OF WOMEN

The government of the People's Republic of China has definitely improved the status of women. Women have been encouraged to come out of the home and into the factories. Legally a woman is equal to a man. She receives equal pay for equal work. She may work in any occupation she chooses, and she has the same opportunity for schooling as a man. A woman may keep her family name and own personal property after marriage. The choice of a marriage partner is hers and there is no need to seek her parents' permission to marry. She has the same right to divorce as her husband. By law men may have only one wife.

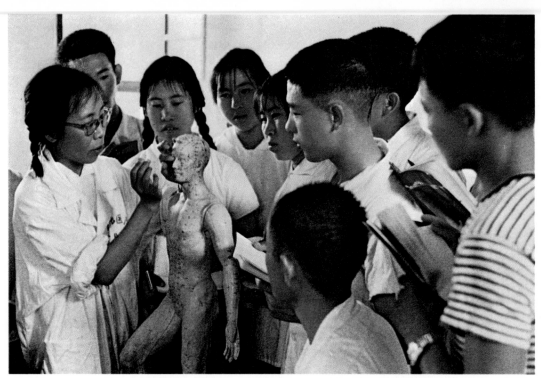

A physician teaches acupuncture to "barefoot doctors" at a rural commune in Shensi Province. Skilled doctors like her are sent into the countryside to train others. Both Western and Chinese medicine are practiced.

Increasing numbers of women are entering the professions. Many of China's doctors are women. Women are found in engineering, educational, scientific, military, administrative, agricultural, and many other fields of work. Women drive trucks and work on construction crews. They also hold important jobs in government, although few women serve on the Central Committee of the Communist party. Women with children can leave them in day-care centers or with older relatives when they work.

More opportunities exist for women who live in urban areas, but the status of women is also improving in the rural parts of the country. In the early 1970s part of the **campaign** to improve women's status centered around the government's effort to discredit the ideas of Confucius. Government representatives taught that Confucian ideas hold back progress and must be wiped out.

However, it is not possible to change traditional attitudes and customs swiftly. Some elements of traditional social behavior may continue in modified form in the People's Republic for some time. Among the millions of Chinese who live in Taiwan, Southeast Asia, Hong Kong, and other places, change is much more gradual.

In the past, the Chinese and other Asians generally thought and acted in terms of the ruler and the ruled. There was the man or woman who ruled and had certain responsibilities. In turn, there were the people who were ruled and had certain duties. The ruler was not chosen by the people, and did not consult them in making decisions. It was their duty to obey commands. The ruler had advisors, and sometimes was controlled by them, but officially and formally there was one ruler.

Confucianists taught that the emperor or empress was responsible for the security and happiness of the people. If he or she failed to carry out this responsibility, the blessing of Heaven would be lost because Heaven thought as the people thought. Thus, the people were told that they had the right to revolt against an unworthy ruler.

ROOTS OF REVOLT

Western sailors and traders who came to China from the 1500s to the 1700s often seemed rough and crude. The Chinese, with their ancient culture and impressive background of achievements, received these Westerners with indifference and even with contempt. The foreigners were kept to such ports as Canton and Macao in southern China. They were not allowed into other parts of the country.

Westerners, particularly the British and French, resented the superior attitude of the Chinese. In the middle of the 1800s, they began to use force to obtain greater freedom to trade. The Chinese were made to sign treaties which opened more ports to the Westerners and gave them the right to settle in China. Special privileges placed them beyond Chinese law. They were subject solely to the representatives of their own governments. Gradually Westerners began to assume greater and greater economic and political control.

Finally the Europeans divided China for themselves into economic **spheres of influence**. Each nation took a section in which it had the exclusive right to trade. The U. S. refused to recognize these spheres of influence. It tried constantly to maintain an open-door policy in China. This meant basically that each country would be free to trade anywhere in the country.

For a long time, the Chinese resisted the influence and pressure of ideas that Westerners brought but finally they gave in. Western methods of government, science, technology, and customs began to spread around the land. Many Chinese began to question their own systems of government, philosophy, and social and economic life. Ultimately, they concluded that if the country was to be free, reform was needed and the Manchu dynasty had to be overthrown.

SUN YAT-SEN

Rebellions broke out in China several times in the last half of the 1800s. However, the Manchus were always able to subdue them.

For centuries, China's rulers were crowned in the Imperial Palace in Peking, shown above after a snowfall. The palace is now a museum. One of the last Manchus to rule China was the Empress Chih Hsi.

Finally, from among the new Chinese there emerged one man, Sun Yat-sen, who was to become known as the father of new China.

Sun was one of the young Chinese who went abroad to study. He was sent to Hawaii where he was converted to Christianity. When Sun returned to China, he found his ideas out of place. He went to British Hong Kong, studied medicine, and became a doctor. He returned again to China and spent his life working for the establishment of a **republican government** in China.

Dr. Sun worked and traveled tirelessly to preach his doctrine of the Three Principles of the People. Through these he tried to adapt and blend the best of Chinese ideology and the best of Western thought and progress.

The first principle was nationalism. It called for the Chinese to think of themselves first as citizens of a nation and only secondly as members of a family or clan. This principle added the virtue of **patriotism** to the traditional Confucian virtues of loyalty, family devotion, and obedience.

The second principle was democracy or **popular sovereignty**. This called for a democratic, representative type of government. It also stressed the duties of each individual toward the state.

The third principle was livelihood. Sun wanted to raise the standard of living for all people. At the same time, he wanted to increase the nation's wealth. He proposed two ways to achieve these goals. One was to divide the land equally among the people. The other was to have government regulate and control the ownership of capital. **Heavy industries** and the communication and transportation systems were to be owned by the government. There were to be progressive income and inheritance taxes.

In 1911 a revolution broke out. Within a few months rebels held most of southern China. The first Chinese republic was proclaimed at Nanking. Sun Yat-sen became its president. Unfortunately, the republic lacked strong organization and the Chinese people had little understanding of democracy. China remained divided among many **factions**, each competing for power.

Frightened by the success of the rebels, the Manchus appointed Yuan Shih-k'ai (YOO-AHN SHIR-KEE), a military leader, as premier. He was to serve under the Manchu emperor, but Yuan wanted to be president of the new republic. He eventually forced the emperor to resign. In an attempt to unify China and preserve the republic, Sun recommended that Yuan be made president in his place. This was done. Yuan, however, had little use for democracy. He ruled as a dictator until his death in 1916. Sun and his followers rebelled but were forced to flee to Japan.

After Yuan's death, China was again divided among the local military chiefs. They kept personal armies, taxed the people, and fought continually among themselves. This situation created terror, chaos, and disorder.

Through the efforts of Sun Yat-sen and later Chiang Kai-shek (jee-AHNG KY-SHEK), the Kuomintang or Nationalist party eventually brought most of China under one republican government. By 1923 Sun was receiving help from the Soviet Communists. He had appealed to other countries for help, but they had delayed. The Soviets, on the other hand, had been quick to see the advantage of having a Communist state in China. They sent organizers, money, and supplies. The Kuomintang was reorganized along Communist lines.

Sun Yat-sen died in Peking in 1925, several years before his dream of a republic headed by his Kuomintang party was realized. His program was carried on by Chiang Kai-shek who was one of his supporters and military leaders.

CHIANG KAI-SHEK

Chiang Kai-shek had begun to support Sun Yat-sen's program as a young military officer. He received much of his military training in Japan and had studied Communist army organization in Russia. He never studied in Western countries.

In 1926, Chiang took command of the Northern Expedition Army of the Nationalist government. This army included Communist and non-Communist forces. By April 1927 Chiang had established a Nationalist government in Nanking. By December 1928, he had reunited most of China under the Nationalist government, which was controlled by the Kuomintang. In mid-1927, Chiang had broken with the Communists in the Kuomintang. After six years of hard fighting, he drove their armies to Yenan in Shensi Province.

Chiang became leader of the Kuomintang, head of state, and

In 1912, Sun Yat-sen became China's first president.

General Chiang Kai-shek's Nationalist government ruled parts of mainland China from 1928 to 1949. What were some causes of his overthrow?

Mao Tse-tung reviews a parade of Red Guards during the Cultural Revolution of the 1960s. How has China changed since 1949?

commander in chief of China's armed forces. His government formally ruled varying parts of China from 1928 until 1949. In that year, after a bitter civil war, the Communists took formal control of mainland China. Chiang and his followers fled to the island of Taiwan or Formosa. He set up a Nationalist government there and claimed that it was the true government of China.

Taiwan, Nationalist China, or the Republic of China, includes 77 islands and 15 million people. From 1945 until 1971 it had a seat on the United Nations Security Council. In 1971 it was expelled from the UN and its permanent seat on the Security Council given to the People's Republic of China. Until his death in 1975, Chiang continued as head of the Nationalist government.

MAO TSE-TUNG

In 1921 Mao Tse-tung had been one of the founders of the Chinese Communist Party. He held a variety of positions in this party as well as in the Kuomintang, which was then allied with the Communists. In 1925 Chiang Kai-shek turned against the Communists and began a campaign to wipe them out. By 1934, he had almost succeeded.

Mao and his followers had retreated 9,600 kilometers (6,000 miles) to Shensi Province. This retreat, known as the Long March, is of great historic importance to Mao's followers. Mao established his headquarters at Yenan and from there the Communists continued their fight against Chiang's Nationalist forces.

In 1931 the Japanese invaded China and the war in China was often a three-way affair. Kuomintang forces fought against both the

Japanese and the Communists. The Communists also fought the Japanese, but continued their efforts to gain control of China.

While the war against Japan continued, greater numbers of Chinese joined Mao's forces. In part, this was because of the moral and economic breakdown which occurred in China as a result of the war. In part, it was because of widespread corruption among local, provincial, and central government officials. And, in part, it was because of the sympathy the Communist party felt for the sufferings of the people.

At the end of World War II, the Communists held strategic positions in various parts of China. A civil war followed between the Nationalist government of Chiang Kai-shek and the Communists under Mao Tse-tung. The Communists won. By 1949 the Communists were in control of mainland China. They established their capital in Peking, the ancient capital of Mongol conquerors and Chinese dynasties.

THE PEOPLE'S REPUBLIC OF CHINA

Mao Tse-tung and his followers established the People's Republic of China in a country that had been torn by rebellions and wars for almost 50 years. Although all their plans have not been successful, Chinese Communist leaders have made giant strides in rebuilding China since 1949. The **Five-Year Plan** that began in 1958 was called the Great Leap Forward and was almost a disaster. Aimed at increasing food as well as industrial production, the plan failed badly and brought about food shortages. Later plans were designed to provide a better balance. As we have seen, farmland was taken away from large landholders and distributed among the peasants on communes. This apparently gives the government better economic and political control over rural areas.

The People's Republic has made steady progress in industrialization, scientific research, and communications. Northern Manchuria is still the primary industrial area. Other large industrial complexes have been established in such places as Peking, Shanghai, Tiensin, and Wuhan. These manufacturing centers are making vehicles, electronic and optical equipment, bridges, machinery, and a host of other products.

The Chinese are training thousands of doctors as well as nurses and medical technicians. Many new hospitals and clinics have been built and staffed. Chinese leaders have placed great emphasis upon preventive medicine. Malaria, venereal diseases, and cholera have been practically wiped out. Chinese advances in nuclear research and in missiles have been widely publicized. What is not widely known is their advanced knowledge in the fields of chemistry, biology, archaeology, and electronics.

There are still many problems for the Chinese to overcome. Despite attempts to limit the birth rate, the population of China continues

This woman operates a lathe at a plant in Port Arthur, Manchuria. Since the 1960s, major industrial centers have been built in Manchuria and in other areas.

to grow at a rate of around 15 million per year. It is estimated that China's population ranges somewhere between 750 and 800 million. Feeding so many people is an enormous task. China now has some of the largest cities in the world. This has caused a drastic housing shortage. In addition, more and better schools are needed to train and educate the millions of people.

THE CULTURAL REVOLUTION   Mao Tse-tung and other leaders who fought to make China a Communist state saw themselves growing old and their work as yet uncompleted. Mao was concerned that some leaders had lost their revolutionary spirit. He was also concerned about China's future when new, young leaders would come to power who did not know the hardships of pre-Communist China. He had apparently long held a belief that a revolution now and then has a cleansing effect upon the people and their political system.

In 1966 Mao began a cultural revolution in China. He wanted to wipe out any foreign influences and aristocratic attitudes that remained. He wanted to remove from power any officials who were becoming like the old Chinese **bureaucrats** and putting themselves above the people. Young followers of Mao, known as the Red Guard, attacked those who showed these old and unMao-like ideas. At times the Red Guard was supported by the army. The Guard roamed the streets, invaded homes, government offices, and factories, and publicly ridiculed and punished those they considered enemies of Mao and his thought. China was torn by fear and hate. A number of Communist officials fell from power during this time.

By 1969 the agony of the Cultural Revolution was over and Mao's position as leader of China was strengthened. The effects of the

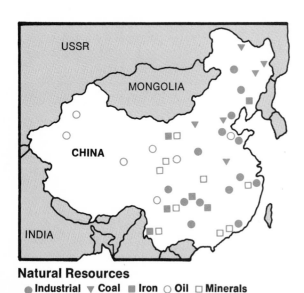

Natural Resources
● Industrial ▼ Coal ■ Iron ○ Oil □ Minerals

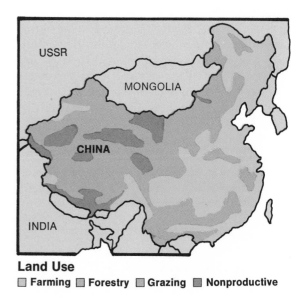

Land Use
□ Farming □ Forestry □ Grazing ■ Nonproductive

Cultural Revolution, however, continued to be felt in many areas of Chinese life into the 1970s. Writers and students began to attack Confucius. They claimed that if the influences of Confucius were not erased, the landlords and **bourgeoisie** would rise to power again.

In 1976 Mao died. The moderates came to power and imprisoned the leaders of the radicals. The future of the People's Republic at home appeared secure. Its policies in international affairs did not change.

A WORLD POWER   Chinese relations with other nations have often been strained. For many years the U.S. supported the Nationalist Chinese and opposed entry of the People's Republic into the UN. In the early years of their rule, Chinese Communist leaders relied heavily on Soviet technological support. In recent years, Chinese national interests have repeatedly come into conflict with those of the USSR. In the 1960s Chinese and Soviet leaders had a serious disagreement over the way communism was developing.

This was a period when the U.S. and the Soviet Union seemed to be coming to a closer, more friendly relationship. The Chinese feared that these two **superpowers** might unite against them. After 1964 when China exploded its first atomic bomb, China began more and more to assume the role of a world power. Chinese leaders sought to influence the developing nations of the world against both the USSR and the U.S. Many of these nations voted in favor of admitting the People's Republic to the UN in 1971.

Mao used young people to strengthen his position as China's leader during the Cultural Revolution. When it was over, he was more powerful than ever. These students are taking part in a swim meet for students in Peking schools.

211

Recently in trying to protect themselves against the Soviet Union, the Chinese have sought better relations with the U.S. President Richard Nixon was invited to visit China in 1972 and the two countries signed several agreements. These provided for diplomatic and cultural exchanges, trade, and visits by journalists, scholars, and ordinary travelers. President Gerald Ford visited China in 1975 and reaffirmed U.S. interest in improving relations with the People's Republic.

TIBETANS

plateau: an area of high, flat land

There are two large concentrations of non-Chinese people within the People's Republic—Tibetans and Mongols. Tibet today has the status of a Chinese Autonomous Region. The Tibetans live on a high plateau surrounded by some of the highest mountains in the world. The Himalayas run along its southern borders. To the east and north are the Chinese. To the south are the people of India, Nepal, and Bhutan.

The Tibetans speak a Tibeto-Burman language. Their religion is a type of Mahayana Buddhism with additions of a local spirit worship. Tibetan monks are known as lamas. For centuries lamas held great economic and political power. The ruler of the country is called the Dalai Lama. In 1959, when the Chinese took control of the country, the Dalai Lama fled to India.

Although it is supposedly a self-governing area, the Chinese have strict control over the country. They have brought an educational system to Tibet and distributed the land more widely to the peasants. They have also encouraged small and medium-sized industries.

MONGOLS

The Mongols ruled China between 1279 and 1368 as part of an empire stretching from Eastern Europe to the Pacific Ocean and Southeast Asia. Under Genghis Khan, they began the conquest that eventually led to the establishment of the Yuan dynasty in China.

After the Yuan dynasty was overthrown, Mongolia remained a part of China for centuries. In the early 1920s, the Mongols of Outer Mongolia expelled the Chinese with help from the Soviet army. Outer

At a festival in Tibet, dancers perform in front of the Potala. This huge monastery was once the home of the Dalai Lama.

The Mongolian people are skillful with horses. These women are racing in an all-army sports meet sponsored by the government.

Mongolia was then established as a socialist state, the Mongolian People's Republic. Ulan Bator became the capital. Mongolia still relies upon the Soviet Union for economic aid to support its 1.5 million people.

Inner Mongolia remained a part of China. There are more Mongols living in China than in the Mongolian People's Republic. The Chinese are fearful of attempts by Mongol nationalists to add Inner Mongolia to their republic. In 1970, parts of Inner Mongolia were assigned to neighboring Chinese provinces. The Chinese hoped by this measure to stop any nationalist movement.

Chapter 6
Korea—A Meeting Place

From very early times the Chinese and Japanese have crossed each other's paths in Korea. Because of Korea's location, it was only natural that this land should serve as a meeting place. It borders China on the northwest and is separated from Japan on the east by a narrow expanse of water. Sometimes the two met in peace, sometimes in anger, but always with far-reaching results for themselves and for the Koreans. For much of its history, Korea has had to fight to preserve its political and cultural independence amid the meddling and ambitions of its two neighbors.

A MIXED HERITAGE

The Koreans are a blend of Chinese and Mongol together with minor strains of other groups. The Chinese first entered Korea hundreds of years prior to the first century A.D.

The cultural **heritage** of the Koreans is predominantly of Chinese origin. Under Chinese influence, Koreans learned to use Chinese

This is South Korea's capital city, Seoul. The buildings in the foreground were designed in the 1300s. Name some ways in which China, Japan, the U.S., and the USSR have influenced Korea.

ideographs, studied Chinese classics, and accepted Confucianism as a guide for their society and their government. The administration of the Korean government was modeled after that of China. The Koreans came to know Chinese drama, art, and poetry. They adapted Chinese architecture and Chinese technological and scientific accomplishments to their own needs. They became Buddhists, Confucianists, and Taoists. But the Koreans modified and enriched whatever they received from other cultures. For example, they created their own versions of porcelains, lacquer, and ceramics.

The Japanese were attracted by the cultural imports from China which the Koreans had adapted. To the Japanese, Korea became a passageway by which they could have contact with the riches of Chinese culture. Also the Japanese began early to think about dominating Korea politically. Even before the first century A.D. there are legends of a Japanese invasion of southern Korea. Tradition also tells of the Empress Jingo who invaded, conquered, and took booty and slaves from Korea around 200 A.D. The Japanese did control portions of southern Korea until about the middle of the 500s A.D. In modern times, the Japanese controlled all of the Korean peninsula from 1910 to the end of World War II.

In the 20th century, two other nations have played important roles in the development of the Koreans—the U.S. and the Soviet Union. As a result of World War II and subsequent actions of the Soviet Union and the U.S., Korea became divided into two parts. North Korea—the Democratic People's Republic of Korea—is governed by Communist leaders and policies. South Korea—the Republic of Korea—has, formally at least, a representative form of government. Both governments desire a **unification** of the country and recently have met officially to discuss ways to achieve this goal. But by reason of geography and history, the Chinese and the Japanese will continue to be concerned with Korean affairs.

Summing Up the Unit

Social Studies Vocabulary

Define: conservatism; mandate; centralize; propaganda; clan; spheres of influence; popular sovereignty; factions; bureaucrats

People

Identify: Confucius; Lao-tzu; Sun Yat-sen; Mao Tse-tung; Chiang Kai-shek

Words

Identify: ideograph; Confucianism; jen; Taoism; Legalism; Theravada, Mahayana Buddhism; bodhisattvas; acupuncture; jade; calligraphy; genealogies; gentry

Questions

1. Describe the feudal system in China.
2. What factors may have caused the great Chinese philosophies to have a practical quality?
3. a. Why is Confucianism considered conservative? b. What are the five fundamental social relationships taught by Confucianism? c. How did Confucianist principles limit the power of Chinese rulers?
4. According to Taoists, what were the two causes of people's suffering?
5. Why was Mahayana Buddhism better suited to the needs of China than Theravada Buddhism?
6. a. List each dynasty and the major artistic achievements of each. b. What is the purpose of art in China today?
7. Describe the traditional Chinese family.
8. Why did the gentry support Confucianism and traditional ways?
9. What changes have occurred in Chinese society since 1949?
10. Where is Nationalist China located?
11. a. What was the purpose of Mao's Cultural Revolution? b. When did it occur? c. Who carried it out?
12. Name the two large groups of non-Chinese people in the People's Republic of China.
13. a. Why does the author call Korea a meeting place? b. How did the Koreans use what they took from other cultures?

Discussion Topics

1. What does "bits of truth are often found in legends" mean? What legends do you know? Is there any truth to them?
2. The Communists have made great progress in building Chinese agriculture and industry. Do you think this progress is likely to continue? Viewed by comparison with China's long history of dynasties and traditions, what advantages and disadvantages does communism have as a form of government for China?
3. For many years the U.S. opposed the entry of the People's Republic of China into the UN. But now China is a member and two U.S. presidents have visited China. Do you think the U.S. change in policy was wise? What caused it?
4. Old age was the best time of life for people in traditional China. Would all societies gain if they gave such respect to the elderly? What status does old age have in the U.S.?
5. The Soviets and the Chinese confront each other along the border between China and the Mongolian People's Republic. Is Mongolia a likely place for trouble to occur between the USSR and China? Why? What would China want in the USSR? What would the USSR want from China? Do you think either side would risk a full-scale war?

Project Ideas

1. Make a map showing changes in the political control of Korea since 1950.
2. Using outside reference materials, write a brief report on one of the following: Chinese warlords; Christian missionaries in China; Sun Yat-sen; Chiang Kai-shek; Mao Tse-tung; the Long March; factors leading to the Communist takeover of the mainland; the Cultural Revolution; the Korean War.
3. Pretend you are a visitor to China. Write a letter home giving your impression of one of the following: the Great Wall; the Forbidden City; women; archaeology; medicine; communes. Outside reading will help you.

Unit IV

Japan

Japan's highest mountain is Mt. Fuji. This woodblock print of Mt. Fuji was made in the 1800s by one of Japan's most famous artists, Katsushika Hokusai. Hokusai's art influenced many European impressionist painters, such as Degas.

The Japanese call their country Nippon, meaning land of the rising sun. Geographically, Japan is made up of about a thousand islands. The land area is small, about the size of California.

In a nation with more than 27,000 kilometers (17,000 miles) of coastline, most Japanese live along or near the sea. Yet they are within view of mountains. Nature has not been kind to the Japanese. Typhoons, tidal waves, earthquakes, and volcanic activity are frequent. About 75 percent of Japan's land is sloped, and much of it is rocky. Only a small part—about one-seventh—of Japan's total land area is suitable for farming. And the soil is naturally poor.

Yet Japan is one of Asia's most important nations. During the past 100 years, it has grown from an almost unknown country to one whose influence is worldwide.

Mystery surrounds the earliest human occupants of Japan. Some scholars believe that **hominids** lived in Japan as early as 500,000 years ago. Others believe that successive waves of people came to Japan from mainland Asia later. Stone tools dating to 16,000 B.C. and earlier have been found. This earliest period is sometimes called the Preceramic period, meaning before pottery-making. The earliest pottery has been dated to about 12,000 years ago.

Chapter 1
Early Japan

JOMON PERIOD

From about 3000 B.C. to around 300 B.C. a more artistic pottery called jomon, which means rope-pattern, was made. This era is known as the Jomon period. The Jomon people built thatch houses over shallow pits. For protection against flooding, they dug trenches around the pits. They made tools and weapons of stone and fish hooks and harpoons of bone.

Some scholars believe that Southeast Asians sailed to Taiwan and Japan about 3000 or 2000 B.C. They brought along their agriculture and knowledge of the use of metals. Other scholars disagree with this claim.

Another early people to come to Japan were the Ainu (EYE-noo) people. It is not known where they came from or when. They may be related to the people of the Jomon period. Slowly other arrivals from Korea and mainland Asia swelled the population of Japan. These new arrivals may have pushed the Ainu northward to the area around Hokkaido. Only a remnant of them remains there today.

YAYOI PERIOD

The Yayoi period was named after a place in Tokyo where remains of a reddish pottery were first found. The Yayoi people who made this pottery were growing rice in paddies by the 200s B.C. A paddy is a field that can be flooded when rice is planted. Paddies show that the Yayoi people understood the uses of irrigation.

The Yayoi people used tools and weapons of bronze and iron. Their pottery was made by turning clay on a wheel rather than by molding the clay by hand. The houses of the Yayoi were built at ground level but some had raised floors. These were much like the wood and thatch dwellings that may be seen in the Japanese countryside today.

Several centuries before the Christian era, the Japanese grouped themselves into clans. Sometimes a Japanese clan included unrelated persons who were adopted into the group. The clans were ruled by chiefs—women as well as men—who had both political and religious authority. Like the Chou emperors, the rulers inherited their power. The ruler of a clan was usually the son or daughter or close relative of the previous ruler. This type of organization became the foundation of Japanese social and political life for many centuries.

Chapter 2
Creators
and Adapters

Japanese artists were making decorative pottery as early as 12,000 years ago. This bowl is from one of Japan's earliest eras, the Jomon period.

By the 300s A.D., one of the competing Japanese clans, the Yamato (yah-MAH-toh), began to gain power in central and southern Japan. Over the next 200 years, they extended their rule to all Japan. The chief of the Yamato clan was both emperor and high priest. He and his successors claimed their power from Shinto, the native religion of Japan. This religion taught that the emperor was of divine ancestry.

According to ancient Shinto legends, Ninigi, the grandson of the Sun Goddess, Amaterasu, came down to rule Japan. He went first to the island of Kyushu carrying three treasures which were given to him by his grandmother. These treasures—a jewel, a sword, and a mirror—became his symbols of sovereignty. One of Ninigi's great-grandchildren, Jimmu Tenno, moved from Kyushu to central Japan. There he established the state of Yamato. Thus, in the year 660 B.C., began the empire of Japan. Jimmu Tenno—Tenno means sovereign of heaven—is traditionally considered Japan's first emperor.

SHINTO

The story of the creation of Japan and the beginning of its long line of emperors is found in two basic Shinto books. These books were written between 700 and 800 A.D., not long after the Japanese learned to write with Chinese characters. It is possible that these books were written primarily to support the position of the ruling Yamato family and the nobles of this period.

DIVINITY IN NATURE   In Shinto, nature is divine. Deities live within rocks, trees, mountains, and in all the forces of nature. Shinto

—which means the way of the gods—identifies these deities by such names as Sun Goddess, Moon God, Mountain Goddess, Fertility God, and Food God.

Shinto teaches that people should be thankful for all the blessings of nature, for birth, growth, and life. Death, decay, and sterility—everything that interferes with these blessings—should be regarded as evil. The most joyous Japanese festivals are those related to the planting, growing, and harvesting of crops.

Ancient Shinto had no shrines except the soaring tree, the quiet stream, and the majestic mountaintop. Sometimes a small but striking natural object—a rock of unusual shape, for example—might be enclosed with sticks. It was later, under the influence of Buddhism, that symbols for the divine were housed in shrines. Today the greatest of these shrines are at Ise (EE-SAY). Every 20 years these shrines are destroyed and erected again with unpainted wood. There is no place for a congregation. Generally, the people approach the outside of the shrine, wash their hands, rinse their mouths, clap their hands, perhaps ring a bell, and make an offering. Then they bow and leave. True Shintoists find divinity outside the shrine, not within.

CLEANLINESS   When Shinto worshipers wash their hands before a shrine, they are really cleansing themselves of dirt. Those who participate in the rituals of Shinto must be physically pure. The deities would be offended if anyone unclean approached them. Sickness, injuries, and physical uncleanliness are some of the things that can soil a worshiper. Shinto is not concerned with moral guilt or impurities beyond the physical. It is actual physical uncleanliness that must be washed away.

LEARNING FROM CHINA

Beginning in the latter part of the 600s A.D., the Japanese made efforts to learn all they could from the Chinese, who were undergoing a period of great creativity under the T'ang dynasty. Over a period of several hundred years, the Japanese sent group after group to learn and bring back all they could of Chinese ideas and creations.

When the visitors returned to Japan, the knowledge they brought with them was put into practice, but not always in a way that the Chinese would understand or approve. The Japanese already had some basic ideas about life and society which they were not prepared to give up.

The Yamato rulers followed the Chinese in establishing a central administration for their government. They divided the country into local government units. The emperor appointed officials to govern these administrative divisions. The new bureaucracy was financed by a land tax. A new capital, called Nara, was built in imitation of the capital of T'ang China.

sterility: in people, the inability to have children; in farming, the inability of land to produce crops

219

Though the system of government was Chinese in form, it was Japanese in spirit. The Chinese administration, both central and local, was staffed by educated people who had passed through a series of difficult examinations. Japanese officials were often chosen because of their rank and the strength of their family connections. The Chinese emperor's power was checked by the right of the people to revolt as well as by Heaven. The Japanese believed that the emperor was divine. He could do no wrong, and therefore there could be no revolt. The new ways of governing were borrowed from China but they were used by the Yamato rulers to strengthen their own position.

Shinto too was affected by Chinese ideas and practices. From Confucianism the Japanese learned to stress forms of behavior and ancestor worship. Confucianism also taught loyalty to superiors, especially the emperor. Certain magical practices of Taoism were also adopted. But the greatest of all influences was Buddhism.

BUDDHISM

As we have seen, the Japanese and Koreans have long been in contact with each other. The Koreans may have carried knowledge of Buddhism and of Chinese writing to Japan as early as the 200s A.D. Certainly by the 500s, the Japanese had been exposed to Buddhism. It was then that a number of Koreans came and stayed in Japan.

Buddhism first clashed with Shinto, just as it had clashed with Chinese ideas when it first appeared in China. But in Japan it was not because people objected to Buddhist beliefs. Buddhism did not threaten to destroy Shinto, for Shinto had few formal rules and teachings. The conflict between Buddhism and Shinto was part of a fight for power. Clans that were warring among themselves for control of Japan chose to attract followers through either Shinto or Buddhism. The supporters of Shinto lost and Buddhism became the religion of the court and the wealthy.

But Shinto remained strong among the common people. Buddhism then began to adapt itself to Shinto, as it had done with the beliefs and attitudes of the Chinese some centuries before. Shinto deities became Buddhist holy ones. Some people proclaimed that the two religions were merely forms of the same religion. Buddhist monks took part in Shinto rituals. Gradually the Japanese became both Buddhists and followers of Shinto.

ZEN Most Japanese Buddhists were and are followers of Mahayana Buddhism. They rely upon the merits and mercy of the Buddhas and the saints for their salvation. But some Japanese felt that they should rely on their own efforts for salvation. They became followers of a form of Buddhism known in Japan as Zen.

Zen is close to the original teachings of Gautama Buddha. It is similar to Theravada Buddhism, which is practiced in Southeast Asia.

This statue of Buddha was made in the 1200s in Kamakura, Japan. This was the capital city of the Kamakura shogunate. By that time, Buddhism had existed in Japan for hundreds of years. Where did Buddhism originate?

The Japanese received their basic ideas about Zen from the Chinese, who started to practice it around 400 A.D. In China it is called Ch'an Buddhism.

To Zen Buddhists, the Buddha-nature is everywhere and it is the purpose of each person to discover and understand this Buddha-nature. Individuals who do will be enlightened. Each person must do it alone. There can be no assistance from others, no matter how devout and saintly they may be. Students cannot find much help in books, in good works or prayer, but only in meditation. This meditation may go on for years before enlightenment comes.

To meditate well, a person must live a quiet, serene, self-disciplined life. It is necessary to conquer oneself and to be simple in tastes and habits. Zen approves of gardening, the study of nature, and the simplicity of the Japanese tea-drinking ceremony. These pursuits are supposed to be helpful in gaining enlightenment. If Zen teachers think that a student is on the verge of enlightenment, they may suddenly shout at or strike the student. This shock may push the individual into enlightenment.

RELIGION AND THE STATE

Buddhism has affected all levels of Japanese life and has played a major role in molding Japanese customs, thought, art, and literature. It has been a comfort, a hope, and a guide for life for scholars and uneducated alike. In addition, ruling groups in Japan used both Buddhism and Shinto to strengthen their power. Both religions worked in the interest of law and order and both taught respect for authority. Gradually the Shinto Sun Goddess became officially recognized as the mother of all the clans. Ultimately the emperor, as her direct descendant, became a god.

By the 1800s, the influence of Buddhism was lessening in Japan. In 1882 Shinto was divided into Sect Shinto and Shrine, or State, Shinto. Sect Shinto was the traditional worship of nature. State Shinto became closely tied to the political life and institutions of the Japanese. Its goal was to encourage patriotism and loyalty to the emperor. Its ties with Japanese politics were not cut until Japan was defeated in World War II.

Chapter 3
Artistry

During and after the 600s A.D., the Japanese were greatly influenced in their culture and their ways of life by the Chinese. During the T'ang dynasty (618-906), many Japanese went to China to study and to learn. In addition to learning the Chinese system of government administration and the art of writing Chinese ideographs, the Japanese looked into city planning and health facilities. The making of porcelains, ceramics, clothing, utensils of every description, and weapons of war were also studied in great detail. The ideas that the returning Japanese brought home were adapted to fit their needs. As with their government system, whatever the Japanese learned or borrowed was changed and given a distinctively Japanese nature.

ARTS AND LITERATURE

One example is the Horyuji (hoh-RYOO-ji) Monastery which was built in the 600s. It is largely Chinese in form but it has a decidedly Japanese artistic touch. The building is both massive and dignified, colorful and light. It seems a natural part of the landscape. The monastery is built of cypress and camphor wood because the Japanese have great quantities of wood but little stone. It is thought to be one of the oldest existing wooden structures in the world.

From 710 to 794, while the capital was at Nara, the Japanese produced enormous amounts of art that was largely influenced by Buddhism. The statues of Buddha have the charm, grace, and simplicity that are characteristic of Japanese art. The materials used were chiefly wood, clay, and bronze. Toward the close of the Nara period, an anthology of poems was collected called the *Manyoshu*. These light, delicate poems were probably written by members of the small noble class of that period.

anthology: a collection in one book of works by different authors

In 794 the capital was moved to Kyoto (kee-OHT-oh). The years from 795 to 1185 are known as the Heian (HAY-yuhn) period. Heian-kyo is another name for Kyoto. Buddhism and Chinese culture continued to inspire the Japanese during this time.

The court life of the Heian period is well-described in *The Tale of Genji.* This novel was written by Murasaki Shikibu, a lady of the court. Its central character is Prince Genji, the son of the emperor. Besides being a well-told story of the life, loves, and thoughts of the prince, the novel is also a vivid picture of Japanese culture and character.

In painting, form was as important in Japan as in China, just as the way of making characters in Japanese and Chinese writing was important. The Japanese borrowed their form of writing from the Chinese. The characters, or ideographs, were and are made with brush strokes and each character is like a small picture. The influence of this picture-writing can be seen in Japanese paintings, where every stroke and line has meaning.

The Japanese, like other people, have used stories from their history as the subjects of plays, novels, and poetry. Japanese history from the 800s to the 1700s provided writers with many themes.

Between 800 and 1100, control of the government slowly passed from the central administration at Kyoto into the hands of military lords outside the capital. These leaders began to organize private armies. The members of these armies made up a warrior class called samurai (SAM-uh-ry), or those who serve. Between the samurai and the lords they served there grew a tradition and a relationship based on loyalty, courage, obedience, and responsibility. The sword was the symbol of this relationship which forms the basis of much of the art and literature of Japan.

Below is a scene from a kabuki play. Kabuki drama began in Japan in the 1600s and is still popular. It combines singing, dancing, and elaborate costumes.

The warrior Yoritomo founded Japan's first shogunate, a feudal system of military government. The system lasted from the beginning of his rule in 1192 until 1867. This portrait of Yoritomo was painted on a silk scroll during his lifetime.

KAMAKURA SHOGUNATE

The powerful lords and clans fought among themselves for control of Japan. From this struggle the Minamoto clans, under the leadership of Yoritomo, eventually emerged as the most influential. Yoritomo established a feudal military government in Japan called a shogunate (SHOH-guh-nuht). This name comes from the title shogun—meaning barbarian-conquering general—which Yoritomo assumed.

The period which started with his rule is known as the Kamakura (kah-MAHK-uh-rah) shogunate (1192-1333). Kamakura is the site of Yoritomo's capital. The emperor was allowed to keep his throne but the shoguns controlled the actual government of Japan for the next 700 years.

The sculpture of the Kamakura period was vigorous and simple, reflecting the tastes of the military overlords. During this period a monk painted *The Nachi Waterfall,* which is an outstanding example of both the Japanese love of nature and of religion. The life of the times is also represented on picture scrolls, many of which still exist.

It was during this period that Zen Buddhism began to flourish. The simplicity and self-discipline required by Zen appealed to the military. The tea ceremony associated with Zen started at this time.

ASHIKAGA SHOGUNATE

The Kamakura shogunate was succeeded by the Ashikaga (ah-shee-KAH-gah) shogunate (1338-1568). This was a time of much civil strife and destruction. But it was also a time when the arts took on a new vigor and new forms. During this period the No drama developed. It evolved from an ancient dance into a play which told a story through dance, music, and some speaking. But dance remains central to No drama. It is primarily through motion and posture that emotions and ideas are expressed. No is still performed today.

During this time several great Japanese painters were at work. Their paintings, influenced by Chinese painters of the Sung dynasty, were in black and white. Two famous painters of this period were Shubun and Sesshu, both of whom lived during the 1400s. Sesshu's work captures the inner idea of a scene with the fewest possible strokes of the brush. His works leave the viewer with a sense of peace and tranquility. His was an art of stark simplicity. No doubt the simplicity of Zen Buddhism influenced him.

Civil strife continued into the 1500s. Japan was divided among many groups, and each wanted to rule. Three Japanese leaders—Nobunaga, Hideyoshi, and Iyeyasu—were outstanding in this period.

civil strife: arguing or fighting among members of one nation

Nobunaga (noh-boo-nah-gah) was called upon by the emperor to restore order and bring unity to Japan. Before this task was completed, Nobunaga was killed by an enemy. Hideyoshi and Iyeyasu were his two lieutenants. Hideyoshi (hee-de-YOH-shee) had great ability and determination. He took command and completed the unification of Japan.

Hideyoshi then dreamed of conquering China. For the Japanese, the road to China ran through Korea, but the Koreans refused to permit peaceful passage. Hideyoshi was forced to fight his way through. This struggle destroyed his army and his supplies. He died before he could achieve his goal.

TOKUGAWA SHOGUNATE

Hideyoshi had wanted to leave his son in control of Japan. To achieve this, a council was formed to rule in his name and Iyeyasu (eye-yeh-yah-soo) was named chairman. But Iyeyasu did not wish to turn the leadership over to Hideyoshi's son. Instead he had himself appointed by the emperor in 1603 as Shogun of Japan. Thus was founded the Tokugawa (toh-koo-gah-wah) shogunate, which lasted until 1867.

Iyeyasu established his capital at Yedo (YED-oh) which is the present site of Tokyo. To maintain control over the great lords, he required them to keep hostages at the capital. These hostages were relatives or important followers of the lords. They had to live in Yedo but were not held as prisoners. However, the threat to their lives was real and assured the shogun that the lords would not try to seize power. Naturally services had to be supplied for these many lords and their families, and a merchant class arose. The wealth of this merchant class eventually became greater than that of the nobles they served.

Much of the art, recreation, and entertainment of the Tokugawa period centered in a section of Yedo called the Yoshiwara (yoh-shee-wah-rah). The Yoshiwara was a world filled with theaters, actors and actresses, dancers, wrestlers, storytellers, and all the colorful people who make a business of providing pleasure. The people of this world became the characters for plays, novels, poems, and the art called ukiyo-e (oo-kee-oh-YAY). This art pictured scenes from that floating world of pleasure. Ukiyo-e is often translated as floating world.

The kabuki (kuh-BOO-kee), or popular drama, began to develop during the Tokugawa shogunate. At first the actors were women, but later only men played parts. Kabuki dramas are all sight, sound, and color. These lively musical attractions still draw large audiences.

Puppet shows known as bunraku (bun-RAHK-oo)—dramatic, realistic, and wonderfully done—became popular at this time. They took the Japanese into a world of vivid play-acting. The puppets seem to be real people enacting a drama of life, not fiction. Some plays originally written for puppets are also performed by live actors and actresses.

Some painters of the Tokugawa period, such as Hishikawa Moronobu (hee-shee-kah-wah moh-roh-noh-boo), painted the people on

The knights of feudal Japan were called samurai. Stories have been written about them for hundreds of years. The woodblock print above was made during the Tokugawa period. It shows a scene from a kabuki play about a clan rivalry.

the streets, passengers on ferry boats, or whatever they saw that reflected life and action. They especially liked to picture rascals, rowdies, and rogues, and to show what they did and how they looked. Their art was colorful and popular.

In the period of the Tokugawa shogunate, the Japanese began to write short poems called haiku (HY-koo), made up of three lines and 17 syllables. The poems were simple but they frequently suggested more than was actually said. The poet Basho in the 1600s was one of the first to write such poems.

THE ARTS TODAY

In the mid-1800s, Japan was forced to open its doors to the rest of the world. Westerners began arriving with new ideas which the Japanese considered, borrowed what they wished, and then made their own.

The modern Japanese novel is, at least in theory, an offshoot of 19th-century French literary movement called realism. However, where the French novelists wrote of humans affected by historical and social influences, the modern Japanese novel is likely to deal with solitary people. The Japanese novel today stresses aloneness as well as loneliness.

The late Yasunari Kawabata is considered one of Japan's greatest

On this page is a scene from the film Rashomon, *directed by Akira Kurosawa. The story takes place in the 700s. This scene shows a sword fight between a samurai (left) and a bandit.*

227

modern novelists. He won the Nobel Prize for literature in 1968. Kawabata was the teacher of another modern Japanese novelist, Yukio Mishima. Mishima shocked the world with his dramatic ritual suicide in 1970. Many viewed his suicide as a protest against the way postwar Japan had developed.

The traditional haiku is still written but modern poets are also borrowing poetic forms from the West. Western forms are not always suitable, however, because of the nature of the Japanese language. Rhythm and rhyme as we know them do not exist in Japanese poetry.

Various international prizes have been awarded to Japanese films. In 1951 *Rashomon* was the first Japanese film to win a Grand Prix at the Venice Film Festival. In spite of the general excellence of Japanese productions, the film industry has suffered as a result of television. Several thousand movie theaters closed between 1960 and 1970. Nevertheless, Japan continues to produce many films of high dramatic and technical quality.

As long ago as the 1600s, a visiting missionary complained that Japanese music was noise. The strangeness of the music is partly due to the musical scales, which are different from those of the West, and partly because of the instruments used. There are three typical instruments. The samisen is a guitarlike instrument with three strings. The koto is a long instrument with 13 strings that is similar to the zither. The shakuhachi is a clarinetlike instrument made of

Music in Japan takes both modern and traditional forms. One classical Japanese instrument is a bamboo flute called a shakuhachi.

bamboo. None of these instruments produce sounds that are wholly familiar to Western ears.

Gagaku is one of the oldest Japanese musical forms. It combines music and dancing and is based on a type of music introduced from China in the 700s. It is still used at the imperial court, and is occasionally performed in public by the court musicians, all of whom are descendants of generations of court musicians. Many of these musicians are also very fine performers of Western music.

Since the 1870s, Western music has been taught in Japanese schools, beginning in the elementary grades. Today all types of Western music, from Bach to the most modern composers, are performed. Western popular music is also widespread, and the Japanese have groups similar to the Rolling Stones. Western musicals like *Hello Dolly* with all-Japanese casts are also popular.

But the Japanese still enjoy their own classical forms of musical theater like the kabuki. Today Japan is making an effort to preserve traditional musical forms. Composers are writing music within the classical Japanese framework.

The influence of Western culture has been felt in dancing as in the other arts. Many Japanese are ardent ballet-goers. In 1912 a ballet master was brought from Italy to train a Japanese troupe. Ballet is now performed not only by traveling companies from the West but also by all-Japanese groups.

Sports fans in Tokyo can choose from such events as a judo tournament (above left) or a home game of the Tokyo Giants (above). How have East and West influenced each other in sports?

229

Chapter 4
Traditional Society and Social Change

Stone lanterns, pagodas, and TV towers are all part of today's Japan.

For many centuries the Japanese, like other Asians, have thought that the good of family, clan, and group was more important than an individual's personal welfare. Great sacrifices were made in order to preserve these social institutions. But there were benefits. In the traditional system, no one was ever alone. Each person had a place—duties and responsibilities—to his or her family and to society.

Today the life of the Asians, especially the Japanese, is in the process of change. Change is slow, however. In the cities, change may appear rapid and complete. But people do not give up overnight the traditions they have lived by for centuries. They cannot shirk their duties without feeling guilt or without being condemned by other members of their society. Japanese may learn to use Western speech, wear Western clothing, and entertain in a Western way publicly and among Westerners. However, they will also talk, dress, act, and think as Japanese in their homes and among fellow Japanese.

The hold of the past is difficult to shake, but the necessity for change appears inescapable. At present the peoples of all Asia are trying to reach a satisfactory **compromise**. They want to retain from the past those ways they cherish while taking on new ways that are essential for survival.

THE FAMILY

The Japanese have been taught to regard themselves as one large family headed by the father of all—the emperor. Within the family, the Japanese find the whole social pattern of their society. Within the family they learn manners, their role in life, and acceptable behavior toward others. Failures on the part of family members traditionally reflect upon the entire family.

The Japanese family, like the Indian, is a patriarchy. The oldest male is the head of the traditional family and represents the family in all official matters. In the past, marriages were arranged, often by a third party. Today some marriages are still arranged, but the younger generation, especially in cities, demands more freedom of choice.

The Japanese love and want children, especially male children, because the family line is carried on by the male. If there are no sons, a younger son of the husband's brother, or the son of another relative, may be adopted. Sometimes if a couple have a daughter but no son, they may adopt a boy who then marries their daughter. He gives up his family name and takes the name of his adopted parents. Some of Japan's great business firms are headed by men who were adopted sons. Of course, the adopted son is chosen very carefully. The continuation of the family is an extremely important matter.

JAPANESE WOMEN

For more than a thousand years, Japanese women were taught that they existed to serve men. But it was not always like this. During the early period of Japan's history, women had the same rights and privileges as men. They were companions rather than subordinates. In ancient Japan women were chiefs of clans, and the Empress Jingu ruled Japan when it invaded Korea. In those days women fought, governed, and led armies into battle.

Around the 500s A.D., the position of women began to change. Japanese women began to be taught that their primary virtues were obedience, devotion to duty, patience, good nature, and self-sacrifice.

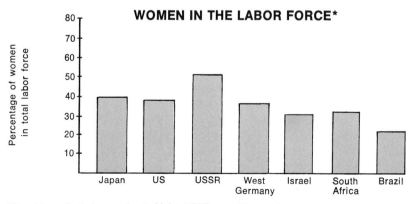

*Countries selected according to highest GNP per culture region.
Source: Based on *Year Book of Labour Statistics 1974*, International Labour Office, Geneva, 1974

231

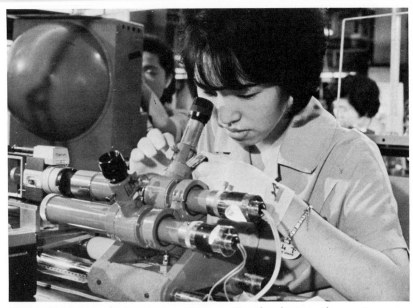

This technician works in a camera factory. Use the chart on the previous page to learn the size of the female labor force in Japan.

Public office and a career outside the home were not for them. These were the privileges and rights of men. A woman's goal in life was to be a good wife and mother. To this end she was trained in the practical matters of the household and was taught the proper way of serving food, of entering rooms, and of greeting guests.

While middle- and upper-class women maintained their dependent position, even with very close male relatives, daughters of farmers lived a different life. They learned to do farm work and helped in the planting and harvesting of crops. Farm women were allowed a greater freedom of association with men because their labor brought them into closer and necessary contact. But the Japanese ideal remained that of delicate, dependent woman.

With the opening of Japan to outside influences in the 1800s, the position of women in society began to improve. After the Meiji (MAY-jee) Restoration in 1868 when the shoguns were removed from power, women were permitted to receive some formal education. But this was intended chiefly to make them better wives and mothers.

However, the Meiji Restoration established a new economy in Japan and the services of women became necessary to the labor force. By the mid-1930s Japanese women were found in many occupations. They became telephone operators, bus attendants, gas station attendants, typists, stenographers, and factory workers. But still the Japanese tried to keep women in their traditional social role. Those who worked in factories, for example, were rarely permitted outside their walls.

Management took the place of parents. Factory women were expected to save their money for a dowry. They were encouraged to use their spare time in preparing trousseaus. The management offered the women classes in traditional subjects which would prepare them to be homemakers. It was impossible, however, to prevent all change.

As early as 1925, a **league** for women's **suffrage** had begun to demand the vote, but Japanese military leaders helped defeat the movement. By the end of World War II, many Japanese women had held jobs outside the home and the experience changed them. They realized that they were able to assume positions of responsibility and equality in society.

With the acceptance of a new **constitution** in 1946 and a revised civil code in 1947, the legal and actual status of Japanese women changed significantly. Legally they were equal to men. The right to vote, to own property, to hold political office, and to seek divorce were theirs. Today Japanese girls must be educated and often study in the same schools as boys. More and more women are attending colleges and universities. Many of them are taking up professional and political careers.

Increasing industrialization and **urbanization** are affecting the size and relationships within families, too. Japanese families are smaller. In cities, particularly, husband and wife live as a nuclear family. In this smaller family unit, the wife is no longer directly and immediately subject to her mother-in-law and the elders of the larger family. By the 1970s four out of every ten working women were married. More and more Japanese women have had to face the problem of combining outside work with family responsibilities.

But much of the past remains. Traditional virtues and customs are still admired and praised. Although the Japanese woman may wear a dress, she retains many kimono manners and traits. Certain traditional patterns of life must be followed if she wishes to keep her status as a good woman, wife, and mother. Japanese women are becoming **modernized**, but they are a blend of their past and their present.

SOCIAL AND ENVIRONMENTAL PROBLEMS

Japan is one of the great industrial nations of the world. The products of Japanese skill and technology are found throughout the world, and their industry continues to grow at a rapid rate. But modernization and industrialization have also brought problems which the Japanese must solve if their future is to remain bright.

Wherever there are areas of industrialization there is growing pollution. The Japanese use the word kogai to cover all environmental pollution and resulting side effects. Kogai is a much-used term in modern Japan.

Today, most Japanese live in cities. Along Japan's coastlines, the

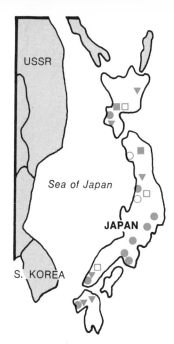

Natural Resources

- ⬤ **Industrial**
- ▼ **Coal**
- ■ **Iron**
- ○ **Oil**
- ☐ **Minerals**

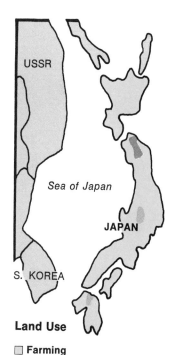

Land Use

- ☐ **Farming**
- ▨ **Grazing**
- ■ **Nonproductive**

scene is one of continuous urban sprawl. This growth of cities and towns has resulted in overpopulation and a housing shortage in some areas.

Japan has taken effective action to combat the problems of overpopulation. The birthrate has declined in recent years. However, because of excellent medical services, increased life span, adequate diet, and improved health education among other reasons, the population continues to increase. But if present trends continue, the population may start to decline after the 1990s.

Chapter 5
Modern Japan

The Japanese system of government has had a long and interesting development. The emperor was central to the political life and thought of the Japanese for most of their history. Today Japan has a representative government. But Japanese culture was shaped during the 1,500 years when the emperor was considered divine.

PUPPET MASTERS

The emperor reigned, but he rarely ruled. Power was exercised in the name of the emperor by some person or group who ruled from behind the throne. This political fact began in the 600s A.D. with the Fujiwara (foo-jee-WAH-rah) family.

To control the emperor, the Fujiwara family married him to a Fujiwara girl. After he had produced sons, they forced him to give up the throne. The head of the Fujiwara family then took the office of **regent** and ruled during the youth of the new emperor. This process was repeated when the young emperor became old enough to father sons.

The Fujiwara family assumed the power of appointing the highest officials of the land, too. As time passed, this power became hereditary to their family. The shoguns—the feudal miliatry **dictators** who succeeded the Fujiwara—continued this policy of ruling from behind the throne. The institution of the emperor was never abolished, but the real rulers were the shoguns. There were even instances of shoguns becoming puppets in the hands of someone behind them.

MILITARY IDEALS From 1192 with the Kamakura shogunate until 1867 when the shogunate system ended, shoguns were supported and assisted by strong military lords. These lords were, in turn, supported and upheld by samurai. Over the years a certain formal relationship developed between the samurai and their lords. Gradually it became an expected pattern of behavior for all Japanese soldiers.

During the Tokugawa shogunate, the code of this relationship was made the basic guide for the lives of all Japanese whether or not they were soldiers. The ideals and virtues of the samurai became the ideals and virtues of all. In the Japanese language there is a term which is used to describe the proper behavior of military men. This term is Bushido (BUSH-ee-doh), which means the way of the warrior.

The virtues of courage and obedience marked Bushido. To lack courage was to lose respect in one's own eyes and in those of one's peers. Superiors had to be obeyed promptly and without doubt or question. Loyalty was valued above all else. The loyalty of a vassal to his lord was more important than all other kinds.

Bushido emphasized the virtues of self-discipline, self-conquest, and self-restraint. Everything should be done in moderation. The ideal man was restrained and touched with simplicity. Bushido included a love of nature. This love of nature was closely related to a deep love for the land. To the Japanese, the wonder of nature and the land of Japan are almost inseparable.

All these teachings of Bushido are part of what the Japanese refer to as their spirit. These teachings supported and strengthened the Tokugawa shogunate. They have in many ways continued to underlie the thinking of the Japanese to the present.

FROM ISOLATION TO EXPANSION

It was not until the Tokugawa shogunate was overthrown in 1867 that Japan began changing into a centralized, outward-looking modern

This silk screen shows a Portuguese ship stopping at a Japanese port. The Tokugawa shoguns decided that Westerners were bringing dangerous ideas into their country. They closed Japan to the West for more than 200 years. What effects do you think this had on Japan? on the West?

235

state. Until that time, the Tokugawas had maintained an attitude of isolationism along with their system of feudalism. For over 200 years Japan had been cut off from much of the world.

The Tokugawa shoguns had feared that any change in the ways of Japanese thinking and action might undermine their authority. Change might come from inside the country, but change most certainly would come from outside. In the 1500s, Westerners had brought different ideas. To prevent any more alien thinking from entering the country, the Tokugawas sealed off Japan. Only one Dutch ship a year and a few Chinese traders were permitted to enter. Even Japanese who were then abroad could not return. If they did, and were discovered, they were killed.

It is impossible, however, to keep a nation completely isolated from the outside world. And it is impossible to prevent the evolution of social, economic, and political change within a country.

The Tokugawas themselves were unknowingly responsible for some of the changes. They established their center at Yedo and forced people to live there. A merchant class arose. As commerce increased, the merchants began to grow rich. The social structure of Japan began to change. The once-powerful feudal lords often found themselves without money and jobs. They could not keep their armies. Their former soldiers roamed about the country, leaderless and penniless. There was a feeling of discontent and an increasing desire for change among many of the samurai. Then Commodore Matthew Perry sailed his U.S. warship into Tokyo Bay in 1853–54.

After Perry's display of power had forced the weak Tokugawa government to sign a treaty, the warships of other Western nations began to come to Japan. The Tokugawa rulers still tried to maintain the isolation of Japan. But this proved to be impossible. When incidents occurred, the Westerners bombarded Japanese cities with their guns. The Japanese found themselves powerless. The samurai decided to learn from those who had humiliated them.

A group of samurai removed the Tokugawa shogun and brought the emperor Meiji to Yedo. This city was renamed Tokyo meaning eastern capital. The move to Tokyo returned the emperor to the center of the country's power.

The reformers emphasized the divinity of the emperor and claimed that the shogun had stolen his position. The government was centralized by forcing all the great lords to deed their lands to it. The country was then divided into large areas similar to states or counties and were governed by officials appointed by the government. The samurai were stripped of their special privileges. All young men were subject to military service. A modern army and navy were set up.

At the same time the reformers started a detailed and systematic study of Western technology, institutions, and science. They adopted a constitution based on that of Germany. Their courts were modeled on those of France. They established a civil service. A banking system was set up along Western lines. Japan began to industrialize. In a

Matthew Perry—shown here in a Japanese print—forced the Tokugawa shogunate to open Japan to the West. Why was he able to do this?

few years Japan, on the surface, had many Western features. These were real features, but they covered a core of basic ideas and traditions that remained very Japanese.

Like the Fujiwara and the shoguns, the samurai ruled from behind the emperor. They were later joined by business interests and bureaucrats. Thus a combination of three groups began to rule Japan: military, bureaucrats, and big business. The militarists were dominant among the three. But all of them were powerful. Sometimes they acted as controls on each other.

Slowly Japanese society began to change. Universal education for both sexes was made compulsory for six years. The basic purpose was not so much to improve the individual for the person's own sake. It was to make the person more useful in the service of the state. In schools pupils were taught the traditional Japanese virtues of obedience, loyalty, and submission to authority.

Japan had political parties, but the relationship between party leaders and their followers was like the one that had existed between lords and their vassals. Personal relations were more important than law or principle.

By the late 1800s, the Japanese were beginning to make their power felt in Asia. In 1895 they defeated the Chinese in war. In 1904-05

Japanese Empire: 1895-1942
☐ **Japan Proper**
— **Extent of Conquest by 1942**

237

Above: the city of Hiroshima after the first explosion of an atomic bomb on August 6, 1945. The blast was so powerful that it burned or poisoned persons four kilometers (2.5 miles) away. People still die from its aftereffects.

they defeated Russia. By 1910 they had incorporated Korea into their empire. By the 1930s they had added great areas of Chinese land to their ever-expanding territory. They dreamed of an empire which would embrace most of East and Southeast Asia.

WORLD WAR II

On December 7, 1941, the Japanese formally launched their great expansionist move by bombing the U.S. naval base at Pearl Harbor in Hawaii. During the first years of the war, the Japanese were very successful. Japanese troops conquered the Philippines. They occupied Hong Kong and much of China, Burma, Singapore, Malaya, French Indochina, Indonesia, and Borneo. They even penetrated the eastern borders of British India.

But their control of these lands was brief. The U.S., assisted by allies from Asia and the West, began to push the Japanese back. Resistance was stubborn. Japanese soldiers had been well-trained in the virtues of Bushido. But they were pushed back island by island until Japan itself was threatened.

The Japanese might have continued to fight except for the development and use of the atomic bomb by the U.S. This bomb was used on the cities of Hiroshima (hir-uh-SHEE-muh) and Nagasaki (nah-gah-SAHK-ee). In a brief moment the A-bomb wiped out most of the life, movement, and structures of great areas of these cities. The will of the Japanese to continue the war was shattered. They asked for peace and surrendered unconditionally to the U.S. on August 14, 1945.

THE NEWER JAPAN

U.S. military forces occupied Japan. Under the command of General Douglas MacArthur, they began a reorganization of the political, economic, and social life of the Japanese. The emperor was persuaded to tell his subjects that he was a symbol rather than a god. State Shinto, which supported the divine-emperor system, was abolished. The Japanese were taught that they were important as individuals, not merely because they were members of a family-state. They were informed that they had certain rights and privileges which were a part of their human nature. Equality before the law was established to protect their rights. These rights could not be done away with at the whim of a ruler or rulers.

Today Japan is one of the world's major industrial nations. Its automobiles, electronic equipment, steel, and textiles are sold around the world.

All these democratic provisions were incorporated into a written constitution. A broad parliamentary form of government was established, with a prime minister and a legislative body consisting of an upper and lower house of representatives. The members of these two houses of parliament are elected by the people. Political parties developed which represent all viewpoints from liberal-democratic to communist.

Since the 1950s, Japan has had a phenomenal rate of economic growth. Between 1960 and 1970, alone, the Japanese gross national product (GNP) rose from around $45 billion to over $166 billion. Japan is the world's largest shipbuilder and one of the major producers of steel and automobiles.

Major industries include electronic equipment (radios and television sets, etc.) and textiles. Japanese investments in other countries include automobile assembly plants in Thailand, South Africa, and Mexico. Japanese foreign interests also range from a pulp mill in Alaska to iron mines in Brazil. The Japanese have also purchased large amounts of real estate in Hawaii and other parts of the world.

Japan is the world's leading shipbuilder. Use the map in Chapter 4 to relate the development of Japan's industry to its natural resources.

Summing Up the Unit

Social Studies Vocabulary

Define: suffrage; constitution; modernization; urbanization

People

Identify: Ainu; Yayoi; Yamato clan; Yoritomo; Iyeyasu; Meiji; Perry; MacArthur

Words

Identify: paddy; Sect, State Shinto; Zen Buddhism; samurai; shogunate; ukiyo-e; kabuki; bunraku; haiku; gagaku; kogai; Bushido

Questions

1. What do paddies tell about the Yayoi people?
2. What organization became the basis of Japanese social and cultural life for centuries?
3. a. Why must the two basic books of Shinto be read carefully? b. What is the Shinto attitude toward cleanliness?
4. a. What changes did the Japanese make in the form of government they borrowed from the Chinese? b. How did Chinese ideas affect Shinto? c. Why was there a conflict between Buddhism and Shinto?
5. How is the influence of ideographs seen in Japanese painting?
6. Describe the relationship between the samurai and the lords they served.
7. Why did Zen Buddhism appeal to the Japanese military class?
8. In No drama how are emotions and ideas expressed?
9. a. How did Iyeyasu control the great lords? b. What was an unexpected result of his method?
10. How are Asians today trying to cope with the need for change in their lives?
11. Describe the traditional Japanese family.
12. a. What impact have industrialization and urbanization had on the Japanese family? b. on Japanese women?
13. Where does Japan's economy rank among world nations?
14. a. Prior to 1867 what two groups supported the shoguns? b. What methods were used to overthrow the shogunate?
15. a. After the Meiji Restoration, what three groups combined to rule Japan? b. What changes did they bring about? c. Describe the relationship of political party leaders to party members.
16. How and when did the Japanese launch their expansionist move?

Discussion Topics

1. Simplicity and restraint are characteristics of Japanese arts. Do you think this traditional aspect of Japanese culture can withstand the impact of industrialization and Westernization? Why or why not?
2. As Japan has built a modern economy, the role of women has changed some, but not entirely. Which do you think is a stronger influence on people's lives: custom and tradition, or economic necessity?
3. Japan has had a phenomenal rate of economic growth. How much of this has been because of Japan's location and natural resources, or because of foreign aid? (See maps in this unit.)
4. Traditional society is changing in India, China, and Japan. Which country do you think has changed the most? Which has changed the least? What evidence supports your answers? What causes of change are similar in India, China, and Japan? How can you account for differences in the rate of change in one country compared with another? Is it reasonable to compare change in different countries?

Project Ideas

1. Make a chart showing the Japanese shogunates in chronological order. Give the major events and artistic accomplishments of each period.
2. Using outside resources, write a brief report on one of the following: the Russo-Japanese war; Japanese conquests in World War II; Bushido and the samurai; industrialization.
3. Make a poster showing elements of Japanese culture—traditional and modern.
4. Write a haiku.
5. Paint a picture in the style of Japanese art.

Unit V

Southeast Asia

A Burmese artist created this cheerful religious portrait on a lacquer tray. Why do you think religion appears in art all over the world?

Southeast Asia is made up of the modern nations of Burma, Thailand, Cambodia, Laos, Vietnam, Malaysia, Singapore, Indonesia, and the Philippines. They spread down a **peninsula** and out into the sea. To the north of the peninsula are India and China, to the west the Indian Ocean, and to the east and south the Pacific Ocean. The islands are separated from each other and from the mainland by several seas and straits. At one time the islands may have been connected to the mainland by **land bridges**.

The political development of Southeast Asia, as it relates to the West, has been increasingly in the news since World War II. However, little attention is usually given to the peoples of this region, their history, their cultural development, and social structure.

242

In modern times the Japanese, the Chinese, and other Asians have borrowed many ideas from Westerners. In borrowing an idea or a product of modern technology, the Asians have also borrowed the words or names used to describe these ideas and products. This spread of ideas and words is called **cultural diffusion**. There seems to be evidence that such a diffusion of knowledge flowed in ancient times from Southeast Asia to other parts of Asia and to Africa.

Some anthropologists, in studying Asian languages, have found that the Chinese language contains a number of words that were originally part of Southeast Asian languages. For example, Southeast Asian words for plow, seed, kiln, ax, pottery, boat, and iron were brought into the Chinese language in ancient times. The borrowing of a word usually means the borrowing of the thing named by that word. Thus, some scholars now believe that the Chinese first learned about such things as plows, seeds, and kilns for baking pottery from the Southeast Asians.

Until recent years it was generally believed that people in the Middle East were the first to develop agriculture around 10,000 B.C. However, some scholars now think that a **prehistoric** people, the Hoabinhians (HWAH-BIN-ee-uhns), in Southeast Asia were among the first to cultivate plants.

The Hoabinhian culture takes its name from the village of Hoa Binh (HWAH BIN) in Vietnam. **Sites** with similar types of artifacts have been found in Thailand, Malaysia, and Sumatra (part of Indonesia). All these sites and the culture revealed by them are called Hoabinhian.

Evidence indicates that as early as 15,000 B.C., the Hoabinhian people may have begun to domesticate wild plants. In addition, they appear to have been making pottery before 10,000 B.C. By 4000 B.C. the Hoabinhians had invented a type of outrigger canoe. They were eating cultivated rice and making copper tools by 3500 B.C. Between 3000 and 2500 B.C., they were working with bronze. It is possible that the Hoabinhian culture was spread to places as far away as the Philippines and Africa. There is evidence that Hoabinhian crops, agricultural techniques, and pottery may have been carried to Japan, Taiwan, and the Philippines as early as 3000 to 2000 B.C.

Around the first century A.D., some Southeast Asians possibly sailed to the island of Malagasy off the east coast of Africa. Through this contact, the Africans of the forest may have learned of crops that were suitable for their soil and climate. It is quite possible that trade contacts existed between the Southeast Asians and the people of the Middle East and Mediterranean regions.

This reconstruction of the past by anthropologists and archaeologists may be supported more strongly as new evidence is found. If so, certain cultural achievements in the Middle East, Africa, and other parts of Asia will be credited to cultural diffusion by Southeast Asians.

Chapter 1
Spread of
a Culture—
The
Hoabinhians

cultivated: crops that are seeded, cared for, and harvested (as opposed to plants that grow wild)

Chapter 2
Religious Beliefs

Originally the Southeast Asians sought the divine in nature. This form of religion is animism. Animists find spirits, sometimes evil, in objects such as trees, stones, mountains, or rivers. Anthropologists have pointed out that animists do not worship these objects. The objects are only symbols of spiritual principles. They represent ideas of good or evil.

The Laotian animists call natural spirits phi. Some spirits are said to cause disease, suffering and even death. Other spirits are good. Almost every Thai village has a spirit guardian, represented in many forms. The Burmese make their offerings to the nat, which is the name they give the spirit whose help they are seeking. Indonesians are careful to try to please the spirits of the volcano, the sea, and the river. The influence of these ancient spirits lingers, though overlaid with the teachings of Hinduism, Buddhism, Islam, and Christianity.

Indian traders brought Hinduism and Buddhism to Southeast Asia. Hinduism did not last, at least not in its pure form; but Buddhism did. By the end of the 500s A.D., Buddhism had become a powerful force in Thailand, Burma, Cambodia, and Sri Lanka. In these lands the people erected imposing stupas and temples. The stories of Buddha's previous lives are carved on the walls, doors, and ceilings. In these lands there are also some magnificent representations of Buddha teaching and meditating. Some of these statues are encrusted with emeralds and placed in temples decorated with gold leaf. In the form called Theravada, Buddhism is today the religion of the majority of people of these countries.

Buddhist shrines with golden domes rise above the countryside in Burma.

Mahayana Buddhism, the more merciful belief, is the Buddhism of the Vietnamese. This is because the Vietnamese received their religious and philosophical thought from the Chinese. Many Vietnamese have also embraced Roman Catholicism, which was brought to them by French missionaries. Most of the Filipinos are also Catholics, the result of the efforts of Spanish priests and missionaries; but a number of them are still animists. In Malaysia, Indonesia, and southern parts of the Philippines, the people are Muslims.

Most of the Southeast Asian nations are located on a peninsula which is bordered by the South China Sea, the Bay of Bengal, and the Gulf of Siam. Today the modern states of Burma, Thailand, Cambodia, Laos, Vietnam, and part of Malaysia occupy the mainland. (East Malaysia is on the northern coast of the island of Borneo.) These countries are home to more than 130 million Southeast Asians.

Chapter 3 Mainland Nations

BURMA: THE BURMESE

The Mon people came to Burma more than 3,000 years ago. They came from the area where China and Tibet meet, and they settled on lands along the Irrawaddy River in what is now lower Burma. There they mixed with unknown peoples who had come before them. After the Mon, other peoples also from the China-Tibet border migrated into the area. They pushed each other down into the broad lowlands of lower Burma or into the mountains around the valleys and plains. Even before the first century A.D., there was a mixing of peoples and a fighting over land in Burma.

Around this time, Indian traders began coming to the region. From these traders the people began to learn about the material and spiritual advances of the Indians. Their society and government became more complex. By the 400s, various kingdoms had arisen in lower Burma.

But the migrations from the north had not ended. A people called Burmans moved into central Burma around the beginning of the 700s. They founded a kingdom called Pagan. Gradually the Burmans extended their political control over most of central and lower Burma. They were influenced by the Mon people to the south, who passed along to them a knowledge of writing and the Buddhist religion. The Burmans began to think of themselves as chosen defenders of Buddhism.

While the Burmans were fashioning their culture, they were being pressed by more people from the north. These were the Thai (TY), mostly from southwestern China who were being pressured by the Chinese. The Shan, a branch of the Thai people, set up a state north of Pagan called the kingdom of Ava. The Shan were gradually drawn to the ways and thinking of the Burmans to the south. The Burmans in turn were influencing and being influenced by the culture of the

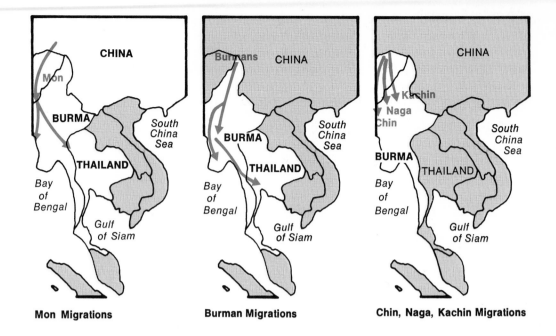

Mon Migrations   **Burman Migrations**   **Chin, Naga, Kachin Migrations**

kingdom of Pegu to their south. The people of Pegu were still much under the influence of Indian civilization.

Throughout the next centuries, there was a continual merging and mixing of people and ideas. Both the people, mostly from Tibet and China, and the ideas, mostly Indian, were changing in the process. In the valleys and on the plains of Burma the Burmese people emerged.

There was also movement in the mountains surrounding the plains. The Chin, Kachin (kuh-CHIN), and Naga (NAH-guh)—all from lands bordering Tibet—occupied parts of the Burmese mountains. These peoples and their ideas were to become a part of the nation now called Burma.

In the early 1800s, the British in their drive to build an empire took over the administration and control of Burma. They held power until 1948, when Burma obtained its independence. After many centuries the blending of peoples and cultures was still not complete. Rival peoples rebelled. This rebellion as well as Burmese Communist activity caused the military to take over the government in 1954 and again in 1962. Since then the government has followed a policy of encouraging patriotism and socialism. Industry and trade were taken away from Indian and Chinese business people and nationalized.

THAILAND: THE THAIS

Thailand (formerly called Siam) takes its name from the Thai people who migrated there from southwestern China. The Thais had been exposed for centuries to the military power and culture of the Chinese to the north of them. Perhaps they had also received some knowledge of Indian civilization from those south and west of their homeland. Between 600 and 700 A.D., they organized the state of Nanchao in Yunnan, China. This state was overrun by Chinese armies around 1000. Finally, after 1200, it was conquered by the Mongols and made part of Kublai Khan's empire.

The Thais had been gradually moving southward even before their Chinese state was conquered. It is thought that the Thais began moving into what is modern Thailand during the 800s A.D. They mixed with the Khmer (kuh-MER) who were already there. These people were to move out and become the ancestors of the Cambodians. At first the Thais gave allegiance to the Khmers and were even soldiers in their armies.

But as the Thais became stronger and more numerous, they began to compete with the Khmers. Then when the Mongols defeated them, another great wave of Thais came out of southwestern China. The newcomers swelled the numbers of Thais struggling with the Khmers. They set up a capital at Sukhothai (soo-koh-TY) in north-central Thailand. In Thai history the period from about 1250 to 1350 is known as the Sukhothai era.

The Thais continued to move southward during this time. Around 1350 they moved their capital to Ayutthaya. In 1767, the Burmese

These Thai people are using sieves to fish for small shellfish in the Mekong River. The Mekong is Southeast Asia's longest river and a source of food for many people. Trace this river on a map.

247

Thai Migrations

destroyed it during one of their invasions. Bangkok became and remains the capital.

During the centuries they were moving southward, and later, the Thais changed in many ways. They took their written language and some political ideas from the Khmers. They intermarried with the Khmers and the Mon people who had also spread into the area. The Thais became Buddhists.

From about the 1600s to the 1800s the Thais were able to play the Western powers, particularly France and England, against each other. Thus they escaped the colonial nets of the Europeans which had caught so many of their neighbors. But they did not escape the influence of Chinese immigrants. Many Chinese came to trade during this period and on into the 1900s.

In this century, the Thais have tried to make their government more democratic, at least formally. In 1932 the king gave up absolute power and a constitutional and **limited monarchy** was established. Actually, the military governed. Since World War II, outside forces—both U.S. and Communist—as well as factions within Thailand have kept the military powerful and the country at unrest. In 1973 a student rebellion unseated the ruling military group and installed a mostly civilian government. The military, however, keeps its power unofficially.

CAMBODIA: THE CAMBODIANS

The Cambodians are descendants of the Khmers. Even before the Khmers, there had been various peoples living in the present lands of Thailand, Cambodia, and Vietnam. Indian traders had also established trading posts in the area. Around the first century A.D., these traders helped to form a state in southern Cambodia known as Funan. Eventually the state spread to the coasts of the Gulf of Siam and the South China Sea. Funan was based chiefly upon sea and river communications. It did not have a powerful government and was held together partly because its people shared the Hindu and Buddhist religions.

To the north of Funan the Khmers—we do not know where they originated—founded the Chenla state. This grew into the great Khmer empire. Between 600 and 1200, the Khmers enlarged their territory and mixed with a number of peoples. They combined Hindu, Buddhist, Chinese, and native cultures with their own. The peak of their development was reached in the 1100s and 1200s. By that time the Khmer empire, with its capital at Angkor, had long since taken over the areas controlled by Funan.

The Khmers had a written language and passed along their alphabet to the Thais. They built reservoirs, stone-surfaced roads, and temples that are wonders of architecture. They made tiles of lead, and everywhere their capital city was adorned with sculpture. The Khmers built

Khmer Migrations

over a hundred hospitals to care for the sick. The Khmers were also remarkable astronomers.

Khmer society was headed by nobles and priests whose positions were based on Hindu and Buddhist teachings. Next were the free middle and lower classes. At the bottom were many slaves. Agriculture was highly developed. The Khmers grew rice and a variety of fruits and vegetables.

But the Khmer empire faded away. It was gradually reduced to about the size of modern Cambodia. A series of wars with the Thai and the Vietnamese, disease, and perhaps bad leadership among other reasons might have caused its decline. In 1432 the capital was moved from Angkor to the neighborhood of Phnom Penh (puh-NAHM PEN), which is the present capital of Cambodia.

The French ended the Khmer empire in 1863 by making Cambodia a French **protectorate**. Politically Cambodia remained associated with the French until it declared itself independent in 1953. During their period as a protectorate, the Cambodians learned the French language, and many of them developed an appreciation for French customs, literature, and culture. But the Cambodians also kept their **national identity** in terms of their religion, customs, and political tendencies.

From 1955 until 1970 Prince Norodom Sihanouk ruled the country. Although officially a **neutral** nation, Cambodia became involved in war when the North Vietnamese used it as a staging area for attacks against South Vietnam. In 1970 Sihanouk was overthrown, and the **monarchy** was abolished. Lon Nol became head of state. Fighting between progovernment forces and Communist **guerrillas** called Khmer Rouge broke out. In April 1975 Lon Nol fled and within weeks the government surrendered to the Khmer Rouge.

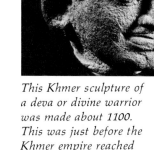

This Khmer sculpture of a deva or divine warrior was made about 1100. This was just before the Khmer empire reached its peak in Cambodia.

LAOS: THE LAOTIANS

The Lao people are of the same family as the Shans of Burma and the Thais. Much of Laotian history is based on **oral tradition**. Perhaps the Lao people started their slow occupation of the land of Laos (LAH-ohs) during the 800s A.D. They gradually overcame the peoples who had come before them into this rough and rugged land. The Lao called these earlier arrivals Kha, which means slave. The land in which the Lao settled was also under Khmer rule and for a time the Lao lived peacefully under them. As Khmer power weakened, however, the Lao assumed more and more control.

During the 1300s a state called Lan Xang—the kingdom of a million elephants—was founded by Fa Ngum. Legend says that there were over 20 earlier rulers, but written records begin with Fa Ngum. He was a great warrior who spent much of his time enlarging the boundaries of Laos. He also made Theravada Buddhism the official religion of the state. But the people tired of his warlike ways, and in 1373 his throne was given to his son, Sam Sen Thai. He was

249

more inclined to peaceful ways and more concerned with the administration of the kingdom.

Succeeding kings in the 1400s and 1500s were preoccupied with defending their land against neighboring people. In the 1700s and 1800s the Laotians split among themselves. Independent tribes and kingdoms dotted the country. The history of that time is one of desperate struggles against the Chinese, the Vietnamese, the Burmese, and the Thais, all of whom tried to take parts of Laos for themselves.

Under French protection in the latter part of the 1800s, Laos enjoyed a period of peace until the end of World War II. Then the Laotians were again divided among themselves by the issues of nationalism, communism, and neutrality. The interested world powers agreed to neutralize Laos in 1962 and set up a coalition government. Fighting between government forces and the Communist Pathet Lao broke out the following year. The conflict continued throughout the Vietnam War. In 1975 the Pathet Lao took control of the government.

Vietnamese Migrations

VIETNAM: THE VIETNAMESE

While the culture of the Burmese, Thais, and Cambodians was heavily influenced by the Indians, the culture of the Vietnamese was strongly influenced by the Chinese. Several years before the Christian era, the Vietnamese migrated—perhaps by force—from southern China to the area around the Red River known as Tongking. This region is now the heartland of northern Vietnam. Between 200 and 100 B.C., the Chinese made this region a part of the Han empire.

Vietnamese political, social, and cultural patterns evolved during this period of Chinese control. Confucianism, the dominant philosophy in China, shaped much of the political and social behavior of the Vietnamese. They accepted Confucian teachings concerning the roles of individuals within family and society. They also accepted the Mahayana Buddhism of China along with some Chinese Taoist ideas and practices. At the same time they kept some of their original animistic beliefs and customs.

Although the Vietnamese accepted many Chinese cultural contributions, they never truly accepted Chinese rule. Throughout the thousand years of Chinese domination, there was continuous friction and even violence between Vietnamese and Chinese. Finally, the Vietnamese drove out the Chinese in 938. But in the Asian tradition of the cultured person, they saved the face of the Chinese. The Vietnamese immediately sent a mission to pay **tribute** to the emperor. From the viewpoint of the Chinese, the payment of tribute was an acknowledgment that China still ruled the area. Thus Chinese honor was preserved, and the Vietnamese obtained self-government.

The rulers of China never really accepted Vietnam's independence.

Kublai Khan, the Mongol ruler of China, sent an army to Vietnam during the 1200s but his forces were defeated. In the 1400s a strong Chinese army was again defeated by the Vietnamese. In each instance the Vietnamese sent envoys to the Chinese capital with soft words and apologies for any inconvenience they had caused. At various times the Chinese repeated their claim to rule Vietnam by demanding payment of tribute.

After they had broken the hold of China on them, the Vietnamese slowly began to conquer their way southward along the coast. The Vietnamese continued south into the Mekong Delta area. That area was then held by the Khmers. Within a short time the Vietnamese took over this southernmost part of Vietnam. The Khmer revolted occasionally, but never successfully.

The Vietnamese have not only fought with their neighbors, but also among themselves. During the 1600s the land was divided into three kingdoms. These kingdoms warred among themselves for over a century. The king of Annam, with the help of the French, finally became the emperor of Vietnam in 1801. Throughout the 1800s the French nibbled away at portions of Vietnam and other areas of Southeast Asia. By 1877 the French had joined most of Vietnam and Cambodia into the Indochinese Union under their control.

During World War II, the Japanese occupied Vietnam. During the occupation, the Communist leader, Ho Chi Minh (HOH CHEE MIN), organized the Viet Minh, League for the Independence of Vietnam, in China. After the Japanese surrendered in 1945, Ho Chi Minh returned to Vietnam, and from Hanoi proclaimed the Democratic Republic of Vietnam. Eventually the French agreed to recognize Vietnam as a free state within the French Union, but fighting broke out between the Viet Minh and the French. The French Indochinese War began in 1946.

After a succession of military losses, the French forces were defeated in 1954. At a multination conference in Geneva that year it was agreed to partition Vietnam temporarily into North and South Vietnam. A Communist government headed by Ho Chi Minh would rule in the North—the Democratic Republic of Vietnam. A government headed by Ngo Dinh Diem came to power in the South—the Republic of Vietnam. Diem, supported by the U.S., refused to participate in the elections of 1956. These elections were intended to provide a single government for both parts of Vietnam. Diem feared that the people would elect Ho Chi Minh and thus make all of Vietnam into a Communist country. In 1957 Communist guerrilla activity began in the South.

During the Vietnam War, the USSR and China sent money and equipment to North Vietnam. The U.S. sent money, supplies, and soldiers to South Vietnam. This 1967 Air Force photo shows U.S. bombs dropping on North Vietnam.

The Vietnamese people were at war almost continuously from 1946 to 1975. This woman's home was destroyed by a North Vietnamese rocket attack on the South Vietnamese capital city of Saigon.

By the 1960s this had escalated into a full-scale civil war. The USSR, China, and other Communist nations supported the North Vietnamese and the Viet Cong guerrillas. The U.S. supported the South Vietnamese government. It provided supplies of all kinds and gradually built up a large U.S. military force in the country. In 1973 an uneasy **truce** was negotiated. Following this truce U.S. forces were withdrawn. Fighting continued. Then, in 1975, the Saigon government surrendered to the Viet Cong and North Vietnamese. All of Vietnam then came under the direction of leaders who professed the same philosophy of communism.

Chapter 4
Part Island, Part Mainland— Malaysia

Malays and Chinese make up the bulk of the population of Malaysia. Some of the Malays have been in Malaysia since prehistoric times. At various times other Malays migrated from Sumatra and Java in Indonesia. They were joined by migrating Chinese and Indians.

Around 2,000 years ago, Indian traders—those familiar faces in Southeast Asia—stopped off in Malaysia on trading trips to Burma, Thailand, and Indonesia. Some of the traders settled in Malaysia and married into Malay families. An Indian-Malay upper class developed. Priests followed the traders and introduced Hinduism and Buddhism into the land. Then during the 1100s or perhaps slightly earlier, other Indians came, and Arabs too. These were followers of Islam. Gradually the Malays became Muslims and have remained Muslims.

Over the centuries, small states headed by rulers called sultans developed in Malaysia. Some of them paid tribute to the Chinese emperors and relied upon them for protection. Some sultans acknowledged the rule of empires based in Sumatra and Java in Indonesia. The strongest of these was the Majapahit (MAH-jah-PAH-hit) empire in Java. During the 1500s the Muslim sultans of Malaysia, aided by Muslim Indians and Arabs, destroyed this empire. After that the Muslim sultans took over more control of Malaysian political and economic life. Trade expanded west and east because Malaysian ports lay across the main sea routes between the Far East and the West.

Many people from the East and the West were drawn to this thriving trading center. Large numbers of Chinese came. They concentrated on making money and, until recently, left politics in the hands of others. The Portuguese came in the 1500s and seized a number of coastal ports. In the 1600s the Dutch seized the ports from the Portuguese. Then in the 1700s the British arrived and established themselves on Penang, an island off the coast of the Malaysian mainland. During the 1800s they took control of the ports. The British expanded their control to cover Malaysian political and economic life. Their power lasted until 1957 when the Malay Peninsula area became the **Federation** of Malaya, an independent country.

In 1963 the island areas of Singapore, Sarawak, and Sabah joined the federation to form Malaysia. Difficulties about territory arose between Malaysia and Indonesia and the Philippines. Fighting broke out between Malaysia and Indonesia but ended when the Indonesian president was thrown out in 1966. Singapore separated from Malaysia in 1965 to become an independent republic. In 1966 the Malaysian government announced that Sabah and Sarawak would be known as East Malaysia. The 11 states that formerly made up the Federation of Malaysia would be known as West Malaysia.

The Malaysians have one of the highest standards of living in Southeast Asia. Their geographic position continues to make their nation one of the leading trading centers of Asia. This is reflected in Malaysia's favorable balance of trade. Rubber and tin make up most of the exports, but Malaysians are widening their export base. They are developing other **natural resources** and encouraging industrialization.

Tension still exists between the Malays and the Chinese Malaysians. The Chinese population continues to dominate the economy of Malaysia while the Malays dominate the politics. Malaysia has a parliamentary government modeled after the British system and a civil service also inherited from the British. Malaysia's foreign policy is one of peaceful coexistence. Its government has called for a neutralization of Southeast Asia. In the meantime a defense arrangement with Great Britain calls for mutual consultation should a threat develop to the security of Malaysia.

Malay Migrations

253

Chapter 5
Island Countries

Singapore, Indonesia, and the Philippines are nations located entirely on islands. The largest islands of Indonesia include Sumatra, Java, most of Borneo (Kalimantan), Timor, Celebes (Sulawesi), and the western half of New Guinea (West Irian). Eleven large islands and more than 7,000 smaller ones make up the Philippines.

These island republics have much in common with the mainland countries of Southeast Asia. Mountains are the main feature of the landscape and rainfall is abundant. The people share many of the same ways of life.

SINGAPORE

The island republic of Singapore is located directly south of the Malay Peninsula. The great majority of the two million people are Chinese. Around 15 percent are Malay. The remainder are divided among Indians, Pakistanis, Eurasians, and Europeans.

For over a century Singapore was governed by the British. It achieved internal self-government in 1959. In 1963 it became part of Malaysia. Two years later, it withdrew and became known officially as the Republic of Singapore.

Singapore is the largest port in Southeast Asia. Merchant and naval ships from all over the world visit it. Much of the tin and rubber of Malaysia and Indonesia passes through the harbor. Singapore is of strategic and economic importance because of its location and role in world trade.

INDONESIA: THE INDONESIANS

A mixture of peoples settled in Indonesia at various times in prehistory. Around the first century A.D., or even earlier, the Indonesian coasts were visited by Indian traders. The Indians built trading centers along the coasts of Borneo, eastern Sumatra, and northern Java, just as they did elsewhere in Southeast Asia. After 100 A.D., Chinese and Arab traders began visiting the Indian centers. By the 300s, these centers were known throughout Asia.

States began to arise on some of the islands, and several of them became large empires. One, called Srivijaya (sree-wee-JAW-yuh), was based on the east coast of Sumatra near Palembang. From about 600 to the 1100s Srivijaya dominated the Malay Peninsula and controlled the sea lanes throughout the region. During the 1200s another great sea power, the Majapahit, arose in east Java. For 300 years the Majapahit had control over much of Java until the Malaysians destroyed the empire.

During this period of the rise and fall of Indian-Indonesian empires, smaller island states were created, destroyed, modified, recreated, and combined again and again. These kingdoms were generally near the coastal trade centers, but there were some inland states too.

During much of this time Indians were dominant, especially in the capitals and the trading ports. They were the merchants. Buddhist priests and monks from India taught and built temples and monasteries. They even counseled government officials. Indians married Sumatrans and Javanese and forged even stronger ties.

The Chinese also came to the Indonesian islands. They were attracted to the profitable and growing trade. Beginning in the 1100s,

many Chinese came to Indonesia to settle and to trade. They were so successful that eventually they controlled much of the economy and resources of Indonesia. They continued to come until recently, when government officials stopped their entry and even expelled many.

The Arabs also came early to this land, for they too were great traders. They brought their Islamic religion along with their trade goods. They were joined by Indian Muslims who came to preach as well as trade, and Islam began to make great advances in Indonesia. It rapidly took the place of Hinduism and Buddhism. By the early 1500s much of Indonesia was Islamic.

During the 1500s Europeans were attracted by the great profits to be made from spices and other goods. The Portuguese came first, followed by the Spanish, Dutch, English, and Danish. The story of trade and politics in Indonesia during the 1600s and 1700s is one of intrigue, struggle, and war. Europeans competed to control and

These are scenes from two capital cities—Singapore (left) and Djakarta. Each city is an important port. Each has areas of wealth and poverty. Compare their histories.

reap the harvest of Indonesia's riches. The main rivalry was between the Dutch and the English. It was finally resolved in a peace treaty giving Indonesia to the Dutch and Malaya to the British. The Portuguese kept a part of the island of Timor.

The Dutch governed Indonesia until 1942, when the Japanese took it during World War II. At the end of the war, the Indonesians proclaimed their country a republic. From then until 1949 they fought with the Dutch to maintain their independence. In 1949 the Dutch formally transferred control of the government to the Republic of Indonesia.

Sukarno became Indonesia's first president. He thought of his role as that of a leader-unifier of the many different people who live in Indonesia. He gave little thought to the future economy of the nation. He spent large sums of money on the establishment of strong military services and on showy buildings and monuments. He was militant in his attempts to increase Indonesian influence in his region of the world. He fought against the establishment of the Federation of Malaysia.

militant: aggressive; eager to force one's views on others

Sukarno preserved his power by playing off the strong Communist party in Indonesia against the military. His power ended after a Communist **coup** in 1965 failed. The military, under the leadership of General Suharto, took control of the country. Sukarno went into forced retirement and died in 1970.

General Suharto became the second president of Indonesia. His leadership brought some stability to Indonesia's political and economic life. Foreign investments have been encouraged. **Inflation** has been slowed. In 1971 the first parliamentary elections since 1955 were held. In power politics Indonesia follows a policy of neutrality.

THE PHILIPPINE ISLANDS: THE FILIPINOS

The story of the Philippines is also an account of the coming of many peoples and the mingling of many cultures. An early Asian Pygmy people, who were later called negritos or little blacks by the Spanish, were among the earliest people to settle in the Philippine Islands. They were followed by a hunting people somewhat like the Malays.

Then, around 8,000 years ago, early Asian peoples crossed over from the mainland and settled on the islands. Over the centuries, Asians continued to cross the sea from the mainland. Among their contributions to the Philippines were houses built on stilts, improved tools, and a knowledge of agriculture. Later Asians introduced methods of working copper, bronze, and gold, and possibly methods of cultivating rice.

Around 500 B.C., the Malays began to stream into the islands. Eventually they became dominant. The Malays brought along their language, ways of dressing, and methods of fishing, farming, and building boats and houses. And they brought some knowledge of Indian advancements—the loom, cotton, and iron manufacture. Indian traders followed or accompanied the Malays. Indian influence is felt especially in language, architecture, and the arts. These streams of people and influences continued through the 500s and 600s A.D.

From around 700 to the 1400s, the Chinese came in numbers. They settled mostly on the large northern island of Luzon. They married the island people and it is estimated that over 10 percent of the Filipinos have some Chinese ancestry. The Chinese came to control a great portion of the trade and wealth of the Philippines.

During the 1400s, followers of Islam came to Mindanao and Palawan, two of the southern islands. These Muslims were mostly Malays, but there were also Indians and Arabs. Along with their religion they brought ideas about social and political life. A number of Filipinos were converted to Islam.

In 1521, sailing under the Spanish flag, Ferdinand Magellan reached the Philippines. About 45 years later the Spanish began their conquest of the islands. They succeeded except in the southern areas occupied by Muslims. For more than 300 years the Spanish ruled. They brought more new ideas and practices to the Philippines. They were Roman Catholics and except for the southern areas, they made the Philippines into a Catholic country. Catholic churches, monasteries, and convents dotted the islands.

The Spanish divided the country into local units of government called barrios. They made the towns and cities into municipalities

Below, college students row on the Pasig River in a tournament sponsored by the Manila Boat Club. In the background is a factory operated by local partners of General Motors, the U.S. company. Why do you think a corporation owned and based in the U.S. would invest in a foreign country?

and established provinces which included barrios and municipalities. Over all these was the central government, which took its orders from Spain. Barrios and provinces are still basic to the political system of the Philippines.

In 1898 the Philippines were given to the U.S. after the Spanish-American War. Americans brought their technical knowledge and the idea of a republican form of government to the Philippines. The Americans separated the **Church** from the **State** and introduced a public school system which has grown rapidly. As a consequence, the modern Republic of the Philippines is, with Japan, among the most **literate** nations in Asia.

Over the years, a kind of partnership developed between Americans and Filipinos. Even the propaganda of the Japanese, who occupied the country from 1941 until 1945, did not destroy this bond. In 1946 the Philippines obtained their independence as the U.S. had promised.

Since independence the Filipinos have passed through some troubling periods. They live in a nation rich with promise. But this promise has never been realized. There has been continuing corruption in

MAJOR EXPORTS AND IMPORTS

Country	Major Export		Total Exports	Major Import		Total Imports
	Commodity	US $ millions		Commodity	US $ millions	
Burma	Rice and Rice Products	59.24	111.94	Machinery and Transport Equipment	50.56	161.63
Thailand	Rice	125.80	518.55	Machinery	476.80	1350.45
Cambodia	Rice	2.96	7.03	Metals and Metal Manufactures	4.23	9.58
Laos	Tin	1.03	2.88	Mineral Products	12.92	45.55
Democratic Republic of Vietnam (North Vietnam)	NO FIGURES AVAILABLE					
Republic of Vietnam (South Vietnam)	Rubber	1.26	1.51	Machinery and Appliances	15.48	98.36
Malaysia	Raw Materials (inedible) excluding Fuels	937.74	2022.63	Machinery and Transport Equipment	610.15	1884.22
Singapore	Raw Materials (inedible) excluding Fuels	588.60	1957.12	Machinery and Transport Equipment	707.16	3100.33
Indonesia	Petroleum and Petroleum Products	446.3	1160.6	Raw Materials and Auxiliary Goods (including Chemicals and Chemical Products, Fertilizers and Weaving Yarns)	376.5	1001.5
The Philippines	Logs and Lumber	249.77	877.31	Non-electric Machinery	235.22	842.58

Source: *The Europa Year Book 1974: A World Survey* (Europa Publications, London)

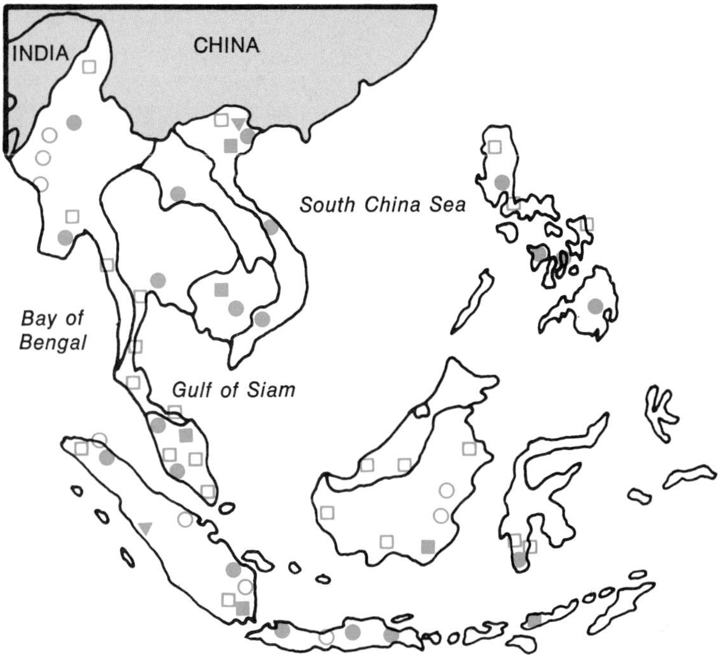
INDIA
CHINA
South China Sea
Bay of Bengal
Gulf of Siam

Natural Resources

● Industrial ▼ Coal ■ Iron ○ Oil □ Minerals

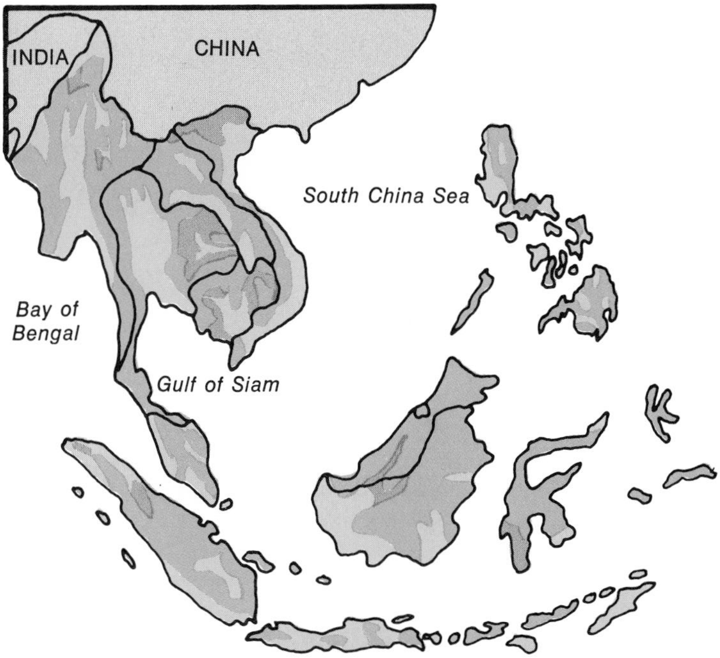
INDIA
CHINA
South China Sea
Bay of Bengal
Gulf of Siam

Land Use

Farming Forestry Grazing

government. The population has grown too rapidly. Wealth and land are controlled by a few people.

In the early 1970s the discontent of many poor and frustrated Filipinos expressed itself in angry mobs and violence. There was guerrilla activity in various parts of the country. The Muslims in the southern part of the islands revolted. In 1972 President Ferdinand Marcos declared martial law. A forced stability was imposed upon the country and a new constitution was adopted. But there remains a long list of economic, political, and social problems to be solved.

Chapter 6
Society

These children attend school in Laos. How is their culture similar to that of other Asian nations? How is it similar to your own?

Southeast Asians practice the joint or extended family found elsewhere in Asia. There are some variations, but the system is still recognizable wherever it is seen. The women of Southeast Asia are familiar with the traditional role of their Asian sisters. They too have been raised to be wives and mothers. The young men know that marriage has a great significance to the family and to the community. Like other Asians, they often accept the wishes of their parents in this matter.

TRADITIONAL COOPERATIVE SPIRIT

There has always been a spirit of helpfulness among Southeast Asians. This spirit has stemmed from their environment, traditions, and religions. From earliest times they have sought to resolve local social conflicts through adjustment and compromise. More often than not they have succeeded. They prefer working together to competing.

People join in constructing community buildings, schools, and clinics, and in building roads, dams, and irrigation canals. They help each other in putting up houses, cultivating fields, and arranging marriages. They are generally ready to assist where help is needed—at funerals, births, and in the many religious and national festivals.

Sometimes the cooperative attitude extends beyond the local community. When the dikes of a river burst people come from many villages to repair the damage. They join in housing the homeless, rescuing the stranded, and feeding the hungry. This spirit of cooperation is an outstanding feature of the society of Southeast Asia. Unfortunately, with more and more people moving to the cities, cooperation is breaking down.

CHANGING WAYS

With modern communication and transportation, contact between people within countries and between countries has become closer. The Southeast Asians like other Asians have found modern life confusing as it begins to affect customs and traditions. They are faced with decisions that are increasingly hard to make. Older villagers, whether in Vietnam or India, thought that life was difficult enough when they had only village and family affairs to consider. Now the village radio tells them of national and international matters. Villages are told that to avoid great trouble, they must change their views. Their rulers must change their policies.

Village meetings are attended by eager young representatives of the central government. These young people urge, and sometimes command, villagers to change their time-honored ways of farming. They sometimes even suggest that the villagers plant new crops and change their eating habits.

Even within the family there is no peace of mind. The government says girls as well as boys must go to school, at least for a while. But it is hard for older people to understand why. To them it appears that young people are not being given a good, sound education. The government and the teachers are spreading strange and troublesome ideas. Young people are encouraged to speak up before their elders. This is a major break with tradition.

The young complain about unsanitary living conditions and a lack of vitamins in the food. They complain of the inefficiency of farming methods. They want to change traditional social attitudes. They speak about marrying for love. Sometimes daughters insist upon going to high school and even the university. Both sons and daughters strongly object when they are told that it is a girl's destiny to get married, raise a family, and manage a household. The older generation finds this all very confusing and troublesome. It is difficult to give up old ways that stretch far back in the time of their ancestors.

Summing Up the Unit

Social Studies Vocabulary

Define: peninsula; land bridges; cultural diffusion; limited monarchy; protectorate; oral tradition; guerrilla; federation; coup; inflation; Church and State

People

Identify: Hoabinhians; Burmans; Thais; Khmers; Sihanouk; Lao; Pathet Lao; Vietnamese; Ho Chi Minh; Malays; Suharto

Places

Locate: the countries of Southeast Asia

Words

Define: animism; sultans; negritos; barrios

⌬ Questions

1. What is the significance of the discoveries at Hoa Binh?
2. What is the leading religion in each of the countries of Southeast Asia?
3. a. Name the people who settled Burma. b. From where did they migrate? c. When? d. What Western nation controlled Burma until 1948?
4. Where did the Thai people originate?
5. The Cambodians are descendants of what people?
6. a. The Lao people are of the same family as what other two groups of people? b. From where did they come?
7. Which Southeast Asian nation has been heavily influenced by Chinese culture?
8. What agreement was reached at the Geneva Conference in 1954 concerning Vietnam?
9. What two groups of people make up the bulk of the population of Malaysia?
10. What nation has one of the highest standards of living in Southeast Asia?
11. Which three Southeast Asian nations are located entirely on islands?
12. a. What is the largest port in Southeast Asia? b. What is its economic and strategic importance?
13. a. In what nations were Indian traders impor-

tant? b. How?
14. a. What nation ruled the Philippines after 1898? b. When did the Philippines become independent?
15. a. What has been the traditional way Southeast Asians have faced problems? b. How is modernization affecting Southeast Asian village life?

Discussion Topics

1. The author states that the borrowing of a word usually means the borrowing of the thing named by that word. Can you name any words you use that demonstrate this? Should people use foreign words, or should they keep their language free of outside influences? Will borrowing of foreign terms lead eventually to the breakdown of a language? (Check reference materials for the French view of this subject.)
2. Pick one of the nations of Southeast Asia and trace the historical events behind current news stories. Can you see how the past influences the present? In what areas of a country's life? How?

Project Ideas

1. Play a map game using places mentioned in this unit. Players must locate them on a wall map within a set time limit.
2. Write a story showing the problems young Southeast Asians might have trying to convince their elders to give up some of their old ways.
3. Write a story from the elder's point of view.
4. Prepare a chart on the nations of Southeast Asia showing ethnic groups, their places of origin, major language, religion, economy, political system, arts.
5. Using an historical atlas or encyclopedia for reference, draw a map showing the routes of Indian traders in Southeast Asia.
6. Using the natural resources and land use maps on page 259 and the "Major Exports and Imports" chart on page 258 form a generalization about the relationship of raw materials to economics. Consider foreign aid in your statement. Would that enable a country to buy what it doesn't have?

For Further Study

General Readings

1. *Ageless Chinese: A History* by Dun J. Li. Charles Scribner's Sons, 2nd ed., 1973. Paperback. Basic history of China to the present, arranged by dynasties.
2. *Ancient China* by Edward H. Schafer and the editors of Time-Life Books. Time-Life Books, 1967. Shang through the T'ang dynasties.
3. *Asian Cultures* edited by Paul Thomas Welty. J. B. Lippincott Co., 1973. Inquiry format.
4. *Buddhism in Chinese History* by Arthur F. Wright. Stanford University Press, 1959. Paperback. A short study of the importance of Buddhism in China.
5. *Caste in India: Its Nature, Function, and Origins* by J. H. Hutton. Oxford University Press, 4th ed., 1963. An attempt by a well-known Cambridge anthropologist to explain the Indian caste system to Westerners.
6. *China in Ferment; Perspectives on the Cultural Revolution,* edited by Richard Baum. Prentice-Hall, Inc., 1971. Paperback. A collection of writings by scholars and government officials from both China and the U.S.
7. *Chinese and Oriental Art* adapted by Michael Batterberry. McGraw-Hill Book Co., 1969. Covers Chinese, Korean, Japanese, and Indian art and their influences.
8. *Chinese Thought from Confucius to Mao Tsetung* by H. G. Creel. University of Chicago Press, 1971. Paperback.
9. *Chrysanthemum and the Sword: Patterns of Japanese Culture* by Ruth Benedict. New American Library, 1967. A study of Japan by a famous anthropologist.
10. *Discovery of India* by Jawaharlal Nehru. Abridged and edited by Robert I. Crane. Doubleday & Co., Inc., 1960. Paperback. An interpretative history of India from the earliest times until World War II. Written while Nehru was a political prisoner of the British.
11. *Everyday Life in Early India* by Michael Edwardes. G. P. Putnam's Sons, 1969. Discusses daily life in India from about the 200s B.C. to 700s A.D.
12. *History of South-East Asia* by D. G. Hall. St. Martin's Press, Inc., 3rd ed., 1968. Paperback.

Emphasizes the importance of Indian influence.
13. *How the Great Religions Began* by Joseph Gaer. New American Library. Paperback. A popular guide to the study of religions.
14. *Japan: The Story of a Nation* by Edwin O. Reischauer. Alfred A. Knopf, rev. ed., 1974. Paperback. A history of Japan emphasizing this century.
15. *Japan before Buddhism* by J. E. Kidder, Jr. Praeger Publishers, Inc., rev. ed., 1966. A review of Japanese archaeology.
16. *Red Star over China* by Edgar Snow. Grove Press, rev. ed., 1968. Paperback. A revision of a 1938 eyewitness report.

Fiction

1. *Bridge Over the River Kwai* by Pierre Boulle. Bantam Books, Inc., 1970. Famous World War II story.
2. *The Good Earth* by Pearl Buck. Pocket Books, Inc., Div. of Simon & Schuster, Inc., 1975. Paperback. Life of peasants in China.
3. *The Hero Machine* by Howard Berk. New American Library of World Literature, Inc., 1967. Air Force in India in World War II.
4. *House of Sixty Fathers* by Meindert DeJong. Dell Publishing Co., Inc., 1969. China during World War II.
5. *Japanese Inn* by Oliver Statler. Random House, Inc., 1961. Paperback. Interweaves history of Japan from the 16th century with the story of a Japanese inn.
6. *Japanese Literature* by Roger Bersihand. Walker & Co., 1965. Paperback. Examples of famous Japanese literature. With commentary.
7. *Passage of Arms* by Eric Ambler. Alfred A. Knopf, 1960. Anti-Communist struggles in Indonesia.
8. *The Sand Pebbles* by Richard McKenna. Fawcett World Library, 1975. Story of China in the 1920s.
9. *They Lived Like This in Ancient China* by Marie Neurath. Franklin Watts, Inc., 1967. Fictionalized account of customs of the times.
10. *They Lived Like This in Old Japan* by Marie Neurath. Franklin Watts, Inc., 1967. Tale of manners and customs.

The Africans

Sub-Saharan Africa's
history and prehistory
are as varied and
colorful as this weaving.
Weavings such as this
are now hung
in museums around the
world. This cloth
from Ghana hangs
in the Textile Museum
in Washington, D. C.

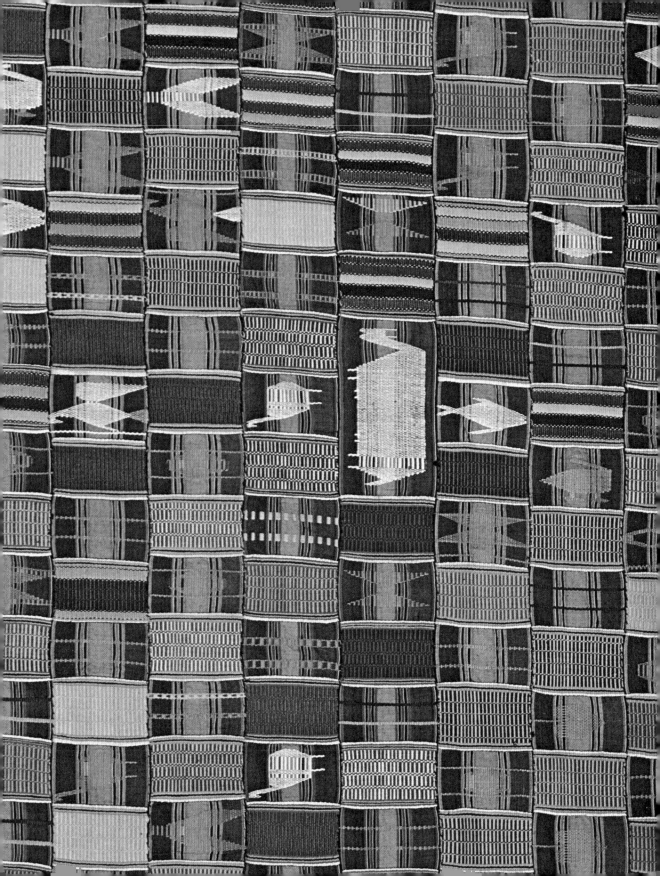

Unit I

The Land and the People

Modern cities are growing at a great rate in Africa. Urban living has been part of the African scene since early times, but the independence movements of the 1950s and 1960s have spurred more and more Africans to move to cities. This is Lagos, the capital of Nigeria.

In the following section on Africa, mainly those countries below the Sahara Desert are discussed. The **nations** of North Africa—Egypt, Libya, Tunisia, Algeria, and Morocco—will not be treated in detail here. In **gene pool**, **religion**, **society**, and **arts**, these **people** are more closely tied to the Arab world of the Middle East. They appear in this section only where the **historical** and **cultural** development of sub-Saharan Africans touch them.

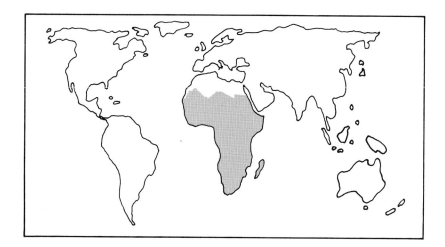

Sub-Saharan Africa itself can be divided into regions: West, Central, South-Central, South-Southwest, Northeast, and East. These are both **geographical** and historical divisions. Like other peoples, where Africans lived has shaped their history and culture. Those who lived on the southern fringes of the Sahara or on the east coast were influenced by Islamic culture. West Africans came more into contact with Europeans. Because of **climate** and landscape, East African agriculture and **trade** were very different from that of the rain forests of Central Africa.

It must be remembered, however, that these divisions are simplifications. Similar **vegetation** and climate regions cut across divisions. In addition, as people moved across and down the continent, their culture went with them. The divisions may, however, make it easier to remember the general location of sub-Saharan Africa's many nations and **territories**.

Sub-Saharan Africa covers about 24.6 million square kilometers (9.5 million square miles). At its widest it is 7,562 kilometers (4,700 miles) across. This is roughly 1.5 times as wide as the continental United States. The central African country of Zaire (ZAIR) is as large as Texas, Colorado, and Alaska combined.

According to the geographical divisions, West Africa includes the modern nations of Nigeria, Benin, Togo, Ghana, Ivory Coast, Liberia, Sierra Leone, Guinea, Guinea-Bissau, Gambia, Senegal, Upper Volta, Mali, Niger, Chad, and Mauritania. Cameroon, Gabon, People's Republic of the Congo, Zaire, Equatorial Guinea, and Central African Empire make up Central Africa. South-Central Africa includes Angola, Zambia, Malawi, Rhodesia, Mozambique, and the Comoro Islands. The South-Southwest includes Namibia or South-West Africa, Botswana, Swaziland, Lesotho, and South Africa. The Northeast includes Ethiopia, Republic of the Sudan, Somalia, and the French Territory of the Afars and the Issas. East Africa includes Tanzania, Kenya, Rwanda, Burundi, Uganda, and the Malagasy Republic.

Chapter 1

Environment and Development

A PHYSICAL MAP OF AFRICA

MOROCCO

Mediterranean Sea

ALGERIA

LIBYA

EGYPT

SAUDI ARABIA

Nile River

SAHARA DESERT

Red Sea

NORTH- EAST

Gulf of Aden

SAVANNAH

Niger River

Blue Nile

WEST

White Nile

RAIN FOREST

RUWENZORI (RAINMAKER) MTS.

Lake Victoria

RAIN FOREST

Congo (Zaire) River

Indian Ocean

GREAT RIFT VALLEY

Atlantic Ocean

CENTRAL

LESSER RIFT VALLEY

EAST

SAVANNAH

SOUTH- CENTRAL

Zambezi River

RAIN FOREST

SAVANNAH

KALAHARI DESERT

Legend
- Mountains
- Deserts
- Rift valleys
- Rain forests
- Savannahs
- Farmland, grazing land, woodlands

SOUTH- SOUTHWEST

CAPE OF GOOD HOPE

A POLITICAL MAP OF AFRICA

Capitals:

1. Luanda	10. Porto-Novo	19. Abidjan	28. Windhoek	37. Pretoria
2. Gaborone	11. Cuidad de Malabo	20. Nairobi	29. Niamey	38. Khartoum
3. Bujumbura	12. Addis Ababa	21. Maseru	30. Lagos	39. Mbabane
4. Yaounde	13. Djibouti	22. Monrovia	31. Salisbury	40. Dar es Salaam
5. Praia	14. Libreville	23. Tananarive	32. Kigali	41. Lome
6. Bangui	15. Banjul	24. Zomba	33. Dakar	42. Kampala
7. Fort-Lamy	16. Accra	25. Bamako	34. Freetown	43. Ouagadougou
8. Moroni	17. Conakry	26. Nouakchott	35. Mogadiscio	44. Kinshasa
9. Brazzaville	18. Bissau	27. Maputo	36. Cape Town	45. Lusaka

For many centuries, Africa's geography played a role in keeping Europeans and Americans in ignorance about the people of the continent's interior. This ignorance resulted in much misunderstanding about the peoples of Africa.

PLATEAU

Sub-Saharan Africa is a giant plateau surrounded by a low coastal plain. Generally the plateau does not slope gently to the ocean. It drops sharply. Thus a cliff-like barrier is created between the coast and the plateau. Few African rivers drain to the sea. Of those that do, many become unnavigable as they reach this barrier. The barrier creates rapids and waterfalls like Victoria Falls on the Zambezi (zam-BEE-zee) River. Because so few rivers have outlets to the sea, there are few harbors for shipping.

The plateau rises in the north and west. It reaches its greatest heights in the east and south. Because much of sub-Saharan Africa lies along or close to the equator, the altitude of the plateau makes it a more comfortable and healthful place to live. This is particularly true in East Africa where the plateau averages 13,000 meters (around 4,000 feet) above sea level. East Africa is one of the few **overpopulated** areas in the sub-Sahara.

Several times in **prehistory**, volcanic activity raised parts of the plateau. This lifting of the earth caused deep fractures, mountains, and depressions. The fractures are called rifts. A chain of them runs from the Red Sea to Mozambique (moh-zuhm-BEEK). The chain divides into the Great or Eastern Rift Valley and the Lesser or Western Rift. In some places the rift is over 750 meters (2,500 feet) deep. The width varies from around 50 to 65 kilometers (30 to 40 miles).

Most of the great lakes of Africa lie on the floor of the rifts. Some of these lakes are Tanganyika (tan-guhn-YEE-kuh), Idi Amin (formerly Edward), Mobutu Sese Seko (formerly Albert), Tana, and Turkana (formerly Rudolf). Lake Victoria in Tanzania (tan-zuh-NEE-

This is a section of the Great Rift Valley in Kenya. The area is primarily used for grazing.

270

uh) is not part of the rift system, but it is the world's second largest fresh-water lake. Only Lake Superior in the U.S. is larger. Africa's lakes provide drinking water and fish. They are used for irrigation and are an important part of Africa's inland transportation network.

Located between Uganda and Zaire are the Ruwenzori (roo-wuhn-ZOHR-ee) or Rainmaker Mountains, Africa's highest mountain range. Lying only about 48 kilometers (30 miles) north of the equator, its highest peaks are snowcapped. There are also mountains scattered along the western, south-central, and southwestern coasts.

The depressions that were made by the earth's movement of the plateau are called basins. Water from surrounding mountains drain into these basins and form rivers. However, about one-third of Africa has no drainage to the sea.

RIVERS

The Nile is the longest river in the world. It runs for over 6,600 kilometers (4,100 miles) and has two branches: White and Blue. The White Nile starts in the Lake Victoria region of Tanzania. The Blue Nile begins in the highlands of Ethiopia and joins the White Nile at Khartoum (kahr-TOOM) in the Republic of the Sudan (soo-DAN). From there they flow together into the Mediterranean Sea.

The main river draining Central Africa's rain forests is the Congo or Zaire. With its dozens of tributaries the Congo (Zaire) provides over 12,872 kilometers (8,000 miles) of navigable waterways. This network provides an easy, cheap means of carrying freight and passengers.

The Niger River starts less than 320 kilometers (200 miles) inland from the Atlantic. It curves northeast and then south finally to reach the ocean after a journey of almost 4,200 kilometers (2,600 miles). The Niger has been a source of food, water, and transportation for generations of West Africans. So important is this river that two African nations are named after it—Niger and Nigeria.

The British explorer Stanley Livingstone named this waterfall Victoria Falls. To Africans, it was Mosi Oa Tunya, meaning thundering smoke. Why do you think Europeans ignored African names and renamed everything?

271

Although African nations are working to industrialize, most Africans still earn their living from the land. These women are picking tea in Tanzania.

CLIMATE AND VEGETATION

Although Africa is developing **industry**, most Africans still make their living as farmers and/or herders. Their livelihoods depend largely on the climate, vegetation, and soil of the area in which they live.

The equator runs about midway between the northern and southern parts of the continent. Similar climate and vegetation zones appear on either side of the equator. Certain major exceptions exist such as the eastern highlands and the mountains. Their higher altitudes modify the climate and vegetation.

In general, however, the northern and southern ends of the continent have slim belts of climate and vegetation similar to that of southern California. Moving south or north are dry plains and deserts. The Sahara covers most of the north. The smaller Kalahari (kal-uh-HAHR-ee) Desert lies in South and Southwest Africa. Desert areas and the semiarid regions that border the deserts go for years without measurable rain. In recent years a severe drought affected the southern edge of the Sahara.

drought: a long period of time without rain

The desert areas merge into regions of grassland and scattered trees called savannahs. North of the equator this area is sometimes called the Sudan (not to be confused with the modern Republic of the Sudan). Savannahs cover almost one-fourth of Africa. These grassy areas average around 50 to 90 centimeters (20-35 inches) of rain a year. But the rain is seasonal. High temperatures and the dry season that follows cause rapid evaporation.

Along the equator lie the tropical rain forests of West Africa and the Congo Basin. Rain forests make up about 10 percent of Africa. In these forests, trees are thick and rain is abundant. More than 250 centimeters (100 inches) a year is not unusual. But the soil is not suitable for **permanent farming**.

Much of Africa's soil is poor. It lacks humus, the organic material in soil which results from the decay of animal or vegetable matter. In addition, in rainy areas, heavy rains wash away nutrients and minerals. This results in thin layers of not very fertile soil.

With this type of soil, a farming method called **slash-and-burn** agriculture is used. Farmers clear a piece of forest or savannah land and plant crops. In a few seasons the fertility of the soil is gone. The farmers move on and repeat the process. Often the trees or grasses are burned and the ashes are used as fertilizer. It may take several years for once-used plots to regain fertility. This method of farming provides a **subsistence living**. Farmers grow enough to live on, but they have nothing extra to sell. In addition, this method requires a great deal of land. With population on the increase, slash-and-burn agriculture may not be possible in the future. Modern African nations are experimenting with various ways to make better use of the land.

In areas where soil is more fertile and animal fertilizers are available, permanent farming is possible. River deltas and valleys, mountain slopes, and some highland regions support permanent farming of **cash crops**. For example, in Nigeria, peanuts are grown. In parts of Ghana and Nigeria cocoa is raised. In dry but fertile areas, rivers and wells provide water for irrigation.

In the drier regions where irrigation is not possible, Africans may depend mainly on herding to earn their living. Cattle, goats, and sheep can survive where crops cannot. The herders are generally nomads. Some wander in savannah and semiarid regions. Others **migrate** between lowlands and neighboring mountains.

Some Africans combine farming and herding. The most extensive areas of **mixed farming** are in the grassy parts of South Africa and southern Rhodesia (roh-DEE-zhee-uh). Mixed farming is also found in Kenya and a few other areas.

RESOURCES

From very early times gold was an important trade item for West Africans. They exchanged it across the Sahara for salt and other goods they did not have. Modern Ghana is still a major source of gold. Gold has also been found in Rhodesia, Zaire, and the Republic of South Africa.

Africa is the major source of the world's diamonds. Most come from South Africa and Zaire. Ghana, Sierra Leone (see-ER-uh-lee-OHN), Angola, Liberia, Tanzania, the Central African Empire, and Botswana (baht-SWAHN-uh) also mine diamonds. Africa also has vast reserves of iron ore. Copper, tin, bauxite, uranium, lead, nickel, and zinc are just a few of the other minerals that have been discovered and are being **exported**. New discoveries are being made every year. The mining and exporting of resources offer great hope for Africa's **economic** future.

Africa also has great potential for hydroelectric power. Harnessing Africa's rivers and waterfalls promises cheap power for homes and industry. Among Africa's hydroelectric projects are those on the Volta River in Ghana, the Orange River in South Africa, and the White Nile in Uganda. Most of Africa's water power, however, is as yet untapped.

The majority of Africa's countries are in the developing stages of their national lives. Most have had independence only since the 1960s. **Capital**, professionals, and **skilled** workers are needed. Lack of these holds back the efforts of African leaders to develop the resources of their countries. But these nations are making great progress toward **modernization**.

CITIES

The rapid growth of **cities** reflects the growing **commerce**, industry, and the political **centralization** of African nations. Africa has had cities since ancient times. Benin (buh-NIN) in Nigeria, Timbuktu (tim-buhk-TOO) in Mali, and Kilwa (KIL-wah) in Tanzania are a few. Some of today's larger cities have grown on the base of what began as trading cities for non-Africans. New cities are growing up in mining and manufacturing areas.

Capitals are having a spectacular growth. This is because of the increasing need of African **governments** for workers. As government employees and their families come to the cities, more services and the people to provide them are needed. Stores, hospitals, schools, and government buildings must be constructed and staffed. Very often trade and industry also cluster around capitals.

As African cities mushroom in size, their freeway systems become as large and complex as any city in the world. This is Abidjan, the capital of Ivory Coast.

While the majority of Africans live and work in the country, thousands come yearly to **urban** areas. Like people elsewhere in the world, they come for jobs, education, and what they hope will be a better life. It will be years before a majority of Africans are city dwellers. But they are moving in that direction.

Chapter 2
Early People

A number of **anthropologists** believe the earliest ancestors of the human family lived in Africa. According to them, the human species developed in Africa and then spread elsewhere. Only time and further investigations will tell if the theory is correct.

Just as there is disagreement about the origins of the human family, disagreement exists about the origins of the people we call Africans. Some anthropologists place Africans into four groups: Bushmanoid, Pygmoid, Negroid, and Caucasoid.

The Bushmanoid group includes Bushmen and a closely related group, the Hottentots. Today they number less than 100,000 and live mostly in southwestern Africa. The Bushmanoids may have been the first human inhabitants of Africa. Their time sequence and place of origin are uncertain. Remains of what may have been their ancestors have been found in East and South Africa.

In the forests of Central Africa members of the Pygmoid group still live as their ancestors did. They hunt and gather food. Like the Bushmen and Hottentots, the Pygmies today are few in number. Some anthropologists believe that the Pygmies, not the Bushmen, were the original Africans.

Most Africans today would be classed as members of the Negroid group. Approximately nine out of ten sub-Saharan Africans belong to this group. By 10,000 B.C. or earlier, their ancestors were living in what is modern Nigeria and elsewhere in West Africa. Whether the Negroid group began in Africa or migrated there is a much-debated question. At present not enough evidence exists to support one theory over the other.

The Caucasoids are also known as Mediterraneans or Afro-Mediterraneans. Their distant ancestors may have migrated to Africa from the Middle East. Remains of this group show that they were in Africa as early as the ancestors of the Negroids. Today Caucasoid descendants include the nomadic herders of North African nations, Ethiopia, and Somalia. Egyptians are also thought to be related to this group.

LANGUAGE DIVISIONS

A clearer way to see the relationship of African groups is by the **languages** they speak. Since prehistory, Africa has experienced sweeping movements of peoples from both inside and outside the continent. As a result, hundreds of different languages developed.

However, certain common elements can be seen in some of them. **Linguists**, therefore, have placed the languages into four major **language families**: Congo-Kordofanian (kor-doh-FAN-ee-uhn), Afro-Asian, Nilo-Saharan, and Khoisan (KOY-sahn).

Congo-Kordofanian or Niger-Congo includes most of the languages spoken by sub-Saharan Africans. Within this grouping are the several hundred Bantu languages. A majority of Africans speak one of these. One of the most commonly spoken is Swahili (swah-HEE-lee). It is found in East Africa and parts of Central and South-Central Africa. Over the centuries, many Arabic and Persian words have become part of Swahili.

Afro-Asian includes the languages of the Ethiopians, Somalians and some North Africans. Ancient Egyptian is an Afro-Asian language. Nilo-Saharan—also known as Sudanic—includes the languages of peoples living in the Sahara, Sudan, and parts of East Africa. The Bushmen and Hottentots speak Khoisan or Click languages. Their neighbors refer to them as Khoi-Khoi people. A few peoples in East Africa also speak a Click language.

The original language of the Pygmies does not belong to any of these language families. It is still spoken today by some Pygmy peoples. Others have blended their original language with that of non-Pygmy neighbors.

Sometimes two other language groupings are included among African languages: Malayo-Polynesian, the main language spoken in the Malagasy Republic, and Afrikaans. Afrikaans was developed by the Dutch who came in the 1600s. It is spoken in southwestern Africa. Many Africans also speak French, English, or Portuguese depending on the European nation that colonized their area.

THE GREEN SAHARA

On a map of Africa the Sahara Desert appears to be the most prominent feature. The Sahara, however, was not always dry and barren. Between 8,000 to 10,000 years ago, the region was one of greenery and water. Giraffe, spotted oxen, wild sheep, ostrich, and other animals grazed over it. Trees grew. Rivers filled with fish cut through it. For several thousand years people made this region their home.

Archaeologists can piece together the life of these Saharan people— they may have been both Mediterraneans and Negroids—from rock paintings recently discovered there. The earliest paintings show a hunting and gathering people. Hunters used bows and arrows, clubs, spears, knives, and throwing sticks. For fishing they used hooks made of bone.

Pictures dated between 4000 and 2500 or 2000 B.C. show people herding cattle, sheep, and goats. They may have learned herding from the people of the Nile River Valley or discovered the method independently. During this time they began using dogs to help them

The Tassili rock paintings were discovered in the Sahara by Henri Lhote. This particular picture shows cattle near huts. The huts are the white ovals. The figures are of women and children working.

hunt. They harvested wild grain, but there is little evidence that they were farmers.

According to the rock paintings, a division of labor existed between men and women. Women are pictured caring for children, cooking, gathering wild grain, herding cattle, and making utensils. Men are shown hunting, fishing, and fighting. They are pictured shaping stone and bone into tools and weapons. Both men and women took part in dances. They had flutes and stringed instruments. The dances may have had religious meaning.

Sometime between 3000 and 2500 B.C. the Sahara began drying up. A slow movement of people and animals out of the region began. By 1500 B.C. the drying-up process had ended. Some people stayed on the few scattered oases that remained. Those who stayed and those who moved northward probably mixed with Egyptians and Berbers, a branch of the Caucasoid or Mediterranean group. Some migrants may have gone eastward to Nubia (NOO-bee-uh)—part of the modern Republic of the Sudan—and to the Horn of Africa. The Horn is the part of Ethiopia and Somalia that extends into the Indian Ocean. Around 1000 B.C. their descendants may have moved into the Eastern Rift region. Some migrants may have gone farther south. They possibly introduced herding to the Hottentots. Others moved south to the savannahs and forests of West Africa. This continuing migration of people may have gone as far as the modern Nigeria-Cameroon border.

This is the Sahara today. The camel caravan is carrying salt. Trade in gold and salt was the basis of much of West Africa's early wealth.

AGRICULTURE

There is some disagreement about when and where Africans south of the Sahara began to farm. There is not enough evidence so far to give a detailed picture.

The information available seems to indicate that farming may have developed in North Africa and the Horn independent of the rest of the continent. The oldest permanent farming settlements so far have been found on the Nile Delta in Egypt. They date to between 5000 and 4500 B.C. One site has been found along the shores of the lake at Fayum (fay-YOOM), southwest of Cairo. There wheat, barley, and flax were cultivated. Flint sickles with wooden handles for harvesting crops have been uncovered. Pottery for cooking and storing grain have also been found. From bones unearthed at the **site**, it appears these farmers raised sheep, goats, and cattle.

Farther south on the Nile, another farming settlement has been found at Badari. Around 4000 B.C. farmers at Badari were cultivating the same crops as those found at older delta sites. They were also using the same kinds of tools. It appears that the knowledge of farming was traveling slowly up the Nile. In the Republic of the Sudan too stone tools similar to those used by Fayum farmers have been found. Authorities believe that the knowledge of farming reached the Sudan

An Egyptian harvests grain. Sickles similar to his were used by the first farmers.

from Egypt between 3500 and 3000 B.C. The early Ethiopians, farther to the southeast, may also have learned about farming wheat and barley from the people of the Nile.

There is no firm evidence, however, that Egyptian farming skills and knowledge moved farther into sub-Saharan Africa. Nor is there evidence that this knowledge moved west and south across the savannahs and the Sahara. Sub-Saharan climate is not suitable for growing wheat and barley, the main crops of the Nile Valley. Considering this, it may be reasonable to assume that the peoples south of the Sahara learned farming methods independently.

Some authorities believe that in West Africa sorghum and millet may have been cultivated as early as 5000 to 4000 B.C. These grains are still the main crops of the western Sudan. By 3000 B.C. West Africans may have been experimenting with growing wild rice and a few other crops.

Where millet and other grains were cultivated and animals were **domesticated**, a continual increase in population occurred. This happened on the savannahs of the western Sudan from about 1500 B.C. onward. The migration of people into this region from the drying Sahara also swelled the population. The making and use of iron tools and weapons improved food production and led to other culture changes.

IRON AGE

The **Iron Age** began in Africa about 500 B.C. with the Kushites of Nubia in what is the modern Republic of the Sudan. The Kushites may have learned iron-making from the Assyrians (uh-SIR-ee-uhns). These Middle Easterners had used iron weapons to drive the Kushites from Egypt. In time, the Kushite capital of Meroe (MER-uh-wee) became a great iron-making center. Knowledge of iron-making may have spread from there southward. By around the first century A.D. iron was being worked along the east and southeast coasts.

In West Africa, people of the Nok (NAHK) culture of central Nigeria were apparently the first to enter the Iron Age. They were making iron tools around 300 B.C. The Nok people may have learned to smelt iron from Carthage, north of the Sahara, rather than from Meroe, to the east. Or the Nok people may have learned to work iron independently.

Iron-making **technology** may have been carried south into the rain forests of Central Africa by the migrating Bantu-speakers. This may have been around the first century A.D.

Iron greatly improved the efficiency of African tools and weapons. Iron-tipped spears made hunting more productive. Iron axes made it easier to chop trees and carve wooden objects. Iron hoes and other farm tools helped to improve farming. In addition, iron objects became valuable items in African trade activities.

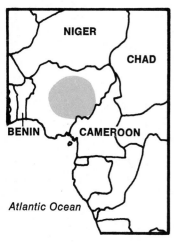

NIGER

CHAD

BENIN   CAMEROON

Atlantic Ocean

■ **Nok Culture,**
   c. 300 B.C. - 200 A.D.

Summing Up the Unit

Social Studies Vocabulary

Define: gene pool; religion; society; arts; geographical; climate; vegetation; prehistory; permanent farming; slash-and-burn farming; subsistence; export; economic; language family; Iron Age

Places

Locate: West, Central, South-Central, South-Southwest, Northeast, East Africa; Great Rift, Lesser Rift valleys; Ruwenzori Mountains; Sahara, Kalahari deserts; rain forest; savannah; Zambezi, Niger, Congo (Zaire), White Nile, Blue Nile rivers

Words

Define: sub-Sahara; humus; hydroelectric; Congo-Kordofanian; Swahili; Afro-Asian; Nilo-Saharan; Khoisan; Malayo-Polynesian; Africans; Horn of Africa

⌐⌐⌐ Questions

1. What effect has Africa's geography had on what others have known about Africans?
2. Why are there few harbors?
3. Why is East Africa overpopulated?
4. Why are Africa's rivers important?
5. Why is much of Africa's soil poor?
6. Why may slash-and-burn farming not be possible in Africa in the future?
7. Where are the most extensive areas of mixed farming in the sub-Sahara?
8. What items offer great hope for Africa's economic future?
9. Africans are making progress toward modernization, despite lack of what three factors?
10. What reasons are given for the growth of Africa's cities today?
11. What disagreements do anthropologists have about early people in Africa?
12. a. What have archaeologists learned about the early Sahara? b. What is their source?
13. What resulted from the Sahara's drying up?
14. What does available evidence indicate about the beginnings of farming in the sub-Sahara?
15. What cultural changes took place in the western Sudan after the 1500s B.C.?
16. What theories are given about the spread of ironmaking among the Kushites?
17. a. Who were the first West Africans to enter the Iron Age? b. Where did they learn to work with iron?
18. What were three consequences of the introduction of iron to Africa?

Discussion Topics

1. Sub-Saharan Africa is a giant plateau with few rivers that drain to the sea. How had this fact affected its history?
2. Africa is rich in minerals and potential hydroelectric power. How do you think these resources can best be developed? What problems must be solved first?
3. The Sahara was not always dry and barren. How can its transformation into a desert be explained? Additional research will be necessary.
4. How Africans earn their livings depends largely on the climate, vegetation, and soil conditions of the area in which they live. How have climatic zones and differences of altitude affected life in different parts of Africa?

Project Ideas

1. Prepare a report on one nation of sub-Saharan Africa. Describe how its geography has affected its population and economy.
2. Write a research paper on Africa's mineral resources as the cause of conflict between Communist and non-Communist nations.
3. Report on recent African discoveries by anthropologists and archaeologists.
4. Plan a trip to Africa. Describe to the class where you will go and what you will see.
5. To become familiar with the physical and political geography of Africa, trace the maps in this unit. After you learn the names and locations of the nations, try to identify them on a blank outline map.
6. Using an atlas or encyclopedia for reference, draw a population distribution overlay for the physical map. Generalize about the relationship of population to geographical features.

Unit II

Kingdoms, Empires, and States

This soapstone sculpture of a head was carved in Sierra Leone sometime during the 1500s or 1600s. What kingdom had arisen in this area by that time?

A number of **kingdoms**, **empires**, and **states** developed in Africa before the coming of the Europeans. **Environment** and location played important roles in their growth.

The available **natural resources** of an area determined the kinds of tools, building materials, art, and **architecture** that developed. Forest peoples, for example, used wood as a material for buildings and artwork. Where wood was scarce, peoples used mud bricks or stone. Environment also influenced the work that people did. Some areas were ideal for settled farming communities. Other regions were more suited to a herding economy.

Location also was a factor. Coastal peoples and those who lived at the edge of the Sahara became traders. Their contacts with the Middle East and North Africa added new features to their cultures. They adopted ideas from these regions and adapted them to their own needs. On the other hand, because of the plateau, peoples of the interior were not greatly influenced by contacts with non-Africans. The European scramble to colonize the continent in the 1800s would change this, however.

From around 3400 to 3100 B.C., fortified settlements began to appear along the Nile River in Egypt. A number of these towns and villages joined together to form two kingdoms—Lower Egypt and Upper Egypt. Lower Egypt was in the delta area that reached north from about Cairo to the Mediterranean Sea. Upper Egypt stretched south to the river's First Cataract, or rapids, at Aswan (ah-SWAHN). Around 3100 B.C. these two kingdoms were united under a single ruler called a pharaoh (FAY-roh).

Chapter 1
The
Northeast

NUBIA

During the Middle Kingdom period (c. 2050-1800 B.C.), one of the pharaohs extended the kingdom southward. He claimed all the area beyond Aswan to the land of the Nubians. The Egyptians had had contacts with the Nubians for many centuries. During the Empire period (c. 1580-1150 B.C.) pharaohs sent a series of invasion forces south. They wanted to control Nubian trade. Eventually Nubia became an Egyptian province.

KINGDOM OF KUSH   Not much is known of Nubia again until the 700s B.C. During this time the Kingdom of Kush (KUHSH) arose among the Nubians. The Kushites built their capital at Napata (NAP-uh-tuh) on the Nile. Around 750 B.C. the Kushites were strong enough to conquer Egypt. Eventually the Kushite king Shabaka became the ruler of Kush and Egypt.

In the mid-600s B.C., Assyrians from the Middle East drove the Kushites back to their Nubian homeland. In the 500s B.C., the Kushites moved their capital from Napata farther south to Meroe. This later period of Kushite development became known as the Meroitic (mer-uh-WIT-ik) **civilization**. Around this time the Kushites began working in iron. Iron objects became part of their trade goods.

The Kushite trade network reached east to ports along the Red Sea and possibly as far southeast as Ethiopia. Kushite cultural influence may have spread as far west as Lake Chad or beyond. The Kushites continued their ties with the Egyptians. Later they developed friendly relations with Egypt's Greek and Roman rulers.

Over the centuries, the Kushites created a civilization which blended elements of these various peoples. Egyptian influence can be seen in temples, palaces, and the pyramid tombs built at Meroe for the royal family. It is also evident in the custom of wrapping the dead in cotton cloth and of placing glass and bronze objects in tombs. Some Kushite ruins also show Roman influence. One ruin is an imitation of a Roman bath. Evidence of contacts with the Arabian Peninsula and even India is apparent in Kushite cloth and **sculpture** designs.

However, Kushites did not lose their African **culture traits**. Royal women played important roles in society and **politics**. Succession to the throne may have come through the female side of the family.

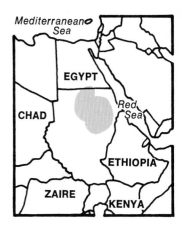

■ **Kingdom of Kush, c. 500 B.C.**

These pyramids were built during the Meroitic period of the Kingdom of Kush. What other peoples built pyramids?

This was common in Africa. Kushites also believed that their rulers were divine. This belief too is part of Africa's long cultural **tradition**.

Beginning around 300 A.D., the Meroitic civilization began to decline. Desert nomads known as Red and Black Noba moved into the kingdom. Evidently some of the nomads passed south through Kush and into the Kingdom of Axum (AHK-soom) in Ethiopia. In 330, the king of Axum marched against the Noba. He chased them into Kushite territory and destroyed both Kushite and Noba towns. In the following centuries, other desert peoples settled among the Kushites. These peoples adapted many Kushite culture traits. From this blending arose three kingdoms in the 500s.

evidently: clearly, obviously

CHRISTIAN KINGDOMS   Nobatia (noh-BAY-shee-uh) was located in the northern region of Nubia between the First and Third Cataracts of the Nile. Makuria (muh-KOOR-ee-uh) was the central kingdom. Alodia (ah-LOOD-ee-uh) was south not far from Meroe.

In the mid-500s these kingdoms were converted to Coptic Christianity. Coptic Christianity had arisen out of a disagreement about whether God as the Son had one nature or two. The Copts believed that Christ had one nature. In the late 200s A.D., Alexandria, Egypt, had become the leading center of Coptic teaching and writing. Religious leaders at Constantinople, however, held that Christ had two natures—divine and human. The Roman Catholic Church called a meeting, the **Council** of Chalcedon (KAL-suh-dahn), in 451 to settle the question. It decided in favor of the teachings set forth by Constantinople. Those who continued to hold the Coptic belief were to be considered heretics. The Copts broke with the Church. However, they continued to make converts in the Nubian kingdoms and in Ethiopia.

From the 600s onward, the Christian Nubian kingdoms grew. Their prosperity was based on trade with Muslim Arabs—followers of Islam—who occupied Egypt at the time. Around the 800s, non-Arab Muslims began to invade the kingdoms for their gold. The kingdoms held out for several centuries. But eventually they were conquered. In the latter part of the 1200s, Muslim rulers were able to take Nobatia. Makuria fell about a century later. Alodia remained independent until the 1400s.

Most Egyptians and people of the Republic of Sudan are now Muslims. Coptic Christianity is very strong in Ethiopia, however. During their years of conquest, the Muslims generally permitted freedom of worship to Christians.

ETHIOPIA

Between 700 and 500 B.C., groups of people crossed the Red Sea from what is modern Yemen to the area known today as Ethiopia. They merged with people already living in the northern highlands. From this mixing of peoples and cultures there developed around 300 to 200 B.C., the Kingdom of Axum.

Axum became a great trading empire. Ivory, tortoise shell, spices, perfumes, and incense among other items passed through the kingdom. Its main port, Adulis (ah-DOO-lis), on the Red Sea, became the center of trade between the Mediterranean Sea and the Indian Ocean. Extensive trade grew with Egypt which was then ruled by Greeks. Greek merchants settled in Axum and began to dominate the kingdom's commerce. Greek became the language of trade and **diplomacy**.

The Ethiopians, however, developed their own language and **script** called Geez (GEE-ez). Among Axumite artistic achievements are steles—large carved stone blocks. Archaeologists believe that these were memorials to important people.

Around 300 A.D., the Axumites invaded Kush to the northwest. They also extended their power east across the Red Sea into the southern part of the Arabian Peninsula. During the 500s, the Persians from what is modern Iran drove them from most of inland Arabia. Ethiopian trade began to decrease. Axum declined. The capital was moved south to Nazaret. In the 600s, Muslim Arabs began moving into the northern and eastern portions of Ethiopia. They made large numbers of converts to Islam.

Around 1100 the Zagwe (ZAHG-wee) from southern Ethiopia seized power. In the 1200s they were driven out. The new rulers were supposedly descended from King Solomon and the Queen of Sheba. They were known as the Solomonian line.

In the 1300s the Ethiopians began a series of **campaigns** to subdue the Muslims. The fighting raged for over a hundred years. In 1527 the Muslims began an all-out war. Ethiopia appealed to Portugal for help. In 1541 the Portuguese joined the Ethiopians to defeat the Muslims. But by this time the empire had split into several kingdoms. It was not until Emperor Menelik (MEN-uh-lik) II came to power in 1889 that the country was once again reunited.

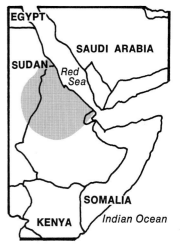

Kingdom of Axum, c. 400 A.D.

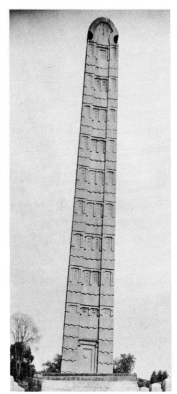

This stele was carved during the period of the Kingdom of Axum. What other peoples carved steles? Why were steles made?

In the 1200s King Lalibela had 11 churches carved out of solid rock in Lalibela, Ethiopia. These are two of the churches. First a rectangular trench was carved, leaving a solid block of rock which was then carved into rooms.

Chapter 2

Central and South Africa

The cultural development of the peoples of Central and South Africa is largely the history of the migrating Bantu-speaking (BAN-too) peoples. The Bantu-speakers also contributed much to the history of the peoples in West and East Africa. Both the Bantus and the many peoples they met changed as a result of these contacts.

One of the most important things that changed about the Bantus was their language. Today there are several hundred variations of the original language. Each language marks its speakers as belonging to a Bantu grouping or family. The term Bantu-speaker places these peoples in a language group, not in a common physical or cultural grouping. Today between 60 and 80 million Africans speak one of the Bantu languages.

BANTU MIGRATIONS

Some scholars believe that the Bantu lived originally in eastern Nigeria south of the Benue River Valley along the border with what is today Cameroon. Other scholars place the original Bantu homeland in the southeast Congo Basin. The Bantu-speakers may have been herders, fishers, and farmers. Authorities are sure they knew about working with iron, however.

No one knows exactly when the Bantu-speaking people began to move from their homeland. Nor does anyone know exactly when

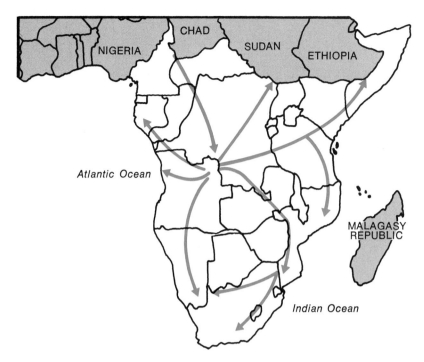

Bantu Migrations

they reached each new area of settlement. Some authorities believe they began to move within the last 2,000 years. Others, however, believe they began their migrations much earlier. They believe the people fleeing the Sahara after 2500 B.C. may have caused the earliest Bantu migrations.

These migrations were not a series of quick, sweeping invasions like those which occurred in Western Europe. The Bantu migrations were gradual movements of small numbers of people. As the population increased in each new area, the groups divided. Some remained, while others moved on. This pattern was repeated many times.

Gradually much of the forest area of Central Africa was settled by Bantu-speakers. They continued south and east along the interior river system. They followed the Congo (Zaire), Kasai (kuh-SY), and other rivers south to the Zambezi River. Gradually, they made their way to the Indian Ocean. The Bantus who reached the east coast may have traveled north as far as modern Somalia. This may have been around the 700s A.D.

Sometime before 400 A.D., some Bantu peoples had gone south into Zambia, Rhodesia, and neighboring regions. By the 1200s, they occupied the southeastern part of what today is the Republic of South Africa. Migrating Bantu-speakers also went southwest into Angola and farther south into what is today Namibia (nuh-MIB-ee-uh).

The Bantu-speakers who migrated eastward may have reached Lake

Some of the Bantu migrated down rivers and along the coasts in dugout canoes much like these.

Victoria by the time the Indian Ocean had been reached. In East Africa, Bantu-speaking peoples became herders. Many of the original Bantus may have been herders. If so, their descendants had given up this way of life as they migrated through the forest regions. Cattle could not survive in the forests because of the tropical climate and diseases. The Bantus in East Africa also cultivated bananas and yams. These crops were probably brought first to the island of Madagascar—part of the Malagasy Republic—by Southeast Asians and then to the African mainland.

Movements of Bantu-speaking peoples continued into the 1800s.

BANTU KINGDOMS

All Bantu-speaking peoples share some culture traits which reflect their common beginnings. For example, **kinship** ties are important. Everyone in a community is descended from a common ancestor. This descent is traced through the mother's side of the family. This is called a **matrilineal** system of descent. Property and inheritance are passed down through the mother's family. Having a common ancestor makes everyone in a community a member of the same **clan**. This kinship system binds members to each other and to their ancestors. Bantu-speaking peoples share the belief that their dead ancestors live among them and watch over them.

Through the centuries, however, differences began to multiply among Bantu-speakers. This happened as the various groups adapted to the environments and peoples they met. They began to develop ways of doing things and **customs** that fit certain areas. Gradually they began to call themselves by various names: Xhosa (KOH-sah),

Sotho (SOH-toh), Zulu, and so on. In Shaba—formerly known as Katanga—a province of modern Zaire, the Luba (LOO-buh) kingdom developed. West of it the Lunda (LOON-duh) kingdom arose. Farther south and west other kingdoms developed along the lower Congo (Zaire) River. Probably the most famous was the Kingdom of the Congo, whose people became known as Congolese.

Still within a kingdom, subgroupings of other peoples existed. They kept ways that marked them as different from the dominant peoples. This fact would have important consequences later.

LUBA AND LUNDA   The Bantus at first generally lived in small villages. In time the villages in an area would multiply. Gradually states were formed. A system of government became necessary. Chiefs were appointed. Sometimes these states grew into kingdoms.

As early as 700 or 800 A.D. people living in the copper-rich area of Shaba were making pottery and working with metal. By the 1100s their copper trade reached to distant parts of Africa. The villages were ruled by family chiefs. They, in turn, were ruled by higher chiefs who were related to them.

According to **oral tradition**, sometime around the beginning of the 1500s, or earlier, Kongolo, a warrior chief from the north, conquered parts of the region. Later he was killed in a struggle with his nephew. The nephew, Kalala Ilunga (kuh-LAH-luh ee-LOON-gah), then joined the scattered villages and states of the region into one kingdom—Luba. Kalala became the king.

A common ruler now bound together the various groups. To the idea of kingship, Kalala added the idea of divinity. He claimed that he was sacred. Only he and his family had the help of the spirits in protecting and guarding the well-being of the people. This claim, of course, kept power in Kalala's family.

The Luba kingdom continued to expand until the mid-1800s when it fell to the Belgians. At its height, Luba extended from Shaba to Lake Tanganyika.

When a Luba king died, his successor could replace minor chiefs, if he wished. Sometimes a displaced chief would become restless and move on. Such an example is the Kingdom of Lunda on the Kasai River to the west. Oral tradition tells that sometime before the 1600s, Rweej, a queen of Lunda, married Kibinda Ilunga (kee-BEEN-duh ee-LOON-gah). He was a Luba chief who had left his homeland. Perhaps under him, but certainly under later rulers, Luba ideas and practices combined with those of the Lunda people.

Like the political and social system of Luba, that of Lunda was based on kinship ties. The elder relatives generally held the positions of authority in the village. The village leader usually was from the village's main family group. He had religious as well as political duties. A council of elders advised him. They, in turn, were governed by district chiefs. The chiefs were the king's tax collectors.

As in Luba, major positions of authority were held by relatives

☐ **Kingdoms of Luba and Lunda**

This is a copper cross made by a Luba craftworker. It was used as part of someone's bride price. A man did not buy a wife, but he did give her family valuables in return for its loss of her services.

of the ruler. However, Lunda rulers appointed some people who were not related to them, for example, chiefs of conquered lands. This insured the chiefs' support and that of their people. The territorial expansion of Lunda was greatly helped by this. At its peak, more than a million people lived under Lunda rule.

MALAWI Sometime around the 1500s, probably before Luba became a kingdom, people from Luba migrated southeast. They may have been the ancestors of people known as Malawi. In the beginning the political system of the Malawi developed differently than that of the Luba. By the mid-1500s, there were a number of Malawi chiefs. Their positions were strengthened when the people began long-distance trade with the east-coast city of Mozambique.

Malawi trade connected the interior with the east coast in the same way that the Luba-Lunda kingdoms connected the interior with the west coast. Gradually a network of trade routes grew which connected the southern east and west coasts from Angola to Mozambique. The routes of the southern savannahs also tied into these trade routes.

In the early 1600s Kalonga Mzura (kuh-LAHN-gah muh-ZOO-rah) became the most powerful of the Malawi rulers. He gained control of the territory from Lake Malawi south to where the Zambezi River empties into the sea. He considered himself no longer a king but an emperor. During his rule, his contacts included the Portuguese who began coming to sub-Saharan Africa in the 1400s. After his death the empire of Malawi gradually declined. By 1800 it had disappeared.

THE CONGO Around the 1100s, states began growing along the lower parts of the Congo (Zaire) River. The greatest of these was the Kingdom of the Congo, or Kongo. Sometime before 1400, Wene (WAY-nay), the son of the chief of the small state of Bungu, conquered an area south of the Congo (Zaire). He and his followers made their rule legal by marrying into the major families they had conquered. Wene took the title manikongo (mah-nee-KAHN-goh), or king. He ruled with absolute authority and was believed to have divine power.

During the 1400s the kingdom grew to include land north of the Congo River. It stretched across northern Angola from the Atlantic Ocean to the Kwango River, where it met the Lunda kingdom. Like other kingdoms in the area, trade was the basis of its economy. Pottery, cloth, and iron goods were traded. The Congolese also farmed. Their main crops were millet and bananas. In the 1600s maize, among other crops from the Americas, was introduced.

The arrival of the Portuguese in 1482 led to divisions within the kingdom. The royal family converted to Christianity. Those who did not convert opposed them. Throughout the 1500s, Portuguese greed for **slaves**, copper, and gold worsened the problems within the kingdom. These and other factors brought about the final division of the

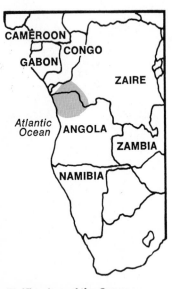

Kingdom of the Congo, 1400s

kingdom around 1664. Local kings and chiefs ruled small areas. The growing influence of merchants, however, undercut their power. By the beginning of the 1800s, little was left of the glory that once was the Kingdom of the Congo.

ZIMBABWE   Between the Limpopo and Zambezi rivers in parts of modern Rhodesia and Mozambique are many groups of stone ruins which Africans call Zimbabwe (zim-BAH-bway). Zimbabwe means houses of stone. These ruins are among the earliest stone structures found south of the Sahara. Elsewhere, wood and mud were the usual materials. The remains of such buildings have long since decayed.

Early in the Christian era, Bantu-speakers moved over this region in their migrations southeast. Perhaps as early as the 400s A.D., some of them began mining gold in the area. These were probably ancestors of the modern Sotho people. These early people also made iron tools, herded, farmed, and made pottery.

Around the 700s, they began trading gold and locally made items with their neighbors. Their trade increased when news of their gold reached east coast traders. It may have been the experience of this trade which moved these people to begin building Zimbabwe sometime before the 1000s. Or they may have begun these buildings much earlier. Some archaeologists have dated the ruins to as early as the 500s A.D.

Builders of the Zimbabwe did not use mortar. They carefully fitted together the stone blocks. The largest of the ruins is known as Great Zimbabwe. It is located near Fort Victoria in Rhodesia. Archaeologists

Prior to the coming of the Europeans, most Africans used the barter system, but some used shells and beads as a medium of exchange. This is a money collar from the Congo.

This is a part of the Temple Ruin at Zimbabwe. Some archaeologists believe it was the home of the ruling chief or king. Between it and the Acropolis is another group of walls and small buildings—the Valley Ruin. Ordinary people may have lived in these.

have named one group of buildings the Acropolis (uh-KRAHP-uh-luhs) because it was built on top of a hill like the Greek Acropolis. It may have been a fort. In the valley below are other stone structures.

Perhaps between 1000 and 1100, the Bantu-speaking ancestors of the Shona (SHOH-nuh) people began settling in the area. They gradually drove out the Sotho. The Sotho moved south to the Transvaal region of South Africa. The Shona took over the gold trade and began to create small states in the area. Then, in the first half of the 1400s, the Monomotapa (muh-noh-muh-TAH-puh) Empire developed.

MONOMOTAPA EMPIRE   Like most Bantu-speaking peoples, the Shona were divided into various clans. Clan unity came from sharing a common ancestor. Among the strongest of these groups were the Karanga (kuh-RAHN-guh). The dominant among the Karanga was the Rozwi (ROHZ-wee). They believed their kings had divine powers. The Rozwi took over the Great Zimbabwe. There and elsewhere, they continued to add to the stone structures that had been built earlier.

One of the Rozwi kings, Mutota (muh-TOH-tuh), began a conquest of the land between the Limpopo and Zambezi rivers around 1440. He gained control of the trade coming to and from the coastal cities. Taxing these goods made him rich. After his death, his son, Matope (mah-TOH-pee), continued the conquests. Matope took much of what is modern southern Mozambique, including Sofala (soh-FAHLuh) and other harbors along the east coast. His empire came to be called Monomotapa.

Monomotapa was divided into provinces. The ruler lived in the north near the Zambezi Valley. This became the center of his government. The other provinces were ruled by relatives and trusted subjects called **vassals**. They paid annual dues to the ruler. Monomotapa was a **feudal** form of government. Like all feudal systems, however, some vassals grew strong enough to challenge their ruler. This happened with a Rozwi vassal named Changa.

Changa ruled a province in the southern part of the empire. After Matope died, around 1480, Changa brought the entire southern part of the empire under his rule. He changed his name to Changamira (CHAN-guh-mee-ruh) and named his empire after himself. Later, after killing the Monomotapa ruler, he gained control of the entire empire. After several years, he too was killed. But his son continued to hold and expand the southern part of Monomotapa. The Changamira kingdom lasted from the late 1600s through the 1700s. Other Bantu-speakers, the Ngoni, destroyed it.

Ultimately, Monomotapa fell not to other Africans but to the Portuguese. Around the beginning of the 1500s, the Portuguese took the coastal city of Sofala. The Portuguese then began to move up the Zambezi River. They were in search of the sources of the gold that flowed into Sofala. At first the Portuguese supported Monomotapa against its rebel vassals. But in return, the Portuguese began to ask more and more from the empire. When the king finally resisted in the 1620s, the Portuguese defeated him. They placed a puppet king on the throne. He ruled as he was directed by the Portuguese king.

■ **Monomotapa Empire, 1400s**

People living along the east coast of Africa have a long history of contacts with non-Africans. The old Ethiopian port of Adulis on the Red Sea was a busy center of commerce. Greeks, Jews, Arabs, and Egyptians among others came there to trade. Farther south—in modern Somalia—was a trading region known in ancient Egyptian writings as the land of Punt.

Over the centuries trade gradually spread farther south. Gold, iron, ivory, and other goods in increasing amounts moved from the interior to the coast. Trading villages grew into cities and then into **city-states**. Muslim Iranians and Arabs played a large role in this expansion of trade. Many of them settled along the coast and on the offshore islands. They blended their culture and customs with the Africans already living there.

People living in the interior of East Africa were not exposed to these continuing outside influences. Traders generally stayed close to the coast. They were interested in the goods coming from the interior. They were not interested in the people who sent them. Thus

Chapter 3
East Africa

East Coast Cities

the people of the interior developed their own ways of life without any great pressure from non-Africans.

COASTAL CITIES

Much of the eariliest knowledge we have of the coastal centers of modern Somalia, Kenya, Tanzania, and Mozambique comes from Greek and Arab writings.

Around 110 A.D., an unknown Greek living in Alexandria wrote *The Periplus* (Guide) *of the Erythraean* (Red) *Sea.* The guide grouped the trading centers along the coast of Tanzania and Kenya under the name Azania (ah-ZAN-ee-uh). The people of Azania exported ivory, palm oil, rhinoceros horn, tortoise shell, and other goods to the southern Arabian Peninsula and India. They exchanged these goods for swords, hatchets, lances, glass, and other items. Not much is known about the social and political systems of east-coast people at this time. They apparently were governed by independent chiefs. Arabs handled most of the trade. By the 700s the trade route had grown to include China.

Monsoon winds played an important part in this trade. From November through March these winds blow from a northeast direction. They carried Arab ships from the west coast of India to the east coast of Africa. From May through September the winds blow in a southeast direction. Arabs and Asians used these winds to return to Asia.

In the 900s, an Arab historian, al-Masudi (ahl-mah-SOO-dee), wrote *Meadows of Gold and Mines of Gems,* after visiting the east coast. From al-Masudi's work, it is clear that the people had become skilled metalworkers and had increased the amount of their trade with Asia. Some of the coast settlements had developed into states. He wrote that the people were ruled by a king who had other kings under him.

In the 1100s, another Arab traveler, al-Idrisi (ahl-id-REE-see), wrote of his visit to the area that is modern Kenya. Trade goods from there went to such distant places as China, Indonesia, and Malaysia. Into the cities came, among other items, Chinese porcelain, Burmese pottery, and Indian cloth and beads. Al-Idrisi was especially impressed by the iron trade. African iron was of excellent quality and easy to shape into blades and tools. Malindi was an important African center for iron.

Major coastal cities of this time included the island-port of Mozambique—for which the nation was later named—Zanzibar and Tumbatu in Tanzania, and Zeila and Berbera farther north in Somalia. Zeila was an outlet for the coffee trade of the Ethiopian highlands. It also traded in goatskins and slaves. Farther south along the Somalia coast were other centers. One of the most important was Mogadishu (mahg-uh-DISH-oo). Mogadishu merchants had trade contacts as far south as Sofala. By the 1200s, the island-city of Kilwa off the Tanzanian coast began to rise above these other cities in importance.

SOURCES OF INFORMATION   Besides Greek and Arab writings, information about early east-coast Africa comes from chronicles written in the various cities. The oldest of these is the *Kilwa Chronicle*. It was written around the first half of the 1500s. Another source of information is oral history or tradition. There is also the information that comes from the work of anthropologists and archaeologists. These sources do not always agree. Often conflicts arise over the time something supposedly happened. For example, disagreement exists over Kilwa's early development.

According to the *Chronicle*, Iranians (Persians), known as Shirazi (shuh-RAHZ-ee), came to Kilwa in the 900s. Archaeologists, however, disagree. Their recent findings indicate that the Shirazi came two centuries later. Archaeologists have found coins in Kilwa which they date to this later period and link to the first Shirazi.

Still other scholars say that no one came directly from Iran to Kilwa. They claim that African descendants of the Iranians moved to Kilwa from earlier settlements in the north. Whatever the final theory will be, it is certain that Kilwa had become an important trading center by the 1100s.

Much of Kilwa's prosperity came when it took over the gold trade of Sofala in the 1200s. The Portuguese who captured Kilwa in 1505 described the city as having three- and four-story stone houses. Gold, pearls, silver, amber, and silk were abundant. The people ate a wide

This is an old ruin in the east coast trading center of Gedi or Malindi. What was the source of wealth of the east coast cities? How important was trade to the development of other areas in Africa? Do you think trade has always played a role in the development of cities?

variety of food: lamb, goat, chicken, rice, millet, oranges, pineapples, limes, and many kinds of vegetables.

MUSLIM INFLUENCE   As early as the 600s A.D., Muslim Arabs had been bringing their religion as well as their goods over the trade routes to Africa's east coast. At first the religious element probably had little impact on the cultural development of the African peoples. It was not until the 800s that Islamic influence began to be felt. More Muslim Arabs came as trade increased.

The Arab traders began to settle permanently along the east coast and marry African women. This mixture of African and Arab peoples came to be known as Swahili. The Swahili were Muslims. They developed their own language, primarily of Bantu origin, with Arabic and some Persian words. Describing Kilwa in the 1300s, Ibn Battuta (IB-un bah-TOOT-tuh), a traveler from Morocco, reported that the Koran, the mosque, Islamic designs in architecture, and other Islamic influences had become part of the daily lives of the people.

It should be remembered that these east-coast cities were not Arab cities. They were African. The Africans living in them adopted Arab and other non-African influences. But the dominant political and social force was African.

KINGDOMS OF THE INTERIOR

Long ago, ancestors of the Hottentots and Bushmen hunted for food in East Africa's interior. Gradually they were pushed out or swallowed up by farming people moving south from Ethiopia. The newcomers spread through the area as far south as Tanzania. Over the centuries other peoples wandered into the Great Rift Valley from the north. Some settled in Kenya. Others moved south of Lake Victoria in eastern Tanzania. They were cattle herders.

Sometime after the 100s A.D., Bantu-speaking peoples began migrating into East Africa from the west. The Bantu mixed with the earlier peoples. Over the next thousand years or so, Bantu-speakers came to occupy all of southern and eastern Tanzania. They also took over the high region of Kenya east of the Great Rift Valley.

In Tanzania and Kenya, the various peoples lived mostly in clusters

This is an example of a Bushman cave painting. Bushmen were early inhabitants of East Africa. Why did they leave?

294

of villages ruled by a chief. They did not develop into kingdoms with a centralized government. Their economy was based mainly on farming. But they traded in such items as salt, iron, and pottery.

KITWARA   In some parts of the Lakes region kingdoms did develop. A non-Bantu-speaking people called Hima (HEE-ma) moved into Uganda around the 1300s. The Hima were herders. They began to dominate the Bantu-speakers already there. Strongest among the Hima clans were the Chwezi (KWEE-zee). The Chwezi became the rulers of a kingdom known as Kitwara (kit-WAH-ruh). This kingdom was divided into districts. Each district was ruled by a subchief. Rule was passed from father to son.

A social system developed based on occupations. Herders held the highest positions. Some people were farmers. Others made pottery or worked iron. All had to give part of their labor as well as other **tribute** to the rulers.

BUNYORO AND BUGANDA   Meanwhile, other people had been moving into the area from the north. Sometime in the 1500s, a branch of these people—ancestors of the modern Luo—replaced the Chwezi as rulers. Their kingdom became known as Bunyoro (bun-YAH-roh).

Gradually smaller kingdoms elsewhere in Uganda came to be ruled by members of the Bunyoro family. One of these kingdoms was Buganda (boo-GAHN-duh). At first Buganda covered a small area centered around Kampala, which later became the capital of modern Uganda. Gradually Buganda's rulers expanded their territory and power. By the 1700s Buganda had become greater in power and **status** than Bunyoro. By the 1890s, Buganda was the greatest state in the interior. Its economy was based on long-distance trade. In Bunyoro and Buganda, the Luo rulers gradually adopted the customs and language of the Bantu whom they governed.

RWANDA AND BURUNDI   South of Uganda, the kingdoms of Rwanda (roo-AHN-duh) and Burundi (bur-ROON-dee) developed. Rulers of both kingdoms came from the Hima people. Tradition states that the first kings were of the Chwezi clan. In the 1400s and 1500s the Tutsi (TOOT-see), also called Watusi (wah-TOO-see), migrated into the area. They took control of the Bantu-speaking Hutu (HOO-too), or Bahutu (bah-HOO-too).

The Hima people brought with them to Rwanda and Burundi their social system. At the top were the herding Hima people. Cattle meant wealth and status and belonged only to the king. However, he gave cattle to various lords to look after. Next were farmers, who were **serfs** for the Hima. At the bottom were the hunting and food-gathering Pygmies. As with the feudal system of Europe, farmers attached themselves to strong lords. In return for their labor, these lords gave them protection and security. Marriage between social classes was forbidden.

295

Chapter 4
West Africa

By 5,000 years ago, West Africans were farming. Over 2,000 years ago, some—the Nok culture in what is modern Nigeria—had entered the Iron Age. The introduction of iron was important to the development of the West Africans. Superior tools and weapons gave them greater control of their environment. The stronger people began to dominate the weaker ones.

At various times between 500 A.D. and the 1700s, a number of states, kingdoms, and empires rose and declined in West Africa. They were based mostly on trans-Saharan trade. They traded gold, ivory, spices, and slaves in return for salt, cloth, metalware, and other items. As this trade grew, it helped to stimulate the growth of cities and states. One of the earliest of these West African states came to be known as the Empire of Ghana.

■ Empire of Ghana,
 c. 300-1076

EMPIRE OF GHANA

Ghana's beginnings may reach back to about 300 A.D. A people called Soninke may have developed and ruled it. The empire's exact boundaries are not known, but it extended into areas which are parts of the modern nations of Mauritania, Mali, Senegal, and Guinea. Ghana's location favored growth and prosperity. It was on a main north-south trade route.

Through Ghana passed the salt traders from the Sahara and North Africa and the gold traders from the south. The West Africans needed salt as much as the Arabs wanted gold. Ghana's king taxed both. Moreover, all gold found within Ghana itself belonged to him. He allowed only limited amounts on the market at any one time. By the 700s Ghana was known as the Land of Gold. Its ruler was described as among the wealthiest in the world.

Ghana's subjects considered their king divine. The position was also **hereditary**. When the king died, he was succeeded by the son of his sister. The various territories conquered by Ghana were generally ruled by local leaders. They paid tribute and provided soldiers to the king. In return, they received protection and were allowed to rule their own areas.

The empire reached the height of its power in the mid-1000s. Then a slow decline began. Revolts from within and attacks from without occurred. The most serious invasion was that of the Almoravid (ahl-muh-RAH-vid) Berbers, an Islamic **sect** from North Africa. The Ghanaian ruler's refusal to become a Muslim angered the Almoravids. They conquered and looted Ghana's capital in 1076. Ghana fought and eventually regained its independence, but the war had seriously weakened it. Territories began to break away. In 1235, what remained of the empire was taken over by Susu, one of its former states.

SPREAD OF ISLAM　During the 600s, Muslim Arabs swept out of the Middle East across North Africa. Many of the people in these areas became Muslims. North African traders carried Islam with them into West Africa. Sometimes—as in the Empire of Ghana—Islam was carried by invading armies.

By the late 1000s, the impact of Islam was very apparent in the savannah region just south of the Sahara. Ghana's kings had kept their traditional religion. But many of their advisors and **ministers** had become Muslims. Kumbi Saleh (KOOM-bee SAHL-uh), Ghana's last capital, was really two towns. Most of the Muslims lived in one. Non-Muslims lived in the other.

During the following centuries, Islam moved even farther into the savannah and forest regions of West Africa. Throughout these areas, the Koran began to be used as the basis for systems of justice and taxation. New buildings resembled those in other parts of the Islamic

These figures are examples of gold work from Ghana. What was the source of Ghana's wealth? How important was trade to Ghana's growth?

world. Since Islam stressed education, schools, universities, and scholars became important. Pilgrimages to Mecca (MEK-uh), the Muslim holy city in modern Saudi Arabia, brought West Africans into contact with peoples from all over the then-known world.

Islamic influence was stronger in cities and towns than it was in **rural** areas. There, many people held onto their traditional ways.

EMPIRE OF MALI

The Empire of Mali achieved its greatness not only by trading in gold and salt as had Ghana, but by actually controlling the sources of these two items. Mali's rulers gained control of both the gold fields and the salt region. Mali eventually covered an area from the Atlantic to the borders of modern Nigeria. Mali's rulers continued the tax practices of Ghana. All goods coming into and leaving the empire were taxed.

Empire of Mali, 1300s

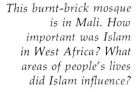

The empire was divided into states. The central region was governed directly by the ruler. He appointed governors—often members of the royal family—to administer parts of this region. Conquered states were generally left under their former rulers. They had to swear loyalty to Mali's ruler. To insure their loyalty, members of their families often had to live in the capital as hostages. The vassal states also had to provide soldiers for the empire's army. These soldiers kept peace and defended the empire. For a time this orderly system resulted in economic prosperity.

The greatest of Mali's rulers was Mansa Musa (MAN-suh MOO-sah, 1312-1337). In 1324, he made a pilgrimage to Mecca. On this journey, Mansa Musa met As-Saheli (ahs-sah-HAYL-ee), a Spanish writer and architect, who returned to Mali with him. As-Saheli built the first mosques and palaces of burnt-brick in the region. His materials and designs greatly influenced future building in West Africa.

During this time, the city of Timbuktu became famous. It endured for almost 1,000 years as part of various empires. At the peak of Mali's and later the Empire of Songhai's power, Timbuktu was known throughout the Islamic world. Early in the 1500s, a young Muslim traveler, Al Hassan ibn-Mohammed (ahl-hah-SAHN IB-un-moh HAM-uhd)—known to the Western world as Leo Africanus (af-ri-KAY-nus)—described the city. He wrote especially of the people's regard for learning. Scholars and students came from far and near to teach and study at Sankore, its university. Graduates of this university established schools of their own.

Like Ghana before, however, Mali became the object of invasions. In the early 1400s, Tuaregs (TWAH-regs), a group of Berbers from North Africa, attacked northern towns in the empire. Revolts occurred within the empire. The most serious of these resulted in the separation of the areas of Timbuktu and Gao (GAH-oh) from the empire. By the late 1400s Mali had lost much of its importance.

This burnt-brick mosque is in Mali. How important was Islam in West Africa? What areas of people's lives did Islam influence?

EMPIRE OF SONGHAI

The Songhai (sahn-GHEE) people of the area around Gao had carved out a kingdom along the Niger River perhaps as early as the 600s A.D. In the 1000s their ruler converted to Islam. In the 1300s the kingdom became, for a time, a vassal state of the Mali. The Songhai people fought and regained their independence. They then began their own territorial expansion.

Sunni Ali (SOO-nee AH-lee), who came to power in 1464, drove out the Mossi people from the area around Timbuktu. He also drove out the Tuaregs. He made the area of the Niger bend and the central savannah the center of his empire. Generally local rulers were not allowed to remain as leaders after their territories were conquered. He appointed his own governors. He also introduced a **bureaucracy** of **civil servants** to run the central government.

Sunni Ali died in 1492. He was succeeded by his son who was deposed by Askia Mohammed (AHS-kee-uh moh-HAM-uhd, 1493-1528). Under Askia Mohammed the Songhai Empire reached the peak of its power and prosperity. He extended its borders in all directions and came to control the sources of gold and salt. Taxes on **imports** and exports brought much wealth into the royal treasury. Unlike Sunni Ali who was tolerant of traditional religious beliefs, Askia Mohammed wanted all his people to become Muslims. He supported the building of mosques and encouraged Islamic teachings throughout the empire.

Askia Mohammed continued the centralization of government. He divided the empire into four regions and appointed trusted officials to govern them. Each region included a number of provinces. No posts were hereditary. Askia Mohammed kept a well-trained army of both cavalry and foot soldiers. When he died, the empire began a slow decline. There were arguments over succession to the throne. Revolts resulted. But it was a Moroccan army that finally destroyed Songhai.

Hoping to gain control of the empire's gold, Sultan Al-Mansur (ahl-mahn-SOOR) sent an army south into the empire. The Songhai army was larger. But its swords, bows and arrows, and spears were no match for the firearms and cannons of the Moroccans. During 1591-1592, the Moroccans overran the main Songhai cities. Other peoples within the empire, including the Mossi and Hausa, took advantage of the situation to revolt. The Moroccans tried to hold onto their gains but could not. They retreated in 1618. By this time, however, the Songhai Empire was gone.

EMPIRE OF KANEM-BORNU

East of the Ghana, Mali, and Songhai empires was one known as Kanem-Bornu (KAH-nem-BOR-noo). Around 850 A.D., the Kanuri (kah-NOO-ree) people established the state of Kanem east of Lake

Empire of Songhai, 1500s

succession: the order in which persons come to authority

299

The wealth of Kanem-Bornu was built on trade. Its position of power was reinforced by a large army. This is one of the ruler's bodyguards. What advances in weaponry were introduced into the army in the late 1500s?

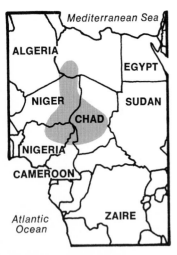

■ **Empire of Kanem-Bornu,**
c. 1550

Chad. Their leaders were members of the Sefuwa clan. Their location in the central savannah area put them at the crossroads of trade.

In 1086 the Kanuri king, Umme Jilma, was converted to Islam. Muslim laws, beliefs, and practices were introduced into the kingdom. This conversion tied Kanem into the cultural and economic community of Islam.

By the mid-1200s, the empire extended north to Fezzan in southwest Libya, east to the interior of modern Chad, and west to Kano in northern Nigeria. It also included Bornu, a territory southwest of Lake Chad. In the late 1300s, Kanem was conquered. The Sefuwa rulers moved their center of government to Bornu. Bornu also became the center of the empire's trade. In the early 1500s, the Sefuwa rulers brought Kanem again under their control.

In 1580, one of the greatest of their rulers came to power—Idris Alooma (EE-drees ah-LOOM-uh, 1580-1610). He introduced firearms and hired Turkish soldiers to train his army. With these new weapons and his armored cavalry, he further enlarged the empire. Idris Alooma built towns in the areas he conquered and placed troops in them to keep peace. He made himself more powerful than the Council of Sefuwa Advisors who previously held as much power as the king.

He continued the spread of Islam. At the end of his rule, Kanem-Bornu was a unified and strong state.

In the mid-1700s a series of internal revolts and outside attacks began to weaken the empire's power. In 1808 the Fulani (FOO-lahn-ee), conquerors of the Hausa States to the west, threatened to overrun the empire. An army from Kanem fought them off. In 1846 the last Sefuwa king died. With his death more than 1,000 years of Sefuwa rule ended.

HAUSA STATES

The area known as Hausaland is located in what is modern northern Nigeria and southern Niger. The Hausa (HOW-suh) people may have been descendants of several peoples. People from the Sahara and others from the Sudan may have come into the area and mixed with the original people. Possibly by around 500 A.D. this new mixture had become the Hausa.

Gradually the Hausa grouped themselves into walled villages. These villages grew into city-states ruled by kings. According to oral tradition, Daura was the first state. Kano (KAH-noh) is the best known historically because of the *Kano Chronicle.*

By 1300 each of the several city-states had well-marked boundaries. They did not form a single kingdom with a central government as did Ghana, Mali, Songhai, or Kanem-Bornu. Instead, they were clusters of settlements, each with a main city. These main cities became the centers of trade and manufacturing. In the 1400s, the cities also became centers of learning. By this time, Islam had reached Hausaland.

In the 1800s, the Hausa States were taken over by the larger Fulani Empire. The Fulani people may have originated in the area between the Niger and Senegal rivers. In the last days of the empire of Ghana,

This photo shows the old section of Kano. Why do you think that the Hausa states never combined into a single centralized government?

301

Yoruba City-States

molten: melted

they began a series of conquests. Over the next several centuries their power grew. After they became Muslims in the early 1700s, most of their conquests were made in the name of Islam.

YORUBA CITY-STATES

The Yoruba (YOH-roo-buh) people speak a Kwa language of the Niger-Congo language family. According to their oral traditions, they trace their origins back to the first king of Ife (EE-fay), a city in western Nigeria. Archaeologists believe they may go back as far as the Nok culture—c. 500 B.C.-200 A.D. Their language may be over 3,000 years old. Today the Yorubas live also in Benin and Togo.

According to one tradition, Ife was founded by a priest-king who had both religious and civil powers. As centuries passed, other Yoruba cities were founded. Oyo (OH-yoh) developed north of Ife around 1000. Benin grew to the southwest. Ife is world famous for its wood, terra-cotta, and bronze sculptures. Ife sculptors used a lost-wax technique that was used in ancient Egypt. In this process, a wax model is surrounded with clay. As molten metal is poured into the clay mold, the melting wax is replaced with the permanent metal.

Benin became the best known of the later Yoruba cities. The people of Benin learned about casting bronze from Ife. The Dutch who visited the city in the 1600s were impressed by the people's skill and the city's size and beauty. They described the great bronze plaques that

The Yoruba city-states became known for their artwork. The animal head is from Nok and the human figure is from Benin. Notice how the neck was built up by applying rows of bronze rings.

graced the pillars of the palace. These plaques were scenes of life in Benin—hunting parties, court musicians, merchants, and acrobats.

During the 1700s, the Yoruba city-states began to decline. **Civil wars**, rivalries between states—especially over the slave trade—and the greediness of rulers caused the decline.

THE ASHANTI UNION

The Ashanti (uh-SHAHN-tee) are one of the Akan-speaking peoples. The first states of Akan-speaking peoples developed along the coast of the Gulf of Guinea perhaps as early as the 1400s. These states were Adansi and Assin. Their prosperity rested on gold. Another early state was Bono-Manso. Later ones near the coast, such as Aguafo, Fante, and the Ga kingdom, were known as the Gold Coast States.

In 1695 the Ashanti leader combined these states into the Ashanti Union of Akan States. The capital was set up at Kumasi (koo-MAH-see). According to tradition, a golden stool came down from heaven to rest in front of the Ashanti leader. His advisor said this meant that the Ashanti chief was to unite the separate states into a **union**. Thus the states began to swear loyalty to the person who was elected to and sat on the Golden Stool of Kumasi.

Once united, the Ashanti started to expand. As they moved south, they met Europeans who were buying slaves. By the 1800s they controlled much of the modern nations of Ghana, the Ivory Coast, and Togo. The British were impressed by the union's power and

☐ **The Ashanti Union, c. 1700**

These brass objects were made by Ashanti craftworkers. What do these figures represent? What can the type of object a culture makes and the materials it uses tell you about its religion, economy, politics, and philosophy?

This is the Golden Stool of Kumasi. According to Ashanti tradition, the stool symbolizes power, bravery, and the welfare of the people.

prosperity. A messenger service operated to all parts of the union. A professional army trained by Germans kept peace. Only after a long and bloody war were the British able to crush the union. That was in 1901.

OTHER STATES AND KINGDOMS

Sometime around the 1100s and 1200s, the Mossi people began developing kingdoms in what is now Upper Volta. They had to fight Mali and Songhai to establish their states. The greatest of the Mossi states was Ougadougou (wahg-uh-DOO-goo). The city that bears that name is now the capital of Upper Volta. In the late 1800s the French conquered the area and added it to French West Africa.

In what is modern Senegal, the Wolof (WOH-luhf) people built a kingdom. When Islam reached the area around 1000, the king converted. Most of the people continued to observe their traditional religion, however. The Portuguese came to Wolof in the 1500s and 1600s. For the next hundred years several European countries fought for control of the kingdom. The French won. In the 1800s, Senegal became the center of French West Africa.

The Kingdom of Dahomey began to develop in the 1600s with the expansion of the Fon people. By the mid-1700s Dahomey controlled the coast between the modern nations of Ghana and Nigeria. The kingdom's major source of income came from the slave trade. Dahomey sold prisoners from its wars with the Ashanti and Yoruba peoples. Many Africans who were brought to the U.S. as slaves came through Dahomey. In a series of wars between 1892 and 1904, the French conquered the kingdom. It too became part of French West Africa.

Summing Up the Unit

Social Studies Vocabulary

Define: kingdom; empire; state; architecture; culture trait; script; kinship; matrilineal; clan; slave; feudal; chronicle; hereditary; sect; minister; civil servant; import

People

Identify: Kalala Ilunga; Rweej; Kibinda Ilunga; Kalonga Mzura; Wene; Matope; Changa; al-Idrisi; Ibn Battuta; Mansu Musa; As-Saheli; Sunni Ali; Askia Mohammed; Al-Mansur; Idris Alooma

Places

Locate: kingdoms of Kush, Axum; Bantu migrations; kingdoms of Luba, Lunda, Congo; Zeila; Berbera; Mogadishu; Kilwa; Mozambique; Sofala; Empires of Monomotapa, Ghana, Mali, Songhai, Kanem-Bornu; Yoruba city-states; Ashanti Union

Words

Identify: Lower Egypt; Upper Egypt; Nubians; Kushites; Coptic Christianity; stele; Zimbabwe; *Kilwa Chronicle;* Swahili; Almoravids; Sefuwa clan; Gold Coast States

⟶ Questions

1. Why did the Egyptian pharaohs extend their power southward?
2. a. Where did Kushite cultural influences and trade contacts extend? b. How did Kushite civilization reflect these outside influences?
3. a. What was the base for prosperity of the Christian kingdoms? b. Why did they decline?
4. a. What do scholars not know about the early Bantu peoples? b. What do they know? c. What culture traits are shared by Bantu peoples?
5. How did Kalala Ilunga keep power within his family?
6. What was the consequence of the Luba kings' successors replacing minor chiefs?
7. a. How did Lunda rulers gain support of the chiefs? b. What was a result of this?
8. How important was trade to Malawi?
9. What caused the divisions within the Kingdom of the Congo in 1482?
10. What form of government did the Monomotapa Empire have?
11. What non-African peoples came to the east coast of Africa to trade?
12. a. Why did a blending of African and non-African cultures occur only in coastal areas? b. How were people in the interior affected?
13. What sources of information are there about early east-coast Africa?
14. a. What was the social system in Kitwara based on? b. Who held the highest positions?
15. What was the base of Buganda's economy?
16. a. Describe the social system in the kingdoms of Rwanda and Burundi. b. How was their system like the feudal system of Europe?
17. Why was the introduction of iron important to the development of West Africa?
18. What was the consequence of the growth of trade in West Africa?
19. Explain the role of salt and gold in Ghana's trade.
20. What impact did Islam have on West African: a. justice and taxation? b. architecture? c. education? d. contacts with non-Africans?
21. What method of power did Askia Mohammed use to strengthen the Songhai Empire?
22. How did Idris Alooma differ from earlier kings in his method of rule in Kanem-Bornu?

Discussion Topics

1. Environment and location were important factors that affected the growth of African kingdoms, empires, and states. What are some examples?
2. What have you learned from this unit that changes ideas or assumptions you had?

Project Ideas

1. Compile a chart of African kingdoms, empires, states, and city-states. List their locations, types of government, dates of existence, trade items, reasons for decline, and any other information you consider important.
2. Write a research report on a kingdom, empire, state, or city mentioned in this unit. Include information about the area today.

305

Unit III

Colonialism

Portuguese forts like this one were the center of busy trade activity on Africa's east coast during the 1500s. Besides being used as trade depots, they showed the force of European power to the Africans.

In the early 1400s Europeans began to look for a sea route to the wealth of Asia. The Portuguese were among the first. They sailed in short jumps south down the west coast of Africa. As they moved down and around the coast, however, the Portuguese discovered the wealth that Africa had to offer. They began to set up trading posts along the coast. The goods they brought back attracted the attention of other Europeans. English, Dutch, and French soon followed the Portuguese to Africa. They too built trading centers along the coast.

In the 1700s Europeans began to explore the interior of Africa. Until then they had been satisfied to buy goods from African and Arab merchants. In the 1800s Europeans began to seize the sources of Africa's trade goods. Because of the **industrial revolution** Europeans needed more **raw materials** and also more **markets** for their manufactured goods. At this time European nations also began setting up **colonial** empires around the world. Like Asia, Africa became caught in European power politics.

It was a number of years before the Portuguese reached the southern tip of Africa. In 1486 while traveling along the west coast of Africa, Bartholomew Diaz's ship was blown out to sea in a storm. When he next saw land, it was to the west rather than to the east. He had rounded the southern end of Africa. The king of Portugal, John II, named this the Cape of Good Hope. He had every hope that the Portuguese would soon reach Asia and take over the spice trade.

Within ten years Vasco da Gama rounded the Cape and reached the east coast of Africa. He crossed the Indian Ocean to southern India. There he traded with Indian merchants for spices. He returned to Portugal in 1499 with two shiploads of spices.

Other Europeans began to follow the routes of the Portuguese. With the exception of Dutch farmers in South Africa, most Europeans stayed along Africa's narrow coastal strip in forts and trading stations. These early Europeans were interested in making money and then going home. They were also afraid of the tropical diseases of the interior such as malaria and sleeping sickness.

More importantly, however, the Africans limited these new people to the coast. The Africans wanted to keep as much of the profits as possible for themselves. By keeping the Europeans on the coast, they could control the flow of trade. Africans could also collect taxes on trade goods as they passed through their territories. Most African trade was in gold, ivory, skins, and food. In return Europeans brought to them tobacco, cloth, alcohol, and later, guns and ammunition.

THE PORTUGUESE

Although other Europeans came to Africa, it was the Portuguese who dominated trade for several centuries. As they traveled down the west coast, the Portuguese came in contact with a number of the empires, kingdoms, and city-states, described earlier.

The Portuguese established diplomatic and trade relations with several of these. Portugal and Benin dealt with each other on the basis of friendly equality for more than a hundred years. The possibility of force often kept the dealings friendly. The Portuguese were very polite when they discovered that rulers of kingdoms like Wolof and Dahomey could command armies of thousands. The Portuguese and other Europeans also came to respect African business sense.

Africans, for their part, learned that a great rivalry existed among Europeans. For a long time they used this knowledge to play European countries off against one another. They tried to keep the Europeans from dominating them through trade or politics.

The Europeans, however, kept looking for weaknesses in the various kingdoms. Whenever an opportunity arose, they used trickery and force to get what they wanted. The Portuguese in East Africa are an example.

Chapter 1
European Impact on African Trade

DECLINE OF EAST AFRICAN RULE   The Portuguese learned of the east-coast cities of Africa after da Gama's trip. For a time they used the coastal cities as stopovers on the way to Asia. But the wealth of the cities soon aroused their greed. Portuguese captains were told to try taking the cities by negotiating with the rulers. If that failed, they were to use force. In 1505 negotiations failed with the ruler of Kilwa. The Portuguese attacked, looted, and destroyed the city. The other cities soon fell.

The Portuguese rerouted trade from India through their island-port of Mozambique off the southern part of the coast. Cities north of Mozambique began to decline. Trade had been their only source of income. The merchants could no longer afford to send caravans to the interior to buy goods. Their income further decreased. As a result, these once strong and wealthy Swahili centers became weaker and poorer. A number of cities turned to smuggling. Sometimes a city would revolt. Such action brought swift punishment from the Portuguese.

Although weakened, many east-coast centers continued in the 1500s under the rule of local leaders. During the 1600s, Oman (oh-MAHN), a city-state on the Arabian Peninsula, was slowly driving the Portuguese out. By the 1700s Oman was the dominant power in much of the Red Sea area. A small revival of trade in ivory and slaves occurred. Little of it was carried on with far Asia, as it had once been, however.

THE SLAVE TRADE

The Europeans did not introduce slavery to Africa. However, they introduced a new economic element to it.

Slavery had existed for many centuries in Africa. But it was different from the slavery later known among Western nations. Africans often took prisoners of war. Sometimes these prisoners were sold or traded back to their own people. Or they were kept as laborers. It was not uncommon for such captives to rise to positions of responsibility. Some even owned property and other slaves.

With the coming of the Europeans and the introduction of guns, the African pattern of slavery changed drastically in some areas. Slaves were traded or sold not to other Africans, but to Europeans for guns and other goods. When one kingdom had guns, it became necessary for other kingdoms to have guns for their security. This was the case with Dahomey, Benin, and the Ashanti Union. An arms race developed and a vicious circle of war and slave trading began.

Europeans were eager to trade guns for people because they needed laborers. They were settling the Americas at the time. There, they opened mines and started plantations. In some areas Europeans used Indian peoples as workers. But European diseases and abuse wiped out whole groups in a short time. In other areas, there were too

This is Regents, formerly a settlement of freed slaves in the British colony of Sierra Leone. What motives do you think prompted the British to abolish slavery in their own colonies and make Sierra Leone a haven for blacks?

few Indians to satisfy labor needs. As a substitute, Europeans began importing Africans to use as slaves.

As the demand for laborers increased in the Americas, slavery became big business. The slave trade lasted for about 300 years. No one knows exactly how many Africans were brought to the Americas. Estimates range from 20 to 50 million. Africans were dragged from their homes or captured in battles. They were marched great distances to the coast. There they were branded and chained together in the hot, cramped holds of slave ships.

A number of British and Americans opposed the slave trade. In the late 1700s, the British colony of Sierra Leone in West Africa was made a refuge for freed slaves. Its capital was named Freetown. After the American Revolution, a number of U.S. states passed laws that forbade the importing of slaves. Some abolished slavery altogether.

Early in the 1800s both Britain and the U.S. passed laws making the slave trade illegal. In 1822 freed slaves from the U.S. landed in Africa in the territory of Liberia. The American Colonization Society had purchased land there for freed U.S. slaves. The settlement was named Monrovia (muhn-ROH-vee-uh) after U.S. President James Monroe. The site is now the capital of Liberia. The colony was declared an independent **republic** in 1847.

But many Europeans continued to operate as slavers. The profits and the difficulty of enforcing the laws against them caused many to risk capture. It was not until late in the 1800s that the slave trade decreased and finally ended. Brazil, for instance, did not abolish slavery until 1888.

CONSEQUENCES   The African slave trade had a number of serious consequences for Africans. The wealth produced by the trade influenced many West Africans to actively engage in the slave trade. They became slave hunters and captured increasing numbers of other Africans. This led to more and more battles, raids, and hostility among African peoples.

To escape the slavers many Africans ran away from their homes. Traditions, families, kinship ties, and villages were torn apart. Because only healthy people would survive as slaves, the youngest and strongest were caught and sold. The old, sick, and weak were left to make out as best they could. Many areas were depopulated. This was especially true in Angola.

depopulated: lost a great number of people from an area

Some African states prospered because of the trade. The location of Benin, Dahomey, and the Ashanti Union, for instance, gave them a **monopoly**. They were between the Africans of the western interior and European slavers on the coast. African economic and political power shifted southward. The huge profits of the slave trade made the coasts and sea routes more important than the trans-Saharan trade routes. As the land routes lessened in importance, so did the savannah kingdoms that were based on them. The forest kingdoms to the south, however, grew in importance as they became part of the new coastal trade.

Arts and **crafts** suffered. The energies of many Africans were used to either escape the slave hunters or to capture other Africans. Moreover, Africans could now get by trade what they had once had to make. A slowdown in African artistry and technology resulted.

The slave trade had consequences for Europeans too. European slave merchants generally remained on the coast. They saw Africans either as slaves or slavers. They neither knew nor were interested in the cultures of the various African peoples. There was no exchange of ideas, no attention given to African history or traditions. It was easier to sell people if they were thought of as property rather than humans.

European slave traders carried their ignorance and prejudice with them to Europe and the Americas. Seeing only this side, other Europeans and Americans developed a distorted picture of Africans. Greed and rationalizations for slavery blocked from view the full scope of African achievements.

Chapter 2
Scramble for Africa

Africa, 1914
- British
- French
- Belgian
- Portuguese
- German
- Italian
- Spanish
- Independent

Atlantic Ocean

Indian Ocean

ALGERIA LIBYA EGYPT SAUDI ARABIA

Red Sea

In the late 1700s and 1800s, Europeans became interested in exploring the African interior. When the slave trade was banned, they began to look for other African goods to trade. The industrial revolution was underway. Greater and greater supplies of raw materials were needed to keep the machines working. Europeans also needed new markets in which to sell the output of their machines. Africa was seen as a possible source of both raw materials and markets.

At this time, too, European governments were beginning to think in terms of empire. A struggle for power among European nations was taking place. Having worldwide colonies, they believed, was one way of increasing a nation's power at home. To European missionaries, Africa presented the possibilities of millions of converts to Christianity. European scientists were curious about the various animals, plants, and resources they might find in Africa.

EUROPEANS MOVE INLAND

The first to enter the interior were explorers and missionaries. Among the adventurers was Mungo Park who, in 1796, was looking for the source of the Blue Nile. In 1827 Rene Caillie (ruh-NAY ka-YAY) followed the Niger River to Timbuktu. In 1848 missionary explorers

Europeans who ventured inland in Africa saw magnificent sights like this one near Malindi, Kenya. Is it correct to call Europeans such as Speke and Burton discoverers? Why or why not? Did they discover Africa's interior or merely explore it?

Johann Rebmann and Johann Krapf of Germany were the first non-Africans to see the Ruwenzori Mountains.

Between 1840 and 1873 David Livingstone, a medical missionary, crisscrossed Africa. His maps helped make South-Central Africa known to non-Africans. When Livingstone had not been heard from for several years, Henry M. Stanley, a U.S. journalist, was sent to search for him. Stanley found him and stayed to explore Africa himself. He crossed Central Africa and explored the course of the Congo (Zaire) River.

Sir Samuel Baker and Florence von Sass explored the White Nile. This husband-and-wife team found the source of the White Nile in a lake they named Albert (now Mobuto Sese Seko). Sir Richard Burton and John Hanning Speke explored Lake Tanganyika. Speke went on to locate the source of the Nile in Lake Victoria. Europeans named lakes and falls after their kings and queens. But the Africans had their own names for them. For example, Victoria Falls is Mosi Oa Tunya (Thundering Smoke). Although these lakes, mountains, and falls were discoveries to Europeans, they were well-known to the Africans who lived or traveled through the areas.

As Africa was explored and mapped, Europeans began to move into the interior and take over. Between 1880 and 1900 Europeans swallowed practically all of Africa. Only Liberia and Ethiopia remained independent. The Europeans used both informal and formal methods.

Many Europeans used the same argument they had used to build empires in Asia and elsewhere. First they ignored the cultures of the peoples they conquered. Then Europeans claimed that they had a mission to bring their way of life to the less-developed peoples of the world. Perhaps some actually believed this. Others used it to conceal their real motive—desire for power and wealth.

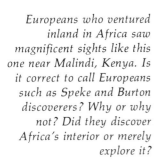

The Sudanese fought for their independence and defeated the British in 1885. Thirteen years later at Omdurman the Sudanese were defeated. Why did Europeans view African resistance as rebellion?

Among those who really believed they were helping the Africans were Christian missionaries. Sometimes, however, the missionaries angered the Africans by their methods. For protection, the missionaries appealed to their national government for troops. Since the governments were interested in taking African territory, the troops were sent to stay. Sometimes European settlers and traders went independently into various parts of Africa. They too asked for help when Africans resisted. Again European governments answered with troops. And again they often stayed.

DIVISION OF AFRICA   Finally in the 1880s European nations divided Africa formally by a **treaty**. Otto von Bismarck had recently **unified** Germany. Like other European leaders of the time, he thought a nation could only be strong if it had an overseas empire. The African continent was the last area in which an empire seemed possible. When Germany turned its attention there, other European nations began to quarrel with Germany and among themselves over territory.

In November 1884 Bismarck called a conference in Berlin to settle the arguments. Fourteen European nations and the U.S. attended. The claim of King Leopold of Belgium to the vast area of the Congo was recognized. It became his personal empire. Other nations, however, were allowed to trade in the Congo Basin and those areas washed by the Nile and Zambezi rivers. Other boundaries were also agreed upon. By February 1885 the Europeans had settled their differences—at the expense of the African peoples.

AFRICAN RESISTANCE   Europeans viewed any African resistance to their plans as rebellion against lawful authority. The Africans saw resistance as defense against invaders.

313

Under their leader Chaka (CHAH-kuh), the Zulus of South Africa fought the Dutch and the British well into the 1800s. Sudanese warriors, called Mahdi (MAH-dee), destroyed British forces at Khartoum in 1885. The British took their revenge in the battle of Omdurman in 1898. Twenty thousand Sudanese died. In Somalia another group of Mahdi resisted the British into the early 1900s. In West Africa, the Ashanti fought the British from 1898 to 1900. The Bunyoro fought back in Uganda.

In West Africa, the Mandingo fought the French for a number of years. King Behanzin of Dahomey was sent to the West Indies for resisting the French. The Germans were forced to conquer the coastal cities of East Africa before they could occupy Tanganyika (part of modern Tanzania). They also had to put down the resistance of the Maji Maji. This area then became known as German East Africa. In German South-West Africa they brutally subdued the Hereros (huh-RAY-rohs).

The Africans fought valiantly. But they were no match for European weapons. In the end the African peoples were forced to come to the best terms they could with the Europeans.

COLONIAL GOVERNMENTS

Similar political and economic reasons drove the various European powers to seize African territory. However, each nation differed in its approach to colonizing and ruling the African peoples.

BRITISH RULE   For the most part, the British did not involve themselves directly in African affairs. They governed indirectly through African rulers. The British wanted law and order. They believed that fewer problems would be created if they did not change traditional ways. Some of the cooperating rulers and their followers were given British titles. A number of their children and other relatives were sent to schools in Great Britain. In this way the British hoped to strengthen the political and economic ties that bound African territories to Great Britain.

Uganda is an example of indirect British rule. As we have seen, the kingdom of Buganda developed around the northern part of Lake Victoria in what is modern Uganda. In 1900 the British made an agreement with the ruler of Buganda. He and his followers were allowed to rule as long as they recognized and supported British authority. As an additional reward, the British gave half of Buganda's land to these few thousand. The British later extended Buganda's rule to include other parts of Uganda.

FRENCH POLICY   In their colonies the French practiced a policy of **assimilation**. They did not think, as some British did, that their African colonies might someday govern themselves. Rather the

This cartoon from a British humor magazine satirizes the European scramble for Africa. The character on the left symbolizes Germany, the one on the right, Italy. Why was Germany suddenly interested in Africa in the 1880s? Why did the rest of Europe fight for a piece of the pie?

French thought that their colonies would become a part of France. In theory, colonial Africans might all become French citizens.

As a beginning, French citizenship was gradually given to all men who were born in certain towns in Senegal. These towns were settled mostly by French and mulattoes, descendants of both French and black Africans. A seat in the French Chamber of Deputies was given to a representative from Senegal.

The long-range aim of the French was to change the culture and traditions of their African colonists. They wanted them to think and act like French. They had some success in training and assimilating an educated elite. After independence, many of these became the leaders and administrators of their former colonies. The vast majority of Africans, however, kept their traditional customs, attitudes, and language. Even the educated elite held to many of their traditional ways.

Because of their long-range goals, the French ruled in a more direct way than the British. A formal chain of command reached from the governor down to the local levels of government. Orders flowed down this chain to the various levels. Reports flowed back to the top through the same channels. At most levels above the local one, administrators sent from France held authority.

315

BELGIAN SYSTEM   In 1885 the Berlin Conference recognized the Congo Free State as ruled directly by King Leopold II of Belgium. It was his personal empire to exploit as he wished. The king developed rubber plantations. In time he began to demand greater and greater outputs of rubber from his Belgian representatives. They, in turn, demanded more and more work from their African laborers. Workers were often whipped and tortured. Workers' families were held as hostages. It was not uncommon to kill laborers if they slowed down. These same methods were used on building projects and in mines.

In the early 1900s these brutalities came to world attention. In 1908 King Leopold was forced to turn over his personal empire to the Belgian government. Some reforms were made. Forced labor was ended. The Belgians began to develop a more humane system of rule. They still exploited the colony, but they realized that satisfied workers produce more. Medical care, homes, clothing, and other benefits were provided.

The Belgians also set up primary and some secondary schools. Most of those who attended school never went beyond the lower grades. A few were sent to technical or vocational training schools. The Belgians wanted to provide enough education so that the Africans could contribute to the development of the colony. But they did not want to provide so much that Africans would become restless and demand change.

PORTUGUESE RULE   Portugal's claims to Mozambique, Angola, part of Guinea, and some islands off the west coast of Africa were recognized by the Berlin Conference.

In their early colonial policies the Portuguese were harsh and brutal. They forced their African colonists to work on farms, plantations, and various work projects. Whippings and beatings were usual. The Portuguese looked upon their colonists as ignorant and uncivilized. The Portuguese believed they needed to be taught discipline and obedience.

Toward the middle of the 20th century, however, Portuguese policies toward their African subjects began to change. This came as a result of African independence movements. The Portuguese did not wish to lose their African territories. It was easier to begin to think of the Africans as part of Portugal. Like the French, the Portuguese started working toward assimilating Africans.

Portuguese citizenship was given to certain Africans. These were the few who had adopted Portuguese customs and language. They were also loyal to the Portuguese government and had become Christians. The vast majority, however, did not give up their traditional beliefs. Even those who converted to Roman Catholicism and adopted Portuguese customs practiced many of their traditional ways.

GERMAN RULE   The Germans took those areas of southwestern Africa which were most desirable for themselves. In Togo and southern Cameroon, they forced the Africans to work on their plantations, rail and road construction, and other public works projects. Wherever African resistance was strong or threatening, the Germans were more flexible. In the northern part of Cameroon where the Muslim Fulani were powerful, the Germans followed the British practice of indirect rule. In Tanganyika, the Germans used Swahilis and Arabs as administrators.

The Germans lost their African territories when they lost World War I. Britain and France divided Togo and Cameroon between them. Britain also took Tanganyika. German South-West Africa was given to the Republic of South Africa. Belgium gained Burundi and Rwanda. In theory, the European nations were to govern these territories under rules set forth by the **international League** of Nations. In fact, they governed them as they governed their own colonies. The League had little power.

ITALIAN AND SPANISH HOLDINGS   Italy and Spain held smaller amounts of African territory. The Italians tried to conquer Ethiopia. Under Emperor Menelik, the Ethiopians defeated them in 1896. The Italians did take Eritrea (er-uh-TREE-uh), now a province of Ethiopia. To the southeast of Ethiopia they controlled a part of Somalia known as Italian Somaliland. They also took over Libya in North Africa.

The Spanish controlled several small portions of Morocco. They also had a larger amount of territory south of Morocco known as Spanish Sahara. South of the Sahara, they held Rio Muni on the mainland and the island of Fernando Po. These two areas are now the country of Equatorial Guinea.

Italian troops march into Axum in 1935. What significance does Axum have in African history?

EFFECTS ON THE AFRICANS

When the Europeans began taking over Africa, they knew little about the variety of peoples who lived there. To Europeans the peoples were Africans—not Zulus, or Masai, or Hottentots, or Yorubas. The cultural and ethnic qualities that made a group different from every other group were ignored. The Europeans were concerned only with exploiting the Africans to European advantage.

The political boundaries drawn at the Berlin Conference cut across common grazing lands, farms, and even villages. This grouping of different peoples within the same borders often led to anger and violence among the Africans. When Europeans discovered this, they used it to make their rule more secure. They pitted one people against another. When independence came, colonial boundaries became the new national boundaries. The disunity and hostility encouraged by the Europeans was not easily forgotten. It continues to hold back the nation-building efforts of modern African leaders.

The Europeans also introduced the Africans to **industrialization** and all it could mean in terms of wealth and luxury. As a result of industrialization, African economies were changed from barter to cash. Before colonization, most Africans exchanged one item for another. A few kingdoms—such as the Kingdom of the Congo—used shells as a **medium of exchange**. And among the east-coast trading centers such as Kilwa coins were used. But these were exceptions.

In some areas colonial administrators now placed a head or a hut tax on the Africans. This had to be paid in cash. In addition, Africans were being attracted to European goods which had to be paid for in cash. To obtain money, the Africans had to work for Europeans. They alone gave cash wages. For many Africans, this meant moving—either alone or with families—from the country to the new cities and industrial centers.

Europeans also brought to Africa the Africans' first look at **nationalism**. This was to prove the undoing of European rule in Africa.

Exploitation of African mineral deposits like this surface diamond mine not only stripped Africa of its resources and put the profits in European pockets, but also changed African social and economic customs. What are some of the changes such exploitation caused?

Summing Up the Unit

Social Studies Vocabulary

Define: raw materials; markets; colonial; republic; monopoly; crafts; treaty; assimilation; international; league; industrialization; medium of exchange; nationalism

People

Identify: Park; Caillie; Rebmann and Krapf; Livingstone; Stanley; Baker and von Sass; Burton and Speke; Leopold II; Chaka

Words

Define: malaria; American Colonization Society; Monrovia; Mahdi; Congo Free State

Questions

1. a. Why did most European traders stay along the coast of Africa? b. Why did the Africans want it this way?
2. How did the Portuguese and Africans deal with each other?
3. What methods did the Portuguese use to weaken the east-coast cities?
4. How did the slavery of the Europeans differ from the slavery that the Africans practiced?
5. Why did Europeans need laborers?
6. What were the consequences of slavery for Africans: a. economically? b. socially? c. artistically?
7. As a consequence of slavery how did Europeans view Africans?
8. Why did many Europeans continue to operate as slavers although a number of British and Americans opposed the slave trade?
9. List five reasons why Europeans began a scramble for control of Africa in the late 1700s and 1800s.
10. What two kinds of Europeans were the first to enter Africa's interior?
11. Describe the informal and formal methods used by Europeans to divide Africa.
12. a. How did Africans react to European plans to control Africa? b. What was the result of African reaction to the Europeans?
13. How did the British and French differ in their approaches to governing their African colonies?
14. a. Why was King Leopold II of Belgium forced to give up his African empire? b. What was the consequence for Africans?
15. Why did Portugal's policy toward its African subjects change in the mid-1900s?
16. a. How did the boundaries of today's African nations originate? b. How do these boundaries sometimes hinder African nations today?
17. What were the results of the introduction of industrialization in Africa?

Discussion Topics

1. Europeans claimed they had a mission to bring their way of life to the less-developed peoples of Africa. But their real motive usually was a desire for power and wealth. To what extent did they achieve their objectives? Were European reasons for colonization based on false assumptions? What were they?
2. Several European powers established colonial empires in Africa. What was the rule of each like? What mistakes did each country make? How did the Africans react to each? How did the Europeans react to their role as colonial rulers?
3. Almost all of Africa was under colonial control. And almost all of Africa is now independent. Why was colonialism in Africa doomed to failure?

Project Ideas

1. Using library references, report on African participation in World War I and on efforts of black Americans to get European powers to consider African independence at Versailles.
2. Read more about the slave trade in Africa. Write a report on the European nations that were involved in it and how they carried it out.
3. Read Rudyard Kipling's poem, "The White Man's Burden." Tell what attitude toward colonialism you think it reveals.
4. Using the map on page 311, locate and list the holdings of Great Britain, France, Belgium, Portugal, Germany, Italy, and Spain in Africa in 1914. Name the independent nations.

Unit IV

Independence and Growth

Mozambique citizens turn out on their Independence Day, June 1975, to welcome home their new president and celebrate the end of Portuguese rule. What events forced the Portuguese to give up their African colonies?

A number of Africans were educated at home in European-run schools. Some were sent to schools in Europe and the U.S. These Africans were exposed to the ideas of **self-government** and nationalism. Everywhere they looked in Africa, however, they saw non-Africans turning Africa's resources into wealth for themselves.

After World War I, more and more ordinary Africans left their villages for mines and industrial centers. They too came in contact with European ideas. During World War II, Africa was an important supplier of materials and troops. Africans in greater numbers began to meet people from other parts of the world. They became increasingly aware of what independence could bring.

At the end of the war, Africans saw Asians gaining freedom from the same colonial powers that ruled them. African leaders began to work openly for independence. The people supported them. Eventually most European governments were forced to surrender their colonies. However, the transition from **colonialism** to independence has not always been smooth. Building a nation of many peoples is not easy. Lack of skilled workers and capital has added to the problems.

At the end of World War II, there were two independent nations in sub-Saharan Africa: Ethiopia and Liberia. In 1957, Ghana, a British colony, gained nationhood. From then on, independence came with a rush. Within a dozen years, most of the sub-Sahara had become independent. By the mid-1970s the last European holdouts were beginning to surrender their power. African movements for independence, world opinion, and the economic drain on European governments were some of the reasons that led to the end of colonialism.

A few places remain under white rule, for example, the Republic of South Africa, and the French Territory of the Afars (AHF-ahrz) and the Issas (ee-SAHZ). Africans say they will fight until black Africans control all sub-Saharan Africa.

Chapter 1
From Colonialism to Independence

FORMER BRITISH COLONIES

Among British possessions with mostly black populations, the change from colony to nation was fairly smooth. After World War II, Great Britain began to make changes that were aimed at moving their colonies toward independence. This was especially true for its West African colonies. Uganda and Tanzania in East Africa also made relatively easy transitions to nationhood. But in areas where many Europeans lived, problems arose. The Europeans were determined to protect their interests. Sometimes, as in Kenya, this led to violence and bloodshed.

Most of the newly independent countries joined the British Commonwealth of Nations. This is a worldwide organization of former British dominions and colonies. These independent nations conduct their own domestic and foreign affairs. But Commonwealth membership gives them many benefits. They write favorable trade agreements with one another and share programs in education and health care.

GHANA'S INDEPENDENCE   The movement for independence in the Gold Coast, now Ghana, was led by Kwame Nkrumah (KWAHM-ee en-KROO-muh). He founded the Convention People's Party (CPP). With the slogan, "Self-government Now," Nkrumah and his followers began using strikes and other—sometimes semiviolent—protests. The British jailed him.

Following its policy of gradual independence, Britain granted the Gold Coast a new **constitution** in 1951. When elections were held, Nkrumah's party won by an overwhelming majority. He was released from jail and became **prime minister**.

Nkrumah and his supporters were not content. Under the new constitution, the British still controlled foreign affairs, finance, and the defense and legal systems. The CPP demanded that the Gold Coast control all its affairs. Finally the pressure became too great and the British withdrew. In 1957 the Gold Coast became independent. It took the name Ghana, after the early West African empire.

GUIDE TO AFRICAN NATIONS

CURRENT NAME	FORMER NAMES*	COLONIAL POWERS*	EARLY HISTORY
Angola	Angola	Portugal	Part of kingdoms of Congo and Lunda
Benin, Republic of	French West Africa Dahomey, Republic of	France	Kingdom of Dahomey
Botswana, Republic of	Bechuanaland	Britain	Early home of Bushmen; later, of Bantu-speaking Tswana
Burundi, Republic of	German East Africa Belgian Trust Territory of Ruanda-Urundi	Germany Belgium	Kingdom of Burundi
Cameroon, Federal Republic of	Kamerun French Cameroons British Cameroons British West Africa Federation of East and West Cameroon	Germany France Britain	May be earliest home of Bantu-speaking peoples
Cape Verde Islands	— —	Portugal	— —
Central African Empire	Ubangi-Shari French Equatorial Africa Central African Republic	France	Home of Sudanic-speaking Banda people
Chad, Republic of	French Equatorial Africa	France	Part of Empire of Kanem-Bornu
Comoro Islands	— —	France	— —
Congo, People's Republic of	French Congo French Equatorial Africa	France	Part of Kingdom of the Congo
Equatorial Guinea, Republic of	Rio Muni; Fernando Po	Spain	Early home of Bantu-speaking peoples
Ethiopia	Abyssinia Empire of Ethiopia	Italy (1936-1941)	Kingdom of Axum; Solomonian Empire
French Territory of the Afars and the Issas	French Somaliland	France	Early home of the Afar and Issa peoples
Gabon Republic	French Equatorial Africa	France	Early home of Pygmy peoples
Gambia, Republic of the	British West Africa	Britain	Early peoples had contacts with empires of Ghana, Mali, and Songhai
Ghana, Republic of	Gold Coast British Togoland British West Africa	Britain	Part of Ashanti Union
Guinea, Republic of	French Guinea French West Africa	France	Part of Empires of Ghana, Mali, and Songhai
Guinea-Bissau, Republic of	Portuguese Guinea	Portugal	Early peoples lived on coast and off-shore islands, away from contacts with great empires

Listed in chronological order, earliest first

Ivory Coast, Republic of	Ivory Coast French West Africa	France	Early home of Baule people
Kenya, Republic of	British East Africa	Britain	Site of east-coast city-states of Mombasa, Faza
Lesotho, Kingdom of	Basutoland	Britain	Kingdom of the Sotho
Liberia, Republic of	Liberia	— —	Early home of Vai and Mandingo peoples; oldest independent nation
Malagasy Republic	Madagascar	France	Settled by peoples from Southeast Asia who brought bananas and canoes to Africa
Malawi, Republic of	Nyasaland Federation of Rhodesia and Nyasaland	Britain	Malawi Empire
Mali, Republic of	French Sudan French West Africa	France	Part of empires of Ghana, Mali, and Songhai
Mauritania, Islamic Republic of	French West Africa	France	Part of empires of Ghana, Mali, and Songhai; conquered by Berbers and Arabs
Mozambique, Republic of	Mozambique	Portugal	Zimbabwe ruins; part of Malawi, Monomotapa, and Changamira empires; site of east-coast cities of Sofala and Mozambique
Namibia (South-West Africa)	German South-West Africa	Germany Union of South Africa	Early home of Bushmen and Hottentots; later of Bantu-speaking Hereros
Niger, Republic of the	French West Africa	France	Part of Bornu; later Empire of Kanem-Bornu; part of Hausa States
Nigeria, Federal Republic of	British West Africa	Britain	May have been home of earliest Bantu-speaking peoples; Nok Culture; part of Hausa States; later part of Fulani Empire; Yoruba city-states of Ife, Oyo, and Benin
Rhodesia (Zimbabwe)	Southern Rhodesia Federation of Rhodesia and Nyasaland	Britain	Zimbabwe ruins; part of empires of Monomotapa and Changamira
Rwanda, Republic of	German East Africa Belgian Trust Territory of Ruanda-Urundi	Germany Belgium	Early home of Pygmy peoples; Kingdom of Rwanda
Senegal, Republic of	French West Africa	France	Part of Empire of Ghana; Kingdom of Wolof
Sierra Leone	British West Africa	Britain	Early kingdoms of Temne and Mende peoples; refuge for freed slaves
Somalia (Somali Democratic Republic)	British Somaliland Italian Somaliland	Britain Italy	Biblical Land of Punt; east-coast city-states of Zeila, Mogadishu, and Berbera

CURRENT NAME	FORMER NAMES*	COLONIAL POWERS*	EARLY HISTORY
South Africa, Republic of	Cape Colony Union of South Africa	Netherlands Britain	Early home of Bushmen and Hottentots; later, of Zulu, Xhosa, and other Bantu-speaking peoples
South-West Africa, *see* Namibia			
Sudan, Republic of the	Anglo-Egyptian Sudan	Britain Egypt	Ancient land of the Nubians; Kingdom of Kush
Swaziland, Kingdom of	Swaziland	Britain	Kingdom of the Swazis
Tanzania, United Republic of	German East Africa Tanganyika Zanzibar British East Africa	Germany Britain	Site of Olduvai Gorge; east-coast cities of Zanzibar, Kilwa, and Tumbatu
Togo, Republic of	Togoland French Togoland	France	Early home of Ewe people
Uganda, Republic of	British East Africa	Britain	Early home of Pygmy peoples; kingdoms of Kitwara, Bunyoro, and Buganda
Upper Volta, Republic of	French West Africa	France	Part of Mossi States; Kingdom of Ougadougou
Zaire, Republic of	Congo Free State Belgian Congo Democratic Republic of the Congo	Belgium	Kingdoms of Luba, Lunda; part of Kingdom of the Congo
Zambia, Republic of	Northern Rhodesia Federation of Rhodesia and Nyasaland	Britain	Early home of Bantu-speaking peoples such as Bemba, Tonga, and Barotsi

Nkrumah was its first president. During the following years he became increasingly **authoritarian**. Several attempts were made on his life. In 1966 while visiting Peking, China, he was overthrown by the military. He lived in exile until his death in 1972. Since 1966 Ghana has had several changes in government—some through elections and some by military takeovers.

SIMILAR COURSE FOR OTHER NATIONS Nigeria's path to independence was similar to that of Ghana. In both nations influential leaders existed who were able to form political parties. Once these leaders had enough support, they were able to bargain with the British. In 1960 Nigeria became independent.

Uganda became independent in 1962. It had a **federal** system of government. Each of the four old kingdoms was considered a sovereign state within the nation. This was done because Buganda was still a powerful force. Buganda's ruler insisted on local control before he would agree to join a national union. In 1966 the federal system was abolished. The following year the national government declared the four kingdoms illegal. Uganda adopted a **republican** form of government. In 1971 a **coup**—military overthrow of the government—deposed the president. A military government was set up. Unrest continued and various attempts at overthrowing the government were made.

When Britain received the former colony of German East Africa after World War I, it changed the name to Tanganyika. Britain governed it under the League of Nations and then under the UN. Independence came in 1961. Zanzibar, an island off the coast of Tanganyika, became independent in 1963. In 1964 the two nations joined to form the United Republic of Tanzania.

The present countries of Cameroon and Togo were formerly German colonies too. During World War I they were occupied and divided between Britain and France. After the war the British and French continued to rule them. In 1956 the British-governed region, known as British Togoland, voted to join the Gold Coast. Together they became the nation of Ghana. The French-governed area voted to become a self-governing republic within the French Community. In 1960 it became an independent republic—Togo.

That same year, the French-ruled part of Cameroon, which was about four-fifths of the territory, became independent as Cameroon. The following year a vote was held in the British-ruled part. The people in the north voted to join Nigeria. Those in the south voted to join the new nation of Cameroon.

Sierra Leone, one of the sub-Sahara's most progressive areas, gained its independence in 1961. Gambia (gam-BEE-uh), one of the smallest African nations, became an independent member of the Commonwealth in 1965. In 1966 Botswana and Lesotho (luh-SOH-toh) gained their independence. Swaziland became independent in 1968.

progressive: advanced; making use of, or interested in, new ideas

VIOLENCE IN KENYA   Kenya gained independence only after a long and sometimes bloody struggle. Starting in 1952, a secret organization known as the Mau Mau fought the governing minority and European settlers. Most of the Mau Mau were Kikuyu (kih-KOO-yoo) people, a branch of Bantu–speakers. The government and the European settlers of the Kenya Highlands fought back. Almost five times as many Africans—approximately 12,000—as European- and government-supporters were killed.

In 1960 under pressure from African leaders, Britain agreed to majority rule by black Kenyans. In 1961 the Kenya National Union party won a majority in the legislature. It was headed by Jomo Kenyatta (joh-moh ken-YAH-tuh). In 1963 Kenyatta became the leader of the new nation. He began easing out European ownership of land and Asian control of trade. Thousands in both groups left. Black Kenyans replaced them.

TROUBLE IN RHODESIA   During the colonial period, Europeans poured into what was known as Northern Rhodesia, Southern Rhode-

Jomo Kenyatta led Kenya's struggle for independence.

Blacks make up the majority of people in Rhodesia. However, white leaders would not allow them adequate representation in the government. Blacks fought for their rights— sometimes with words, sometimes with actions. This is Joshua Nkomo, leader of the Zimbabwe African People's Union.

sia, and Nyasaland (ny-AS-uh-land). These areas have large mineral resources.

In 1953 the territories of Northern Rhodesia and Nyasaland and the self-governing colony of Southern Rhodesia joined in a **federation**. The European settlers of Southern Rhodesia dominated it. Black Africans—especially in Southern Rhodesia and Nyasaland—saw the federation as an attempt to interfere with their march toward independence. They pressured Britain into breaking up the federation in 1964. Northern Rhodesia became the independent nation of Zambia. Nyasaland became the independent nation of Malawi. Both came under control of their black African majorities.

Britain did not grant independence to Southern Rhodesia, however. Its European settlers refused to give black Africans adequate representation in the government. Black Africans make up about 95 percent of the population. With the end of the federation, Southern Rhodesia became known simply as Rhodesia. Black Africans, however, call it Zimbabwe for the stone ruins of the early African state.

In 1965 Rhodesia declared itself independent of Britain. Britain claimed the action was illegal. The UN agreed and ordered all trade with Rhodesia to stop. But some countries, such as the Republic of South Africa and Portugal, continue to do business with Rhodesia. Leaders of Africa's black nations demand that Rhodesia's black Africans be given majority rule. Zambia and Tanzania allow their countries be used as bases for **guerrilla** operations against Rhodesia.

In 1974 representatives of Rhodesia's white minority government and leaders of the nationalist movement met in Zambia. They agreed on a broad program of reform. Voting privileges were to be extended gradually to greater numbers of black Rhodesians. In 1975 more talks were held. These centered on the possibility of a federation of black- and white-ruled areas in Rhodesia.

A SPECIAL CASE: THE REPUBLIC OF SOUTH AFRICA

The Republic of South Africa is still ruled by a white minority. In 1652 the Dutch East India Company sent colonists to the Cape of Good Hope. They were to grow vegetables and other food to supply ships traveling between Europe and Asia. The Hottentots and Bushmen living in this area were pushed north. The Dutch came to be known as Boers (BOHRZ), which is Dutch for farmers.

The Boers began moving inland. In the 1700s they met Bantu-speakers who had moved south. The Bantu-speakers, among them the Xhosas and Zulus, fought the Dutch and later the British for over a hundred years. Ultimately they were defeated.

In the late 1700s the British came looking for favorable places to settle along the sea routes. In 1806 they seized the colony. Many of the Boers came to resent British control. In a journey known as the Great Trek of 1836, Boers went northeast to find new homes.

They founded the states of Natal (nuh-TAL), Orange Free State, and Transvaal (trans-VAHL).

The British moved into and took over Natal in 1843. The Boers might have lived undisturbed in their other states, but diamonds and then gold were discovered in Transvaal in the late 1800s. Many non-Dutch poured into the area. The Boers closed their land to outsiders. This action angered the British. The British and Boers fought several wars. By 1902 the Boers were defeated. Their states came under British rule. The entire area became the Union of South Africa in 1910. In 1961 South Africa gained its independence.

This is an example of apartheid—separate entrances to the local post office.

APARTHEID   Afrikaners (af-ri-KAHN-uhrs)—descendants of Dutch and other European settlers—were determined to keep black Africans from participating in the government of South Africa. Between 1926 and 1947 the ruling whites passed a series of **segregationist** laws. Known as apartheid (uh-PAHR-tayt), this system keeps Europeans, Asians, black Africans, and Coloureds separate from each other. Coloureds are people of mixed European and African ancestry. The different groups must live in separate areas. They must attend separate social gatherings. Certain jobs are forbidden each group.

Where economics is involved, however, the South African government can be flexible. Africans work in European houses. Africans, Asians, and Coloureds work in European-owned factories, mines, and businesses. Ironically, the Japanese are not classified as Asians because of the benefits they contribute to South Africa's economy.

South Africa has been severely criticized for its apartheid policy. Black Africans elsewhere are especially angered by it. They, together with a number of non-African nations, refuse to buy South African goods. They demand that others support their boycott. In the mid-1970s a **coalition** of African and other countries voted to deny South Africa a seat in the UN General Assembly. But criticism and boycotts have had little effect on South Africa's leaders. The nation's trade with many of its critics is small. Its important customers continue to do business.

BANTUSTANS   South Africa's rulers have tried to quiet the country's black majority. They are setting up areas where black South Africans can have self-rule. These areas are called Bantustans (ban-tu-STANS). In Bantu this means homeland. Supposedly, each of the main groups of African peoples within South Africa will have a homeland. Africans from the Bantustans can work in South Africa with temporary workers' permits. By the mid-1970s, a number of these homelands had been set up.

NAMIBIA (SOUTH-WEST AFRICA)   Namibia was formerly the German colony of German South-West Africa. At the end of World War I South Africa received control of it through a League of Nations

327

In 1958 Sekou Toure of Guinea defied French President Charles de Gaulle and led his nation to complete independence.

The UN sent troops such as these into the Congo (Zaire) during the fighting among rival factions in the early 1960s.

mandate. In 1966 the UN ended the mandate. South Africa refused to recognize Namibia's independence. During the mid-1970s, however, South Africa indicated that it might eventually give up Namibia. Black Africans were calling for immediate independence.

THE FRENCH COMMUNITY

France's colonies gained their independence more rapidly than those of Britain did. After World War II France, like Britain, began to feel the economic burden of keeping a colonial empire. So it allowed its African possessions to determine their own futures. In 1958 French President Charles de Gaulle invited France's colonies in Africa to join France in what he called the French Community. In general, the colonies would control their domestic affairs. However, France would handle foreign affairs, finance, and defense. A constitution was drawn up and submitted to a vote of the people of the various territories.

De Gaulle made it clear that any nation which voted "no" would receive immediate independence. But it would receive no future help from France. The people of Guinea, under the leadership of Sekou Toure (SEH-koo too-RAY), were the only ones to vote "no." De Gaulle kept his promise. Guinea was given immediate independence. But it was stripped of all French property that could be removed—even the desks in government offices. Economic assistance was cut off. Guinea was plunged into economic chaos for some years.

The other French-ruled territories agreed to de Gaulle's proposal. But they were impressed by Sekou Toure's courage. They demanded more and more independence. By the end of 1960 France had recognized the full independence of all its former colonies. Some dropped out of the French Community. Those which have remained are very sensitive to French interference. France continues to provide economic aid. But it has no power to force policy on its former territories.

BELGIUM'S FORMER COLONIES

Years of guerrilla activity were necessary before some European governments gave up their colonies. Even after a colonial government withdrew, peace did not always come immediately. The former Belgian Congo is one such example.

The Republic of Zaire, as it has been known since 1971, covers a large part of Central and South-Central Africa. The Belgian officials who took over the colony from King Leopold thought that a little education plus a few material benefits would keep their rule and profits secure. And they did for a time. But the Congolese began rebelling in the late 1950s. Pressured by revolts and world opinion, Belgium granted independence to the Congo in 1960.

Joseph Kasavubu (kah-suh-VOO-boo) became the first president. Patrice Lumumba (loo-MOOM-buh) was the first premier. Lumumba wanted a strong central government. Kasavubu was more moderate in his views. He wanted a loose federation of provinces.

Belgian officers still commanded the army. The army soon revolted against them. The soldiers elected their own leaders and began **terrorizing** the people, especially Belgians. Thousands fled. The province of Shaba, then Katanga, under Premier Moise Tshombe (moy-SEH CHAHM-bay), seceded. UN forces were brought in to put down the revolt. Tshombe was finally defeated and exiled in mid-1963.

In 1960 Colonel Joseph Mobutu (moh-BOO-too) seized power after a quarrel between Kasavubu and Lumumba. Lumumba was deposed and later killed. In 1961 Mobutu turned the government over to Kasavubu. In 1964 Kasavubu invited Tshombe to return from exile and become premier. He did this as a gesture of national unity. But it failed. Former Lumumba supporters rebelled. Belgian forces, who were flown in by U.S. transports, crushed the revolt. This action angered other African leaders. They saw it as an act of **imperialism**. Opposition continued. Tshombe again went into exile. In 1965 Mobutu seized power. He brought order, stability, and some prosperity to the country.

Belgium's other colonial holdings, Ruanda-Urundi, gained independence in 1962 as two nations. Ruanda became a republic—Rwanda. Urundi, renamed Burundi, became independent as a **monarchy**. In 1966, Burundians overthrew the monarchy. A republic was proclaimed.

INDEPENDENCE FOR PORTUGAL'S COLONIES

The Portuguese were the first Europeans to settle in Africa. They were among the last to leave. Although guerrillas had fought them for years, the Portuguese held on. In 1974, however, a more liberal group of leaders overthrew Portugal's colonial-minded government. Soon after taking office, General Antonio de Spinola, the new Portuguese leader, promised independence to the colonies.

Guinea-Bissau (GIN-ee bis-SOW)—formerly Portuguese Guinea—was the first of Portugal's territories to gain its freedom. It had been in the hands of guerrillas since 1973. When Spinola took office, these militants demanded and were granted independence. The Cape Verde Islands voted in 1975 to join in a union with Guinea-Bissau.

Since the early 1960s, three African guerrilla groups in Angola worked to overthrow the colonial government. These groups fought among themselves as well as with the Portuguese. When Portugal announced that it would grant independence to Angola, other African leaders persuaded the warring groups to unite. In early 1975 the leaders of the three organizations signed an agreement with Portugal. A **provisional government** was established that would prepare Angola for complete independence later in the year. But fighting continued and in August Portugal took over the government again. In November

Once he took power in the Congo and settled the war, Joseph Mobutu began an Africanization program. He changed the name of the country to Zaire and his own name to Mobutu Seso Seko. He enouraged the Zairese to discover and preserve their African heritage.

329

Angola was given its independence. It faced an uncertain future as **factions** continued fighting for control. All sides were receiving **foreign aid** which made possible the continued conflict.

Guerrillas had been fighting for Mozambique's freedom since 1964. The main group of nationalists was the Mozambique Liberation Front (Frelimo). In 1974 a series of meetings were held between Frelimo leaders and the Portuguese. As a result, Frelimo leaders set up a temporary government. Complete independence came in June 1975.

Chapter 2
Nation Building

Since independence African nations have followed many different paths. Some have had able leaders. Others have been plagued with many and violent changes in government. Some nations have a favorable location and valuable resources to exploit. Others have a poor environment and few natural resources. Many of the new nations have one thing in common, however. They are faced with dealing with the rivalries of the various peoples within their borders. This makes economic and social progress difficult.

CIVIL WARS

When independence came, most of the new nations kept their colonial boundaries. When outside enemies existed—the Europeans—the African peoples within these borders had been able to unite. But once independence had come and the Europeans were gone, unity broke down. The hostility Europeans had encouraged began to tear apart some of the nations. For example, groups turned against each other in Nigeria, Burundi, and Rwanda.

Within Nigeria are 200 different **ethnic groupings**. Among the largest are the Hausa, Fulani, and Kanuri people of the north. In the west are the Yoruba and Edo. In the east are the Ibo (EE-boh), Ibibio (ih-BIB-ee-oh), and Ijaw peoples. After independence, the suspicions and distrust of the various peoples began to surface.

Northern and western regional leaders were accused of vote frauds and corruption. The Ibos of the east were especially angry. They believed that other regions were receiving most of the revenue from their area's oil resources. In 1966 Ibo army officers staged a coup. In the course of the coup many western and northern leaders were killed. Later in the year army officers from the north headed another coup. All government power was placed in the hands of a supreme military council. The country was divided into 12 ethnically based states and a federal district for the capital, Lagos. Each state was given a military governor.

In 1967 the eastern region seceded and declared itself an independent country—the Republic of Biafra (bee-AF-ruh). Nigerian troops invaded it. The war continued until 1970 when Biafra surrendered. During the fighting, thousands, mostly Ibos, were killed. Since that time,

After its civil war, Nigeria began to rebuild. Special attention was given education and social services.

the Nigerian government has followed a policy of rehabilitating the eastern region. A general amnesty was proclaimed. The future of the nation depends on the ability of the various groups to work together.

MILITARY TAKEOVERS

A growing number of African governments have been taken over by the military. Military groups have seized power in Nigeria, the Central African Empire, Uganda, Somalia, Ghana, and Ethiopia among others. A number of reasons have moved these groups to overthrow their governments. Most seem to have been angered by the worsening economic and political conditions of their countries. In some cases deposed leaders had used their positions to reward their **kinfolk** and supporters. In other instances former leaders simply were not able to govern effectively.

Since its liberation by the Allies in 1941, Ethiopia too has been disturbed by internal revolts. After World War II, Emperor Haile Selassie (hy-lee-suh-LAS-ee) made some efforts to bring his country into the modern age. He imported technicians and experts in various fields. More schools were opened. A small number of students began to receive a university education. The armed forces were better trained. Better agricultural methods were introduced. A more equal distribution of land was attempted. But the gains were small.

By the early 1970s Ethiopia was still a feudal state. The emperor held all power. In return for their support, he shared some power with wealthy followers in the countryside. Most Ethiopians, however, lived in poverty. The feudal lords opposed any **reforms** that might disturb their status. The clergy of the Coptic Church also fought reform. They too owned great parcels of land.

Through 1973 and 1974 conditions grew worse. Drought and **famine** hit the northern and central provinces. Fighting broke out between government troops and Muslim rebels in the province of Eritrea. The Muslims wanted independence. Finally in 1974 the military removed Haile Selassie from power. Many of his supporters were shot. Reforms that supposedly would redistribute the wealth were set up. There is much to be done, however.

AFRICAN SOCIALISM

Some African leaders have chosen **socialism** as a way to gain national unity and further economic development. Socialism is the government ownership and control of the **means of production** and distribution of goods.

Modern Africans, however, have added a traditional African element to form their own concept of socialism. The relationships among kinfolk have long been basic to African peoples. Land has traditionally been thought of as the common property of a people, its clans, and

Burundi and Rwanda have also experienced civil wars. Above, soldiers raise the flag of the newly independent kingdom of Burundi in 1962. The Tutsi people became dominant. Since then, the government has had to fight violent attempts by the Hutu to take control. What are the historical reasons behind this conflict?

331

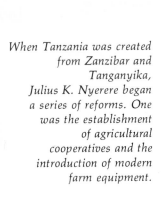

When Tanzania was created from Zanzibar and Tanganyika, Julius K. Nyerere began a series of reforms. One was the establishment of agricultural cooperatives and the introduction of modern farm equipment.

families. Cooperation was all-important. Africans added this idea of kinfolk to socialism. To them, socialism now means all peoples within a nation working and sharing. Such an example is Tanzania.

Julius K. Nyerere (ny-uh-REHR-ee), the first president, introduced a form of socialism which he called ujamaa (oo-jah-MAH). In Swahili this means a family feeling for each other. Nyerere has extended this meaning to apply to all the peoples in Tanzania. He wants everyone to work together for the common good. In rural areas, this goal took the form of **cooperative** and communal farms and other agricultural projects. In other areas, banks, businesses, and even privately owned buildings were taken over by the government.

AFRICAN AUTHENTICITY

Some leaders are trying to build national unity by awakening their people's interest in their own **heritage**. Zaire's president, Mobutu Sese Seko, called for a program of national authenticity—a return to genuine Africanness—to do this. In 1971 he had the country's name changed from the Democratic Republic of the Congo to the Republic of Zaire. Zaire is the original name for the Congo River. The river was renamed Zaire. The people are now Zairese instead of Congolese. Lake Albert is now Lake Mobutu Sese Seko. The copper-rich province of Katanga became Shaba. This is the Swahili word for copper. Mobutu wanted his people to have African rather than European names. As an example, he changed his own name from Joseph Desire Mobutu to Mobutu Sese Seko.

In 1971 a coup led by General Idi Amin (ee-DEE ah-MEEN) took control of Uganda. The following year he began an Africanization program. He expelled all Asians who worked in trade, education, and government. British firms operating in Uganda were **nationalized**. Amin followed the example of Zaire in replacing European place names with African ones. Lake Edward, for instance, is now Idi Amin.

ONE-PARTY SYSTEMS

Leaders of the new nations discovered that the unity of political purpose their people had shown against the Europeans soon split apart. It seemed that the various postindependence political parties represented only local interests. National leaders felt that so many parties threatened national unity and economic development. After a time some leaders declared that only one party could exist within their countries.

The leaders did not view this move as undemocratic. Membership in the one party was open to everyone. Past membership in another party could not bar anyone from joining the new one. Leaders felt that if everyone worked within the same party, the good of the country would be better served.

bar: prevent, forbid

UNITY

Soon after independence, various African nations began setting up organizations for mutual help. One of the first was the Common African, Malagasy and Mauritanian Organization (OCAM). By the mid-1970s it had an airline known as Air Afrique, a merchant fleet, shared postal and telegraph services, and a variety of cultural, technical, and educational programs.

The Organization of African Unity (OAU) includes all but two African countries. Rhodesia and South Africa do not belong. The OAU was founded in 1963. Its goals are the promotion of the political, cultural, scientific, and economic interests of its members. One of the organization's major aims has been to end colonialism in Africa.

In 1967 the East African Community was founded. It consists of Kenya, Uganda, and Tanzania. Under the community are a development bank, postal and telecommunications services, railway administration, and an airline. East and Central African nations have set up various customs unions. One includes the nations of Benin, Ivory Coast, Niger, Upper Volta, and Togo. Besides export and import rules, this union also coordinates national laws dealing with labor, health, finance, and justice. Guinea, Mali, Mauritania, and Senegal have organized to promote the development of the Senegal River.

The various inter-African organizations were set up because the new nations have found that a number of problems can be better handled jointly. Greater benefits for individual nations are possible if various countries pool their resources. Less chance of conflict exists if there is a regional organization to settle disagreements.

All independent black African nations are members of the UN. Most also participate in the activities of the UN's specialized agencies such as the World Health Organization (WHO). A number of nations are associated states of the European Economic Community (EEC). **Tariff** and economic aid benefits come with association in this group.

This is the conference room of the Africa Hall in Addis Ababa, Ethiopia. It is the headquarters of the Organization of African Unity.

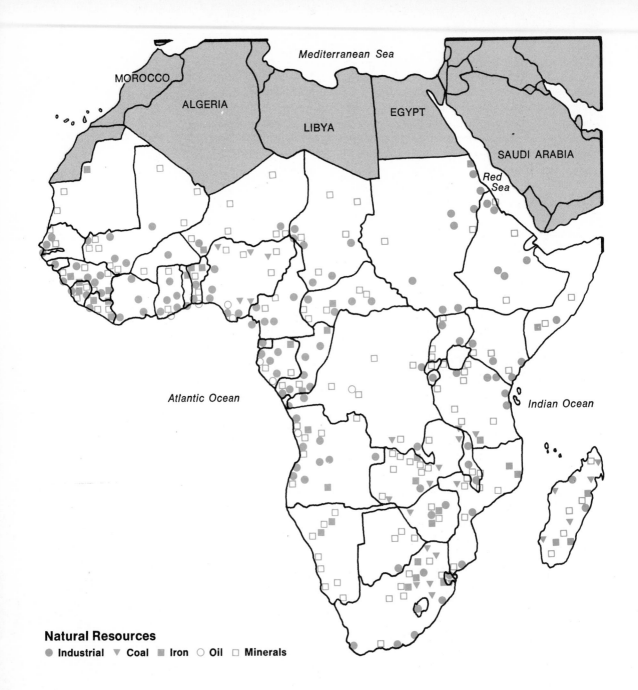

Natural Resources

● Industrial   ▼ Coal   ■ Iron   ○ Oil   □ Minerals

ECONOMIC GROWTH

Traditionally, Africans of the sub-Sahara have been subsistence farmers. They took from the land only enough to support themselves. They rarely had or needed a **surplus**. If anything extra was produced, it was usually exchanged within the farming village.

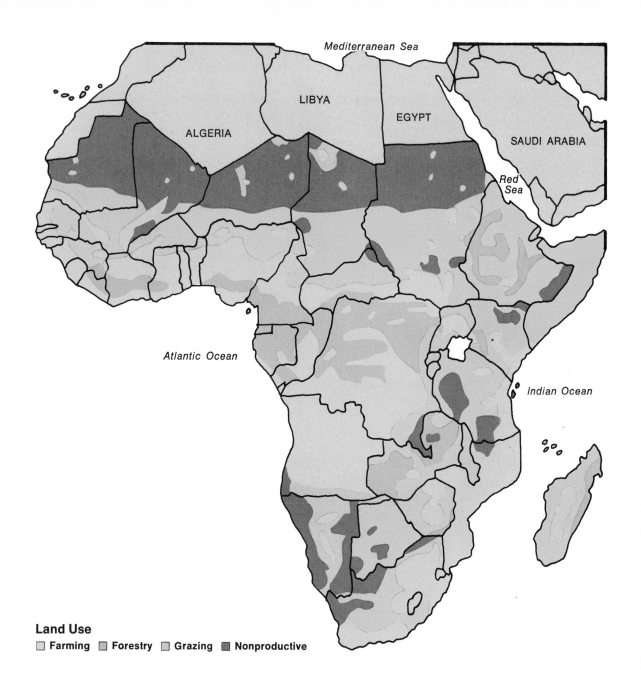

Land Use
■ Farming ■ Forestry ■ Grazing ■ Nonproductive

Europeans introduced modern agricultural methods. They terraced
and fertilized the land and began to raise crops and livestock for export.
Europeans also began to exploit Africa's mineral resources. Europeans
provided the technology and money. Africans provided the labor.
European settlements grew up around mines and industrial centers.

335

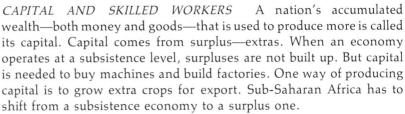

Commerce grew as merchants arrived to provide services and goods needed by these new groups of people. Cities and ports rose to handle the increasing exports and imports. In some areas, dams were built to generate power to run the machines and light the cities.

As we have seen, Europeans introduced a cash **economy** into Africa. The wages paid to Africans, however, were much lower than those for Europeans. But even this smaller amount stimulated Africans to buy **consumer goods**. Since independence, Africans have been demanding consumer goods in increasing amounts.

The economic growth of sub-Saharan Africa has been held back by a number of factors. Better use of natural resources is necessary. More capital and more people trained for management and business are needed. Efficient transportation and **communications** systems have to be developed. Because of these reasons, African nations generally follow a policy of **national planning**. Projects are decided upon and carried out on orders from national leaders. Money is invested where leaders think it should be. Leaders feel that only a coordinated national program will benefit the whole nation.

African nations are benefiting from the struggle among stronger nations for world power and influence. This railroad was built with labor and aid from China. Can you find any similarities between 20th-century foreign aid programs and the 19th-century policy of spheres of economic influence?

CAPITAL AND SKILLED WORKERS   A nation's accumulated wealth—both money and goods—that is used to produce more is called its capital. Capital comes from surplus—extras. When an economy operates at a subsistence level, surpluses are not built up. But capital is needed to buy machines and build factories. One way of producing capital is to grow extra crops for export. Sub-Saharan Africa has to shift from a subsistence economy to a surplus one.

By the mid-1970s most African nations had not been able to do this. As a result, they had not built up the necessary capital for expansion. They still depended in large part on foreign aid. France aids the nations that are members of the French Community. Where strategic and economic advantages are involved, France also helps some countries that are no longer members. Great Britain aids former British colonies, especially members of the Commonwealth of Nations. Political and economic conditions within a country, however, influence the amount and type of aid. When Uganda nationalized British interests, Britain reduced its aid.

Canada, the U.S., West Germany, and some other Western nations have also given assistance in various forms. The Communist nations, headed by the USSR and the People's Republic of China, have given aid to selected nations. Generally these are countries whose leaders have strong pro-Communist leanings. China built and largely financed the railroad linking Zambia to the port of Dar es Salaam (dahr-es-suh-LAHM), Tanzania. It is one of the largest foreign aid projects undertaken by the Chinese. China and the USSR have also sent experts and advisors to the People's Republic of the Congo.

Until independence most technical, management, and business positions were held by non-Africans. As nations became independent,

One problem African nations face is lack of skilled workers. Some nations have fewer problems in regard to this. The young woman above is working in a textile factory in the Ivory Coast.

many of these trained people left. Today most Africans are still subsistence farmers. Less than one percent of the population have a high school education. There are some skilled and **semiskilled** laborers. Many of these are contract workers. They travel to the industrial and mining areas of East and South Africa. When they have enough money to meet their needs, they return to their villages. Their wages go into the economies of their home countries. But wages are so small that the impact is little.

AGRICULTURAL RESOURCES To produce agricultural surpluses, sub-Saharan nations must make the land more productive. They need to make more use of irrigation systems, fertilizers, and modern tools and farming methods. As we have already seen, permanent farming will have to replace slash-and-burn agriculture. Wherever possible, farmers will have to plant a greater variety of crops.

Those countries that do grow surplus crops for export often depend on one or a few products for export. For example, Niger and Senegal rely on peanuts and cotton for their cash crops. A limited or **one-crop economy** can be a disaster for a nation. The harvest could be bad or the price on the world market for that crop could fall.

Africa's agricultural output is often affected by weather conditions. When a drought hits, production is sharply reduced. This happened in the late 1960s and early 1970s in Chad, Senegal, Mali, Mauritania, Niger, and Upper Volta. The nomads and farmers who live along the southern edge of the Sahara Desert in these countries suffered the most. This area is called the Sahel (sah-HAYL). Sahel comes from an Arabic word meaning borderland.

Overpopulation in the area made the six-year drought worse. People and animal populations had doubled over the preceding 25 to 30 years. Overgrazing, **erosion**, and the drought turned poor land into desert. Around 650,000 square kilometers (250,000 square miles) of this region became part of the Sahara. Many animals and people died. Survivors fled to cities and towns. With the loss of their livestock, the nomads lost their way of life.

This disaster strained the economies and political stability of the various countries that govern parts of the Sahel. Senegal was badly hit. The Senegalese lost perhaps 40 percent of their livestock. More than half their millet and sorghum crops were destroyed. Mauritania's agricultural production also was affected. Fortunately the nation has rich deposits of iron ore and copper. Niger, Upper Volta, and Chad were not so fortunate. The drought badly hurt their attempts at economic progress.

MINERAL RESOURCES   As we have seen, Africa is rich in minerals. These resources are beginning to play major roles in the economies of a number of nations. Mauritania's iron and copper deposits have been developed greatly since independence. Botswana at one time was considered a very poor country. But because of its recent exploitation of diamonds, copper, and nickel, millions of dollars are pouring into the country.

The wealth produced from mining there and in other sub-Saharan nations is stimulating growth in other parts of their economies. By using the capital produced by mining and agricultural exports, nations will be able to build factories. Over the next decade manufacturing will become increasingly important. The Ubungo Farm Implements Factory in Tanzania is one such example.

TRANSPORTATION AND COMMUNICATIONS   Transportation and communications are also vitally important to Africa's future economic growth. Several nations, such as Mali, Zambia, Niger, and the Central African Empire have no outlets to the sea. Much of Africa is far from highways, railroads, and rivers. Roads generally are poor. Until recently no attempts were made at coordinating transportation systems between or even within nations. Among the reasons were geographic features, such as deserts and rain forests, and a lack of money.

Steps are being taken to solve the problem, however. The Trans-African Highway will connect the east and west coasts. The Trans-Saharan Highway will connect West Africa with the northern coast. The Tanzam Railroad connects Zambia with the Tanzanian coast. The Central African Empire signed an agreement with the Republic of the Sudan in 1971 for construction of a railroad between the two nations. The CAE also hopes to have a rail line to Cameroon and Gabon to the west.

With the completion of the Pan-African Telecommunications Network, communications should improve greatly. The regional sharing of air, rail, postal, and telegraph services also brings the various nations closer together.

Among the nations exploiting their resources is Botswana. The impurities of the ores that it mines are removed in smelters. The worker above is pouring out this worthless material, called slag.

Workers carry copper ingots to storage. Refer to the map on page 334 for the other minerals African nations have.

Summing Up the Unit

Social Studies Vocabulary

Define: self-government; colonialism; authoritarian; coup; monarchy; foreign aid; ethnic group; kinfolk; famine; socialism; nationalize; national planning; semi-skilled; one-crop economy

People

Identify: Nkrumah; Jomo Kenyatta; de Gaulle; Toure; Kasavubu; Lumumba; Tshombe; Mobutu; Haile Selassie; Nyerere; Amin

Words

Define: British Commonwealth of Nations; Mau Mau; Boers; Great Trek; Afrikaners; apartheid; Coloureds; Bantustans; French Community; ujamaa; OAU; contract workers; Sahel

Questions

1. List three of the reasons that led to the end of colonialism in Africa.

2. How did the population of the British colonies that had less difficult changes to nationhood differ from those where there was trouble?

3. Describe the course that Ghana and Nigeria took to independence.

4. Why was the independence movement in Kenya a long and sometimes bloody struggle?

5. a. Why did the UN order all trade with Rhodesia stopped in 1965? b. What position do black African leaders hold regarding Rhodesia?

6. a. Who did the Boers fight in South Africa? b. Why?

7. a. In which aspects of South African life is apartheid most rigidly enforced? b. When is it flexible? c. Why?

8. Why has the boycott of South Africa had little effect?

9. What is the purpose of the Bantustans?

10. Why did France's African colonies gain their independence more rapidly than those of Britain?

11. Why did Portugal promise independence to its African colonies in 1974?

12. a. What factors have caused African nations to follow different paths since independence? b. What one thing do many have in common? c. What problem has this caused?

13. Why do many new African nations have a problem with hostility among various peoples within their national boundaries?

14. What conditions led to an internal revolt in Ethiopia in 1974?

15. How has tradition been used to support socialism in Tanzania?

16. a. What is Zaire's program of national authenticity? b. What examples are given?

17. Describe Uganda's Africanization program.

18. a. What reasons have been used by African national leaders to justify one-party political systems? b. Why do the leaders not view this as undemocratic?

19. Why have the various inter-African organizations been established?

20. Why was subsistence farming satisfactory for sub-Saharans before colonial times, but not since independence?

21. What factors are needed to speed economic growth in sub-Saharan Africa?

22. Why is there a shortage of workers with technical, management, and business skills?

23. What is needed to make agriculture more productive?

24. What steps have been taken to solve Africa's transportation and communication problems?

Discussion Topics

1. Some African nations have enjoyed political stability. Others have had frequent changes in government. How can you explain this?

2. South Africa's rulers tried to quiet the black majority by setting up Bantustans. What are the pros and cons of this policy when viewed in connection with apartheid?

3. Biafra's attempt to become an independent nation was put down in a very destructive war. How did this war illustrate the problems of African nationalism?

Project Ideas

1. Report on recent economic developments in one sub-Saharan nation.

2. Stage a debate on the whether the U.S. should intervene through aid or troops to prevent a Communist takeover in an African nation. How much danger is there of African nations becoming Soviet or Chinese satellites?

Unit V

Tradition and Change

African nations, like many nations in the world, are a mixture of old and new, traditional and changing. This photo is a good example. What elements of modern and traditional ways are apparent? Is complete change necessary?

The transition from colonialism to independence brought great changes to many Africans. Before the coming of the Europeans, Africans felt a deep relationship with their land and their groups. Life was known, certain, and secure. Then Europeans came and forced change on them. Independence, the world market economy, and the technology of the late 20th century are forcing more change.

Adapting to new ways is never easy. And problems arise when conditions force people to change. But more and more Africans believe that change is necessary. They are trying, however, to make those changes within an African framework. They are merging the old and the new into their own kind of future.

Africans traditionally have thought of themselves not as individuals but as members of a group. From birth they are part of a community. Their joys and sorrows are all shared. What happens to one happens to the group. And what happens to the group happens to each member. Understanding this relationship is basic to understanding African society.

ETHNIC GROUPINGS

Today we speak of Africans as Ghanaians, Nigerians, Tanzanians and so on. These are names that came with independence. But below the national level, Africans group themselves ethnically. Such a grouping is sometimes known as a **tribe**. However, the term has taken on a somewhat negative meaning. Therefore, we prefer to use the term ethnic grouping, or simply a people. Such groupings are usually identified by a number of common factors: language, culture, social and political ties, and geographical region. Underlying these common features is a shared religious experience.

Persons are born into an ethnic grouping. They cannot become part of it by moving from one region to another. Sometimes the group may consist of millions of members. The Hausa people of West Africa number 15 million. Or the group may be very small. The El Molo people of Kenya are only a few dozen.

In Africa today there are between 800 and 1,200 different peoples. Sometimes groups cut across national boundaries. The Fulani people, for example, live in Nigeria, Senegal, and Cameroon. As we have seen, placing different peoples within national boundaries has led to tension and conflict.

To unify nations which include many different peoples, leaders have to consider the interests of each group. The larger the group the more consideration it is shown. Having the support of a large group can provide a person with a base for political office.

Within an ethnic grouping, subgroupings exist. The subgrouping is called a clan. Clan members are those persons who claim to be descended from a common ancestor. African clans often have hundreds and even thousands of members. Some of the ancestors may have lived in remote times. They are known only through **legends** and **myths**. Others lived in later times and are better known. All those who claim the same ancestor claim each other as relatives.

Those members who trace their descent down the same side of the family belong to the same **lineage** (LIN-ee-ij). Within a clan there may be several lineages. In Africa, descent may be traced through either the mother's or the father's side of the family. If descent is traced through the mother's side, it is called a matrilineal (ma-truh-LIN-ee-uhl) system. If descent is traced through the father's side, it is called **patrilineal** (pa-truh-LIN-ee-uhl). Members of the same lineage and clan cannot marry. For this reason children cannot be

Chapter 1
Traditional
Society

Africans are of many peoples or ethnic groupings. This woman is a member of the Kanuri people of northeastern Nigeria. Nigeria has at least 11 other large ethnic groupings and many smaller ones.

While the extended family is the general rule in the country, the nuclear family is the trend in the new African cities.

members of both their mother's and father's lineage and clan. They belong to one or the other. In a few places exceptions to this exist.

In West, Central, and South Africa the matrilineal system is common. The family centers around the mother and the mother's brother. The sons of rulers do not inherit the ruling office. The son of the sister of the ruler inherits the office. Sons do not inherit their father's property either. They inherit the property of their mother's brother, their uncle. Children are sent at an early age to live in the home of their uncle. His home becomes their home. It is the uncle's duty to care for them, teach them, and later see that they have suitable marriage partners. The Ashanti people of Ghana and the Ivory Coast among others follow this system.

The patrilineal system is more widespread in Africa. Political office, property, and wealth are inherited by the father's children. Thus they remain within his family. His wife, the children's mother, does not have as important a **role** as in the matrilineal system.

THE FAMILY

The family is the basic unit of the ethnic grouping. In traditional Africa a child's immediate family is large. It may include grandparents, married and unmarried sons or daughters, and children of married ones. This is the **extended family**. Within the family, children learn their rights and responsibilities. They learn that family members work together for the good of the whole group. Individuals may farm separate pieces of land, but they help each other. When harvests are poor, they share.

Children are very important in African families. A mother braids her daughter's hair as mothers around the world have for centuries. Only the style varies.

As children grow older, they are expected to help. Young girls care for old people or younger children. They may also learn a skill such as weaving that will enable them to earn money. They may learn to buy, sell, and trade goods in market towns. Women, particularly in West Africa, are skilled merchants. The women of Togo, for example, handle much of that nation's textile trade. Boys learn farming, fishing, and herding. Women, however, do much of the farm work. Fathers also teach their sons their own particular trade—carpentry, blacksmithing, or wine-making, among others.

INITIATION CEREMONIES   In traditional Africa, as children reach the age of adolescence, they undergo initiation (in-ish-ee-AY-shun) ceremonies. These ceremonies mark the end of childhood and the beginning of adulthood. They are usually for boys. Among some peoples, girls also have initiation **rituals**.

Initiation varies from place to place. In general, however, it prepares young people to assume adult roles in their grouping. Initiation is not a single ceremony. The period of initiation may last from several weeks to several months. Often the individual's bravery and discipline are tested. In all instances, the individual is expected to show indifference to pain and hardship.

During the rituals, the full meaning of a group's kinship is explained to the candidate. In a way a group is a secret society. It has beliefs and a history that are revealed only to full members, that is, adults. These secrets must be kept for life. To become full members, individuals have to prove themselves mature and responsible. That is the purpose of initiation rituals.

The traditional African family pattern is the extended family. Cooperation is a characteristic of this system. Here young women in Upper Volta work in the family's fields.

AGE SETS   Among some peoples, initiation also prepares boys for entrance into an age set. The boys who are being initiated are not necessarily from the same clan, but are about the same age. Age sets are common among those peoples who need cooperation regardless of family or clan ties. For example, herders have age sets. They need to help one another look for water and grazing land. They also cooperate in protecting their cattle from wild animals and thieves.

During initiation one person in an age set will emerge as the leader of the age set. This is a post he will hold for life. Members of an age set develop strong and lasting relationships with each other. Until they marry, age-set members often live together in a special area. They help each other when needed and, if necessary, fight side by side. In time they move as a unit to higher levels of authority in their community. Eventually, they become elders and senior advisors. Under them, like a ladder, are other age sets. As each age set moves up, the next lower age set fills its place.

Age-set groupings cut across family and clan lines. But members often become related by marrying sisters or cousins of other age-set members. The age-set system helps unify a people. It lessens jealousies and divisions that sometimes arise between families and clans.

In Africa today initiation rituals are that part of traditional life that has experienced the most drastic change. Pressure from missionaries and national governments have caused many rituals to be modified.

MARRIAGE

Because family is so important in African society, marriage is a matter of concern not only to those being married, but to their families too. Some parents start looking for suitable mates for their children while their children are still young. A boy or girl may be engaged at an early age although the marriage takes place much later. This custom is common in traditional societies around the world. Many families, however, wait until the young reach mid- or late teens before arranging a marriage.

The family generally considers their son's or daughter's feelings about a mate. If a person dislikes the one selected, the family will look for a more suitable choice. Sometimes a young person meets someone he or she likes and asks the family's approval to marry. If a person wishes to marry someone of whom the family disapproves, the individuals may choose to run away. Among traditional Africans this can cause serious problems. Among other things, the couple loses the security and protection of the group. Families and individuals all try to avoid pushing matters to so serious an end.

Once both families agree to the marriage, the family of the groom usually gives gifts to the father of the bride. These gifts are called bridewealth. The amount and type depend on the custom, wealth, and status of the families. East Africa's herding peoples give gifts

of cattle. West and Central African farming peoples may give farm tools, goats, or chickens.

Actual marriage rituals vary from one people to another. In some places, relatives of the bride and groom visit for several days in one or both of the families' communities. Sometimes the elders bless the marriage. All the elements of the ceremony stress the importance of the marriage to the community of relatives.

When the couple has a child, they will fulfill the main purpose of their marriage. They will have added to the next generation in the kinship system.

ELDERS

As parents grow older, their authority and influence within the family and clan usually increase. Africans value older people. They believe that wisdom comes with age. In a matrilineal system, the mother's influence grows. In a patrilineal system, the father's influence increases. If he is of exceptional ability, the father may become a clan chief. Whether they reach high positions or not, elders are often consulted about community problems. Preserving the ways and customs of their ancestors is of primary importance to them. They want to keep alive and strong the kinship ties that give order and security to their community.

In traditional societies the young learn about their past—their folklore—from village elders. Today in Tanzania this is still true, but with a difference. Formal education is considered necessary, but the Tanzanians are also trying to preserve their past. These students are on a field trip to learn about local history from a village elder.

345

Chapter 2
Religion

These Coptic Christians are taking part in an Epiphany procession in Lalibela, Ethiopia. Epiphany commemorates the visit of the Three Kings to the Christ Child.

Traditionally religion has been a vitally important part of African life. Religious ceremonies were community affairs in which all members took part. Local leaders often had religious as well as political roles.

Today millions of Africans still practice traditional religions. However, the degree to which they are observed depends on the particular group. Among many peoples, modern medicine, technology, and education challenge traditional beliefs. Many people are in the process of adapting their old ways and beliefs to the demands of the modern world. But among those peoples whose traditional ties are strong, especially in rural areas, traditional religions are still influential.

However, many young people are forced to move to urban or mining areas to find work. They no longer live as part of a lineage, a clan, or a people. They are suddenly individuals far from the rituals and customs that form their cultural and religious heritage. Christianity and Islam have made great numbers of converts among these and other Africans. These two religions, however, have long histories in sub-Sahara Africa.

TRADITIONAL RELIGIONS

The traditional religions of Africa are as varied as the hundreds of peoples who live there. However, there are some beliefs and rituals that are common to many peoples: belief in a Supreme Being, in a middle level of divinities, in ancestor spirits, and in life after death.

THE CONCEPT OF GOD   Central to African religions is the idea of God as Creator. But after Creation, God withdrew. The affairs of earth and its people were left to lesser divinities and to ancestor spirits. Various peoples have different explanations for this. Basically, however, the reasons are the same. The attitudes and actions of humans were so unpleasant that they drove God away.

This is similar to the Biblical story of Adam and Eve. By their actions they angered God and God drove them from the Garden of Eden. In a real sense God withdrew protection from them. Traditional Africans hold a like view. For example, the Barotse people of Zambia call God Nyambi. Nyambi fled to the sky to get away from a person called Kamonu. Kamonu had made a spear and killed animals. Nyambi did not approve of this.

LESSER DIVINITIES   Humans are not left completely without protection, however. They have lesser divinities to help them. The divinities which are worshiped vary from people to people. Often, however, the divinities are identified with nature. They may live in mountains, forests, rivers, or in animals such as snakes. Storms, thunder, lightning, the sun, the moon, and other works of nature are controlled by them. These divinities are often thought of as having human characteristics and of having once enjoyed human pleasures. Ogun, for example, is the Yoruba god of iron. The Yoruba people believe that when he was human, he was a hunter.

At certain times of the year and during times of trouble, animals are sacrificed to the divinities. They usually live in sacred shrines. The people around Kano in Nigeria have a divinity that lives in a tree. The tree is encircled with a wall. Only the guardian of the shrine and other authorized persons may enter. Black goats, dogs, and fowl are sacrificed to this divinity. Among a number of peoples, black is regarded as a sacred color.

sacrificed: offered to a deity

If the sacrifices or offerings are not made, the community can expect trouble. According to an old legend, the empire of Ghana fell because one year the great snake Bida did not receive its annual sacrifice. Historically Africans have sacrificed the things they valued most: cattle, sheep, goats, chickens, and even humans. They also made offerings of grains and vegetables.

ANCESTOR SPIRITS   Ancestor spirits are closest to the everyday concerns of traditional Africans. Ancestors have died in a physical sense, but as spirits they are still present to their descendants. Ancestors generally stay near the community or even the house in which they lived. They will remain as long as they are remembered. Some Africans carve figurines into which the spirits can go. Sometimes a spirit enters an animal.

For most traditional Africans, their present attitudes, customs, duties, and responsibilities began with their ancestors. Thus traditional ways cannot be ignored or lightly discarded. Ancestors will protect and help their descendants if they are honored with rituals

347

Masks and costumes are an important part of African traditional religions. These figures are on their way to the Dama festival of the Dogon people of Mali.

and ceremonies. If the rituals are not observed, ancestors take their revenge. Among many people the young are not told the history of their clans and, therefore, their ancestors until their initiation. At that time they are warned that trouble awaits them if they stray from the ways of the ancestors.

Obedience to traditional ways has provided stability and security for the various African peoples. It has tended, however, to discourage change. Reliance on ancestors is found among other cultures besides African ones. For thousands of years the Chinese practiced ancestor reverence. They too believed that their welfare depended on the respect and honor shown their ancestors.

SPECIALISTS   Traditional African religions have their special people as Christianity has its ministers and priests and Judaism, its rabbis. Among these special people are the guardians of the shrines of local divinities. The guardians may be either male or female. Like the ancient Greeks and Romans, African community leaders and individuals consult the guardian for advice. The people believe that he or she has the power to communicate with the spirit. A guardian learns from the spirit the cause of someone's troubles and what must be done to end them.

Traditional Africans believe that mediums, diviners, and rainmakers also possess special powers. Mediums serve as contacts between the world of the living and the spirit world. Mediums are mostly women. The spirit speaks through the medium while the medium is in a trance. The medium gives advice and foretells the future. Diviners who are usually men also foretell the future. But they use omens and symbols. An omen is an occurrence or phenomenon such as an eclipse or the way sacred stones fall when the diviner throws them. A symbol represents or suggests something else. A lion, for example, may symbolize strength. Rainmakers supposedly have the power to bring rain or sometimes to stop it.

Another group of specialists are medicine men and women. They play a variety of roles in traditional African religions. They heal both physical and spiritual illness. Sometimes they are called herbalists. As apprentices they learn about the medicinal properties of a variety of herbs, roots, fruits, and minerals. Like modern medical doctors, they also understand that certain physical ills are brought on by the mind. They use rituals to cure these.

CHRISTIANITY

Christianity came early to Northeast Africa. Ethiopians were converted in the 300s A.D. The majority of Ethiopians and a small number of Egyptians still practice Coptic Christianity. Elsewhere in the Sudan and northern Africa, Islam almost stamped out Christianity beginning in the 600s.

Christianity came late to the rest of sub-Saharan Africa. In the

1400s and 1500s, Portuguese and Spanish traders brought missionaries with them. The missionaries established churches along the west coast. Not many Africans became Christians, however. Toward the end of the 1700s, a number of former slaves who had converted began moving to Liberia and Sierra Leone. From these areas Christianity began to spread along the west coast and into the interior.

During the early 1800s, European missionaries began going into the interior to set up missions and convert Africans. Some of them, including David Livingstone, became famous explorers. In the late 1800s European and U.S. missionaries accompanied the new colonial rulers. As colonial power spread, the number of missionaries and their converts increased.

Many Africans saw Christianity as part of colonialism. The missionaries were mostly Europeans; so were the colonial rulers. Colonial officers generally gave aid and even military support to missionaries. In mission schools European—not African—languages, history, and culture were taught. Despite these actions, millions of Africans over the years converted to some form of Christianity. The reasons were both spiritual and material. It is estimated that the total number of Christians in sub-Saharan Africa is between 50 and 70 million. This includes those who belong to the major Christian churches. It also includes members of the estimated 5,000 or so independent African Christian churches.

Both missionary churches and independent African churches are attempting to make Christianity more African in form and content. They want it to be more rooted in African social and religious traditions. Those attitudes and practices which come from European tradition and are not part of **doctrine** are being removed. Baptizing Roman Catholics with African names instead of saints' names is one such practice. Christianity, Africans believe, should be related to the everyday life of the people. It should follow the way that traditional African religions have been and are related to African life.

ISLAM

Islam swept across North Africa during the 600s and 700s. In the following centuries it moved into West African communities along the southern fringe of the Sahara. It moved more slowly across the savannahs and into the forest areas of West and Central Africa. Islam spread up the Nile River to what is modern Sudan and Ethiopia. Today most of the Sudanese are Muslims. Ethiopia has a substantial minority of Muslims. At the same time Islam was spreading across North Africa, Arab and Persian traders were carrying it to the east coast of Africa. Somalia gradually became almost entirely Muslim. For centuries, however, Islam stayed in the trading centers and cities of the east coast. It began to reach the interior only in the 1800s. Today there are somewhere between 70 and 100 million Muslims on the African continent.

substantial: large; important

349

Many Africans are Muslims. These are praying at a mosque in Kano, Nigeria. How did Islam come to Africa? When? In what part of Africa is Nigeria? How much influence has Islam had?

Islam came to Africa without a color barrier. Muhammad is believed to have married an African woman to teach his followers that Islam was without **prejudice**. Wherever Islam spread, it merged with the traditional customs and practices of the people. Since Africans already believed in one God, they had little difficulty in accepting this key teaching of Islam. Many African converts initiate their young, but they include passages from the Koran—the sacred book of Islam—at the ceremony. Evil spirits are driven out with prayers from the Koran.

In a number of African nations Islam is also a political force. Some countries like Somalia and Mauritania have made Islam the **state religion**. In other countries, such as Senegal and Mali, Islam was used as a rallying point in the fight for independence. In Nigeria, the Muslims of the northern area exercise great influence on government policies. Islam has also tied the Africans to a worldwide community of over 500 million Muslims. Increasingly large amounts of money and aid from Arab countries are coming to Africa through this tie.

Some Muslims are beginning to believe that they too must adapt their ways to the forces of change and modernization. Some Muslims are opposed to polygyny—the practice of having more than one wife—which Islam permits. Others say that Africa's Muslim leaders should do more to encourage education among the young.

JUDAISM AND HINDUISM

Followers of Judaism lived in Egypt and northern Africa long before the first century A.D. Alexandria was a famous center of Jewish learning. A number of Berbers converted to Judaism. Judaism also has a long history in Ethiopia. The first Jews came to the area in the 500s A.D. Today about 50,000 Jews live there.

In various parts of Africa, there are large communities of Hindus. Almost all are originally from India. There are very few African converts. The Hindu **caste** system is a barrier to conversions. One must be born into a caste. Exceptions are sometimes made for African women who marry Hindus. They generally take the caste of their husbands.

The lives of many Africans have changed through their contacts with non-Africans. Some changes came through attending European-run schools. Other changes came through working for Europeans. In the cities and **towns** which grew around mining, manufacturing, and shipping centers, Africans from rural areas learned new **life-styles**. During World Wars I and II, many Africans were recruited into Western armies and navies and sent to other areas of the world.

Since independence, outside influences are even more forceful. Through trade and foreign aid, African countries are becoming more closely tied to non-African nations. As Africans move toward industrialization and **urbanization**, more of their traditional patterns will change or be adapted to new ways. The question is how much and how useful will change and adaptation be.

EDUCATION

Traditionally family, lineage, and clan were responsible for educating the young. It was within kinship groups and age sets that young people learned their history and roles in life. Some exceptions to this informal education existed. Along the east coast, Muslims set up schools where African students learned to read and write Arabic and/or Swahili. These schools, however, were usually limited to teaching Islam. Social roles or a people's heritage were not included.

The real changes in African education began with European Christian missionaries. They opened schools across the continent. These schools were primarily for converting Africans to Christianity. But they also taught the culture and technology of the West. Some schools were supported by the colonial governments.

The results of this type of education on Africans were many. In some ways the educational system resulted in cultural conflicts. Africans learned more about Europe than about their own continent. They began to value European cultures and ideas more than those of their own peoples. The French tried to replace African cultures with French culture. Perhaps the British did not deliberately try to make African students into British copies. But their students learned to speak English with a British accent and adopted British attitudes and customs.

In other ways European-based schooling prepared Africans for independence and modernization. Africans learned about such political ideas as self-government and nationalism in these schools. They learned that by controlling their own economies, they would benefit more than if colonial powers controlled them.

Since independence, many governments have been pouring money into their educational systems. African leaders seem to believe that modern education is the key to the future. Most of the money has been spent to build primary schools. But students trained at high school, college, and university levels are also needed. Building and

Chapter 3
Changing Social Patterns

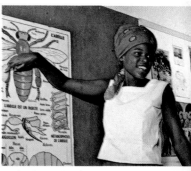

In higher education, the areas of law, medicine, and engineering are stressed over such things as the arts and history. Why do you think this is so? Above a teacher explains a fact in entomology, the branch of zoology dealing with insects.

supporting such large educational systems place great economic burdens on nations. Resources are few. Needs are many.

Because of the economic factors, wide differences in the quantity and quality of education exist among African countries. In Mali, less than 10 percent of the young are in school. In Ghana, 60 percent of its elementary grade children are in school. Yet only 20 percent of its high school population are enrolled.

In most African countries, education is more available in the cities than in the country. A lack of trained teachers adds to the problems. Some African countries, such as the Ivory Coast and Nigeria, are using television to reach greater numbers of their citizens. Other countries are using radio and correspondence courses.

For African nations at this time, providing the right kind of education—not just providing education—is vital. Vocational training is essential. However, in countries where higher levels of education are available, many young are interested only in the kind of education that will get them government jobs. Government jobs have high status. While skilled workers are desperately needed, the bureaucracy in many countries is becoming overcrowded and inefficient. Graduates who have come from the country do not want to return even though few jobs exist in the city. To return home would seem an admission of failure. They are reluctant to return to the country even to teach.

IMPACT AND CONFLICT The ideas and practices which come from the new educational system are having a great impact on Africans.

The young especially are greatly influenced. Their new attitudes often bring them into conflict with their families, clans, and peoples. In other instances, the young have been led to examine and rediscover the value of their own cultures. Still other people are trying to adapt the new ways to their old customs and beliefs.

Cultural conflicts take many forms. A young man might declare he no longer believes in the power of the clan's ancestor spirits. He would then be forbidden to take part in his clan's religious rituals. Such disbelief threatens the very foundation of the clan's traditional religious and social organization.

As we have seen, the traditional purpose of marriage was to produce as many children as possible. Marriage insured the continuation of family, lineage, and clan. If a couple refuses to have more than two children, the family's future is threatened.

Conflict may also arise when a young man leaves his wife in the village and goes to the city to work or study. When they meet again, the ways of one may seem strange to the other. The man might even appear to be ashamed of his wife. This affects the well-being of the marriage which affects the well-being of the clan.

URBANIZATION

In Africa, as in other parts of the world, towns and cities are centers of change. Government and industry cluster in them. Residents are constantly exposed to a variety of customs and behaviors, opinions

Cities are increasing in size and number in Africa. These are government buildings in Nairobi, the capital of Kenya. Why have cities grown up around the new capitals?

RURAL-URBAN SHIFT IN GHANA

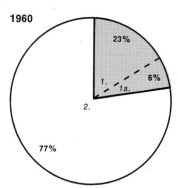

1960

23%

1.
6%
1a.

2.

77%

1960 Population: 6,726,820

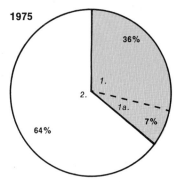

1975

36%

1.

2.

1a.

7%

64%

1975 Population: 9,904,000

1. **Urban (including Accra)**

1a. **Accra Metropolitan Area**

2. **Rural**

Source: *Demographic Yearbook, 1963* and *Demographic Yearbook, 1973,* copyright, United Nations (1964, 1974). Reproduced by permission

Zambia is training workers to fill gaps in its industries. Trainees receive two-year courses in such skills as carpentry, electricity, or plumbing. This man is learning to be a welder. What industries would need welders?

and attitudes. Most Africans, however, continue to live in rural areas. There the traditional ways of life are still strongly held. But as more and more people move to towns and cities, they are caught up in a new experience.

They live and work with many different peoples who have different customs and beliefs. Their lives now are run by the clock and not by the seasons as they were in the country. City dwellers often have to change from wearing traditional clothes to wearing Western ones. They may live with relatives, but they are not surrounded by family as they were in their villages. They are not under the constant watch of their elders. At the same time the city provides many opportunities to wander from traditional ways.

Many workers are required to join a labor union or other kind of organization associated with their job. This is not the kinship grouping they have known. These unions and other associations may be composed of many unrelated people. Nor is it like the traditional age sets. People of all ages belong.

Urban living has not entirely displaced ethnic groupings, however. Associations of those who belong to the same people have been organized in some cities. These organizations teach newcomers the ways of the city and help them to find jobs. They also provide help for unemployed group members.

The first generation, especially, of city dwellers go back to their old homes for marriages, deaths, births, and religious celebrations. Thousands of contract laborers, such as those who work in South

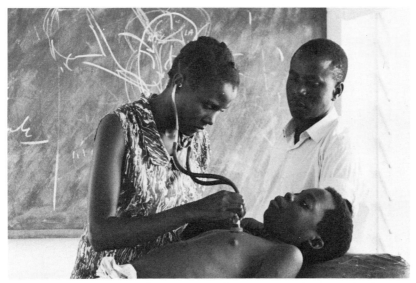

With industrialization, modernization,, urbanization, and increased education have come improvements in health care. Does this progression seem inevitable? Why? This picture also shows the changing status of women.

Africa, return to their homes at the end of their contracts. But the ties are not all one way either. When relatives come to visit the city, they expect to stay with city relatives. Relatives who come seeking a job or further education stay with relatives. The obligations of kinship require city dwellers to help members of their clan if possible.

Today second-, third-, and fourth-generation Africans are being born and are growing up in the new towns and cities. These later generations are not so closely tied to the traditional ways as earlier generations were, or rural Africans continue to be. Their education and experiences are very different from the traditional patterns. For example, these new Africans were probably brought up in a **nuclear** rather than an extended family. The authority of clan and lineage elders is unknown to them. They may have visited their ancestors' villages, but the way of life may have seemed strange. These new Africans are concerned with careers and national and international events.

WOMEN

Throughout history women have played important roles in a number of African societies. Some scholars believe that the women of the old Nubian kingdoms held considerable power. Various empires were ruled by queens. In many cultures women acted as advisors to kings and chiefs. Among the Ashanti people, sisters and mothers of rulers often held the real power. Oral histories tell of women who served

African women have always played important roles in the family and in society. Since independence they have been involved in national and international politics. This is Annie Jiagge of Ghana at the UN.

This is another African representative to the UN, Jeanne Martin Cisse from Guinea.

as generals and led warriors into battle. As we have seen, a number of peoples practiced, and still practice, the matrilineal system in which inheritance comes through the mother's side.

In African religions, mediums are usually women. Women also serve as rainmakers and diviners. Besides motherhood and household chores, African women are farmers and merchants. In West Africa, especially, they play—as they have for centuries—important roles in trade.

In modern Africa, women are also playing increasingly important roles in politics. Annie Jiagge was the first woman judge and Supreme Court Justice in Ghana. She also served as the Chairwoman of the UN Commission on the Status of Women. Angie Brooks became the first African woman to serve as President of the UN General Assembly. In her own country of Liberia she has held a number of government positions. Dr. Irene Ighodaro of Nigeria is known throughout the world for her work in medicine and education. Margaret Kenyatta, daughter of President Jomo Kenyatta of Kenya, worked with her father for the independence of that country. Since independence she has held a number of government positions including mayor of Nairobi, Kenya's capital.

Modern African women are doctors, nurses, teachers, and engineers. Often they do these things while raising a family and keeping house.

Some African women, especially Muslim ones, still lead lives centered around the home. Many still spend their lives within the boundaries of their villages. But growing numbers of African women are assuming additional roles.

This woman is a carpet designer in Mauritania. What historical basis is there in Africa for women's involvement in economics, politics, and medicine?

Among many peoples of West Africa there exists a long tradition of visual arts such as weaving, sculpture, and metal casting. Along the east coast until recently, creativity was more likely to be expressed in the spoken word and in music.

The arts of some peoples reflect non-African influences. Their many centuries of contact with Islam is evident in the works of the Hausa and Fulani, for example. European elements have had their greatest impact on modern African literature. Many writers use French or English rather than an African language. Non-African influences are also being felt in the contemporary visual arts. Some African artists are adapting Western styles and techniques to traditional subject matter.

Chapter 4
Creativity

EARLY ART

Many early African art objects, especially those made of wood, have been lost. Dampness, termites, and wars have destroyed them. For the most part only works of metal, clay, or soapstone have survived.

We do have some knowledge of very early African creativity, however. Among the art which has survived are rock and cave paintings found from the Sahara to South Africa. The oldest of these are in the Tassili plateau in southern Algeria. As we have seen, ancient artists painted and carved scenes from their daily lives on cave walls and rocks.

In sub-Saharan Africa, the oldest surviving art comes from the village of Nok in northern Nigeria. There, in the 1940s, terra-cotta—fired clay—heads of both humans and animals were discovered. Found with them were some iron tools. The earliest of these have been dated to between 400 and 300 B.C. As we have seen, scholars believe that this may have been the earliest date for making iron in West Africa. The influence of the Nok culture continued in the region after its decline around 200 A.D.

The Nok culture may have inspired artists of the later city-state of Ife. As we have seen, Ife **artifacts** include works in bronze, wood, terra cotta, and ivory. The artists of Ife passed along their knowledge and techniques to other peoples in West Africa, especially those of Benin.

This terra-cotta head is from the Nok culture. How long did the influence of this culture last? Why do you think people imitate the art styles of others?

VISUAL ARTS

The Portuguese who came to West Africa in the late 1400s took back to Europe carved figurines and ceremonial masks. Objects such as these are still important in traditional African art. This art has been, and still is, deeply rooted in the religious life of the various peoples. These objects are not made for beauty alone or as a means of self-expression for the artist. They are made for religious or ceremonial purposes.

Masks may represent a spirit or divinity or force of nature. Humans

Much of African art is tied to traditional religions. Masks such as the one above from the Kuba culture of Zaire are worn in ritual dances. These masks also influenced artists of other cultures such as Picasso. The man on the right is carving a figurine. Some traditional religions believe that the spirits of ancestors live in such figurines.

wearing the masks symbolize the beings or ideas. When worn during a funeral rite, the masks may serve as a bridge between the living and the dead. They are also worn among some peoples during initiation rituals. The Ibo people of Nigeria wear masks for many events—festivals, rituals, dramas, and even public holidays such as Nigeria's Independence Day. Some masks are abstract representations of the human head. Others combine human and animal features. Still others may represent ideas such as beauty or ugliness.

Generally, carved figurines also have religious meaning. Some people, like the Dogons of Mali, carve these figurines to serve as places in which ancestor spirits can live. Some are used as carriers of the spirits of unborn babies. And some are carved as symbols to bring fertility, strength, or other power to the bearer.

Traditional African artists use many materials for their carvings: wood, ivory, soapstone, and clay. Masks are often carved wood. But they may be made of animal skins, cotton or other fiber, or shells. Besides masks and figurines, boxes for cosmetics and jewelry, cups and other containers, headrests, chairs, stools, shutters, and doors and also carved. Even many of the pulleys used by weavers in such areas as Mali, Benin, the Ivory Coast, and Guinea are decorated with carvings.

Where natural materials—clay, raffia, and so on—are available, pottery, baskets, weavings, and leather goods are made. Leatherwork is found especially among herding peoples. The Ashanti and Baule people of West Africa have long worked with gold. Bronze, silver, brass, and copper are among the other materials used by African artists.

Besides masks and figurines, African artisans also carve heads. The one above is from Senegal. Most of Africa's buildings are made of materials such as mud-dried bricks or wood. Why? Why has this made archaeology difficult in this area?

ARCHITECTURE

Mention has already been made of the great stone buildings made by the Nubians and people of Zimbabwe. These structures are tributes to the technical knowledge and sense of design of these peoples.

In most areas today—except in the large towns and cities—buildings are still made of the most easily available materials. In rural communities, stone buildings are rare. Clay or mud is used. Some peoples use straw, reeds, or wood. Round houses of straw are common among some Sudanese and East African peoples. The Dogon people of Mali build multistory square houses of mud. The Ndebele people of South Africa decorate the outside walls with colorful geometric designs.

The buildings that are going up in the new cities belong to the school of design known as international. They look very much like glass skyscrapers in large cities elsewhere in the world.

DANCE AND MUSIC

African dancing is highly symbolic and tied to traditional religions. There are dances for rain, a good harvest, a successful hunt. Dances are also performed to thank the spirits that guard the community. In many communities, there are dances of sorrow at a death. And at times people dance just for the joy of life.

Dancing is a community act, since the reason for the dance generally concerns all members. Among some peoples, however, such as the Watusi of Burundi, persons are trained as professional dancers.

Drums and gourd rattles often provide the rhythms for dancing.

Rhythm is basic to all music. And complex rhythm is the trademark of African music. It is not easy for some non-Africans to appreciate fully the music and dancing of African peoples. African music is polyrhythmic. That means that there may be three, four, five, or more rhythms going at the same time. Dancers represent the various rhythms by moving different parts of their bodies to different rhythms. Arms, legs, head, shoulders, and trunk each move to a different rhythm. Great skill and practice are needed by the dancers.

African music has strongly influenced the music of many peoples throughout the world. Some modern Latin American and North American music, for example, reveals a strong African influence.

ORAL LITERATURE

Over the centuries most African literature has been oral. **Epics, myths,** poems, stories, and **proverbs** have been handed down from one generation to the next by word-of-mouth. Certain members of each community memorize the tales from their elders. They in turn pass them on to the next generation.

Some African peoples south of the Sahara developed written languages. The people of Nubia and the Vai and Banum people of the Guinea coast had scripts. The Nyungwe people of the Zambezi River area reportedly once had a written language. There may have been other peoples who had written languages. But if the writings were on materials such as wood, leather, or skins, the manuscripts were lost through decay. For the most part, people have had to rely on storytellers.

All over sub-Saharan Africa storytellers still recite their tales. They do not simply entertain; they also teach. They recite their peoples' legends about the creation of the world and humans. The Ashanti of the Ivory Coast and Ghana, the Masai of Tanzania and Kenya, the Bushmen and Hottentots of South Africa, and the many peoples of Central Africa all have their oral traditions of creation. Epic tales of the exploits of ancestors and local heroes are also passed on by word of mouth. Among these are the great struggle between Sundiata (sun-dee-AH-tuh), a Mandingo chief, and Sumanguru Kante (soo-man-GOO-roo KAHN-tuh), ruler of the Kingdom of Susu. Another tale concerns the ancestor of the Yoruba people, Oduduwa (oh-DOO-doo-wah). He was the first ruler of Ife.

Other African tales are about small animals who outsmart bigger and stronger enemies. **Fables** of the clever spider are found throughout West and Central Africa. There are also tales about the hare and the tortoise. Apparently Africans have long admired those whose intelligence enables them to overcome the greater physical strength of others. Through symbolism these tales teach listeners that cunning and cleverness can outwit injustice and evilness. Some experts think that Aesop (EE-sop), whose *Fables* are known throughout the world, was from Ethiopia.

Music is also very much a part of traditional African religions and life in general. What part does music play in African religious and social life? What makes African dance so complex? This drum is from Ghana.

Some of Africa's oral traditions deal with the exploits of ancestors and local heroes. Most of these are warriors. Will figures like this track star become the subjects of new traditions? Do people always need heroes? Why?

In traditional Africa, storytelling is a community activity. The storyteller, usually an elder of the village, will act out all the parts of the story. Sometimes sound effects or music are used too. Very often the audience will sing any songs that are part of the tale. Often listeners will comment on the action of the story. The tale is after all part of their past and their present.

Africans also have an oral tradition of truths and useful sayings. These are usually described as proverbs. They also have a treasury of riddles, songs, and poetry whose origins have been lost in time.

MODERN LITERATURE

The education and local circumstances of writers influence their choice of topics. Many of the writers were educated under the French, English, or Portuguese colonial systems. Many continue to write in the language of their former rulers.

WRITERS IN FRENCH   As early as the 1930s Africans writing in French began comparing the values of the West with those of Africa. They concluded that there was a naturalness and warmth in African culture that Western culture lacked. African culture was more in harmony with nature and with life. It seemed to them that Western culture was cold and exploitive. It had had a brutal impact on Africans and their cultures. These themes came to be grouped under the general heading of Negritude (NEG-ruh-tood).

Among the best known writers of the school of Negritude was the poet Leopold Sedar Senghor (lay-oh-POLD SAY-dahr SAHN-gohr). He later became the first president of Senegal. He, along with poets Aime Cesaire (eh-MAY say-ZAHR) of Martinique and Leon

This is Leopold Senghor, poet and politician.

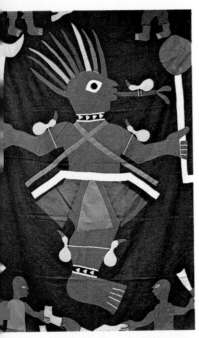

Weaving is one of the many arts that are practiced in Africa today. This tapestry is from Benin and tells a story. The figure represents a king. For what other kinds of art objects have the cities of the Republic of Benin been famous?

Damas of French Guiana, founded the African literary magazine *Presence Africaine.* Other well-known Negritude poets include Birago Diop and David Diop, also of Senegal. Several novelists from Cameroon also based their writings on the themes of Negritude. Ferdinand Oyono protested the French claim that their African colonists were just another part of France and that educated Africans were really French. France, he said, was exploiting Africans in its own interests.

More recent African writers in French have not been so concerned with Negritude. They do not claim to speak for all Africans. Among these writers is Camara Laye, whose book *Dark Child* is considered to be one of Africa's best autobiographies. The poems of the Congolese Tchicaya U Tam'si speak of his sorrows and those of his people.

WRITERS IN ENGLISH   Many Africans writing in English base their works on social, economic, or political themes. One of their great literary centers is in Nigeria. Among Nigerians, Ibo writers have been especially productive. Perhaps the best known is Chinua Achebe. In three of his novels, *Things Fall Apart, No Longer at Ease,* and *Arrow of God,* he deals with the clash of old and new values. Another Ibo writer, Onuora Nzekwu, also deals with this conflict. Dilim Okafor-Omali examines especially the causes of such conflicts in *A Nigerian Villager in Two Worlds.*

Among Nigeria's poets is Christopher Okigbo who died in the Biafran civil war. Other well-known Nigerian writers include Nkem Nwankwo, John Pepper Clark, and Gabriel Okara. Probably the most famous African playwright is Nigerian Wole Soyinka. In his plays he pokes fun at strutting school teachers and so-called prophets. He also criticizes the idea of Negritude and African **dictators**.

West Africa too has its writers. Gladys Casely-Hayford of Ghana was writing in the early 1900s. Two of Ghana's playwrights are Efua Sutherland and Ama Ata Aidoo. Sutherland founded the Ghana Society of Writers and the Ghana Experimental Theater. She is known in the U.S. for *Playtime in Africa,* a children's book. Lenrie Peters of Gambia and William Conton and R. Sarif Easmon of Sierra Leone also write in English.

During the 1960s several East African writers came into prominence. James Nguigi of Kenya wrote several works which explore the problems of harmonizing old and new ways. *Weep Not Child* and *The River Between* are two of these. In *Song of Lawino* Okot p'Bitek of Uganda portrays the troubles an uneducated wife has in understanding the ways of her educated husband.

South African writers are caught up in the anger and anguish of living in an apartheid society. Ezekial Mphahlele examines this theme in his autobiography *Down Second Avenue.* Alfred Hutchinson and Bloke Modisane have also described their experiences in autobiographies. James Matthews and Peter Abrahams have written on this subject too. In "Me Colored," Abrahams uses poetry to examine the conflict that comes from being part black and part white. Matthews explores the legal restrictions of apartheid in the short story "The Park." The problems of race relations have also been portrayed by novelist Alex La Guma and playwright Lewis Nkosi.

WRITERS IN AFRICAN LANGUAGES   Not all African literature is in the language of Europeans. Africans are also writing in their own languages. During the 1920s and 1930s, Thomas Mofolo wrote several novels in the Sotho language. One of these, *Chaka,* was the first historical novel in modern African literature. Poets B. W. Vilakazi and J. L. Dube wrote in Zulu. S. E. K. Mqhayi wrote poems in his Xhosa language. All these are Bantu languages.

The modern Yorubas of Nigeria and Benin have a strong literary tradition in their native language. In the 1940s Daniel O. Fagunwa began writing novels in Yoruba. Another writer in Yoruba is I. O. Delano. Herbert Ogunde writes plays in this language.

The earliest known Swahili writings date to the 1600s. Until the 1800s the only Swahili literature was poetry. Its themes were mostly religious. In the 1800s some poets began to write on other subjects. Two 20th-century Swahili poets are Sheikh Amri Abedi and Mathias E. Mnyampala. James Mbotela and Muhammad Saleh Abdullah Farsi wrote novels in Swahili. Perhaps the best-known Swahili writer is novelist Shaaban Robert.

This painting is by a modern Ghanaian artist, Poto Poto. What is the subject matter? When were the earliest African paintings done?

363

Summing Up the Unit

Social Studies Vocabulary

Define: legend; myth; lineage; patrilineal; role; extended family; ritual; doctrine; prejudice; state religion; caste; urbanization; nuclear family; epic; proverb; fable

People

Identify: Jiagge; Brooks; Ighodaro; Margaret Kenyatta; Senghor; Laye; Achebe; Soyinka; Sutherland

Words

Define: initiation ceremony; age set; bridewealth; divinities; ancestor spirits; omen; symbol; herbalist; Tassili Plateau; Nok culture; terra cotta; polyrhythmic; Negritude

Questions

1. a. How do persons become part of an ethnic grouping? b. What are some things that members of such a group have in common?
2. Describe the matrilineal system of kinship.
3. When do young Africans learn the full meaning of a group's kinship?
4. What advantages do age sets have?
5. Why are marriages usually arranged, or at least approved, by families?
6. Why are older people important in African society?
7. a. How have traditional religions been a vitally important part of African life? b. To what degree are these religions practiced today? c. What is the concept of God in traditional African religions?
8. a. Why do traditional Africans honor ancestors with rituals and ceremonies? b. How is obedience to traditional ways that is aided by ancestor worship both bad and good?
9. Why did Christianity and colonialism appear to many Africans to go together?
10. Why have so many Africans accepted Islam?
11. a. In traditional Africa, who was responsible for educating the young? b. When did the real changes in African education begin? c. Why do wide differences exist among African nations in the availability of education? d. Why is the right kind of education vital for African nations now?

12. What new experiences are people faced with when they move to urban areas?
13. How have kinship ties been affected by urbanization?
14. a. How have women been important in African history? b. What roles do they play today?
15. How do the arts of some African peoples reflect non-African influences?
16. What types of art objects have been widely used for religious and ceremonial purposes?
17. a. What is a trademark of African music? b. Name two areas of the world that have been influenced by African music.
18. What types of literature make up African oral tradition?
19. Negritude writers used: a. what language? b. what themes?
20. What are themes of modern African writers?

Discussion Topics

1. Placing different peoples within national boundaries has led to tension and conflict in African nations. Would it be possible, or practical, for each ethnic grouping to have its own nation? If this were so, what would be some of the pros and cons?
2. Ancestor worship has been practiced by both Africans and Chinese. What comparisons can you make between them?
3. How would you assess the impact of European-based schools on Africans? What did such schools teach? Were there schools in Africa prior to the coming of Europeans? What did they teach?
4. Examine the chart on page 354. What does it tell you about the change in Ghana's population over a 15-year period? If the trend continues, what problems can you foresee in Ghana's future?

Project Ideas

1. Prepare a report on: Islam and Africans; the Falasha Jews of Ethiopia; Christianity.
2. Arrange a bulletin-board display of African art and architecture.
3. Using library references write about the impact of African art on cubism.
4. Find pictures of African village life and city life. Describe to the class the contrasts that you note.

For Further Study

General Readings

1. *Africa and Africans* by Paul Bohannan and Philip Curtin. Natural History Press, 1971. Paperback. An excellent concise introduction to African cultures.

2. *Africa and the West: Intellectual Responses to European Culture* ed. by Philip D. Curtin. University of Wisconsin Press, 1972. Paperback. Seven essays by various authors presenting African views of the West during the past century.

3. *African Art* by Frank Willett. Praeger Publishers, Inc., 1971. Paperback. Interesting, informative, and comprehensive.

4. *African Cultures* ed. by Paul Thomas Welty. J. B. Lippincott Company, 1973. Readings book. Inquiry format.

5. *African Genesis* by Robert Ardrey. Dell Publishing Co., Inc., Paperback. A theory of the beginnings of mankind in Africa.

6. *The African Genius: An Introduction to African Cultural and Social History* by Basil Davidson. Atlantic Monthly Press, 1970. Paperback. A cultural analysis of modern Africa by a respected author.

7. *African Heritage* by Jacob Drachler. The Macmillan Co., 1969. Paperback. Selection of tales by both Africans and non-Africans designed to give an intimate look at the past and present of Africans; beautifully done.

8. *Africa in Social Change* by P. C. Lloyd. Penguin Books, Inc., 1975. Paperback. Focuses on West Africa, where the interaction of traditional institutions with European ones has existed longest.

9. *The African Nettle: Dilemmas of an Emerging Continent* ed. by Frank L. Meyer. B.F.L. Communications, Inc., 1965. Problems in modern Africa.

10. *African Culture Speaks* by Ladislas Segy. DaCapo Press, Inc., 4th rev. ed., 1975. Paperback. A purely artistic look at the sculpture of Africa.

11. *Africans and Their History* by Joseph E. Harris. The New American Library, Inc., 1972. Paperback. Excellent account of the history and life of Africans.

12. *Ancient African Kingdoms* by Margaret Shinnie. The New American Library, Inc., 1970. Paperback. Brief and informative.

13. *The Autobiography of an Unknown South African* by Naboth Mokgatle. University of California Press, 1975. Paperback. A gripping tale of the modern history of South Africa.

14. *Black Cargoes: A History of the Atlantic Slave Trade, 1518–1865* by Daniel P. Mannix and Malcolm Cowley. Viking Press, Inc., 1965. Paperback.

15. *A Glorious Age in Africa* by Daniel Chu and Elliot Skinner. Doubleday & Co., Inc., 1965. Paperback. Fascinating story of Central Africa from the 700s to the 1500s.

16. *A History of the African People* by Robert W. July. Charles Scribner's Sons, rev. ed., 1974. Paperback. Sub-Saharan history concentrating on the pre-European period.

17. *Horizon History of Africa* ed. by Alvin M. Josephy *et al.* American Heritage Publishing Co., 2 vols., 1971. Many authors contributed to this book. Contains sections on primary source documents and covers the cultural as well as historic life of Africa. Illustrated: maps, charts, photographs.

18. *Islam in Africa* by James Kritzeck and William H. Lewis. Van Nostrand Reinhold Co., 1969. Survey by a number of writers on the past development and present status of Islam in Africa.

19. *Life Nature Library Series* by various authors. Published by Time-Life Books, A Division of Time, Inc. Silver Burdett Co. Special reference to Africa: *Early Man* and *Land and Wildlife of Africa.*

20. *Lonely African* by Colin M. Turnbull. Simon & Schuster, Inc., 1968. Paperback. Sensitive portrayal of Africans in a transitional period.

21. *Ms. Africa: Profiles of Modern African Women* by Louise Crane. J. B. Lippincott Co., 1973. Presents the new African women.

22. *The Political Awakening of Africa* by Rupert Emerson and Martin Kilson. Prentice-Hall, Inc. Paperback. African leaders and intellectuals speak about their problems, opinions, and hopes. A selection of materials not widely available.

23. *Oral Literature in Africa* by Ruth Finnegan. Oxford University Press, Inc., 1970. Very important in understanding African cultural history.

Fiction

1. *A Man of the People* by Chinua Achebe. Doubleday & Co., Inc. Paperback. Politics in Nigeria.

2. *Meeting with a Stranger* by Duane Bradley. J. B. Lippincott Co., 1964. Changing ways in Ethiopia.

The Western Europeans

The Benedictine abbey of Mont Saint Michel, off the coast of France, is an example of Gothic architecture. Parts of it were built in the 700s and the rest in the 1200s. Besides its religious and artistic significance, it also played a role in Europe's military history. William the Conqueror and Harold of England met there before the Norman invasion of England in 1066. During the Hundred Years War, the abbey was beseiged several times but never captured.

Unit I

The Land and the People

This bronze horse and chariot and gold disk were made in Denmark around 1000 B.C. Like early Greeks and Romans, Danes believed the sun was driven around the earth.

Europe is the western section of the Eurasian landmass. The boundary between Europe and Asia has traditionally been the Ural Mountains in the Soviet Union. Today, however, the entire Soviet Union is treated as a separate **geographic** unit. Since World War II the rest of Europe has been divided into two parts—Western Europe and Eastern Europe. This division was made for **political** reasons. Eastern European countries have **Communist governments** while those in Europe are non-Communist.

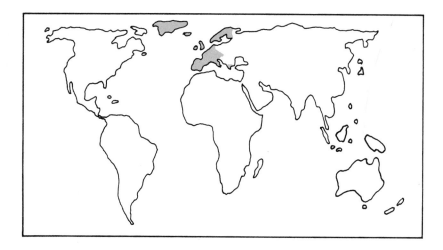

Western Europe covers 26 **nations** and dependent states and over 5.2 million square kilometers (2 million square miles). The Atlantic and the Arctic oceans border Europe on the west and the north. The Mediterranean Sea forms its southern border. Many small **peninsulas** jut out from Europe and numerous islands fringe its coasts. Thus, despite its small size, Western Europe has a coastline of about 64,000 kilometers (40,000 miles).

As a result of its position and its many excellent harbors, Europe became a major **trade** and **commercial** center. At its nearest point, across the Strait of Gibraltar, Europe is only 12.8 kilometers (8 miles) from Africa. For centuries Western Europeans have also had contact with the Middle East and Asia.

Chapter 1
The
Landmass

MOUNTAINS AND PLAINS

The mountain ranges of Western Europe developed over three different time periods. The oldest, the Atlantic range, is found throughout the United Kingdom, Ireland, and Norway. These mountains date from the ice age and have been gradually worn down by **erosion**. The second range forms the hills and mountains of West Germany, Spain, and France.

The last group to be formed were the Alps. They form the boundary between France and Italy and cover most of Switzerland, Austria, and parts of southern West Germany. Two offshoots are the Pyrenees (PIR-ih-neez) between Spain and France and the Apennines (AP-uh-nynz) running southward down the Italian peninsula.

The Alps are the youngest of the Western European mountain ranges. They are also the highest and rockiest. While in the past they have been a barrier to trade and **communications**, the Alps have not kept out invaders.

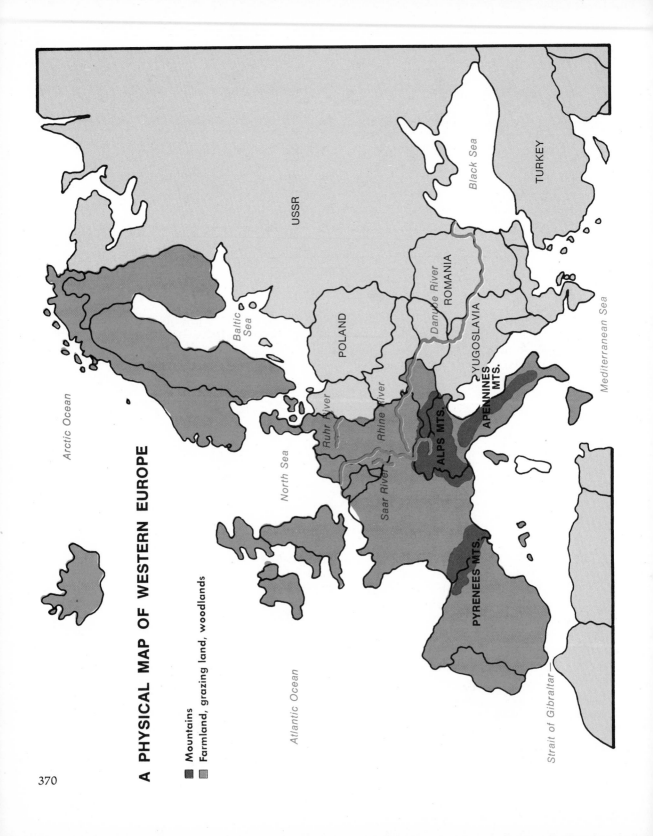

A PHYSICAL MAP OF WESTERN EUROPE

■ Mountains
■ Farmland, grazing land, woodlands

Arctic Ocean

Atlantic Ocean

North Sea

Baltic Sea

USSR

POLAND

Ruhr River

Rhine River

Saar River

Danube River

ROMANIA

YUGOSLAVIA

Black Sea

TURKEY

Mediterranean Sea

ALPS MTS.

APENNINES MTS.

PYRENEES MTS.

Strait of Gibraltar

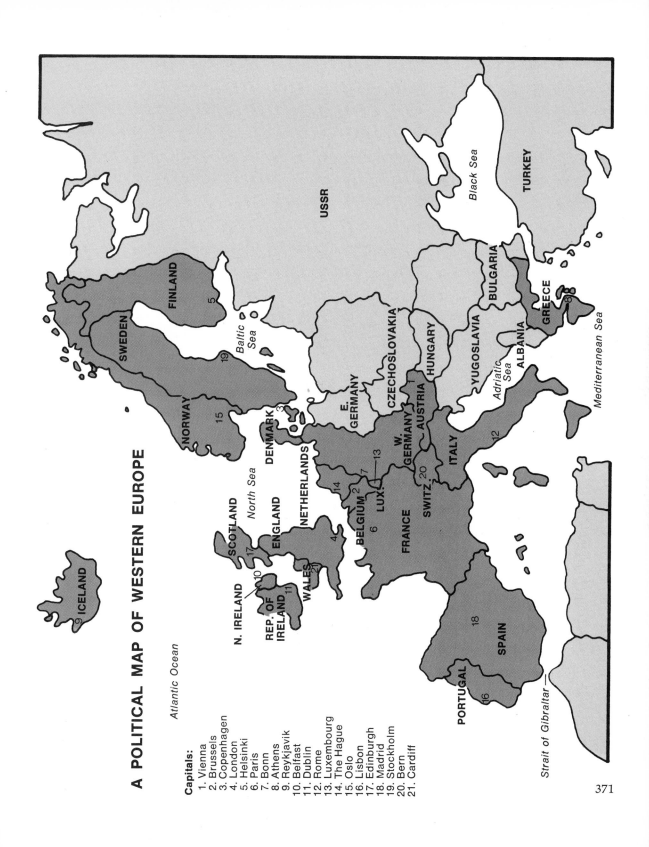

A POLITICAL MAP OF WESTERN EUROPE

Capitals:
1. Vienna
2. Brussels
3. Copenhagen
4. London
5. Helsinki
6. Paris
7. Bonn
8. Athens
9. Reykjavik
10. Belfast
11. Dublin
12. Rome
13. Luxembourg
14. The Hague
15. Oslo
16. Lisbon
17. Edinburgh
18. Madrid
19. Stockholm
20. Bern
21. Cardiff

Atlantic Ocean

ICELAND

NORWAY

SWEDEN

FINLAND

USSR

Baltic Sea

North Sea

SCOTLAND

N. IRELAND

REP. OF IRELAND

WALES

ENGLAND

NETHERLANDS

DENMARK

E. GERMANY

W. GERMANY

BELGIUM

LUX.

FRANCE

SWITZ.

AUSTRIA

CZECHOSLOVAKIA

HUNGARY

ITALY

YUGOSLAVIA

Adriatic Sea

ALBANIA

BULGARIA

GREECE

TURKEY

Black Sea

Mediterranean Sea

SPAIN

PORTUGAL

Strait of Gibraltar

371

Through passes in the Alps like this one, Roman armies came to conquer Switzerland. Today the Alps provide the Swiss with income in winter from tourists who come to ski and in summer from those who come to mountain climb.

Northwest of the mountains is the Northern European Plain. Large portions of France, Belgium, the Netherlands, Denmark, and parts of England, Sweden, and Finland lie within this region. The plain has very fertile soil and contains some of the most productive farmland in the world. Although continental Europe suffers from a severe shortage of oil resources, it is generally rich in minerals, especially coal and iron. However, these **natural resources** are not found in all countries.

NATURAL REGIONS

Western Europe's mountain ranges have created four natural regions. These four areas are the western, northern, central, and southern regions.

The British Isles (England, Scotland, Wales, Northern Ireland, the Republic of Ireland, and many small islands), Belgium, Luxembourg, the Netherlands, and France are included in the western natural region of Western Europe. These countries have a temperate, humid **climate**. This is because of the North Atlantic Drift. The drift is an ocean current, part of the Gulf Stream, which brings warm water across the North Atlantic Ocean. The western winds pick up this warm water and carry it overland where it falls as rain. Thus the climate is milder than the northerly location would suggest. It is also very moist and damp.

The islands of this area are separated from the rest of Europe by the English Channel. These lands were once part of the continent but sections became submerged in an earlier age. The isolation of the British Isles has greatly influenced its **history** and development.

France has many good seaports and rivers for trade, rich soil for farming, and natural resources for **industry**. Although most of its borders are protected by mountains or seas, France's northeast corner is part of the Great Northern Plain. This section has been a weak spot in France's defense. Invading armies have found it very inviting.

Wedged in the northwest corner between Germany, France, and the North Sea are the Low Countries: Belgium, the Netherlands or Holland, and Luxembourg. Their location has been both a blessing and a problem. The harbors and rivers of Belgium and the Netherlands have made them cultural and commercial centers. These same harbors and rivers have also made them targets for invaders. The Netherlands has also had to fight the sea. The Dutch have built dikes, canals, and windmills to keep back the water and reclaim vast areas of land for agriculture.

The northern region of Western Europe includes Norway, Sweden, Denmark, Iceland, Greenland, and Finland. The whole area, which is composed of two major peninsulas and many islands, is generally known as Scandinavia. However, only Norway and Sweden are actually on the Scandinavian peninsula.

Most of Scandinavia has long cold winters and short cool summers. Large sections of Norway, Sweden, and Finland are part of the subarctic. The land there is covered by evergreen trees and has a short growing season. Farther north lies tundra where little in the way of crops can be grown because the soil is frozen most of the year.

Most of Norway and Sweden is covered by mountains although Sweden is part of the Northern European Plain. Since the climate and soil are not suited to most types of farming, Norwegians and Swedes depend on wood products, mining, fishing, and shipping for their livelihood.

Denmark forms part of the Jutland peninsula and contains many islands. While its land is flatter than the rest of Scandinavia, the soil is not particularly fertile. The Danish **economy** depends on fishing, livestock, and dairy products. The island of Greenland belongs to Denmark and lies almost entirely within the Arctic Circle.

Iceland is the westernmost point of Europe. Except for a few coastal areas, Iceland is covered by ice fields and volcanic mountains. Its climate, however, is relatively mild because of the North Atlantic Drift. Most of Iceland and Greenland are inhabited. The few hundred thousand people who live there fish, graze animals, or mine.

Finland, although technically not a part of Scandinavia, has been linked for centuries to the Scandinavians through a common history.

Southern Finland is flat with thousands of lakes. The north is mountainous. The Finns earn their living from the forest and the sea.

The countries of central Western Europe are West Germany, East Germany, Switzerland, Austria, and the principality of Liechtenstein (LIK-tuhn-styn). Their winters are colder and their summers hotter than the coastal areas.

Since World War II Germany has been divided into two parts. Non-Communist West Germany is a very modern, industrialized, and wealthy nation. The rich coal and iron mines of the Ruhr and Saar valleys have been the foundation of Germany's **industrialization**. A network of rivers cheaply transports goods across the continent or north to the Baltic Sea. Northern Germany is a flat plain. The central area is forested highlands while the south is covered by the Bavarian Alps.

Austria adjoins Germany in the south. Although 75 percent of its land is covered by mountains, Austria has an agricultural economy. Liechtenstein is located entirely in the Alps between Austria and Switzerland.

Switzerland, in the midst of the Alps, is bordered by Germany, France, Austria, Liechtenstein, and Italy. Within Switzerland lie the sources of most of the important rivers in Europe. The Swiss have harnessed them for hydroelectric power. Because Switzerland possesses few minerals and generally poor soil, the Swiss have had to develop and depend on **technological**, manufacturing, and commercial enterprises. Today Switzerland has one of the highest **standards of living** in Europe.

The southern part of Western Europe contains Spain, Portugal, Greece, Italy, and the small states of San Marino, Andorra, Vatican City, and Monaco. Except for the mountain regions, southern Europe's climate is very similar to that of southern California. The summers are long, hot, and dry while the winters are mild with a rainy season.

Spain and Portugal lie on the Iberian (eye-BIR-ee-uhn) Peninsula between the Atlantic Ocean and the Mediterranean Sea. Spain covers the major portion of the peninsula. These two countries have been isolated from the rest of the continent by the Pyrenees. In some ways, Spain and Portugal have been more influenced by the **culture** of nearby Africa.

Although both nations are primarily agricultural, farming is hindered by poor rocky soil and lack of rain. However, agriculture is possible on coastal plains and in fertile river valleys. Some of the crops grown are oranges, grapes, and olives. Portugal has an important fishing industry and Spain has some rich mineral deposits. Both countries, however, are industrially and technologically behind the rest of Europe.

Italy forms a boot-shaped peninsula between the Mediterranean and Adriatic seas. In northern Italy between the Alps and the Apennines lies the fertile Po Valley. This is the site of Italy's richest farm-land and of major industry and manufacturing. The center of Italy, between the Arno River and Rome, has some agriculture but is best known as the nation's **intellectual** and artistic heartland. Southern Italy is agricultural but is the poorest region of the country.

Greece, on the Balkan Peninsula, is a mountainous country. The soil has been greatly eroded over the centuries. As a result, agriculture is limited and the Greeks depend on grazing and fishing.

grazing: way of raising cattle, sheep, goats by feeding them on grass

San Marino in the Italian Apennines is agricultural. Andorra, which is situated on the French-Spanish border in the Pyrenees, makes its living raising sheep. Monaco is in the southeast corner of France on the Mediterranean Sea and is best known for its gambling casino at Monte Carlo. Vatican City is located within the Italian city of Rome. The pope, the head of the Roman Catholic Church, lives there.

RIVERS

Europe's rivers form a vital transportation network. Many of Europe's **cities** such as Rome and Paris were built on rivers.

The most important river is the Rhine, which flows through the industrial center of Europe to the North Sea. The Rhine connects the Ruhr industrial basin with the Dutch port of Rotterdam and has been crucial to Germany's development. Through a series of canals,

Paris is named for the Parisii, fishers who were in the area when Romans came in 52 B.C. Above is the part of Paris known as Ile de la Cite, site of the Palace of Justice and Cathedral of Notre Dame.

the Rhine is also connected with the main rivers of France and Belgium.

Also important are the Danube and Rhone rivers. The Danube flows east from the Alps to the Black Sea while the Rhone moves south to the Mediterranean. The Danube's course is through agricultural lands.

The rivers in the Mediterranean countries are generally unsuitable for navigation. They tend to have irregular courses and are dry during the summer but flooded in the winter.

Norway has deep sheltered bays called fjords (fee-ORDS). These have become tourist attractions and are also major sources of hydroelectric power. Most of the rivers in Scandinavia have so many waterfalls that they are difficult to navigate. They do, however, provide hydroelectric power.

Chapter 2
Early Cultures

Does a new radiocarbon dating for Stonehenge seem to be important to you? Does it affect in any way your attitude toward "history as unchanging?"

The cultures described in this chapter appeared, developed, and most had disappeared before written history began. In the west and north they occupied the British Isles, Norway, Sweden, Denmark, Iceland, Greenland, and Finland. In central Europe they were found in West Germany, Switzerland, Austria, and Liechtenstein. In southern Europe sites of **prehistoric** cultures have been found in parts of Spain and Portugal, Italy, Greece, and the islands of the western Mediterranean.

Archaeologists have pieced together the story of early Europeans from many sources. Of course, much is still unknown. Sometimes a theory must be changed as more information is discovered. This happened with **radiocarbon dating**. Before radiocarbon dating was corrected, archaeologists generally believed that all cultural developments originated in the Middle East. Through trade and **colonization** all skills and knowledge spread from there to the rest of the world. New datings now appear to show that some developments occurred first in Europe.

Not all archaeologists accept the idea that cultures developed independently in Europe. However, many agree that new ways of dating **artifacts** solve some problems. Pre-Greek and pre-Roman Europeans were once viewed as barbarians. Now we know that peoples in Western Europe had developed various cultures before those of Greece and Rome.

MEGALITH BUILDERS

Excavations of **sites** in northern Europe reveal the presence of a reindeer-hunting **people** in the area about 10,000 B.C. Tools of reindeer bone and antlers as well as bone and amber carvings have been found. Some among these people were plant-gatherers who added to their diet with wild foods.

Exactly how early peoples made the change from food-gathering to farming is unknown. Experts believe that farming was established as a way of life in Western Europe between 4500 and 4000 B.C. Small groups of farmers lived in **villages** and cultivated the land around them.

By around 3500 B.C., farming peoples in various parts of Europe were building with megaliths—massive stones. Megalithic structures have been found from Scandinavia to the Mediterranean Sea. They are important to the study of the development of a people because they show the evolution of **architectural** and engineering skills.

Some megalithic structures were used as tombs. But other megalithic structures, generally described as monuments, become more impressive the more we know about them. We do not know the exact purposes for many of them, but we can guess.

The most famous monument is Stonehenge, in England. Many archaeologists believe that Stonehenge was built as an **astronomical** observatory. Calculations on a computer show that the groups of stones align with various events in the sky. Gerald S. Hawkins, an astronomer, has shown that eclipses of the moon could have been predicted using the arrangements of stones at Stonehenge. Since the people who built Stonehenge were farmers, the study of the heavens would be important to them. They could then predict the change of seasons.

The building of monuments like Stonehenge required knowledge of what we call mathematics and geometry. It also required the cooperation of large numbers of people from many villages. At the time villages were small, possibly 10 to 50 people. One scientist calculated that 80 people using ropes of hide could move a 4.5 metric-ton (5-ton) stone. Some of the stones weighed ten times that much.

Stonehenge was built in three stages. It is believed to have been begun about 2700 B.C. and completed about 2000 B.C. Until radiocarbon dating, most archaeologists thought that Stonehenge was built or inspired by Greek **civilization**. The new dating shows that Stonehenge was completed before the beginning of the Mycenaean (my-SEE-nee-uhn) civilization—the second stage in the development of Greek civilization.

METALWORKERS

Sometime after 6000 B.C. people began to use metals. The first metal objects were made of copper. Experts generally have believed that the working of copper began in the Middle East and spread to Europe. However, ancient copper mines have been found in Eastern Europe and some archaeologists believe that the techniques for working copper developed there independently.

A long time passed between the first use of copper and its use on a large scale. Even after the working of copper was widely known, the use of stone tools continued. The **Stone Age** and the **Copper Age** overlapped in various places for many years. As with stone tools there were several stages in the development of the use of metals.

Although Eastern Europe is discussed in another section, the prehistory of Europe would not be complete without noting the first European metal culture. It began as early as 5000 B.C. in the lower Danube Valley, in modern Hungary and Yugoslavia. By about 3000 B.C. the Copper Age there had passed into the **Bronze Age**.

One center producing bronze objects was near present-day Prague, Czechoslovakia. Evidently a trade network existed between it and other cultures since objects made there have been found throughout Europe.

Beginning about 1800 B.C., in its Bronze Age, Italy had a variety of cultures. The Remedello culture seems to have been related to the metal cultures of the Danube. Between about 1700 and 1500 B.C., in the Po Valley, villages were built on pilings and surrounded by walls built of wooden stakes. In the lower Alps rock carvings have been found showing a mountain culture. The people seemed to have been driven into the higher areas by pressure from new groups settling on the plains to the south.

In Italy the Bronze Age drew to a close and the **Iron Age** began about 1000 B.C. Two peoples were influential—the Villanovans and the Etruscans (ih-TRUHS-kuhns). Both practiced cremation and placed the ashes of their dead in tombs.

The Danes traded amber for tin and copper and learned to make bronze. This bronze comb was crafted in Denmark about 1000 B.C.

The Etruscan tombs were underground chambers that seemed to be built as homes for the dead. The tombs were usually on a hill opposite the city of the living. Tomb walls were decorated with colorful paintings of the Etruscans feasting, dancing, and playing musical instruments. After 500 B.C. the Etruscans were absorbed by the Romans.

Etruscans decorated the walls of their homes as well as their tombs.

One of the earliest ironworking cultures in Europe was first identified by the discovery of a large cemetery near Hallstatt, Austria, in Central Europe. It is thought that the Hallstatt people used iron objects as early as 1000 B.C. The earliest known iron furnace in Europe was found there.

Their cemeteries tell much about the Hallstatt people. Bodies were buried wearing long belted cloaks fastened with brooches. Weapons of bronze and iron surrounded the bodies. Women were also buried with daggers. The Hallstatt people appear to have dominated northern Europe during the early Iron Age. Britons may have learned iron working from them.

From about 500 B.C. a culture known as La Tene rose to power

This is an aerial view of an Iron-Age hill fort in Dorset, England. Note the rows of earth fortifications.

in this area. The La Tene people were Celts. Roman statues show their warriors as tall and blonde with long drooping mustaches. Some of their chiefs were buried with their chariots as well as other riches. These people conquered central Europe and most of France. They raided Spain, Italy, Greece, Asia Minor (modern Turkey) and sacked Rome in 390 B.C.

As the Romans became more powerful they pushed northward into Celtic **territory**. About the same time, peoples from Scandinavia began **migrating** and raiding southward. The influence of the Celts had disappeared by 50 B.C.

By about 2500 B.C. copper was in use in northern Europe, in Britain and in France. By about 2000 B.C. Britain had entered the Bronze Age. As a result, Britain experienced an increase in trade. Tin was needed for making bronze, and Britain had large tin deposits. This encouraged trade and brought wealth to the area.

Society seemed to be developing **classes**. A few people had gained wealth and **status**. Before Stonehenge was completed, there were signs of the existence of chiefs or tribal leaders. During the Bronze Age chiefs appear to have increased in power and wealth.

By the late Bronze Age there were numerous hill-forts surrounded by earth embankments. Sometimes the embankments were surrounded by stone walls, sometimes by ditches. Protection was needed, either from invaders or from other settlements. Artifacts of this period include axes, metal vessels, tools, swords, and shields. By 500 B.C. iron was being produced in Britain.

In Denmark, Norway, and Sweden settlements extended far north. Communities lived by farming, hunting, or fishing. The climate was too cold to permit an economy based only on crops.

Rich amber deposits were found in Denmark and led the ancestors of the Danes to develop a rich trade in this stone. Amber was highly prized in Europe. The Scandinavians transported amber and furs to the south in return for gold, copper, and tin. Eventually they became skilled metalworkers who made axes, swords, shields, ornaments, and huge, graceful, curved trumpets. They also made statues apparently used in religious worship. One is a bronze horse and six-wheeled chariot bearing a golden sun figure.

The wealth of the Scandinavians declined by about 500 B.C. To the south the Celts blocked their trade routes. The climate of northern Europe was becoming very wet and cold. This combination makes living unpleasant and also affects the production of crops and livestock.

Groups of Scandinavians began to migrate southward. The migrations were a series of conquests and settlements. The Goths, probably from Sweden, and the Burgundians, also thought to be from Sweden, moved into northern Germany. The Langobards or Lombards from southern Sweden pushed into central Europe. Eventually they moved into Italy, and by the 400s A.D. they would defeat Rome itself.

Summing Up the Unit

Social Studies Vocabulary

Define: peninsula; erosion; natural resources; culture; archaeologists; artifacts; radiocarbon dating; sites; civilization; Copper, Bronze Ages; society; classes

People

Identify: Etruscans; Hallstatt; La Tene; Celts; Goths; Burgundians

Places

Locate: Strait of Gibraltar; Alps, Apennine, Pyrenees mountains; western, northern, central, southern Europe; Ruhr, Saar, Rhine, Danube rivers

Words

Define: North Atlantic Drift; Low Countries; Scandinavia; fjord; megalith

Questions

1. What factor has greatly influenced the history and development of the British Isles?
2. a. What part of France's border is the weakest spot in its defense? b. Why?
3. What are the advantages and disadvantages of the Low Countries' location?
4. a. What do Norwegians and Swedes depend on for their livelihood? b. Why?
5. a. What regions of Germany are the foundation of its industrialization? b. Why?
6. Why have the Swiss had to develop and depend on technology, manufacturing, and commerce?
7. Why have Spain and Portugal been more influenced by the culture of Africa than of Europe?
8. a. Which one of Europe's rivers is most important? b. Why?
9. Why are the rivers of the Mediterranean countries generally unsuited for navigation?
10. What have archaeologists learned from the corrected radiocarbon dating?
11. Why are megaliths important in studying the development of a people?
12. Why would the Stonehenge builders need to study the heavens?
13. What kinds of artifacts help archaeologists to learn about a people?
14. Why did Britain experience an increase in trade during the Bronze Age?
15. How did amber benefit the early Danes?
16. Why did the Scandinavians migrate?

Discussion Topics

1. Western Europe, despite its small size, has topographic features and a location favorable for trade. What geographic advantages have aided Western Europeans? How have Western Europe's mountains, rivers, plains, and climate affected trade?
2. Western Europe contains many nations. How might the geography of Europe have influenced this division into so many nations?
3. Some cultures are known to us through their tombs. What can tombs tell us about the way people lived and about their beliefs? When using archaeological evidence to analyze a culture, what cautions should investigators use? How have limitations of archaeological evidence affected the way Chapter 2 is written? Find examples in the chapter and explain.
4. Stages of cultural development are named for the materials used in making tools: Stone, Copper, Bronze, Iron. Why are such materials used to identify levels of cultural development? Would other materials such as wood decay? Why isn't pottery used to label cultures? Does it decay? Do additional research to answer these questions.

Project Ideas

1. Using materials such as clay or salt dough, make a relief map of Western Europe showing the geographical features mentioned in Chapter 1.
2. Draw a sketch or make a model of a megalithic site such as Stonehenge.
3. Using outside materials, write a brief report on one of the following: radiocarbon dating; megalith builders; how archaeologists learn about a people.

Unit II

The Glory of Greece

Athens practiced a form of limited democracy. Only men could vote. Ballots were stones, balls, or shells. In the above detail of a vase painting, Athena, the patron of Athens, watches over the voting.

Almost 5,000 years ago the Indo-Europeans (not a culture but a **language** grouping) began the westward advances that led them throughout Europe. Some of them settled the rugged land that is modern Greece. Their descendants founded **city-states**. Often these states struggled among themselves. Sometimes, however, they were able to join against common enemies.

In a few short centuries Greece's political power declined, to be replaced by that of Rome. However, Greek achievements remain. The Greeks are regarded as the developers of many fields of knowledge: **philosophy**, geometry, areas of the natural and physical sciences, and medicine. They are also recognized as talented sculptors, builders, writers, and the developers of a **limited democracy**.

Around 2500 B.C. or earlier the ancestors of the Greeks started on a series of migrations southward into the peninsula of Greece. These peoples did not settle an uninhabited land. As early as 3000 B.C. people had come from Asia and settled eastern parts of the peninsula and some of the nearby islands, including Crete.

Chapter 1
The Road
to Democracy

CRETANS

The island of Crete lies across the entrance of the Aegean (ih-JEE-uhn) Sea. By the time the Indo-European invaders came into contact with them, the Cretans had developed a highly sophisticated civilization. Its principal city was Knossos (NAHS-uhs). Some historians call this civilization Minoan (muh-NOH-uhn) after an ancient Cretan king, Minos. Others think of Cretan society as the center of the entire area washed by the Aegean Sea and refer to the culture that developed as Aegean.

sophisticated:
highly developed and complex (as opposed to simple and natural)

The Cretans lived well. They had hot and cold running water, bathrooms, and elaborate furniture. They protected their valuables with metal locks and keys. The plastered interiors of their homes were colorfully decorated with paintings called frescoes. This technique of painting on wet plaster is still used today.

We have learned much about Cretan culture from their art. The Cretans were fond of dancing, as well as boxing, racing, and other sports. There was one sport, however, in which the Cretans seem to be unique. That was bull-leaping. Cretan paintings show men and women leaping over a bull's horns, turning handsprings on its back, and landing upright behind the bull.

From their paintings, it appears the Cretans were slender, short, and had dark, curly hair. The women wore hats, tight jackets and long, bell-shaped skirts. Women apparently held a high position in Cretan society. The chief **deity** of the Cretans was a goddess who was often represented in gold or ivory statues holding a snake. Cretan art also reveals that the people had a feeling for nature and peace. They did not portray scenes of war but pictured landscapes, sports, and festivals.

The Cretans were among the earliest sea traders. Their journeys took them to Egypt, Phoenicia (fy-NEESH-ee-uh)—the general area of Lebanon, Syria, and Israel—and lands bordering the Aegean Sea. Their trade goods included vases, enameled bronze daggers, rings, and other items made of gold, silver, and bronze. Trading brought the Cretans to the shores of mainland Greece.

MYCENAEANS

Although others had entered the Greek peninsula before them, the Achaeans (uh-KEE-uhnz) who arrived about 2000 B.C. came to dominate the trade and government of the area. Near the sea they met

Besides the subject of a poem by Homer, the siege of Troy became the theme for other artwork. This large pottery container is decorated with a relief of the Trojan horse. What does the phrase "Trojan horse" mean?

the Cretans. The result was the rise of a new civilization called Mycenaean, after the first Achaean site to be excavated.

The Mycenaeans built walled cities and worked in bronze. The products of their trade—bronze daggers, beads, and pottery—have been found in the western parts of Europe, on the islands of the Aegean, and in the Middle East.

Around 1400 B.C. the Mycenaeans captured Knossos and ruled it until 1100 B.C. Scholars differ about the dates, but it is certain that the Mycenaeans ruled the Aegean around this time. Two great **epics** testify to this.

The poems narrate the story of the Mycenaean expedition against the rival city of Troy in Asia Minor. One poem, the *Iliad* (IL-ee-uhd), tells of the siege of Troy, which possibly happened between 1250 and 1170 B.C. The other epic, the *Odyssey* (AHD-uh-see), relates the adventures of the warrior-hero Odysseus (od-DIS-yoos) as he tries to return home from Troy. These epics are thought to have been written by the blind Greek poet Homer. Their composition is dated sometime between the 800s and the 500s B.C. The epics are the chief written descriptions of the events and life of the earlier time.

siege: surrounding a place in an effort to capture it

Neither the walled cities on the mainland nor the waters around Crete could protect the Bronze-Age civilizations of the Mycenaeans from later tribes. One group called Dorians came to dominate Greece and much of the Aegean. Some scholars believe that the Dorians were responsible for the destruction of Knossos around 1100 B.C.

CITY-STATES

The descendants of the Achaeans, Dorians, and other peoples who settled the peninsula have come to be known as Greeks. These early Greeks created an unusual system of government for themselves.

On the hills and rocky coasts, the Greeks built forts which gradually grew into city-states. The Greek word for city-state is *polis;* the word **politics** comes from it. The Greeks acknowledged no authority over the individual or the city except that of the tribal leader. The basic social groupings of the Greeks were the family and the **clan**. These were part of a larger **kinship group** known as a people or a tribe. Those outside the kinship group were considered possible enemies to be raided. The position of the tribal leader became that of king. The clan leaders became nobles.

Beyond the small area of valley, coast, and mountain controlled by each city, there were other city-states that were equally proud and jealous of their independence. As a result, the peninsula was the scene of battles and shifting **alliances** for centuries. Geography was in part responsible for the development of small city-states. The self-reliance and separateness of the Greeks were strengthened by the rough, mountainous countryside.

There were, however, a few occasions when city-states temporarily cooperated. One was the Olympic Games. Every four years Greeks gathered together for five days of athletic contests. The earliest re-

The Greeks placed great emphasis on sports and physical fitness. Why would a state be concerned with the physical well-being of its people?

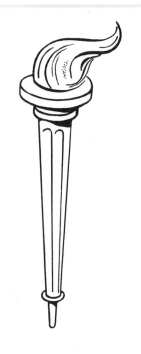

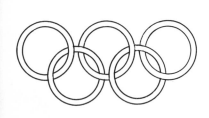

The modern Olympic Games begin with the lighting of the Olympic flame from a torch that is carried from Olympia Valley in Greece. The five interlocking rings appear on the official Olympic flag.

corded date of these games to honor Zeus (ZOOS)—the father of deities and humans—is 776 B.C. The games consisted of foot races, chariot races, discus and javelin hurling, the broad jump, and other displays of physical fitness. Wreaths of olive branches or laurel were placed on the heads of winners. More honors awaited the victors when they returned to their city-states.

At first Greek women were not allowed to take part in or watch the Olympic Games. There is evidence to suggest, however, that they set up games of their own, the Heraea. These were held every four years too.

The city-states had other reasons besides jealousy for their inability to form a national government. Different city-states placed their emphasis on different values and **life styles**. Sparta and Athens are good examples of the wide differences that existed among city-states.

SPARTA Sparta was located in the southern part of Greece called Peloponnesus (pel-uh-puh-NEE-suhs). The Dorians, ancestors of the Spartans, had migrated there from the north. By 600 or 500 B.C. the Spartans ruled the entire area of Peloponnesus. They ruled because their bodies and minds had been toughened and shaped for war since childhood.

While yet a baby, the Spartan boy was examined by his elders. If he met their standards of physical fitness, he was permitted to live. Others not so lucky were taken to a hillside or cave and left to die. At the age of seven the Spartan began the severe training designed to make him into a soldier.

He was given too little food so that he would be forced to steal. This training taught the Spartan soldier how to live off the land when he was fighting in the field. The boy who was caught stealing was whipped. If he whimpered, he disgraced himself. The Spartan had to learn to endure pain and insults in silence. The young Spartan male was given only a single piece of cloth to wear in both summer and winter and no shoes. He marched, fought with weapons, wrestled, and hardened his muscles with gymnastics. He was instructed to speak little; his deeds in war would speak for him. At the age of 20 he became a full citizen of Sparta. Spartan women were trained to accept political responsibilities and had a voice in public affairs. When men were away at war, they ran the city.

At the age of 30 a Spartan man married. His wife had also been taught to keep her body healthy and sound for child-bearing and for work. Her first loyalty was to Sparta. The ideal Spartan woman was one who asked first whether Sparta had won or lost. Only afterward did she ask about the life of her husband or sons.

Fighting was the primary job of Spartan men. Everything else, including making money, was secondary. **Slaves** worked the fields, which were given to each citizen equally. In a sense, however, the Spartans too were slaves. Although their city was governed by men whom they elected, Spartan men and women existed for the state alone. Spartans lived to fight, to breed, and to die for the glory and preservation of Sparta.

ATHENS   The citizens of Athens, on the other hand, enjoyed discussing arts and politics and preferred to serve the state by choice rather than force. Athens was located in the district of Attica in east-central Greece. Ionians had settled the area around 2500 B.C.

The early Athenians were ruled by kings and later by nobles who governed for their own benefit. Most of the citizens owned little land. Only men were citizens. The fields that they worked as tenants produced scarcely enough to pay their rent. Some tenants were forced to work for their creditors almost as slaves. Merchants, laborers, independent farmers, and sailors were no better off.

creditors: people to whom one owes money or goods

Beginning around the 600s B.C., some men began to step forward and offer themselves as the solution to the Athenians' problems. The Athenians called them tyrants. A tyrant's rule could be good or bad, short or long.

The tyrant Draco gave the Athenians their first written code of law around 621 B.C. Draco's law was unreasonably severe. Even a minor theft was punishable by death, and the law leaned in favor of the nobles.

Solon, who assumed power in 594 B.C., advanced the Greeks along the path to **democracy** and **economic** reform. He cancelled all debts, freed those already enslaved because of debt, and placed a limit on the amount of land a person could own. He urged farmers to take up other trades where the land was crowded.

Solon opened the Assembly, one of the governing bodies of Athens, to the poor and the unpropertied. Formerly only male citizens with property had been members of this group. Solon increased the power of the Assembly by giving it a **council** of 400 members elected by the Assembly. The members of the council could propose laws and reforms to the highest ruling body of Athens, the Council of Areopagus (ar-ee-AHP-uh-guhs). This council was composed of great nobles.

Cleisthenes (KLYS-thuh-neez), another good tyrant, came to power in 508 B.C. He had a deep sense of obligation and concern for the welfare and freedom of the Athenians. Every male citizen over the age of 20 became a member of the Assembly. The power of the Assembly was enlarged. A Council of Five Hundred was established, which became the chief administrative and executive body. Its members were chosen by lot from all male citizens over 30.

The above shows two sides of a coin minted about 413 B.C. in the Corinthian colony of Syracuse on the island of Sicily. The area is now part of Italy.

BEYOND THE SHORES   The people of Athens, Corinth, and other city-states began very early to be sea traders. Between 750 and 500 B.C. the Greeks built trading posts along the shores of the Mediterranean and beyond.

They colonized the islands of the Aegean Sea and the coasts of Asia Minor bordering the Aegean. Greek **colonies** dotted the edges of the Black Sea and included the city of Byzantium (buh-ZAN-shee-uhm, modern Istanbul). The Greeks moved westward to Sicily where they built Syracuse and then to the mainland of Italy. Naples was originally a Greek city. The Greeks had so many cities and settlers in this area that it came to be known as Great Greece.

Later the Greek city-state of Corinth began to dominate the trade of the western Mediterranean. The Greeks colonized southern France. Their city of Massilia later became the French city of Marseilles (mar-SAY). The Greeks were the first to locate a **town** on the site of Nice (NEES). They even dared to plant settlers on the shores of North Africa, which had been for centuries the territory of the Phoenicians.

It was not difficult to recruit Greeks for trading posts and colonies. The Greeks found it difficult to make a living on the barren hillsides and mountainous land of their peninsula. Also much of the best soil was owned by nobles and the wealthy. The Greeks were fast increasing and further crowding the already scarce patches of tillable soil.

WAR AND A LEAGUE OF CITY-STATES

Around 492 B.C. the Persians governed the land from northeast India to the shores of the Aegean Sea. The Persians generally left their subjects in peace if they acknowledged Persian rule and paid **tribute**. The Persians offered this same treatment to the Greek city-states on the coasts of Asia Minor. But it was not in the Greeks to acknowledge the rule of anyone else. They were supported and encouraged in this attitude by those at home.

In 490 B.C. the Persian king, Darius, sent a force against Greece. Although outnumbered, the Greeks defeated the Persians on the plain of Marathon. Ten years later under a new king, Xerxes, the Persians marched once more against the Greeks. In the land battle at Thermopylae (thuhr-MAHP-uh-lee) and especially in the naval battle of Salamis, the Persians paid a heavy price in soldiers and equipment. Revolts at home and the approach of bad weather, among other reasons, caused Xerxes to return to the Middle East.

The Persians had badly frightened many of the Greeks living in Asia Minor and in the Aegean. Since the Persians had been defeated mostly by the courage and cleverness of the Athenians, the other city-states asked Athens to form a **league** of city-states. The league would serve as protection against future attacks. The Athenians accepted. Eventually the league numbered over 200 city-states.

The Athenians began a fleet-building program assisted by the other city-states. Soon Athens was the leading naval power in the eastern Mediterranean. As Athenian naval power grew, their commerce, industry, and city also grew. The power of the Athenians restrained their foes, but it disturbed their allies. The other Greek city-states

This helmet is called Corinthian. It was developed in the city-state of Corinth during the 500s B.C. Later, Corinth joined with other city-states to fight Athens' growing power.

suspected that Athens might use its new strength to dominate them. When they tried to withdraw from the league, the Athenians would not permit it. Occasionally, the Athenians even used force to keep them within the league.

The Athenians brought the league's treasury to their own city. They extorted tribute from the other cities and regarded them as parts of their **empire** rather than as equals. By now the Athenians had come under the rule of Pericles (PER-uh-kleez).

☐ **Athens in the Age of Pericles, c. 450 B.C.**

AGE OF PERICLES

The period between 461 and 429 B.C. is often called the Age of Pericles because his leadership and words express the spirit of the time. Under Pericles, early democracy for Athenians reached its fullest flowering. It should be noted, however, that according to a modern definition of democracy, this was a limited form. Women and slaves had no voice in the way things were run. Only men were citizens.

About 45,000 men were considered citizens of Athens. Decisions could be made if there were at least 6,000 at the open-air meetings of the Assembly. The Assembly made the laws for the city-states, decided on matters of war or peace, and approved **treaties** and the city's budget. Any citizen could express his opinion.

The Assembly was much too large to administer Athen's affairs effectively. Therefore, daily business was undertaken by the Council of Five Hundred. These men were chosen by lot from the various demes or districts into which Athens was divided. The English word democracy comes from this word.

The Council of Five Hundred was further divided into ten committees of 50 members each. These committees took turns in handling the affairs of the city for one-tenth of the year. No man could be

by lot: to decide something by chance; for example, to choose straws to see who does something

Alexander the Great fought and defeated Darius III (far right) and his Persian armies three times between 333 and 330 B.C. The final defeat opened

a member of the council for more than two years. Thus the vast majority of male Athenians had the opportunity of acting as officials of their government during their lives.

Some officials could be reelected to their posts. The most important of these officials were the generals. Each year the Assembly chose ten generals to oversee the armed forces. If a general was found to be a successful and effective leader, he might be elected over and over again. Pericles was chosen 30 times.

The Athenians trusted justice from the many, but not from the few. Each year the demes elected 6,000 citizens over 30 years old to sit on juries. When cases were to be heard, the 6,000 met. From them large numbers were chosen by lot to hear and judge the various cases. The number needed for a single case might range from 200 to 2,000.

The Athenians reasoned that if the number were large enough there was less chance that the jurors might be swayed by bribery, threat, or prejudice. The jurors determined the guilt or innocence of the parties and also fixed the penalty.

As has been stated, the Greek system had flaws. Women had no political rights. Slaves were not considered citizens and had no share in Athenian freedoms. Foreigners were permitted to live in the city-state, but they were not allowed to own land. Only rarely were foreign men permitted to become citizens.

Athenian men who lived in the city found it easier to attend Assembly meetings than the farmers who lived in the countryside. Thus, the Assembly came to be dominated more and more by city-dwellers. But for its time, the Athenian experiment in rule by ordinary citizens—even a limited number—was daring. Its success provided an example for future states.

Alexander's way into India. These two illustrations are mosaics. Mosaics are made by cementing together bits of colored stone or glass.

CULTURAL MERGING

There had been contacts between the Greeks and people in the Middle East for centuries. But in the 400s B.C. these contacts increased. The groundwork for the merging of cultures was laid by the decline of Athens beginning in 431 B.C. In that year the Peloponnesian War began between a rival league started by the Spartans and the Athenian league. By 404 B.C. Athens was in ruins, the fleet and the orchards destroyed, and thousands killed by plague and war.

The victory of Sparta over Athens, however, did not bring peace. The Spartans were overthrown by Thebes. Thebes, in turn, lost its dominance after a short time. Soon there was no city-state powerful enough to rule all Greece. This weakness attracted a clever, strong ruler to the north—Philip of Macedon.

The Macedonians (mas-uh-DOH-nee-uhnz) were a mixture of Greek and other cultural groups from the north. From the time Philip became king in 359 B.C., he schemed to unify Macedon and Greece. In the decisive battle of Chaeronea (ker-uh-NEE-uh) in 338 B.C., Philip overthrew the combined forces of Athens and Thebes and became overlord of Greece. In 336 B.C. he was murdered by an assassin his wife had allegedly hired.

Philip was succeeded by his son Alexander, whose military exploits earned him the title Alexander the Great. Alexander dreamed of uniting the world into one empire. He united for a brief time much of the area from Macedon to India and part of the Middle East.

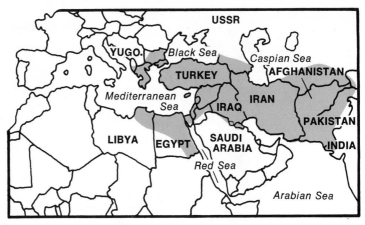

Empire of Alexander the Great

Alexander attempted to blend the **customs** and **institutions** of the Greeks with those of the peoples he conquered. He stressed the ties that bind people together rather than the differences that separate them. He brought the Greeks and Middle Easterners together, and their ties continued long after his death in 323 B.C.

After the death of Alexander, Macedonia could not control Greece. Many of the less powerful cities wanted to form leagues that would give them the strength of unity yet continue their local independence. Two such leagues were formed. Each had a **central** government, a **senate**, and an **assembly** of all the citizens of each city-state. Each league also had an army and a navy.

The central government had little authority other than the power to establish armed services and to tax. The bulk of political power was kept in each city-state. The formation of these leagues was an experiment in a **federal** system of government.

Unfortunately, the Greeks failed to find strength in unity. Athens and Sparta, the two strongest city-states, refused to join a league. The empire-building Romans from the western part of the Mediterranean moved in. By the mid-100s B.C. the Romans were the rulers of Greece.

Chapter 2
Beliefs
and Ideas

The period between 500 and 338 B.C. saw the greatest developments in Greek civilization. Some scholars think that the Age of Pericles was the golden expression of the **era**. The later period between 338 and 133 B.C. is generally referred to as the Hellenistic Age. During this age the thought and culture of the Greeks and Middle Easterners were meeting and blending. The results were new outlooks on humanity and nature, new forms of art, and great advances in science and medicine.

GOD AND GODDESSES

The Greeks believed in a family of gods and goddesses that could protect and aid them in their daily lives. Their chief deities were believed to live on Mount Olympus in northern Greece. These deities were considered to be immortal and had powers far superior to those of humans. The Greeks had to be careful at all times not to offend them. Their anger was extremely fierce and dangerous.

Zeus was the father of the gods and goddesses. Hera, his wife, was the guardian goddess of women and marriage. Poseidon (puh-SY-duhn), a brother of Zeus, was god of the sea. Another brother, Pluto, was the god of the underworld where most people went after death. Aphrodite (af-ruh-DYT-ee) was the daughter of Zeus and the goddess of love and beauty.

Each locality and city-state had its special gods and goddesses who were honored as founders and protectors. A very close relationship existed between the people and these deities. For example, Athena, the goddess of wisdom, was the patron of Athens. The Athenians felt themselves to be the wisest of Greeks because of her. When the Athenians performed their duties to the **state** well and avoided arguments among themselves, they believed they could count on Athena's aid. In honoring her, the Athenians were performing civic as well as religious duties.

The Greeks believed that at shrines sacred to certain deities they could ask and receive answers about the future. The gods or goddesses often answered through the mouth of a priest or priestess, and the answers were known as oracles. The priest or priestess and the shrine itself were also called oracles. Apollo, a son of Zeus, was particularly helpful in advising men at his shrine in Delphi (DEL-fy). He was the guardian of music, poetry, and healing and was also the god of light.

This is the Theseum, a temple built in the mid-400s B.C. to honor Hephaestus, the god of fire, and Athena, the goddess of the arts. According to legend, Hephaestus was a blacksmith who crafted the golden throne of Zeus.

The religious beliefs of the early Greeks had a strong influence upon their literature, art, and architecture. The Olympic Games grew out of ceremonies honoring Zeus. Some of the greatest Greek **sculptures** were portrayals of their deities. Among the finest Greek public buildings were temples. Many Greek poems were hymns honoring and praising the gods and goddesses. Greek drama had its beginnings in religious festivals.

However, the Greek idea of the deities changed over the years. Human qualities became more apparent. The more philosophic and sophisticated Greeks took the gods and goddesses less seriously in a **religious** sense. They gradually transformed them into literary and philosophical symbols.

THINKERS

The Greeks came to believe there was a rational explanation for the existence of the universe and of humans. They were determined to reason out that explanation.

In the 500s B.C. some Greeks in Asia Minor began to search for a single substance that was basic to all material things. At various times water, air, and fire were suggested. However, several Greeks, one of whom was Democritus (dih-MAHK-ruh-tuhs), declared that all matter—everything that can be seen and felt—was composed of invisible particles called atoms.

By the 400s B.C. Greeks were becoming more interested in human existence than in the basic stuff of matter. They wanted to know more about themselves so they could live happier and more useful lives. A group called Sophists, or wise people, believed that truth is relative. What is beautiful, true, just, and good for one may not be seen as such by another in another place and at another time. These Sophists saw the world as a jungle. For them might made right.

Many Sophists were teachers. They taught pupils how to speak, debate, and discuss in a way that would help them succeed whether or not they spoke the truth. Other Greeks, however, challenged the ideas of the Sophists. Among them were Socrates, Plato, and Aristotle.

SOCRATES   Students listened to Socrates (SAHK-ruh-teez) and were impressed by what he said and how he lived. He left no writings, but Plato, his disciple, wrote about him.

Socrates would ask his listeners a series of questions. He would continue the questioning until the people would contradict themselves or could no longer answer. By his questions he hoped to lead people to gain an understanding of themselves and to discover the truth. Perhaps his greatest teaching was summed up in the words "Know thyself."

Socrates was opposed to the Sophists, for they used words to deceive. And they failed to admit ignorance of what they did not know. Socrates said there was an ultimate truth and a correct course of action for each individual. It was true and right wherever or whenever the individual lived. Further, each person has the ability to discover it.

Socrates' method of seeking the truth gained him enemies among the Athenians. He was brought to trial and accused of misleading youth and blaspheming the deities. He was found guilty. When he refused to leave the city or to stop teaching, he was condemned to death. In 399 B.C., at the age of 70, he ended his life by drinking a cup of hemlock—a deadly poison.

blaspheming: speaking about sacred people or things in a disrespectful way •

PLATO   Plato was a student of Socrates and founder of a school, the Academy. His writings—called dialogues—were discussions among fictional people on such subjects as government, religion, and justice.

Through his characters Plato presented his philosophy. He reasoned that the material world is in a constant state of change. Nothing in it ever remains the same. An object described today may have changed by tomorrow and the description would no longer be true. Thus Plato came to believe that knowledge could never be gained simply from what could be observed in the material world.

The Greeks tried to understand the world around them through religion, philosophy, and science. Many of their ideas have lasted for 2,000 years. This is a view from the temple of Poseidon at Cape Saunion in central Greece.

It was possible, however, to discover a perfect, unchanging world of universal truths. These truths Plato called Ideas and they represented perfection. They could not be understood by observing the real world but could be grasped only by the mind. Only there could perfect Truth, Beauty, and Justice be found.

In *The Republic,* one of his more famous dialogues, Plato described an ideal government and society based on courage, wisdom, and moderation. It was governed by philosopher-kings. The next class was composed of soldiers and **artisans**. Farmers and merchants made up the third class. The classes did not depend upon birth or wealth but upon ability developed through education. In Plato's **republic** there were no slaves, and all things were held in common.

Aristotle was a student of Plato. Compare and contrast Aristotle's ideas on government with those of Plato.

ARISTOTLE   When Aristotle (AR-uh-staht-uhl) was 17, he became a student in Plato's Academy. Later Aristotle served for seven years as tutor to Alexander the Great. When he returned to Athens he founded a school known as the Lyceum.

Aristotle was more concerned with the material world than Plato had been. He did not believe, as Plato did, that the world of ideas or ideals was separate from the real world. To Aristotle the world of material things and the world of ideas were equally real and true.

Another important part of Aristotle's thinking was the describing of things, based on similarities and differences. He was one of the first thinkers and scientists to use a systematic method of description and analysis. Aristotle applied this systematic method in studying a variety of subjects. As a biologist, he collected facts about natural life which he organized, classified, and distinguished according to groups. Before he wrote a work called *Politics,* he analyzed the **constitutions** of 50 city-states.

According to his findings Aristotle came to believe that civilized people could not exist outside a state of some kind. He believed that the best state was somewhere between an oligarchy—government by a few—and a democracy. The middle class—neither the too rich nor the too poor—would control it.

During the Middle Ages in Europe, Aristotle's writings were accepted as a standard authority. The influence of Aristotle's methods of reasoning can be seen in the *Summa Theologica* that Thomas Aquinas wrote in the 1200s A.D. The latter's work is still influential within the Roman Catholic Church. Aristotle's influence can also be seen in the research methods used by modern scientists and scholars.

OTHER PHILOSOPHIES   Later Greek philosophers were not always interested in discovering truth. Zeno, who founded Stoicism, was an Athenian who taught around 300 B.C. Zeno and his followers wanted peace of mind. They found it in resignation, duty, and self-discipline. They believed that everything that happened to people, bad or good, was for the good of the universe. It was useless for people to rebel against the evils that came to them. People did not direct their lives. If they wanted peace of mind and happiness, they must accept whatever happened to them.

The Stoics also taught that there was a unity among people and that all should live together in tolerance and equality. They spoke out against slavery and war and they urged all to take an active part in public affairs. They believed in the existence of a natural law by which principles of right and wrong are discoverable through reason.

The Epicureans (ep-ih-kyoo-REE-uhns) believed that humanity's purpose was to avoid pain. They took their name from their founder, Epicurus (ep-ih-KYOOR-uhs), who lived in Athens around 300 B.C. Epicureans believed that there was neither reward nor punishment after death, only nothingness. They urged people to seek what pleasure they could find here and now. They were especially interested in the pleasure that comes from a tranquil and serene mind. They cautioned people to seek this pleasure in moderation. Excess would bring pain.

The Cynics, contemporaries of the Epicureans, believed that living a virtuous life was all-important. Everything else was useless.

The Skeptics did not believe that a person could have definite knowledge about anything. There was no use in seeking absolute truth or knowledge because it could never be obtained. They said a person should abandon the search and suspend judgment. Then peace of mind would follow.

THE ARTS

The Greeks discovered that one of the essentials of excellence was to do nothing in excess. Their temples, theaters, and public buildings were ideals of moderation and balance.

The Greeks, like the Egyptians, used columns instead of arches to support the flat roofs of their buildings. They used three types: Doric, Ionic, and Corinthian. The Doric column was the simplest in design and the Corinthian, the most elaborate. One of the finest examples of Doric columns is found on the Parthenon, the temple to Athena on the Acropolis in Athens.

The Greeks also carved columns in the form of human figures. One such example is the Porch of the Maidens on one side of the Erechtheum. This temple is on the north side of the Acropolis.

Among the greatest of Greek sculptors was Phidias (FID-ee-uhs), who lived during the 400s B.C. He carved the massive statue of Athena that stood within the Parthenon. Phidias also carved the great statue of the seated Zeus at Olympia, the site of the Olympic Games. This statue was considered one of the seven wonders of the ancient world. Phidias was artistic advisor to Pericles in his efforts to make Athens a center of beauty. Praxiteles (prak-SIT-uh-leez) and Myron, both of whom worked in the 300s B.C., were also well-known sculptors.

According to Greek mythology, Athena was the goddess of war, wisdom, arts, and crafts. She was the special patron of Athens. This bronze statue of Athena was made in the 300s B.C. and stood in Piraeus, the port city of Athens.

Greek theaters were open-air constructions called amphitheaters. The seats were set in the natural bowl of a hillside and curved around three sides of the stage.

On stage, two or three male actors, dressed in elaborate costumes, spoke through masks and walked on raised shoes to make them seem taller. Only males performed on the Greek stage, so some were trained to play the parts of females. There was no scenery. At times a chorus—a group of singers and speakers—described events that were happening off stage. They explained the background of the play or told a part of the story.

During the festival of Dionysus (dy-uh-NIS-uhs), the Athenians attended plays for three successive days. Beginning at sunrise they might watch as many as nine plays each day. At the end of the day they were asked to select the best play—an honor to which every playwright aspired.

Greek plays explored the struggles of people to free themselves from the flaws in their characters. It was these flaws that caused individuals to do evil thus setting in motion forces that returned evil

for evil. Among the Greek dramatists of the 500s and 400s B.C. whose works are still performed are Aeschylus (ES-kuh-luhs), Sophocles (SAHF-uh-kleez), and Euripides (yoo-RIP-uh-deez).

The Greeks balanced their tragedies with comedies that poked fun at the important and the disliked. The most famous of the comedy playwrights—also called satirists—was Aristophanes (ar-uh-STAHF-uh-neez). In *The Clouds* Aristophanes ridiculed Socrates. The philosopher is shown talking from a basket suspended in midair. Aristophanes implies that Socrates' words were impractical and full of hot air. Only those whose feet are firmly planted on the ground have wisdom and common sense.

Although in ruins, the Parthenon, above left, is still a good example of Doric architecture. The temple's decoration was designed by the sculptor Phidias. Above right, modern Greeks still attend performances of ancient Greek plays. Today, however, women play the female roles as in this production of Euripides' play, Hippolytus.

HELLENISM: IMPACT ON SCIENCE

Upon the death of Alexander the Great in 323 B.C., his empire was separated into three parts. Macedonia continued to control some Greek city-states. Egypt was ruled by the Ptolemy (TAHL-uh-mee) family. The Seleucids (suh-LOO-sidz) governed the rest of the Middle East. The latter two ruling houses were descended from Alexander's generals. After this time there emerged from the blending of cultures begun by Alexander a culture known as Hellenistic or Greeklike. Hellas was the name the Greeks used for their own country.

Alexandria in Egypt, Antioch in Syria, island cities of the Aegean, and cities in Asia Minor became centers of Hellenistic culture. Hellenistic sculptors carved the world-renowned statues of *Venus de Milo* and *Nike of Samothrace*. Tragedies and comedies continued to be written. The greatest advances, however, were made in the sciences.

Greek scholars of this period, with the help of knowledge gained from the Middle East, came to various conclusions about the stars that were way ahead of later Europeans. Aristarchus (ar-uh-STAHR-kuhs) of Samos, who lived during the 200s B.C., discovered that the earth and the other planets revolve around the sun.

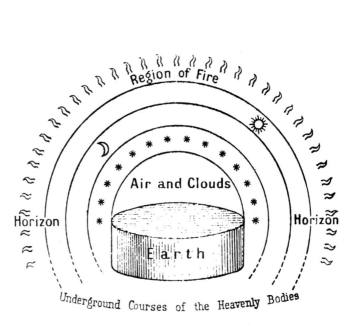

Greek science did not begin with the Hellenistic period. Anaximander, for example, who lived from 611 to 547 B.C. is credited with designing a sundial and introducing mapping. Above is his description of the universe.

Eratosthenes (er-uh-TAHS-thuh-neez), a contemporary of Aristarchus, knew the earth to be spherical, not flat. Fifteen hundred years before Columbus he claimed that if one sailed west from Spain one would eventually reach the coasts of India. He calculated the earth's circumference to within 80 kilometers (50 miles) of its actual size.

In the 100s B.C. Hipparchus (hip-AHR-kuhs) invented the astrolabe —a device used in navigation—that Columbus used in a modified model. Hipparchus charted the heavens and knew the approximate distance of the earth from the moon as well as the moon's diameter.

Around 300 B.C., in his school at Alexandria, Euclid drew upon earlier Greek and Middle Eastern ideas to state the basic principles of geometry. Students still study Euclidean geometry. Other Hellenistic mathematicians developed trigonometry.

Archimedes (ahr-kuh-MEED-eez) was one of Euclid's students. He continued the mathematical work of his teacher and uncovered various laws of physics, including the principle for determining specific gravity. Archimedes knew the use of the pulley and the lever. He once used them to pull a loaded ship out of the sea and rest it on the beach by himself. He also established the basic principle of the modern conveyor belt.

Hero, another inventor, lived in Alexandria in the 100s B.C. His long list of inventions included a fire engine and a steam engine.

Hippocrates (hip-AHK-ruh-teez), known as the father of medicine, believed that sickness came from natural causes rather than from the anger of a god. Hippocrates formulated the Hippocratic Oath which outlines the responsibilities of a doctor and which medical school graduates still take.

During the later Hellenistic period there were many who advanced the art of healing. Among the best known was Herophilus (hih-ROF-uh-luhs) who lived around the 200s B.C. From his careful study and examination of the human body, he made many discoveries. He learned that (1) blood is pumped from the heart through arteries to the entire body; (2) the pulse is important in revealing sickness; (3) a relationship exists between the nerves and the brain; and (4) the brain is divided into many sections, each with its own function in controlling various parts of the body.

Erasistratus (er-uh-SIS-trah-tuhs), in the 200s B.C., investigated the workings of the body so thoroughly that he might be called the father of physiology. He fought against the practice of removing blood from a person's body to bring about a cure. However, this practice, known as leeching, continued in the West until modern times. Hellenistic doctors performed surgery and prescribed drugs to deaden pain.

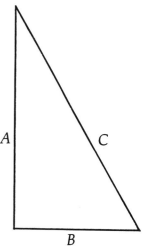

Pythagoras was also a pre-Hellenistic scientist. He lived during the 500s B.C. and developed the Pythagorean Theorem. According to the theorem, the square of c (hypotenuse) equals the sum of the squares of a and b.

AT HOME AND AT WORK

The Greeks were not obsessed with the material comforts of life. Their interest in moderation affected their day-to-day living as well as their artistic and philosophical works. Their daily life was simple and focused toward the practical.

The Greeks lived in small, plain houses that were tightly packed along narrow lanes. The houses often were built of sun-dried brick. Only a painted door brightened the outside. The door faced a lane, which sometimes smelled of garbage. There were no drains or sewer system. Water had to be carried from wells. Furniture was kept to a minimum. The houses were lighted with olive oil lamps.

The Greeks ate and dressed simply, too. They generally ate fish, onions, and barley cakes. Their breakfast was often only bread, and they washed down their food with a mixture of wine and water.

The men draped themselves in rectangular cloths called tunics,

401

which they pinned at the shoulders and belted at the waist. When they went out they merely threw another piece of cloth over their shoulders. Women dressed in a similar fashion, but their tunics were longer. Both men and women wore sandals.

The family unit consisted of husband and wife, all unmarried children, and married sons and their wives and children. A married woman lived with the family of her husband. The father was the absolute head of the household.

He arranged the marriage of his daughters, although he usually consulted with his wife. A girl was usually only 14 or 15 years old when she married, and she rarely saw her husband before the marriage. The father gave each daughter a dowry, which had been agreed upon with her future husband's family. Women in Greek society stayed mostly in the home. They spent their time weaving, spinning, cooking, and managing the house. They did not go to banquets with their husbands. Even when a man entertained at home, a wife was expected to keep out of sight.

The rather limited life of Greek women did not represent a scorn for them. The Greek deity of wisdom was a female, Athena. Women characters played central roles in Greek drama. Sappho, who wrote in the 600s B.C., is considered one of Greece's greatest poets. But in general, within the Greek social system, woman's place was considered to be in the home rather than in public.

At the age of six or seven, Greek children whose parents could afford it were sent to private schools. Schooling consisted of reading, writing, public speaking, literature, mathematics, and music. A well-balanced Greek needed a healthy body as well as a healthy mind, so boys also learned to hurl the discus, throw the javelin, jump, race, and wrestle. Girls learned gymnastics.

If the family could afford it, a boy at 14 went on to advanced studies in government and astronomy among other fields. If his family was poor, a boy was apprenticed to his father. At 18 young men entered the armed forces for a year. At 19 they were admitted to full citizenship. Upon the death of the father, all sons shared equally in the inheritance.

Most Greek city-dwellers owned small businesses. They were potters, blacksmiths, weavers, tanners, food merchants, or metal workers. There were very few large manufacturers. Some Greeks were **exporters**. Although barley and wheat were grown, much grain still had to be **imported**. Greek soil was poor, and farmers could not produce enough to feed the people. As a result overseas trade grew. In exchange for foodstuffs Greeks traded olive oil, wine, silver articles, and products made from imported raw materials.

In general Greeks worked only for what was necessary to support themselves and their families. Business was not their whole life. They took an active role in public affairs, and they spent much of their time exchanging ideas.

This picture of a young man writing on a clay tablet is on the inside of a kylix, a two-handled drinking cup. The Greeks decorated their cups, vases, pitchers, and various jars and containers. Much of what we know of the early Greeks comes from such objects. Why would people decorate everyday items like these?

Summing Up the Unit

Social Studies Vocabulary

Define: city-state; philosophy; limited democracy; deity; epic; kinship group; alliance; life-style; council; colony; league; tribute; state; empire; senate; central government; federal; artisan; constitution

People

Identify: Homer; Solon; Darius; Pericles; Philip of Macedon; Alexander the Great; Socrates; Plato; Aristotle; Zeno; Archimedes; Sappho

Places

Locate: Aegean, Ionian, Mediterranean seas; Athens; Corinth; Sparta; Asia Minor

Words

Define: frescoes; Olympic Games; Heraea; tyrant; oracles; dialogues; oligarchy; Hellenism; amphitheaters; astrolabe; tunic

☞ Questions

1. a. From what source have we learned about Cretan culture? b. What have we learned?
2. What do epics like the *Iliad* and the *Odyssey* tell us about the early Greeks?
3. a. What effect did geography have on the development of the city-states? b. Why did the Greeks develop city-states rather than one national government?
4. a. Why did the Greeks establish trading posts and colonies? b. Where?
5. Why did the Persians fight the Greeks?
6. a. How did the Athenians become leaders of the league of city-states? b. What trouble did this create?
7. Why was early Athenian democracy described as limited?
8. Who were the Macedonians?
9. How was the formation of less-powerful city-states into leagues an experiment in a federal system of democracy?
10. a. What did the Greeks believe about their deities? b. Over the years, how did the Greeks' ideas about their deities change?
11. What ideas about truth were held by: a. the Sophists? b. Socrates? c. Plato? d. Aristotle? e. the Skeptics?
12. What examples are given to show that early Greek scholars reached conclusions about astronomy that were far ahead of later Europeans?
13. a. Why did overseas Greek trade grow? b. What goods did the Greeks trade?

Discussion Topics

1. Athens reached the peak of its power and democracy when it headed the league of city-states in the Age of Pericles. What were the reasons for Athenian greatness at that time? What mistakes and flaws soon brought about the downfall of the Athenians?
2. Both military service and participation in the affairs of government were responsibilities of Athenian citizens. Do you think democracy developed in Athens because of warfare, or in spite of it?
3. The Greeks believed that nothing should be done in excess. Moderation and balance were important. How was this idea reflected in Greek philosophy, art, architecture, and drama? How did this attitude affect the daily lives of the Greeks?
4. The Athenians trusted justice from the many but not from the few. What were the strengths and weaknesses of the Athenian experiment in rule by ordinary citizens? Were they really ordinary citizens? Were their interests different from those of immigrants, slaves, and women? Does democracy have similar strengths and weaknesses today? Why or why not?

Project Ideas

1. Read some Greek myths and summarize for the class the ones you found interesting.
2. List ten English words of Greek origin.
3. Write a report on one of the following: Plato; Aristotle; Socrates; Diogenes; Greek drama; Greek contributions to the arts or sciences.
4. Using outside sources, make a chart comparing the society and politics of Sparta with that of Athens in Pericles' time.

403

Unit III

The Greatness of Rome

Remains of Roman rule can be seen throughout Europe, North Africa, and into the Middle East. This Roman aqueduct is in France.

During the days of its greatness, Rome ruled an empire that stretched from the borders of Persia (modern Iran) and the deserts of Africa to the banks of the Danube and Rhine rivers and to southern Scotland. At their best, the Romans showed a high sense of duty and sacrifice and a feeling for others. They displayed tolerance and a sense of the practical in governing the many peoples of their empire.

But the cycle of empire, like that of humans, is one of growth, maturity, aging, and decay. The strength of the Romans gradually waned. Roman rule passed into other hands. The empire was divided and ruled in the West by Germanic peoples and in the East by the Byzantine emperors. The center of the Christian Church in the West, however, remained in Rome.

Sometime after 2000 B.C. groups of migrating peoples discovered the passes through the Alps that separate Italy from the rest of western Europe. For more than a thousand years, members of these groups straggled through the passes to settle the Italian peninsula. Some lingered in the rich green valley of the Po River. Others continued down the western plains that lay between the Apennine Mountains and the Tyrrhenian (tuh-REE-nee-uhn) Sea.

Among the groups that moved southward were a people called Latins. The plain they settled was called Latium. This plain is immediately south of the Tiber (TY-buhr) River. The Latins were the ancestors of the Romans, and their early developement was greatly influenced by the Etruscans, Greeks, and Carthaginians (kahr-thuh-JIN-yuhnz).

ROMAN BEGINNINGS

The Etruscans are among the mystery people of history. Some scholars believe they were a people long native to Italy. Others believe that they came from the Middle East, perhaps from Asia Minor. All are certain, however, that by the 600s and 500s B.C. the Etruscans were firmly settled in the western portion of Italy.

They lived in an area known as Etruria (ih-TRUR-ee-uh) just north of the Tiber River and the plain of Latium. The plain was already occupied by the Latins who were farmers. The Etruscans lived in walled cities with paved streets. They designed arches for their gates and domes for their buildings and laid underground sewers. They dressed in fine clothes and wore jewelry. Their wealth came from trade and from iron mines. From some time before 600 B.C. until 510 B.C., the Etruscans ruled the Latins.

Greeks had come to Italy around 750 B.C. and settled in colonies on the peninsula south of the Latins and on the island of Sicily. From them the Latins learned the alphabet which the Greeks had received from the Phoenicians and modified. The later Romans further modified the alphabet, and it is upon this alphabet that the Indo-European languages are based. The Greeks also taught the Latins about many of their deities.

The Latins also came into contact with the Carthaginians, settlers of an early Phoenician colony in North Africa across from Sicily. The Carthaginians established trading posts and colonies in western Sicily and on the islands of Sardinia and Corsica off the west coast of Italy.

The Latins learned much from these other cultures. As they learned, they adapted, adjusted, and grew until they were the people we know as Romans. They took their name from the city of Rome, which the Etruscans had built some 24 kilometers (15 miles) inland on the Tiber River. The growth of Rome was due in part to its river location which helped it grow into a trading center.

Around 510 B.C., the Romans drove the Etruscans from the city.

Chapter 1
The Road
to Empire

Ancient Italy
- Etruscans
- Latins
- Greeks

These three warriors are the handle of a lid for a bronze container. The piece was crafted in the 300s B.C.

Thus began an expansion that continued until the name of Rome was known and feared in Europe, Africa, the Middle East and parts of Asia.

WAR AND CONQUESTS

The Romans started in Italy on the road to empire. They made allies of the friendlier peoples and enlisted their help in conquering the more hostile ones. Often they offered the conquered peoples special privileges and even citizenship in return for help. The Romans first gave citizenship to those who lived around Rome. As the empire grew, citizenship was extended to the many peoples within its far-reaching borders. Whether friend or former foe, once the Romans made an alliance with a people, they never willingly let them go. By 264 B.C. the Romans held all of Italy south of the Po River.

When the Romans had gained control over this territory, they looked with suspicion at Carthage. Its influence reached the boundaries claimed by Rome. Nor was Carthage pleased with the nearness of so ambitious a neighbor. Between 264 and 146 B.C. the Carthaginians and Romans tested each other in three wars. The Romans called these the Punic Wars (PYOO-nik)—from the name they called the Carthaginians.

At the end of the Third Punic War the Romans leveled Carthage. To prevent any further animal or vegetable growth, they plowed the site with salt. Thus Carthage's centuries of glory came to an end.

As a result of the Punic Wars, North Africa and Spain became Roman provinces. Kingdoms and cities tumbled before Roman arms and demands. By the year 133 B.C., the Romans could truly call the Mediterranean "our sea." All the people who lived on the shores of that sea were Roman subjects.

THE REPUBLIC

In the late 400s B.C. while the Romans were changing the political appearance of Italy, their own political appearance was changing. When they overthrew the Etruscans they set up a republic. At that time there were two classes of people: patricians and plebeians. Patricians (puh-TRISH-uhns) were the few wealthy property owners. The majority were plebeians (pleh-BEE-yuhns)—artisans, citizen-farmers, soldiers, and the poor. Women had no legal status. Their social status depended on the rank of first their fathers and later their husbands.

The expansion of Rome was due in large measure to its citizen-farmer-soldier class. During the early republic Romans were required to serve in the army. They were expected to provide helmet, shield, sword, and iron-tipped javelin. Discipline was harsh. Any honor a soldier received was an honor to his entire family. Any disgrace was also a disgrace upon his family.

PATRICIANS AND PLEBEIANS At the head of the republic were two officials known as consuls. In the early days consuls were always patricians. They were chosen by the patrician-dominated senate. Although the consuls were empowered to veto each other's acts, they did nothing that would lessen the political influence of their own class. Sometimes, during a war or civil emergency, the consuls, with senate consent, would appoint a **dictator** to govern for a maximum of six months. He too was always a patrician.

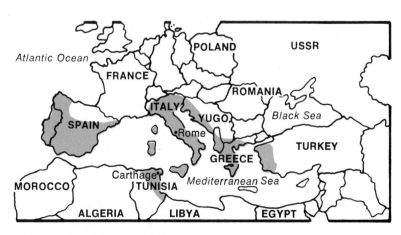

■ **Roman Republic, c. 133 B.C.**

Below the consuls was the senate. It was composed of 300 members who were selected by the consuls. Members were appointed for life. Patrician consuls and senators had the power to veto all decisions of the Assembly of Centuries. In this assembly plebeians had some representation. However, it too was dominated by patricians.

Through the assembly, patricians were able to elect members of their own class to official positions, such as consuls, praetors, and censors. Praetors (PREET-uhrz) were judges who occasionally acted as consuls when the consuls were absent from Rome. The censors took the census and decided who could or could not be a citizen. Two censors passed judgment on the morals of Roman citizens and made the lists of citizens from which senators were selected.

census: the official counting and collecting of information about its people by a government

During the several centuries that the Romans were expanding in Italy, the plebeians were advancing in their rights as citizens. Because patricians dominated the Assembly of Centuries, plebeians established the Assembly of Tribes. This assembly had the right to participate in making laws and in electing officials. The plebeians elected ten tribunes from their ranks, and they had the power to veto any act of a magistrate or judge.

Gradually plebeian power and social conditions improved. Around 450 B.C. the plebeians managed to get the unwritten laws of Rome set down upon 12 tablets. This gave them additional protection from

Today the Roman Forum is in ruins. But during the peak of Roman power, it was the center of government for the Republic and later the Empire.

patrician judges who often interpreted the unwritten laws in the interests of their own class. In 445 B.C. plebeians gained the right to marry into the patrician class. In 367 B.C. they won the right to be selected as consuls. By 300 B.C. plebeians were eligible for all public and religious offices of the republic.

The divisions between patrician and plebeians eventually became less sharp. In 287 B.C. patricians and plebeians were joined in a new assembly. This group made laws for everyone. Gradually the two classes merged, and new classes arose.

FOUR CLASSES   During the later years of the republic and the period of the empire, the Romans became divided into four new classes: aristocrats, equites, farmers and workers, and slaves. The aristocrats, who were few in number, mostly held high government positions. The equites (EK-wuh-teez) were originally members of the Roman cavalry. From their high military rank, they developed into a privileged social class. They were moneylenders and speculators in grain, wine, and oil. They bought government contracts, collected taxes, owned ships and gladiator schools, and were the large merchants.

The farmers and workers were the ordinary citizens. But many were the poor wards of the state—who numbered over 300,000 toward the end of the republic. The slaves were the lowest class. There were approximately 1.5 million in Italy during the latter days of the republic. They produced most of the Romans' food, worked in their industries, and made the lives of the wealthy more comfortable.

Sometimes slaves were branded, whipped, and chained at night. For some of the educated slaves, life was more fortunate. They worked as tutors, secretaries, and managers of businesses. At times they had owners who treated them humanely and even gave them their freedom. A few were able to earn money and buy their freedom. These were a small minority, however. More often the Romans feared their slaves. In 104 B.C. rebellious slaves devastated the island of Sicily. In 73 B.C., under the leadership of Spartacus, 70,000 slaves kept Italy in turmoil for more than a year.

RISE OF THE EMPIRE

From 133 to 27 B.C. the Romans continued to extend their territory. But the republican system of government was dying. Bribery was normal. The buying and selling of offices had become routine. Tax collecting was a profitable profession for the collectors. Governors ruled their **provinces** for the purpose of retiring to Rome with loot and bags of gold. The rich used hundreds of thousands of slaves to work their lands and factories.

Small free farmers could not compete with cheap slave labor. The farmers saw their holdings and homes being taken over by large landlords. Former owners of little pieces of land frequently sought refuge in Rome and became part of the mass of unemployed. Ex-soldiers, who returned from wars that made other men rich, discovered their families scattered and their homes gone. They too swelled the mass of Rome's poor.

Though many Roman citizens were poor, their votes were still important. They were wooed by honest and dishonest office-seekers alike with bread, money, games, and circuses. For centuries humans, animals, and fortunes were sacrificed in the arenas to satisfy the mobs of Rome.

Out of the uncertainty and wretchedness of this period, some people rose to greatness, and some fell. Reformers like the Gracchi (GRAK-eye) brothers, Tiberius and Gaius, wanted to make the republic more democratic by decreasing the economic and political power of the wealthy. First Tiberius and later Gaius proposed limits on the amount of land that could be owned by any one family. They urged that farmers who had lost their lands be resettled in colonies abroad or on state-owned lands in Italy.

The Gracchi brothers also suggested that Rome's poor be permitted to buy grain at or below cost from the state. They also wanted to reduce the power of the senate and expand Roman citizenship. Their proposals and actions angered the leaders of Rome. Tiberius was murdered and Gaius driven to suicide by the rich who would have suffered from their reforms.

A period of **civil war** followed. On one side were the supporters of increased senate power; on the other were opponents of the senate. Into the fighting came Gaius Marius (MER-ee-uhs) and Lucius Cornelius Sulla (SUHL-uh). Both military men, they started the **tradition** of rule by the military. Marius abolished the citizen-soldier army and replaced it with soldiers serving for a fixed period of time and paid by their general. A soldier's loyalty was transferred from the state to his general. From this new relationship there sprang one of the most famous of all Romans—Julius Caesar.

JULIUS CAESAR   At first Caesar shared the rule of Rome with two other men, Gnaeus Pompey (PAHM-pee)—called Pompey the Great —and Marcus Licinius Crassus (KRAS-uhs). Crassus was soon killed in war, leaving Pompey and Caesar. Each wished to rule alone. Pompey had gained great popularity in Rome by conquering Syria and Jerusalem. Caesar too knew that the way of the soldier was now the way to permanent power.

While consul in 59 B.C., Caesar had himself appointed governor of the territory called Gaul (approximately modern France). In 58 B.C. Caesar started a **campaign** that in nine years brought what is now Holland, Belgium, France, part of Germany, and part of England under Roman rule. He sent back to Rome progress reports on his victories. These reports were collected as *Commentaries on the Gallic Wars.*

approximately: about, almost

Caesar's success disturbed his rival, Pompey, and others who were jealous and fearful of his rising power. In 49 B.C. he was asked to resign his office and return to Rome without his army. Suspicious of the senate's intentions, he set out with the army. A messenger from the senate met them at the River Rubicon (ROO-bih-kahn), which separated Gaul from Italy. The messenger said that the senate would consider Caesar a rebel if he entered Italy with his army. Caesar crossed the river with the army and marched on to capture Rome.

Caesar followed Pompey to Greece and defeated him. Caesar then crossed to Africa and placed Cleopatra on the throne of Egypt. He returned to Rome and in 45 B.C. was given full power to rule Rome as a dictator for ten years. Caesar carefully chose his officials and checked on them with inspectors. Reforms were introduced to make the system of tax collection more honest and efficient. Caesar returned land to the landless and thus lifted the morale of the people. He offered citizenship to those who lived outside Italy and thus knit the empire closer together.

Caesar also had other interests. He had the calendar changed to correct its errors. This reformed calendar was used by Europeans until the Gregorian corrections were made in the 1500s A.D. Some nations continued to use the Julian calendar until the early 1900s. The month of July is named for Julius Caesar.

Leaders like Caesar arouse fear and envy. A group of Romans, including Caesar's friend Brutus, murdered him on the Senate floor on the Ides (15th) of March, 44 B.C.

OCTAVIAN AND MARC ANTONY   The struggle to possess the power of Rome continued. Marc Antony, who spoke eloquently over Caesar's body, wanted Caesar's authority. Octavian, grandnephew and heir of Caesar, also desired power. Some wished to restore authority to the senate. Marc Antony and Octavian joined forces and defeated the senators' army. The two then divided Roman territory. Marc Antony ruled the East and Octavian the West.

Octavian made his headquarters in Rome. Marc Antony ruled from Egypt, where Cleopatra remained as queen. For a time there was peace. But plots, jealousies, and rivalry arose between the two. In 32 B.C., at the urging of Octavian, the senate stripped Marc Antony of his authority. War was formally declared against Egypt. It was really a war between the forces of Marc Antony and those of Octavian.

In the summer of 30 B.C. Octavian conquered Egypt. Marc Antony committed suicide. Cleopatra also killed herself to avoid having to walk as a prisoner before the people of Rome.

Thus Octavian became supreme in Rome. Under his rule the republic died, and the Roman Empire began. The forms of the republic were kept. However, the actual power was held by one man—the emperor. The senate kept its name and membership, but it confirmed the successor chosen by the reigning emperor or by the military.

Julius Caesar used his role as a soldier to rise to power. What other leaders have used their military positions to gain control of government?

This inscription in Latin and Neo-Punic (bottom) is the dedication for a Roman theater built in 1-2 A.D. in what is modern Libya.

PAX ROMANA

When Octavian was given the title Augustus—Exalted One—by the senate in 27 B.C., he began a 200-year period of stability and prosperity called the Pax Romana (PAKS roh-MAHN-uh) or Roman Peace. The empire's frontiers were protected by well-trained and well-led soldiers. Roman security was reinforced by stone walls built across southern Scotland and along the Rhine and Danube rivers.

The Romans administered their widespread territory very well. They interfered little in the local affairs of their subjects. The Romans asked them only to pay taxes, fill their quotas of soldiers, acknowledge the emperor, and keep the peace. Having done this, the Romans left their subjects to follow their accustomed ways of life.

The Romans used other methods to keep the loyalty of their subjects and to tie the empire together. They began to extend the privilege of citizenship to subjects in the provinces. By the middle of the 200s A.D., thousands called themselves citizens of Rome, although they had never seen the city and were not of Latin ancestry. Roman subjects were also brought closer together by the network of Roman roads, Roman law, and a general use of the Latin and Greek languages. They were further united by one monetary system, one capital, and one emperor. Thus the Romans were able to fashion and preserve their empire for centuries.

Chapter 2
Beliefs and Ideas

The Romans took the thoughts and works of the Greeks and others of the Mediterranean area and blended them with their own ideas. For example, much of the knowledge we have of Greek sculpture is from Roman copies.

However, the Romans were creators as well as adapters and preservers. They invented instruments for surgery and passed on to later Europeans a tradition of public hospitals and public hygiene. They built a legal system which people continue to use. Roman domes, arches, and amphitheaters are still copied, and the foundations and routes of Roman roads are still in use. Roman writings are still read for their style and view of life.

Latin is the base of the Romance languages of the Indo-European **language family**: French, Spanish, Italian, Portuguese, and Romanian. Also, many Latin words have been incorporated into English, German, and other languages.

SPIRITS AND DEITIES

The Romans were originally animists or spirit worshipers. During the early years of the republic, Romans were concerned mostly with their families and farms. The spirits in which they believed were

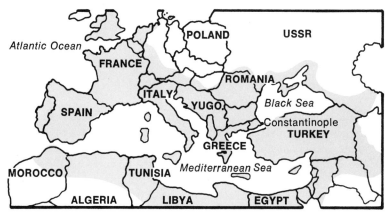

☐ **Roman Empire at Its Peak, c. 117 A.D.**

closely associated with these two areas. Dead ancestors as well as objects were parts of this spirit world. The male head of the family had an obligation to sacrifice to the spirits and to assume leadership in the family's religious ceremonies.

The most important of the Roman spirits was Vesta, the spirit of hearth and fire. As hearth and fire were central to the Roman household, so Vesta was the center of Roman worship. As their civilization developed, the Romans symbolized the larger grouping of their national family by building a temple for Vesta in Rome. There this spirit was placed as the guardian of the hearth of the total Roman family. Within this temple a sacred fire always burned, attended by six vestal virgins. The virgins were among the most honored and respected of Romans.

Spirits who protected the household and its fortune were called lares (LAR-eez). Other spirits called penates (puh-NAYT-eez) guarded the storerooms. There were also spirits that watched over grain from its sowing to its storing. These spirits were as numerous as there were steps in the production of food.

The Romans honored all their spirits with ceremonies and festivals. Later Romans began to attribute human shapes and human needs and feelings to the spirits. This was in part a result of the Romans' long association with the Greeks. The Romans began to mix Greek gods with their own. Zeus became the Roman god Jupiter, and Hera became the Roman goddess Juno. Aphrodite was known to the Romans as Venus. The Greek messenger of the gods, Hermes, was changed to Mercury.

But the Romans also accepted deities from other peoples. They accepted the cult of Mithra from the Persians, the Egyptian goddess Isis (EYE-suhs), and Cybele (SIB-uh-lee), the fertility goddess from Asia Minor, among others. After the first century A.D., some also

413

Around the 700s B.C. the Latins came in contact with the story of the Greek god Dionysus, the god of wine. The later Romans borrowed the myth, and their god became known as Bacchus. The worship of Bacchus was in direct opposition to the philosophy of the Stoics. What was Stoic philosophy?

accepted the God of the Christians. Before the breakup of the Roman Empire in the 400s A.D., the deities of many peoples had found a place in Roman temples.

THE STOIC APPEAL

The Romans also found that the philosophies of others were adaptable to their own needs. Greek ideas were especially interesting. Greek scholars were brought to Rome, and Romans went to Greece to study.

The Romans of the republic were most influenced by the Stoics. The Stoic insistence on the obligations of citizens appealed to the Romans who had their own ideas of duty and public-spiritedness. The Stoic idea of the unity of people agreed with the Roman idea of empire. A natural law that applied to all peoples supported the Romans who were expanding their rule over so many.

One of those who were attracted to the teachings of the Stoics was Cicero (SIS-uh-roh). He studied law in Rome and philosophy in Greece. He became one of Rome's greatest lawyers and orators and held many important government offices. Cicero believed in the Roman Republic and was often opposed to the imperial policies of Caesar.

Cicero accepted the idea of a natural law and believed that a virtuous life was in accord with it. Individuals derived their rights from the natural law which was above human **institutions** like the state. He advised people to pursue virtue, be indifferent to pain and grief, to cooperate with each other, and always be guided by reason. Cicero's teachings had a great influence on the development of Roman law.

Seneca (SEN-ih-kuh) was born in Cordoba, Spain, but studied and lived most of his life in Rome. He was a patrician, a teacher, and chief advisor to the Emperor Nero (54-68 A.D.). He was also an author of scientific writings, a playwright, and a philosopher. He believed that there was a divine force directing all things to some final and good end. This divinity was shared by all humans. For this reason Seneca held that there were essentially no class distinctions among people. Romans should treat their slaves decently because they too were part of humanity. Seneca urged all to use their reason to practice the good life and to remain calm and untouched by troubles.

Another Stoic philosopher was Epictetus (ep-ik-TEET-uhs). He was a slave from Asia Minor who was brought to Nero's court and later freed. Like Seneca he believed that a divine force was guiding the universe to a particular end. It was the duty of humans, he said, to direct their will in accordance with this divine plan. It was important that people recognize which things were within their control and which things were not. People could fulfill their own desires and make their own choices. However, they should not be upset by matters beyond their control. People could have peace of mind and true freedom only when they renounced those things that were beyond them.

Emperor Marcus Aurelius was both a soldier and a follower of Stoicism. Does this statue portray both sides of his character? If so, how?

In turn, people had to be prepared to accept and endure whatever misfortunes came to them.

A firm believer in the disciplined life of the Stoics was the Emperor Marcus Aurelius (aw-REEL-yuhs, 161-180 A.D.). In his life and his writings, *The Meditations of Marcus Aurelius,* he taught the importance of duty and virtue. For much of his life he fought on the frontiers of the empire, and he knew the hardships that duty often requires. He related in his *Meditations* that he was often tempted to remain under his blankets in the cold early morning. But when he thought of the ordered purpose for which he was destined, he threw off his warm coverings and began his day. He was aware of the demands of humanity and of the need to give of himself and his property.

LAW

The Romans had a deep feeling and respect for law. Their law was based upon tolerance and reason. Many modern legal ideas such as partnerships, private property, innocent until proven guilty, and contracts were first expressed by the Romans.

The first Roman code of law, called the Twelve Tables, was written down about 450 B.C. It was designed for the simple farm life of the early republic. However, life did not remain simple for long. As the Romans expanded their empire, they expanded their law. They adapted it to meet the **customs** of their new subjects and the teachings of the Stoics. They also wanted to insure that justice was given in every case. Praetors were flexible in interpreting the law for each case that came before them. Their interpretations became precedents for other praetors to follow and upon which to base further interpretations. The Roman law grew in much the same fashion that later English common law grew—daily, gradually, and practically. Cicero's teachings on natural law and rights of individuals helped to bring reason to the administration of Roman justice.

The Romans did not force their law upon the people they conquered. But in time most of the people of the empire came to accept Roman law as suitable and just. Even after the fall of the empire, many continued to use it. All the later European countries were affected by Roman law but its greatest impact was on Italy, France, Spain, and the countries of Latin America. Roman law is still the basis of their legal systems.

THE ARTS

The Romans did not confine themselves to philosophy and law. They also made significant contributions to literature, art, and architecture.

Roman writers sometimes imitated Greek comedies and other forms of Greek literature. The two best-known Roman playwrights, Terence and Plautus (PLAWT-uhs), drew heavily from the Greeks. They lived during the mid-point of the republic.

Virgil (VUHR-juhl) was influenced by the Stoics. He was also influenced by a sense of the destiny and greatness of Rome. His finest creation is the epic poem, the *Aeneid* (ih-NEE-uhd). It tells the **legendary** story of Aeneas who escaped the ruin of Troy by the Greeks. After much wandering and many adventures, he settled in Italy where his descendants founded the city of Rome. Although the *Aeneid* is similar to the *Odyssey* and the *Iliad* of Homer, it is not an imitation. Virgil brought his own unique style to its creation.

Horace wrote poetry and prose. He condemned neither pain nor pleasure but believed that the person of moderation was the happiest. He advised others to hope when things looked bad and to worry a little when everything was going right. This attitude and way of behaving he called the Golden Mean.

Another Roman poet, Ovid, was more concerned with human pleasure than with morality. Livy wrote a history of Rome that is famous for its style, but scholars question its accuracy. All these writers lived around the time of Augustus, often referred to as the Augustan or Golden Age of Rome.

Writers after this period were not so talented. There were exceptions, among them Juvenal and Tacitus. Juvenal satirized the vices of Rome under the empire. Observing the hypocrisy and dishonesty of his time, he once remarked, "Honesty is praised and starves."

satirized: criticized or poked fun at people's ideas or actions

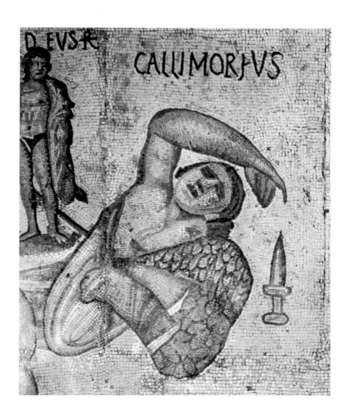

By the end of the Roman Republic, fights between gladiators were a favorite form of entertainment. This mosaic shows a wounded gladiator dropping his dagger. Why might this type of game appeal to the masses of poor Romans?

Tacitus (TAS-uht-uhs) was the best of the Roman historians. In *Germania,* he wrote a classic description of the early Germans. He compared the hardiness and simplicity of the Germans with the softness of many Romans. He scorned the decay and luxury of his society. Tacitus was upset by the shallowness of education and the delight of the Romans for chariot racing and the circus. He feared the evil times that would follow the Roman pursuit of luxury and easy living. It should be noted, however, that the Roman Empire continued for another 300 years.

Although Roman paintings and works of art in bronze and marble are still admired, the Romans are best remembered as builders. They

The Appian Way, which ran south 589 kilometers (366 miles) from Rome to Brindisi, was begun in 312 B.C. Parts of it are still used. The Pantheon was originally a temple. Christians used it as a church. Now it is a national shrine. The marble columns in the above photo are Corinthian in design. The only light comes through an opening in the dome.

made their buildings massive and strong. Still standing in Rome are the walls of the Colosseum (kahl-uh-SEE-uhm), where thousands of ancient Romans watched scenes of bloodshed and violence. The Romans built huge baths where rich and poor went to bathe and gossip. On warm summer evenings, modern Romans can gather to listen to opera at the baths built by the Emperor Caracalla.

The Romans often capped their buildings with domes. During the rule of the Emperor Hadrian (HAY-dree-uhn, 117-138), the domed Pantheon (PAN-thee-ahn) was built. The diameter of its rotunda is exactly equal to its height from floor to ceiling. Within their buildings the Romans placed statues of their emperors and famous people. Sometimes their statues showed depth of character and realism. However, Roman creations done in the style of the Greeks do not compare with Greek originals.

Unlike the Greeks, who designed with columns, the Romans used the arch in their buildings, bridges, and aqueducts—structures for carrying water. The Romans also built arches to commemorate military victories.

The Romans were very interested in hygiene and used great amounts of water. No one in those early times built as many—or as many lasting—aqueducts as the Romans. They built them wherever they settled, in the Middle East, North Africa, Spain, and elsewhere. An aqueduct still standing in southern France is around 275 meters (900 feet) long and over 45 meters (150 feet) high. The Romans also laid underground sewers and constructed latrines, which were sometimes made more attractive with marble facing. By draining swamps the

Romans made land more useful and life more healthful.

The Romans also built bridges and roads. The roads were of stone and sometimes of lava blocks. They were built to last and were laid throughout the empire. Over these roads Roman legions tramped, messengers hurried, and trading carts plodded. Many modern European roads are laid over old Roman ones. The Romans also made road maps for the convenience of travelers.

CHANGES IN FAMILY LIFE

During the early days of the republic, Romans lived in a modest manner. Their lives centered around the family. Within the family, the Romans learned certain basic values. They learned to respect authority and tradition and to feel responsibility for their families. However, they were prepared to sacrifice their personal interests if called upon by the greater Roman family—the state.

In the beginning of the republic, the father's authority was absolute. He was the head of the household. The household included unmarried children and married sons and their families. Family property was held in the father's name. After his death it was passed to his sons—not his daughters—in equal shares. By the time of the empire women had gained greater rights and could inherit property.

Originally the primary duty of Roman women was the bearing and raising of children and the care of the home. With the coming of the empire, upper-class women enjoyed greater freedom. Even before that a woman exercised great influence over her husband and family.

Above left is an outside view of the Colosseum in Rome. At right is the interior. The Colosseum was built for fights between gladiators and humans and animals. By the 1400s Romans had begun using it as a source of building materials. Today the Colosseum is a major tourist attraction.

419

How did the life of Roman women differ from that of Greek women?

She helped entertain at home and frequently went out with her husband on business and social engagements. She was often consulted on family decisions and played a part in the education of her children. The Romans did not provide free schooling but private schools were open to both boys and girls.

The poor—the vast majority of Roman citizens—could not afford to give their children any formal education. Besides attending private schools, wealthy Romans were sometimes taught at home by an educated slave or a private tutor. After graduation a son might go to one of the famed schools of Greece for a time. Octavian, who ruled as Augustus, was a student there when his granduncle, Julius Caesar, was murdered.

Chapter 3
Decline of the Roman Empire

As the Roman Empire declined, the pattern of later European life was shaped by three forces: Greek and Roman cultural **heritage**; Christianity; and German political customs and social institutions. The merging of these three characteristics marked the period known historically as the European Middle Ages or **medieval** period. Traditionally the medieval period is considered as the years between the early 400s and the 1400s. However, the transition from the Roman to the medieval way of life was not an abrupt change. It was a gradual process over several centuries.

THE FINAL STAND

Shortly after 180 A.D., quarreling between military **factions** for the throne of Rome caused discord and disunity within the empire. From 180 to 284, 26 men became emperor. Of these, 25 were assassinated, and the empire was gravely weakened.

The decline of Rome was delayed for some years by the able rule of two emperors, Diocletian (dy-uh-KLEE-shuhn, 284-305) and Constantine (307-337). Diocletian was a strong-willed administrator and **reformer** who changed the empire. He **centralized** the government while dividing the empire into a greater number of provinces. The provinces were grouped into 13 administrative units called dioceses.

The entire Roman Empire was then divided into two parts. The Latin-speaking part included Gaul, Spain, Britain, North Africa, and Italy. The other part was made up of Greek-speaking areas and included Greece and the Middle East. Diocletian chose a co-emperor to govern the western division, while he spent much of his time in the eastern portion of the empire. Diocletian's reforms were continued and completed under Constantine.

In 313 Constantine legalized Christianity by the Edict of Milan. Until this time, Christians had been persecuted or not depending upon the emperor and the political condition of the empire. Romans were generally tolerant of all religions. However, a number of Romans regarded Christians as enemies of the state. Christians refused to offer incense and wine before the statue of the emperor and to serve in the Roman army. But Christianity was spreading widely even before it was legalized by Constantine. Under one of Constantine's successors, Theodosius (thee-uh-DOH-shee-uhs, 378-395), the worship of all other gods was forbidden. Christianity was made the supreme religion.

Constantine built a second capital for the Roman Empire on the site of the ancient Greek colony of Byzantium, and named it Constantinople. Constantine governed alone for a period. Later it became the practice to have two emperors—one in Rome, the other in Constantinople. The emperor who lived in Rome ruled the dying portion of the empire. A slow decay had been weakening Rome's inner strength for several centuries.

INNER WEAKNESS   The morality of the Romans had weakened as their power and wealth increased. Though Roman leaders paid lip service to the old virtues of responsibility and simplicity, their personal lives were often selfish and corrupt.

The number of poor continued to increase and their lives grew more miserable. They became accustomed to living on handouts from the government. The government was near bankruptcy. Taxes were raised again and again to meet the costs of government, the military, and feeding the poor.

Under Diocletian and later emperors, occupations became **hereditary**. The worker was bound to the fields he worked or the industry he served. He could not move away, and his sons inherited his occupation. This policy encouraged disinterest in work and a **caste** system. Plagues depopulated large areas of Italy. There was a lack of vigor and self-reliance among the Romans. They had little will or desire to resist the roving peoples who moved into the western regions of the empire.

INVADING PEOPLES   The Danube and Rhine rivers generally marked the eastern boundaries of the European portion of the Roman Empire. Peoples had been living beyond these rivers to the shores of the Baltic Sea for centuries. The resources of their land could not keep pace with their rapidly increasing numbers. Branches of these peoples occasionally broke away and moved southward into central Europe and southern Russia.

During the centuries of Roman rule, some of these Germanic people settled in lands under Roman control. Some even became soldiers in Roman legions. As we have seen, the Roman historian Tacitus praised their family life, loyalty, and courage in contrast to the immorality of Romans.

Invasions of the Huns, c. 300s-500s A.D.

At their peak, the Romans were able to withstand the pressure of these peoples. But as Roman will and firmness weakened, greater numbers of Germans—or Teutons (TYOOT-uhnz)—took over territories the Romans had once called their own. Often these groups had little choice. Their lands had been invaded by the Huns, savage warriors from Central Asia who had already swept into India and China.

Eventually the Huns were not content to raid the Germans and Slavs. Under the leadership of Attila, who boasted that he was the scourge of God, they wanted all Europe. The eastern emperor paid them to stay away from Constantinople. In 451 the Huns moved into Gaul, but were defeated. The following year they marched against the city of Rome. The tale is told that they were stopped from robbing and burning Rome by Pope Leo the Great. In any event, Attila died, a plague killed many of the army, and the Huns left Italy.

Scattered and fleeing before the Huns, the trickle of Germans into the Roman Empire became a flood. The first peoples to overpower the Romans were the Visigoths—West Goths. The Visigoths had moved from their Baltic homes to the shores of the Black Sea around 200 A.D. There the Huns swept down on them. The Visigoths fled across the Danube into the eastern portion of the Roman Empire.

In 378 the Visigoths and Romans fought at Adrianople, north of Constantinople. The Visigoths won and continued to wander and plunder in eastern Europe. They moved west and settled an area in southern Gaul. Eventually they moved into Spain and added much of this country to the land they ruled.

Many other Germanic peoples moved into Europe. The Romans had neither the confidence nor power to stop them. A German leader, Odoacer (OHD-uh-way-suhr), removed the co-emperor from Rome in 476. This date is used to mark the end of the Roman Empire in the West. The Ostrogoths—East Goths—then moved into Italy. Under

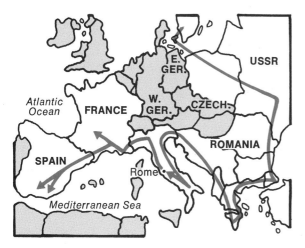

Invasions of the Visigoths, c. 300s-500s A.D.

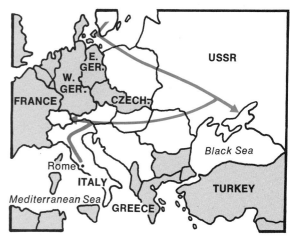

Invasions of the Ostrogoths, c. 300s-500s A.D.

their king, Theodoric (thee-AHD-uh-rik), they governed Italy for a time.

Earlier, a group called Vandals had moved across Gaul and down into southern Spain, burning and looting as they went. In 429 they took land in North Africa. They built a navy and used it to capture and plunder Rome in 455. The word vandalism comes from their name.

The Angles, Saxons, and Jutes were Germanic peoples that raided from the shores of the North Sea to Britain. In the early 400s, after the Roman legions had been recalled to Rome, the king of Britain called upon these peoples for help against invaders. The Germans came to stay and eventually to rule the Britons. Two Scandinavian groups—Burgundians and Lombards—had reached and settled in southern Europe by about this time.

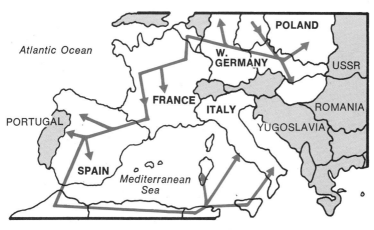

Invasions of the Vandals, c. 400s A.D.

CHANGES IN WESTERN EUROPE

The many years of invasion and rule by the Germanic tribes brought gradual changes in the social, political, and economic life of Europe. These new peoples were warriors, farmers, and herders. Their laws, customs, and social relationships were suited to this way of life. They did not need cities. They had not developed an economic and social structure based upon peaceful commerce.

During the period of invasion **the arts**, **crafts**, commerce, and education suffered. But as the groups settled down, a merging of Roman and Germanic ways took place. The systems of **feudalism** and manorialism that developed in medieval Europe were a blending of the customs of these two cultures.

During this period the Christian Church was emerging as a strong organized institution. In monasteries and churches many ideas and works of the past were preserved. Moreover, the Byzantine Empire, which rose in the East, preserved for later generations much of the best of earlier civilizations.

Chapter 4
The
Byzantine
Empire

When Constantine chose the site for the eastern capital of the Roman Empire, he chose well. Constantinople, formerly Byzantium, was in an important location. It lay along the Bosporus, a narrow waterway between the Black Sea and the Sea of Marmara, across from Asia Minor. The city was the crossroads of trade routes between Asia and Europe. Three sides of the city were surrounded by water. The fourth side was well-protected by strong walls.

Within a short time, Constantinople became so powerful that it surpassed Rome in importance. Although the empire in the West fell, the eastern provinces survived for another thousand years. The people of the eastern Roman Empire considered themselves Roman,

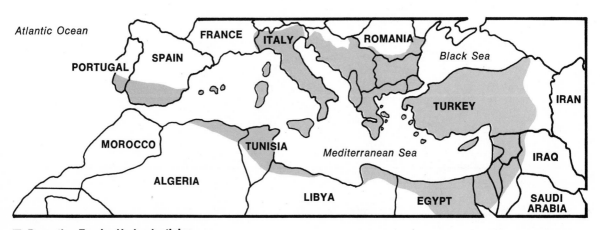

Byzantine Empire Under Justinian

but they were more Greek and Middle Eastern in their cultures. They spoke a form of Greek. Because they differed culturally from the Romans, they are referred to as Byzantines (BIZ-uhn-teens).

EMPERORS

Although the Byzantines eventually ruled a vast area, they were never able to regain the glory or possessions of the earlier Roman Empire. Under their many capable rulers, however, the empire prospered.

Justinian (juh-STIN-ee-uhn, 527-565) was probably the most noteworthy of these emperors. His wife Theodora was so influential in his decision making that she was considered co-ruler. Many portions of the divided Roman Empire were reunited by these two. Byzantine soldiers retook North Africa from the Vandals, Italy from the Ostrogoths, and the southern part of Spain from the Visigoths. Roman law from the time of Emperor Hadrian was resurrected, codified, and preserved for future generations.

Emperor Heraclius (her-uh-KLY-uhs, 610-641) recaptured the provinces that had been taken by the Persians in the Middle East. Basil I (867-886) and his successors held off the Arabs who had found

These mosaics of the Emperor Justinian and Empress Theodora were made in the 500s. What reasons can you give to explain why Byzantine rulers wanted to enlarge the empire?

codified:
arranged items in a system

425

unity and a mission in their conversion to Islam. Constantinople was besieged twice, but the Byzantines saved their capital both times. The empire, however, had shrunk considerably since the time of Justinian.

A century later Basil II (976-1025) began a series of conquests. He defeated the powerful Bulgarians, protected the poor, and encouraged trade. By the time of his death, Basil had restored the empire to almost the full glory of its ancient days.

A COMMERCIAL CENTER

Trade poured into the empire from everywhere. Furs, hides, ivory, gold, silver, spices, jewels, slaves, wine, and foods of all varieties came into the city daily from far and near. Constantinople ranked among the most prosperous trading centers of the world. One of the largest sources of income was from the manufacture of silk. Silk became so valuable to the economic life of the Byzantines that it was placed under government control.

Not everyone profited from the growing wealth of the empire, however. Throughout much of the life of the empire, the poor were made poorer and even enslaved by landowners and merchants. A small farmer's land would be seized if the taxes were not paid or the crops failed.

Some of the better rulers attempted to curb the growing power of the big landowners. But the growth of great landholdings and the complaints of the poor became a permanent part of the empire. The independence of many small farmers was lost, and this loss weakened the empire. It affected the morale of those from whom the emperor drew his soldiers.

RELIGIOUS ATMOSPHERE

The Byzantines, like many members of the Roman Empire, were Christians. And Christianity was an important part of their lives. From the emperor down to the most ordinary citizen, religious matters were discussed and debated as fiercely as politics. Often, issues were both religious and political in nature.

At first it was only natural for Christians to think of the bishop of Rome as holding a central position in the organization of the Church. Rome had long been the center of government power. The authority of the bishop of Rome, who was later called pope, was strengthened by the doctrine of Petrine supremacy. This doctrine states that the pope is the divinely appointed head of the Church. He is the successor of Peter, to whom Christ had given leadership of the Church.

Some early popes vigorously asserted their authority, at least in the western part of Europe. The Eastern Christians, however, did not accept the supreme authority of the Roman pope. They gradually began to look to both the patriarch and the emperor living in Constantinople as their leaders. The patriarch was the highest church official in the Eastern Empire.

The emperor was not considered divine, but he was supported by the divine. He was regarded by his subjects as God's agent on earth. He had more voice in religious affairs than the patriarch whom he selected. But there were some limits beyond which an emperor could find it unwise to go. A struggle over icons illustrates this point. Icons are pictures of the Virgin Mary, Jesus, and the saints. When one emperor tried to remove icons from Byzantine worship, he encountered such resistance that he was forced to restore them.

Christians of the eastern and western parts of the former Roman Empire drifted apart. As time passed, the eastern Christians began to refer to their church as the Eastern **Orthodox** or Greek Orthodox Church to distinguish it from the Roman Catholic Church. They used the Greek language instead of Latin in church ceremonies.

The Byzantines preserved and added their own comments to ancient Greek writings on science and philosophy. Eastern Orthodox monks did much of this work, as did Roman Catholic monks in the West. However, there was a difference. The Byzantines were actively using the knowledge the monks were recording. In the West the monks were not using the knowledge, only preserving it for later Europeans to build upon. Arab scholars were using the stored knowledge of the empire before Westerners knew the works existed.

In the 800s Byzantine missionaries went out to convert the Slavs and other peoples of eastern Europe and Russia. The Byzantine missionary brothers, Sts. Cyril and Methodius, invented an alphabet still used by the Soviets, the Serbs of Yugoslavia, and the Bulgarians. It is called the Cyrillic alphabet in honor of Cyril.

The depths of Byzantine religious feeling can be seen in the Church of Saint Sophia in Constantinople. It was built by the Emperor Justinian in the 500s and is a blending of Greek, Roman, and Middle Eastern influences. The exterior was designed simply except for its magnificent dome. The interior was decorated with paintings, gold leaf, and mosaics. After the Turks took Constantinople in 1453, they copied the style of this church in their own buildings.

Byzantine artists also fashioned exquisite icons for public and private worship. Byzantine artists and craftworkers worked in colored marble and ivory. They illustrated manuscripts with vivid miniature paintings and elaborate letters. They turned out a wealth of articles in gold, silver, and precious stones. Through their commercial system, Byzantine products were carried throughout Western Europe, Russia, and the Middle East and were often imitated.

FALL OF THE EMPIRE

Political differences between the popes in Rome and the Byzantine emperors existed as early as the 700s. The Byzantine emperor removed

Justinian built the church of Saint Sophia in Constantinople (modern Istanbul) to honor the patron of wisdom. Under the Ottoman Turks in the 1400s, it became a mosque— a Muslim place of worship. In 1935 Turkey made it a museum for Muslim and Christian art. Do you know of any other governments that have made places of worship into museums?

areas of the Balkan peninsula (modern Yugoslavia, Romania, Bulgaria, Albania, Greece, western Turkey) from the authority of the pope and gave them to the patriarch. Friction continued in later centuries as the Normans from France invaded southern Italy. These invaders took Byzantine churches and territory and placed them under the authority of the pope.

Then a dispute over doctrine arose between the two branches of Christianity. They could not agree over the interpretation of the Trinity—the threefold nature of God. In 1054, a **schism** (SIZ-uhm)—or formal division—split the two on this point. The breach still exists.

However, in the late 1000s, mutual concerns brought the Roman Catholic and Eastern Orthodox churches together briefly. The Muslim Seljuk Turks were making inroads into the Holy Land (modern Israel) and the Byzantine Empire. Beginning in 1096 and lasting into the late 1200s, Europeans went on a series of crusades to regain the Holy Land. The Byzantines joined in hopes of holding onto their own territory and regaining what they had lost.

However, in 1204 the Fourth Crusade went to Constantinople instead of the Holy Land. The crusaders plundered the city as though it were the stronghold of a hated enemy. The Byzantines regained Constantinople in 1261, but their power was considerably reduced. The empire declined as others around it increased in strength. In Asia Minor, the Ottoman Turks grew stronger. In 1453 Constantinople fell to the Turks and with it the Byzantine Empire. No one offered help. Constantinople is known today as Istanbul and is still part of Turkey.

Summing Up the Unit

Social Studies Vocabulary

Define: dictator; civil war; tradition; campaign; language family; institutions; customs; heritage; medieval; factions; hereditary; the arts; crafts; feudalism; orthodox; schism

People

Identify: Julius Caesar; Pompey; Marc Antony; Octavian (Augustus); Marcus Aurelius; Virgil; Tacitus; Diocletian; Constantine; Odoacer; Justinian; Theodora

Words

Identify: Punic Wars; patricians; plebeians; consuls; praetors; censors; equites; Pax Romana; Romance languages; Golden Mean; aqueducts; vandalism; Cyrillic alphabet

⌨ Questions

1. a. Who were the Latins? b. What peoples influenced their early development? c. How?
2. a. In building their empire, how did the Romans deal with other peoples? b. Compare their methods with those of the Athenian League.
3. How did the patricians hold their political control in Rome?
4. a. How did the plebians advance their rights as citizens? b. How did their power and social conditions improve?
5. Describe each of the four classes of Romans during the Republic and Empire periods.
6. What change made by Gaius Marius brought about military rule?
7. How did Caesar strengthen his control?
8. During the Pax Romana, what methods were used to keep the loyalty of Roman subjects and tie the people of the empire together?
9. a. Which Greek gods and goddesses were comparable to Roman ones? b. What Stoic ideas appealed to the Romans? c. What Stoic ideas did Epictetus stress? d. How did Marcus Aurelius put into practice what he believed as a Stoic?
10. How was the growth of Roman law similar to that of English common law?
11. How did Greek writers influence Roman ones?
12. In describing the Germans, how did Tacitus compare them with the Romans?
13. How did Roman buildings differ from Greek ones?
14. How did family life change from the early days of the Republic to the Empire?
15. What three forces shaped the pattern of European life after the Roman Empire declined?
16. Why hadn't Christianity been legalized before the Edict of Milan?
17. What reasons are given for the decay that weakened Rome's inner strength?
18. What changes in Western Europe were caused by the invasions and rule of Germanic peoples?
19. How did the loss of land by small farmers weaken the Byzantine Empire?

Discussion Topics

1. Julius Caesar was a strong leader who brought about needed reforms. But he aroused fear and envy. Is it good for a country to have so strong a leader? Why or why not?
2. The Romans were great warriors. What qualities of Roman greatness resulted from war? How did warfare weaken Rome? What can be learned from the history of Rome about the assets and liabilities of an emphasis on military power?

Project Ideas

1. List ten words of Latin origin.
2. Make a poster showing the most important achievements of the Romans.
3. Using outside sources, prepare a report on one of the following: Roman myths; Roman law; Roman government; Christianity in the Roman Empire; Byzantine art and architecture.
4. Make a poster showing elements of Byzantine culture.

Unit IV

The Medieval Scene

Some crusaders were more interested in what they could take for themselves than in fighting Muslims. Why were castles like this one necessary?

From the late 400s through the 1000s, Europeans struggled to survive as monarchs, knights, and raiders divided and subdivided Europe. They found their solutions in Catholicism, feudalism, and manorialism. For centuries the Roman Catholic Church provided stability and helped ordinary people to accept their hard lives. Feudalism and manorialism also provided stability. However, they limited the loyalty and interest of the people to a small piece of land.

After the 1000s, the crusades, trade, greater wealth, growing population, the rise of cities—all reduced the power of feudal lords. The period from around 1100 to 1450 is often described as the later Middle Ages. It may also be viewed as the preface to a new era, a time of awakening. An economically powerful middle class began to experiment with national assemblies and **parliaments**. Kings used intrigue and force to centralize the power of emerging nations in their own hands. There was movement, change, and inquiry in the air.

For several centuries after the fall of Rome the peoples that swept over the empire in the West continued moving across Europe. In the early Middle Ages there were no strong native rulers or national states to protect the people from the invaders. Both the rulers and the states arose gradually. Some arose from the invaders themselves and some in reaction to them.

Chapter 1
Stability
Amid
Instability

FRANKS

Among the last and most important of the Germanic peoples to come from east of the Rhine were the Franks. Under their king, Clovis, they established themselves as rulers of much of the area known as Gaul, later France. Clovis became a Christian in 496 and encouraged the conversion of his people. From this time onward close cooperation existed between the Franks and the Roman Catholic Church.

The Franks ruled for several centuries but eventually their kings neglected their duties. High officials in the palace took over the real functions of the king. One of the greatest of these officials was Charles Martel. In 732 he saved the Franks by defeating an army of Muslim Arabs and Moors at the battle of Tours. The Moors were North Africans who had converted to Islam and captured Spain. Martel had no title other than mayor of the palace. His son Pepin, however, took the title of king and ruled from 751 to 768.

At this time the Lombards were threatening to take much of Italy. The pope called on Pepin for help. Pepin marched into northern Italy and defeated the Lombards who were forced to return some of the lands they had seized. These lands became known as the Papal States, and were under the rule of the pope until 1860.

Pepin's son, Charlemagne (SHAHR-luh-mayn), extended the territory of the Franks until it included much of the western portion of the old Roman Empire. In 800 Pope Leo III crowned Charlemagne emperor of Rome. Once again an emperor ruled most of the West, but he was a Frank, not a Roman. This event marked the beginning of what became the Holy Roman Empire. The **nationality** of its rulers changed from Frankish to German, and the size of its territory varied considerably before its end in the early 1800s.

Charlemagne was able to hold his huge empire together by the strength of his personality and ability. He placed various parts of his empire under counts and dukes. He supervised them closely by sending royal investigators to check on them each year.

While Charlemagne lived the system worked, and it continued to work under his son Louis. But on the death of Louis, the empire was divided among his three sons. One son received the territory of approximately what is now Germany and another son received much of what is now France. The third son received the title of emperor and the territory of northern Italy, Belgium, the Netherlands,

Charlemagne's Empire

Luxembourg, and the rest of France.

This division brought constant war to Europe. The middle **kingdom** was eventually absorbed into the eastern part. The central government was weakened as local lords asserted their independence. The breakdown of authority was hastened by continued invasions from various directions. The most terrifying raiders were the Vikings.

VIKINGS

The Vikings were a group of Scandinavian people. By 900 the Norwegian branch of the Vikings had settled Iceland. In 930 the Icelanders drew up a constitution and created a **general assembly**. Under Eric the Red, Icelanders traveled to Greenland. Eric's son, Leif, sailed farther west to the North American coast. But the visit of the Vikings to America made no lasting impression. It was in England, Ireland, and on the continent that the Vikings had a lasting effect.

The Danes, another group of Vikings, conquered large portions of England during the 800s and 900s. The Anglo-Saxons resisted. Alfred the Great, king of the West Saxons (871-899), was able to unite most of England against the Danes. The Danes were able to hold only the eastern third of the country. Between 1016 and 1018, a Dane named Canute conquered England and ruled a northern em-

Invasions of the Vikings, c. 700s-1000s A.D.

HIC EXEVNT CABALLI DENAVIBVS · ET HIC MILITES FESTINA VERV NT HE

pire that included Norway, Denmark, and England. His line did not last, and in 1042 a Saxon, Edward the Confessor, seized power.

By the early 900s another branch of the Vikings, the Normans, had settled a part of northwestern France along the Seine (SAYN) River. This area is known as Normandy. In 1066 Normans, led by William, Duke of Normandy—later called William the Conqueror—crossed to England. They defeated the forces of King Harold at the battle of Hastings and began their long rule of England. Over the centuries the traditions, languages, and customs of the Anglo-Saxons and the Norman French mixed and evolved into a new culture.

The Normans did not stop their conquests with England. In the 1000s they moved into the Mediterranean and formed the Kingdom of the Two Sicilies from southern Italy and the island of Sicily. This kingdom endured until the mid-1800s. The Normans also played a leading role in the conquest of Constantinople in 1204 and settled a few areas and islands along the Balkan peninsula.

The Vikings did not spare even Ireland. The Irish were Celts and were related to the early Britons. They had been converted to Christianity in the 400s by St. Patrick. Under the leadership of the Church the arts flowered from about 700 to 1000. From Irish monasteries monks took Christianity and learning to Britain and parts of the European continent.

From around 800 to 1000 the Vikings fought over the land. They were eventually defeated and absorbed by the Irish. In the process Ireland became disunited. In the 1100s the Norman English took advantage of this and forced their rule on parts of Ireland. This began a conflict that still exists between English and the Irish.

By 1000 the beginnings of modern European states could be seen in faint outline. There were independent units called England, Scotland, Ireland, Wales, Denmark, Norway, and Sweden. The German Otto I had been crowned Holy Roman Emperor and extended his rule to include northern Italy. France had a king although in reality he governed only a very small portion of what is modern France. There were Christian kingdoms in northern Spain, but the Muslims controlled much of Spain.

On September 26-27, 1066, William the Conqueror and a fleet of 3,000 ships crossed the English Channel from Normandy to England. Within three months, William was king. Above is a section of the Bayeux Tapestry. According to legend, Matilda, William's wife, embroidered it.

This medieval woodblock print shows a church procession. Printing pictures from woodblocks was an important art form during the Middle Ages. The method was first developed by the Chinese in the 700s A.D.

THE ROMAN CATHOLIC CHURCH

Amid the puzzle of scrambled political authorities and the uncertainties of existence, there stood an unshakable institution in Europe—the Roman Catholic Church. It gave stability to the lives of medieval people and hope to their future. By the 1000s, throughout most of Europe the non-Christian was an oddity. And the rare person who denied Christian truths was considered a heretic.

The Church conditioned people to look at life very differently from the way the earlier Greeks and Romans had. The welfare of the soul became of greater importance than the body. This was shown in the medieval acceptance of the troubles of earth. Life on earth was a period of testing and waiting, a preparation for a better life after death. Because of this attitude, the early Middle Ages was an age of acceptance rather than doubt. People endured rather than rebelled. Most did not question their short life span, their poor living conditions, the feudal system, and **secular** or clerical authorities.

ORGANIZATION As Christians increased in numbers, they set up an organization for their church. They followed Roman political divisions in governing their widely spreading churches and congregations. A local group of Christians became a parish. The bishop appointed a pastor to take care of it. The bishop himself governed a territorial unit called a diocese, which incorporated many parishes. Several dioceses were grouped within a **province**. At the head of the province was an archbishop who lived in the provincial capital. The position of cardinal grew out of the function of the early priests who served in the city of Rome. They became advisers to the bishop of Rome who later became known as the pope. After 1059 cardinals had the power to elect new popes.

As we have seen, through the doctrine of Petrine supremacy the pope possessed the authority of God on earth. During the Middle Ages strong and able popes molded the Roman Catholic Church. Pope Gregory the Great (590-604) expanded the membership of the Church. His missionaries converted the Lombards in northern Italy, the Anglo-Saxons in England, and the Visigoths in Spain. Leo III (795-816) asserted the political power of the pope by crowning Charlemagne emperor. The pope crowned the emperor, but the emperor claimed the right to confirm the election of the pope.

As in the eastern empire, politics began to play a large part in religious matters. In the 1000s Gregory VII forced the emperor of Germany, Henry IV, to do penance for opposing the pope's authority. Henry had to travel to Italy and stand outside the papal residence, barefoot and robed in burlap, for three wintry days. Innocent III (1198-1216) regarded kings and emperors as his subordinates.

The pope had weapons to enforce his power. Chief of these were excommunication and interdict. Excommunication was the cutting off of an individual from the sacraments of the Church. Fellow Catholics were told to avoid this person. Interdict was excommunication applied to an entire country or region rather than to an individual.

If punishment, or the threat of punishment, is to be effective, it must be fitted to time and circumstance. The Europeans during this period were very religious people. They feared that their souls would burn in hell forever if they died while excommunicated. And Europeans—whether nobles, merchants, or **serfs**—wanted no part of a life without the comfort of the Church. Consequently, the mere threat of these punishments was usually sufficient to bring the disobedient into line.

The cardinals, archbishops, and bishops came most frequently from the nobility while parish priests were peasants. However, an intelligent man of a peasant family could sometimes rise to a high position in the Church. The Church offered one of the few ways for sons of the lowly to become educated and gain power.

Because popes, cardinals, archbishops, bishops, and priests lived and worked in the world, they were known as secular clergy. Those men who chose to retire from the world and live in prayer were called monks. They lived in monasteries where strict rules governed their lives.

The monks had various duties besides prayer. They cultivated orchards, reclaimed swampland, and devised and used the best farming practices then known. They made clothes, tools, and leather goods. Some monasteries became famed for their wine and beer. Monasteries were often used as inns by travelers. They were also the charitable centers of Europe. From the monks the poor could get clothes and food.

The Benedictine monks, founded in the 500s by St. Benedict, were also a missionary order. They traveled over Europe trying to convert people to Christianity. In the 1200s two other religious orders were founded, known as Franciscans and Dominicans after their founders, St. Francis of Assisi and St. Dominic. The members of these groups, generally called friars, went into the world to minister to spiritual and physical needs and to make converts.

Women too founded and joined religious orders to lead lives of prayer or to do charitable work. Often the women's organizations followed the patterns established for monks. St. Clare, for instance, adapted for her own convent the rules her friend St. Francis had used for the Franciscans. Women also established hospitals, orphanages, and asylums. Some of the convents were schools.

During this period the Church and clergy became closely identified with education. Not all the lower clergy were poorly educated. Some were teachers and scholars. Monks, especially, kept learning alive in the Middle Ages. In the silence of monasteries, monks studied,

The room where monks copied manuscripts was called a scriptorium from the Latin word scribo, to write. In this print, the artist has also shown monks painting and designing a new church. Why was the work of copying important?

meditated, wrote, and copied what they thought to be the best of the ancient classics. By copying the works, they preserved them and also increased the number available for study. Nevertheless, it should be said that because of their preoccupation with spiritual affairs, medieval copyists destroyed ancient manuscripts they considered opposed to Christian teachings.

Monasteries began to collect documents and manuscripts. These collections eventually became libraries. The monasteries also began teaching students. During the early Middle Ages these libraries and schools were often the only ones to be found in most of Europe.

PROBLEMS OF POWER   As the Middle Ages wore on, some people began to question the Church. They did not usually doubt its teachings, but often doubted the rightness of the actions of some clergy. It was difficult to trust a bishop or cardinal who seemed more interested in advancing his own power and wealth than in spiritual matters. Some popes appeared to work only for the advancement of a particular king or the possession of a certain piece of land. The welfare of the Christian community appeared secondary.

FEUDALISM

Besides the Roman Catholic Church, feudalism and manorialism helped the people adjust to the **decentralized** life of medieval Europe. Feudalism was a political and military system. Manorialism was an economic system.

Charlemagne unified a great portion of Europe for a time. But after the division of his empire, local areas moved toward independence. Kings, queens, and nobles rose to power by seizing and giving away land as they wished. They granted landed estates called fiefs (FEEFS) to others in return for money and help in war. Sometimes small landholders, frightened by powerful neighbors, surrendered their land to a powerful, but friendly, landholder for protection. The holder of the fief was a **vassal**; the grantor of the fief was a lord. In reality the person who owned an estate could be a woman or a man. Daughters and widows could and did inherit property. Vassals, who could also be men or women, did not own the land. They only had use of it.

FIEFS   Over the years the legal use and possession of fiefs became hereditary, passing from father to son or daughter. In the case of clergy, possession and use of land remained under control of the clergy or a Church organization.

The name vassal was an honorable title. Theoretically, every noble was a vassal to someone above him or her. The ruler was the exception. He or she sat at the top of the feudal pyramid. Beneath them were lesser nobles and beneath them the many knights and ladies.

The grant of a fief was a contract that placed responsibilities upon both landholder and vassal. The holders promised to protect the vassal and to administer justice in cases where his or her judgment was necessary. The vassal promised to remain loyal and faithful to the landowner and to give aid when needed. This aid was usually military. Vassals provided and equipped soldiers for battle and paid their expenses while at war. Since military expenses were heavy, such aid was usually limited to a certain number of days per year. Should the lord be captured in battle, the vassal had to contribute to the ransom.

These obligations reflect the chief activity of the period—war. Little wars were constantly being waged to gain glory, to kidnap the rich for ransom, or to extend borders.

KNIGHTS   War was the pastime of men called knights, and a test of courage for their trainees called squires. A man did not inherit knighthood. He earned it. At an early age he became a page in his lord or lady's household. When he reached his teens, he became a squire and learned the use of arms. He was assigned as a servant to a knight whom he accompanied into battle. When the squire had proven himself in battle, he was knighted in a formal ceremony.

By becoming a knight a man did not become less human. Contrary

This Spanish woodblock print of an armored knight on horseback dates from the 1500s. Introduction of gunpowder in the 1300s in Western Europe made armored knights on horseback impractical. Eventually they were replaced by foot soldiers and rifles.

to the popular idea of chivalry, the touch of the sword did not change character or create abilities. A man did not suddenly become loyal to the death or unable to live without honor. The knight was a man of his times—times when strength of arms was more important than education.

When there were no real wars, the knights kept in shape by staging tourneys. These were warlike games in which two groups of knights battled. One of the favorite tests of strength was the joust. Two riders fought to unseat each other with lances. The knights also took pleasure in hunting.

MANORIALISM

By the 1000s much of Europe was divided into thousands of farming units called manors. Agriculture was the basis of the economic life of the Europeans at this time. The relationship between those who worked on the manor and the owner is called manorialism.

The vassal who held the fief lived in the main building of the manor. Sometimes it was a castle. In the early Middle Ages in England, the castle often was only a combination of earthworks and wood. Later the castle became a menacing-looking building of high, thick stone walls surrounded by a wide, deep moat. A drawbridge that was drawn up at night or during an attack was the only way across. The drawbridge led into the castle yard. Around the yard were castle buildings which included stables and rooms for knights, servants, and guests. The woman of the manor supervised the manor house as well as educated her sons and daughters. When her husband was away or if she inherited the estate, she supervised the entire manor.

Around the manor in scattered communities lived serfs. Serfs were not slaves. They were bound to the manor under a general set of customs with obligations placed on both serf and fiefholder. Serfdom was passed from father to son but women worked in the fields along with the men. There were at all times some free men and women who had their own small bits of land.

A typical manor included a mill to grind grain, a central oven, a blacksmith shop, pasture land, and fields. Surrounding this settlement was often a forest that separated the manor from the outside world. These forests often harbored outlaws. By the 1100s manors were usually self-sufficient. They bought little from the outside world except salt, iron, and stones for the mill. Sometimes the landholder might purchase luxury items such as spices or fine cloth. But these cost money and even nobles had little ready money.

The homes of the serfs and their families were one-room huts with thatched roofs. The walls were sometimes wood, sometimes stone. If there was no fireplace, the fire was built on the dirt floor. Smoke filtered out through little openings in the roof. These people owned a few pots, perhaps a spindle and a loom, a bag of straw for a bed,

439

Monks decorated the manuscripts they copied. The first letter of a new section would have a picture painted through it. Above is such a letter from a copy, made in the 1400s, of the work Natural History *by the Roman naturalist, Pliny (23-79 A.D.).*

a wooden plank or two for a table, a few rough dishes and utensils. At night the serf and his family shared their hut with their animals.

The ordinary people ate black bread, cheese, occasionally eggs, cabbage, and a few other vegetables. In northern Europe serfs might drink beer, in the south sour wine. Nobles had the same diet, but with the addition of meat. At times wandering players, acrobats, and storytellers entertained in the district. There were also holidays, usually religious ones, when everyone might rest. But in general the life of a serf and his family was one of back-breaking toil.

RIGHTS AND DUTIES Serfs were assigned strips of land in the manor fields. The number of fields per manor varied from two to five according to the area and the kind of crops that were grown. Wheat was grown in the warmer climates and barley, oats, and rye in colder ones.

Within each field the landholder and each serf had several strips. The average size of a strip was about .4 hectare (one acre). Each year one entire field was allowed to remain unplanted while the others were planted with spring and autumn crops. Thus, in a three-field system, every third year one field was left to regain its fertility.

In addition to the cultivated fields, there was also common land on the manor. Everyone could use the meadows for grazing cattle and could gather wood from the forest for fuel and building purposes.

Besides their own land, serfs were required to cultivate the land assigned to the landholder. In addition, serfs were obliged to pay dues—grain, ducks, chickens, a pig, or other farm goods—depending upon the custom of the particular manor. In later centuries a fixed sum of money was required. The landholder also demanded fees for the use of the village bake oven, mill, winepress, brewery, and blacksmith shop.

The workers on the manor did have a certain degree of security, however. They would continue to farm the land no matter to whom the fief was given. Also among landholders there was the idea of noblesse oblige (noh-BLES uh-BLEEZH)—high rank and high birth carry with them an obligation to deal honorably with those of lower rank. Landholders usually accepted their responsibility toward the people of their manor. They fed them in times of **famine**, protected them during wars, helped them in sickness, and supported them in old age—although it should be noted that the average life span was short.

The later Middle Ages saw political, economic, and social change in Europe. The growth of cities, trade, wealth, **capital**, and the development of banking began to change the manorial and feudal systems. Change in terms of political rights was much slower in coming, but England was taking steps in that direction. And the face of Europe was changing. Slowly the fragments of a shattered Roman Empire were being pulled together into new national states.

Chapter 2
Changing Times

GROWTH OF COMMERCE

Trade did not cease entirely after the fall of the Roman Empire. Some merchants and peddlers risked the dangers of robbers to travel from manor to manor to sell goods the manors could not produce. Frequently a market town served several manors.

There was also the yearly fair. Sometimes the fair lasted for a few days, sometimes for several weeks, depending upon the time and place. Merchants came from far and near to display their goods. People from the manors and the surrounding neighborhood came to look, to admire, to haggle, and to buy. The fair was also a time of festivity. Acrobats and tumblers performed, plays were given, music was played, and a holiday mood prevailed.

Beginning in the 1100s the pace of trade steadily increased. As sea and land routes expanded and became safer, more traders dared to travel them. One of the reasons for this expansion of trade was the crusades.

This broadsword once belonged to a crusader. Broadswords were double-edged and longer than the old Roman swords.

THE CRUSADES The crusades began as military expeditions to free the Holy Land from the control of the Seljuk Turks. In the 600s Arab Muslims had taken Palestine from the Byzantine Empire. But Islam preached tolerance toward Christians and Jews so the Muslims permitted them to visit and live in Palestine.

Years later the Seljuk Turks from Central Asia invaded and conquered much of Asia Minor and the Middle East. These Turks had been converted to Islam but did not practice tolerance. When the Turks threatened Constantinople itself, the Byzantine emperor asked Rome for help. Pope Urban II responded in 1095 by urging a crusade against the Turks in the Holy Land. Many Europeans answered the call.

People became crusaders for various reasons. They were told that if they were killed in battle their sins would be forgiven and they would go directly to heaven. Debtors had their debts cancelled. Criminals were pardoned. Others thought of the riches they might obtain. Still others were attracted by the promise of adventure.

There were eight crusades between 1096 and 1270. They ended without finally achieving their purpose. By the late 1200s the crusaders had been driven from all the areas in the Holy Land they had taken. The crusades, however, had certain lasting effects which the crusaders had not foreseen when they set out with the cry "God wills it!"

The crusades may have speeded the movement of people to towns. Some feudal lords began to sell special privileges to towns under their control in return for money and equipment to outfit soldiers. The crusades did provide some impetus to the growth of a middle class and further reduce the power of the nobles. The crusades gave Europeans a better knowledge of geography and stimulated their spirit of adventure. Through their contacts with the Byzantines and Muslims, Europeans came to realize that there was much that they did not know.

NEW TRADE ROUTES Many European trading centers were pushed to the limit to furnish supplies for the crusaders. The cities of Italy—Venice, Genoa, Pisa and others—provided ships to transport many of the crusaders to the Middle East. The ships returned filled with drugs, perfumes, spices, jewels, silk, dyes, and other products which the Europeans gradually came to value. The Venetians built great merchant fleets and sent them to England and Flanders carrying Eastern goods. The merchants of Genoa, Pisa, and other Italian cities roamed the Mediterranean and elsewhere with their cargoes.

On the shores of the North and Baltic seas, cities such as Hamburg, Lubeck, and Bremen grew prosperous and powerful through trade. In the latter part of the 1200s, the merchants of these cities established a **confederation** known as the Hanseatic (han-see-AT-ik) League. In time it grew to over 80 cities.

The confederation provided protection for merchants, supplied lighthouses, maps of harbors, and other navigational aids, and standardized weights and measures. The league sent its own **diplomats** abroad, had its own flag, and made treaties with other powers. The Hanseatic League continued into the 1700s when it declined in power and finally vanished.

Trade routes tied all parts of Europe together. Wool went from England to the cities of Flanders, northern France, and Italy to be woven into cloth and reexported. Fleets of ships took salt from the coast of France to the Baltic Sea and to Scandinavia where it was used to preserve fish for export. Wine was carried in great quantities from southern to northern Europe.

RISE OF BANKING   Trade led to the growth of banking. Business became increasingly complex and traders began traveling great distances for long periods of time. Letters of credit and documents of exchange—similar in idea to credit cards—became necessary so that traders could conduct their business more easily. Merchants also increased their wealth by lending money to kings, nobles, and Church officials. In return for financial help, merchants received special privileges and political favors. They also began to charge interest on the money they loaned.

This picture of Marco Polo leaving Venice is from an English manuscript of the 1400s. Polo set out for China about 1271. He did not see Venice again for 24 years. His book, Description of the World, *became an important guide in the 1400s. But during his own life, Europeans did not believe his tales. What attitude on the part of Europeans does this show?*

This Portrait of a Banker *was painted about 1530 by the Flemish portrait painter Jan Mabuse. How did the crusades promote the rise of banking?*

During the early Middle Ages the charging of interest was forbidden by the Roman Catholic Church. Moneylending, therefore, became one of the few occupations open to Jews. However, the growth of business and the need for capital was changing the Catholic Church's attitude toward moneylending. From around 1250 to 1450, groups of people began changing money from one currency to another, lending it, keeping it safe, and transporting it from one region to another. These groups became the first European bankers.

The greatest and earliest bankers were Italian. They emerged in Rome and other Italian cities, but perhaps the most famous of the banking cities was Florence. It was the home of many banking families—the Peruzzi, the Bardi, and the Cerchi among others. The bankers of Florence transported money for kings and popes. They kept money on deposit and made loans for commercial and political ventures. They issued bills of exchange payable elsewhere. The Florentine bankers laid the foundations for modern banking systems. From Italy the banking business spread to other areas of Europe. In the 1400s the Fugger (FOO-gur) family of Augsburg, for example, founded a financial empire of enormous prestige and wealth.

GROWTH OF TOWNS AND CITIES

The expansion of trade, wealth, and capital as well as population hastened the growth of towns during the later Middle Ages. Fourteenth-century towns and cities were usually small by modern standards. Populations ranged from 5,000 to 10,000 people. But even this relatively small number of persons found themselves packed tightly within the protecting walls of the city. Of course, cities such as Paris and London, which were very old, had many more people.

Townspeople solved the problem of space by building upward. They built their houses with four, five, and six stories. To gain additional space, each story was extended a little farther out so that the top floors of facing buildings almost met over the narrow streets. This gave the townspeople more space but it also made life hazardous for passersby. It was not uncommon for those living on upper floors to empty their garbage out the windows.

Most towns of the 1300s lacked sewers and drainage systems. Rotting garbage and other refuse were a breeding ground for disease. Drinking water was often polluted so city dwellers drank beer, ale, and wine. The fire department was a volunteer bucket brigade. It was not very effective. Once a fire started among the tightly packed houses, it quickly spread from one dwelling to another. There was also danger at night from robbers. The police were usually aged men who were of little help in a fight with a thief.

Yet life in the towns and cities was generally better than the serfdom of the manor. There were opportunities for advancement in the towns.

bucket brigade: a chain of people organized to pass buckets of water from a water source to a fire

Above is the Ponte Vecchio (Old Bridge) across the Arno River in Florence. During the Middle Ages, Florence prospered as the center of Europe's wool trade.

As towns grew in size, more services were required to meet the expanding needs of townspeople and those of the surrounding area.

GUILDS Shoemakers, tailors, embroiderers, masons, carpenters, goldsmiths, silversmiths, weavers, spinners, bakers, and other craftworkers responded to the growing needs. As their numbers increased, they began to organize into guilds. The membership of a guild included anyone working in the craft—women as well as men. Some guilds were made up exclusively of women. Women exercised great economic and social independence at this time; they could own and dispose of property as they wished.

Guilds fixed wages, hours, working conditions, and even the price that could be charged for products. They disciplined members who violated rules. Guilds also acted as welfare agencies. In time guild members developed high standards of excellence and full membership was reserved to experts known as masters. Those who wanted to

This tapestry showing the legendary Semiramis, Queen of Babylon, was made in Flanders about 1480. Until about the 1500s, guilds included women. Some guilds were made up only of women.

be master workers had to undergo a long period of training. There were also merchant guilds which regulated and protected the general trade of the town.

NEW PRIVILEGES   Gradually the people of the growing towns and cities obtained greater liberties and privileges from the one who ruled them. Often they bought these privileges with their new wealth. At times they took them by force.

Sometimes rulers granted privileges to cities because of their service. In Spain, for instance, the rulers of Leon and Castile granted special charters to cities that protected the frontiers against the Moors. During the 1200s and 1300s there were a number of such self-governing cities in Spain—Madrid, Barcelona, and Seville among them.

Around this time townspeople in France, Germany, and England were also gaining freedom from feudal control. They gradually were released from a number of obligations, including payment of feudal dues. They gained the freedom to buy and sell as they chose. They could organize their own courts of law. A number of towns, like those in Spain, gained the right of **self-government**. The type of government varied from city to city. It ranged from rule by a few wealthy merchants to government by elected officials. Often the privileges enjoyed by the people of the city extended into the neighboring countryside.

THE MIDDLE CLASS

With the development of cities a new and powerful social group arose.

It became known as the Third Estate or middle class to distinguish it from the other two estates or classes: the nobility and the clergy. The power of the middle class was centered in the cities and founded on its new freedoms: knowledge and wealth. Representatives of the new middle class were received at royal councils and gained a voice in assemblies, diets, and parliaments.

In 1302 Philip the Fair of France invited town representatives to an assembly called to gain support for him in a dispute with Pope Boniface VIII. The king had claimed the power to tax the clergy. This was the first meeting of the Estates-General of France. It was also the first time that people other than French nobility and clergy took part in an assembly of national importance. During this period representatives of cities began to appear in the diet or Reichstag (RYKS-tahk) of Germany, in the Parliament of England, and in the Cortes of Castile.

dispute:
disagreement

The primary reason that the rulers requested middle-class representatives at these meetings was money. Kings and queens needed money. One way to raise it was through taxation and grants. Clergy and nobility were traditionally exempt from taxation. However, the middle class owned property that was subject to taxes. In return for agreeing to requests for funds, the middle class began to require additional privileges and rights from rulers.

By 1357 middle-class power had reached the point where the ruler of France was forced to accept proposals which gave the middle class equal power with others in government. But this was the peak of French middle-class political power. From the 1400s through the 1600s the Third Estate gradually declined in influence. The king was becoming all-powerful.

CENTRALIZATION: FRANCE

During the 1400s French kings were attempting to secure their throne and expand their rule. They had an especially hard task because feudalism was very strong in France. In addition, French kings found themselves fighting both the English and their own nobles.

From 1337 to 1453 the English and the French fought a series of wars which together are known as the Hundred Years' War. The fighting stemmed chiefly from English claims to the French throne and French territory. In 1337 the English king, Edward III, formally claimed the throne of France and sent an army to Normandy. The French refused to acknowledge this claim.

During the early part of the war, English armies made great gains. At the battle of Crecy (kray-SEE) in 1346, gunpowder and English foot soldiers with longbows routed the armored knights of the French. The fighting ability of armored knights on horseback was ending.

During the course of the war chaos and disorder spread over France. It was also the time of the bubonic plague, or Black Death, which struck down millions in England and on the Continent.

447

After the battle of Agincourt (AJ-uhn-kohrt) in 1415, Henry V of England was granted the French crown. But upon his death in 1422 war broke out again. At first the English seemed successful. Then, in 1428 the French gained courage and unity behind a girl called Joan of Arc. She had been led, she said, by visions and voices telling her to drive out the English. Under her leadership the French began to win. She was captured by the English and burned at the stake as a heretic in 1431. But by this time the French under Charles VII (1422-1461) were able to throw out the English.

Joan of Arc who lived in the 1400s provided the subject for this portrait done in the 1800s. Which of Joan's qualities might have moved an artist to paint her?

The French state became more strongly centralized than ever under the next king, Louis XI (1461-1483). Control of much of France passed from the nobles to the crown. By the time of his death, Louis had increased the size of France and greatly strengthened the position of the king.

WIDER REPRESENTATION: ENGLAND

This centralization of power in the hands of the king was not the trend in England. The story begins with the conquest of Anglo-Saxon

England by William the Conqueror, Duke of Normandy, in 1066.

William imposed his own type of feudal system on England. He took away much of the land that had belonged to Anglo-Saxon nobles and gave it to his personal followers. However, he did not completely trust these nobles. The manors he gave them were widely scattered. William also required that the nobles take an oath of allegiance to him. Decentralization of authority was basic to the feudal system, but the new Norman ruler wanted as much power as possible in his own hands.

William's successors continued to try to lessen the power of the nobles. Henry I (1100-1135) began to pay his officials salaries which made them more dependent upon him. He also established a royal court and a treasury which audited the accounts of the kingdom. Henry established one system of law for all his subjects. It incorporated much from both Anglo-Saxon and feudal customs and practices.

WRITS, JUDGES, JURIES   Henry II (1154-1189) continued to improve the processes of the law. He made writs—written orders in the king's name—available to his subjects at a moderate price. These writs made it possible to bring cases into royal courts for inquiry and judgment. Many major crimes were declared offenses against the king's peace, and the offenders were tried by royal judges.

Henry II sent judges into the countryside to try cases. Judges were assigned to hold court along regular routes at regular times. They were called circuit judges. That name is still used in the United States.

To assist the judges in uncovering cases, the king appointed juries in each district. These juries consisted of respected persons who gave the judges the names of individuals they thought had committed crimes. Today in the U.S. we have grand juries that similarly decide whether or not there is sufficient evidence to bring a person to trial.

The king also gave authority to a jury of 12 men to function as sworn witnesses to the facts in cases concerning land. This is the origin of the jury system. In time juries came to be used to decide criminal cases. The jury is now a fixed institution in British and U.S. courts. The replacement of private feudal law by the king's law assisted in the breakdown of English feudalism. The feudal system was dying but not the power of the nobles. Their role was merely changing.

MAGNA CARTA   Henry II was succeeded by his son, Richard the Lion-Hearted (1189-1199). During most of his reign Richard was out of the country fighting against the French and later against the Turks in the Middle East. Richard's brother, John, followed him on the throne (1199-1216).

King John aroused the anger of his nobles by trespassing on their rights. They organized against him and on June 15, 1215, at a place called Runnymede, they forced him to sign a document known as the Magna Carta (mag-nuh KAHRT-uh), or Great Charter.

In its main provisions King John promised: that he would not impose

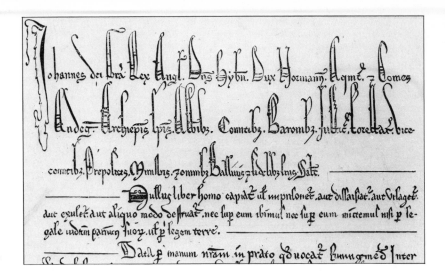

This is a section of the Magna Carta. *What rights did this charter give the English? Why was it unusual?*

unusual taxes without the consent of his council; that the city of London could keep its old privileges; that no free person could be imprisoned, banished, or deprived of property unless it was the judgment of a jury of peers or equals; and that he, the king, must give justice to all.

The Magna Carta also guaranteed various personal rights of English men and women, mostly in the noble class. However, its importance for future people lay in its definition of the king's power. The king was not above the law. He could be forced to obey it.

DEVELOPMENT OF PARLIAMENT   John's son, Henry III (1216-1272), also antagonized the nobles. He appointed foreigners, mostly Italian and French, to high positions and made great financial demands on the nobility. The nobles rebelled. They gained control of the king's council and appointed a committee that issued the Provisions of Oxford. This document surrounded the king with a council of 15 nobles and required him to accept their advice. They called this council Parliament and declared it should meet three times a year.

When Henry failed to fulfill his agreements, civil war broke out. In 1264 the barons under Simon de Montfort (MAHN-fuhrt) defeated the king, and a new government was established under de Montfort. In 1265 he held an assembly which included the great lords, clergy, knights, and burgesses, or representatives, of the towns. Two knights represented each county, and the more important towns sent two burgesses.

The knights were the **rural** ruling class. They had become moderately well-to-do landowners who were midway on the feudal social scale. For years they were of great help to the kings and fiefholders in the local areas where they lived. Starting about 1254, they began

450

to participate in assemblies dealing with national matters, especially financial matters. From that time onward it became customary to invite them to the assemblies. The assembly of 1265, however, was the first one to which representatives of towns were invited. The growing influence of towns in national affairs was now recognized in England as it was elsewhere in Europe.

As the 1300s and 1400s moved along, the kings were forced to call more and more upon Parliament for money. Money was needed to govern and wage war. The members of Parliament learned to use this need as a bargaining weapon.

As they found their interests moving closer together, the knights and burgesses began to work together. They started meeting away from the lords and high clergy. This happened as early as 1332. Thus the Parliament of England slowly came to be divided into the House of Commons, where the knights and burgesses met, and the House of Lords, for the nobles and high clergy. This division still exists. However, over the centuries the Commons has become the stronger of the two groups.

OTHER KINGDOMS

During this time strong kings were developing in other parts of Europe. The Moors were slowly being pushed out of the kingdoms of northern Spain. In 1469 the marriage of Ferdinand of Aragon and Isabella of Castile brought these two kingdoms together in the fight against the Moors. The last Moorish stronghold fell in 1492. Shortly afterward Spain was united under a line of strong rulers.

Portugal also came to be governed by able rulers. In Scandinavia, Sweden and Denmark became separate kingdoms. Norway had been a separate kingdom since about 900. During the 1300s it was united with Denmark. In 1814 as a result of the Napoleonic Wars it was given to Sweden. From the mid-1100s until 1809 Finland was part of Sweden. In 1809 the Russians were powerful enough to take Finland. It remained a grand duchy under the rule of the czar until 1917 when the Finns rebelled.

In central and eastern Europe there was the Holy Roman Empire. Its emperors were elected by the archbishops and rulers of four of the more powerful German-speaking states. The empire was roughly the central and eastern sections of Charlemagne's former empire.

But it was not unified. Until the 1800s the empire remained a league of independent German-speaking states and northern Italy. The title of Holy Roman Emperor carried great prestige but little real power. There were always quarrels and disputes between the emperor and the pope.

Some emperors were constantly meddling in northern Italy and arousing the suspicions of the pope. This was the case in the reign of Frederick Barbarossa (1152-1190)—known as Red Beard—and that of his successor, Frederick II.

■ Holy Roman Empire, c. 1000

Chapter 3

Artisans, Artists, and Philosophers

This stained glass window called Holofernes Crossing the Euphrates *dates from 1246. According to the Book of Judith in the Bible, Judith killed Holofernes, a Babylonian general, in order to save her people, the Hebrews.*

The works and thoughts of medieval people very much reflected the world in which they lived. Many of their creations were works of the hands. Often religion was the source of their inspiration. Gothic cathedrals, plays based on the Bible, and philosophical thought are some examples of medieval creativity. But there was also a lighter side as shown in the poetry, romances, and music of the time.

LANGUAGES AND LITERATURE

Throughout the Middle Ages, Latin was a spoken language in Europe. It was used by the Roman Catholic Church, schools, and educated people. Much of the literature of the time was written in Latin. This literature often dealt with religious subjects. But poetry and tales that were secular—nonreligious—in content and tone were also written in Latin.

Latin, however, was the language of only the educated. The ordinary people spoke **dialects** of various tribal languages. During this period national or **vernacular** (vuhr-NAK-yuh-luhr) languages were developing. French, Spanish, and Italian came into being. They were based largely on a corrupted form of Latin. German, the Scandinavian languages, and English were also developing.

Some of the earliest examples of European literature composed in the vernacular appeared during the Middle Ages. Among these are *Beowulf*, an Anglo-Saxon poem of the 900s, and the Norse sagas of the 1100s. There were also the French *Song of Roland* which dates from the 1100s and the Spanish *Poem of the Cid* from the 1200s.

Romances—tales in prose and poetry in the vernacular—were also written during this period. In England, some of the most popular were about King Arthur and his court. Tales, poems, and songs dealing with chivalry were especially pleasing to lords and ladies who identified with these themes of adventure. But the rising middle class were delighted with works which satirized their rulers. The tales of Reynard the Fox poked fun at chivalry and were very popular with them.

The main dramatic forms of the medieval period were religious in nature. These were the mystery, miracle, and morality plays. Mystery plays first appeared about the early 900s. They were based on stories from the Bible, both the Old and New Testaments. The plays from the New Testament were usually about Christ. In the beginning mystery plays were acted by the clergy and were presented in churches. Later, musicians' guilds staged them.

Miracle plays date from a somewhat later period. They dealt with the lives, miracles, and martyrdoms of saints or with the life of the Virgin Mary. Although miracle plays were first presented by the clergy, later the guilds may have performed them. Like mystery plays, miracle plays were a casualty of the different tastes of the Reformation and the Renaissance.

About the beginning of the 1400s a new form appeared—the morality play. In these plays, the characters are abstractions such as Vice, Riches, Faith, Charity, or Death. For example, in *Everyman*, the most famous morality play, when Death comes for Everyman, he seeks help from those whom he considers his friends, including Riches. They all refuse to go with him. At last he calls upon Good Deeds, who is weak through long neglect. Good Deeds agrees to go with Everyman and be his guide. In England of the 1500s the morality plays were enlarged, became more elaborate, and influenced some Elizabethan dramatists.

Beginning around 1090, a group of poets and singers flourished which provided almost the only music and literature not religious in nature. They played for the nobles who were their patrons. In southern France, northern Italy, and northern Spain, these poet-singers were called troubadours (TROO-buh-dohrs). In northern and central France trouveres (TROO-verz) were writing and singing similar material. During the same period and later, in Germany, the minne-singers (MIN-ih-sing-uhrs) were popular.

These poet-singers wrote and sang of love, war, and politics. They enjoyed a freedom of speech surprising for the period. The decline and eventual disappearance of the troubadours was the result of religious persecution in the 1200s.

Playing cards like this one first came into use in Europe in the 1200s. This one dates to about 1440. Lancelot was a knight in King Arthur's court. Can you explain how interest in a subject such as knights might become the basis of works in many art forms?

453

GOTHIC ARCHITECTURE

Prior to 1100, Europeans imitated the Roman style of architecture. They built churches, palaces, town halls, and houses with thick walls, narrow windows, heavy pillars, and rounded arches. The windows were small and few because the builders feared that too many windows would weaken the walls. The walls would not be able to withstand the weight of the roof and the building would collapse. This architecture—known as Norman in England and Romanesque on the continent—gives a general impression of heaviness.

But between the mid-1100s and 1500, the northern Europeans developed a style of architecture that became known as Gothic. This is the name the Italians of the later Renaissance gave it. They felt that the design was barbarous like the Goths or northern Europeans who had designed it. According to the Italians, the northern Europeans

Throughout the Middle Ages, the Roman Catholic Church dominated the religious and cultural life of Western Europe. Its teachings and beliefs were expressed in music, painting, plays, and architecture. This Gothic cathedral was built in the 1200s in Chartres, France.

had corrupted the classical Greek and Roman styles. Regardless of the Italians' dislike, Gothic buildings have an air of lightness, spaciousness, and a sense of soaring about them.

Gothic buildings had steeply slanted roofs and tall spires. The walls were higher and narrower than those of Roman buildings. These walls were braced on the outside by pointed stone arches called flying buttresses. These braces enabled the walls to withstand the outward thrust from the weight of the roof.

Another characteristic of Gothic architecture is the size and number of windows. Very often Gothic buildings, particularly later ones, appear to be mostly glass with very little stonework. Church windows began to be made of stained glass. Small pieces of colored glass were fitted together to show Biblical stories and lives of saints.

Statues of saints adorned the inside and outside of the churches. Contrasted to them were grotesquely carved devils and creatures called gargoyles. These were used as spouts to carry rainwater from the roof.

With the coming of the Renaissance, classical Roman and Greek forms were revived. Buildings in the Gothic style were no longer built.

SCHOOLS AND UNIVERSITIES

The number of people who had the opportunity to study during the Middle Ages gradually increased over the years. In the early period, Alfred the Great of England and Charlemagne provided schools for the wealthy. After the 1000s schools became more commonplace. Girls and boys attended them together in some areas. The schools were generally associated with religious institutions such as cathedrals, monasteries, and convents.

The early education of a student centered on the study of the seven liberal arts: Latin, rhetoric, logic, arithmetic, geometry, astronomy, and music. After the 1100s students could go on to a university if they had the ambition, will, and money. Universities began as guilds of students and their teachers who banded together to gain and protect their rights and privileges. Among the best known universities were those of Bologna (buh-LOHN-yuh) and Salerno in Italy, Oxford in England, and the University of Paris in France. Bologna specialized in law, Salerno in medicine, and both Oxford and the University of Paris in theology and the liberal arts.

In the next 400 years, at least in Italy, women began to attend, take degrees from, and teach at universities. There is evidence that women lectured in Spain during the rule of Queen Isabella. Even if women did not attend universities, their education was not neglected. They were educated in convents and by tutors. Women of the noble class often taught their children, and a number of women like Catherine of Genoa (1447-1510) were philosophers and scholars.

This stone monster called a gargoyle overlooks the city of Paris from atop Notre Dame Cathedral.

455

In the universities students might continue their studies of the liberal arts or work in the areas of medicine, law, and theology. By the 1300s students could receive degrees: bachelor's, master's, and if the area was theology, medicine, or law, a doctorate. The study of medicine was not greatly advanced until the later Middle Ages. Because of the deep religious beliefs of the times, theology was considered the most important of subjects, and many students studied it. Theology and law were of great advantage to the ambitious student. Both could lead to a career in the service of the ruler or the Church.

THINKERS

In the latter half of the 1100s, the works of Aristotle and the writings of the Muslims on philosophy, theology, and medicine became available to the Europeans. These created great controversy. Some medieval philosophers began to wonder about their long-cherished ideas and beliefs.

During the Middle Ages philosophy and theology were closely related. The combined study of the two led to the system of philosophy called scholasticism. The two who were most prominent in founding this philosophy were the Dominican friars Albertus Magnus and Thomas Aquinas (uh-KWY-nuhs). Albertus Magnus attempted to reconcile and combine the philosophy of the Greeks and Muslims with the **doctrines** of Christianity. Thomas Aquinas was his pupil.

Aquinas was convinced that the teachings of Catholicism were supported by reason. Acting on this idea, he wrote the *Summa Theologica* in which he showed the errors in Aristotle while pointing out the truths. He combined Aristotle's thought and Christian teachings. By his writings Aquinas made Aristotle acceptable and respectable to medieval thinkers.

There were other medieval philosophers, however, who did not believe that reason could be used to explain religious beliefs. Chief among these was William of Ockham. Ockham believed that universal truths existed only as ideas. They had no reality. Ockham believed that each question should be considered in its own terms, not as part of a universal truth. He was, therefore, in opposition to the followers of Aristotle. They looked for great general truths.

Roger Bacon, an English friar, disagreed with any reasoning that began by accepting something as true on the basis of authority or faith. He believed that experience was important. First one must prove by experimentation that an idea is factually correct. Then one can reason to a conclusion. This is the method that is used by scientists today. Through his own personal experimentation, Bacon made some startling predictions about the future. He foresaw the submarine, the mechanized ship, the automobile, and the airplane. They may not be today exactly as he imagined them, but he sketched the general outline of what was to come.

Thomas Aquinas believed that the teachings of Catholicism could be proven by reason. What elements of Aristotle's philosophy do you think appealed to Aquinas?

Summing Up the Unit

Social Studies Vocabulary

Define: parliament; nationality; kingdom; general assembly; secular; province; decentralization; feudalism; vassal; serf; confederation; treaty; self-government; dialect; vernacular

People

Identify: Clovis; Charles Martel; Charlemagne; Joan of Arc; William the Conqueror; Simon de Montfort; Thomas Aquinas; Roger Bacon

Words

Define: Papal States; heretic; parish; excommunication; interdict; secular clergy; monks; friars; manorialism; fiefs; noblesse oblige; guilds; writs; burgesses; troubadours; Gothic

⌕ Questions

1. Describe Charlemagne's method of power.
2. Where did the Vikings have the most lasting effect?
3. Name the modern states that were apparent by the year 1000.
4. How did medieval Roman Catholics view life differently than the early Romans and Greeks?
5. a. How did the medieval popes gain so much power and authority? b. Why were the Church and clergy closely identified with education?
6. How did the granting of fiefs help to determine feudal obligations between lord/lady and vassal?
7. Describe the rights and duties of serfs.
8. How did the crusades affect trade?
9. How did trade influence banking?
10. What factors hastened the growth of towns in the later Middle Ages?
11. a. How did guilds evolve? b. How did they help and protect their members?
12. a. How did town and city people gain greater privileges? b. What were the privileges?
13. a. How did the middle class gain power? b. How did they use this power?
14. How did the Hundred Years' War weaken feudalism and strengthen the power of the French monarchs?
15. How did the distribution of power between monarchs and nobles in England and France differ?
16. What role did English towns assume beginning in the late 1200s?
17. a. How did the English Parliament become divided into two houses? b. Name the houses.
18. How did the works and thoughts of the Middle Ages reflect the lives of the people?
19. a. Describe the main forms of medieval drama. b. What happened to each form?
20. What effect did the works of Aristotle and Muslim Arabs have on medieval Europeans?

Discussion Topics

1. The medieval Church conditioned people to accept the troubles of earth. How did this attitude support feudalism? How did feudalism encourage this attitude of acceptance?
2. While political power in Europe was becoming fragmented, the Roman Catholic Church was developing an organized administrative system headed by strong popes. How were these two trends related?
3. Latin was a living language in Europe throughout the Middle Ages. But its use in literature eventually gave way to vernacular languages. Why?
4. Feudalism was accepted because it offered protection, yet the chief activity of lords and vassals in the feudal period was war. How can warfare explain the rise and decline of feudalism? Consider the new weaponry introduced at the end of the period.
5. The crusades were an opening wedge for the end of the Middle Ages. How?

Project Ideas

1. Imagine you are a serf in the Middle Ages. Describe a typical day.
2. Using library sources, write a paper on one of the following: the Holy Roman Empire; guilds; knights; the Magna Carta; Gothic architecture; medieval literature.
3. Draw a map of a typical medieval manor.
4. Design a chart showing the relationships between people in the feudal system or in the manorial system.

457

Unit V

The Renaissance

Creation of the Stars and Planets *is one of 21 scenes from the Bible that Michelangelo painted on the ceiling of the Sistine Chapel in the Vatican.*

The period from around 1350 to about 1600 is usually labeled the Renaissance (ren-uh-SAHNS), which means rebirth. Some writers have described the Europeans of this period as being born again through their discovery of early Greek and Roman culture.

The Renaissance was an attitude of mind that was concerned with the art of living rather than the art of dying. This attitude encouraged creativity, inventiveness, and inquiry. This unit will deal with the arts and sciences of the Renaissance as well as with the religious upheaval of the period—the Reformation (ref-uhr-MAY-shuhn). The Reformation was an attempt at purifying the doctrines and practices of the Roman Catholic Church.

It should be remembered that names such as Middle Ages, Italian Renaissance, and Northern Renaissance are only handy labels. Some scholars view the Renaissance as a continuation of the Middle Ages. Others see it as a break with the old and a beginning of the modern. Still other scholars consider the Renaissance as a time of transition. Elements of the dying medieval era existed along with the first breaths of the modern age.

For centuries Europeans had quietly accepted the hardships of their lives as a preparation for life after death. By the 1300s, however, they were beginning to question this attitude. This was partly because of the rediscovery of the works of Greek and Roman philosophers. The early Greeks and Romans found beauty in humanity and believed that humans might find happiness on earth. The Europeans were attracted by this emphasis on the physical world. They began to discover this beauty and potential for happiness themselves. The Europeans did not lose their religious spirit. However, they started to believe that life on earth was important and good in itself.

As the Renaissance unfolded, this attitude of questioning and seeking increased in depth and intensity. Renaissance Europeans became convinced that a person was entitled to immediate satisfaction on earth. They centered their attention upon human wants and interests. For this reason they are described as humanists.

Chapter 1
Humanism

ITALY

The first humanists were Italian. The Italians had long been acquainted with the Byzantines and Muslims who had preserved much of the Greek and Roman heritage. The merchants of Venice, Genoa, and Pisa specialized in trade with them. These cities, as well as Florence and Milan, became so wealthy and powerful that they were almost independent city-states. There was no central government in Italy at this time.

Around the mid-1300s leaders of some of these city-states began to show an interest in art and literature. Along with some of the popes, they tried to outdo one another in obtaining Greek and Roman writings. Increasing numbers of Italians studied these ancient works with their attention to life on earth. Italian writings began to reflect this Greco-Roman influence. In their works many Renaissance writers criticized the excesses of the clergy and the conditions of society.

WRITERS AS SOCIAL CRITICS   One such writer was Dante Alighieri (DANT-ee al-uhg-YEAR-ee) of Florence. The first two sections of his *Divine Comedy* tell of an imaginary trip through Purgatory and Hell guided by the Roman poet Virgil. Many famous people are encountered on the journey. Dante tells their stories as a means of pointing out the vices of his times. The third section describes the poet's entrance into Paradise guided by an ideal woman, Beatrice.

Instead of following the practice of his time and writing in Latin, Dante wrote in his native tongue, the Tuscan dialect. (Tuscany is the area of Italy where the ancient Etruscans settled.) Gradually Italian writers began using the Tuscan language and it became the language of all Italians.

Other important writers of the time were Petrarch and Machiavelli. Petrarch (PEE-trark) who lived during the 1300s, is sometimes called

This Madonna and Child *is by Giotto. One of the earliest Renaissance painters, he is considered the most important artist of the 1300s.*

the father of humanism. He was a collector of old manuscripts, traveler, student of archaeology, and lyric poet. He was also a critic of the medieval viewpoint.

Niccolo Machiavelli (mak-ee-uh-VEL-ee) was a political philosopher. Italy of the early 1500s was divided and in disorder. Machiavelli decided that a ruler could use any means necessary to bring about peace and stability. He ignored morality and advised those who wanted power to seek it without concern for right or wrong. He expressed many of his ideas in *The Prince.* Machiavelli saw humans as they often actually are, rather than the ideal of how they should be. For many years he was a leading figure in the government of Florence.

ART AND ARTISTS While medieval artists had often produced their works as offerings to God, the artists of the Renaissance were often hungry for fame and material rewards. Although Giotto (JEE-aht-oh) worked with religious themes, he wanted all to know that the work was his, and he wanted good payment for it.

The new wealth of the period worked in favor of artists. The rich and mighty—popes, kings, nobles, and rich merchants—competed for their services. Artists were often richly supported and showered with official positions, money, and favors.

Some Renaissance artists continued to paint religious themes, but with a new approach. In their works they stressed the human qualities of people. Even the most spiritual ideas came to be expressed in terms of physical and worldly beauty. In this fashion, Fra Angelico depicted Biblical subjects and scenes from Christian tradition and teaching. Massacio (muh-ZAHCH-ee-oh) portrayed the drama of human emotional and spiritual life. One of his greatest works reflects the tragedy of Adam and Eve as they are driven out of the Garden of Eden. Raphael Santi has been called the perfect painter because of the harmony and balance of such works as *Madonna of the Chair* and *Sistine Madonna*.

Other Renaissance artists like Sofonisba Anguisciola (ahn-GWEE-shoh-lah) responded to the emphasis upon individuals and their worldly activities by painting portraits. They pictured church officials, kings, queens, nobles, and wealthy merchants and their families. The paintings were more than likenesses. They attempted to express the personalities of their subjects.

Many artists of the Renaissance found their inspiration in Greek and Roman art which was very realistic. They studied anatomy and learned to depict the human body in all its beauty. Some painted the gods and goddesses of Greek and Roman mythology. Botticelli (baht-uh-CHEL-ee) painted the *Birth of Venus* and portrayed the deities in springtime. Scenes of important contemporary events also interested Renaissance painters.

Botticelli painted Birth of Venus *over a hundred years after Giotto worked. Do you see any difference in style between the two men? Is the use of light different? Is one figure more life-like than the other? Since both men were Renaissance painters, how can you explain any differences?*

This is a sketch of a flying machine from one of Leonardo da Vinci's many notebooks. He was a scientist and inventor as well as an artist of unusual talent.

In that age of artistic greatness, none was greater than Leonardo da Vinci, Michelangelo, and Titian. Leonardo da Vinci (dah-VIN-chee) had many talents. His paintings such as *The Last Supper* and the *Mona Lisa* are widely acclaimed. He was also a natural scientist and inventor. He kept notebooks in which he sketched plants, animals, and inventions that ranged from two-level highways to airplanes.

Michelangelo (my-kuh-LAN-juh-loh) thought and worked in gigantic dimensions. Lying on his back he painted the story of the Creation on the ceiling of the Sistine (SIS-teen) Chapel in the Vatican. It took him four years to complete the painting. Michelangelo was also a sculptor. Among his works are the statues *David* and *Moses,* and, for a chapel of the Medici family, the figures *Night, Day, Dawn,* and *Twilight.* Michelangelo also designed the great dome of St. Peter's Cathedral in Rome.

Titian (TISH-uhn) is credited with having painted a picture a month for 80 years. He used vivid colors, and painted many subjects: madonnas, battles, nobles, merchants, and popes.

Around the 1400s, oil paints came into wide use. Until this time, paintings had been done chiefly with tempera—colored powder mixed with egg whites, milk, or other liquid. Tempera paints were applied to a surface which had been prepared with a coat of glue. The paints were almost transparent, and very beautiful effects could be achieved. But it was necessary to work quickly before the paints dried. Once the paints were applied, it was very difficult to make changes.

Oil paints, on the other hand, were very slow-drying. This made it possible for artists to work more slowly and carefully. Because oil paints were not transparent, mistakes could be painted over. The techniques of oil painting were developed in northern Europe but their use was common throughout Europe.

Renaissance artists experimented with new techniques. They wanted to give a three-dimensional quality to the flat surface of their pictures. They did this by the skillful use of colors and detail and by contrast between light and shade.

CLASSICAL ARCHITECTURE The architecture of the Renaissance followed classical lines. Architects were commissioned to design palaces and churches which reflected ancient Greek and Roman forms. As a result the buildings of this period show many Greek columns and Roman arches and domes.

The best known example of this style is St. Peter's Cathedral in Rome, which is the largest church in the world. Although Michelangelo designed the dome, Bramante (bruh-MAHNT-ee) and Palladio (puh-LAHD-ee-oh) designed the rest of the building. Palladio was the most influential architect of the Renaissance. Publication of his work *Four Books on Architecture* kept his influence alive for the next two centuries.

Above is a self-portrait of da Vinci done about 1512.

MUSIC   Since very little ancient Greek or Roman music existed to revive, Renaissance music continued to develop medieval forms. The most noteworthy contributions were in musical instruments and in composition. The violin and the harpsichord were developed and instrumental music became as important as vocal music. The oratorio —a religious drama set to music—appeared around this time. It combined vocal and instrumental music and foreshadowed modern opera.

Many composers were at work during this period but the greatest was Palestrina (pal-uh-STREE-nuh). An organist and choirmaster at the Vatican, his works were primarily religious.

St. Peter's Church in Rome dates from the 1500s and 1600s. What feature of Greek and Roman architecture can you find in this building? What brought about the Renaissance interest in ancient architecture?

IMPORTANCE OF PRINTING

The philosophy of humanism spread so widely during the later Renaissance because the Europeans had perfected the art of printing. The Chinese had first discovered the principle of printing in the 100s A.D. They carved their writings on blocks of wood which were then inked and pressed against silk or other material. In the 1000s movable type was invented in China. However, because of the many characters in the Chinese language, movable type was impractical at the time.

Europeans were still copying manuscripts by hand. This meant that very few books were produced. Also errors crept into works as they were copied again and again. In the 1440s, however, a German named Johann Gutenberg developed a method of molding individual letters

463

This woodblock print of the humanist Erasmus was done by Albrecht Durer. The top inscription gives the name of the subject, the artist, and the information that the painting was done during Erasmus' life. The date is 1526. The second inscription says, "His writings depict him even better."

from metal. The letters were arranged in a frame, then inked. A sheet of paper was pressed on them. These molded letters could be reused over and over. Gutenberg's metal type revolutionized book-making.

Printing presses were much faster and more accurate than hand copyists. At first, printed books were very expensive and only the rich could afford them. Eventually, however, printing made it possible to produce inexpensive books that appealed to a wide reading public. Printing contributed to the growth of **literacy**.

NORTHERN EUROPE

The Renaissance spread northward from Italy. By the 1500s it had reached across northern Europe. Some scholars believe that even without the knowledge of Italian writings, England, France, the Netherlands and other countries would have developed humanism. By the 1500s these countries had reached a degree of economic, social, and political growth that encouraged the rethinking of attitudes about life.

WRITERS   Erasmus (ih-RAZ-muhs), a Dutch scholar, was one of the greatest humanists. He believed that evil came only from ignorance and the human tendency to make mistakes. Erasmus was ever aware and respectful of the potential in humanity. He cited Jesus, Socrates, and Cicero among others as examples of the best in human nature. He traveled throughout Europe and taught at some of its finest universities. Erasmus criticized the laxity of the clergy. The title of one of his most famous works, In Praise of Folly, indicates his sense of humor and satire.

Erasmus also published a New Testament in Greek. It differed in some ways from the official Roman Catholic version in Latin called the Vulgate. These differences raised doubts in the minds of some about the accuracy of the official version.

In England, Geoffrey Chaucer (CHAW-suhr) wrote The Canterbury Tales. This is a collection of 25 tales told by pilgrims on their way to Canterbury. Although the works belong to the period considered the later Middle Ages, they are Renaissance in tone. Through descriptions of the pilgrims and their stories, Chaucer satirizes the clergy, the wealthy, and the code of chivalry. Chaucer wrote in Middle English, the form of English spoken at the time, rather than in Latin. Thomas More, also of England, criticized society in a work called Utopia. Utopia (yoo-TOH-pee-uh) means a place where society is perfect. The word utopian has come to mean an idea considered impossibly idealistic.

In France, Francois Rabelais (rab-uh-LAY) urged people to live naturally, joyfully, and honestly. In his novels, Rabelais created two giants, Gargantua and Pantagruel who lived life to the fullest. France also produced Michel de Montaigne (mahn-TAYN). The easy conversational style of his Essays has had considerable influence on world literature. Montaigne is considered the creator of the personal essay.

NATIONAL LITERATURE   By the 1500s popular languages had replaced written and spoken Latin. Although this vernacular literature was focused on and influenced by classical humanism, it was very nationalistic. Epics and dramas were especially suited to this theme. Foremost among these writers was Spain's Miguel de Cervantes (suhr-VAN-teez). In *Don Quixote,* Cervantes satirizes the ideals of medieval chivalry.

Although the Renaissance did not reach England until the 1500s, its spirit quickly captured the feelings of writers. By this time the Middle English of Chaucer had developed into the modern English with which we are familiar. This period in English history is known as the Golden Age of English literature or the Elizabethan Age, after Queen Elizabeth I.

Poetry blossomed during the Elizabethan Age with such poets as Edmund Spenser and John Donne. Spenser composed *The Faerie Queene* which celebrated Elizabeth's reign. Donne wrote metaphysical poetry—poetry that is concerned with philosophical problems such as matter and spirit. Some of his poetry was religious in nature. He influenced a group of contemporaries who wrote about the same subjects and who experimented with rhythms and stanza forms.

It was in drama, however, that Elizabethan literature reached its high point. Christopher Marlowe made a major contribution by adapting blank verse—unrhymed poetry—to drama. He is best known for his plays *Doctor Faustus* and *Tamburlaine.* Ben Jonson is remembered for his comedies and court masques. Masques are fanciful productions with music, dance, and elaborate costumes and scenery.

However, one playwright stands above all other English dramatists: William Shakespeare. No dramatist before or since has approached his scope, dramatic ability, inventiveness, or graceful use of the English language in his plays, songs, and sonnets. Among the many plays attributed to Shakespeare are tragedies such as *Hamlet, Othello, King Lear;* comedies, *Twelfth Night, Midsummer Night's Dream;* and histories, *Richard II,* and *Henry VI, Parts I-III.*

Historical plays were very popular at this time. Like ancient Greeks and Romans the Elizabethan English wanted to know about their earlier history. Eight of Shakespeare's ten historical plays deal with England between 1397 and 1485. The plays chronicle the rise of the house of Tudor, the royal family to which Elizabeth I belonged.

ARTISTS   The Renaissance also affected the artists of northern Europe. During the 1400s, the Low Countries produced painters who were noted for the detail of their work. Jan van Eyck created the delicately intricate Ghent altarpiece.

More than Italian artists, Low Country artists began to picture ordinary people and scenes from everyday life in their paintings. This is known as genre (ZHAHN-ruh) painting. Pieter Brueghel (BROO-

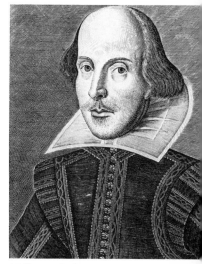

William Shakespeare is considered the greatest playwright in the English language, because of the variety and quality of his works.

Shakespeare's plays were performed in the Globe Theater (above model) and others like it. The theaters were adapted from the design of inn courtyards. These were, in fact, the first theaters.

guhl) the Elder is considered a good example of a genre painter.

Albrecht Durer (DYUR-er), Lucas Cranach, and Hans Holbein (HOHL-byn) the Younger are among the best known of the German painters of this era. Durer was noted for his engravings and wood cuttings. Cranach's work combined classical and religious elements and was greatly influenced by the Reformation. Holbein concentrated on portrait painting. He served at the court of Henry VIII of England where he portrayed many of Henry's wives. Levinia Teerling, a Flemish artist, is credited with painting one of the few known portraits of Elizabeth I.

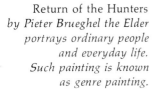

Between 1520 and 1600 there arose a branch of classical painting known as mannerism. By 1520 artists began to feel that art had reached perfection. Many of the younger artists tried to surpass the older established artists with new and different techniques. At times these techniques took unusual forms as the artists exaggerated and distorted shapes. Two of the most famous mannerist painters were Tintoretto and El Greco—the Greek.

Tintoretto created paintings that were full of energy and action. El Greco was born in the island of Crete, but worked in Italy and later in Toledo, Spain. His works show elongated forms and express a feeling of gloom and anguish. Many of El Greco's paintings were of a religious nature.

Return of the Hunters by Pieter Brueghel the Elder portrays ordinary people and everyday life. Such painting is known as genre painting.

Chapter 2
Science and Technology

These are instruments of Nicolaus Copernicus' time. On the wall is an astrolabe. To the right is an astronomical globe and to the left, a triquetrum, used for measuring altitudes in astronomy.

Renaissance people began to question their ideas about the world of nature and the physical laws which they believed governed the universe. They looked at the world with new awareness and asked new questions. The old answers were no longer satisfactory. For example, Leonardo da Vinci observed that plains were formed by soil washing down mountains to the lowlands. It seemed to him that long periods of time were needed to build up a plain. However, the majority of people of the time believed that the earth was only a few thousand years old.

Technology made great advances during this period. In addition to the printing press, Europeans gained a knowledge of geology and mining and improved shipbuilding, charts, and navigational instruments. These advances widened their horizons and stimulated them to even greater efforts to know themselves and their **environment**.

ASTRONOMY

Nicolaus Copernicus (koh-PUHR-nih-kuhs) was a Polish astronomer who studied in Italy. Because astronomical instruments were limited, astronomers used mathematics to help them form theories about the universe. Copernicus could not make his mathematics agree with the popular theory that the earth was stationary and the planets and stars revolved around it. Copernicus believed that the earth and other

popular: accepted by the general public

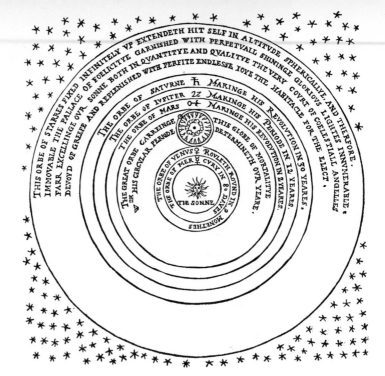

Copernicus did not publish his work, On the Revolution of Heavenly Bodies, *until shortly before his death. This woodblock print shows Copernicus' theory of the universe. How does it differ from that of the early Greek, Anaximander? What was the popular belief in Copernicus' day about the universe? Why?*

bodies moved around the sun. His publication of *On the Revolution of the Heavenly Bodies* in 1543 marks the beginning of the **revolution** in science.

The popular theory of the universe had first been stated by the Greek astronomer Ptolemy in the 100s A.D. His theory had been accepted for hundreds of years because it fitted well with the view of humans as the crowning achievement of creation. Because his ideas were so revolutionary, Copernicus delayed publication of his book for some years.

In the 1600s, Galileo Galilei (gal-uh-LEE-oh gal-uh-LAY-ee), an Italian, constructed a telescope and saw moons revolving around the planet Jupiter. His observations supported the theory of Copernicus. For publishing these **radical** findings he was brought before the Inquisition. The Inquisition was a Church court set up as early as the 1200s to discover, investigate, and prevent heresy. It operated at different times in different countries with varying degrees of brutality. Threatened by punishment, Galileo promised to remain silent about his observations.

Giordano Bruno, a Dominican monk, carried the ideas of Copernicus much further. In one of his books, Bruno claimed there were many suns in the universe. Each had several planets revolving around it. Bruno even suggested that these planets might be inhabited. He was burned alive for publishing this supposed heresy.

Two other astronomers of this period deserve mention. Tycho Brahe (TEE-koh BRAH), a Dane, made careful observations and measurements to determine the position of planets revolving around the sun. His assistant, Johannes Kepler, stated laws that explained the orbits of planets.

Because of expanding knowledge in the field of astronomy, the Julian calendar, which had been used since Roman days, was found to be inaccurate. In 1582 Pope Gregory XIII ordered that the calendar be set back ten days. Thus the new Gregorian calendar would correspond exactly with the solar year.

APPLIED SCIENCE

Mathematicians had long known about Roman and Greek arithmetic and geometry. They borrowed Arabic numerals and algebra from the Muslims. However, the late Renaissance saw much original work by Europeans in the areas of finance, warfare, weights, and measures.

Those working in physics and metallurgy in the 1500s were also interested in practical goals. Zacharias Janssen, a Dutch lensmaker, invented a compound microscope about 1590. As a result of his invention, telescopes became widely available.

Geography also made great advances. This was a result of Europeans' enthusiasm for overseas exploration and commerce. Gerhard Kremer, known as Mercator (muhr-KAY-tuhr), established a geographical laboratory and drafting institute at the University of Louvain. He invented maps using a projection or view of the world which still bears his name. Mercator also improved the quality of geographical instruments and maps.

LIFE SCIENCE

Medical science was held back to some extent by the so-called new learning of the period. Instead of relying on their own observations, physicians returned to the works of the early Greek physicians Hippocrates and Galen (GAY-len). Although their findings were remarkable for their times, their theories were often in error.

Andreas Vesalius (veh-SAY-lih-uhs), a Flemish physician, was one of the first to challenge Galen's theories on anatomy. Vesalius published an important work on anatomy and demanded that the study of anatomy be part of medical training. He was outraged at the practice of surgery by barbers. He felt that surgery should be performed only by physicians. William Harvey, an English physician, traced the system of blood circulation in the human body. He was the first to recognize that the heart acted as a pump.

J. B. van Helmont made great strides in chemistry with the discovery of carbon dioxide. He was also the first to distinguish gases from solids and liquids. Konrad von Gesner, a Swiss naturalist, laid the foundations for modern botany and zoology with his observations of plant and animal life.

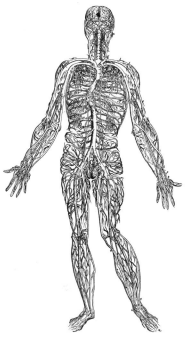

A Chart of Veins *illustrates Andreas Vesalius' view of the human circulatory system. This woodblock print was made in the workshop of the Renaissance artist Titian and is reproduced from a book published in 1543. This was the same year that Copernicus published his theory of the universe. The works of Copernicus mark the beginning of modern astronomy; those of Vesalius, the beginning of modern anatomy.*

Chapter 3
The Reformation

Others before Martin Luther (above) had asked for reforms within the Roman Catholic Church. But historians consider Luther's actions the beginning of the Reformation. What factors—religious, social, and political—brought it about?

The atmosphere of the Renaissance had its effects on the Roman Catholic Church. During the Middle Ages the Church was able to enforce spiritual and political supremacy over Europe. The popes were capable and strong. Feudalism was the accepted way of life. However, as kings and queens gained power, they dreamed of empires and national states.

Rulers often began to see the popes as threats to their political and economic strength. They envied the vast holdings of the Church which were exempt from royal taxation. And they quarreled with the popes over control of certain lands. Rulers were also annoyed that clergy accused of crimes could be tried only by the Church. In addition, growing numbers of clergy and lay people criticized the lax lives of clergy and nuns. It was not long before questions arose about the very doctrines which the clergy preached but did not practice.

WEAK AND DIVIDED PAPACY

Papal prestige and authority had been shaken when, from 1309 to 1377, a succession of popes lived in Avignon, France, rather than in Rome. In Avignon (a-veen-YOHN) the popes were subject to the influence of French rulers. This period is sometimes known as the Babylonian Captivity. The citizens of Rome and other European countries resented French domination of the papacy.

When the papacy was returned to Rome, a quarrel arose between French and Italian factions. The French cardinals elected a rival pope who again moved to Avignon. There were now two popes. Each excommunicated the other and called him false. European Christians were faced with deciding who was the true pope. Their choice was often determined by political consideration.

The period of the divided papacy (1378-1417) is usually referred to as the Great Schism. In 1415 a Church council met at Constance, Germany, to settle the question. The council was also supposed to bring about a reform within the Church. After several years of debate and discussion, the council managed to have one man elected pope. However, little was done about reform.

REFORMERS

As early as the 1300s there had been demands for reform. John Wycliffe (WIK-lif), a friar and teacher at Oxford, England, declared that the Church should give up all its wealth. He believed that the clergy were unnecessary. The Bible was the only authority necessary for Christian teachings. Wycliffe's writings were widely read and accepted.

One of the people he influenced was John Huss, a Bohemian. Huss also attacked the clergy but did not believe that the Bible was the final authority. Huss was excommunicated. By order of the Council of Constance he was burned at the stake as a heretic.

MARTIN LUTHER A hundred years later the Reformation began. On October 31, 1517, Martin Luther nailed his Ninety-five Theses to the door of All Saints' Church in Wittenberg, Saxony. The document attacked certain teachings of the Roman Catholic Church.

Luther was a priest and a professor of theology. He had also studied law for a time. Luther was in good standing in the Church until he proclaimed his Theses. He felt forced into this action by the extravagant claims of a monk named Tetzel (tet-SUHL). Tetzel was trying to raise money by selling indulgences.

The Church taught that sinners who wished their sins forgiven had to confess them with sorrow to a priest. The priest gave sinners penance to do to show their sorrow. Sinners would then receive pardon from the priest, acting as God's representative. This is the sacrament of penance. But penance might not be enough to allow people to enter Heaven. After death people might have to undergo further punishment in Purgatory. All or part of their punishment could be removed by good works or by saying special prayers. It drew upon all the unused merit accumulated in their lives by Jesus, Mary, and the saints. This pardoning of punishment in Purgatory was called an indulgence.

In his eagerness to obtain money Tetzel went beyond the Church's doctrine on indulgences. Luther attacked the commercialism of Tetzel in buying sinners out of Purgatory. But Luther also attacked some of the basic teachings of the Church.

This woodcut cartoon was made about 1520. It satirizes the practice of selling indulgences. What is an indulgence? Was Luther excommunicated because of his stand against this practice? Or were there other reasons?

Church officials reacted swiftly and harshly. In 1518 Luther was asked to retract some of the statements in the Theses. He refused. In a debate with the theologian John Eck in 1519, Luther was asked if he accepted the authority of popes and Church councils. Luther replied that their authority was not necessarily final. The controversy became bitter. In 1520 the pope condemned the teachings of Luther. Luther burned the condemnation.

Luther was excommunicated and declared an outlaw. He was asked once again if he would retract his words and teachings. He refused. Unless he could be proven wrong by Scripture, he would take back nothing. Frederick III, the ruler of Saxony, protected Luther. Other German princes came to his support.

Luther's writings were widely read and accepted, especially in
northern Germany. He taught that Christians could find salvation

through faith alone. Clergy, although helpful, were not essential to salvation. For guidance Christians need only read the Bible. To help people in finding this guidance, Luther translated the Bible into German. Luther's own writings were also in the vernacular. By his insistence on reading the Bible, Luther helped the spread of literacy in Germany.

Luther also wrote on secular topics. His writings supported the authority of the German princes and helped to stir up German **nationalism**. Luther was displeased that the Germans paid taxes to Rome. He urged the princes to stop this economic drain and to throw off the authority of the pope. Some German princes already resented sharing their authority with an Italian and responded eagerly to Luther's words. These princes became Lutherans. They declared Lutheranism the official religion of their states, and seized Church property. It was the custom of the time for people to follow the religion selected by their rulers. The only alternative was to overthrow the ruler.

When the Holy Roman Emperor Charles V forced his diet to declare the Lutheran doctrine to be heresy, a number of Lutheran princes protested. It is from their protests that the word Protestant comes. Wars broke out between Protestants and Catholics in Germany. They were ended in 1555 by the Peace of Augsburg. By this time Lutheranism was established in northern Germany and Catholicism in southern Germany.

Lutheranism quickly spread beyond the borders of the German states. In slightly more than ten years it became the official religion of Denmark and Norway. A short time later it also became the **state religion** of Sweden.

JOHN CALVIN   In Switzerland Ulrich Zwingli (TSWING-lee), a humanist, began a quieter Protestant movement. He saw no need for priests, incense, candles, or other decorations. These he considered superstitions. He also denied the worth of indulgences.

Under the leadership of John Calvin, Protestantism made rapid progress in Switzerland. From there it spread to France, Scotland, Holland, Hungary, southern Germany, and other parts of Europe.

In 1536 John Calvin had published *Institutes of the Christian Religion.* This book provided the foundation for a form of Protestantism often referred to as Calvinism. Calvin believed that stained-glass windows, altars, incense, and other symbols could distract the Christian from direct communication with God.

Calvin became all-powerful in the city of Geneva. He forbade dancing, card-playing, fancy clothing, and worldliness. He regarded religion as very serious and thought people should approach it in a serious manner. No one could be sure of salvation. Thus it was necessary for all to search their consciences constantly and to strive always to live moral lives.

Once the Reformation began, many different religions sprang up in Europe. One was founded by John Calvin. What did Calvin preach? Why do you think people were attracted to Calvinism?

People came to Geneva from all over Europe to hear Calvin and then return home to spread his words. The French who returned to France converted many of the middle class of the towns and cities. These Protestants became known as Huguenots (HYOO-guh-nahts). A series of wars lasting almost 50 years were fought between Huguenots and Roman Catholics. Finally in 1598 the Edict of Nantes (NANS) gave Huguenots political rights and some religious freedom.

John Knox came to Geneva from Scotland. In 1559 Knox returned to Scotland to found the Calvinist Presbyterian Church which replaced Catholicism. From Scotland Calvinist ideas flowed into England and influenced people called Puritans. They were among the first settlers of the English colonies in New England. Puritan thinking and way of life left a deep imprint on these colonies and through them on the United States.

THE ENGLISH

In England, as in Germany, politics and religion were mixed. The fate of the house of Tudor—and with it the unity of England—was eventually to hang in the balance.

From 1307 to 1485, the power of Parliament continued to grow. Reacting to the economic disaster caused by the Hundred Years' War and the bubonic plague, it seized greater control of financial policy. Parliament's most dramatic use of power came in 1399. The Houses of Lords and Commons deposed King Richard II and replaced him with Henry of Lancaster.

The Lancastrian line lasted until 1485. From 1455 to 1485, however, two branches of the royal house fought to gain the throne. The conflict—known as the Wars of The Roses—was finally resolved by Henry Tudor. In 1485 he claimed the throne as the heir of the Lancasters. He married Elizabeth, heiress of the house of York, thus uniting the two opposing branches. With his reign Henry VII broke the power of the nobles. When Henry died, he left his kingdom with a full treasury and well along the road to centralization. His son, Henry VIII, ascended the throne in 1509 at the age of 18. It was during his reign that England broke with the Roman Catholic Church.

HENRY VIII   Henry VIII needed a male heir to ensure the future of the house of Tudor. But he had no son by his wife, Catherine of Aragon. When Henry requested an annulment so that he might marry Anne Boleyn, the pope hesitated. Catherine had powerful political connections. She was the daughter of Ferdinand and Isabella of Spain and the aunt of the Holy Roman Emperor, Charles V. Moreover, Henry had already received a papal dispensation to marry Catherine because she was the widow of Henry's brother. In the Roman Catholic Church permission is needed before such a marriage can take place.

annulment: cancellation; a doing away with an agreement as if it never existed

474

For a time Henry VIII was a champion of Catholicism. He was given the title Defender of the Faith for a pamphlet he wrote attacking Luther. But when the Church stood in the way of Henry's desire for power, he rebelled against it. This painting is by Hans Holbein the Younger.

Henry, however, would not tolerate hesitation. With the help of the new archbishop of Canterbury, Thomas Cranmer, an English church court annulled Henry's marriage. In 1534 Henry obtained from Parliament the Act of Supremacy. This made the monarch head of the Church in England and cut all ties with the pope. Henry was excommunicated in 1538. He took his new wife, but she produced a daughter. Henry's third wife Jane Seymour gave him his son. In all Henry had six wives.

Henry used the Act of Supremacy to further his other political and economic interests. He took away the properties of monasteries and convents. Some properties he kept for himself; others he gave to loyal followers. Henry tightened his control over all affairs of the English nation. When Henry VIII died, his ten-year-old son Edward VI took the throne. England was now stronger and more centralized than ever.

Edward reigned for only a few years. However, during this time, Edward's advisors carried England even farther along the Protestant way. These men were heavily influenced by Calvinism and Lutheranism. The trend toward Protestantism was curtailed by Edward's successor Mary.

Mary was Henry's daughter by Catherine of Aragon. She was a devout Catholic and was married to Philip II of Spain. Mary tried to restore England to Roman Catholicism and to allegiance to Rome. But she ruled for only five years. She was succeeded by Elizabeth I, the daughter of Henry VIII and Anne Boleyn.

ELIZABETH I   During her 45-year reign (1558-1603), Elizabeth I brought England some of its greatest prestige. She set about making England a sound and prosperous country. She had been raised a Protestant and she renewed the task of making England a Protestant nation.

During Elizabeth's reign, the Thirty-Nine Articles were published. These set forth the doctrines of the Church of England—or Anglican Church—which became the official English Church. State taxes supported it. A number of the ceremonies and beliefs of Catholicism were kept but its head was the ruler of England, not the pope.

At this time Calvinist influences were pouring into England. However, Elizabeth practiced a policy of religious tolerance. She wanted to keep her realm free of the religious wars which were making chaos of much of the Continent. Persecutions of Catholics were for political rather than religious reasons.

CONSEQUENCES

The Reformation left permanent marks on European history. It contributed to the disappearance of the medieval way of life. It strengthened the position of the middle class. This middle class became the base of future European democracies. The German **sociologist** and economist Max Weber reasoned that the Reformation's stress on saving, thrift, and hard work contributed to the growth of **capitalism**. He cited the Dutch, Germans, English, and New England Yankees to support his argument.

It is probable that the Reformation also strengthened the growing feeling of **nationalism** in Europe. The religion of a people became closely identified with the politics of their state. Rulers were often suspicious of subjects who followed a religion different from their own or from that of the majority. After the mid-1500s, Europeans began to refer to their nations as either Catholic or Protestant.

THIRTY YEARS' WAR   Political and religious differences soon turned into conflict—the Thirty Years' War. It began in 1618 between the Protestants of Bohemia and their Catholic rulers, the Hapsburgs. Ill will between the Catholics and Protestants contributed to its beginning, but political and economic factors prolonged it.

Sweden, Denmark, German Protestant territories, France, and other nations interfered for purely political reasons. They feared the power of the Hapsburgs who ruled the Holy Roman Empire, Austria, Spain, and several other European nations. For example, Catholic France at this time was under the guidance of Cardinal Richelieu (RISH-uh-loo). Richelieu wanted the Hapsburgs weakened so that they would not threaten France's rising power.

Hapsburg counts had made their home originally in Switzerland in the 1000s. Over the years, their wealth and influence increased. In the late 1200s Rudolph of Hapsburg was elected Holy Roman emperor. Through skillfully arranged marriages, the Hapsburgs managed to dominate much of Europe.

Acting on Richelieu's advice, France entered the war against the Hapsburgs. It did not matter that both nations were Catholic. France's entry greatly reduced the strength of the Hapsburgs. Eventually all the participants became weary and exhausted. The Treaty of Westphalia (wes-FAYL-yuh) ended the conflict in 1648.

France got what it had wanted. The Hapsburgs declined and the power of France increased. The treaty guaranteed independence to all 300 German princes. They could make peace or war and handle their own diplomatic relations without the Holy Roman Emperor.

This pen and ink drawing shows one battle of the Thirty Years' War. The siege of Nordlingen, Germany took place in 1634. A Swedish army defending Protestantism attacked an army supporting Catholicism. The Swedes were defeated, but other armies took their places.

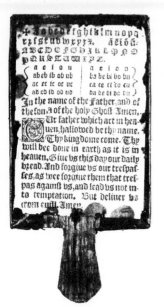

Protestantism encouraged its followers to read the Bible. Because of the need to be able to read, education grew during the 1500s. Above is a hornbook. It is the typical way Elizabethans were taught reading. The alphabet is at the top, followed by the vowels, various combinations of vowels and consonants, and then prayers.

The war left Germany a divided land and delayed **unification** for 250 years. It did, however, contribute to the rising power of Prussia, whose Hohenzollern (HOH-uhn-zahl-ern) rulers were later to unite Germany. In 1618 the territories of Brandenburg and East Prussia were united as Prussia. Under Frederick William the Prussians won some important victories in the closing days of the Thirty Years' War. The Treaty of Westphalia gave Prussia considerable territory which added to its strength.

Sweden obtained lands along the Baltic Sea. Holland and Switzerland were formally recognized as independent countries. France gained Alsace on the German border.

German Calvinists were given the same privileges as Lutherans and Catholics. Prior to this time, Calvinism was not recognized within German territory. Protestant princes who held Church lands in 1624 were permitted to keep them.

DIVISIONS WITHIN PROTESTANTISM   At first the aim of Protestantism had been to remove practices and doctrines which seemed to cloud the teachings of Jesus. Protestants maintained that they were restoring the simplicity and purity of Christianity. In searching out this purity, they stressed the spirit rather than the letter of the law.

Protestants differed among themselves, however, in determining which beliefs and practices were foreign to Christian tradition. Many Protestants—for instance, the Calvinists and the Puritans—felt that such objects as statues and incense were foreign. The Anglicans, however, found these objects and practices to be within Christian tradition. Most Protestants denied that the confession of sins was necessary. But a number of Anglicans believed it essential. These differences led to divisions within Protestantism. These divisions became formalized into many different denominations.

COUNTER-REFORMATION   The Protestant Reformation did not leave the Roman Catholic Church unchanged. In addition to Martin Luther, there were many other Catholics who called for reform. These voices were finally answered in the Council of Trent. This council met a number of times between 1545 and 1563 and restated the important doctrines of Roman Catholicism. It also accomplished many reforms within the Church.

The education of priests was improved. The religious education of lay people was strengthened. Decrees were published concerning the sacraments, indulgences, the veneration of saints and so forth. These were meant to clarify Church teachings. The council also strongly affirmed the supremacy of the pope.

The Counter-Reformation, as the movement was known, helped to give the Roman Catholic Church much of its modern shape. The period of reforms continued until the end of the Thirty Years' War.

Summing Up the Unit

Social Studies Vocabulary

Define: literacy; revolution; radical; state religion; capitalism; nationalism; unification

People

Identify: Petrarch; da Vinci; Gutenberg; Shakespeare; Calvin; Elizabeth I; Hapsburgs

Words

Define: Renaissance; Reformation; humanists; Elizabethan Age; metaphysical; blank verse; genre; mannerism; Huguenots; Puritans

Questions

1. a. What did the humanists believe? b. Why were the first humanists Italian?
2. What were the characteristics of Italian Renaissance writings?
3. a. How was the attitude of Renaissance artists different from that of medieval artists? b. How did the wealth of the era favor them?
4. Describe how works of the following reflect a humanistic viewpoint: a. Machiavelli; b. Giotto; c. Anguisciola; d. Botticelli.
5. What new materials and techniques did Renaissance artists use?
6. a. What lines did Renaissance architecture follow? b. What was the result?
7. In which two areas of Renaissance music were the most noteworthy contributions made?
8. What impact did printing have on: a. humanism? b. the growth of literacy?
9. What factors influenced northern humanism?
10. How did the writings of the following reflect a Renaissance tone: a. Dante? b. Erasmus? c. Chaucer? d. Rabelais? e. Cervantes?
11. Why were historical plays popular in Elizabethan England?
12. a. How did genre painters of the Low Countries differ from Italian artists? b. Why did the mannerists break with classical painting?
13. Why were Copernicus and Galileo viewed as heretics?
14. What effect did the advances in technology have on Renaissance people?
15. a. Why did Renaissance rulers view popes as threats? b. How was the authority of the popes weakened by their living in Avignon?
16. a. Why was Luther excommunicated? b. Why did some German princes support him? c. How did his writings stir up German nationalism?
17. What did Henry VIII accomplish by obtaining from Parliament the Act of Supremacy?
18. a. What permanent marks did the Reformation leave on European history? b. How did the Reformation strengthen nationalism?
19. Why did divisions arise in Protestantism?
20. What effect did the Reformation have on the Roman Catholic Church?

Discussion Topics

1. Italian Renaissance artists were supported by popes, rulers, and the rich. Was this essential to Italy's artistic achievements? Is similar patronage needed today to support the arts?
2. The Renaissance was a time of transition when elements of the dying medieval era existed along with the first breaths of the modern age. What medieval characteristics continued during the Renaissance? What was new?
3. Renaissance artists portrayed people as more lifelike. How did this reflect the attitude of the Renaissance? Would this type of art have been possible in the Middle Ages?
4. Erasmus believed that evil comes only from ignorance and human mistakes. How does this philosophy exemplify the Renaissance? Can it be applied to modern attitudes toward good and evil? On what do modern people base their ideas of good and bad?

Project Ideas

1. Write a biography of one of the following: Michelangelo; da Vinci; Dante; Erasmus; Shakespeare; Copernicus; Galileo.
2. Find pictures of Renaissance art and architecture and use them to give an illustrated lecture on trends mentioned in Chapter 1 or make a poster on the same theme.

Unit VI

Exploration and Competition

This engraving shows the English fleet lined up to protect the English coast against the Spanish Armada. What factors led to this battle in 1588?

From the 1400s to the 1700s Europeans launched voyage after voyage of discovery which took them all over the world. These explorations brought changes to Europe as well as to those lands the Europeans visited, seized, and colonized.

At first, most Europeans believed that the world was flat and that frightening beasts lived in the unknown waters. They had no desire to gamble their lives and money on sea ventures. Others, however, thought of the seas as paths to trade and wealth, to the conversion of souls, and to exciting adventure. Their willingness grew out of the atmosphere of the Renaissance. As more people were influenced by the Renaissance, its spirit spread and infected other Europeans.

Meanwhile, European rulers were involved in protecting their interests at home. They schemed to take or defend territories in Europe that they regarded as vital to their existence and power. From the 1500s onward, European interests were so interlocked that wars usually raged across the Continent.

Portugal, Spain, the Netherlands, France, and England led the age of exploration. Their ships sailed in all directions. Their explorers charted unfamiliar seas and claimed great parts of the lands they reached. Often these claims resulted in disagreements and conflict.

Chapter 1
Explorers

PORTUGUESE

Prince Henry of Portugal was a religious man who wanted to spread Roman Catholicism. He was also a practical man who wanted part of Venice's **monopoly** of the spice trade.

In those days without refrigeration, meat spoiled quickly. Spices were essential for seasoning meat so that people could eat it. The main source of spices was Asia. On their way from Asian fields to European merchants the spices passed through the hands of many traders. By the time the Venetians bought them, the cost of the spices was more than 20 times their original value.

Henry determined to break the Venetian monopoly and gain the profits of the spice trade for Portugal. He assembled a fleet of ships and prepared to find a direct sea route from Portugal to Asia. Because of his great interest in exploration, Henry is remembered in history as Henry the Navigator.

In the early 1400s Henry's captains began to sail in short trips down the west coast of Africa. As they went along they established trading posts. Henry died before his captains reached the source of the spices; however, Portuguese rulers who came after Henry continued to encourage exploration.

In 1486 Bartholomew Diaz, a navigator, was caught in a storm along the African coast. When he next sighted land it was to the west rather than to the east. He had rounded the southern tip of Africa. The Portuguese were so hopeful that the spice trade would soon be theirs that King John II named this area the Cape of Good Hope.

A few years later, Vasco da Gama rounded this cape, reached the east coast of Africa, and crossed the Indian Ocean to southern India. There he filled two ships with spices. When he reached Lisbon two years later, in 1499, his spices were worth 60 times the cost of the voyage.

The Portuguese continued exploring, trading, and setting up trading stations in strategic areas of the world. Pedro Cabral sailed west and reached Brazil in 1500. He immediately claimed it for Portugal.

It was the European custom at the time to claim the people who lived on the land as well as the land itself. It did not matter how great was the civilization of the people claimed. Unless they had the weapons to withstand European force, they were taken over. European rulers generally feared only fellow Europeans.

Unfortunately European rivalries often spilled over into the newly claimed lands. The Portuguese and the Spanish requested the pope to settle their dispute over one area in particular—South America.

Prince Henry of Portugal never made a voyage himself, but he encouraged others to explore. What was the European attitude toward peoples in other parts of the world? How did others view Europeans? See the unit on China in this book for comparison.

The Portuguese received all lands within a line 300 miles east of the Cape Verde Islands. The Spanish received everything west of this line. In effect, South America was divided between them. A year later, in 1494, the Treaty of Tordesillas (tord-uh-SEE-yuhs) shifted the line farther west. The Dutch, French, and English refused to accept this division. They took everything they could, east or west of the line.

Although they traded elsewhere, the main effort of the Portuguese was in Asia. They established a base of operations in Goa on the western shore of India, which they kept until recent years. From there they fanned out to Sri Lanka, Malaysia, Indonesia, Macao on the China coast, and even to Japan. They had little influence on most of the people with whom they traded. However, for a number of years they were the only Europeans the Asians knew. Besides trade, the Portuguese were interested in converting the Asians. Some of the first European missionaries to these lands were brought by the Portuguese.

Portuguese trading posts were gradually taken over by the Dutch, English, and others who followed the sea routes the Portuguese had first explored. Ultimately only a few areas remained in Portuguese hands.

SPANISH

Like the Portuguese, the Spanish wished to spread Roman Catholicism to others. They also desired the wealth that exploration brought. In their first venture, Christopher Columbus reached the American continent, and the Spanish were on their way to a worldwide empire.

Columbus, of Genoa, Italy, was convinced that the earth was round. This belief had been held by a number of early Greeks. However, their work had been ignored so Columbus had difficulty in finding anyone to finance a voyage to prove this theory. Finally, he convinced Queen Isabella of Spain that he could reach the Far East by sailing west. In spring 1492 Columbus set out westward with three ships. On October 12 he sighted land.

Columbus thought he had reached the Indies. Indies—or East Indies—was the name Europeans gave to India and various island areas of the Far East. Actually Columbus had landed on one of the Bahama islands. He sailed on to see what are now known as Cuba and Santo Domingo before returning to Spain. He took back some Indians as well as some unfamiliar plants and animals.

The Spanish were disappointed that Columbus had not brought back spices. However, they were excited about what he had found. He returned three times with settlers to start colonies. When he died in 1506, Columbus still thought he had reached the Indies. In 1513 Balboa crossed the narrow strip of Panama. When he saw the ocean, he realized that Columbus had discovered a new land and not the Indies.

Although Christopher Columbus' voyages made others wealthy, he received little for his efforts. At one time he was imprisoned for supposed mismanagement of his governorship in the New World.

In 1519 Ferdinand Magellan, a Portuguese in the service of Spain, set out with five ships and 243 sailors. He sailed through the dangerous passage at the southern tip of South America—later named the Strait of Magellan—and entered the Pacific. He crossed it as far as the Philippine Islands where he died fighting the inhabitants. His sailors continued across the Indian Ocean and around the Cape of Good Hope. At last, in 1522, one ship with 18 men arrived back in Spain. They were all that remained of Magellan's expedition but they had proved that the Earth was round.

The Spanish went on to claim and colonize large areas in North and South America as well as the Philippines. From these new lands, gold and silver poured into Spain's treasury. These riches of the New World were used to further Spain's interests in Europe.

DUTCH

The Dutch were industrious, thrifty people. By the 1500s their cities and ports were centers of industry, banking, and trade. Their ships were familiar sights in all the ports of Europe.

Dutch ships roamed the world. By around 1600 the Dutch had 10,000 ships on the seas. They were building them at the rate of one a day.

In the 1500s, Holy Roman Emperor Charles V added the Netherlands to his large empire. Later it became a part of the empire of his son, Philip II, who ruled Spain. During this time the Dutch in the northern part of the Netherlands became Calvinists which angered the Catholic Philip. He sent armies against them and cut back their religious and political privileges. The Dutch resisted. They fought under William the Silent, Prince of Orange. Although William was assassinated before freedom was won, he is considered the founder of the Dutch Republic.

In 1579 the Dutch of the seven northern provinces formed the Union of Utrecht (YOO-trekt). In 1581 these provinces declared their independence as the Republic of the United Netherlands. However, their independence was not **formally** recognized until the Treaty of Westphalia in 1648.

formally: officially

From the late 1500s until the late 1700s the Dutch roamed the seas in their privateers and merchant ships. They attacked Spanish and Portuguese shipping and trading posts. Their greatest triumph was the capture of the spice trade of the Indies from the Portuguese. The Dutch seized most of the islands of what is modern Indonesia. The Portuguese were able to hold only Timor.

The area became a rich island empire for the Dutch. They introduced coffee plantations and developed production of rubber, palm oil, and sugar among other items. Dutch merchants formed the Dutch East India Company and channeled their overseas business through it. So strong was Dutch control that the East Indies remained Dutch possessions until the end of World War II. In 1949 after bitter fighting the area became independent as the Republic of Indonesia.

The Dutch did not confine themselves to Asia. They also sailed to the New World. They whaled in the Arctic and searched for a northwest passage to the Indies through North America. On such a trip Henry Hudson sailed up the river which now bears his name as far as present-day Albany, New York. The Dutch settled the present site of New York and called it New Amsterdam. They also found their way into the Caribbean and fought over the islands. They struggled with the Portuguese for a part of Brazil and lost.

In Africa the Dutch planted a colony on the Cape of Good Hope. Descendants of the Dutch still make up the majority of the white population of the Republic of South Africa.

ENGLISH

The English were late in starting their voyages of exploration. Once under way, however, they continued until they had built an empire upon which the sun never set. The empire began in 1497. In that year the English hired the Italian explorers John and Sebastian Cabot to search for a northwest passage to the Indies. They explored the North American coast from Hatteras to Labrador. Their expedition laid the foundation for Great Britain's later claim to the coastline.

In the 1500s the English, however, were primarily interested in the trade of Asia, not in colonizing the New World. They focused on India. For many years the English operated through a private company of investors called the East India Company. In return for the profits, this company raised the money and provided ships and supplies for voyages. Queen Elizabeth I chartered the company in 1600 and gave it a monopoly of all eastern trade.

By the late 1600s the company was well established in Madras, Bombay, and Calcutta. During this period Mogul power in India was breaking down. The English took advantage of this opportunity to set the rulers of states against each other. In this way the English were able to expand their political and economic power. They also weakened French influence in the area.

Eventually, through the efforts of Robert Clive and the British East India Company, the British controlled a substantial part of India. The company put armies into the field and governed India much as if it were the real government of the country. However, this commercial company was not equipped to rule a country so complex and vast as India. In 1858, the British crown took over the country and governed it for British interests.

Although the English had been active in India since the 1500s, it was not until the mid-1700s that their power became dominant. Robert Clive brought the area into the British Empire.

In the meantime the British explored other parts of Asia. They took Sri Lanka, Malaysia, Burma, North Borneo, Hong Kong, and other Asian islands.

The profits the British gained from trade were enormous. They stimulated British industry and the growth of one of the world's largest merchant and war fleets. The British, like other European powers of the period, insisted that its goods travel only its ships. In addition, the colonies could sell their raw materials and other products only to Great Britain. They were permitted to buy only British-manufactured goods. This system was based on the theory of **mercantilism**.

According to mercantilism, the country that had the most gold and silver was the wealthiest and strongest. One way of obtaining this position was to sell goods to other countries. In order to have enough goods to sell, a country like Great Britain without many natural resources had to monopolize the trade of its colonies. This monopoly of trade would eventually be one reason for the revolt of Britain's American colonies.

The English began their North American empire in 1607. In that year under the leadership of Captain John Smith, the first permanent English settlement was started at Jamestown, Virginia. In 1620 a shipload of Pilgrims crossed the Atlantic on the *Mayflower* and landed at Plymouth, Massachusetts.

Gradually a line of British colonies grew along the eastern coast of the present-day U.S. from Georgia to Maine. By the 1700s these colonies had built an economy founded on agriculture and supported by growing trade with England and the West Indies. The growth of the colonial economy, however, never really satisfied the British. They had hoped to make a much larger profit from their North American colonies.

The British also explored and claimed land in South America and a number of Caribbean islands. In America and in India, however, they found the French to be fierce rivals.

FRENCH

The French claimed vast stretches of territory in various parts of the world. For a time they held Canada and much of what is present-day U.S. west of the Mississippi. The state of Louisiana takes its name from land that was named for King Louis XIV.

During Louis' reign and under the guidance of his finance minister, Jean Baptiste Colbert, the French also formed an East India Company. It competed in India against the British. The French first established a trading post at Pondicherry near Madras on the southern coast of India. From there their trade routes fanned out across India.

In both North America and India, competition between the French and the British often led to conflict. By 1763 the French hold on parts of India had been weakened. They could still trade in India, but they

had no fortified areas there. In that year they also lost Canada to
the British.

Chapter 2
Monarchs and World Empire

*Charles V as the Holy Roman Emperor ruled one of the largest empires in
the world. The symbols of his office were an orb and scepter.*

Some historians believe that the age of exploration was the force
that brought about the **industrial revolution**, Western-oriented global
unity, and the growth of capitalism. Certainly this period contributed
to far-reaching developments in politics, economics, science, and
industry. However, these changes came slowly.

While explorers were seeking out distant lands, European monarchs
were fighting among themselves over territory at home. European
rulers were very suspicious of one another. The more powerful one
became, the greater the fear and suspicion of the others. If one ruler
became too powerful, the others joined together to attack him or
her before they were attacked.

CHARLES V: HOLY ROMAN EMPEROR

One of the greatest of the European rulers was Charles V (1500-1558)
who became Holy Roman Emperor at 19. He was a member of the

Hapsburg family. Through his Spanish mother, he inherited the possessions of Spain. From his father he inherited Burgundy and the Low Countries. From his grandfather he inherited the Austrian empire of the Hapsburgs which included half of Italy, Germany, Austria, and part of Hungary. The wealth of the Americas poured into his treasury. He commanded large armies of soldiers and officials. But the people he governed allowed him no peace.

The Turks plunged deep into Hungary and threatened the city of Vienna. The French threatened the empire's western borders. Rebellious Italian nobles plotted independence. A revolt of Lutheran princes threatened to tear Germany apart. Abroad, the English, Dutch, and pirates plundered Charles' treasure ships and attacked his colonies.

Charles managed to hold the borders of his empire until 1555. Then, exhausted by his efforts, he divided his possessions between his brother Ferdinand and his son Philip. Charles retired to a monastery where he spent the last two years of his life.

PHILIP II OF SPAIN

Philip's share of his father's inheritance included parts of Italy, France, the Spanish Americas, the Philippines, and the Low Countries. His uncle, Ferdinand, inherited the remainder of the empire, including Austria and Germany.

Philip II (1556-1598) had two goals: to make Spain first in world importance and to stamp out Protestantism. He saw Protestantism as a threat to both his political and religious purposes. He used the Inquisition in Spain and in the Netherlands to root it out.

It was at this time that the Dutch declared their independence, held off Philip's soldiers, and destroyed many of his ships. The Moors in Spain revolted. Subduing them drained Philip's treasury and his resources. In 1580 Philip seized the vacant Portuguese throne. To defend Portugal's overseas empire he was forced to spread his sea power thin. Portuguese possessions and ships were additional prey that had to be protected from the Dutch, French, and English.

In 1554 Mary, the daughter of Henry VIII of England, had married Philip. A year earlier, she had become queen of England. She and Philip attempted to restore Roman Catholicism to England. This action aroused the anger of the English who by then were determined to be independent of the pope. When Elizabeth became queen at Mary's death in 1558 she supported the Church of England. She also supported sea raiders like Francis Drake and John Hawkins. These privateers kept England's enemies off balance and filled the English treasury with gold and silver.

In 1588 Philip sent an armada of ships to destroy the English pirates and to remove Elizabeth. The armada was supposed to be invincible. But Elizabeth's captains destroyed most of Philip's fleet. They were superior sailors and had better guns. A freak storm in the English Channel helped too. From that time on, Philip's enemies became

Queen Elizabeth I—the Armada Portrait *is by the Flemish painter Gheeraerts. The Protestant Gheeraerts fled to England from Catholic Flanders. Flanders is now part of Belgium and France.*

more daring and confident. Spanish sea power began to decline. As the Spanish declined, French power increased.

HENRY IV OF FRANCE

Under the title Henry of Navarre, Henry IV of France had been the leader of the Huguenots. But when the throne of France became vacant, he embraced Catholicism. The majority of French people were Catholics. Henry realized that in order to win the throne over his rivals he would have to become a Catholic. In 1589 Henry's plan succeeded, and he became King Henry IV.

Henry ruled as a wise and tolerant king. With the help of an able Huguenot, the Duke of Sully, Henry proclaimed a policy of religious tolerance that ended the civil wars between Catholics and Protestants. In 1598 he issued the Edict of Nantes which gave Huguenots freedom to worship as they pleased. It also permitted them self-government and allowed them to keep their forts.

Henry was also interested in the welfare of his people. Under Sully's guidance, industry and commerce were encouraged. The expansion of overseas colonies was stimulated. Quebec, Canada, was founded during this period. Henry IV was assassinated in 1610 but he left France prosperous and more centralized than ever.

489

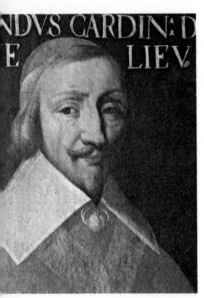

Cardinal Richelieu was more interested in furthering France's power than in meeting the spiritual needs of the country's Catholics. What facts can you find to support this statement?

LOUIS XIII AND CARDINAL RICHELIEU

Louis XIII (1610-1643) was nine when his father, Henry IV, died. While he was a child, his mother, Marie de Medici, was regent, and France weakened. But when Cardinal Richelieu became Louis' advisor, the country became one of the most powerful in Europe. Richelieu worked for the glory of France and his king. Not even the Church's interests were permitted to interfere with increasing the power of France. Under Richelieu's guidance, Louis XIII embarked upon an ambitious foreign policy. As we have already seen, France's role in the Thirty Years' War helped decrease the power of the rival Hapsburg family.

At home, Huguenots could continue to worship in peace. However, they lost their self-government and their fortified towns and cities were destroyed. Under Richelieu's direction, the power of nobles was also curbed. They were watched over by members of the middle class, who were sympathetic to the king. Supervisors were appointed to oversee government at the local level.

Richelieu also contributed to the cultural growth of France. He established the French Academy in 1635 to guard the purity of the language and encourage French literature. The Academy still functions.

LOUIS XIV

At the age of five, Louis XIV (1643-1715) inherited the French throne. During his reign France reached even greater heights of power. The rule of Louis XIV was given a sound foundation by Cardinal Mazarin (maz-uh-RAN), who continued the policies of Richelieu. After Mazarin's death, Louis himself assumed control of France.

Louis had excellent advisors. One was Jean Baptiste Colbert, the finance minister who guided the formation of the French East India Company. He filled the treasury, improved the economy, and encouraged the establishment of overseas colonies.

Louis also had capable military commanders. Much of his reign was dominated by war. Between 1667 and 1713 Louis fought four wars. At various times most of Europe was combined in alliances against France. The other nations of Europe feared France because it was stronger than any individual country. However, France was not stronger than certain combinations of countries.

By his wars Louis wanted to expand the territory of France and to increase its power. When the fourth war was settled in 1713 by the Treaty of Utrecht, Louis had made some gains. However, he also was forced to make some concessions. France lost many of its overseas and European possessions. The financial burden upon the French for Louis' wars was severe.

Under Louis XIV, the content and style of French culture became part of the cultures of other European countries. Visitors to France saw performances of plays by Moliere, Racine, and Corneille. French became the second language of educated Europeans and the language of diplomacy.

DIVINE RIGHT MONARCHY   Louis XIV is an example of those monarchs who believed that their power was absolute. He and other European monarchs of the time thought that they ruled by divine right: God had planned their birth and position in life. They considered themselves to be God's agents on earth. Their subjects had a duty to obey their commands without questions. Opposition to royal power was, to their thinking, opposition to God.

Some subjects, however, did not think that a monarch's will was always God's will. The nobility, clergy, and rising middle class clung to privileges more ancient than the rights of a monarch. A monarch who trespassed upon these privileges frequently met opposition. The theory of **divine right monarchy**, however, hastened the centralization of government then under way in Europe.

FORERUNNERS OF GLOBAL WAR

During the 1600s and 1700s wars among European powers were not confined to Europe. They spread to the colonies, although often under other names. The wars fought by England, France, and Spain in North America are examples of this extension of European wars.

When Charles VI, Holy Roman Emperor, died in 1740, his daughter Maria Theresa inherited the Austrian throne. Frederick II of Prussia and some German princes thought this an opportunity to take some

491

Empress Maria Theresa discusses policy with her minister of state, Count Wenzel von Kaunitz. Was the desire for power the major reason European monarchs fought each other from the 1500s through the 1700s?

of the Hapsburg territory. The war moved from small beginnings to a full-scale conflict. Most of the great powers of Europe became involved. The conflict spread to the Americas. There it set the French and Spanish allies of Prussia against the English and the Dutch, who supported Maria Theresa. When the war ended in 1748, Frederick II received Silesia which had been ruled by Maria Theresa.

Maria Theresa wanted revenge upon the Prussians. She gathered Spain, France, Sweden, Russia, and Saxony into an alliance against Prussia. Supported by this combination, she started in 1756 what was known to Europeans as the Seven Years' War. England supported Prussia. In North America, the French once again fought against the British in the French and Indian War. Both European and American conflicts were settled in 1763 by the peace of Paris.

No European lands changed hands. In America, however, the French gave to the British their land in Canada and all the land they had claimed east of the Mississippi. Spain was forced to give the territory of Florida to Britain. Great Britain became dominant in North America from the east coast to the Mississippi River.

By the end of the Seven Years' War, the British were supreme overseas. Much of the credit for the vigor of the British must go to William Pitt, who was **prime minister** several times during the 1750s and 1760s. Pitt brought direction and spirit to the British fight for empire.

Summing Up The Unit

Social Studies Vocabulary

Define: monopoly; mercantilism; industrial revolution; divine right monarchy; prime minister

People

Identify: Henry the Navigator; Bartholomew Diaz; Vasco da Gama; Cabral; Balboa; Magellan; William the Silent; Colbert; Charles V; Philip II; Louis XIV; Richelieu; Maria Theresa

Words

Identify: Treaty of Tordesillas; Indies; Union of Utrecht; British East India Company; armada; Edict of Nantes

🗝 Questions

1. List the two reasons for which Prince Henry of Portugal assembled a fleet.

2. a. What was the European custom during the age of exploration regarding the people who lived on the lands Europeans claimed? b. Whom did Europeans fear?

3. What two things did the Portugese hope to do in Asia?

4. What did the Spanish hope to accomplish with their explorations?

5. How did Spain use its New World riches?

6. a. What method of power did the British East India Company use to control India? b. Why did the British crown take control of India?

7. What effects did British overseas trade have on its economy?

8. Why did the British monopolize the trade of their colonies?

9. Competition in North America and India led to conflict between what two nations?

10. What factors do some historians believe were brought about by the age of exploration?

11. During the age of exploration, what happened if one European ruler became too powerful?

12. a. What were Philip II's two goals for Spain? b. How did he set about furthering them?

13. a. Why did Henry of Navarre become a Catholic? b. What method of power did Henry IV use in ruling France? c. How successful was he?

14. Which was Richelieu's primary interest—France or the Catholic Church?

15. How did Louis XIV use each of the following to become more powerful: a. finances? b. wars? c. diplomacy? d. rule by divine right?

16. After the Seven Years' War, which European nation had become the leading colonial power?

Discussion Topics

1. Why did Portugal and Spain enter the race for world power first, while France and England came later? What advantages and handicaps did each contender have? Why did Britain become the leading colonial power?

2. Exploration and colonization began during the Renaissance and accompanied the Protestant Reformation and the rise of modern nations. How were these developments connected? How can they help to explain colonial rivalries?

3. The wars among European powers during the 1600s and 1700s were not confined to Europe, but extended to colonies. How was Britain's location an advantage in the wars that were fought both on the European continent and in other parts of the world?

Project Ideas

1. Prepare a report on: the British East India Company; Dutch struggle for independence; Dutch development of the East Indies; the Huguenots.

2. Draw a map showing: Portuguese, Spanish, English, Dutch, or French colonial empires at their height.

3. Make a time-line of rulers of major European countries during the 1500s and 1600s. Include significant events at home and abroad during their reigns.

4. Read and write a book report on *Armada* by Garrett Mattingly. Can you detect a bias on the part of the author? In your report, consider whether a historian can be totally unbiased in his/her work.

5. Research and report on what happened to the armada after the storm.

Unit VII

Exploding Ideas
and Revolutions

The pace of political and scientific change was rapid in the 1600s and 1700s. Above, the physicist Isaac Newton is pictured analyzing a ray of light.

During the 1600s and 1700s drastic changes were occurring in the European attitudes toward government. The spirit of the Renaissance had set the Europeans in motion. The pace of discovery and change gradually speeded up over the years.

The changes in politics resulted from and, in turn, contributed to economic and social change. However, progress did not move at the same rate in each country. Sometimes change exploded in violent revolutions which quickly ended the established order. In other countries, there was a more or less peaceful evolution into something new. Reaction and progress were often found side by side within a country. Thus the rate of progress was often painfully slow.

The English did not win a greater share in their government overnight. It took centuries for their rights to become part of English custom and law. Their slow growth of freedom began in the late Middle Ages when Parliament started its long evolution. In this same period the laws were made uniform in England. Justice came to be better administered. The idea of juries began to take form. In addition, many ancient privileges were restated and confirmed. Many of these had to do with the rights of women to inherit, own, and dispose of property.

Because the Tudor rulers of the 1500s—from Henry VIII to Elizabeth I—wanted the power for themselves, they did not increase the privileges of the English people. However, the Tudors were wise enough to realize that they could not reduce existing rights without causing trouble.

The Stuart kings, James I (1603-1625) and Charles I (1625-1649), who succeeded the Tudors, were not so sensitive. Under them, there was a constant tug-of-war between the will of the king and the will of Parliament.

STUARTS versus PARLIAMENT

James I followed Elizabeth on the throne of England. James believed that he ruled by divine right and that his authority was absolute. This belief angered the members of Parliament. They believed that they possessed certain rights, including control of finances and a voice in foreign policy.

James also angered Parliament by discriminating against the nonconformists or Puritans. Puritans had influence both inside and outside Parliament. At the time Puritans included Low Church Anglicans, Presbyterians, Congregationalists, and those influenced by John Calvin's teachings. James' policies toward them caused some to emigrate to Holland and later to the Americas. Others stayed in England to oppose James both secretly and openly.

emigrate: to leave one country for another

James was usually in need of money because of his extravagance and because of the **inflation** of this period. Parliament, however, was not inclined to grant him money. James dismissed Parliament and ruled without it for some years.

Upon the death of James I, Charles I succeeded his father. He was even more convinced of rule by divine right than James had been. But Charles found it necessary to call Parliament into session to raise money. In 1628 before the members would give it to him, they forced him to agree to the Petition of Right.

The Petition of Right became another foundation stone in the rights of the English people. In this petition, the following limits on the king were approved: no taxes would be collected without the consent of Parliament; martial law could not be applied in time of peace; the English could not be forced to house soldiers in their homes;

and no person could be imprisoned without a trial.

Charles agreed to the conditions, but he was furious. After he received his money, he dismissed Parliament. He refused to call it back into session for another 11 years. To obtain money he imposed heavy taxes on towns and levied heavy fines.

Charles, like his father, hated the Puritans. He persecuted them so severely that many more emigrated to the Americas. He had those who opposed him brought before the Star Chamber, a court that tried people without a jury. Charles especially angered the Scots. When they invaded England, Charles was forced to call Parliament together once again to raise funds. The Parliament which convened in 1640 was in a rebellious mood. The House of Commons was controlled by Puritans. They passed legislation stating that Parliament could not be dismissed without its consent. They also outlawed the special courts that Charles had set up to collect fines. Charles agreed to these laws but later tried to arrest some of the leaders of the House. They escaped. Civil war broke out and Charles fled London in 1642.

King Charles I of England believed in rule by divine right. What does this mean? Can you name other rulers throughout history who believed in divine right monarchy?

Oliver Cromwell, a member of Parliament in 1628 and 1640, became the leader of the Puritans. Above is the warrant issued for Charles I's death. Cromwell's signature is in column one.

OLIVER CROMWELL

Charles was ultimately defeated by the Roundheads. They were so called because they cut their hair short to distinguish themselves from the long-haired Cavaliers who supported Charles I. The Roundheads were under the leadership of Oliver Cromwell. In 1649 they had Charles beheaded for treason.

That a monarch could be executed for treason was an entirely new idea. Until this time only a person who conspired against the monarch was considered a traitor. No one had ever acted on the idea that a monarch might be a traitor to the people.

Oliver Cromwell (1599-1658) changed England into a commonwealth ruled by a council. Later he became a dictator under the title Lord Protector. He and the Puritans had been helped in their overthrow of the king by the more moderate Protestants—Presbyterians and Low Church Anglicans. They wanted a constitutional monarchy rather than a complete overthrow. But Cromwell controlled the army, and his will was carried out. He could have been king, but he refused the title.

Cromwell tried to maintain and increase English power on land and sea. He fought against Spain and seized Jamaica in the Caribbean. He beat the army of the Scots and savagely put down a rebellion in Ireland.

When Cromwell died, he was succeeded by his son Richard. He lacked his father's strength and could not control the English who wanted an end to strict Puritan rule. In 1660 Parliament, supported by the army, recalled Charles II from exile.

constitutional monarchy: rule by a king or queen whose powers are limited by a constitution

497

THE RESTORATION

The period between 1660 and 1688, marking the reestablishment of the **monarchy** in England, is known as the Restoration. Two Stuarts, Charles II and after him James II, ruled during this time. They were the sons of Charles I.

Charles II did not argue with Parliament. He had had enough of exile. Life in England became gayer. Theaters, dancing, card playing, and other pleasures forbidden by the Puritans were once again permitted. But the English were suspicious of Charles' friendship toward France and of his leaning toward Roman Catholicism.

James II ascended the throne on the death of Charles and ruled from 1685 until 1688. James was publicly a Catholic. In 1687 he granted freedom of worship to Catholics and dissenters. Dissenters were Protestants who did not follow the Church of England. Many English thought that James was scheming to return England to Catholicism and to restore the former authority of the monarchy. A faction in Parliament known as the Whigs decided to change rulers. They began what is known as the Glorious Revolution.

THE GLORIOUS REVOLUTION

The Whigs were a group of lords and wealthy merchants. They negotiated with Mary, the Protestant daughter of James II, and her husband, the Dutch prince, William of Orange. They accepted the Whig offer to come to England and occupy the throne. William landed in 1688 with 14,000 soldiers. James had no support and fled to France. Before formally accepting the reign of William and Mary, Parliament had them agree to a Bill of Rights.

BILL OF RIGHTS   This Bill of Rights stated among other items that laws could not be suspended without the consent of Parliament. Taxes for the use of the crown could not be set without Parliament's approval. Parliament's agreement was needed to maintain a standing army during peacetime. Freedom of speech could not be questioned, nor could books be censored. Parliament should meet frequently. The use of excessive bail and fines as well as cruel and unusual punishment should be outlawed. The Bill of Rights had a deep effect upon the writers of the U.S. Constitution. A number of the rights in this bill were incorporated into the first ten amendments to the Constitution.

In 1689 Parliament also passed the Act of Toleration. This allowed freedom of worship to all Protestants who were not Anglican. However, it did not include Roman Catholics.

ACT OF SETTLEMENT   The Act of Settlement confirmed the supremacy of Parliament over the monarch. This act spelled out who would inherit the throne if William and Mary, or Mary's sister Anne, died without heirs. The throne would go to the son of Sophia, granddaughter of James I and wife of the Elector of the German house of Hanover. This happened.

After the deaths of Mary and William, Anne was named queen. During Anne's reign (1702-1714), England and Scotland were united as Great Britain. When Anne died childless, George of Hanover started a new line of English rulers.

During this time, parliamentary government continued to evolve. Political parties arose. The monarch began to choose **cabinet** ministers from the majority party. Thus the leaders of the majority party gradually came to control the executive as well as the legislative branch of English government.

Parliament gained other powers, such as those of declaring war and removing bad judges from the bench. Custom turned into an unwritten law that no act of Parliament could be vetoed by a monarch. By the mid-1700s, the English had erected the government structure which continues to the present.

Chapter 2
Science and Philosophy of the Enlightenment

The successes of science in the 1600s and 1700s helped stimulate inquiry and faith in the scientific method. The belief in natural science progressed slowly through the 1600s and peaked in the Age of Reason or the Enlightenment of the late 1600s and early 1700s.

The Enlightenment was more a state of mind than an actual movement. As in the Renaissance people questioned old values and tried to find ways of correcting abuses in church, state, and society. Of course, the church, state, and society were those which had evolved during and since the Renaissance.

In general the Enlightenment was founded on the principles of naturalism, rationalism, progress, and humanitarianism. Naturalism was a belief in science and natural law. Rationalism said that human reason could determine the principles of natural law and people should live according to them.

Progress and humanitarianism expressed a belief in the rights of the individual and the possibility for the perfection of society. Society could become perfect if people always used reason and thus could gain a greater knowledge of the natural law. From these principles came serious efforts to promote peace and to reform government, society, and education.

NATURAL SCIENCE

The 1600s was a period of transition in Western European thought. The discoveries of Copernicus, Kepler, and Galileo became the foundations for research. Many scientists were at work. Their patient labor, careful experiments, and bold thinking produced great advances

This microscope was made in the 1600s for a wealthy patron of the sciences.

in technology. A deeper understanding of the solar system and a clearer picture of the complexities of the human species emerged.

Scientists turned away from supernatural explanations to natural science and the scientific method. They believed that a natural order existed in the universe. This order was governed by laws of nature which could be scientifically observed.

Scientific development was encouraged by the founding of organizations. Both the English Royal Society and the French Academy of Sciences were established during this period. As had the arts during

the Renaissance, science came under the patronage of kings and queens.

One of the foremost figures of the period was Sir Isaac Newton. His work *Principia* explained gravity—why objects fall and why planets revolve around the sun instead of wandering through space. Newton's law of motion verified the work of Copernicus and became the basis for still later scientific investigations.

Robert Boyle and Antoine Lavoisier (luh-VWAH-zee-ay) are considered the founders of modern chemistry. Through careful experi-

This woodblock print shows Antoine Lavoisier analyzing the elements of air. According to the text, which element did he name?

mentation, Boyle discovered the relationship of the volume of gas to pressure. This is known as Boyle's Law. Boyle distinguished a number of elements and compounds and worked on chemical reactions and analysis. Joseph Priestley discovered oxygen which Lavoisier named. Lavoisier also introduced quantitative analysis to chemistry. He showed that although the state of matter may be changed, its quantity is untouched.

Work in mineralogy progressed during this period but geology did not exist as a separate science until the work of James Hutton. He believed that by studying the different layers of the earth, scientists could determine the earth's age. Contrary to the popular ideas of his day, Hutton believed that the earth was very old.

During the 1600s and 1700s, medical science progressed rapidly. The work of Giovanni Morgagni (mohr-GAH-nyee), an Italian physician, on the nature of disease earned him the title father of pathology. Edward Jenner, an English doctor, discovered a vaccine for smallpox, one of the greatest killers of the time.

Advances were also made in biology. A Dutch naturalist, Anton van Leeuwenhoek (LAY-vuhn-huk), made simple microscopes and described tiny cells of living matter. His discoveries started a field of research called microbiology. Robert Hooke (1635-1703) studied the structure of plants and coined the word cell. In Sweden, Carl Linnaeus (luh-NEE-uhs) founded the modern study of biology and established the present system of classifying plants and animals.

Continued development of scientific instruments helped promote discovery and accuracy. For example, Gabriel Fahrenheit (FAH-ren-hyt), a German physicist, devised a mercury thermometer. His method of measuring temperature is still used.

This is a reproduction of Gabriel Fahrenheit's thermometer. His differed from earlier ones because he used mercury instead of alcohol. Mercury is more accurate.

RATIONALISM AND RELIGION

The scientific triumphs of the 1600s and 1700s deeply influenced the religious and intellectual thought of the period. Writers, scientists, and thinkers developed an attitude toward religion known as deism (DEE-iz-uhm). Deism is incorrectly thought to be the same as atheism (AY-thee-iz-uhm), the belief that there is no god. Deists, on the contrary, believed that God created the world and the natural laws that govern its operations. After creation, God withdrew. The world was left to run according to its natural laws.

Deists believed that there was never any supernatural interference, such as miracles, in the functioning of the world or in the lives of humans. Therefore, people should occupy themselves with a natural, rational religion. Because God and all that God has made is good, there is no place in life for superstition, persecution, or intolerance.

Deism was not an organized religion with ritual and ceremony. While deism appealed to certain individuals, it was too impersonal for most people. A number of new religious movements appeared. The two most important were Methodism and Quakerism.

This portrait bust of Voltaire was sculpted by Jean-Antoine Houdon. What characteristics of Voltaire does Houdon appear to have captured?

In Methodism, John Wesley presented a doctrine that was more personal than deism but less formal than Anglicanism. George Fox founded the Society of Friends who are popularly called Quakers. They rejected ceremonies and religious symbols such as statues. They opposed war and refused to bear arms.

THE PHILOSOPHES   Some of the greatest intellectuals of the Enlightenment considered themselves deists. Among them were the philosophes (FEE-luh-zofz) of France.

The philosophes were not true philosophers in that none of them created a system of philosophy as had Aquinas or Aristotle. Rather, the philosophes shared a belief in the ability of reason to solve problems and to correct abuses. They also shared a hatred of intolerance, ignorance, superstition, and persecution. At least, this was their official position. Some, for example, Voltaire and Rousseau, could be very intolerant of anyone who disagreed with them. The ideas of the philosophes were extremely important in stirring up the French Revolution and giving it direction.

Francois Marie Arouet, known as Voltaire (vohl-TAIR), was a master of satire. On several occasions his sharp wit resulted in exile or prison. In *Philosophical Letters,* Voltaire praised the workings of the English political system which he had observed during one of his exiles. Other of his works that show the spirit of the philosophes are *Poem on Natural Law* and *Essays on the Manners and Spirit of Nations.*

Jean Jacques Rousseau (roo-SOH) came to national attention in 1750 when he won an essay prize from the Academy of Dijon. The topic the Academy had chosen was whether the arts and sciences had improved the morals of humankind. Rousseau took the position that people had been corrupted by the arts and sciences. This was an unusual viewpoint for the 1700s. Rousseau presented further ideas in his essay *The Origin of Inequality Among Men,* in a study on educational theories called *Emile,* and in his chief work, *The Social Contract.*

In *The Social Contract,* Rousseau maintained that all people are free and equal. All social and political forms must have as their aim the protection of the rights of the individual. The people are sovereign. Monarchs ruled not by divine right but because this right was given to them by the people. Rousseau upheld the idea that the people should choose their own rulers.

In the 1740s, Denis Diderot (dee-DROH) was commissioned to work on a French translation of an English encyclopedia. Diderot, one of the philosophes, saw the project as an opportunity to unite into one collection all the efforts and talents of his age. He convinced his publisher to start on an entirely new encyclopedia instead of a translation. Nearly every well-known person in the arts and sciences —many of whom were Diderot's friends—contributed to the *En-*

cyclopedia. Also known as *Descriptive Dictionary of the Sciences, Arts, and Crafts,* the work is a chronicle of the learning and spirit of the Enlightenment.

INFLUENCES ON THE AMERICAN REVOLUTION   The thought of the Enlightenment spread across Europe and found its way to the New World. Of the French writers of the 1700s, Montesquieu (mahn-tuhs-KYOO) had the strongest influence upon the Americans who wrote the Constitution. Montesquieu was trained for the legal profession and eventually became a judge. However, like the philosophes, he was deeply stirred by the scientific advances of the period.

In 1748, after 20 years of study, Montesquieu published *The Sprirt of the Laws.* In this work he analyzed different laws and constitutions. They ranged from ancient ones to those of his own time. From his findings, Montesquieu recommended that government powers be separated into legislative, judicial, and executive branches.

The American Declaration of Independence states one of the most important theories of the English writer John Locke. In *The Treatises of Government,* he said that people have the right to freedom of speech and of worship. Locke also believed that people are sovereign and that government is responsible for their welfare. If the rights of the people are abused or threatened, the people have the right to overthrow the government.

OTHER PHILOSOPHERS   Not all philosophers of the Enlightenment were deists, but most were greatly influenced by the interest in science of the time. Rene Descartes (day-KAHRT) of France believed that although the human body is governed by natural laws, the mind and soul are not. Descartes based his system of philosophy on logic. His motto became "I think, therefore I am."

In England Thomas Hobbes developed the philosophy of materialism. He believed that people were only matter and motion. Thus the study of human beings could be approached through science. The materialistic views of the 1600s were further developed by David Hume. He believed that experience is the only source of knowledge. His philosophy is known as empiricism (im-PIR-ih-siz-uhm).

Emmanuel Kant was perhaps the greatest philosopher of the time. He attempted to bring together rationalism and empiricism. He outlined his theories in such works as the *Critique of Pure Reason.*

SOCIAL SCIENCES

During the 1600s and 1700s, natural law and laws of science were applied to the study of people. History was one of the first disciplines to make use of the new scientific techniques of critical scholarship. Giovanni Vico (VEE-koh) of Italy analyzed early Greek and Roman

Rousseau (top) believed that arts and sciences had corrupted people. Why was this an unusual view for the Age of Enlightenment? Descartes (bottom) believed people could use reason to find truth. Compare this to Aristotle's philosophy.

sources and decided that many were not accurate. Along with Montesquieu, he attached importance to environment and climate as forces that shape history.

The scientific method was also applied to law, and there emerged a group of scientific jurists. One of the most famous was Jeremy Bentham who is credited with the philosophy of utilitarianism. Bentham believed that things should be judged according to their usefulness. He advocated "the greatest happiness of the greatest number." He spent much of his life working for legal reform based upon his theory.

WOMEN AND BLACKSTONE'S COMMENTARIES   William Blackstone's *Commentaries on the Laws of England* proposed that English law be based on scientific principles. This work was to become the cornerstone of the English and American legal systems.

Unfortunately portions of the *Commentaries* did much to erode the legal status of women. Since the Middle Ages when women had been independent entities, their rights had been slowly decreased. Blackstone codified the process. Blackstone stated that the legal existence of a woman was suspended during her marriage. All possessions belonged to her husband. The husband was even the guardian of their children.

Blackstone probably intended these *Commentaries* to be used for the protection and benefit of married women. However, later writers have cited them to show the historical subjection of all women to men. It was not until the present century that some of the laws created by Blackstone's work were replaced by woman's **suffrage** and equality under the law. In France the later Napoleonic Code had the same effect on women's rights as Blackstone's work had.

subjection:
being under the power
or control of another

Chapter 3
The French Revolution and Napoleon

In France the worship of reason reached its high point during the French Revolution. A goddess of reason was seated on the high altar of the Cathedral of Notre Dame in Paris. However, men such as Montesquieu, Voltaire, and Rousseau did not intend to overthrow the French monarchy. They wished only to reform abuses. The philosophes hoped to change the French monarchy to one like that of England. They wanted a government in which the monarch's power was limited and where the people were represented in a parliament. However, to save the nation, some people felt it necessary to destroy the system.

DISCONTENT

Louis XIV and Louis XV had squandered the treasury of France upon wars and displays of magnificence. The burdens of taxation fell heavily upon the middle class and the poor. The people looked bitterly at

the extravagance of the king and queen, nobles, and clergy, none of whom paid taxes.

Many of the literate French had read Voltaire's satiric attacks on the privileges of the upper class. They knew Montesquieu's idea of the separation of powers. Many of them believed with Rousseau that humans were basically good. Society had corrupted them. The French found in the newly formed U.S. a model of government by, for, and of the people.

By 1789 the French were ready for change. In that year a desperate Louis XVI called a meeting of the Estates-General. He needed money urgently. The Estates-General was the French legislative assembly. It had not met for 175 years.

The First Estate represented the clergy. The Second Estate was the nobility. The Third Estate was the rest of France—the commoners—and had twice as many representatives as the other two estates combined. The three estates traditionally voted as separate units, each with one vote. Thus the **conservative** clergy and nobility could outvote the commoners two to one.

So long as this method of voting was followed, the Third Estate had little hope of pushing through their reforms. They wanted the three estates to meet together in a national assembly where the ballots of individual representatives would be counted. In this way, the commoners could—with some support from **liberal** clergy or nobility—outvote the other two estates.

Louis refused to allow this. However, the commoners were not

The Palace of Versailles, southwest of Paris, was begun by Louis XIV in 1661. Later monarchs added to it. The best architects, artists, and landscapers were used in its design and decoration. In 1789 the Estates-General met there to consider Louis XVI's money request.

505

to be denied. They declared themselves to be the National Assembly and took an oath that they would not disband until they had written a new constitution. Louis gave in and ordered representatives of all three estates to meet as the new National Assembly.

NATIONAL ASSEMBLY

In an effort to exercise control, the king secretly began bringing troops into Paris. When the people of Paris learned this, they turned into a mob. The mob stormed and captured the Bastille (ba-STEEL), a fortress-prison which had become a symbol of the wrongs done to commoners by the ruling class. This happened on July 14, 1789. The date is now celebrated as Bastille Day and to the French it marks the beginning of their independence.

The Revolutionary tricolor—a flag of blue, white, and red—soon flew over the city of Paris. Throughout France revolution spread. Hated nobility were driven from castles and chateaus. Officials were killed.

The Bastille dates to the 1300s when it was used as a fortress. Later it was turned into a jail for political prisoners. The storming of the Bastille marked the beginning of the French Revolution.

Records of debts were burned. The slogan of the Revolution became liberty, equality, and fraternity.

Meeting in an atmosphere of change and violence, the National Assembly swept away the ancient feudal structure of government. Serfdom and special obligations to royalty and church were abolished. The privileges of the old governing class were removed. Anyone could now hold public office. Everyone would be taxed.

These sweeping changes were capped with a statement known as the Declaration of the Rights of Man. This document proclaimed the principles of the Revolution. It followed in the tradition of the English Bill of Rights and the American Declaration of Independence. It made all men equal before the law. Every man had a right to participate in the making of this law either personally or through representatives. No man could be arrested or imprisoned except in cases prescribed by law. Women were excluded from politics. In 1790 the Girondist revolutionary Condorcet wrote "The Admission of Women to Full Citizenship," deploring this situation.

In 1791 the National Assembly wrote a constitution for France which turned the absolute monarchy into a limited one. A government of three separate branches—executive, legislative, and judicial—was established, following the principles of Montesquieu. Thinking they had finished their job, the members of the National Assembly disbanded in 1791. Later a Legislative Assembly was elected according to the rules set down in the new constitution.

LEGISLATIVE ASSEMBLY

The moderate middle class was opposed in this Legislative Assembly by more radical groups led by Jean Paul Marat (mah-RAH), Georges Jacques Danton (dahn-TOHN), and Maximilien Robespierre (ROHBZ-pyeer). The radical leaders wanted a republic rather than a **limited monarchy**. They were helped by the success Prussia and Austria were having against the French on the battlefield. Rulers of these two nations had feared the French Revolution might inspire their own people to revolt. They organized an army to restore the **absolute monarchy** in France.

Emotions flared in Paris. A mob attacked the palace. The king fled to the protection of the Legislative Assembly. The Austro-Prussian army continued to move toward Paris. Radicals killed several thousand **royalists** and clergy imprisoned in Paris. Their actions have become known as the September Massacres of 1792. In this atmosphere, the assembly called for a new National Convention to draw up another constitution.

NATIONAL CONVENTION

The new National Convention governed France from 1792 to 1795.

Three major groups sat in the convention: the Girondists, the Jacobins, and those called the Plain of the Marsh. The Girondists (juh-RAHN-duhsts) were the more conservative **republicans** and represented the upper middle class. The Jacobins (JAK-uh-buhns) represented part of the middle class and the more radical elements among the peasants and workers. The members of the Plain of the Marsh shifted between these two groups.

The Girondists controlled the convention until about the middle of 1793. Under their leadership, the monarchy was abolished. Louis XVI was tried, convicted, and executed for treason. Under Girondist leadership, however, France suffered great military losses. These losses, along with a lack of capable and determined leadership, weakened the Girondists. The Jacobins were able to capture leadership.

Under such leaders as Robespierre, the Jacobins established a revolutionary government. It was headed by two committees—the Committee of Public Safety and the Committee of General Security. These committees administered the government, waged war abroad, and kept peace at home. A revolutionary tribunal hunted out and tried suspected enemies.

Because of its harshness against its enemies, the government of the Jacobins has frequently been called the Terror. Many people suspected or accused of treason were shot or beheaded by the guillotine. Those who died by the guillotine included the queen of France, Marie Antoinette, leaders of the Girondists like Danton, and thousands of royalists and others. The revolutionary government ended in July 1794 when a group called the Thermidorians (thur-muh-DOR-ih-uhnz) seized power. They were fearful of Robespierre and more moderate in their politics. Robespierre and his chief followers were sent to the guillotine.

In 1795 members of the National Convention put into effect a new republican constitution. They established a legislature of two houses and placed the executive power of the government in the hands of five men, known as Directors. Their government, known as the Directory, controlled France from 1795 until 1799. It was not a particularly honest or efficient ruling group. In 1799 Napoleon Bonaparte, a man of unusual military ability, dismissed the Directors with the help of the army. In the same year he became the First Consul of France. In 1804 he proclaimed himself emperor.

Marie Antoinette, once queen of France, is bound and awaiting judgment. Is this how you expect to see a queen—even one about to be executed? Does this drawing reflect the French Revolution's idea of equality? How?

NAPOLEON BONAPARTE

Among the French, Napoleon is still regarded as one of their greatest heroes. Napoleon centralized the government, improved communications, and introduced a system of public education. With the Napoleonic Code he unified the laws of France. Although based on old Roman law, the code also contained principles born of the Revolution.

Napoleon continued the process which the Revolution had started of turning the French provincial into the French national. When the revolutionary government drafted men for the armies, it appealed to their love of France and of the principles of liberty, equality, and fraternity. These appeals developed in the French a spirit of **patriotism** and nationalism.

During his leadership Napoleon also appealed to this love of country. The French were constantly reminded that they were being asked to fight for the glory and honor of their nation. Thus the citizens of France became conscious of the oneness of their culture and their land.

RISE TO POWER   Napoleon Bonaparte was born on the French island of Corsica. He studied at military schools in France. During the Revolution he rose quickly to the rank of brigadier general. In 1796 he was given command of the French forces fighting the Austrians in Italy. His marriage to Josephine de Beauharnais (boh-ahr-NAY), who had influence with the Directory, and his military record helped obtain this appointment.

During a swift campaign Napoleon won a reputation for military genius and skillful **diplomacy**. The successful end to the war gave France command of much of northern Italy. This left France with only one military opponent—Great Britain. Napoleon persuaded the Directors to approve his plan of an expedition to the Middle East. He thought he could strike a heavy blow at Britain by hurting its trade in the East.

The Middle Eastern campaign went badly at first. Admiral Nelson, a British naval hero, destroyed Napoleon's fleet in 1798. Napoleon's communication and supply lines from France were cut. However, the following year French troops were able to defeat the Turkish allies of the British. Napoleon left his army and returned to France where he and his followers seized power. They set up a government known as the Consulate. Napoleon became First Consul and ruled France as such from 1799 to 1804.

CONSUL   By diplomacy and war, Napoleon was able to defeat his enemies. The Austrians, who again had gone to war against France, asked for peace in 1801. In 1802 Great Britain made peace.

Napoleon then turned toward the Americas. He dreamed of a vast colonial empire built around Haiti in the Caribbean and the Louisiana Territory. The latter he had forced Spain to give to France in 1801. However, Napoleon's costly wars in Europe, the continued resistance of the Haitians, and yellow fever among his troops changed his plans. In 1804 Haiti was able to win its independence. In 1803 Napoleon was forced to sell the Louisiana Territory to the U.S. for $15,000,000. Reluctantly Napoleon had to discard his scheme of an overseas empire.

At home, however, Napoleon was more successful. He reorganized

Napoleon Bonaparte posed for this portrait by the neoclassical painter Jacques Louis David in 1810. This was 11 years after Napoleon first came to power. What methods did he use to gain and keep power in France?

Empire of Napoleon, 1812

Atlantic Ocean

NORWAY

FINLAND

SCOTLAND

SWEDEN

USSR

North Sea

Baltic Sea

ENGLAND

POLAND

W. GER.

FRANCE

ITALY

ROMANIA

YUGO.

Black Sea

CORSICA

SPAIN

BULGARIA

SARDINIA

TURKEY

Mediterranean Sea

SICILY

☐ Ruled by or Allied to France
☐ Independent Nations

and centralized the government. His economic reforms brought greater prosperity to France. Secure in the affection and support of his people, Napoleon asked for their approval to become emperor.

EMPEROR In 1804 the pope came to Paris to crown Napoleon in the Cathedral of Notre Dame. When the pope was about to place the crown on Napoleon's head, Napoleon took it and crowned himself. The power expressed by this gesture was not lost on the Europeans. From 1804 to 1815 Emperor Napoleon I was dominant in Europe. During these years he was busy with war and conquest. His greatest enemy was Great Britain.

War broke out between Britain and France again in 1805. Napoleon prepared to cross the channel and conquer Britain with the help of his ally, Spain. Britain, however, had more experienced sailors and better ships. At the battle of Trafalgar, off the coast of Spain, Admiral Nelson destroyed many French and Spanish ships without the loss of a British vessel. With Nelson's victory, Britain controlled the seas and Napoleon found the English Channel impossible to cross.

Napoleon turned his attention to the interior of Europe. Between 1805 and 1807 he defeated the Austrians, Russians, and Prussians. Napoleon reached the summit of his glory in 1807. In that year by the Treaty of Tilsit, he and Czar Alexander I divided Europe between them. By this settlement Napoleon became either directly or indirectly the ruler of Europe to the borders of Russia, the Ottoman Empire, and Sweden.

In the meantime, Britain had established a blockade of Napoleon's empire. Although British goods were smuggled into the continent, the industries and economies of France and other European nations suffered. Napoleon's policies of economic control and his taking of money and material to support his wars were draining these countries of their resources. Napoleon's continual nibbling at parts of Europe further angered the Spanish, Austrians, Prussians, and Russians.

In 1808 France invaded Spain. Spanish civilian fighters began to use hit-and-run tactics against the French. This kind of war came to be known as **guerrilla** warfare. The British sent forces under the command of the Duke of Wellington to help the Spanish. The Peninsular War drew 300,000 French troops. But even so large a number of soldiers was not enough for a French victory.

Then Napoleon made one of his biggest mistakes. In 1812 he tried to conquer Russia. He assembled an army of 500,000 soldiers and marched into Russia. The strategy of the Russians, however, consisted of one long retreat. The French could not keep their army supplied because the Russians burned everything as they retreated. By the time Napoleon reached Moscow his troops had been reduced by a third. The Russians had lost few soldiers.

The Russians withdrew beyond Moscow and set fire to the city.

blockade: a military tactic to keep ships from entering or leaving another nation's ports

Napoleon flees Moscow as hundreds of thousands of his troops die in the snow. This scene was painted by Jan Chelminski, a Polish painter of the early 1900s. What characteristics of Napoleon might interest a later artist in painting him?

The French were without shelter. With supplies running out, winter coming, and the czar refusing to meet his terms, Napoleon began a retreat. Lack of discipline among his discouraged troops, the long march, winter, and Russian attacks killed more than three-fourths of Napoleon's army.

Encouraged by Napoleon's failures in Spain and Russia, all of Europe entered into a **coalition** against him. In October 1813 he was defeated at the battle of Leipzig (LYP-sig) in Saxony. The following April coalition forces occupied Paris and the Emperor Napoleon abdicated. He was exiled and given the small island of Elba, off the coast of Italy, to rule.

CONGRESS OF VIENNA

With Napoleon in exile, representatives of the leading monarchs of Europe assembled for the **Congress** of Vienna. Although a meeting of all representatives never took place, much work was done in committees. Britain, Austria, Prussia, and Russia emerged as the chief powers at the Congress. Clemens Metternich, prime minister of Austria, was the dominant figure. Through skillful diplomacy, Talleyrand, who had been a leading diplomat under Napoleon, obtained very easy peace terms for France.

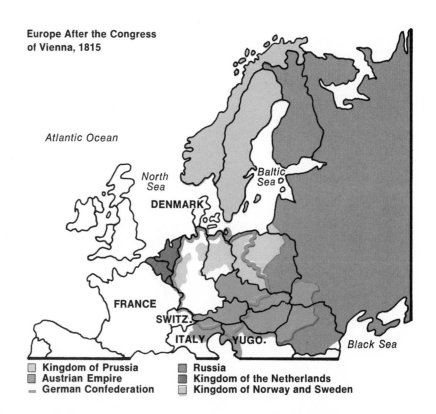

Europe After the Congress of Vienna, 1815

Atlantic Ocean

North Sea

Baltic Sea

DENMARK

FRANCE

SWITZ.

ITALY YUGO.

Black Sea

☐ Kingdom of Prussia
☐ Austrian Empire
▬ German Confederation
■ Russia
■ Kingdom of the Netherlands
☐ Kingdom of Norway and Sweden

One of the chief aims of the Congress was the restoration of the monarchs who had been overthrown by Napoleon. King Louis XVIII came to power in France. Monarchs were also returned to the thrones of the Netherlands and several German and Italian states. Another objective was the establishment of alliances among European nations. These would insure a **balance of power**. In this way no single nation could become powerful enough to threaten the others.

As a result of the Congress of Vienna, the map of Europe was redrawn. Territories were swapped without regard for inhabitants. Rulers and politicians were interested only in payment for losses suffered at the hands of Napoleon.

Belgium and the Netherlands were combined into the Kingdom of the Netherlands. Denmark, who had fought with Napoleon, was forced to give Norway to Sweden, who had fought against Napoleon. Poland was carved up among Austria, Russia, and Prussia. Austria also took some Italian states. Finland was given to Russia. The Holy Roman Empire was replaced by a confederation of German states. Prussia took part of Saxony and other lands along the Rhine River.

Napoleon, however, was not yet finished. In March 1815 he escaped from Elba and returned to France. The people rallied to his cause. Once again the coalition formed against him. On June 18, 1815, at the battle of Waterloo, Belgium, he was again defeated. Napoleon was exiled to the small island of St. Helena in the South Atlantic where he died in 1821.

While the 1600s and 1700s saw new developments in government, science, and philosophy, the artistic and literary movements were not so deeply influenced. They continued in the classical style of previous centuries. Artists and writers continued to look to early Greece and Rome for inspiration. Classicism in the 1600s came to be known as baroque (buh-ROHK) and in the 1700s as rococo.

Chapter 4
The Arts

BAROQUE

The term baroque is used for the period from about 1600 to around 1750. In some countries baroque style appeared earlier than in others, and disappeared earlier. The word itself means misshapen pearl, thus something rare, unusual, or strange.

ART AND ARCHITECTURE Baroque style in art is characterized by bold sweeping curves and sharp color contrasts. Painters and architects tried to capture a feeling of movement and space. Baroque, first seen in Italy around 1600, developed from the earlier mannerist style. The most typical baroque art and architecture appeared in Germany, Italy, Austria, Spain, and France. In England, the style

Above is The Mill *by Rembrandt.*
To the right is The Artist in His Studio
*by Jan Vermeer. From the description
in the text, what characteristics
of baroque art can you find
in these two paintings?*

arrived later and never became as widespread as it was on the Continent.

The Flemish painter, Peter Paul Rubens was among the first and greatest of the baroque artists. His use of color and portrayal of skin color are especially noteworthy. Even though he employed many assistants, the number of paintings that are all his own is astounding: portraits, hunting scenes, enormous murals of religious events, village feasts, and scenes from mythology. His paintings are full of color and life.

Sir Anthony Van Dyck, a pupil of Rubens, is considered the founder of the English school of portraiture. He painted portraits of the English royal family, members of the aristocracy, and other notables. His work had an elegance and quality that was new to England.

One of Spain's greatest painters, Velasquez (vuh-LAS-kuhs), lived during this period. At first, he painted chiefly religious or domestic subjects. Later his paintings became less detailed and naturalistic. Two centuries later his style would influence the French impressionists. Velasquez himself appears to have been influenced strongly by the earlier Titian.

Among the Dutch artists of the time were Franz Hals, Jan Vermeer, and Rembrandt van Rijn (RYN). Hals' works are alive with color and cheerfulness. His interest in good living is reflected in the subject matter of many of his paintings. In contrast to Hals, Vermeer painted

scenes of quiet home life. Rembrandt is considered one of the world's master painters. He was a careful observer of life and an excellent storyteller. Whether he depicted a scene from the Bible or a scene from his local village, he painted with both sympathy and understanding.

In France the long reign of Louis XIV (1643-1715) coincided with much of the baroque period. One of the great French baroque painters was Charles Le Brun. Although Le Brun did paint portraits, his chief work was that of interior decorator. Louis XIV entrusted him with decorating the palace of Versailles (vuhr-SY). Le Brun painted some ceilings and murals himself. Mostly, however, he designed tapestries, furniture, chandeliers, art objects, and even door handles and locks for the palace. For nearly 30 years he supervised the artists and craftworkers who made Versailles a palace worthy of the Sun King, as Louis was called.

In Italy baroque architecture originated with Bernini (buhr-NEE-nee) and Borromini (bohr-roh-MEE-nee). Both were employed by the Vatican and both worked on St. Peter's Cathedral. Bernini designed the colonnade and square in front of the cathedral.

The grand and decorative style of baroque architecture quickly spread across Europe. This excessive decoration characterized such buildings as Frederick the Great's palace at Potsdam in modern East Germany. In many places baroque soon was transformed into the elaborate rococo style.

In England in the 1600s the first great architect was Inigo Jones. He had visited Italy and studied the buildings of the earlier Palladio. When Jones returned to England, he began to use Palladio's principles of design. The Banqueting Hall in Whitehall Palace, London, is considered Jones' finest work. His buildings mark English architecture's break with medieval tradition.

From left to right are Portrait of an Officer *by Franz Hals;* The Needlewoman *by Velasquez; and,* Head of One of the Three Kings *by Peter Paul Rubens.*

515

Sir Christopher Wren designed St. Paul's Cathedral in 1675. He followed classical style. Compare it with the picture of St. Peter's Church, page 463, built along classical lines during the Renaissance.

Christopher Wren further developed classical architecture in England. In 1665 Wren traveled to France where he met Bernini. Bernini's designs and the buildings that were being constructed in and around Paris had a great influence upon Wren. When Wren returned home he was asked to submit a plan for remodeling St. Paul's Cathedral. At that time it was the largest medieval cathedral in Europe. However, St. Paul's was completely destroyed in the Great Fire of London in 1666. Wren was then commissioned to rebuild St. Paul's. The cathedral he designed is a huge yet perfectly proportioned example of the classical style.

MUSIC   Italy dominated music throughout the 1600s. The most outstanding achievement was the growth of opera. Often operas of this period were based on classical themes. Monteverdi and Scarlatti (skahr-LAH-tee) were among the major operatic composers. The peak of Italian baroque instrumental music came with Vivaldi (vih-VAHL-dee).

The operatic form spread to Germany when Heinrich Schutz composed the first German opera. An Italian, Lully (loo-LEE) is credited with founding French opera. French opera made elaborate use of ballet and chorus. Henry Purcell is generally regarded as the greatest English composer of the period. Among his many musical pieces is the short opera, *Dido and Aeneas.*

LITERATURE   In literature baroque meant a flowery style. The greatest baroque literature was written in France and England.

Under Louis XIV, French literature enjoyed a golden age. Three dramatists, Corneille (kor-NAY), Moliere (mohl-YAIR), and Racine (ruh-SEEN) were at work. In classical tragedies like *Le Cid,* Corneille glorified the concept of duty. Racine followed the classic style in such works as *Phedre.* Unlike Corneille and Racine, Moliere's comedies satirized human weaknesses.

In Puritan England the most notable literary works were those of John Milton. After Shakespeare, he is considered the greatest English poet. His work reflects his religious and political interests. Among his best known poems are *L'Allegro, Il Penseroso,* and the epic *Paradise Lost.*

Many English nobles had gone into exile in France while the Puritans had been in power. There, the nobles had been impressed by the elaborate scenery and stage machinery of French theaters. When they returned to England, at the time of the Restoration, they brought back some of these ideas. As a result, the staging of English plays became more elaborate.

The greatest writer of tragedy of this period was John Dryden. His most famous play, *All for Love,* is based on the story of Antony and Cleopatra. Today Restoration tragedies are likely to seem pompous and dull. This is not true, however, of the comedies of the period. Called comedies of manners, they satirize society and its customs.

ROCOCO

Rococo evolved from the baroque style. This new style was lighter and less formal than baroque. Rococo was popular from 1720 to about 1770, especially in France. There this period is also called Louis XV.

ART AND ARCHITECTURE   By about 1720 an evolving rococo style was becoming evident in France. Free-flowing lines in long or short S- and C-curves were being used. Designs were being based on natural forms—flowers, shells, and animals. Eventually, as a result of the growing trade with Asia, Chinese designs began to appear in art and furniture.

Rococo was essentially light-hearted, cheerful, and even superficial. It expressed the mood of a society that was reacting to the ceremony of the earlier baroque period. A characteristic of the 1600s was the glorification of **Church and State**. If baroque can be called a religious style—and in Europe in the 1600s the sovereign was very close to a deity—then rococo is a worldly style.

Jean Antoine Watteau (wah-TOH) of France, in spite of his early date, painted pictures that capture the very spirit of rococo. Misty delicate outdoor settings are filled with young nobles, men and women, dressed as shepherds. They appear to be living in a world devoted to pleasure. Francois Boucher's (boo-SHAY) paintings also portray a gaiety and luxury typical of the period. Soft tones of blues and pinks predominate in his pictures.

Not all artists of an era paint in the prevailing style. There are always exceptions. One such exception to rococo style was William Hogarth. He was the first truly English artist and he does not fit into any school or style. Many of his paintings are social commentaries. They are satirical or express a moral. Hogarth's portraits often seem to be comments on the character of the sitter rather than a picture of the sitter's appearance. He refused to flatter his subjects, and therefore was not very popular.

Sir Joshua Reynolds had little in common with his contemporary Hogarth, either artistically or intellectually. Reynolds was a product of his period. His portraits give the subjects an air of aristocratic elegance. This was probably one reason for his popularity. Reynolds established and became the first president of the Royal Academy of Arts. English art thus came under the patronage of the royal family.

MUSIC   The influence of rococo is also apparent in music. Musical works were lighter in mood than those of the baroque period. There was more emphasis on melody. Music historians refer to music of the later 1700s as classical.

In 1710 German-born George Frederick Handel arrived in London. Handel had been thoroughly trained in all forms of musical composition. His output was enormous and varied. At first he composed operas in the Italian style but later turned to oratorios. His masterpiece, the

Madame de Pompadour
*by Francois Boucher is an
example of the rococo
use of soft colors. What
other characteristics
of rococo art can you see
in this picture?*

Messiah, is now a traditional Christmas piece. For nearly 40 years Handel was a major influence on English music.

The German, Johann Sebastian Bach, although writing music in the 1700s was baroque in style. Bach attempted through his work to show his religious devotion. Among his most famous compositions are the *Mass in B Minor* and the *St. Matthew Passion*.

Also important during the 1700s were Wolfgang Amadeus Mozart (MOHT-sahrt) and Franz Joseph Haydn (HYD-uhn), both of Austria. Mozart was writing music by the age of six. During his short life, he composed more than 600 works including concertos, symphonies, and operas. Haydn composed more than a hundred symphonies as well as the oratorios, *The Creation* and *The Seasons*.

NEOCLASSICISM

In the first half of the 1700s excavations were begun at the ancient Roman cities of Herculaneum (huhr-kyuh-LAY-nee-uhm), and Pompeii (pahm-PAY). Both cities had been buried in 79 A.D. by an eruption of Mount Vesuvius (vuh-SOO-vee-uhs). The rediscovery of these two cities aroused a strong interest in things ancient.

ART AND ARCHITECTURE   In the 1700s Robert Adam established a neoclassical style in architecture. It was based upon many actual models and architectural designs found in Pompeii. The style was light and elegant. It contrasted sharply with the more stately designs of Palladianism. The influence of Adam and his three brothers was felt not only in architecture and interior decoration but also in furniture design, silver, jewelry, and carpets.

In painting neoclassicism aimed at simplicity, beauty, and nobility. Artists portrayed the virtue, courage, and patriotism which they believed were characteristic of ancient Greeks and Romans. Like Hogarth, neoclassicists expressed a moral in their paintings. Unfortunately, they lacked Hogarth's wit. Neoclassicists also glorified the political ideals of first the French Revolution and later the Napoleonic era.

Important neoclassical works were painted by Jacques Louis David (dah-VEED). David developed a rigid, cold style very different from that of his teacher, Boucher. David painted not for the court or the

The above is a line of music from Fugue in A-flat *for organ by Johann Sebastian Bach. Although Bach lived most of his life in the 1700s (1685-1750), his work was baroque in character. Overlapping of trends and time periods is a drawback in grouping people into schools of thought. As a student can you see any advantages to learning artists or thinkers by common characteristics? The lute is a Middle Eastern instrument that became popular in Europe.*

519

aristocracy but for the middle class. He wanted to preach a moral and to spread the new political ideals. For example, *The Battle of the Romans and Sabines* was a plea to end state factions and to live in peace and harmony. Elisabeth Vigee-Lebrun (vee-ZHAY-luh-BRUN), a contemporary of David, was at one time the official portrait painter of Marie Antoinette. Her later works reflect the influence of neoclassicism.

LITERATURE   Most of the best known English literature of the 1700s was prose. Alexander Pope's poetry was the great exception. Style and form were of utmost importance to the prose writers. The writing was elegant and polished. However, it was firmly rooted in logic and common sense, characteristics of the Age of Reason.

A good illustration are the works of Jonathan Swift such as *Gulliver's Travels.* His prose is marked by a clear style, logical development, and satire. The leading figure of the latter half of the 1700s was Samuel Johnson. His *Dictionary of the English Language* became the model for all succeeding dictionaries. His work had a tremendous impact on the development of the English language.

During the early 1700s in England, literature and the theater ceased to be the exclusive interest of the nobility. The Glorious Revolution of 1688 ruined the supporters of King James. Many went into exile with him. During the same time, the rising middle class became supporters of the new monarchs, William and Mary.

The middle class became the new elite. They began to attend the theater and patronize the arts. From this point on the English middle class began to color society with its values. The team of Joseph Addison and Richard Steele wrote for this group. In their periodicals *The Tatler* and later *The Spectator,* they preached goodness, learning, and good manners.

Middle-class theater-goers objected to the often bawdy plays of the Restoration. The comedy of manners became proper, genteel, and sentimental to the point of tears. For years this new comedy of tears played English stages. The first writer to rebel was Oliver Goldsmith with *She Stoops to Conquer.* Later Richard Brinsley Sheridan brought satire back to the theater with *The Rivals* and *School for Scandal.*

The 1700s also witnessed the growth of a new literary form—the novel. The novel was patterned after the style and type of works of Swift and Daniel Defoe, who wrote *Robinson Crusoe.* The first novel was *Pamela* by Samuel Richardson. It became so popular that such works soon followed as Henry Fielding's *Tom Jones,* Tobias Smollett's *Roderick Random* and *Humphrey Clinker* and Laurence Sterne's *Tristram Shandy.*

Horace Walpole and Anne Radcliffe developed the Gothic novel. They used mystery, terror, and castles to create a mood for their sentimental romances.

In an illustration from Jonathan Swift's Gulliver's Travels, *Gulliver inspects the Lilliputian army. Although considered by many to be a children's story, Swift's work is an attack on English society and government of the early 1700s. Why do you think art is used as propaganda? Is satire propaganda?*

Summing Up The Unit

Social Studies Vocabulary

Define: inflation; conservative; limited monarchy; absolute monarchy; royalist; republican; patriotism; coalition; balance of power

People

Identify: Newton; Hutton; van Leeuwenhoek; Linnaeus; Wesley; Voltaire; Rousseau; Diderot; Descartes; Rubens; Velasquez; Rembrandt; Wren; Lully; Milton; Boucher; Hogarth; Reynolds; Bach; Handel; David; Pope; Johnson; Defoe

Words

Identify: naturalism; rationalism; humanitarianism; Quakers; philosophes; deism; materialism; empiricism; utilitarianism; First, Second, Third Estates; Directors; baroque; comedy of manners; rococo; neoclassicism; comedy of tears; novel

⌐ Questions

1. How did James I anger Parliament?
2. a. Why did Charles I agree to the Petition of Right? b. What limits did it set?
3. Why was the idea that prompted Charles I's execution so unusual?
4. What was the Restoration?
5. What caused the Glorious Revolution?
6. What changes were made by: a. Glorious Revolution; b. Bill of Rights; c. Act of Settlement?
7. How did the English government continue to evolve during the first half of the 1700s?
8. Relate science to the Enlightenment.
9. a. On what four principles was the Enlightenment based? b. What efforts resulted from it?
10. Why did scientists turn to natural science and the scientific method?
11. a. How did Montesquieu influence the U.S. Constitution? b. What theory of Locke is stated in the U.S. Declaration of Independence?
12. How did Blackstone's *Commentaries* erode the legal status of women?
13. a. How did the philosophes want to change the French monarchy? b. Why didn't they succeed?
14. In seeking change, how were the French influenced by: a. actions of the nobility; b. ideas of the philosophes; c. the U.S.?
15. Why did the Third Estate want a national assembly?
16. a. What form of government did the National Assembly create? b. What form did radicals want?
17. a. What did Girondists do? b. What did the National Convention of 1795 do?
18. Why do the French regard Napoleon as one of their greatest heroes?
19. State two goals of the Congress of Vienna.
20. What were the roots of baroque art?
21. What was the outstanding musical achievement of the baroque period?
22. a. What are the characteristics of baroque literature? b. rococo music? c. neoclassical literature?
23. Why did the staging of English plays become more elaborate?
24. Why is rococo called a worldly style?
25. What caused the interest in things ancient in the 1700s?
26. What effect did the development of the English middle class as the new elite have?

Discussion Topics

1. What would the deists and philosophes think of the world today? Would they believe in reason as much today as they did in their own time?
2. The Congress of Vienna aimed at ensuring a balance of power through alliances. Is this the best way to achieve peace? Are there others?

Project Ideas

1. Write newspaper headlines describing events of the Glorious or French revolutions.
2. Listen to music of some of the composers mentioned in this unit. Describe how the music reflects the period in which it was composed.
3. Arrange a class exhibit on the arts of the baroque, rococo, and/or neoclassical periods.
4. Write a brief report on: Stuart rule; the Puritans; the Quakers; the Cavaliers; the French Revolution; Congress of Vienna. Highlight the most important people in each movement.

Unit VIII

Machines and Materialism

This 1876 engraving shows four inventions of the industrial revolution: a steam-driven printing press, telegraph, locomotive, and steamboat.

The widespread industrialization of modern Western society began during the industrial revolution. This revolution started in England at the end of the 1700s and spread to Western Europe and America. Although the term revolution is used, the process was more evolutionary than revolutionary. The rise of industry took place over several centuries and its growth continues.

The essential change during the so-called industrial revolution was the introduction of machinery into all areas of economic life. This caused the change from an agricultural and commercial society to an industrial mechanized one. The way persons earned their livings changed. In turn, the economic, philosophical, artistic, and social framework of Western society changed.

Prior to the industrial revolution most people earned their living by farming, handcrafts, or both. Farmers were still using the methods of their ancestors. Most manufacturing was done at home by hand and sold in surrounding communities. Since there was little money in circulation, people continued to use the barter system. Transportation was slow and inadequate. Most people never left the area where they were born. In addition, at birth people inherited a place in their family's social class. There was little they could do to improve their status.

Several significant changes made the industrial revolution possible. The advances in science made during previous centuries were finally being put to use. The exploration and colonization efforts of earlier centuries were beginning to show results. A strong commercial system had been created and a business class established. In general the potential for making money was increasing. At the same time greater political freedom for the middle class was spreading, especially in England.

Chapter 1
The Industrial Revolution

ENGLAND AS THE HUB

The industrial revolution began in England because certain conditions there were favorable to it. The English possessed the needed transportation, capital, labor, resources, markets, and techniques.

The English of the later 1700s lived on an island defended by the finest navy in the world. A great merchant fleet supplied its needs. Communications within England were excellent. The island kingdom was small and crisscrossed by roads and canals.

The atmosphere in which the English conducted their business was becoming increasingly free. A large surplus of wealth was building up. The English were interested in schemes and investments which would use the surplus profitably and thus continue to pile up wealth. The demands of markets at home and abroad were growing. Speedier methods of production were needed. The English found this solution in machines.

REVOLUTION IN AGRICULTURE   One of the first areas to feel the impact of new machinery and new ideas was agriculture. The resulting changes increased production and freed farmworkers for factory jobs. Yet larger populations could be fed.

In the late 1700s England changed from an open-field system of farming to an enclosed system. Since medieval times farmers had cultivated small plots of land and shared a common pasture. With enclosure these small plots were grouped into large farms. Agricultural output and efficiency were increased. But many farmers lost their land and were forced into the cities to find work.

At the same time many inventions and discoveries contributed to the efficiency of farming practices. Jethro Tull had invented a horse-drawn cultivator for loosening the soil and a drill for planting seeds. Charles Townshend found that wheat, turnips, clover, and barley could be planted in alternate years to improve the fertility of the soil. The discovery that crops could be rotated made it unnecessary to let land remain unplanted every other year.

During this time more scientific approaches to the breeding of animals were discovered. Among the pioneers in scientific animal breeding was Robert Bakewell who developed new breeds of sheep and cattle. He learned that inbreeding—breeding back into the same bloodlines—could be used to improve animals. Through his experiments it became possible to produce larger animals, thereby increasing the supply of meat. For the first time, meat became an important part of the diet of average people.

INDUSTRIALIZATION   Until the late 1700s most of England's manufacturing was done by small shopkeepers, craft workers, or people who combined farming or another occupation with handwork. These people were under contract to a manufacturer who furnished the raw materials and paid them for their labor. This practice was known as the domestic system.

But hand labor was too slow to keep up with the demands of trade, especially in cotton cloth manufacturing. In 1733 John Kay patented an instrument for weaving called the flying shuttle. With this shuttle, cloth could be woven faster than the thread could be spun.

This was the beginning of the multiplication of inventions which increase more and more rapidly with time. The invention of one machine for an industry leads to the invention of another and another and so on. This pattern has led to our present high level of technology and may produce an even higher level in the future.

Eli Whitney's cotton gin (left) is an example of a machine created to fill a need. The earlier invention of the spinning jenny (right) by James Hargreaves made it possible for large amounts of cotton to be spun quickly into thread. But until the cotton gin, cotton could not be cleaned fast enough to keep the jennies running efficiently.

This is James Watt's first steam engine. How did the use of water power and then of coal quicken the pace of the industrial revolution?

The next invention in the textile industry was James Hargreaves' spinning jenny. It spun thread many times faster than the old spinning wheel could. Then Richard Arkwright harnessed water power for spinning and Samuel Crompton improved on Arkwright's invention. Weavers soon found that they could not keep up with the spinners. But in the 1780s, Edmund Cartwright found a method of using water to power looms. The production of cotton textiles soared.

Increased production methods created a shortage of raw cotton fiber. The seeds of the cotton plant had to be removed by hand. Then in 1793 Eli Whitney, an American, developed a machine to remove the seeds. This invention—the cotton gin—increased production about 50 times. The gin was later improved so that it became a thousand times more productive than the average worker.

As the above examples show, when hand labor was found to be too slow, people began to look for new sources of machine power. A way to power machines by the water of rivers and streams was discovered. In 1769 a Scot named James Watt invented an engine that could provide power without using running water. His steam engine ran on coal. This discovery allowed manufacturers greater freedom in selecting sites for factories. And more factories could be built. People began to work full time in factories. What had been an extra source of income as handwork became a full-time job.

Fortunately Great Britain had a major source of coal and the British

In the Bessemer method of making steel, the hot metal is poured into a converter (left). The converter is tilted up and hot air blown through it (right).

quickly learned efficient mining techniques. Once a suitable fuel was found, a strong, durable metal for building machines was needed. Machines had many movable parts which had to withstand continuous strain. Steel, which is made from iron ore, is the strongest metal. Steel had been known since ancient times but it was very expensive. It could be made only in small quantities. The earliest kind of steel was probably made in a crucible, a large container which could be heated to a very high temperature. However, this process had been lost.

In 1740 Benjamin Huntsman rediscovered the technique. But steel was still very expensive. In the 1850s Henry Bessemer of England and William Kelly, an American, both experimented with blasting air through molten iron to remove impurities and make steel. At about the same time, Robert Mushet of England discovered that the addition of the metal manganese strengthened steel.

Steel could now be produced cheaply and in large quantities. Coal, iron, and steel became the basic ingredients of the industrial revolution. As production increased, machines were needed to make other machines. Thus began the machine-tool industry. At the same time it was necessary to standardize parts for machines. Worn-out parts had to be replaced easily and cheaply. These interchangeable parts made mass production a reality.

SPREAD OF INVENTIONS

From England the industrial revolution rapidly spread to Western Europe and the U.S. In these countries other people continued to build upon and improve the foundations laid in England.

The iron plow had been known since ancient times. However, few new farm machines were introduced before the agricultural revolution. Following upon British inventors, Americans began to contribute to the changes in agriculture. In the 1830s Cyrus McCormick patented a reaper. Steam-powered threshing machines for harvesting grain came into use. In 1837 John Deere introduced a steel plow. Besides being stronger than iron plows, the steel plow had a self-cleaning surface. This enabled farmers to make clean, even furrows in the soil.

Machines were also invented to improve transportation. An American, John Fitch, built a steam-driven ship in 1787. But it was Robert Fulton who popularized steamboats. He operated the first successful commercial steamboat in 1807. Soon steam was propelling ships on rivers and seas in all parts of the world. Around 1825 George Stephenson ran a steam-powered locomotive on iron rails in England. This was the beginning of railroads which have played a vital role in improving communications and transportation. The internal combustion engine, which Europeans had first developed, was improved by American inventors. This engine led to the development of the automobile and airplane.

In 1832 instant long-distance communication became a reality. Samuel F. B. Morse, an American, used the discoveries of the Italian Volta and Ampere of France to build an electrical telegraph. Later, communications were greatly improved with the invention of the telephone by Alexander Graham Bell and Marconi's wireless, which grew into radio.

George Eastman further improved photography which had been invented by Niepce (NYEPS) and Daguerre (dah-GAIR) of France. Thomas Edison perfected the electric light and invented the phonograph and motion picture among other items. George Westinghouse made railroads safer by designing air brakes. Whole new industries, such as food canning and tire manufacturing, were born.

This is a model of Thomas Edison's first successful light bulb.

Once machines were housed in factories, the face of Europe really began to change. In order to make a living, workers now had to spend most of the day in factories. People began to build their homes or rent rooms near their jobs. Food merchants, shoemakers, and a variety of other tradespeople were needed to serve these workers. Soon a local government was needed to preserve law and order. Gradually these communities became cities. Where cities already existed, factories turned them into overcrowded slums.

SOCIAL CHANGE

The first factory workers came from among the poor, the landless, and the children. But gradually workers began to pour into factory towns from the countryside. They crowded together in rows of small dingy houses. Although wages were very low, people were completely

Chapter 2
The Machine and Change

527

This is the city of Leeds, England, in 1885. Note the closely packed houses. The city is still an industrial center, manufacturing farm tools, glass, leather goods, and woolens.

dependent upon them. Husbands, wives, and their children all had to work in order to exist. At this time upper- and middle-class women were taught that their proper place was in the home. Lower-class women were raised with this ideal, but the industrial revolution forced them to work in factories to support their families.

Working conditions were bad for men and women but worse for children. Child labor was encouraged because there was no need to pay children much. The machine received more attention than its human operator—adult or child. The machine was more valuable. There was always a pool of unemployed from which new laborers could be hired. Factories bred poverty, slums, disease, **illiteracy**, and death.

There were many individuals and groups who reacted to the human suffering of the times. One was William Booth. Seeing the miserable life of London slum-dwellers, he founded the Salvation Army to help them. Many national governments recognized the role that education would play in a machine-dominated future. At this time, education was made free and compulsory, at least up to a certain level. The laws did not stop child labor, however. They merely widened the gap between the middle class and the poor.

ECONOMIC UPHEAVAL

International affairs rarely intruded on the farm or in the small shop. The farmer and the shopkeeper managed to get enough food to eat and clothes to wear. Each had a limited but steady market. But when the farmer and shopkeeper moved to the city and the factory, they were affected by everything that affected the output of machines.

There were many such factors: overproduction and underdemand; a revolution or war which cut off raw materials; financial instability

within a country which made it difficult to obtain credit. Booms and depressions introduced new problems into economic life. Factories were often closed and workers laid off. Unemployment and job security became major issues.

A new class of people known as **capitalists** was created. They owned the capital—land, factories, mines. By the mid-1800s, money was becoming more and more important. Money was needed to buy, improve, house, and replace machines. Few people had enough money to do this. They had to borrow it from banks and governments. Still more money was needed to keep up with expanding needs, growing competition, and increasing costs of labor, raw materials, and transportation.

Business people found the money they needed by selling stock in their companies to the public. Profits, in the form of dividends, were distributed among those who had bought stock. A new world of corporations and stock exchanges emerged. It became possible to earn a living not by working at a job but by investing money.

NEW POLITICAL FORCES

Two major political forces—the middle class and labor unions—emerged from the changes caused by the industrial revolution. In England the middle class of merchants, bankers, and manufacturers began to exercise political power during the 1800s. This class was able to win greater voting privileges and representation in the House of Commons. By 1918, most men over 21 and women over 30 had the right to vote. The voting age for women was lowered to 21 in 1928. The battle for woman's suffrage had been fought over a 40-year period. It was won largely through the efforts of Emmeline Pankhurst and her daughters, Christabel, Estelle, and Adela.

529

The industrial revolution brought lower-class women out of the home and into the factory. At right is Emmeline Pankhurst, a major force in gaining the right to vote for English women. Suffrage was fought for and won largely by the middle class. Why do you think the fight might not have seemed important to women such as these mill workers?

The unions arose as workers became increasingly angry and frustrated with the insecurity of their jobs and their working and living conditions. Recognizing the need for unity and collective action, workers banded together. They formed unions which negotiated for them with business owners.

Because **unions** had the power of numbers behind them, they were able to improve working conditions and wages and reduce the number of working hours. Benefits for injured and aged workers, the ill, and the unemployed were obtained. Once workers were organized collectively, they became politically powerful. Their votes began to be heard in government.

INTERNATIONAL EFFECTS

The increased wealth and efficiency of the industrial revolution also produced far-reaching effects in international relations. Capitalists began to look to other parts of the world for trading partners or potential suppliers of raw materials. However, some Western Europeans did not act as though these nations were equals. They wanted to gain economic concessions by dominating less developed countries. The mid-1800s saw the beginning of economic imperialism. The major industrialized nations divided the world into **spheres of influence**. Each controlled certain portions of the world for its own profit.

Industrial strength became the key factor in determining the balance of power between nations. Industrialized powers had the upper hand in negotiations and war. War was more deadly and destructive than ever. Technology was used to make such mechanized weaponry as the repeating rifle and the machine gun.

SOCIOECONOMIC THEORIES

The industrial revolution also influenced the way people viewed their government and its relationship to the **socioeconomic**—social and economic—system. Several methods for organizing society to cope with the problems of the new era sprang up.

LAISSEZ-FAIRE CAPITALISM   Capitalism, as we have seen, was an economic system born of the industrial revolution. An outgrowth of capitalism was a theory called **laissez-faire**. This was the belief that government should not impose economic controls or interfere in any way with workers and their employers.

Its chief disciple was Adam Smith. In his book *Wealth of Nations* he argued that competitive self-interest would regulate the economy. Most of the capitalists and middle class of the 1800s lived by laissez-faire principles. Today, however, the doctrines of complete capitalism and laissez-faire have been greatly modified.

SOCIALISM   **Socialism** was a major force in the modification of capitalism. It opposed capitalism in an effort to represent and remedy the problems of workers. According to socialists, the government should intervene in social and economic areas of life.

Socialists believe that all people should own the **means of production**—factories, farms, mines—and the means of distribution—railroads, trucking lines, ships, or other transportation systems. Since the government represents all the people, socialism meant government ownership and management of production and distribution.

Several kinds of socialism developed over the years. Early experiments were usually of a communal type. Robert Owen established a model industrial village at New Lanark, Scotland. In France early advocates of socialism included Saint-Simon (san-see-mohn), Charles Fourier (FOOR-ee-ay), and Louis Blanc. Saint-Simon promoted an industrialized state headed by scientists and engineers. Fourier advocated a utopia of self-supporting economic units of 1,620 people. He believed that people would naturally select jobs that interested them. Economic balance would be maintained while freedom of choice was preserved. Blanc believed strictly in "from each according to his abilities, to each according to his needs." He attempted to establish national workshops in France in 1848 but was unsuccessful.

Later socialist efforts developed into many of the socialist and labor parties of today. The Fabians, an English socialist group under the leadership of Beatrice and Sidney Webb, laid the basis for the British Labour party. The Fabians worked for change through political parties and legislatures.

advocates: people who argue for or favor something

This drawing recreates a meeting of several members of the Fabian Society: from left, playwright George Bernard Shaw; the society's founders, Beatrice and Sydney Webb; and political scientist Graham Wallas.

COMMUNISM   **Communism** was a more radical and revolutionary kind of socialism. It also grew out of the industrial revolution. Communists were followers of Karl Marx. A German, Marx was forced to flee his own country because of his radical activities. He formed many of his ideas while observing the problems of the machine age in England.

The foundations of communism were presented by Marx and his collaborator Friedrich Engels in the *Communist Manifesto* published in 1848. Later Marx expanded his ideas in *Das Kapital.*

collaborator: one who works with another

Marx believed that history was a series of class struggles. The haves fought with the have-nots. Marx predicted a class struggle between capitalists and workers as a result of the industrial revolution. The workers would finally revolt and become the ruling class. They would then control the means of production and a socialist state would exist. Eventually there would be no need for a state; it would cease to be.

Marx felt that violence was to be used only if absolutely necessary. However, later followers of Marx, particularly Lenin in the Soviet Union, adopted violence as the major way of imposing communism. Marx's theories have greatly influenced the modern world. Today they are practiced in varying degrees in the Soviet Union, Eastern Europe, the People's Republic of China, and several other countries.

Today the European worker is frequently a member of a moderate socialist or labor party. However, most European countries also have a communist political party. It is usually a minority party but in France and Italy the communist political party has millions of members.

In the 1800s, as in the previous 200 years, science had a great influence on art and philosophy. New fields of scientific investigation opened up. More and more areas of life seemed to be explained by science. People began to view themselves differently. Philosophical thought was changed by this and in turn contributed to the change. For many philosophers spiritual values became meaningless. Material things, those things that could be detected by the senses, were all-important.

Chapter 3
Scientific and Philosophic Thought

NATURAL SCIENCE

Scientific developments had grown steadily through the 1600s and 1700s. However, the 1800s were dominated by vast advances in experimental and applied science. Science became more specialized. It was centered on the practical and the profitable.

Physicists began to study the power of heat and called the new science thermodynamics. Interest in this field was a result of work done on the steam engine. Benjamin Thompson and James Joule (JOOL) worked in this area. William Thomson, Lord Kelvin, made the Kelvin scale of temperature. He also worked on the laying of the Atlantic telegraph cables.

Work in the science of optics was done by Helmholtz of Germany and Foucault (foo-KOH) of France. Foucault's work improved the quality of lenses. This led to developments in photography and the creation of finer scientific instruments.

Some of the most exciting scientific developments in the 1800s were in the field of electricity. Much of the work was based on the discoveries of Volta of Italy. Volta worked with electric charges and gave his name to the volt, a unit of electricity. By the 1800s electricity was beginning to have important industrial and commercial use. Andre Ampere discovered important principles of electricity. Michael Faraday constructed the first dynamo and made possible the development of the generator. James Maxwell worked out a theory of electromagnetism. Maxwell's work was confirmed by the experiments of Heinrich Hertz. In the process he created electromagnetic waves now known as radio waves.

In 1895 Wilhelm von Roentgen (RENT-guhn) discovered the X ray. Marie and Pierre Curie (kyoo-REE) investigated radioactivity and discovered radium. Their work opened up a new field of research and was important in the development of the atomic bomb.

Industry served as a major force in the development of chemistry. As new materials for industry were sought, it became necessary to know the composition of things. Great strides were made when the difference between organic (living) and inorganic (nonliving) matter was discovered. Friedrich Wohler (VOH-luhr) in Germany was the first to synthesize an organic compound. His work was furthered by Liebig (LEE-big), who developed artificial fertilizers. The commercial possibilities of these discoveries were soon felt as synthetic dyes, drugs, and rubber appeared.

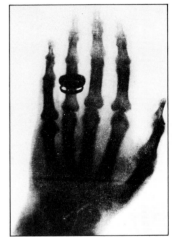

This is one of the first x rays ever made. It was taken by Wilhelm von Roentgen, the discoverer of the X ray.

In the 1830s Sir Charles Lyell published *Principles of Geology.* This work stated that it had taken millions of years for wind, ice, and other forces of nature to shape the present features of the earth. This had been Hutton's theory in the 1700s. However, Lyell's work was more scientifically sound and better presented.

A short time later evidence appeared that humans had lived during these early geological ages. In 1846 fossil remains were found in the Somme Valley in France. In 1856 remains of a prehistoric person were discovered in the Neander Valley in Germany. Four skeletons of a different type were unearthed at Cro-Magnon, in France, in 1868. These discoveries stimulated **anthropological** research.

The development of a theory of evolution was one of the most dramatic events of the 1800s. It opened new horizons for exploration and changed the way people viewed themselves. It affected science, philosophy, literature, religion, and politics.

One of the first to put forward an evolutionary theory was Jean Lamarck, a French naturalist. He believed in the inheritance of acquired characteristics; that is, biological changes developed by organisms during their lifetimes are transmitted to their offspring. But Lamarck did not account for the great length of time needed for change.

The theory of evolution did not gain major recognition until 1859. In that year Charles Darwin, the major naturalist of the day, published *The Origin of Species.* In his book Darwin observed that all living

Besides discoveries in electricity, Michael Faraday worked in the field of optics and discovered several chemicals. Here he is shown lecturing to the Royal Society of London, organized under the patronage of Charles II in 1660.

things had evolved from ancient beginnings. He also expressed the theory that those kinds of plants and animals had lived which were best suited to survive. Less hardy ones had died out. Darwin called this survival-of-the-fittest process natural selection.

Darwin based his theory on observation of the natural world and on the theories advanced by the economist Thomas Malthus. Malthus argued that poverty was unavoidable. Population increased at a geometric progression (1, 2, 4, 8, 16, etc.) while food supply increased at an arithmetic progression (1, 2, 3, 4, 5, etc.). Thus he saw life as a struggle among ever more populous nations for the supply of food.

Since the publication of Darwin's observations, science has continued to probe the mysteries of evolution and heredity. Later findings such as those of August Weismann (VY-smahn) have clarified the beliefs of Lamarck and Darwin. Only those characteristics already in the genes of the parents are inherited by their children.

clarified:
made clear or
understandable

Gregor Mendel, an Austrian monk, and Hugo De Vries (duhv-REES) of Holland were led by their research to the belief that evolution occurs quickly. Mutations occur within a single generation. The offspring are markedly different from the parents.

The field of medicine made great progress during the 1800s. Advances multiplied rapidly. Louis Pasteur of France discovered the world of germs and learned that many bacteria could be killed by heat. Pasteur and Robert Koch of Germany worked independently. However, they arrived at the same conclusion—germs were the cause of many diseases. Pasteur invented the process of pasteurization of milk and developed vaccines against rabies and anthrax. Koch identified the bacilli that cause tuberculosis and cholera.

Joseph Lister's work reduced the danger of infection after operations. He believed that instruments and wounds should be washed with a solution of carbolic acid. The use of antiseptics grew out of Lister's practices. Florence Nightingale pioneered in the training of nurses.

Until the 1800s scientists had not considered the mind as part of the total physical being. Nor that it could be studied and analyzed in much the same way that other parts of the body are studied. It was Wilhelm Wundt (VUNT) of Germany who established **psychology** as a science. He stressed the importance of the experimental method in studying human behavior.

PHILOSOPHY

The dominant philosophy of the late 1800s was materialism. It grew out of the scientific and industrial achievements of the period. This philosophy expressed the view that science could cure the ills of humanity. Machinery, technology, and social politics would bring the good life. Spiritual and intellectual values were ignored while materialists sought worldly goods and actions. The name applied not only

535

to philosophers but to anyone who was concerned with material goods.

The concept of evolution dominated the thought and writings of the 1800s. Some people saw Darwin's survival of the fittest displayed in the social system of the times. One of these was Herbert Spencer who viewed the rich as the thrifty, the intelligent, and the strong. The unfit and less able were the poor.

But not all philosophers were materialists. Georg Wilhelm Friedrich Hegel (HAY-guhl) of Germany was an idealist. In contrast to materialism his philosophy was concerned with the mind and spiritual values. He believed that progress occurred through a process called dialectics: a situation (thesis) gives rise to an opposite situation (antithesis). The two blend to form a third situation (synthesis). The synthesis then becomes a thesis, and the whole process begins again. Karl Marx borrowed Hegel's dialectic theory, but turned it upside down. Where Hegel believed that each stage of history was shaped by ideas, Marx's dialectical materialism stressed matter over mind.

Some philosophers presented a pessimistic view of human nature. They focused on the beginnings of the human race and the animal nature of humankind. Such attitudes gave rise to a philosophy of the will. The concept was first set forth by Arthur Schopenhauer (SHOH-puhn-haw-uhr) of Germany. He believed humans responded only to the forces of appetite and passion.

Friedrich Nietzsche (NEE-chee), a German philosopher and poet, believed people could control these passions, but not through religion. According to him, religion kept people from taking full command of their lives. Instead of relying on the authority of religion, Nietzsche believed that people should use their courage, strength, and loyalty to realize their full human potential. The Nazis were later to misinterpret Nietzsche. They used his philosophy to support their belief in a master race.

SOCIAL SCIENCES

Natural science also contributed to developments in the social sciences, especially sociology. Scholars began to apply the scientific method to the study of human behavior. Social scientists tried to combine and apply the knowledge of several different areas in their work. Field investigations and sociological studies were conducted. Statistics were employed as a tool of measurement.

Auguste Comte is considered the father of **sociology**. He was also the originator of positivism, a philosophy based on observable facts. Comte wished to reform society according to scientific facts. He rejected the idea of natural rights, disliked ordinary people, advocated force, and made humanity the new god of his philosophy.

Comte's theories influenced and were expanded by John Stuart Mill. Mill developed what became known as liberal positivism. He preached reform on the basis of empiricism. His work was a combination of the earlier theories of utilitarianism and humanitarianism. It was also a forerunner of state socialism.

Mill was also a champion of women's rights. In 1869, in *The Subjection of Women* he examined the ideas expressed by Blackstone in his *Commentaries.* Mill proposed that women had the right to legal equality with men. He wanted all signs of women's subjection eliminated and the right to vote given to them. Almost 80 years earlier, Mary Wollstonecraft had written the first **feminist** piece, *Vindication of the Rights of Woman,* calling for equality under the law.

Goya's work Execution of May Third *was inspired by Napoleon's occupation of Spain. Goya influenced various schools of art far into the 1900s.*

Chapter 4
From Romanticism to Post-impressionism

The 1800s saw new trends in literature, art, and music. The first half of the century was dominated by romanticism. By midcentury this glorification of nature, the supernatural, and the emotional was being replaced by realism. By then the industrial revolution and the resulting changes were being felt in the arts. Realism was an attempt to combine the science and philosophy of the era with the arts.

ROMANTICISM

The arts in the 1700s had been dominated by classicism. Near the end of the century some artists and writers began to revolt against classical forms and subjects. The revolt climaxed in the 1800s and became known as the romantic movement. In general the romantics rejected ancient Greek and Roman influences. They turned instead to nature and the simple things of life for inspiration. Some developed an interest in **folklore** or the Middle Ages. People began to look to their own national heritage for inspiration.

The philosophy of the romantics was influenced by such thinkers of the 1700s as Rousseau and Kant. Rousseau's natural person became the romantic ideal. Kant's emphasis on moral duty, spirit, and will became very important. However, it was the idealistic philosophy of Hegel that spoke for the romantic movement.

The romantic movement was also marked by an increased interest in religion based on faith. This is in contrast to the deism of the 1700s. The Roman Catholic Church especially experienced a revival during the early 1800s.

LITERATURE   Romanticism had its greatest impact on the literature of England, France, and Germany. Poetry became the most important literary form. The subject matter of poetry expanded. Descriptions of nature, feelings, and the simple life became the sources for poems.

English romantic poetry had its roots in the 1700s. James Thomson's *The Seasons* was one of the early works to describe the beauties of nature. Thomas Gray's poem *Elegy Written in a Country Churchyard* dealt with simple human emotions. William Cowper's *The Task* glorified country living. Robert Burns immortalized Scottish folk songs in his poetry. Burns, of a peasant family, wrote in dialect and became a celebrity in his own time. To his contemporaries he symbolized the natural person.

The beginning of the 1800s witnessed the first generation of true romantic poets. Among these were William Wordsworth and Samuel Taylor Coleridge. As young men both had been radicals in the tradition of the French Revolution. Because they believed in the wisdom of ordinary people and preferred the natural life of the country, they chose to live in the Lake Country of northern England. They have since become known as the Lake poets.

The second generation of romantic poets, Lord Byron, Percy Bysshe (BISH) Shelley, and John Keats saw the world differently than had the first generation. Generally they rebelled against or felt disgust at politics. Their poetry was highly emotional.

Although not so important as the poems of the period, some noteworthy English novels were being written. Sir Walter Scott gave historical accounts of romantic adventure and chivalry in such works as *Kenilworth* and *Ivanhoe*. Mary Wollstonecraft Shelley wrote the novel *Frankenstein,* published in 1818.

In Germany romanticism was preceded by a movement that came to be called *Sturm und Drang* or Storm and Stress. Artists were caught up in a revolt against classicism. One of the most notable writers was Johann Wolfgang von Goethe (GUHR-tuh). His sorrow over an unhappy love produced the sensitive and gloomy novel *The Sorrows of Young Werther.* However, Goethe is best known in the English-speaking world for his drama *Faust.* A close friend of Goethe and a forerunner of romanticism was Friedrich von Schiller. He was a novelist, dramatist, and national revolutionary.

One of the characteristics of the romantic movement was an interest in folklore. Two German scholars, Jacob and Wilhelm Grimm, gathered and published a collection of German folk stories under the title *Grimm's Fairy Tales.*

Of the French romantics one of the most interesting was the poet, dramatist, and novelist, Victor Hugo. Hugo was a republican who fled his native land when Louis Napoleon became emperor in 1852. Of Hugo's works, the novel *Les Miserables* is probably the most famous. Other well-known French romantic novelists include George Sand, pen name of Amandine Dupin, and Alexandre Dumas (dyoo-MAH). Sand was famous for her work for women's rights. Dumas wrote exciting adventure stories such as *The Three Musketeers.*

ART AND ARCHITECTURE   Romantic artists renounced the cold style of neoclassicists. They painted pictures that conveyed mood. Often, as in the case of Francisco Goya (GOY-yuh), paintings were social documents as well.

Joseph Turner went through several styles in his art. From painting subjects from history and mythology in the baroque style, he went to expressing abstract ideas through masses of color. His work influenced painters of the later impressionist school. This painting is called Rain, Steam, and Speed.

Ludwig von Beethoven was the major figure in music at the turn of the 19th century. He used what he had learned from his teachers—among them, Mozart and Haydn—and added his own talents for arrangement and development of form. For example, he put a chorus in a symphony finale.

Goya, a Spaniard, combined both realism and romanticism in his work. As court painter, he painted many royal portraits. However, he also painted ordinary people. He used wit and satire to interpret the character of his subjects. After Napoleon invaded Spain, Goya's interests changed. In *The Disasters of War* he depicted the evils and suffering caused by war.

English painters John Constable and Joseph Turner were also part of the romantic movement. Constable was the first landscape painter to realize the importance of working from a sketch made on the spot. Spontaneity is one of the chief characteristics of his works. Turner painted not what he saw but what he remembered or imagined. His paintings are masses of light and color. Turner's works were to have considerable influence upon the French impressionists later in the 1800s.

In France patronage of the arts was no longer in the hands of the aristocracy. Members of the old nobility were in exile or living in poverty on their country estates. When the political situation became more stable, a new upper class appeared. They were rich bankers and industrialists. They liked and bought pretty pictures. To succeed an artist had to paint to please them.

Romantic ideals did not translate very well into architecture. But between 1830 and 1870 a Gothic revival was in full swing in England and throughout Europe. The renewed interest in Gothic buildings inspired the restoration of many medieval churches including the Cathedral of Notre Dame in Paris.

MUSIC Romanticism had a major impact on music. Composers began to express their emotions and imagination in their music. Often they turned to national events, poetry, or nature for their subject matter. Romantic music was dominated by German composers. Foremost was Ludwig van Beethoven (BAY-toh-vuhn).

Other outstanding romantic composers include Franz Schubert, Carl Maria von Weber (VAY-buhr), Felix Mendelssohn, Robert Schumann, Frederic Chopin, and Franz Liszt. Weber was one of the first composers to use nationalism as a theme for opera.

REALISM

To a small degree classicism and romanticism continued into the second half of the 1800s. However, a new force began to affect literature, art, and music—realism. Realists rejected romanticism and portrayed everyday life as they believed it really was. They examined in detail ordinary people and their problems, especially those arising from the industrial revolution.

Realists analyzed the implications and effects of these problems on the individual, the family, and the levels of society. Most writers saw people as caught in the web of society and struggling for their very existence.

LITERATURE   The effects of realism can be seen in the literature of England, France, and to some extent Germany, Scandinavia, and Spain during this time. Realism and psychological or sociological analysis generally dominated the English novels. Charles Dickens served as the English conscience. In his novels he portrayed the social ills caused by industrialization. Dickens displayed a sense of humanitarianism and the ability to create unforgettable characters. Works such as *Oliver Twist* and *David Copperfield* did much to change existing social conditions.

William Makepeace Thackeray and John Galsworthy were realists in their portrayal of the English upper classes. Mary Ann Evans, under the pen name of George Eliot, wrote about English rural life. Works such as *Silas Marner* and *The Mill on the Floss* reflect her concern for social and moral problems.

However, in terms of style, the finest realistic novelists of the period were George Meredith and Thomas Hardy. Meredith's novels probe human psychology and describe the relationship of the individual to society. Meredith used a selective type of realism. He did not attempt to record every detail. Hardy, on the other hand, was a strict realist. He was also a pessimist in his study of character and environment.

Jane Austen, although writing during the earlier romantic period, was actually a realist. In her novels she recorded in great detail the everyday lives of characters in her society.

Although English literature during the Victorian age—the reign of Queen Victoria (1837-1901)—was dominated by the realistic novel, other philosophies and styles appeared. One of the best examples of later romantic writing is the work of Robert Louis Stevenson. Stevenson was a world traveler whose voyages and love of adventure inspired such tales as *Treasure Island* and *Kidnapped.* Charlotte Bronte created *Jane Eyre.* Her sister Emily wrote *Wuthering Heights.* Both are Gothic in style.

Poetry flourished in England along with the novel. Alfred, Lord Tennyson admired the classical and the romantic. Works such *Idylls of the King* show both influences. Robert Browning created the dramatic monologue in which a character tells his or her own story. Browning's work shows his grasp of the motives behind human behavior. Browning was married to the poet Elizabeth Barrett.

In his works Rudyard Kipling expressed the attitudes of English **imperialism**. He provided interesting insights into colonial life in India. He is at his best as a storyteller in such works as *Kim* and *The Jungle Book.*

A favorite dramatist of the period and a dominant literary figure in both the late 1800s and the early 1900s was George Bernard Shaw. Shaw was a realist with a message. He preached reform through science. He joined the Fabian Socialists and often used his plays for social **propaganda**. His wit saved much of his work from dullness.

In France a few writers, such as Edmond Rostand in *Cyrano de Bergerac,* continued the romantic movement. However, French litera-

George Bernard Shaw's life (1856-1950) spanned a number of schools of writing. But his style and subjects changed little.

Above is Honore de Balzac *by the sculptor Auguste Rodin.*

ture was dominated by realism. The greatest novelist and founder of the French realistic novel was Honore de Balzac. Although he wrote about people at all levels of French society, he was especially accurate with his descriptions of the middle class as in *Le Pere Goriot.*

Other realists were Gustave Flaubert (floh-BAIR), Guy de Maupassant (moh-puh-SAHN), and Emile Zola. Using a simple, direct style, Maupassant showed remarkable insight and wit in his many short stories. Zola created novels based on contemporary discoveries about heredity and the influence of the environment. He believed in naturalism and was a political activist and reformer.

In Scandinavia, the Norwegian Henrik Ibsen was writing provocative dramas. He was a realist who portrayed the social and economic conflicts of the modern world in works such as *A Doll's House.* Ibsen's influence is evident in the works of the Swedish dramatist August Strindberg.

In Spain during this time, several writers were writing in the realistic style. Among these were Benito Perez Galdos and Emilia Pardo Bazan. Galdos wrote about contemporary life in a multivolume series of novels. Bazan wrote novels and short stories.

ART　　During the later 1800s, as the upper middle class began to decorate their houses there was a great demand for art works. Paris became the art capital of the world. The most famous painters were either French or came to Paris to study and work. Their efforts mark the beginning of modern art.

The developments in art closely paralleled those of the literary movement. Artists too rejected neoclassicism and romanticism. They chose instead to paint nature realistically. Their works are characterized by attention to exact detail.

As early members of the realist school, Corot (kuh-ROH) and Millet (mee-YAY) combined realism with a touch of romanticism. Both loved nature. Corot concentrated on landscapes while Millet painted peasant scenes.

The acknowleged master of realism, however, was Courbet (kur-BAY) who painted very detailed pictures. He was a political activist and many of his works are social protests. In the same spirit Daumier (DOH-mee-ay) used caricatures of people to make political and social protests. He influenced other artists to use cartooning to satirize political and social conditions. Their works were reproduced in the many journals that flourished during this period.

During her lifetime, Rosa Bonheur (boh-NUHR) of France gained fame both in Europe and in the U.S. for her realistic paintings of animals. Another French artist who enjoyed much acclaim in his lifetime was Henri de Toulouse-Lautrec (tu-loos-loh-TREK). Toward the end of the 1800s, he captured the mood of the cafes and night life of Paris. His paintings made the poster a work of art.

insight: understanding of a situation or a person

This is an example of Toulouse-Lautrec's poster art. The subject, Jane Avril, was a dancer. Toulouse-Lautrec was also a book illustrator and print maker.

MUSIC With few exceptions music continued to be romantic. In the latter half of the 1800s this romanticism became increasingly nationalistic. Many composers turned to folk music and folklore for inspiration.

Opera continued to dominate Italian music. The aria or sung monologue became the most important part of the opera. The outstanding operatic composers of the period were Rossini, Donizetti, Bellini, Verdi, and Puccini (poo-CHEE-nee).

In France the tradition of a national opera was established with Gounod (GOO-noh), Bizet, and Jules Massenet (mas-uh-NAY). During this time, Jacques Offenbach created the operetta with such works as *La Vie Parisienne* and *La Belle Helene.* Operetta is comic opera. Following Offenbach, Johann Strauss, Jr., of Vienna, and the English team of William S. Gilbert and Arthur S. Sullivan firmly established the operetta as a popular musical form.

Hector Berlioz and Cesar Franck made original contributions to French symphonic music. Both were romantics and wanted their music to express emotion. Berlioz expanded the use of orchestra. Camille Saint-Saens (san-SAHNS) chose to follow a more classical style. He composed a number of symphonic poems, including *Danse Macabre* (Dance of Death).

German music during the later 1800s was dominated by the works of Richard Wagner (VAHG-nuhr) and Johannes Brahms. Wagner revolutionized opera by treating it as a musical drama. To him, the story, music, singing, and scenery should form a whole. Wagner's operas are romantic spectaculars full of emotion. He intensified German nationalism by using German folklore for themes. Brahms also wrote nationalistic music, but rejected the theatrical aspects of Wagner's works.

Later, Richard Strauss broke with the German romantics to develop a more modern musical style. In his choice of themes he was influenced by the philosophy of Nietzsche.

Vienna, the capital of the Hapsburg empire, was the music capital of the late 1800s. Gustav Mahler (MAH-luhr) held the post of conductor of the Viennese Opera House while he composed his symphonies. Johann Strauss, besides writing operettas, made the Viennese style of waltz popular. He composed such works as *The Blue Danube* and *Tales from the Vienna Woods.*

Nationalism was dominant in the work of Scandinavian composers. Edvard Grieg used the folklore of his native Norway for inspiration. Jean Sibelius (suh-BAYL-yuhs) based many of his works, most notably *Finlandia,* on ancient Finnish epics. The most important Danish composer was Carl Nielson.

Spanish composers also turned to their history and folklore for themes. Manuel de Falla (FAH-yuh) gained international fame. His early works featured the folklore of the province of Andalusia.

In his ten symphonies, Gustav Mahler enlarged the number of performers needed in an orchestra. He used choruses and added vocal solos to symphonic music.

543

Claude Monet was especially interested in the effects of light in creating mood. This is his painting of Old St. Lazare Station *in Paris.*

IMPRESSIONISM

As a movement impressionism lasted from about 1870 into the 1900s. It was most apparent in art, especially in painting. It combined and was influenced by several elements.

Technical advances in photography made many artists feel there was no longer any need to recreate reality. If one wanted realism, one could take a picture. The impressionists chose to capture on canvas one moment in the ever-changing world of nature. They did not concern themselves with social messages or storytelling. They conveyed their personal feelings or impressions of a scene. For inspiration they turned to the romantics, to Velasquez and El Greco of Spain, and to Japan which had recently been opened to the West.

Manet (mah-NAY), an early impressionist, was especially influenced by the Spanish. Other notable impressionists were Pissaro, Monet, Degas (duh-GAH), Renoir (ren-WAHR), and Berthe Morisot (maw-ree-ZOH). Joaquin Sorolla y Bastilda (suh-ROL-yuh-ee-bah-STEE-duh) of Spain, a later impressionist, is noted for his use of sunlight. Ignacio Zuloaga (zoo-luh-WAHG-uh), also of Spain, is known particularly for his landscapes and bullfight scenes.

In music, impressionism was a revolt against the restraints of the classical and romantic schools. Instead of following precise musical rules, it became concerned with expressing fleeting moods. Impressionist music attempted to create a mood by breaking away from the usual melody and chord patterns.

Foremost of the impressionist composers was Claude Debussy (deb-yu-SEE) of France. His symphonic poem *Afternoon of a Faun* is an outstanding example of musical impressionism. The influence of impressionism is evident to some degree in the music of Isaac Albeniz (ahl-BAY-nees) and Enrique Granados of Spain, Ottorino Respighi (ruh-SPEE-gee) of Italy, and Frederick Delius of England.

POSTIMPRESSIONISM

Postimpressionism is the term applied to the works of a group of artists who wished a more individualistic style than impressionism offered. There was no particular unity to the school. The artists moved beyond impressionism to express their personal perceptions in their own way.

Paul Cezanne (say-ZAN), one of the greatest postimpressionists, exerted a major influence on modern art. He was a superb technician who combined the best of several centuries of art. During his lifetime he moved from impressionism to the depiction of more solid forms and masses.

This is L'Estaque *by Paul Cezanne. Can you see any differences in style between this and the impressionist work on the opposite page? Are there differences in the use of light, the colors used, shapes, forms?*

Paul Gauguin painted this self-portrait in 1889. What differences do you see between this painting and the postimpressionist work of Cezanne on the preceding page?

palette knife: knife used to mix or spread paint

While Cezanne displayed little emotion in his work, Paul Gauguin (goh-GAN) and Vincent van Gogh tried to express their innermost feelings. Gauguin, a well-to-do French stockbroker, deserted his family, and fled to the South Pacific island of Tahiti. His works are characterized by bold lines and colors. The Dutch van Gogh led a troubled life, plagued by fits of madness that ended in suicide. His paintings combine bright colors and violent strokes made with a palette knife.

Suzanne Valadon carried postimpressionism well into this century by continuing to paint in this style until the late 1930s.

Sculpture also reflected the developments in science, literature, and art. The foremost sculptors of the late 1800s were the Belgian Constantin Meunier (moon-YAY) and August Rodin (roh-DAN) of France. Meunier was a realist whose goal was to portray the laborer's role in industrialization. Statues like *The Mower* and *The Mine Girl* helped people realize the dignity of physical work.

Rodin cannot be put into a particular school. At various times and in different works, he has been considered a realist, romantic, and impressionist. He admired the classics, yet his works reflect the realism of his times and the interest in human nature. He is considered the first modern sculptor.

Summing Up The Unit

Social Studies Vocabulary

Define: illiteracy; international; capitalists; unions; spheres of influence; socioeconomic; laissez-faire capitalism; socialism; means of production; communism; psychology; sociology; feminist; folklore; imperialism; propaganda

People

Identify: Tull; Watt; Booth; the Pankhursts; Adam Smith; the Webbs; Marx; Roentgen; Darwin; Malthus; Nightingale; Wundt; Comte; Mill; Goethe; Goya; Constable; Turner; Beethoven; Dickens; Meredith; Hardy; Ibsen; Shaw; Courbet; Offenbach; Wagner; Grieg; Debussy; Manet; Cezanne; Rodin

Words

Define: open-field system; enclosure; domestic system; Bessemer process; materialism; dialectics; positivism; romanticism; realism; Victorian Age; aria; postimpressionism

Questions

1. What made the industrial revolution possible?
2. What conditions in England caused the industrial revolution to begin there?
3. How did increased agricultural production help to make the industrial revolution possible?
4. Using examples from the text, explain how the invention of one machine for an industry led to a multiplication of inventions?
5. Why was the steam engine better than water power for industry?
6. Why was the beginning of the machine-tool industry important?
7. a. What areas of life were improved by the industrial revolution? b. What new industries grew up?
8. What widened the gap between the middle class and the poor?
9. What factors affected machine output?
10. What made it possible to earn a living by investing money?
11. a. What two political forces emerged from the industrial revolution? b. What power did each exercise?
12. How did the industrial revolution affect international relations?
13. How did the discoveries of the following lead to further scientific developments: a. Foucault; b. Faraday; c. the Curies?
14. Why was the development of a theory of evolution so important in the 1800s?
15. How did natural science contribute to developments in the social sciences?
16. Who influenced the romantics?
17. What effect did the industrial revolution and its resulting changes have on the arts?
18. How did the rise of a new upper class affect the arts in France?
19. Why did advances in photography cause some artists to turn away from realism?

Discussion Topics

1. Changes in agriculture helped to make the industrial revolution possible. How? Does industrialization of underdeveloped countries depend on farm productivity today? Why or why not?
2. The industrial revolution produced far-reaching effects in international relations. Can they still be seen today? Where? What are they?
3. How have trends in the arts—romanticism, realism, etc.—been affected by political and economic developments? Is the opposite true?

Project Ideas

1. Make a model or draw a detailed sketch of an invention of the industrial revolution. Explain the consequences it has had.
2. Write a short play about the troubles of the poor in England during the industrial revolution. Use works such as Dickens' novels for reference.
3. Listen to music of some of the composers mentioned in this unit. Explain how the music reflects the trends of the times.
4. On the basis of outside reading, write a brief report on: Malthus's theory; Adam Smith; Dickens; the Fabians.

Unit IX

Europe Warred
and the World Followed

War has been the occupation of peoples for centuries. It has also been the subject of many works of art. In some eras artists glorified war and war heroes. In other periods they painted the cruelty and destruction of war. This is Pablo Picasso's Guernica *(1937, May-early June). It symbolizes the terror and death caused in the bombing of the town of Guernica during the Spanish Civil War (1936-1939).*

Like many peoples throughout history, the Europeans have often wasted their energies and resources in war. For centuries they fought among themselves and with each other on the Continent. In the 1600s Europeans extended their quarrels to their colonies overseas. During the 1800s Europeans were engaged in almost constant unrest and war. In 1914 European fighting exploded into global warfare.

Many factors were at work in the 1800s drawing the Europeans into war. The reasons Europeans fought were many and complex. Nationalism, imperialism, the arms race, and various alliances were intensifying ancient jealousies. In addition, the end of one war often provided reasons for fighting a new one. The events surrounding and immediately following the French Revolution and Napoleon's reign became such a link in the continuous chain of European wars.

Chapter 1
The Forces
of War

NATIONALISM

The word nationalism means a sense of the unity, exclusiveness, and common interests of a people. At its best, nationalism preserves the independence and culture of each nation-state. It can mean the same as peaceful patriotism—love of the ideals, culture, and history of one's country. But nationalism can also be misused by the ambitious and misguided. It can be an excuse for violence, hatred, and the extension of one nation's power over another.

Under feudalism Europeans lived in many small groups each under the rule of a lord or lady. The loyalties of each group were directed toward their particular feudal lord or lady. They did not identify with the larger group with whom they shared a geographic area and a common language and culture. But in the later Middle Ages, larger territorial groupings were formed. A sense of national consciousness began to grow. National economies, national literature, and a feeling of common culture and tradition began to develop.

By the late 1700s nationalism was playing a major role in shaping modern nations. The French Revolution and Napoleon's military campaigns intensified the national consciousness of the French. Europeans who came under French attack became more conscious of their separateness and of their need for internal unity and self-government. Words such as, "I am French," "I am English," "I am Swedish" took on a definite meaning. By the mid-1800s the Germans and the Italians had yet to achieve this feeling of nationalism. Before the end of the century, however, they too had developed **national identities** and nation-states.

REVOLUTIONS OF 1848 The Congress of Vienna which had settled European boundaries after Napoleon's defeat, had been dominated by the philosophy and spirit of the Viennese minister of foreign affairs, Klemens Metternich. Metternichism—or the Vienna System, as his policy came to be known—was a reaction against the liberal spirit of the French Revolution. Metternichism was an attempt to restore complete political authority to the monarch. Any movement toward liberal reform was ignored or suppressed. For the first half of the 1800s most of Europe was dominated by Metternichism.

However, opposition was growing. Under the pressure of the indus-

The July Revolution or Revolution of 1830 in France was the result of the dissatisfaction of working- and middle-class people with Charles X's policies. Here citizens are attacking militia.

trial revolution, workers began to demand reforms. Movements for national unity and constitutional government were developing. Occasionally the conflicting forces of Metternichism and liberalism erupted in violence.

After Napoleon's defeat the monarchy had been restored to France. The throne was first held by Louis XVIII who was succeeded by his brother, Charles X. Neither monarch was popular. Discontent increased. Under the disguise of social reform, a small group of business people engineered the Revolution of 1830. In what is known as the July Monarchy, they placed Louis Phillipe, the Citizen King, on the throne. All legislative power was held by an elected assembly. However, the assembly represented only the wealthy.

This attempt at constitutional government failed. Louis Philippe was able to assume almost absolute control. His reign became increasingly conservative. All opposition was suppressed.

dissenters: those who disagree with official policy

Since freedom of the press had been denied by Louis Philippe, banquets were held as forums for dissenters. In February 1848 the government ordered the cancellation of one such banquet. Rioting broke out. Many government troops refused to support the king unless reforms were made. Finally Louis Phillipe abdicated.

A provisional government was established. National elections with full male suffrage were to be held in April. Prior to the elections, the government established national workshops, the idea of socialist Louis Blanc. They were originally an effort to help the unemployed, but the workshops soon turned into a huge public relief system. The taxes required by such a project alarmed the middle class and many peasants in the provinces. When elections were held the conservatives won a majority. The workshops were closed. Paris workers rioted.

Excited by the French, Europeans elsewhere rose up against their governments. In Vienna Metternich himself was overthrown. The peoples of the Austro-Hungarian Empire saw this as an opportunity to free their countries. However, they were never able to unite. As each group—Hungarians and various Slavic peoples—tried separately to win their national freedom, they were crushed by the Austrian army.

The Italians also revolted against Austrian rule at this time. They too held their freedom for only a short time. The spirit of revolution spread to Germany. Radicals met in an assembly and formed a confederation of German states under a constitutional monarchy. Their efforts collapsed when Frederick William of Prussia rejected the throne.

The Revolutions of 1848 were followed by a period of reaction. It appeared as if the reformers' efforts had failed completely. But in reality desire for constitutional government and nationalism had been firmly established in Europe.

FROM FRENCH EMPIRE TO REPUBLIC   But change in policy sometimes lags far behind change in philosophy. A case in point is France. After the riots, the French National Assembly drew up a democratic constitution. Presidential elections were scheduled for December 1848. On a platform of law and order, the French elected as their new president Louis Napoleon Bonaparte, the nephew of Napoleon. Louis Napoleon spent the next four years gaining popular support for himself. By 1852 he had assumed absolute control and by popular vote proclaimed himself Emperor Napoleon III. The Second French Empire was born.

During his reign, Napoleon III established a **dictatorship**. Censorship was imposed and most **civil liberties** were denied. However, the period was one of great industrial and economic growth. Hospitals were built, Paris was beautified, and a major transportation system of railroads and steamships was created.

However, his real interest was in foreign affairs. Through his foreign policy, Napoleon III hoped to glorify both France and himself. He also hoped to quiet his critics at home by focusing their attention abroad. However, his failure to build a French empire in Mexico united the opposition. Eventually his aggressive foreign policy caused his downfall. Outmaneuvered by the German chancellor, Otto von Bismarck, Napoleon III declared war on Germany in 1870. The Germans united and defeated the French within a few months. Napoleon III was captured and later went into exile.

The treaty that resulted from the Franco-Prussian War demanded

Napoleon III ruled France from 1848 to 1871. Compare and contrast his policies and methods of controlling the people with those used by Napoleon Bonaparte.

that France surrender Alsace-Lorraine and pay $1 billion in damages. German troops remained in France until the sum was paid. The war and the treaty terms humiliated the French and created a bitter rivalry between the two nations. The French began stockpiling weapons and waited for a chance to avenge themselves. These factors were a major force in bringing about World War I.

The Third French Republic was established according to the constitutional laws of 1875. The French adopted a parliamentary system with power resting in the hands of the premier. The republic was especially unstable. The major reason for this was the number of political parties that existed. Since no single party usually held a majority, it was necessary to form a coalition government of several parties. As soon as one group withdrew its support, the government collapsed. As a result France had 50 changes in government between 1871 and 1914.

THE IRON CHANCELLOR   Otto von Bismarck, known as the Iron Chancellor, became chief minister of Prussia in 1862. He believed that larger political problems were settled ultimately by iron weapons and bloodshed. Bismarck, however, could be a cautious and clever diplomat. He knew the value of making concessions when he could not gain his ends directly or immediately.

Prussia had begun its rise to power under the leadership of its ruling family, the Hohenzollerns, during the Thirty Year's War. After the invasion of the German states by Napoleon's armies, the spirit of nationalism began to grow. When Bismarck became chief minister, Prussia was one of 38 German states in a confederation dominated by Austria. Bismarck set about freeing these states and uniting them under Prussian leadership. First, Bismarck made his army into one of the best in Europe. He then made an agreement with France and Italy that they would remain neutral in case of a Prussian war with Austria. In 1866 when his army was ready, he provoked Austria into declaring war on Prussia. In seven weeks of fighting, Bismarck's army defeated the Austrians. Prussia was now supreme in Germany. All but four of the German states united with Prussia in a North German confederation.

In 1871, after Prussia defeated France in the Franco-Prussian war, the German Empire was declared. William of Prussia became kaiser (KY-suhr) or emperor. The German states that had remained outside the confederation now joined in the new empire. Bismarck had worked well with William I but his grandson William II eased Bismarck out of power in 1890. William II was not so farseeing or skilled a diplomat as Bismarck. Under his rule, Germany was eventually led into World War I.

ITALY UNITED   Italian unification was brought about by the efforts of three people: Giuseppe Mazzini (maht-TSEE-nee), idealist,

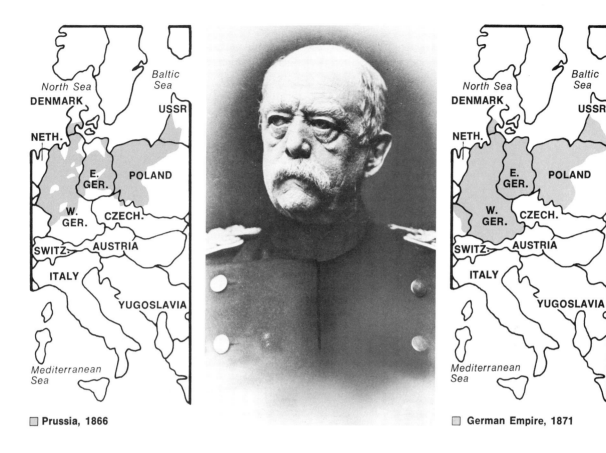

□ Prussia, 1866

□ German Empire, 1871

scholar, and poet; Giuseppe Garibaldi (gar-uh-BAWL-dee), sailor, farmer, and activist; and Camillo di Cavour (kuh-VUR), aristocrat, diplomat, and government leader. Although they differed in their methods and the type of government they wanted—Mazzini and Garibaldi wanted a republic and Cavour a limited monarchy—all three were nationalists.

Mazzini spent much of his life in exile or prison. While in exile in Switzerland he organized a secret society known as Young Italy. In 1848 his followers seized Rome and Venice and founded republics. However, the cities were recaptured by the Austrians with French help. Mazzini fled to Switzerland again but his dedication continued to inspire others.

Garibaldi was a member of Young Italy. When discovered by the police, he escaped to Latin America where he fought beside the nationalists there. He returned to Italy in 1848 to help found a republic in Rome. When the republic fell, he went into exile but returned in 1854. Several times after that he took an active part in Italian politics. Garibaldi was not interested in title, glory, or wealth. He only wanted a unified Italian nation where Italians could live free and self-governing.

Otto von Bismarck created the German Empire from a confederation of states. What methods did he use? How did the theory of nationalism influence him?

553

Italy in 1852 Before Unification
- ☐ **Kingdom of Sardinia**
- ☐ **Kingdom of the Two Sicilies**
- ☐ **Papal States**

Giuseppe Garibaldi is wearing a red shirt, his famous uniform, in this 1860 photograph.

Cavour schemed and planned for Italian unity among the ruling houses of Europe. In 1852 he became prime minister of the Kingdom of Sardinia. Besides the island of Sardinia, the kingdom included a region in northeastern Italy called Piedmont. Cavour aimed to make his kingdom powerful enough to drive Austria from Italy. By doing this he would be able to put his king, Victor Emmanuel II, on the throne of a united Italy.

Cavour made an agreement with Emperor Louis Napoleon of France. If Austria declared war on Piedmont, France would help Italy. As a reward, France would receive the Austrian lands of Nice and Savoy. Cavour then provoked Austria into declaring war on Piedmont. The combined French and Italian forces drove the Austrians from northern Italy. They would have continued but uprisings of revolutionaries in northern Italy frightened Louis Napoleon. He made a separate peace with Austria. The northern Italian states were now strong enough to form with Sardinia the Kingdom of Italy.

Italy still was not unified, however. The Kingdom of the Two Sicilies and the Papal States remained outside. But the fires of nationalism were still burning. They were reflected in the Redshirts, the followers of Garibaldi. In 1860 he led a thousand of them in an invasion of Sicily. The people of the Kingdom of the Two Sicilies rallied around him. Within a short time Garibaldi controlled all of southern Italy. He then prepared to march on Rome and the other papal states.

Cavour was fearful that this move would bring France and Austria into the fight on the side of the pope. Cavour met Garibaldi in Naples and persuaded him to surrender the southern territories to him. This surrender made it possible to unite northern and southern Italy. Garibaldi again returned to private life. Victor Emmanuel II became king of all Italy except for the city of Rome. In 1871 Italian forces were able to occupy Rome and make it their capital.

With the unification of Germany and Italy, nationalism was triumphant in much of Europe. Now secure at home, Europeans turned their view outward.

IMPERIALISM

In the mid-1800s another great era of European expansionism began. The leaders of Germany, France, Italy, Belgium, and Great Britain looked beyond their continent. They saw lands that were tempting in their military weaknesses and potential wealth. Europeans began a policy of acquiring these lands for themselves.

This competition for empire intensified European rivalries. The more powerful nations obviously were at an advantage. It was natural, therefore, that each nation should strive to increase its own power in every way possible. One way was to acquire territories for use as military bases in strategic parts of the world.

Economic forces also contributed to the outward drive of European nations. The growing industries of Europe needed greater amounts of raw materials and larger markets for their products. Overseas possessions provided many opportunities for safe and profitable investment of surplus capital. In addition, manufacturers and merchants could sell their goods in their nation's colonies without paying **tariffs.** The nations of Europe had raised tariff walls—duties on imports into Europe—and refused to allow other nations to trade in their colonies. The British, however, following the philosophy of laissez-faire capitalism, were an exception. They allowed a policy of free trade.

Many Europeans also felt that they had a mission to bring European civilization to the so-called backward peoples of the world. This viewpoint was held sincerely by some and tongue-in-cheek by others. However, it was loudly and frequently expressed by Europeans as well as by some of the people of the newly acquired areas. It did not matter that many of the peoples had cultures far older than that of the Europeans. Under this pretext European nations took over territories in Africa, the Middle East, and Asia.

The Europeans were so successful at gaining territory that by the beginning of the 1900s they dominated most of the world. But they paid a heavy price in anxiety, suspicion, and fear. In no area was the price higher than in their mounting military budgets.

THE ARMS RACE

In the latter part of the 1800s the Europeans started an arms race which in this century has become worldwide. Under Prussian leadership, the Germans demonstrated the advantage of a general staff to plan and organize for war. They also proved the value of a reserve army. All able-bodied men were drafted for duty, trained, and then returned to civilian life. They could be called up whenever needed.

By the end of the 1800s, the German army was still the best but the British had the best navy. By the 1890s, however, the Germans wanted to surpass the British navy. To maintain naval superiority the British were forced to build more and more ships. Then the French and Americans began building up their navies.

Industries arose to produce better and greater quantities of arms. National budgets were increased to meet increased defense needs. The arms race, far from bringing a sense of security to nations, only added to their tenseness. Ultimately arms were not enough.

ALLIANCES

In order to increase their power, the nations of Europe began to form alliances. First Germany proposed a defensive alliance with Austria-Hungary. According to the alliance, either country would come to the aid of the other if attacked by a third nation. Austria-Hungary agreed and the pact became known as the Dual Alliance. Germany then turned to Italy and proposed the same conditions. Italy agreed. The Dual Alliance became the Triple Alliance.

France was now alone in Europe. It frantically sought allies to counterbalance those of Germany. So long as Bismarck had controlled the diplomacy of Germany, he had managed to keep France without allies. But the policies of William II unwittingly helped bring Russia and France together. Britain, fearful of Germany's growing strength, also sought an alliance with France. This became known as the Triple **Entente.** By 1907 two great power blocs faced each other in Europe.

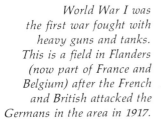

Perhaps none of the nations of Europe wanted war. Yet they all wanted things they could not have without war—more territory, more wealth, more power. And they set the stage for war by forming alliances and engaging in an arms race.

WORLD WAR I

World War I was the first war fought with heavy guns and tanks. This is a field in Flanders (now part of France and Belgium) after the French and British attacked the Germans in the area in 1917.

World War I mushroomed from the assassination of Archduke Franz Ferdinand, heir to the Austro-Hungarian throne. He was killed on June 28, 1914, by a Bosnian nationalist. Bosnia was an Austrian province on the Adriatic Sea. The Serbians thought Bosnia should belong to them.

Bosnia and Serbia, (both now part of Yugoslavia) along with Ro-

mania, Bulgaria, Albania, and Greece, were part of that section of southeast Europe known as the Balkans. The Balkans were considered a powderkeg. Nationalist feelings were often violently expressed there and these outbursts attracted the attention of larger powers. Germany was interested because it wanted to run a railroad through the Balkans to Constantinople and on to Baghdad and the Persian Gulf. This railroad would give Germany an overland route to the trade of the Middle East and Asia.

Britain was interested because such an undertaking would threaten the Suez Canal, which the British considered their lifeline. Britain also did not want either Germany or Russia meddling with Turkey or the Middle East. Russia was interested because the Turks controlled the only channel between the Black and Mediterranean seas. In addition, many of the people of the Balkans were Slavs. The Russians, who were predominantly Slavic, regarded them with a protective eye. Austria-Hungary was interested because the Balkans were along its southern boundaries. Any desire for national independence there threatened Austria-Hungary.

This was the situation when Archduke Franz Ferdinand was shot. Austria-Hungary immediately demanded reparations from Serbia. The Serbians refused to meet these demands. Austria-Hungary then declared war on Serbia. The Russians mobilized and Germany declared war on Russia. When the French refused to state whether or not they would remain **neutral,** Germany declared war on France. The Belgians remained neutral. However, the easiest land passage to France was through Belgium. Germany invaded Belgium. As a result Britain declared war on Germany and Austria-Hungary. World War I had begun.

Italy had been secretly promised some spoils from the war if it would join France, Britain, and Russia. Italy deserted the Triple Alliance. France, Italy, Britain, and Russia came to be known as the Allies. Japan saw an opportunity to profit and joined them. Romania and Greece also joined the Allies. Turkey and Bulgaria joined Germany. Germany and the nations associated with it became known as the Central Powers. The war leaped overseas to the British dominions and drew in Canada, Australia, and New Zealand among others. In 1917 the U.S. entered the conflict. Thus the globe was encircled by war.

For much of the four years that the war lasted, it was a struggle for a few patches of muddy, gun-beaten land on the eastern front of France. Soldiers lay in trenches protected by barbed wire. Patrols ventured cautiously beyond the wire to probe the enemy's position. The British built and used tanks which proved to be powerful weapons in trench warfare. The Germans in turn developed great gun power. Some of their guns had a range of 113 kilometers (70 miles) and could knock out steel and concrete fortifications.

Both sides built airplanes. It was in this war that nations began to learn the possibilities of air power. Sea power was also important.

World War I was also the first war in which airplanes were used. This is a photograph of an aerial dogfight. Military people learned the importance of what other kind of power besides air power in World War I?

spoils: property or land taken from the losing side in war

German submarines—called U-boats—sank millions of tons of shipping and killed thousands of people. But the British ruled the surface of the sea and were able to bottle up the German navy. Overseas the Allies were victorious. Germany lost its island and colonial possessions in Africa and Asia.

In Europe the tide of war turned when the U.S. threw its power behind the Allies. Gradually the nations on Germany's side began to ask for peace. The German people rebelled and forced the kaiser to abdicate. On November 11, 1918, the chancellor of the new German socialist government signed an armistice, or **truce**.

GROUNDWORK FOR A NEW WAR

World War I, like all wars, left misery and disaster. Improved weapons had made it more destructive than any previous war. Of the 65 million men and women mobilized, nearly 8.5 million were killed. Over 20 million were wounded. The battlefields, especially in France, had been torn and pitted. Forests had been stripped by exploding shells. Shells which failed to explode made the land dangerous to farm for years afterward. Economies were shattered, political life was disrupted, and society was in disorder.

U.S. President Woodrow Wilson said this war must be "a war to end wars" and pleaded for the need to make "a world safe for democracy." As a guideline for peace negotiations, Wilson formulated a program which became known as the Fourteen Points. Among other things he called for freedom of the seas, freedom to trade, a reduction of armaments, and the establishment of a worldwide organization, the League of Nations, to insure peace. Some among the Allies did not agree with all of Wilson's Fourteen Points but his idea of a League of Nations was carried out.

Germany was forced to submit to harsh terms. In the Treaty of Versailles that ended the war Germany was required to pay $5 billion in two years. In 1921 the total bill was set at $33 billion. Germany had to return Alsace and Lorraine to France and agree to leave the Rhineland unfortified. The Saar Valley—rich in coal deposits—was to be administered by the League of Nations.

Some German territory was given to Belgium and another slice to Denmark. Poland received a corridor of land which cut Prussia in two. All German colonies were divided among the victors to be administered under the supervision of the League of Nations. Germany's army was limited, the general staff was disbanded, and the manufacture of arms was restricted. In 1919 Germany tasted the bitter fruits of defeat. This bitterness was one cause that led to World War II.

The Treaty of Versailles, like the Congress of Vienna, changed the face of Europe. New states were added. The territories of defeated nations were cut up. Austria and Hungary were split. Austria became

European Alliances, 1914

☐ **Triple Entente Nations (France, England, Scotland, Wales, N. Ireland, Rep. of Ireland, USSR)**

Triple Alliance Nations:
☐ **Germany**
☐ **Austria-Hungary**
☐ **Italy**

NORWAY

SWEDEN

North Sea

Baltic Sea

DENMARK

NETHER-LANDS

Atlantic Ocean

BELGIUM
LUX.

SWITZ.

SPAIN

Black Sea

BULGARIA

GREECE

Mediterranean Sea

ALBANIA

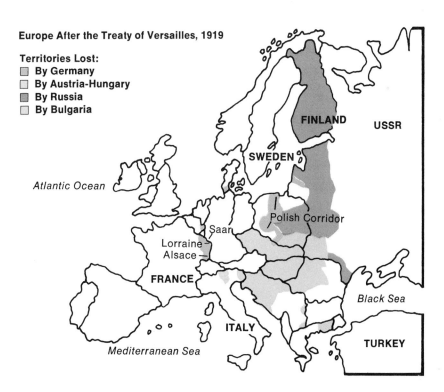

Europe After the Treaty of Versailles, 1919

Territories Lost:
☐ **By Germany**
☐ **By Austria-Hungary**
☐ **By Russia**
☐ **By Bulgaria**

FINLAND

USSR

SWEDEN

Atlantic Ocean

Polish Corridor

Saar

Lorraine

Alsace

FRANCE

Black Sea

ITALY

Mediterranean Sea

TURKEY

559

a small republic. Hungary became a kingdom without a monarch. The new nations of Czechoslovakia and Yugoslavia were created to satisfy Slavic nationalism. Four new states—Finland, Estonia, Latvia, and Lithuania—split from Russia and were recognized as independent. Though the treaty makers tried to follow nationality lines in drawing borders, it was impossible. A number of minorities were left in other countries. German minorities in these countries were later to give Hitler an excuse for his invasions.

Chapter 2
The Rise
of Dictators

Benito Mussolini addresses his followers. This photograph was taken in 1932—ten years after he took power. What factors helped Mussolini's rise?

Political, economic, and social conditions, especially in Germany and Italy, worsened after the war. These conditions plus the problems created by the Treaty of Versailles eventually led to the rise of **authoritarian** regimes. These factors would also lead eventually to World War II.

The freedoms that Woodrow Wilson had hoped would grow out of the war could not live in the poverty and despair of postwar Europe. Instead the slogan of Mussolini's Fascists (FASH-uhsts) rang out across the Continent: "Believe! Obey! Work!"

MUSSOLINI AND FASCISM

The Italians were discontented and frustrated after World War I. Although they were among the victors, they had not received all the territory they had been promised. In addition, Italy suffered from inflation, labor unrest, unemployment, and terrible poverty. The

Italians looked to their government for help. But the government changed hands rapidly as one group after another failed to cope with the nation's problems. The king was only a figurehead.

Then into their lives came Benito Mussolini (moo-suh-LEE-nee). He told the Italians that he had the answers to their problems. Follow him, he told them, and he would make them proud members of a powerful nation.

Il Duce (DOO-chay), the leader—as Mussolini was often called—was the son of a blacksmith and a schoolteacher. He had joined the Socialist party in the early 1900s. When the party refused to support Italy's entrance into World War I against Germany, Mussolini broke with it. From 1915 to 1917 he fought in the Italian army.

Amid the postwar chaos of Italy he organized the Fascist party. Army veterans and frustrated nationalists became the backbone of the party. The Fascists—sometimes known as Blackshirts—were anti-Communist and anti-Socialist. They fought with both groups, breaking up their meetings and silencing their speakers.

Mussolini became so powerful that in 1922 Victor Emmanuel III asked him to become prime minister. By 1924 the Fascists ruled everywhere in Italy. For the next 20 years Mussolini did not win or hold power by free elections. The Fascists turned Italy into a **totalitarian state**.

The Chamber of Deputies and the Senate were kept. But it was Il Duce who ruled through his Grand Council of the Fascist party. Men of various occupations—farmers, industrial workers, and so on—were grouped into 13 syndicates or corporations. Each of these syndicates was represented in the government. (This differed from countries like the U.S. where people were represented geographically and on the basis of numbers.) The Italian syndicates were all controlled by Mussolini as minister of corporations. This system is sometimes referred to as a corporate state. Private property existed, but it was always subject to seizure and use by the state.

Under Fascist rule, the material life of the Italians improved. But the price was high. Opponents of Fascism were constantly in danger of arrest. Political prisoners were often tortured, killed, or sent to prison camps. Strikes by workers attracted a number of followers from among the middle class and the large industrialists. Fascists restored order, discipline, and a feeling of security to many Italians. Like other peoples throughout history the Italians traded freedom for security.

In foreign affairs, Mussolini wanted to build a new Roman Empire. The Italian army, navy, and air force were strengthened and prepared for war. In 1935 Italy invaded and occupied Ethiopia. Mussolini also joined Hitler in meddling in the Spanish Civil War in the 1930s. Mussolini dreamed of a great empire that would be his if he and Hitler won World War II. Mussolini's ambitions, however, brought only death to himself and defeat to his country. His own people hanged him toward the end of the war.

figurehead: a person who has the title of ruler but no power

561

During Francisco Franco's 34 years in power, he supported the wealthy. He was against social change and economic reforms aimed at the poor. Censorship was imposed. Those who opposed him were jailed.

CIVIL WAR AND FRANCO

Long before the 1930s Spain had lost its status as a great power. The decline of Spain had begun when the great armada that Philip II sent against England was destroyed in 1588. By the mid-1800s the Spanish overseas empire—once the greatest in the world—had shrunk. Uprisings, independence movements, and defeat in wars with other nations led to the loss of most of Spain's holdings. As the flow of gold, silver, and other wealth from the colonies decreased, Spain became a weak nation. Throughout the 1800s and into the 1900s internal conflicts and economic problems affected the Spanish.

Most of the people were of the working class and desperately poor. Antagonisms and conflicts grew between the poor and the few wealthy. These few were the large landowners, the military, and the clergy. Thousands of Spanish turned to socialism, communism of various kinds, and **republicanism**. All of these were part of the political left in Spain. In 1931 a republican-socialist government came to power and proclaimed Spain a republic.

The new leaders separated Church and State. They turned the Roman Catholic schools into secular institutions. The breakup of large landed estates was planned. Other changes in the traditional political, economic, and cultural structure of Spain were attempted. But the divisions continued to widen between **leftists** and **rightists**. Divisions among leftists themselves arose.

In 1936 leftists including Communists united in a Popular Front and won the election. The rightists, or Nationalists, fearing the end of a system and a way of life they believed in, attempted to overturn the government. General Francisco Franco became their leader. This attempt led to a bloody civil war which lasted from 1936 to 1939.

General Franco was supported by the same groups which had supported the monarchy: landowners, military, and clergy. There was also a strong rightist party called the Falange. Founded in 1932, it modeled itself along the lines of the Italian Fascist party. The members of this party brought additional support to Franco. Further, Mussolini and Hitler saw in Franco a welcome ally in their drive for power.

They sent Franco help in the form of weapons, tanks, airplanes, and soldiers. The Soviet Union entered the struggle on the side of the republican armies. Liberals and leftists from many parts of the world fought in international brigades against Franco's forces. Thus, for nearly three years an international struggle **of ideologies** was waged on Spanish soil. The Spanish Civil War became a prelude to World War II.

In 1939 General Franco occupied Madrid and began the rule of the caudillo (kaw-THEE-yoh), or strong man. He held the posts both as chief of state and head of the Falange party. The Cortes or parliament was kept, but its power was subordinated to that of General Franco. In 1947 Franco proclaimed that Spain was to become a monarchy after his death or retirement. In 1969 he chose Prince Juan Carlos

Bourbon, grandson of King Alfonso XIII who abdicated in 1931, to succeed him. In 1975 Franco died. Juan Carlos was crowned king and immediately eased some of Franco's harsher rules.

HITLER AND NAZISM

Immediately after World War I, the Germans had established the Weimar (VY-mahr) Republic. It had an elected president and parliament of two houses. In the lower house—known as the Reichstag—parties were represented in proportion to the number of votes they had received. The upper house—the Bundesrat—represented the 17 states of Germany. The premier or prime minister was called the chancellor. He came from the majority party in the lower house as did his cabinet.

The Weimar Republic had a stormy history. Economic conditions made life a nightmare. Parties representing all shades of opinion from extreme right to extreme left multiplied rapidly. The communists were suppressed when they attempted to take the government by force. The monarchists also tried and were stopped. Liberal leaders were murdered. Strikes became commonplace. Unemployment soared. Money became cheaper than the paper it was printed on. No nation experienced inflation as bad as that of Germany.

It is estimated that in 1923, 25 cents of U.S. money was worth one trillion German marks. The smallest bill printed in Germany was five million marks. Germans collected their salaries in large bags. For those who had their savings in bonds, banks, and pensions, there was disappointment and despair. Their money, which had formerly been worth hundreds and thousands of dollars, was now worth a few cents.

The government was able to curb inflation in 1924 by introducing a new monetary system. Conditions improved a little until 1929. Then a worldwide depression struck. The Germans were hit especially hard. Seeking an answer to their problems, they started to turn in growing numbers to the extremists of the right and left. The rightist party of Adolf Hitler—the National Socialist German Workers' party or Nazis—made great gains.

Hitler was born in Austria in 1889. He fought in World War I, won an Iron Cross for bravery, and rose to the rank of corporal. He rebelled at the terms of the Treaty of Versailles and joined those who wanted to overthrow the republic. It was during this postwar period of unrest that Hitler joined the Nazis.

Hitler promised the German people improvements in their welfare, security, and economy. He preached repeal of the Versailles treaty and the return of lost territories and colonies. He told the people that they were a master race, the great and pure Aryans. All who were not Aryans were inferior. (The Aryans were an ancient Indo-European language group. If they had ever been a gene pool, it

On September 1, 1939, Adolf Hitler (arrow) announces the beginning of what was to become World War II. Claiming that the Polish had fired first, Hitler said he had decided to send the German army into Poland.

had been mixed with others for thousands of years.) Many Germans believed Hitler, Der Fuhrer (FYOOR-uhr) or the leader. His party became the largest in the Reichstag. In 1933 President Paul von Hindenburg appointed Hitler chancellor of Germany. The Nazis quickly seized full power.

Germany became a centralized, totalitarian state ruled by Hitler and the Nazi party. The Nazis controlled every area of German life. Concentration camps were built. People whom Hitler did not like, feared, or could use as scapegoats were shifted to the camps. The Jews were singled out for special hatred. By the end of World War II, Nazi concentration camps had become places of horror where gas ovens had killed over six million Jews. Communists, socialists, Roman Catholics, and liberals also suffered under the Nazis.

Hitler's goal was world empire. First, however, he wanted to regain the territories which Germany had lost in the previous war. In 1936

scapegoats: people who are made to take the blame for something others have done

Hitler tested the British and the French by sending troops into the Rhineland. This part of Germany was supposed to remain unfortified according to the Treaty of Versailles. Nothing was done to stop Hitler.

Hitler had begun to build his Nazi party in Austria, Czechoslovakia, and wherever there were German minorities. Nazi parties in these countries prepared the way for Hitler. He entered Austria in March 1938 and proclaimed it part of the German Reich. Next he declared that the three million Germans in Czechoslovakia must belong to Germany.

Neville Chamberlain, then prime minister of Great Britain, went to Germany and met with Hitler at Munich. In the hope of preventing war, Chamberlain yielded to Hitler's demands. Czechoslovakia was taken apart as Germany, Poland, and Hungary claimed portions of it as their own. The Munich Pact became synonymous with appeasement, that is, unresisting surrender.

In 1939 Hitler made a pact with Stalin, the Communist dictator of the USSR. They pledged **nonaggression** toward each other and divided eastern Europe between them. Then on September 1, 1939, Hitler invaded Poland. Two days later Britain and France declared war on Germany. World War II had begun.

Through her diary, Anne Frank has come to symbolize the millions of Jews who died under Nazi persecution. She and her family went into hiding in 1942 in the Netherlands when the Nazis overran the country. Discovered in 1944, she died in a concentration camp. Above is the city of Warsaw, Poland, after numerous Nazi bombing raids in September 1939.

WORLD WAR II

France and Britain were not as well-prepared for war as Germany. During the years after World War I, the French declined in power. The economy of France was weak. Inflation became a curse. The French population declined. A great fortification complex of steel,

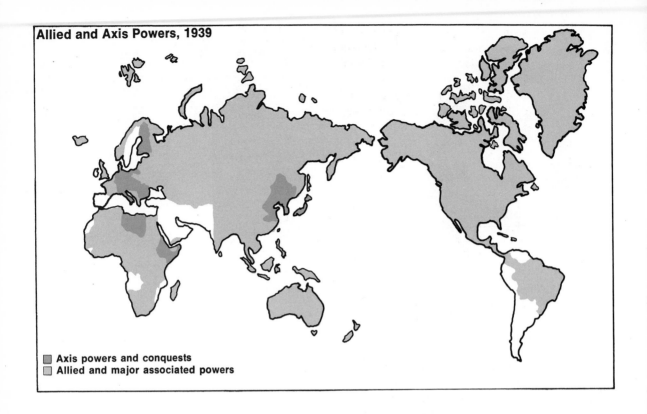

Allied and Axis Powers, 1939

■ Axis powers and conquests
□ Allied and major associated powers

stone, and guns called the Maginot (mazh-uh-NOH) Line was supposed to guard the French borders against the Germans. In their blind trust, the French neglected to consider the possibility of a new kind of war. When it came, France was surprised and unprepared.

The only ally France could depend on was Great Britain. But the British had their own problems. They too had experienced political and economic difficulties during the postwar years. Most British investments abroad had been spent to fight World War I. The British were losing markets to the U.S. and Japan. Taxes after the war fell heavily upon the great fortunes and great estates. In British factories, old machines needed to be replaced by more efficient ones. The colonies and overseas territories increasingly demanded more freedom to run their own affairs. All these matters demanded financing and attention. Little attention was paid to preserving the efficiency of the military.

While the French and the British moved into and around the Maginot Line, Hitler moved quickly elsewhere. In April 1940 he conquered Norway and Denmark. This victory so startled the British that they requested Neville Chamberlain's resignation. Winston Churchill became prime minister. Then with screaming dive bombers and roaring tanks, Hitler took Holland, Belgium, and Luxembourg in quick succession.

The Germans rolled the British forces back to the beaches of Dunkirk on the French side of the English Channel. The British managed to evacuate most of their forces, but much of their equipment was left on the beach. Then the Germans turned on the French army and flanked the Maginot Line. On June 22, 1940, the French signed an armistice with Germany. In the meantime, Italy had entered the war on the side of Germany. In September 1940 the Japanese joined Hitler and Mussolini.

Britain was now fighting alone. After besieging the British with a week of bombing, Hitler offered them peace. The British could keep their empire but Britain would have to recognize the dominance of Germany and Italy. Churchill refused. The British fought on.

On December 7, 1941, the Japanese bombed Pearl Harbor in Hawaii and thus brought the U.S. into the war. The Japanese quickly seized Burma in Southeast Asia, the Philippines, and a number of other Pacific islands. The Germans had invaded the Soviet Union on June 22, 1941. These two events gave the British two powerful allies. This combination of forces was to bring about the eventual defeat of Hitler.

In fall 1942 the British stopped the Germans in North Africa. The Americans landed and joined forces with them. By February 1943 the German army attacking Stalingrad was forced to surrender. The Germans were defeated in Africa in May 1943. Two months later, the Allied armies landed in Sicily. Mussolini was forced to resign

Allied naval forces took a heavy loss at the start of World War II. This is a picture of the bombing of Pearl Harbor which brought the U.S. into the war.

Smoke rises over Nagasaki, Japan, after being hit by an atomic bomb on August 9, 1945. The use of the bomb there and at Hiroshima ended the war. How do you feel about the use of the bomb?

as prime minister and fled to German protection in northern Italy. The new Italian government declared war on Germany. But the Germans made it difficult for the Allies to take Italy north of Rome.

By the beginning of 1944 the German armies on the eastern front were forced back to Poland. On June 6, 1944, the Allies landed on the beaches of Normandy, France. By August they were in Paris. The Soviets launched an attack from the east. By April 1945 Soviet and U.S. armies met in Germany. On May 7, 1945, the Germans surrendered unconditionally.

Then the Allies turned their attention to defeating the Japanese. The Japanese had it all their own way until spring 1942 when the naval battles of the Coral Sea and Midway Island turned them back. Under the overall command of General Douglas MacArthur, the Allies began gradually to leap from island to island toward the Philippines and Japan. In October 1944 the Americans landed in the Philippines and in six months recaptured them.

It was on August 6, 1945, however, that the single most important event of the war occurred. The U.S. dropped an atomic bomb on the Japanese city of Hiroshima. Three days later another bomb hit the city of Nagasaki. The next day the Japanese asked for peace. On September 2, 1945, they signed an unconditional surrender aboard the USS *Missouri* in Tokyo Bay. World War II had officially come to an end.

Summing Up The Unit

Social Studies Vocabulary

Define: national identity; liberalism; dictatorship; civil liberties; tariff; truce; authoritarian; totalitarian; leftist; rightist; ideology; nonaggression

People

Identify: Blanc; Louis Napoleon; Bismarck; Mazzini; Garibaldi; Cavour; Franz Ferdinand; Woodrow Wilson; Mussolini; Franco; Hitler; Churchill

Places

Locate: Alsace-Lorraine; Saar Valley; Polish Corridor

Words

Define: Metternichism; kaiser; Triple Alliance; Fourteen Points; syndicates; corporate state; caudillo; chancellor; Weimar Republic; master race; appeasement

⚷ Questions

1. a. How can nationalism be used for peaceful purposes or be abused? b. How did national consciousness begin to grow as feudalism declined?
2. How did the French Revolution and Napoleon's military campaigns intensify nationalism?
3. What peoples revolted against the Austrians in 1848?
4. a. Why did Napoleon III stress foreign policy? b. How did this policy bring his downfall?
5. How did the Franco-Prussian war help to bring about World War I?
6. What flaw in the French political system caused the Third Republic to be unstable?
7. How did Bismarck use his belief in bloodshed and diplomacy to make Prussia supreme?
8. a. How did Mazzini, Garibaldi, and Cavour differ? b. How were their policies alike?
9. Why did European nations engage in imperialism by acquiring territories?
10. Why did the nations of Europe begin to form alliances?
11. From what incident did World War I mushroom?
12. Why were the following interested in the Balkans: a. Germany? b. Britian? c. Russia? d. Austria-Hungary?
13. How did the Treaty of Versailles change the face of Europe?
14. Why were the Italians discontented after World War I?
15. What positions did Mussolini's Fascists take toward: a. communism? b. political parties? c. private property? d. military power?
16. Why was the Spanish Civil War an international struggle?
17. a. What promises did Hitler and his Nazi party make to the German people? b. How did he abuse Jews? c. for what purpose?
18. Why were France and Britain poorly prepared to fight Hitler?
19. What was the single most important event in World War II?

Discussion Topics

1. Nationalism has played a major role in shaping modern nations and world events. Why? How can an understanding of nationalism help to explain recent developments in Africa and Asia?
2. World War I left misery and disaster. If European leaders could have foreseen how much destruction the war would cause, do you think they would have avoided it? Why or why not? How important was the desire for power?

Project Ideas

1. Prepare a report on one of the political leaders mentioned in this unit. Tell why he was a strong leader, the methods he used, and why you think he was a success or failure.
2. Imagine you are a member of the Allied or Central powers in World War I. Stage a classroom debate justifying your country's entrance into the war.
3. Draw a map showing Germany in 1939, 1941, and after World War II.

Unit X

The New Europe

The degree of Europe's prosperity after World War II is shown in this photo of an indoor shopping mall in Hamburg, West Germany. Hamburg was bombed out during the war but was rebuilt. Its harbor, rail system, and industries make it one of West Germany's most important cities.

Since the end of World War II, change has been an important feature of European life. The war left Europe in ruins. Within ten years, however, prosperity had returned. By the early 1970s wealth was more evenly distributed among European social classes than ever before. Greater educational opportunities and an increase in jobs among other factors contributed to this. So did the establishment of large national welfare systems.

Other changes are evident in Europe. The attitudes of Europeans toward war and each other were changed by the horror of World War II. Europeans wanted no more wars among themselves. The importance of cooperation is stressed. Since 1945 European nations have actively participated in and formed international and regional organizations. Nationalism, however, remains a strong force. Economic and political competition is not dead. But Europeans negotiate their problems today rather than fighting over them.

World Wars I and II speeded up technological and scientific advances. These discoveries have changed the way Europeans live and work. European arts and philosophy reflect the new social patterns.

World War II left an even more torn up Europe than the previous world war had. Thousands of tanks and millions of soldiers fought over much of Western and Eastern Europe. Weaponry had been vastly improved since World War I. Bombs were larger and long-range bombers could carry them great distances. No longer was war limited to fields, forests, and villages. Heavily populated cities became targets.

When the war was finally over, millions of Europeans were homeless. Countless numbers suffered from illness, lack of food, war-related injuries, and despair. Where the Nazis had ruled, millions of Jews had been killed. The war had drained Europe of much of its wealth and energy. The tremendous task of rebuilding was beyond the Europeans' own abilities. They needed help and that help came from the U.S.

Chapter 1
Cooperation—
Legacy of
World War II

TRUMAN DOCTRINE AND MARSHALL PLAN

At the end of the war, the Soviet Union controlled Eastern Europe. It also occupied eastern Germany and ruled part of Berlin. Communist and non-Communist forces were battling for control of Greece. Turkey was threatened by a Communist takeover. Communist parties were growing powerful in France, Italy, and other Western European countries. The promises of communism were becoming more attractive to Europeans because they were suffering from economic and social chaos. A number of European and U.S. leaders believed that Communists might eventually dominate all Europe. To prevent this, U.S. leaders announced two major programs.

In 1947 President Harry S. Truman began the Truman Doctrine. Through it the U.S. would provide aid to those nations fighting the loss of their countries to armed minorities and outsiders.

The second policy came to be known as the Marshall Plan. Named after then Secretary of State George C. Marshall, it was designed to bring about the economic recovery of Europe. Under this plan, the U.S. sent billions of dollars worth of raw materials, food, machinery, and other items to Europe. With this help, Europeans were able to raise their standards of living and contain the spread of Soviet influence in Europe.

NORTH ATLANTIC TREATY ORGANIZATION

In 1950 Canada and the U.S. joined ten European nations to form the North Atlantic Treaty Organization (NATO). Today there are 13 European members (Belgium, Denmark, France, Great Britain, Iceland, Italy, Luxembourg, The Netherlands, Norway, Portugal, Greece, Turkey, and West Germany). In the beginning the purpose of NATO was to keep the Soviet Union and its allies from attacking any member nation. The heart of the treaty states that "an armed attack against one or more of them in Europe and North America

571

shall be considered an attack against all."

 Even though tensions between Communist and non-Communist nations have cooled down, the aim of NATO continues to be primarily one of security. Members contribute air, land, and naval forces. Under the NATO agreement the U.S. keeps several hundred thousand troops in Europe. In recent years serious problems over policy have arisen between some European members and the U.S. Some members of the U.S. Congress have called for a drastic reduction of U.S. armed forces stationed in Europe. A number of European members of NATO, however, fear any withdrawal of U.S. forces.

UNITED NATIONS

In April 1945 representatives of 50 nations—many of them European countries—met to draw up a charter for a United Nations (UN). These countries believed that only an international organization dedicated to cooperation could save the world from another war. Among the purposes of the UN are: to maintain international peace and security; to settle international disputes by peaceful means; and to develop friendly relations among nations based upon respect for the equal rights and self-determination of peoples.

The charter also calls for international cooperation in solving the

These are the United Nations buildings in New York. At left is the General Assembly; center, Conference Building (low building) and Secretariat (tall building); right, Dag Hammarskjold Library. What are the other agencies of the UN? Where are they located?

THE UNITED NATIONS AND ITS SPECIALIZED AGENCIES

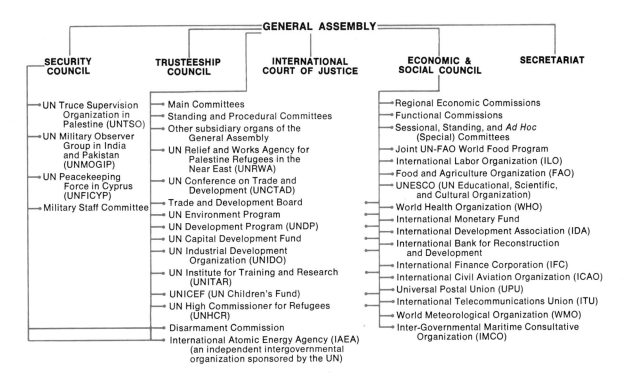

GENERAL ASSEMBLY

SECURITY COUNCIL

- UN Truce Supervision Organization in Palestine (UNTSO)
- UN Military Observer Group in India and Pakistan (UNMOGIP)
- UN Peacekeeping Force in Cyprus (UNFICYP)
- Military Staff Committee

TRUSTEESHIP COUNCIL

INTERNATIONAL COURT OF JUSTICE

- Main Committees
- Standing and Procedural Committees
- Other subsidiary organs of the General Assembly
- UN Relief and Works Agency for Palestine Refugees in the Near East (UNRWA)
- UN Conference on Trade and Development (UNCTAD)
- Trade and Development Board
- UN Environment Program
- UN Development Program (UNDP)
- UN Capital Development Fund
- UN Industrial Development Organization (UNIDO)
- UN Institute for Training and Research (UNITAR)
- UNICEF (UN Children's Fund)
- UN High Commissioner for Refugees (UNHCR)
- Disarmament Commission
- International Atomic Energy Agency (IAEA) (an independent intergovernmental organization sponsored by the UN)

ECONOMIC & SOCIAL COUNCIL

- Regional Economic Commissions
- Functional Commissions
- Sessional, Standing, and *Ad Hoc* (Special) Committees
- Joint UN-FAO World Food Program
- International Labor Organization (ILO)
- Food and Agriculture Organization (FAO)
- UNESCO (UN Educational, Scientific, and Cultural Organization)
- World Health Organization (WHO)
- International Monetary Fund
- International Development Association (IDA)
- International Bank for Reconstruction and Development
- International Finance Corporation (IFC)
- International Civil Aviation Organization (ICAO)
- Universal Postal Union (UPU)
- International Telecommunications Union (ITU)
- World Meteorological Organization (WMO)
- Inter-Governmental Maritime Consultative Organization (IMCO)

SECRETARIAT

basic economic, social, and cultural problems of people. Another purpose is to work toward insuring freedom for all without regard to race, sex, language, or religion.

The main organizations of the UN are the General Assembly, Secretariat, Economic and Social Council, Trusteeship Council, International Court of Justice, and Security Council. Each member nation is represented in the General Assembly and has one vote. The Secretariat administers the UN. The Economic and Social Council oversees the improvement of worldwide social and economic conditions. The Trusteeship Council watches over people and territories that are not yet independent. The International Court decides on disputes brought before it by members and gives advisory opinions on matters of international law.

The Security Council handles international disputes and tries to settle them peacefully. This council is composed of 15 members. Ten are elected for two-year terms by the General Assembly. The other five Council members—the U.S., USSR, People's Republic of China, Great Britain, and France—are permanent.

These five were made permanent members because they were the most powerful countries in the world. Each possesses veto power. If any one of the five votes against a proposal, the Council cannot

administers:
manages

573

act. Thus in this Council the UN recognizes the reality and continuing privileges of power. Over the years permanent members have exercised this right whenever they felt an action was not in their **national interest**.

UN members represent the majority of the world's independent nations. As in the Security Council, these members base their voting on national interests. It is not uncommon for members to vote in blocs. For example, the European nations might band together to vote the same way on a proposal. At other times regional groupings such as the Asians and the Africans may join to swing their combined strength for or against an action. In still other instances no bloc voting takes place.

ROLE OF THE UN TODAY   It is true that no new world war has broken out since the founding of the UN. But since 1945 the world has been on the brink of global war several times. Regional and local wars have been fought almost continuously. Critics have claimed that it is not the UN which has prevented world war. Rather it is the fear of the consequences of such a war. A number of countries now have nuclear weapons. The U.S. and the USSR supposedly have enough bombs to destroy life many times over.

Supporters of the UN believe that it has a role to play in maintaining a more peaceful and secure world. They say it provides a neutral place for opposing groups to meet and discuss differences. Hopefully with the help of middle parties in these discussions a peaceful agreement can be reached. Supporters also point out that forces under the UN flag have helped preserve peace between warring groups. Critics, however, say that UN peacekeeping forces are of no use if one or other of the groups is determined to continue fighting.

Perhaps the most effective work of the UN has been done by its specialized agencies. A number of their headquarters are in Europe. The Food and Agriculture Organization (FAO) is centered in Rome. UN Educational, Scientific, and Cultural Organization (UNESCO) is headquartered in Paris. The International Atomic Energy Agency (IAEA) is in Vienna. The World Health Organization (WHO), International Labor Organization (ILO), International Telecommunications Union (ITU), and World Meteorological Organization (WMO) are all in Geneva. Much of the work of the special agencies is successful because it is not directly concerned with political or security affairs. Rather the agencies are concerned with more concrete activities in the physical and scientific fields.

REGIONAL ORGANIZATIONS

In the years following World War II, a number of European leaders decided that their governments should work together on questions of regional interest. Many Europeans hoped that the result would be a politically linked Europe—the United States of Europe or the Federated States of Europe. A number of countries began to join together in regional organizations.

The first organization was the Council of Europe founded in 1949. Eighteen European countries and Turkey are members. The Council's purpose is to propose and support cooperation in economic, social, or political matters among members. The Council has made decisions in a number of areas including social security, human rights, and extradition.

The European Convention on Human Rights was established in 1953. Most of the member nations of the Council of Europe belong. The purpose of the convention is the protection of the rights of individuals within member states. Individuals or groups may appeal decisions beyond their national courts. Appeals may reach to the Commission on Human Rights. If not solved there, a case may go to the Committee of Ministers, the decision-making body of the Council of Europe. Final appeals go to the European Court of Human Rights.

In 1959 the European Free Trade Association (EFTA) was formed. Its members originally included Austria, Denmark, Norway, Great Britain, Portugal, Sweden, and Switzerland. Finland and Iceland later

extradition:
a government's turning over of a person charged with a crime to the government where the crime was committed

In 1975 the British held a referendum to determine whether or not to stay in the European Common Market (EEC). Here officials watch the ballots being counted. The outcome, by a 2-1 margin, was approval to stay in the Common Market. Why would citizens be interested enough in membership in the Market to demand a popular vote on it?

575

became members. The Benelux Economic Union which included the Netherlands, Belgium, and Luxembourg was founded around this time.

EUROPEAN COMMUNITY   In 1951 Belgium, Italy, Luxembourg, France, the Netherlands, and West Germany joined to create a common market for coal and steel. Under a plan offered by Robert Schuman of France, they formed the European Coal and Steel Community (ECSC). The organization was designed to remove all obstacles to coal, iron ore, and steel trade among members. Such obstacles were tariffs, quotas, and import restrictions. The ECSC dealt also with the movement of coal and steel workers from one member country to another. Another aim of the organization was to bring Germany and France closer together economically.

In 1957 the same six nations set up the European Atomic Energy Community (Euratom). Euratom supports nuclear research and helps build nuclear power plants in Europe. At the same time, the European Economic Community (EEC) began operations with the same six nations.

In 1973 Great Britain, Ireland, and Denmark joined. A number of British groups questioned the effect of Britain's move on its economy. The EEC also has associate members—Greece, Turkey, and several African countries. The EEC provides various kinds of aid to the developing countries associated with it.

The EEC's goal is the removal of all barriers to the free movement of goods, capital, and people among member nations. The EEC also wants common tariff and economic policies. The organization has met a number of its goals. The flow of capital and people among members has increased. Their transportation and communication systems have improved. These have contributed greatly to the prosperity which followed the EEC's establishment.

The EEC, ECSC, and Euratom are grouped together within a common political framework known as the European Community. The agencies of the Community are the Council of Ministers, Commission, Court of Justice, and European Parliament.

The Council decides on policy. Its members are appointed by their governments and reflect the official views of their nations. The members of the Commission, on the other hand, represent the interests of Europe as a whole. They suggest legislation for the Community.

The Court of Justice is like a supreme court. It interprets the meaning of the various treaties and agreements that the Community makes. The Court also handles questions of jurisdiction and disputes between the Community's various agencies. Its decisions are final. Members of the European Parliament are chosen by the parliaments of member states. This parliament has no power to make laws or decisions. It is only an advisory body.

Natural Resources

● Industrial ▼ Coal ■ Iron ○ Oil □ Minerals

Land Use

☐ Farming ☐ Forestry ☐ Grazing ☐ Nonproductive

Throughout the 1960s French President Charles de Gaulle blocked any attempt by the European Community to become an independent economic and political unit. In 1972 President Georges Pompidou of France refused the Dutch request that members of the European Parliament be elected directly by the people. By the mid-1970s the possibility of European political unity seemed unlikely. Nationalism was still a strong force but the necessity of economic cooperation was apparent to Europeans. And it is in this area that cooperation continues.

COMMONWEALTH OF NATIONS

As we have seen, Europeans in the late 1400s began to carve out worldwide empires for themselves. The Portuguese were the first, followed by the Spanish, Dutch, English, and French. With the exception of the Spanish, these empires remained largely intact until late into this century. It was only after World War II that colonies began gradually to win independence. A few areas were still ruled by European governments in the mid-1970s.

Of the former colonies, some have chosen to continue their ties with their former rulers. This is done through voluntary associations. Among such groups are the French Community and the Commonwealth of Nations. The French Community is largely an association between France and African nations and has been discussed in the African section of this book.

The Commonwealth of Nations is made up of former dependencies of Great Britain. In the mid-1970s there were 34 members. They are not tied to the Commonwealth by formal treaties and may make their own foreign policy. However, certain material benefits come from Commonwealth membership. Members negotiate favorable trade agreements with each other. Developing nations within the group receive aid from richer members. Various agencies provide a system of cooperation in such areas as education, health care, and scientific research. Among the original members were Australia, New Zealand, and Canada.

AUSTRALIA   About 50,000 years ago people came to Australia from what is today called Indonesia. They were the ancestors of Australia's first inhabitants, the aborigines. Aborigines were and, for the most part, still are hunting and gathering nomads. Since 1948 government policy has encouraged them to enter the mainstream of Australian society. The government has also encouraged them to keep as many of their traditional ways as they wish. The aborigines are skilled and creative artisans who make bark paintings, rock carvings, and woven baskets and mats.

In 1770 Captain James Cook claimed Australia for Great Britain. The British saw the remote continent as a place to send convicts from their overcrowded jails. The first shipment of prisoners and guards

arrived in 1788. They soon discovered that Australia was ideal for raising sheep. Increasing numbers of free settlers began coming. By the end of the 1860s, the British stopped sending convicts.

In 1851 gold had been discovered. The promise of quick wealth drew people from all over the world. Those who could not find gold turned to farming and raising fruit. Australia's environment made agriculture difficult. Although Australia has a land area more than two-thirds as large as the mainland U.S., nearly 40 percent is wasteland. There were many failures and disasters, and the colonists demanded government help. Over the next decades the government built roads, railroads, ports, and public utilities and encouraged new industries. These developments drew even greater numbers of people.

In 1901 the six separate colonies of Australia were united into a commonwealth. Its legislative body—Parliament—consists of two houses: the Senate and the House of Representatives. The prime minister who heads the government and his cabinet are chosen from the majority in the House. Trade unions exercise considerable power in Australian politics. They have pressured the government into adopting many social measures. Among these are pensions for the aged, health and unemployment insurance, and assistance to widows and children.

NEW ZEALAND   About 1,250 miles southeast of Australia lie the islands of New Zealand. In area New Zealand is about the size of the states of North and South Carolina and Virginia.

A people known as Maoris (MOW-rees) from the Pacific area of

These photos are of track events at the Commonwealth Games. The games are held to promote friendship among member nations. The runners are from Canada, Kenya, New Zealand, Australia, and Tanzania. Is sports a common cultural denominator?

579

Polynesia settled the islands several centuries before the Europeans. In 1642 Abel Tasman, a Dutch navigator, reached the islands and named them New Zealand. The British began exploring the area in the 1700s. In 1840 they **annexed** the islands.

The royal governor signed a treaty with the Maoris which was supposed to protect their land rights. British settlers did not honor the treaty. Between 1860 and 1872 the Maoris waged a series of wars. They lost, but through the years they have gained a place of importance in national life. Today Maoris are about 10 percent of the population.

In 1853 a constitution was adopted for New Zealand. Power was placed in a single House of Representatives. The prime minister and cabinet are chosen from among the majority party. In 1893 New Zealand became the first democracy in which women could vote. The government built railroads, roads, public utilities, and communications facilities. Today the government provides a number of social services. Among these are old-age pensions, unemployment benefits, and accident and health insurance. New Zealanders are generally neither extremely wealthy nor extremely poor. More than many of the other Commonwealth nations, New Zealand has kept close ties with Great Britain.

CANADA   Archaeological knowledge of most of Canada's Indians is scanty. But Indians were living in the area thousands of years before Europeans arrived. They lived mostly in central and northern Canada although some roamed the subarctic region. Today almost 300,000 Canadians consider themselves Indians. Most live on reserves. The Indians own the reserves, but the government provides schools and health services.

In 1534 Jacques Cartier (KAHRT-ee-ay) claimed the St. Lawrence River in eastern Canada and the lands around it for France. In 1608 Samuel de Champlain established a settlement called Quebec on the river. This became the heart of the colony of New France. Under the determined will of Louis XIV soldiers and settlers were sent to the colony in increasing numbers. French villages and towns gradually lined the St. Lawrence valley.

The British took control of the area in 1763 at the end of the French and Indian War. By that time the language, customs, and religion of France were firmly established. The British were forced to pass the Quebec Act to reassure its newly acquired French Canadian subjects. Among other things the act allowed them to keep their legal code and their customs. They were also permitted freedom of worship. The present desire of French Canadians for a separate state has its roots in this early history of the dominance of French culture.

However, the rest of Canada is thoroughly British in law, language, and ways. British colonists settled the rest of the eastern coast as well as the western provinces.

After 1763 Canada evolved rather peacefully into a self-governing country. Several small uprisings against British rule occurred but slowly the huge area came under one government. By the British North America Act in 1867 the British government approved self-rule for Canada.

Canada has a federal system of government like that of the U.S. Each of the ten provinces has its own government with the power to govern and legislate for itself. There are also two territories which are administered by commissioners appointed by the national government. The national government has a legislature of two houses: the Senate and the House of Commons. The prime minister and the cabinet are selected from the majority party of the House. Members of the Senate are appointed for life by the cabinet.

Atomic energy is being used in Europe to produce electricity. This plant is in France. How does Euratom promote the peaceful uses of atomic energy?

Chapter 2
Contemporary Technology and Thought

Throughout this century, scientific achievements have continued to mount at an astonishing rate. Breakthroughs have come from team research. Individual scientists no longer work alone in laboratories. Universities, industry, and governments support science centers with the massive resources necessary for research. Often discoveries that began in Europe were further developed in the U.S. Between and after World Wars I and II, many European scientists, especially Jewish ones, immigrated to the U.S.

At first advances in physics and chemistry dominated science. Immediate practical use was made of them. This century opened with the first transatlantic cablegram. Since then radio, television, videotape, and cassettes have been developed. Today satellites transmit live broadcasts to all parts of the world. This century has also seen such improvements in transportation as mass-produced automobiles, propeller-driven airplanes, jets, rockets, turbo-driven trains, and nuclear-powered ships. For many people the computer seems to symbolize the entire age. Computers make possible the fast and easy storing, sorting, retrieving, and computing of data.

Because of scientific developments, a revolution in life-styles has occurred. Household appliances and conveniences have given a new ease to modern life and freed many women from their traditional roles. Air conditioning and central heating provide maximum climate control. Plastics and synthetic materials have created entire new industries. These, in turn, have changed the look of fashions and home furnishings.

However, these developments have not spread evenly across all levels of European society. All cannot afford the conveniences provided by modern science and technology. Although the standard of living in many countries remains low, the impact of **modernization** has and is changing the look of Europe and many European attitudes.

THE ATOMIC AGE

The beginning of the 1900s saw several discoveries which revolutionized modern science and had far-reaching effects on society. Physicists studied light waves, X rays, electricity, and other forms of energy and saw that they were related. In Germany Max Planck developed a theory to explain how energy was conserved, expended, and released.

From the time of the ancient Greeks there had been those who thought that all matter was composed of atoms. However, they believed these atoms could not be destroyed or divided. Now it was discovered that the atom could be split. From this fission tremendous amounts of energy were given off. Albert Einstein, a German who immigrated to America, developed the concept of a relationship between matter and energy.

Further discoveries built on and expanded the work of Planck and Einstein. Ernest Rutherford, a British physicist, conceived a theory of the structure of the atom. Niels Bohr of Denmark was able to reconcile this theory with Planck's work. Einstein's formula was proven correct when the atomic bomb was made. The bomb was developed under the direction of Italian physicist Enrico Fermi at the University of Chicago during World War II.

Peacetime uses of atomic energy have also been developed. It can be a source of power or part of medical treatments. For better or worse the development of atomic energy has changed the way war is waged and international relations are conducted. It has also changed the very fabric of peacetime life.

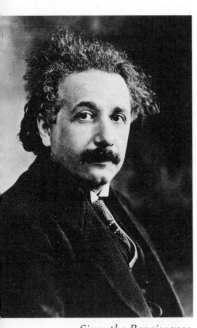

Since the Renaissance, science has become very practical. For example, Albert Einstein's work on the quantum theory contributed to the invention of talking movies.

MEDICAL SCIENCE

This century has also become the age of medical wonders. Medicine has wiped out many diseases, extended the lives of people, and provided insights into the workings of the human body. Progress has been so great in extending life expectancy that **overpopulation** has become a serious problem. Medical science has responded with the development of various forms of birth control.

Medical research too has spread across national boundaries. Many European discoveries were reinforced or enlarged by scientists in the U.S. and elsewhere. The era of wonder drugs began with the discovery and development of penicillin by Alexander Fleming, Ernst B. Chain, and Howard W. Florey in Great Britain. Their work was followed by a stream of discoveries such as sulfa drugs and cortisone, and diphtheria and tetanus vaccines.

The discovery of insulin by Frederick Banting and Charles Best of Canada has meant a normal life for most diabetics. Polio, once a deadly crippler, is practically unknown today as a result of the vaccines created by two Americans: Jonas Salk and Albert Sabin. Measles too is far less common through the work of John F. Enders.

In recent years the transplanting of human organs has been increasingly successful. The first heart transplant was done by Dr. Christiaan N. Barnard of South Africa in the late 1960s. Although heart transplants are beset by many problems, transplants of other organs are more common. They appear to have great potential as still another means of extending life.

Knowledge about the origin of life and the secrets of heredity increased when Francois Jacob, Andre Lwoff, and Jacques Monod of France discovered how the activities of body cells are regulated. Another breakthrough in genetics came with the discovery of the structure and function of deoxyribonucleic acid (DNA). This is the basic ingredient in genes. British scientists Francis H. C. Crick and Maurice H. F. Wilkins, along with the American James D. Watson, solved this mystery.

PSYCHOLOGY AND PSYCHIATRY

Psychology is the study of the mental, emotional, and behavioral processes of people. Psychiatry deals with the treatment of problems in these areas. Psychiatrists are medical doctors with a speciality in psychiatry. Some psychologists, called clinical psychologists, treat patients with psychiatric methods, but they are not medical doctors. Various schools of psychological theory developed during this century. Each tried to explain human actions and responses to environment.

Ivan Pavlov, a Russian, was influenced by the teachings of Wundt, the founder of psychology as a science. Pavlov experimented with the reactions of animals. In one series of experiments with dogs, he fed them only after ringing a bell. After a period of time Pavlov discovered that the dogs' mouths would water on merely hearing the bell. He called this response an example of a conditioned reflex. Pavlov suggested that conditioned reflexes were the key to all human behavior. Today some psychologists and psychiatrists believe that if humans are exposed for a long enough time to certain conditions, they will eventually respond to them in an almost automatic way.

FREUD   Others do not think of behavior merely as the response to outside influences. They conceive of humans as individuals with basic inner drives—such as self-preservation, sex, and power. The first and most famous member of this school was Sigmund Freud (FROYD). He was a Viennese doctor and the founder of psychoanalysis.

Freud saw every person as different from every other person. However, people shared in common the need to express their basic inner drives. If prevented from doing so, people bury the drives or desires in the unconscious part of their minds. The drives are not dead. Frequently they reveal themselves in abnormal behavior and mental disorders. Freud recommended that each case be treated on an individual basis by an analyst, a specially trained psychiatrist. Analysts use methods such as free association and dream interpretation to help patients see hidden reasons for their behavior.

Freud believed that when an individual recognized the long-buried reasons for his/her behavior, the patient would be helped. Originally Freud's work was received with great hostility. However, many psychiatrists and psychologists have come to believe that his method and solution were essentially correct. His theories, they feel, need to be evaluated in terms of the society in which he formed them. Freudianism has had a tremendous influence on the development of psychology and psychological treatment. It has also deeply influenced 20th-century drama, literature, medicine, and the social sciences.

While agreeing with Freud on many points, a number of psychiatrists and psychologists rejected his emphasis on sex as the major drive. One of these was a Viennese colleague, Alfred Adler. Adler began a school of individual psychology. He insisted that all personality disorders stem from inferiority complexes and the need to make up for them.

Another psychiatrist who broke with Freud was Carl Jung (YOONG) of Switzerland who founded analytical psychology. Jung believed that self-preservation rather than sex is the strongest drive in humans. Others like Erich Fromm and Karen Horney—both of whom left Germany—believe that the economic structure of society must be considered as an influence on mental health.

During this early period of psychological development, some American psychologists were involved in experimental psychology. They were concerned only with facts that could be measured by tests. They were interested in the stimulus-response (action-reaction) characteristics of human behavior. The behavioral school developed. The

Sigmund Freud was the founder of a branch of psychiatry called psychoanalysis. What other aspects of 20th-century life did Freud influence?

Gestalt (guh-SHTAHLT)—shape or form—school of psychology originated in Germany under Max Wertheimer (VERT-hy-mer). Later most of the major Gestaltists moved to the U.S. The Gestaltists studied the organization of perceptions, how people interpret what they see. For psychologists to concentrate only on the physical aspects of behavior seemed to Gestaltists to ignore the total person.

LEARNING AND CHILD PSYCHOLOGY   Another important aspect of current psychology is the development and growth of child psychology. Freud's belief in the importance of early childhood years helped stimulate research in this area. Anna Freud founded the school of child psychoanalysis. Her father was Sigmund Freud.

Field theory, a variation of Gestalt psychology, was developed by Kurt Lewin. Lewin expanded Gestalt thinking and showed a greater concern for the motivation of actions and the pressures of society on behavior. The Gestaltist emphasis on perception led him to work in the areas of learning, memory, and problem solving.

Jean Piaget (PYAH-zhay), in his Geneva laboratory, studied the development of children's thought processes. Piaget's work and the extensive research done on learning theory have had great influence on the educational systems of both Europe and the U.S.

THERAPY TODAY   Today many therapists prefer to develop their own minisystems of theory and technique. They do not follow one school. As a result, a wide variety of methods are used. The various theories can be grouped under the label humanist psychology.

A common approach to psychotherapy treats the symptoms of a problem rather than the whole personality, as in analysis. This method takes anywhere from a few visits to over a year. Analysis can take four or five years or longer. Some psychiatrists too have had success with the use of drugs. Others have used Pavlov's conditioning ideas to change behavior patterns. This is called behavior modification.

The progress of modern psychology has had great impact not only on those with mental disturbances but also on education, industry, and government. Through the publication of works written for the general public, modern psychology is also affecting the way people see themselves and each other.

SOCIAL AND PHILOSOPHIC THOUGHT

The application of scientific methods to social problems had begun in the 1800s. By the early 1900s sociologists, political scientists, and anthropologists were using observation, statistics, and controlled conditions to analyze social problems. We have already seen how this led to behaviorism in psychology. In philosophy Bertrand Russell of Great Britain attempted to combine philosophy and science. He developed the concept of mathematical or symbolic logic.

Some philosophers, however, questioned the value of science and reason. One group led by Jacques Maritain (mar-ee-TAN) placed the

Jean Piaget has spent over 40 years studying how children learn. He and his co-workers have written over 30 books on the subject. However, as in many branches of the social sciences, not all researchers agree.

spiritual above the material in importance. Maritain wanted to apply the principles of Thomas Aquinas to modern life. Pierre Teilhard de Chardin (tay-YAR duh shar-DAN), a French Jesuit and paleontologist, tried to unite the spiritual and the scientific in his thinking.

Other philosophies evolving during the 1900s were less concerned with spiritual or Christian values. Several were atheistic or agnostic. They either believed in no God or that God could not be known. Henri Bergson believed in what he called the *elan vital* (ay-LAHN vee-TAL) or life force. To Bergson, the life force could only be known through human instinct and emotion, not reason. This life force created powerful individuals and made human progress possible.

Out of war-torn France of the 1940s emerged a philosophy of doubt called existentialism. It was founded by Jean-Paul Sartre. Sartre's thought was influenced by the work of the Danish theologian, Soren Kierkegaard (KIR-kuh-guhrd). Kierkegaard believed that people have to find truth within themselves. Sartre and the existentialists maintained that the only certainty is human existence and experience. Sartre's philosophic works such as *Being and Nothingness* and *No Exit* have been a major force in modern literature and thought.

Chapter 3
The Contemporary Arts

The contemporary arts have reflected the revolutionary, political, social, and scientific events of the 1900s. Since World War I artistic and literary efforts have been filled with feelings of confusion and doubt. The century has produced no central theme or dominant school in literature, art, or music. If anything the era has been one of isms. Although styles of past centuries continued in varying degrees, this century gave rise to futurism, surrealism, functionalism, and abstractionism to name a few.

Some artists have attempted to interpret the modern world according to religious values. Others have tried to make sense of it according to political or sociological values. To others science is supreme. Underlying most works are the theories of Freud on the workings of the unconscious mind.

LITERATURE

In 1909 F. M. Marinetti, an Italian writer, proclaimed what he called futurism in the arts. The futurists rejected everything from the past. They wanted to create an art and literature that would glorify the new and future world of the machine. Although many artistic and literary developments of the period were not called futurist, they contained many elements characteristic of futurism. Any work that attempted to break away from traditional and conventional standards was futurist in feeling. Futurist ideas eventually revolutionized not only the content of the arts but also their form.

In the late 1800s Marcel Proust of France had experimented with a literary style that later came to be known as stream of consciousness. In his 16-volume work *Remembrances of Things Past,* Proust examined the smallest detail of events in an effort at total recall of experiences. Proust was not popular in his own time but has had considerable influence on modern literature.

James Joyce, an Irish writer who moved to the Continent, refined the stream of consciousness style. Stream of consciousness describes writing in which the unstructured thoughts of a character are related as the person thinks them. Joyce's works are difficult to understand because he writes as people think—on various levels of the mind. Many of Joyce's works were originally banned because of their frankness. Virginia Woolf used stream of consciousness to probe the feelings of her characters in such works as *To the Lighthouse.*

Even when the form remained traditional, the content was often looked at in a new way. Although poetry remained rich in imagery, it was psychologically oriented to a great extent. Some of it reflects the theme of disillusionment with the modern world. The early works of T. S. Eliot, a naturalized Briton, convey this mood. He later found comfort in religion. Eliot's work is very complex and filled with literary allusions. Dylan Thomas of Wales wrote poetry and prose that reflect both a Christian and a Freudian influence. Other well-known modern British poets include Dame Edith Sitwell, W. H. Auden, and Robert Graves.

Some British prose writers have looked upon the future with wonder or fear. H. G. Wells was fascinated with science as a means to human progress. He was a utopian in many of his works but is best known for science fiction stories such as *The Time Machine.* Aldous Huxley, on the other hand, satirized scientific values in *Utopia* and *Brave New World.* George Orwell defended personal freedom and opposed authoritarianism in his satires *Animal Farm* and *Nineteen Eighty-Four.*

Nationalism continued to be an important influence in some countries and among some writers. A group of Spanish writers of the early 1900s have come to be known as the "Generation of 98." Juan Ramon Jimenez (hee-MAY-nuhs), Antonio Machado (mah-CHAH-doh), and Jose Martinez Ruiz (roo-EEZ) (pen name, Azorin) were among those who were affected by Spain's defeat in the war of 1898. Their works reflect a concern for nature and the folklore of their native provinces. A more recent writer was the versatile Federico Garcia Lorca (gahr-SEE-uh LOR-kuh). A poet and playwright, he was killed in the Spanish Civil War.

During the early 1900s, Ireland produced a number of major playwrights, prompting the term Irish Renaissance. Among the well-known writers were William Butler Yeats, John Millington Synge (SING), Lady Augusta Gregory, and Sean O'Casey. Yeats, an Irish nationalist, used Irish folklore in his works. Along with Synge he was cofounder of the Abbey Theater in Dublin, the national theater of Ireland. Synge's plays capture the life and spirit of the Irish peasants. Lady Gregory was a director of the theater. She wrote folk history plays and, like Synge's people, her characters speak in peasant dialect.

The Scandinavians have preserved much of their old Norse literature. The Edda, a collection of poems about early Norse heroes and gods, the poetry of the scalds (ancient poets), and the epic sagas are still used as sources for themes by many Scandinavian writers.

Sigrid Undset's *Kristan Lavransdatter* pictures Norway in the Middle Ages. Selma Lagerlof of Sweden used Scandinavian folklore in the *Gosta Berlings Saga* and *The Wonderful Adventures of Nils.* Par Lagerkvist (LAHG-uhr-kfist) despite a simple writing style deals with the spiritual, political, social, and moral questions of the modern age. Johannes Jensen (YEN-sin) of Denmark showed a Darwinian influence in *The Long Journey* and other works. Halldor Laxness established a new literary tradition in modern Iceland. His works reflect both spiritual and communist values.

After World War II, existentialism played an important role in French literature. Besides Sartre, the major existentialist writers have been Albert Camus (kah-MYOO) and Simone de Beauvoir (bohv-WAHR). Camus' *The Plague* speaks for the need for courage against all odds. Beauvoir has stood as a champion of women's rights in her own life and in such works as *The Second Sex.*

A major figure of modern German literature was Thomas Mann (MAHN). He gained recognition for his first novel *Buddenbrooks* in which he traces the rise and fall of a German family. With the Nazi takeover, Mann fled Germany to the U.S.

PAINTING

Modern art is characterized by great diversity and individuality. Artists have been highly innovative in their development of new approaches and techniques. No longer are many artists concerned with merely storytelling or subject matter. Freud and sometimes current political and social events have influenced their choice of themes. The primary quality of most modern work is its visual impact. A number of schools have sprung up, but most have lasted only a short time. Artists have outgrown them in their search for better methods of self-expression.

FAUVISM   The first important art movement of the 1900s was fauvism (FOH-viz-uhm), which means wild beasts. It lasted from about 1903 to 1907. The fauves did not wish to convey a message. They wanted simply to paint pleasant happy pictures. They used bold colors but often did not paint objects in their natural color. Sky could be

This is Madame Matisse *by Henri Matisse. What characteristics of fauvism can you see in this painting?*

red or green. The fauves also exaggerated and distorted forms. The originator of fauvism was Henri Matisse (ma-TEES). Other well-known fauves were Raoul Dufy (DYOO-fee) and Georges Roualt (roo-OH).

CUBISM   Both Georges Braque and Pablo Picasso had originally worked with the fauves. In 1907, however, they broke away and developed cubism. This style had both an immediate and a long-term impact on modern art. Braque (BRAK) and Picasso rejected representational art; that is, art that shows what an object or person actually looks like. Cubists attempted to depict the form and shape of objects geometrically.

Undoubtedly the most influential and innovative artist of this century has been Picasso. As a young man he left his native Spain to study in Paris. His works progress through many stages and periods of development. His early work, known as his Blue Period, is conventional in form. He then turned to cubism. Picasso's work was influenced by Cezanne, Spanish sculpture, and African masks.

During the early 1920s Picasso's style changed again to neoclassical. His figures were huge and dignified. During the later 1920s and 1930s his paintings had a feeling of life about them even though they were not representational. As a result of the civil war, Picasso vowed never to return to Spain while Franco was in power. He remained in France until his death in 1973. During his life he was politically active. He painted the dove that has become the symbol for peace movements throughout the world.

Pablo Picasso drew this charcoal sketch of a violin about 1912. This was during his cubist period. He changed his style several times during his career. What other styles influenced his works?

DADAISM   Dadaism—meaning rocking horse—was a radical art movement that developed in Switzerland under Jean Arp. The dadaists were disillusioned with the modern world. They rejected all traditional art forms; they wanted no form. A major dadaist was Marcel Duchamp (dyoo-SHAHN). Conventional life and art were ridiculous to him. His most famous picture, *Nude Descending a Staircase,* created a major sensation when it was first shown. It was controversial because of its technique, not its subject matter. One cannot see a human figure in the painting.

EXPRESSIONISM   In contrast to fauvism and cubism there emerged a new movement in Germany known as expressionism. To expressionists, a painting was an expression of emotion and feeling. The expressionists used color and distorted forms to convey emotion.

The pictures of the German Emil Nolde (NOHL-duh) and the Norwegian Edvard Munch (MOONGK) reflect an honest attempt to portray suffering, pain, and the world's sorrows. As a result their paintings are very somber. Those of Paul Klee (KLAY) and Franz Marc are less gloomy and more symbolic than that of other expressionists. The work of Gabriele Munter and Marianne von Werekin also belong to this group.

This picture by Edvard Munch is called The Cry. *Can you explain the feeling that this picture seems to express to you? How do the various elements—colors, shape, use of light—bring about this feeling?*

SURREALISM   Influenced by Freud's theory of dreams, a movement known as surrealism developed in Paris in the 1920s. Surrealists claimed there was a reality more real than what we can see. This reality was the world of our unconscious mind where dreams originated. Freud thought that in our dreams the barriers of control and will are broken down. Primitive and childlike qualities possessed by all of us emerge. The surrealists wanted to probe the unconscious and to capture this world of dreams through painting.

Two groups emerged from surrealistic thought. In one group were Salvador Dali (DAH-lee) and Giorgio de Chirico (duh KIR-ih-koh). They gave strange and unusual titles to their pictures such as Dali's *Apparition of Face and Fruit-dish on a Beach.* Dali's work is filled with a weird sense of confusion. Mysterious fantasy creatures are placed next to ordinary objects.

The other group of surrealists, with such artists as Max Ernst, developed automatism. They no longer wanted to consciously create art. Instead they let their brushes wander over the canvas. The results were considered the efforts of the subconscious mind of the artist.

Joan Miro (ZHWAHN-mee-ROH), although a surrealist, developed a simple individual style of his own. He used vivid colors and geometric forms.

591

OTHER ARTISTS   Two artists who really belong to no particular
school are the Italian Amedeo Modigliani (moh-deel-YAHN-ee) and
the Dutch Piet Mondrian (MON-dree-ahn). Modigliani worked in
Paris and was influenced by the cubists and African art. His most
typical paintings are portraits of elongated figures with expressionless
faces. Mondrian was an abstractionist. He used straight lines, black,
white, and the primary colors to form geometric patterns, primarily
crosses and rectangles. His compositions have had a major influence
on modern architecture and commercial design, including clothing.

ABSTRACT EXPRESSIONISM   During the 1930s and World War II,
many European artists settled in the U.S. From the merging of the
styles of these older European artists with younger American artists
a new movement known as abstract expressionism grew. One important painter was Hans Hofman. Others were Jackson Pollack and
Mark Rothko. Paintings were free-form masses of color or had some
recognizable shapes.

Since then American artists have dominated such new art movements as pop art, minimal art, and new realism. These styles subse-

This is Mark Rothko's Blue, Orange, and Red. *Compare abstract expressionist
Rothko's use of color with that of impressionist Monet, page 544.*

quently spread to Europe, and influenced such artists as England's Francis Bacon and France's Jean Dubuffet (dyoo-buh-FAY). Bacon combines cubism, surrealism, and expressionism. In Dubuffet's effort for naturalism, his work looks like scribbles.

SCULPTURE

Influenced by the movements in modern painting, sculptors also rebelled against conventional techniques. A great variety of styles—classical, abstract, primitive, and pop—has resulted. While still using the human figure as subject, many sculptors have experimented with form and shape. Sculptors have also worked with the many new materials available as a result of technological advances. Aluminum, rubber, stainless steel, and junked auto parts are some of the new materials of sculpture. Eric Gill of England sculpted religious figures, although his techniques were modern. The Stations of the Cross in Westminister Cathedral are his work. Aristide Maillol (may-YOL) of France continued in the neoclassical tradition but turned to primitive Greek art for inspiration.

Some sculptors, such as Ernst Barlach of Germany, were influenced by the expressionists. Barlach and Wilhelm Lehmbruck, another German sculptor, created pieces that are reminiscent of earlier Gothic sculpture. Different in style is the work of Kathe Kollwitz (KAH-tee KOHL-wits). Figures such as *Tower of Mothers* and *Bread* reflect the suffering of war-torn Germany.

Gothic art also influenced Albert Giacometti (jahk-uh-MET-ee) of Switzerland. He created elongated, somewhat distorted, figures in bronze. Giacometti attempted to keep the original shape of his material while only suggesting his subject. Jacob Epstein (EP-styn), an American who lived and worked in England, started as an abstractionist but became more traditional. Some of his work reflects African influences.

British sculptors, Henry Moore and Barbara Hepworth also experimented with abstract techniques. Moore attempted to bring together new materials, shapes, and ideas. The concepts of space and how to show three-dimensional quality fascinated him. His most characteristic pieces are huge, reclining figures.

Among the most impressive Scandinavian works are the figures of Gustav Vigeland (VEE-guh-lahn) in Sculpture Park, Oslo, Norway; of the Icelandic sculptor, Einar Jonsson (YOHN-suhn), and the Swedish sculpture, Carl Milles. Milles, a disciple of Rodin, is well known for his fountains and human figures.

ARCHITECTURE

Historically architecture has been one of the slowest arts to change. Modern architecture was no exception. It grew gradually, building on the principles of the past and adapting to the changing needs

Albert Giacometti only attempted to suggest the subject of his sculptures. This is his Walking Man. Besides a figure in motion, does it express any other feeling to you? What? What people and schools influenced modern sculptors?

of modern life. Architects experimented with new types of materials such as steel and reinforced concrete and new construction techniques. Architects such as Henri van de Velde of Holland and Americans, Louis Sullivan and Frank Lloyd Wright were among the first.

However, modern architecture was given its greatest impetus from the rapid industrialization and **urbanization** of the 20th century. For a time it appeared that engineering would replace architecture. At first modern skyscrapers were created by engineers not architects.

The conflict between technology and design was finally resolved by a group of architects headed by Walter Gropius (GROH-pee-uhs). Gropius and his colleagues founded the Bauhaus school of architecture in Dessau, Germany. The Bauhaus group believed that architecture and engineering could benefit one another. The appearance of a building should correspond to its purpose. To them any building that was functional was beautiful. Gropius wrote several books explaining his views on functionalism. He was followed as director of the Bauhaus by Ludwig Mies van der Rohe (mees-vahn-duh-ROH) who designed the Seagram building in New York.

This is Finlandia House designed by Alvar Aalto. The international style in architecture is often considered all windows. But as often as not, the buildings have few or no windows.

Modern architecture—sometimes called international style—can be seen all over the world. It is generally characterized by geometric form and emphasis on function. Modern architects have discarded elaborate decoration. They prefer the quality of their materials and design to be the only decoration. As a result modern buildings have a clean simple streamlined look.

Foremost among European architects was Swiss-born Le Corbusier (luh kor-byoo-ZYAY) (Charles Edward Jeanneret). He was also interested in city planning. German-born Eric Mendelsohn of England was influenced by expressionism. Some of his buildings resemble modern sculpture. In Holland J. J. P. Oud (OUT) was influenced by Mondrian. In Finland Alvar Aalto (AHL-tuh) began to experiment with multilevels, skylights, and the use of natural materials. One of his most famous buildings is Finlandia House in Helsinki.

Between the two world wars, much experimentation took place in furniture design and construction. Designers were influenced by the ideas of functionalism. Steel tubing as the base of chairs and tables made furniture sturdier and more practical.

After World War II women, as the major consumers, were looking for more time-saving ways of operating a house. Designers responded by giving them new materials—foam rubber, molded plywood, synthetics, and plastics—and new designs—modular and multiple-use furniture. These sleek, clean-lined styles of furniture and home furnishings are easy to care for and fit the needs of modern life. Major contributors to modern design are Scandinavia, Italy, and Germany.

MUSIC

The traditional methods and romantic nationalism of the music of the 1800s continued to some extent into the 20th century. Richard Strauss remained the dominant figure in German music. The English composers Ralph Vaughn Williams and Benjamin Britten used traditional techniques. Folklore and historical events influenced their choice of themes.

As the 1900s progressed, however, many changes occurred in music. U.S. and Latin American composers began to gain recognition. Many European composers moved to the U.S. As composers communicated and were influenced by one another, international styles began to develop.

Another interesting development has been the growth of electronic music. French-born Edgard Varese (vuh-RAYZ) pioneered in the field. His work is characterized by its dissonance or noise. Karlheinz Stockhausen uses only electronic devices to produce his music. The tape recorder and electronic instruments like the Moog Synthesizer have opened up a whole new world of possibilities for the modern composer.

Chapter 4
Changing Social Patterns

During the days of the Roman Empire, the site of modern Frankfurt was a Roman outpost. Today the city is a busy manufacturing and commercial center. With its wealth has come pollution.

Today Europe is one of the most highly industrialized areas in the world. Some countries, of course, are more advanced industrially than others. But on the whole Europeans enjoy a higher standard of living than most people. Industry is increasing. The food supply is more than adequate. Educational opportunities are opening up for more and more students.

But industrialization brings problems as well as benefits. **Pollution** dirties Europe's cities, streams, rivers, and countryside. By the mid-1970s inflation was again eating into European wages, savings, and pensions. Some Europeans, such as the Italians, have lived with continuous political and economic crises since World War II. Such uncertainty sometimes moves Europeans to look to authoritarian parties like the Communist party for leadership.

So far modernization has had little effect on the structure of marriage and close-knit family life. Like other peoples of the world, Europeans cling to traditions until change is forced upon them. And change is being forced on them. Like others, Europeans are finding themselves adapting to the patterns that the late 20th century is bringing.

NATIONALITIES

Although Western Europe covers about 2.5 percent of the world's total land area, over 330 million people live there. It is the most densely populated area of the world. Further, these millions of people are divided among 26 countries. The term European masks the variety of languages and cultures within the region. In addition within Europe's 26 countries live more than 30 ethnic groups. These groups insist on maintaining their separate identities.

For example, Belgium is composed mainly of two groups—Flemings and Walloons. The Flemings live mostly in northern Belgium and speak Dutch. The Walloons live mainly in southern Belgium and speak French. Each group values its language and customs and demands equal recognition from the national government. Belgian politics is often torn by conflict.

The Bretons of France hold secret meetings, toast the autonomy of the province of Brittany, and occasionally turn to violence. The Welsh of Great Britain proclaim loyalty to the English Crown but have never given up their national identity. Nor have the Scotch. Through their Scottish National Party, they elect members to the British Parliament. In 1974 the party ran on a platform of self-government and won 30 percent of Scotland's vote.

autonomy: self-governing; independent

Not all ethnic groups desire independence. But most do want to keep their cultural traditions and language alive. This is becoming more difficult. The Common Market which promotes travel, trade, and job opportunities between countries exposes more and more Europeans to other cultural traditions. So does European television which transmits programs across national borders.

To these factors must be added the millions of people who have come from outside Europe to live and work. The growing industrial power of the Netherlands, West Germany, and France requires large numbers of workers. As a result the recruitment of cheap labor from other countries began. Workers from Turkey, Yugoslavia, Morocco, Italy, and elsewhere came and with them came their customs. Generally, the Germans, Dutch, and French look down upon these workers as inferior in culture. Tensions develop especially when a slackening of the economy causes unemployment. Then the citizens of the countries call for the ouster of foreign workers.

In Switzerland, for example, non-Swiss make up about 18 percent of the population. Attempts have been made to force them to leave. In 1974, at the height of the period of worldwide inflation, an amendment to the constitution was proposed to limit the number of foreigners to 500,000. If passed, more than half the foreign residents would have had to leave the country. The amendment was defeated.

Women in the late 1960s and early 1970s were becoming strong political forces at home and abroad. At left is Francoise Giroud, Secretary of State for the Status of Women. Next is Annemarie Renger, president of the West German

WOMEN

About one third of Europe's paid workers are women. Increasing educational opportunities are giving more of them a chance to enter the professions—medicine, law, and education. However, opportunities are still fewer than for men.

For the most part women hold the lowest paying jobs. In most European countries they earn less than men. It is estimated that in Sweden women make 15 percent less and in Britain about 45 percent less. A number of countries have laws requiring equal pay for equal work, but few enforce the laws. West German Minister for Health, Dr. Katharina Focke, indicated that in economic crises women are the first fired.

Some Europeans believe that women should limit their new activities to such matters as health services, cultural and social work, and family problems. These people believe jobs in business and industrial management are too difficult.

Nevertheless, more women are entering politics. A few of the women who hold public office are Margotta Aananen, Finnish Minister of Cultural and Scientific Affairs; Nathalie Lind who has been both the Danish Minister of Social Affairs and the Minister of Justice and Cultural Affairs; and, Helga Petersen of Denmark, a member of the International Court at the Hague. Traditionally, Scandinavian women have had the greatest degree of equality with men in Europe.

Bundestag. Margaret Thatcher became the first woman to head a major British political party. At right is Helvi Sipila of Finland who became Assistant Secretary-General for Social and Humanitarian Affairs at the UN.

In Great Britain in 1975, Margaret Thatcher was elected to head the Tory party. She was the first woman to lead a major English political party. Annemarie Renger was the first woman president of the West German Parliament. The importance of the women's movement was officially recognized when, in 1974, Valery Giscard d'Estaing, President of France, appointed Francoise Giroud State Secretary in charge of women's affairs.

SOCIAL SERVICES

In the past wide gaps in social services such as education and health care existed between the rich and middle classes and the poor. Richer Europeans could, of course, pay for any service they needed. The rest had to get by with what they could afford. National governments did little for them. Since World War II, however, national governments have been taking more and more responsibility for social services. The result is increased taxes for their citizens.

Great Britain, for instance, has moved far in providing for all kinds of social services. Its compulsory insurance program covers a wide range of needs. Maternity and sick care, unemployment and industrial accident benefits, pensions for the aged, widows, and orphans, and death benefits are some of the items covered. The National Health Service gives free medical and hospital care. Small fees are charged for dental work and prescriptions. Under the Family Allowance Act

compulsory: ordered by law to do something; not voluntary

Strikes and marches have become a part of European political life. These demonstrators are gathered before the Eiffel Tower in Paris. The tower was built in 1889 to commemorate the French Revolution.

the government gives a certain amount of money for each child of compulsory school age. Education is free and all children from 5 to 16 must attend.

Denmark, Norway, and Sweden also have various forms of social security, health insurance, old-age pensions, and unemployment insurance. Over 20 percent of Sweden's total national income is put back into its social welfare system.

Other countries provide some welfare services but not to the same extent. People are demanding increasingly better services. Strikes, and sometimes demonstrations and riots, bring these demands forcibly home to the current government. Socialist and Communist parties have made greater welfare benefits the foundation of their election platforms. Their programs attract millions of voters from outside their membership. In order to stay in power and keep peace, a number of governments have been forced to increase welfare services.

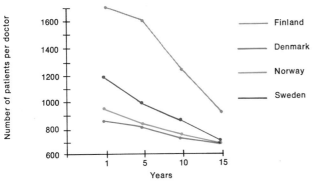

SELECTED HEALTH CARE OVER A 15-YEAR PERIOD

	Finland	Denmark	Norway	Sweden
1	2,455	5,172	3,769	5,910
5	3,104	5,650	4,346	7,359
10	3,797	6,550	4,847	8,840
15	5,087	7,203	5,667	11,290

Source: *The Europa Year Book 1974: A World Survey* (Europa Publications, London); reproduced by permission of the copyright holder, World Health Organization, from: *World Health Statistics Annual, Volume III, 1966 and 1971*, and *Annual Epidemiological and Vital Statistics, 1956 and 1961.*

RELIGION

The majority of Europeans are formally Christians—either Roman Catholic or a Protestant denomination. As we have seen throughout European history, a close relationship existed between religious and secular authorities. This relationship was generally regulated by written agreements or treaties. The rights and obligations of both Church and State were spelled out. Often tensions developed in the interpretation of these agreements. In the ages when faith was unquestioned and the Church was strong, religious authorities could retain control in these disputes. But many modern Europeans are questioning religious teachings and the role of organized religion in their lives. For example, Italians in the early 1970s passed a law making divorce legal. Prior to this the teachings of the Roman Catholic Church had been strong enough to defeat such a law.

Many Europeans keep their membership in a particular denomination but seldom participate in its activities. Both Catholic and Protestant church leaders declare that they are in a period of religious crisis. Increasing numbers of people, particularly among the young, are looking elsewhere for moral and spiritual guidance. Eastern religions and philosophies are especially appealing to them. Millions of Europeans, however, continue to follow the traditional beliefs and practices of Judaism or Christianity.

Like many people in the world today, Europeans are confronted with the problems and benefits that accompany change. Villages are no longer so far from cities; pollution is spreading over the countryside. Education is more available, but unemployment is increasing. Luxuries are more plentiful, but they still are out of reach of many Europeans. Wages are higher and so are taxes. As technology continues to advance, how will Europeans accept and adapt to the changes? How rapidly? How much of their traditional ways will they lose? How much will they retain?

601

Summing Up the Unit

Social Studies Vocabulary

Define: national interest; neutral; modernization; overpopulation; urbanization; pollution

People

Identify: Einstein; Pavlov; Freud; Jung; Russell; Orwell; Mann; Picasso; Giacometti; Hepworth; Le Corbusier

Words

Define: aborigine; computer; DNA; conditioned reflex; Gestalt; behavior modification; humanist psychology; existentialism; futurism; stream of consciousness; Irish Renaissance; Generation of '98; fauvism; cubism; surrealism; expressionism; dadaism; abstract expressionism; Bauhaus group; international style

⌐ Questions

1. What were the aims of the: a. Truman Doctrine? b. Marshall Plan?
2. What was the original purpose of NATO?
3. a. What are the purposes of the UN? b. Name the main organizations of the UN and the purpose of each.
4. What have supporters and critics of the UN said for and against its peacekeeping ability?
5. a. What is the purpose of the ESCS? b. EEC?
6. What benefits derive from membership in the Commonwealth of Nations?
7. Why is this century called the age of medical wonders?
8. How does the training for psychology differ from that for psychiatry?
9. How did Freud influence the surrealists?
10. How did functionalism resolve the conflict between engineering technology and architectural design?
11. What ethnic groups have separate identities in: a. Belgium? b. France? c. Britain?
12. Why is it becoming more difficult for European ethnic groups to keep their cultural traditions and language alive?
13. a. Why do millions of people migrate to Europe today? b. Why has this caused tensions?
14. In what part of Europe do women have the greatest degree of equality?
15. a. What nations of Europe provide the most welfare services? b. Why have governments increased welfare services?

Discussion Topics

1. Since the end of World War II, wealth has become more evenly distributed among European social classes. What have been the causes and consequences of this redistribution?
2. Europeans share with Americans in developing science. Can modern science be considered any more American than European? Or does scientific achievement ignore national boundaries? Does science advance because of, or in spite of, national policies? In what ways can governments encourage or discourage science?
3. Has atomic energy changed international relations for better or for worse?

Project Ideas

1. Write a report on the life and work of a scientist or artist mentioned in Unit X.
2. Make a collage showing changes in home furnishings in this century.
3. Read one of the books by Huxley or Orwell mentioned in Chapter 3. Describe the dangers the author sees in a world changed by science.
4. Write your own science-fiction account of the future as you imagine it will be.
5. Make a poster display on European cities. Use pictures that contrast the old sections and those with modern architecture.
6. Stage a panel discussion on the changing roles of women in Western Europe and the U.S.
7. Study the land use and natural resources maps on page 577. Select one nation and write a brief essay on how its natural resources have helped shape its history.
8. Research and write a report on the use of atomic energy in Europe. Compare European practices with those of U.S. power plants. Is atomic power as controversial a subject in Europe as it is in the U.S.?

For Further Study

General Readings

1. *Age of Exploration* by John R. Hale. Time-Life Books, 1966. Interaction of cultures.
2. *Age of Faith* by Anne Fremantle. Time-Life Books, 1966. Introduction to the Middle Ages. Illustrated.
3. *The Age of Ideas: Eighteenth-Century France* by George R. Havens. Free Press, 1965. Paperback. Contributions of eight philosophers.
4. *The Ancient Greeks: An Introduction to Their Life and Thought* by M. I. Finley. Viking Press, Inc., 1963. Paperback.
5. *Dawn of European Civilization* by V. G. Childe. Alfred A. Knopf, Inc., 6th ed., rev. ed., 1958. Paperback. Standard account.
6. *Everyday Life in Renaissance Times* by Eric R. Chamberlin. G. P. Putnam's Sons. Paperback.
7. *First Industrial Revolution* by Phyllis M. Deane. Cambridge University Press, 1966. Paperback. Analysis of the industrial revolution in England.
8. *Garibaldi and His Enemies* by Christopher Hibbert. New American Library, 1970. Paperback. A detailed but lively account.
9. *Greek Art* by John Boardman. Praeger Publishers, rev. ed., 1973. Paperback. A concise history. Illustrated.
10. *Guns, Sails and Empires: Technological Innovation and the Early Phases of European Expansion 1400-1700* by Carlo Cipolla. Funk & Wagnalls Co. Military aspects of exploration.
11. *Hitler and Nazism* by Louis L. Snyder. E. M. Hale & Co., 1961.
12. *The Industrial Revolution and Nationalism* by Willis Linquist. (Vol. XII of *The Universal History of the World* edited by Irwin Shapiro). Western Publishing Co., Inc., 1966. Influence of the industrial revolution on new democracies and the rise of nationalism.
13. *Knights of the Crusades* by Jay Williams and M. B. Freeman. American Heritage Publishing Co., 1962. Illustrated.
14. *Roman Women: Their History and Habits* by J. P. Balsdon. Greenwood Press, Inc., 1975. Study of roles of Roman women. Includes biographies.
15. *Shakespeare and His World* by Ivor Brown. Henry Z. Walck, Inc., 1964. Short account of life in Shakespearean England.
16. *Spain in America* by Charles Gibson. Harper & Row Publishers, Inc., 1968. Paperback. Survey.
17. *Western European Cultures* edited by Paul Thomas Welty. J. B. Lippincott Company, 1973. Readings. Inquiry format.

Fiction

1. *Age of Chivalry* by Thomas Bulfinch. Airmont Publishing Co., Inc. Paperback. A retelling of important medieval legends.
2. *Armada* by Garrett Mattingly. Houghton Mifflin Co. Paperback. Study of the people and politics behind the "Invincible Armada."
3. *The Battle of Waterloo: The End of an Empire* by Manuel Komroff. Macmillan Publishing Co., Inc., 1964. The battle and its significance.
4. *Ben Hur* by Lew Wallace. McGraw-Hill Book Co., 1962. Classic story of early Christianity.
5. *Greek Gods and Heroes* by Robert Graves. Dell Publishing Co., Inc. Paperback. Retelling of Greek myths.
6. *Kenilworth* by Walter Scott. E. P. Dutton & Co., Inc., 1972. Paperback. Renaissance in Britain.
7. *North to Freedom* by Anne Holm. Harcourt Brace Jovanovich, Inc., 1974. Paperback. Children escape from Nazi-occupied land.
8. *Shield Ring* by Rosemary Sutcliff. Henry Z. Walck, Inc., new ed., 1972. A young Viking girl against the backgrouund of the last Viking attempt to conquer Britain.
9. *Siege and Fall of Troy* by Robert Graves. Dell Publishing Co., Inc. Paperback. Easy-to-read account based on Homer.
10. *Tale of Two Cities* by Charles Dickens. Pendulum Press, Inc., new ed., 1974. Paperback. London and Paris during the French Revolution.
11. *Winged Watchman* by Hilda Van Stockum. Farrar, Straus & Giroux, Inc., 1963. World War II in Holland.
12. *Wonderful Winter* by Marchette G. Chute. E. P. Dutton & Co., Inc. Story of London in Shakespeare's time.

The
Russians
and
Eastern
Europeans

These distaffs are examples of Russian folk art. Distaffs are used in spinning raw wool into yarn and flax into linen fiber. These are part of the collection in Moscow's Folk Art Museum. Why do you think people would spend so much time and talent in decorating tools?

Unit I

Russian Land and Early People

This gold comb shows Scythian warriors, nomads who lived in what is now the USSR. The comb was made to order by a Greek in the 300s B.C. for sale to a Scythian. Trade was common between the two peoples.

Geography has played an important role in shaping the **culture** of the Russians and the Eastern Europeans—the people of Poland, Czechoslovakia, Bulgaria, Romania, Hungary, East Germany, Yugoslavia, and Albania. Sometimes these people were protected from invaders and conquerors by mountains, deserts, or **climate**. At other times the steppes of Central Asia and the plains of the Danube and of other rivers were roadways for invaders. The **history** of this region has often been one of struggle among many **ethnic groups**.

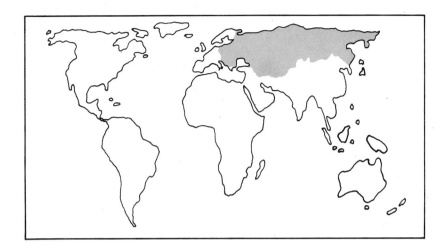

The Union of Soviet Socialist **Republics** is made up of 15 **states** or republics. The largest of these is Russia, which was the name of the entire country before the Communists came to power. Today, for most people the terms USSR, the Soviet Union, and Russia are used to mean the same country. These names will be used interchangeably throughout the following pages.

The Soviet Union is the world's largest **nation** in terms of land space. It covers one-sixth of the globe. Its area of approximately 22.3 million square kilometers (8.6 million square miles) is about two and one-half times that of the United States.

Russia's entire northern border rims the Arctic Ocean. This extremely northern location has been very important in Russia's development. Winter is the nation's longest season. Some of the coldest temperatures on earth outside the North and South poles occur there. The long severe winters limit the amount of food that can be grown. However, winter has also been one of Russia's strongest weapons against invaders.

VEGETATION AND CLIMATE REGIONS

One way to study the land of the Soviet Union is to divide it by zones of **vegetation** and climate. Another is by geographical regions. The USSR can be divided into four vegetation belts that span the width of the country: tundra, forest, steppe, and desert.

The northernmost of these belts, next to the Arctic, is the tundra. This is a huge, nearly flat land with almost no trees. The winters there are long and dark. The summers are short and cool. The soil is frozen except for a short time in the summer when moss and small shrubs grow. Very few people live there. Those who do, earn their living by herding reindeer.

Chapter 1
The World's
Largest
Nation

607

A PHYSICAL MAP OF THE USSR AND EASTERN EUROPE

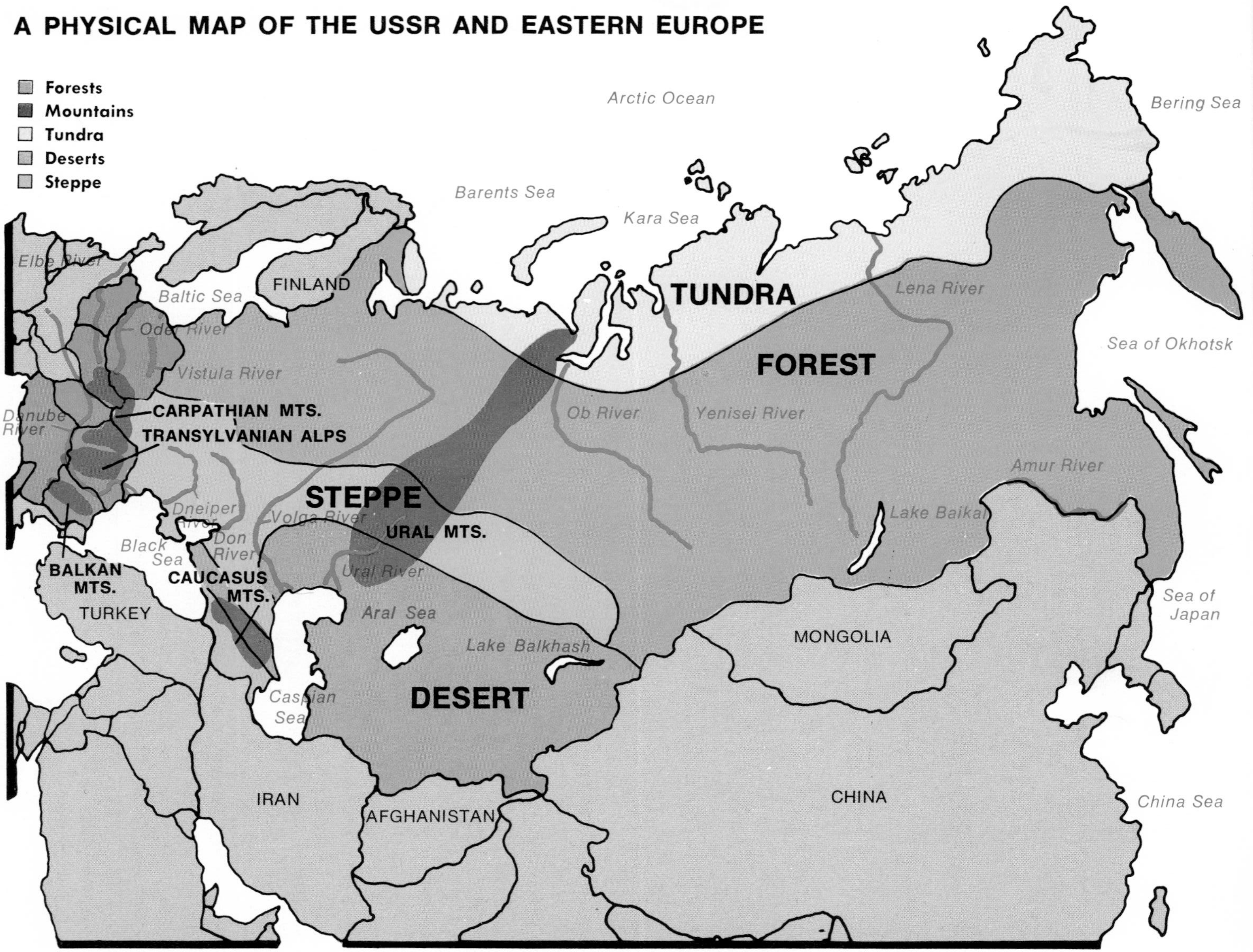

Forests
Mountains
Tundra
Deserts
Steppe

Bering Sea

Sea of Okhotsk

Sea of Japan

China Sea

Amur River

Arctic Ocean

Lena River

Lake Baikal

MONGOLIA

CHINA

TUNDRA

FOREST

Kara Sea

Yenisei River

Barents Sea

Ob River

Lake Balkhash

DESERT

STEPPE

URAL MTS.

Ural River

Aral Sea

AFGHANISTAN

FINLAND

Vistula River

CARPATHIAN MTS.

TRANSYLVANIAN ALPS

Volga River

Caspian Sea

IRAN

Baltic Sea

Oder River

Don River

Dnieper River

CAUCASUS MTS.

Elbe River

Danube River

Black Sea

BALKAN MTS.

TURKEY

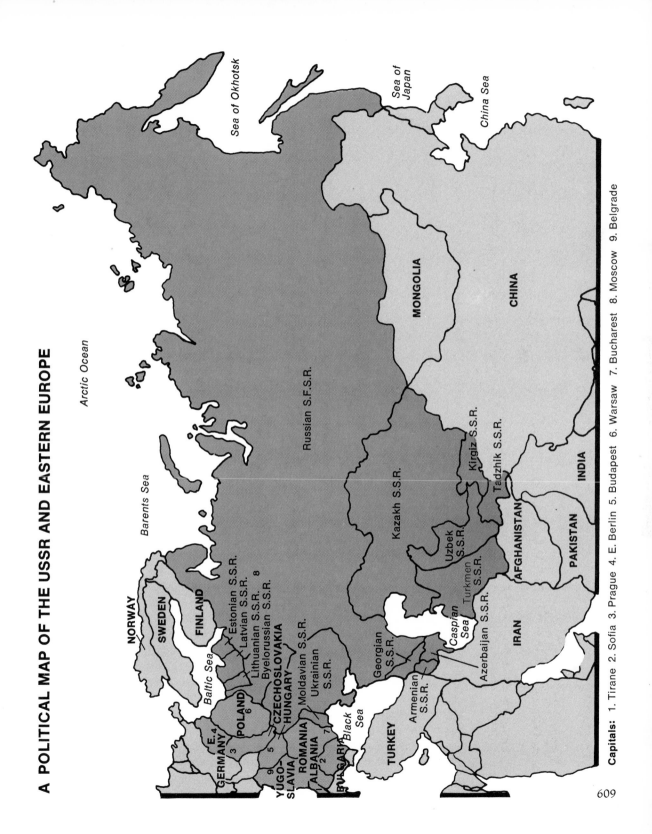

A POLITICAL MAP OF THE USSR AND EASTERN EUROPE

Arctic Ocean

Sea of Okhotsk

Sea of Japan

China Sea

Barents Sea

NORWAY

SWEDEN

FINLAND

Baltic Sea

Russian S.F.S.R.

MONGOLIA

CHINA

Estonian S.S.R.

Latvian S.S.R.

Lithuanian S.S.R. 8

Byelorussian S.S.R.

E. 4 GERMANY

POLAND 6

CZECHOSLOVAKIA

HUNGARY

Moldavian S.S.R.

Ukrainian S.S.R.

YUGO-SLAVIA

ROMANIA

ALBANIA 2

BULGARIA

Black Sea

Georgian S.S.R.

Armenian S.S.R.

Azerbaijan S.S.R.

Caspian Sea

Turkmen S.S.R.

Uzbek S.S.R.

Kazakh S.S.R.

Kirgiz S.S.R.

Tadzhik S.S.R.

TURKEY

IRAN

AFGHANISTAN

PAKISTAN

INDIA

3

5

9

7

1

Capitals: 1. Tirane 2. Sofia 3. Prague 4. E. Berlin 5. Budapest 6. Warsaw 7. Bucharest 8. Moscow 9. Belgrade

609

The forest zone is actually two regions. Evergreens grow in the most northern area called the taiga (above). In the mixed forest belt, many kinds of trees

Russia's forest is the largest continuous forest area in the world. It covers about half the Soviet Union. The people who live there make their living from timber and furs.

Below the forest is the steppe (STEP), a vast treeless plain. In some places the steppe is covered with grass that grows taller than a rider on horseback. The steppe extends about 6,400 kilometers (4,000 miles) from the European part of Russia into western Siberia. It is bordered by mountains on the east and the south. The Ural Mountains run down the middle.

The steppe area has been, and continues to be, one of the most important regions in the Soviet Union. Because of its fertile soil, it is known as the Soviet breadbasket. Wheat is one of the chief crops grown there. Most of the 240 million people of the USSR live in this region. And it is by way of the steppes that most of the invaders have come to Russia.

The southernmost zone is a desert region that stretches from the Caspian Sea to Mongolia. The people who live there are generally nomads who wander from place to place in search of pasture for their herds. In the past, very little could be grown there because of the lack of water. But today, with modern methods of irrigation, some

grow. This photo was taken at Kuznetsk, a settlement of Soviet geologists about 500 kilometers (300 miles) southwest of Moscow.

farming of crops is possible. The area has become the major cotton producer of the Soviet Union.

GEOGRAPHICAL REGIONS

The USSR can also be divided into four geographical regions: European Russia, Siberia, Central Asia, and the Transcaucasus.

The Ural Mountains and the Ural River are generally considered to be the dividing line between European Russia and the rest of the USSR in the north. These mountains do not form a serious barrier because they are low and easily crossed. There are no particular differences between the people or the land on either side of the mountains.

Siberia occupies the northern third of Asia. It stretches from the Ural Mountains in the east to the Pacific Ocean in the west, and from the Arctic Ocean in the north to Mongolia and Manchuria in the south. Almost all the climate and plant variations of the USSR are present in Siberia.

Much of Siberia is a land of long cold winters and short summers. The temperatures there are extreme and can range from 90° below

These log cabins will house workers on the new Baikal-Amur Railroad. A branch of the Trans-Siberian, it will open Siberia's southeast region to development.

zero in the winter to 90° above zero in the summer. In the far north is the tundra. The eastern section of this belt is the most mountainous region of the USSR. Most of this region is still undeveloped. The whole eastern portion is too cold for agriculture of any kind. Large portions of the region known as the Soviet Far East have been claimed by the Chinese. However, the Soviets continue to hold it, especially because of the importance of the port city of Vladivostok (vlad-uh-vuh-STAHK).

To the south of the tundra, fur-bearing animals roam the forest. Below the forest are the grasslands. Still farther south lies fertile farmland.

Siberia has been compared to the early American West as the home of a rugged frontier society. It has been a place of refuge for peasants fleeing their brutal landlords. Under both czars and Communists it has been used as a prison and slave-labor camp for millions of criminals and political prisoners.

Siberia did not open up for voluntary settlement until the Trans-Siberian Railroad was begun in 1891. It took 26 years to complete the railroad. Today it stretches 9,243 kilometers (5,777 miles) from Moscow to Vladivostok, an eight-day ride.

Only about one-tenth of the Soviet people live in Siberia. Most of these have settled near the railroad in the south and in the west where there is rich farmland. However, the main value of Siberia lies in the tremendous mineral and other **natural resources** that have been discovered there. The government is trying to develop these resources and bring more people and **industry** to Siberia.

Below Siberia lies Central Asia. This is fertile steppe with some desert. Its southern, western, and eastern borders are mountainous. They stretch from the Caspian Sea in the west to Lake Baikal in Siberia.

The Caucasus Mountains run east to west between the Black and Caspian seas. They are the dividing line between Asia and Europe in southwestern Russia. The area between the seas and below the mountains is called the Transcaucasus (trans-KAW-kuh-suhs). Geographically this area is part of Asia, but the people are a mixture of Europeans and Asians.

RIVERS

One other physical feature of the Soviet Union is of great importance. The USSR is for the most part landlocked. There are over 48,000 kilometers (30,000 miles) of coast. But much of it can be used only on a limited basis. For example, except for a few ports, the Soviet shoreline on the Arctic and Pacific oceans is frozen most of the year. The Baltic, Black, and Caspian seas are almost completely landlocked.

Therefore, the Russians have had to depend on their rivers for **communication** and **trade** with other **peoples**. Luckily some of the major rivers of the world flow through the USSR. These have been Russia's highways for hundreds of years. Although railroads, trucks, and airplanes are now used for transportation, the rivers still remain the most vital communication links in Soviet life.

Four of the longest rivers in the world flow through Siberia. The Ob, Yenisei, and Lena rivers cross its vastness northward to the Arctic Ocean. The Amur River wanders east along part of the Chinese border and empties into the Sea of Okhotsk.

Among the major rivers in western Russia are the Dnieper (NEE-puhr), on which the city of Kiev (KEE-yef) is located; the Don, in the middle of European Russia; and the Volga, which is the longest river in Europe.

The Volga is the most important of the Soviet waterways. It begins north of Moscow, capital of the USSR, and winds south to the Caspian Sea. The Volga is used not only to carry people and products but also to generate electricity. Through a series of canals it is connected with many other rivers. But the Volga is more than a river to the Soviets. It has been called the Main Street of Russia. Many songs and stories have been written about the Volga. One of the most famous is the "Song of the Volga Boatmen."

Moscow, the USSR's capital, is built on the Moscow River. Factories and high rises dot its skyline. The city manufactures vehicles, machinery, and textiles.

Chapter 2
A Sweep of Peoples

This rock painting—petroglyph—was made by an unknown Neolithic artist in the Kazakhstan Republic at least 5,000 years ago.

In ancient times before there were national boundaries to cut people off from one another, they lived and moved wherever the land, climate, and plant and animal life were favorable. They followed the changing seasons and the changing fortunes of their neighbors. Travel was by the easiest routes—along rivers, through mountain passes, and across flat lands.

The history of the area now known as the Soviet Union and Eastern Europe has been one of **migrations**. Peoples moved constantly out of Central Asia and pushed westward across the steppes. Others came out of the west and pushed eastward. Still others came up from the south. Peoples collided and fought each other. Those who survived among the losers fled farther west or east to settle other lands.

As a result of these invasions and subsequent migrations, many peoples were forced across European Russia and down into what have become the modern nations of Eastern Europe. The progress of these peoples—the Serbs, Croats, Bulgars, Magyars, Moravians, Poles, Romanians, and Albanians—will be discussed later.

FIRST SETTLERS

The earliest evidence of human life in Russia dates from the **Old Stone Age** which in Russia lasted from 30,000 B.C. to about 3000 B.C. No remains of **hominids** before the **Cro-Magnon** type have as yet been discovered.

From archaeological digs in Siberia, it appears that Cro-Magnon people were spread across Siberia from the Yenisei River to Kamchatka by 30,000 B.C. No scholar is certain about where these people originated. One theory is that they traveled northward from China. The people were hunters who killed such game as reindeer, antelope, mammoth, and fox. They ate the meat, cured the hides for clothes and tents, and used the bones for fuel, tools, and ornaments.

The earliest finds in European Russia date from about the same time. House **sites** and **artifacts** such as tools and ornaments carved from bone have been found. Sites that date to about 20,000 years ago have also been discovered along the banks of the Don River. These early people, like those in Siberia, were hunters. No one knows where they came from, but they seem to have come on foot in search of game.

Over the centuries the hunters learned to **domesticate** animals, especially the horse. The horse enabled them to move faster and hunt better. Farming also began to develop.

Farther south in the area where the forest and the steppe meet, people were living in **villages** by 8000 B.C. Between 2000 and 1000 B.C. the people of this area entered the **Copper** and then the **Bronze Age**. Their artifacts indicate that their weapons and tools were not so advanced as those of their neighbors. However, they had wide trading contacts. There is evidence that the people of this region did not enter the **Iron Age** until the 600s B.C. At this time, hunting, fishing, and waging war were still the major occupations.

EARLY MIGRATIONS

From 1000 B.C. to 500 A.D., one people after another spread across Russia. Little is known about the life of these early people. They were slow to develop an organized **society** and a written **language** of their own. The little we do know comes from the few artifacts that have been found and from writings of some of their neighbors.

The first of these migrants were called Cimmerians. They ruled southern Russia from about 1000 B.C. to 700 B.C. when they were overrun by the Scythians.

The Scythians (SITH-ee-uhnz) were a nomadic people who came out of Central Asia. They established an **empire** around the Black Sea and in the lower areas along the Don and Dnieper rivers.

During Scythian rule, the Greeks founded **colonies** on the northern shores of the Black Sea. The Scythians served as merchants and police for the Greeks. Greek **culture** spread among them. They began to admire Greek art and skills. The Scythians imitated what they liked and became known for their beautiful cups, bowls, and ornaments made from silver and gold.

The Scythians were able to preserve their empire until about 200 B.C. when they were overthrown by the Sarmatians. The Sarmatians —from what is modern Iran—controlled the area for the next 400 years.

Around 200 A.D. the Goths, a Germanic people, moved eastward and conquered the Sarmatians. The Goths settled in the region north of the Black Sea. However, their rule lasted only a short time. In 372 the Huns swept in from the steppes of Asia in an attempt to conquer the Goths. This attack caused the Goths to split into two groups. The Visigoths moved west into the Roman Empire in order to escape. The Ostrogoths were finally conquered.

nomadic people: people who wander from place to place to find grazing land and water for their herds

615

HUNS

There was no group of people during this period who frightened the Germans and Romans more than the Huns. They were a fierce nomadic people who rode out of the steppes to threaten all Europe. The Huns were expert riders and hardened from childhood to harsh weather. They dressed in animal skins and lived off the land. Anybody or anything in their path was destroyed.

Around 200 B.C. the Huns swept into China. They occupied northern China for a century. The Chinese added to the length of the Great Wall to keep them from the rest of the country. Four hundred years later the Huns were moving west. In 372 A.D. they scattered the Goths in Russia and started the waves of migration that finally destroyed the Roman Empire.

Under their greatest leader Attila, the Huns almost succeeded in conquering Europe. They came close to the gates of Rome itself. But Attila died in 453. A plague killed many in his army and the remaining Huns rode back to their homeland in the eastern steppes. Their empire, in turn, had been invaded by another nomadic people called the Avars. The Avars were to influence the migration of the Serbs and Croats and the development of Hungary.

SLAVS

These silver objects of dancing men and a lion were made by Slavs in the Ukraine in the 500s or 600s A.D.

Although the people of the Soviet Union and Eastern Europe have evolved from a long mixing of peoples, most of them are of Slavic origin. They are known today by various names—Russians, Poles, Czechs, Slovaks, Serbs, Croats, Romanians, Albanians, and Slovenes. The beginnings of the Slavs are still unclear. But some aspects of their early life and development are known.

The Slavs emerged as a distinct group about 600 B.C. They were primarily hunters and fishers although they raised some crops. They lived in villages of about 20 families. The land was owned in common and all food and supplies were shared.

These early Slavs lived for hundreds of years in the areas of what are now eastern Poland, Byelorussia (White Russia), and probably the western Ukraine. Around the first century A.D. they began to spread west, south, and east and win control of vast territories.

The Slavs who moved west went toward the Vistula (VISH-chuh-luh) Basin. They were the ancestors of the Poles, Czechs, and Slovaks. The southern Slavs traveled beyond the Carpathian Mountains of southern Russia and into the Balkan **Peninsula**. Their descendants are the Slovenes, Serbs, and Croats of Yugoslavia. The eastern Slavs moved north and northeast into the forests of present-day Russia. These Slavs are the ancestors of the Russians who today form the major ethnic group in the USSR. This movement of Slavs took place over many centuries.

Summing Up the Unit

Social Studies Vocabulary

Define: vegetation; climate; natural resources; peoples; migrations; artifacts; culture; domesticate; empire

People

Identify: Scythians; Goths; Huns; western Slavs; southern Slavs; eastern Slavs

Places

Locate: Arctic Ocean; European Russia; Siberia; Central Asia; the Transcaucasus; Ural Mountains; Amur, Ob, Lena, Yenisei, Volga, Don rivers; Moscow; Black Sea

⟳ Questions

1. What countries make up Eastern Europe?
2. What are the various names by which the Soviet Union is known?
3. Name the four belts of vegetation and climate in the USSR.
4. What area of Russia has served as a major invasion route?
5. Name the four geographical regions into which the USSR can be divided.
6. What is Siberia's main value to the USSR?
7. Why are the USSR's rivers more useful than its coastline for communication and trade?
8. The text states: "The history of the area known as the Soviet Union and Eastern Europe has been one of migrations." What reasons does the author give for this fact?
9. a. What is the ethnic origin of most of the people of the Soviet Union and Eastern Europe? b. By what various names are these peoples known today?

Discussion Topics

1. The Soviet Union has a variety of climates and types of vegetation. How can climate and vegetation affect where people choose to live? Use the text to support your answer.
2. The Ural Mountains are low and easily crossed. If the Urals were higher and few passes existed through them, how might the history of Russia have been different?
3. The Soviet government is working to develop Siberia's resources and bring people and industry to Siberia. If these efforts are successful, what benefits will they bring to the USSR?
4. Hunters in early Russia domesticated the horse. Why would horses be useful in Russia?
5. Archaeologists can recreate the way a people lived from the artifacts found at their sites. Using the text as a reference, how would archaeologists know that the people of the forest and steppe area did not have tools and weapons that were as advanced as those of their neighbors?
6. Between 1000 B.C. and 500 A.D., the various peoples in Russia were slow to develop an organized society and written language. What possible reasons could explain these facts? The material under "Civilizations and Cities" in the *Beginnings* section of this book will help you in forming your opinions.

Project Ideas

1. Superimpose a map of the U.S. and Canada on a map of the USSR to compare their sizes and latitudes. Using a reference such as an atlas or encyclopedia, explain how winds, the location of mountains, and distances from oceans—as well as latitude—cause both similarities and differences between the climate and vegetation of the USSR and those of North America.
2. Imagine you are a passenger on the Trans-Siberian Railroad. Describe your eight-day journey from Moscow to Vladivostok.
3. Trace the physical map of the USSR and Eastern Europe from the text. Draw a possible migration route for each of the following: Scythians, Goths, Huns. Show mountains, rivers, and vegetation belts.
4. Write a report on the work Soviet archaeologists have done on the Scythians.
5. Make a relief map using salt dough or clay showing the length of the Trans-Siberian railroad and its branches.

Unit II

The Rise of the Russian State

Russian royalty had a vast treasure of gold and jewels such as this crown, orb, and scepter. The Communists keep them on display in museums. Why do you think the Communists preserve these symbols of the past?

The USSR and Eastern Europe share borders with three large and very different culture areas. To the west are the countries of Western Europe, whose histories were shaped by the traditions of ancient Greece and the Roman Empire. To the east and the south are Asia and the Middle East. Through contact with these the peoples of Russia and Eastern Europe met the Byzantine Empire and the expanding world of the Muslims.

The Russians were slow to develop a distinct culture. The constant invasions and the many ethnic groups that settled in the area held them back. They were late in forming a unified government and in achieving a **national identity**. National identity is a sense of the oneness of a people who hold a common land, **economy**, culture, and language. It was not until the 1400s that a stable Russian state was actually established. Even after that there were periods of chaos. Unity and stability were finally established only under the rule of strong czars and czarinas.

From among the various **tribes** that migrated to the Russian steppes, one group of people emerged to dominate the others. These were the eastern Slavs.

From 600 to 800 A.D., the eastern Slavs fought for land with the peoples that were already there. The Slavs won and settled along the rivers. Because of their location, they became traders. By the 800s, they had developed a prosperous business in honey, wax, furs, and slaves. Their goods were sent over a river road extending from the Baltic to the Black Sea, along the western Dvina River to Lake Ladoga, then to the Volga River and into the Caspian Sea. Important trading towns, such as Novgorod (NAHV-guh-rahd) in the north and Kiev in the south, grew up along these vital river routes.

Chapter 1
Kiev
and Moscow

KIEV: THE FIRST STATE

Because of its location on the main trade route between the Baltic and Black seas and the Byzantine Empire, Kiev grew into the most important trading center. It also gained political importance. Its grand prince became the most powerful leader among the Slavs. Kiev tried to unify the other cities, but the cities preferred to rule themselves.

At about this time, the Khazars began to threaten Slavic land and trade. The Khazars were originally Turkic people who had settled in southern Russia between the Volga and Don rivers by the 700s A.D. They began to demand taxes from the Slavs living in this region and from any Slav trader passing through.

The Slavs were too disorganized to fight very well. According to Russian tradition, the Slavs turned to a group of warrior-traders called Varangians (vuh-RAN-jee-uhns) for protection. Some scholars believe that the Varangians actually conquered the Slavs.

In either case, **archaeological** findings verify that during the 700s, the Varangians were navigating, trading, and plundering the Russian rivers. They came across the Baltic Sea from present-day Sweden. These people were related to the Vikings who invaded England and France and who came to North America around 1000 A.D.

The Varangians gained control over many Slavic trade routes and built fortified settlements to insure their continued control. Because of the leadership, military, and administrative abilities of the Varangians, many of the Slavs bought their services for protection.

According to tradition, Oleg, a Varangian chieftain, took over Kiev and brought the surrounding peoples under his rule around 862 A.D. He combined Slav and Varangian forces. Gradually, the **institutions** and culture of the Varangians fused with those of the Slavs. Something new and unique was formed and came to be known as Russian.

CITY-STATES   Kievan Russia still did not form one country united under a single ruler. Instead there was a loose **alliance** of several **city-states** under the leadership of the Grand Prince of Kiev. Each

Kievan Russia, 1054

city-state or **town** was ruled by a prince who was a great Varangian warrior. The prince was expected to protect his town. In return he received a share of the town's profits from trade.

Kievan Russia was divided into several **classes**. At the top was the prince. Directly below him were his warriors. The next group was made up of the large landowners. Their power increased as farming became more important.

The majority were free people who earned their living farming, hunting, and lumbering. They had few rights, were subject to military service, and had a difficult time in simply earning a living. Below them were the **slaves**, with no rights. These included prisoners of war and Slavs who sold themselves to pay their debts.

INFLUENCES OF TRADE   From the 800s through the 1100s, Kievan Russia continued to prosper as a trading center. For a share of the profits, the princes protected river traffic from Asian peoples. The latter were really river pirates who demanded huge sums of money for safe passage.

The Russians built up a prosperous trade with the Byzantine Empire. The Russians would send furs, wax, honey, wood, fish, and grain in return for wine, jewelry, perfume, glassware, and silk. In addition, after the 700s, the only safe trade route between the Byzantine Empire and Western Europe was through Russia. Muslim warships roamed the Mediterranean and Black seas. The Muslims controlled North Africa and Spain and were chipping away at the Byzantine Empire itself. Thus, although the river route through Russia was longer, it was safer.

From their trading contacts, the Russians were exposed to both Western European and Byzantine influences. They were especially attracted to the culture of the Byzantine Empire. Originally the Byzantine Empire was the eastern portion of the Roman Empire. In 330 the Roman emperor Constantine had established Constantinople as the eastern capital of the empire. When the empire in the west fell in the 400s, Constantinople (modern Istanbul) was able to hold the eastern empire together. By the 800s, the eastern empire had shrunk to only Asia Minor.

However, Byzantine culture was still flourishing. It influenced the Russians in their **religion**, **architecture**, and art. Eastern Orthodox Christianity was the official religion of the Byzantine Empire and in 988 became the official religion of the Russians too.

This resulted in several benefits for the Russians. The religious tie strengthened the already existing commercial link between the Russians and the Byzantines. Moreover, the Eastern Orthodox religion strengthened the power of the Russian rulers. Since the religion taught that all power comes from God, to disobey the ruler—God's representative—was to sin.

The Orthodox religion also gave the Russians the beginnings of a sense of national identity. All Russians now shared some beliefs and practices in common. In the centuries to come, disaster would overtake the political structure of the country. However, the structure of the Church would provide stability for the people.

Under the influences of increasing trade and the Byzantine Empire, Kievan Russia enjoyed its Golden Age. In 1019 Yaroslav (yuh-ruh-SLAHF) the Wise inherited Novgorod and extended his control until, in 1036, he became the Grand Prince of Kiev. During his rule, Kiev became a city of splendor and wealth.

After Yaroslav's death in 1054, however, the kingdom was weakened by fighting among his sons. His grandson, Vladimir Monomakh (VLUH-dih-mihr muh-nuh-MAK), was able to reunite the city-states. His death, however, signaled the beginning of further **civil wars.** These were to drain Kievan Russia of its soldiers. By the 1200s when the Mongols swept into Russia, there was no group strong enough to withstand them.

In Western Europe the 1300s saw the beginning of the Renaissance. The basis of modern Western **civilization** was being laid. But these changes would not affect the Russians. Mongol rule would cut them off from Europe.

MONGOL INVASION AND RULE

The Mongols or Tatars were a group of loosely organized peoples in the northeastern steppes of Asia. They were great warriors, but fought constantly among themselves. In the late 1100s there was born among them one who was destined to become the greatest of their leaders—Temuchin. He later took the name Genghis Khan (JENG-gihs KAHN) which means ruler of the universe.

Under the iron command of Genghis Khan, the wandering peoples became disciplined followers. Peace came to the lawless steppes. However, Genghis Khan exacted peace at a heavy price. A city that he wanted had two alternatives: to fight or to surrender. The Khan spared cities when they submitted.

But if the cities refused, he spared no one. His successive victories, his terrible revenges, and his power spread fear far and wide. The mention of the name Mongol was enough to paralyze people with fear. This terror was the Mongols' **psychological** weapon for success in battle.

Another reason for the Khan's success was that he always determined the strengths and weaknesses of his enemy. Before striking at the West, he sent a scouting expedition to look over western Europe and adjoining lands. Around 1221-1222, while this force was camped in the southern part of the Ukraine, the Russians attacked. The Mongols were only a small force, but they fought back and destroyed the Russians.

Because they were so few, the Mongols left Russia. When they

The Russians adopted the Byzantine style in making icons, portraits of religious figures. This is a 14th-century portrait of St. Barbara, a patron saint of builders.

Genghis Khan ruled by terror. What did the Mongols learn about this method of government?

returned in 1237, they were under the leadership of Batu (BAH-too), Genghis Khan's grandson, and they meant to stay. They were called the Golden Horde because of the splendor of the tent in which Batu lived. Starting in 1237 and for about six years, the Mongols fought and conquered Kievan Russia and parts of modern Poland, Hungary, Yugoslavia, and Bulgaria. Batu found the land rich and populous. He reduced it to poverty and burned Kiev to the ground.

The Mongols soon discovered, however, that the dead and the poor are not able to pay tribute or provide soldiers. The Mongols began to encourage trade, discourage lawlessness, and promote the growth of cities. Their capital, Sarai, was located on the lower part of the Volga River. There the Mongols received **tribute**, issued orders, and ruled with firmness. But they showed some tolerance.

Russian princes were allowed to keep their titles and land so long as they gave money and obedience to their Mongol masters. The princes became the tax collectors and peacekeepers for the Khanate, or empire of the Golden Horde. This sharing of power was eventually to lead to the downfall of the Mongols.

MOSCOW: BEGINNING OF THE CZARS

In the early days of Russian history, Moscow was an unimportant place deep in the Russian forest. During Mongol rule, however, it began to grow in importance. Through marriages, mortgages, and inheritances, the princes of Moscow gradually enlarged their land-holdings and their power.

By the early 1300s, Ivan I had obtained the exclusive right to collect tribute from the other Russian princes for the Mongols. Thus the attention of all Russia was turned toward Moscow as the seat of power. Finally, Ivan the Great in 1480 declared Russia free of Mongol control. This date marks the rise of Moscow to its place as capital of Russia and begins the age of the czars.

IVAN THE GREAT Ivan the Great (1462-1505) married Zoe, the niece of the last Byzantine emperor. (In 1453, the Byzantine Empire fell to the Turks.) Because of his marriage, Ivan claimed for himself the rights and personal power of a Byzantine emperor. He claimed, like an emperor, that he received his right to rule directly from God. He assumed the Byzantine title of autocrat—a ruler with complete power over his subjects—and called himself czar or tsar. In Russian this means caesar or emperor. Ivan **centralized** the operations and power of **government** in his own hands.

Ivan surrounded himself with Byzantine **ritual** and ceremony. He took the Byzantine symbol of the double eagle for his own seal. **Status** and manners became extremely important in obtaining office and in conducting oneself in Russian society.

The **traditions** that Ivan established found an ally in the Eastern

Orthodox Church, a great and growing force in Russia. Formerly the Church had looked to Constantinople for guidance and leadership. But with the fall of the empire, the leaders of the Russian Church found they had to set up their own center in Moscow. Mutual interests kept the czar and the Russian Orthodox Church tied together.

This scene is from the 1946 film Ivan the Terrible, *which was directed by Sergei Eisenstein. Eisenstein was one of the world's greatest filmmakers. Why would an artist choose a theme from a nation's past?*

IVAN THE TERRIBLE   Ivan IV (1533-1584), known as the Terrible, continued to concentrate power in the hands of the czar. He broke the power of the old nobles and encouraged the rise of a new class of military-service landholders. These landholders received their land from the czar in return for military service in time of need.

The Mongol invasion had divided Russia. The people east of the Dnieper River fought those west of the river—Poles, western Russians, and Ukrainians among others. This land between Germany and Russia, a large section of Eastern Europe, was a battleground for centuries. Ivan took advantage of this to expand Russian borders. He tried to open a door on the Baltic Sea but was stopped by the Poles and the Swedes. He did drive the Mongols from along the middle Volga and brought the territory to the Caspian Sea under Russian rule. He opened Siberia and the steppes all the way to the Pacific Ocean.

From boyhood, Ivan had found himself surrounded by intrigue and attempts at assassination. Gradually he became convinced that he could trust no one. He began to strike out at those around him and to punish suspected offenders harshly. The least suspicion that someone was disloyal often resulted in the death of the suspect and the suspect's family.

Under orders from Ivan, police roamed the countryside with power to punish suspected traitors. Ivan capped some of the extremes of his rule by causing the death of his eldest son. In a fit of temper Ivan hit his son so hard that he killed him. Despite Ivan's excesses, some historians today regard the long-term good he did for Russia as greater than his evil. They question whether he was any more terrible than William the Conqueror of England or others faced with the disloyalty of powerful nobles.

Boris Godunov is
the subject of an opera
by the 19th-century
composer Moussorgsky.

FROM PEASANT TO SERF   Ivan was succeeded by his second son, Theodore I (1584-1598). A weak ruler, he was influenced by his brother-in-law, Boris Godunov (GOOD-uh-nof). Together they continued Ivan's policy of keeping peasants on the land they farmed. In the past, peasants had contracted with landlords to work the land and to pay so much in produce after each harvest. But the peasants always had the right to leave. From the time of Ivan on, however, it became more and more difficult for peasants to change landlords.

Eventually, in 1649, the peasants were bound to the soil as **serfs**. This meant they were no longer free. They were the property of the landholder. If the land changed owners so did the serfs. With its military-service landholders and its serfs, Russia was taking on the elements of a feudal society. This was several centuries after the countries of Western Europe had abandoned the feudal system. **Feudalism** in the West had declined as **commerce** had increased. But in Russia in the 1600s, land was becoming more important.

Theodore had no heir, and Boris Godunov (1598-1605) was elected czar by an **assembly** which he had carefully selected. At Boris's death, several men claimed the throne. From about 1605 to 1613 civil war, famine, and an invasion by the Poles kept Russia in turmoil. This period is referred to as the Time of Troubles.

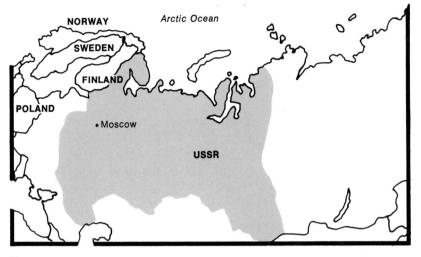

☐ **Russia, 1613**

Chapter 2
Expansion
Abroad—
Unrest
at Home

Frightened by the Time of Troubles, an assembly of nobles convened in 1613 to elect a new czar. They wanted someone who could unite Russia. Michael Romanov (roh-MAHN-uhf), a distant relative of Ivan the Terrible, was chosen. This event marks the beginning of the 300-year rule of the Romanovs.

During this time the Romanovs changed Russia from a disorganized backward nation into a major world power. They built an empire that spread from Eastern Europe to the Pacific Ocean. The czars became interested in Western Europe. The nation was brought more and more under the influence of the West. Russia became important in European **diplomacy**.

Although fascinated by the technological and artistic achievements of Western Europe, the czars did not adopt the political practices of the West. Some of these nations were unseating rulers, or at least limiting their power. However, Russian rulers were growing stronger. They were gaining absolute control over their subjects.

PETER THE GREAT

Michael Romanov (1613-1645) started improving relations with Europe. He opened Russia to foreign trade and encouraged European craftworkers to immigrate. This trend toward the Europeanization of Russia was furthered by Michael's son Alexis (1645-1676). However, it was Alexis' son, Peter, who marked the real beginning of the Russian movement outward.

immigrate: to enter a foreign country

Peter became czar at 17. Known as Peter the Great, he ruled Russia from 1689 to 1725. Bright and eager, he had a passion for the practical and useful. He loved to tinker and work with his hands. This fondness

Although he spent a year abroad, Peter did not realize the centuries that had been needed for the technology he saw. This painting of Peter in Holland was done by V. A. Serov 200 years later, in the late 1800s.

for manual labor never left him. He was a practical joker, but could be quite cruel. He tortured his eldest son to death because he suspected him of treason.

Before Peter's reign, Russian rulers had been suspicious of foreigners. Although they were curious about foreigners and allowed them to live in Russia, they kept them **segregated**. Only a few loyal Russian officials were allowed to do business with them. For centuries ordinary Russians had known foreigners chiefly through invasions. It was only natural that they should be fearful. But Peter was not afraid. He had spent much of his youth wandering through the foreign quarter of Moscow. There he had developed an interest in Western **technology**, especially shipbuilding and military service.

EUROPEAN TRIP   After he became czar, Peter visited Western Europe. He did not travel in the grand manner of a king. Instead, he went under an assumed name. He worked for a time as a carpenter in the shipyards of Holland and England and studied the technical advances that he saw all around him.

Peter and the Russians with him were amazed at the progress in Western Europe. They realized how far behind Russia was. Peter determined to **modernize** his country within his lifetime. However, he was not interested in the new European ideas of government. He was interested only in the developments that would advance Russia's technology. He had no intention of endangering his personal power.

Peter's trip was cut short by the news that some military officers had revolted. They wanted a voice in the government. Peter hurried back to Moscow and the revolt was crushed. The rebellious officers were executed.

MODERNIZATION EFFORTS   Once he had firmly established his power, Peter started his program to change Russia. His first step was to extend Russian territory. Russia needed ports if it was to expand its commerce and, therefore, its wealth and power. Peter originally wanted to fight the Turks in order to secure a warm-water port. However, he could find no other European country to help him. So he decided to seek a port in the north. After making secret **treaties** with Poland and Denmark, Peter declared war against Sweden.

The Russians were badly defeated in the beginning of the war. But Peter modernized his army. He equipped it with new weaponry, disciplined the soldiers, and gave them a sense of duty. He also built the first Russian navy and used it on the Baltic. In 1709 Russia defeated Sweden and became a major power in northern Europe. By the end of the war in 1721, Peter had gained his port on the Baltic and had secured the territories of Livonia, Estonia, and part of Finland. Except for a brief two years, Peter waged war throughout his 36-year rule. Besides a warm-water port, he wanted more land in Central Asia.

One of Peter's greatest dreams was to build a capital that would be modern and European. He chose a site on the Baltic coast for his capital, St. Petersburg, now called Leningrad. Although thousands died that the city might rise in the swamps and marshes, Peter was determined to have his window to the West. St. Petersburg became a European-Russian city, where Western culture, thought, and achievements merged with those of Russia.

Men were able to keep their beards if they paid a tax and carried a beard license.

Peter also made changes in many phases of Russian life including the way the people looked. When he returned from Europe, Russian men were still wearing long coats and full beards. Peter insisted that all coats be shortened to knee length. Anyone found wearing a long coat was forced to kneel and have it cut off at the knee. Beards were sacred to the Russians but Peter insisted that they be cut off. Anyone caught with a beard had it immediately removed by scissors or razor.

Western European forms of administration were copied. Government officials were placed under committees. Peter imposed the same committee system on the Church. He did not want anyone to rank near him in power, not even the head of the Church. He bound the serf more tightly to the soil. He took a census of his people and imposed a head tax on every person in Russia.

In 1700 Peter instituted use of the Julian calendar throughout Russia. Until then, Russians had used an ancient calendar which at that time placed them in the year 7208. The Julian calendar was already incorrect by 11 days in 1700, but at least the year was the same as the Gregorian calendar used throughout Western Europe. Russia finally abandoned the Julian calendar after the 1917 Revolution.

627

*During Catherine's rule
Russia continued
to expand abroad,
while many new towns
were built at home.*

CATHERINE THE GREAT

Peter the Great died in 1725 without appointing an heir to succeed him. From 1725 until 1762, several rulers were seated and unseated by a group of nobles known as the Palace Guard. The only one who lasted any length of time was Czarina Elizabeth who ruled from 1741 to 1762. She chose as her successor her nephew Peter, Duke of Holstein, who was a grandson of Peter the Great.

In 1744 a German princess named Sophia was chosen to marry him. Sophia was converted to the Russian Orthodox religion and was renamed Catherine. Peter was crude, incompetent, and possibly insane. He became czar in 1762. A few months later, after a palace revolt, Catherine was placed on the throne. Peter mysteriously died not long after.

Catherine II ruled from 1762 to 1796. Although born a German, she tried to make herself over into a Russian. She hoped to make her adopted country a major European power. During her long rule, she accomplished many of her goals and earned the name Catherine the Great.

CONQUEST AND RUSSIFICATION   Catherine continued to expand Russia's territory. She warred with the Turks and took from them the northern coast of the Black Sea. On three occasions Russia joined with Austria and Prussia to rob Poland of its land and divide the spoils among themselves. Russia received the largest share including Poland's capital, Warsaw. Under Catherine's leadership, Russia fought to gain land and retain power in Finland. She also took the Crimea from the remnants of the Mongols and added the entire Ukraine to Russia.

The conquest of these lands brought many new peoples into Russia. Catherine wanted these conquered peoples to become part of Russian society. To accomplish this, she established a program called Russification. This meant that the people had to speak Russian, join the Russian Orthodox church, and pledge loyalty to the crown. The conquered peoples fought back in an effort to keep their own ethnic identities and ways of life. However, Russification continued as official government policy.

FRENCH INFLUENCES   Catherine welcomed foreigners and their ideas to Russia. She read and wrote Russian, German, and French and was a patron of **the arts**. She especially admired the French and took them as her model. She hoped to make the Russian court as elegant and splendid as that of France. She corresponded with some of the greatest thinkers of her day including Voltaire, the French philosopher.

However, as sympathetic as Catherine may have been to the ideas of Western Europe, she made little effort to reform her government.

Built for Peter, the Great Palace near Leningrad was enlarged during Catherine's reign by Bartolomeo Rastrelli. World War II left the palace and gardens in ruin. The Soviet government rebuilt and restored them.

The small **reforms** that she attempted did not reach down to the majority of her subjects, the serfs. Nobles, landlords, and **intellectuals** advanced, but the peasants remained in slavery.

In 1773 a revolt of Cossacks—fierce warriors who lived in southern and eastern Russia—and serfs broke out. It was a bloody rebellion that was quickly put down. After this, Catherine reorganized local government somewhat but she continued to exercise absolute power.

In 1789, during Catherine's reign, the French Revolution began. Its ideas of liberty, equality, and fraternity spread into other countries and caused great unrest. The **revolution** temporarily weakened France and gave other nations a chance to grab new territories. As a result, a series of wars broke out across Europe. Although the French Revolution disgusted Catherine, she kept Russia out of wars. She did not want to endanger her power.

fraternity: a feeling of closeness because of shared interests and goals

At Catherine's death in 1796, she was succeeded by her son Paul. Known as the mad czar, he was assassinated in 1801. It was Catherine's grandson, Alexander, who made Russia a truly great European power.

ALEXANDER I

To many people, Alexander I is a riddle. He was raised by Catherine to be an **enlightened despot**; that is, a ruler with absolute power who uses it for the benefit of his or her subjects. Alexander's Swiss tutor presented him with the more **liberal** ideas then current in Western Europe. But from his father, Paul, Alexander learned a love of power

629

Constant war had turned
Alexander I's interest
from the philosophy of
the Enlightenment to
Christianity. What were some
ideas of the Enlightenment?

and the military. When he came to the throne, Alexander was a mixture of Russian and European influences. Historians are unable to agree on whether he really believed in liberal principles or was simply very clever at holding onto his power.

Alexander's reign (1801-1825) began with several reforms. He freed many prisoners, abolished torture as a punishment, allowed foreign books to be sold, arranged a system to free serfs, formed a committee to draw up a **constitution**, and set up another committee to consult with him. These reforms were pushed aside, however, when Alexander joined Britain, Austria, and Prussia in war against Napoleon.

NAPOLEON IN RUSSIA   After the French Revolution, Napoleon Bonaparte came to power in France and engaged in a series of wars. In 1805 Russia joined the fight against Napoleon. Although the Russians fought well, they were badly defeated on several occasions. In 1807 Alexander and Napoleon met in Prussia and signed the Peace Treaty of Tilsit. However, neither side kept the agreement.

In June 1812 Napoleon invaded Russia. The Russian leaders knew their soldiers could not defeat Napoleon's armies, so they retreated farther and farther into Russia. As they retreated, they burned the land behind them. The French were unable to live off the land and they did not carry supplies with them. When Napoleon reached Moscow in September, he found the city deserted and in flames.

Napoleon stayed in Moscow until late October, trying to reach a settlement with the Russians. They refused to surrender. Afraid of the approaching winter, Napoleon began to pull back his army. However, the French were too deep inside Russia and did not start their retreat soon enough. The terrible Russian winter caught them without supplies and shelter. As a result, the French army was almost destroyed. It is estimated that 300,000 died on the march out of Russia.

After Napoleon's defeat in Russia, Alexander joined the other European rulers in their struggle against the French emperor. Napoleon was defeated once and for all in 1815.

During the Congress of Vienna, the peace conference that followed, Alexander played an important role. He had become the most powerful ruler in Europe. He asked the Allies to form a Holy Alliance for the purpose of maintaining peace. The Allies were suspicious, and the Holy Alliance had little effect on European **politics**.

SECRET SOCIETIES   When Alexander returned home from Vienna, he found Russia in serious trouble. Ways had to be found to finance the government and the costly wars he had just waged. Alexander reorganized the government into bureaus for greater efficiency and unity. The conquest of new lands had brought many more foreign peoples into Russia. Under the slogan "One church, one government, one language," Alexander continued Catherine's policy of Russification.

Discontent spread. Many nobles and educated Russians had seen the progress of Western Europe. They felt that Alexander should return to the reforms he had dropped in 1805. They wanted a constitution, public education, the freeing of serfs, and limits on the czar's power. Many of these people formed secret societies to work for reform. Alexander paid little attention to these groups. If they were discovered, however, the members were exiled.

REBELLION AND REPRESSION

When Alexander died in 1825, he was succeeded by his younger brother Nicholas I (1825-1855). Nicholas was not popular, especially among the reformers. On December 26, 1825, when the Russian troops were to take the oath of loyalty to the new czar, they revolted. The revolt was put down quickly, and the leaders were exiled to Siberia. But Nicholas was frightened. He increased the use of censorship, and his police to try to control his subjects.

Despite Nicholas's efforts, two groups—the Slavophiles (lovers of things Slavic) and the Westernizers—preached various reform ideas. Both of these groups were loyal Russians. But they felt that great changes were needed to modernize Russia. However, they could not agree on how to accomplish these changes.

The Slavophiles wanted to do away with Western culture. They claimed that it was corrupt. Only by following and preserving Russian **customs** and traditions could progress be made. The Westernizers were admirers of Peter the Great and of Western culture. They believed that Russia could advance only by imitating the ideas and reforms of Western Europe. Although these groups were not active **revolutionaries**, knowledge of their ideas spread among the people.

In foreign affairs, Nicholas continued the czarist policy of expansion. He sent troops into Poland, Hungary, and against the Turkish Ottoman Empire. Nicholas won a great deal of land in the Balkans. But in 1853 the Crimean War broke out between Russia and the Ottoman Empire. This time the British, French, and Austrians joined the Turks. Nicholas died during the Crimean War and left his son, Alexander II (1855-1881), the task of ending it. The Russians were defeated and had to return a large part of the land they had taken from the Turks.

Alexander and the Russians were stunned by their defeat. Alexander realized that Russia had to advance into the 19th century in order to remain a force in European affairs. So he began to make the necessary changes. The most famous of these was the Emancipation Act in 1861 in which he freed the serfs. Freedom, however, did not improve their lives. Now all land belonged to the village and sections were assigned to families. A family could not move away without asking the village **council's** permission.

Alexander established town councils with elected representatives.

Nicholas I tightened control over Russia. His son, Alexander II, tried to enact reforms. Neither was successful. What do you think might account for this?

631

He reformed the courts, began building railroads, started new industry, and organized a banking system. He also improved education by setting up primary schools for the freed serfs. He continued to expand Russian territory by conquering Central Asia. However, to pay some of his bills, he sold Alaska to the United States.

Unfortunately, Alexander's efforts at reform seemed to please no one. Some people felt his reforms went too far. Others felt they did not go far enough. This discontent led to rebellion throughout Russia. Russian nobles offered to lead the peasants in revolt. Several attempts were made on Alexander's life. In 1881, he was assassinated by a **terrorist's** bomb.

Alexander's son, Alexander III (1881-1894), shared none of his father's liberal views. It made no difference to the new czar that Alexander II had been murdered by terrorists and not by liberals. In his father's death he saw what he thought would be the natural outcome of liberalism. Thus, the reign of Alexander III was one of the most repressive in modern history with regard to human rights.

Nicholas II (1894-1917) succeeded his father and was to be Russia's last czar. He also tried to stop ideas of reform and freedom. But, like previous czars, he would fail.

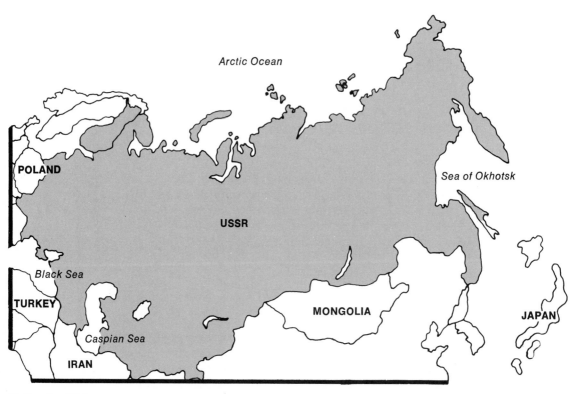

■ **Russia, 1914**

Summing Up the Unit

Social Studies Vocabulary

Define: national identity; city-states; classes; tribute; traditions; serfs; feudalism; commerce; technology; intellectuals; enlightened despot; council; liberal; terrorist

People

Identify: Varangians; Mongols; Genghis Khan; Boris Godunov; the Romanovs; Alexander I; Napoleon Bonaparte; Nicholas I

Places

Locate: Caspian, Baltic, Black seas; Kiev; Sweden; Finland

Words

Identify: Byzantine Empire; czar; Russian Orthodox Church; Time of Troubles; window to the West; Congress of Vienna; secret societies; Ottoman Empire

⌫ Questions

1. What advantage did the Kievans have for becoming traders?
2. In what three ways did the Russians benefit by adopting the Byzantine religion?
3. What changes came about when the Mongols were overthrown?
4. a. How did Ivan the Terrible extend Russian rule? b. How did these methods increase his own power?
5. In the hands of Theodore I and Boris Godunov, how did Ivan's methods contribute to the establishment of a feudal society in Russia?
6. a. How was Peter the Great's knowledge of the West different from that of ordinary Russians? b. How did his knowledge of the West change Russian life?
7. a. Catherine the Great extended Russia's territory at the expense of what four peoples? b. Russification required these people to become Russian in what three ways?
8. How did reforms desired by the Slavophiles differ from those wanted by the Westernizers?

Discussion Topics

1. Many empires have been built on trade. Kiev is one such example. Why was its location so important? Why did it become less important than Moscow in the long run? What other advantages did Moscow have that Kiev didn't? Why do you think the merchants of Kiev didn't resist the Mongols the way the princes of Moscow did?
2. As feudalism declined in Western Europe, it took hold in Russia. Why did Russia adopt such a system when Western Europe was abandoning it?
3. Peter the Great wanted to advance Russia's power and greatness. Which of his accomplishments helped Russia most? Did his changes harm Russia? If so, in what ways? Do you think he should be called Peter the Great?
4. Alexander I arranged a system to free the serfs but later gave up the idea. Why do you think he changed his mind?
5. Most of the czars tried to kill ideas of reform and freedom. Would it have been possible for them to bring about democratic reforms in Russia and still keep their power? Could they have prevented the Communist takeover in Russia? Do you think such a takeover inevitable?

Project Ideas

1. Write a biographical sketch on one of the following: Genghis Khan; Ivan the Great; Ivan the Terrible; Peter the Great; Catherine the Great; Alexander I.
2. Using reference materials, write a report on one of the following influences on Russia: the Byzantines; the Germans; the French.
3. Draw a series of maps showing the stages of territorial growth of the Russian empire.
4. Write an essay, supported by research, on one of the following topics: why the czars and czarinas of Russia were able to gain dictatorial power; the comparative importance of Middle Eastern, Asian, and Western European influences on Russia; how Russia became an empire; the effectiveness of Russian strategy against Napoleon; the effects of the French invasion on Russian nobility and serfs.

Unit III

Communism in Russia

This is a section of the USSR's flag. The red background symbolizes revolution. The joined hammer and sickle stand for the union of farmers and industrial workers. The star represents the Communist party.

During the 1800s and early 1900s, many ideas from Western Europe circulated among the Russians. Included were ideas about human rights: the right to decent living conditions, the right to share in the government, and the right to live without fear and oppression.

These ideas fanned the flames of discontent that were spreading in Russia. In the countryside angry and desperate peasants burned and looted the estates of their landlords and then fled. In the cities they found still more reason to be dissatisfied. Wages were low, housing was substandard, and working conditions were nearly unbearable. Moving among the people were revolutionaries who were determined to change the government. Some were willing to do this by force. In 1917 they were finally successful.

The theory of **communism** was originally developed by two German revolutionaries, Karl Marx and Friedrich Engels. Their ideas are contained in the *Communist Manifesto,* written by Marx and Engels in 1848, and *Das Kapital,* written by Marx in 1867. The **philosophy** they developed has been, and continues to be, the basis of revolutionary movements throughout the world.

Chapter 1
The Fight
for Power

KARL MARX AND COMMUNIST THEORY

Marx and Engels interpreted history according to economics. Throughout history, different economic systems have developed. The first was based on slavery, the next on serfdom, and the latest on capitalism. **Capitalism** means the private ownership of the **means of production**—factories, railroads, machines, land, and so on.

According to Marx and Engels, in each period, one class—the slave owner, the feudal lord, the capitalist—was the exploiter. At the same time, the exploited—the slaves, the serfs, the workers—were struggling to gain a greater share of wealth and power. History, Marx claimed, is a continuous struggle between classes. It is a conflict between those who have and those who have not.

Marx believed that the final struggle was coming. It would be between the capitalists and the proletariat (proh-luh-TER-ee-uht), that is, the workers. The workers would eventually overthrow capitalism. It would then be replaced by communism in which the means of production would be owned in common by the community.

Marx came to these conclusions after seeing the factory workers of Western Europe, especially of England. They worked long hours under bad conditions for very low wages, while owners of factories grew rich. The owners were able to make huge profits because they sold goods for high prices while paying low wages. Marx believed that an item was only worth the labor that went into its production. In that case, the workers were entitled to the full profit of what they produced. Capitalists were unnecessary.

According to Marx, the lives of the workers would not improve until the governments, which were controlled by the capitalists, were overthrown. Although this would happen eventually, Marx preached immediate revolution. This would be the first stage on the way to achieving the perfect society.

After the workers had overthrown the capitalists and seized the means of production, they would become the rulers. They would set up a **dictatorship** of the proletariat. The **state** would become unnecessary. It would wither and die. All workers would produce according to their abilities and be rewarded according to their needs. To Marx, this was the ultimate and best system in humanity's evolving life.

However, before communism could exist, Marx thought that there had to be a propertied middle class, the **bourgeoisie** (burzh-wah-ZEE). Marx further believed that communism would come first to highly

Karl Marx was a member of the middle class. How might this have shaped his view that communism needed a middle class?

The last of the Romanovs sat for this family portrait in 1913, 300 years after the first Romanov took the throne. The family was executed in 1918.

industrialized countries. Yet communism was first put into practice in Russia—an agricultural society with almost no middle class.

NICHOLAS II AND THE MARCH REVOLUTION

The last czar, Nicholas II, (1894-1917) lacked foresight. Although conditions throughout Russia were growing worse, he insisted on expanding Russian territory eastward. Nicholas wanted a warm-water port, and he was ready to overrun Manchuria and Korea to get it. However, Japan wanted the same territory. In 1904 the Russians went to war against the Japanese and were defeated. This defeat, by a nation whom the Russians considered a third-rate power, caused open opposition to the czar.

From the opposition three groups arose who were committed to reform. The Social Democrats were followers of Marx. They wanted to improve conditions for industrial workers. In 1903 they split into two **factions**. The Mensheviks (MEN-chuh-viks), favored gradual change. The other faction was called Bolsheviks (BOHL-shuh-viks). Led by Nikolai Lenin (LEN-uhn), they wanted immediate revolution and establishment of a dictatorship of the proletariat.

The second major group was the Socialist Revolutionary party. It wanted all land taken from the large landholders and given to the peasants. The members of this party were terrorists who waged open warfare.

The third organization was the Union of Liberation, which contained many professional people and Westernizers. They wanted a constitution that would promote democratic aims. These three groups added to the discontent in the country—a discontent that often burst into violence.

BLOODY SUNDAY　　The violence, however, was not always caused by the people. On a Sunday morning in January 1905, the workers of St. Petersburg, with their wives and children, marched in a peaceful procession to the czar's palace. They were asking for better working conditions and better government. Nicholas gave the order to fire on the marchers and then left. Hundreds were wounded.

The Russians were horrified. Strikes and mutinies occurred across the country. In St. Petersburg and Moscow, workers formed soviets—the Russian word for councils—to organize and direct the strikes. Many of these people were Mensheviks and Bolsheviks from the Social Democratic party. Later that month a general strike brought the nation to a standstill and became known as the Revolution of 1905.

The strikes frightened Nicholas. He promised reforms, including an assembly called a Duma (DOO-muh) to help write new laws and a constitution for the country. From 1906 to 1916 four sessions of the Duma were called, but they made small progress toward easing conditions. Nicholas had recovered from his fright and given little power to the Duma. However, the assembly gave many critics of the czar a platform from which to speak.

THE TURNING POINT　　It was World War I that changed the course of Russian history. In the late 1800s, the Russian government had

Russians flee as soldiers fire on their march to the Winter Palace. This was Bloody Sunday, the beginning of the first nationwide Russian revolt.

637

joined an alliance with Great Britain and France against Germany and Austria. But when the war came in 1914, Russia was unprepared. Many soldiers marched into battle unarmed. Thousands were killed, wounded, or captured by the Germans. At home, the war drained the country of its scarce resources. Serious shortages of food, fuel, and labor occurred.

The people looked to the czar for hope, but they saw only an indecisive man. When the war continued to go badly for the Russians, Nicholas went to inspect the front. He left the government in the hands of Czarina Alexandra and Gregory Rasputin. Rasputin (ras-POO-tuhn) was a monk who supposedly had faith-healing powers.

faith-healing powers: the ability to cure illness through prayer

He had helped Nicholas's son who suffered from hemophilia, a rare blood disease. Alexandra was convinced that Rasputin had been sent by God and she faithfully followed his advice—good or bad. Rasputin's influence on the czarina was distastrous for the country. In 1916 a group of nobles murdered him.

Because the czar was doing nothing to help them, the people took action. On March 8, 1917, a food riot broke out in Petrograd (formerly St. Petersburg). This quickly turned into a general strike and marked the beginning of the Russian Revolution. Within a few days, conditions had grown so desperate that Nicholas abdicated. The rule of the Romanovs had ended.

The leaders of the Duma set up a **provisional government** until elections could be held. However, the new government faced tremendous problems. They were made worse by trying to keep Russia in the war and provide domestic reform at the same time. Unrest continued to grow. As the provisional government wavered, the soviets became more powerful. They opposed the war and spread feelings of defeatism in the country. At this time, Lenin stepped in.

LENIN AND THE BOLSHEVIK REVOLUTION

Lenin was a long-time Communist revolutionary. Through his oldest brother, Alexander, Lenin first saw the revolutionary movement in action. When Lenin was 16, Alexander was hanged for his part in a plot to kill the czar. After his brother's death, Lenin himself became a revolutionary. In 1896 he was arrested and sent to Siberia for three years.

From Siberia he went into exile in Switzerland where he edited the Social Democrat newspaper. Lenin wrote a great deal, and one of his best-known works is *Imperialism, the Final Stage of Capitalism.* When the Social Democrats split in 1903, Lenin led the Bolsheviks while in exile. He came back to Russia during the Revolution of 1905 but stayed only a short time. He returned in 1917 with the help of the Germans who hoped he could take Russia out of the war.

LENIN'S VIEW OF MARXISM   Lenin concentrated on the revolutionary aspects of Marxism. He emphasized that the workers would

This painting, Lenin Proclaims Soviet Power, *was painted during Lenin's time. Its style is called socialist realism. The artist, V. A. Serov, also painted* Peter in Holland. *Could an artist glorify a czar and the revolution too? Could both paintings glorify the revolution?*

never be free until the capitalists and their governments had been overthrown by violent revolution. He felt, however, that the workers would never be able to do this by themselves. The revolution would have to be organized and led by trained professional revolutionaries. The Communists have used this reasoning as a justification for their power ever since. Unlike Marx, Lenin felt that Communist revolutions would and could occur in industrially undeveloped countries such as Russia. They were, in fact, prime targets.

THE REVOLUTIONARY IN ACTION   When Lenin returned to Russia, the nation was in chaos. Food and fuel shortages continued. People were rioting. Soldiers were deserting. As the provisional government grew weaker, the soviets gained strength with the help of Lenin and the Bolsheviks. Frightened by this, the provisional government had many Bolsheviks arrested. Lenin went into hiding for a time but returned with a promise of land for the peasants, control of the factories for the workers, peace for all, and a takeover of the government.

devised: made up

In the meantime the provisional government had scheduled national elections for November 25. Lenin knew the Bolsheviks were not strong enough to gain a majority in the elections. So he devised a daring plan to bring the Bolsheviks to power. On November 6, 1917, the Bolsheviks called a strike. Soldiers, sailors, and armed workers, called the Red Guard, marched on the government buildings. They arrested the officials of the provisional government and took control of the government. They met little resistance.

Two days later the All-Russian Congress of Soviets met in Petrograd. Those who opposed the Bolsheviks walked out. This left control of the soviets in the hands of Lenin and the Bolsheviks. When the elections were held later in the month, the Bolsheviks received only one-fourth of the vote. But when the new assembly was convened, Lenin and the Red Guard disrupted it and sent everyone home. Thus, in three moves the Bolsheviks had gained control of the nation. Once in power, they changed their name to Communists.

The Communists first made peace with Germany. They then began a fight to preserve and enlarge the power they had seized. As a result, civil war raged in Russia for the next three years. It pitted the White Army—which included supporters of the czar—the regular army, and the landowners, against the Communist Red Army. Although the White Army received troops and supplies from Britain, France, Japan, and the U. S., they were finally defeated by the Red Army. By the end of 1920, the Communists ruled all of Russia.

THE NEW SOVIET STATE   The Communist government should have been established as a dictatorship of the proletariat. However, it soon became apparent that this really meant the dictatorship of Lenin and the Communist party. To strengthen their power, Lenin and the Communists began a program of removing anyone who opposed them. Czar Nicholas and his family were executed to prevent their rescue. Nobles and landlords were murdered.

In 1918 government by constitution had been established. The soviets were to be the basis of local government, and they would elect a national **congress**. The national congress would, in turn, appoint a **cabinet** under the leadership of Lenin. Since the Communist party was the only party allowed, everyone in the government would be a Communist or a sympathizer. Thus, Lenin was the leader of both the Communist party and the government.

The new government took over all the factories, banks, mines, and land. In Communist theory, the workers owned the factories and the land, but in practice everything was controlled by the government. The people received wages. However, the wages were low and the people were little better off than they had been under the czars. By 1921, Lenin realized that his system of communism was not working, and he developed a New Economic Policy (NEP)—a combination of capitalism and **socialism**. The peasants were able to keep some of their produce and sell it themselves. The factory workers received higher wages and some shops were even returned to private ownership.

In January 1923 Lenin had the name of the country changed from Russia to the Union of Soviet Socialist Republics (USSR). At that time there were only four members, but by World War II the Soviet Union had brought 11 more **territories** into the USSR. The Russian Soviet Federated Socialist Republic (RSFSR) was and is the dominant member of the Union. Each republic has a Communist party and government of its own but is responsible to and closely watched by the Communist party of the entire union. Over 100 **nationalities** live within the republics.

After Lenin's death in 1924 a three-year stuggle for power developed between Leon Trotsky (TRAHT-skee) and Joseph Stalin (STAHL-uhn). A fundamental disagreement existed between the two men over the course communism should take.

TROTSKY versus STALIN

Lev Davydovich Bronstein, known as Leon Trotsky, was a Ukrainian Jew from a well-to-do family. His father was a landowner with several employees and servants. Nevertheless, Trotsky devoted his life to the revolution. He was exiled to Siberia for his activities but escaped. He lived abroad from 1902 to 1917. When the revolution began, he went to Petrograd. There he joined Lenin and the Bolsheviks and became second in command. It was Trotsky who organized the Red Guard. He later commanded the Red Army and led it to victory during the civil war. He gained fame as the negotiator of the peace treaty with Germany that ended Russia's role in World War I.

Trotsky became commissar or **minister** for foreign affairs under Lenin and one of Lenin's most trusted friends. He believed in a world revolution of workers. Since Russia was an **underdeveloped** nation, he felt that it could not succeed as a Communist country until there was a worldwide revolution of workers.

Stalin, on the other hand, was convinced that world revolution would come only after communism had been made strong in Russia. He believed Russia could accomplish this by itself.

Joseph Stalin was born in the province of Georgia near the Black Sea. He was the son of a shoemaker. He originally planned to be a priest but was expelled from the seminary because of his Marxist beliefs. Historians disagree over his role in the revolution. All that is certain is that after the revolution Lenin appointed him commissar for national minorities. By 1922 Stalin had become general secretary of the Communist party. As secretary he made many friends and appointed them to high places. In this way he developed a following within the party.

When Lenin died, the choice for new party leader was between

This photo of Leon Trotsky at about age 25 is from Russian police files. Trotsky had been arrested by the Czarist government for his activities.

641

Trotsky and Stalin and their opposing points of view. While Trotsky was very bright, Stalin was cunning and shrewd. It was Stalin who had built up a major following. By playing one side against the other, he was able to take command of the Communist party and thus become dictator of the Soviet Union.

By 1927 Stalin had Trotsky expelled from the party and sent into exile. Between 1927 and 1940 Trotsky wrote a series of books and articles opposing the Stalin dictatorship. In 1940 Trotsky was assassinated, presumably by an agent of Stalin.

Trotsky's ideas can be traced in a direct line back to Marx. His ideas were part of the movement that promoted the **unification** and revolution of workers throughout the world. The movement was called the **International** Workingmen's Association or International. It was started by Karl Marx in 1864. However, because of disagreements it soon fell apart. A second attempt was made in 1889 at Brussels.

The second International collapsed because of World War I. When the Bolsheviks came to power, they organized the third International or Comintern. The Comintern, under Russian domination, was organized to help other countries overthrow capitalist governments. It supported the Chinese Communists in the 1920s. By 1943 the Comintern was officially disbanded. Trotsky had organized his own International in Mexico in 1937 but it had died with him.

Chapter 2
Party and Government

In theory, the Soviet Union has a constitutional government. In practice, the country is a dictatorship under the Communist party. Describing this system, Lenin referred to the party as the brains and the government as the body. The Communist party leads the country and makes the decisions, but it created a large government structure to carry out its orders.

The Communist leaders wrote a constitution providing for a **representative government** for several reasons. Through the constitution, the leaders were able to state their basic philosophy and goals. They were able to proclaim that they lived under a constitutional system. But constitutions can always be interpreted to fit the purposes and actions of those who control the country. Stalin never permitted the constitution to limit his activities.

PARTY ORGANIZATION

The Communist party is the only political party permitted in the Soviet Union. The Communists claim there is no need for any other party, since no one is being exploited. It is only through the party that people can attain positions of power and status. Party membership is limited. The Communists believe that if the party becomes

PARTY AND GOVERNMENT STRUCTURE

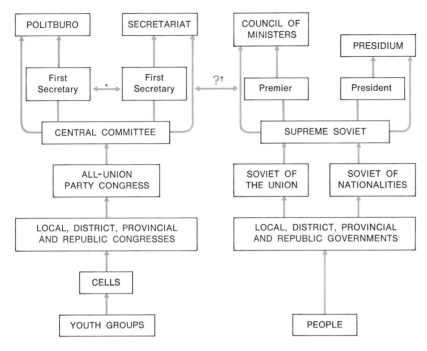

*Most powerful person in government.

†First secretary may be Premier also.

too large, there will be too many disagreements. The quality and discipline of the party will suffer. The party has grown through the years and today over 14 million people hold full party membership. However, this is only 5 percent of the population.

The usual way to become a member is to join the Communist-sponsored youth organization as a child. In the Pioneers (ages 9-14) and the Komsomol (ages 14-20)—the All-Union Lenin League of Communist Youth—young people learn to be good party members and are able to show their abilities. If the young Communists show talent for administration, for carrying out orders, and acting as an example for others, they have a good chance of rising high in the party.

Starting at the foundation of the party are the approximately 360,000 cells of party members. A cell is formed when there are more than three party members. Every Communist must belong to a cell, and these cells honeycomb the whole of Soviet society. Members of cells elect representatives to city or district congresses. They in turn elect representatives to **provincial** congresses who elect representatives to congresses in each republic.

Above these is the All-Union Party Congress, which meets at least once every four years. It is made up of representatives from the republic congresses. The All-Union Party Congress elects the Central Committee, which meets every six months. It contains the major party leaders and is the main executive or policy-making group. The Central Committee then selects a smaller group called the Politburo to actually run the party. The Politburo decides all domestic and foreign policy. It has 15 members and six alternates.

At the top of the Politburo is the first secretary of the party who is also the head of the Secretariat. The Secretariat carries on all administrative business for the party. Through subordinate secretaries the first secretary controls the Communist party and thus the Soviet Union. Stalin became the first secretary in his struggle with Trotsky. In the 1960s, Leonid Brezhnev replaced Nikita Khrushchev in the same post.

domestic policy: government programs that affect a nation at home

GOVERNMENT STRUCTURE

The important leaders of the Communist party occupy the key positions in the government. The placement of Communists in high governmental offices insures that the policies of the party also become the policies of the government. All questions about Soviet life—commerce, agriculture, transportation, conditions of work, housing, and social and cultural life—are first discussed and decided in the top levels of the party.

The people elect the members of the Soviet of the Union and the Soviet of Nationalities. The Soviet of the Union has one deputy for every 300,000 people. The Soviet of the Nationalities has 32 deputies from each of the Union's 15 republics. There are also a few additional ones from smaller territories. These two houses make up the Supreme Soviet of the USSR. In theory, this is the highest lawmaking body in the Soviet Union. In reality it meets two weeks each year to approve new laws that the party has already decided upon.

The Supreme Soviet elects the 33 members of the Presidium, which acts for it when it is not in session. The head of the Presidium is called the president of the USSR. The Supreme Soviet also appoints a group called the Council of Ministers, which is the administrative part of the government. There are 80 different ministries and committees within the Council of Ministers. They see to various parts of Soviet life and are presided over by a chairperson or premier who is the actual head of the government. Occasionally, the post of premier and first secretary of the Communist party are held by the same person, as happened with both Stalin and Khrushchev.

The Supreme Soviet is also responsible for the election of members to the Supreme Court of the USSR. Each republic, province, district, and town has a similar structure of government and courts including a council of ministers and a supreme soviet.

The Communist party places its members in important positions

Lenin looks down as delegates to the All-Union Party Congress approve party policy.

by controlling the selection of candidates for election to the Supreme Soviet. The party also controls the elections. Candidates to be placed on the ballot are carefully screened. One person is finally offered for each position. Generally the candidates are Communists. Some non-Communists are given a place on the ballot, but they are a small percentage.

Voters are required by law to vote. Almost all eligible Soviet citizens vote. On election day voters may either mark their official ballots in an open voting place or go to a secret voting place. If they vote secretly, it is assumed that they are crossing out the name of the official candidate and writing in another name. Use of the secret ballot makes a citizen the object of official suspicion. Few voters are this daring, and the official candidates are elected overwhelmingly. Thus, the great majority of the Supreme Soviet are Communists who have been chosen by the party. Naturally, they will elect or appoint ruling party members to key government posts.

With the defeat of Trotsky and the approval of the 15th Communist Party Congress, Stalin became the undisputed dictator of the Soviet Union. Like Peter the Great, Stalin saw that Russia was far behind the nations of Western Europe. He determined to change the Soviet Union into a major industrial state within his lifetime.

Chapter 3
Change in Direction

STALIN AS FIRST SECRETARY

To accomplish his goal, Stalin discarded Lenin's economic policy and began the first of his **Five-Year Plans**. These Five-Year Plans provided for a planned economy in which all the means of production and the items and quantity to be produced were controlled by the government. This system is called **central planning**.

Stalin moved even farther away from basic Communist theory. He

started a capitalistic system of reward and punishment. If factory managers did not meet government quotas, they were punished. If workers produced more than their quota, they were rewarded with higher wages and paid vacations.

Stalin concentrated his efforts in the area of **heavy industry**: steel, machines, and equipment for making machines. Since he paid little attention to **consumer goods**, the life of the average Russian did not improve much.

Stalin's Five-Year Plans faced serious problems. The USSR had a very poor transportation system and few **skilled** workers. Also vast portions of the Soviet Union were still undeveloped. Stalin put great effort into the development of such areas as Siberia and the Arctic.

COLLECTIVIZATION AND PURGES   The success of Stalin's industrialization program, however, hinged on the agricultural system of the country. Most people in the Soviet Union still made their living by farming. Stalin needed workers for his factories, but he also needed high agricultural production. The Soviets had to grow enough farm produce to feed themselves and have a **surplus**. They were already **exporting** farm products but Stalin wanted more. He needed a large surplus to exchange for modern machinery.

To increase farm production Stalin ordered the peasants to merge their small farms into huge collective farms run by the government. This meant that large farm machinery could be used. The amount of food produced would increase, and the rate of increase could be controlled by the state. The peasants would work the farms together and share the profits.

Most Russian peasants had always hoped to own their own farms. Many had fought for the Communists because the Communists had promised them land. After the revolution, many had received land, but now they were being ordered to give it up. They refused. Stalin responded by executing thousands of rebellious peasants and sending thousands more to labor camps in Siberia.

Conditions grew worse as Russia experienced a severe famine in 1932-1933. In the end Stalin won and the farms became collectives. However, the peasants were allowed to keep some livestock and a little piece of ground for growing vegetables.

It was during this time that Stalin became especially fearful of opposition. He sent his secret police, the NKVD, to spy on and arrest anyone who disagreed with him. This activity climaxed in the purges of 1935-1936. Hundreds of thousands were either executed or sent to Siberian labor camps. The smallest disagreements, even false charges, were used against people. Execution or exile became convenient tools for officials who wished to get rid of personal enemies.

Left: Joseph Stalin taking a stroll in 1925. Can you find any similarities between his government and that of the Romanovs?

The victims included the lowliest peasants as well as high-ranking party members.

Stalin replaced party officials with his own people. In this way he was able to build a police state in which no one dared oppose him. In the midst of this terror, Stalin had the Constitution of 1936 written. This constitution is the legal basis of the Soviet government as it is today.

WORLD WAR II   While Stalin worked to industrialize the Soviet Union and strengthen his power, he tried to avoid conflicts with other countries. During the 1930s, Stalin became fearful of Hitler's rise in Germany and Japan's expansion in the East. Stalin tried to persuade Britain and France to join him in an alliance against Hitler. They refused. Hoping that Hitler might leave the Soviet Union alone, Stalin signed a **nonaggression** pact with Germany in 1939. As a result of one of its clauses, they divided Poland between them.

The pact gave Stalin more time to prepare his nation for war. He became convinced that despite their agreement Hitler was going to attack Russia. To protect Russia's borders, Stalin seized Estonia, Latvia, Lithuania, Moldavia, and part of Finland. He hoped this additional land would act as a buffer between Russia and Germany. His desire to increase Soviet territory also prompted this move.

In June 1941, two years after the pact, Hitler's armies overran the buffer zone and invaded Russia. The USSR entered World War II on the side of the British and the French. Although the Soviets had been preparing for two years, they still were not equipped to meet the German armies head-on. Instead they used the same methods that their ancestors had used against Napoleon. This was the **scorched-earth policy** in which they destroyed everything in front of the invading army. The terrible Russian winter caught the Germans without supplies.

In the meantime, the U.S. had joined the war against Germany and was sending supplies to its Soviet ally. In 1942 the Germans sent reinforcements into Russia. They were stopped by the Soviet army. The turning point of the war came in February 1943 at Stalingrad. The Soviets virtually destroyed the German army. Then they relentlessly pushed the Germans back through Eastern Europe until, in May 1945, the Soviets entered the German capital, Berlin. At the same time the Allies invaded Europe, fought their way across France, and into Germany. The war in Europe was over.

During the war Stalin had met several times with Winston Churchill, the British **prime minister**, and U.S. President Franklin Roosevelt. In these conferences Stalin promised to help the Allies against Japan once the war with Germany was over. It was decided that control of Germany be divided among the USSR, the U.S., Britain, and France. Stalin agreed to participate in the founding of the United Nations. He insisted, as did the U.S., that the major nations have veto power in the Security Council and that the USSR be a permanent member of the Council.

THE COLD WAR   The Soviet Union emerged from World War II as a **superpower**. It was the strongest nation in Europe and second only to the U.S. in the world. Stalin chose this time to begin his own policy of expansion. He wanted to spread communism and to protect Soviet borders from future invasions. He began a policy that was to place large sections of Europe under Communist domination.

After the war, Stalin refused to withdraw his armies from the Eastern European countries through which they had fought. In each country he developed Communist parties. With the help of the Soviet army he placed party members in power. He thought of these nations as Soviet **satellites**, meaning that they were minor bodies linked in orbit to the main body of the USSR. He signed special treaties and economic agreements with them. Europe thus became divided into two blocs—free nations and Communist nations. The Soviet Union and its satellites began to shut themselves off from the rest of the world. Winston Churchill described their action as the lowering of an iron curtain between East and West.

U.S. leaders were especially displeased with Stalin's policies. They requested free elections in Eastern Europe, but the Soviets were determined to maintain their power. From these conflicts developed a period of mutual distrust and antagonism known as the **cold war**. The U.S. formulated a policy of containment to hold back Communist expansion. It provided economic, political, and sometimes military aid to countries faced with Communist takeovers.

antagonism: hostile feelings

Out of this containment policy grew such U.S.-sponsored programs as the Truman Doctrine, which stopped Communism in Greece and Turkey, and the Marshall Plan, which provided economic aid to Western Europe. It also brought about the unification of the British, French, and U.S. sectors of Germany and the founding of the North Atlantic Treaty Organization (NATO) in 1949. This organization was set up for the mutual defense of the U.S., Canada, and ten nations of Western Europe. The Soviets responded by establishing their own programs such as the Communist Information Bureau (COMINFORM) and the Council for Mutual Economic Assistance (COMECON). With the nations of Eastern Europe, the Soviets formed the Warsaw Pact as a defense against NATO.

At home Stalin moved decisively too. The war had left the Soviet Union almost in ruins. As many as 20 million Russians may have died. Stalin introduced his fourth Five-Year Plan. He seized machinery from East Germany, Austria, and Eastern Europe and sent it back to Russia. He used captured German scientists and technicians to help rebuild his war-torn nation. He drove the Soviet people relentlessly. Thousands were sent to slave-labor camps. When he died in 1953, Stalin had rebuilt the Soviet Union and left it with a recovered economy. He had accomplished much but at a terrible price.

FROM COEXISTENCE TO DETENTE

Since Stalin had carefully disposed of any rivals, his death left a gap in Communist leadership. At first a collective leadership was formed in which several men shared power. It included Georgi M. Malenkov, premier or chairman of the Council of Ministers, Lavrenti P. Beria, head of the secret police, and Nikita S. Khrushchev (kroosh-CHOF), who became the first secretary of the Communist party. Beria was arrested the same year, tried, and executed on charges of conspiring to take full control of the Soviet Union.

A power struggle then developed between Malenkov and Khrushchev which resulted in Malenkov's resignation in 1955. He was replaced by Nikolai A. Bulganin, who lasted until 1958 when he was forced to resign. Khrushchev emerged as the sole leader of the Soviet Union. He was both premier and first secretary.

KHRUSHCHEV   Nikita S. Khrushchev had been a coal miner before he became a member of the Communist party in 1918. During the revolution he was active in the Ukraine. He later rose to power in both the Communist party of the Ukraine and the Communist party of the Soviet Union. He used many of the same methods Stalin had used in his rise to power. He made many friends and placed them in high positions. He was trusted by Stalin and worked faithfully for him.

But once Khrushchev was in power, he changed many of Stalin's policies of terror. He realized that times had changed and so should

Every May 1—May Day— the Soviets parade their armaments through Red Square in Moscow. Why would they want other nations to see their weapons?

649

the face of communism. He began a policy of revisionism or change known as de-Stalinization. When Malenkov and Bulganin were forced to resign, they were not executed. They were merely demoted. In 1956, at the 20th Communist Party Congress, Khrushchev denounced Stalin as a dictator, murderer, and a bad leader.

During his rule, Stalin had history books rewritten to glorify himself, placed statues, paintings, and pictures of himself all over the country, and had cities and streets renamed for him. In 1961, at the 22nd Communist Party Congress, Khrushchev attacked Stalin for these actions, or what he called "the cult of personality." Khrushchev had the pictures removed, the history books rewritten, and the names changed again. Stalin's body, which had been placed with Lenin's in a tomb on Red Square, was moved to a simple grave site.

Khrushchev tried to improve the life of the average Soviet citizen. He continued to emphasize industrial development but added consumer goods to the list. However, the Soviet economy was not geared for both consumer goods and heavy industry.

Another problem that Khrushchev faced was lagging farm production. The collective farms were not yet providing enough food. Agricultural products still could not be exchanged for foreign capital. Also there was no extra food for the Soviets themselves in case of a bad crop year, or series of years. Khrushchev made many changes in farm administration, but his biggest effort to increase production was the virgin lands program. He selected sections of southern Siberia and Central Asia to be turned into major food producing areas. To do this, student volunteers and thousands of farm workers were shipped to collective farms in these regions. However, the program did not work immediately, and Soviet agricultural problems remained unsolved.

In world affairs, Khrushchev became a goodwill ambassador for the Soviet Union. He traveled all over the world including the U.S. to promote communication and trade between Communist and free nations.

In 1956 Khrushchev declared a policy of **peaceful coexistence** in which total war was to be avoided. He felt that Communist interests could be expanded by other means. The struggle with capitalist nations would be carried on in the fields of economics, politics, or, if necessary, by limited warfare among third-party nations. He began to use foreign aid to Third World nations—the underdeveloped countries of the Middle East, Asia, Africa, and Latin America—as a weapon against the U.S.

Crises still occurred in Soviet foreign relations. Confrontations occurred with the U.S. over Cuba and the divided Germany. In Germany Khrushchev responded by building the Berlin Wall in 1961. But he was forced to remove Russian missiles from Cuba by President John F. Kennedy the following year.

However, the most bitter dispute that occurred during Khrushchev's

Khrushchev gestures with an ear of corn on his trip across the U.S. in 1959. Compare and contrast his trip with Peter's to the West in the late 1600s.

period in office developed within the Communist bloc. Because the Soviet Union had been the first Communist state, Soviet leaders considered themselves the leaders of world communism. But as other countries became Communist, these countries began to argue with the USSR's claim to leadership. They wanted to promote their own policies. The Chinese Communists became the most vocal opponents of the Soviets. They argued that war was inevitable if capitalism was to be overthrown. They also wanted to actively support Communist activities in Third World nations.

Their private disagreement became public at the 22nd Communist Party Congress in 1961 when the Chinese walked out. Albania joined them. The Soviets withdrew their **foreign aid**. The Chinese, who greatly needed the help, resented this action. Since the early 1960s, the Soviets and Chinese have engaged in bitter battles. Sometimes the battles are waged with words. But fighting has broken out several times along the common border between the Soviet Union and the People's Republic of China.

BREZHNEV—KOSYGIN   Despite improved relations with the West —such as a treaty ban on nuclear weapons tests—many of Khrushchev's policies were not popular among other Communist leaders. The break with the Chinese, the Cuban missile crisis, and problems in his agricultural and industrial programs forced Khrushchev to retire in 1964.

The Politburo once again turned to collective leadership and placed several men in positions of power. The two most influential were Leonid I. Brezhnev, head of the Communist party, and Aleksei N. Kosygin, premier of the government.

Brezhnev (BREZH-nef) had been educated as a metallurgist. During World War II he became active in the Communist party of the Ukraine. With the backing of Khrushchev, he moved up through party ranks as a secretary to various committees. He became a member of the Politburo in 1957 and was president of the Soviet Union from 1960 to 1964. This is a position of status but no power. In 1964 he became first secretary of the Communist party.

Kosygin (kuh-SEE-guhn) specialized in economics and industrial planning. He fought in the Red Army during the Russian civil war of 1917-20. He became a member of the Communist party in 1927. He served on the Politburo and Central Committee until 1952. He was out of power until 1957 when he again became a member of the Politburo.

Brezhnev and Kosygin continued many of Khrushchev's policies but emphasized efficiency and achievement. They modified some aspects of central planning. Factories were to be judged on the basis of their profits, not on how much they produced. The eighth Five-Year Plan set more realistic goals for the economy. Brezhnev and Kosygin tried to achieve a better balance between the production of consumer

In 1960 Khrushchev came to the UN. During an angry debate, he pounded the desk with his shoe. When order was restored, he left the shoe for all to see. Why?

651

Brezhnev (right) and Kosygin are both from the middle class. Discuss this in terms of Marx's theories.

goods and heavy industry. As a result, the **standard of living** in the Soviet Union rose slowly.

 Through the 1960s, Brezhnev and Kosygin continued the policy of peaceful coexistence. They were, however, always anxious to promote the interests of the Soviet Union and communism. Despite their efforts to work with the West, they showed no weakening of their hold on their satellites. This was demonstrated in 1968 when Soviet troops went into Czechoslovakia to stop the movement toward greater personal freedom. The struggle between China and the Soviet Union continued as each tried to exercise control over the Communist world. Each also tried to win over the Third World nations.

 During the late 1960s and early 1970s, Brezhnev emerged as the chief Soviet leader. His ideas went beyond Khrushchev's policy of peaceful coexistence. Brezhnev showed a willingness to maintain world peace through **detente**—a policy of relaxing international tensions through negotiations. Although conflicts occurred between the U.S. and the Soviet Union, major crises were avoided. Sometimes both sides used their influence to achieve a peaceful settlement. One instance was in the Middle East.

In the 1967 Six-Day War, the Soviets supported the Arab cause while the U.S. backed Israel. Despite the Arab defeat, the Soviets continued to arm the Arab nations for the next six years. In fall 1973 war broke out again between Israel and Egypt and Syria. Throughout the war, the Soviets airlifted supplies to the Arab states, and the U.S. supplied Israel. A cease-fire was finally achieved at the urging of the USSR and the U.S.

The policy of detente was strengthened in the early 1970s by several summit conferences between Brezhnev and U.S. presidents. Trade agreements and the Strategic Arms Limitation Treaty (SALT) to limit nuclear weapons were signed. To promote detente among European countries, the Soviets also participated in the continuing Conference on Security and Cooperation in Europe in the 1970s.

Summing Up the Unit

Social Studies Vocabulary

Define: communism; capitalism; means of production; bourgeoisie; provisional government; socialism; central planning; heavy industry; consumer goods; surplus; nonaggression; scorched-earth policy; superpower; cold war; peaceful coexistence; detente

People

Identify: Nicholas II; Bolsheviks; Marx; Engels; Lenin; Stalin; Trotsky; Khrushchev; Brezhnev; Kosygin

Words

Communist Manifesto; Das Kapital; dictatorship of the proletariat; Bloody Sunday; Duma; soviets; Red Guard; Red Army; commissar; third International; NKVD; NATO; COMINFORM: COMECON; Warsaw Pact; SALT

Questions

1. How did Marx believe capitalism would be overthrown? b. What kind of countries did he believe would fall to communism first?
2. a. What were three effects of World War I on the Russian homefront? b. What began the Russian Revolution?
3. How did Lenin's government differ in practice from Marxist theory?
4. By what methods did Stalin become undisputed dictator of the Soviet Union? b. Over what did Stalin and Trotsky disagree?
5. a. What is the organizational structure of the Communist party? b. of the government? (Use the chart as reference.)
6. How does the practice of Soviet government differ from its constitution?
7. a. What was Stalin's goal for the Soviet Union? b. How did it affect the lives of the people? c. The lack of what two factors created problems for the Five-Year Plans?
8. a. How did Stalin expand his power at home? b. abroad?

9. a. Name one similarity between Stalin's and Khrushchev's rises to power. b. Name five ways in which their policies differed.
10. How did Brezhnev and Kosygin's leadership resemble Khrushchev's? b. In what way did Brezhnev's differ from Khrushchev's?

Discussion Topics

1. Karl Marx claimed that workers would no longer be exploited once communism replaced capitalism. Workers would receive the full profit of what they produced. Has communism in the USSR supported Marx's view? Why or why not? If workers are still exploited, who are the exploiters?
2. When Lenin returned from exile in 1917, he brought along several promises. Did Lenin's communism accomplish the things he promised?
3. Marx interpreted all history according to his theory of struggle between economic classes. Can all change in history be explained entirely by economic reasons? Are noneconomic factors also important? If so, what are these other factors?
4. The USSR has a different type of government in practice than it has in theory. How does the role of the Communist party account for this?

Project Ideas

1. Give an oral report on one of the following describing how he affected or changed communism in Russia: Marx, Lenin, Trotsky, Stalin, Khrushchev, Brezhnev.
2. Hold a debate on peaceful coexistence, detente, and arms limitations between the U.S. and USSR. Plan the debate so that the pros and cons of using a tough approach by the U.S. versus a cooperative one are brought out. Consider these questions: Why have the U.S. and USSR been opponents in the cold war? Is it in the best interests of each nation to ease international tensions and limit the arms race? Can both nations agree to limit arms without endangering their security? If agreements are reached, can the two nations trust each other to keep the agreement? If so, how can either nation be sure of the other? If not, why not?

653

Unit IV

Life in the Soviet Union

St. Basil's Cathedral in Red Square, Moscow, was built by Ivan the Terrible to celebrate his victory over the Mongols. Today it is a museum.

The Russian Revolution brought more than a change in rulers. The new Communist leaders wished not only to reshape the forms of government but also to shape a new kind of society. This society would conform to the teachings of communism and would produce a new kind of person—the ideal Soviet citizen. To create this ideal, all non-Communist influences would be stamped out. Despite these efforts, differences continue to exist.

Lenin established the new Soviet state on a Communist economy. However, he found it unsatisfactory and modified it with his New Economic Policy. When Stalin rose to power, he began his Five-Year Plans. He set as his goals rapid industrialization and high agricultural production. At the time, it was considered very daring to try long-range planning of a nation's whole economy.

Today through its centrally planned economy the Soviet state owns and controls all the nation's resources—mines, factories, the transportation system, and power plants. The state also owns or controls most of the retail trade, the marketing system, domestic and foreign commerce, and most of the land. There is, however, still some personal property in the USSR. People may own automobiles and home furnishings but not the land on which their houses are built.

Chapter 1
The Economy

AGRICULTURE

Agriculture is the weakest part of the Soviet economy. The country cannot produce enough food to feed its expanding population. This is true even though one-third of the total labor force are farm workers.

Part of the problem is the geographical location of the Soviet Union. Where the land is fertile, the rainfall is uncertain. One year may bring an abundance of rain, and the next year a drought. Also much of the land lies above 50° north latitude where crops can be grown only in the short summer periods. Soviet scientists are working to develop quick-growing crops and improve land use and irrigation. But the process is slow and frustrating.

Despite these geographical limitations, Russia exported farm products before World War I. Since Stalin forced Soviet farmers onto collectives, the Soviet Union has turned into an **importer** of farm products.

Today there are two kinds of farms in the Soviet Union, the collective and the state. On collective farms, a number of families work together. Each farm is run by a chairperson who makes sure the farm delivers its quota as assigned by the state. Also a farmer cannot move from a collective without the chairperson's permission.

The collective's produce is sold to the state at a price fixed by the state. The state then sells the produce to consumers through state-operated stores. A small amount of collective farm produce may be sold on the open market. The money is shared among the farmers. Fees for insurance, building, and the cost of machinery and certain other items are deducted and the farmers share any money left.

Soviet leaders have found that the collective farm system does not provide enough incentive to farmers to produce the quantity and quality desired. Farmers need to work for more than the good of the state and the small uncertain profits of communal labor. For this reason, members of collective farms are permitted to have private gardens. These gardens vary in size according to the region of the USSR.

communal: public, shared

The director of an experimental farm looks over the harvest. Collectives and state farms have never produced enough food to satisfy Soviet needs.

Farmers may grow vegetables, or whatever else they can eat or sell. Farmers are also permitted to own a cow, several sheep, a pig, and all the poultry they can raise. The products of these backyard gardens are sold on the open market rather than in state stores.

The average size of state farms is around 30,000 hectares (75,000 acres). On state farms members are paid like factory workers. Each is paid according to the kind and amount of work done. Besides monthly wages, workers are entitled to paid vacations, sick pay, and a pension. The Soviets have found this kind of farm to be more productive than collectives.

Since agriculture has remained such a problem, Soviet leaders have been forced to give it a high priority. When Khrushchev was in power, he made reforms designed to improve working conditions and morale. He increased prices for produce. Instead of the central planning committee in Moscow telling farmers what and how to plant, local authorities were given the choice of planting what they thought was best suited to their particular climate and soil. These reforms helped. However, Khrushchev did not solve the farm problem, and this failure contributed to his downfall.

Under Brezhnev and Kosygin, the production of collective farms has improved. Quotas were lowered and wages were increased significantly. As a result, workers began to give as much time to the collectives as they gave to their private plots. However, as recently as the early 1970s, the USSR had to import large amounts of grain.

PLANNERS AND INDUSTRY

The industrialization of the Soviet Union had begun before the Communist takeover. By World War I the USSR was the fifth-ranking industrial nation in the world and possessed a growing number of engineers and scientists. The move to industrialize was helped by the enormous natural resources of the Soviet Union. It possesses every metal needed for industry except tin. Its deposits of coal, iron ore, and oil are huge.

Since Stalin Soviet leaders have used central planning to establish goals for industry. The top planning commission is located in Moscow. Below it are regional councils that coordinate the plans of all industries in the region. Next in line are the local factories. Plans go up from the lower levels, and plans come down from the higher levels. The plans which come down from Moscow are the ultimate authority for each factory. They set the yearly quotas and production plans. The government expects its directions to be followed because the state owns all factories.

Soviet leaders have concentrated on building industries to serve other industries rather than people. Until recently they were not concerned with producing consumer goods. Power plants and dams, trucks, machine tools, and military equipment were emphasized. The government said the people could sacrifice for the future.

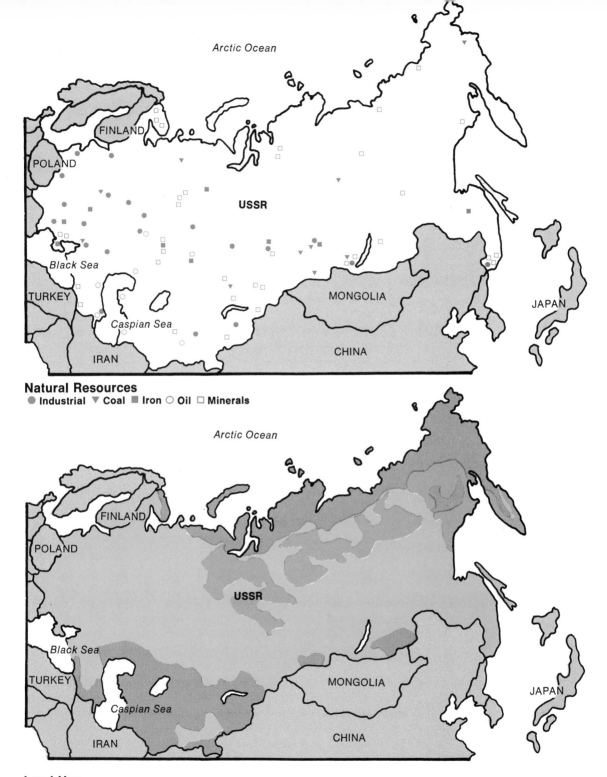

Natural Resources
● Industrial ▼ Coal ■ Iron ○ Oil □ Minerals

Land Use
▫ Farming ▪ Forestry ▪ Grazing

After devising the Periodic Chart, Dmitri Mendeleev continued his research. This drawing shows him making a balloon flight in 1887 to study the atmosphere.

Because of the emphasis upon building for the future, ordinary citizens of the USSR have a low standard of living compared to U.S. citizens. Soviet wages are low, and the workers are not permitted to strike to raise them. Officials explain that a strike is impossible. The workers would be striking against themselves because ultimately they own the factories in which they work.

Unions do exist in the USSR, and they are free to complain about work conditions, poor cafeteria food, and similar matters. **Unions** are also used to help settle disputes and to promote production. There is little unemployment in the Soviet Union. The person who does not work does not eat.

Many consumer goods still are not available. Those that can be found are often very expensive and poorly made. A person usually has to wait several years to get a car or refrigerator, if he or she can afford it. As a result a black market has grown up to supply the great demand for consumer goods. Anyone caught dealing in the black market, however, is severely punished. It should be noted that the standard of living has risen since the time of the czars.

Under Brezhnev and Kosygin, some **decentralization** of the economy has occurred. More freedom is now given to plant managers in terms of what and how much they produce and the number of workers in their plants. Many factories are now judged on the basis of how much of their product is sold and how much profit is made. Workers receive part of the profits as incentive pay. Old-line **bureaucratic** planners fear decentralization. They see it as a threat to their power and speak of creeping capitalism. However, in industry the Soviet Union now ranks second only to the U.S.

TECHNOLOGY AND SCIENCE

In 1725 the Imperial Academy of Sciences was founded in Russia to promote scientific achievement. This is one of the oldest scientific groups in the world.

Under the czars, Russia produced such great scientists as Mendeleev, Metchnikoff, and Pavlov. In 1869 Dmitri Mendeleev created a system for classifying chemical elements according to their atomic weight and properties. Ilya Metchnikoff received the Nobel Prize for medicine in 1908. His research showed how white blood corpuscles fight and kill bacteria within the body.

Probably the best-known Russian scientist is Ivan Pavlov who won the Nobel Prize in 1904 for physiology. Pavlov studied conditioned reflexes and used dogs to show how habits are learned unconsciously. His work made a major contribution to psychology and the theory of learning.

When the Communists took control of the government, many scientists and technicians left Russia. However, the Soviet government has done a great deal to encourage scientific work. They reorganized

To encourage the study and development of Siberia, the USSR's Academy of Sciences has built a science city near Novosibirsk, in the Siberian wilderness. In the background are apartments for research scientists.

the Imperial Academy into the Academy of Sciences of the USSR. This academy controls research in fields as varied as science, engineering, literature, and history. The Soviet government funds most research and has built and equipped great scientific laboratories. Scientific research has become a part of the Five-Year Plans. This action stopped people from duplicating one another's work but it also hampered experimentation.

Soviet science is oriented toward the practical. Scientists and technicians are used to solve specific problems in industry, weaponry, and agriculture. For example, a great deal of work is done on trans-

The first man and the first woman in space were Soviet citizens. Yuri Gagarin and Valentina Tereshkova each orbited the earth in the early 1960s.

portation, **pollution**, food supplies, and fuel and energy. By the 1970s, the Soviets were experimenting with water heaters, refrigerators, portable wells, heaters, and air conditioners operated by solar energy. Sometimes, however, scientists can be hindered by too much planning.

To ease this situation and yet continue to solve practical problems, the Siberian branch of the Academy of Sciences established a science city near Novosibirsk (noh-voh-suh-BIRSK). The center contains separate institutes for each of the sciences. Each institute is free to experiment as much as its members want. The goal is the study and development of Siberia.

Siberia holds great natural resources which the Soviet Union needs. It is believed that their discovery and development for industrial use is possible only through science. This plan is proving so successful that other science cities are being planned.

The Soviets have demonstrated their greatest scientific skill in the fields of military weaponry and space technology. During World War II, Stalin became aware that both the U.S. and Germany were developing atomic weapons. He used all available Soviet resources to develop this power. In 1949 the first Soviet atomic bomb was exploded. This was followed by the explosion of a hydrogen bomb in 1951.

Russians were the first to launch a space craft. In 1957 they put aloft Sputnik I. They followed this with Yuri Gagarin's orbit of the earth in 1961. In 1963 the Soviets sent the first woman, Valentina Tereshkova, into space. Although the Soviets did not reach the moon first, they have landed spacecrafts, obtained lunar dust and rock samples, and returned them to earth. In 1975 they launched a joint space venture with the U.S. These scientific achievements have won worldwide acclaim for the Soviet Union. However, they have been a heavy drain on its economy.

Chapter 2
Society

Under communism the Soviet Union has produced its own unique society. Most Soviet citizens have a similar standard of living and are entitled to equal social welfare benefits, such as free medical care. Supposedly there is freedom of opportunity. One's ability is all that is important. Education is encouraged and free to everyone. Soviet women participate fully in all areas of Soviet society. However, the Soviet Union does have differences. It is a nation of many peoples. There are over a hundred ethnic groups within its 15 republics.

NATIONALITIES

Seventy-five percent of the Soviet population are Great Russian, Byelorussian, or Ukrainian. These three groups are Slavic in origin. The other 12 republics represent other major nationality groupings. They were set up to give a sense of self-determination to non-Slavs. However, it is chiefly the descendants of the Slavs who rule and enjoy the better life.

The largest group in the Soviet Union is made up of Great Russians. They live in the largest republic, the Russian Soviet Federated Socialist Republic or Great Russia. It stretches across the northern part of the USSR from the Ukraine to the Bering Sea and includes Siberia. Russia's largest city, Moscow, is located within this republic. It is from there that the Communist party rules. The language and customs of the Great Russians dominate the rest of the Soviet Union.

Byelorussia, or White Russia, is located on the steppes between Great Russia and Poland. The Ukraine—or Little Russia—is the section of the Soviet Union just north of the Black Sea. This was the first home of Russian culture. Kiev, the first Russian capital, is now the capital of the Ukraine. The Ukrainians, while similar to the Great Russians and Byelorussians in language, religion, and customs, are very independent. Since the 1300s they have fought various countries for their freedom. Under Soviet rule they continue to be restless.

As Russia expanded its borders, many non-Slavic peoples became part of the country. The history of a number of these peoples goes back farther than that of the Slavs. They have their own language, culture, and customs. Over the centuries, the non-Slavs became resentful and bitter as the Slavs and later the Russians came to dominate them. Under the policy of Russification, they were frequently persecuted.

Many of these groups joined the Revolution of 1917. They saw in the downfall of the czar an opportunity to be independent again. But the Communists soon imposed their own rule. Non-Slavs could have cultural but not political independence. They were permitted to teach their languages in schools and use them in newspapers. They could keep their styles of dress, their arts, and their customs so long as they did not interfere with communism. However, the content of education and writing and the economic way of life had to be Communist.

Many of these groups, however, wanted more than the Communists allowed. When the Germans invaded the Soviet Union in World War II, some of these groups—such as the descendants of the Mongols in the Crimea—joined them. When the German armies retreated, the Soviet rulers took their revenge. The rebellious groups were uprooted from their homelands and scattered throughout the USSR. Recently some have been allowed to return to their lands.

Through the government and the Communist party of each republic, the nationalities are being bound ever more closely to the national state of the Soviet Union. In addition, indoctrination in the party line, teaching the same material in all schools, and the migration of Slavic peoples throughout the USSR are loosening ethnic ties.

Along with Great Russia, Byelorussia, and the Ukraine, the four republics of Moldavia, Estonia, Latvia, and Lithuania (lith-uh-WAY-nee-uh) lie within the European area of the Soviet Union. Moldavia

Ukrainian girls in native dress and an old man of Turkmenistan in his wool cap reflect their ethnic origins.

is on the Romanian border. The people speak a form of Romanian and share much of the cultural **heritage** of the Romanians.

Estonia, Latvia, and Lithuania are on the Baltic Sea. These tiny countries have been dominated for centuries by the Poles, the Swedes, and the Russians. After World War I they declared their independence but were retaken by the Soviet Union in 1940. The U.S. government does not recognize Estonia, Latvia, or Lithuania as socialist republics. Primarily agricultural areas, they enjoy one of the highest standards of living in the USSR. Each republic has its own language.

The Transcaucasus is the home of many ancient peoples. Lying between Europe and Asia, its population is a mixture of both. In 1936 the Transcaucasus was divided into three republics—Armenia, Georgia, and Azerbaijan. Armenia (ahr-MEE-nee-uh), on the Turkish-Iranian border, has a long history of invasion and persecution. Georgia has its own language, which is unrelated to any other known language in the world, and its own alphabet. The people of Azerbaijan (AH-zuhr-by-jahn) speak a Turkic language and are primarily Muslims.

The area that comprises the Central Asian republics was originally known as Turkestan. For centuries Russia, China, Iran, and Afghanistan fought over it. The land became part of Russia in the 1800s when the czars expanded southward. The people are descendants of Turkish nomads. They had not divided themselves into separate regions until they were forced to do so by the Communists. The various nationalities are similar, but the Soviet government emphasizes their differences. The Central Asians are still primarily nomads. However, the Soviet government is trying to settle them on farms. But the effort is meeting with resistance. It wants the people to identify with the state rather than with their tribes. The five republics are: Kazakhstan (kuh-zak-STAN), Turkmenistan (turk-me-ni-STAN), Uzbekistan (uz-bek-i-STAN), Tadzhikistan (tah-jik-i-STAN), and Kirgizia (kir-GEE-zhee-uh). All are Turkic-speaking except for Tadzhikistan. There the people speak a form of Persian.

The people are predominantly Muslim, and their culture is closely tied to their religion. While not encouraging the religious aspects, the Soviet government has tried to keep alive the cultural heritage of the region. Each republic has been encouraged to develop its own distinct written language with Russian as a second language. This along with increased **literacy** has produced a native literature.

Artistically, this area is famous for its beautiful carpets and architecture. The architecture is best seen in the mosques—Muslim buildings of worship—which the republics are preserving.

ECONOMIC AND SOCIAL GROUPINGS

According to Communism history is an unfolding drama of conflict between different classes in society. The triumph of communism would mean the abolition of classes and the disappearance of conflict. But people do not always evolve according to a formula. New classes

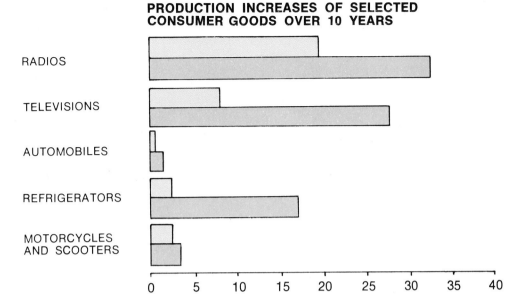

PRODUCTION INCREASES OF SELECTED CONSUMER GOODS OVER 10 YEARS

RADIOS

TELEVISIONS

AUTOMOBILES

REFRIGERATORS

MOTORCYCLES
AND SCOOTERS

0   5   10   15   20   25   30   35   40

Number of goods per 1000 population

Source: *The Europa Year Book 1974: A World Survey* (Europa Publications, London); *Information USSR*, compiled and edited by Robert Maxwell (Pergamon Press, 1962)

have emerged in the Soviet Union. There may not be private ownership of the means of production, but there are those who control production. And they are the upper class.

At the top of Soviet society are the members of the Politburo and the Presidium, the members of the Council of Ministers, and ranking Communist leaders and officials. At this level also are generals and the most outstanding artists, writers, and scientists. They are few— less than one percent of the population. They live in fine houses or apartments, are driven in chauffeured cars, and have villas in the country or at the seaside.

The next group consists of the second level of Communist leaders. These are managers of industry, the planners, high officials, engineers, university professors, artists, and scientists. They too are well paid and have country houses. They vacation in mild climates, attend operas and ballets, and generally enjoy the good life. This is the Soviet middle class. They are slightly less than one-tenth of the total population of the country.

Lower down are the men and women who are technicians, factory supervisors, better paid clerks, and others of similar rank. They make up the lower middle class. Often they live with their families in an apartment in the city or in a small house in a village. In the city two or more families may share an apartment. Each family has one room and shares the kitchen and the bathroom. Sometimes older buildings lack modern conveniences. Many high-rise apartment buildings have no elevators. A telephone is a real luxury.

663

At the end of a long cold winter, Russians, like many other peoples, take to the outdoors at the first hint of spring.

Meat, eggs, and vegetables are expensive. Both the husband and wife must work in order to meet expenses. After paying for food and rent, there is little money left for entertainment. However, many kinds of entertainment like movies and the theater are free or very cheap. The Soviet people also spend much of their time reading. Many books are available although all must be approved by the government. The lower middle class makes up between 30 and 40 percent of the population.

At the bottom of the social scale are the poor workers and farmers. These people do not starve, but their life is hard. They must budget very carefully, and the daily routine of making a living occupies much of their time. However, many of them feel that their standard of living is improving. They hope the future of their children will be even better.

Because there are economic differences in the Soviet Union, there are also social differences. These differences result in growing gaps between the classes. Members of a group tend to follow similar ways of life and to associate only with others of that group. Through education and/or membership in the Communist party, it is possible to climb to a higher level. Young, ambitious, loyal, intelligent Communists have a good chance of raising themselves and their families to the upper levels of Soviet society.

SOVIET WOMEN

Equality for women in the USSR is a reality. They make up more than half of the total labor force. There are few fields of labor, skilled or unskilled, professional or nonprofessional, in which women do not work. Over 70 percent of the doctors and teachers of the USSR are women. Women are a sizeable minority in engineering, in the technology of agriculture, and in economics. Women are also playing a part in the Communist party and Soviet government. They have risen high in the ranks of both. They also sweep streets, shovel snow, drive tractors, and dig ditches. And they receive equal pay for equal work.

Women **monopolize** the medical profession. In recent years Soviet health care has improved significantly. Epidemic diseases, such as cholera, have been virtually wiped out. Infant and maternity care have improved greatly. Venereal disease has been controlled. The life expectancy in the Soviet Union is now 70 years of age. Medical care, including hospitalization, is provided free by the state. Medicine can be purchased at a minimal cost. Doctors are employed by the state but may practice privately if they wish. However, they are taxed heavily for this extra income.

epidemic diseases: diseases that quickly spread among a group

The Soviet government has encouraged women to work for several reasons. During World War II, the Soviet Union lost an estimated 20 million people. This left five women for every man. As a result there was an acute labor shortage. Women were needed to fill the vacancies. Today many women work to help support their families. But most importantly, the Soviet government considers women a valuable national resource that should be used.

Men and women are treated equally under Soviet law. They may marry or vote when they are 18. Divorce is granted automatically if both partners agree and there are no children. Property is divided equally between husband and wife. If children are involved, the matter must go to a people's court for a ruling. A month is usually provided for reconciliation. If agreement cannot be reached, a divorce is granted. The court then decides who should have custody of the children and how the property should be divided.

Like many other modern working mothers and wives, Soviet women have problems in taking care of their families. The state has tried to ease their burden. There is a network of government-run nurseries and kindergartens where working mothers may take their small children for the working day. Parents pay part of the cost of these schools, but the majority of the cost is paid by the state.

The Soviet government gives financial assistance and prestige to mothers. Pregnant women are given paid maternity leaves and cannot be fired from their jobs. Women with large families are given special awards. A child allowance is paid to mothers after their third child. Abortion, however, is legal.

EDUCATION

Under the czars, most Russians were **illiterate**. After the Revolution, education became of major importance. The Communists wanted the USSR to become an industrialized country and a world power. Soviet leaders also wanted to produce the New Soviet Citizen. This person would have to be taught proper Communist values. To achieve these purposes, the people would have to be able to read and write. Today the Soviet Union has achieved almost total literacy. In fact, reading has become a national pastime in the Soviet Union.

All schools in the Soviet Union follow a course of study prepared by the Ministry of Education. Soviet students generally have a longer school day and year than U.S. students do. Most Soviet students begin their education in state-operated nurseries and kindergartens. At the age of seven they are enrolled in a four-year primary school. After that, they go to an incomplete secondary school for another four years. Most students do not go beyond this level.

Students who stop their schooling after ten years can never hope to rise to very high positions. Even secondary or high school graduates cannot look forward to much advancement. It is university graduates for whom the future holds greatest promise. Entrance requirements are very difficult. Admission is based on the student's school record, entrance examinations, and political reliability. Students who are lucky enough to enter a university and study engineering or one of the sciences are given special living allowances.

The Soviet Olympic ice hockey team lines up for a photo. Ice hockey began in Canada, but the Russians have won many world championships.

Soviets compete in many sports. Here a speed skater and a cross country ski racer show their determination. Do you think governments should support athletes?

At this higher level, the Communists are chiefly interested in producing engineers and scientists. These are the main roads to advancement. The Soviet Union produces more scientists than the U.S. and three times as many engineers. The humanities are neglected.

SPORTS

The Soviet people in general are athletic. Sports are emphasized in schools, youth groups, at work, and on vacation. The government believes that physical fitness and good health produce better workers and soldiers. It sponsors physical fitness programs under the slogan "Ready for Labor and Defense." Soviet workers do exercises on their work breaks instead of drinking coffee.

As can be expected in their climate, the Soviet people are great fans of skiing, ice hockey, and skating. They also enjoy hunting, fishing, and swimming. Their beaches are mobbed in summer and many Russians swim in outdoor pools in winter. The national sport is soccer, and most Soviets are devoted fans of some soccer team.

Through its youth organizations, the government supervises all athletics. Officials are able to select and train the best youths. These then compete in such world competitions as the Olympic Games. The Soviets, especially women athletes, have been very successful in these events. All athletes in the Soviet Union are considered amateurs, but those groomed for competition are supported by the government.

Chapter 3
Religion

The Cathedral of the Annunciation was built by Ivan the Great. It stands within the walls of the Kremlin in Moscow. The Kremlin—which means fort—was once the home of the royal family and later of the Soviet government. In 1955 the entire area was made a museum.

Kievan Russia gained great wealth through its trade with the Byzantine Empire. At the same time, the Russians opened themselves to the attractions of Byzantine civilization, especially its religion.

The official religion of the Byzantine Empire was Eastern Orthodox Christianity. Originally Christianity had been united. But between 313 A.D., when the Emperor Constantine made Christianity the official religion of the Roman Empire, and 1054, eastern and western Europeans had gradually drifted apart. They disagreed over their politics, their cultures, and the interpretation of their religion. In 1054 a split occurred between eastern and western Christians. The eastern Christians followed the patriarch in Constantinople, and the western Christians obeyed the pope in Rome.

Originally the Russians had chosen to follow the Orthodox Christianity of the Byzantine Empire. In the split the Russians remained loyal to the Orthodox Church.

THE RUSSIAN CHURCH

The Russians had worshipped nature until around the 980s when Prince Vladimir I of Kiev became a Christian. He wanted his people to follow some religion but he was unable to choose among the Muslim, Jewish, and Christian faiths. He sent out an expedition to find the best religion for his people.

These men went to religious services all over the known world. They reported to Vladimir that the most magnificent ceremonies were held at the Orthodox Cathedral of St. Sophia in Constantinople. The ritual, sincerity of worship, and beautiful churches of the Eastern Orthodox faith overwhelmed Vladimir's agents. After Vladimir was baptized a Christian, he had his subjects baptized. Eastern Orthodox Christianity became the official religion of Russia.

Russian life was vastly changed by the Orthodox Church. Morals, family and national attitudes, laws, language, literature, and art were all shaped and colored by the Russians' conversion. The Russians had no written language of their own, so they used the Slavic or Cyrillic (suh-RIL-lik) alphabet created by Byzantine missionaries. Byzantine priests opened schools and taught religion, reading, and writing. It was from these schools that the first Russian literature was produced. First came religious books and next historical works such as the *Primary* **Chronicle**. The Russians also began to use the ancient Roman laws that the Byzantines had preserved. The Russians codified the laws and called the system the *Russkaya Pravada.*

THE CHURCH AND THE CZARS   With the development of the Russian state and of the power of the czars, the Church grew stronger. It developed close ties with the government. During the Time of Troubles the Church provided unity and kept learning and culture alive.

However, with the beginning of the Romanov **dynasty**, changes occurred within the Orthodox Church that were to tear it apart. The Church emphasized ritual and ceremony. Many peasants and clergy believed that any change in this ritual would be heresy. In 1652 Czar Alexis appointed as head of the Church in Russia, Patriarch Nikon, who began certain reforms. The real split, however, came the following year when the Ukraine became part of Russia.

The Ukrainians demanded some changes if they were to join the Russian Orthodox Church. Patriarch Nikon agreed to a **compromise**, but thousands of Russians left the Church rather than change.

These dissenters came to be called Old Believers. The Old Believers were persecuted by both the Church and the government. Thousands were tortured and killed. Old Believers considered it their mission to preserve the old and traditional forms of the Russian Church. They could not agree, however, and split into various small groups. Descendants of these groups still live in Russia today.

When Peter the Great became czar, he abolished the position of patriarch. Instead he established a synod, or group of men loyal to him, to govern the Church. Under Alexander I, the Orthodox, Old Believers, and Roman Catholics agreed to teach that the czar was

heresy: a conflict with the official teaching of a religion

chosen by God to rule. The people were to consider the czar their Little Father.

Because of their close link with the czar, the clergy grew into a powerful class. Monasteries became centers of culture and education. Monks became owners of large tracts of land. As their wealth increased, they became more closely tied to the nobility. This had a corrupting influence on the Church.

The life of parish priests, however, was very different. They were generally very close to the peasants. They themselves were peasants. To support themselves and their families, they worked in the fields alongside their parishioners. However, because some parish priests were uneducated, they could not always provide the religious training that the people needed. Sometimes their religion bordered on superstition. Occasionally priests led or joined the people in various revolts. For the most part, however, the Church supported the czars and their policies.

COMMUNIST PERSECUTION The Communists believe the basic assumptions of religion to be false. They consider religion to be as Karl Marx described it: "the opium of the people." They disliked the clergy and hated the Church because it had been tied to the czars. When the Communists came to power, they **nationalized** Church property, seized Church valuables, forbade priests to teach, sent many into exile, and imprisoned others. Churches were made into museums or taxed so heavily that they closed.

Persecution continued under Stalin. For a time the children of priests could not obtain a university education. Nor could children under 18 be taught religion except at home and in groups of three or less. Only people who cared little for their careers and their lives dared to practice religion openly.

When World War II broke out, relations with the Church improved. Support from all the people was needed if the enemy were to be defeated. It was unwise for the government to antagonize any part of the population. Since that time, persecution has eased. However, the Soviet government still discourages religion. Religious organizations must register with the government and are then investigated. If a person attends religious services, the government sends someone to try to persuade him or her to stop. Children are not allowed to receive religious instruction. The Church is allowed only three schools in which to train its priests.

Because of the persecution, the number of people who are members of the Russian Orthodox Church is unknown. Estimates vary from 25 to 45 million. Because of fear many do not practice their religion openly. However, religious activity appears to be on the increase. Some groups are openly demanding religious freedom.

Russia's policies of expansion brought many new peoples and new religions into the Soviet Union. From Catherine the Great on, rulers tried to force these people to accept the Orthodox Church. Many, however, continued to practice their own religions. Later the Communists made it as difficult for them as for members of the Orthodox Church. Yet the Armenians and Georgians each have their own churches. Roman Catholicism and several Protestant denominations are also represented in the Soviet Union. But Judaism and Islam are the most important religions.

JUDAISM

The Jews, as a group, have been especially persecuted. Before the rise of Kievan Russia, there were groups of Jews, including the Khazars, living in the area. During the 1500s many Jews settled in Poland and the Ukraine. In the 1600s the Cossacks killed thousands of them. When these areas became part of Russia, the persecutions continued.

Jews were allowed to live only in certain places in Russia. They were not permitted to join some professions. Usually they could not own land and only a limited number were allowed to go to school. Jews could not observe their Sabbath, which falls on Saturday, because they were supposed to work. At times their synagogues and schools for training rabbis were closed.

Periodically, these persecutions became violent. They then became known as pogroms (POH-gruhms), a Russian word meaning devasta-

Only a few synagogues are open in the USSR. In the early 1970s, Jews who attended services sometimes faced hostile crowds when they left.

tion. During a pogrom, Russians would turn on their fellow Jewish citizens, burn their houses, and kill thousands of them. The pogroms became especially violent during the 1880s and just before the Russian Revolution. The czars tried to blame the Jews for the social unrest. During pogroms, several million Jews fled to other countries, especially the U.S. Many Jews, such as Trotsky, participated in the Revolution. However, during his purges, Stalin killed many of these revolutionaries. When the Nazis invaded the USSR in World War II, they massacred many more Jews.

Between two and three million Jews still live in the Soviet Union. This is the largest number outside Israel and the U.S. Anti-Semitism is still strong, however. Few Jews are allowed to hold government positions, but they have produced some of Russia's leading scientists and artists.

Since the USSR has generally followed a pro-Arab policy in the Middle East, many Jews have not been allowed to emigrate to Israel. The U.S. has voiced strong protests against this policy. Many groups within the U.S. actively support a movement to free Soviet Jews.

ISLAM

When Central Asia was conquered by the czars in the 1800s, millions of Muslims became citizens of Russia. At that time they were severely persecuted. Many fled. Today, however, Muslims are the second largest religious group after the Orthodox Church. They number about 20 million.

Like other religious groups, Muslims have difficulty in practicing their religion, especially their feast of Ramadan. During Ramadan, they are supposed to fast for a month. The Communists claim this interferes with work. Muslims also have difficulty in observing their day of assembly, which falls on Friday, and in going to their mosques to pray several times a day. Many mosques have been closed.

Chapter 4
The Arts

Prior to the time of Peter the Great, the Russian arts were closely tied to the Orthodox Church and the Byzantine Empire. Russia also had a strong folk culture. When Peter became czar, he ended Russia's isolation from Western Europe. Western culture, however, reached only the educated classes. Catherine the Great continued to bring Western influences into Russia. But Russian rulers were quick to censor any foreign ideas that might interfere with their power. They also executed or sent into exile artists who opposed them.

Russian cultural achievements reached their peak in the 1800s. Much of this work, especially in literature, spoke out against the czars and demanded government reform.

After the Revolution, artists were told that their works should reflect

Communist ideals. In the 1930s, through the Ministry of Culture, Stalin took control of the arts. He and ministry officials decided what would and would not be published or shown. The Union of Writers was established in 1932. All Soviet writers who wanted to publish had to belong.

Stalin and the Communist party advocated a policy of socialist realism. According to this philosophy, the only purpose of art was to glorify communism and to inspire Communist ideals. Art had to be understandable and available to everyone. It should reflect the reality of the socialist state. This concept of socialist realism characterizes and restricts Soviet artists to this day.

WRITERS AS SOCIAL CRITICS

The Russians have a rich treasury of great literature. One of their greatest writers is Alexander Pushkin who lived from 1799 to 1837. One of his ancestors was an African prince who had been presented as a gift to Peter the Great. The latter freed him. Pushkin wrote about the life and history of the Russian people. One of his best works is *Boris Godunov.* Pushkin laid the foundation of Russian national literature but was forced to live in exile because of his liberal ideas.

The greatest writers of the 1800s used their works to expose the political and social corruption of czarist Russia. One of these writers was Nikolai Gogol, who is considered the father of the Russian novel. In *Dead Souls* he dealt with such issues as serfdom and in the play *The Inspector-General* with the corruption of the government.

Ivan Turgenev, a follower of Gogol, also dealt with the hardship of the serfs in *A Sportsman's Sketches.* This work was considered vital in gaining the emancipation of the serfs. In his masterpiece, *Fathers and Sons,* Turgenev studies the impact of Western thought on Russia. This period also produced Anton Chekhov. Chekhov portrayed the inactivity and stagnation of the nobility in *The Cherry Orchard.*

Perhaps the two greatest Russian writers were Feodor Dostoevski and Count Leo Tolstoy. In his youth Dostoevski (dahs-tuh-YEF-skee) was a member of a secret society. He was caught and sentenced to

Dostoevski (left) was one of Russia's greatest writers. Beside him is part of the handwritten manuscript for his novel The Brothers Karamazov. *I. Repin, the 19th-century realist, painted the portrait of composer Moussorgsky.*

673

Solzhenitsyn talks to the press in Switzerland after his deportation. Why do you think Soviet leaders deported him rather than exiling him to Siberia? What does this say about Soviet politics?

death. As he stood before the firing squad, an order came from the czar, reducing his sentence to four years at hard labor in Siberia. The hardships he experienced there gave him a great sympathy toward the underprivileged. He became convinced that the most miserable creature could be saved. His novels, *The Idiot, The Possessed, The Brothers Karamazov,* and *Crime and Punishment,* deal with the themes of guilt, crime, and redemption.

Tolstoy was a Russian noble whose masterpiece *War and Peace* grew out of his own wartime experiences. In *War and Peace* Tolstoy sought to demonstrate the futility of war. He crusaded for social justice but believed in nonviolence. His works influenced Gandhi of India. Tolstoy tried to free and educate his own serfs. At one point, he was ready to divide his property among the poor, but his family stopped him. He spent his final years working in the fields, mending shoes, and writing. He refused to accept anything he had not earned.

When the Communists took over, many writers fled. One was Ivan Bunin (BOON-yuhn) who went to France and wrote against communism. He was the first Russian writer to win the Nobel Prize for literature. He received it in 1933 for *The Gentleman from San Francisco.*

In 1958 Boris Pasternak received the Nobel Prize for literature for *Doctor Zhivago.* After he had written *Doctor Zhivago,* a novel of Russian life before and after the Revolution, he submitted it for publication in the USSR. The Soviets refused because Pasternak had criticized the excesses of communism. But the novel was published in Italy despite Russian protests. Under government pressure, Pasternak had to refuse the Nobel Prize. The Writer's Union expelled him.

Today perhaps the best-known Soviet writer is Aleksandr I. Solzhenitsyn (sohl-zhuh-NEET-shun). After World War II, Solzhenitsyn was sentenced without trial to eight years of hard labor; this was followed by exile in Central Asia. His crime was writing a letter critical of

Stalin. From his experiences he wrote *One Day in the Life of Ivan Denisovich.* It was published in the Soviet Union with Khrushchev's approval and describes the misery of one day in a Stalinist labor camp. Two other works, *The First Circle* and *The Cancer Ward,* deal with his experiences as a prisoner and an exile. *The Gulag Archipelago* is his first nonfiction work and is a three-part indictment of the Communist system of police terror. These later works had to be published outside the Soviet Union.

indictment: an accusation or strong criticism

CENSORSHIP   Under Stalin writers who showed too much originality or expressed criticism of the regime were risking exile or death. Soviet writers stayed close to the party line and the triumphs of socialism. After Stalin died, Soviet writers began to grow more daring in their novels and books, especially those critical of Stalin. This period became known as the thaw. However, Soviet writers were required to stay within limits and were still under the control of the Writers Union.

One of the best-known writers to emerge during this time was Yevgeny Yevtushenko (yef-GEN-ee yef-tuh-SHENG-koh). He became famous for his poem "Babi Yar," which exposed Soviet anti-Semitism. Khrushchev gave him permission to publish "Stalin's Heirs," an outspoken criticism of Stalinism. Since Khrushchev's resignation, Yevtushenko has had trouble periodically with the party over his works. But he has been allowed to travel abroad to read his poetry.

Restrictions on writers tightened in the late 1960s, especially after the 1968 Czechoslovakian uprising. To avoid censorship, some writers try to publish their works in the underground press or smuggle them out to the West. In 1966 Yuli Daniel and Andrei Sinyavsky were tried and sentenced to labor camps for smuggling out their works. Worldwide protests over this incident were ignored by the Soviet government. Other writers, who feel they cannot work under such censorship, flee to the West.

In the 1970s a new round of restrictions and physical persecutions began with the publication in the West of Solzhenitsyn's book *The Gulag Archipelago.* His friends were beaten, his family was harassed, and his life was threatened. The Soviets finally deported him in 1974.

THE FINE ARTS

Painting and **sculpture**, like literature, have been hampered by Communist insistence on socialist realism and conformity. Artists are reluctant to experiment for fear that their works will not be accepted and that persecution will follow. The Soviets have made no significant contribution to painting. Their works are mainly realistic murals depicting the Soviet worker. Two famous Russian-born artists, Vassily

The Bolshoi Theater Ballet dates to the late 1700s. Here the company performs Nutcracker *by the 19th-century composer Peter Tchaikovsky.*

Kandinsky and Marc Chagall, left Soviet Russia to work elsewhere.

However, the artistic treasures of the past are preserved by the Communists. Orthodox churches with their beautiful icons have been turned into museums as have the palaces of the czars. The Soviet government inherited one of the finest collections of paintings in the world.

THE PERFORMING ARTS

Theater and filmmaking too have been held back by socialist realism. Since the government owns and controls all forms of communication—theaters and film studios as well as newspapers and television and radio stations—it insists that the party line be followed. This usually means that the media are used for **propaganda** purposes, not for artistic works. On the Soviet stage either the classics or works about the glories of communism are performed. While Soviet actors are very skillful, Soviet plays tend to be dull.

classics: works of art that are considered of lasting importance

For generations the world has paid tribute to Russian achievements in music. The works of such renowned composers as Tchaikovsky, Rimsky-Korsakov, and Moussorgsky are heard everywhere. More recently, the composers Prokofiev, Shostakovich, and Khachaturian have received critical praise. Although he left the Soviet Union, Igor Stravinsky made major contributions to modern music.

The Russians are considered supreme in ballet. Both the czars and the Communists have supported this art form. The Russian Imperial School of Ballet has produced such great dancers as Anna Pavlova, Vaslav Nijinsky, and Maya Plisetskaya. Many Soviet cities have their own ballet companies, but the finest of all performs in the Bolshoi Theater in Moscow. Among Soviet dancers competition to become a member of this group is keen.

Summing Up the Unit

Social Studies Vocabulary

Define: union; decentralization; bureaucratic; literacy; chronicle; compromise; nationalize

People

Identify: Mendeleev; Pavlov; Pushkin; Dostoevski; Tolstoy; Solzhenitsyn; Yevtushenko; Kandinsky; Chagall; Moussorgsky; Tchaikovsky; Pavlova

Places

Locate: the 15 Soviet Socialist Republics

Words

Academy of Science of the USSR; Sputnik I; mosques; Old Believers; pogroms; Union of Writers; socialist realism; the thaw

Questions

1. a. What areas of the economy are controlled or owned by the government? b. by individuals?
2. a. Give two reasons why agriculture is the weakest part of the Soviet economy. b. How do collective and state farms differ? c. Why haven't collective farms been very successful?
3. a. Who plans production for the Soviet economy? b. What type of production has been emphasized? c. What effect has this had on ordinary Russians?
4. a. Which republic dominates the others? b. Why? c. How are the various nationality groups being tied to the national state?
5. a. What social classes exist? b. Why?
6. a. What is the position of women in the Soviet Union? b. Why?
7. Why was literacy an important goal for the communists?
8. What is the role of sports in Soviet life?
9. a. What major religions are practiced in the USSR? b. How did the Russian Orthodox Church contribute to the power of the czars? c. What was the pre-World War II communist attitude toward religion? d. Why did it change during the war? e. What is it now?

10. a. Name the major influence on the arts under the czars. b. under the communists. c. Compare the czars' treatment of artists with that of the communists.
11. How has socialist realism affected artists?

Discussion Topics

1. There are growing gaps between the classes in the USSR's classless society. Why is this so? How do the economic and social classes of the Soviet Union compare with those classes in the U.S.? Do you think differences between classes in the U.S. are growing larger or smaller? Do classes in the two countries exist for the same or different reasons? Should a government encourage or discourage class differences? Is it possible to have a classless society?
2. Compare the chart on consumer goods with the natural resources map. What resources are needed to produce the goods listed? Are these same resources needed to produce articles for heavy industry? What do you think about favoring heavy industry over consumer goods?
3. The USSR uses sports to promote group loyalty and identification and produce better workers and soldiers. Also, althletes who compete in international events are government-supported. Do you think a government should encourage or use sports for its own purposes?

Project Ideas

1. Report on recent developments in the movement to allow Soviet Jews to emigrate.
2. Read Yevtushenko's poem "The City of Yes and the City of No." Does the poem seem to reflect aspects of the Russian character or experience? Is it also universal?
3. If you have seen the musical, *Fiddler on the Roof,* describe it for the class. What does the story tell us about the traditions and problems of Russian Jews? If possible, play the music for the class.
4. Make a list of prominent Americans of Russian ancestry. Include their professions and accomplishments.

Unit V

Eastern Europe

Eastern European nations are becoming more industrial, but agriculture is still important. Above are farmers at a collective in Hungary.

Perhaps no area in the world has been more strongly affected by its location than Eastern Europe. For centuries the countries of this area have been used as battlegrounds. They have been caught in power struggles among Western European countries and between Western Europe and czarist Russia. Turks, Germans, Austro-Hungarians, and Russians have overrun and carved up Eastern Europe many times. Only between world wars in this century were Eastern European countries able to achieve political independence. That did not last.

After World War II, the Soviet Union took control of most of the countries and imposed Communist governments on them. Six of these countries—Poland, Czechoslovakia, Bulgaria, Romania, Hungary, and East Germany—are now tied politically, economically, and militarily to the Soviet Union. Albania is closely allied to the People's Republic of China. Yugoslavia has been following an independent policy.

Despite the instability and turmoil, Eastern European peoples have developed a strong sense of nationalism. They take great pride in their countries and struggle valiantly to keep their national identities.

Geographically, Eastern Europe can be divided into the Baltic Plain, the Danube River Basin, and the Balkan Peninsula. The Baltic Plain runs 480 kilometers (300 miles) from the Baltic Sea in the north to the Carpathian Mountains in the south. This is open land with no natural eastern or western boundaries. The area is a natural invasion route.

South of the Baltic Plain lies the Danube River. It winds through great portions of Eastern Europe and has been a major transportation route for both traders and armies. The Danube River Basin is the land on either side of the river. It is the most fertile region in Eastern Europe. Below this area is the Balkan Peninsula, ringed on three sides by the Adriatic, Aegean, and Black seas.

POLAND

Poland—officially the Polish People's Republic—lies between the Baltic Sea and the Carpathian Mountains. It is part of the Baltic Plain and until recently was primarily an agricultural country. The Oder and Vistula are its two major rivers. Warsaw, the capital, is located on the Vistula. The province of Silesia (sy-LEE-zhee-uh) contains large deposits of coal and iron ore, which are helping Poland to industrialize today. The country also has valuable zinc and rock-salt deposits.

Poles are descendants of a Slavic people known as the Polanie. They were first united in the 900s under Mieszko (MYESH-koh), who founded the Piast (PYAHST) dynasty. Mieszko was baptized in 965 and established the Roman Catholic Church throughout Poland. This common religion was a unifying force among the Poles. It also marked a difference between them and the Orthodox Russians.

The Piast dynasty expanded its domain until in 1138 it split Poland. The country was not reunited again until 1320 under Ladislas I. His son, Casimir the Great, was the last and greatest of the Piast dynasty. He encouraged commerce and learning. When he died in 1370 without an heir, the throne passed to King Louis of Hungary.

When Louis died in 1382 with no male heir, Polish nobles arranged for his granddaughter, Jadwiga (yahd-VEE-gah), to be crowned queen. Jadwiga married the Grand Duke of Lithuania. This marriage united Poland and Lithuania and established the Jagellon (yah-GEL-uhn) dynasty, which ruled from 1386 to 1572. In 1410 Ladislas II, Jadwiga's husband, drove the Prussians from northern Poland. During the Middle Ages a band of Germans known as the Teutonic Knights had seized the area and added it to the Prussian state they were building.

In the late 1600s the Poles reached the height of their military power. They defeated the Russians and in 1683, under King John III Sobieski, saved Europe from invasion by Turks.

In the 1700s, however, the Poles fell victim to the schemes of their neighbors Prussia, Austria, and Russia. In 1772 these nations divided Poland among themselves. Twenty years later a new division of Poland

Thaddeus Kosciusko led a peasant army against the Prussians, Russians, and Austrians in 1794 in a fight to prevent the third partition of Poland. The revolt was defeated.

was made between Russia and Prussia. During this time, Thaddeus Kosciusko (kahs-ee-UHS-koh), returned from America where he had fought in the Revolution. Kosciusko formed a peasant army to fight the invaders. At first it was victorious, but eventually Kosciusko was captured and the movement collapsed.

Austria objected to the second partition and in 1795 a third one was made. As a result, Poland no longer existed as a nation. But it remained a reality in the hearts of Polish patriots. Many Poles fought and died in an effort to reestablish a united Poland.

When Napoleon was in power, the Duchy of Warsaw was created and it lasted from 1807 to 1813. After Napoleon's defeat, the Congress of Vienna united Poland with Russia but allowed it to have its own constitution. In 1830 and again in 1863 the Poles revolted against the Russians. The constitution was abolished and the revolts were crushed. The Poles were subjected to intense Russification.

It was not until 1918 that the Poles again received some land and independence. Danzig, Poland's Baltic seaport which had been a source of friction for centuries, was made an independent city. The **League** of Nations, an international peace-helping group, was to supervise it. Poland was given access to Danzig through a strip of land that ran through Germany. This became known as the Polish Corridor and was to be the source of future conflict between the two nations.

In 1939, Germany and Russia plotted the **partition** of Poland again. When the Poles rejected Hitler's demand that Danzig be turned over to Germany, German troops invaded Poland on September 1, 1939. World War II had begun. A few weeks later the Soviets also invaded Poland. Germany and the USSR divided the nation between them. Two years later Hitler attacked the Soviet Union. Eventually Soviet troops turned back the Germans and completely occupied Poland.

Throughout the war, conferences were held at Tehran, Yalta, and Potsdam by leaders from Britain, the U.S., and the Soviet Union. Eastern Europe and Poland were principal topics. As a result of these conferences, the USSR took 181,300 square kilometers (70,000 square miles) of Polish territory in the east. About 11 million Poles lived there. In return, Poland was given about 101,000 square kilometers (39,000 square miles) of former German territory in the west.

The Soviets were not satisfied. Polish Communists were placed in power by the Red Army. At Yalta, Churchill and Roosevelt agreed to recognize this provisional government. When elections were held, the Communist-controlled police spread terror throughout the country. By 1947 Poland was completely under Communist control and bound to the USSR politically and economically. In 1955 Poland joined the Warsaw Pact.

The Poles do not succumb easily to suppression, however. On several occasions Polish workers have organized demonstrations to protest economic and political conditions. In 1956 workers in Poznan marched through the streets demanding food. This riot brought the return of Wladyslaw Gomulka (vwad-DEE-swahv goh-MOOL-kuh), a Polish Communist leader who had been exiled from the party by Stalin. Gomulka tried to meet the needs of the workers and keep the Soviets from intervening. However, in the early 1970s more riots forced Gomulka to resign. He was replaced by Edward Gierek (GEER-ik) who made some changes.

intervening: interfering, or coming between

The Polish people have been more successful than other Eastern Europeans in toppling governments and bringing about reforms. For centuries the Poles have shown an independent spirit and a pride in their country and culture no matter who governed them. At present they may be tied to the Soviet Union, but those ties are as flexible as they can make them.

CZECHOSLOVAKIA

Czechoslovakia is not a large country. It covers an area about the size of New York State. Economically its industry and coal and iron ore deposits make it an important country. Completely landlocked,

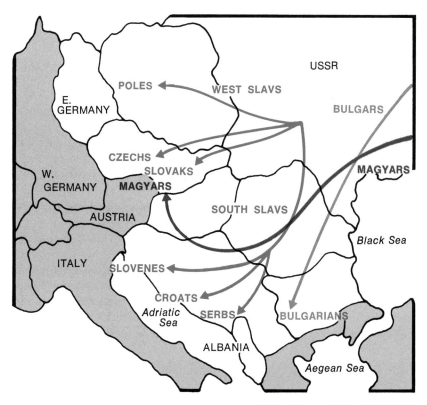

Migrations, 500-1000 A.D.

681

it shares its borders with several other nations and lies within the Danube River Basin.

During the first six centuries A.D., groups of western Slavs moved into this area and seized control from earlier inhabitants. By the 800s the Czechs and Slovaks—who now make up the majority—combined the territories of Bohemia, Moravia, and Slovakia into the Great Moravian Empire. At the time both the Roman Catholic and Eastern Orthodox churches were trying to convert the Moravians. However, because of the powerful influence of the neighboring Germans, the Moravian Empire was converted to Roman Catholicism.

In the early 900s the Magyars—a people from what is modern Hungary—defeated the Moravian Empire and ruled Slovakia. In the 1100s Bohemia became part of the Holy Roman Empire. This empire —ruled by German-speaking emperors—occupied large and varying portions of Europe between 962 and 1806. Through a series of marriages and wars, the three areas of Bohemia, Moravia, and Slovakia were joined to the Austrian and Hungarian possessions of the Hapsburg family in the 1600s. In 1848 the three areas revolted against Austrian rule but were unsuccessful. Austria continued to rule until its defeat in World War I. As part of the peace settlement, Czechoslovakia became an independent country in 1918. Because of the long rule of other countries, there were large groups of Hungarians, Germans, Poles, and Ukrainians in the country.

Thomas G. Masaryk (MAHS-uh-rik), and Eduard Benes (BEN-esh) were the founders of the new republic. Masaryk became its first president. As an independent and **democratic** country, Czechoslovakia had a history of about 20 years.

In 1938 Great Britain, Italy, and France agreed to the division of Czechoslovakia to appease Hitler and avoid war. The agreement— known as the Munich Pact—allowed Hitler to take Czechoslovakia's best lands and industry on the pretext that Germans lived in these areas. In 1939 Hitler dissolved the new state and formed Slovakia. The rest of the country was divided among Germany, Hungary, and Poland. In 1945 the Soviet Army occupied Czechoslovakia. The native Germans were exiled. The pre-1938 borders of the country were restored, and a **coalition** government was established.

Because the other political parties could not cooperate, the Communists were able to seize power. By 1948 the country was Communist dominated and had a constitution modeled after that of the Soviet Union. Its official name became Czechoslovak Socialist Republic.

While other Soviet satellites experienced some loosening of control after Stalin's death, Czechoslovakia did not. As a result many Czechs fled to the West. In 1968 a power struggle within the Communist party overthrew First Secretary Antonin Novotny. Alexander Dubcek succeeded him and tried to liberalize the government. He introduced reforms and expanded **civil liberties**.

These measures disturbed Soviet leaders and the more **conservative** among his Soviet neighbors. In August 1968 troops from the USSR,

Thomas G. Masaryk fought for Slavic rights against the Austro-Hungarians. His son, Jan, fought the Communist takeover of Czechoslovakia. In 1948 Jan died mysteriously.

Poland, Bulgaria, and East Germany occupied the country. Dubcek was deposed and his reforms were stopped. However, no Czech Communist would form a new government. Dubcek was returned to power under the watchful eyes of 50,000 Soviet Army troops. In an effort to have Soviet troops removed, Dubcek tried to be cooperative. By 1969, however, he had been replaced as party leader by Gustav Husak.

Since the Communist party in Czechoslovakia had supported Dubcek, Husak began a purge of party members. Censorship was reimposed, and the political and economic structure was reorganized. This display of tightened rule was meant to be a lesson to other Soviet satellites.

purge: to remove people who oppose the government—by jailing them, sending them out of the country, or murdering them

BULGARIA

Bulgaria—officially the People's Republic of Bulgaria—is part of the Balkan Peninsula. Primarily an agricultural country, it has fertile soil and a moderate climate. Its main exports are grains, tobacco, potatoes, and fruit. An underdeveloped country, it is attempting to build up its industry.

Bulgaria takes its name from an Asian people known as the Bulgars. They invaded the country during the 600s A.D. and mixed with the Slavic people already there. The Slavs and Bulgars merged to form the first Bulgarian Empire around 680. They were part of the Byzantine Empire from 1018 to 1185 but later founded a second empire of their own. In 1396 Bulgaria was conquered by the Turks, who ruled it for the next 500 years.

Historically, the Bulgarians were never as suspicious of Russia as other Eastern European nations were. The Bulgarians often looked to Russia for help. During the late 1800s, the Russians helped the Bulgarians to overthrow the Turks. The Bulgarians also practiced the same Orthodox Christianity as the Russians. The Bulgarians have been Christians since the 800s. However, as a result of the long Turkish rule, there are about 75,000 Muslims in the country.

In 1908 Bulgaria became an independent country with its own czar. In an effort to gain an outlet on the Aegean Sea, it became involved in two Balkan wars against Turkey (in 1912 and in 1913). Bulgaria was defeated each time. It was on the side of Germany during both world wars and lost great pieces of territory as a result. At the end of World War II, Soviet troops occupied the country. The **monarchy** was abolished in 1946, and a Communist government was established. Bulgaria has joined the Soviet Union in many economic ventures and is a member of the Warsaw Pact.

ROMANIA

Romania—the Romanian People's Republic—is part of the Danube River Basin. It is a mountainous region crisscrossed by the Carpathian

Above is a fishing port in Bulgaria on the Black Sea. On the right is a synthetic fiber plant in Romania. How can industry stimulate economic growth?

Mountains and the Transylvanian Alps. Romania has some excellent natural resources, including oil. Although an economically underdeveloped country, it is rapidly developing manufacturing industries.

Romania has a long history. It was first inhabited by an ancient people known as Dacians. They were conquered and ruled by the Romans from about 101 to 274 A.D. Romania was later invaded by the Goths, Huns, Avars, Slavs, and Magyars. The influences of these people as well as the Greeks and the later Turks can be seen in the Romanian language.

During the Middle Ages, the Romanian provinces of Moldavia and Walachia formed independent nations. However, by the 1500s all Romania was under the control of the Turks. Despite one attempt at independence, the Romanians were controlled by the Turks until 1878. Prior to independence, Romania was the scene of repeated conflicts between the Turks and the Russians. Later the Romanians had to fight the Russians who periodically pushed into Romanian territory.

At the beginning of World War I, Romania declared itself **neutral**. Eventually, it joined the Allies against Germany. In World War II Romania again attempted to remain neutral. However, when Germany forced Romania to give up land, the king abdicated. Under its new leader, General Ion Antonescu (YON an-tuh-NES-koo), Romania fought on the side of Germany. But as Germany met defeat, King Michael overthrew Antonescu and joined the Allies. Romania was later occupied by Soviet troops. The Soviets used their usual methods —police and army—to place the Communist party in power. King Michael abdicated in 1947.

Initially, Romania had very close economic, political, and military bonds with the Soviet Union. However, this policy gradually changed during the 1960s. Romania declared itself free to trade with anyone and free to run its own government. Under Nicolae Ceausescu (koo-zee-ES-koo) a new constitution was written and relations with the U.S. and West Germany were resumed.

HUNGARY

Hungary—the Hungarian People's Republic—lies on the western edge of the Danube River Basin. Like Czechoslovakia, Hungary is a land-locked nation. It is primarily an agricultural land. In recent years, however, industry has expanded and industrial exports are becoming increasingly important.

Slavs and Germans first settled the area. They were overcome in the late 800s by the Magyars, who had originally come from the steppes of Central Asia. In 1001 Hungary was united under King Stephen I.

In the 1200s the country was invaded by the Mongols, who were driven out with the aid of the Holy Roman Empire. Between 1458 and 1490, Hungary achieved unity under Matthias Corvinus. In the 1500s the country was conquered by the Turks. In the 1600s the combined efforts of the Hungarians and Austrians drove them out. Hungary then came under Austrian domination for almost 200 years. In 1848 the Hungarians under Lajos Kossuth (LAW-ohsh KAH-sooth) revolted unsuccessfully. In 1867 Hungary was made part of the dual monarchy of Austria-Hungary with the ruling family of Austria in power.

In World War I Austria-Hungary fought on the side of Germany. With defeat the empire fell apart. Control of Hungary passed to revolutionaries. For a few brief months in 1919, Hungarian Communists ruled under the Bolshevik leader, Bela Kun. They were ousted by Admiral Miklos Horthy who set up a monarchy with himself as **regent**.

After the war, Hungary experienced severe financial troubles. It had also lost large amounts of territory as a result of the peace treaty. Through agreements with Hitler, Hungary managed to regain part of this land.

In World War II Hungary joined with Germany to invade the Soviet Union. The Hungarians were badly defeated and asked for peace. Germany then invaded Hungary only to be pushed out by Soviet troops. By 1945 the Soviets had conquered all of Hungary.

The Soviets kept troops there while elections were held. The Hungarian Communists gained a little more than one-fifth of the vote and formed a coalition government with the other parties. In less than a year, however, the Communists had seized complete control. By 1947 Hungary had a government patterned after Soviet Russia.

Through the early 1950s, Hungary experienced serious economic problems. Several changes in government resulted. Dissatisfaction with the economic and political system reached a crisis stage in 1956. The Hungarians rebelled. They gained control for a short time and made Imre Nagy (NOJ) premier.

Soviet tanks and troops sped into Hungary to put down the revolt. Thousands, including Nagy, were imprisoned or executed. Almost 200,000 people fled. The rebels were brave, daring, and almost successful, but they were poorly armed and could not withstand the hundreds of thousands of Soviet troops and tanks. The Soviets reorganized the government under Janos Kadar, the first secretary of the Hungarian Communist party. The Soviets were infuriated by the Hungarian rebellion. It had been necessary for them to show the steel hand with which they control their satellites.

Hungary is quiet now. Living conditions have improved. Through the 1960s several changes in government occurred. In 1967 Jeno Fock (YEH-nuh FOHSH) became premier and announced more freedom for the country. However, the Soviets keep a close watch on Hungary.

YUGOSLAVIA

The Socialist Federal Republic of Yugoslavia lies on the Balkan Peninsula along the Adriatic Sea. Yugoslavia forms part of the Danube River Basin but is essentially a mountainous country. It has rich mineral resources and extensive forests. Today its people are divided almost evenly between agricultural and industrial workers.

Yugoslavians are a mixture of various ethnic groups—Serb, Croat, and Slovene among others. As a result of the many diverse tribal origins and the many nations that have ruled them, Yugoslavians have many different languages and religions. The nation has been divided and ruled by Austria-Hungary, Bulgaria, Montenegro, and Serbia. The latter two are now Yugoslavian republics. The area was also conquered and governed by the Turks. It was not until after World War I that one independent nation was formed.

The country was called the Kingdom of the Serbs, Croats, and Slovenes. Peter I of Serbia ruled. The name Yugoslavia was adopted in 1929. The young nation had a difficult time as each group jealously guarded its ethnic, religious, and **linguistic** identity.

In 1941 the Germans invaded and occupied the country. From then until near the end of World War II, Yugoslavia was a place of conflict. A national liberation movement was established under the leadership of Communist Josip Broz (YOH-sef BROHZ), later known as Marshal Tito. As head of the **Partisans**, he led a **guerrilla** war against the Germans. In 1945 he proclaimed the country a republic.

Yugoslavia was in ruins. Tito attempted to reorganize and rebuild the country along Communist lines. He later revised his thinking. He put most operations on a profit basis and eventually did away

Sarajevo was the site of the assassination of Archduke Franz Ferdinand in 1914, which started World War I. The city's many mosques were built under Turkish rule, from the 1400s to the 1800s.

with collective farms. Tito refused to bow always to the will of Stalin in foreign policy or to have his domestic policies dictated by the USSR. The USSR denounced him in 1948 for this independence. An international Communist effort was organized to unseat him. Plans were made to destroy the Yugoslavian economy through a trade blockade.

Tito survived these attacks and began a neutralist policy in the cold war. He accepted aid from the U.S. and other non-Communist countries and continued his independent line of acting.

When Khrushchev came to power, he embarked upon a policy of winning Marshal Tito back into the Communist bloc. He apologized for the policies of Stalin and offered to work more cooperatively. In 1955 Khrushchev visited Yugoslavia in an attempt to restore relations. Tito did not return completely to the Soviet Communist camp, but relations improved between the two countries.

Compare and contrast Marshal Tito's policies with those of other Eastern European leaders.

Yugoslavia was traditionally an agricultural country. Tito tried to change it into a more industrialized nation. Gradually the economy is becoming more balanced, and the standard of living is improving. The country continues to need and accept outside economic help.

ALBANIA

The People's Republic of Albania is the smallest of the Communist countries. It is a mountainous land on the Balkan Peninsula along the eastern coast of the Adriatic Sea. Albania is an extremely poor agricultural country with almost no industry.

Albania was fought over for many centuries. Both the Greeks and the Romans conquered it. During the Middle Ages it was invaded

Workers on an Albanian collective pick tobacco. How can a surplus agricultural economy help a country to industrialize?

by the Goths, Bulgarians, Slavs, and Normans and finally became a part of the Byzantine Empire. Despite the attempts of Scanderbeg (1403?-1468), an Albanian patriot, Albania was conquered and ruled by the Turks for over 400 years. It finally became an independent nation in 1912 during the First Balkan War.

During World War I, Albania was occupied by Italians, Austro-Hungarians, Serbs, and French. It did not achieve independence again until 1925. Ahmed Bey Zogu took power that year and made himself King Zog I.

Albania was invaded and occupied by Italian and German troops during World War II. In the middle of the war, fighting broke out between non-Communist troops and Communist forces led by Enver Hoxha. With the defeat of Germany, Albania became a Communist country under General Hoxha's control.

Initially, Albania allied itself with the Soviets. However, it broke off relations with the USSR in 1961. Albanian leaders disagreed with the idea of peaceful coexistence. They insisted that war with the capitalist countries was inevitable and condemned many of Khrushchev's policies. Albania withdrew from the Warsaw Pact.

Albania and the People's Republic of China joined in alliance. Albania is not a strong country and has had problems with Yugoslavia over territorial claims. These, however, were settled by treaty. Although Albania is small, it can be annoying to the larger powers. They dare not move against it because of its powerful Chinese ally.

EAST GERMANY

After World War II, Germany was divided into two parts. The eastern part was occupied by the Soviets; the western, by the Allies—Great Britain, France, and the U.S. In 1955 the Allies recognized the area they had occupied as an independent republic. It became the Federal Republic of Germany, commonly referred to as West Germany. West Germany covers about 248,600 square kilometers (96,000 square miles), including the Bavarian Alps, Rhine Valley, and the Ruhr industrial region. In 1949 East Germany had become known officially as the German Democratic Republic. It has a territory of about 106,200 square kilometers (41,000 square miles), most of which is level ground.

In East Germany the Soviets set up a political and economic structure similar to that of the Soviet Union. Although East Germany is recognized as a sovereign country by the USSR, the Soviets continue to influence its affairs. They keep an estimated half million soldiers and huge supplies of military equipment there. East Germany is very important to Soviet power in Europe.

A major source of friction between the USSR and the West has been Berlin, the former capital of Germany. Berlin lies within what was the Soviet occupied zone of Germany. According to an agreement

sovereign country: one that is free and independent

688

reached at the end of the war, the city was divided into sectors. The USSR, the U.S., France, and Britain were each to govern one sector. The sectors governed by the Allies are called West Berlin. That part governed by the USSR is known as East Berlin.

Under Soviet direction, the Communist leaders of East Germany tried to harass Western powers into leaving Berlin. In 1948 they closed the surface supply routes from West Germany. West Berlin was so blockaded that all supplies had to be delivered by air. This became known as the Berlin Airlift. The Western powers stubbornly maintained their legal right to be in Berlin.

Through the Marshall Plan, the U.S. helped the West Germans build their war-torn nation into a prosperous country. The Soviets neglected the economic development of East Germany. For years the standard of living remained much lower there than in West Germany. Because of this and the lack of freedom, there has been a continuous migration from East Germany to West Germany. An estimated four million people have left. At least half were under 25 years of age. Many were professionals—engineers, doctors, and skilled technicians.

East German leaders took various measures to stop the escape of workers. In 1961 they sealed off East Berlin and East Germany from the West with walls and barbed wire. In the Berlin area this barricade became known as the Berlin Wall. Fewer East Germans got through, but there were those who still tried. Some were lucky, and some were shot and left to die where they fell.

When the Soviet Union began its policy of detente, it pressured East German leaders into a similar policy. In the 1970s the two Ger-

The Brandenburg Gate, shown above at left, was built in 1791 as a tribute to Prussian military might. It stands in East Berlin behind the Berlin Wall. Many East Germans, like the soldier above, have risked their lives to escape.

manies signed their first treaty, thus easing access to West Berlin, and both Germanies were admitted to the United Nations. The USSR, Britain, France, and the U.S. approved an agreement on the status of West Berlin. But the Berlin Wall still stands.

Chapter 2
Life

Prague, the capital of Czechoslovakia, has been an important city since the 1300s. Czechoslovakia has a higher standard of living than most of its neighbors.

After Communist leaders took control in Eastern Europe, they attempted to change economic and social systems to fit Soviet ideals. But at the local level there existed no support for communism.

In trying to impose their system on countries that already had traditional ways of life, the Soviets met with many failures. However, hard-line Communists kept control as long as Stalin and his secret police were in power. With the coming of Khrushchev's policy of revisionism, there was a reawakening of **nationalism** among Eastern Europeans.

Despite the people's resistance, the Soviets have left their imprint on Eastern European life. Today there exists side by side a mixture of the traditional and modern, capitalism and communism, and national and Soviet-imposed culture.

SOCIETY

As a result of the numerous migrations and invasions of the area, great differences exist among the peoples of Eastern Europe. Large minority groups live within most countries. Generally they speak different languages, practice different religions, and follow different customs from those of the majority group.

The Slavs are the major group in Eastern Europe and they are split between western and southern Slavs. The Poles, Czechs, and Slovaks are descended from the western Slavs. The southern Slavs were ancestors of the Bulgarians, Serbs, Croats, Slovenes, and Macedonians. Other ethnic groupings, scattered among several countries, include Germans, Magyars, Romanians, Albanians, Gypsies, Greeks, and Turks. Most of these peoples speak their own languages. Several branches of the Indo-European **language family** are represented—Balto-Slavic, Germanic, Romance, and Albanian. Most groups use a Slavic-based language, however.

RELIGION   The variety in Eastern Europe is also reflected in the many religions practiced there. Religion has always played a major role in the lives of Eastern Europeans. In most countries Church and State were very closely linked. After the Communist takeover, Church lands were seized, schools closed, and clergy imprisoned. The Roman Catholic Church suffered most because it commanded the loyalty of almost half the people. Catholics were especially influential in Poland, Hungary, Czechoslovakia, and parts of Yugoslavia.

The Communists claimed that the Catholic clergy had collaborated with the Germans, and they moved against many of their high-ranking members. In Hungary, Josef Cardinal Mindszenty was arrested, tried, and sentenced to life imprisonment in 1949. He was freed in the revolution of 1956, and fled to the U.S. embassy for asylum. In 1973 Communist authorities allowed him to go to Rome.

Today the Church is still closely watched, but a policy of coexistence seems to have emerged. In general, churches are open and the people are free to attend. However, Communists continue to try to undermine the influence of religion, especially among the young.

The other major religious groups—the Orthodox Christians and the Muslims—have had a less difficult time but they too are supervised. The Orthodox Church, which tends to be a national church, has large followings in Bulgaria, Romania, and Yugoslavia. Albania is the only European country that is predominantly Muslim, although Yugoslavia and Bulgaria have large Muslim populations.

Prior to World War II, Eastern Europe was the home of many Jews. However, the Nazis almost destroyed the Jewish population. Before World War II, one out of every 20 Hungarians was a Jew. By the mid-1950s only one out of every 100 was.

political asylum: protection in a foreign country from one's enemies at home

Poland was the scene of the greatest massacres of Jews. Over three million were slaughtered at the Auschwitz concentration camp. One of the most horrifying scenes of the war occurred in the Warsaw ghetto. Over 50,000 Jews died there defending themselves against the Nazis. Under the Communists, anti-Semitism has continued.

THE ECONOMY

Before World War II, the peoples of Eastern Europe relied primarily on agriculture for their living. At the end of the war much of Eastern Europe had been left in ruins. When the Communists came to power, they imposed the Soviet system on all countries. Industry was nationalized and put under the direction of central planners. Heavy industry was given top priority. Most farms were collectivized.

Through 1953, the plans were generally successful. Industrial production more than doubled. Then serious problems began to arise. Shortages of everything from labor to capital appeared. Farmers bitterly resented the collectivization of their farms and produced less. A lack of attention, funds, and equipment also hampered agricultural production.

The revolts and upheavals of the 1950s can be partially traced to the economic situation. A general reorganization and reordering of priorities resulted. The standard of living was to be raised. Industrial development was to assume a less important role.

Both Poland and Yugoslavia returned to privately owned farms in the early 1950s. As a result, farm production increased. Today many of the other Eastern European countries are attempting to modify their farm collectives. Like the Soviets, they have learned that they must provide greater incentives if production is to increase.

incentives: rewards for doing something

Despite limitations and setbacks, Eastern Europe now ranks fourth in the world in industrial production. It comes after the U.S., the USSR, and Western Europe. Since the 1950s local managers have been given increased independence and responsibility. Competition and profits are stressed. At first this created problems. Only a few people had been trained for management positions.

The industrial development of the Eastern European nations varies considerably. Czechoslovakia is one of the most developed. Two-thirds of its national income comes from industry rather than agriculture. Poland and Hungary are moderately industrialized, although Hungary is limited because of its lack of minerals. Bulgaria, Romania, and Albania are all underdeveloped.

To strengthen Eastern Europe's economic ties to the USSR, the Soviets formed the Council for Mutual Economic Assistance known as COMECON in 1949. All the satellite countries except Albania belong. Through it the Soviet Union has been able to control Eastern European trade, resources, and production to fulfill its own needs. As a result, the economic development of Eastern Europe has been held back.

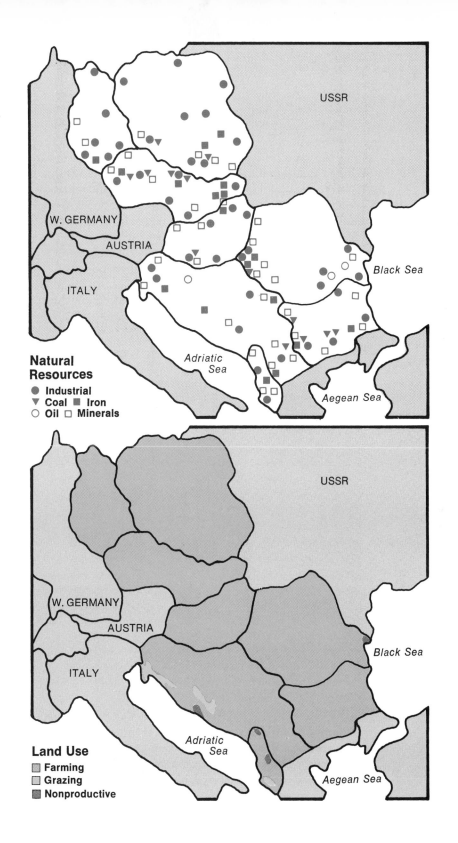

Natural Resources
- ● Industrial
- ▼ Coal ■ Iron
- ○ Oil □ Minerals

Land Use
- Farming
- Grazing
- Nonproductive

USSR

W. GERMANY

AUSTRIA

ITALY

Black Sea

Adriatic Sea

Aegean Sea

USSR

W. GERMANY

AUSTRIA

ITALY

Black Sea

Adriatic Sea

Aegean Sea

THE ARTS

Folklore was and is the core of Eastern European culture. This includes the folk dances, songs, stories, dress, art, and handicrafts that characterize the various peoples of Eastern Europe. In the 1800s with the rise of nationalism and romanticism—a movement that used nature and the emotions as themes—many Eastern European writers and composers turned to their native folklore for inspiration. They emphasized **patriotic** values and pride in their nations in a moving and emotional style. This period produced an outpouring of literature and music that expressed the desire of Eastern Europeans for independence.

The Poles were especially productive. One example is Adam Mickiewicz (mits-KYAY-vich) who was both a poet and a revolutionary. He spent part of his life exiled in Russia for his political activities. He wrote *Pan Tadeusz*, an **epic** poem about Poland during the Napoleonic wars.

Folk music is still a vital part of the cultures of many countries. Above, Romanian musicians entertain at a festival. Why do you think ethnic heritage and tradition remain important to so many people?

Polish nationalism achieved its greatest expression, however, in the music of Frederic Chopin. His polonaises and mazurkas were inspired by Polish folk music and dances. Ignace Jan Paderewski (pad-uh-REF-skee), a pianist and composer, was the first premier of the newly formed Poland in 1918.

Czech composers also took most of their inspiration from their nation's folk music. Bedrick Smetana (SMET-uhn-uh) established a national musical style. He gained fame for his symphonic poem *The Moldau* and his opera *The Bartered Bride.* Anton Dvorak (duh-VOR-zhahk) used folk music in his *Slavonic Dances,* but is best known for the *New World* Symphony which he composed while in the U.S. Gustav Mahler and Leos Janacek (YAHN-uh-chek) are also renowned Czech composers.

Hungarian composers also used their music to express nationalist feelings. Franz Liszt is famous for his *Hungarian Rhapsodies.* Later Hungarian composers include Zoltan Kodaly (KOH-dy) and Ernst von Dohnany (DOH-nah-nyee). One of the most influential composers of modern music has been Bela Bartok.

influential: having the power to change the thinking or actions of others

Two of the best known writers of pre-Communist Eastern Europe belong outside the tradition of nationalism. They are Joseph Conrad, born in Poland, and Franz Kafka of Czechoslovakia. Conrad left Poland and became a British citizen. He used his experiences in the British navy in such works as *Lord Jim.* Kafka, in novels such as *The Trial* and *The Castle,* deals with the dilemma of modern people as they seek salvation.

When the Communists seized power, they imposed their concept of socialist realism on the arts. Under the police state and system of censorship developed by Stalin, creative expression was stifled. In the 1950s and 1960s, however, a revival of nationalism occurred. The revolts that shook Eastern Europe were followed by a great rebirth in the arts. Often writers and artists were the leaders of the rebellions. The arts became vehicles for protest rather than for Communist propaganda. The theory of nationalist realism—an emphasis on the national interest—was developed.

The degree of its success varied from country to country depending on each government's policies of artistic freedom and **ideological** conformity. In Albania, Hoxha continued heavy censorship. East Germany's government also suppressed protests.

In general, the thaw—as it was known in the USSR—occurred throughout Eastern Europe. For the most part the works that poured forth were preoccupied with the past. Eastern Europe had seen tremendous upheavals and undergone great change since the beginning of World War II. Many writers and artists seemed to go through several stages in their exploration of the past. Their first interest was with the Nazis and their treatment of the Jews. Next Stalinism and the cult of personality were probed. This was replaced by the expression of a surrealistic, or unreal, world. Throughout there has been a rejection of things Soviet and a turning toward Western ideas and style.

One of the most interesting results has been a revival of poetry in Hungary. Hundreds of books of poetry are published each year. Hungarian television and radio programs feature poetry readings.

During the 1960s film production experienced a major rebirth. It started in Poland with such films as *Ashes and Diamonds* and *The Age of Illusion.* These depict the disillusionment and alienation of modern men and women. However, filmmaking reached its peak when the state-owned film company in Czechoslovakia began to lose money. Restrictions were lifted and filmmaking fell almost entirely to intellectuals.

In 1966 the Czech film *The Shop on Main Street* won an Academy Award for its portrayal of the plight of Jews in Eastern Europe. In 1968 the Czech film *Closely Watched Trains* won an Academy Award. Czech films became almost documentaries. They attempted to deal with people's struggles with such things as society and love.

The theater also thrives in Eastern Europe, especially in Poland, Czechoslovakia, and Romania. In these countries it is used for national protest or as a means to escape life's realities. Czechoslovakia has produced a series of leading dramatists whose plays are generally concerned with political issues. Satire is very popular.

In the mid- and late 1950s a thaw also occurred in music. The leader, Witold Lutoslawski, split with the Communist realists in his *Concerto for Orchestra.* Composers up until then were not supposed to experiment. One of the most esteemed composers of the new wave is Krzysztof Penderecki of Poland. One of his major works, *Suite for Hiroshima,* is electronic music.

There are many struggling artists in Eastern Europe. Under the Communist system, there are no wealthy art buyers or even many art galleries. As a result, most artists find it impossible to earn a living by their work, unless they sell to the state for export. The state then sets the price of the work and determines how much the artist will receive. The state also has the right to censor works.

One of the most outstanding and original painters in Poland today is Tadeusz Brozowski. Among the best-known sculptors from Eastern Europe are Constantin Brancusi who was born in Romania but worked in Paris, and Ivan Mestrovic of Yugoslavia.

Despite the efforts to rebuild after World War II, no noteworthy Communist style in architecture or city planning has developed. Communist cities tend to be drab and boring in their sameness. They possess little charm except where the architecture from another era remains. This can be explained partly by the scarcity of materials and the need for rapid building because of housing shortages. But it may also be because of the restrictions on imagination and vision which are so much a part of Communist life.

At left is an example of 20th-century art. The Romanian Constantin Brancusi made this sculpture out of polished bronze and named it Bird in Space. *Why do you think he chose this title?*

Marie Sklodowski Curie, a Polish chemist and physicist, discovered the elements polonium and radium. She became Professor of Physics at the Sorbonne in Paris and won two Nobel Prizes.

SCIENCE

Artistic achievement has generally outweighed scientific achievement in Eastern Europe. However, Poland is famous as the home of the 16th-century astronomer, Nicolaus Copernicus. Copernicus established that the earth rotates around the sun. Until then the popular theory was that the earth was the center of our planetary system. Modern **astronomy** is based on the Copernican system.

Poland was also the birthplace of Marie Sklodowski Curie. She and her French-born husband, Pierre, were awarded a Nobel Prize in 1903 for their work on radioactivity. In 1911, Marie Curie alone received the Nobel Prize for research with radium.

In 1938 Yugoslavian chemist Leopold Ruzicka (ROO-zhich-kuh) shared the Nobel Prize in chemistry for his work in synthesizing musk. It is an important ingredient in perfume. Jaroslav Heyrovsky (HAY-rof-skee) of Czechoslovakia won the Nobel Prize for chemistry in 1959.

Summing Up the Unit

Social Studies Vocabulary

Define: partition; coalition; civil liberties; conservative; guerrilla; language family; folklore; patriotic; epic; propaganda

People

Identify: John Sobieski; Kosciusko; Masaryk; Dubcek; Ceausescu; Kossuth; Nagy; Tito; Mindszenty; Curie

Places

Locate: the eight East European countries

Words

Identify: Polish Corridor; Tehran, Yalta, Potsdam conferences; Munich Pact; Berlin Airlift; Berlin Wall; *The Bartered Bride*; *Slavonic Dances*; *The Trial*; *Lord Jim*

ᴄᴏ Questions

1. a. How has the geography of Eastern Europe affected its politics and economics? b. Name the peoples that are descended from western Slavs. c. From southern Slavs. d. What other peoples live in the area? e. Why so many?
2. What major religions are practiced?
3. a. What was the pattern of communist takeover in six countries? b. Give two examples. c. Name the countries in which local communists took control. d. Which country has lost the most citizens by migration to the West?
4. a. Name three countries that have followed courses independent of the USSR. b. Which is independent of both the USSR and China?
5. How did Stalin control nationalism in Eastern Europe during his rule?
6. a. On what was the economy of Eastern European nations based before World War II? b. What changes have taken place since then? (Use the maps as reference.)
7. a. What aspect of Eastern European culture lent itself to nationalsim in the arts? b. What was the effect of socialist realism in Eastern Europe? c.

Through what stages have the arts in Eastern Europe passed since the thaw?
8. a. What arts have flourished? b. How does state control of the arts affect artists?
9. a. What is the state of science in Eastern Europe? b. Name three important scientists and their contributions.

Discussion Topics

1. Explain how Eastern Europe came under Soviet control at the end of World War II. Should the U.S. have supported independence for the nations of Eastern Europe? How?
2. Large minority groups live within most Eastern European nations. How has the presence of mixed populations affected nationalism in these countries? Would it be better for ethnic groups to have their own countries? Are there advantages to mixing peoples? What?
3. The theater in Eastern Europe is used as a means of national protest. Why do you think the governments allow this?

Project Ideas

1. Kossuth, Paderewski, and Masaryk have been honored on U.S. postage stamps. Write a brief report telling why they were chosen. If possible, make a poster with the stamps.
2. Arrange a class exhibit on the nations of Eastern Europe. Use materials such as maps, photographs, travel posters, and items made in these countries. Include lists or pictures of people important in government, the arts, science, education, and sports.
3. Prepare an illustrated report on one of the ethnic groups in the U.S. that came from Eastern Europe. What customs, traditions, etc., have they given to this country?
4. Play for the class records or tapes of music by composers mentioned in this unit. Explain how the music reflects the national character of each composer's country.
5. Make a current-events scrapbook on Eastern Europe. State the importance of the events making news and how they relate to this unit.

698

For Further Study

General Readings

1. *Eastern Europe: Czechoslovakia, Hungary, Poland* by Godfrey Blunden. (Life World Library Series). Time-Life Books, rev. ed., 1969. Past and contemporary history. Illustrated.

2. *The Governments of Communist East Europe* by H. Gordon Skilling. Thomas Y. Crowell Co., 1966. Paperback. Communism at work.

3. *The Land and People of Czechoslovakia* by Elvajean Hall. J. B. Lippincott Company, rev. ed., 1972. Traces the Czechs and Slovaks from the 10th century. Illustrated.

4. *The Land and People of Hungary* by Emil Lengyel. J. B. Lippincott Company, rev. ed., 1972. The section on life and customs is particularly useful.

5. *The Land and People of the Balkans* by Dragos Kostich. J. B. Lippincott Company, rev. ed., 1973. Account of the people of Albania, Bulgaria, Romania, and Yugoslavia.

6. *Last Stand at Stalingrad* by Edward R. Sammis. Macmillan Co., 1966. An exciting account of the battle that marked the turning point on the eastern front during World War II.

7. *Makers of the Red Revolution* by Olivia Coolidge. Houghton Mifflin Co., 1963. About the major figures of the revolution.

8. *Russia: A Short History* by Michael T. Florinsky. Macmillan Co., 2nd ed., 1969. Emphasizes the personal aspects.

9. *Russia: The Story of a Nation* by William Habberton. Houghton Mifflin Co., 1965. Considers industry, agriculture, education, and religion in addition to political events.

10. *Russia and the West Under Lenin and Stalin* by George Kennan. New American Library, Inc. Paperback. An outstanding analysis of Soviet-Western relations during the period.

11. *Russian and Eastern European Cultures* ed. by Paul Thomas Welty. J. B. Lippincott Company, 1973. Readings on customs, the arts, economics, politics, and philosophies of the area. Inquiry format.

12. *The Russian Marxists and the Origins of Bolshevism* by Leopold H. Haimson. Beacon Press, 1966. Paperback. Traces the origins of Lenin's party to the Revolution of 1905.

13. *Rumania: Russia's Dissident Ally* by David Floyd. Praeger Publishers, Inc., 1965. A journalistic account of Romania's changing relationship with Russia from 1945-1965.

Fiction

1. *Azef* by Roman Gaul. Doubleday & Co., Inc., 1962. Terrorist activities of the Social Revolutionary Party in Russia.

2. *The Black Earth* by Hans Habe. G. P. Putnam's Sons, 1952. Communism comes to Hungary.

3. *Bridge on the Drina* by Ivo Andric. Macmillan Co., 1959. World War II in Yugoslavia.

4. *Candlesticks and the Cross* by Ruth F. Solomon. Pocket Books, Inc., 1974. Treatment of the Jews in Russia in the 20th century.

5. *Catherine the Great* by Katherine Scherman. Random House, Inc. 1957. Fictionalized biography.

6. *Daily Life in Russia Under the Last Tsar* by Henri Troyat. Macmillan Co., 1962. Life in Russia in 1903.

7. *Eighty-seven Days* by Andrew Angarsky. Alfred A. Knopf, 1963. The 1917 Revolution from the viewpoint of the White Russians.

8. *A Gift for Genghis Khan* by F. J. Alberts. McGraw-Hill Book Co., 1961. Story of Mongol life.

9. *Medieval Russia's Epics, Chronicles, and Tales* by Serge Ginkowsky. E. P. Dutton & Co., Inc., 1963. Paperback. A collection of legends and history from the 1000s to the 1600s.

10. *No Man's World* by Martin Caidin. E. P. Dutton & Co., Inc., 1967. The Soviet Union and the United States compete in space exploration.

11. *One Day in the Life of Ivan Denisovich* by Alexander Solzhenitsyn. New American Library, Inc. Paperback. A day in the life of an inmate in one of Stalin's forced labor camps.

12. *Peter the First* by A. N. Tolstoi. Macmillan Co., 1959. Fictionalized biography.

13. *St. Petersburg* by Andrew Biely. Grove Press, 1959. Paperback. The story of the Revolution in 1905.

14. *Thousand Hour Day* by W. S. Kuniczak. Dial Press, Inc., 1966. The resistance efforts of Poland during World War II.

The
Latin
Americans

Gold objects such as this
Chimu vest tempted
Europeans to come to the
New World in search
of treasure. Some took
the riches and left. Others
stayed to settle the land
they seized from the
Indians. More came and
brought with them blacks
from Africa. All blended
their ways to make the
Latin American culture.

Unit I

The Land and Ancient Peoples

There are many farms and villages on the shores of Lake Atitlan, Guatemala.

Geographers divide the New World into two continents: North America, which reaches to the southernmost tip of Panama, and South America. **Culturally** and **historically**, however, it is more accurate to divide the area into North America and Latin America. North America, in this case, includes only Canada and the United States. Latin America refers to Mexico and all the countries between it and the southern tip of South America. The hundreds of islands in the Caribbean Sea are also part of this **culture region**.

The terms Central America and Middle America are also sometimes used to label parts of this larger area. Central America is the mainland between Mexico and the South American continent. Middle America includes Central America, Mexico, and the Caribbean islands.

Latin America was settled by three waves of people: **prehistoric** Asians, whose descendants came to be known as Indians; Europeans, mostly Spanish and Portuguese; and Africans. The most visible influences today in Latin America are those of the Spanish and Portuguese. They brought their **languages**, **arts**, **society**, and **religion**. The contributions of Indians and blacks blended with those of the Europeans to create a unique culture we call Latin American.

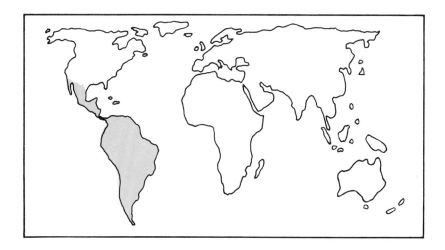

Latin America is made up of 26 nations and 18 dependent states. Several of the Caribbean islands are independent. Some are possessions of other countries. A great variety of physical features—mountains, plateaus, rain forests, deserts, plains, and rivers—mark the vastness of this region. There are also great differences in the kinds and uses of the material resources found throughout the area.

Chapter 1
The
Environment

MEXICO

Mexico, the United Mexican States, is a **federation** of 29 states, two **territories,** and a **federal** district. The district is Mexico City, the nation's capital. Mexico is the largest of the Middle American nations and the third largest country of Latin America.

The Sierra Madre—part of the same chain as the U.S. Rocky Mountains—forms two mountain ranges that run along the east and west coasts. Between them is a fertile plateau that averages 1,500 to 2,400 meters (5,000 to 8,000 feet) above sea level. The central and southern parts of this plateau produce much of Mexico's food. A variety of crops including corn, wheat, rice, oats, barley, and beans can be grown. Because of its rich soil and temperate **climate**, most of the country's major cities are located there. The Valley of Mexico, where Mexico City is located, lies in the plateau.

The northern half of Mexico is mostly desert. For part of the length of Mexico the coastal climate is suitable for growing cotton, sugar, and coffee. The Yucatan (yoo-kuh-TAN) Peninsula forms part of the southeast coast. Areas of this **peninsula** are dense with rain forests.

Traditionally Mexico has had a strong agricultural **economy**. However, in recent years it has become an industrial nation. The basis of its **industry** is mining and oil. Mexico leads the world in the production of silver and also mines large quantities of gold.

SIERRA
MADRE
MTS.

Gulf of Mexico

Atlantic Ocean

*Gulf
of
California*

*Yucatan
Channel*

YUCATAN
PENINSULA

Yucatan

VALLEY
OF MEXICO

Caribbean Sea

*Lake
Nicaragua*

*Panama
Canal*

Orinoco River

RAIN
FOREST

Magdalena River

Pacific Ocean

Amazon River

*Lake
Titicaca*

ATACAMA-PERUVIAN
DESERT

Parana River

ANDES
MTS.

Uruguay River

Rio de la Plata

PAMPAS

▨ Mountains
▨ Deserts
▨ Rain forests
▨ Pampas
▨ Farmland, grazing land, woodlands

CAPE HORN

704

A PHYSICAL MAP OF LATIN AMERICA

Capitals:
1. Nassau
2. Bridgetown
3. Belmopan
4. San Jose
5. Havana
6. Santo Domingo
7. San Salvador
8. St. George's
9. Guatemala City
10. Port-au-Prince
11. Tegucigalpa
12. Kingston
13. Mexico City
14. Managua
15. Panama City
16. San Juan
17. Port of Spain
18. Buenos Aires
19. La Paz
20. Sucre
21. Brasilia
22. Santiago
23. Bogota
24. Quito
25. Cayenne
26. Georgetown
27. Asuncion
28. Lima
29. Paramaribo
30. Montevideo
31. Caracas

A POLITICAL MAP OF LATIN AMERICA

CENTRAL AMERICA

Below Mexico are the six Central American **nations** of Costa Rica, El Salvador, Guatemala, Honduras, Nicaragua (nik-uh-RAHG-wuh), and Panama and the **self-governing** colony of Belize (buh-LEEZ), formerly British Honduras. At its widest, Central America is less than 965 kilometers (600 miles) across. In Panama where the Panama Canal connects the Caribbean Sea and the Pacific Ocean, the land narrows to about 80 kilometers (50 miles).

On the east and west coasts of Central America are low plains. Between them lie highlands. The climate of the coastal lowlands is hot and humid. Most of the population lives in the higher regions where temperatures are milder but where there is less rainfall.

Like most of Middle America, the economies of these nations are based on agriculture. Lumber as well as such tropical crops as bananas, coffee, sugar, cacao, and cotton are the most important products. Some areas in Middle America stress one crop, such as sugar or bananas, for export. This dependence on a **one-crop economy** sometimes leads to problems.

Buyers in the world **market**—not sellers—have traditionally set the price of a commodity. If there were a worldwide scarcity, the price would be high. If there were a **surplus,** the price would be low. But Middle Americans could be the victims as well as the winners in such a system. Bad weather or crop disease could destroy an entire harvest of any of the countries.

Because of the uncertainty of their economies, Central American nations lack the **capital** to build up their own industries. They must look to other countries for manufactured goods such as machinery, vehicles, and other products of iron and steel.

ISLANDS OF THE CARIBBEAN

The islands of the Caribbean are often called the West Indies. This name was given to them when Columbus thought he had discovered islands off the coast of India.

The islands are divided into the Greater Antilles (an-TIL-eez) and the Lesser Antilles. Cuba, Jamaica, Hispaniola (his-puhn-YOH-luh), and Puerto Rico make up the Greater Antilles. East of Puerto Rico are the Virgin Islands. Some of these islands are U.S. possessions. Great Britain claims others. The Lesser Antilles is an arc of many small islands lying at the eastern end of the Caribbean. They are divided into three major groups: the Windward Islands, the Leeward Islands, and the Netherlands Antilles.

Independent nations among the islands are the Bahamas, Barbados (bahr-BAYD-ohs), Cuba, the Dominican Republic, Haiti, Jamaica, Grenada, and the two-island nation of Trinidad-Tobago.

Most of the islands have agricultural economies. Because most fall

Costa Rica's economy in the areas of both agriculture and industry has been improving steadily. Above, a young man picks coffee beans, one of the nation's important exports.

within the tropics, coffee, bananas, cacao, sugar, and lumber are among the major products. Jamaica, however, is developing a strong industrial economy because of its mineral deposits. Since the discovery of oil, Trinidad-Tobago has begun to move toward **industrialization.** Tourism is also important in the West Indies.

SOUTH AMERICA

South America has 12 percent of the world's land area, but only 5 percent of its population. Most of the people are concentrated in plateau or plains areas or along the coasts. **Overpopulation** in these regions is a serious problem. The independent nations of South America are Argentina, Bolivia, Brazil, Chile, Colombia, Ecuador, Guyana (GY-an-uh), Paraguay, Peru, Uruguay, and Venezuela. French Guiana (gee-AN-uh) is a French colony. Surinam (SUR-uh-nam) is a **self-governing** territory of the Netherlands.

The Andes Mountains are among the most impressive geographical features of South America. They extend 7,200 kilometers (4,500 miles) along the western coast of the continent from Venezuela to Cape Horn. Only the Himalayas of Asia are higher. Mount Aconcagua (ak-uhn-KAHG-wuh) in western Argentina at an altitude of approximately 6,960 meters (22,832 feet) is the highest peak in the Western Hemisphere. Over millions of years volcanic activity split the Andes into two or three parallel ranges in some places. Volcanoes and earthquakes still shake the area. Residents of Lima (LEE-muh), Peru, are used to frequent earth tremors. Occasionally, as in 1974, earthquakes are severe.

Rain forests cover much of Brazil and are found in a few other parts of South America. In these forests the trees grow into tangled masses of green. The sun cannot penetrate this thick ceiling of leaves, but rains can. Rains fall almost daily in these forests. The soil is

Bogota is the capital and largest city in Colombia. It is set high in the Andes where several rivers meet. Why are many of the world's largest cities located on rivers?

easily exhausted. Cultivation for even a few years, along with the heavy rains, robs the soil of the minerals which make it fertile. For this reason, the Indians who live there practice **slash-and-burn farming**. They cut trees and burn them to clear the land. In a few years, when the land wears out, the Indians move and begin again.

For the most part, South Americans, like Middle Americans, have avoided the rain forests. However, **government** and private industry are working to change this, especially in Brazil. They have set up several programs to bring agriculture and industry to the area that the Amazon River drains. Within its 5.2 million square kilometers (two million square miles), the basin has many products of present or potential value—rubber, oil, medicinal herbs, and minerals.

In contrast to the rain forests, South America also has areas of desert. Brazil, Argentina, Chile, and Peru all have regions where rain seldom falls. The largest is the Atacama (at-uh-KAHM-uh)—Peruvian Desert. It extends almost 2,900 kilometers (1,800 miles) along much of the coast of Peru and northern Chile.

In the Atacama section in Chile miners dig tons of nitrates—used in the manufacture of fertilizers—and copper ore from the earth. In the Peruvian section people live along the river valleys where they use irrigation systems to grow food.

Most of South America's food, however, is raised on its plains and plateaus. The main occupation of South Americans, like that of Middle Americans, is agriculture. South America's most productive farmland lies within Argentina in an area of fertile plains. Called pampas, these plains make up about one-third of the country. There, wheat and other crops grow in soil that washes down from the mountains. The flatness of the pampas prevents **erosion,** but allows for the buildup of rich mountain soil. Besides grain, cattle are raised in the area.

Brazil, Uruguay, and Paraguay also have fertile plains for grazing cattle and growing wheat, corn, barley, oats, and other grains. In the Andean countries crops are planted on the high plateaus and terraced mountainsides.

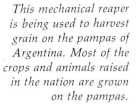

This mechanical reaper is being used to harvest grain on the pampas of Argentina. Most of the crops and animals raised in the nation are grown on the pampas.

RIVERS   Rivers are more important in South America than in Middle America. The Amazon is among the greatest rivers of the area and the world. It extends for over 6,400 kilometers (4,000 miles). Only the Nile River in Africa is longer—by a few hundred kilometers. But the Amazon holds more water than the Nile.

With its 10,000 tributaries—some of them over 1,600 kilometers (1,000 miles) long—the Amazon drains about 40 percent of the South American continent. The tributaries begin in Peru, Bolivia, Venezuela, Colombia, Surinam, Guyana, French Guiana, Ecuador, and Brazil. In all, the Amazon empties one-fifth of the total river water of the world into the Atlantic Ocean.

The Amazon is navigable by ocean steamer and riverboat as far inland as Iquitos, Peru, over 3,200 kilometers (2,000 miles) from the coast. The Amazon Basin to which the river gives its name is located in western Brazil and parts of Colombia and Peru. The basin is mostly rain forest.

The next largest river system is formed by the Parana River of Paraguay and Brazil and the Uruguay River of Uruguay and Brazil. It empties into the Rio de la Plata, a bay, and then the South Atlantic between Uruguay and Argentina. The Orinoco (ohr-uh-NOH-koh) River waters the great plains of southern and central Venezuela and tributaries in Colombia. Another large river system is the Magdalena in Colombia. It flows northward and empties into the Caribbean.

South Americans are working to make their river systems more usable. They are building deep-water channels to improve river transportation. New dams will generate electricity and provide flood control. Irrigation systems will make more land available for farming. Most importantly, the efficient use of both the Orinoco and the Amazon will open up vast resources in the interior.

The geography of Latin America is one of many contrasts. On the left is a copper mine in the Atacama desert. Above is the green Amazon Basin. The Brazilian government is working to bring people and cities into the basin. How might that affect the area's environment?

709

Chapter 2
Early Peoples

The Americas were among the last areas of the earth to be settled. People did not walk the lands of the Western Hemisphere until hundreds of thousands of years after humans were living in Africa, Asia, and Europe.

Archaeologists still debate when the first **people** arrived in the Americas. Past estimates have varied from 12,000 to 50,000 years ago. Recently, however, some archaeologists have uncovered evidence which leads them to think that humans may have lived there over 100,000 years ago. It is generally agreed, however, that some time before 10,000 B.C. and over an extended period of time people traveled from Asia across a land bridge that connected Siberia with Alaska. By about 10,000 B.C. water had covered the land bridge. The area is now known as the Bering Strait.

HUNTERS

The first travelers from Asia were hunters. They were following herds of mammoths, horses, camels, and other big game that were looking for grazing land. The early peoples did not **migrate** in one group but in successive waves. They spread downward through North and Middle America into South America. Archaeologists believe that by 7000 B.C., at least, the migrants had reached the tip of South America.

As they followed the herds, groups of migrants became separated from one another. According to where they finally settled, they developed different physical types. The Indians of the high Andes are shorter and have larger chests than the Indians of the lowlands. The larger chests developed because it is difficult to breathe in high altitudes.

A variety of languages developed. It has been estimated that there were over 1,800 languages spoken in Middle and South America in the pre-Columbian era. Pre-Columbian means before Columbus.

Although the prehistoric groups became separated, they usually went through similar stages in their development. However, in different areas these stages took place at different times. Archaeologists do not agree on the names for each stage. But each is distinguished by the kinds of tools that were made and used at that time.

The early hunters came during the **Old Stone Age**. They used tools similar to those used in other parts of the world in that age. These were large crude stone or bone tools. Hunters did little to improve the stone or bone beyond the form in which they found it. They did not know how to sharpen the edges to make points.

In the next stage hunters began to sharpen and shape their tools. Darts and stone knives have been found among the remains of extinct animals. This stage dates from about 20,000 to 10,000 B.C.

In the third stage, the pace of change increased. During this time, the use of food-grinding tools became widespread. This stage lasted from about 9000 to 5000 B.C. For some time these early people probably had been eating wild plants along with their meat. Archaeologists believe that food gathering had begun around 15,000 B.C. The big game animals were disappearing either because of changes in climate or from overkilling by the hunters. Gathering and preparing plants for food were becoming more important. To make these tasks easier, new kinds of tools were developed.

NEW WORLD FARMING

As people began to rely more and more on plants for food, they found that some plants grew better than others. They learned that if seeds from these plants were gathered and planted, harvests would be larger. Gradually these first Americans went from plant gathering to planting. During this development there seems to have been a certain amount of borrowing and adapting of materials among regions.

MEXICO   So far the earliest remains of **domesticated** plants in the New World have been found in northern Mexico. These were pumpkins and peppers dating from 7,500 to 9,500 years ago. Archaeologists have estimated that by 6000 B.C. cotton and squash were being farmed. By 5000 B.C. a very small type of corn was being grown. Within 1,600 years beans had been added to the list.

These early farmers were still seminomads. They cleared the land and planted crops, but moved on when the soil was worn out. Archaeologists believe that it was not until around 1500 B.C. that people were living in permanent **villages**. By then farmers were producing hardier plants and had developed better ways of farming. The Valley of Mexico and the Yucatan Peninsula appear to have been the first areas to support a settled agricultural life.

SOUTH AMERICA   Less is known about early agriculture in South America. The evidence of earliest domesticated plants dates to about 4500 B.C. Between 3000 and 2500 B.C., cotton, squash, and beans were being grown along the coast. Corn seems to have been introduced from Middle America about 1500 B.C. or earlier. Root plants like the sweet potato originally were domesticated in the rain forests of the Amazon and the Orinoco basins. They spread through the Caribbean.

By about 1000 B.C., settled agriculture was a way of life in Middle and South America. Pre-Columbian farmers domesticated over a hundred crops. They apparently did this independent of Old World developments. Animals did not play an important role in the development of New World farming. Only the dog, guinea pig, llama, and turkey were domesticated.

As the people of the New World settled down to farming, they began to make pottery. They found that they needed containers to prepare and store food. Pottery developed in Ecuador and Colombia about 3000 B.C. From there it appears to have spread northward to Mexico where similar styles and techniques have been discovered.

Corn became part of the diets of the people of Mexico around 5000 B.C. The earliest corn was even smaller than the variety shown above. This was found with prehistoric remains in South America.

OLD WORLD CONTACTS

The early pottery of Ecuador—named after Valdivia (val-DEEV-ee-uh) where it was first discovered—seems to show a strong Asian influence. It suggests that people from other cultures came to the Americas before Columbus in 1492 or even before the Vikings in about 1000 A.D. There are many such pieces of evidence.

Pre-Columbian medical practices, mummification, pyramid building, and some other **artifacts** are similar to ones found elsewhere in the world. Reed boats used by fishing peoples on Lake Chad in Africa and on Lake Titicaca (tit-uh-KAHK-uh) in Peru are similar.

Chinese records indicate that around 500 A.D. a Chinese Buddhist monk came to the Americas. He sailed down the coast of California to Mexico and possibly to Central America. He spent some time there before returning home to write about his adventures.

UNIQUE DEVELOPMENTS By considering ocean currents and the seaworthiness of ancient crafts, experts have shown that such contacts were possible. The voyage from Morocco to Barbados in 1970 by the *Ra II*, a reconstruction of an ancient Egyptian reed boat, further showed this. It was captained by the Norwegian **anthropologist**-explorer, Thor Heyerdahl (HAY-uhr-dahl).

But these early contacts, if they occurred, were isolated events. The visitors did not deeply influence the cultural developments of pre-Columbian peoples. Pre-Columbian agriculture developed without the plow. No culture used the wheel—except on toys. And in only limited ways did these peoples use iron. Yet they built beautiful **cities**, ruled vast **empires**, and created dramatic works of art.

This is an example of Valdivia pottery. It is similar to Japanese pottery of the same period, 3000-2500 B.C.

A modern-day resident of the Andes poles his reed boat across Lake Titicaca the way his ancestors did for centuries. These boats are similar to ones used on Lake Chad in Africa.

Summing Up the Unit

Social Studies Vocabulary

Define: geography; culture region; federation; territory; peninsula; one-crop economy; overpopulation; slash-and-burn farming; erosion; Old Stone Age; domesticate; A.D.; artifacts; anthropologist; city; empire

Places

Locate: Sierra Madre; Valley of Mexico; Yucatan Peninsula; Caribbean Sea; Panama Canal; Pacific, Atlantic oceans; Andes Mountains; Cape Horn; rain forest; Atacama-Peruvian Desert; pampas; Rio de la Plata; Amazon, Parana, Orinoco, Magdalena rivers

Words

Define: Central America; Middle America; Indians; rain forest; West Indies; pampas; pre-Columbian

⌐ Questions

1. a. Where are most of Mexico's major cities located? b. Why?
2. What type of vegetation is found on the Yucatan Peninsula?
3. How has Mexico been able to move from an agricultural to an industrial nation?
4. Why is most of Central America's population concentrated in its higher regions?
5. What problems can result from dependence on a one-crop economy?
6. a. What type of economy do most of the Caribbean islands have? b. Which two nations are developing new economies? c. How?
7. a. Where are most of the people concentrated in South America? b. What problem has this caused?
8. Why is the soil of Brazil's rain forests easily exhausted by cultivation?
9. a. How are South Americans working to make their rain forests more usable? b. their river systems?
10. How do South Americans use their deserts?
11. When do archaeologists think the first people arrived in the Americas?
12. a. Why did early hunting groups develop into different physical types? b. What example is given in the text?
13. Where have the earliest remains of domesticated plants been found in the New World?
14. What plants were grown in the various areas of Middle and South America in pre-Columbian times?
15. By when was settled agriculture a way of life in Middle and South America?
16. Why did people begin to make pottery?
17. How important were animals in the development of New World farming?
18. a. What evidence suggests that there were early contacts between the Old and New Worlds before Columbus? b. What three examples suggest that the contacts did not have much influence?

Discussion Topics

1. Latin America contains a great variety of geographic features. Which of these are advantages and which are disadvantages for the Latin Americans? Why?
2. Most of Latin America's population that lives within the tropics is concentrated in higher regions. How has this affected the use of Latin America's lands and natural resources?

Project Ideas

1. Make a list of useful plants native to the Americas and unknown to Europeans before Columbus. List plants that were brought to the Americas from other parts of the world.
2. To become familiar with the political and physical geography of Latin America, trace the maps in this unit. Include the place names mentioned. Draw another map and from memory add the various places.
3. Using an atlas or encyclopedia for reference, draw a population distribution map of Latin America. Include rivers, mountains, deserts, rain forests, and pampas. Relate population to physical features and climate.

713

Unit II

Pre-Columbian Civilizations

The Castillo at Chichen Itza has 91 steps on each of its four sides. They lead to a temple. What other peoples built pyramids? Were they temples too?

Millions of people lived in Middle and South America before Columbus arrived. They represented hundreds of **tribes**, cultures, and language groups. Where the people had settled down to farming, the food supply had become more certain and plentiful. As a result, the population increased. More people lived in larger settlements.

Permanent farming made possible the development of the complex **civilizations** of southern Middle America and the Andes Mountains. These two areas became the two most intensely farmed regions of pre-Columbian America. Trade played an important role in these civilizations.

However, not all pre-Columbian peoples were farmers or traders. Many—like the Puelches (PWEL-chays) of the pampas and the Araucanians (uh-raw-KAHN-ee-uhns) of the southern Andes—were nomads. They lived by hunting, fishing, and seed gathering. In the rain forests of Brazil and the Caribbean islands, people such as the Arawaks (AR-uh-wahks) and the Caribs used slash-and-burn farming.

For a long time, authorities believed that the Aztecs of Mexico and the Incas of Peru had the most highly developed civilizations in the New World. But because of recent discoveries, we know that there were great civilizations before these two. The earlier New World cultures predate Buddhism in India, the Confucian Age in China, the Golden Age of Greece, and Etruscan rule in Rome. Perhaps the earliest of these cultures was that of the Olmecs of Mesoamerica. Archaeologists use the term Mesoamerica to refer to the area of southern Mexico and Central America.

OLMECS

Sometime before 1200 B.C. a people whom archaeologists call Olmec (OHL-mek) were developing a farming culture along the southern coast of the Gulf of Mexico. The soil of these humid lowlands is ideal for farming. Corn, beans, and squash were probably raised.

Archaeologists have found several Olmec ceremonial centers in the region. These centers were not cities. People lived near the centers and used them for religious ceremonies. The major **sites** are at La Venta, San Lorenzo, and Tres Zapotes. All the centers have large pyramids, earth mounds, huge stone heads, and steles (STEE-lees)— large stone columns with a form of **hieroglyphic** (HY-uh-ruh-glif-ik) writing on them. This writing has not as yet been decoded. The Olmecs had also worked out a calendar.

Olmec religion seems to have centered around worship of a half-human, half-jaguar god of fertility. Many finely carved jade figures of this god have been found.

An outstanding feature of the centers is the huge stone heads. The largest head is 2.7 meters (9 feet) high and weighs 18 metric tons (20 tons). The heads are wearing hats that look much like football helmets. Archaeologists believe that they may have been worn for protection. From other artifacts it appears that the Olmecs played some type of ball game. The game may have had a religious meaning.

The Olmecs had to be clever engineers as well as skilled sculptors to fashion these heads. The stone had to be brought to the centers from as much as 80 kilometers (50 miles) away. For part of the trip the stones probably were floated on rafts. For land passage the people had to drag them. The Olmecs had neither horses, oxen, nor wheeled vehicles. Also, they did not have metal tools. They used stone tools to sculpt these heads and carve and drill their jade figures and beads.

Between 1200 and 200 B.C. Olmec influence spread widely. It is not known whether the Olmecs conquered other peoples or spread their art styles and knowledge by **trade** and/or **colonization.** Olmec influence became so widespread in Mexico and Central America that it is considered the base culture of Mesoamerica. Later cultures, including that of the Mayas, used and improved on Olmec cultural features such as its calendar and hieroglyphics. Some scholars believe

Chapter 1
Mesoamerica

ceremonial:
belonging to a ceremony, which is a series of formal acts, such as a wedding

☐ **Olmec Civilization,**
   c. 1200s-200s B.C.

The Olmec head above wears what looks like a helmet. Archaeologists believe that the Olmecs played some type of ball game that required a protective covering for the head. At right are the remains of a Mayan ball court at Copan, Honduras. The Mayan empire rose as the Olmecs declined. The Mayas played a game much like soccer. They batted a rubber ball back and forth by hitting it with their bodies.

that Olmec influence can even be seen as far south as Peru. The jaguar god of Peru's Chavin (CHAH-veen) culture may possibly have been an adaptation of the Olmec god. Possibly the two cultures were joined by a sea route.

Most of the major Olmec discoveries have been made since the 1940s. In comparison, European archaeology was almost a hundred years old by then. As archaeologists continue to study Olmec sites, more of the mystery surrounding these early people may be solved.

The influence of the Olmec culture began to decline about 200 B.C. Its people and monuments were overshadowed by a more powerful culture to the south—that of the Mayas.

MAYAS

When the Spanish arrived on the Yucatan Peninsula in the 1500s, they found the remains of the Mayan (MY-uhn) civilization. In their eagerness to remove all traces of non-Christian worship, they destroyed much of what they found. Monuments and other artifacts were smashed. Many manuscripts were destroyed. A few were stored away and forgotten. Recently these few were rediscovered. Scholars are trying to decode them. Hopefully these records will tell how the Mayas were able to develop their society in the unlikely **environment** of a rain forest. Rain forests have the least favorable climate and soil in which to build a civilization.

Meanwhile archaeologists are at work uncovering Mayan temples and monuments that have been blanketed by centuries of jungle growth. These experts have been able to determine that the Mayan civilization went through several stages. It may have begun as early as 500 B.C. The greatest stage of its development lasted from about 300 to 900 A.D. During that time, Mayan cultural centers stretched from the Yucatan Peninsula into what are modern Guatemala, Honduras, Belize, and El Salvador.

From the evidence of artifacts some Mayas were traders. Most, however, were farmers. Despite the harshness of the environment, they were very successful. Their crops supported a large population and a **class** of priest-scholars.

It is not known if the Mayas had monarchs or even if their cultural centers were united with one another. They might have been independent **city-states** like those of ancient Greece. Archaeologists are not even certain if the sites were actually cities. They might have been only ceremonial centers. Remains of temples, marketplaces, amphitheaters, ball courts, and even astronomical observatories have been found, but no houses. Archaeologists believe that priest-scholars lived near the outer limits of the centers. The majority of people lived in nearby villages around their fields.

This stele was found at Piedras Negras, Guatemala. Archaeologists believe the figures to be that of a priest-ruler and his wife.

SCIENCE AND ART   In mathematics and **astronomy** the Mayas were more advanced than their European counterparts. Although they had no telescopes, their astronomers had worked out the movement of planets and stars. They could accurately predict eclipses. By the 600s A.D. the Mayan calendar was more accurate than the Gregorian calendar that was adopted in Europe in the 1500s.

The Mayas also developed the most complex writing system in the New World—a form of ideographs—which they carved on steles. These monuments may contain records of important events or descriptions of daily life. So far scientists have been able to decode only the dates.

The Mayas cut limestone blocks to build their temples and monuments. They also made bricks, and used mortar and stucco. Their buildings have a massive appearance and are decorated with columns, stairways, and elaborate carvings. Some buildings are over 60 meters (200 feet) high. Like the Olmecs, the Mayas had neither metal tools nor wheeled vehicles.

Temple murals detail Mayan ceremonial and daily life. The Mayas worshiped **deities** that were connected with the harvest. There were rain, soil, sun, and corn gods, and a moon goddess.

DECLINE   No one knows why the culture of the Mayas came to an end. Their calendar stops about 900 A.D. They stopped building then too. Half-finished temples were left to crumble. If a natural disaster occurred, there is no trace of it. Neither is there evidence of an

**Mayan Civilization,
c. 500s B.C.-1200s A.D.**

invasion. Perhaps an epidemic, a drought, or the wearing out of the soil caused the sudden decline. Or perhaps the people rebelled against their leaders for some as yet unknown reason.

The Mayan culture survived in the highlands of Guatemala but under increasing pressure from a warlike people, probably the Toltecs (TOHL-teks) of northern Mexico. Their influence is recorded by a change in art styles and themes. Skulls, warriors, and feathered serpents appear. Human sacrifice became an important part of religion. Wars between centers became frequent.

About 1000 A.D. the Toltecs also took control in the northern Yucatan. They ruled from the old Mayan center of Chichen Itza (chee-chen eet-SAH). Mayas were able to regain control about 1200 A.D. but the 200-year influence of war remained. The centers in the Yucatan too fought numerous wars among themselves.

By the time the Spanish arrived in the 1500s, the Mayas had lost their dominance in Mesoamerica. Today about 1.5 million of their descendants live in Central America.

TEOTIHUACANOS

About the time that the early Mayan culture was developing in southern Mexico, another civilization was developing north of present-day Mexico City. It began in an area of the Valley of Mexico called Teotihuacan (TAY-oh-tee-wah-kahn).

People were living in the region by 300 B.C. or earlier. But some archaeologists believe that Teotihuacan and the civilization that bears its name developed about 2,000 years ago. Over the centuries the city of Teotihuacan came to rival any city of Europe in size, splendor, and planning. Estimates of the city's population, at the height of its influence, range from 60,000 to 200,000. Teotihuacan spread across nearly 21 square kilometers (8 square miles). Wide avenues, temple pyramids, palaces for priests and nobles, and houses for **artisans** and traders filled the city. Smaller communities grew out from it.

Of its architectural features, Teotihuacan is best known for the Pyramids of the Sun and of the Moon. They are located at either end of the Avenue of the Dead. The Pyramid of the Sun was built of adobe bricks and covered with stone. Possibly 10,000 workers labored 20 years to build it.

Some archaeologists believe that Teotihuacan may have been the largest city in Mesoamerica. Its prosperity was built on its trading network. This network spread Teotihuacan's influence from Guatemala in the south to the U.S. Southwest.

About 400 A.D. the Teotihuacanos began a series of wars of conquest. Sometime between the 600s and 900s A.D., enemies—probably Toltecs from the north—burned the city. It never again regained its importance.

Teotihaucan was possibly the largest city in Mesoamerica. The large grassy area in the foreground was once a giant market. Behind it are the Pyramids of the Sun and Moon. How important was trade to the economy of Teotihuacan?

TOLTECS

Other peoples—Zapotecs, Totonacs, and Mixtecs, to name a few—came to power in pre-Columbian America and then fell. The people they conquered regarded them as barbarians. The invaders usually had a less well-developed culture. As has often happened, however, the invaders accepted many of the ways of the peoples they conquered. But they also left their own cultural mark on the conquered. As we have seen with the Olmecs, none of the cultures totally disappeared. Elements reappeared in one form or another in one culture or another. This fact is also illustrated by the merging of Mayan and Toltec cultures.

The origins of the Toltecs are as yet unknown. But archaeologists believe that around 750 A.D. the Toltecs built the city of Tula north of Teotihuacan. It is believed that at first the Toltecs were ruled jointly by a priest and a civil leader.

Ultimately the two leaders and those they represented argued over policy. The followers of the civil leader favored war. They won, and the Toltecs began a series of conquests. They carried their empire to the Yucatan and Guatemala. They took control of the lowland Mayas and Chichen Itza. There they mixed their art styles with those of the Mayas. The Toltecs extended their rule throughout central Mexico.

The Toltec empire was probably larger than that of the later Aztecs. Even if their actual rule was not so widespread, their influence was. Toltec copper bells have been found as far north as the U.S. Southwest. By 1200 A.D. internal differences, disease, and a new wave of invaders caused the empire to fall.

■ **Toltec Civilization, c. 750 A.D.**

☐ **Aztec Civilization,
c. 1200s-1520 A.D.**

AZTECS

We know more about the Aztecs than about any of the other Meso-american cultures. Many written accounts—both Aztec and Spanish—give details of Aztec civilization. Some of these records were written at the time of the Spanish conquest. Others were written shortly afterward.

From their own records we know that the Aztecs were originally one of the Chichimec (chee-chee-MEK) tribes that lived in the barren lands of northern Mexico. The name Aztec comes from the area where they lived, Aztlan (AZT-lahn). In the late 1100s A.D. they wandered south into the fertile Valley of Mexcio. By the mid-1200s the Aztecs were forcing out the Toltecs. After a few generations, the Aztecs themselves were being forced farther south by new invaders. In 1325 they came upon islands in a salt-water lake.

According to Aztec legend, the god Huitzilopochtli (WEET-see-loh-poh-chit-lee) had told them that they would someday be a great people. But they must follow his advice: Seek out good land. Plant corn and beans. War only when strong enough to conquer. Make sacrifices of war captives. The Aztecs would know that they had found the right place when they came upon a small island. They would find an eagle perched on a cactus. In its beak would be a serpent.

When the Aztecs arrived at the lake, they supposedly found these signs. They built a city that they called Tenochtitlan (tay-notch-tit-LAHN)—Cactus in the Rock. (Today the lake is gone but Mexico City stands on the dry lake bed.) The Aztecs planted corn, pumpkins, beans, tomatoes, and peppers, among other crops. As they prospered, they began conquering nearby tribes. Tenochtitlan soon became a great city-state. Through a **confederation** of city-states, the Aztecs spread their power and influence throughout central and southern Mexico. Their empire ultimately included some five million people.

POLITICS AND SOCIETY **Political** and social organization within the Aztec confederation was complex. At its head was a ruler whom the later Spanish called an emperor. The nation itself was made up of many **states**. Each was divided into a number of districts called calpullis. A calpulli might contain a few dozen families or a few hundred. Each calpulli was ruled by a group of household heads. They in turn were ruled by a chief whom they selected. Land was owned in common by the calpulli. At marriage each man was given a share to work. What he produced was his, but the calpulli kept the land.

The Aztecs had a rigid class system. At the top was a small group of priests and nobles. The next level was made up of commoners and was the largest segment of the population. But within this group were further divisions. **Skilled** artisans held the highest position. At the lowest social level were the **slaves**. People became slaves because they were prisoners of war, criminals, or debtors. Sometimes a slave could gain freedom or even own other slaves.

segment:
portion or part

720

This is a reproduction from the Codex Mendoza. *The* Codex *dates from around the time of the conquest and describes Aztec history. This scene seems to depict the class structure of Aztec society. What clues can you find to support this assumption?*

THE ECONOMY   Aztec economy was based on agriculture. The Aztecs dug elaborate irrigation systems for their fields. In marshy areas, they built floating gardens using the rich soil deposits under the water. To make these islands, they dug square or rectangular ditches. Then they filled the enclosed areas with mud. The mud was held in place with tree branches or cane. Their main crop was corn.

Besides farmers, Aztecs were skilled artisans and traders. They produced a variety of items in wood, feathers, textiles, gold, silver, jade, and other semiprecious stones. Not all the **natural resources** or foodstuffs needed to support the Aztecs were found near Tenochtitlan. Trade thus became an important part of Aztec life.

Often, however, **raw materials** became the reason for war. Once people were captured they became part of the empire and had to pay **tribute** to the emperor. The tribute was usually in the form of materials not found near Tenochtitlan.

WAR AND RELIGION   The principal god of the Aztecs, Huitzilo- pochtli, was the god of war. Many Aztec religious ceremonies required human sacrifice. This was to fulfill another part of the legend. Usually the victims were captives taken in war. Sometimes a war was waged simply to obtain such victims.

The training of soldiers began at an early age. It was the responsibility of the calpulli to train its young men. And each had a school for the purpose. Aztec weapons were limited to wooden clubs, javelins, bows and arrows, and slings. For protection Aztec soldiers wore helmets and armor made of heavily padded cotton. A single battle usually determined the victor.

Aztec religion was concerned with death and the end of the world. The Aztecs believed that the world had been destroyed and remade several times. They believed that a final destruction could be prevented by human sacrifice. Sometimes several thousand victims were killed in a single ceremony.

When the Aztec empire was less than 200 years old, the Spanish arrived in the New World. At that point, the Aztec empire was still expanding. Would the Aztecs have been more successful than earlier peoples in holding together an empire? We shall never know. For when the Spanish murdered Montezuma II (mahn-tuh-ZOO-muh) in 1521, they replaced Aztec power and civilization.

This is a reproduction from the Codex Mendoza. *The men appear to be warriors. How important were warriors to the continuing strength of the Aztec empire?*

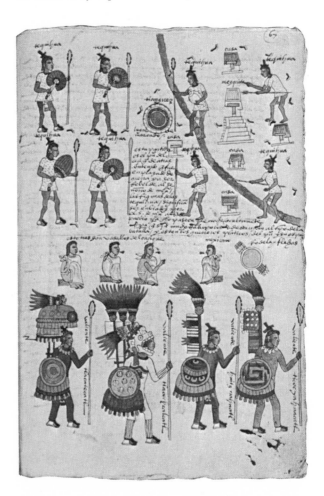

722

Andean cultures are those cultures that evolved in western South America before the Spanish conquest. They developed along the mountains and coastal area from southern Ecuador through Peru, Bolivia, and Colombia into northern Chile. Like those of Mesoamerica, the Andean cultures were based on agriculture. The later ones had large **urban** areas and, among the Incas especially, a high degree of **centralized government**.

PRE-INCAN CULTURES

All we know of pre-Incan peoples is what archaeologists have found. And there are various interpretations of what the artifacts mean. We know for certain, however, that early in their development Andean peoples began farming. They also learned metalworking, and became skilled weavers and stone carvers. So far, however, no traces of scientific accomplishments have been found. Neither calendars nor written material like Mayan steles has yet been discovered.

Very little archaeological work was done in the area before World War II. The expense of sending expeditions and the difficult working conditions kept archaeologists away. Also because of a lack of records, it was difficult to know where to explore. The study of Spanish histories of the New World and new techniques such as aerial surveys have helped solve this problem.

CHAVIN The Chavin (CHAH-veen) culture is considered the oldest Andean culture. Other societies existed before it. However, not enough evidence has been found to call any of them a specific culture. Some archaeologists believe that the Chavin culture began about 1400 B.C. Others date it to around 1000 B.C.

The Chavin people built ceremonial centers, not cities. The people lived around the centers in small communities. The centers may or may not have been linked by a central government. However, Chavin influences, in terms of religion and art styles, have been discovered in northern and central Peru and along the southern coast. It is possible that missionaries spread its art while carrying the message of the Chavin religion. Religion and art were closely tied.

A jaguar god may have been part of their religion. Designs and figures with catlike features are prominent on Chavin pottery, textiles, and metalwork. This god may have been an adaptation of the Olmec god. The most impressive features of the ceremonial centers are massive, elaborately carved temples. The best-known center is at Chavin de Huantar in northern Peru, over 3,000 meters (10,000 feet) above sea level. Several structures remain, including a stone temple with many rooms and corridors. Chavin influence seems to have declined around the 400s B.C.

Between 200 B.C. and the 400s A.D. many different groups competed for land and power in the Andes. Simple scattered farm villages became parts of larger social and/or political units.

Chapter 2
The Andes

This bowl made in the shape of a jaguar was found at Chavin de Huantar. What other people used a catlike figure in their art?

☐ **Chavin Civilization, c. 1000s-400s B.C.**

SOUTHERN ANDES   Around 200 B.C., people on the Paracas (puh-RAHK-uhs) Peninsula of southern Peru began developing a culture. So far its weavings are the most impressive aspect to be unearthed. Most that have been found are cloaks wrapped around mummies. The weavings are adorned with brilliantly colored birds, fish, animals, and gods. The themes seem to be religious. Various weaving techniques were used and some pieces have over a hundred different colors. The Paracas culture appears to have lasted until 400 A.D. However, its artistic influence can be seen in later periods. The same kinds of woven designs, although more stylized, are found on Nazca (NAHS-kah) textiles.

The Nazca culture also developed along the desert coast of southern Peru. Nazca weavings are not as helpful in tracing Nazca life or religion as is its pottery. The Nazcas adapted Paracas woven designs just as they borrowed and adapted Paracas pottery styles. But while the Paracas people painted designs on pottery after firing, the Nazcas learned to add the color before. In place of the catlike faces on Paracas bowls, Nazca pottery shows scenes or objects from daily life.

The Nazcas have created what seems to be Peru's most baffling archaeological mystery. On the dry plains around the Palpa Valley, north of Nazca, are giant lines made in the shapes of animals and geometric forms. The Nazca lines, which may possibly be 1,500 to 2,000 years old, were first spotted less than 50 years ago, from an airplane. Archaeologists have wondered about the meaning of the lines, and why the people made them so large. An entire pattern can never be seen at one time.

It is believed that the Nazcas later came under the influence of the Tiahuanaco (tee-uh-wuh-NAH-koh) people farther inland.

Sometime after 200 B.C. and before 600 A.D. on the border between modern Peru and Bolivia the great ceremonial center of Tiahuanaco rose. Most of the city is in ruins today, but the Gateway of the Sun still stands. It is adorned with what may have been Tiahuanaco's major god. He has a large square face and tears falling from his eyes. Throughout the center, carvings of this god and his winged messengers are found on temples, stones, and doorways. This design is found over northern Chile and northwestern Argentina to northern Peru. Evidently it was religious conversions rather than military force that spread Tiahuanacan influence. For a yet unknown reason the center was abandoned around 1000 A.D.

NORTHERN ANDES   The Huari (WAH-ree)—or Wari—empire rose and fell during part of the life span of the southern center of Tiahuanaco. Huari helped to spread Tiahuanacan designs into the central and northern Andes. The culture began about 600 A.D. in the highlands between Tiahuanaco and what is modern Lima, Peru. For the next 400 years Huari dominated the Andes. Like Tiahuanaco its influence may have been more religious and artistic than political. Like Tiahuanaco it too was abandoned about 1000.

COLOMBIA

ECUADOR

PERU

BRAZIL

Paracas Peninsula   Tiahuanaco

Pacific Ocean

CHILE

☐ Huari Empire, c. 600-1000 A.D.

Above left is a pottery dove from the Nazca culture. To the right is a Mochica portrait jar of a religious figure. Both cultures used their pottery to describe objects and scenes from daily life. Why would people take such care and use so much talent to make an ordinary item such as a jar?

At about this time the Andes people were beginning to settle in walled urban areas. However, the economy was still agricultural. People may have moved into cities to have more farmland or to be better able to defend their fields. As in Mesoamerica, war was becoming an important part of life. No longer were cultural influences spread through trade as in Mesoamerica or religion as in the Andes. Conquering armies brought political, social, and artistic ideas.

One of the greatest pre-Inca civilizations was that of the Mochica (moo-CHEE-kuh). In about 200 B.C. a people began to build a city in the Moche Valley along the northern coast of Peru. Ultimately the culture had a number of cities, ceremonial centers, irrigation systems, and forts. It appears that Mochica society was agricultural and had a class society in which warriors ranked high. Archaeologists believe that war in defense of the fields was common.

One piece of evidence used to support this theory is Mochica pottery. Its designs and style developed along lines similar to the Nazca. The Mochicas too portrayed scenes from their daily lives. However, they developed a unique design—the portrait jar. It was fashioned in the shape of humans or animals. Many that have been found represent warriors or other officials. Sometime between 600 and 800 A.D. the Mochica culture declined.

The Chimu (CHEE-moo) empire rose on the base of the Mochica culture. In the 1300s the people of Chimu in the Moche Valley began to expand beyond its borders. For the next hundred years they waged highly successful wars. Chimu economy was agricultural. The mountains were terraced and a vast irrigation system was built. Larger cities had walled areas for defense. Forts dotted the fields.

Mochica-Chimu Civilizations
— **Mochica, c. 200s B.C.-800s A.D.**
▨ **Chimu, 1300s-1460 A.D.**

725

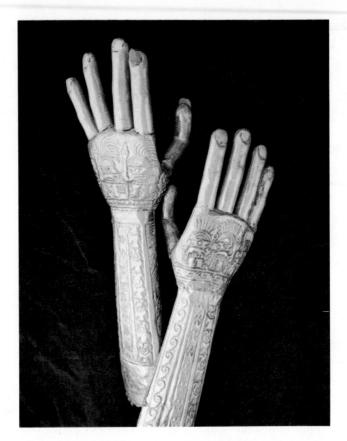

The peoples of the Mesoamerican and Andean cultures had been working in metals for centuries before the Europeans came. This is an example of Chimu goldwork. Human and animal figures as well as abstract designs were beaten into the gold. What figures can you identify on these hands?

The Chimus set up a strong political organization. They resettled conquered peoples close to the center of the empire. In this way the captured were surrounded by subjects friendly to the Chimus. Loyal settlers were moved into the new distant territories. A system of roads made **communication** between various parts of the empire possible. The Chimu empire fell about 1460 when its leader was captured by the Incas.

INCAS

Like the Aztecs, the Incas had a relatively low level of **technology** and political organization until they began conquering other peoples. The Incas apparently learned much about roads, irrigation systems, and administration from others, especially the Chimus. By the time the Spanish arrived, the Incas ruled an empire that included all of Peru and stretched north into Ecuador, south into Bolivia and Chile, and east to the border of Argentina. It included a population estimated at between four and seven million people. At one time the word Inca was applied only to the ruler. The Spanish, however, used it to describe the entire culture.

Little is known about the Incas before the 1200s A.D. The records that describe them after that time must be read with caution. The Inca rulers had history made up to glorify themselves and their family. According to legend, the first ruler—Manco Capac and his sister Mama Ocllo—were created by Inti, the sun god. Manco then founded the city of Cuzco (KOOS-koh), which became the capital of the empire. The Incas believed that their ruler was descended from the gods and was himself a god. According to **tradition**, one **dynasty** ruled from the time of the empire's founding until its end at the hands of the Spanish.

ORGANIZATION   Archaeologists believe that the Incas were originally a small group in the Cuzco Basin of the central Andes. In the early 1400s as the population increased, the Incas began to spread beyond the basin. They preferred to persuade non-Inca peoples to become subjects voluntarily. However, if they refused, the Incas fought. Conquered peoples were allowed to keep their rulers. But the people as a group were resettled among loyal subjects. The new citizens could keep their religions as long as they also worshiped Inca gods. They also had to learn Inca customs and Quechua (KECH-uh-wuh), the Inca language.

Today we would call the Inca empire a **totalitarian** state. The emperor made all political and religious laws for his subjects. For administrative purposes, the empire was divided into four districts. The governor of each was a member of the emperor's family and was directly responsible to the emperor. Each district was divided into smaller districts, each with a governor. Under him were local officials. They conducted the census, recorded wealth, and set tax rates. With this system, the emperor knew at all times the exact condition of every part of the empire.

All land was owned by the emperor but worked by the people. Its products were divided into three parts. One part was kept by the

Machu Picchu is one of the largest examples of the Inca culture to be found. It is set high in the Andes, not far from Cuzco. Its ruins include a temple, a fort, and walled terraces. The Incas raised crops on these terraces.

727

community. Products of the second part were used in religious ceremonies and to support the priests. The third part was for the use of the ruler and the **bureaucracy**. A portion of this, however, was stored away. In times of drought or crop failure, the emperor would send some of this emergency supply to the needy areas.

Efficient communication throughout the empire contributed to Inca success. A network of highways extended over 16,000 kilometers (10,000 miles) from the coasts of the Pacific to the rain forests of the Amazon. Two main roads ran parallel for the length of the empire. Small roads connected them. Wherever the route crossed mountain chasms or rivers, suspension bridges were built. A special staff kept the roads clear and in repair.

Messengers carried news from one part of the empire to another over these roads. Roadside stations were located one day apart. Fresh runners and food were supplied by the people who lived nearby. The stations also served as rest houses for travelers.

TECHNOLOGY   The Incas inherited much of their technology from earlier peoples. But they adapted and expanded these ideas to their own needs. Under Inca management, agriculture was improved and intensified. They expanded the use of terracing for growing crops, especially potatoes. Fertilizer was used extensively. By enlarging irrigation systems, more land was brought into production.

The Incas created their empire without the aid of a written language as far as we know at present. However, they kept exact numerical records by means of the quipu (KEE-poo). The quipu is a rope with knotted cords hanging from it. Quipus were used as memory aids by the messengers who traveled the highways on state business.

Despite their military strength, **diplomacy**, and organization, the Inca empire came to an end in 1533. In that year the Spanish marched into Cuzco.

The Incas had no writing system but used quipus instead. Quipus were made of one long rope with shorter ropes knotted to it and shorter ropes tied to these. The knots were used to show units, tens, and hundreds. The cords were dyed. Each color represented a different item such as land or tribute.

Summing Up the Unit

Social Studies Vocabulary

Define: permanent farming; civilizations; site; hieroglyphic; trade; colonization; city-states; deities; artisans; confederation; skilled; raw materials; tribute; urban; communication; totalitarian state; bureaucracy; diplomacy

Places

Olmec Civilization; Gulf of Mexico; Mayan, Toltec, Aztec civilizations; Tenochtitlan; Chavin civilization; Paracas Peninsula; Tiahuanaco; Huari Empire; Mochica, Chimu civilizations; Inca Empire; Cuzco

Words

Define: Mesoamerica; stele; calpulli; Andean cultures; portrait jar; Quechua; quipu

☞ Questions

1. a. The culture of what people is thought to be the oldest in Mesoamerica? b. Where was the culture located? c. What special skills did the people have?
2. a. What evidence is there to call Olmec a base culture? b. How did the culture spread?
3. a. When were the first Olmec discoveries made? b. How does this compare with European archaeology?
4. Why did the Spanish destroy much of the Mayan civilization?
5. Why is the environment in which the Mayas developed their society described as unlikely?
6. a. What have archaeologists been able to determine about the Mayas? b. What do they not know about the Mayas?
7. How were the Mayas more advanced than their European counterparts?
8. a. What deities did the Mayas worship? b. All of them were connected with what activity?
9. a. What evidence is there of a sudden decline of Mayan culture? b. What possible answers are offered for that decline? c. Where did Mayan culture survive? d. What does Mayan art tell us about changes in the culture that survived?
10. a. What city do archaeologists believe may have been the largest in Mesoamerica? b. What was the basis of its prosperity?
11. What evidence is there that Toltec influence was widespread?
12. Why do we know more about the Aztecs than about any of the other Mesoamerican cultures?
13. a. Trace the wanderings of the Aztecs. b. What geographic feature caused their wanderings?
14. How did the Aztecs spread their power and influence throughout Mexico?
15. Describe the class system of the Aztecs.
16. a. Why did trade and war become important parts of Aztec life? b. Why did the Aztecs practice human sacrifice?
17. What do we know about pre-Incan peoples?
18. a. Which Andean culture is considered to be the oldest? b. Why?
19. What evidence is there that Tiahuanacan influence was spread by religious conversions rather than military force?
20. What methods did the Chimus use to control their empire?
21. What did the the Incas learn from others, especially the Chimus?
22. What methods did the Incas use to control their empire?
23. a. What effect did communication have on the Inca empire? b. How did the Incas improve agricultural production?

Discussion Topics

1. No one knows why the Mayan culture ended. What explanation of the ones offered in the text seems most reasonable to you?
2. The Teotihuacanos built great temple pyramids. To do this what features of wealth, power, and organization must have been necessary?
3. Underlying the Aztec religion was a depression and an obsession with death. How might conditions of Aztec life have caused such a fear?

Project Ideas

1. Make a chart listing Mesoamerican and Andean cultures. Include names, time periods, and other information under these headings: Politics, Class System, Economy and Technology, War, Religion, Arts, Other Accomplishments. What comparisons do you notice from the information?
2. Using the maps in this unit, make a combined map of Mesoamerican and Andean cultures.

Unit III

Coming of the Europeans

Like other conquistadores, Vasco Nunez de Balboa claimed land and people in the name of God and his monarch. This statue of Balboa stands in Panama City. Why did Europeans believe they had a right to claim the land they explored?

The European discovery of the Americas was an accident. It was the result of efforts during the 1400s to find a sea route to the riches of the Orient. Neither the Spanish nor the Portuguese wished to create new nations. Nor were they interested in learning about the peoples they found. The European conquerors, regardless of **nationality**, treated the Indians as objects to rob.

Between 1500 and 1800 the British, French, and Dutch fought with the Spanish and Portuguese for control of parts of Latin America. Along the northeastern coast of South America, they took three territories known today as Surinam, Guyana, and French Guiana. They also claimed some of the islands of the Caribbean. In Middle America the British seized land known today as Belize. The Spanish and Portuguese, however, held on to the largest portions of Latin America.

On his first voyage to the New World, Christopher Columbus sighted San Salvador (Watling Island) in the Bahamas, and the island of Hispaniola (modern Haiti and the Dominican Republic). The first people he met were the Arawaks who were friendly to him. Believing that he had reached the Indies, he called these people Indians. He captured some and loaded them aboard his ship for display in Spain. Some of his crew remained on Hispaniola.

In 1493 Columbus brought about 1,500 colonists with him. They hoped to find gold quickly so that they could return to a life of luxury in Spain. Columbus thought they should farm.

When Columbus arrived at Hispaniola, he found that the Spanish he had left were dead. During his absence they had mistreated the Indians. In self-defense the Indians killed them. The new Spanish arrivals hunted down and killed the Indians. Columbus founded another **colony,** Isabela, which became the first permanent European settlement in the New World.

CONQUISTADORES

In all Columbus made four voyages to the New World looking for the Asian mainland. Although he never brought back great riches, his discoveries sparked interest in the New World. A group of explorers known as conquistadores (kon-KEES-tuh-doh-rez)—Spanish for conquerors—began coming. For the possibility of gold these adventurers fought mountains, rivers, jungles, cold, heat, and Indian resistance. If they found treasure, they were permitted to keep the larger share. The rest went to the Spanish monarch.

In time the Spanish began claiming the land as well as its mineral resources. They also claimed the people living on the land. They were following the European **custom** at the time. Unless non-Europeans had the weapons to withstand European force they became European subjects. The reasons were cultural, religious, and economic. The level of civilization of the claimed people did not matter. By European standards, these foreigners were not civilized. They were not Christians. In addition, they were sitting on land and minerals worth fortunes to the Europeans.

This attitude toward the Indians can be seen from the beginning of European influence in the New World. Almost all the conquistadores served first on the islands of the Caribbean. There the Arawaks and Caribs were wiped out in about a century. This attitude was also true of the Portuguese in Brazil. In fact, it was true of European colonists around the world from the 1500s on.

MEXICO   By 1515 the Spanish controlled Hispaniola, Puerto Rico, Cuba, and other islands. Cuba became the base of operations for the conquest of the mainland. In 1517 Francisco Hernandez de Cordoba left Cuba in search of slaves to replace the island's Indians.

Chapter 1
The Spanish

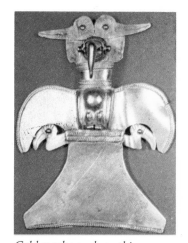

Gold works such as this tempted the Spanish into exploring the lands of the New World. When they found the peoples who made these objects, the Europeans seized their land and valuables and killed them or made them slaves on their estates.

He landed on the Yucatan Peninsula where he found ruins of the Mayan civilization. News of his discovery soon spread.

Within two years Hernan Cortes (kor-TEZ), the most successful of the Mexican conquistadores, sailed to the Yucatan. He had about 600 men with him. Early in his expedition Cortes gained the help of a woman called Malinche (mah-LIN-chuh) by the Indians. The Spanish called her Dona Marina (mah-REE-nah). She was an Aztec who had been sold as a slave to the Mayas. She spoke both the Mayan and Aztec languages.

Dona Marina acted as an interpreter for Cortes. With her help he learned that the Aztecs were hated by their subjects because of their cruelty. Cortes promised to help the Indians overthrow the Aztecs. Knowing that he was outnumbered even with Indian allies, Cortes burned his ships. In this way his men had to fight to survive.

Word of Cortes' arrival reached the Aztec ruler, Montezuma, long before Cortes reached Tenochtitlan. Montezuma believed that Cortes fulfilled an ancient Aztec prophecy. To him Cortes was the white god Quetzalcoatl (ket-SAHL-koh-ah-tuhl) who had once walked among the Aztecs, but then returned home. According to the prophecy, when the god came back, the empire would fall.

Montezuma was frightened, but he welcomed Cortes. With Dona Marina's help, Cortes was able to use Montezuma's fear to his own advantage. Within a short time he had made the Aztec ruler his voluntary prisoner. Ultimately Montezuma was killed. By 1521 Cortes had conquered the Aztecs. They fought valiantly but were no match for the horses, guns, and tactics of the Spanish. The Aztec empire came to an end with the destruction of Tenochtitlan.

CENTRAL AMERICA   In 1513, Vasco Nunez de Balboa, a Spanish explorer, journeyed across the Isthmus of Panama. When he reached the Pacific Ocean, he claimed it and all the lands that it washed for the Spanish Crown. A colony was established. It became the springboard for the conquest of South America.

In 1523 Cortes sent Pedro de Alvarado (day al-vuh-RAHD-oh) to what is modern Guatemala. He became captain-general of the colonial settlement there. Honduras, a dense jungle to the south, became part of the Captaincy-General of Guatemala in 1539. At that time and for the next 300 years Guatemala also included lands that are today Nicaragua, Honduras, Costa Rica, and El Salvador.

FALL OF THE INCA EMPIRE   Stories of rich civilizations prompted the conquistadores to explore the Andes of present-day Peru. Francisco Pizarro (puh-ZAHR-oh) set out to find such a **kingdom**. When he arrived in the empire of the Incas in 1531, he found a **civil war**. The followers of two men were fighting over which would be the new emperor. One of the men was Atahualpa (aht-uh-WAHL-puh) who ruled the northern part of the empire. The other was his half-brother Huascar (WAHS-kahr), ruler of the southern part.

Atahualpa heard of Pizarro's arrival, and asked for his help. Pizarro answered by making him a prisoner. In exchange for his release Atahualpa promised Pizarro a room filled with gold and another filled with silver. While still a prisoner, Atahualpa arranged for the death of his brother. The Spanish later tried and executed him for Huascar's murder. He was also found guilty of plotting against the Spanish.

With the fall of the Inca capital, the empire began to crumble. Pizarro and his army carried away Atahualpa's ransom. When news of Inca gold and silver spread, Spanish began coming in great numbers.

COLONIZATION

By the mid-1500s, the Spanish controlled much of the territory of South, Middle, and North America. They had explored from Florida to California and from Mexico to Chile. Claiming and exploring the lands was only the first step. Colonizing it and converting the Indians was the next. Some Indians in remote parts of the New World were able to keep their culture. Most, however, came under direct European influence.

Neither the Spanish Crown nor the Roman Catholic Church had been able to exercise authority over the early settlements in the Caribbean. By the time Cortes had completely conquered Mexico, however, both the Crown and the Church had become powerful influences. The new rulers had to Christianize the Indians. In addition they were expected to change the Indians into Europeans. This fitted in well with the colonists' plans.

Atahualpa (above) was the last Inca. His death came as a result of the efforts of the Spanish under Francisco Pizarro (below) to seize Inca gold and silver.

After the conquistadores came those who were willing to work the land for its natural resources. Some farmed, others mined. At first they used Indian labor. As these peoples died from disease and abuse, the Europeans replaced them with blacks. In this picture, slaves work a gold mine.

Cortes and Pizarro wanted only gold and silver. The Spanish who followed wanted the profits of the vast agricultural lands of the Indians. To work these lands efficiently, however, the Spanish needed a cheap and plentiful labor force. This force became the Indians themselves. But the landholder needed a way of controlling them. The encomienda (ayn-kohm-YAHN-dah) system—supported by the Church and the Crown—provided the means.

Laws governing the encomienda—or land-grant system—described the rights and responsibilities of both the Spanish and the Indians. Spanish landholders would develop the land for their own profit. In return they were to educate and provide for the welfare of the Indians living on it. The landowners could use Indian labor as a tax for taking care of them.

Legally the Indians were free. They were, however, considered wards of the Spanish Crown. The Spanish thought the Indians were by nature lazy and sinful. Thus they were required to live in settlements under Spanish control. In this way they could be taught good habits. Abuses of the system were frequent. Indian homes were destroyed and ancient customs forbidden. The Indians were not allowed to travel without permission. They were forced to work long hours without wages. Great numbers of Indians died in the West Indies, Mexico, and Peru.

To the missionaries who came with the conquistadores the New World was a spiritual conquest. In their eagerness to convert the Indians, they destroyed temples and forbade **rituals**. They set up missions as the ideal of what the encomienda could be. Spanish administrators valued the missions because they kept the Indians peacefully occupied. The Indians cultivated the fields and gardens and made the missions almost self-supporting. But the missionaries saw their ideal distorted by the great landholders.

In the West Indies the encomienda caused such hardship that the clergy led the fight to destroy the system. **Reformers** like Father Bartholome de Las Casas (day lahs-KAHS-uhs) attacked the system's worst feature—forced labor. The system gradually died out. By 1720 it had been abolished everywhere in Latin America except Chile. Some historians believe that by then the Indian population of Latin America had been reduced by as much as 80 percent.

As early as 1501, the Spanish in the Caribbean had begun to look for people other than Indians to use as laborers. In that year the first Africans were brought to the island of Hispaniola as slaves. By 1528 Africans were being imported into South America. Within 15 years they were being used as slaves in Central America.

ADMINISTRATION

The original Spanish explorations and conquests were a result of individual action. Columbus, Cortes, and Pizarro were all soldiers of fortune. Gradually the government in Spain realized that their conquests had placed a huge territory under its authority.

In 1535, the Crown divided Spanish America into two administrative units called viceroyalties. A government headed by a viceroy was set up for each. The Viceroyalty of New Spain was centered in Mexico and included parts of Central America and the present-day southern U.S. The Viceroyalty of Peru was headquartered in Lima and included most of Spanish South America. In the 1700s the Viceroyalty of Peru was divided twice again. The administrative units had become too large to govern effectively. The new territories were the Viceroyalty of New Granada and the Viceroyalty of La Plata.

The missionaries who traveled with the conquistadores baptized Indians by the thousands. Most did not understand what was happening. Later priests were more careful to explain the teachings of Christianity. The Francisco Cantona Chapel in Quito, Ecuador, was built in 1669 with money given by Atahualpa's nephew.

735

Viceroyalty of New Spain

Gulf of Mexico

Viceroyalty of New Spain

Treaty of Tordesillas (1494)

Atlantic Ocean

Caribbean Sea

Viceroyalty of New Granada

Pacific Ocean

BRAZIL

Viceroyalty of Peru

Viceroyalty of La Plata

☐ **Spanish Colonial Administration, 1790**

These are the front and back of a Spanish coin called a piece of eight. Gold and silver of the New World were sent to Spain and minted into millions of such coins.

In addition to the viceroyalties, there were also regions governed by captaincy-generals. Chile, Cuba, Guatemala, and Santo Domingo (Hispaniola) were ruled in this manner. The captains-general were only slightly less powerful than the viceroys. Both ruled Spanish America in an **authoritarian** way. The only appeal to their decisions was to the king in Madrid. This was costly and time-consuming.

The important posts in the colonies were held by peninsulares, those who had been born in Spain. The term means from the peninsula (of Spain). Below them in rank were creoles (KREE-ohls). They were the descendants of the original Spanish colonists. They owned plantations or profitable trading businesses. The creoles were angered by domination of the Crown and peninsulares in colonial affairs.

Persons of Spanish and Indian blood were called mestizos (mes-TEE-zohs). Persons of Spanish and African blood were called mulattoes (moo-LAT-ohs). Mestizos, mulattoes, Indians, and African slaves had nothing to say about government.

The small group of peninsulares and the few creoles who held any power used it to make themselves and Spain richer. So long as the colonies produced wealth for Spain and provided markets for Spanish goods, those in power had little interest in the welfare of the ordinary colonist. But in the late 1700s, some colonists began to think about changing the situation.

In 1500 a Portuguese captain, Pedro Alvarez Cabral (kuh-BRAHL), reached the coast of northeast Brazil and claimed it for Portugal. According to Cabral, he had been blown off course while on the way to India. But historians suspect that Cabral set out to claim New World land for Portugal. Cabral based his claim on the Treaty of Tordesillas. This treaty was signed in 1494 by Spain and Portugal under the direction of the pope. It divided the uncharted world between the two.

It took many years and many expeditions before the Portuguese began colonizing Brazil in earnest. The area was neglected because trade with the Far East appeared more profitable. Thus, the development of Brazil as a colony was very different from the Spanish experience. It was different in another important way too. Once the Spanish had defeated the Aztecs and Incas, they were able to use the Indian organizations as a base for their own colonies. However, no strong organized Indian states existed in Brazil, only small scattered groups.

EXPLORATION AND COLONIZATION

At first Cabral thought that he had discovered a large island. In reality the land that he claimed covers about half the South American continent. In the beginning the Portuguese claimed only a narrow coastal strip. During the first few years only occasional Portuguese traders visited the area. They were looking for wood, similar to Asian brazilwood, used to make red dye. The French began to take advantage of Portugal's lack of interest in Brazil. They tried to win the Indians to their side and gain Brazil's resources.

In 1532 the Portuguese king sent a force to drive out the French. He then divided Brazil into a number districts called captaincies. He gave these grants of land to wealthy Portuguese. In many ways the captaincies were like the Spanish encomiendas. The land involved, however, was many times larger. The landholders agreed to find settlers and promote farming and trade. They also were to fight off invaders and guard the spiritual well-being of the Indians.

Some of the captaincies were never started. Others, because of the great cost, did not have the funds needed to support them until they could become self-supporting. Within a short time, all but a few had failed. However, they had attracted settlers to Brazil. A number of **towns**, ranches, and businesses had been built along the coast.

In 1549 the king appointed a captain-general as governor of all Brazil. He was to make the colony profitable and stop French interference. The new captain-general set up his headquarters at Bahia (buh-HEE-uh) (modern Salvador) in the northeast. The introduction of sugar cane in the 1530s had made this area the center of Brazil's economy. The environment of the northeast was highly suitable for this crop. In the 1700s when Brazilian prosperity shifted from sugar to minerals, the capital was moved to Rio de Janeiro (REE-oh-day-zhuh-NER-oh), closer to the mines.

Chapter 2
The
Portuguese

promote:
bring about, encourage

This painting shows a group of Portuguese nobles arriving in Brazil to set up their captaincies. Why did the captaincy system fail in Brazil?

The captain-general brought with him Jesuit missionary priests. The Jesuits were the first Europeans to brave the wilderness. They set up mission villages for the Indians in remote areas of the Amazon River. Thousands of Indians were baptized, gathered into fortified settlements, and taught religion and farming. These missions provided a place of safety for the Indians against slave raiders. They also became outposts of Portuguese political and economic influence.

The Jesuits vigorously opposed slavery for the Indians. Landowners who were expanding their estates resented Jesuit control of Indian labor. Some of the mission settlements were becoming wealthy sugar plantations. They were competing with the landowners for profits. The wealthy finally united against the Jesuits and had them driven from the colony in 1759.

PROSPERITY

By the early 1600s many of the forests of northeastern Brazil had been cleared for giant sugar plantations. Brazil soon became the world's leading producer of sugar. More and more people were needed to work the cane fields and to open new territories. A labor shortage soon developed. The Indians in Brazil, as in Spanish America, were not able to withstand European diseases and abuse. The Portuguese had to look elsewhere for workers. Slavery seemed the solution.

The first slaves were brought from Africa in the 1530s. By 1585 several thousand had been imported. Through the years, as Brazil's economy shifted from one product to another, the number of slaves increased. Over a 300-year period more slaves were brought to Brazil than to any other area in the Americas. It was six times the number brought to the U.S.

However, the number of slaves alive in Brazil at any one time does not reflect this. The death rate was very high and the birthrate low. New slaves were gotten by **importing** more adult blacks rather than by encouraging births. The importing of slaves ended in 1850. But slavery was not abolished until 1889.

The Portuguese were less conscious than other nationalities of the status of slaves. Until the 1700s Brazil had more Africans than Europeans. Portuguese men often had children by black women. Unlike the Spanish or English they recognized these half-black, half-white children as their own. Mulattoes became clerks, supervisors, and priests.

But slavery is still slavery. During this period escaped slaves fled to the interior and established settlements. The Portuguese tried to capture them, but many put up strong resistance.

During the 1600s, Brazil was gaining in population and prosperity. The authority of the Portuguese king was growing weaker and more distant. By the mid-1600s the Brazilian colonists themselves had to drive the Dutch from Brazil. The Dutch had been attracted to Brazil by the success of its sugar industry. By then the great landholders actually ruled.

From the end of the 1600s to the end of the 1700s adventurers, mostly from Sao Paulo (sawn-PAW-loo), explored the interior. Some

Portuguese Colonial Administration, 1790

Many times between 1530 and the mid-1600s, Brazil's colonists had to drive out French, Dutch, and British forces. The Portuguese gave them no aid. In 1565 this fleet of Brazilians sailed to Rio de Janeiro to fight the French.

This polychrome—many colors—and gilt wooden statue is of St. Peter as Pope. It stands in a church in Sao Paulo. The statue is done in the baroque style. Baroque art began in Europe in the 1600s and was very ornate and colorful.

went to prospect for gold and precious stones. Gold rushes, like one in Minas Gerais (mee-nuh-zhuh-RYS) in 1695, attracted people from the coastal cities and southern Brazil. Mining camps and boom towns became common. Many people stayed to establish permanent settlements. In the north, cattle ranchers pushed outward.

However, Indian-hunters called bandeirantes did more than any other group to establish Portuguese rule in the interior. They are credited with extending the borders of Brazil to their modern limits. The bandeirantes captured and sold Indians as slaves. They were themselves part Portuguese and part Indian. For their hunts they traveled in bands of from 50 to several hundred. Occasionally members dropped out of the hunt, kept some slaves, and began a settlement. Some of Brazil's modern estates were begun by bandeirantes.

Bandeirantes also began the gold rush in 1695. The discovery of gold was most fortunate because it came just as Brazil's sugar industry was declining. Cheaper West Indian sugar was driving the Brazilian product from the market. In the 1720s there was a diamond boom.

For many years Brazil's prosperity was based on slavery and sugar. This picture shows slaves operating a sugar mill. Gold replaced sugar, and diamonds replaced gold. How long did slavery remain legal in Brazil?

Summing Up the Unit

Social Studies Vocabulary

Define: nationality; colony; custom; kingdom; civil war; rituals; reformers; authoritarian; town; import

People

Identify: Cortes; Malinche; Montezuma; Balboa; Pizarro; Atahualpa; Huascar; Cabral

Places

Locate: Viceroyalties of New Spain, Peru, New Granada, La Plata; Treaty of Tordesillas line

Words

Define: conquistadores; encomienda system; viceroyalty; captaincy-general; peninsulare; creole; mestizo; mulatto; bandeirante

⚷ Questions

1. Why did the conquistadores come to the New World?
2. How can the conquistadores' attitude toward the Indians be explained?
3. Why were the Aztecs hated by their subjects?
4. Why did Montezuma fear Cortes?
5. a. What conflict within the Inca empire did Pizarro use to his advantage? b. How?
6. How were the Indians affected by the encomieda system?
7. How did Spanish administrators regard the missions?
8. Why did the Spanish government set up viceroyalties?
9. Why did creoles dislike peninsulares?
10. What was Spain's attitude toward the ordinary colonist in the New World?
11. Upon what did Cabral base his claim of Brazil for Portugal?
12. In what two ways did Portugal's New World colonization differ from that of Spain's?
13. Why did Bahia become important to the Brazilian economy?
14. Why did the Jesuits set up missions in the Brazilian wilderness?
15. a. How did the Portuguese solve their labor shortage? b. Why were more slaves brought to Brazil than to any other area in the Americas?
16. What was the Portuguese attitude toward the status of slaves?
17. a. Which group was most influential in establishing Portuguese rule in the interior? b. How?

Discussion Topics

1. Montezuma and Atahualpa led powerful empires yet they were conquered by Cortes and Pizarro. Why do you think they were unable to cope with the Spanish?
2. The conquistadores sought wealth and land; the missionaries came for spiritual conquest. How did the attitudes of these two groups toward the Indians differ? Did the missionaries aid the Indians or the Spanish political conquest?
3. Laws governing the encomienda described the rights and responsibilities of both the Spanish and the Indians. Why were abuses of the system frequent? What was wrong with the system?
4. The development of Brazil as a colony was very different from the Spanish experience. In what ways? How does Brazil today, as a result of its colonial experience, differ from the Spanish nations of Latin America?

Project Ideas

1. Imagine you are a newspaper reporter. Write an article evaluating the influence of Spanish and Portuguese colonization on the character of Latin America today.
2. Make a chart showing the political chain of command and the class structure of Spanish America. Include all levels of power from top to bottom.
3. Write a report on one of the following: the conquistadores; Jesuit missions; the encomienda system; African slave trade in the New World; Spanish gold and silver mines in the New World.

Unit IV

Wars of Independence

Jose de San Martin leads his army through the Andes to fight the Spanish in Chile. San Martin wanted to free Latin America. He had no personal ambition.

The American and French **revolutions** in the late 1700s began to make the people of Latin America restless and daring. The respect for human dignity which gave birth to these revolutions appealed to them. Latin Americans began to rebel against their foreign rulers.

Between 1810 and 1824 all of Spain's mainland possessions gained independence. Brazil became independent of Portugal in 1822. Unlike the Spanish colonies, however, it set up a **monarchy**. It was not until 1889 that Brazil introduced a **republican** form of government.

In the Caribbean blacks as well as European descendants shared the anger and dissatisfaction of their mainland neighbors. Today only a few islands in the Caribbean and tiny sections of Central and South America remain under Dutch, British, or French control.

The wars of independence were preceded by several generations of unrest and discontent. One of the early revolts against Spanish rule occurred in Peru. It was led by Tupac Amaru II (too-PAHK ah-MAH-roo) who claimed to be a direct descendant of the last Inca emperor, Tupac Amaru I. In the late 1500s Tupac Amaru I had ruled the short-lived Neo-Inca empire. The Spanish murdered him.

Two centuries later, the Spanish recognized Tupac Amaru II's rank and gave him wealth and a title. Jesuits educated him. But Tupac Amaru rejected the life of luxury the Spanish offered him. He chose instead to identify with the Indians. He protested their forced labor in mines and on farms but was ignored. In 1780 he organized an army. By showing Indian strength, Tupac Amaru hoped to force the Spanish to reform their colonial system.

Instead the Spanish captured, tortured, and brutally murdered him. The Indians were shocked into action. Although they had few weapons, they tried to drive the Spanish from Peru. Some 80,000 Indians and Spanish died in the two years of fighting that followed.

NATURE OF THE REVOLUTIONS

Through the years the mestizos and creoles became more and more dissatisfied with Spanish rule. Mestizos, who were part Indian and part European, were denied by both. Yet their numbers grew rapidly and they collected into separate settlements. Often a mestizo village sprang up between a European town and a nearby Indian settlement. Mestizos became traders and were an important link between the two cultures. Mestizos also became wholeheartedly Latin American. No European monarch could claim their loyalty. When the wars of independence came, they were ready. The leaders of the revolts, however, were usually creoles.

It should be noted that the creoles were primarily interested in gaining power for themselves. They were not particularly concerned with improving the conditions of the lower classes. The protection of creole interests was a dominant factor in the revolutions. It was also a factor in determining the course the new nations would take.

Between 1799 and 1815 European nations were fighting Napoleon Bonaparte and the French. In 1808 Napoleon's troops took Spain. The Spanish king was overthrown and Napoleon's brother came to power. The viceroys tried to continue their rule as before. However, the events in Europe were the signal for rebellion in Spain's colonies.

Except in Mexico, the wars began as revolts within cities. City councils in the larger cities tried to assume governing power over their local areas. In 1810 Buenos Aires (bway-nuh-SAR-eez), the largest city in southern South America, declared itself independent of the Viceroyalty of La Plata. This marks the beginning of the 15-year independence movement in Spanish America.

Chapter 1
Spanish South America

Independent South America, 1825

◼ Gran Colombia
◼ Peru
◻ Bolivia
◼ Chile
◼ Argentina
◼ Paraguay

FRANCISCO DE MIRANDA

Like many leaders of
Latin American independence
movements, Francisco
de Miranda was a creole.
What do you think about his
surrender to the Spanish?
Would you have been
disillusioned? Was Miranda
simply being practical?
This painting was done
while Miranda
was in a Spanish jail.

Francisco de Miranda (day muh-RAHN-dah) was one of the early leaders of the independence movement. He was a creole, born in Caracas, capital of modern Venezuela. In 1772 Miranda became a captain in the Spanish army. His career was clouded by a charge of misusing army funds. He escaped to the newly founded United States of America where he met a number of leaders of the young republic. He became fired with the idea of freeing his homeland from the Spanish.

For years Miranda traveled throughout Europe seeking help for his plan. In 1792-93 he fought in the French Revolution. Finally in 1806 with soldiers recruited in North America, Miranda landed on the coast of Venezuela to begin the revolution. The attempt failed and he escaped to London. The city welcomed him. At that time Britain was the only nation fighting Napoleon. The British were also supplying **guerrillas** in Spain. At the urging of Simon Bolivar (see-mohn buh-LEE-vahr), a fellow Venezuelan, Miranda returned home in 1810. In 1811 Venezuela was declared independent and Miranda was made **dictator**.

The Venezuelan revolutionists began to write a **constitution**. It was modeled after that of the United States and influenced by the French Declaration of the Rights of Man. But the Spanish had not given up. In 1812 they attacked Miranda's forces. Afraid of a costly defeat, Miranda surrendered. His followers were disillusioned. They deserted him and allowed the Spanish to capture him. He died in a Spanish prison in 1816.

SIMON BOLIVAR

Simon Bolivar—known as the Liberator—was also a wealthy creole. He was born in Caracas in 1783. He traveled widely in Cuba, Europe, and the U.S. Inspired by liberal ideas, he dreamed of a free, united Latin America.

Bolivar worked to bring about Venezuela's first declaration of independence in 1811. He joined Miranda's forces. Although Miranda was imprisoned, Bolivar was allowed to go free. In 1813 he returned to retake Caracas but was forced to flee the next year. The war with Napoleon that had been occupying Spain had ended. Troops were sent to put down the rebels in the colonies.

Bolivar fled to Jamaica and then Haiti. In 1817 he landed in Venezuela again. Along the lower Orinoco River, he trained recruits. Some of these were cowboys from the Orinoco Plain as well as a number of blacks. In 1819 with about 3,000 troops, Bolivar began a march to Bogota, the capital of the Viceroyalty of New Granada. He felt that if he could capture the Spanish capital, he would seriously hurt Spanish morale.

morale: good feelings

Bolivar's army had to march hundreds of kilometers across the rugged snow-capped Andes. At Boyaca, 97 kilometers (60 miles) from Bogota, they fought a large Spanish army and were victorious. A few days later Bolivar rode into Bogota and declared it free. He became the president of the new **republic** of Gran Colombia. During his lifetime this included the modern states of Colombia, Ecuador, Panama, and Venezuela.

Bolivar's dream would not be realized until all the Spanish armies were out of South America. In 1821 he advanced into Venezuela and drove most of the Spanish forces from the region. Jose Antonio de Sucre (SOO-kray), Bolivar's comrade, defeated another Spanish force and occupied Quito (KEE-toh), Ecuador, in 1822.

In July 1822 Simon Bolivar and Jose de San Martin (day san mahr-TEEN) met at Guayaquil (gwy-uh-KEEL), Ecuador. San Martin had led the struggle for liberation in Chile and southern Peru. Their conferences did not bring agreement. Among other differences, both wanted to add Ecuador to their territories. San Martin withdrew rather than risk endangering the independence movement.

Within two years with Sucre's help, Bolivar had driven the Spanish from the mountains of Peru. The fight at Ayacucho (eye-uh-KOO-choh) in 1824 was the final battle for independence in South America. A separate state named Bolivia in honor of Bolivar was formed in what had been Upper Peru. Bolivar had indeed kept his oath: all Spanish South America was free. However, by the time of his death in 1830 Bolivar's dream of a united Latin America was dead.

745

This is a painting of Simon Bolivar. Contrast Bolivar's desires with those of San Martin. Does San Martin's unselfishness make him a better man than Bolivar? Were Bolivar's personal desires and those for Spanish America intertwined?

Several factors contributed to Bolivar's failure to unite Latin America. The new governments were having trouble financing themselves. Jealousy and a scramble for power among leaders tended to drive the sections of Gran Colombia farther apart. And there was Bolivar himself. He set up a life term as president for himself. He also tried to create a constitutional system that would put complete government control in the president's hands. By assuming dictatorial power, Bolivar set a precedent. Many rulers in Latin America's future would repeat it.

JOSE DE SAN MARTIN

The area which today includes Argentina, Paraguay, Uruguay, and Bolivia was separated from Peru in 1776 and became the Viceroyalty of La Plata. It was there in 1778 that Jose de San Martin was born. Just as Bolivar was the liberator of northern South America, San Martin was the liberator of the south.

San Martin, the son of a Spanish official, was educated in Madrid for a military career. He served in the Spanish army in Europe and in North America. When he returned to his home in 1812, he was already a successful commander. San Martin offered his services to the government of Buenos Aires, which had proclaimed its independence. Unlike Venezuela, the territory of Buenos Aires had not been recaptured by the Spanish. However, while a Spanish force remained nearby in Chile and Peru, Buenos Aires was not safe.

San Martin organized an expedition against the Spanish force. In contrast to Bolivar, San Martin had no ambition to be a ruler. He only wanted South America to be free. This sincerity attracted many. Chilean exiles, revolutionists from the area governed by Buenos Aires, and some out-of-work soldiers from Europe rallied to San Martin. Among those who joined him was Bernardo O'Higgins.

Two years before Bolivar made his successful march to Bogota, San Martin scaled the Andes with his army. In February 1817 he met and defeated the main Spanish army not far from Santiago, the present capital of Chile. San Martin entered the city in triumph. Refusing the leadership of Chile, he stepped aside for O'Higgins.

Gradually the Spanish troops were cleared from northern Chile. The formal independence of Chile was declared on February 12, 1818. San Martin then turned his attention to freeing southern Chile, and uniting the two sections. A decisive defeat of the Spanish in April 1818 made this possible.

After freeing Chile, San Martin moved on to Peru. Realizing that their army could not march across the Atacama Desert, the rebels began to build a navy. With ships stolen from the Spanish or bought from foreigners, O'Higgins and San Martin blockaded the ports. The Spanish viceroy left Lima and took his armies to the mountains. San Martin entered Lima in July 1821 and received from its citizens the title Protector. On July 28, 1821, Peru was declared a free and independent country. The Spanish forces, however, remained in the mountains.

In 1822 San Martin and Bolivar met at Guayaquil. Since the two could not agree on how one would help the other, San Martin quietly withdrew. He went into exile in Europe and died there in 1850. As we have seen, Bolivar ultimately freed Peru.

Chapter 2
Mexico's Struggle

What has been said about the dissatisfaction of creoles and mestizos in South America can also be said of these classes who lived in Mexico in the Viceroyalty of New Spain. There the creoles too felt that they should control their own affairs. When Napoleon occupied Spain in 1808, many began to work for independence. However, the first open rebellion was an Indian revolt in 1810.

EARLY MOVEMENTS

Miguel Hidalgo (ee-DAHL-goh), a parish priest, was among the first to fight for the poor. His parishioners in Dolores, a small town north of Mexico City, were mostly Indians and mestizos. Hidalgo believed that along with their spiritual welfare, their material life needed to be improved. He introduced silk manufacturing and new, efficient farming methods. The **philosophies** of the Enlightenment and the French Revolution greatly influenced his thinking.

Father Miguel Hidalgo led the first revolt against the Spanish in Mexico. In what century and where in Spanish America did other priests attack government policies?

When Napoleon deposed the king of Spain, secret societies were organized in New Spain to fight the Spanish. Hidalgo belonged to one such group. Instead of escaping when the authorities discovered the society, Hidalgo rang the church bells in Dolores. With Grito de Dolores—cry of Dolores—he proclaimed the beginning of the revolution against Spanish rule. This was on September 16, 1810.

Hidalgo was neither a military leader nor a good organizer. But he became the center of an army of 60,000 rebels, mostly Indians. Hidalgo's followers fought with clubs, knives, and their hands against the weapons of the Spanish. For a time they were successful. They captured several large cities and **provinces** and came near Mexico City. Hidalgo set up a government for the freed territories. Slavery was abolished. The Indians were given back their land.

By 1811 creoles and peninsulares had become frightened by Hidalgo's political policies. They sided with Spanish forces and called for an end to the revolution. A disciplined and well-equipped army defeated Hidalgo's followers. Hidalgo was shot. Although the Grito de Dolores movement did not free Mexico, September 16 is celebrated as Mexican Independence Day.

Another Mexican priest, Jose Maria Morelos (moh-RAY-lohs), continued the struggle. He had joined the revolt in 1810. When Hidalgo was defeated, Morelos became the leader. By 1813 he had captured enough territory near the western coast that he declared Mexico independent. Morelos set up a government that went further than Hidalgo's program. Neither the army nor the Roman Catholic Church were to enjoy any special privileges. Everyone, regardless of class or race, was to have equal rights. The large estates were to be broken up and given to the people.

Again the program of the rebels frightened the wealthy. They supported the Spanish and in 1815 Morelos was captured and killed.

INDEPENDENCE

In 1821 Spain experienced a revolt of its own. **Liberals** forced the king to accept a constitution. These events frightened the wealthy in New Spain. They were afraid that the liberal ideas of the new Spanish ruling party would change their way of life. The creoles and peninsulares decided it was time to act.

Agustin de Iturbide (day ee-tur-BEE-day), a creole who had fought for the Spanish cause, became their agent. In February 1821, he deserted the Spanish and signed an agreement with a guerrilla leader. Iturbide was supported by the wealthy and the rebels. The Spanish forces were forced to surrender and Mexico became independent.

Once the Spanish had been defeated, the **coalition** fell apart. Iturbide declared himself emperor and promised to rule under a liberal constitution. However, unrest and poor administration forced him to abdicate in 1823. Mexico was proclaimed a republic.

YEARS OF DICTATORSHIP

The republic did not last long. The political **factions** could not agree on a centralized government or a federal system like that of the U.S. Those who supported **federalism** finally won. In 1824 a president was elected. The votes were cast not by the people but by the state legislatures.

The next few years were chaotic. In 1832, by playing the liberals against the **conservatives**, Antonio Lopez de Santa Anna was elected president. He soon seized power as dictator and ruled until 1855. During that time, political and economic troubles were constant. Santa Anna waged a series of battles over the territory of Texas. They ended with the loss of Texas to the U.S. in the Mexican-American War. The economy of Mexico could not afford such long-term military expeditions. In 1855 Santa Anna was forced to step down.

BENITO JUAREZ

In 1858 Benito Juarez (buh-NEE-toh HWAHR-ayz)—a man held by Mexicans to be their finest liberal reformer—became president of Mexico. He was born of a poor Indian family in 1806. He managed to receive an education and become a lawyer. For a time he served as a state governor and his term in office was a model for the rest of Mexico.

A year before Juarez was elected president, Mexico had adopted a new, liberal constitution. The federal system was restored. The influence of the army was to be reduced. The large landholdings of the Church were to be broken up. But powerful forces including the Roman Catholic Church were opposed to the constitution. For three years liberals and conservatives battled in a civil war. When the liberals won in 1861, Juarez was again president. Mexico was almost bankrupt. Juarez stopped all repayments of loans to European creditors for two years.

France, one of the creditor nations, tried to take control of Mexico. In 1864 the emperor Napoleon III sent his cousin, the young Austrian archduke Maximilian, to Mexico as emperor. French troops were sent to support his claim. The U.S. objected. This was a violation of the Monroe Doctrine which President James Monroe had issued in 1821. The **doctrine** was a warning to European countries to keep out of the Western Hemisphere. The effectiveness of the U.S. objection was limited at this time, however. The U.S. was busy with the Civil War.

Juarez joined the Mexican army. A long series of small battles was fought. After the Civil War, the U.S. used its influence to bring about the withdrawal of the French. Napoleon abandoned Maximilian. The Mexicans executed him. In 1867 Juarez once again became president. The liberals were supreme. Juarez was finally free to carry out the constitution's liberal program of reform. But the attempt at reform lasted only a few years.

Orphaned at three, Benito Juarez managed to receive an education and become a lawyer. From 1847 to 1852, he was governor of the state of Oaxaca. His term in office was a model for later officials. Why do you think the wealthy objected to Juarez's reforms?

END OF REFORM

In 1872 Juarez died. For four years Mexico enjoyed republican government. Then in 1876 a revolt occurred. From 1877 to 1910 Mexico was under the dictatorship of Porfirio Diaz (por-FEE-ryoh DEE-ahs). Occasional revolts forced him from power, but he always regained control.

During this time, any attempts at **land reform** or improvements in the **standard of living** of the mestizos and Indians died. The laws that Juarez had hoped would remove the large estates from the Church were used against the Indians. The laws called for forced sale of corporate landholdings. Diaz applied these laws to the Indian peoples that still held land in common. The tribes were considered **corporations** as much as the Roman Catholic Church. In this way, the government took away the Indians' ancient landholdings. These lands were then sold to anyone with enough money. If the Indians resisted, the army stepped in.

The Indians were reduced to peonage. Under the system of peonage workers found themselves bound to the land by debt. Like North American miners who had to buy everything from the company store, peons were forced to buy everything from the landowners. Prices were high and wages low. The peons remained constantly in debt.

CENTRAL AMERICA

Five of the modern nations of Central America—Guatemala, Nicaragua, Honduras, El Salvador, and Costa Rica—were part of the Captaincy-General of Guatemala. In 1821 they peacefully declared their independence. The following year they united with Mexico under Iturbide. After Mexico became a republic, the five nations set up their own federal system. It was called the United Provinces of Central America.

A capital was established in Guatemala City but each state had its own president. Slavery was abolished. But the benefits of the revolution were felt mainly by the creoles and the Roman Catholic Church. For the next several years, liberals and conservatives quarreled over the turn the revolution had taken.

In 1829 civil war broke out. Liberals gained control and ruled until 1837. During this time the privileges of the Church were taken away. In 1838 an Indian revolt occurred and the federation collapsed. Toward the end of the 1800s, Guatemala tried a number of times to reunite the states by force. It was never successful.

From the beginning of Brazil's history as a colony, the Portuguese Crown had had little control over it. Wealthy Brazilians exercised power. Because Portugal's economy had become more and more dependent on colonial exports, the Portuguese king did little to restrict them. By the mid-1700s Portugal had declined considerably from its past trading glories. It needed the money Brazilian exports brought in. At that time Brazil's plantation economy was the most profitable in the New World.

EARLY REBELLIONS

Brazil never experienced any revolts that affected the entire colony. From time to time, however, Brazilians rebelled. One of the earliest was a slave uprising. In 1633 slaves escaped into the interior and set up the Republic of Palmares. At one time an estimated 20,000 runaways lived in the republic. It had an organized government headed by a king. Palmares remained a refuge for many years. Finally in the 1690s a Portuguese military expedition destroyed it.

A desire for economic freedom prompted another Brazilian uprising. In 1789 the citizens of Minas Gerais rebelled. Most of them worked in the gold and diamond mining operations of the province. The Portuguese king lowered their wages to make a greater profit for Portugal. A group formed to protest this action. Its leader was Jose da Silva Xavier or Tiradentes (teer-uh-DEN-tes), the tooth puller.

Mexico and United Provinces of Central America, 1825

■ Mexico
□ United Provinces of Central America

Chapter 3
Brazil's Development

☐ **Empire of Brazil, 1825**

Besides voicing workers' complaints, Tiradentes called for the abolition of slavery. He also asked that factories and a university be built in Minas Gerais. His demands attracted a small group of followers. The rebels were quickly and violently subdued. Tiradentes was taken prisoner and later executed.

ROYALTY IN EXILE

The beginning of the wars of independence in the Spanish-ruled parts of Latin America had been signaled by Napoleon's conquest of Spain. However, Napoleon's threat to Portugal had a very different effect on the course of Brazilian independence. When Napoleon invaded Portugal in 1807, the Braganzas (brah-GAN-zahz)—Portugal's royal family—fled to Brazil. Led by Queen Maria, they gathered thousands of followers and court officials. These, the treasury of Portugal, art, jewels, and a huge library were put aboard a fleet of 37 ships. The Brazilians enthusiastically welcomed them. They expected that Brazil's importance to the Portuguese empire would finally be recognized.

The Brazilians were not disappointed. Joao (ZHWOWN), who became king when his mother Maria died, declared Brazil an equal partner with Portugal in the empire. In effect, Brazil became the seat of Portuguese power; Rio de Janeiro became the capital of Portugal.

However, the Brazilians paid a price for this recognition. King Joao's family had escaped with the help of the British. As a reward, King Joao opened Brazilian trade to all nations, especially Britain. Several British companies opened trading posts. The economy of Brazil boomed. The British dominated Brazil's **commerce** for more than a century. They also exercised influence on Brazil's internal politics.

As early as 1826 the British began demanding that the Brazilian slave trade be stopped. Their reasons were economic as well as humanitarian. The British had outlawed slave trade in their territories in 1807. But then they found their West Indian sugar trade was having difficulty competing with the price of Brazilian sugar. Brazil's sugar plantations were run by slave labor. The Brazilians eventually outlawed the importing of slaves in 1850.

King Joao tried to encourage the expansion of industry so that Brazil could vary its economy. It was still based largely on one-crop and raw material exports—like sugar and diamonds. A printing press, public library, hospitals, and medical and law schools were set up. However, Joao removed Brazilian-born officials and replaced them with Portuguese. This angered the Brazilians.

FROM COLONY TO EMPIRE   After Napoleon fell from power in 1815, liberal forces began to emerge in Portugal. By 1820 they were demanding many reforms. Joao had to return to Portugal if he wanted to keep his throne. At the same time, Brazilians were demanding more rights. They wanted limits placed on the powers of the king.

In Rio de Janeiro Joao's son Pedro told the people that the constitution which was being written in Portugal would be acceptable to Brazilians. But conditions grew worse. In 1821 King Joao left for Portugal. He took with him much of Brazil's treasury. Prince Pedro remained in Brazil to act as **regent**, that is, he ruled in his father's name. The Portuguese Cortes or **parliament** began to limit the freedoms of the Brazilians. They wanted to return Brazil to the **status** of a colony. The Cortes ordered Pedro back to Portugal. It feared that he might lead a Brazilian revolt.

Under the leadership of Jose Bonifacio, the Brazilians persuaded Pedro to stay and rule as a constitutional monarch. Pedro ripped the Portuguese colors from his uniform and declared "Independence or death!" On September 7, 1822, he declared Brazil independent.

THE EMPIRE

The transition from colony to independent nation was more orderly in Brazil than in any of the former Spanish-ruled nations. But freedom from European rule did not bring social reform to the former colonies of either Spain or Portugal.

The rule of Emperor Pedro I was not a happy one. Among other things he governed without consulting the elected chamber of deputies. In 1831 regents took control of the government and ruled for Pedro's son until 1840.

Pedro II was only 15 years old when he became emperor. During the nearly half century of his reign, Dom Pedro—as he was called— gave new direction to Brazil. He encouraged inventors, investors, and builders. But some Brazilians grew restless under Pedro's long rule. The plantation owners were beginning to be very influential in Brazilian politics. Some feared for the country's future and their own interests if Pedro's daughter Isabel should succeed him. As it was, while Pedro was out of the country, Isabel had freed the slaves.

Besides losing the support of the former slaveowners, Pedro also lost favor with the Roman Catholic Church and the army. The Church was angry at Pedro's attitude toward religion. The military wanted officials appointed that were favorable to its goals. In November 1889 a military **coup** toppled Pedro II. It was done without violence and the royal family was exiled to Europe.

BEGINNING OF THE REPUBLIC

From its earliest days as a republic, Brazil was contolled by the military. Officers took the key positions in government. A constitution—modeled after that of the U. S.—was adopted in 1891.The constitution could be suspended, however, for grave reasons. Although a president was elected, the military kept its newly won influence. It acted as a watchdog over the president and the opposition.

Dom Pedro II ruled Brazil from 1840 to 1889. So long a reign made some of his subjects restless. His overthrow by the military was an example of the importance the military has played and continues to play in Latin America.

Chapter 4
Independence in the Caribbean

The first area to win its independence in Latin America was neither a Spanish nor a Portuguese colony but a French one—Saint-Domingue (san-duh-MANG, modern Haiti). It occupied the western third of the island of Hispaniola. The French had seized the area from Spain in the early 1600s. Of the remaining Spanish colonies in the New World, the Dominican Republic—the other part of Hispaniola—gained independence during the **era** of revolutions on the mainland. Spain, however, was able to keep the islands of Puerto Rico and Cuba until the end of the 1800s.

LIBERATION OF HAITI

Saint-Domingue was one of France's most profitable colonies. It **exported** sugar, coffee, indigo, and spices. By 1788 the colony had a half million black and mulatto slaves. They were ruled by 32,000 French creoles. In addition there were about 24,000 free blacks and mulattoes.

When the French Revolution broke out in 1789, the creoles tried to take control of the island's government from French officials. The creoles used arguments drawn from the philosophes. But terms like liberty, equality, and fraternity also appealed to blacks and mulattoes —free and slave. While the creoles and free mulattoes attempted to bargain for self-rule, the slaves rebelled.

TOUSSAINT L'OUVERTURE   Perhaps as many as 100,000 slaves participated in the revolt. Plantations were burned. Many French and mulattoes were killed or fled the country. Pierre Toussaint L'Ouverture (TOO-sahn-LOO-vuhr-tyur), a former slave, gained control and disciplined the rebels. Fighting continued throughout 1791 and 1792. In 1793 the French government abolished slavery in the colony. In the meantime both Spain and Great Britain were attempting to take over the island. Toussaint and his followers joined with the French to fight them.

abolished:
did away with

In 1799 Toussaint found himself at the head of Saint-Domingue's government. A civil war had broken out and his side had won. However, Toussaint ruled in the name of France. He could not bring himself to declare the colony independent.

In 1801 Toussaint was appointed governor-general by France. A year later Napoleon decided to return his Caribbean possessions to their former colonial status. He wanted to restore slavery and direct French rule. Napoleon ordered an invasion of Saint-Domingue. The expedition was a failure. However, Toussaint was captured and died in a French prison.

On January 1, 1804, Jean-Jacques Dessalines (DAYS-uh-leen), once a general under Toussaint, declared Saint-Domingue independent. The nation was renamed Haiti, the original Arawak name for the island.

INDEPENDENCE   Dessalines ruled for only two years. Once freedom had been gained, blacks and mulattoes fought against each other. In 1806 Dessalines was killed in a mulatto revolt. Then Henri Christophe (KREE-stof), another aide under Toussaint, tried to bring order to the nation and improve its standard of living. The plantation system of the French did not seem adaptable to independence. Most of the people turned to small-scale farming and grew only enough for survival. This is called **subsistence farming**.

After the death of Christophe in 1820, foreign investors gained greater and greater control over the island. The Haitian government was forced to borrow money from them to support the people. Yet the money did not help. Violence was frequent, especially with the neighboring Dominican Republic. Within Haiti itself national leadership changed 21 times between 1820 and 1915. The lack of public education and social services reflected Haiti's increasing poverty.

In 1915 President Woodrow Wilson landed U.S. troops in Haiti. Supposedly, they came to restore order, improve the welfare of the Haitians, and make certain that Haiti repaid its loans. The Haitian government and the U.S. signed a treaty setting a time limit on U.S. occupation. Haitians resented the intervention. They felt the troops were really there to protect U.S. investments.

Elections were held and a new constitution adopted. However, Haitians staged a revolt against some of the tactics used by U.S. Marines. The revolt was put down. In 1934 the U.S. withdrew according to its agreement. But it continued for some time to control and influence the Haitian economy.

Toussaint L'Ouverture led the first successful revolt against colonialism in Latin America. What was different about the leadership of this revolt as opposed to the revolts on the mainland? The photo on the right shows U.S. Marines in Haiti. Why did foreign countries intervene in domestic affairs in Latin America in this century?

755

The old tensions between blacks and mulattoes surfaced from time to time. In the 1950s President Paul Magloire was able to provide a brief period of harmony. However, official corruption and disillusionment with the government caused another change in leadership. Dr. Francois Duvalier (dyoo-VAL-yay)—called Papa Doc by his people—succeeded Magloire in 1957 and ruled as a dictator with the aid of a private army. Papa Doc died in 1971. His son, Jean-Claude, succeeded him as president for life.

DOMINICAN REPUBLIC

The eastern two-thirds of Hispaniola was known as Santo Domingo to its Spanish rulers. Because of developments in the European wars against Napoleon, Santo Domingo was given to France. But the actual transfer of the colony never took place. The Haitians overran the colony. However, the Spanish regained it with British help. In 1821 Santo Domingo declared its independence as the Dominican Republic.

Again the Haitians overran their neighbors and ruled until 1844. During this time slavery was abolished. In 1861 the president of the Dominican Republic invited Spain to rule. This was to protect the Republic from the Haitians. Within four years Spain withdrew. The continual fighting was too great a drain on the Spanish treasury. The next 40 years saw more revolutions and economic problems for the Republic. Increasingly control was taken over by foreign interests.

In 1905 the U.S. took over administration of customs revenue and loaned the country money. Political unrest continued and the U.S. established a military government there in 1916. The U.S. left in 1924 after **democratic** elections were held and a new president took office.

Rafael Leonidas Trujillo Molina took control as dictator in 1930. Trujillo (troo-HEE-yoh) remained in power until he was assassinated in 1961. After his death, the first free elections in 32 years were held.

Free elections were new to residents of the Dominican Republic after 32 years under the dictatorship of Rafael Trujillo. What elements do you think led to a dictatorship in the Dominican Republic?

But rival political groups fought among themselves for the next three years. Full-scale civil war broke out in 1965. Once again the U.S. intervened in Dominican affairs. Fearing that the latest uprising was Communist-inspired, President Lyndon B. Johnson sent forces to put down the revolt. Order was restored and a **provisional government** was created. Elections in 1966 brought a constitutional government to the country.

PUERTO RICO

In 1508 Juan Ponce de Leon began the conquest of Puerto Rico. For most of its early history the island was a military outpost of Spain. Taxes raised elsewhere in Spanish America supported it. Its economy consisted mainly of subsistence farming and cattle raising. The census of 1765 listed approximately 40,000 Spanish and 5,000 slaves. Blacks, mulattoes, and whites mingled freely. The island had become a haven for runaway slaves from nearby colonies. By 1800 the population had more than tripled. Puerto Rican products such as coffee and sugar were becoming important on the world trade market.

Between 1810 and 1824 Spain was busy trying to put down rebellions in Mexico, Venezuela, and its other New World colonies. Fearful of losing Puerto Rico, too, Spain extended full Spanish citizenship to the islanders in 1812. This and other reforms and Puerto Rico's economic importance to Spain created great hopes among Puerto Ricans. However, by the mid-1800s Spain had tightened its control over the island.

Angered by these new restrictions, some Puerto Ricans rebelled in 1868. El Grito de Lares—the cry of Lares as the revolt was called—was quickly defeated. Yet the uprising won some reforms. For example, slavery was abolished.

CHARTER OF AUTONOMY In 1895 a revolt in Cuba against Spanish rule caused revolutionaries to become active again in Puerto Rico. Unrest was widespread but nonviolent. In 1897 Puerto Ricans won

Buildings such as El Morro fortress in San Juan remind Puerto Ricans of their Spanish heritage. What other ethnic groups have contributed to the heritage of Puerto Ricans?

757

a charter of autonomy or self-rule for themselves. It had been gained through bargain and **compromise** among Puerto Rican political parties and the Spanish government. The Puerto Ricans were to elect a parliament and a **cabinet**. Spain was to appoint a governor-general. However, all acts of the governor or the Crown affecting the island had to be approved by parliament and/or the cabinet.

One of the great national leaders to emerge from Puerto Rico's **campaign** for independence was Luis Munoz Rivera (moon-YOHS ruh-VAY-rah). Unfortunately, the reforms that he worked for were short-lived. Two months after Puerto Rican self-rule went into effect, the U.S. and Spain went to war. In July 1898 the U.S. invaded and occupied Puerto Rico. The war ended in August. By October the island belonged to the U.S. and had a military government.

LIMITED SELF-GOVERNMENT   In 1900 the U.S. Congress passed the Foraker Act giving Puerto Rico a civilian government. Most officials were U.S. citizens, however, not native Puerto Ricans. They were appointed by the president of the U.S. In 1917 Puerto Ricans themselves were made U.S. citizens and allowed to elect their own **senate**. However, the president continued to appoint most officials. During the 1920s and 1930s Puerto Ricans continued their struggle for home rule.

The 1930s especially were a time of violent protest. Puerto Ricans were fighting not only for political principles, but for their survival. The worldwide depression of the time brought great hardship to most Puerto Ricans. There were a few wealthy families whose fortunes were based on large agricultural estates. Most of the wealth, however, belonged to outsiders—mainland U.S. citizens. Puerto Rico's problems were intensified by a population explosion.

These events gave rise to a strong **nationalist** movement for immediate independence. Sympathetic members of the U.S. Congress twice introduced independence bills into Congress. Both times they were defeated. Most legislators felt that the economy had to be improved before the status of the island could be settled.

In 1940 Luis Munoz Marin (muh-REEN) became the leader of the Popular Democratic party and made great strides toward home rule. His father had led the campaign for self-rule in the 1890s. The first native-born Puerto Rican governor was appointed in 1946. Two years later Munoz Marin became the first locally elected governor. In 1952 Puerto Rico became a self-governing U.S. territory, the Commonwealth of Puerto Rico.

THE COMMONWEALTH   Puerto Rico is neither a state nor a colony. It is a free community of U.S. citizens who govern and administer their affairs within the structure of U.S. They have a senate and a house of representatives whose members are elected every four years. The governor is also elected for a four-year term.

The U.S. administers Puerto Rico's foreign relations, defense,

postal, and customs services. Until the end of the draft in 1973, Puerto Rican men were subject to military service. Puerto Ricans do not pay federal income tax and they cannot vote for a U.S. president. They do not have voting representation in the U.S. Senate or House of Representatives. But they elect a commissioner who serves on House committees as a nonvoting member.

In 1967 the island's voters were asked to choose among commonwealth status, independence, or statehood. They voted to continue as a commonwealth. Less than 1 percent of the voters chose independence. However, the independence movement did not die. It was still very active in the 1970s.

Under Munoz Marin's leadership Puerto Rico launched Operation Bootstrap. The aim was to pull the island up by its bootstraps from poverty to prosperity. Munoz Marin realized that the island had to move from one-crop agriculture—sugar cane—toward industrialization. He offered ten-year tax exemptions to encourage U.S. businesses to build factories there. Today Puerto Rico has an industrialized economy. Sugar is still important, but it accounts for only about one-fifth of the island's income. The standard of living has greatly improved. However, unemployment is still high. This causes a flow of migrants each year to the U.S. mainland in search of work.

This oil refinery is just one example of the industry that Operation Bootstrap helped bring to Puerto Rico. How have the investments made in Puerto Rico by U.S. firms since the 1950s been different from the investments of the 1930s?

CUBA

After Cuba was discovered by Columbus, it became the base of operations for Spanish conquistadores. As the mainland opened up, Cuba served as the supply depot for ships traveling between the New World and Spain. Control of Cuba meant control of the gateway to the southern New World.

By the end of the 1700s, however, Cuba was attracting settlers for its own sake. Cuba's plantations were flourishing. Tobacco, cattle, coffee, and especially sugar were being raised in great quantities. Slavery was widespread. Besides Europeans and slaves, there were many free mulattoes.

depot: a place for storing supplies, especially military ones

759

Throughout the 1800s there were various attempts by Cubans to free their land from Spanish rule. The last one was led by Jose Marti (right) and Antonio Maceo. Marti was a creole, and Maceo, a mulatto. Why do you think the social class of the leaders made a difference in the direction that movements and their later governments took?

While the colonies on the Latin American mainland rebelled, Cuba remained quiet for the most part. Many of its plantation owners and wealthy merchants were creoles. And like creoles in Mexico they feared the influence of liberal ideas. Instead of seeking change, wealthy Cubans tried to keep Cuba as it was.

Around the mid-1800s some creoles began to favor **annexation** by the U.S. By then European nations had abolished or were leaning toward abolishing slavery in their colonies. Cuban plantation owners feared that the Spanish might soon free the slaves in Cuba. The Cubans saw an ally in the plantation system of the southern U.S. Moreover, the U.S. was replacing Spain as Cuba's major market. Some U.S. citizens managed to interest the U.S. government in buying Cuba. However, Spain was not interested in selling.

Events seemed to climax in the Ten Years' War (1868-1878). A group led by Carlos Manuel de Cespedes (SAYS-pay-days) demanded independence and an end to slavery. Spain answered with troops. When the revolt was put down, the Spanish promised reforms. Slavery was to be abolished.

Many Cubans were not satisfied. In February 1895 fighting broke out again. This time the revolt was led by Jose Marti, a creole, and Antonio Maceo (mah-SAY-oh), a mulatto ex-slave. Marti was killed in May, and the war dragged on. The economy of Cuba suffered greatly. U.S. citizens worried about their investments.

In 1898 President William McKinley sent the USS *Maine* to Havana to protect U.S. citizens. When the battleship was destroyed, allegedly by the Spanish, the U.S. declared war on Spain. The war ended three months later with Spain's defeat. As part of the peace **treaty**, the victorious U.S. took Cuba. In 1902 Cuba was declared independent and Cubans elected their first president. Cuba, however, was destined for a stormy future.

Summing Up the Unit

Social Studies Vocabulary

Define: revolution; republican; guerrilla; dictator; constitution; liberal; coalition; faction; federalism; land reform; standard of living; corporation; status; coup; subsistence farming; provisional government; nationalist; annexation

People

Identify: Tupac Amaru II; Miranda; Bolivar; San Martin; Hidalgo; Iturbide; Santa Anna; Juarez; Maximilian; Tiradentes; Dom Pedro; Toussaint L'Ouverture; Dessalines; Christophe; Duvalier; Luis Munoz Rivera; Marti

Places

Locate: Gran Colombia; Mexico; United Provinces of Central America; Empire of Brazil; Cuba

Words

Define: Grito de Dolores; peonage; Republic of Palmares; El Grito de Lares; charter of autonomy; Foraker Act; Operation Bootstrap

Questions

1. Why had mestizos and creoles become increasingly dissatisfied with Spanish rule?
2. When creoles led revolts, what was their main objective?
3. What events in Europe signaled rebellion in the Spanish colonies?
4. a. Where did the independence movement in Spanish America begin? b. When?
5. Ideas for the Venezuelan constitution came from what two sources?
6. What was Simon Bolivar's dream?
7. a. Where was the final battle for independence in South America? b. When?
8. What factors contributed to Bolivar's failure to keep Gran Colombia united?
9. a. Who was the liberator of the south? b. How was he different from Bolivar? c. What happened when the two men met at Guayaquil?
10. a. What events in Spain affected New Spain in 1821? b. How? c. Why?
11. a. Who led the successful effort in 1821 to force the Spanish to surrender in New Spain? b. What title did he give himself? c. What happened then?
12. Why did the Mexican republic not last long?
13. What happened to Mexico during the rule of Antonio Lopez de Santa Anna?
14. a. What nation tried to control Mexico in the 1860s? b. How? c. Why?
15. How did Diaz reduce the Indians to peonage?
16. a. What Latin American nations were once the Captaincy-General of Guatemala? b. Why did the United Provinces of Central America collapse?
17. Why did the Portuguese Crown have very little control over Brazil as a colony?
18. What effect did Napoleon's threat to Portugal have on the course of Brazilian independence?
19. a. What was the first area to win its independence in Latin America? b. When?
20. What was the U.S.'s role in the Dominican Republic between 1905 and 1924?
21. a. What step did Spain take to keep from losing Puerto Rico in 1812? b. Why were the 1930s a time of especially violent protest in Puerto Rico?
22. a. While the mainland colonies rebelled, why did Cuba oppose change? b. Why did some Cubans favor annexation by the U.S.?

Discussion Topics

1. Independence movements in Spanish America were generally led by creoles who wanted control over their own affairs. Could Spain have retained the loyalty of creoles by wiser policies, or was revolt inevitable?
2. Bolivar dreamed of a free and united Latin America. Could Latin Americans have gained much advantage from being united? What would the disadvantages have been?
3. As mainland nations gained their independence, Cuba remained a Spanish possession. Why do you think Spain kept Cuba but lost the rest of the Americas?

Project Ideas

1. Write a report on one of the persons listed in the **People** section in the first column.
2. Write a brief military history of one of the wars of independence.

761

Unit V

The Evolving Political Scene

This is a political poster from Chile. What do you think it means?

Since the beginning of the independence movements, Latin Americans have tended to center their support and their governments in the person of a strong leader. Often this person, known as a caudillo (kaw-THEE-yoh)—a Spanish word meaning chieftain—was a member of the military. A caudillo ruled alone. In recent years, the **junta** (HOON-tuh)—a group of several military officers—has become a common form of government. Juntas have power in Brazil, Chile, and Peru. Often one person, sometimes a civilian popular with the people, serves as a figurehead for the junta. Most Latin Americans live under military rule or constant threat of a military takeover.

Adding to Latin America's political instability has been foreign intervention. Although Latin Americans were able to win political independence, they were not so successful in winning economic independence. As we have seen with Haiti and the Dominican Republic, foreigners through investments have exercised varying amounts of control over Latin American governments.

At one time or another, and often for very long periods of time, caudillos have ruled every nation in Latin America. As we have seen, Mexico had General Porfirio Diaz, the Dominican Republic had General Rafael Trujillo, and Haiti had Papa Doc Duvalier. Although the pattern of strong rule has remained constant, the personalities of caudillos have varied greatly. But all caudillos have had one thing in common. They have exercised absolute and unlimited power.

Why was and is there such a widespread dependence on authoritarian leadership in Latin American society? Although Brazil did not fight for its independence as Spanish America had, some of the same factors gave rise to authoritarian rule in Brazil.

Chapter 1
Rise
of
Caudillos

BASIS OF POWER

When independence came, ordinary citizens were not prepared to govern themselves. They had no experience. Long before the Spanish conquest, Indian chiefs and kings had exercised absolute authority. The Spanish and Portuguese who replaced the native rulers governed in the same way. They taught black, mestizo, and mulatto men and women that the laws and the government which controlled them were not their concern. Rules came from above.

When the Latin Americans broke free from Spanish control, the leaders of the revolts were usually creole men. They were the wealthy, educated landowners, merchants, and military. When independence came, this small group simply replaced the foreign rulers and continued to govern from above. When Brazil proclaimed its independence in the 1880s, the same kind of people came to power.

Considering the lack of political experience of the ordinary people, the rulers could always say that the people were not ready for a republican form of government. Then the rulers could agree that they had to create a system in which they ruled with unquestioning authority. Only in Mexico and Haiti did independence result in some social change. However, the death of Juarez in 1872 ended Mexico's reforms for several decades. Haiti's revolution was successful for one reason. The blacks who began it were able to keep the new government from falling into creole hands.

The European pattern of settlement also encouraged the power of the privileged. In Argentina and Brazil, especially, the small number of European descendants were scattered over wide areas. A few families acquired vast landholdings. They were able to dominate not only the laborers on their estates but the small towns that sprang up around them. After independence these people used their wealth and local authority as a base from which to widen their power.

Religion also reinforced belief in the need for central authority. The Spanish and the Portuguese felt they had a mission to convert their new subjects to Catholicism. The Roman Catholic Church

Emiliano Zapata was one of many who fought for power in Mexico.

preached strict obedience and acceptance of authority. Once converted, the Spanish and Portuguese did not want the blacks and Indians exposed to heresy. Latin Americans were isolated from ideas which might cause them to question religious authority. Religious and civil authority were closely connected in these countries. If religious authority were questioned, civil authority might be challenged as well. After independence, religion continued to be used to reinforce the authoritarian tradition.

Another factor that encouraged the rise of caudillos was a demand for law and order after the bloodshed and chaos of the wars of independence. Cities, villages, and farmlands had been destroyed. Ports had been blockaded and business interrupted. Transportation and communication systems had to be restored or built. Outlaws and groups of unemployed soldiers roamed the countryside. These needs seemed more important than insuring freedoms which few people had heard about.

THE STATUS QUO

To maintain stability, order, and security has been the excuse of every caudillo and junta that has seized power in Latin America. It is also a convenient excuse for those who wish to hold on to their own privileges. Most of the rulers have been concerned with preserving the status quo (stayt-uhs-KWOH). That is, they wish to keep society and the economy the way they are. The rich continue to control the wealth. The poor continue to be poor. Education is limited to the wealthy.

This is a general picture of the development of authoritarian rule in Latin America in the 1800s and into this century. The hold of the upper class on wealth, lack of education for the majority, acceptance of authority, and the call for law and order still operate in favor of caudillos and juntas. But Latin America is a varied area and there are exceptions. One such is Mexico.

MEXICO'S REVOLUTION

After Juarez's death, Porfirio Diaz came to power as dictator in 1876. By the early 1900s the Mexicans were increasingly discontented with his rule. When Diaz declared himself reelected in 1910, armed bands organized against him. Diaz was forced to resign. Francisco I. Madero (muh-DER-oh), a liberal, was elected president. But in three years General Victoriano Huerta (WERT-uh) seized power.

Civil war broke out. Madero's supporters rallied around Venustiano Carranza (kahr-RAHN-sah). Meanwhile Francisco "Pancho" Villa (VEE-yuh), a bandit, began to claim land south of Mexico City. A folk movement of peasants and **intellectuals** grew up around him. Soon a coalition made up of Villa, Carranza, and Emiliano Zapata (sah-PAH-tah) among others was fighting the government. Huerta

The leaders of the Revolution of 1914 sit for their portrait. Mexico was to endure several more stormy years, but by the 1940s the nation was politically and economically stable. Industrialization was making rapid progress.

was forced to resign and the rebels formed a new government. Land was to be redistributed and the conditions of factory workers improved.

Early in 1915 a bloody battle took place between Villa's forces and an army raised by one of the other revolutionaries. Carranza assumed the presidency. By this time the political and economic machinery of the nation had broken down completely. Private armies were fighting the national army. Crime was widespread.

Just as Carranza set about restoring order, Villa invaded U.S. territory and killed 16 Americans. Villa had become angry by President Woodrow Wilson's recognizing Carranza's government. Wilson sent U.S. troops into Mexico.

Order gradually returned to Mexico. In 1917 a new constitution was written. The government broke up large estates and divided them among the peasants. Unlike other Latin American countries, mestizos, not creoles, came to dominate politics. The Mexican government acted to restore and preserve Indian monuments. The Indians' pride in themselves and in their ancestors was encouraged.

The revolution destroyed the tradition of the caudillo. All men and women are guaranteed the right to vote. Mexican presidents now take their power from the office they hold.

The struggle for power between rivals for control of Mexico involved U.S. forces in 1916. These troops are marching across the New Mexico-Mexico border.

Chapter 2
Radical versus Conservative Change

⚬─

Two world wars and the worldwide depression of the 1930s have had their impact on the economies and social awareness of Latin Americans. As nations industrialize, the middle class grows. More people are being educated and are learning about political, social, and economic rights. Latin American leaders no longer find it so easy to preserve the status quo. Citizens are beginning to express their impatience with the old forms of government.

Occasionally protesters use terror activities such as kidnappings to try to unseat the government. Urban guerrilla tactics like those of the Tupamaros began in Uruguay and have spread to other Latin American nations. But not everyone is seeking sudden or **radical** change. There is still a conservative right that believes either in no change or change that is slow and gradual.

ARGENTINA

The politics of Argentina show the effects of the depression and World War II. From 1852 until 1930, Argentina had regular elections and a democratic government. Then in 1930 the nation fell victim to the worldwide depression.

The army which had long been the guardian of Argentina's presidency became in 1930 the instrument of revolution. The military took control and a long succession of president-military officers followed. None stayed in power very long. Then in 1943 Colonel Juan D. Peron took over but ruled through a figurehead. In 1946 he assumed the presidency himself and ruled for nine years.

Peron set the country on the road to industrialization. One consequence was the rise of labor **unions.** Unlike some leaders, Peron did not outlaw these labor groups. He used them as a base for his own power. He increased wages and fringe benefits. He **nationalized** the railroads and used government money for public works. While he protected workers' rights, he outlawed such rights as freedom of the press and freedom of speech. He abolished the clause in the constitution which prevented him from succeeding himself as president.

Peron's wife, Eva, helped him to win support. She acted as **minister** of health and labor. Women's rights and welfare programs were her special concerns. She organized women workers and helped women gain the vote. She was highly effective. When she died in 1952, the Argentine working class wept for her.

Peron ultimately lost the support of the army when he threatened to organize his followers into an armed militia. He also lost favor with the Roman Catholic Church when he tried to weaken its position. Peron was deposed by a junta in 1955 and fled into exile.

The next 18 years saw worsening political and economic conditions in Argentina. Elections were ignored as military leaders turned elected officials out of office. By the 1970s unemployment and **inflation** were high. But Peron's supporters were very strong and active. In 1972,

Juan Peron (left) after his reelection in 1952 as president of Argentina listens while Eva Peron addresses a crowd of supporters. How important was Eva Peron to her husband's career?

one of them, Hector Campora, won the presidency. Peron returned to Argentina. Campora resigned. Peron was elected president.

In 1974 Peron died and was succeeded by his widow Isabel. Violence by various groups of Peronist followers, **Marxists**, and government security forces caused the new president to declare a state of siege. She was ousted by a junta in early 1976.

CUBA

Aside from Mexico, only one other Latin American nation in this century has had a revolution that has brought complete and far-reaching changes. That nation is Cuba.

Cuba has a strategic location in relation to the U.S. It lies at the mouth of the Gulf of Mexico, between the other Caribbean islands and the U.S. Although Cuba became an independent nation in 1902, the U.S. feared that a foreign power might try to seize it. To prevent this, the U.S. had the Platt Amendment written into the Cuban constitution. According to the amendment, Cuba could not run up too large a foreign debt. The U.S. could step in at will to preserve order and maintain Cuban independence. In addition, Cuba was to sell or lease sites for U.S. naval and refueling stations.

Between 1902 and 1933 Cuba experienced a series of shaky or do-nothing dictatorships. Civil disorder was frequent. On three occasions U.S. troops were sent. The problems that caused the unrest were economic and social as much as political. Most Cubans were very poor. They resented the fact that a few Cubans held the nation's wealth. They also resented U.S. businesses that were making large profits from Cuban resources without sharing the wealth with Cuban workers. Small groups of Cubans protested, but they had no power.

In 1933-34 Fulgencio Batista y Zaldivar (buh-TEES-tuh ee zahl-DEE-vahr), an army sergeant, led a military coup. Though others ruled in name, Batista ruled in fact for 25 years. He restored order but ended all political opposition. The economy prospered but social problems continued to grow. Revolutionaries tried several times to overthrow Batista, but failed—until Fidel Castro. In December 1956 Castro, his brother Raul, and Ernesto "Che" Guevara (CHAY gay-VAH-rah) began a rebellion. After two years of guerrilla warfare, Batista was overthrown. By January 2, 1959, Fidel Castro was in control.

CASTRO AND COMMUNISM   Castro instituted sweeping land reforms. A **central planning** board was set up. Sugar and tobacco production and cattle lands were nationalized. Castro also nationalized banks, industries, and foreign-owned companies. The greatest number of the latter were owned by the U.S. The U.S. cut off diplomatic relations with Cuba. Castro was left without a source of **foreign aid** and without Cuba's largest market for sugar. Castro turned to the Soviet Union for help.

In 1960 Castro announced publicly that he was a **Communist**. Aid came immediately from Communist-bloc nations. Castro began to support the cause of the USSR against the U.S. The U.S. set about overthrowing Castro's government. In 1961 Cubans trained in the U.S. and Guatemala landed on the southern coast of Cuba in a poorly planned invasion. They were overwhelmed by Castro's forces. The operation—known as the Bay of Pigs invasion—was a failure.

In fall 1962 the U.S. learned that the Soviet Union was delivering nuclear missiles and other weapons to Cuba. President John F.

Cuban soldiers guard a downed plane during the Bay of Pigs invasion. Do you think the U.S. should have backed this attempt by Cuban citizens to capture their government? Would they have tried without U.S. support?

Kennedy publicly called upon the Soviet government to put an end to their "threat to world peace." He stated that any missile coming from Cuba would be considered an attack by the Soviets. The U.S. would return the attack on the USSR, not on Cuba. The missiles were removed.

Castro's support of communism shocked many Latin American governments. Every country except Mexico broke diplomatic relations with Cuba. But many, if not most, Latin American countries have those rebels who are trying to imitate Castro's revolution in their own countries. His success showed them that radical revolution was possible. Castro supports some of these activities with money. He also brings recruits to Cuba to be trained in revolutionary tactics. They are taught the use of weapons and also trained in public health and land-reform policies.

By the late 1960s Castro appeared to be playing a more independent role within the Communist bloc. He has openly condemned the economic policy of the USSR toward Latin America. Cuba's **ideological** war with the U.S. has also lost some of its intensity. By the 1970s the two governments had reached agreements on several issues, including airplane hijacking.

EFFECTS OF THE REVOLUTION   Even Castro's critics admit that he has improved the living standards of most Cubans. Education is free and available to everyone. In 1958 almost one-third of Cuba's workers were unemployed. Today there is full employment. Public

Fidel Castro (right) welcomes Communist party chief Leonid Brezhnev to Havana. What is the relationship between Cuba and the USSR today? Between Cuba and the U.S.?

health care has been greatly improved. Every Cuban has the right to proper diet and to decent housing.

The price for a better standard of living has been high. Families have been uprooted. Most of Cuba's upper and middle classes lost their land and wealth. Many chose exile, often in the U.S., to life in Cuba. Those who remained and opposed the Castro government often were sent to prison. Executions were part of the revolution.

LEFTIST PARTIES

Most Latin American **leftist** parties are political rather than revolutionary. **Socialist** and Marxist parties as well as the Communist party are considered leftist. In any country a number of leftist parties of varying philosophies may exist and compete for followers. Venezuela alone has at least three small Communist parties. To increase their strength, Communist parties sometimes work with other socialist or Marxist parties. Such a combination is called a front party.

In Chile in a municipal election in 1963 the Communists formed a coalition with the Popular Action Front. The Front candidate polled more than one-fourth of the votes cast. More recently Salvador Allende (ah-YEN-day), a Marxist, was the successful presidential candidate of Chile's Popular Unity coalition. It consisted of several leftist parties.

In recent years leftists have been gaining members from among those angered by the U.S. role in Latin America. The Cuban revolution has encouraged many who are seeking radical change. Radical change can be achieved in various ways, however. Peru is an example of a leftist government that came to power without violence.

PERU In 1968 members of a military junta set out to cure some of Peru's problems. They stepped in when the Peruvian government seemed to be giving a U.S.-owned oil company too many privileges. The junta felt that the government was being generous at the expense of Peruvian citizens.

The new government made drastic reforms in the economic structure of the nation. Old agricultural estates were turned into **cooperatives**. Foreign-owned companies were forced to expand their investments. The oil company was nationalized. These reforms were made without violence. But the ability of the junta to continue in power depends on its continued appeal to Peru's poor. By the mid-1970s most people still lived a subsistence existence. The gap between promise and reality for them will have to lessen. A new junta came to power in 1975, but the elements of the revolution did not change.

CHILE The government of Salvador Allende was another example of a leftist government that came to power without violence. Allende was the first freely elected Marxist president in the Western Hemisphere. But unlike Peru, members of Chile's military turned against Allende.

During the 1800s Chile was among the most stable of Latin American nations. Its economy was based on nitrate production. Like Peru, most land and wealth was held by a few hundred families. Most of the people were poor, but unlike Peru, there was a middle class. World War I brought changes. The nitrate market declined, and massive unemployment resulted. The government was unable to ease the nation's troubles. Workers and the middle class protested this ineffectiveness. So the military entered politics. A junta took control and dismissed **congress**. A new constitution gave supreme power to the president. Chile was not to see another coup for 48 years.

Although no military takeovers occurred, Chile did not enjoy peace. Industrialization and inflation fed the unrest. When Allende took office in 1970, he called for the equalization of income and landholdings. His reforms were aimed at helping the very poor. They were taken, however, at the expense of the middle class. This caused work slowdowns and strikes by doctors and taxi drivers among others. A rash of **right**-wing **terrorist** activities occurred.

By fall 1972 Chile's economy had been badly hurt. Foreign credit had been withdrawn. Many countries equated Marxism with communism. They were afraid of supporting another Castro-like government in Latin America. Antigovernment activity quickened. It ended with the overthrow of Allende by a rightist junta and Allende's death.

To his defenders, Allende was a victim of middle-class interests, the military, and U.S. **imperialism**. The involvement of the U.S. Central Intelligence Agency (CIA) in the overthrow added to this view. His opponents felt that his Marxism was destroying the legal, social, and economic fabric of Chile.

TUPAMAROS What may happen when leftist political parties do not succeed? Sometimes they become revolutionaries as the Tupamaros (too-pah-MAH-rohs) of Uruguay have done. The name Tupamaro is derived from Tupac Amaru, the Inca who led a rebellion in the Viceroyalty of Peru.

Salvador Allende, the first freely elected Marxist president in Latin America, speaks to supporters at a May Day rally. What groups of Chileans did Allende's policies anger? What did they do about him?

derived:
comes from (as a name)

Although the price for wool fell in the 1950s, many Uruguayans could not change their way of making a living. It is from these people like the man above that the Tupamaros gained their support.

During the 1950s Uruguay's economy had begun to weaken. World prices fell for its major exports—wool and meat. At the same time government bureaucracy was growing rapidly, absorbing more and more tax money. Ordinary citizens were becoming increasingly frustrated at their lack of rights and money. A variety of leftist groups who were demanding reforms were organized. In the 1962 elections a coalition of leftist parties won only two seats.

Many leftist Uruguayans withdrew support from the electoral process. They believed that those who held power would never peacefully agree to share it. Armed struggle was the only way to bring about socialism. The result was the Tupamaros.

In the early 1970s the government toughened its attempts to stamp out the Tupamaros. The guerrillas became more violent. The military stepped in and set up a civilian front through which to rule. The revolutionaries seem in retreat. Some of the original leaders are dead or in jail. But there are still thousands of Tupamaro sympathizers in Uruguay. They could keep the movement alive as long as the country's social and economic problems are unresolved.

ARGUMENTS FOR SLOW CHANGE

Some Latin Americans truly believe that the rule of the so-called new liberators would be worse than the present system. The more democratic and concerned among them admit, however, that changes need to be made. The wealth must reach more of the people. While this is done, however, military leaders of such countries as Chile and Peru argue that they must retain power. Military force, they believe, is the only defense against a takeover by Communists or other leftists.

Many Roman Catholic Church officials agree. They have seen what the Communists have done to the Church in Cuba. Other Church officials, however, feel that in the long run the new radicals can be stopped only by democratic and social reforms. They plead for a more liberal Church policy that does not appear to support the status quo.

A growing number of nonrevolutionary Latin Americans are trying to achieve reforms through democratic means. In some countries, non-Communist Christian Democratic parties campaign on strong reform platforms. In other countries these parties are more conservative in their approach.

There are as many solutions to Latin America's social, political, and economic problems as there are opposing groups.

Chapter 3
Hemispheric Relations

While Spain ruled its American colonies, political unity existed among the four viceroyalties of the New World. Once independence was gained, however, this unity fell apart. Brazil—a Portuguese colony—did not suffer from this problem for several reasons. The nation had always been ruled as one country of several provinces. In addition, the royal house of Braganza was a unifying influence. In the person of Dom Pedro, Brazilians were able to find a focus for their loyalty. No other person or group could command the support of a following large or powerful enough to split Brazil. But Portuguese Brazil was isolated from Spanish Latin America.

DISUNITY

Some factors that caused the fragmenting of the former Spanish colonies were geographic. Others were cultural or political. The size of the area, the mountains, rain forests, and swamps made travel and communication difficult. Like Europeans before the **industrial revolution**, most Latin Americans knew only their own locality, rulers, and neighbors. They knew little of other people and places.

Differences in the composition of population also separated the people of the various countries. In Argentina, Uruguay, Costa Rica and Chile the descendants of Europeans were the most numerous. Indians were in the majority in Bolivia, Mexico, Ecuador, and Peru. In some countries, such as Nicaragua, Honduras, El Salvador, Venezuela, Colombia, and Chile, a large number of people were mestizos. Descendants of the Portuguese ruled Brazil although many Brazilians were Indians, blacks, and mulattoes. Blacks dominated Haiti. Blacks and mulattoes made up a large part of the population of Panama and Cuba and other Caribbean islands.

Ambitious and power-hungry leaders were also a fragmenting factor. Many of them were eager to divide up and rule the new countries. As we have seen, internal power struggles dissolved the United Provinces of Central America and Bolivar's Gran Colombia.

At times wars were fought over territory. Uruguay originated as a buffer state between Brazil and Argentina in 1828. In the War of the Pacific (1879-1884), Chile took a rich mineral region from Bolivia.

buffer state: neutral nation lying between rival nations

In 1903 Brazil acquired another piece of Bolivia. Paraguay and Bolivia fought over the Gran Chaco in the early 1940s.

PAN-AMERICANISM

Some Latin Americans, however, have tried to keep Bolivar's dream of a united Latin America alive. Movements for regional and continental cooperation have appeared regularly since the late 1800s. One of the first was the Pan-American Union.

The First International Conference of American States was held in Washington, D.C., in 1889-90 as a result of the efforts of U.S. Secretary of State, James G. Blaine. The purpose was to create closer ties among the nations of the Western Hemisphere. Every nation except Canada and the Dominican Republic was represented.

The most concrete result was the creation of the International Association of American Republics. It was to act as a clearinghouse for the exchange of scientific, economic, and cultural information. In 1910 it became known as the Pan-American Union.

In 1948 the Organization of American States (OAS) was established on the foundations of the Pan-American Union. One aim of the OAS was to protect member nations from aggression. It provides means for the peaceful settlement of disagreements and promotes regional cooperation. Another aim is to improve the social and material welfare of the citizens of its 23 member nations.

Among its actions has been the removal of Communist Cuba from active membership. In 1965 the OAS sent troops into the Dominican Republic to establish order during a civil war. In 1969 the OAS intervened in the fight between Honduras and El Salvador. In the early 1970s the organization was restructured. Three councils were set up to deal with the areas of organization, economics and society, and education, science, and culture.

In addition to the OAS, there have been other attempts at cooperation and unity among Latin American nations. In 1951, the Organization of Central American States was formed. The Central American Common Market (CACMO) was established in 1960.

Another common market was formed in 1969 when an economic association of Andean nations was established. Venezuela, Colombia, Chile, Bolivia, Ecuador, and Peru banded together. They have a combined market of over 65 million people.

LATIN AMERICA AND THE U.S.

The long history of relations between Latin America and the U.S. has not always been even. Friendship and ill-will, understanding and misunderstanding, progress and retreat have marked it. Common elements, however, tie the two areas together. More often than not, self-interest has torn them apart.

The Mexican-American War created hardships not only for Mexicans living in Mexico but also for those who lived in the areas that the U.S. took in the Southwest. What are some of the current problems of Mexican Americans that can be traced to the outcome of this war? This is a scene of the Battle of Molina el Rey.

THE MONROE DOCTRINE   In the beginning the U.S. sympathized with and encouraged the Spanish wars of independence. In 1823, through the Monroe Doctrine, President James Monroe tried to keep Europeans from reimposing their rule. He warned them that the Americas were not to be looked upon as areas of possible future colonization.

In time, however, the U.S. itself began to use the Monroe Doctrine as a cloak for its own expansion. In the 1830s and 1840s U.S. settlers in the Spanish territories of California and the Southwest and expansionists within the U.S. wanted to take these territories. President James K. Polk agreed that the Monroe Doctrine prevented transfer of New World territory to a European state. However, it did not forbid changes in ownership among the nations of the Western Hemisphere.

Between 1835 and 1848, Texas was the object of a series of struggles and finally the Mexican-American War. As a result of the Treaty of Guadalupe Hidalgo (GWAH-duh-loop-ee ee-DAHL-goh), Mexico lost Texas. It also lost the areas that are now the states of California, Nevada, Utah, and parts of Arizona, Colorado, New Mexico, and Wyoming. In return the Mexican government received $15 million. Eight years later—in the Gadsden Purchase—the U.S. bought the rest of Arizona and New Mexico for $10 million.

THEODORE ROOSEVELT   By the mid-1800s Europe was becoming highly industrialized. Merchants and manufacturers needed raw materials. They were also looking for areas in which to loan or invest surplus money. Latin America had great sources of raw materials and good loan and investment possibilities.

Naturally Europeans expected the repayment of loans and regular returns on their investments. In a number of cases, however, Latin American governments borrowed money that they either could not

Colonel Theodore Roosevelt poses with his Rough Riders atop San Juan Hill, Cuba, during the Spanish-American War. What events led to this war?

or would not repay. Whenever this occurred, as it did in Venezuela in 1902, European creditors were furious. Their governments threatened the offending nations with blockades. U.S. officials became alarmed. They saw this as an opportunity for European powers to further their interests at the expense of Latin America. In addition, the position of the U.S. in the hemisphere could be weakened and U.S. investments endangered.

In 1895, before a gathering of world leaders, U.S. Secretary of State Richard Olney declared: "God has marked the American people as His chosen Nation to finally lead to the regeneration of the world . . . We are trustees of the world's progress, guardians of the righteous peace." Olney's words became the basis for aggressive U.S. foreign policy.

President Theodore Roosevelt acted with special energy and determination in regard to Latin America. He believed equally in the Monroe Doctrine and the words of Olney. In 1904 he combined the two and declared the Roosevelt Corollary to the Monroe Doctrine. According to his policy, whenever a nation in the Western Hemisphere failed to pay a just debt, the U.S. would assume supervision of that country. Payment would be assured. In other words the U.S. would police by force the countries of the Western Hemisphere in economic matters. As we have seen, U.S. troops took possession of Haiti and the

Dominican Republic and interfered in their domestic policies.

Roosevelt's intervention in Panama had more lasting consequences.  The U.S. had made an agreement with Colombia to finish a canal that the French had started in the Colombian province of Panama. At one time Panama had been independent. Panamanians (pan-uh-MAY-nee-uhns) saw prosperity ahead if they were free again when the canal was built. In 1903 they rebelled. However, they had only a small untrained force and needed outside help. Roosevelt sent a warship, thus discouraging the Colombians from fighting. Panama quickly proclaimed its independence.

The U.S. recognized the new government and signed a treaty for construction of the canal. Panama received $10 million at once. An annual rental fee was established. In return the U.S. received complete control of a 16-kilometer (10-mile) wide canal zone. Although the rental fee has been increased several times, recent years have seen strong anti-American feelings in Panama. Panamanians want an end to U.S. control of the Canal Zone and payment of the operating fees to themselves.

GOOD NEIGHBOR POLICY Latin Americans came to resent the U.S. Its investments in Latin America were growing. Many people became convinced that the U.S. was following a policy of political and economic imperialism. After World War I, Latin American governments became enthusiastic supporters of the **League** of Nations. They hoped that a strong world organization could restrain U.S. influence. But the League did not last.

A ship passes through the Culebra Cut of the Panama Canal. How did the U.S. gain control of the Panama Canal Zone? What is the present status of U.S.-Panama relations?

In the 1920s, the U.S. tried to assure Latin Americans that it had no imperialistic designs on their area. After his election in 1933 President Franklin Roosevelt set about this in earnest. He developed what was known as the Good Neighbor Policy. In a treaty with other American nations the U.S. agreed that no country had the right to interfere in the affairs of another. Many of the old one-sided treaties were done away with. When troubles arose in various countries, the U.S. did not intervene. In 1934 the U.S. pulled out of Haiti as promised.

The years between 1933 and 1945 were relatively free of tension. The Good Neighbor policy was especially critical during World War II. After Asian sources were cut off, the U.S. was able to buy essential war materials like copper, tin, and rubber from Latin America. Many people began to see the possibility for a new spirit of cooperation.

SUPPORT OF THE STATUS QUO   But hopes proved short-lived. After the war the U.S. was accused of supporting dictatorships like those of Trujillo in the Dominican Republic and Batista in Cuba. These leaders allegedly oppressed their own people in order to protect and further U.S. business interests. Groups that supported social and land reforms received criticism and no U.S. financial help. The U.S.-supported overthrow of Arbenz Guzman's liberal regime in Guatemala in 1954 seemed to prove this. The Guatemalan government had started to give to peasants much of the land of the U.S.-owned United Fruit Company.

However, it was the threat of Cuban communism that brought about some cooperation between Latin America and the U.S. The **Alliance** for Progress was President John F. Kennedy's program for containing Castro's appeal. The program called for large-scale U.S. aid. The money was to be matched by equally large amounts from participating countries. It was meant to pay the cost of a peaceful social revolution. Along with the economic development, the Alliance was to promote democratic and social justice. Ironically, one of the first projects the Alliance supported was Guatemala's land reform law.

Ten years of the Alliance for Progress accomplished little. Some of its inspiration was lost when Kennedy was killed. It failed too, because the traditional landowning class in Latin America resisted change. In addition the U.S. compromised its aims even as they were announced. From the beginning it cooperated with conservative and military elements. The Alliance spent $10 billion. Two-thirds of it went to military rulers or military-controlled governments. Much of the money went for weapons and not for social reform.

When President Lyndon B. Johnson sent marines into the Dominican Republic in 1965, a new wave of anti-U.S. feeling spread across Latin America. The administration of Richard M. Nixon did little to lessen that bitterness. During his term the Central Intelligence Agency supported groups opposed to Allende's government in Chile. Since Nixon the U.S. has tried to reassure Latin Americans, but they still view the U.S. with suspicion.

A Guatemalan peasant carries his merchandise to market. The land reform programs of the 1950s in Guatemala, which would have helped poor people like him, were stopped with U.S. help. What do you think about the U.S.'s intervening in another country's domestic affairs?

Summing Up the Unit

Social Studies Vocabulary

Define: junta; intellectual; radical; unions; nationalize; minister; inflation; Marxist; central planning; foreign aid; Communist; ideological; leftist; socialist; cooperative; congress; rightist; terrorist; imperialism

People

Identify: Madero; Huerta; Zapata; Carranza; Villa; Juan Peron; Eva Peron; Batista; Fidel Castro; Allende; Guzman

Words

Define: caudillo; status quo; Platt Amendment; Bay of Pigs invasion; Tupamaros; OAS; Monroe Doctrine; Treaty of Guadalupe Hidalgo; Gadsden Purchase; Panama Canal Zone; Good Neighbor Policy; Alliance for Progress

Questions

1. Why were ordinary citizens not prepared to govern themselves in Latin America?
2. With independence, what class of people gained political power?
3. How did the European pattern of settlement encourage the power of the privileged?
4. How were religious and political leaders alike in dealing with the people?
5. What has been the excuse of every Latin American caudillo and junta that has seized power?
6. What changes did Carranza's government bring about in Mexico?
7. What were Juan Peron's policies?
8. a. What reforms did Castro institute? b. What have been the good and bad effects of Cuba's revolution?
9. What kinds of economic changes have been made by the military junta in Peru?
10. Why did the military in Chile turn against Allende?
11. a. What excuse do military leaders in Chile and Peru give for retaining power? b. What is the Roman Catholic Church's position?
12. What geographic, cultural, and political factors caused the fragmenting of the former Spanish colonies into many nations?
13. What was the purpose of the Pan-American Union?
14. How did the U.S. apply the Monroe Doctrine differently in the 1830s and 1840s than it did in the 1820s when first written?
15. Why did the Alliance for Progress accomplish little?

Discussion Topics

1. Considering the history of U.S.-Latin American relations, would you trust the U.S. if you were a Latin American?
2. In the past the U.S. has supported military rulers in Latin America. Do you think this has been a wise policy for the U.S.? What arguments can be given for and against it?
3. Peron tried to promote industrialization in Argentina. Was his policy wise? Or did it ignore Argentina's natural economic advantages by turning away from an agricultural economy?
4. Could the U.S. have used its influence to avoid a Communist takeover in Cuba by using different policies than it used? Was U.S. opposition to Castro justifiable? according to whose interests?
5. U.S. business interests have large investments in Latin America. Has U.S. business helped Latin America, or has it done more harm than good? What position do you think the U.S. government should take toward U.S. investments abroad?
6. How do you think military takeovers affect the economy of a nation? Will economic progress be initially retarded? Consider Chile, Peru, and Argentina.

Project Ideas

1. Imagine you are a citizen of a Latin American country. Write an editorial praising or criticizing the military takeover of your country.
2. Using library references, write a report on one of the following: the Alliance for Progress; the Cuban missile crisis; Panama Canal; U.S.-Mexican diplomatic relations.
3. If you know someone who has lived in or visited Latin America, arrange to interview her or him. Report to the class on his or her observations.

Unit VI

Society in Transition

As a society changes, big differences such as land reform attract attention, yet little things change too—toys, for example. The Indian man and child above are dressed the way their ancestors dressed for hundreds of years, but they are playing with a late 20th-century frisbee.

Although the struggles for independence ended European rule, they did not lift Indians, blacks, and people of mixed **gene pools** from the bottom of the social scale. However, as the nations of Latin America move toward industrialization and **urbanization**, change is coming. Two emerging groups—a rapidly growing middle class and a large urban working class—are beginning to exercise power.

Greater numbers of people are being educated. More women are working outside the home. Land reforms are breaking up the great landholding systems which contributed to the poverty of most Latin Americans. Within the Roman Catholic Church, people are beginning to call for reform. Latin American society is in transition.

From the beginning of the colonization of Latin America, two well-defined social classes existed: European landowners and Indian and black laborers.

Among the Europeans themselves there soon arose class divisions. American-born descendants of Spanish or Portuguese were considered socially inferior to European-born colonists. Between the classes of Spanish and Portuguese and their laborers gradually emerged the mestizos. These Spanish-speaking offspring of Europeans and Indians were considered above the Indians because they were part European. However, because they were part Indian, they were considered socially inferior to the Spanish. This was also true of mulattoes. The Portuguese had a more casual attitude toward birth as a factor in determining class.

With independence, of course, the distinction between American-born and European-born Spanish and Portuguese disappeared. The new upper class included anyone with money and all-European ancestors. The two usually went together. Independence did little for Indians, blacks, mulattoes, and mestizos. They remained at the bottom of the social system—often in peonage.

MODERN SOCIAL STRUCTURES

In most Latin American nations today, the same small upper class still holds the wealth. Their families have owned the large landholdings since colonial days. Now these few also hold key positions in industry and government. The successful children of later immigrants from Europe, Asia, and the Middle East also rank high in Latin American society today.

In some nations, such as Argentina and Uruguay, the growing middle class is becoming important. It is made up of doctors, lawyers, government clerks, and other white-collar workers. Education has made the middle class possible. In its attitudes and manners the new middle class tends to identify with the upper class.

Most Latin Americans, however, belong to the lower class. They are subsistence farmers, field workers, laborers, and artisans. Wages are low and the future often seems hopeless. These people usually have little or no education.

SOCIAL MOBILITY   Even though the movement for social change is great in Latin America, there is, as yet, little **social mobility**—movement from one social class to another. Occasionally a poor person may rise to the middle class through education. Or a middle class professional may rise to the upper class. But this does not happen often. For upward social mobility it is a person's dress, speech, education, and wealth that are important. Immigrants perhaps have had the best chance of moving up the Latin American social ladder.

It is estimated that more than ten million immigrants entered Latin

Chapter 1
Social
Patterns

white-collar workers:
people who are paid weekly or monthly salaries instead of working for an hourly wage

America from about 1885 to the mid-1900s. Over four million may have come from Italy alone. Others came from Spain, Portugal, Germany, France, Ireland, and the countries of Eastern Europe as well as the Middle East and Asia. They went mostly to Mexico and countries in the temperate zone—Argentina, southern Brazil, Chile, and Uruguay.

Of all the Latin American countries, Brazil offers the greatest chances for upward mobility. The experience of the Japanese in Brazil is an example. They began arriving in large numbers about 1908. Today there are more than a half million in the country. They came first as laborers on coffee plantations, mostly in the state of Sao Paulo. They soon abandoned the harsh working conditions of the plantations and turned to other ways of making a living. They began to grow cotton, jute, and pepper. They started a poultry industry and modernized commercial fishing. Soon the Japanese were leaders in many areas of agricultural development. In addition, because they immigrated as families, the Japanese formed stable **rural** communities.

After World War II the Japanese began moving into urban areas. The move signalled a cultural change among them. On the farms, much of their Japanese culture as well as their language had been kept. In the cities they were exposed to Brazilian culture. They exchanged the Japanese language for Portuguese. Many young Japanese took jobs outside agriculture. They became engineers, economists, and doctors, and members of the middle class.

EDUCATION

One way to stimulate social and economic change is through education. Some nations have long traditions of mass public education. About 90 percent of the people of Argentina and Uruguay are **literate**. But in nations such as Ecuador, Haiti, and Peru scarcely one-fourth of the people receive an education. Overall, about half the population of Latin America can read and write.

Indians make up the largest percentage of the poor. Will education enable this girl to achieve upward mobility? Do you think upward mobility is always desirable?

Higher education has expanded most rapidly. Argentina, Brazil, Colombia, Peru, and Mexico combined have more than a hundred universities. Why are medicine, law and engineering stressed in developing countries? Here a professor talks with students.

In the late 1960s, the presidents of the Latin American nations pledged a coordinated effort to improve education. The program was to be carried out through the OAS. Education was encouraged and attempts were made to upgrade it at every level. But the process is slow and costly. The least-developed countries have few schools. Those few are generally located in cities.

Across most of Latin America only a fraction of young children attend school for more than a year. Although national leaders pledged their support, progress has been interrupted often because of political and economic troubles. Moreover, Latin America's population is expanding so quickly that each year additional hundreds of thousands of children reach school age. As a result governments must give education larger shares of their budgets to maintain existing standards.

Higher education has expanded more rapidly. Argentina, Brazil, Colombia, Peru, and Mexico combined have more than a hundred universities. They are preparing students to be lawyers, doctors, engineers, and other professionals. Like many developing nations, Latin American countries recognize that their educational systems must train people who can develop the economy. Therefore, these schools concentrate on subjects such as mathematics and medicine are stressed over literature and history.

Mexico is an example of a nation that has made educational and economic progress at the same time. Like land reform, education was a goal of the revolution of the early 1900s. After the revolution, massive literacy campaigns were organized. Classes were set up for adults and children. Barns, churches, and other buildings became temporary classrooms while schools were being built. Educational opportunities expanded at every level. For a long time it was difficult to find qualified teachers and harder still to pay them. By the mid-1970s more than three-fourths of the population were able to read and write. Schools were teaching the Indian as well as Spanish **heritage** of Mexico. Perhaps the most important accomplishment of education has been the realization that everyone should have an opportunity to attend school.

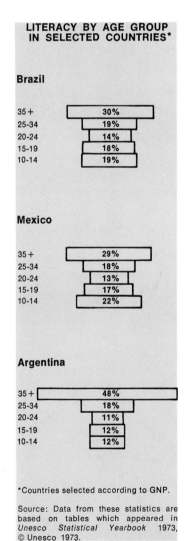

LITERACY BY AGE GROUP IN SELECTED COUNTRIES*

Brazil

35 +	30%
25-34	19%
20-24	14%
15-19	18%
10-14	19%

Mexico

35 +	29%
25-34	18%
20-24	13%
15-19	17%
10-14	22%

Argentina

35 +	48%
25-34	18%
20-24	11%
15-19	12%
10-14	12%

*Countries selected according to GNP.

Source: Data from these statistics are based on tables which appeared in *Unesco Statistical Yearbook* 1973, © Unesco 1973.

783

From the beginning of the conquest, the church was often the largest and most impressive building in a settlement. This church is in Colombia and is an example of Spanish colonial architecture.

RELIGION

Most of the people of Latin America are Roman Catholics. The Spanish and Portuguese were as earnest in their desire to convert the Indians and slaves as they were to colonize the land. Wherever explorers and settlers went, they were usually accompanied by missionaries. Colonial and later national governments and Church officials worked closely together. Roman Catholicism was virtually a **state religion**. In Spanish colonial territory it was the only religion permitted.

Indians were sometimes converted in mass baptisms. They were called Catholic before they understood the meaning of the word. Sometimes the Catholicism they practiced was heavily influenced by pre-Columbian beliefs and attitudes. This is still true.

Most of the descendants of the Africans who were brought to the New World also became Catholics. They too kept many beliefs and ways of the religions they had practiced in Africa. This influence is especially evident among the Brazilian blacks of the Bahia region and the Haitians. Most of the Europeans who migrated to Latin America in the 1800s were Catholic.

A few Latin Americans have accepted Protestant Christianity. Some Protestant denominations have been very active as missionaries, especially among Indians and blacks. In remote regions, such as the Amazon Basin, missionaries often combine their religious message with clinics and schools. Some communities of Coptic Christians and Muslims exist, expecially in coastal cities. There are influential Jewish communities in several countries.

OPPOSITION AND REFORM   Many Latin Americans have resented the closeness of the Catholic Church and the State in Latin America. They see the Church as an obstacle to progress.

In the past the Church taught people to accept life as they found it. Since the mid-1950s, however, a movement of Catholic lay people and clergy has challenged this. It is concerned with labor, land reform, and the strengthening of political democracy. It has produced a split in the Catholic Church in Latin America. In the 1800s and early 1900s, liberal political parties fought for separation of **Church and State**. They were anticlerical but not necessarily anti-Catholic. However, they were often accused of being opposed to the Church. This charge still hangs over some political parties and groups.

In Brazil the Archbishop of Recife, Dom Helder Camara, has been one of the supporters of social and political reform. He sees the role of the Catholic Church as an agent of change. Only his position saves him from the tortures of the Brazilian junta. In Colombia Camile Torres Restrepo, a priest and sociologist, sought an even more active role. "I am a revolutionary as a Colombian, as a sociologist, as a Christian, and as a priest," he said. He joined the National Liberation Army, a guerrilla group. Torres was killed in a fight with Colombian army troops in 1966.

These priests are only two examples of the restless attitude among many Catholics in Latin America today. As society changes, so do its **institutions.** Thus the Church reflects many of the stresses which also appear in the political system.

Roman Catholicism in Latin America is both changing and remaining the same. On the left is an example of an age-old tradition—the Good Friday procession—being carried out. On the right is Dom Helder Camara, the Archbishop of Recife, who represents the forces of change in the church.

The changes in Latin American society have affected native Americans the least. They still live according to the traditions of their ancestors even though the social, economic, and political base of their way of life was destroyed long ago. They are unsure about adopting European ways because their experience with those in power has seldom been good. They fear change. Do you think this fear is reasonable?

THE FAMILY

Traditionally the family has been an important social and economic institution in Latin America. Today families remain important and close. The traditional **extended family** is still found among many upper and middle-class Latin Americans. Everyone may not live under the same roof, however. But important questions are still discussed among family members. Businesses are often family enterprises. When problems arise that might reflect upon family pride, the members present a united front to the public.

The father is the head of the family. From a legal and public point of view, he is the most important family member. He makes the final decision in all important questions, and even many minor ones—social, political, and economic. Male activities are highly valued

Machismo is the basis of Latin American society. How does this picture show machismo? Why do you think women are barred by social convention—not law—from such activities? Are these unwritten rules reasonable?

786

throughout Latin America. Women have no place in them—not even as spectators at soccer games.

WOMEN

To understand the present status of women in Latin America it is necessary to understand one of the values of Latin American society—machismo (mah-CHEEZ-moh). The term comes from the Spanish word macho, meaning manliness. It is an attitude that always implies the superiority of men. Those who believe in machismo regard women as inferior. Women are to be treated as personal property and are useful for bearing children and keeping house. Violence toward and the humiliation of women may even be featured in Latin American literature as acceptable male behavior.

Slowly attitudes toward women are changing and their status is improving. As a general level of prosperity rises, opportunities for women increase.

There have been famous and powerful women in Latin America throughout its history. During the Spanish conquest many translators for the Spanish were Indian women. Dona Marina or Malinche who helped Cortes is one example. In this period an Arawak, Anacaona, led her people against the soldiers that Columbus had left during his first voyage. She was later captured and hanged by the Spanish.

The Spanish and Portuguese, however, traditionally kept women shielded from the public. Colonial Latin American houses were designed to protect the unmarried woman from contact with men outside her family and close friends. Her bedroom was in the inner part of the house and its windows were barred. She went out only to attend church or for social reasons. When she did go out, she was chaperoned by a trusted older woman.

Marriages were arranged. The ideal wife cared for her husband and took care of his household. She was quiet, obedient, and understanding of her sometimes wayward husband. She did not interfere in his business or political affairs.

IDEAL versus REALITY   There were always exceptions to this ideal of the secluded and pampered woman. Even if the ideal were accepted by the common people, they could not follow it. Poor people had neither servants nor large homes in which women could be **segregated**. Even among the wealthy, the ideal was seldom achieved completely. Some upper-class women were well-educated and took an active part in society.

Sor (Sister) Juana Ines de la Cruz was among the first Latin American poets. She was born in Mexico in 1651. Sor Juana once described in an essay how she had learned to read at the age of three. She criticized the attitude toward women and the lack of education for them. She devoted her life to study and had a personal library of over 4,000 books.

Although the women's movement in Latin America was late in starting, it is now very active. Mexico City hosted the UN conference on women in 1975, International Women's Year. Here Aurelia Guadalupe Sanchez describes the goals of feminism.

Not all women are enjoying the benefits of increasing opportunities for women. The nation and whether a woman lives in a city or a village will determine her opportunities. This is a rope seller in an outdoor market in Ecuador. What do you think are the chances of her improving her standard of living?

In the 1800s during the struggle for independence there were many heroines. Some were executed for their activities. Marina Dolores Bedoya de Molina was active in the independence movement in Guatemala. Josefa Ortiz played a similar role in Mexico. In later years when men marched off to fight, as in the War of the Pacific (1879-1883), women took over many of their jobs. In farming areas, women always shared the labor.

FEMINISM   The **feminist** movement in Latin America did not begin until after 1900. Women's rights and opportunities there still lag behind those of women in Europe, Canada, and the U.S. In recent years, women have been gaining greater status, but conditions vary greatly from country to country. Technical training and equal employment are not available everywhere, especially in rural areas. In general the rate of **illiteracy** is higher for women than for men. In Argentina, an industrialized society with a sizable middle class, education for women is generally approved of. Half of the nation's dentists, 30 percent of its architects, and 22 percent of its medical doctors are women.

In 1928 the Inter-American Commission of Women was formed. Its purpose was to promote the civil, political, and economic rights of women in all American states. The Commission's first task was gaining **suffrage** for Latin American women. Before 1942 women could vote in only five Latin American countries. In 1961 Paraguay became the last country to withhold this right from women.

Since 1966 the Commission has been working on a long-range program to use education to improve the status of women. It is working to include rural women in the development of their communites. The work of women folk artists is being popularized. Another goal of the Commission of Women has been to include legal protection for women in the codes of its member states. Through this, discrimination against women would be outlawed. Sixteen Latin American nations have women's bureaus to look after the legal and social welfare of working women.

In some Latin American countries women have found positions of leadership. Eva Peron and Isabel Peron are two examples. Celicia Guerrero de Ciappa, a professor of education, was a candidate for president of Uruguay in 1971. Maria Eugenia Rojas de Morena was a strong candidate for the presidency of Colombia in 1974. However, these women are still exceptions. Political, economic, and social freedoms are still dreams for most Latin American women.

The process of **modernization**—the attempt to bring life up to date with the late 20th century—is most evident in the cities of Latin America. In some nations, such as Argentina, Brazil, Chile, Mexico, and Uruguay where most people are city-dwellers, movement from a traditional to a modern society is far along. The upper, middle, and urban working classes seem to benefit first. But among the lower class—about 80 percent of all Latin Americans—modernization is just beginning.

Chapter 2
Economic Development

LAND REFORM

Almost half the people of Latin America still earn their living from agriculture. But farming methods are generally inefficient and unproductive. Before 1950 only one nation—Mexico—was trying to improve agricultural methods. Beside the low level of technology, the problem of land ownership has held back agricultural growth.

Large landholdings in Latin America had their origin in the practice of rewarding loyalty with large land grants. In no other area of the world is so much land owned by so few people. In Argentina 2 percent of the estates cover 60 percent of the nation. Similar situations exist in other countries. Not only do a few people control most of the land, it is usually the best land. With the current level of technology, too little fertile land exists outside these big estates to support the growing population. At best the crops of the small landholder are only enough to feed the family. There is no surplus to sell.

The movement for land reform has a long history. One of the most successful was the Mexican reform in the 1920s. It was part of the social revolution which continued beyond the fighting. Mexico redistributed land in two ways. It divided large estates into workable units and gave them to individuals. It also delivered land grants to entire communities. This communal arrangement was based on the Aztec system of land organization.

The government soon found that it was not enough to give land to the people. They needed instruction, seeds, equipment, and credit. By the 1950s land reform was working. Agricultural production had increased. The standard of living was higher. The average life expectancy had risen. In some areas, rural residents had health care and schools for the first time.

credit: a loan against which a person can borrow, or charge goods and services

Natural Resources

- ● Industrial
- ▼ Coal
- ■ Iron
- ○ Oil
- □ Minerals

U.S.

Gulf of Mexico

Atlantic Ocean

Caribbean Sea

Pacific Ocean

U.S.

Gulf of Mexico

Atlantic Ocean

Caribbean Sea

Pacific Ocean

Land Use
- Farming
- Forestry
- Grazing
- Nonproductive

Almost half of all Latin Americans earn their living from agriculture. Here a family is plowing and planting potatoes in the highlands of Peru.

When Fidel Castro began land reform in Cuba, he built upon Mexico's experience. Cuba, however, did not divide any land among individuals. The estates which were taken from private owners or companies were operated by workers as cooperatives. All were placed under government supervision. The land reforms begun in Chile in 1971 favored cooperative units. But Chile also shared an alternative solution with Brazil.

Brazil's program does not attempt to destroy the old landholdings. Instead the government is setting up colonies within Brazil's interior. Ideally, the colonization program will accomplish four goals. First, unsettled lands will be brought into production. Second, the resources in the interior will begin to be tapped. Third, poor rural Brazilians, especially from the northeast, will have a chance to improve their living conditions. And fourth, colonies will receive some of the people who might otherwise migrate to already crowded industrial centers.

PROBLEMS   The problems surrounding land reform are many. For those who follow Mexico's pattern, great areas of land must be acquired from current owners. Few landholders willingly give up the source of their wealth and prestige.

Colonization requires vast sums of money too. Land must be cleared and roads built. The colonists must be taken to the new areas, and then given financial aid until they become self-supporting. Most of the colonization schemes guarantee government-financed educational and health services. Moreover, the new land may not be productive. Brazil discovered this. Once the **vegetation** was cleared from the rain forests, the soil quickly wore out.

Much of the money needed for these projects must come from industry. Industry has to support land reform in order to have a market for its own goods. In addition, urban and industrial growth are dependent to some extent on rural areas. Farmers must produce enough to feed themselves and to provide city dwellers with low-cost food. If a surplus of foodstuffs exists, it can be expected to bring in capital for expansion.

INDUSTRIALIZATION

Since the worldwide depression of the 1930s, industry has been considered the key to modernization. Until then, the economies of most Latin American nations depended upon the export of a few agricultural products or minerals. Tin from Bolivia, oil from Venezuela, coffee from Brazil and Colombia, all were sent to foreign processing plants. Latin Americans then had to import the finished products at high prices. When the depression hit, foreign nations stopped buying raw materials.

After World War II, Latin Americans were determined to avoid such economic disaster again. One nation after another adopted policies favoring industrial growth. Governments offered tax incentives and direct money grants to industry. They established **tariffs** to protect new local industries against the products of foreign competitors. They also allowed foreigners to invest heavily in industry. Brazil, Mexico, and Chile began to exploit their own natural resources.

In the beginning industrial development was rapid but not widespread. It tended to concentrate in a few cities, usually national capitals. Latin Americans began to produce enough of two items—textiles and foodstuffs—for their own needs. Predepression marketing arrangments were kept for some raw materials. Sugar, rubber, coffee, and cacao among others were still sent abroad for processing. But more favorable trade agreements were written. As industry grew, so did government participation in it. Soon services such as transportation and communication, which help industrial development, were under government control.

By the early 1970s, three nations—Argentina, Brazil, and Mexico—accounted for 80 percent of Latin America's industrial production. Chile, Colombia, Peru, Uruguay, and Venezuela together accounted for another 17 percent. All other Latin American nations combined shared the remaining three percent.

Foreign investors, especially from the U.S., have spurred Latin America's industrial growth. They focused on Mexico, Brazil, and South American nations along the Caribbean. More recently Japanese investments in Brazil are balancing those of the U.S. there. In combination, these investments make Brazil the largest industrial complex in South America. Brazil's manufactured goods range from trucks and tractors to transistors and computers. And industrial growth is spurring agricultural growth. Coffee is still Brazil's largest export crop but Brazil now harvests more sugar than Cuba, and is second only to the U.S. in soybeans.

PROS AND CONS   Industrialization is solving some problems, enlarging others, and creating new ones. It diversified the economies of various Latin American countries. And it introduced flexibility and economic independence. The industrial nation is no longer dependent

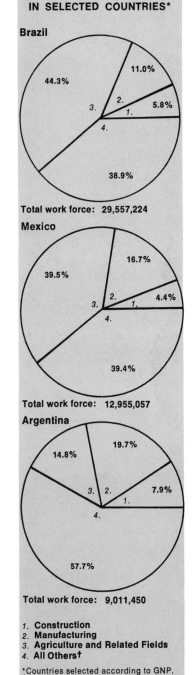

EMPLOYMENT BY INDUSTRY IN SELECTED COUNTRIES*

Brazil

44.3% · 11.0% · 5.8% · 38.9%

Total work force: 29,557,224

Mexico

39.5% · 16.7% · 4.4% · 39.4%

Total work force: 12,955,057

Argentina

14.8% · 19.7% · 7.9% · 57.7%

Total work force: 9,011,450

1. **Construction**
2. **Manufacturing**
3. **Agriculture and Related Fields**
4. **All Others†**

*Countries selected according to GNP.
†Includes mining, utilities, retail trade, etc.

Source: Based on *Year Book of Labour Statistics*, 35th edition, 1975, © International Labour Office, Geneva (Switzerland) (1975).

*Latin America has an
abundance of natural re-
sources. Various
nations are beginning
to exploit them. The welder
is working in a plant
in Sao Paulo, Brazil's new
industrial center.
The oil rig is in Ecuador.
Refer to the map on page 790
to see what are the resources
of each nation.*

on the size of a single harvest. Nor is it dependent on the world market price for a single product. Local consumers have a wide range of manufactured goods from which to choose. More Latin Americans can be better dressed and fed than in the past.

Industrialization is also intensifying one of Latin America's oldest problems—the concentration of wealth in the hands of a few. Yet industry has stimulated growth among the middle class. A sizable white-collar and an even larger blue-collar middle class now exists. In the long run these two groups may radically affect the way wealth is distributed. Because they live in and near the centers of power—the cities—they can use their numbers to affect policies. Political power is shifting away from the old landed **aristocracy** to the cities.

URBANIZATION

Since World War II, cities in Latin America have grown faster than those in any other part of the world. Argentina, Chile, and Uruguay are among the 15 most urban nations of the world. Venezuela, Costa Rica, Peru, and Paraguay are only slightly behind.

Urban growth has come from two major sources: population growth and migration. Latin America's very high birthrate has been the greater cause. The growth rate is not as high in cities as in rural areas, but the survival rate is higher. Urban babies benefit from better health care and medical facilities.

Some of the migrants to the city are from outside the nation. But most are from rural areas within the same country. Most are young. They are usually illiterate, inexperienced, and unskilled. Some are lucky and find work although the wages are very low. Some do not. Even those who find jobs live in poverty. But they remain because whatever faint hope the city offers is better than the certain poverty of the countryside.

The contrast between the middle class housing in the foreground and the squatter settlement on the mountain is common in Latin America's cities. Why? How do squatter settlements begin? What are governments trying to do about them?

Most migrants live in patched-together shacks of wood scraps and discarded trash on the hillsides and lowlands around the cities. They search garbage dumps for food and building materials. They have no running water, sewers, or electricity. Most of these areas should be called squatter settlements, not slums. Few people in these settlements arrived there directly from the countryside. They lived first in rented rooms or stayed with relatives.

They went to the squatter settlements when they could not afford, or could not find, permanent housing. Squatter settlements usually begin as an invasion of unoccupied land. They represent a demand for the right to own and improve property when existing housing is not available. On the average, 40 percent of the people in Latin American capitals live in such settlements.

Many governments are trying, but they cannot build low-cost housing as rapidly as the people need it. In Venezuela, for example, the Caracas skyline is dotted with massive low-rent apartment buildings. But public housing falls far behind the need. Nor have governments been able to build enough schools or provide adequate health services. Disease and malnutrition are widespread in the cities.

The creative arts of Latin America reflect the influence of the three major **ethnic groups** that settled its nations. In some regions, especially along the west coast of South America, the Indian influence is most strongly felt. In other areas Africans have provided the dominant cultural expression. The Bahia region of Brazil and several islands of the Caribbean show their influence. In still other regions, Spanish and Portuguese influences are most evident.

Chapter 3
Creativity

WEAVING

Weaving may very well be one of the oldest arts of the Western Hemisphere. It had reached a high level of development in the Andes long before pottery appeared. The early Andean people knew the

795

basic weaves—plain, patterned, looped pile, and tapestry. They spun llama fleece and cotton fibers for their materials. The beauty of Nazca and Paracas textiles has already been mentioned.

The art of weaving is still carried on today by many Latin Americans, especially in Peru, Bolivia, Mexico, and Guatemala. Woven articles such as belts and sashes are prominent parts of the garments woven and worn by the Indians. Using hand looms, Guatemalan weavers produce beautiful designs, many of which are pre-Columbian. Patterns vary from one region to another. By studying the design it is possible to tell where a weaving was done.

Feather work is a unique contribution of the Aztecs to world art. Only a few pre-Columbian feather pieces remain today—some shields and headdresses. After the Spanish conquest, the Indians created religious scenes that were actually feather mosiacs. The art of working with feathers began to disappear in the 1800s. It is almost gone today. Some traces of the art can be found in rugs and coverlets produced by modern Mexican artisans.

METALWORK

Latin American metalwork probably began among the Andean cultures of South America. Masks, weapons, breastplates, and helmets have been found in the Moche Valley. The early people there worked in gold, silver, and copper. In Colombia, gold and platinum were used. Gold was widely used by the ancient metalworkers of Cocle (koh-KLAY) who created pendants and other objects of exceptional quality.

Early metalworkers used many techniques, including wire coiling, casting, and inlaying. So highly perfected was the metalwork of the Incas that in the 1600s a Spanish priest wrote a book on their technology. It became a reference for people elsewhere in the world who worked with metals.

In several areas of Latin America today metalwork is still an important means of expressing creativity. In Mexico, Taxco has been known since colonial times as the City of Silver. Originally it was so named because of the silver mines found in the area. Today the city still has the title because of the many silversmiths there.

MUSIC

Into the creation of Latin American music have gone the folk songs of the Indians, the drum rhythms and chants of the Africans, and the melodic moods of the Spanish and Portuguese.

The Indians who lived in pre-Columbian Latin America already had a definite musical style when the Spanish arrived. Among Aztec instruments were drums, rattles, flutes, and horns made of conch shells. The Andean peoples used long-tubed panpipes, flutes, and other wind instruments. They made their instruments from cane or the bones of llamas. Modern counterparts of these early Indian instruments are still used along the west coast of Latin America.

When the Spanish came, they introduced stringed instruments such as the guitar, harp, and violin. The Indians combined these instruments with their own to create exciting new sounds.

With the blacks came a third musical tradition. African influences are especially strong along the east coast of Brazil and on many of the Caribbean islands. Although black musicians have not made as much use of the harp and violin as the Indians, they do use the guitar and a wide assortment of drums. Trinidad is the home of the calypso and the limbo. The lyrics of calypso songs are witty and often satirical. They may contain political or social comment. The limbo is a dance which may have had its origins in ancient African ritual. The dancer passes under a bar—sometimes flaming—which is gradually lowered during the dance. The bar sometimes is held less than a foot from the floor.

Many modern dances have originated in Latin America. The samba is an African dance that was modified in Brazil. The beguine (buh-GEEN) began among the black people of the islands of Martinique and St. Lucia. Cuban blacks gave the rhumba to the world. The conga is another Latin American dance of African origin.

Trinidad is also the home of a relatively new instrument—the steel pan—a consequence of modernization. The pan is made from an empty steel oil drum. Four types which correspond to the human voice can be made: soprano, alto, tenor, and bass. When the pans are played together, they form a pleasing sound that has become very popular.

This Andean boy makes the miles to market pass more quickly by playing his pipe.

There are also a number of Latin American composers of more formal music. Often they use folk music in their compositions. The symphonies of Mexico's Carlos Chavez glorify his Indian heritage. He used Indian themes and rhythms and in works such as *Toccato for Percussion Instruments.* Brazil's Heitor Villa-Lobos (AY-tohr vil-uh-LOH-buhs)—perhaps the most famous of Latin America's composers—makes use of folk themes in his works. *Bachianas Brasileiras,* for instruments and chorus, blends the classical style of Bach with the flavor of Brazilian folk music.

Many Latin American countries have important symphony orchestras. Rio de Janeiro and Buenos Aires have two of the world's leading opera companies. Argentina's Alberto Einastera, composer of the opera *Don Rodrigo,* is world-famous.

Latin America has produced many instrumental performers and singers of exceptional talent. Among these are pianists Claudio Arrau of Chile, Jesus Maria Sanroma of Puerto Rico, and Guiomar Novaes of Brazil; singers Bidu Sayao, also of Brazil, and Teresa Carreno of Venezuela; and violinist Jamie Loredo of Bolivia. The Pablo Casals Festival in Puerto Rico each summer attracts musicians from all over the world.

FESTIVALS   Festivals with music and dancing are a part of Latin American life. Some aspects of the festivals have their roots in pre-Columbian times. Dancing was always a very important part of ancient Indian rituals. Many dances were unique to a particular people such as the pole dance of the Aztecs. After the Indians were converted to Christianity, some adapted their earlier rituals to the new religion. Native costumes and music were kept, but the themes took on Christian elements. What may have been an Aztec war dance became one showing saints fighting devils.

A band of steel pans plays the music of Trinidad. How is the steel pan a consequence of modernization?

Peruvian Indians celebrate a festival in Cuzco, once the capital of the Inca Empire. How have traditional Indian and Christian themes been blended in various festivals?

The people of Rio de Janeiro take to the streets during carnival. Across the country, people celebrate. What is the reason for this festival? How is Brazil's past a part of the celebration?

Not all festivals have Christian significance, however. The festival of Alacitas in Bolivia is still purely Indian. Its continued celebration reveals the strength of the Indian heritage in Latin America.

Alacitas is a week-long celebration held in late January. Its theme is good luck. People buy a small dwarf-like figure called an ekeko and load it with tiny items. Usually the ekeko is scarcely visible beneath miniature pots and pans, trucks, sacks of food, baskets, and brooms. The idea of the festival is that everything bought in miniature during the festival week will become a reality during the year. To bring luck, the figure must be given away.

Some of the most exciting festivals are those that precede Ash Wednesday, the beginning of Lent in Christian churches. The most famous is the carnival of Rio de Janeiro. During carnival, business stops, and government comes to a standstill. For a few days the streets belong to everyone—rich and poor. Rio's carnival reflects the cultural influences of all the various Brazilian peoples. Even the brief period of Dutch rule in the northeast is recalled in some of the costumes. Rio's carnival is repeated on a smaller scale in almost every city and town in Brazil.

PAINTING

As we have seen, pre-Columbian peoples painted murals and pottery and wove intricate designs in their textiles. But in colonial Latin America the painters often were trained in Europe. They brought European influences to their work. Many churches and public buildings of the 1600s and 1700s as well as the paintings and sculptures found in them show a strong baroque influence. They are very ornate.

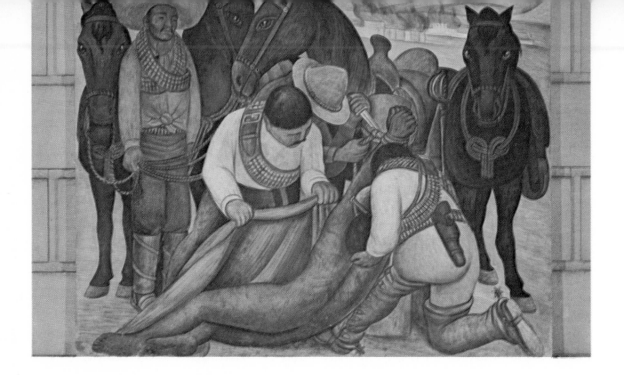

Diego Rivera painted Liberation of the Peon *as an attack on Mexico's old social and economic system. Revolutionary soldiers are cutting the rope from the wrists of a peon. His body shows the scars of the landlord's whip. The master's house is in flames. Rivera's message is that the revolutionaries will right the wrongs done by the landowners. Do you think that art should be used for propaganda?*

Religious themes dominate these works. The great cathedrals and monasteries are filled with paintings of Christ, the saints, and scenes from the Bible. Cristobal de Villalpando of Mexico painted a number of noteworthy religious paintings. Some decorate the sacristy of the great cathedral in Mexico City.

A few of the early artists used the world around them for their themes. Frans Post painted scenes of life in northeastern Brazil while it was occupied by the Dutch.

Toward the end of the 1700s and in the 1800s, Latin American artists began to show a sense of nationalism in their choice of subjects. Although the European tradition lingered, it was never again strong. The new artists depicted battle scenes and the leading figures of the independence movements. Today many of these works hang in public buildings across Latin America.

In the early 1900s, a group of artists emerged who sought to teach reform through their works. Perhaps the most important were Diego Rivera and Jose Clemente Orozco (oh-RAW-skoh) of Mexico. They, along with other Mexican artists, painted murals with historical meaning. Many of the artists had fought in Mexico's revolution and they captured in their art what they had seen.

Rivera's murals tell of Mexico's legends, traditions, and history. He wanted ordinary people, most of whom were illiterate, to know and appreciate their past, both Spanish and Indian. He hoped to give to all Mexicans the feelings of nationalism he felt. His works speak of the ideals of the revolution and the progress that it would bring.

Where Rivera expresses hope in his world, Orozco is more pessimistic. He hated the brutality which people inflict on each other. The sufferings of Mexico's Indians moved him to paint the evil of which humans are capable. Orozco wanted his paintings to shock. And they do. Although he used life as he saw it in Mexico as the base of his work, Orozco's paintings are universal in their themes.

David Alfaro Siqueiros (si-KAY-rohs) also painted pictures with social messages. In some of his works, he has curved the wall to create a feeling that the viewer is actually part of the scene.

Newer Latin American artists use a wide variety of styles ranging from traditional to the most extreme abstract expressionism. The works of Emilio Pettoruti are cubist in technique. The style of Rufino Tamayo (tuh-MY-oh), a Mexican, is bright and colorful. Haiti has produced a number of artists such as Hector Hyppolite and Wilson Bigaud, whose works are marked by directness and simplicity in style and theme.

ARCHITECTURE

From what we have learned, we know that pre-Columbian peoples were capable and sophisticated builders and city planners. Their influence is evident in some present-day Latin American **architecture**, especially in Mexico. University City in Mexico City is a complex of modern buildings. Many of them show the impact of early Indian creativity not only in the architecture but in the ornamentation and

This sculpture is called The Builders *and stands in Brasilia, Brazil's new capital. The city was planned and built in the country's interior as a way to unify the nation.*

murals that decorate them as well. The international style of architecture has also had an impact on Latin American building.

In house design, Spanish and Portuguese styles dominate. The colonial settlers built their houses facing inward. Rooms led into a central patio or courtyard. High windows and surrounding walls created a feeling of privacy. Many contemporary houses reflect this design element.

In Brazil, the city of Ouro Preto, in the state of Minas Gerais, was a product of the gold rush of the 1700s. The city is now a national monument. Its ornate cathedral and modest adobe houses are examples of colonial Portuguese architecture. In an effort to preserve original buildings, no heavy traffic is allowed on the city's streets. New buildings must follow a strict building code to preserve the colonial look of the city.

The Mexican government is also trying to preserve its Spanish architecture. The colonial city of Taxco also is a national monument. It dates from the time of Cortes. New buildings must conform to the existing colonial style. The Spanish architecture of Mexico City is the oldest in the New World. The city was begun on the Aztec capital, Tenochititlan. Today it blends Spanish and ultramodern styles.

Many modern Latin American architects have welcomed the challenge of rapid urbanization and modernization. They view it as an opportunity to influence the total environment. Exciting and original designs have resulted. In Caracas, the Helicoid is an example. It is an enormous commercial center in the downtown area. The buildings are set along 4.8 kilometers (3 miles) of interlocking roads.

The main square of Lima, Peru, is an example of Spanish colonial architecture. All settlements were built around a square. On one side was the church. Opposite it were government buildings. Businesses and homes lined the other sides.

Brasilia (bruh-ZIL-yuh), the new capital of Brazil, is another example. In 1960, Brazil moved its capital inland to what had once been a barren isolated plain. Rio de Janeiro, the former capital along the east coast, was believed to be too far from the interior. An inland capital was seen as a unifying force for the country. It would also be a stimulus to the development of the interior.

Oscar Niemeyer (NEE-my-uhr), Brazil's most famous architect, was given the contract to design Brasilia's government buildings. He also had final authority over the design of all other structures. Under his direction, architects have created impressive buildings of concrete, glass, steel, and bronze. Two of the most imaginative are the bowl-like structures which house Brazil's two chambers of deputies.

Very different in style from colonial architecture is Brasilia's Chamber of Deputies designed by Oscar Niemeyer. But Brasilia in the 1960s was as much a frontier as the New World had been to Europeans in the 1500s.

LITERATURE

Just as the English spoken in the U.S. has changed from that of England, so have Spanish and Portuguese undergone changes in Latin America. For example, the Spanish of Argentina shows the influence of the country's large Italian population. Both Spanish and Portuguese have incorporated many words of Indian origin. Almost all the names for New World fruits, plants, and animals are Indian words.

Besides Paraguay where Guarani is spoken by a majority of the people, Indian languages are still spoken in Guatemala, Colombia, Peru, Bolivia, Honduras, and Venezuela among other nations. Some nationalists view this as an obstacle to progress. They want everyone to speak only Spanish. But others see the continued use of Indian languages as a way to preserve Indian cultures.

The Aztecs, Mayas, and Incas had their own literary traditions long before the Europeans arrived. Theirs was largely an oral literature. When the Spanish came, they learned the spoken language of the Indians, wrote grammars, and recorded Indian literature. They used letters of the Spanish alphabet to represent sounds of Indian words.

This is the opera house at Manaus, Brazil. Its interior walls are decorated with paintings illustrating scenes from Jose Martiniano de Alencar's O Guarani.

A Dominican priest, Francisco Ximinez (huh-MAY-nays), recorded a version of the *Popul Vol* both in Spanish and in the Quiche languages. This is the story of the creation of the universe and the beginning of people as believed by the Quiche-speaking Mayas of Guatemala.

EUROPEAN INFLUENCES   In the early 1800s, a literary style called romanticism swept Europe. Romanticism looked to the emotions, nature, and the simple things of life for themes. Probably the finest of the Latin American romantic writers was the novelist Jose Martiniano de Alencar (a-LAYNG-kar). He is known for his deep feelings toward the Indians and the land of his native Brazil. His novel, *O Guarani,* written in 1857, concerns the love of an Indian and a Brazilian of European descent. Scenes from this novel decorate the walls of the opera house in Manaus, Brazil.

Ruben Dario was the pen name of Feliz Ruben Garcia Sarmiento of Nicaragua. He was both a poet and a diplomat. His experiments with themes, verse forms, and language revolutionized Spanish literature. He wrote several books of verse and prose. Dario introduced modernism into the Latin American literary tradition. Modernists revolted against the style and themes of romanticism.

REGIONALISM   Dario and other writers of the late 1800s and early 1900s helped to awaken an awareness among Spanish Americans of the ties that bound them together. Jose Marti of Cuba, Jose Asuncion Silva of Colombia, Jose Enrique Rodo of Uruguay, and Manuel Gutierrez Najera of Mexico emphasized the common cultural bonds of Latin Americans. They stressed that this unity reached beyond physical and political differences.

Until this century, most Latin American writers wrote as though they were not part of the world in which they lived. Unlike the artists such as Rivera and Orozco, the writers did not believe it their purpose to write about the common people. They thought of their writing as being far removed from the commonness of life. They had little social consciousness. But as the century wore on, Latin American writers changed their attitude. The development of an interest in **regionalism** and national character was an important first step.

One aspect of regional thinking was a common belief that the U.S. was a threat to the cultural and political life of Latin America. An example of this attitude can be found in the interpretations of the work of the Uruguayan Jose Rodo.

In his essay "Ariel," written in 1900, Rodo called upon Latin American youth to maintain a high cultural level. He pointed out that the U.S. feeling for liberty and its technical genius might be imitated by Latin Americans. On the other hand, North American cultural values were not to be accepted uncritically. Many readers believed that Rodo intended to contrast a materialistic U.S. and a culturally superior Latin America. This interpretation led many Latin Americans to think of the U.S. as culturally inferior. This attitude

still persists among some Latin Americans today.

Other writers expressed a bitter fear of U.S. foreign policy. Jose Marti, the Cuban revolutionary, was fearful that the U.S. would attempt to seize Latin American nations. Ismael Enrique Artigas of Colombia lashed out at Yankee offenses against Latin Americans. Francisco Garcia Calderon of Peru wrote about Anglo-Saxon invaders.

In recent years, more and more writers are following the tradition of realism and describing actual conditions. They are attempting to do through their writing what recent Mexican artists have done through their murals.

One such writer was Joaquim Maria Machado de Assiz (ma-SHA-doo day a-SEES). Born in poverty, his talent took him to the height of success in Brazil. He founded the Brazilian Academy of Letters and wrote numerous poems and books. His urban novels are realistic in style. Some of his works—*Dom Caosmurro* and *Epitaph of a Small Winner*—have been translated into English.

Within the past several decades, a number of Latin Americans have won **international** fame for their works. The Chilean poet Gabriela Mistral was awarded the Nobel Prize for literature in 1945. Miguel Angel Asturias of Guatemala wrote a bitter protest against political and social conditions under a dictatorship in *Mr. President.* Asturias won the Nobel Prize for literature in 1967.

Another Chilean poet, Pablo Neruda, received the same award in 1971. Neruda's poetry ranges from lyrics to passionate pleas for social commitment. Gabriel Garcia Marquez, author of *One Hundred Years of Solitude* and Julio Crotazar, who wrote *Hopscotch,* have also gained international attention. Piri Thomas is a well-known Puerto Rican writer.

In recent years, more and more Latin American writers have turned their attention to the problems of the world. With their increased awareness, some have entered politics. At left Gabriela Mistral talks to reporters in her role as a Chilean diplomat. At right Pablo Neruda campaigns for president of Chile in 1969.

social commitment: sense of responsibility to improve the conditions of society

Summing Up the Unit

Social Studies Vocabulary

Define: urbanization; social mobility; heritage; state religion; Church and State; institution; segregated; feminist; illiteracy; suffrage; modernization; tariff; aristocracy; ethnic group

People

Identify: Chavez; Villa-Lobos; Post; Rivera; Orozco; Siqueiros; Niemeyer; Ximinez; Alencar; Dario; Rodo; Marti; Mistral; Asturias; Neruda; Thomas

Words

Define: upward mobility; machismo; squatter settlements; calypso; limbo; samba; beguine; carnival; Guarani; Quiche; modernism

☜ Questions

1. With independence, what was the only class distinction in Latin America that disappeared?
2. a. Who make up the growing middle class? b. What has made this middle class possible? c. In what nations is it important?
3. What people make up the lower class?
4. a. What factors are considered important for upward social mobility? b. What country offers the greatest chances for upward mobility?
5. a. What is one way to stimulate social and economic change? b. What two problems do governments face in providing education?
6. What has produced a split in the Roman Catholic Church in Latin America?
7. a. Describe the traditional family in Latin America. b. How has machismo affected the status of women in Latin American life? c. Which class of people were least able to segregate women? d. Why? e. What is the status of women's rights and opportunities in Latin America at present?
8. What two factors have held back Latin America's agricultural growth?
9. a. How has land reform in Cuba differed from Mexico's experience? b. Describe Brazil's colonization efforts.
10. What problems surround land reform?
11. How did the depression of the 1930s encourage industrialization in Latin America?
12. What two sources have contributed to Latin America's urban growth?
13. What three ethnic groups have influenced the creative arts in Latin America?
14. What was the status of music in pre-Columbian Latin America?
15. a. What style in painting developed around the 1900s? b. What is the present status of art in Latin America?
16. a. How does modern Latin American architecture reflect Indian influences? b. What are some countries doing about their colonial architecture? c. Why do many modern Latin American architects welcome the challenge of rapid industrialization and modernization?
17. a. What European influences are evident in Latin American literature? b. How do some modern Latin American writers reflect an interest in regionalism? c. What is the predominant style today in Latin American literature?

Discussion Topics

1. What problems stem from Latin America's class structure? Can anything be said in defense of it? How are class distinctions being changed? Is greater social mobility desirable? What kinds of problems could arise with greater mobility?
2. What advantages would Latin America gain from a higher literacy rate? What new problems might arise?
3. Study the graphs on page 783. Which nation has the highest literacy rate for people over 35? How do you account for this?
4. Refer to the employment charts on page 793. How do you account for Argentina's low agricultural work force while the country has South America's most productive farmland?

Project Ideas

1. Write an essay on the stereotyped image of Latin America. Show the flaws in this image.
2. Listen to Latin American music. If possible, bring tapes or records to class of music that demonstrate the influences of the three ethnic groups: Indian, European, and African.
3. Arrange a class exhibit on the arts of Latin America. Use as many visuals as possible.

For Further Study

General Readings

1. *Ancient America* by Jonathan Norton Leonard and Editors of Time-Life Books. Time-Life Books, Illustrated. A Division of Time Inc., 1967.

2. *Ancient Mexico: An Introduction to the Pre-Hispanic Cultures* by Frederick A. Peterson. G. P. Putnam's Sons, 1962. Paperback. Includes material on many cultures.

3. *Art Before Columbus* by Andre Emmerich. Simon & Schuster, Inc., 1963. On native pre-Columbian art.

4. *Bernal Diaz: Historian of the Conquest* by Herbert Cerwin. University of Oklahoma Press, 1963. Biography of Diaz who was an eyewitness to the conquest of the Aztecs and left an account.

5. *The Borzoi Reader in Latin American History* by Helen Delpar. Alfred A. Knopf, Inc., 2 vols., 1972. Paperback. Vol. I covers from the colonial period to independence and Vol. II covers the 1800s and 1900s.

6. *Brazil: The Land and People* by Rollie E. Poppino. Oxford University Press, Inc., 2nd ed., 1973. Paperback. An overview.

7. *Broken Spears: The Aztec Account of the Conquest of Mexico* by Miguel Leon-Portilla. Beacon Press, 1962. Paperback. Presents the Aztec account of the conquest of Mexico.

8. *Chilean Revolution* by Regis Debray and Salvador Allende. Random House, Inc., 1971. Paperback. Besides the author's essay on the Chilean revolution, the book also contains his conversations with President Allende in 1971.

9. *Complete Bolivian Diaries of Che Guevara and Other Captured Documents* by Ernesto Che Guevara and ed. by Daniel James. Stein & Day Publishers, 1968. Paperback. The diary of a famous revolutionary in modern Latin America.

10. *Cuba in Revolution* ed. by Rolando E. Bonachea and Nelson P. Valdes. Doubleday & Co., Inc., 1972. Paperback. An overview of the Cuban revolution and the post-revolutionary society.

11. *The First Americans: The Pre-Columbian Civilizations* by G. H. Bushnell. McGraw-Hill Book Co., 1968. Paperback. A brief survey. Illustrated.

12. *Five Letters of Cortes* tr. by Morris J. Bayard. W. W. Norton & Co., Inc., 1969. Paperback. A collection of five dispatches sent by Cortes.

13. *Latin America, A General History* by John Edwin Fagg. The Macmillan Co., 2nd ed., 1969. A comprehensive work with good information about the Europeans' arrival in America.

14. *Latin American Cultures* ed. by Paul Thomas Welty. J. B. Lippincott Co., 1973. Readings.

15. *The Maya* by Michael D. Coe. Praeger Publishers, Inc., 1966. Paperback. A history of the Maya civilization.

16. *Mexico Before Cortez: Art, History and Legend* by Ignacio Bernal, tr. by Willis Barnstone. Doubleday & Co., Inc., rev. ed., 1975. Paperback. An art and cultural history of a region of many civilizations.

17. *The Military and Society in Latin America* by John J. Johnson. Stanford University Press, 1964. Paperback. Traces the importance of the military in Latin American politics.

18. *New World Beginnings: Indian Cultures in the Americas* by Olivia Vlahos. The Viking Press, Inc., 1971. Paperback. Covers early Indian cultures in South and North America.

19. *Race Mixture in the History of Latin America* by Magnus Morner. Little, Brown and Co., 1967. Paperback. A look at the historical mingling of races in Latin America.

20. *A Short History of the West Indies* by J. H. Parry and P. M. Sherlock. St. Martin's Press, Inc., 3rd ed., 1972. Paperback. An excellent introduction to the history of the West Indies

21. *Why Peron Came to Power: The Background of Peronism in Latin America* by Joseph R. Barager. Alfred A. Knopf, Inc., 1968. Paperback. An account of Juan Peron, of Argentina, and his followers.

Fiction

1. *Pedro Martinez* by Oscar Lewis. Random House, Inc., 1964. Paperback. The peasants of Mexico during revolution in the 1800s.

2. *The Maya; Indians of Central America* by Sonia Bleeker. William Morrow & Co., Inc., 1961. A tale of the early Mayans.

3. *Star Mountain and Other Legends of Mexico* by Camilla Campbell. McGraw-Hill Book Co., 2nd ed., 1968. Legends of the Aztecs, Mayans and Toltecs.

SOCIAL STUDIES VOCABULARY/GLOSSARY

absolute monarchy: government in which power rests completely in the hands of a king or queen.

A.D.: in the year of our Lord (Latin: anno Domini).

alliance: a joining together of groups by a formal agreement to promote their mutual interests.

annexation: the addition of territory to a nation or state.

anthropologist: one who practices anthropology.

anthropology: the study of people, their place in the natural world, their cultural development, and their differing ways of living and behaving.

archaeologist: one who studies archaeology.

archaeology: the study of the cultures of prehistoric and historic peoples through their remains such as tools, weapons, pottery, buildings, and writings.

architecture: the planning and construction of buildings.

aristocracy: the upper class in society; usually, nobles.

artifacts: objects made either by hand or machine.

artisan: a trained or skilled worker; a craftworker.

arts, the: music, literature, painting, sculpture, dance, etc.

assembly: a meeting of people for a specific purpose; often, a lawmaking body.

assimilate: to become like others in customs and attitudes.

assimilation: the act of becoming like others in customs and attitudes.

astronomy: the science that studies the sun, moon, stars, planets, and other heavenly bodies.

authoritarian: believing in complete obedience to authority—for example, a government—instead of personal freedom.

balance of power: the spread of authority or control so that no one nation or combination of nations has enough power to control other nations.

B.C.: before the birth of Christ.

bourgeoisie: the middle class.

Bronze Age: a stage in the development and use of metals when people made bronze tools and weapons.

bureaucracy: collectively, the departments or bureaus that administer a government.

bureaucrat: a member of a bureaucracy.

C. (circa): around.

cabinet: a group of advisors that helps a chief executive or monarch in administering a government.

campaign: a series of related activities, often military or political, directed toward a certain goal.

capital: accumulated wealth, both money and goods, that is used to produce more wealth.

capitalism: an economic system in which the land, machines, factories, and other means of production are privately owned. Goods and services are produced for profit in a free, usually competitive, market.

capitalist: one who supports capitalism.

cash crop: a crop that is raised for profit rather than subsistence.

cash economy: an economic system in which money is used to get goods and services.

caste: a social system in which people are grouped according to occupation, wealth, heredity, religion, or some other characteristic.

central planning: the coordinating of economic, social, or political goals by a national government.

centralization: the concentration of control, administration, and so on, in one authority.

chronicle: an account of events written in the order that they occurred; a history.

Church and State: the religious and secular institutions of a nation existing together and in competition for the people's loyalty.

city: a densely populated area that usually cannot produce its own food and lives by trade.

city-state: an independent community made up of a city and the surrounding area.

civil disobedience: a form of protest against government in which people use non-violent means to resist authority.

civil liberties: the rights of people to act and speak as they wish without government interference, providing they do not harm others.

civil servant: one employed in the civil service.

civil service: government employment that does not include the military, elected officials, or the heads of government bureaus or departments.

civil war: war between sections of the same state or nation.

civilization: a level of cultural development that includes a food-producing base, increasing centralization of political and religious authority, monumental buildings, and often, but not always, the development of writing and written records.

clan: those people within an ethnic group who claim to be descended from a common ancestor.

class: a grouping of persons according to similar social and economic status.

climate: the generally existing weather conditions of a region.

coalition: a voluntary joining together of interest groups, political parties, or nations for a purpose.

cold war: conflict between nations through the use of diplomatic, psychological, or economic means rather than military force.

colonialism: a national policy that approves of taking control of the politics and economies of weaker peoples.

colony: a territory over which a nation claims the right of possession and over which that nation exercises political and economic control.

commerce: the large-scale buying, selling, or exchanging of goods.

communications: the exchange of ideas and information by means such as telephone, telegraph, radio, television, etc.

communism: an economic system in which the community or government owns the means of production such as lands and factories. The right of individuals to own the means of production is partly or entirely denied. Marxism.

communist: a person who supports communism.

compromise: settlement of a conflict by having all parties agree to giving up some of their demands.

confederation: a government system which results from the loose joining of states into a union. The states give up some of their powers.

congress: a meeting; usually of a lawmaking body.

conservatism: the practice of preserving what is already established; the opposition to change.

conservative: one who favors conservatism.

constitution: a document that contains the procedures, laws, and principles used for governing a nation or state.

consumer goods: those goods which are bought by people for their own use rather than for producing other goods and services.

cooperative: an enterprise—farm or store—owned by and operated for its members; members share the profits in proportion to the amount of business they do with it.

Copper Age: a stage in the development and use of metals when people made copper tools and weapons.

corporation: a group acting legally as an individual for purposes of commerce.

council: a group of people who may make

laws or advise a ruler; it may be formal or informal.

coup: a sudden, violent overthrow of a government by a small group.

crafts: the arts or trades, such as carpentry, that require skill with the hands.

Cro-Magnon: prehistoric people who appeared about 40,000 years ago; part of the species Homo sapiens.

cultural diffusion: the spread of culture traits or characteristics such as baseball from one cultural group to another.

culture: the tools and other objects people make and use, their language, religious beliefs, customs, values, folklore, ways of eating and dressing, and their everyday activities; the way a particular group of people has adapted to its particular environment and background.

culture region: an area in which people of different cultural groups have adapted to their surroundings in similar ways.

culture trait: a characteristic held in common by members of a culture.

custom: a usual way of acting in a particular situation, as sending birthday cards.

decentralization: the distribution of power and administration among a number of agencies rather than concentration in the hands of one person or small group.

deity: god or goddess.

democracy: a form of government in which the people rule either directly or through elected representatives.

detente: a policy of relaxing international tensions through negotiation.

dialect: a speech pattern of language, such as the Southern dialect of American English, that is characteristic of a certain region or group within a larger culture group.

dictator: a person who exercises absolute authority and unlimited power over a nation or a state.

dictatorship: a system of government in which one person exercises absolute authority over a nation or a state.

diplomacy: conduct of affairs between nations; the skill in such relations.

divine right monarchy: a government in which the monarch's power is believed to come directly from God.

doctrine: a position or principle taught by a church, government, or other group.

domesticate: to tame, as an animal; to refine a wild plant into one that can be cultivated as a crop.

dynasty: a succession of rulers who are of the same family line.

economic: pertaining to the economy.

economy: a system for producing, distributing, and consuming goods and providing services.

empire: a state, territory, or group of states ruled by a single government; ruler is often called an emperor or empress.

enlightened despot: a ruler with absolute power who uses it for the benefit of his/her subjects.

entente: an agreement of understanding between two or more nations.

environment: all the outside influences and conditions, such as weather and geography, that affect the continuing development of people.

epic: a long narrative poem about the adventures of a great hero.

era: a period of time marked by a significant event.

erosion: a gradual wearing away of soil by water or wind.

ethnic group: a group of people who share a common culture, social and political ties, and/or geographic region.

export: to send goods to another country to sell.

extended family: a family that includes father, mother, unmarried and married children and their families, grandparents, uncles, aunts, and cousins.

fable: a story, usually about animals, that is meant to teach a lesson.

faction: a group of people within a larger organization whose opinions and aims disagree with the larger group.

famine: a severe shortage of food.

federal: a system of government in which separate states unite under a central organization that controls matters of mutual concern. Each member, however, retains control over local affairs.

federation: the government system that results from a union of separate states in which each state keeps its own sovereignty, or authority.

feminism: the belief that women should have the same political, economic, and social rights as men; the movement that supports this belief.

feudalism: an economic, social, and political system in which upper-class landowners give to lower-class laborers protection and the use of their lands. In return, the laborers give military or other service to the landowner.

Five-Year Plan: a program that outlines, over a five-year period, government policy, usually economic development.

folklore: the tales, legends, beliefs, customs, and traditions of a people.

foreign aid: economic aid in the form of money, goods, advisors, or services that one nation gives to another.

front: a group formed to fight for political or economic goals; a person or group used as a cover for the activities of a second person or group.

gene pool: collectively, all the genetic (hereditary) units that determine traits in the biological makeup of organisms in an interbreeding population.

general assembly: a lawmaking body.

geography: the study of the earth's surface, its physical features, political and natural divisions, natural resources, climate, peoples, land use, industries, and products.

guerrilla: a member of an independent group that carries on raids and harrassments against an enemy.

heavy industry: the manufacture of steel, machines, transportation equipment, and the machinery used for making machines.

hereditary: traits passed biologically from one generation to the next.

heritage: an inheritance; that which is passed from one generation to the next.

hierarchy: a group that is organized into ranks, one above the other.

hieroglyphics: pictures or symbols that represent letters, words, ideas, or sounds.

history: the study of the past; an account of past events.

hominid: a member of the family of primates to which humans belong.

Homo erectus: literally, upright person; an extinct primate group related to modern people. Includes the types Java and Peking.

Homo sapiens: literally, intelligent person; the primate group to which modern people (Homo sapiens sapiens) belong. Includes the extinct Neanderthal and Cro-Magnon.

ideology: a political or social philosophy of a group.

illiteracy: the condition of being unable to read or write.

imperialism: a nation's policy of extending economic or political control over other nations, sometimes by force.

import: to bring goods into a country to sell them.

industrial revolution: the change from a farming to an industrial economy that took place in England from the mid-1700s to the mid-1800s.

industrialization: the change of an area's economic system from one based on agriculture or trade to one based on industry.

industry: a branch of economic activity, such as business, finance, or manufacturing.

inflation: an increase in the price of goods and services.

institution: any established organization, law, custom, or practice.

intellectual: one who places value on knowledge, on the arts, and on the use of reason   811 in forming opinions.

international: between or among nations.

Iron Age: a stage in the development and use of metals when people made iron tools and weapons.

junta: a group of people, often military, who join to control a government.

kinfolk: relatives.

kingdom: an area ruled by a king or queen.

kinship group: a group in which all members are related.

laissez-faire capitalism: an economic policy that claims the government should not impose economic controls or interfere in any way between workers and employers.

land bridge: a narrow strip of land that connects two larger bodies of land.

land reform: steps taken, usually by a government, to bring about a fairer distribution of farmland.

language: all the words used by a people to communicate among themselves.

language family: languages which have their base in the same source.

league: a union of two or more peoples, groups, or nations to promote matters of mutual interest.

left, the: those who favor complete and sometimes sudden social, political, and/or economic change; opposite of right.

leftist: one who supports complete and sometimes sudden social, political, and/or economic change; opposite of rightist.

legend: a story, passed from one generation to the next; it may or may not be true.

liberal: one who is not bound by established ways of doing things in politics, society, or religion; one who favors progress or reform.

liberalism: a philosophy that favors progress or reform.

life-style: the way a person lives.

light industry: the manufacture of textiles, handcrafted articles, foods, and other items which do not require massive machinery and complex assembling.

limited democracy: a system of government in which the freedoms and responsibilities of the people are restricted by law.

limited monarchy: a system of government in which the rule of a monarch is restricted by law.

lineage: the line of descent from one or both sides of the family—father and/or mother.

linguist: one who makes a scientific study of languages.

linguistics: the scientific study of languages.

literacy: the condition of being able to read and write.

mandate: an order or command; a League of Nations commission to a member nation to administer a colony or territory.

market: where goods are sold, bought, or bartered.

Marxism: the political, economic, and social doctrine of Karl Marx. After a class struggle, the workers revolt against the ruling class. They then control the means of production, and a socialist state is formed. Eventually the state becomes unnecessary and ceases to exist.

Marxist: one who believes in Marxism.

matrilineal: tracing descent through the mother's side of the family.

means of production: factories, railroads, and other transportation systems; machines, mines, land, and so on.

medieval: relating to the Middle Ages.

medium of exchange: something—for example, money—that represents a standard of value and is accepted in exchange for goods and services.

mercantilism: an economic theory that the nation with the most gold and silver is the strongest.

Middle Stone Age: a stage in the cultural development of early prehistoric people in which they began to depend on plant gathering rather than hunting for food.

migration: the movement of people from one country or region to another.

minister: a diplomat who represents his/her government in a foreign nation; one appointed to head a government department.

mixed farming: agriculture in which crop raising is combined with herding.

modernization: the adoption by a country of modern ways and views.

monarchy: a government headed by a hereditary ruler such as a king/queen or emperor/empress.

monopoly: exclusive control or possession of a product or service.

myth: a legendary story, often religious, that gives an account of some event such as the origin of a people.

nation: a grouping of peoples within specific boundaries into a large political, economic, and social unit.

national identity: a sense of the oneness of a people who share the same land, economy, culture, and language.

national interest: something that is of concern to a nation as a whole.

national planning: the coordination of economic, social, and political goals by the national government.

nationalism: a loyal or patriotic feeling for one's own nation.

nationality: a group of people sharing a language and customs and either living in or having ancestors who came from the same country.

nationalize: to transfer control or ownership of private land or industry to the national government for the benefit of its citizens.

natural resources: water, mineral deposits, animals, forests, etc.

Neanderthal: one early form of Homo sapiens.

neutrality: the position of refusing to take sides or become involved in a situation.

New Stone Age: stage in the cultural development of early prehistoric people when they began to grow crops and domesticate animals.

nonaggression: the policy of not attacking or using force.

nuclear family: a family that includes only father, mother, and their children.

Old Stone Age: oldest stage in the cultural development of early prehistoric people; simple forms of pebbles were used as tools.

one-crop economy: farming system in which a single crop is the basis of the economy.

oral tradition: customs, legends, myths, etc., handed down from one generation to the next by word of mouth; spoken as opposed to written tradition.

orthodox: in agreement with the accepted view, especially in religion.

overpopulation: a condition that exists when a population is so large it places a burden on the environment.

parliament: a lawmaking body.

partisan: one who strongly supports a cause, person, faction, or party.

partition: division into parts.

patrilineal: tracing descent through the father's side of the family.

patriotism: a strong sense of loyalty to one's own country and its causes.

peaceful coexistence: living together peaceably; not in a state of conflict.

peninsula: land that is almost surrounded by water.

people, a: all the persons who belong to an ethnic group.

permanent farming: farming in one location.

philosophy: the study of knowledge, existence, or morality; the results of such a study organized into a system.

politics: the art and science of government; the activities and organizations through which people and political parties seek power or control of a government.

pollution: dirtying of the environment.

polygyny: the practice of having more than one wife.

popular sovereignty: government power or control that is subject to the wishes and demands of the people.

prehistory: the time before writing was developed.

prejudice: hatred or intolerance of others; an unfavorable opinion formed without knowledge.

prime minister: leader of a government.

propaganda: information or news used by a government, person, or group to influence the opinions and beliefs of others.

protectorate: nation or state that depends on a stronger country for defense and the conduct of foreign affairs. It is not a possession of the more powerful country.

province (religious): a district ruled by an archbishop; (political): a subdivision of a country.

provisional government: temporary control of a state.

proverb: wise or useful saying.

psychology: study of the mind and its activities.

radical: one who favors extreme change in government or society.

radiocarbon dating: method for determining the age of remains of ancient cultures.

raw material: a material such as foodstuffs or coal which is used in the manufacture of other goods.

reform: a change for the better.

reformer: one who seeks to improve conditions by removing existing evils.

regent: one who rules in place of another who is absent, too young, or disabled.

regionalism: pursuit of interests that are of special concern to a region.

religion: a system of beliefs about the supernatural.

representative government: government in which lawmaking power is given by the people to those elected to act for them.

republic: a government in which the officials and representatives who rule are elected by the people.

republicanism: the policy that supports a republican form of government.

revolution: a fundamental change or complete overthrow of the existing order of a government, political system, or society.

right, the: those who favor keeping things as they are or returning to what existed in the past; conservatives.

rightist: one who supports the right.

ritual: a ceremony; an established way of doing something.

role: the part one has or plays in a social group.

royalist: one who supports government ruled by a monarch.

rural: of the countryside.

satellite (political): a small country that follows a more powerful one in matters of policy.

schism: a formal division, especially within a church.

scorched-earth policy: the practice of destroying everything in the path of an invading army.

script: writing.

sculpture: a piece of art carved, cast, or modeled with material such as stone, metal, clay, wax, wood, etc.

sect: a group of people who are united by certain ideas, beliefs, and opinions; often a religious group.

secular: not religious.

secularism: a policy of concern with matters that are not of a religious nature.

segregate: to keep peoples separate from each other by law or by custom.

segregation: the condition of being separated from others.

self-government: government of, by, and for the people.

semiskilled: having some training or ability.

senate: a lawmaking group.

serf: in the manorial system, the lowest ranking person on a manor; one bound to the land.

site: in archaeology, the place where an excavation is done.

skilled: trained, specialized; having expert ability.

slash-and-burn farming: farming system in

which land is cleared and burned to make it workable.

slave: a person who is owned by another person.

slavery: the practice of owning slaves.

social mobility: freedom to move from one social class to another.

socialism: a system of social organization in which the people own and control all the major means of production.

society: any group of people who have a shared culture and identity.

socioeconomic: combining social and economic elements.

sociology: the study of the development, organization, and functioning of human society.

sphere of influence: area in which a powerful nation exercises political and economic control over less powerful nations.

standard of living: the average level of goods, services, luxuries, etc. that a person or group uses in daily living.

state: a group of people organized under one government and living within a definite territory.

state religion: a religion that is supported by a government.

status: the ranking or standing of a person or a group in relation to other people or groups.

Stone Age: stage in the cultural development of early prehistoric people when they used stone tools.

subsistence farming: small-scale farming in which people grow only enough food for survival.

subsistence level: the minimum level at which people can live and still have food, shelter, and clothing.

suffrage: the right to vote.

superpower: one of the most powerful nations of the world.

surplus: more than is needed.

tariff: tax on imports and exports.

technology: the practical and industrial arts and the applied sciences of a society.

territory: area under the administration of a ruler, nation, state, etc.

terrorist: one who uses violence and fear of violence to gain certain ends.

totalitarian state: a state in which every part of life—economic, religious, social, educational, etc.—is controlled by the government.

totalitarianism: a political policy that does not permit opposing political parties to exist.

town: a settled area larger in size and population than a village but smaller than a city.

trade: commerce; buying, selling, or bartering goods and services.

tradition: an established custom, practice, or way of doing something that is handed down from one generation to the next.

treaty: a formal agreement between nations.

tribe: a people who share a common language, religion, social and political ties, and who are united under one leader.

tribute: a forced payment of money by one nation, ruler, or group to another in return for protection or as a guarantee of peace.

truce: a temporary stopping of a fight or war by an agreement of the opposing sides.

underdeveloped nation: a nation that has not reached an economic level high enough to insure an adequate standard of living.

unification: the bringing together of separate areas into a unified nation.

union: a grouping together of nations, states, or individuals, for a particular purpose.

urban: of the city.

urbanization: the change of an area from a rural to an urban environment.

vassal: in the feudal system, one who, in exchange for land and protection, promised loyalty and military or other services to a lord or lady.

vegetation: plant life.

vernacular: the language of a particular region.

village: a collection of households, smaller than a town.

ACKNOWLEDGEMENTS

Walter R. Aguiar, P. O. Box 328, New York, New York 10011: 2, 712T, 714, 716L,R, 725L,R, 727, 735, 757, 778, 788B, 792, 798B, 804. Albright-Knox Art Gallery, Buffalo, New York: Charles Clifton Fund 59; Bequest of Arthur Michael 249. Else Sackler, Courtesy of The American Museum of Natural History 303. Courtesy of the American Numismatic Society, New York 387, 736. Archives Photographiques—Paris 50B. Courtesy of the Art Institute of Chicago 544. Art Reference Bureau 382, 475, 491, 537, 545; Scala-Art Reference Bureau 458; Alinari-Art Reference Bureau 462B; Reproduced by kind permission of His Grace the Duke of Bedford 489; Reproduced by Courtesy of the trustees of the National Gallery, London 539. Ann Atene 187, 386T,B, 401, 634. The Bettmann Archive 60, 127, 236, 278, 318, 358L, 434, 436, 438, 448, 450, 455, 472, 477, 483, 485, 487, 492, 494, 499, 500, 501, 503B, 506, 508, 511, 516, 519L, 525, 526, 530L,R, 532, 533, 534, 540, 541T,B, 542, 543, 550, 636, 680, 697, 734, 740B, 742, 748, 760, 765T,B, 775; Springer/Bettmann Film Archive 565L. Photo Bibliotheque Nationale Paris 481, 732. Black Star: Yves de Braine 585. Bodleian Library colour filmstrip 161C: 443; colour filmstrip 113D: 721, 722. Lee Boltin 66. Greta and Norman Britan 702, 719. Courtesy of *China Pictorial*, People's Republic of China 191, 203, 204. Cincinnati Art Museum: J. J. Emery Fund 420; The John Omwake Playing Card Collection on permanent loan to the Cincinnati Art Museum from The United States Playing Card Company 453. Colombian Information Service 784. Compix 330, 562, 564, 805L,R. Culver Pictures 86T, 89, 90L,R, 93, 309, 313, 315, 473, 551, 557. John B. Davis 293, George M. Davis 221, 247, 260. Leo de Wys Inc.: 333; J. M. Bertrand 362; Peter Dublin 360; Victor Englebert 277, 283; Helmut Oizinger 358R; Andre Picou 274,

363; K. Shuster 312. Courtesy Ibarra Dimasalang 257. DPI, Inc.: Jerry Frank/DPI 301, 340, 341; M. Lee/DPI 350. *Ebony* Magazine 300. Edison National Historic Society (photo provided by Edison Electric Institute) 527. Editorial Photocolor Archives 16B, 17B, 18T, 21T,B, 32, 38, 47, 76, 83, 114, 121, 131T, 396, 417, 418L, 440, 456, 461, 462T, 490, 668; Bruce Anspach 68L; D. W. Funt 62; Martha Guthrie 9; Jan Lukas 393; Susan McKinney 68R. Eliot Elisofon Archives, Museum of African Art: Courtesy of Paul and Ruth Tishman 297; Courtesy of the Nigerian Government, Department of Antiquities 302L. Courtesy of Field Museum of Natural History, Chicago 302R. Courtesy of the Consulate General of Finland in New York 594. By permission of the Folger Shakespeare Library, Washington, D.C. 464, 465T; Model by John Cranford Adams and Irving Smith on loan to the Folger Shakespeare Library 465B; 470, 478, 480. Rare Book Department, Free Library of Philadelphia 520. French Government Tourist Office 375, 454. S. L. H. Fuller 306. THE GRANGER COLLECTION, New York 468. David Hallinger 780, 785L. The Higgins Armory Museum, Worcester, Massachusetts 388, 442. Hirshhorn Museum and Sculpture Garden, Smithsonian Institution 592, 593. Historical Pictures Service, Chicago 85, 86B, 96. Historical Society of Pennsylvania 746. Honolulu Academy of Arts, Gift of Charles M. and Anna C. Cooke Trust Fund, 1946: 446. Information Service of India 157, 171R, 173. Interfoto MTI, Hungary 622. Italian Government Travel Office 463L,R. Courtesy of Janus Films, 745 Fifth Avenue, New York, N. Y. 10022 (212-753-7100) and Museum of Modern Art/Film Stills Archive 166, 227. Consulate General of Japan, N.Y. 228, 229L, 240. Japan National Tourist Association 223. Konran/Media, Inc. 266, 353,

788T, 794L, 802T. Kunsthistorische Museum, Vienna 466, 514R. Library of Congress 522, 776. Magnum: 786T; Robert Azzi 31, 113; Micha Bar-Am 124; Bruno Barbey 73, 101, 505, 799; Ian Berry 30, 298, 348; Werner Bischoff 797; Rene Burri 14BL, 106, 108, 148, 359L, 709R; Cornell Capa 11B, 707; Robert Capa 110, 111; Elliott Erwitt 49; Leonard Freed 122; Burt Glinn 126, 135, 140, 165, 255L; Mark Godfrey 244; Charles Harbutt 120, 798T; Erich Hartmann 15T; Sergio Larraine 709L; Erich Lessing 18B, 24–25, 42, 52, 276, 338B, 368, 378, 384, 385, 404, 425L, 433, 467, 604–605; Ingeborg Lipmann 771; Bernard Lipnitzky 102; Constantine Manos 11T, 629; Rick Merrons 794R; Inge Morath 20, 78, 129T, 694; J. P. Paireault 762; Marc Riboud 98, 180; Sepp Seitz 65; David Seymour 61; Marilyn Silverstone 169. Ray Manley Photo 338T. Margaret Mead, *Blackberry Winter, My Earlier Years,* William Morrow, 1972 (p. 149): 8. The Metropolitan Museum of Art: Rogers Fund, 1913: 51; The Crosby Brown Collection of Musical Instruments, 1889: 164; Gift of Edith Root Grant, E. W. Root, and Elihu Root, Jr., 1937: 503T; Gift of Joseph W. Drexel, 1889: 519R. Monkmeyer: 58, 71, 74, 104, 131B, 184, 351, 712B, 803; WHO by J. Abcede 355T; Dee and Walter Banker 796; Omar Bessim 33; Hilda Bijur 337; Pierre Boucas for WHO 129B; Eric L. Brown 35; Paul Conklin 708, 772, 783; John Feily 419R; Toge Fujihira 342, 782; Dr. N. T. Gidel 44; Dieter Grabitzky 802B; Maury Greenberg 759; Ursula Mahoney 366–367; Theodore Theologos 706. Photograph Courtesy Museum of the American Indian. Heye Foundation. 731. Pablo Picasso. *Guernica.* (1937, May-early June). Oil on canvas, 11' 5½" × 25' 5¾". On extended loan to The Museum of Modern Art, New York, from the artist 548. Courtesy of the Museum of Primitive Art, New York 280. Courtesy of Na-

816

tional Bank of Detroit Money Museum 287, 289. National Gallery of Art, Washington: Ailsa Mellon Bruce Fund 444; Gift of Chester Dale 515R; Chester Dale Collection 502, 546; Samuel H. Kress Collection 460, 509; Andrew W. Mellon Collection 515L,C; Widener Collection 514L. National Gallery, Oslo 591. The National Gallery of Scotland 518. National Portrait Gallery, London 496, 497L. Nelson Gallery-Atkins Museum, Kansas City, Missouri (Nelson Fund) 160, 304. Jorge Neumann Lima-Peru 700–701; Gold Museum of Peru-Foundation Miguel Mujica Gallo 726. New Zealand Consulate General, New York 579L,R. Organization of American States (OAS) 482, 733T,B, 738, 739, 740T, 753, 755L, 777, 801; Pan-American Union 764. Embassy of Pakistan 177. Photo Courtesy of Pan American World Airways, Inc. 150. Embassy of Panama 730. Philadelphia Museum of Art: The Joseph Lees Williams Memorial Collection: Bequest of Mrs. Mary A. Williams 134; Purchased by subscription supplemented by the Lola Downin Peck Fund 226; Given by Mrs. Clement Biddle Wood 452; The Smith, Kline and French Laboratories Collection 469; The Louise and Walter Arensberg Collection 587, 590, 696; Given by Mr. and Mrs. Herbert Cameron Morris 800. Photo Researchers: Frederick Ayer 372; Bruce Brander 282; Jules Bucher 255R; Victor Englebert 346; Jack Fields 242; Carl Frank 408; T. D. W. Friedman 7L, 271; Farrell Grehan 428; Fritz Henle 430, 445; Tibor Hirsch 690; George Holton 294, 357; Diana Hunt 284L; Russ Kinne 376; R. McCabe 399R; Susan McCartney 155; Tom McHugh 14T (Field Museum, Chicago), 14BL, 16T; Roland and Sabrina Michaud 661B; E. Orel 395; Carl Purcell 332; Diane Rawson 270; Frank Schreider 272, 343; Taylor 678; Leonard von Matt 379, 390, 391, 406, 411, 415, 418R, 419L, 425R; Hans von Meiss 290; Rapho/Photo Researchers: Dominique Berretty 581; John Bryson 654, 661T; G. Cranham 13; Ray Ellis 320; Georg Gerster 19, 284R, 380, 412; Don Getsug 399L; Hubertus Kanus 613; Paolo Koch 214; John Veltri 398. Radio Times Hulton Picture Library 497R, 528–529, 682. The Romanian Library 684R. Credit Caracciolo and Banoun/Photographs by Scala New York/Florence 286, 344, 356B, 359R. Dr. Ruben H. Segal 230. Sekai Bunka Photos 197, 216, 218, 224, 229R, 232, 235, 239. The Smithsonian Institution Photo No. 49,918: 133; No. 73-11288: 524L; No. 44699-A: 524R. Courtesy of the Smithsonian Institution, Freer Gallery of Art, Washington, D.C., 138–139, 163, 190, 193, 195. SOVFOTO: 618, 621, 623, 626, 628, 630, 631, 637, 641, 646, 656, 659BL, 673L,C,R, 687T; EASTFOTO 146, 182, 186, 198, 201, 206L,R, 208, 209, 212, 213, 684L, 686, 687B; Erich Lessing from SOVFOTO 606; NOVOSTI from SOVFOTO 612, 614, 616, 624, 627, 645, 649R, 659T; TASS from SOVFOTO 554, 610–611, 635, 639, 649L, 652, 658, 659BR, 664, 666, 676, 769. *Madame Matisse/The Green Line*, Henri Matisse, © SPADEM, Paris, 1977, the Royal Museum of Fine Arts; J. Rump Collection, Copenhagen: 589. SPORTS ILLUSTRATED photo by Neil Leifer © Time Inc. 361. James B. Steele 795. Stock, Boston: Erik Anderson/Stock, Boston 7R; Richard Balzer/Stock, Boston 211; Owen Franken/Stock, Boston 6TR,B, 570, 596; Jim Holland/Stock, Boston 4–5,7C,26, 115; Bohdan Hrynewych/Stock, Boston 69; Eric Simmons/Stock, Boston 17T; Frank Siteman/Stock, Boston 55; Cary Wolinsky/Stock, Boston 64. TEXTILE MUSEUM, Washington, D.C. 264–265. United Nations 144, 152,171L, 174, 328B, 355B, 572. UNICEF photo by Horst Cerni 345; by J. F. Schiano 352; by Marc and Evelyne Bernheim 354. U.S.D.A. photograph 711. Official United States Air Force photographs 238, 251, 568. Official U.S. Navy photograph 567. United States Olympic Committee 386T,B. University Museum of the University of Pennsylvania 15B, 40L,R, 50T, 189, 192, 402, 414, 717, 723, 728. Courtesy of the Embassy of Venezuela 744. Wide World Photos 99, 100, 103, 105, 175, 176, 207T,B, 252, 317, 325, 326T,B, 327, 328T, 329, 331, 336, 356T, 361B, 553, 556, 560, 565R, 575, 584, 598L,R, 599L,R, 600, 650, 651, 667L,R, 671, 674, 689L,R, 755R, 756, 767, 768, 785R, 786B. Yerkes Observatory photograph 400, 582.

INDEX

Pages references to illustrations are in italics.

Abbasid dynasty, 80–81, 82, 83, 132
Abd-al-Wahhab, 103–04
Abdul Abbas (caliph), 80
Abdul Hamid (sultan), 90
Abdullah (king of Jordan), 108
aborigines, Australian, 578
Abraham, 54, 55, 71, 72, 162
abstract impressionism, 592–93, 801
abstractionism, 586, 592
Abu Bakr (caliph), 77
Abu Dhabi, 126
Academy (Plato), 395, 396
Academy of Sciences (USSR), 659
acculturation, 8–9
Achaeans, 383–85
Achebe, Chinua, 362
Acropolis (Greece), 398
Acropolis (Zimbabwe), 290
Act of Settlement, 498–99
Act of Supremacy, 475
Act of Toleration, 498
acupuncture, 190, 204
Aden, Gulf of, 26, 27
Adrianople, 85, 422
Adriatic Sea, 374, 556, 679, 686
Adulis (port), 283
Aegean Sea (and region), 85, 383, 384, 388, 399, 679, 683
Aeneid, 416
Aeschylus, 399
Aesop, 360
Afars and the Issas, French Territory of the, 267, 321, 322
Afghanistan, 27, 30, 32, 44, 95, 662
Africa: cities of, 274–75; colonialism in, 306–18; creativity of, 357–63; early peoples of, 275–78; economy, 333–38, 352; environment, 261–74; Guide to African Nations, 322–24; independence for, 320–29; kingdoms, empires and states of, 280–304; nation-building, 330–38; nations of, 267; religion, 346–50; society, 341–45, 350–56
African authenticity, 332
Afrikaans (language), 276
African socialism, 331–32
Afrikaners, 327
Afro-Asian languages, 34, 276
Afro-Mediterraneans, 275
age sets, 344
Agincourt, battle of, 448
agriculture: in Africa, 273, 334–35, 337–38; in Asia, 151, 217; in Australia, 579; Aztec, 721; and

growth of cities, 21; in Latin America, 703, 706, 708, 789, 792; and manorialism, 439; in Middle East, 32, 39, 120–21; revolution in, 523–24, 526; in Southeast Asia; 243, 256; in USSR, 646, 650, 655–56, 662; in Western Europe, 374, 375. See also farming.
Ahmose I (pharaoh), 48
Ahura-Mazda, 61
Ainu (people), 217
Akan (language), 303
Akbar, 162–63
Akkadians, 40, 41
Albania, 651, 678, 687–88, 691, 692, 695
Albanians (people), 614, 616
Albertus Magnus, 456
Alencar, Jose Martiniano, 804
Alexander I (czar), 510, 629–31, 669–70
Alexander II (czar), 89, 631–32
Alexander III (czar), 632
Alexander the Great, 45, 46, 56, 61, 171, 390, 391–92, 396, 399
Alexandra (czarina), 638
Alexandria, Egypt, 45, 69, 92, 126, 282, 292, 350, 399–401
Alexis (czar), 625, 669
Al Fatah, 112
Alfonso XIII (king of Spain), 563
Alfred the Great, 432, 455
Algeria, 26, 33, 70, 78, 93, 105, 117, 128, 357
Al Hassan ibn-Mohammed, 298
Ali (caliph), 77, 81
al-Idrisi, 133, 292
Al Khwarizmi, 133
Allah, 72, 73, 74, 76
Allende, Salvador, 770, 771, 778
Alliance for Progress, 778
Al-Mansur (sultan), 80, 299
al-Masudi, 292
Almoravid Berbers, 296
Alps, 369, 372, 374, 376, 378
Al Razi, 133
Alsace-Lorraine, 552, 558
Alvarado, Pedro de, 733
Amazon River, 708, 709, 711, 784
Ambrose, St., 70
Amenemhet III (pharaoh), 48
Amenhotep IV (pharaoh), 48, 60
American Colonization Society, 309
Amorites, 41
Ampere, Andre, 527, 533

amphitheater, 412
Amur River, 613
Anacaona, 787
ancestor spirits, 347–48
anchorite (Hinduism), 155
Andalusia, 543
Andean cultures, 723–28, 796
Andes Mountains, 707, 710, 714, 724, 727, 733, 745, 747
Andorra, 374, 375
Angkor, 248, 249
Angles (people), 423
Anglican Church, 476, 478, 502. See also Church of England.
Anglo-Saxons (people), 432–33, 435, 448, 449, 453
Angola, 267, 273, 285, 288, 316, 322, 329–30
animism, 243, 412
Anne (queen of England), 498–99
anthropology: and culture, 8; dating remains, 15; divisions of, 7; meaning of, 7; reconstructing past, 13; and social groupings, 10–11; special terms, 7–8
Antigonus, 46
Antioch, Syria, 45, 69, 134, 399
anti-Semitism, 672, 675, 692
Antonescu, Ion, 684
Antony, Marc, 411, 517
apartheid, 327, 362, 363
Apennine Mountains, 369, 375, 405
appeasement, 565
aqueducts, 46, 404, 418
Aquinas, Thomas, 397, 456, 502
arabesque, 131
Arabia, 70–71, 103–04, 283
Arabian Peninsula, 27
Arabian Sea, 26, 39, 151
Arabic (language), 34, 66, 80, 132, 133, 276, 294, 351
Arabic (numerals), 133, 469
Arabic (script), 100, 131
Arab-Israeli conflict, 106, 108–09, 111–13, 118–19, 652
Arab League, 122
Arab socialism, 102
Arabs: ancestry of, 71; and Byzantine Empire, 425–26, 427; culture, 122; defined, 34; and Islam, 71–72, 77, 79, 130; in Ottoman Empire, 87; Palestinian, 111–13; unity among, 34, 102, 122; and Western culture, 133–34
Arafat, Yasir, 112, 113

Aramaeans, 52, 54, 56
Aramaic (language), 34, 54
Arawaks (people), 714, 731, 787
archaeology: dating prehistoric remains, 16; defined, 7
archbishop, 69, 435
Archimedes, 401
architecture: African, *282, 283, 284,* 289, 294, 297, 298, 359; Assyrian, 43; baroque, 515; Byzantine, 427; Chaldean, 44; Chinese, 191–92, 195; and civilization, 20; classical, 516; contemporary, 593–95; Eastern European, 696; Egyptian, 49; Etruscan, 405; Gothic, *366,* 452, 454–55; Greek, 394, 398; of India, 151, 158–60; international style, 126, 359, 595, 802; Islamic, 130–31; Japanese, 222; Khmer, 248–49; Latin American, *784,* 801–03; Mesoamerican, 717, 718, 723; Middle Eastern, 126; Mogul, 164; neoclassical, 519; Norman, 454; Persian, 45; Renaissance, 462; rococo, 517–18; Roman, 412, 416, 417–18, 454; Romanesque, 454; Soviet, 662; Sumerian, 39–40; Western European, 377
Arctic Ocean, 611, 613
Ardashir I, 46
Argentina, 707, 708, 724, 726, 766–67, 773, 781, 782, 783, 788, 789, 793, 794
aria (music), 543
Aristarchus of Samos, 400
Aristophanes, 399
Aristotle, 45, 134, 394, *396–97*
Arkwright, Richard, 525
armada (Spanish), *480,* 488, 562
Armenia, 36, 81, 90, 662, 671
Arthur (king of England), 453
arts: African, 280, 302, 303, 310, 357–63; Assyrian, 43; baroque, 513–14, 799; Byzantine, 427; Chinese, 187, 191–92, 196–97; and civilization, 20; classicism in, 513; contemporary, 586, 589–93; Cretan, 383; development of, 19; Eastern European, 696; Greek, 394, 398–99; of India, 158–60, 164–65; Islamic, 130–32; Japanese, 222–29; Latin American, 799–801; medieval, 452; neoclassical, 519–20; Renaissance, 459–62, 465–66; rococo, 517–18; Roman, 416; romanticism and, 539–40; Russian, 672; Soviet, 662, 673–76; Western European, 424, 537, 545
Aryans (people), 44, 151, 152, 167, 563–64

Ashanti (people), 303, 342, 355, 358, 360
Ashanti Union of Akan States, 303, 308, 310, 314, 322
Ashikaga shogunate, 225
Ashurbanipal (Assyrian king), 43
Asia: cities of, 144, 147–48; creativity, 158–65, 190–98, 222–29; environment, 140–48; nations of, 141; religion, 152–57; 218–22; 244–45; society, 166–71, 199–204, 230–33, 260–61
Asia Minor, 38, 380
Askia Mohammed, 299
Asoka (ruler of India), 157
As-Saheli, 298
Assyria (and Assyrians), 42–43, 49, 54, 56, 59, 278
astrolabe, 133, 400, *467*
astronomy: Arab, 132–33; Chaldean, 44; Chinese, 194; Egyptian, 49, 51; Khmer, 249; Mayan, 717; medieval Europe, 455; modern, 697; Renaissance, 467–69; Stonehenge, 377; Sumerian, 40
Asturias, Miguel Angel, 805
Aswan, 281; High Dam, 30, 102, *103,* 115
Atacama-Peruvian Desert, 708, 747
Atahualpa, 733
Ataturk, Mustafa Kemal, 91, 92, 99–100, 108
Athens, 386, 387–89, 390, 393, 397, 398
Atlantic Ocean, 369, 374, 486, 533, 709
Atlas Mountains, 31
atomic bomb, 211, 238–39, 533, 568, 582, 660
atoms, 161, 394, 582
Attila, 422, 616
Augsburg, 444; Peace of, 473
Augustine, St., 70
Augustus (caesar), 412, 420
Aurangzeb (Mogul ruler), 164
Australia, 557, 578–79
Austria: and Congress of Vienna, 512, 513; Hapsburg rule, 477; and Holy Roman Empire, 488; and Napoleon, 509, 510, 630; Nazis in, 565; and Ottoman Empire, 88; and Poland, 628, 679, 680; and Prussia, 552; Triple Alliance, 638
Austria-Hungary: alliances, 555–56; and Balkans, 557, 686; and Congress of Berlin, 89; creation of, 685; and Czechoslovakia, 682; and Metternich, 551; separated, 688; and Slavic people, 91; and World War I, 91, 558
Avars (people), 616, 684

Avicenna, 133
Avignon, France, 470–71
Axum, *317;* Kingdom of, 282, 283
Ayacucho, battle of, 745
Ayyubid dynasty, 82, 84
Azerbaijan, USSR, 662
Aztecs, 715, 719–22, 732, 789, 797, 798, 803

Babylonia, 41–44, 56, 59, 63
Babylonian Captivity (Jews), 56; (papacy), 471
Babur (Mogul ruler), 162
Bach, Johann Sebastian, 519
Bacon, Roger, 456
Badari, Egypt, 277
Baghdad, Iraq, 80, 81, 82, 83, 126, 132, 133, 557
Bahamas, The, 482, 706, 731
Bahia, Brazil, 737, 784
Bahrain, 27, 36, 39, 95, 96
Bahutu (people), 295
Baker, Samuel, 312
Bakewell, Robert, 524
Balboa, 482, *730,* 733
Balfour Declaration, 110
Balkans: and Byzantine Empire, 427; Crimean War, 631; nationalism in, 89; nations of, 428, 683, 686, 687; Normans in, 433; and Ottoman Empire, 88–89, 91, 631; and Russia, 89, 631; wars in, 91, 683, 688; and World War I, 557
Baltic Sea, 374, 612
Balto-Slavic languages, 691
bandeirantes, 740
Bangladesh, 141, 147, 178
banking, 441, 443–44, 529, 540
Bantu-speaking peoples, 278, 286, 295, 325, 326; early history, 322, 323, 324; kingdoms, 286–91; languages, 276, 284, 294, 363; migrations, 284–86, 294
Bantustans, 327
Barbados, 706, 712
Barbary States, 93
Bardi family, 444
Bar Mitzvah, 65
baroque, 513–14, *740,* 799
Barotse (people), 324, 347
barrios, 257
Bartered Bride, The, 695
Basho, 227
Basil I (Byzantine emperor), 425
Basil II (Byzantine emperor), 426
Bastille, 506
Basutoland, 323
Batista, Fulgencio, 768, 778
Bauhaus group, 594
Baybars (Mameluke sultan), 84
Bay of Pigs invasion, 768
bazaars, 126

Bechuanaland, 322
bedouins (nomads), 71, *122,* 125
Beethoven, Ludwig van, 540
beguine (dance), 797
Behanzin (king of Dahomey), 314
behavior modification, 585
Belgian Congo, 313, 322, 324, 328
Belgium: African colonies, 287, 316, 317, 322, 324, 328; and Congress of Vienna, 513; and Holy Roman Empire, 431; imperialism of, 554; in World War I, 91, 557, 558; in World War II, 566
Belize, 706, 717, 730
Benelux Economic Unit, 576
Benes, Eduard, 682
Ben-Gurion, David, 110, 111
Benin (city-state), 274, 302, 307, 308, 310, 323
Benin, Republic of, 302, 304, 307, 308, 310, 314, 322, 333, 357, 358, 362, 363
Bentham, Jeremy, 504
Berbera (city-state), 292, 323
Berbers (people), 78, 79, 276, 296, 298, 323
Beria, Lavrenti, 649
Berlin, 571, 647, 688–89; airlift, 689; wall, 650, 689, 690
Berlin Conference (1884–85), 313, 316, 318
Berlin, Congress of (1878), 89
Bessemer process, 526
Bhagavad-Gita, 153
Bhutan, 212
Bhutto, Zulfikar Ali, 178
Biafra, 330, 362
Bible, 53, 62–63, 66, 67, 70, 72, 82, 347, 452, 453, 464, 471, 473
Bill of Rights, English, 498, 507
Bismarck, Otto von, 313, 551, 552, *553,* 556
Black Sea, 26, 376, 612, 613
Blackstone, William, 504, 537
Blanc, Louis, 531, 550
blank verse, 465
Bloody Sunday, 637
Blue Nile River, 271, 311
boat people, 144
bodhisattvas (Buddhism), 190
Boers, 326–27
Bogata, Colombia, *707,* 745, 747
Bohemia, 471, 476, 682
Boleyn, Anne, 474, 476
Bolivar, Simon, 745–46
Bolivia, 709, 723, 724, 726, 745, 746, 773, 774, 793, 796, 803
Bolsheviks, 636, 637, 638, 639, 640, 641
Boniface VIII (pope), 447
Bonifacio, Jose, 753
Booth, William, 528

Borneo, 238, 245, 254
Bosnia, 89, 556
Bosporus, 85, 424
Botswana, 267, 273, 322, 325, 338
Boucher, Francois, 518, 519
Bourguiba, Habib, 106
Boyaca, battle of, 745
boycott, 112
Braganza family, 752, 773
Brahe, Tycho, 468
Brahman (caste), 166–68, 174
Brazil, 793, 802–03; colonialism in, 737–39, 792; development of, 751–53; empire in, *752, 753;* independence, 742, 753; land reform, 792; modernization, 789; politics, 762; Portuguese in, 737–40
Bretons (people), 597
Brezhnev, Leonid, 644, 651, 652, 656, *769*
bride-price, 127
bridewealth, 344
British Commonwealth of Nations, 325, 336, 497, 578–81
British East India Company, 96, 172, 485
British Honduras, 706
British Isles, 53, 372, 373, 376
British North America Act, 581
British Togoland, 317, 322, 325
Britons (people), 379, 423, 433
Bronze Age, 17, 36, 378, 380, 384, 615
Brooks, Angie, 356
Buddha, Gautama, 156, 159, 189–90, 192, 220, *221,* 222, 244
Buddhism, *6;* and arts, 222, 244; in China, 158, 182, 189–90, 192, 194; history of, 156; in India, 159, 161; in Japan, 158, 219, 220–22; in Korea, 158, 214; in Southeast Asia, 158, 244–45, 248, 252, 255; spread of, 157–58; teachings of, 156–57
Buenos Aires, 743, 746, 747
Buganda Kingdom, 295, 314, 324
Bulganin, Nikolai, 649, 650
Bulgaria, 45, 89, 91, 426–28, 557, 622, 683, *684,* 686, 688, 691, 692
Bulgars (people), 614, 683
Bundesrat, 563
bunraku, 226
Bunyoro Kingdom, 295, 314, 324
burgesses, 450–41
Burgundians (people), 380, 423
Burma, 141, 158, 238, 242, 244, 245–46, 486, 567
Burmans (people), 245–46
Burton, Richard, 312
Burundi Kingdom, 295, 317, 322
Burundi, Republic of, 267, 322, 329, *331,* 359

Bushido, 235, 238
Bushmanoids, 275
Bushmen, 275, 276, 322, 323, 324, 326, 360
Byelorussia, USSR, 616, 660, 661
Byzantine Empire, 70, 404, 459, 683, 688; and crusades, 82, 428, 442; decline of, 427; emperors, 425–26; falls, 85, 622, 623; in North Africa, 79; and Ottoman Empire, 85, 428; and Persia, 46; rise of, 424–25; influence on Russia, 619–21; and Seljuk Turks, 81–82, 428
Byzantium, 70, 388, 421, 424

Cabot, John and Sebastian, 484
Cabral, Pedro Alvarez, 481, 737
Caesar, Julius, 410–11, 420
Caillie, Rene, 311
Cairo, 85, 126, 131, 277
Calcutta, 144, 485
calendar: Chinese, 196; development of, 17; Gregorian, 133, 411, 469, 627; Julian, 411, 469, 627; Mayan, 717; Muslim, 72, 74, 133; Olmec, 715; solar, 133
caliph (title), 77, 79, 80
calligraphy, 193
calpulli, 720, 722
Calvin, John, 473–74, 495
Calvinism, 473–76, 478, 484
calypso (song), 797
Cambodia, 141, 195, 242, 244, 247, 248–49
Cambyses, 44
Cameroon, 267, 277, 284, 316–17, 322, 325, 338, 341, 362
Canaan (and Canaanites), 53, 55, 56; language of, 34
Canada, 336, 486, 487, 492, 557, 571, 580–81
Canon of Medicine, 133
cantor, 65
Canute, 432
Cape Horn, 707
Cape of Good Hope, 307, 326, 481, 483, 484
Cape Verde Islands, 329, 481
capital: accumulating, 529; and industrialization, 117; and industrial revolution, 523; and subsistence level economy, 336
capitalism: and communism, 635; creation of, 529; growth of, 487; international effects of, 530–31; laissez-faire, 531; and Reformation, 476; and socialism, 531
captaincies (Brazil), 737, 738
captaincy-generals, 733, 736
Caracas, 744, 745, 795, 802
Caribs (people), 714, 731, 773
Caribbean Sea, 702, 706

carnival, 799
Carranza, Venustiano, 764–65
Carthage, 53, 79, 278, 405, 406
Cartier, Jacques, 580
Cartwright, Edmund, 525
Casimir III (the Great, Polish king), 679
Caspian Sea, 26, 27, 610, 612
caste system, 152, 155, 161, 166–68, 176, 350
Castro, Fidel, 768
Catal Huyuk, 36
Catherine of Aragon, 474, 476
Catherine II (the Great, czarina), 628–30, 670, 672
Caucasoids, 275, 277
caudillo, 562, 762-65
Cavaliers, 497
Cavour, Camillo di, 553, 554
Ceausescu, Nicolae, 685
Celebes, Indonesia, 254
Celts (people), 380, 433
censors, Roman, 408
Central Africa, 267
Central African Empire, 267, 273, 322, 331, 338
Central America, 702
Central American Common Market, 774
Central Asia, 612, 650, 662, 674
Central Committee (USSR), 643, 644, 651
Central Europe, 374
Central Powers, 91, 95, 557–58
Cerchi family, 444
Ceylon, see Sri Lanka.
Cezanne, Paul, 545, 546, 590
Chad, Republic of, 267, 300, 322, 337, 338
Chaeronea, battle of, 391
Chagall, Marc, 124, 135, 676
Chaka (Zulu leader), 314
Chaldeans (people), 43
Champlain, Samuel de, 580
chancellor, 563
Changa (emperor), 291, 323
Chandragupta, 157
Chanukah, 56
Charlemagne, 431, 435, 437, 451
Charles I (king of England), 495–97, 498
Charles II (king of England), 497, 498
Charles V (Holy Roman emperor), 473, 474, 484, 487–88
Charles VI (Holy Roman emperor), 491
Charles VII (king of France), 448
Charles X (king of France), 550
charter of autonomy, 757–58
Chaucer, Geoffrey, 464
Chavin de Huantar, 723
Chiang Kai-shek, 207–08, 209

Chichen Itza, 714, 718, 719
Chichimec (people), 720
Chile, 707, 708, 724, 726, 737, 746–47, 762, 770–71, 773, 774, 778, 782, 789, 792, 793, 794
Chimu empire, 700, 725–26
China: ancient, 181–82; Buddhism in, 158, 182, 189–90, 192, 194, 221; Ch'ing dynasty, 196; Chou dynasty, 181–82, 191, 197; cities, 147; communism in, 202–04, 207–212, 532, 651; contacts with Arabs, 133; creativity, 190–98; European influences in, 196, 202, 205; Han dynasty, 185, 189, 191, 197, 250; Manchus in, 196, 205, 207; Ming dynasty, 195–96; and Mongolia, 213; Nationalist, 207, 208, 209, 211; philosophies, 182–89; republic declared, 207, 209; revolutions in, 205–11; and Russia, 662; Shang dynasty, 181, 191, 197; society, 199–204; and Southeast Asia, 245, 246, 248, 250–52, 254, 255, 257; Sui dynasty, 190; Sung dynasty, 193, 194–95; T'ang dynasty, 190, 193–94, 219, 222; in UN, 208, 211, 573; and U.S., 212; and USSR, 211, 212, 651, 652; in World War II, 238; Yuan dynasty, 195, 212
Ch'ing dynasty, 196
chivalry, 439, 453, 464, 465, 538
Chou dynasty, 181–82, 191, 197
Christianity: in Africa, 282–83, 288, 311, 348, 349; in Asia, 172, 202; in Balkans, 90; in Byzantine Empire, 426–27, 668; and crusades, 82, 442; differences within, 69–70; early church, 68–69; founded, 67; and Islam, 58, 442; and Judaism, 58; legalized, 69, 420; and medieval philosophy, 456; missionaries spread, 196, 202, 436, 734, 784; orthodox, 88, 428, 668, 683, 691; in Ottoman Empire, 87; and Protestantism, 478; in Roman Empire, 414, 420–21, 426; schism within, 428; spread of, 67–68, 421; in Southeast Asia, 244, 245; teachings of, 67, 69–70; in Western Europe, 404, 424, 433, 434–37, 451. See also Coptic Christianity; Eastern Orthodox Church; Roman Catholic Church; Russian Orthodox Church; names of individual denominations.
Christophe, Henri, 755
Chuang-Tzu, 186
Churchill, Winston, 566, 567, 647,

648, 680
Church of England, 488, 498. See also Anglican Church.
Chwezi (clan), 295
Cicero, 414, 464
Cimmerians (people), 615
cities: and civilization, 20–21; and family life, 128; and industrial revolution, 527–28; in Middle Ages, 430, 444, 446; and organized society, 21; and stages of cultures, 19; and trade, 21, 36; and war, 571
city-states: African, 291–92, 301; Aztec, 720; Greek, 385–89, 399; Italian, 83, 459; Mesopotamian, 39, 41; Russian, 619–21
clans, 11
classicism, 513, 537–38, 540
Cleisthenes, 387
Cleopatra, 46, 411, 517
clergy: development of, 69; English, 451; French, 447, 451, 491, 505; and feudalism, 437; and Islam, 74; Luther on, 473; monks, 435–36; problems within, 470, 471; Renaissance, 459, 464; in Russia, 669–70; secular, 435–36
Click languages, 276
Clive, Robert, 485
Clovis (Frankish king), 431
Colbert, Jean Baptiste, 486, 490
collectives, 646, 655–56, 692
Colombia, 709, 711, 723, 731, 745, 774, 777, 783, 785, 789, 793, 803
colonialism: and acculturation, 7; 172; and industrial revolution, 523; and missionaries, 349
Coloured (apartheid), 327
Columbus, Christopher, 482, 706, 731, 735, 759
comedy of manners, 517, 520
comedy of tears, 520
Comintern, 642
commerce, 402, 424, 426, 523, 624
commissar, 641
Common African, Malagasy, and Mauritanian Organization, 333
common market: Europe, 576, 597; Latin America, 774
communes, 202, 203, 209
communism: in Africa, 336; in Albania, 651, 678, 688; and the arts, 672–76, 695; in Asia, 173; in Bulgaria, 683; in Burma, 246; in Cambodia, 249; and capitalism, 635; in China, 197–204, 209–11; in Cuba, 768–69; in Czechoslovakia, 682, 683; development of, 532; in Eastern Europe, 690–92, 695–96; in East Germany, 689; in Hungary, 685;

in Indonesia, 256; in Laos, 250; in Latin America, 778; Marx and, 635–36; in Middle East, 101; in Poland, 680–81; and religion, 670, 691; in Romania, 684–85; and society, 661, 662, 664; in Southeast Asia, 256; in Thailand, 248; in USSR, 640, 642–44, 662–65, 670–76; in Vietnam, 251–52; in Western Europe, 562, 571, 572, 600; workers and, 640; world, 651; and Yugoslavia, 686–87. *See also* Communist party.

Communist Information Bureau (COMINFORM), 648

Communist Manifesto, 532, 635

Communist party (Soviet): and Brezhnev-Kosygin, 651–53, 656, 658; and government, 640, 642–44; and Khrushchev, 649–51, 656; and Lenin, 640–41, 645; and nationalities, 662; organization of, 642–44; and Stalin, 642, 645–49, 655, 656; structure of, *643;* and Trotsky, 641–43, 645

Comoro Islands, 267

composite art, 130

computers, 582

Comte, Auguste, 536

conditioned reflex, 584, 658

Condorcet, 507

Confucian Canon, 183

Confucianism: and Buddhism, 190; influence of, 185, 189; in Japan, 220; in Korea, 214; origin of, 182; teachings of, 183–86, 205; in Vietnam, 250

Confucius, 183, *184,* 204, 211

Congo Basin, 284, 313

Congo, Democratic Republic of, 324, 332. *See also* Zaire.

Congo Free State, 316, 324

Congo, Kingdom of, 287, 288–89, 318, 322, 324

Congo, People's Republic of, 267, 322, 336

Congo-Kordofanian languages, 276

Congo (Zaire) River, 271, 285, 287, 288, 312, 332

Congregationalists, 495

Congress of Berlin, 89

Congress of Paris, 89

Congress of Vienna, 512–13, 549, 558, 630, 680

conquistadores, 731–34, 759

Constable, John, 540

Constantine (Roman emperor), 69, 70, 420, 421, 620, 668

Constantinople, 70, 82, 85, 91, 92, 282, 421, 422, 424, 426, 427, 428, 433, 442, 620, 668, 691

Consulate, French, 509

consuls, Roman, 407–08

contract workers, 337, 354–55

Cook, James, 578

Copernicus, Nicolaus, 467–68, 499, 500, 697

Copper Age, 17, 378, 615

Coptic Christianity, 282–83, 331, 348, 784

Corinth, 387, 388

corporate state, 561

Corsica, 405, 509

Cortes, Hernan, 732, 733, 734, 735, 802

Cortes (Spanish), 444, 562

Corvinus, Matthias, 685

Cossacks, 629, 671

Costa Rica, 706, 733, 751, 773, 794

cotton gin, *524–25*

Council for Mutual Economic Assistance (COMECON), 648, 692

Counter-Reformation, 478

covenant, 62

Courbet, Gustave, 542

Crassus, Marcus Licinius, 410

Crecy, battle of, 447

creoles, 743, 744, 747, 748, 751, 754, 760, 763; defined, 736

Crete, 36, 53, 383, 384

Crimean War, 89, 631

Croats (people), 614, 616, 686, 691

Cro-Magnons, 14–15, 16, 35, 534, 614

Crompton, Samuel, 525

Cromwell, Oliver, 497

Cromwell, Richard, 497

crusades, 82, *83,* 84, 428, 430, 441–42; consequences of, 82

Cuba, 706, 772; communism in, 768–69; independence, 760; land reform in, 792; revolution in, 767–68; Spanish in, 482, 731, 737, 757, 759–60; and U.S., 650, 651, 760, 768–69; and USSR, 650

Cuban missile crisis, 650, 651, 768–69

cubism, 590, 592, 801

Cultural Revolution, 197, 198, 210–11

culture, *4;* and anthropology, 7–8; and change, 8; dating remains of, 15; and environment, 140; and geography, 19; importance of knowing a people's, 6; stages of, 15–16, 17

cuneiform, 40, 43

Curie, Marie, 533, 697

Curie, Pierre, 533, 697

Cushitic languages, 34

Cynics, 397

Cyrillic alphabet, 427, 669

Cyrus of Persia, 44, 56

czar (title), 622–23, 625

Czechoslovakia, 378, 565, 616, 650, 652, 681, 682–83, 691, 692, 695, 696, 697

Dacians (people), 684

dadaism, 590

Dahomey, Kingdom of, 304, 307, 308, 310, 314, 322

Dahomey, Republic of, *see* Benin, Republic of.

Damascus, Syria, 54, *71,* 77, 126, 131, 132

damask, 132

Dante Alighieri, 459

Danton, Georges Jacques, 507, 508

Danube River, 376, 378, 679

Danube River Basin, 679, 682, 683, 685, 686

Dardanelles, 85, 92

Darius (the Great, king of Persia), 38, 44, 54, 61, 157, 388

Darwin, 534–35, 536, 588

Das Kapital, 532, 635

David (king of Judah), 56

David, Jacques Louis, 519, 520

Debussy, Claude, 545

Declaration of the Rights of Man, 507, 744

Deere, John, 527

Defoe, Daniel, 520

de Gaulle, Charles, 105, 328, 578

deism, 501, 502

deities: early Arabian, 71, 72; Aryan, 152; Aztec, 732; Cretan, 383; Egyptian, 59–61; Greek, 383, 386, 393–94, 405; Hindu, 154; Mayan, 717; Mesoamerican, 716, 717, 723, 724; Olmec, 716; Roman, 412–13; Semitic-speaking peoples, 59; Shinto, 218–19, 220; Sumerian, 39–40

Delhi, India, 153, 162

democracy (origin of term), 389

Democritus, 394

dendrochronology, 15

Denmark, 255, 376, 380, 432–33, 451, 476, 513, 558, 566, 571, 576, 588, 598, 600, 627

denominations, Protestant, 478

deoxyribonucleic acid (DNA), 583

Descartes, Rene, 503

Dessalines, Jean-Jacques, 754–55

de-Stalinization, 650

dharma (Hinduism), 155

dialect, 140, 452, 459, 538, 588

dialectics, 536

dialogues (Plato), 395, 396

Diaspora, 56, 66, 109, 111

Diaz, Bartholomew, 307, 481

Diaz, Porfirio, 750, 763, 764

Dickens Charles, 541

dictatorship of the proletariat, 635, 636, 640

Diderot, Denis, 502
dig, 7
diocese, 69, 420, 435
Diocletian (Roman emperor), 420
Directory (French), 508, 509
divine right monarchy, 491, 495
divinities, 347
Dnieper River, 162, 613, 615, 624
Dogon (people), 358, 359
domestication: of animals, 17, 18–19, 36, 181, 278, 615, 711; of plants, 17–18, 243, 711
domestic system, 524
Dominican Republic, 706, 731, 744, 754, 755, 756, 762, 763, 777, 778
Dom Pedro, 753, 773
Don River, 613, 615, 619
Dorians (people), 384, 385, 386
Draco, 387
Drake, Francis, 488
drama: baroque, 517; in China, 198; contemporary, 588; in Eastern Europe, 696; Elizabethan, 453, 465; English (1700s), 520; Greek, 394, 398–99, 402; in India, 153, 160; in Japan, 223, 225, 226; medieval Europe, 453; realism in, 541; Restoration, 517; Roman, 416; Scandinavian, 542; Soviet, 676
Dubcek, Alexander, 682, 683
Duma, 637, 638
Dutch, see Netherlands.
Dutch East India Company, 326, 484
Duvalier, Francois, 756, 763
Dvina River, 619

earth: age of, 501, 534; early concepts of, 400, 467–68, 482; Copernican theory, 467–68, 697; rotation of, 161; size of, 400
East Africa, 267
East African Community, 333
Eastern Europe, 110, 368; creativity, 694; economy, 692; early history, 83, 378, 624; nations of, 606, 678; post-World War II, 571; and Warsaw Pact, 648. See also nations.
Eastern Orthodox Church, 70, 427–28, 620, 622–23, 668–69
Eastern Rift Valley, 270, 277
Eastern Slavs, 616
East Goths (people), 422–23
East Germany, 515, 648, 678, 688–90, 695. See also Germany.
East Indies, 482
East Pakistan, 177, 178
East Prussia, 478
Eck, John, 471
Economic and Security Council,

UN, 573
economics: and capitalism, 531; and communist theory, 635; and imperialism, 554; and the industrial revolution, 528–29; and manorialism, 437; mercantilism, 486
Ecuador, 707, 709, 711–12, 723, 726, 745, 773, 774, 782
Edict of Milan, 69, 420
Edict of Nantes, 474, 489
Edo (people), 330
education: in Africa, 337, 351–53; in Asia, 148; in China, 202–03, 210; Christian, 436–37; in Cuba, 769; and the Enlightenment, 499; in France, 508; in Great Britain, 600; in India, 171; and industrial revolution, 528; and Islam, 99, 297; in Japan, 233, 236; in Latin America, 781–83; in Middle Ages, 455–56; in Middle East, 120–21; and missionaries, 351; Roman, 420; theories of, 585; in USSR, 660, 666–67; in Western Europe, 424, 601
Edward I (the Confessor, king of England), 433
Edward III (king of England), 447
Edward VI (king of England), 475–76
Egypt: Alexander the Great and, 45, 49; ancient, 35, 38, 47–49, 53, 275, 277–78, 383; Arab-Israeli conflict, 112–13, 652; Aswan High Dam, 30, 102, 103, 115; economy, 102, 117; European domination, 92; Fatimid dynasty, 80, 81, 82; Mamelukes in, 84; nationalism, 102–03; Ottoman conquest of, 82, 85, 87; Persians in, 44, 49; Ptolemaic dynasty, 45, 399; republic declared, 102; as Roman province, 46, 411; and Sudan, 324; and World War II, 92
Einstein, Albert, 582
Elburz Mountains, 30
El Grito de Lares, 757
Elizabeth (czarina), 628
Elizabeth I (queen of England), 465, 476, 485, 488, 489, 495
Elizabethan Age, 465
El Salvador, 706, 717, 733, 751, 773, 774
Emancipation Act (Russia), 631
embargo, 118–19
Empire Period (Egypt), 48–49, 52, 60, 281
empiricism, 503, 536
enclosure (farming system), 523
encomienda system, 734–35

energy: atomic, 582; crisis, 33; and matter, 582; solar, 660
Engels, Friedrich, 532, 635
England: Anglo-Saxons in, 432–33; evolution of rights in, 448–51, 495–99; explorations of, 484–86; and France, 447–48; Glorious Revolution, 498–99; becomes Great Britain, 499; and Holy Roman Empire, 488; Magna Carta, 449–50; in Middle Ages, 443, 446, 453–55; monarchy in, 448–51, 495–99; Parliament develops, 450–51; Reformation in, 474–76; Renaissance in, 464; Restoration in, 498; Seven Years' War, 492; Vikings in, 432–33. See also Great Britain.
English Channel, 373, 488, 510, 567
English language, 276, 362–63, 412, 452, 464, 520
Enlightenment, 499, 747
enlightenment (Buddhism), 156, 157, 190, 221
environment: and cultural geography, 19; and history, 504; and population, 19–20; and standard of living, 20
Epictetus, 414
Epicureans, 397
epistle, 68
Equatorial Guinea, 267, 317, 322
equites, Roman, 409
Erasistratus, 401
Erasmus, 464
Eratosthenes, 400
Eric the Red, 432
Eritrea, 317, 331
essential self (Hinduism), 154
Estates-General, 447, 505
Estonia, 560, 627, 647, 661–62
Ethiopia, 13, 34, 267, 275, 276, 282–83, 291, 292, 312, 317, 321, 322, 331, 348, 349, 360, 561
Etruscans (people), 378–79, 405, 407, 459
Euclid, 400
Euphrates River, 31, 38, 39, 41, 43
Euripides, 399
Europe, see Eastern Europe; Western Europe; names of nations.
European Atomic Energy Community (Euratom), 576
European Coal and Steel Community (ECSC), 576
European Economic Community (EEC), 333, 576
European Free Trade Association (EFTA), 575
European Russia, 611, 613, 614
excommunication, 70, 435
existentialism, 586, 588
Exodus, 55, 62

extended family, 126, 169, 199, 200, 202, 260, 342, *344*, 355, 786; defined, 11
expressionism, 590

Fabian Society, 531, *532*, 541
factories: and economy, 528–29; growth of, 527; and industrial revolution, 525, and mass production, 526; and social change, 527–28; working conditions in, 528
Fahrenheit, Gabriel, 501
Faisal (king of Saudi Arabia), 104
family: in Africa, 342–45, 353, 354; in China, 189, 199–202; and Confucianism, 184–85; Greek, 402; in India, 169–70; in Japan, 230–31, 233; in Latin America, 786; in Middle East, 126; in Rome, 419; as social unit, 10–11; in Southeast Asia, 260; in USSR, 665; in Western Europe, 596
Fa Ngum (Laotian ruler), 249
Faraday, Michael, 533, *534*
farming: in Africa, 272–73, 334, 337; in ancient Egypt, 49; in Asia, 144, 145, 147; in Eastern Europe, *678*, *687*, 692; in Latin America; 708, 711, 712, 714, 717, 723, 755, 792; in Middle East, 30, 31, 114–15; origin of, 17–18; and population growth, 18; Roman, 409, 410; in USSR, 610–11, 612, 615, 620, 646, 650, 655–56; and urban life, 36; in Western Europe, 373, 377, 380, 523, 526–27. *See also* agriculture.
Farouk (king of Egypt), 102, 134
Fascism, 560–61
Fatima, 78, 81
Fatimid dynasty, 80, 81, 82
fauvism, 589–90
fedayeen, 112
Ferdinand I (Holy Roman emperor), 488
Ferdinand II (king of Aragon), 451, 474
Fermi, Enrico, 582
Fernando Po (island), 317, 322
Fertile Crescent, 31, 32, 114
feudalism: in China, 181–82; and commerce, 624; in East Africa, 295; in Ethiopia, 331; in Japan, 236; Monomotapa, 291; in Russia, 624; in Western Europe, 424, 430, 437–39, 449, 507, 549
fiefs, 437–39
filmmaking, 165–66, 198, 228, *623*, 696

Finland, 373, 374, 575, 598; after Congress of Vienna, 513; independence, 560; and Russia, 451, 627, 628; and USSR, 647
Firdausi, 132
First Dynasty (Egypt), 47
First Estate (France), 505
First Zionist Congress, 110
Fitch, John, 527
Five Books of Moses, 62, 63
Five Pillars of Islam, 73–74
fjords, 376
Flemings (people), 597
Flemish (language), 514
flying shuttle, 524
Fock, Jeno, 686
folklore, 132, 135, 161, *345*, 538, 539, 543, 588, 595, 694
Fon (people), 304
Food and Agriculture Organization, UN (FAO), 574
Foraker Act, 758
Formosa, 208
fossil, 13
Foucault, 533
Fourier, Charles, 531
Four Noble Truths, 156–57
Fourteen Points (Wilson), 558
Fox, George, 502
France, 372, 373, 531, 571, 573, 576, 591; and Africa, 304, 306, 314, 317, 322–24, 328, 351; alliances, 556; arms race, 555; and Austria, 507, 553; and Canada, 580; and Congress of Vienna, 512-13; and Egypt, 92, 112; exploration and colonization, 481, 482, 486-87; Franks in, 431–32; French Community, 325, 328, 336, 578; and Germany, 551-52, 682; under Henry IV, 489; and Holy Roman Empire, 431–32, 477; Hundred Years' War, 447-48; imperialism, 554; in India, 172, 486; and Latin America, 730, 737; under Louis XIII, 490; under Louis XIV, 490-91; in Middle Ages, 443, 446, 453, 455; and monarchy, 447, 491, 513; Moors in, 79; and Napoleon I, 508-12, 549, 550, 630; and Napoleon III, 551; nationalism in, 549-51; Normans in, 433; in North Africa, 104-07; and Ottoman Empire, 88-89, 631; and Prussia, 551-52; Reformation in, 473-74; Renaissance in, 464; Revolution, 504-09, 549, 629; Revolution of 1830, 550; Revolutions of 1848, 551; Romans in, 410, 416, 418; and Russia, 630, 638, 640; Seven Years' War, 492; socialism in, 531; in Southeast Asia, 249-51; Third Republic, 552; Thirty Years' War, 476, 478; World War I, 91, 557, 688; World War II, 565, 566-68, 647
Franco, Francisco, 562, 590
Franks (people), 79, 431
Franz Ferdinand (Austrian archduke), 91, 556, 557
Frederick I (Barbarossa, Holy Roman emperor), 451
Frederick II (the Great, Holy Roman emperor), 451, 491–92, 515
Frederick III (ruler of Saxony), 472
Frederick William, 478
Frederick William IV (king of Prussia) 551
French Academy, 490
French Academy of Sciences, 500
French Community, 325, 328, 336, 578
French Equatorial Africa, 322
French East India Company, 486, 490
French Guiana, 362, 707, 709, 730
French Guinea, 322
French Indochina, 238, 251
French language, 276, 361–62, 412, 452, 490, 597
French Morocco, 94
French West Africa, 304, 322, 323, 324
frescos, *76*, *83*, 383
Freud, Anna, 585
Freud, Sigmund, 584, 585, 586, 589, 590
friars, 436
Fugger family, 444
Fujiwara family, 234
Fulani (empire), 301–02, 323
Fulani (people), 301, 317, 330, 341, 357
Fulton, Robert, 527
functionalism, 586
futurism, 586

Gabon, 267, 322, 338
Gadsden Purchase, 775
gagaku, 229
Galen, 134, 469
Galileo Galilei, 468, 499
Gama, Vasco da, 172, 307, 308, 481
Gambia, 267, 322, 325, 362
Gandhi, Indira, 175
Gandhi, Mohandas K. (Mahatma), 168, 173–74, 674
Ganges River, 141, *155*
Garibaldi, Giuseppe, 553, 554
Gaul, 410, 411, 420, 422, 423
Gaza Strip, 113
Geez (language), 283
genealogies, 194, 200

General Assembly, UN, 113, 356, 573

Generation of '98, 588

Geneva, 473, 474, 574; Conference, 251

Genghis Khan, 83, 162, 195, 212, 621–22

genre painting, 465–66

gentry, 200–02

geographical race, 12–13

George I (king of England), 499

Georgia, USSR, 81, 641, 662, 671

German East Africa, 314, 322, 323, 324, 325

Germanic peoples, 404, 421–23, 424, 431, 615, 685

German language, 412, 452, 473, 691

German South-West Africa, 314, 323, 327

Germany: and Africa, 313, 314, 316–17, 322, 323, 324, 327; alliances, 555–56; and Balkans, 557; as confederation of states, 551; and Congress of Vienna, 513; divided, 650, 688; empire created, 552, 553; and France, 551–52; part of Holy Roman Empire, 451; imperialism in, 554; and League of Nations, 680; in Middle Ages, 446, 447, 453; nationalism in, 549, 551; Nazism in, 563; Reformation in, 472–73; and Russia, 638, 647; Thirty Years' War, 476–78; in World War I, 91, 557–58, 560; in World War II, 565–68, 660, 688. *See also* East Germany; West Germany.

Gesner, Konrad von, 469

Ghana, 267, 273, 274, 303, 321, 322, 324, 325, 331, 342, 352, 356, 360, 362, *363*

Ghana, Empire of, 296, 301, 322, 323, 347

Giacometti, Albert, 593

Gibraltar, Strait of , 53, 94, 369

Gibran, Kahlil, 134

Gierek, Edward, 681

Gilbert, William S., 543

Gilgamesh Epic, 59

Giotto, 460

Girondists, 507, 508

Glorious dynasty (China), 195

Glorious Revolution, 498, 520

God: in African traditional religion, 346–47; and Christianity, 58, 586; and deism, 501; and Islam, 58, 72; Jesus and, 67; and Judaism, 58

Godunov, Boris, 624

Goethe, Johann Wolfgang, 538–39

Golan Heights, 112, 113

Gold Coast States, 303, 321, 322

Golden Horde, 622

Golden Mean, 416

Gomulka, Wladyslaw, 681

Good Neighbor Policy, 777–78

Gothic architecture, 454–55

Goths (people), 380, 615, 616, 684, 688

government: and cities, 21; and communism, 640; and economy, 531; and the Enlightenment, 499, 503; changing attitudes in European, 494; early Greek, 387, 389–90, 392; and labor unions, 530; in Middle Ages, 446, 447; Plato on, 396; representative, 173, 450–51; and society, 531; and socioeconomic systems, 531–33

Goya, *537*, 539–40

Gran Chaco, 774

Gran Colombia, 745, 746, 773

Great Britain, 380, 571, 573, 575, 576, 578, 597, 599; and Africa, 303–04, 314, 317, 321, 322–24, 325, 336, 351; and Canada, 580; and Congress of Vienna, 512; creation of, 499; and Egypt, 92, 102, 112, 557; imperialism, 554–555; in India, 172, 177; and Iran, 94–95, 101; and Latin America, 730, 752; and Middle East, 95–96; and Napoleon, 509, 510, 511, 744; and North America, 484; and Palestine, 111; and Ottoman Empire, 88–89, 631; and Russia, 630, 638, 640; and slavery, 309; in Southeast Asia, 246, 253, 254; and World War I, 91, 557–58; and World War II, 565, 566–67, 647. *See also* England.

Great Charter, 449

Greater Antilles, 706

Great Leap Forward, 209

Great Moravian Empire, 682

Great Northern Plain, 373

Great Rift Valley, 270, 294

Great Russians, 660, 661

Great Trek (Boers), 326

Greece, 374, 375, 428, 576; and Africa, 281, 291; and Albania, 687; ancient, 382–402; Balkan Wars, 91; in Eastern Europe, 691; and Egypt, 283; Hellenistic Age, 392; and Middle East, 45–46, 391–92; and Persia, 44, 388; philosophies, 456, 459; and Renaissance, 461; religion, 70, 393–94, 427; and Romans, 405, 413, 414; Truman Doctrine, 571; and World War I, 557

Greek language, 50, 70, 283, 412, 420, 425, 427, 464

Greek Orthodox Church, 70, 427

Greenland, 373, 376, 432

Gregory I (the Great, pope), 435

Gregory VII (pope), 435

Gregory XIII (pope), 469

Grenada, 706

Grieg, Edvard, 453

Grito de Dolores, 748

groundwater, 115

Guadalupe Hidalgo, Treaty of, 775

Guarani, 803

Guatemala, 706, 733, 751, 768, 778, 788, 796, 803, 805

Guatemala, Captaincy-General of, 733, 735, 751

guilds, 445–46, 453, 455

Guinea, 267, 296, 316, 322, 328, 333, 360

Guinea-Bissau, 267, 322, 329

Gupta dynasty, 159–61

Gutenberg, Johann, 463–64

Guyana, 707, 709, 730

Guzman, Arbenz, 778

Hadith, 72

Hadrian (Roman emperor), 418, 425

Hafiz, 132

Hagiographa, 62, 63

haiku, 227, 228

Haile Selassie, 331

Haiti, 509, 706, 731, 745, 755–56, 762, 763, 773, 776, 778, 782, 784, 801

Hallstat culture, 379

Hammurabi, 41

Handel, George Frederick, 518–19

Han dynasty, 185, 189, 191, 197

Han Fei-tzu, 188

Hangchow, China, 194

Hanseatic League, 442–43

Hapsburg family, 86, 87, 88, 476–77, 488, 490–91, 543, 682

Harappan culture, 151

Hardy, Thomas, 541

Hargreaves, James, *524*, 525

Harold (king of England) *366*, 433

Harsha, 161

Harun al-Raschid, 132

Hasmonean dynasty, 56

Hassuna, 36

Hastings, battle of, 433

Hatshepsut, 52

Hausa (people), 299, 301, 330, 341, 357

Hausa States, 301–02, 323

Hawkins, John, 488

Hebrew (language), 34, 54, 63, 119

Hebrews, 52, 54–56

Hegel, Georg Wilhelm Friedrich, 536, 538

Hegira, 72

Heian period, 222
Hellenism, 399–401
Helmholtz, 533
Helmont, J. B. van, 469
Henry I (king of England), 449
Henry II (king of England), 449
Henry III (king of England), 450
Henry V (king of England), 448
Henry VII (king of England), 474
Henry VIII (king of England), 474–75, 476, 488, 495
Henry IV (Holy Roman emperor), 435
Henry IV (king of France), 489, 490
Henry (the Navigator, Portuguese prince), 481
Hepworth, Barbara, 593
Heraclius (Roman emperor), 425
Heraea, 386
herbalists, 348
heredity, 161, 535, 583
Hereros (people), 314, 323
heretics, 434
Hero of Alexandria, 401
Herophilus, 401
Hertz, Heinrich, 533
Herzegovina, 89
Herzl, Theodore, 110
Hidalgo, Miguel, 747–48
Hideyoshi, 225
hieroglyphics, *21*, 50, 715
Hima (people), 295
Himalaya Mountains, 144, 156, 212
Hinayana Buddhism, 189
Hindenburg, Paul von, 564
Hindi (language), 163
Hinduism: in Africa, 350; and Buddhism, 156; and caste system, 155, 167–68; Gupta dynasty, 159–60; history and teachings of, 152–55; sacred writings of, 153, 158; in Southeast Asia, 244, 248, 252
Hindustani (language), 10
Hipparchus, 400
Hippocrates, 401, 469
Hispaniola, 706, 731, 736, 754, 756
Hitler, Adolf, 110, 560–62, 564–67, 647, 680, 685
Hittites (people), 41, 42, 48, 52, 53, 61
Hoabinhians (people), 243
Hobbes, Thomas, 503
Ho Chi Minh, 251
Hogarth, William, 518, 519
Hohenzollerns, 478, 552
Holbein, Hans, 466, *475*
Holland, 373, 410, 495, 566; as independent nation, 478; and Reformation, 473. *See also* Netherlands.
Holy Alliance, 630
Holy Land, 82, 428, 442

Holy Roman Empire: beginning of, 431; and Bohemia, 682; and Charles V, 484, 487–88; and Charles VI, 491; end of, 513; and Frederick I and II, 451; Hapsburgs, 477; and Luther, 473; and Ottoman Empire, 86
Homer, 384, 416
Honduras, 706, 717, 733, 751, 773, 774, 803
Hong Kong, 204, 206, 238, 486
Hooke, Robert, 501
Horace, 416
Horn (of Africa), 277
Horthy, Miklos, 685
Hottentots (people), 275, 276, 277, 294, 318, 323, 324, 360
householder (Hinduism), 155
House of Commons, 451, 474, 496
House of Lords, 451, 474
Hoxha, Enver, 688, 695
Hsai dynasty, 181
Huang Ti, 181
Huari empire, 724
Huascar, 733
hudas, 135
Hudson, Henry, 484
Huerta, Victoriano, 764
Huguenots, 474, 488, 490
Huitzilopochtli, 720, 721
Hulagu Khan (Mongol ruler), 83, 84
humanist psychology, 585
humanists and humanism, 460, 463, 464, 465, 473
humanitarianism, 499
Humayun, 162
humus, 273
Hundred Years' War, *366*, 447, 474
Hungary, 87, 378, 488, 558, 560, 565, 616, 622, 631, 678, 682, 685–86, 691, 692, 695
Huns (people), 189, *422*, 615, 616, 684
Huntsman, Benjamin, 526
Hurrians (people), 41–43, 52
Husak, Gustav, 683
Huss, John, 471
Hussein (king of Jordan), 108, 112–13
Hutton, James, 501, 534
Hutu (people), 295, *331*
hydroelectric power, 274
Hyksos, 48

Iberian Peninsula, 374
Ibibo (people), 330
ibn-Abdul-Aziz (king of Saudi Arabia), 104
ibn Battuta, 294
ibn Saud, (king of Arabia), 104
Ibo (people), 330, 358, 362
Ibsen, Henrik, 542

Iceland, 373, 376, 432, 571, 575, 588
ideographs, 181, 193, 213–14, 223, 717
Idi Amin, 332
Idi Amin, Lake, 270, 332
Idris Alooma, 300
Ife (city-state), 302, 323, 357, 360
Ighodaro, Irene, 356
Ijaw (people), 330
Ikhnaton (pharaoh), 60–61
imam (title), 78, 109
Imperial Academy of Sciences, Russia, 658, 659
imperialism, 329, 530, 541, 554–55
impressionism, 514, 544, 545
Incas, 715, 726–28, 733, 803
India: and early Africa, 281, 292; Alexander the Great in, 391; Aryans in, 152; caste systems of, 166–68; creativity of, 158–64; early history, 141, 147, 149, 152; Europeans in, 171–72, 307, 308, 485–87; government, 174; Gupta dynasty in, 159–61; imperialism in, *172*; independence, 171–75; Mogul Empire in, 131, *150*, 162, 176, 485; partition of, 177; Persians in, 44, 388; religion, 152–58; society, 166–71; and Southeast Asia, 245, 254, 255, 256; and World War II, 238
Indian Ocean, 141, 144, 277, 285, 286, 307, 481, 483
Indians (of the Americas): defined, 702; pre-Columbian civilizations, 714–28; exploitation of, 730, 734–35; influence on arts, 795–99; and Spanish conquests, 730–38. *See also* names of individual peoples.
Indies, 482, 484
Indo-European language family, 9–10, 34, 38, 41, 44, 54, 152, 382, 383, 405, 412, 563, 691
Indonesia, 144, 158, 238, 244, 245, 253, 254, 255–56, 292, 482, 484, 578
Indus River, 39, 44, 141; civilization, 151
industrialization: and architecture, 594; and art, 546; and families, 127; and geography, 20; and imperialism, 554; and society, 541
industrial revolution: and acculturation, 9; and the arts, 540; cause of, 523; and colonialism, 306, 311; and economics, 528–29; in England, 523–26; and government, 531–33; international consequences of, 530–31; and labor reforms, 549–50; and

politics, 529–30; and social change, 527–28; and socio-economic systems, 531–33
initiation ceremonies, 343–44
Innocent III (pope), 435
Inquisition, 468, 488
Inter-American Commission of Women, 788
interbreeding, 12
interdict, 435
International Association of American Republics, 774
International Atomic Energy Agency (IAEA), 574
International Court of Justice, UN, 573
International Labor Organization (ILO), 574
international style (architecture), 126, 359, 595, 802
International Telecommunications Union (ITU), 574
International (USSR), 642
Ionian Sea, *389*
Ionians (people), 387
Iqbal, Mohammed, 176–77
Iran, 27, 30, 31, 32, 33, 38, 78, 80, 117, 118, 131–32; nationalism in, 100–01; and Ottoman Empire, 83–86; outside interest in, 94–96; Safavid rule, 85. *See also* Persia.
Iran, Plateau of, 30
Iraq, 27, 30, 31, 32, 33, 34, 36, 43, 55, 80, 83, 85, 112, 117, 118, 122; British mandate in, 95; military coups in, 106–07
Ireland, 369, 372, 432, 433, 576, 588
Irish Renaissance, 588
Iron Age, 17, 278, 378, 379, 615
iron curtain, 648
Irrawaddy River, 141, 245
Isaac, 54
Isabella (queen of Castile), 451
Isabella (queen of Spain), 66, 455, 474, 482
Ishmael, 71
Islam: in Africa, 283, 294, 296–97, 299, 348, 349, 350; and arts, 130–32; beginning of, 71; divisions within, 77; and education, 120, 297; in Egypt, 26; and holy wars, 81; in India, 162; and marriage, 127; and nationalism, 99; in North Africa, 26, 349; orthodox, 131, 135; and Ottoman Empire, 91; in Pakistan, 176–77; in Persia, 61; Shia sect, 77–78; in Southeast Asia, 244–45, 252–53, 255, 257; spread of, 78–79; and Sufism, 74; Sunni sect, 77; teachings of, 71–74; and tolerance, 442; in USSR,

671, 672; Wahabism, 103–04; and Western culture, 133–34, 469; without color barrier, 350; and women, 128–30, 356. *See also* Muslims.
Ismail, 85
Israel (Hebrew leader), 55, 71
Israel, Kingdom of, 56
Israel, 27, 31, 32, 34, 36, 44, 53, 55, 56, 103, 122, 135; and Arab-Israeli conflict, 111–13, economy, 119–20; modern nation created, 56, 111. *See also* Palestine.
Israelites, 55, 56
Istanbul, 126, 127, 388, 428, 620. *See also* Byzantium; Constantinople.
Italian language, 412, 452, 459
Italian Somaliland, 317, 323
Italy, 93, 317, 322, 323, 369, 374, 375, 376, 378, 380, 422, 425, 431, 513, 571, 576; and Fascism, 560–61; Kingdom of, 554; in Middle Ages, 443–44, 453; nationalism in, 549, 551–52; Renaissance in, 459–62; unification of, 553–54; and World War I, 557, 560–61; and World War II, 93, 567, 688
Iturbide, Agustin de, 748, 751
Ivan I (ruler of Russia), 622
Ivan III (the Great, czar), 622
Ivan IV (the Terrible, czar), 623–25
Ivory Coast, 267, *274*, 303, 323, 333, *337*, 342, 351, 358, 360
Iyeyasu, 225

Jacob, 54, 55
Jacobins, 508
jade, 192
Jadwiga (queen of Poland), *679*
Jagellon dynasty, 679
Jamaica, 497, 706–07
James I (king of England), 495, 499
James II (king of England), 498
Japan, 144, 145, 146, 147; and China, 193, 208–09, 219–20, 222; creativity, 222–29; early, 217; economy, 240; Europeans in, 482; expansion of empire, 225, 238; government, 239–40; isolation of, 236; and Korea, 214; Meiji Restoration, 232, 236; modern, 234–40; politics in, 237; religions of, 218, 220–22; and Russia, 636, 640, 647; shogunates, 224; society, *9.* 230–33, 236; and Southeast Asia, 243, 256; Western influence on, 227, 229, 230, 236; and World War I, 557; and World War II, 222, 223, 238–39, 251, 567, 568

Jarmo, 36
Java, 14, 195, 252, 253, 254, 255
Jehovah, 62
jen (Confucianism), 183
Jenner, Edward, 501
Jericho, 35, *36*
Jerome, St., 70
Jerusalem, 56, *58*, 67, 81, 82, 83, 111, 112, 126, 410
Jesus Christ, 63, *66*–68, 72, 162, 282, 478
Jews, 784; and Arab–Israeli conflict, 109–13; in Africa, 350; in Alexandria, 350; Babylonian Captivity of, 56; in Eastern Europe, 671, 691–92, 696; and Islam, 442; and World War II, 564, 571, 691–92. *See also* Hebrews; Israel; Judaism.
Jiagge, Annie, 356
Jimmu Tenno, 218
Jingo (empress of Japan), 214, 231
Jinnah, Mahomed Ali, 177
Joan of Arc, 448
Joao (king of Portugal), 752–53
John II (king of Portugal), 307, 481
John (king of England), 449
John III Sobieski (king of Poland), 87, 679
Johnson, Samuel, 520
Jomon period, Japan, 217, *218*
Jones, Inigo, 515
Jordan, 27, 30, 31, 32, 35, 44, 104, 108, 112–13, 122, 125, 135
Jordan River, 32, 53
Joule, James, 533
Juan Carlos, 562–63
Juarez, Benito, 749–50, 763, 764
Judah, Kingdom of, 56
Judaism; in Africa, 350; and Bible, 62–63; Conservative, 63–64; and Greek philosophy, 66; Orthodox, 63–64; Reform, 64; and the Talmud, 63; teachers and students, 65; and the Torah, 63; in USSR, 670–71; in Western Europe, 601. *See also* Hebrews; Jews.
Judges (Israelites), 56
Jung, Carl, 584
jury system, 449, 450, 495
Justinian (Byzantine emperor), 425, 427
Jutes (people), 423
Juvenal, 417

Kaaba, 71, 72, 74
kabuki, *223*, 226, 229
Kachin (people), 246
kaiser (title), 552
Kalahari Desert, 272
Kalala Ilunga, 287
Kalidasa, 160

Kalonga Mzura, 288
Kamakura shogunate, 223, 234
Kandinsky, Vassily, 675–76
Kanem-Bornu, Empire of, 299–301, 322, 323
Kano (state), 301, 347, *350*
Kano Chronicle, 301
Kant, Emmanuel, 503, 538
Kanuri (people), 299–301, 330
Karanga clan, 290
karma (Hinduism), 154
Kasai River, 285, 287
Kasavubu, Joseph, 328–29
Kassites (people), 41, 42
Kay, John, 524
Kazakhstan, USSR, *614, 662*
Kelly, William, 526
Kenya, 267, *270,* 273, 292, 294, 323, 325, 332, 341, 360, 362
Kenyatta, Jomo, 325, 356
Kenyatta, Margaret, 356
Kepler, Johannes, 469, 499
Kha (people), 249
Khalid (king of Saudi Arabia), 104
Khan, Yahya, 178
Khan, Sayyid Ahmad, 176
Khayyam, Omar, 133
Khazars (people), 619, 671
Khmer Rouge, 249
Khmers (people), 247–49, 251
Khoisan language, 276
Khrushchev, Nikita, 644, 649–51, 656, 675, 687, 688, 690
Khufu (pharaoh), 49
kibbutzim, 120–21
Kibinda Ilunga, 287
Kiev, USSR, 613, 619–21, 622, 661
Kievan Russia, 619–22, 668, 671
Kikuyu (people), 325
Kilwa, 274, 293, 294, 308, 318
Kilwa Chronicle, 293
Kirgizia, USSR, 662
Kitwara, Kingdom of, 295, 324
knights, 437, 438–39, 450–51
Knossos, 383, 384
Knox, John, 474
Koch, Robert, 535
kogai, 233
Komsomol, 643
Kongolo, 287
Koran, 72–73, 77, 81, 99, 103, 104, 120, 127, 131, 162, 164, 294, 297, 350
Korea, 144, 158, 213–14, 217, 225, 238, 636
Kosciusko, Thaddeus, 680
kosher, 64
Kossuth, Lajos, 685
Kosygin, Aleksei, 651, *652,* 656
Krapf, Johann, 312
Kremer, Gerhard, 469
Kshatriya (caste), 166, 167

Kuan I-wu, 188
Kublai Khan (Mongol ruler), 195, 247, 250–51
Kumbi Saleh, 297
Kun, Bela, 685
Kuomintang, 207, 208
Kush, Kingdom of, 278, 281-82, 283, 324
Kuwait, 27, 33, 95, 96, 115, 117, 118, 119
Kwa (language), 302

labor: contract workers, 337, 354-55; forced, 316; hand, 524, 525; and industrial revolution, 523; migratory, 597; and political parties, 531; shortage of, and slavery, 308-09
labor unions, 529, 530
Ladislas I (king of Poland), 679
Ladislas II (king of Poland), 679
laissez-faire capitalism, 531, 554
Lamarck, Jean, 534, 535
Lancaster, House of, 474
land reform: in China, 209; in Cuba, 792; in Egypt, 102; in Guatemala, 778; in Iran, 101; in Latin America, 780, 789, 792; in Mexico, 750, 765, 789, 792; in Middle East, 115
languages: of Africa, 275-76, 363; of Asia, 140, 243; and culture, 34; of Egypt, 47; of Eastern Europe, 691; of Ethiopia, 283; Inca, 727; of India, 10, 163, 165; Indus Valley, 151; Khmer, 248; of Latin America, 803; Malay, 256; of Mesopotamia, 40, 41, 44; of Middle East, 33-34; of pre-Columbian Americas, 710; Thai, 248; of Tibet, 212; of USSR, 661; vernacular, 452-53; in Yugoslavia, 686. *See also* name of language.
language families, defined, 9
Lao (people), 249
Laos, 141, 242, 245, 249–50, *260*
Lao-tzu, 186
La Plata, Viceroyalty of, 735, 743, 746
Las Casas, Bartholome de, 735
La Tene culture, 379–80
Latin alphabet, 100
Latin America: creativity, 795-805; early peoples of, 710-12; economy, 789; environment, 703-09; Europeans in, 730-40; independence struggles, 742-60; industrialization, 793; politics in, 762-78; pre-Columbian civilizations in, 714-28; religion in, 784-85; society, 780-88; urbani-

zation, 794-95. *See also* names of nations.
Latin language, 134, 412, 420, 452, 455, 459, 465
Latins (people), 405
Latvia, 560, 647, 661, 662
La Venta, 715
Lavoisier, Antoine, 500-01
law: Byzantine, 669; Draco's, 387; and the Enlightenment, 504; English, 495-96, 504, 537; European, 99, 101; Hammurabi's code, 41; Islamic, 78, 99, 101, 104, 128; and Legalism, 188; in Middle Ages, 449, 455-56; of Moses, 63; Napoleonic Code, 504, 508; Roman, 46, 408-09, 412, 414, 416, 425, 669; Soviet, 644, 665
Laye, Camara, 362
League of Nations, 95, 317, 325, 327, 558, 680, 777
Leakey, Louis S. B., Mary, and Richard E., 13, 14
Lebanon, 27, 31, 32, 120, 125, 134, 383; and Arab-Israeli conflict, 112; and Arab unity, 122; civil wars in, 107; French mandate, 95
Le Brun, Charles, 515
Le Corbusier, 595
Leeuwenhoek, Anton van, 501
Leeward Islands, 706
Legalism, 182, 188-89
Legislative Assembly, 507
Leipzig, battle of, 512
Lena River, 613
Leningrad, 627, *629*
Lenin, Nikolai, 532, 636, 638-39, 640, 641, 650
Leo Africanus, 298
Leo I (the Great, pope), 422
Leo III (pope), 431, 435
Leopold (king of Belgium), 313, 316
Lesotho, 267, 323, 325
Lesser Antilles, 706
Lesser Rift Valley, 270
liberal positivism, 536
Liberia, 273, 309-10, 312, 321, 323, 349, 356
Libya, 26, 33, 48, 78, 93, 107, 300, 317
Liebig, 533
Liechtenstein, 374, 376
Lima, Peru, 707, 724, 735, 747
limbo (dance), 797
Limpopo River, 289, 290
Linnaeus, Carl, 501
Lister, Joseph, 535
Li T'ai-po, 194
literature: African, 357, 360-63; baroque, 517; Chinese, 194-96,

197; contemporary, 586-89; Eastern Europe, 695; Egyptian, 51; French, 490; Greek, 394; of India, 158, 160, 165; Islamic, 132; Israeli, 135; Japanese, 222-23, 227-28; Latin American, 787; 803-05; Middle Ages, 452-53; Middle Eastern, 134, 135; realism in, 541-42; Renaissance, 459; romanticism in, 538-39; Roman, 416-17; Russian, 669, 672, 673-74; Soviet, 673, 674
Lithuania, 560, 647, 661, 662, 679
Little Russia, 661
Livingstone, David, 312, 349
Livonia, 627
Livy, 417
Locke, John, 503
Lombards (people), 380, 423, 431, 435
London, 444, 450, 496, 515, 516, 518, 744
Long March (China), 208
Lon Nol, 249
Lord Jim, 695
Louis XI (king of France), 448
Louis XIII (king of France), 490
Louis XIV (king of France), 486, 490-91, 504, 515, 517, 580
Louis XV (king of France), 504, 517
Louis XVI (king of France), 504, 508
Louis XVIII (king of France), 513, 550
Louis (Holy Roman emperor), 431
Louis (king of Hungary), 679
Louis Napoleon, *see* Napoleon III
Louis Philippe (king of France), 550
Low Church Anglicans, 495, 497
Low Countries, 373, 465, 488
Lower Egypt, 47, 281
Luba, Kingdom of, 287, 288, 324
Lully, 516
Lumumba, Patrice, 328-29
Lunda Kingdom, 287-88, 322, 324
Luo (people), 295
Luther, Martin, *470,* 471-73
Lutheranism, 473, 475-76, 478, 488
Luxembourg, 372, 373, 432, 566, 571, 575, 576
Lyell, Charles, 534

Macao, 205, 482
MacArthur, Douglas, 239, 568
Macedonia, 45-46, 391-92, 399
Maceo, Antonio, 760
Machiavelli, Niccolo, 459-60
machismo, 787
Madagascar, 286, 323
Madero, Francisco I., 764
Magdalena River, 709
Magellan, Ferdinand, 172, 257, 483
Magellan, Strait of, 483

Magloire, 756
Magna Carta, 449-50
Magyars (people), 682, 684, 685, 691
Mahabharata, 153, 158, 165
Mahayana Buddhism, 189-90, 192, 212, 220, 250
Mahdi, 78, 314
Mahmud II (Turkish sultan), 88
Maimonides, Moses, 66
Majapahit empire, 253, 254
Maji Maji, 314
Malagasy Republic, 243, 267, 276, 286, 323
malaria, 209, 307
Malawi, 267, 288, 323, 326
Malaya, 238, 256; Federation of, 253
Malayo-Polynesian language, 276
Malay Peninsula, 253, 254
Malays (people), 252-53, 254, 256
Malaysia, 141, 158, 242, 245, 252-53, 256, 292, 482, 486
Malenkov, Georgi, 649, 650
Mali, Empire of, 297-98, 299, 304, 322, 323
Mali, Republic of, 267, 274, *298,* 333, 337, 338, 350, 352, 358, 359; early history, 296, 323
Malinche, 732, 787
Malthus, Thomas, 535
Mamelukes, 83-84, 85
Manchu dynasty, 196, 205, 207
Manchuria, 196, 209, 611, 636
mandates, League of Nations, 95, 327-28
Mandingo, 314, 323, 360
Manet, Edouard, 544
Manichaenist sect, 61, 69
Mann, Thomas, 589
mannerism (art), 466, 513
manorialism, 424, 430, 439-41
Mansa Musa, 298
Maoris (people), 579-80
Mao Tse-tung, 197, 208, 209, 210
Marat, Jean Paul, 507
Marconi, Guglielmo, 527
Marcos, Ferdinand, 260
Marcus Aurelius (Roman emperor), 415
Maria (queen of Portugal), 752
Maria Theresa, 491-92
Marie Antoinette, 508, 520
Marmara, Sea of, 84, 424
marriage: in Africa, 344-45, 353; in China, 199; in early Greece, 402; in India, 170; in Japan, 231; in Latin America, 787; in Middle East, 127; in Southeast Asia, 260; in Western Europe, 596
Marshall Plan, 571, 648, 689
Marti, Charles, 79, 431
Marti, Jose, 760, 804, 805

Martinique, 797
Marx, Karl, 532, 536, 635, 638, 639, 642, 670
Marxism, 638-39, 770, 771
Mary (queen of England), 488, 498-99
Masai (people), 318, 360
Masaryk, Thomas G., 682
master race, 536, 563
materialism, 503, 535, 536
mathematics: and astronomy, 467; Chinese, 194; Egyptian, 49, 51; Hellenistic, 400-01; in India, 161; Mayan, 717; of megalith builders, 378; Muslim, 133; Sumerian, 40
Matilda (queen of England), *433*
Matope, 290-91
Mau Mau, 325
Mauritania, 79, 105, 267, 333, 337-38, 350, *356;* early history, 296, 323
Maurya dynasty, 157, 161
Maximilian (archduke), 749
Maxwell, James, 533
Mayas, 715, 716-18, 719, 731, 803, 804
Mazarin, Cardinal, 490
Mazzini, Giuseppe, 552-53
McCormick, Cyrus, 527
Mecca, 71, 72, 74, 85, 104, 130, 131, 297, 298
Medes (people), 43
Medici, Marie de, 490
medicine: in Africa, 348; in China, 190, 194, 209; in Egypt, 51; during Enlightenment, 501; Greek, 382, 469; Hellenistic, 401; in India, 161; medieval, 455-56; modern, 583; Muslim, 133; in Renaissance Europe, 469; in Russia, 658; Sumerian, 40; in USSR, 665
Medina, 72, 77, 85
Mediterraneans (people), 275, 276, 277
Mediterranean Sea, 26, 27, 369, 376; early states, 38, 52-56
megalith builders, 377-78
Mehemet Ali, 92
Mehmed II (Turkish sultan), 85
Meiji Restoration, 232
Meir, Golda, 130
Mekong River, 141, *247,* 251
Memphis, Egypt, 786-87
Mendel, Gregor, 535
Mendeleev, Dmitri, 658
Menelik II (emperor of Ethiopia), 283, 317
Menes (pharaoh), 47
Mensheviks, 636, 637
mercantilism, 486

Mercator, 469
Meredith, George, 541
Merneptah (pharaoh), 54
Meroe, 278, 281, 282
Mesoamerica, 715-22
Mesolithic period, 16
Mesopotamia, 31, 38-40, 52, 53, 151
Messiah, 63-64, 67, 68, 78, 109
mestizos, 743, 747, 773, 781; defined, 736
Mestrovic, Ivan, 696
metals and metalworking: in Africa, 292; Andean cultures, 723; in Asia, 151; discovery of, 17, *18*; in Japan, 217; in Latin America, 796-97; in Philippines, 256; in Western Europe, 378-79
metaphysical poetry, 465
Metchnikoff, Ilya, 658
Methodism, 501-02
Metternichism, 549, 550
Mexican-American War, 749, 775
Mexico: dictatorship in, 749; empire in, 551, 749; independence movement, 747-48; revolutions in, 764-65; Spanish in, 733-35; and U.S., 775
Mexico, Gulf of, 715
Mexico, Valley of, 703
Michael (king of Romania), 684
Michelangelo, *458*, 462
Middle Ages: art and architecture of, 454-55; banking in, 443-44; Church in, 434-37; craft guilds in, 445-46; education, 455-56; feudalism, 437-39; languages in, 452; literature of, 453-54; manorialism in, 437, 439-41; middle class in, 430, 446-47; philosophy of, 397, 456; political life in, 447-51; towns and cities of, 444-45; trade and cities, 441-44
Middle America, 702
middle class, 430, 443, 446-47, 453, 476, 491, 529, 635-36
Middle East: ancient kingdoms and empires of, 28-56; creativity of, 130-35; defined, 26; economy, 114-22; environment, 26-32; industrialization in, 117; nationalism in, 99-106; politics in, 106-13; religion in, 58-74; society in, 124-30. *See also* nations.
Middle Kingdom (Egypt), 48, 51, 60, 281
Mideast, 26
Midhat Pasha, 90
mihrab, 130, 131
Mill, John Stuart, 536-37
Milton, John, 517
Minamoto clan, 224

minaret, 131
Minas Gerais, 740, 751-52, 802
Ming dynasty, 195-96
Ministry of Culture, USSR, 673
Ministry of Education, USSR, 666
Minoan civilization, 383
Miranda, Francisco de, 744-45
Mistral, Gabriela, 805
Mitanni (people), 41, 52
Mithra, cult of, 413
Mixtecs (people), 719
Mobutu Sese Seko, 332
Mobutu Sese Seko, Lake, 270, 312
Mochica culture, 725
model village, 147
modernism, 804
Mogadishu, 292-93, 323
Mogul Empire (India), 131, *150*, 162-64, 176, 485
Mohammad Riza Pahlevi, 101
Mohenjo-Daro, 151
Moldavia, 647, 661-62, 684
Mombasa, 323
Mon (people), 245, *246*, 248
Monaco, 374, 375
Mongolia, 83, 144, 213, 610, 611
Mongols: in China, 195, 247; empire of, 83-84, 212; in Hungary, 685; in India, 162; in Middle East, 83, 84; in Russia, 621-22, 624, 628, 661
monks, 435-36
Monomakh, Vladimir, 621
Monomotapa Empire, 290-91, 323
Monophysites, 69
monotheists, 80
Monroe Doctrine, 749, 775, 776
Monrovia, Liberia, 310
monsoons, 145, 292
Montenegro, 89, 91, 686
Montesquieu, 503, 504, 505, 507
Montezuma II (Aztec emperor), 722, 732
Montfort, Simon de, 450
Moors, 79, 431, 446, 451, 488
Moravia, 614, 682
More, Thomas, 464
Morelos, Jose Maria, 749
Morgagni, Giovanni, 501
Morocco, 26, 294, 597, 712; Barbary States, 93; early history, 299; European domination, 93, 94, 317; independence movement, 104, 105; religion in, 78
Morse, Samuel F. B., 527
Moscow, 511, 612, 613, 622-23, 630, 637, *649*, *654*, 656, 661, *668*
Moses, 55, 56, 62, 63, 72
mosques, 73-74, 130-31
Mossadegh, Mohammad, 101
Mossi (people), 299, 304, 324
motion pictures, 527

Mozambique, 267, 270, 288, 289, 290, 292, 308, 316, 323, 330
Muawiyah, 77, 78, 79
Muhammad, 71-73, 77-78, 162, 350
Muhammad Ali (Mehemet Ali), 92
mulattoes, 739, 754-55, 759, 773, 781; defined, 736
Munich Pact, 565, 682
Munoz Marin, Luis, 758, 759
Munoz Rivera, Luis, 758
Murad I (Turkish sultan), 84
Mushet, Robert, 526
music: of Africa, 359-60; Arabic, 133, 134; baroque, 516; Chinese, 197-98; and communism, 696; contemporary, 595; of Eastern Europe, 694, 695; folk, 538, 543, 694-95, 797, 798; impressionism in, 545; in India, 158, 164; in Japan, 228-29; of Latin America, 360, 797-98; nationalistic, 540, 695; medieval, 452, 453, 455; of Middle East, 135; Renaissance, 463; rococo, 518-19; romanticism and, 540; Soviet, 676
Muslims: in Africa, 282-83; contributions of, 133-34, 469; in Eastern Europe, 683, 691; in India, 174; meaning of name, 72; and non-Muslims, 134; in North Africa, 26; in Pakistan, 175-76; in Spain, 433; in Southeast Asia, 244-45, 252-53, 255, 257, 260; in USSR, 622. *See also* Islam.
Mussolini, Benito, 560-62, 567-68
Mutota (Rozwi king), 290
Mycenaeans, 378, 383-84
Myron, 398

Nagy, Imre, 686
Namibia, 267, 285, 323, 327-28
Nanak, Guru, 174
Napoleon: career of, 509-13; and Haiti, 754; and Moscow, 630; and nationalism, 509, 549; and Portugal, 752; and Spain, 512, 743, 744, 745, 747, 748; wars of, 92, 451, 510-12, 630, 694, 745
Napoleon III, 539, 551, 749
Napoleonic Code, 504, 508
Nara, Japan, 219, 222
Nasser, Gamal Abdul, 102-03, 108, 122
national authenticity, 332
national consciousness, 549
nationalism: in Africa, 318, 351; in art, 694, 800; in Asia, 173, 206; in Balkans, 89, 91, 557; in Eastern Europe, 678, 690, 694; in literature, 588; in Middle East, 99-106; in music, 540, 543, 694; in Ottoman Empire, 90; and

Reformation, 473; in Western Europe, 549-52, 570, 578
Nationalist party (China), 207
nationalist realism, 695
naturalism, 499
natural selection, 535
Nazca culture, 724, *725*, 796
Nazism, 536, 563, 564, 565, 589
Ndebele (people), 359
Neanderthals (people), 14, 16, 34, 35
Near East, 26
Nebuchadnezzar, 43, 44, 54, 56
negritos, 256
Negritude, 360-62
Negroids, 275, 276
Nehru, Jawaharlal, 174-75
Nelson, Horatio, 509, 510
neoclassicism, 519-20, 539, 542, 590
Neolithic Age, 17
Neo-Punic language, *412*
Nepal, 144, 145, 158, 212
Nero (Roman emperor), 414
Neruda, Pablo, 805
Netherland Antilles, 706
Netherlands (Dutch): in Africa, 276, 306, 307, 314, 324, 326-27; in Brazil, 799, 800; explorations of, 483-84; and Holy Roman Empire, 431, 484, 488; in India, 172; and Latin America, 730; in Malaysia, 253; and Ottoman Empire, 88; Renaissance in, 464; Republic created, 484, 488; in Southeast Asia, 255-56. *See also* Holland.
New Babylonian Empire, 43-44
New Granada, Viceroyalty of, 735, 745
New Guinea, Indonesia, 254
New Spain, Viceroyalty of, 735, 747
New Stone Age, 17
New Testament, 63, 67, 68, 72, 453, 464
Newton, Isaac, *494*, 500
New Zealand, 557, 578, 579-80
Ngo Dinh Diem, 251
Ngoni (people), 291
Nicaragua, 706, 733, 751, 773, 804
Nicholas I (czar), 631
Nicholas II (czar), 636-38, 640
Niemeyer, Oscar, 803
Niepce, Joseph, 527
Nietzsche, Friedrich, 536, 543
Niger, 267, 271, 333, 337, 338; early history, 323
Niger-Congo languages, 276, 302
Nigeria, 267, 273, 275, 277, 278, 284, 296, 300, 302, 323, 324, 325, 330-31
Niger River, 271, 299, 301, 311
Nightingale, Florence, 535
Nikon, Patriarch, 669

Nile River and Valley, 30-32, 45, 49, 271, 276, 281, 313; and ancient Egypt, 38, 47, 48, 278; source of, 312
Nilo-Saharan languages, 276
Ninety-Five Theses, 471-72
Nineveh, *42*, 43
nirvana, 156-57, 190
Nkrumah, Kwame, 321, 324
NKVD, 646
No (drama), 225
Noble Eightfold Path (Buddhism), 157
noblesse oblige, 441
Nobunaga, 225
Nok culture, 278, 302, 357
Normandy, 433, 447, 568
Normans (people), 428, 433, 449, 688
North Africa, 26
North Atlantic Drift, 372
North Atlantic Treaty Organization (NATO), 571-72, 648
North Borneo, 486
Northeast Africa, 267
Northern Europe, 373
Northern Ireland, 372
Northern Rhodesia, 324, 325, 326
North German Confederation, 552
North Korea, 214
North Vietnam, 249-52
Norway, 369, 373, 376, 380, 432, 433, 473, 513, 542, 543, 566, 571, 575, 588, 590, 593, 600
novel, 520
Novotny, Antonin, 682
Nubia, 48, 49, 277, 278, 281, 324, 355, 360
nuclear family, 128, 202, 233, *342*, 355; defined, 11
nuclear power, 576, 582
nuclear weapons: limiting, 652; test ban on, 651
Nyasaland, 323, 324, 326
Nyerere, Julius K., 332
Nyungwe (people), 360

obelisks, 50
Ob River, 613
Octavian (Roman emperor), 411, 412, 420
Oder River, 679
Odoacer, 422
Oduduwa (Ife ruler), 360
Offenbach, Jacques, 453
O'Higgins, Bernardo, 747
oil, 94, 96, 101, 104, 127; impact of, in Middle East, 117-19; reserves in Middle East, 33
Old Believers (Russia), 669
Old Kingdom (Egypt), 48, 49-50, 51, 59

Old Stone Age, 16, 18, 614, 710
Old Testament, 54, 55, 59, 63, 67, 72, 453
Olduvai Gorge, 13, 324
Oleg (Russian prince), 619
oligarchy, 397
Olmecs (people), 715-16
Olney, Richard, 776
Olympic Games: ancient, 385-86, 394; modern, *666*, 667
Oman, 27, 95, 96, 117, 119, 135, 308
Omar (caliph), 77
Omdurman, battle of, *313*, 314
omens, 348
Ommaid dynasty, 77, 79-80, 81
open-door policy, 205
open-field system, 523
Operation Bootstrap, 759
oracles, 393
Organization of African Unity (OAU), 333
Organization of American States (OAS), 774, 783
Organization of Arab Petroleum Exporting Countries (OAPEC), 118-19
Organization of Central American States, 774
Organization of Petroleum Exporting Countries (OPEC), 118-19
Orinoco River, 709, 711, 745
Orozco, Jose Clemente, 800, 801
Orwell, George, 588
Osman I (Ottoman ruler), 85
Ostrogoths, 422-23, 425, 615
Othman (caliph), 77
Othman I (Ottoman ruler), 85
Otto I (Holy Roman emperor), 433
Ottoman Empire (and Ottoman Turks): and Balkan Wars, 91; and Byzantine Empire, 85, 428; decline of, 86-87; and Eastern Europe, 87, 683, 684, 686, 688; in Egypt, 92; expansion of, 85; and North Africa, 93; peak of power, 85-86; reforms in, 88, 90; revolts against, 90; rise of, 84; and Russia, 87, 88, 89, 627, 628, 631, 679; and Young Turks, 90-91. *See also* Turkey.
Ougadougou, Kingdom of, 304, 324
outcastes (caste), 167, 168
Ovid, 417
Owen, Robert, 531
Oyo (city), 302, 323

Pacific Ocean, 172, 483, 567, 611, 624, 706, 728, 733
paddy, rice, 217
Pagan, Kingdom of, 245
Pahlevi dynasty, 100-01
Pakistan, 141, 147, 151, 152, 175-77

Palembang, Indonesia, 254
Paleolithic Age, 16
Palestine, 48, 56, 67, 78, 88, 95, 108, 109–13
Palestine Liberation Organization (PLO), 113
Palladio, 462, 515, 516, 519
Palmares, Republic of, 751
pampas, 708, 714
Panama, 482, 706, 773, 777
Panama Canal, 706, 777; Zone, 777
Pan-Americanism, 774
Pankhurst, Emmeline, Christabel, Estelle, and Adela, 529
Pan-Slavism, 89
Pantheon, 418
papacy (and popes): and Byzantine Empire, 70, 426, 427, 428; created, 69; divisions within, 470–71; and England, 475, 476; and Holy Roman Empire, 451; home of, 375; and ·Luther, 473; in Middle Ages, 470, 473; in Renaissance, 459, 460; supremacy of, 426, 435, 478. See also names of popes.
Papal States, 431, 554
papyrus, 21, 51
Paracas, 724, 796
Parana River, 709
Paraguay, 707, 708, 709, 747, 774, 788, 794, 803
pariah (caste), 167
Paris, 375, 444, 504, 506, 507, 516, 540, 542, 551, 568, 574
Paris, Congress of, 89
Paris, Peace of (1763), 492
parish, 435
Park, Mungo, 311
Parliament, English, 450–51, 474, 495–99
Parsis, 61
Parthenon, 398
Parthians, 46
Partisans (Yugoslavia), 686
Passover, 55, 62, 67
Pasteur, Louis, 535
Pataliputra, 158
Pathet Lao, 250
patriarch, 70
patricians, 407, 408, 409, 414
Paul (czar of Russia), 629
Pavlova, Anna, 676
Pavlov, Ivan, 583–84, 658
Pax Romana, 412
Pedro I (emperor of Brazil), 753
Pedro II (emperor of Brazil), 753
Pegu, Kingdom of, 246
Peking, 14, 195, 209
Peloponnesian War, 391
Peninsular War, 511
peonage, 750–51, 781
Pepin (Frankish king), 431

Pericles, 389–90, 398
Peron, Eva, 766, 789
Peron, Isabel, 767, 789
Peron, Juan D., 766–67
Persian Empire (and Persians): Arab Muslims overthrow, 46; and Axum, 283; and Byzantine Empire, 46, 425; decline of, 45; extent of, 38, 44; and Greece, 388; in India, 157; and Islam, 132; Parthian rule in, 46; and Phoenicians, 54; rise of, 44; and Roman Empire, 56; Sassanian dynasty in, 46; Seleucid rule, 46. See also Iran.
Persian Gulf states, 95
Persian language, 10, 34, 132, 163, 276, 294, 662
Peru, 707, 723–28, 733–35, 743, 745, 746, 762, 770, 771, 774, 782, 783, 793, 794, 803
Peru, Viceroyalty of, 735, 771
Peruzzi family, 444
Peter (duke of Holstein), 628
Peter I (the Great, czar) 625–28, 631, 672, 673
Peter I (king of Serbia), 686
Petition of Right, 495
Petrarch, 459–60
pharaoh (title), 47, 49–50, 281
Phidias, 398, 399
Philip II (king of Spain), 476, 484, 488, 562
Philip of Macedon, 391
Philip IV (the Fair, king of France), 447
Philippine Islands, 17, 141, 158, 172, 238, 243, 245, 256–58, 488
Philistines, 56
Philo of Alexandria, 66
philosophes, 502, 503, 747, 754
philosophy: Chinese, 182–89; of the Enlightenment, 502, 503; Greek, 382, 394–97, 459; Jewish, 66; medieval, 456; modern, 585–86; Roman, 414–15, 459; and romanticism, 538; and science, 585; Western Europe, 533, 535–36, 585–86
philosophy of the will, 536
Phoenicians, 52–54, 56, 78–79, 383, 388, 405; language, 34
physics, 401, 469, 533, 581, 582
Piast dynasty, 679
Picasso, Pablo, 548, 590
Pioneers (USSR), 643
Pitt, William, 492
Pizarro, Francisco, 733, 734, 735
Plain of the Marsh, 508
Planck, Max, 582
plants; classification of, 501; domestication of, 17–18, 243, 711
Plato, 134, 394, 395–96

Plautus, 416
Platt Amendment, 767
plebeians, Roman, 407–09
Pnom Penh, 249
Po Chu-i, 194
pogram, 671–72
Poland, 513, 558, 565, 568, 614, 616, 622, 628, 678–81, 682, 691, 692, 694, 696, 697
Polish Corridor, 558, 680
Politboro, 643, 644, 651, 663
political parties: in Africa, 333; in England, 499; in Latin America, 770–73; in Western Europe, 531, 532
political science, 585
Polo, Marco, 195, 443
Polynesia, 580
polyrhythmic, 360
Pompeii, 519
Pompey (the Great), 410, 411
Pompidou, Georges, 578
Ponce de Leon, Juan, 757
Pontic Mountains, 30
pope, see papacy.
Pope, Alexander, 520
Po River and Valley, 375, 378, 405, 406
portrait jar, 725
Portugal: in Africa, 288, 291, 293, 304, 306, 307–08, 316–17, 322, 323, 329, 357; in Bahrain, 96; in Brazil, 737–39, 742, 751; empire, 578; explorations of, 172, 481–82; in India, 172; in Japan, 235; in Latin America, 781; in Malaysia, 253; medieval, 451; in Southeast Asia, 255; and Spain, 488
Portuguese Guinea, 322, 329
Portuguese language, 276, 803
positivism, 536
postimpressionism, 545–46
Potsdam Conference, 680
Praxiteles, 398
Preceramic period, 217
pre-Columbian, 710
Presbyterianism, 474, 495, 497
Presidium (USSR), 644, 663
Priestley, Joseph, 501
Primary Chronicle, 669
printing: in China, 193, 196, 463; in Europe, 463–64
Protestantism, 70, 473–76, 478, 488, 497, 498, See also Reformation and denominations.
Proto—Indo-European languages, 9
Provisions of Oxford, 450
Prussia, 553; and Congress of Vienna, 512, 513; and France, 507, 551–52; and Germany, 555; and Ottoman Empire, 88; and

Poland, 679–80; and Russia, 628, 630; Seven Years' War, 492; and Thirty Years' War, 478; and World War I, 558

psychology, 535, 583–84, 658

Ptolemaic dynasty, 46, 399

Ptolemy (astronomer), 468

Puelches (people), 714

Puerto Rico: autonomy, 757–58; as commonwealth, 758–59; creativity, 798, 805; early history, 757; economy, 759; limited self-government, 758; Operation Bootstrap, 759; and Spain, 731, 757; and U.S., 758–59

Punic Wars, 406–07

Puritans, 474, 478, 495, 496, 497, 498, 517

Pygmies, 256, 275, 295, 323, 324; language of, 276

Pygmoids, 275

Pyrenees Mountains, 369, 374, 375

Pythagoras, *401*

Qajar rulers, 94

Qatar, 27, 95, 96

Quakerism, 501–02

Quraysh (people), 77

Quebec, 489, 580

Quechua (language), 727

Quiche (language), 804

quipu, 728

Quito, Ecuador, *735*, 745

rabbi, 65, 671

Rahman, Mujibur, 178

rain forests, 272, 707–08

Rajputs, 167

Ramadan, 74, 672

Ramayana, 152, 153, 158, 165

Ramses II (pharaoh) *47,* 55

Ramses III (pharaoh), 48

rationalism, 499

realism, 227, 537, 540–43, 544, 805; nationalist, 695; Soviet, *639,* 673, 676

Rebmann, Johann, 312

Red Army (Russia), 640, 641

Red Guard (Russia), 640, 641

Red Sea, 27, 30, 45, 48, 71, 92

Reformation: Calvin and, 473–74; consequences of, 476–78; in England, 474–76; Luther and, 471–73; and papacy, 470–71

Reichstag, 447, 563, 564

reincarnation (Hinduism), 154

religion: in Africa, 346–48, 357–58; Andean cultures, 723, 724; arts and, 460–61; in Asia, 212, 214; Aztec, 721–22; in Byzantine Empire, 426–27, 668; in China, 182, 187, 189; and civilization, 20; in Eastern Europe, 679, 683,

686, 691–92; in Egypt (ancient) 59–61; and the Enlightenment, 501–02; in India, 151–58; in Latin America, 784–85; in Mesoamerica, 715, 717, 718; in Middle East, 58–74; early Roman, 412–14; in Russia, 620–21, 669–70; in Southeast Asia, 244; in USSR, 668–72; in Western Europe, 601. *See also* names of religions.

Rembrandt, 514–15

Remedello, 378

Renaissance: and arts, 460–63; 465–66; defined, 458; in Italy, 458, 459–63; in Northern Europe, 458, 464–66; and printing, 463–64; and Reformation, 470; science and technology, 467–69

Restoration, 498, 517, 520

Revelation, 68

Rhineland, 558, 565

Rhine River and Valley, 375–76, 404, 412, 421, 431, 513, 688

Rhodesia, 267, 273, 285, 289–90, 323, 325–26, 333

Richard I (the Lion-Hearted, king of England), 449

Richard II (king of England), 465, 474

Richelieu, Cardinal, 477, 490

Rio de Janeiro, 737, 752, 753, 790, 803

Rio de la Plata, 709

Rio Muni, 317, 322

Rivera, Diego, 800, 804

river of sorrows, 144

Riza Shah, 100–01, 108

Robespierre, 507, 508

rococo, 513, 517–18

Rodin, Auguste, *541,* 546, 593

Rodo, Jose Enrique, 804

Roentgen, Wilhelm von, 533

Roman Catholic Church: and Coptic Christianity, 282; in Africa, 349; Counter-Reformation, 478; in Eastern Europe, 682, 691; in England, 474–76, 498; and explorations, 481–82; in Latin America, 733, 748, 751, 763–64, 766, 772–73, 780, 784, 785; Luther and, 471–73; in Middle Ages, 434–37, 456; organization of, 434–35; Renaissance and, 470; in Southeast Asia, 245, 257; split with Eastern Church, 426–27, 428; in USSR, 671; in Western Europe, 538, 601. *See also* Christianity.

Roman Empire: and the arts, 416–19; beginning of, 405–06; Christianity in, 68, 69; decline

of, 420–23; in Egypt, 411; influenced by Greeks, 413, 414, 416, 418; and Julius Caesar, 410–11; law, 416, 425; in the Middle East, 46, 56; in North Africa, 79, 405, 406–07; and Octavian, 411; Pax Romana, 412; rise of, 409–10; philosophy, 414–15, 459; religion, 412–13; size of empire, 404; society, 419–20; wars and conquests, 406–09

Roman Republic, 407–09

Romance languages, 412, 691

Romania, 89, 91, 614, 616, 683–85, 691, 692, 696

Romanian language, 412, 684

Romanov dynasty, 625, 630, 638, 699

romanticism, 537–40, 542, 543, 694, 804

Rome, 375, 404–06, 410, 411, 416, 431, 462, 553, 554, 568, 574, 668; decline of, 424; Huns in, 422; medieval, 444

Roosevelt, Franklin D., 647, 680, 778

Roosevelt, Theodore, 776–77

Roosevelt Corollary, 776

Rosetta Stone, 51

Roundheads, 497

Rousseau, Jean-Jacques, 502, 504, 505, 538

Rozwi (people), 290

Ruanda-Urundi, 322, 323, 329

Rub'al Khali, 30

Rubens, Peter Paul, 514, *515*

Rudolph of Hapsburg, 477

Ruhr Valley, 374, 375, 688

Russell, Bertrand, 585

Russia: and Afghanistan, 95; and Alexander I, 629–30; becomes USSR, 641; and Byzantine Empire, 620–21; under Catherine the Great, 628–29; communism in, 634–41; and Congress of Vienna, 512, 513, 630; creativity of, 672; early history, 614–16; and Eastern Europe, 679, 680, 683, 684; Europeanization of, 625; and Finland, 451; and Iran, 451; under Ivan IV, 623–24; and Japan, 237–38; Kievan, 619–21; Mongols in, 621–22, 624; Moscow's rise, 622; and Napoleon, 510, 511–12, 630; and Nicholas II, 636; and Ottoman Empire, 87, 88, 89, 627, 628, 631; and Peter the Great, 625–28; repression and rebellion in, 631–32; revolution in, 638–41; Romanov rule, 625, 630, 638, 699; Time of Troubles, 624–25; Varangians in, 619; and World War I, 91,

641. *See also* Union of Soviet Socialist Republics.
Russian language, 662
Russian Orthodox Church, 620–21, 623, 627, 668–71
Russian Soviet Federated Socialist Republic, 641, 661
Russification, 628, 630, 661, 680
Russo-Turkish War, 89
Rutherford, Ernest, 582
Ruwenzori Mountains, 271, 312
Rwanda, Kingdom of, 295, 323
Rwanda, Republic of, 267, 317, 323, 329
Rweej, 287

Saadi, 132
Saadi Gaon, 66
Saar Valley, 374, 558
Sabah, 253
Sabin, Albert, 583
sacraments, 68, 69, 435, 478
Sadat, Anwar, 103, 108
Safavid dynasty, 85
Sahara Desert, *26*, 272, 276, 284, 301, 337–38; once green, 276–77
Sahel, 337–38
Saint Domingue, 754
St. Lucia, 797
St. Petersburg, 627, 637
Saint-Simon, 531
Saladin (Egyptian sultan), 82
Salamis, 388
Salk, Jonas, 583
samba (dance), 797
Sam Sen Thai, 249–50
samurai, 223, *226*, 234–35, 236, 237
Sanchi Stupa, 158–59
Sanhedrin, 67
San Lorenzo, 715
San Marino, 374, 375
San Martin, Jose de, *742*, 745, 746–47
sannyasi (Hinduism), 155
San Salvador, 731
Sanskrit (language), 10
Santa Anna, 749
Santo Domingo, 482, 756, 737
Sappho, 402
Sara, 71
Sarawak, 253
Sardinia, 405; Kingdom of, 554
Sargon I (king of Akkad), 40
Sargon II (king of Assyria), 43
Sarmatians (people), 615
Sassanian dynasty, 46
Saud family, 104
Saud III (king of Arabia), 104
Saudi Arabia, 27, 30, 33, 35, 71, 105, 112, 115, 122, 125, 135; nationalism in, 103–04; oil reserves in, 33, 117–18

Saul of Tarsus, 69
savannahs, 272
Savoy, 554
Saxons (people), 423, 432–33
Saxony, 471, 492, 513
sayyid, 127
Scanderberg, 688
Scandinavia, 373
scheduled castes, 168
schism, 428
scholasticism, 456
Schopenhauer, Arthur, 536
Schuman, Robert, 576
science: in China, 194, 196, 209; in Eastern Europe, 697; and the Enlightenment, 499–501; Hellenistic, 399–400; in India, 161; and the industrial revolution, 523; Islam and, 132–33; modern, 581–83; 19th century, 533–35; Renaissance and, 467–69; in USSR, 658–60
Scotland, 372, 404, 412, 433, 473–74, 496, 497, 498, 531, 597
scribes, 50, 51, 194
Scythians (people), *606*, 615
Second Dynasty (Egypt), 47
Second Estate (France), 505
Second French Empire, 551
Secretariat, UN, 573
Secretariat (USSR), *643*, 644
secret societies, 630–31
Sect Shinto, 222
secular clergy, 435–36
Security Council, UN, 101, 108, 573–74
Sefuwa clan, 300
Seleucia, 45
Seleucid dynasty, 56, 399
Seleucus, 46
Selim I (Turkish sultan), 85, 93
Selim II (Turkish sultan), 87
Selim III (Turkish sultan), 88
Seljuk Turks, 81, 83, 428, 442
Semitic languages, 34, 38, 40, 41, 42, 43, 47, 53, 59
senate, Roman, 407–08, 410, 411
Senegal, 267, 296, 304, 315, 323, 337, 338, 341, 350, 361
Senegal River, 301, 333
Senghor, Leopold Sedar, 361
Serbia, 89, 91, 556, 557, 686
Serbs (people), 427, 614, 616, 686, 691
Serbs, Croats, and Slovenes, Kingdom of, 686
serfs and serfdom: in Middle Ages, 439–41; in Russia, 624, 629, 630, 631, 635, 673, 674
Seti I (pharaoh), 55
Seven Years' War, 492
Sevres, Treaty of, 91

Shaba province, 287, 329, 332
Shabaka (king of Kush), 281
Shah Jahan, 131, *150*
Shakespeare, William, 465, 517
Shan (people), 245, 249
Shang dynasty, 181, 191, 197
Shastri, Lal Bahadur, 175
Shaw, George Bernard, *532*, 541
sheikh (title), 96, 127
Shia sect, 77–78, 80, 85
Shinto, 218–22, 239
Shirazi, 293
shogunate, 224
Shona (people), 290
Shrine Shinto, 222
Siam, Gulf of, 245, 248
Siberia, 610, 611–12, 624, 638, 641, 646, 650, 660, 661, 674, 710
Sicily, 80, *387*, 388, 405, 409, 433, 586
Sierra Leone, 267, 273, 323, 325, 349, 362
Sierra Madre, 703
Sihanouk, Norodom, 249
Sikhism, 174
Silesia, 492, 679
Sinai Peninsula, 30, 112, 113
Singapore, *140*, *255*, 238, 242, 251, 253, 254, 256
single society, 12
Sinkiang, 144
Siqueiras, David Alfaro, 801
Six-Day War, 112, 652
Skeptics, 397
Skulh people, 34–35
slavery and slave trade: and Africa, 288, 303, 304, 308–10; in Assyria, 43; in Brazil, 738–39, 751, 752; in Caribbean, 754, 757, 759, 760; consequences of, 310–11, in Egypt, 51, 55; and economics, 635; in Greece, 386, 389, 390; and Islam, 80; opposition to, 309; in Roman Empire, 409; in Russia, 620; in Saudi Arabia, 104; in Spanish America, 735
Slavonic Dances, 695
Slavophiles, 631
Slavs (people): and Austria, 91, 551; in Balkans, 557; and Byzantine Empire, 427; eastern, 616–20; in Eastern Europe, 679, 682, 683, 684, 685, 688, 691; and nationalism, 89, 560; southern, 616, 691; union of, 91; in USSR, 660–61; western, 616, 682, 691
Slovakia, 682
Slovaks (people), 616, 682, 691
Slovenes (people), 616, 686, 691
Smith, Adam, 531
socialism: African, 331–32; in Asia, 173; and capitalism 531; in

Egypt, 102; kinds of, 531–33; in Latin America, 770; in Syria, 107; in recent Western Europe, 600

socialist realism, 685

society, 6, 10–12; in Africa, 341–45, 351–56; and the arts, 540, 541; in China, 199–204; in Eastern Europe, 691–92; and economy, 531; and the Enlightenment, 499; and the industrial revolution, 527–28; in Japan, 230–33, 236; in Latin America, 778, 780–82, 786–89; in Middle East, 125–30, 134; Plato on, 396; in Southeast Asia, 249, 260–61; utopian, 464; in USSR, 660–67; in Western Europe, 596–600

socioeconomic theories, 531–33

Socrates, 394–95, 399, 464

Sofala, 290–91, 293, 323

Solomon, 56, 283

Solon, 387

Solzhenitsyn, Aleksandr, 674–75

Somalia, 267, 275, 276, 285, 291, 292, 314, 317, 323, 331

Songhai, Empire of, 299, 304, 322, 323

Soninke (people), 296

Sophia of Hanover, 498–99

Sophists, 394, 395

Sophocles, 399

Sotho (language), 363

Sotho (people), 287, 289, 290, 323

South Africa, Republic of, 285, 317, 326–27, 333, 484; apartheid policy, 321; Bantustans, 327; government, 326–27; white rule, 321, 327

South Africa, Union of, 324, 327

South America: environment, 707–08; exploration of, 481–82, 483; nations of, 707. *See also* names of nations.

South-Central Africa, 267

Southeast Asia: economy, 258; early history, 243; environment, 144, 145; history and government, 245–60; nations of, 242; religion, 244–45; society, 260–61. *See also* names of nations.

Southern Europe, 374

Southern Rhodesia, 325–26

Southern Slavs, 616, 691

Southern Yemen, 109, 119

South Korea, 214

South-Southwest Africa, 267

South Vietnam, 251–52

South-West Africa, 316, 317

Southwest Asia, 26

Soviet of Nationalities, 644

Soviet of the Union, 644

Soviet realism, *639*, 673, 676

Soviet Union, *see* Union of Soviet Socialist Republics.

soviets, 637, 638, *639*, 640

Soyinka, Wole, 362

space technology, 660

Spain: 70, 422, 423, 425; in Africa, 317, 322; civil war, 561–62, 588, 590; explorations of, 172, 482–83; and Franco, 562–63; Hapsburg rule, 477; Islam in, 66, 79, 131, 433; and Latin America, 488, 728, 730–36, 742, 743, 756, 757, 781, in Middle Ages, 446, 451, 453; and Napoleon, 509, 510, 511, 540; and Philip II, 488–89; Romans in, 46, 418, 420; Seven Years' War, 492; in Southeast Asia, 255, 257

Spanish-American War, 258, 760

Spanish language, 412, 452, 803

Spanish Morocco, 94

Spanish Sahara, 94, 105, 317

Sparta, 386–87, 391

Speke, John Hanning, 312

sphinxes, *47*, 50

spinning jenny, *524*, 525

Sputnik I, 660

squatter settlements, 795

squire (knighthood), 438

Sri Lanka, 145, 158, 195, 244, 482, 486

Srivijaya, Empire of, 254

Stalin, Josef, 565, 640–42, 644, 670, 672, 675, 687, 690, 695

Stalingrad, 568, 647

Stanley, Henry M., 312

Star Chamber, 496

State Shinto, 222, 239

status quo, 764, 766, 773, 778

stele, 283, 715, 717

Stephen I (king of Hungary), 685

steppes, 30, 615

Stoicism, 397, 414–15, 416

Stone Age, 15–16

Stonehenge, *376*, 377–78, 380

Strategic Arms Limitations Treaty (SALT), 652

stream of consciousness, 587

Stuart, House of, 495, 498

subcastes, 168

sub-Saharan Africa, 267

Sucre, Jose Antonio de, 745

Sudanic languages, 276, 322

Sudan (region), 272, 276, 301

Sudan, Republic of, 267, 277, 278, 314, 324, 338, 348, 349

Sudra (caste), 166, 167

Suez Canal, 27, 92, *93*, 102, 557; and Arab-Israeli conflict, 112

Sufism, 74

Suharto, 256

Sui dynasty, 190

Sukarno, 256

Sulawesi, Indonesia, 254

Suleiman I (the Magnificent, Turkish sultan), 85–86, 87

Sully, Duke of, 489

sultan (title), 81, 253

Sumanguru Kante, 360

Sumatra, Indonesia, 195, 252, 253, 254, 255

Sumer, 38, 39–41, 42, 59

Sundiata (Mandingo chief), 360

Sung dynasty, 193, 194–95

Sunna, 72, 77, 99

Sunni Ali, 299

Sunnite sect (Islam), 77, 85

Sun Yat-sen, 202, 206–07

Supreme Court (USSR), 644

Supreme Soviet, 644, 645

Surinam, 707, 709, 730

surrealism, 586, 591

Susu, Kingdom of, 296, 360

Sutherland, Efua, 362

Swahili (language), 276, 294, 332, 351, 363

Swahili (people), 294, 308, 317

Swaziland, 267, 324, 325

Swazis (people), 324

Sweden, 372, 373, 575, 600; and Congress of Vienna, 513; in Middle Ages, 433, 451; and Russia, 624, 627; and Seven Years' War, 492; and Thirty Years' War, 476, 478

Switzerland, 369, 374, 376, 473–74, 477, 478, 590, 597

symbols, 348

synagogue, 63, *671*

syndicates, 561

Syria, 27, 30, 31, 42, 45, 48, 53, 54, 61, 68, 77, 78, 83, 84, 85, 112, 125, 383, 399, 410; Arab-Israeli conflict, 112–13, 652; French mandate, 95; military in, 107

Tacitus, 417, 421

Tadzikistan, USSR, 662

Tagore, Rabindranath, 165, 168

Tahiti, 546

Taiwan, 204, 208, 217, 243

Talleyrand, 512

Talmud, 63

Tamerlane, 84, 162

Tanganyika, 314, 317, 324, 325

Tanganyika, Lake, 270, 287, 312

T'ang dynasty, 190, 193–94, 219 222

Tang Chu, 186

Tangier, 94, 105

Tanzania, 274, 292, 293, 314, 324, 325, 326, 332, 333, 336

835

Taoism, 194, 220, 250; and Buddhism, 190; in Korea, 214; origin of, 182, 186; teachings of, 186–87
Tao Te Ching, 186
tariffs, 333, 554, 576, 793
Tasman, Abel, 580
Tassili Plateau, 357
Tatars (people), 621
Taxco, Mexico, 796, 802
taxes and taxation: in Africa, 318; in Assyria, 43; in Byzantine Empire, 426; of clergy, 447, 470; in England, 450, 476, 495, 498; in France, 505; in Great Britain, 566; and Islam, 74; and the Magna Carta, 450; in the Roman Empire, 411, 412, 421; in Russia, 627
Tehran Conference, 680
Tell Al Ubaid, 39
Temuchin, 621
Ten Lost Tribes of Israel, 56
Tenochtitlan, 720, 721, 732, 802
Ten Years' War (Cuba), 760
Teotihuacan, 718, 719
Terence, 416
terra-cotta, 357
Terror, the (Russia), 508
Tetzel, Johann, 471–72
Teutonic Knights, 679
Thai (people), 245, 246–47, *248,* 249
Thailand, 147, 242, 245, 246–48
thaw (USSR), 675, 695, 696
Theodora (Byzantine empress), 425
Theodore I (czar), 624
Theodoric (Ostrogoth king), 423
Theodosius (Roman emperor), 421
theology, 70, 455–56
Theravada Buddhism, 189, 220, 244, 249
Thermidorians, 508
Thermopylae, 388
Third Estate (France), 447, 505
Third Republic (France), 552
Third World, 650, 651, 652
Thirty-Nine Articles, 476
Thirty Years' War, 476–77, 490, 552
Thomas, Piri, 805
Thompson, Benjamin, 533
Three Principles of the People (Sun Yat-sen), 206
Thutmose III (pharaoh), 48, 52
Thutmose IV (pharaoh) *24*
Tiahuanaco, 724
Tiber River, 405
Tibet, 83, 144, 158, 212, 245, 246
Tibeto-Burman languages, 212
Tigris River, 31, 38, 39, 41, 42, 43, 45
Tilsit, Treaty of, 510, 630
Timbuktu, 274, 298, 299, 311
Time of Troubles, 624–25, 669

Timor, Indonesia, 254, 256, 484
Timur, 162
Tiradentes, 751–72
Titian, 462
Titicaca, Lake, 712
Tito, Marshal, 686–87
Togo, 267, 302, 303, 316, 324, 325, 333
Togrul Beg, 81
Tokugawa shogunate, 225–27, 234, 235, 236
Tokyo, 144, 217, 225, 236
Tolstoy, Leo, 673, 674
Toltecs (people), 718, 719, 720
Torah, 62, 63, 65
Tordesillas, Treaty of, 482, 737, *739*
Totonacs (people), 719
Toure, Sekou, 328
Toussaint L'Ouverture, Pierre, 754
Townshend, Charles, 524
trade: African, 278, 281, 283, 291–92, 296, 300, 307, 308; Aramaean, 54; Aztec, 721; Bangladesh, 178; Byzantine Empire, 426, 668; China, 205; and cities, 21; Cretan, 383; and crusades, 82–83; Etruscan, 405; free, 555; Greek, 383, 402; in India, 252; Indus Valley, 151; in Latin America, 793; Mesoamerican, 714, 715, 717; during Middle Ages, 430, 441–44; in Middle East, 35–36, 557; and natural resources, 17; and Phoenicians, 53; and rivers, 144; Roman, 405; in Russia, 619–21, 625, 668; in Southeast Asia, 248, 252–56; Sumerian, 39; and urban life, 36; in USSR, 613; in Western Europe, 377, 378, 380, 481–82, 486
Trafalgar, battle of, 510
Transcaucasus, 611, 613, 662,
Transjordan, 95, 108
Transylvanian Alps, 684
Transvaal, 290, 327
Tres Zapotes, 715
Trial, The, 695
tribune, Roman, 408
Trinidad-Tobago, 706–07, 797
Trinity, 67, 69–70, 428
Tripartite Treaty of Alliance, 101
Triple Alliance, 556, 557
Triple Entente, 91, 556
Tripolitan Wars, 93
Trotsky, Leon, 641–42, 645, 672
troubadours, 453
Troy, 384, 416
Trujillo, Rafael, 756, 763, 778
Truman Doctrine, 571, 648
Trusteeship Council, UN, 573
Tshombe, Moise, 329
Tuaregs (people), 298, 299

Tudor, House of, 465, 474, 495
Tu Fu, 194
Tula, Mexico, 719
Tull, Jethro, 523–24
Tumbatu, 292, 324
tunics, 401
Tunis, Tunisia, 86
Tunisia, 78, 80, 93, 105–06
Tupac Amaru, 743, 771
Tupamaros, 766, 771–72
Turanians (people), 90
Turkestan, USSR, 662
Turkey: military takeover, 107; modernization of, 99–100; nationalism in, 99; and Truman Doctrine, 648; and World War I, 91, 557. *See also* Ottoman Empire.
Turkic language, 81, 662
Turkic people, 90–91, 619
Turkmenistan, USSR, 661, 662
Turner, Joseph, 540
Tuscany, 459
Tutsi (people), 295, 331
Twelve Tables, 416
Two Sicilies, Kingdom of, 433, 554
tyrants, in Greece, 387
Tyrrhenian Sea, 405

Uganda, 267, 274, 295, 314, 324–25, 331, 332, 333, 336
Ugarit, 53
ujamaa, 332
ukiyo-e, 226
Ukraine, 616, 621, 628, 660, 661, 669, 671
Ultimate Reality (Hinduism), 154
Umme Jilma (Kanuri king), 300
underground, 111
Union of Soviet Socialist Republics (USSR): the arts, 672–76; and China, 207, 211, 212; and Cuba, 768–69; and Eastern Europe, 680, 683, 684–90, 692; economy, 655–60; environment, 606–14; government structure, 643, 644–45; and India, 175; and Middle East, 27, 101, 102, 109, 112; name changed, 641; religion, 668–72; science and technology, 658–60; society, 660–67; and Vietnam, 252; and World War II, 565, 567–68, 647–48, 661, 672; since World War II, 571, 573, 648–52. *See also;* communism (USSR); Communist party (Soviet); Russia.
Union of Utrecht, 484
Union of Writers (USSR), 673
United Arab Emirates, 95, 96, 117, 126
United Nations, 111, 112, 325, 327, 329, 356, 690; charter, 572–73;

organizations, 573–74; purposes, 572; special agencies, 573–74
United Nations Educational, Scientific, and Cultural Organization (UNESCO), 574
United Netherlands, Republic of, 484
United Provinces of Central America, 751, 773
United States: and Africa, 336; and Arab-Israeli conflict, 112, 113; and arms race, 555; and Chile, 771; Constitution, 498, 503, 744; and Cuba, 650, 767, 768–69; and Dominican Republic, 756, 757; and Haiti, 755; and Latin America, 774–78; legal system, 449; and Mexico, 749, 765; and oil embargo, 118–19; and Puerto Rico, 758–59; and Philippines, 258; and slavery, 309; and Tripolitan Wars, 93; and UN, 573; and USSR, 652, 662; and Vietnam, 251–52; and West Germany, 688; and Western Europe, 571–72; and World War I, 91, 557–58; and World War II, 238, 567, 647–48, 660
universities and colleges: in Africa, 298; in China, 203; in India, 161, 165; Islamic, 79; medieval, 455; in USSR, 666. *See also* education.
untouchables (caste), 167
Upanishads, 153
Upper Egypt, 47, 281
Upper Volta, 267, 304, 324, 337, 338
upward mobility, 781–82
Ur, 39, 40, 41
Ural-Altaic languages, 34
Ural Mountains, 368, 610, 611
Ural River, 611
Urban II (pope), 82, 442
Urdu (language), 163
Ur-Nammi (legal code), 41
Uruguay, 707, 708, 747, 771–72, 773, 781–82, 789, 793, 794, 804
Uruguay River, 709
utilitarianism, 504
utopian socialism, 531
Utrecht, Treaty of, 490
Utrecht, Union of, 484
Uzbekistan, USSR, 662

Vai (people), 323, 360
Vaisya (caste), 166, 167
vandalism, 423
Vandals (people), 79, 423, 425
Varangians (people), 619–20
vassals, 181, 437–39
Vatican City, 374, 375, *458,* 462, 463, 515

Vedas, 152–53, 158, 160
Velasquez, 514, *515,* 544
Venezuela, 707, 709, 744, 745, 770, 773, 774, 776, 793, 794, 795, 803
Venice, 83, 87, 88, 228, 442, 459, 481, 553
Versailles, Treaty of, 558–60, 563, 564
Vesalius, Andreas, 469
viceroyalty, 735
Victor Emmanuel II (Italian king), 554
Victor Emmanuel III (Italian king), 561
Victoria (queen of Great Britain), 541
Victoria Falls, 270, *271,* 312
Victoria, Lake, 270–71, 285–86, 294, 312, 314
Victorian Age, 541
Vienna, 86, 87, 488, 543, 574, 630
Vienna, Congress of, 512–13, 549, 558, 630, 680
Vienna System, 549
Viet Cong, 252
Viet Minh, 251
Vietnam, 242, 245, 249, 250; civil war in, 252; partition of, 251
Vikings (people), 432–33, 619
Villa, Francisco "Pancho," 764–65
Villanovans (people), 378
Vinci, Leonardo da, 462
Virgil, 416, 459
Virgin Islands, 706
Visigoths (people), 422, 423, 435, 615
Vistula River and Basin, 616, 679
Vladimir I (Russian prince), 668
Vladivostok, 612
Volga River, 613, 619, 622, 624
Volta, 527, 533
Voltaire, 502, 504, 505, 628
von Sass, Florence, 312
Vulgate (Bible), 70, 464

Wagner, Richard, 543
Wahabism, 103–04
Walachia, 684
Wales, 372, 433, 587
Walloons (people), 597
Wari empire, 724
War of the Pacific, 773, 788
Warring States Period, 182
Warsaw, *565,* 628, 679, 692; Duchy of, 680
Warsaw Pact, 658, 680, 683, 688
Watt, James, 525
Watusi (people), 295, 359
Webb, Beatrice and Sidney, 531, *532*
Weimar Republic, 563
Weismann, August, 535
Weizmann, Chaim, 110, 111

Wellington, Duke of, 511
Welsh (people), 597
Wene (Congo ruler), 288
Wesley, John, 502
West Africa, 267
West Bank (Jordan River), 112
West Berlin, 688, 690
Western Europe: defined, 368; early cultures, 376–80; environment, 369, 372–76; explorations of, 480–92; government, changing attitudes of, 494–13; and industrial revolution, 522–33; in Middle Ages, 430–56; nations of, 368; Renaissance in 458–79. *See also* names of nations.
Westernizers, 631, 636
Western Rift Valley, 270
Western Slavs, 616, 682, 691
West Germany, 369, 374, 376, 571, 576, 596, 598, 599; created, 688. *See also* Germany.
West Goths, 422
West Indies, 486, 706, 734, 740, 752
Westinghouse, George, 527
Westminster Abbey, 593
West Pakistan, 177, 178
Westphalia, Treaty of, 477, 478, 484
West River, China, 141
Whigs, 498
White Army (Russia), 640
White Nile River, 271, 274, 312
White Russia, 616, 661
William I (the Conqueror, king of England), *366, 432,* 433, 449, 624
William II (emperor of Germany), 556
William III (of Orange, king of England), 498–99
William and Mary, 520
William of Ockham, 456
William of Prussia, 552
William the Silent, prince of Orange, 484
window to the West, 627
Windward Islands, 706
Wolof, Kingdom of, 307
Wolof (people), 304
women: in Africa, 277, 281–82, 342, 343, 348, 355–56; and Blackstone's *Commentaries,* 504, 537; in China, 199, 203–04; and Confucianism, 185; as consumers, 595; in Egypt (ancient), 51–52; in Egypt (modern), 102; and English law, 495, 504; and equality, 504; and feudalism, 437; and French politics, 507; in Greece (ancient), 386, 389, 402; in guilds, 445, *446;* Hammurabi's code and, 41; in India, 169–71; and industrial revolution, 528; in industry, *209, 232,*

530; in Iran, 101; and Islam, 128–30, 356, in Japan, 231–33; in labor force, *231;* in Latin America, 766, 780, 787–89; and Magna Carta, 450; and manorialism, 439; in medieval Europe, 455; and Napoleonic code, 504; in religious orders, 436; in Roman Empire, 407, 419–20; in Southeast Asia, 260; in space, first, 660; in Turkey, 100; in USSR, 660, 665, 667; in Western Europe, 598–99

Wordsworth, William, 538

World Health Organization (WHO), 333, 574

World Meteorological Organization (WMO), 574

World War I: armistice, 558; casualties, 558; Allies, 91, 92, 684; causes of, 552, 556–57; Central Powers, 91; League of Nations, 95

World War II, *570;* in Africa, 320; and atomic bomb, 582; causes of, 558, 560; in Eastern Europe, 683, 684, 685, 686; and Egypt, 92; end of, 568; and Japan, 222, 233, 238, 239, 256, 567; and Jews, 564, 571, 691–92; and Latin America, 778; in Middle East, 101; and Spanish civil war, 562; and USSR, 641, 665, 670, 672; and Western Europe, 565–67

World Zionist Organization, 110

Wren, Christopher, 516

writing: in Africa, 360; calligraphy, 193; in China, 181; development of and civilization, 20; in Egypt, 47, 50–51; and government, 21; and history, 21; ideographic, 181, 193, 213–14, 223, 717; in Japan, 223; oldest known, 40; origins of, 21

writs, 449

Wuhan, China, 209

Wundt, Wilhelm, 535, 583

Wycliffe, John, 471

Xerxes, 388

Xhosa (language), 363

Xhosa (people), 286, 324, 326

Ximinez, Francisco, 804

x-ray, 533, 582

Yahweh, 62

Yalta Conference, 680

Yamato clan, 218, 219–20

Yangtze River, 141

Yaroslav the Wise, 621

Yayoi period, 217

Yedo, 225, 236

Yellow River, China, 141

Yellow Sea, 162

Yemen, 109, 112, 120, 122, 135

Yemen Arab Emirates, 27

Yemen Arab Republic, *see* Yemen.

Yemen, Democractic Republic of, *see* Southern Yemen.

Yenan, China, 208

Yenisei River, 613, 614

yeshivas, 65

Yevtushenko, Yevgeny, 675

Yoritomo, 224

Yoruba (city-states), 302–03, 323

Yoruba (language), 363

Yoruba (people), 302, 314, 318, 330, 347, 360, 363

Yoshiwara, 226

Young Italy, 553

Young Turks, 90–91

Yuan dynasty, 195, 212

Yuan Shih-k'ai, 207

Yucatan Peninsula, 703, 711, 716, 717, 718, 719

Yugoslavia, 691, 696, 697; created, 560; and Tito, 686–87

Yunnan Province, China, *146, 247*

Zagros Mountains, 30

Zaire, 267, 273, 287, 324, 328, 332

Zaire (Congo) River, 271, 285, 287, 288, 312, 332

Zambezi River, 270, 285, 288, 289, 290, 291, 313, 360

Zambia, 267, 285, 324, 326, 336

Zanzibar, 292, 324, 325

Zapata, Emiliano, 764

Zapotecs (people), 719

Zeila, Somalia, 292, 323

Zen Buddhism, 220–21, 224, 225

Zend-Avesta, 61

Zeno, 397

ziggurat, 39–40

Zimbabwe, 289–90, 323, 326

Zionism, 110

Zog I (king of Albania), 688

Zoroastrianism, 61

Zulu (language), 363

Zulu (people), 287, 314, 318, 324, 326

Zwingli, Ulrich, 473